NX 12

For Beginners

Tutorial Books

Contents

Introduction

Welcome to the *NX 12 for Beginners* book. This book is written to assist students, designers, and engineering professionals. It covers the important features and functionalities of NX using relevant examples and exercises.

This book is written for new users, who can use it as a self-study resource to learn NX. In addition, it can also be used as a reference for experienced users. The focus of this book is part modeling, assembly modeling, drawings, sheet metal, and surface design.

Topics covered in this Book

- Chapter 1, "Getting Started with NX 12", introduces NX. The user interface and terminology are discussed in this chapter.

- Chapter 2, "Sketch Techniques", explores the sketching commands in NX. You will learn to create parametric sketches.

- Chapter 3, "Extrude and Revolve features", teaches you to create basic 3D geometry using the Extrude and Revolve commands.

- Chapter 4, "Placed Features", covers the features, which can be created without using sketches.

- Chapter 5, "Patterned Geometry", explores the commands to create patterned and mirrored geometry.

- Chapter 6, "Additional Features and Multibody Parts", covers additional commands to create complex geometry. In addition, the multibody parts are also covered.

- Chapter 7, "Modifying Parts", explores the commands and techniques to modify the part geometry.

- Chapter 8, "Assemblies", explains you to create assemblies using the bottom-up and top-down design approaches.

- Chapter 9, "Drawings", covers how to create 2D drawings from 3D parts and assemblies.

- Chapter 10, "Sheet Metal Design", covers how to create sheet metal parts and flat patterns.

- Chapter 11, "Surface Design", covers how to create complex shapes using surface design commands.

- Chapter 12, "NX Realize Shape", helps you to create complex shape using freeform modeling.

Chapter 1: Getting Started with NX 12

Introduction to NX 12

NX 12 is a parametric and feature-based system that allows you to create 3D parts, assemblies, and 2D drawings. The design process in NX is shown below.

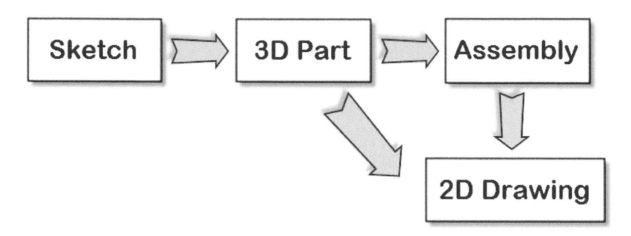

In NX, parameters, dimensions, or relations control everything. For example, if you want to change the position of the hole shown in figure, you need to change the dimension or constraint that controls its position.

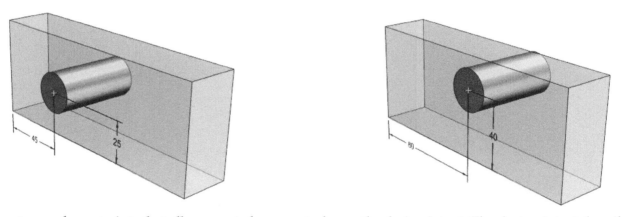

The parameters and constraints that allow you to have control over the design intent. The design intent describes the way your 3D model will behave when you apply dimensions and constraints to it. For example, if you want to position the hole at the center of the block, one way is to add dimensions between the hole and the adjacent edges. However, when you change the size of the block, the hole will not be at the center.

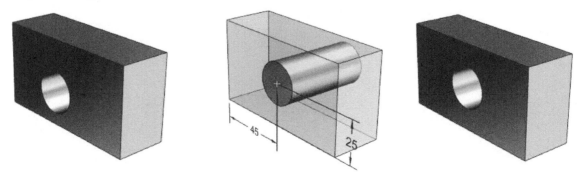

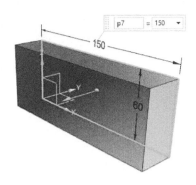

You can make the hole to be at the center, even if the size of the block changes. To do this, you need to delete the dimensions and apply the **Midpoint** constraint relationships between the hole point and the horizontal and vertical edges. Now, even if you change the size of the block, the hole will always remain at the center.

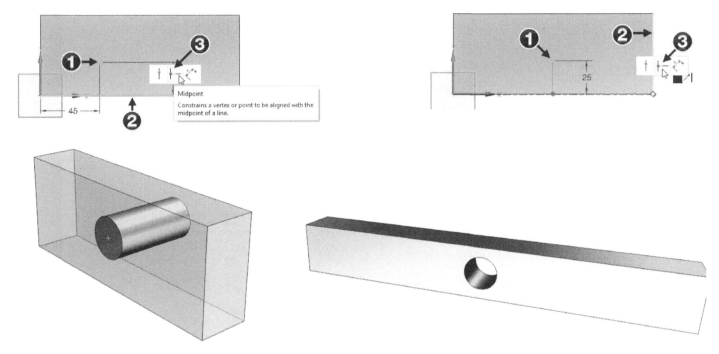

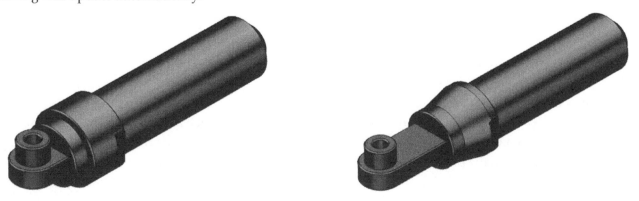

The other big advantage of NX is the associativity between parts, assemblies and drawings. When you make changes to the design of a part, the changes will take place in any assembly that it is a part of. In addition, the 2D drawing will update automatically.

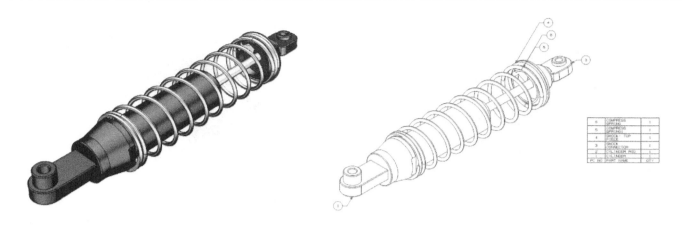

Starting NX 12

To start **NX 12**, type **NX 12.0** in the search box available on the taskbar. Select NX 12.0 from the search results; the NX 12.0 application window appears. On the Application Window, click **Home > New** to open the **New** dialog. On this dialog, click the **Model** template, and then click **OK**. The files created in NX have an extension *.prt*.

User Interface

The following image shows the **NX 12** application window.

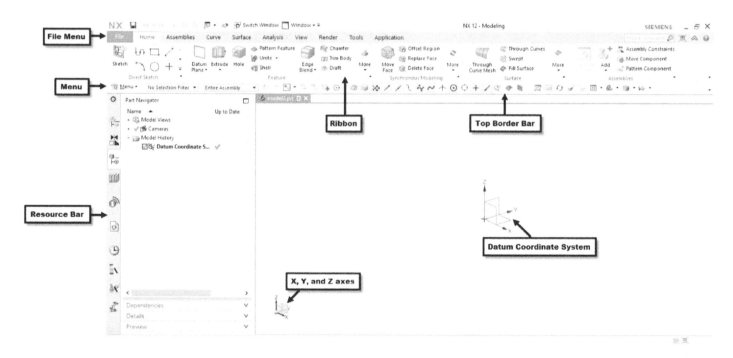

Various components of the user interface are:

Quick Access Toolbar

This is located on the top left corner. It has some commonly used commands such as **Save, Undo, Redo, Copy**, and so on. You can add more commands to the **Quick Access Toolbar** by clicking on the down-arrow next to it, and then selecting commands from the pop-up menu.

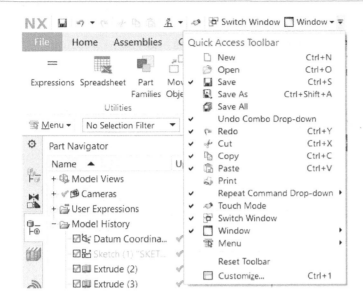

File Menu

The **File Menu** appears when you click on the **File** button located at the top left corner of the window. The **File Menu** has a list of self-explanatory menus. You can see a list of recently opened documents under the **Recently Opened Parts** section. You can also switch to different applications of NX using the File Menu.

Ribbon

A ribbon is a set of commands, which help you to perform various operations. It has tabs and groups. Various tabs of the ribbon are:

Home tab

This ribbon tab contains the commands such as **New, Open, Help,** and so on.

Home tab in the Model template

This ribbon tab has the commands to construct 2D and 3D features.

Analysis tab

This ribbon tab has the commands to measure objects. It also has commands to analyze the draft, curvature, and surface of the model geometry.

Home tab in Sketch Task environment

This ribbon tab has all the sketch commands. It is available in a separate environment called Sketch Task environment.

Tools tab

This ribbon tab has the commands to create expressions, part families, movies, fasteners.

View tab

This ribbon tab has the commands to modify the display of the model and user interface.

Render tab

This ribbon tab has the commands to generate photorealistic images.

Assemblies tab

This tab contains the commands to construct an assembly.

Drafting template ribbon

In the **Drafting** template, you can generate orthographic views of the 3D model. The ribbon tabs in this template contain commands to generate 2D drawings.

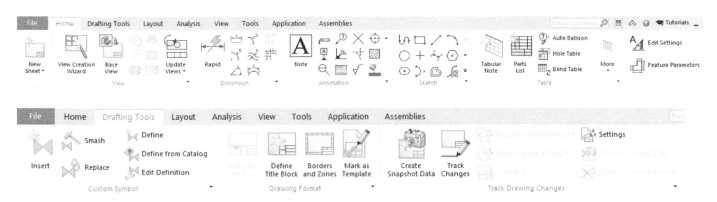

Sheet Metal ribbon

The commands in this ribbon help you to construct sheet metal components.

Some tabs are not visible by default. To display a particular tab, right-click on the ribbon and select the tab name from the list displayed.

You can also add a ribbon tab by opening the **Customize** dialog.

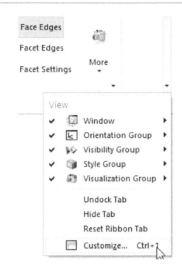

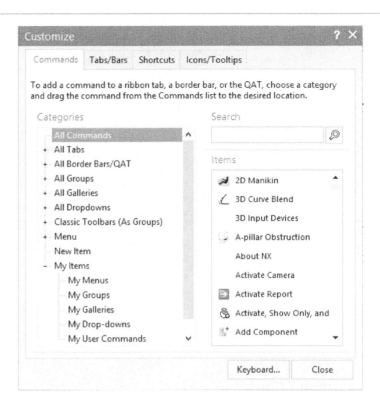

Ribbon Groups and More Galleries

The commands on the ribbon are arranged in various groups depending upon their use. Each group has a **More Gallery**, which contains additional commands. Click on the **More** option of a group to display the gallery.

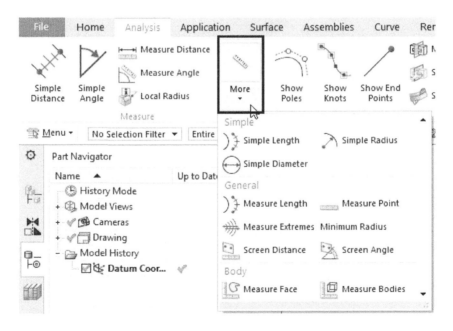

You can add more commands to a ribbon group by clicking the arrow located at the bottom right corner of a group; a drop-down appears. Select the name of the command to be added to the group.

Command Finder

The **Command Finder** bar is used to search for any command. You can type any keyword in the **Command Finder** bar and find a list of commands related to it.

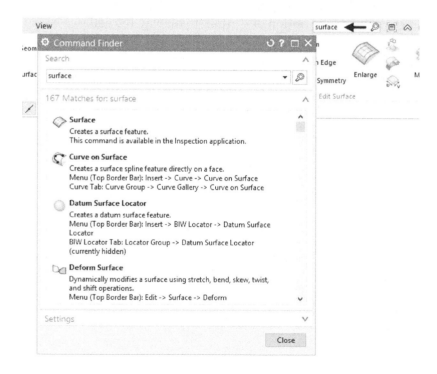

Top Border Bar

This is available below the ribbon. It has all the options to filter the objects that you can select from the graphics window. It also has some options to change the display of the model in the graphics window.

Menu

Menu is located on the Top Border Bar. It has various options (menu titles). When you click on a menu title, a drop-down appears. Select any option from this drop-down.

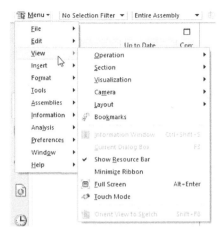

Status bar

This is available below the graphics window. It shows the prompts and the action taken while using the commands.

Select object for sketch plane or double-click axis to orient

Resource Bar

This is located on the left side. It has all the navigator windows such as Assembly Navigator, Constraint Navigator, Part Navigator, and so on.

Part Navigator

Contains the list of operations carried while constructing a part.

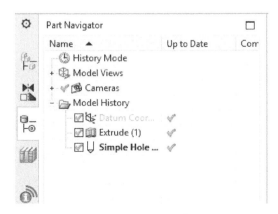

Roles Navigator

The **Roles** Navigator has a list of system default and industry specific roles. There are two types of roles: Content and Presentation. A content role is a set of commands and ribbon tabs customized for a specific application. For example, the **CAM Express** role has a set of commands used for performing manufacturing operations. This textbook uses the **Advanced** content role.

A Presentation role is an arrangement of the commands in the user interface. NX 12 provides you with four Presentation roles: **Default**, **High Definition**, **Touch Panel** and **Touch Tablet** roles. This textbook uses the **Default** presentation role. The **High Definition** role displays large icons suitable for 4K High definition screens. The other two roles help you to use NX on a Touch screen PC or tablet.

Touch Panel role

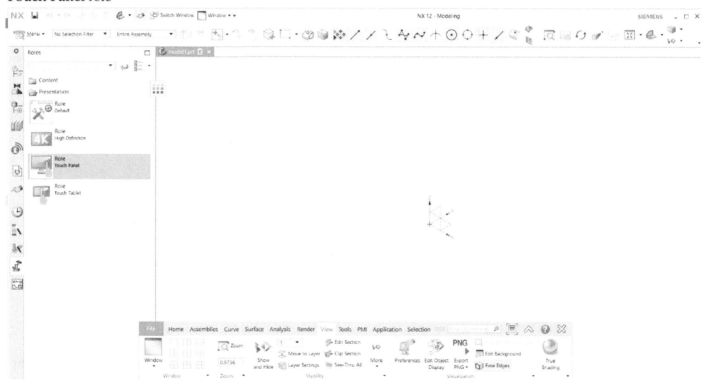

Touch Tablet role

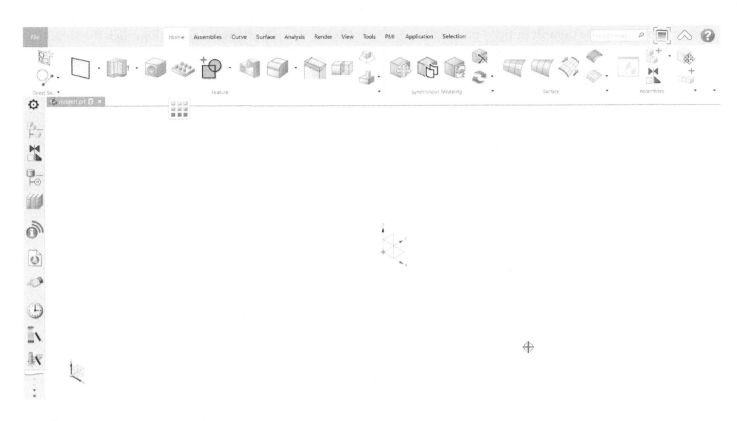

Dialogs

When you execute any command in NX, the dialog related to it appears. A dialog has of various options. The following figure shows various components of a dialog.

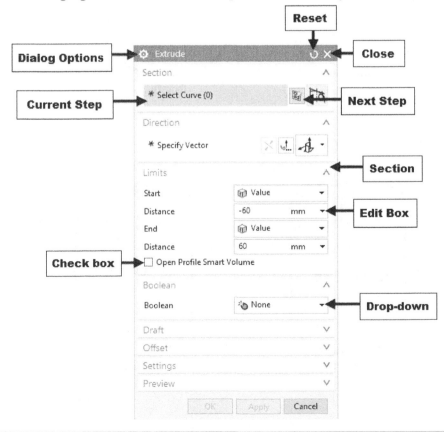

This textbook uses the default options on the dialog. If you have made any changes to a dialog, click the **Reset** button on the dialog; the default options appear.

Mouse Functions

Various functions of the mouse buttons are:

Left Mouse button (MB1)

When you double-click the left mouse button (MB1) on an object, the dialog related to the object appears. Using this dialog, you can edit the parameters of the objects.

Middle Mouse button (MB2)

Click this button to execute the **OK** command.

Right Mouse button (MB3)

Click this button to open the shortcut menu. The shortcut menu has some selection filters and options to modify the display of the model.

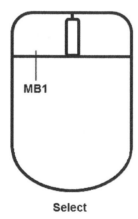

Select

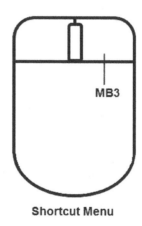

Shortcut Menu

Rotate

The other functions with combination of the three mouse buttons are:

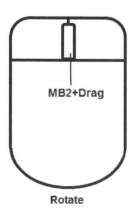

Rotate

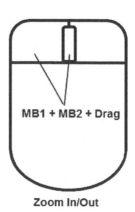

Zoom In/Out

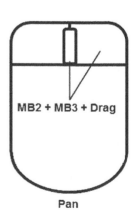

Pan

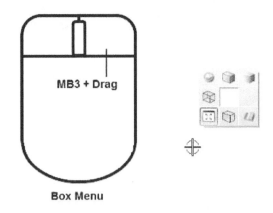

Box Menu

Edit Background

To change the background color of the window, click **Menu > Preferences > Background**. On the **Edit Background** dialog, click the **Plain** option to change the background to plain. Click on the **Plain Color** swatch. On the **Color** dialog, change the background color and click **OK** twice.

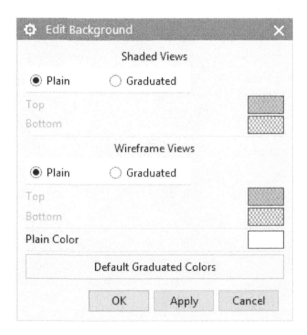

Shortcut Keys

CTRL+Z	(Undo)
CTRL+Y	(Redo)
CTRL+S	(Save)
F5	(Refresh)
F1	(NX Help)
CTRL + SHIFT + Z	(Zoom)
CTRL + R	(Rotate)
CTRL+M	(Starts the Modeling environment)
CTRL+SHIFT+D	(Starts the Drafting environment)
CTRL+SHIFT+M	(Starts the NX Sheet Metal environment)

CTRL+ALT+M	(Starts the Manufacturing environment)
X	(Extrude)
CTRL+1	(Customize)
CTRL+D	(Delete)
CTRL+N	(New File)
CTRL+O	(Open File)
CTRL+P	(Plot)

NX Help

NX offers you with the help system that goes beyond basic command definition. You can access NX help by using any of the following methods:

- Press the F1 key.
- Click on the **NX Help** option on the right-side of the window.

Questions

1. Explain how to customize the Ribbon.
2. What is the design intent?
3. Give one example of where you would establish a relationship between a part's features.
4. Explain the term 'associativity' in NX.
5. List any two procedures to access NX Help.
6. How can you change the background color of the graphics window?
7. How can you activate the Box Menu?
8. How is NX a parametric modeling application?

Chapter 2: Sketch Techniques

This chapter covers the methods and commands to create sketches used in the part-modeling environment. The commands and methods are discussed in context to the part-modeling environment. In NX, you can create sketches in two environments: Part and Sketch task environment. You will learn to create sketches in both the environments.

In NX, you create a rough sketch, and then apply dimensions and constrains that define its shape and size. The dimensions define the length, size, and angle of a sketch element, whereas constrains define the relations between sketch elements.

The topics covered in this chapter are:

- Sketching in Part and Sketch Task Environments
- Use constraints and dimensions to control the shape and size of a sketch
- Learn sketching commands
- Learn commands and options that help you to create sketches easily

Sketching directly in the Part environment

Creating sketches in NX Part environment is very easy. You have to activate the **Sketch** command, and then define a plane on which you want to create the sketch. To do this, click **Home > Direct Sketch > Sketch** on the ribbon. Next, click on any of the Datum Planes located at the center of the graphics window. On the **Create Sketch** dialog, click **OK** to start the sketch. You can now start drawing sketches on the selected plane. After creating the sketch, click **Home > Direct Sketch > Finish Sketch** on the ribbon to finish the sketch.

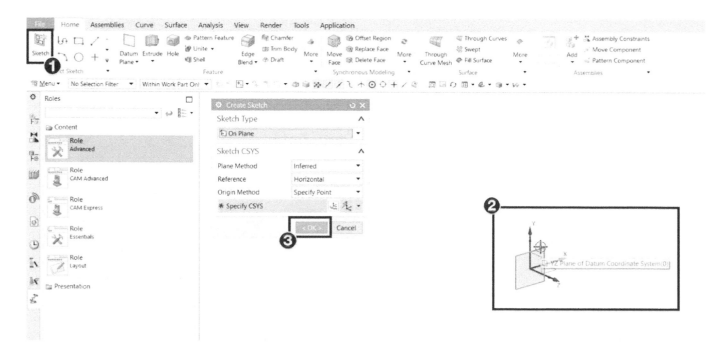

Sketching in the Sketch Task environment

The Sketch Task environment is used to create sketches only to complete a specific task. For example, if you want to create a sketch to construct an *Extrude* feature, activate the **Extrude** command (On the ribbon, click **Home > Feature > Extrude**), and then click on a Datum plane. The Sketch Task environment will be active. You will notice that the **Profile** command is also activated, by default. You can start sketching lines or select any other sketching command. After completing the sketch, click **Home > Sketch > Finish** on the ribbon to come out of the Sketch Task environment.

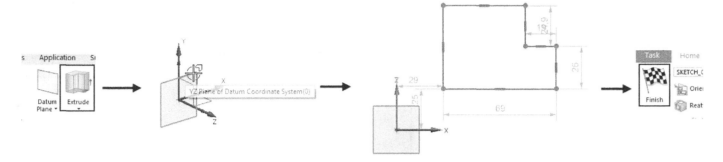

Draw Commands

NX provides you with a set of commands to create sketches. These commands are located on the **Direct Sketch** panel of the **Home** ribbon.

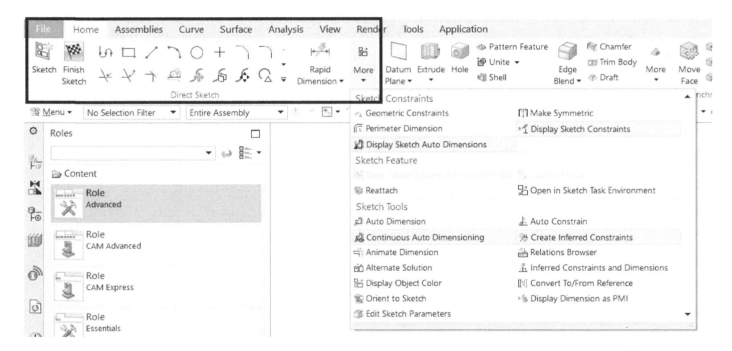

The Profile command

This is the most commonly used command while creating a sketch. To activate this command, click **Home > Direct Sketch > Profile** on the ribbon. As you move the pointer in the graphics window, you will notice that a box is attached to it. It displays the X and Y coordinates of the pointer. To create a line, click in the graphics window, move the pointer and click again. After clicking for the second time, you can see that an end point is added and another line segment is started. This is a convenient way to create a chain of lines. Continue to click to add more line segments. You can right-click in the graphics window and click **OK**, if you want to end the chain. You will notice that the **Profile** command is still active. You can create another chain of line segments or press Esc to deactivate this command.

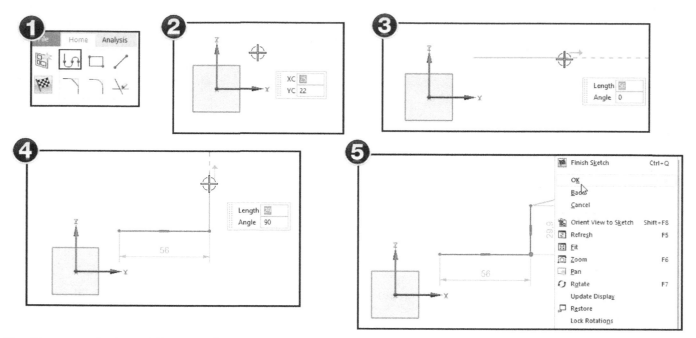

Tip: To create a horizontal line, specify the start point of the line and move the pointer horizontally; a dotted horizontal line appears. Click the on the dotted line to create a horizontal line. In addition, the Horizontal constraint is applied to the line. You will learn about constraints later in this chapter. Likewise, you can create a vertical line by moving the pointer vertically and clicking.

The **Profile** command can also be used to draw arcs continuous with lines. Click the **Arc** icon on the **Profile** dialog to draw this type of arc. The figure below shows the procedure to draw arcs connected to lines. To switch from tangent arc to normal or vice-versa, move the pointer to the end point of the previous line.

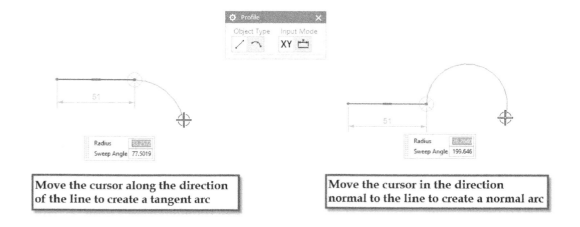

| Move the cursor along the direction of the line to create a tangent arc | Move the cursor in the direction normal to the line to create a normal arc |

To delete a line, select it and press the **Delete** key. To select more than one line, click on multiple line segments; the lines will be highlighted. You can also select multiple lines by dragging a box from left to right. Press and hold the left mouse button and drag a box from left to right; the lines inside the box boundary will be selected.

The Arc command

This command creates an arc using two methods: **Arc by 3 Points** and **Arc by Center and Endpoints**.

The Arc by 3 Points method

This method creates an arc by defining its start, end, and radius. Activate the **Arc** command (click **Home > Direct Sketch > Arc** on the ribbon). On the **Arc** dialog, click the **Arc by 3 Points** button, and then click to define the start point of the arc. Click again to define the end point. After defining the start and end of the arc, you need to define the size and position of the arc. Move the pointer and click to define the radius and position of the arc.

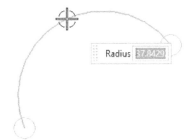

The Arc by Center and Endpoints method

This method creates an arc by defining its center, start and end. Activate the **Arc** command and click **Arc by Center and Endpoints**. Click to define the center point. Next, move the pointer and you will notice that a dotted line appears between center and the pointer. This line is the radius of the arc. Now, click to define the start point of the arc and move the pointer; you will notice that an arc is drawn from the start point. Once the arc appears the way you want, click to define its end point.

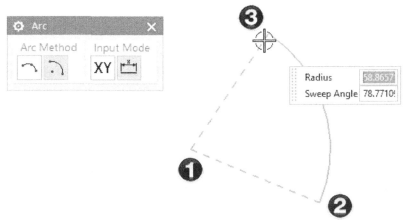

The Rectangle command

This command creates a rectangle using three different methods: **By 2 Points**, **By 3 Points**, and **From Center**.

The 2 Points method

This method creates a rectangle by defining its diagonal corners. Activate the **Rectangle** command (On the ribbon, click **Home > Direct Sketch > Rectangle**). On the **Rectangle** dialog, click **By 2 Points** and click to define the first corner. Drag the pointer and click to define the second corner. You can also type-in values in the **Width** and **Height** boxes attached to the pointer.

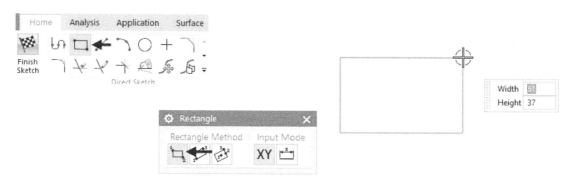

The 3 Points method

This method creates an inclined rectangle. The first two points define the width and inclination angle of the rectangle. The third point defines its height.

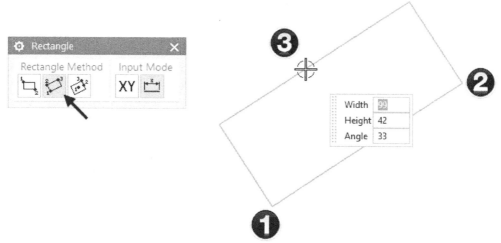

The other procedure to create a 3 Points rectangle is to specify the first corner. Next, type-in a value in the **Angle** box. Press the Tab key and type-in values in the **Width** and **Height** boxes. Click in the graphics window to create the rectangle.

The From Center command

This method creates a rectangle by defining three points: center of the rectangle, and mid and endpoints of the height. Activate the **Rectangle** command and select the **From Center** button on the **Rectangle** toolbar. Specify the centerpoint of the rectangle, move the pointer, and click to define the width and orientation angle of the rectangle. Move the pointer and click to define the height of the rectangle.

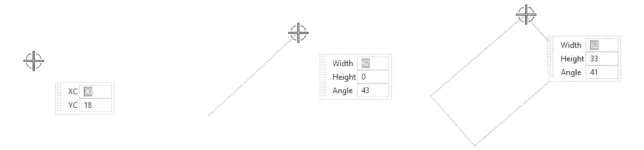

⃝ The Circle command

This command creates a circle using two methods: **Circle by Center and Diameter** and **Circle by 3 Points**.

⊙ The Circle by Center and Diameter method

This is the most common way to draw a circle. Activate the **Circle** command (click **Home > Direct Sketch > Circle** on the ribbon) and click **Circle by Center and Diameter** on the **Circle** dialog. Click to define the center point of the circle. Drag the pointer, and then click again to define the diameter of the circle.

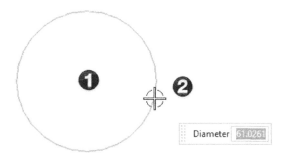

⃝ The Circle by 3 Points method

This method creates a circle by using three points. Activate the **Circle** command and click **Circle by 3 Points** ⃝ on the **Circle** dialog. Select three points from the graphics window. You can also select existing points from the sketch geometry. The first two points define the location of the circle and the third point defines its diameter.

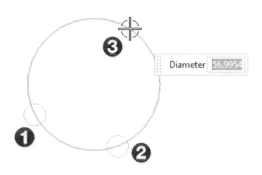

The Polygon command

This command provides a simple way to create a polygon with any number of sides. Activate this command (On the ribbon, click **Home > Direct Sketch > More Curve > Polygon**) and click in the graphics window to define the center of the polygon. As you move the pointer away from the center, you will see a preview of the polygon. To change the number of sides of the polygon, just click in the **Number of Sides** box on the dialog and enter a new number. Next, press the ENTER key to update the preview.

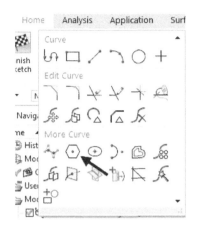
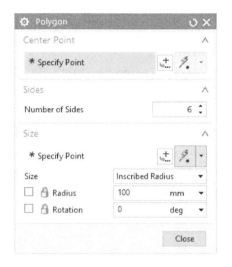

Now, you have to define the size of the polygon. On the dialog, the **Size** menu has three options to define the size of the polygon: **Inscribed Radius**, **Circumscribed Radius**, and **Side Length**. If you select **Inscribed Radius**, the pointer will be on one of the flat sides of the polygon. If you select **Circumscribed Radius**, a vertex of the polygon will be attached to the pointer. Click in the window to define the size and angle of the polygon. You can also define the size and angle of the polygon by entering values in the **Radius** and **Rotation** boxes on the dialog.

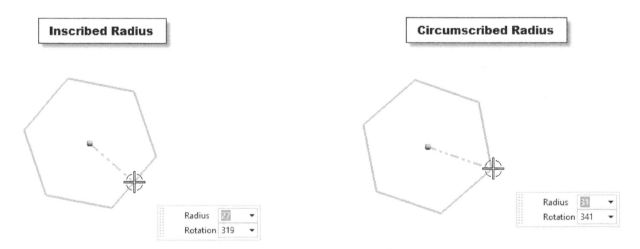

If you select **Side Length**, then you have to define the length and angle of one side a polygon. Type-in values in the **Length** and **Rotation** boxes and press Enter to create the polygon.

The Ellipse command

This command creates an ellipse using a center point, and major and minor axes. Activate this command (On the ribbon, click **Home > Direct Sketch > More Curve > Ellipse**) and click to define the center of the ellipse. On the **Ellipse** dialog, type-in values in the **Major Radius** and **Minor Radius** boxes. You can also drag the arrows attached to the ellipse to define the major and minor radius.

On the dialog, type-in a value in the **Angle** box or drag the angle modifier on the ellipse to define the rotation angle of the ellipse. On the dialog, click **OK** to create the ellipse.

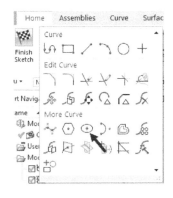

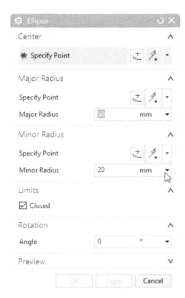

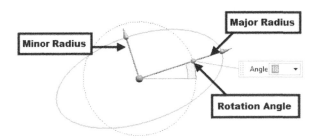

The Studio Spline command

This command creates a smooth B-spline curve using two different methods: **Through Points** and **By Poles**. B-Splines are non-uniform curves, which are used to create smooth shapes.

The **Through Points** method creates a smooth spline passing through the points you select.

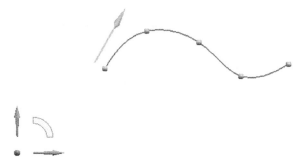

In the **By Poles** method, you will define various points called as poles. As you define the poles, grey lines are created connecting them. The spline will be drawn tangent to these lines.

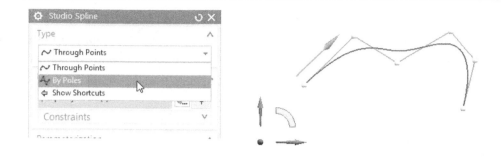

You can also use the **Close Curve** option to create a closed curve.

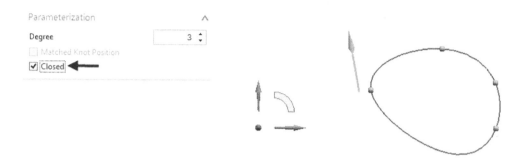

On the dialog, click **OK** to complete the studio spline.

The Rapid Dimension command

It is generally considered a good practice to ensure that every sketch you create is fully constrained before creating solid features. The term, 'fully-constrained' means that the sketch has a definite shape and size. You can fully-constrain a sketch by using dimensions and constraints. As you create sketches in NX, some dimensions are added to the sketch elements. These dimensions are called Driven dimensions and they do not have any control over the sketch geometry. If you want these dimensions to control the shape and size of the sketch geometry, you have to convert them into Driving dimensions. Driving dimensions are so named because they drive the geometry of the sketch.

You can add Driving dimensions to a sketch by using the **Rapid Dimension** command. You can use this command to add all types of dimensions such as length, angle, and diameter and so on. This command creates a dimension based on the geometry you select. For instance, to dimension a circle, activate the **Rapid Dimension** command, and then click on the circle. Next, move the pointer and click again to position the dimension; you will notice that a box pops up. Type-in a value in this box, and then press Enter to update the dimension.

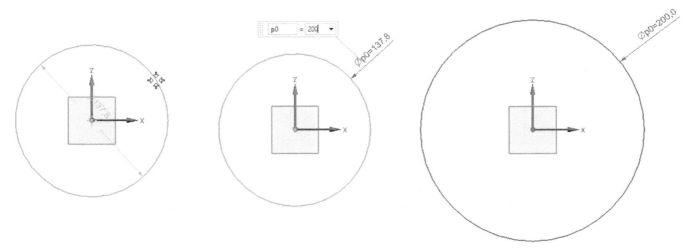

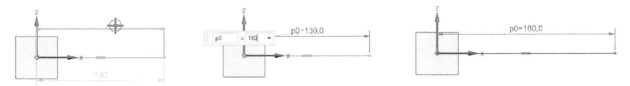

If you click a line, the **Rapid Dimension** command automatically creates a linear dimension. Click once more to position the dimension, and then type-in a value and press Enter; the dimension will be updated.

On the **Rapid Dimension** dialog, click **Close** to deactivate the **Rapid Dimension** command.

Linear Dimensions

NX allows you to create various types of linear dimensions. Select a line and click on the **Horizontal Dimension** icon on the Contextual toolbar; a horizontal dimension is created.

Select a line and click the **Vertical Dimension** icon on the Contextual toolbar; a vertical dimension will be created.

If you want the true length of the line, select the line and click the **Parallel Dimension** icon on the **Contextual Toolbar**. Next, double-click on the dimension, type-in a value in the box, and press Enter; the dimension is updated.

Angular Dimension

The procedure to create an angle dimension is similar to that of linear dimensions. Select two lines that are positioned at an angle to each other. Click the **Angular Dimension** icon on the Contextual Toolbar. Double-click on the angular dimension, type-in a value, and press Enter.

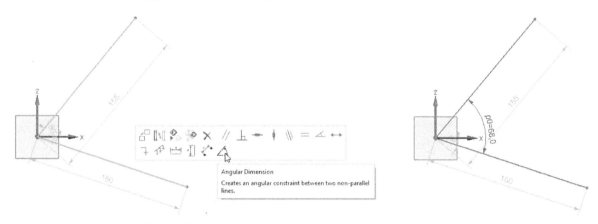

Over-constrained Sketch

When creating sketches for a solid or surface feature, NX will not allow you to over-constrain the geometry. The term 'over-constrain' means adding more dimensions than required. The following figure shows a fully constrained sketch. If you add another dimension to this sketch (e.g. diagonal dimension), the **Update Sketch** message pops up. It shows that the dimension over constrains the sketch. If, you click **OK**, all the dimensions in the sketch will become red.

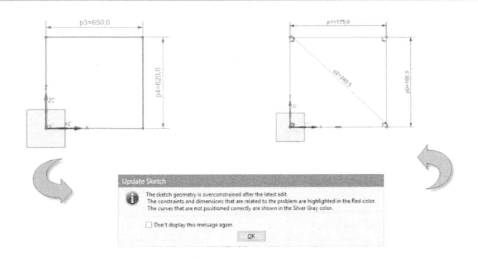

Now, you have to make one of the dimensions as a Reference dimension. Click on the diagonal dimension and select **Convert to Reference** on the contextual toolbar. The **Convert Dimension to Reference** message appears. Click **OK** to convert the dimension to reference. The reference dimension will be in brown color. Now, if you change the value of the width, the reference dimension along the diagonal updates, automatically. Also, note that the dimensions which are initially created will be driving dimensions, whereas the dimensions created after fully defining the sketch are driven dimensions.

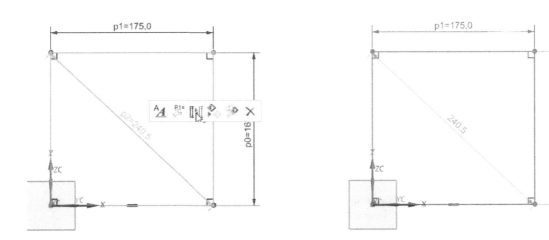

Continuous Auto Dimensioning

NX creates dimensions automatically when you draw a sketch. However, if you do not want dimensions to be created automatically, then deactivate the **Continuous Auto Dimensioning** command (on the ribbon, click **Home > Direct Sketch > More > Continuous Auto Dimensioning**).

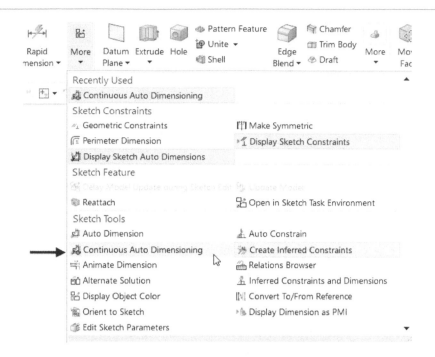

You can also hide the already created continuous auto dimensions by deactivating the **Display Sketch Auto Dimensions** button (Click **Home > Direct Sketch > More > Sketch Constraints > Display Sketch Auto Dimensions**). You can activate this button, if you want to display the auto dimensions.

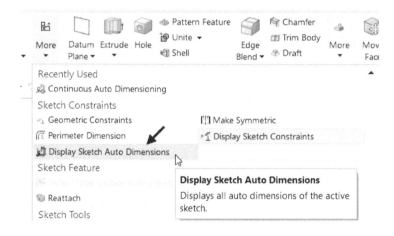

Geometric Constraints

Geometric Constraints are used to control the shape of a drawing by establishing relationships between the sketch elements. These geometric constraints can be applied using the **Geometric Constraints** command (On the ribbon, click **Home > Direct Sketch > Geometric Constraints**) or with the help of Contextual Toolbar.

Coincident

This constraint connects a point with another point. Select the points to be made coincident and click the **Coincident** icon on the Contextual Toolbar. The selected points will be connected.

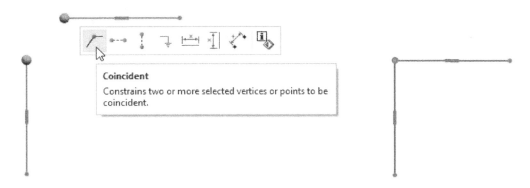

Point on Curve

This constraint makes a vertex or a point to be on a line, curve, arc, or circle. Select a curve and point, and click **Point on Curve** on the Contextual Toolbar. The point will lie on the curve or the curve extension.

Tangent

This constraint makes an arc, circle, or line tangent to another arc or circle. Select a circle, arc, or line. Select another circle, arc, or line. On the **Contextual Toolbar**, click the **Tangent** button; both the element become tangent to each other.

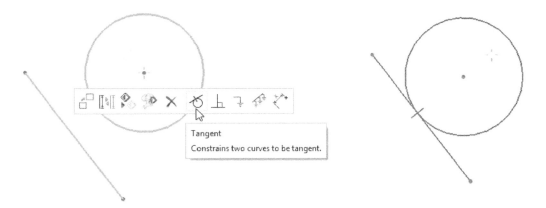

Parallel

This constraint makes two lines parallel to each other. Select two lines from the sketch and click **Parallel** on the Contextual Toolbar. The under constrained line is made parallel to the constrained line. For example, if you select a line with vertical constraint and a free to move line, the free-to-move line becomes parallel to the vertical line.

Concentric

This constraint makes the center points of arcs, circles or ellipses coincident. Select a circle or arc from the sketch. Select another circle or arc, and then click **Concentric** on the Contextual Toolbar. The first circle/arc will be concentric with the second circle/arc.

Horizontal

This constraint makes a line horizontal. Select a free-to-move line, and then click **Horizontal** on the Contextual toolbar; the line is made horizontal.

Vertical

This constraint makes a line vertical. Select an under-constrained line, and then click Vertical on the Contextual toolbar.

Equal Length

This constraint makes two lines equal in length.

Equal Radius

This constraint makes circles or arcs equal in radius.

Perpendicular

This constraint makes two lines perpendicular to each other. Select two lines from the sketch, and click the Perpendicular icon on the Contextual Toolbar. The two lines will be made perpendicular to each other.

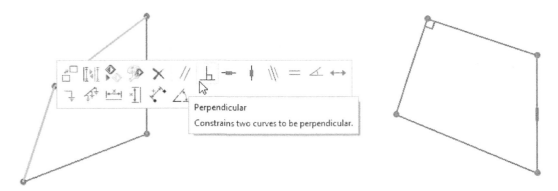

Collinear

This constraint forces a line to be collinear to another line. The lines are not required to touch each other.

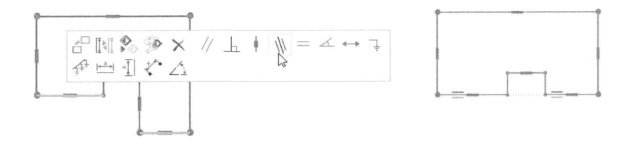

Midpoint

This constraint forces a point or vertex to be aligned with the midpoint of a line. Click on a point or vertex, and then click on a line. Select **Midpoint** from the Contextual Toolbar.

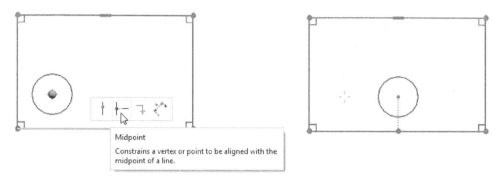

Horizontal Alignment

The **Horizontal Alignment** constraint aligns the two selected points horizontally. Select the points to align horizontally, and then click the **Horizontal Alignment** button on the Contextual Toolbar.

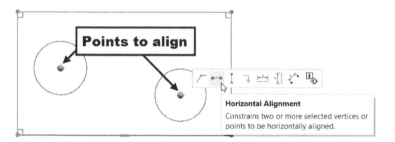
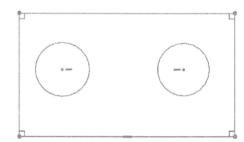

Vertical Alignment

The **Vertical Alignment** constraint aligns the two selected points vertically. Select the points to align vertically, and then click the **Vertical Alignment** button on the Contextual Toolbar.

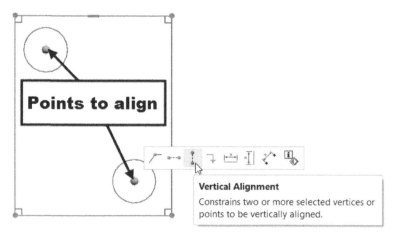
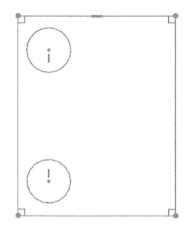

Constant Length

This constraint fixes the length of a selected line. Select a line and click the **Constant Length** button on the Contextual Toolbar.

Click and drag the sketch elements connected to the line; the size of the connected elements changes but the length of the line remains constant.

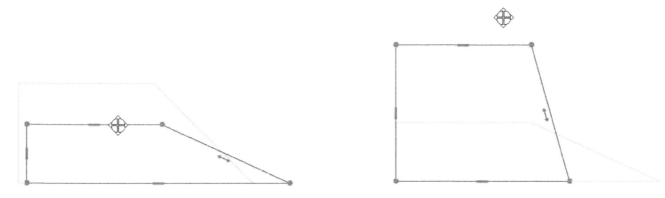

Constant Angle

This constraint fixes the angle of a selected line. Select a line and click the **Constant Angle** button on the Contextual Toolbar.

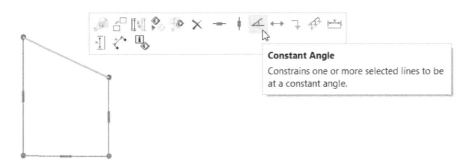

Constant Angle

Constrains one or more selected lines to be at a constant angle.

Click and drag the sketch elements connected to the line; the size of the sketch elements changes but the angle of the line remains constant.

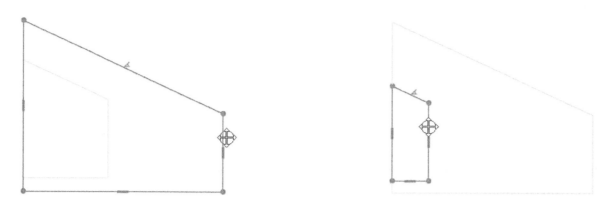

Non-uniform scale

This constraint scales a spline in horizontal or vertical direction. Select a spline and click **Non-uniform scale** on the Contextual toolbar.

Activate the **Rapid Dimension** command, and then select the two end points of the spline. Change the dimension value; the spline is scaled along the direction of the dimension.

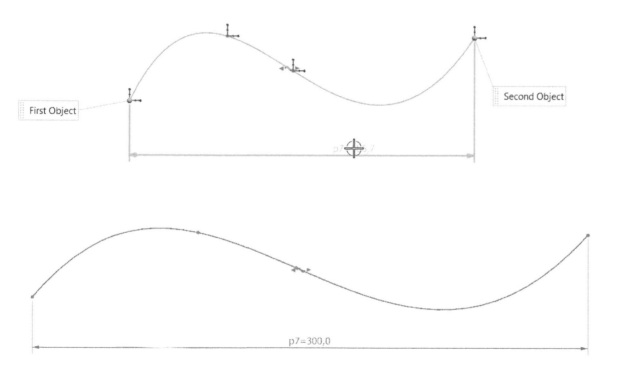

Uniform scale

This constraint scales a spline in both horizontal and vertical direction. Select a spline and click **Uniform scale** on the Contextual toolbar.

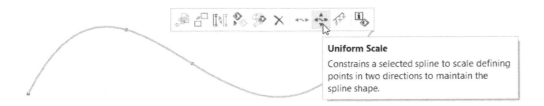

Uniform Scale

Constrains a selected spline to scale defining points in two directions to maintain the spline shape.

Activate the **Rapid Dimension** command, and then select the two end points of the spline. Change the dimension value; the spline is scaled uniformly in both horizontal and vertical directions.

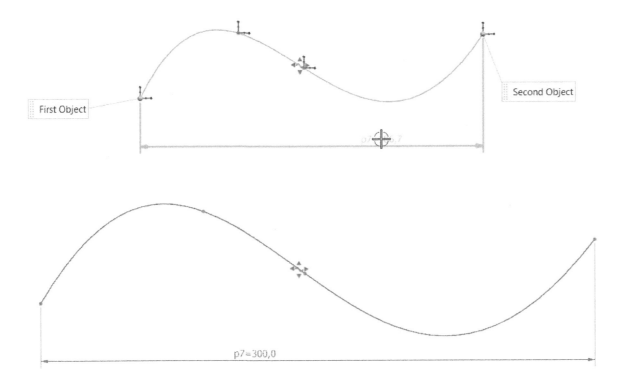

Make Symmetric

This command makes two objects symmetric about a line. The objects will have same size, position and orientation about a line. Activate this command (On the ribbon, click **Home > Direct Sketch > More > Make Symmetric**) and click on the first object. Click on the second object, and then define a symmetry centerline. The two objects will be made symmetric about the centerline. The Make Reference option on the Make Symmetric dialog converts the the centreline into a reference object.

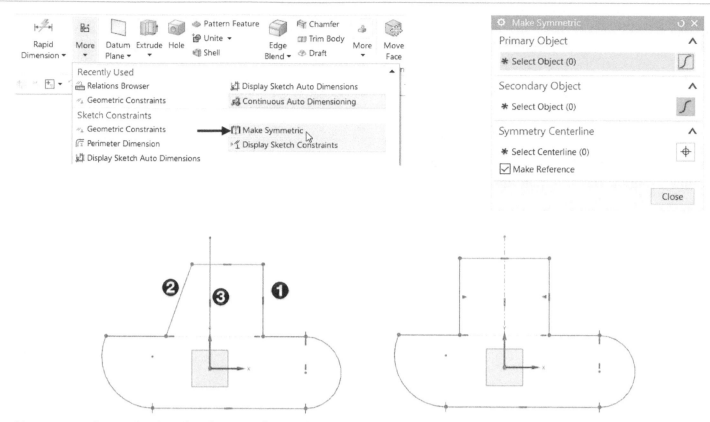

You can continue selecting the objects to be made symmetric object the previously selected centreline. Close the dialog after applying the symmetric constraint.

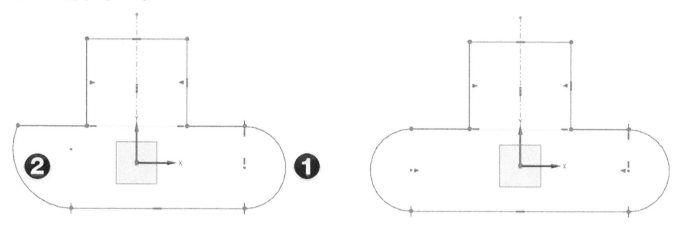

Create Inferred Constraints

Constraints can also be applied automatically by activating the **Create Inferred Constraints** command. Activate or deactivate **Create Inferred Constraints** by clicking **Direct Sketch > More > Create Inferred Constraints** on the ribbon. With this command turned on, constraints are applied automatically when the sketch elements are created. You can define which constraints to apply automatically by using the **Inferred Constraints and Dimensions** dialog. On the ribbon, click **Home > Direct Sketch > More > Inferred Constraints and Dimensions**. On the **Inferred Constraints and Dimensions** dialog, select the constraints to be created while sketching elements.

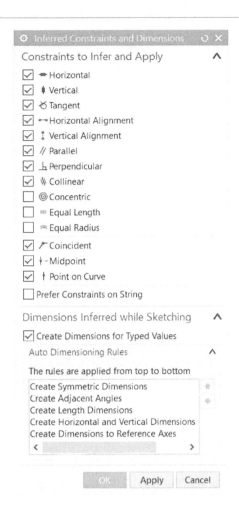

Under the **Dimensions Inferred while Sketching** section, define the order in which the automatic dimensions are applied. Check the **Create Dimensions for Type Values** to create driving dimensions, when you create sketches by typing exact values. Click **OK** to close the dialog.

By default, you cannot create the inferred alignment constraints in NX 12. In order to do so, you need to check the **Create Alignment Constraints** option in the **Customer Defaults** dialog. To open this dialog, click **File > Utilities > Customer Defaults**. On the **Customer Defaults** dialog, click **Sketch > Inferred Constraints and Dimensions** in the tree view. Next click the **Constraints** tab and check the **Create Alignment Constraints** option. Click **OK** on the **Customer Defaults** dialog; the **Customer Defaults** message box pops up showing that the changes to customer defaults options do not take effect until you have restarted your NX session. Click **OK** on the **Customer Defaults** message box, and then restart the NX application. Now, you can start creating the alignment constraints by inferring.

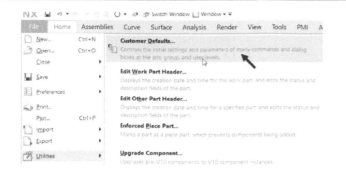

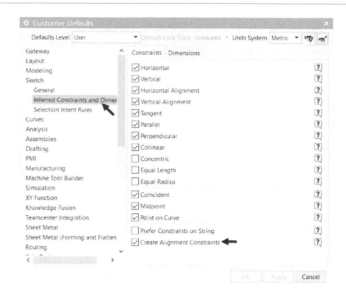

Display Sketch Constraints

As constraints are created, they can be viewed using the **Display Sketch Constraints** button (On the ribbon, click **Home > Direct Sketch > More > Display Sketch Constraints**). When dealing with complicated sketches involving numerous constraints, you can deactivate this button to turn off the display of all constraints.

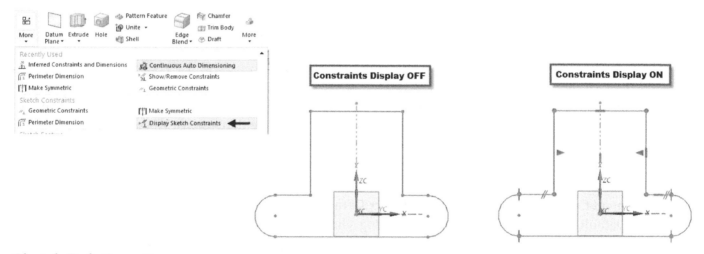

Sketch Relations Browser

The **Sketch Relations Browser** dialog helps you to view all the constraints in the sketch, their status, and elements associated with them. Activate the **Sketch Relations Browser** (On the ribbon, click **Home > Direct Sketch > More > Relations Browser**). On the **Sketch Relations Browser** dialog, select **Scope > All in Active Sketch** to view all the constraints and dimensions in the active sketch. Next, select **Top-level Node Objects > Curves** to display all the curves available in the sketch in the form of nodes. Next, expand each curve node to view all the constraints related to it. The **Status** column displays the status of each curve: **Fully Constrained** ●,
Partially Constrained ◑, or **Over Constrained** ⊗. Right click on the curve node and select **Fit View to Selection**; the select curve is zoomed in the graphics window.

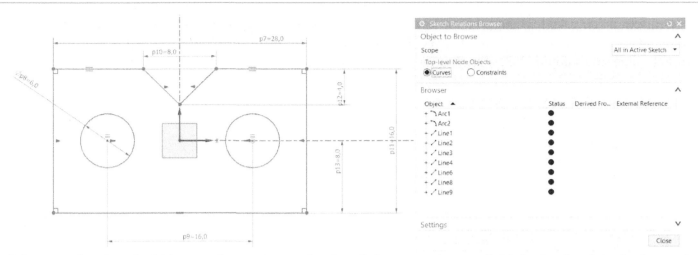

Select **Top-level Node Objects > Constraints** to display all the constraints available in the sketch in the form of nodes. Next, expand each constraint node to view the curves related to it. Right click on a constraint and notice a shortcut menu with different options. These options are self-explanatory.

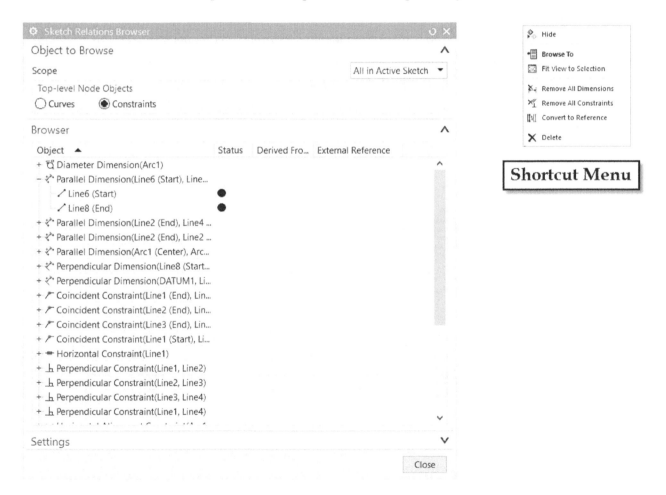

Close the **Sketch Relations Browser** dialog.

Alternate Solution

This command gives alternate solutions for different dimensions and constraints applied between sketch elements.

For example, if you want to change the side of the linear dimension shown in figure, activate the **Alternate Solution** command (On the ribbon, click **Home > Direct Sketch > More > Alternate Solution**). Click on the linear dimension to see the alternate solution. Likewise, you can see alternate solutions for geometric constraints.

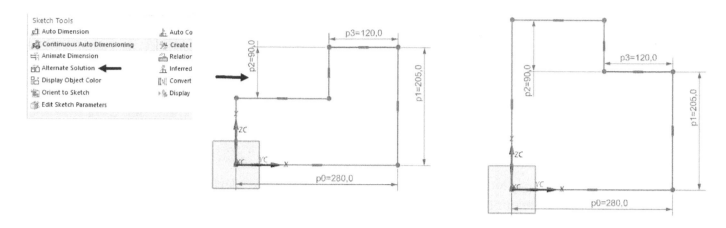

Convert to Reference

This command converts a sketch element into a reference element. Reference elements support you to create a sketch of desired shape and size. To convert a sketch element to the reference element, click on it and select **Convert to Reference** on the contextual toolbar. You can also convert it back to a sketch element by clicking on it and selecting **Convert to active**.

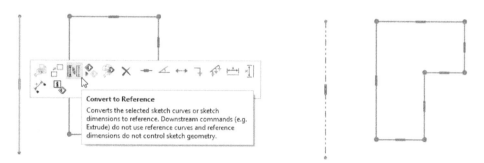

The Fillet command

This command rounds a sharp corner created by intersection of two lines, arcs, circles, and rectangle or polygon vertices. Activate this command (On the ribbon, click **Home > Direct Sketch > Fillet**) and select the elements' ends to be filleted. Type-in a radius value in the **Radius** box and press Enter. The elements to be filleted are not required to touch each other.

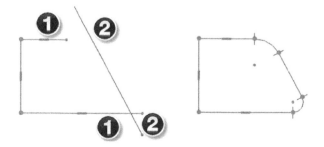

You can also drag the pointer across the elements to apply a fillet to them.

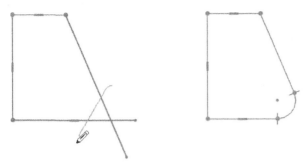

By default, the elements are automatically trimmed or extended to meet the end of the new fillet radius. You can use the **Untrim** ⌐ option on the dialog, if you do not want to trim or extend the elements as necessary. Click the **Untrim** option on the dialog, and then select the elements forming a corner. Move the pointer, and then click to create the fillet. Notice that the elements are not trimmed at the corner.

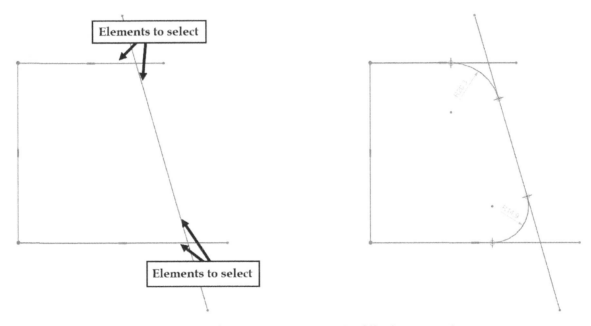

Use the **Delete Third Curve** option, if you want to create the fillet between three curves.

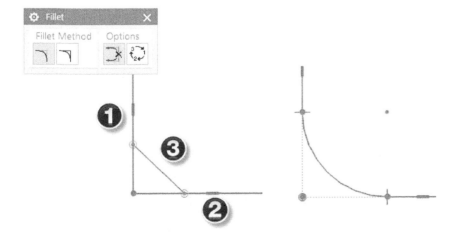

Use the **Create Alternate Fillet** option, if you want an alternate solution.

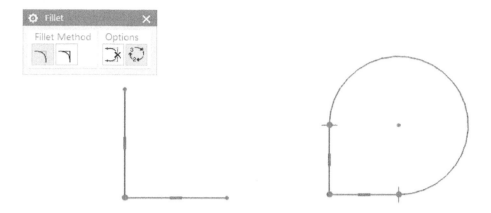

The Chamfer command

This command replaces a sharp corner with an angled line. Activate this command (On the ribbon, click **Home > Direct Sketch > Chamfer**) and select the select the elements' ends to be chamfered. Type-in the chamfer angle in the **Distance** box and press Enter.

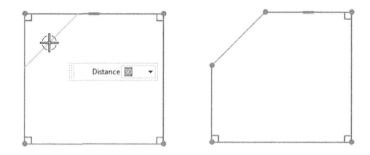

The Quick Extend command

This command extends elements such as lines, arcs, and curves until they intersect another element called the boundary edge. Activate this command (On the ribbon, click **Home > Direct Sketch > Quick Extend**) and click on the element to extend. It will extend up to the next element.

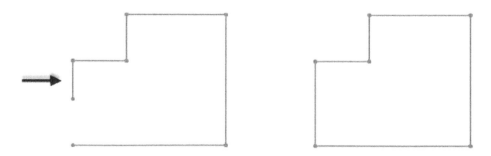

The Quick Trim command

This command trims the end of an element back to the intersection of another element. Activate this command (On the ribbon, click **Home > Direct Sketch > Quick Trim**) and click on the element or elements to trim. You can also drag the pointer across the elements to trim.

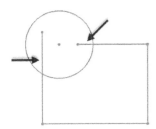 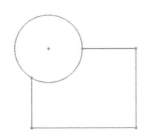 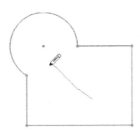

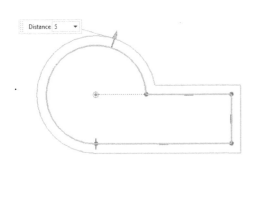 **The Make Corner command**

This command trims and extends elements to form a corner. Activate this command (On the ribbon, click **Home > Direct Sketch > Make Corner**) and select two intersecting elements. The elements will be trimmed and extended to form a closed corner.

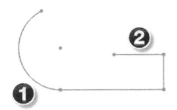 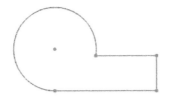

The Offset Curve command

This command creates a parallel copy of a selected element or chain of elements. Activate this command (On the ribbon click **Home > Direct Sketch > Offset Curve**) and select an element or chain of elements to offset. After selecting the element(s), type-in a value in the **Distance** box. On the **Offset Curve** dialog, click the **Reverse Direction** button to reverse the side of the offset. Check the **Symmetric Offset** option to create a parallel copy on both sides. Set the **Cap Options** to **Arc Cap** to create arcs at the corners. On the dialog, click **OK**. The parallel copy of the elements will be created.

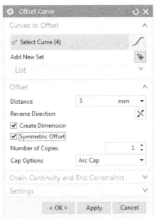 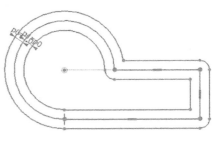

Examples

Example 1 (Millimeters)

In this example, you will draw the sketch shown below.

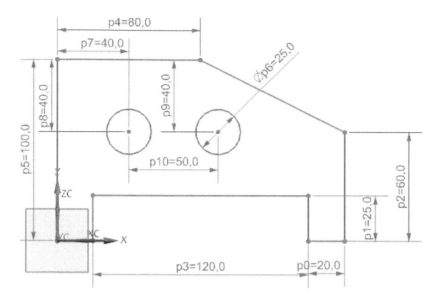

1. Start **NX 12** by clicking the **NX 12.0** icon on your desktop.
2. On the ribbon, click **New**.
3. On the **New** dialog, set **Units** to **Millimeters**. Click **Model**, and then click **OK**. A new NX file starts in the **Modeling** mode.
4. To start a new sketch, click **Home > Direct Sketch > Sketch** on the ribbon.
5. On the Datum Coordinate System, click on the XZ plane.

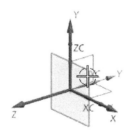

6. On the **Create Sketch** dialog, click **OK** to start the sketch.
7. On the ribbon, click **Home > Direct Sketch > Profile**.
8. Click on the origin point to define the first point of the line.
9. Create a closed loop by selecting points, as shown below.

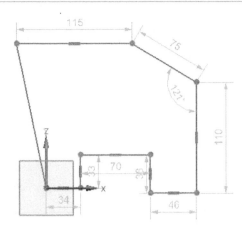

10. Click on the two horizontal lines at the bottom. Select **Collinear** from the context toolbar; the selected lines become collinear.

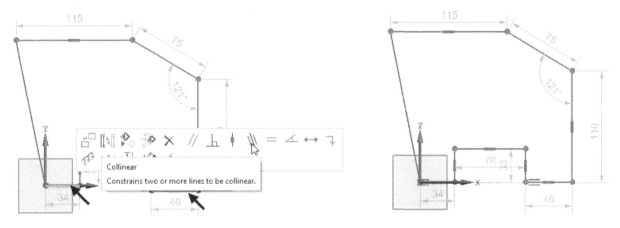

11. Click on the two horizontal lines at the bottom. Select **Equal Length** from the context toolbar; they become equal in length.

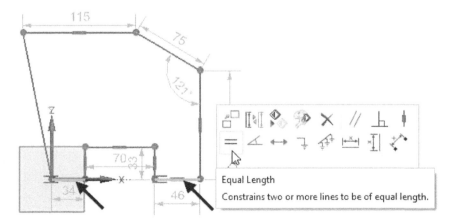

12. Select the small vertical lines, and then click the **Equal Length** icon to make their lengths equal.

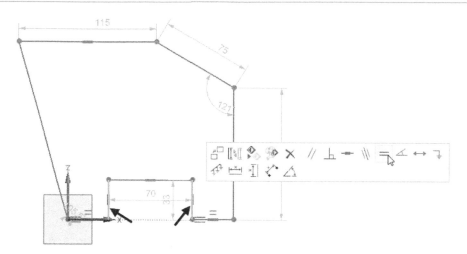

13. Select the inclined line on the left side and click the **Vertical** icon.

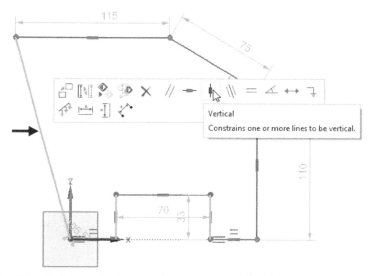

14. Double-click on the linear dimension of the lower horizontal line. Type-in **20** in the dimension box and press Enter.

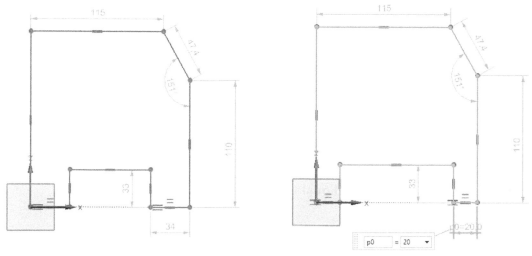

15. Double-click on the linear dimension of the small vertical line. Type-in **25** in the dimension box and press Enter.

16. Likewise, change the dimension values of the right vertical line to 60. Close the **Linear Dimension** dialog.

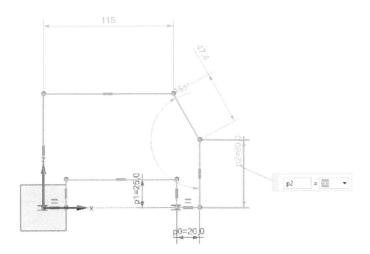

17. On the ribbon, click **Home > Direct Sketch > Rapid Dimension**. On the **Rapid Dimension** dialog, set **Method** to **Inferred**.
18. Click on the top horizontal line and position the dimension.
19. Type-in 80 in dimension box and press Enter.
20. Likewise, apply a linear dimension to the bottom horizontal and left vertical lines. The dimension value are 120 and 100, respectively.

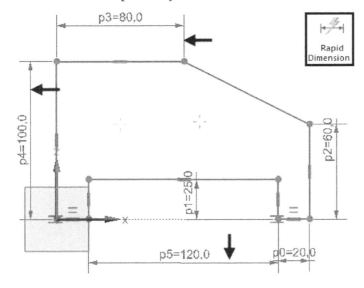

21. On the ribbon, click **Home > Direct Sketch > Circle**. Click inside the sketch region to define the center point of the circle. Move the pointer and click to define the diameter. Likewise, create another circle.

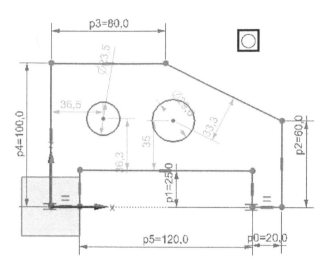

22. Select the two circles and click **Equal Radius** on the Context Toolbar. The diameters of the circles will become equal.

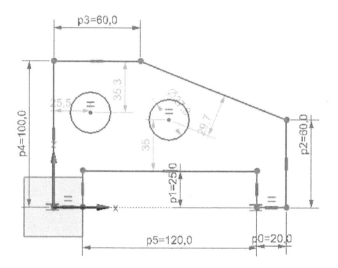

23. Create other dimensions between the circles and the adjacent lines, as shown below.

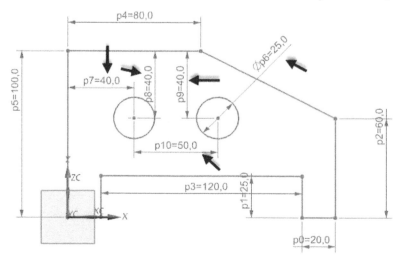

24. On the ribbon, click **Home > Direct Sketch > Finish Sketch**.

25. Click the **Save** icon on the **Quick Access Toolbar**.

26. On the **Name Parts** dialog, type-in **C2_example1** in the **Name** box and click the folder icon. Define the location and file name, and then click **OK** twice to save the part file.
27. Click **Close Window** on the top right corner to close the part file.

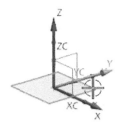

Example 2 (Inches)

In this example, you will draw the sketch shown below.

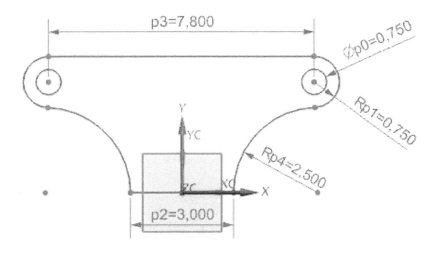

1. Start **NX 12** by clicking the **NX 12** icon on your desktop.
2. On the **Quick Access Toolbar**, click the **New** icon.
3. On the **New** dialog, set the **Units** to **Inches** and select the **Model** template. Click **OK** to start a new part file.
4. To start a new sketch, click **Home > Direct Sketch > Sketch** on the ribbon.
5. On the Datum Coordinate System, click on the XY Plane. Click **OK** to start the sketch.

6. Activate the **Profile** command (On the ribbon, click **Home > Direct Sketch > Profile**).

7. Click in the second quadrant of the coordinate system to define the start point of the profile. Drag the pointer horizontally and click to define the endpoint.

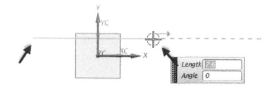

8. On the **Profile** dialog, click the **Arc** icon.
9. Take the pointer to the endpoint of the line and move it upwards right. Click to create the arc.

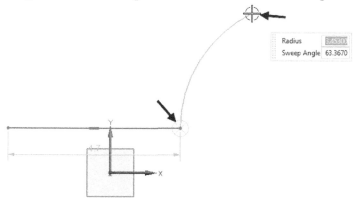

10. Again, click the **Arc** icon on the dialog.
11. Take the pointer to the endpoint of the arc and move it upwards right.
12. Move the pointer toward left and click when a vertical dotted line appears, as shown below.

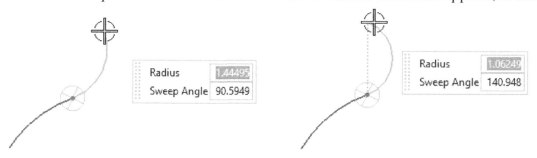

13. Move the pointer toward left and click to create a horizontal line.
14. Click the **Arc** icon on the dialog. Take the pointer to the endpoint of the arc and move it downward left.
15. Move the pointer toward right and click when a vertical dotted line appears, as shown below.

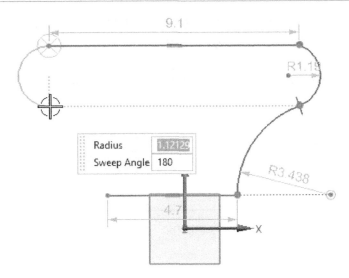

16. Click the **Arc** icon on the dialog. Move the pointer toward downward right and click on the origin to close the sketch.

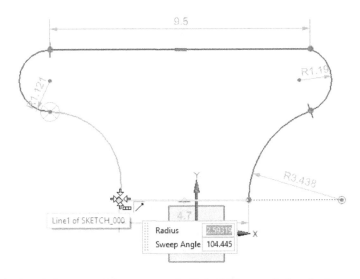

17. Click the right mouse button and click **OK** to end the chain.
18. Activate the **Circle** command and draw a circle inside the loop.
19. Click on the circle and the small arc. Click **Concentric** on the Context Toolbar. The circle and arc are made concentric.

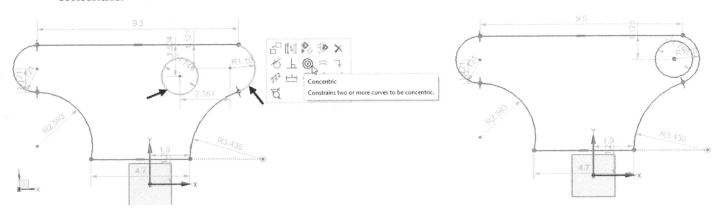

20. Likewise, create another circle concentric to the small arc located on the left side.
21. On the ribbon, click **Home > Direct Sketch > More > Make Symmetric**.
22. Click on the large arcs on both sides of the Y-axis.
23. Click on the Y-axis located at the center. The arcs are made symmetric about the Y-axis.
24. Likewise, make the small arcs and circles symmetric about the Y-axis.

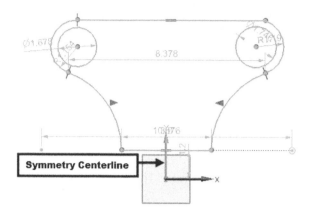

25. Apply the **Equal Radius** constraint between the two circles.
26. Apply the **Collinear** constraint between the bottom horizontal line and the X-axis.

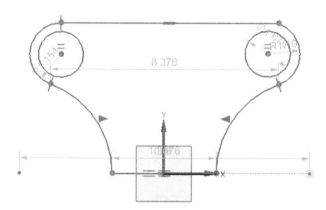

27. Activate the **Rapid Dimension** command and apply dimensions to the sketch in the sequence, as shown below.

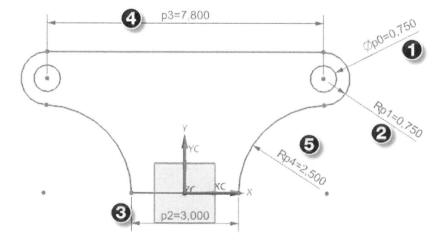

28. On the top border bar, click the **Fit** icon to fit the drawing in the graphics window.
29. Click **Finish Sketch** on the ribbon to complete the sketch.
30. To save the file, click **File > Save > Save**.
28. On the **Name Parts** dialog, type-in **C2_example2** in the **Name** box and click the folder symbol. Define the location, file name, and click **OK** twice to save the part file.
31. To close the file, click **File > Close > All Parts**.

Questions

1. What is the procedure to create sketches in the Part mode?
2. List any two sketch constraints in NX.
3. Which command creates dimensions automatically while creating a sketch?
4. Describe the method to create an ellipse.
5. How do you define the shape and size of a sketch?
6. How do you create a tangent arc using the **Profile** command?
7. Which command is used to apply different types of dimensions to a sketch?
8. List any two methods to create circles.
9. How do you create a fillet with an alternate solution?

Exercises

Exercise 1

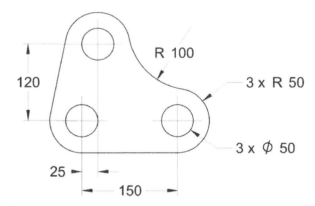

Exercise 2

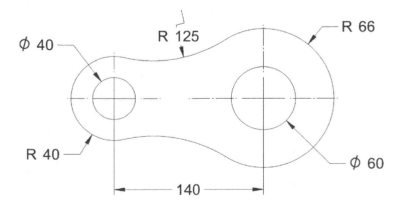

Exercise 3 (Inches)

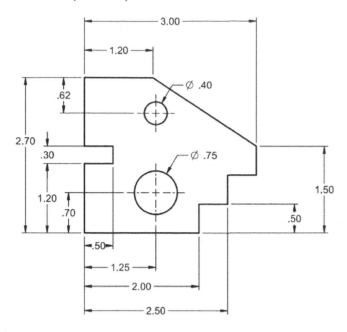

Chapter 3: Extrude and Revolve Features

Extrude and revolve features are used to create basic and simple parts. Most of the times, they form the base for complex parts as well. These features are easy to create and require a single sketch. Now, you will learn the commands to create these features.

The topics covered in this chapter are:

- *Constructing Extrude and Revolve features in the Modeling template*
- *Creating Reference Planes*
- *Additional Options in the Extrude and Revolve commands*

Extrude Features

Extrude is the process of taking a two-dimensional profile and converting it into 3D by giving it some thickness. A simple example of this would be taking a circle and converting it into a cylinder. Once you have created a sketch profile or profiles you want to *Extrude*, activate the **Extrude** command (On the ribbon click **Home > Feature > Extrude**). Click on the sketch profile to add thickness to the sketch. Type-in a value in the **End** box and press Enter to create the *Extrude* feature.

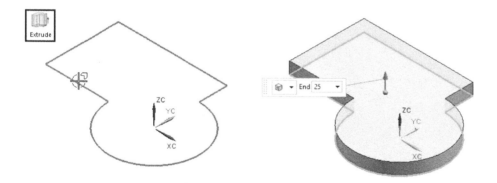

You can use the **Symmetric Value** option on the dialog to add equal thickness on both sides of the sketch.

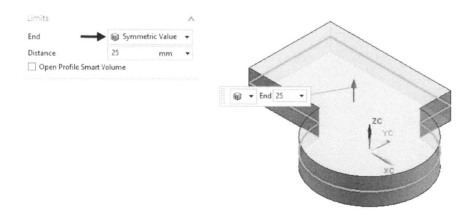

On the dialog, click **OK** to complete the *Extrude* feature.

Revolve Features

Revolve is the process of taking a two-dimensional profile and revolving it about a centerline to create a 3D geometry (shapes that are axially symmetric). While creating a sketch for the *Revolve* feature, it is important to think about the cross-sectional shape that will define the 3D geometry once it is revolved about an axis. For instance, the following geometry has a hole in the center. This could be created with a separate *Cut* or *Hole* feature. But in order to make that hole part of the *Revolve* feature, you need to sketch the axis of revolution using a reference line so that it leaves a space between the profile and the axis. By default, the reference elements of the sketch are not displayed in the Modeling window. To display the reference line, click the right mouse button on the sketch in the Part Navigator, and then select **Settings** 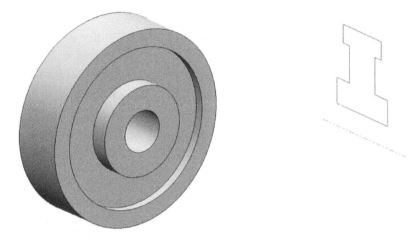. On the **Sketch Settings** dialog, check the **Display Reference Curves** option in the **Inactive Sketch** section. Next, click **OK** to display the reference line.

After completing the sketch, activate the **Revolve** command (On the ribbon, click **Home > Feature > Design Feature Drop-down > Revolve**). Click on the sketch to define the section of the *Revolve* feature. On the dialog, click **Specify Vector** under the **Axis** section. Click on a line to define the axis of revolution. The sketch will be revolved by full 360 degrees. If you want to enter an angle of revolution, type-in a value in the **End** box attached to the preview and press Enter. On the dialog, click **OK** to complete the *Revolve* feature.

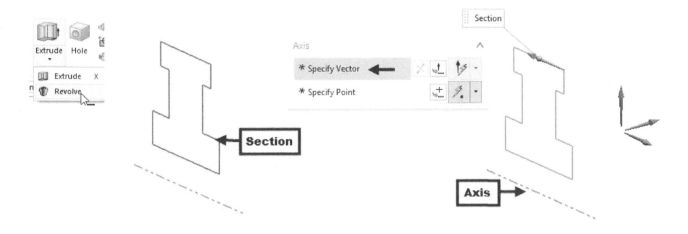

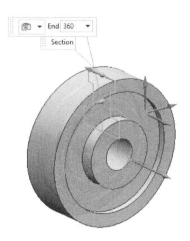

Datum Planes

Each time you start a new part file, NX creates default Datum planes along with the Datum coordinate system, automatically. Planes and coordinate system make up a specific type of features in NX, known as Datum features. These features act as supports to your 3D geometry. In addition to the default Datum features, you can create your own additional planes and coordinate systems too. Until now, you have known how to create sketches on any of the default datum planes. If you want to create sketches and geometry at locations other than default datum planes, you can create new datum planes manually. You can do so by using the **Datum Plane** command.

At Distance

This method creates a datum plane, which will be parallel to a face or another plane. Activate the **Datum Plane** command (click **Home > Feature > Datum Plane** on the ribbon). On the **Datum Plane** dialog, set the **Type** to **At Distance** and select a flat face. Click and drag the arrow that appears on the plane (or) type-in a value in the **Distance** box and press Enter. On the dialog, click the **Reverse Direction** button to flip the plane to other side of the model face. If you want to create more than one parallel plane, then type-in a value in the **Number of Planes** box on the dialog.

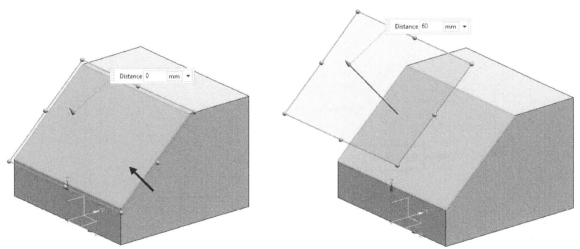

On the dialog, click **OK** to create the **At Distance** plane.

At Angle

This method creates a plane, which will be positioned at an angle to a face or plane. Activate the **Datum Plane** command and select **Type > At Angle** on the **Datum Plane** dialog. Select a flat face or plane. Next, click on an edge of the part geometry to define the rotation axis. Type-in a value in the **Angle** box and press Enter.

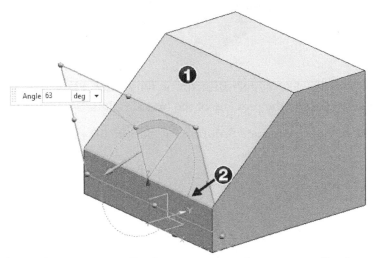

On the dialog, select **Angle Option > Perpendicular** to create a plane perpendicular to the selected face. Select **Angle Option > Parallel** to create a plane parallel to the selected face.

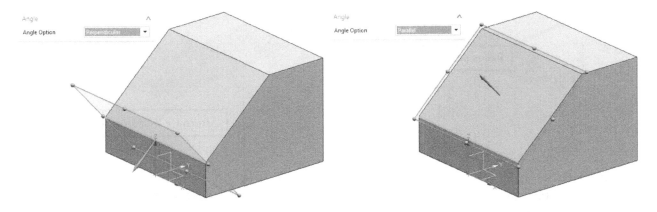

Bisector

This method creates a plane, which lies at the midway between two selected faces. You can also create a plane passing through the intersection point of the two selected planes or faces. Activate the **Datum Plane** command and select **Type > Bisector** on the **Datum Plane** dialog. Click on two faces of the model geometry which are parallel to each other. Click **OK** to create the bisector plane.

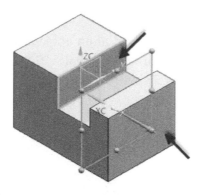

Activate the **Datum Plane** command select **Type > Bisector** on the **Datum Plane** dialog. Select two intersecting faces or plane from the graphics window; the preview of the bisector plane appears. On the dialog, expand the

Plane Orientation section and click the **Alternate Solution** button; the plane orientation changes. Click to create the bisector plane.

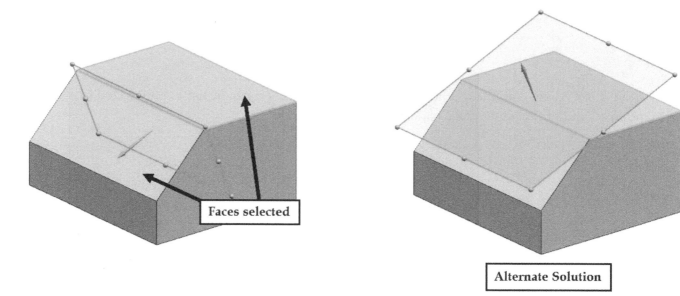

Faces selected

Alternate Solution

Curves and Points

This method creates a datum plane passing through three points. Activate the **Datum Plane** and select **Type > Curves and Points** on the **Datum Plane** dialog. Select three points from the model geometry. A plane will be placed passing through these points.

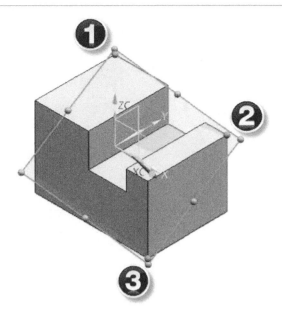

Tangent

This option creates a plane tangent to a curved face. On the **Datum Plane** dialog, click **Type > Tangent** and select a curved face. A plane tangent to the selected face appears.

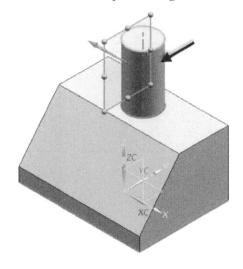

On Curve

This method creates a datum plane, which will be normal (perpendicular) to a line, curve, or edge. On the **Datum Plane** dialog, click **Type > On Curve** and select an edge, line, curve, arc, or circle. Next, select an option from tnhe **Location** drop-down (For example: **Arc Length**). Drag the pointer and click on a point to define the location of the plane (or) type-in a value in the **Arc Length** box and press Enter.

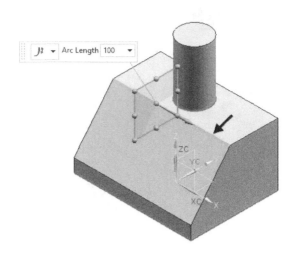

Datum CSYS

This command creates a new coordinate system in addition to the default one. Activate this command (click **Home > Feature > Datum/Point Drop-down > Datum CSYS** on the ribbon). The Dynamic WCS appears on the default coordinate system. Click on the Translate handle (arrow) and drag the pointer. Click on a point to position the coordinate system.

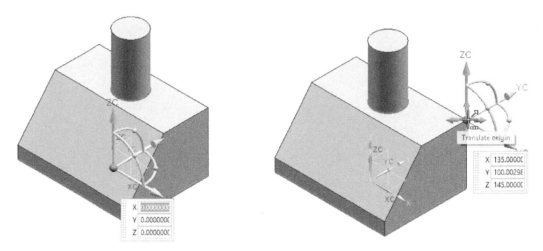

Drag the XC, YC, or ZC handles to translate the Dynamic WCS along X, Y, or Z-axis, respectively. Drag the small dots on the coordinate system to rotate it about X, Y, or Z-axis, respectively. On the dialog, click **OK** to create a new datum coordinate system.

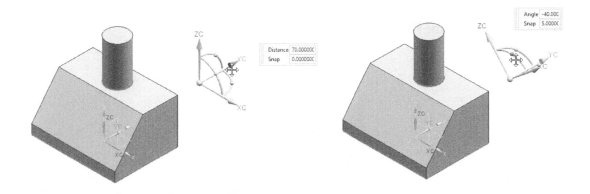

Additional options of the Extrude command

The **Extrude** command has some additional options to create a 3D geometry, complex features, and so on.

Boolean

When you extrude a sketch, the **Boolean** options determine whether the material is added, subtracted or intersected from an existing solid body.

Inferred

This option adds or removes material from the part geometry. If you extrude a sketch into the part geometry, the material will be removed. Likewise, if you extrude the sketch in the direction away from the part geometry, the material will be added.

Unite

This option adds material to the geometry.

Subtract

This option removes material from the geometry.

Intersect

This option creates a solid body containing the volume shared by two separate bodies.

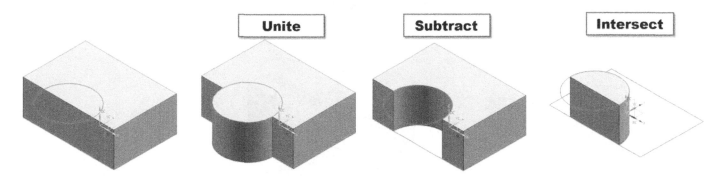

None

This option creates a separate solid body. This will be helpful while creating multi-body parts.

Limits

On the **Extrude** dialog, the **Limits** section has various options to define the start and end limits of the *Extrude* feature. These options are **Value, Symmetric Value, Until Next, Until Selected, Until Extended,** and **Through All**.

The **Until Next** option extrudes the sketch through the face next to the sketch plane.

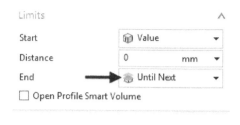

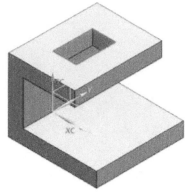

The **Until Selected** option extrudes the sketch up to a selected face. Ensure that the sketch will lie on the selected face, if projected.

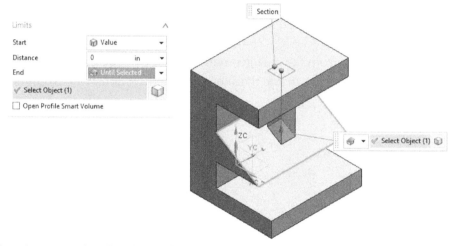

The **Until Extended** option extrudes the sketch from the sketch plane up to the extended portion of the selected face.

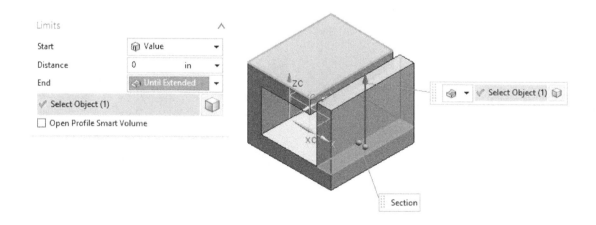

The **Through All** option extrudes the sketch throughout the 3D geometry.

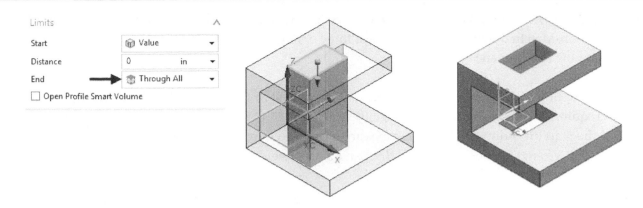

Open Profile Smart Volume

This option creates an *Extrude* feature using an open profile. It extends the profile to meet the adjacent edges. Activate the **Extrude** command, and then click on the open profile. On the dialog, select **Limits > Open Profile Smart Volume** and set the **Boolean** type to **Inferred.** Under the **Direction** section, click the **Reverse Direction** button.

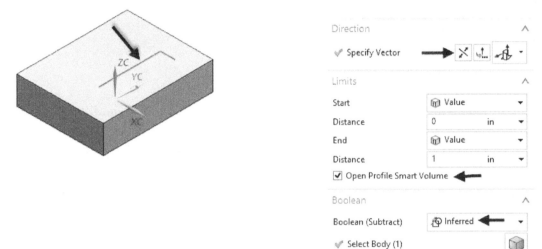

A preview of the *Extrude* feature appears. Double-click on the horizontal arrow to change the material side. On the dialog, type-in a value in the **End Distance** box and press Enter.

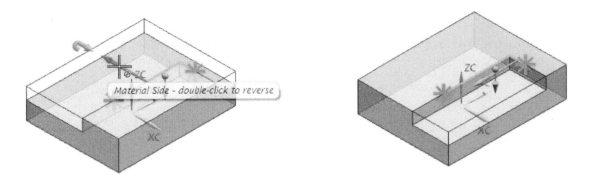

Draft options

The **Draft** options will help you to apply draft to the extrusion. There are five draft options under the **Draft** section of the **Extrude** dialog: **From Start Limit**, **From Section**, **From Section-Asymmetric Angle**, **From Section-Symmetric Angle**, and **From Section-Matched Ends**. Note that the last three options are available only when you extrude the sketch on both sides of the sketch plane.

The **From Start Limit** option applies a draft to the extrusion from the start limit. Note that the sketch plane and Start Limit are not required to be same. You can change the start limit of the extrusion by entering a value in the Distance box below the Start drop-down. The draft angle can be changed dynamically using the arrow that appears on the geometry. A positive angle applies an inward draft and a negative angle applies an outward draft.

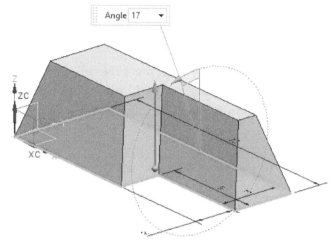

The **From Section** option applies a draft to the extrusion from the sketch plane. In addition, different draft angles can be applied to multiple faces of the extrusion. Select **Angle Option > Multiple** and you will notice that multiple arrows appear on the side faces of the extrusion. Different angles can be applied dynamically using these arrows.

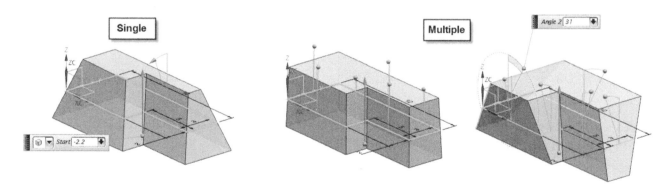

The **From Section-Asymmetric Angle** option applies different draft angles to either sides of the sketch plane.

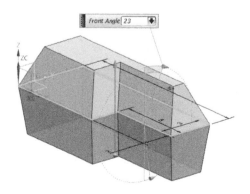

The **From Section-Symmetric Angle** option applies a draft symmetrically in both sides of a sketch plane.

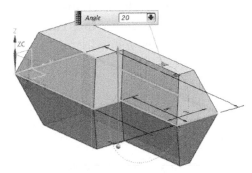

The **From Section-Matched Ends** option applies a draft to both sides of the extrusion such that the top and bottom faces match each other.

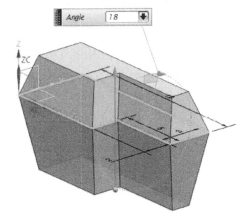

Offset options

The **Offset** options will help you add thickness to the selected sketch. There are three offset options: **Single-Sided**, **Two-Sided**, and **Symmetric**. These three types of offsets are explained in the images shown next.

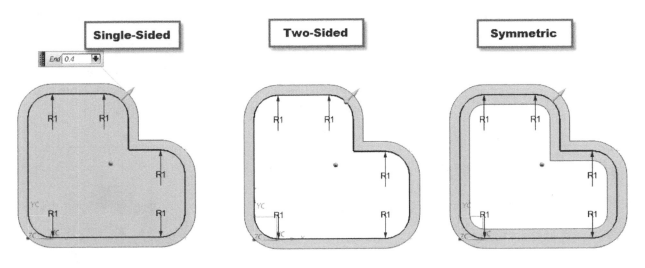

View Modification commands

The model display in the graphics window can be determined using various view modification commands. Most of these commands are located on **Top Border Bar** or on the **View** tab on the ribbon. These commands can also be accessed from contextual menu, shortcut menu, or box menu in the graphics window. The following are some of the main view modification commands:

.

⬚	**Fit**	The model will be fitted in the current size of the graphics window so that it will be visible completely.
⬚	**Pan**	Activate this command and press the left mouse button. Drag the pointer to move the model view on the plane parallel to screen.
 ↻	**Rotate**	Activate this command and press the left mouse button. Drag the pointer to rotate the model view. You can select the model edges or curves to rotate about them. You can also type-in a rotation angle.
⬚	**Zoom**	Activate this command and drag a rectangle. The contents inside the rectangle will be zoomed.
 ⬚	**Perspective**	This command allows you to change between the perspective and parallel projection of the model.
⬚	**Fit View to Selection**	This command fits the selected objects in the graphics window.
 ⬚ Zoom 1.0000 Zoom	**Zoom Scale**	Type-in a value in this box and press Enter; the model view is zoomed in or out based on the value that you entered. Note that this box is available only on the **View** tab of the ribbon.
⬚	**Shaded with Edges**	This represents the model with shades along with visible edges. 

	Shaded	This represents the model with shades without visible edges.	
	Wireframe with Hidden edges	This represents the model in wireframe. The hidden edges are not shown.	
	Wireframe with Dim edges	This represents the model in wireframe. The hidden edges are greyed out.	
	Static Wireframe	This represents the model in wireframe along with the hidden edges.	
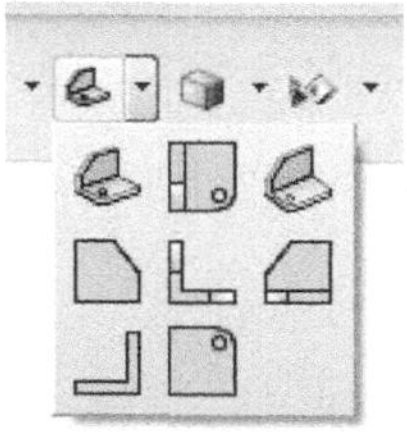	**Orient View Drop-down**	Use this drop-down to change the model view orientation.	

Examples

Example 1 (Millimeters)
In this example, you will create the part shown below.

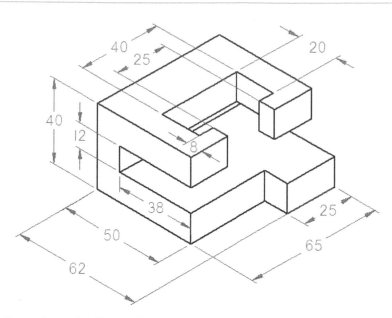

Creating the Base Feature

1. Start **NX 12**.
2. On the ribbon, click **Home > New**.
3. On the **New** dialog, select **Units > Millimeters**. Click the **Model** template, and then click **OK**.
4. On the ribbon, click **Home > Direct Sketch > Sketch**.
5. On the Datum coordinate system, click the XZ plane. Click **OK** on the **Create Sketch** dialog.

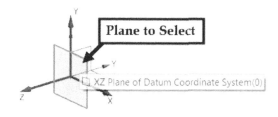

6. On the ribbon, click **Home > Direct Sketch > Rectangle**.
7. Click the origin point to define the first corner of the rectangle.
8. Move the pointer toward top right corner and click to define the second corner.
9. On the ribbon, click **Home > Direct Sketch > Rapid Dimension.**
10. Select the horizontal line of the rectangle, move the pointer upward, and then click.
11. Type 50 in the dimension box and press Enter.
12. Select the vertical line of the rectangle, move the pointer horizontally, and then click to position the dimension.
13. Type 40 in the dimension box and press Enter.
14. Click **Close** on the **Rapid Dimension** dialog.

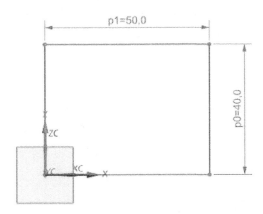

15. On the ribbon, click **Home > Direct Sketch > Finish Sketch**.
16. To change the view orientation, click on the **Orient view** drop-down available on the Top Border Bar, and then select **Isometric**.

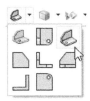

17. On the ribbon, click **Home > Feature > Extrude**. Click on the sketch.
18. On the **Extrude** dialog, under the **Limits** section, click **Start > Symmetric Value**.
19. On the dialog, type-in **32.5** in the **Distance** box and press Enter. Click **OK** on the **Extrude** dialog to complete the *Extrude* feature.

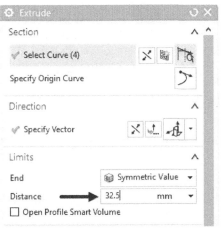
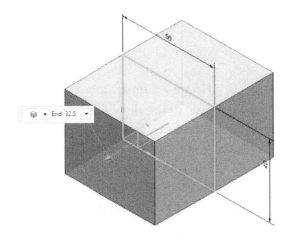

Creating the Cut throughout the body

1. Activate the **Extrude** command and click on the front face of the part geometry. Make sure that you click near the lower left corner. This defines sketch origin at the lower left corner.

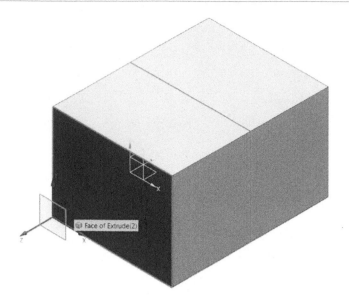

2. On the ribbon, click **Home > Curve > Rectangle**.
3. Click on the upper portion of the right vertical edge.
4. Move the pointer diagonally toward bottom-left, and then click.

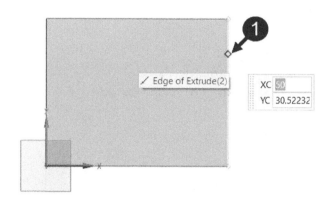
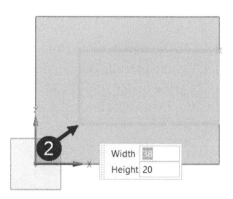

5. On the ribbon, click **Home > Constraints > Rapid Dimension**.
6. Select the horizontal line of the sketch, move the pointer vertically and click.
7. Type 38 in the **Dimension** box and press Enter.
8. Select the vertical line of the sketch, move the pointer horizontally and click to position the dimension.
9. Type 12 in the Dimension box and press Enter.
10. Click **Close** on the **Rapid Dimension** dialog.
11. Click the on midpoint of the left vertical line of rectangle, and the midpoint of the left vertical edge of the model face.

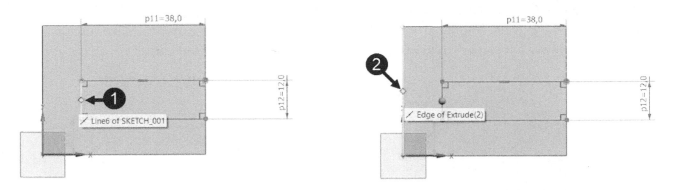

12. Select **Horizontal Alignment** from the Contextual Toolbar; the two selected midpoints are aligned horizontally.

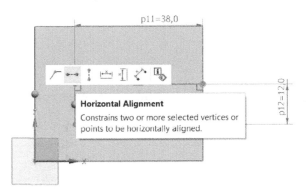
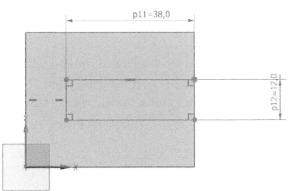

13. On the ribbon, click **Home > Sketch > Finish**.

14. On the dialog, select **End > Through All**. Under the **Boolean** section, select **Boolean > Subtract**.

15. If the extrude handle points toward front, then click the **Reverse Direction** ✕ button under the **Direction** section.

16. Click **OK** to create the cut throughout the part geometry.

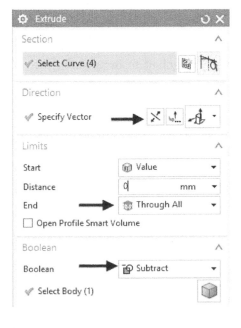
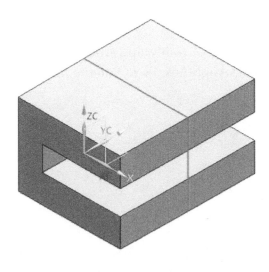

Creating the Cut up to the surface next to the sketch plane

1. Activate the **Extrude** command and click on the top face of the part geometry. Make sure that you click near the lower left corner. This defines the sketch origin at the lower left corner.

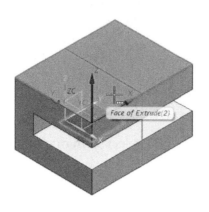
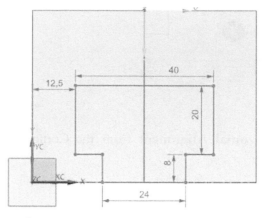

2. Activate the **Profile** command, if not already active.
3. Click the lower horizontal edge of the model face, as shown.
4. Move the pointer horizontally toward right and click. Note that the Horizontal ⟶ glyph appears above the line when you move the pointer horizontally.

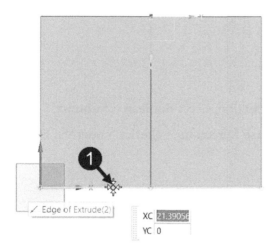
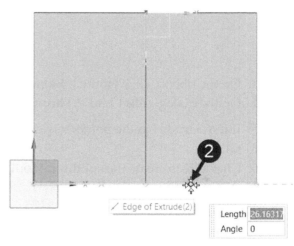

5. Move the pointer vertically upward and type 8 in the **Length** box attached to the pointer. Press Tab and enter 90 in the **Angle** box. Press Enter to create a vertical line with a dimension.

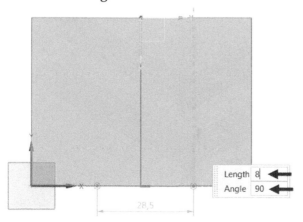

6. Move the pointer horizontally toward right and click.
7. Move the pointer vertically upward, type 20, press Tab. Type 90 and press Enter.
8. Move the toward left, type 40 in the **Length** box and press Tab. Type 180 in the **Angle** box and press Enter.

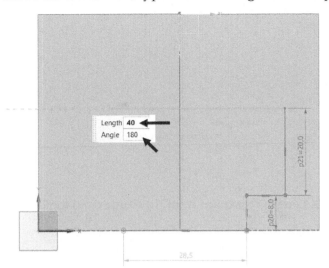

9. Likewise, create other two lines, as shown. Close the **Profile** dialog.

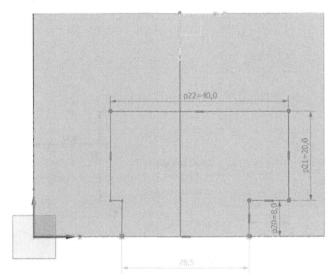

10. Select the two horizontal lines, as shown. Select the **Equal Length** constraint from the Contextual toolbar.

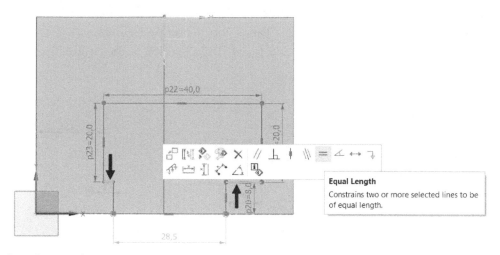

11. Select the two lines, as shown. Select the **Equal Length** constraint from the Contextual toolbar.

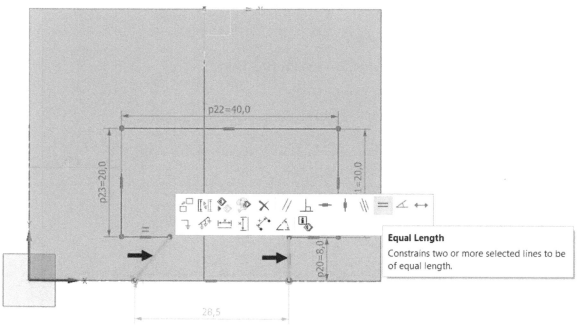

12. Select the line, as shown. On the Contextual toolbar, select the **Vertical** constraint (leave this step if the **Vertical** constraint is already applied).

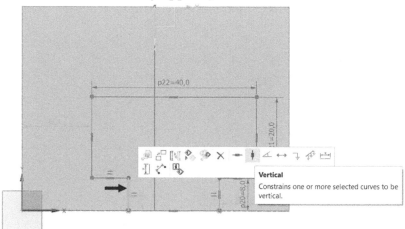

13. On the ribbon, click **Home > Constraint > Rapid Dimension**. Select the bottom horizontal line of the sketch, move the pointer downward, and click. Type 24 in the **Dimension** box and press Enter. Close the **Rapid Dimension** dialog.

14. Select the midpoints of the upper horizontal line and the horizontal edge of the model face. Select the **Vertical Alignment** constraint from the Contextual toolbar.

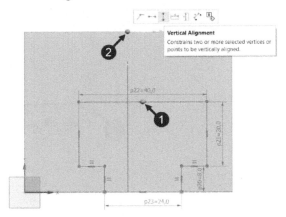 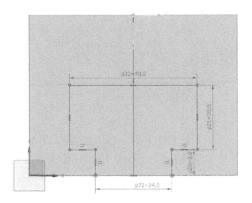

15. On the ribbon, click **Home > Sketch > Finish**.

16. On the **Extrude** dialog, click **End > Until Next**. Under the **Direction** section, click the **Reverse Direction** button.

17. Under the **Boolean** section, click **Boolean > Subtract**. Click **OK** to create the cutout feature until the surface next to the sketch plane.

 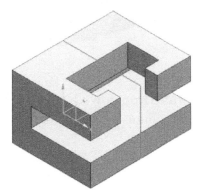

Extruding the sketch up to the Extended Surface

1. Activate the **Extrude** command and click on the horizontal face, as shown in figure. Make sure that you click near the lower right corner. This defines the sketch origin at the lower right corner.

2. Draw a rectangle. Apply dimensions and finish the sketch.

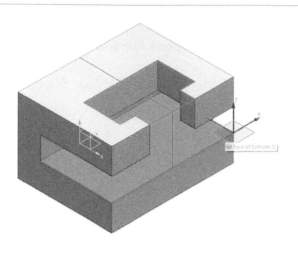

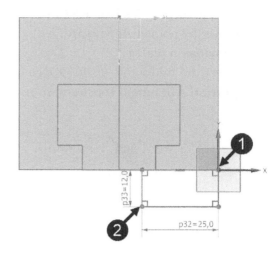

3. On the **Extrude** dialog, click **Boolean > Unite**.

4. Click **End > Until Extended** and select the bottom face of the part geometry.

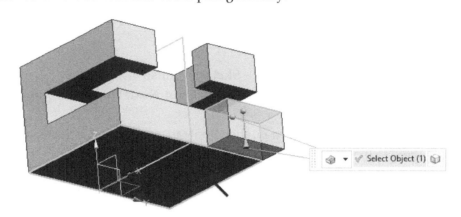

5. Click **OK** to complete the part.

6. On the Top Border Bar, click **Show/Hide Drop-down > Show and Hide**.

7. On the **Show and Hide** dialog, click the minus (-) symbol next to **Sketches**. Close the dialog.

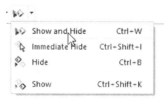

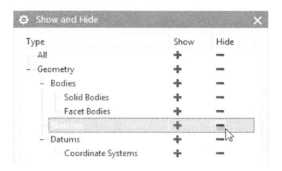

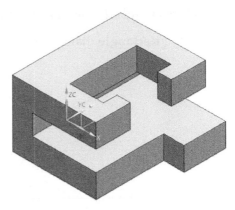

8. Save and close the file.

Example 2 (Inches)

In this example, you will create the part shown below.

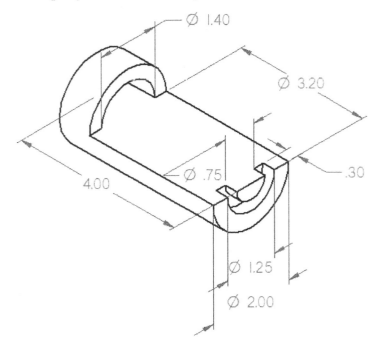

Creating the Revolved Solid Feature

1. Start **NX 12**.
2. On the **Quick Access Toolbar**, click **New**; the **New** dialog appears.
3. On the **New** dialog, click **Units > Inches** and select the **Model** template. Click **OK** to close the dialog.
4. On the ribbon, click **Home > Direct Sketch > Sketch**.
5. Select the XY plane from the Datum Coordinate System. Click **OK** on the **Create Sketch** dialog.

6. On the ribbon, click **Home > Direct Sketch > Rectangle** ⬚. On the **Rectangle** dialog, click the **By 3 Points** icon. Specify the three points of the rectangle, as shown. Close the **Rectangle** dialog.

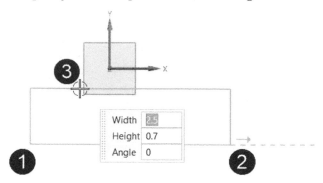

7. Select the midpoint of the lower horizontal line, and then select the Y-axis of the sketch. Next, select the **Point on Curve** constraint on the Contextual Toolbar.

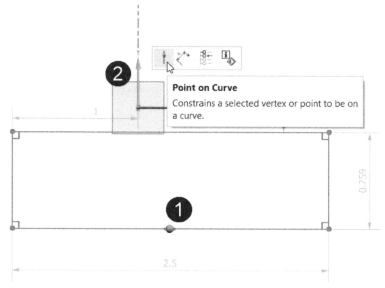

8. Select the X-axis of the sketch and the top right end point of the rectangle. Select the **Point on Curve** constraint from the Contextual Toolbar.

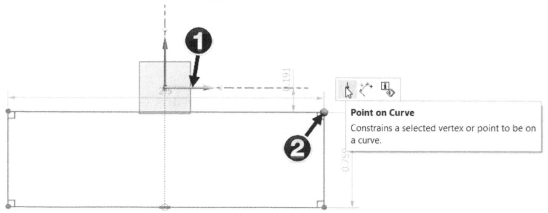

9. Apply dimensions to the sketch, as shown.

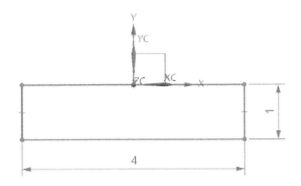

10. Finish the sketch. Press the **End** key to change the model orientation to Isometric.
11. Activate the **Revolve** command (On the ribbon, click **Home > Feature > Design Feature** Drop-down > **Revolve**) and click on the sketch.
12. On the **Revolve** dialog, click **Specify Vector** and click on the line passing through the XC-axis.
13. On the **Revolve** dialog, under the Limits section, type-in **180** in the **Angle** box below the **End** drop-down. Click the **Reverse Direction** button under the **Axis** section, if required. Click **OK** to create the *Revolve* feature.

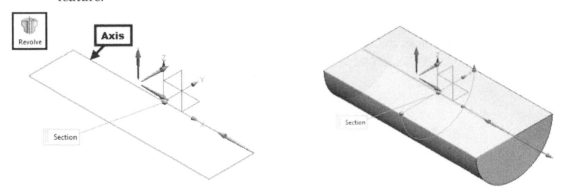

Creating the Revolved Cut

1. Activate the **Revolve** command and click on the top face of the part geometry.
2. Draw the sketch on top face and apply dimensions. Finish the sketch.

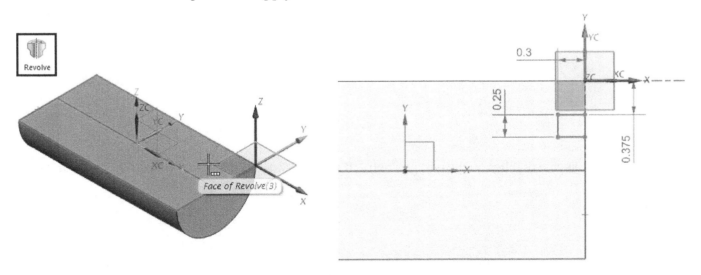

3. Click on the X-axis vector to define the axis of the revolution.

4. Click on the origin of the datum coordinate system to define the axis origin.
5. Type-in **180** in the **End** box and click the **Reverse Direction** button under the **Direction** section.
6. Under the **Boolean** section, click **Boolean > Subtract**.
7. Click **OK** to create the revolved cutout.

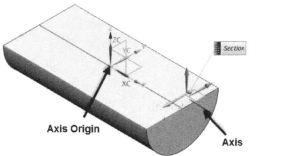
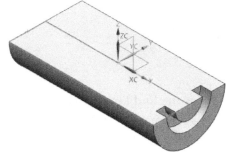

Adding a Revolved Feature to the model

1. Activate the **Revolve** command and click on the top face of the part geometry.
2. Draw a sketch and click **Finish** on the ribbon.
3. On the ribbon, click **Boolean > Unite**.
4. Click on the **Specify Vector** option under the **Axis** section of the **Revolve** dialog. Click on the X-axis of the triad to define the axis of rotation and click on the origin to define the axis origin.

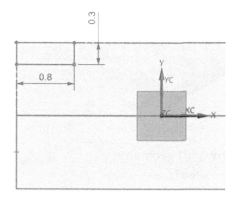
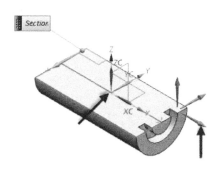

5. Type-in **180** in the **End** box and click **OK** to add the *Revolve* feature to the geometry.
6. On the Top Border bar, click **Show/Hide Drop-down > Immediate Hide**.

7. Click on the sketch that lies on the part geometry. It will be hidden immediately. Close the **Immediate Hide** dialog.

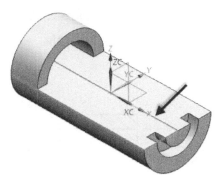 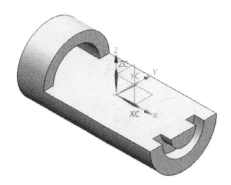

8. Save and close the file.

Questions

1. How do you create parallel planes in NX?
2. What are the **Draft** options available on the **Extrude** dialog?
3. List any two **Limit** types available on the **Extrude** dialog.
4. How do you extrude an open profile in NX?
5. List any two Boolean operations.
6. How do you create angled planes in NX?

Exercises

Exercise 1 (Millimeters)

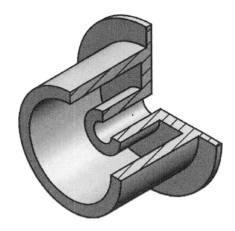

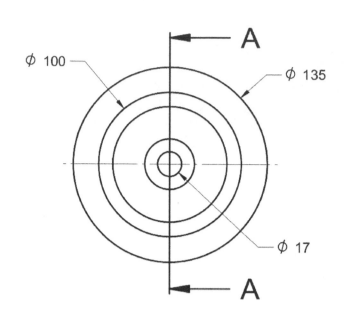

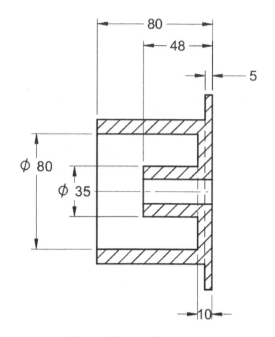

SECTION A-A

Exercise 2 (Inches)

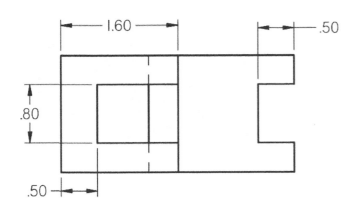

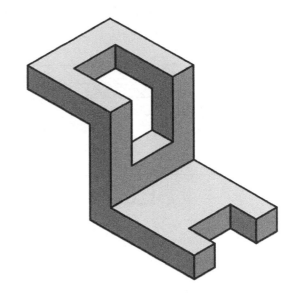

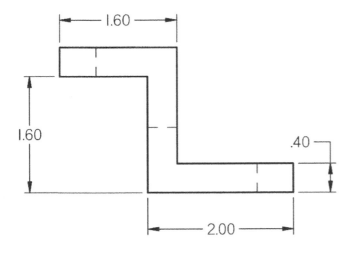

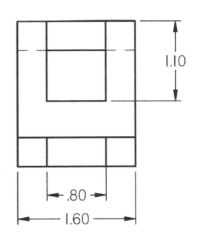

Exercise 3 (Millimeters)

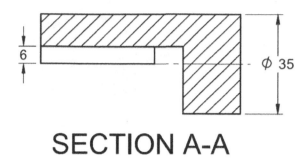

SECTION A-A

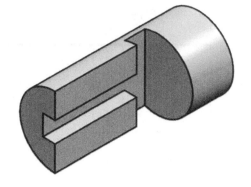

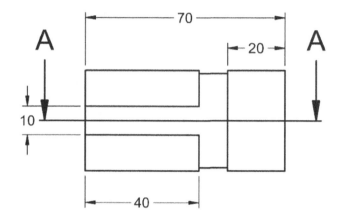

Chapter 4: Placed Features

So far, all of the features that were covered in previous chapter were based on two-dimensional sketches. However, there are certain features in NX that do not require a sketch at all. Features that do not require a sketch are called placed features. You can simply place them on your models. However, to do so, you must have some existing geometry. Unlike a sketch-based feature, you cannot use a placed feature for a first feature a model. For example, to create a *Blend* feature, you must have an already existing edge. In this chapter, you will learn how to add placed features to your design.

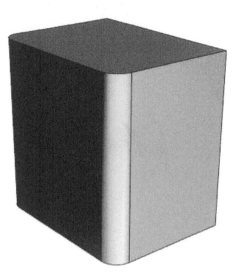

The topics covered in this chapter are:

- *Holes*
- *Threads*
- *Slots*
- *Blends*
- *Chamfers*
- *Drafts*
- *Shells*

Hole

As you know, it is possible to use the *Extrude* command to create cuts and remove material. But, if you want to drill holes that are of standard sizes, the **Hole** command is a better way to do this. The reason for this is it has many hole types already predefined for you. All you have to do is choose the correct hole type and size. The other benefit is when you are going to create a 2D drawing, NX can place the correct hole annotation, automatically. Activate this command (Click **Home > Feature > Hole** on the ribbon) and you will notice that a dialog pops up. There are options in this dialog that make it easy to create different types of holes.

Simple Hole

To create a simple hole feature, select **Type > General Hole** on the **Hole** dialog. Under the **Form and Dimensions** section, select **Form > Simple**. Type-in a value in the **Diameter** box and select the **Depth Limit** type. If you want a through hole, select **Depth Limit > Through Body**. If you want the hole only up to some depth, then select **Depth**

Limit > Value, and then type-in a value in the **Depth** box. The **Depth To** drop-down in the **Form and Dimensions** section has two options to define the depth of the hole: **Cylinder bottom** and **Cone Tip**. The **Cylinder bottom** option applies the **Depth** value to the cylindrical portion of the hole. The **Cone Tip** option applies the **Depth** value to the entire hole up to the bottom tip. The **Tip Angle** box defines the angle of the cone tip at the bottom.

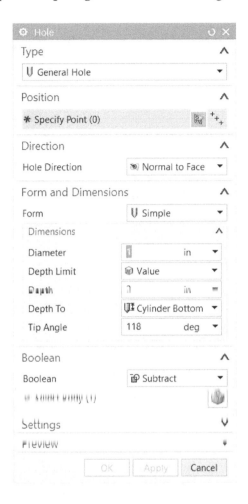

On the dialog, click **Specify Point**, and then click on a face. Place points on the face and add dimensions to define their position. On the ribbon, click **Home > Sketch > Finish**.

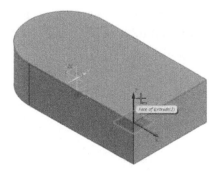
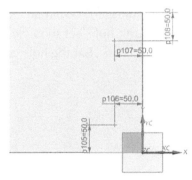

The holes will be created normal to the selected face. If you want to create holes at an angle or along a specified vector, then set the **Hole Direction** to **Along Vector**. Select the **Two Points** option from the drop-down next to the Specify Vector option. Next, select two points from the graphics window. Click **OK** to create the holes.

First Point

Second Point

Counterbored Hole

A counterbore hole is a large diameter hole added at the opening of another hole. It is used to accommodate a fastener below the level of workpiece surface. To create a counterbore hole, select **Form> Counterbored**. Next, define the diameter, counterbore diameter, and counterbore depth. Specify the settings in the **Depth Limit** and **Depth To** drop-downs. Type-in a value in the **Tip angle** box, to define the angle of the V-bottom.

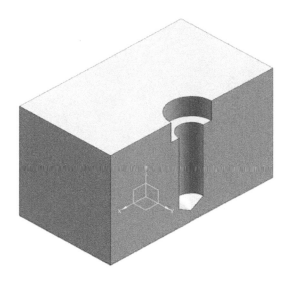

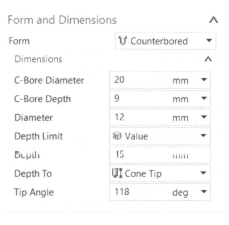

Countersunk Hole

A countersunk hole has an enlarged V-shaped opening to accommodate fastener below the level of work piece surface. To create a countersunk hole, set the hole **Form** to **Countersunk**. Type-in values in the **Diameter**, **C-Sink Diameter**, and **C-Sink Angle** boxes. Set the hole depth and end condition.

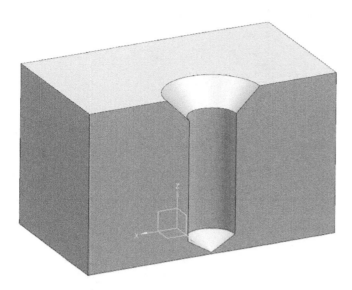

Form and Dimensions		∧
Form	Ṽ Countersunk	▼
Dimensions		∧
C-Sink Diameter	30	mm ▼
C-Sink Angle	90	deg ▼
Diameter	15	mm ▼
Depth Limit	🔟 Value	▼
Depth	45	mm ▼
Depth To	Ṳ̈ Cone Tip	▼
Tip Angle	118	deg ▼

Tapered Hole

Tapering is the process of decreasing the hole diameters toward one end. A tapered hole has a smaller diameter at the bottom. To create a tapered hole, set the hole **Form** to **Tapered**. Type-in a value in the **Diameter** box, and then simply enter the taper angle in the **Taper Angle** box. After defining the taper, specify the hole depth.

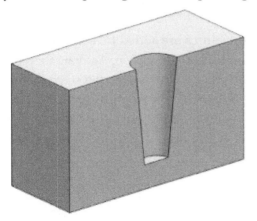

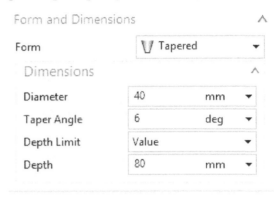

Form and Dimensions		∧
Form	Ṽ Tapered	▼
Dimensions		∧
Diameter	40	mm ▼
Taper Angle	6	deg ▼
Depth Limit	Value	▼
Depth	80	mm ▼

Threaded Hole

To create a threaded hole feature, set the hole **Type** to **Threaded Hole**. Under the **Forms and Dimensions** section, set the **Thread Dimensions** settings and thread **Handedness**. Set the hole limits and end condition in the **Dimensions** sub-section. If you want to provide a relief, then expand the **Relief** section and check the **Enable** option. Likewise, enable or disable the **Start Chamfer** and **End Chamfer**.

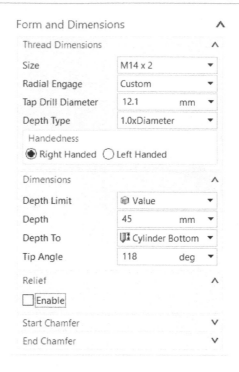

Thread

This command adds a thread feature to a cylindrical face. The thread features are added to a 3D geometry so that when you create a 2D drawing, NX can automatically place the correct thread annotation. Activate this command (click **Home > Feature > More > Thread** on the ribbon). The **Thread** dialog pops up on the screen. To create a symbolic thread, set the **Thread Type** to **Symbolic** and click on a cylindrical face of the part geometry. The thread parameters are automatically updated on the **Thread** dialog. If you want to apply a standard thread, then click **Choose From table** on the dialog and select a standard thread. Note that you need to select a standard thread that matches the diameter of the cylindrical face. Next, click **OK**.

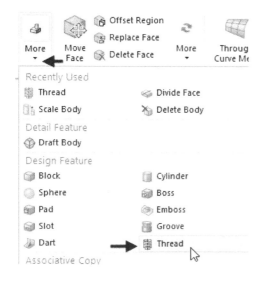

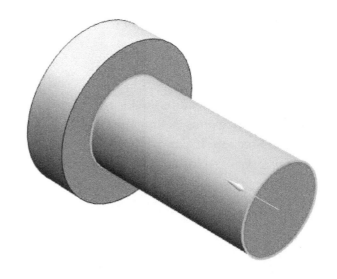

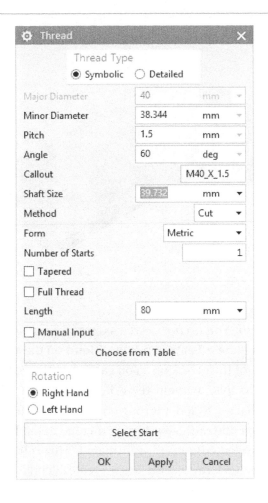

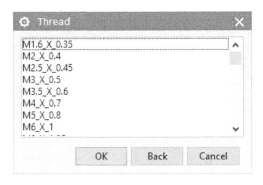

On the **Thread** dialog, set the other parameters such as **Method**, **Form**, **Number of Starts**, **Length**, and **Rotation**. Click **OK** to apply the symbolic thread.

To create a detailed thread, set the **Thread Type** to **Detailed** and click on the cylindrical face. On the **Thread** dialog, define the thread parameters and rotation. Click **Select Start** and click on an end face to define the start point of the thread. Click the **Reverse Thread Axis** button, if required. Click **OK** to complete the thread feature.

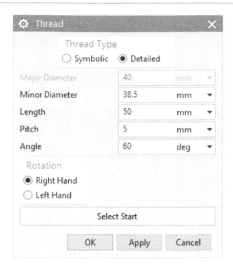

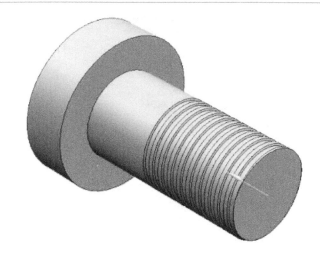

Edge Blend

This command breaks the sharp edges of a model and blends them. You do not need a sketch to create a blend. All you need to have is model edges. Activate this command (click **Home > Feature > Edge Blend** on the ribbon) and select edges. As you start selecting edges, you will see a preview of the geometry. You can select the edges, which are located at the back of the model without rotating it. To do this, activate the **Allow Selection of Hidden Wireframe** ⊗ button on the Top Border Bar. By mistake, if you have selected a wrong edge, you can deselect it by holding the Shift key and selecting the edge again. You can change the radius by typing a value in the **Radius** box displayed on selected edge. As you change the radius, all the selected edges will be updated. This is because they are all part of one instance. If you want the edges to have different radii, you must create blends in separate instances. Select the required number of edges and click **OK** to finish this feature. The *Edge Blend* feature will be listed in the Part Navigator.

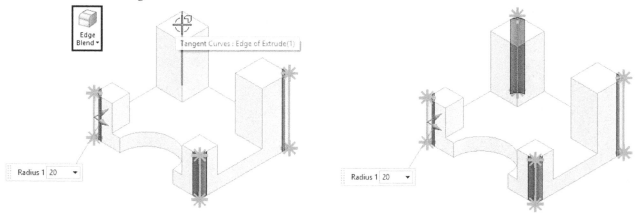

Curvature Continuous Blends

By default, the edge blends are tangent to adjacent faces. However, if you want to create a blend that is curvature continuous with the adjacent faces, then select the **G2 (Curvature)** option from the **Continuity** drop-down on the dialog. Next, type-in a value in the **Radius 1** and **Rho 1** boxes. The edge blends with different rho values are shown below.

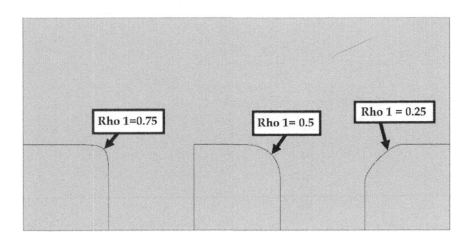

Variable Radius Blend

NX allows you to create a blend with a varying radius along the selected edge. Activate the **Edge Blend** command and click on the edge to blend. On the **Edge Blend** dialog, expand the **Variable Radius** section and click **Specify Radius Point**. Define the variable radius points on the selected edge. Drag the arrows to change the radius value at each location. Check the **Soft Radius change at End** option, if you want a smooth transition between the variable radius points.

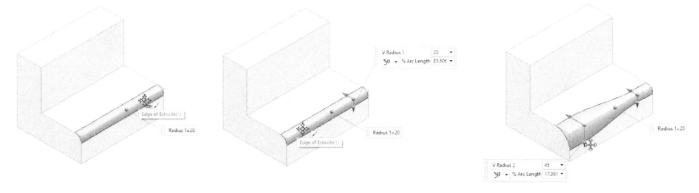

Corner Setback

If you create an edge blend on three edges that come together at a corner, you have the option to control how these three blends are blend together. Activate the **Edge Blend** command and select the three edges that meet together at a corner. On the **Edge Blend** dialog, expand the **Corner Setback** section and click **Select End Point**. Now, click on the vertex where the three blends meet. You will notice that three arrows appear at the corner. Drag these arrows to change the setback distances dynamically (or) type-in values in the individual setback boxes.

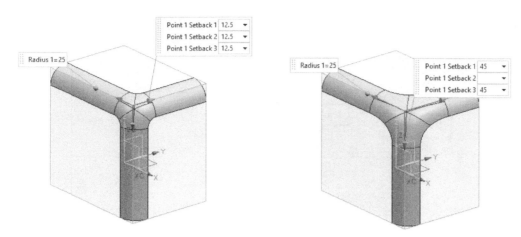

The **Corner Setback** drop-down in the **Corner Setback** section has two options: **Include with Corner** and **Separate from Corner**. The **Include with Corner** option includes the setback with the corner. The **Separate from Corner** option creates a separate setback from the corner, as shown.

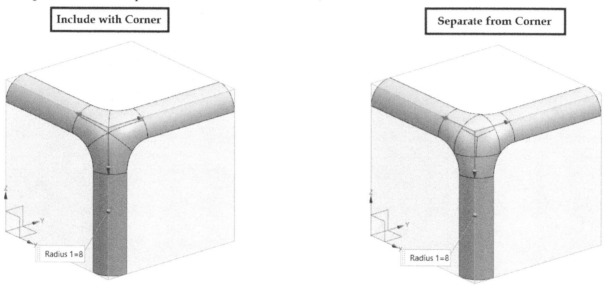

Stop Short of Corner

If you want the edge blend to stop short of the corner, then expand the **Stop Short of Corner** section and click **Select End Point**. Click on a corner vertex of the selected edge and drag the mouse. The blend will be stopped at the distance specified by dragging the mouse.

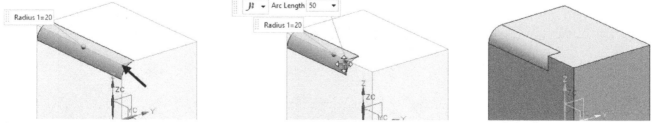

The **Limit** drop-down in the **Stop Short of Corner** section has two options: **Distance** and **Blend Intersection**. The **Distance** option is used to limit a blend up to a selected point. The **Blend Intersection** option is used to stop two blends from intersecting at a corner. You need to select the intersection point of the two blends, as shown.

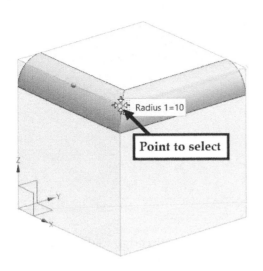

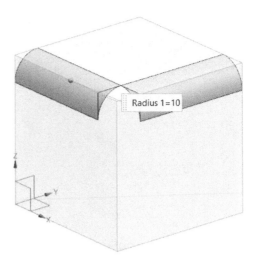

Length Limit

NX allows you to limit the length of an edge blend using a limiting object. To do this, expand the **Length Limit** section and check the **Enable Length Limit** option. Next, select an option from the **Limit Object** drop-down. You can select **Plane, Face** or **Edge** from this drop-down. For example, select the **Plane** option, and then click on the edge selected to create the blend; a plane appears on the edge at the selected point. Click and drag the center point of the plane to define it position. You can also type-in a value in the **Arc Length** box that appear on the selecting the centerpoint of the plane.

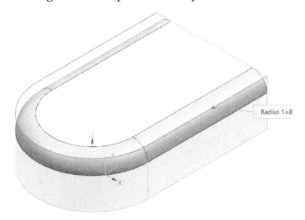

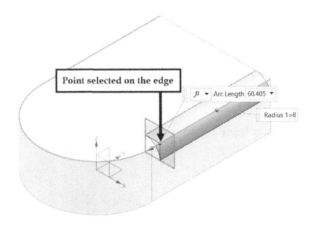

If the limiting plane intersects the blend at multiple points, then click the **Specify Trim Location Point** option in the **Length Limit** section, and the click on the portion to keep.

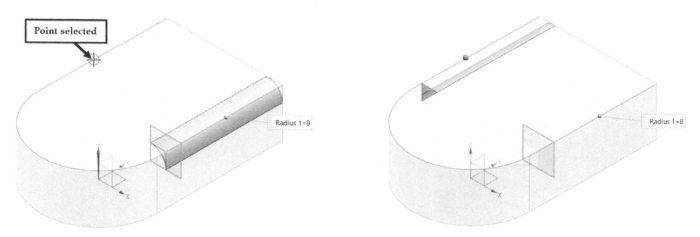

If you select the **Edge** option from the **Limit Object** drop-down, you need to select an edge to define the limit object. The edge fillet will be limited up to the selected edge.

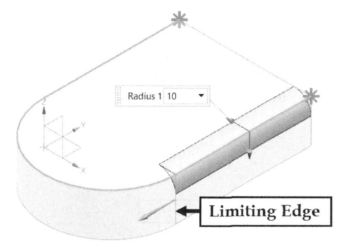

If you select the **Face** option from the **Limit Object** drop-down, then select a face from the model geometry.

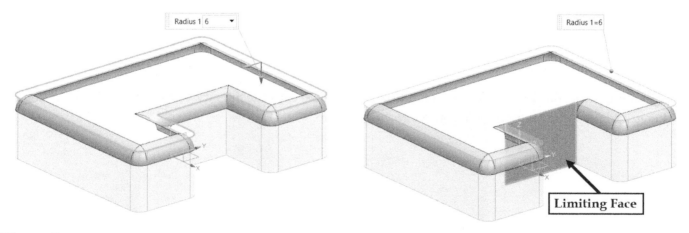

Chamfer

The **Chamfer** and **Edge Blend** commands are commonly used to break sharp edges. The difference is that the **Chamfer** command adds a bevel face to the model. A chamfer is also a placed feature. Activate this command (click

Home > Feature > **Chamfer** on ribbon) and select **Cross Section > Symmetric**. Select the edge to chamfer and type-in a value in the **Distance** box and press Enter to create the chamfer. Click **OK** to complete the chamfer.

Asymmetric chamfer

If you want a chamfer to have different setbacks on both sides of the edge, then select **Cross Section > Asymmetric** on the dialog. Type-in values in the **Distance 1** and **Distance 2** boxes on the dialog and select the edge to chamfer. If you want to switch the setback distance, then click the **Reverse Direction** button on the dialog.

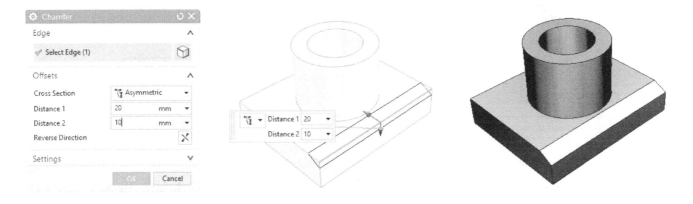

Offset and Angle chamfer

This option lets you to create a chamfer by defining its distance and angle values. On the **Chamfer** dialog, select **Cross Section > Offset and Angle** and click on the edge to chamfer. Type-in values in the **Distance** and **Angle** boxes and click **OK**.

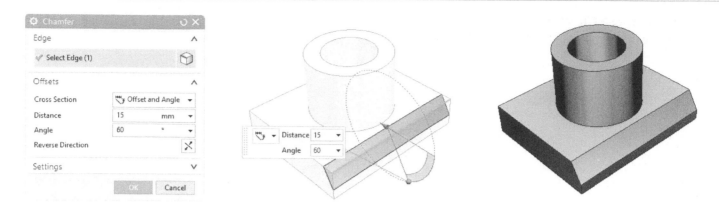

Draft

When creating cast or plastic parts, you are often required to add draft on them so that they can be molded easily. A draft is an angle or taper applied to the faces of components so that they can be removed from a mold easily. The following illustration shows a molded part with and without draft.

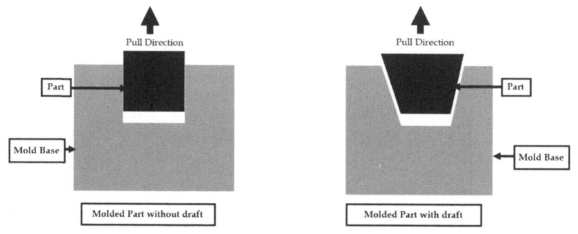

When creating *Extrude* features, you can predefine the draft angle. But most of the time, it is easier to apply the draft after the features are created. Activate the **Draft** command (On the ribbon, click **Home > Feature > Draft**). On the **Draft** dialog, select **Type > Face** and click on the X, Y, or Z-axis to define the draft direction.

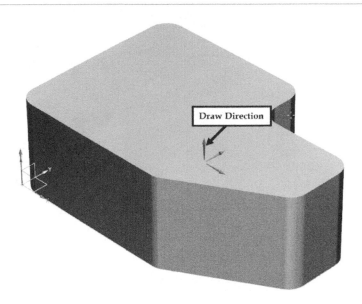

On the Draft dialog, select **Draft Method > Stationary Face**. Select a face, which will act as a reference plane (stationary face) for the draft. The draft angle will be measured with reference to this face. After selecting the reference plane (stationary face), click **Faces to Draft > Select Face**. Select the faces to draft and type-in a value in the **Angle** box. If you want to flip the draft direction, then click the **Reverse Direction** icon under the **Draw Direction** section.

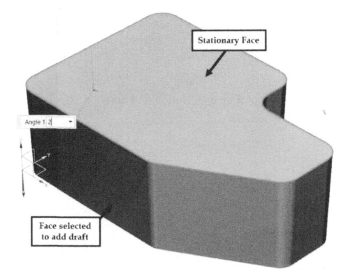

Shell

The **Shell** is another useful command that can be applied directly to a solid model. It allows you to take a solid geometry and make it hollow. This can be a powerful and timesaving technique, when designing parts that call for thin walls such as bottles, tanks, and containers. This command is easy to use. You should have a solid part to use this command. Activate this command from the **Feature** group (On the ribbon, click **Home > Feature > Shell**). On the **Shell** dialog, select **Type > Remove Faces, then Shell** and select the faces to remove. Type-in the wall thickness in the **Thickness** box that appears on the model. Click the **Reverse Direction** button to specify whether the thickness is added inside or outside the model. Click **OK** to finish the feature.

If you want to shell a portion with a different thickness value, expand the **Alternate Thickness** section and click **Select Face**. Select the outer face of the portion to which you want a different thickness value. Type the alternate thickness value in the **Thickness 1** box.

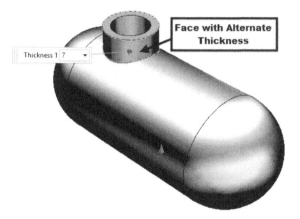

If you want to shell the solid body without removing any faces, then select **Type > Shell All Faces** on the dialog. Click on the solid body and type-in a value in the **Thickness** box.

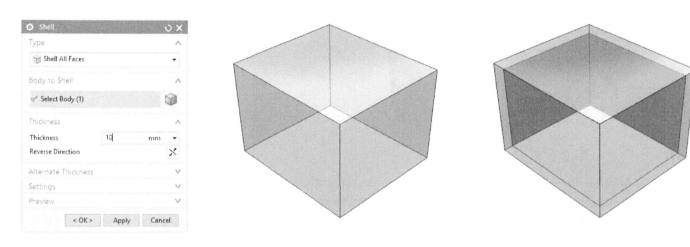

Examples

Example 1 (Millimetres)
In this example, you will create the part shown below.

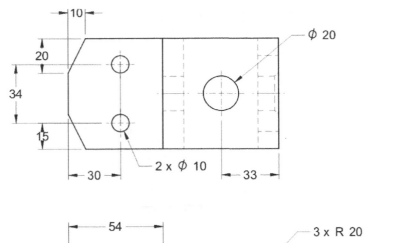

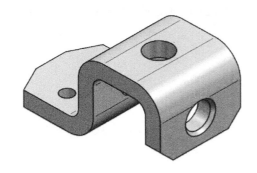

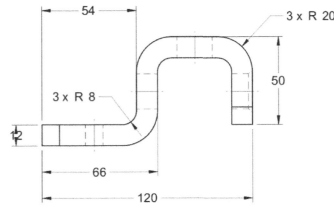

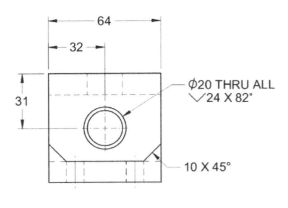

1. Start **NX 12**.
2. On the ribbon, click **New**. On the **New** dialog, select **Units > Millimeters** and double-click the **Model** template.
3. On the ribbon, click **Home > Feature > Extrude**.
4. On the Datum Coordinate System, select the XZ plane. Draw the sketch shown in figure and create the Extrude feature of 64 mm thickness.

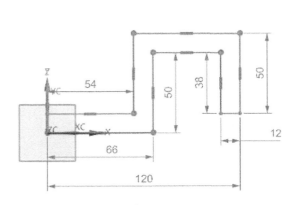

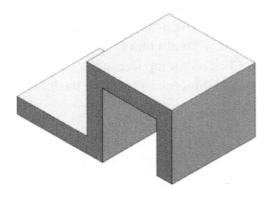

5. On the ribbon, click **Home > Feature > Hole**.
6. On the **Hole** dialog, select **Type > General Hole**.
7. Under the **Form and Dimensions** section, select **Form > Countersunk**.
8. Set the **C-Sink Diameter** and **C-Sink Angle** values to **24** and **82**, respectively.
9. Set the **Diameter** value to **20** mm.
10. Set the **Depth Limit** value to **Through Body**.

11. Click on the right-side face of the part geometry. A point is placed on the selected face.

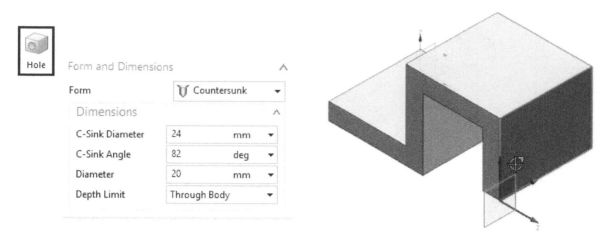

12. Add dimensions to define the point location. Click **Finish** on the ribbon.
13. Click **OK** to complete the hole feature.

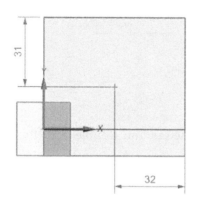

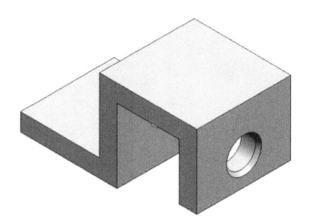

14. Activate the **Hole** command and select **Form > Simple** on the **Hole** dialog.
15. Set the **Diameter** value to 20 mm.
16. Set the **Depth Limit** type to **Through Body**.
17. Click on the top face of the part geometry.
18. Add dimensions to define the location of the hole. Click **Finish**.

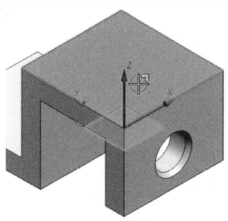

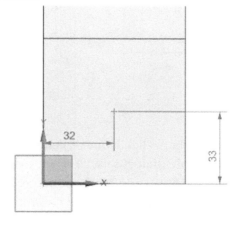

19. Click **OK** to close the dialog.

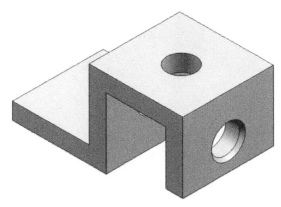

20. On the bottom-left corner of the graphic window, click the Z-axis of the coordinate system and set the **Angle** value to 90. This changes the view orientation of the model.

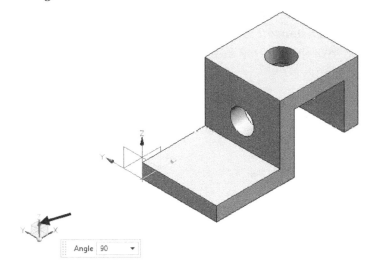

21. Activate the **Hole** command. On the **Hole Options** dialog, select **Form > Simple** and type-in **10** in the **Diameter** box.
22. Click on the lower top face to place a point for the hole location. Place one more point and add dimensions to define the location of the holes. Click **Finish** on the ribbon.

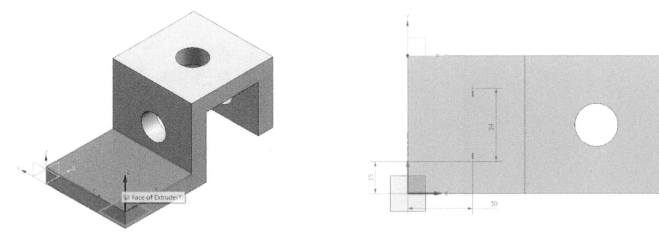

23. Click **OK** to complete the hole feature.

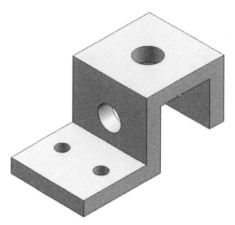

24. Click **Home > Feature > Chamfer** on the ribbon.

25. On the **Chamfer** dialog, select **Cross Section > Asymmetric**.

26. Set the **Distance 1** and **Distance 2** values to **10** and **20**, respectively.

27. Click on the side edge of the selected face, as shown in figure.

28. Click **Apply** on the dialog.

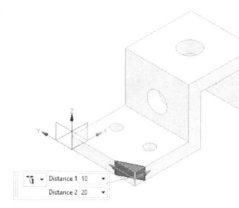

29. Click on the rare side edge and click the **Reverse Direction** button.

30. Click **OK** to apply the chamfer.

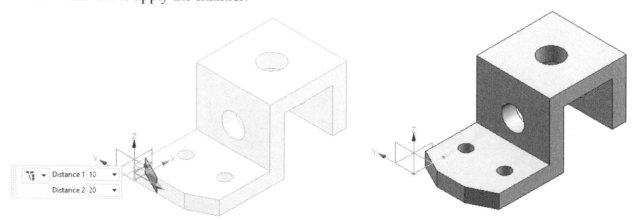

31. Click **Home > Feature > Edge Blend** on the ribbon.

32. On the **Edge Blend** dialog, select **Shape > Circular** and type-in **8** in the **Radius 1** box.

33. Select **Continuity > G1 (Tangent)** from the **Edge** section of the dialog.

34. On the Top Border Bar, activate the **Allow Selection of Hidden Wireframe** ⬙ icon.

35. Click on the horizontal edges of the geometry, as shown below.

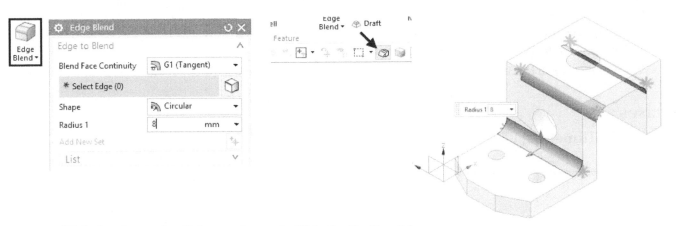

36. Click **Apply** on the dialog and type-in 20 in the **Radius 1** box.
37. Click on the outer edges of the model, as shown below. Click **OK** to complete the edge blend feature.

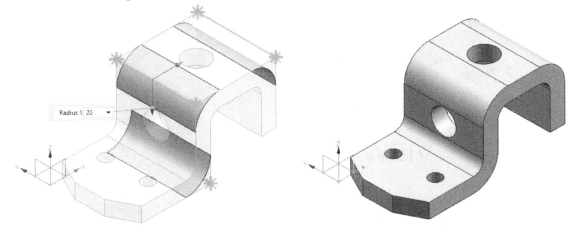

38. On the Top Border Bar, click **Orient View Drop-down > Isometric** to change the orientation of the model view to Isometric.
39. Click **Home > Feature > Chamfer** on the ribbon.
40. On the **Chamfer** dialog, select **Cross Section > Symmetric**.
41. Click on the lower corners of the part geometry.
42. Type-in **10** in the **Distance** box and press Enter. Click **OK** to chamfer the edges.

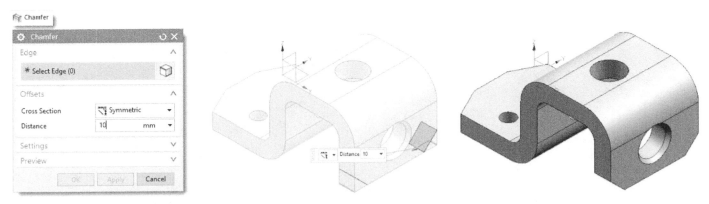

43. Save and close the file.

Questions

1. What are placed features?
2. Which option allows you to create a chamfer with unequal setbacks?
3. Which option allows you create a variable radius blend?
4. When you create a thread on a cylindrical face, the thread diameter will be calculated automatically or not?

Exercises

Exercise 1 (Millimetres)

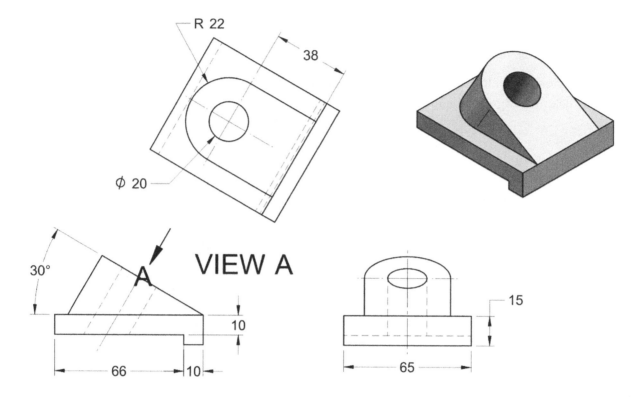

Exercise 2 (Inches)

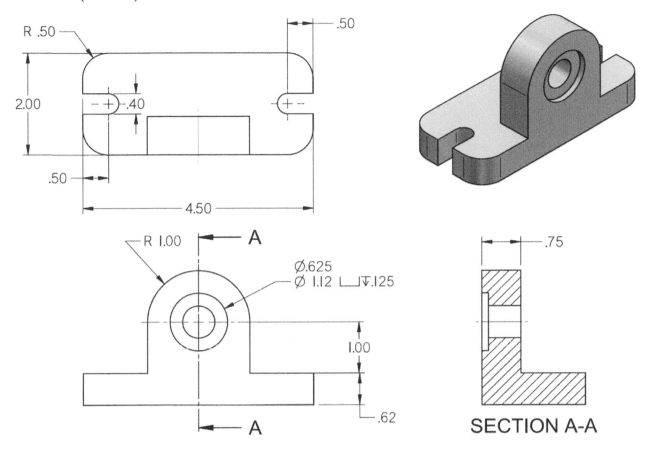

Chapter 5: Patterned Geometry

When designing a part geometry, oftentimes there are elements of symmetry in each part or there are at least a few features that are repeated multiple times. In these situations, NX offers some commands that save your time. For example, you can use mirror features to design symmetric parts, which makes designing the part quicker. This is because you only have to design a portion of the part and use the mirror feature to create the remaining geometry.

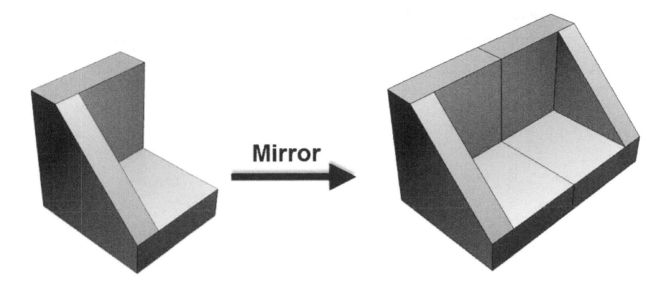

In addition, there are some pattern commands to replicate a feature throughout a part quickly. They save you time from creating additional features individually and help you modify the design easily. If the design changes, you only need to change the first feature and the rest of the pattern features will update, automatically. In this chapter, you will learn to create mirrored and pattern geometries using the commands available in NX.

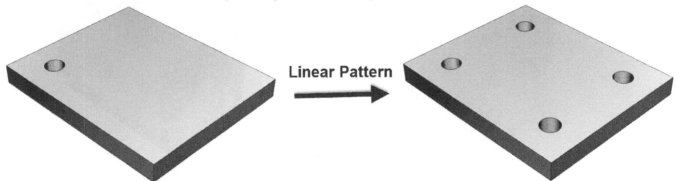

The topics covered in this chapter are:

- *Mirror* features
- *Linear Patterns*
- *Circular Patterns*
- *Along Curve Patterns*
- *Helical Patterns*

Mirror Feature

If you are designing a part that is symmetric, you can save time by using the **Mirror Feature** command. Using this command, you can replicate individual features of the entire body. To mirror features (3D geometry), you need to have a face or plane to use as a reference. You can use a model face, default plane, or create a new plane, if it does not exist where it is needed.

Activate the **Mirror Feature** command (click **Home > Feature > More > Mirror Feature** on the ribbon). On the part geometry, click on the features to mirror, and then click **Select Plane** on the **Mirror Feature** dialog. Now, select the reference plane about which the features are to be mirrored.

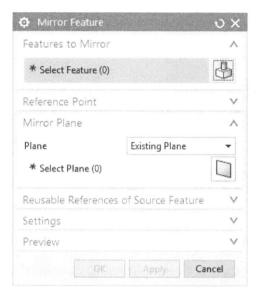

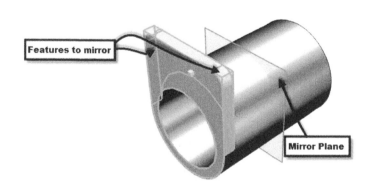

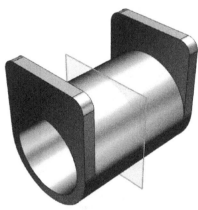

Now, if you make changes to the original feature, the mirrored feature will be updated automatically.

Mirror Geometry

If the part you are creating is completely symmetric, you can save more time by creating half of it and mirroring the entire geometry rather than individual features. You can accomplish this by using the **Mirror Geometry** command. Activate this command (On the ribbon, click **Home > Feature > More > Associate copy > Mirror Geometry**) and click on the solid part. On the **Mirror Geometry** dialog, click **Specify Plane** and select the face about which the geometry is to be mirrored. Click **OK** to complete the mirror geometry.

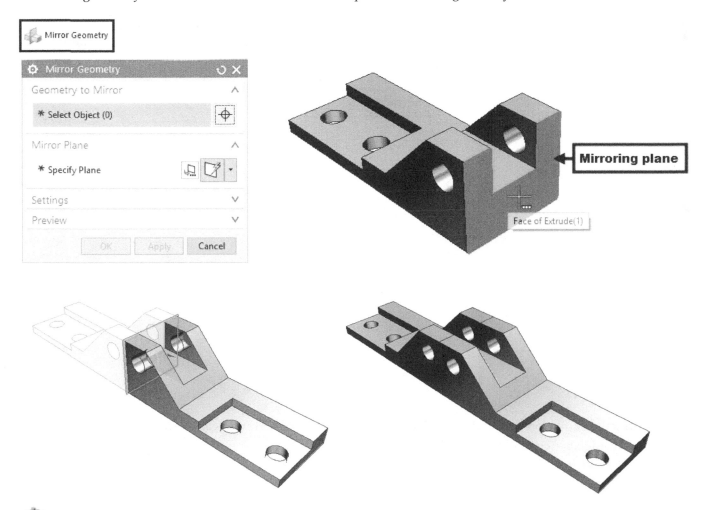

Pattern Feature

This command replicates a feature using different layouts such as linear, circular, polygonal, spiral, along curve, and randomly arranged points. Activate this command (on the ribbon, click **Home > Feature > Pattern Feature**).

The following sections explain the different pattern layouts that can be created using the **Pattern Feature** command.

⠿ Linear Layout

To create a pattern in a linear layout, you must first activate the **Pattern Feature** command (On the ribbon, click **Home > Feature > Pattern Feature**). On the **Pattern Feature** dialog, under the **Pattern Definition** section, select **Layout > Linear**. Select the feature to pattern from the model geometry and select **Direction 1 > Specify Vector**. On the part geometry, click on an edge (or) select the X, Y, or Z axis to define the direction 1 of the linear pattern. You will notice that a pattern preview appears on the model. Now, select **Spacing > Count and Pitch** on the dialog and set the parameters of the pattern (**Count** and **Pitch Distance**). Check the **Symmetric** option, if you want to pattern the feature on both sides.

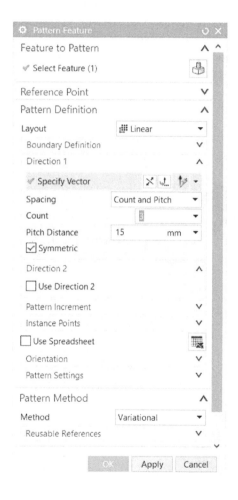

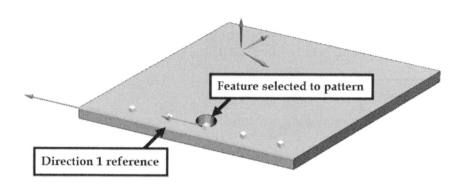

Under the **Direction 2** section, check the **Use Direction 2** option to pattern the feature in the second direction as well. Click on an edge to define the second direction of the pattern. Set the parameters (**Count** and **Pitch Distance**) of the pattern in direction 2.

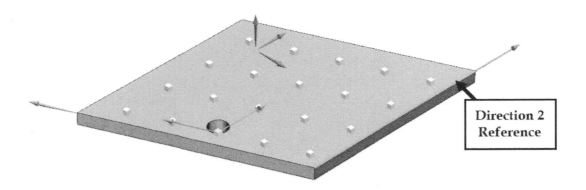

If you want to suppress an instance of the pattern, click the right mouse button on it and select **Suppress**.

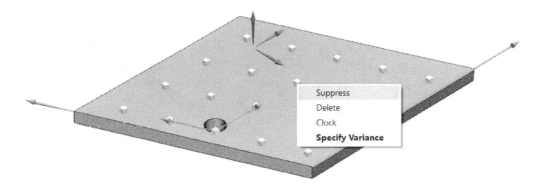

Select **Spacing > Count and Span** on the **Pattern Feature** dialog, if you want to enter the instant count and total spacing along the direction 1 or direction 2.

Select **Spacing > Pitch and Span**, if you want to enter the distance between individual instances of the pattern and total spacing along the directions.

Select **Spacing > List** and add multiple set of the instances along a single direction using the **Add New Set** button. You can define different spacing value for each set.

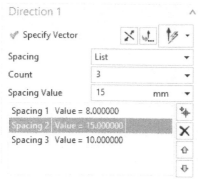

On the **Pattern Feature** dialog, click **OK** to complete the pattern.

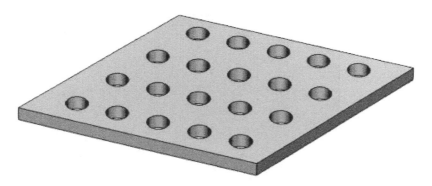

✦ Circular Layout

On the **Pattern Feature** dialog, select **Layout > Circular** to pattern the selected features in a circular fashion. Select the feature to pattern from the model geometry. Under the **Rotation Axis** section, click **Specify Vector** and select the X, Y, or Z axis to define the axis of the rotation. Usually, the axis of rotation is perpendicular to the plane/face on which the selected feature is placed. Click on a point to define the location of the rotation axis.

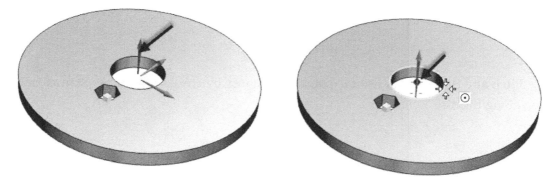

Under the **Angular Direction** section, select **Spacing > Count and Span**. Type-in values in the **Count** and **Span Angle** boxes.

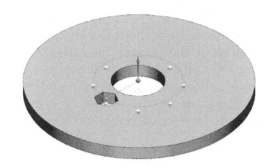

Select **Spacing> Count and Pitch,** if you want to type-in the count and the angle between individual instances.

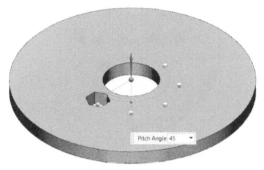

Select **Spacing > Pitch and Span**, if you want to type-in the angle between individual instances and the total angle of the circular pattern.

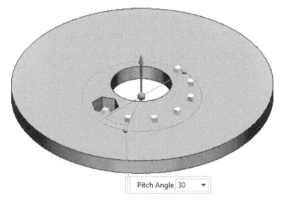

Under the **Orientation** section, select **Orientation > Same as Input** to pattern the feature with the original orientation. Select **Orientation > Follow Pattern** to change the orientation of the instances, as they are patterned in the circular fashion. Click **OK** to complete the circular pattern.

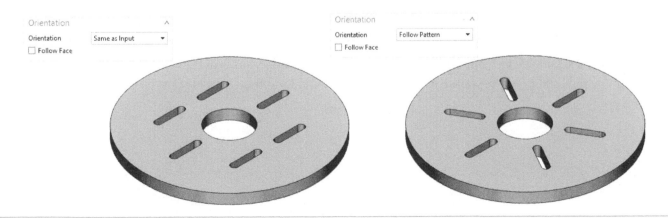

Create Concentric Members

The **Pattern Feature** command has options to radiate the circular pattern. On the **Pattern Feature** dialog, expand the **Radiate** section and check the **Create Concentric Members** option to view the options to radiate the circular pattern. Select **Spacing > Count and Pitch**, and type-in values in the **Count** and **Pitch** boxes. The **Count** and **Pitch** values specify the number of concentric members and distance between them, respectively. On your own, examine the other options in the **Spacing** drop-down as they are explained earlier in the **Linear Layout** section. Select/deselect the **Include First Circle** option to show or hide the first circle of the pattern.

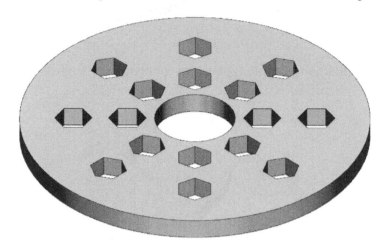

⟳ Along Layout

The **Along** option creates a pattern along a selected curve or edge. On the **Pattern Feature** dialog, select **Layout > Along**, and then click on the feature to pattern. Under the **Direction 1** section, click **Select Path** and select a curve or edge. For this example, select the **Offset** option from the **Path Method** drop-down. If the path has tangent continuous curves, then select **Curve Rule > Tangent Curves** on the **Top Border Bar**. Now, you can select the path in a single click.

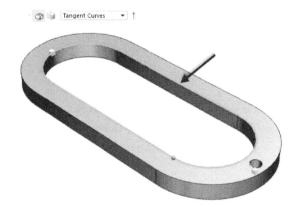

Under the **Direction 1** section, select **Spacing > Count and Span**. Type-in values in the **Count** and **%Span By** boxes. You have to enter **100** in the **%Span By** box to create pattern along the complete curve.

Helical Layout

The **Helix** option creates a pattern along a helical path. Select the feature to pattern from the model geometry and select **Layout > Helix**. Under the **Rotation Axis** section, click **Specify Vector** and define the axis of the helical pattern. Select a point to define the position of the axis. Under the **Rotation Axis** section, click the **Reverse Direction** button to reverse the helical pattern, if required.

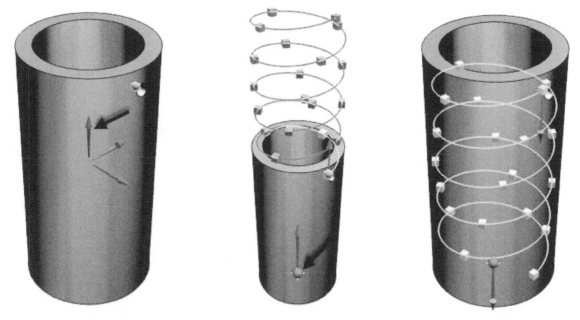

Under the **Helix Definition** section, define the **Direction** and select **Helix Size By > Count, Helix Pitch, Turns**. Type-in values in the **Count, Helix Pitch, Turns** boxes. Click **OK** to complete the helical pattern.

Examples

Example 1 (Millimetres)

In this example, you will create the part shown below.

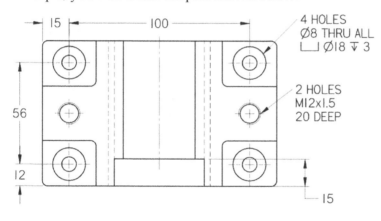

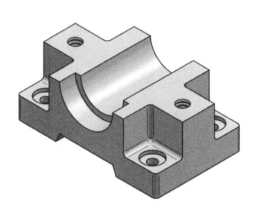

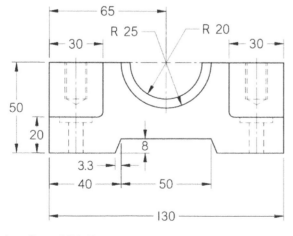

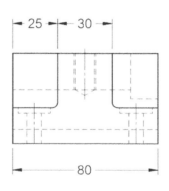

1. Start **NX 12**.
2. Open a new file using the **Model** template.
3. Activate the **Extrude** command and click on the XZ plane.

4. Create a rectangular sketch, add dimensions to it, and then click **Finish** on the ribbon.
5. On the **Extrude** dialog, select **Start > Symmetric Value** and type-in **40** in the **Distance** box.

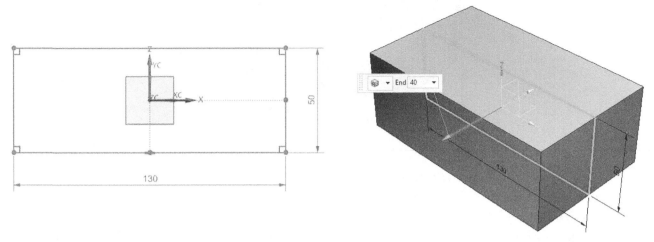

6. Click **Apply** to complete the *Extrude* feature.
7. Click on the top face of the part geometry at the location, as shown in figure. Next, draw the sketch, as shown.
8. Create the *Cutout* feature of **30 mm** depth.

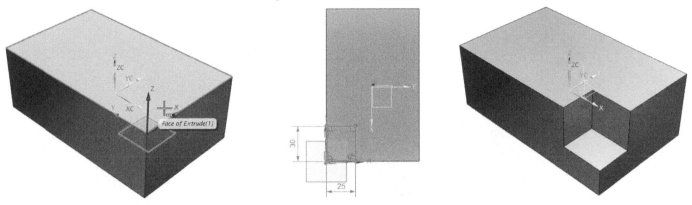

9. Activate the **Hole** command and place a counterbore hole on the *Cutout* feature.

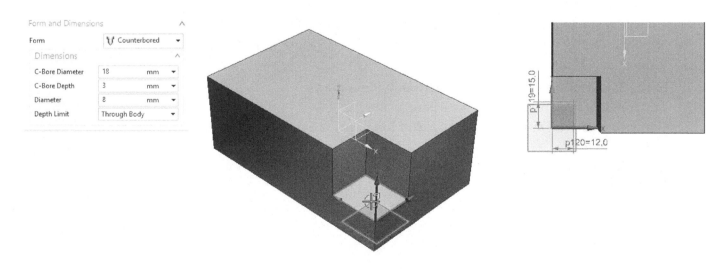

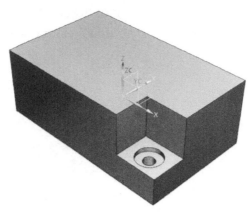

10. Click **Home > Feature > Pattern Feature** 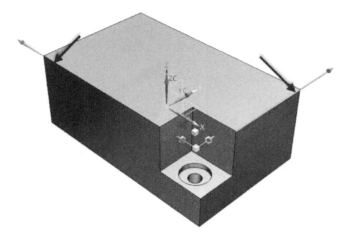 on the ribbon.
11. Click on the *Cutout* of the part geometry.
12. On the **Pattern Feature** dialog, select **Layout > Linear**.
13. Under the **Direction 1** section, click **Specify Vector,** and then click on the top front edge of the part geometry.
14. Under the **Direction 2** section, check the **Use Direction 2** option and click on the top side edge of the part geometry.

15. Under the **Direction 1** section, select **Spacing > Count and Span**.
16. Type-in **2** and **100** in the **Count** and **Span Distance** boxes, respectively.
17. Under the **Direction 2** section, select **Spacing > Count and Span**.
18. Type-in **2** and **55** in the **Count** and **Span Distance** boxes, respectively. Click **Apply** to complete the pattern feature.
19. On the **Pattern Feature** dialog, select **Layout > Reference** .
20. Click on the counterbored hole of the part geometry.
21. Under the **Pattern Definition** section, select **Reference > Select Pattern**, and then select the linear pattern from the model.
22. Select dot displayed on the counterbored hole to define the base instance of the reference pattern.

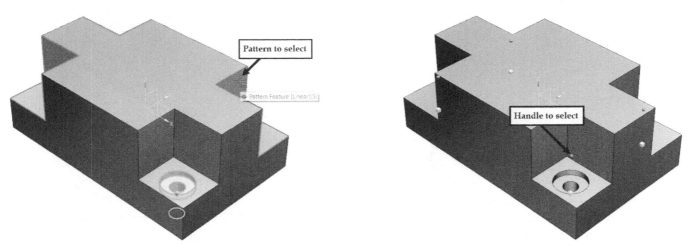

23. Under the **Pattern Method** section, select **Method > Simple**. Next, click **OK** to create the reference pattern.

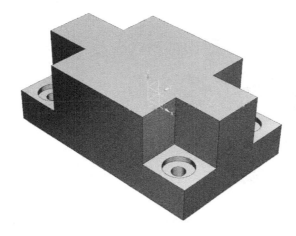

24. Activate the **Hole** command and select the midpoint of the top front edge.
25. On the **Hole** dialog, set the parameters in the **Form and Dimensions** section.

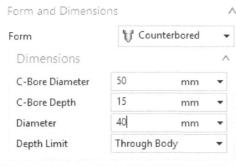

26. Under the **Direction** section, select **Hole Direction > Along Vector**.

27. Select the **Inferred Vector** option under the **Direction** section.

28. Select the Y-axis vector to define the direction in which the hole will be created.

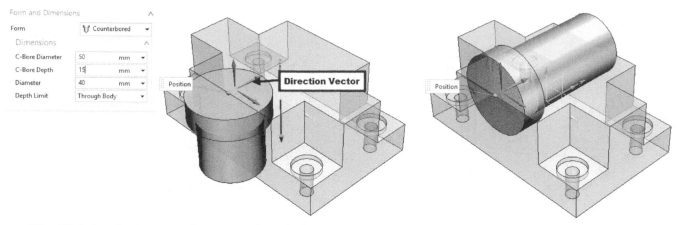

29. Click **Apply** to create the counterbore hole.

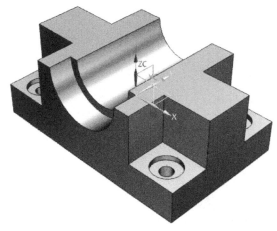

30. On the **Hole** dialog, select **Type > Threaded Hole** .
31. Under the **Form and Dimensions** section, set the parameters, as shown in figure.

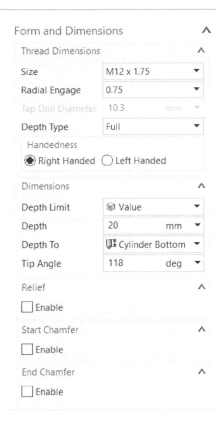

Form and Dimensions ∧

Thread Dimensions ∧

Size	M12 x 1.75 ▼
Radial Engage	0.75 ▼
Tap Drill Diameter	10.3 mm ▼
Depth Type	Full ▼

Handedness
◉ Right Handed ○ Left Handed

Dimensions ∧

Depth Limit	⑪ Value ▼
Depth	20 mm ▼
Depth To	⊔⌶ Cylinder Bottom ▼
Tip Angle	118 deg ▼

Relief ∧
☐ Enable

Start Chamfer ∧
☐ Enable

End Chamfer ∧
☐ Enable

32. Click on the top face of the part geometry and add dimensions to locate the hole.

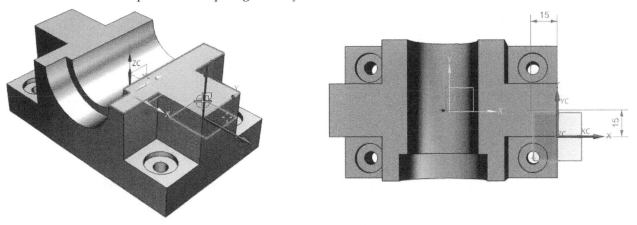

33. Click **Finish** on the ribbon. On the dialog, click **OK** to complete the threaded hole feature.

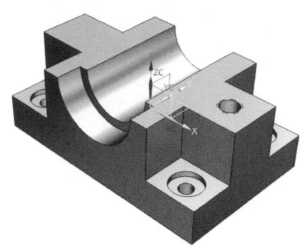

34. On the ribbon, click **Home > Feature > More > Mirror Feature**.
35. Click on the threaded hole on the part geometry.
36. On the **Mirror Feature** dialog, expand the **Settings** section and check the **Maintain Thread Handedness** option.
37. Under the **Mirror Plane** section, click **Select Plane**, and then click on the YZ plane. Click **OK** to complete the mirror feature.

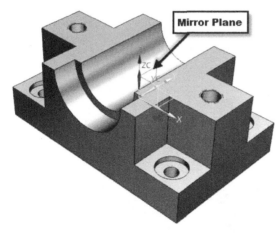

38. Draw a sketch on the front face of the pat geometry. Note that you should apply the Symmetric constraint between the two inclined lines and the Z axis of the coordinate system. Next, create a *Cutout* throughout the geometry.

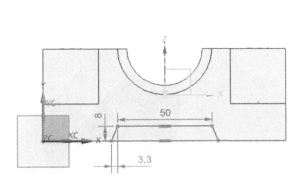

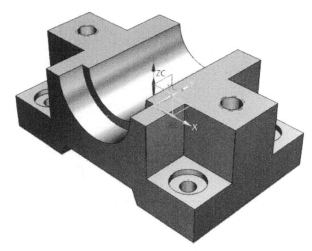

39. Blend the sharp edges of the geometry. The blend radius is 2 mm.

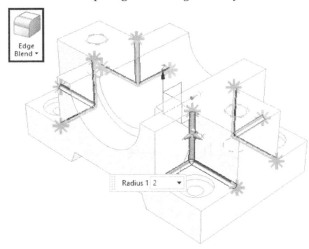

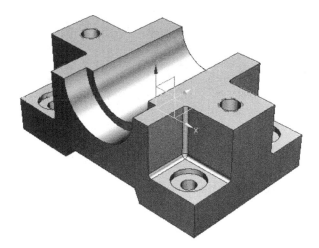

40. Save and close the part file.

Questions

1. Describe the procedure to create a mirror feature.
2. List any two layouts to create patterns.
3. What is the difference between the **Mirror Feature** and **Mirror Geometry** command?
4. Describe the procedure to create a helical pattern.
5. List the methods to define spacing in a linear pattern.

Exercises

Exercise 1 (Millimetres)

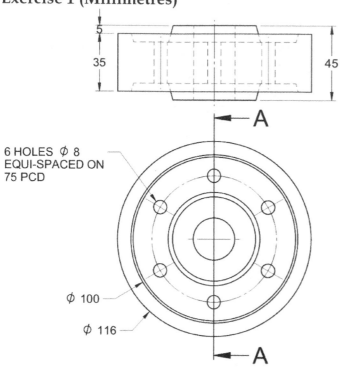

6 HOLES ⌀ 8
EQUI-SPACED ON
75 PCD

⌀ 100

⌀ 116

5

35

45

⌀ 50

⌀ 25

10 25

15° TYP

SECTION A-A

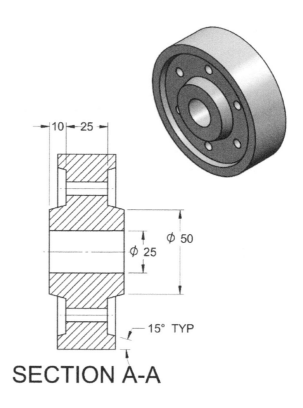

Exercise 2 (Inches)

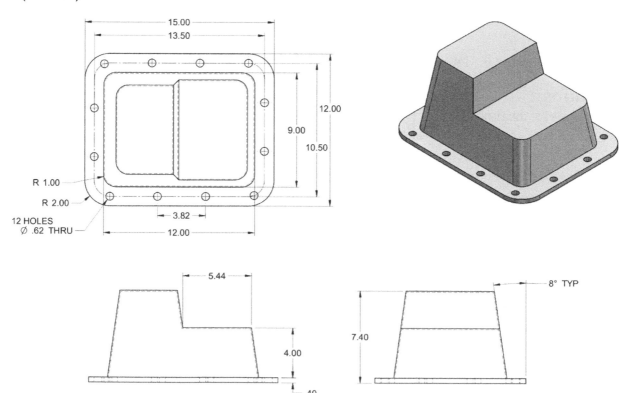

15.00

13.50

12.00

9.00

10.50

R 1.00

R 2.00

12 HOLES
⌀ .62 THRU

3.82

12.00

5.44

4.00

.40

7.40

8° TYP

SHEET THICKNESS = 0.079 in

Chapter 6: Additional Features and Multibody Parts

NX offers you some additional commands and features which will help you to create complex models. These commands are explained in this chapter.

The topics covered in this chapter are:

- *Ribs*
- *Slots*
- *Multi-body parts*
- *Split bodies*
- *Boolean Operations, and*
- *Emboss features*

Rib

This command creates rib features to add structural stability, strength and support to your designs. Just like any other sketch-based feature, a rib requires a two dimensional sketch. Create a sketch, as shown in figure and activate the **Rib** command (click **Home > Feature > More > Design Feature > Rib** on the ribbon). Select the sketch; the preview of the geometry appears. You can add the rib material to either side of the sketch line or evenly to both sides. Set the **Dimension** type to **Symmetric** to add material to both sides of the sketch line. Type-in the thickness value of the rib feature in the **Thickness** box. You can click the **Reverse Rib Side** button to change the direction of the rib.

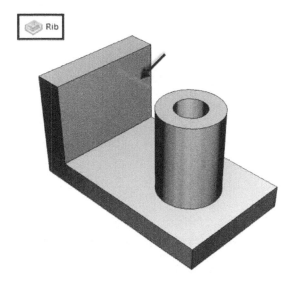

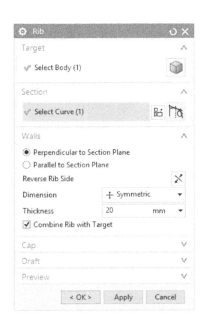

You can define the direction of the rib feature by using the **Perpendicular to Section Plane** or **Parallel to Section Plane** option.

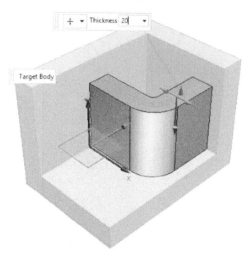

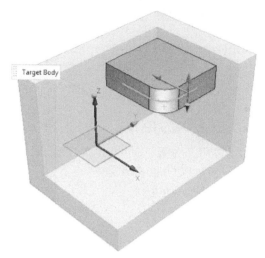

To draft to the rib feature, select **Draft > Draft > From Cap** on the **Rib** dialog, and then type-in a value in the **Angle** box. Note that the **Draft** section available only when you select the **Perpendicular to Section Plane** option.

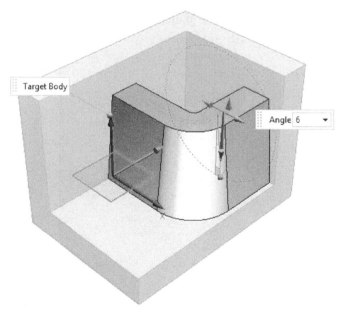

You can use a sheet body to cap the top face of the rib feature. To do this, select **Cap > Geometry > From Selected** on the **Rib** dialog and click on the sheet body, as shown.

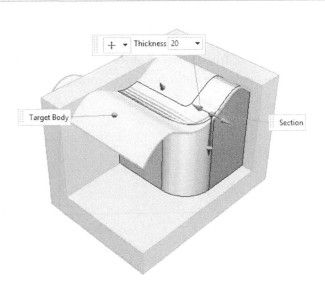

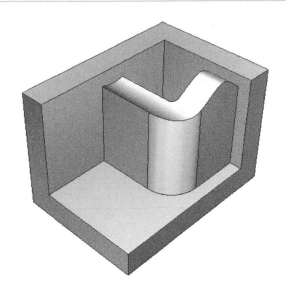

Multi-body Parts

NX allows the use of multiple bodies when designing parts. This opens the door to several design techniques that would otherwise not be possible. In this section, you will learn some of these techniques.

Creating Multibodies

The number of bodies in a part can change throughout the design process. NX makes it easy to create separate bodies inside a part geometry. Also, you can combine multiple bodies into a single body. In order to create multiple bodies in a part, first create a solid body, and then create any sketch-based feature such as extruded, revolved, or swept feature. While creating the feature, ensure that you set the **Boolean** type to **None**.

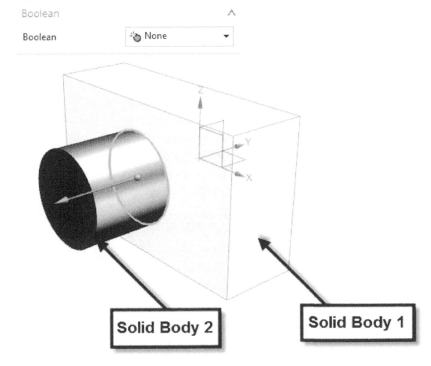

Split Body

The **Split Body** command can be used to separate single bodies into multiple bodies. This command can be used to perform local operations. For example, if you apply the shell feature to the front portion of the model shown in figure, the whole model will be shelled. To solve this problem, you must split the solid body into multiple bodies (In this case, separate the front portion of the model from the rest).

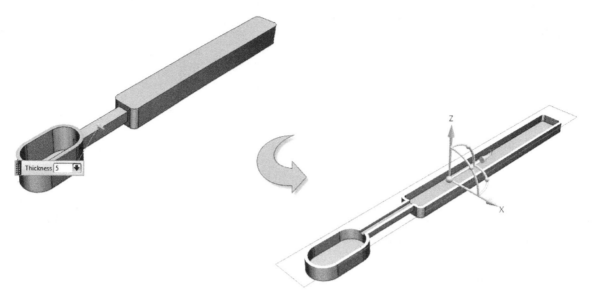

To split a body, you must have a splitting tool such as planes, sketch elements, surface, or bodies. In this case, a surface can be used as splitting tool. Activate the **Split Body** command (click **Home > Feature > More > Trim > Split Body** on the ribbon) and select the solid body from the graphics window. On the **Split Body** dialog, select **Tool > Tool Option > Extrude** and click **Select Curve**. Click on the curved edge to define the section curve. As you click **OK**, an extruded surface will be created and eventually the body will be split into two separate bodies.

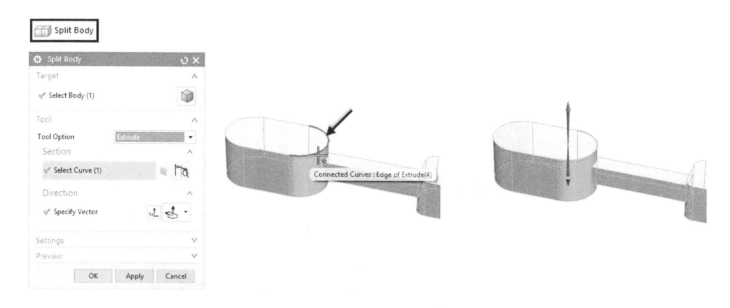

Now, create the shell feature on the split body.

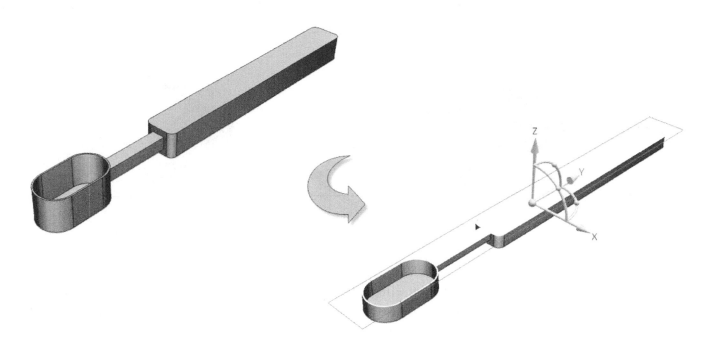

Unite

If you apply blends to the edges between two bodies, it will result in a different result as shown in figure. In order to solve this problem, you must combine the two bodies using the **Unite** command. Activate this command (click **Home > Feature > Combine Drop-down > Unite** on the ribbon) and select the bodies. Click **OK** on the dialog to unite the bodies. Now, apply blends to the edges.

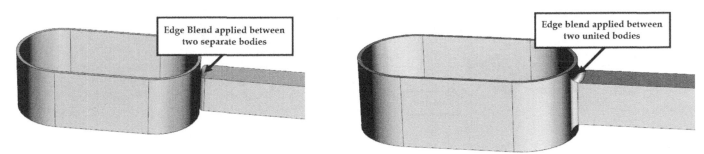

Intersect

By using the **Intersect** command, you can generate bodies defined by the intersecting volume of two bodies. Activate this command (click **Home > Feature > Combine Drop-down > Intersect** on the ribbon) and select two bodies. Click **OK** to see the resultant single solid body.

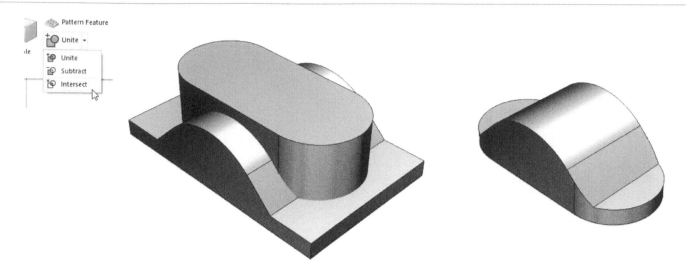

Subtract

This command performs the function of subtracting one solid body from another. Activate this command (click **Home > Feature > Combine Drop-down > Subtract** on the ribbon), and then select target body and the tool body. Click **OK** to subtract the tool body from the target.

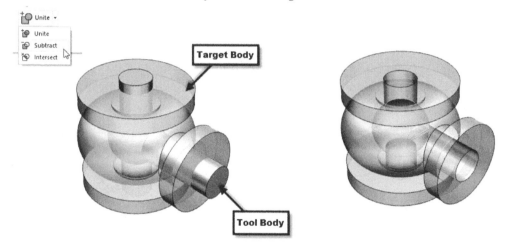

Emboss Body

This command allows you to change the shape of a solid body by using another solid body. The solid body that is changed is called the target body and the solid body that causes the change is called the tool body. To do this, you must have two solid bodies in a part. Activate the **Emboss Body** command (click **Home > Feature > More > Combine > Emboss Body** on the ribbon) and select the target and tool bodies. On the **Emboss Body** dialog, click **Select Region Object** and click on a portion of the tool body to define the side on which the body is embossed. Type-in values in the **Clearance** and **Thickness** boxes. Click **OK** on the dialog to complete the emboss body.

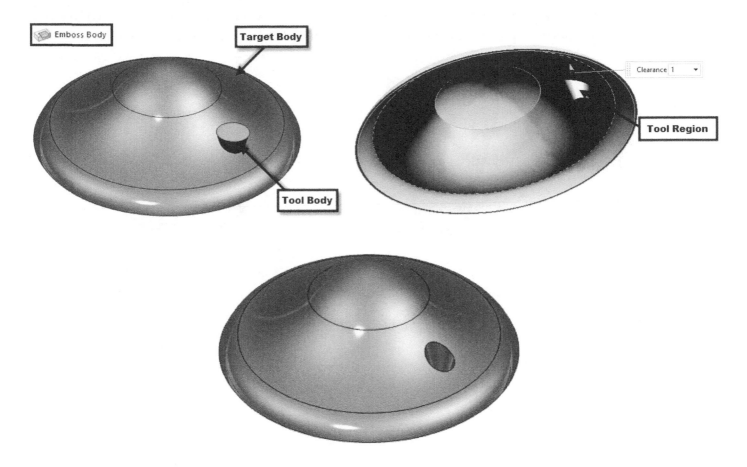

Swept Volume

This command removes material or creates an intersection solid by sweeping the volume of a solid body along a planar or non-planar curve. To sweep a volume, first create the target body and the tool path, and then create the tool body. Note that you should create the target and tool bodies as separate bodies (Set the **Boolean** option to **None**). The tool path should be created on the target face. The target face can be planar or non-planar. Also, note that the tool path and the axis of the tool body should intersect each other.

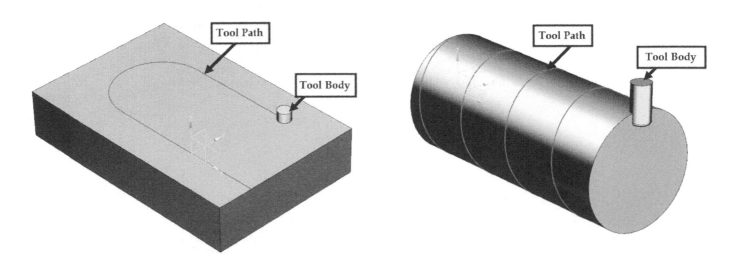

The tool body should be cylindrical or revolved solid with blend edges. However, you are not required to blend the edge of the tool body for the planar tool path. Examples of tool bodies are shown in figure below.

The following figure shows some examples of tool bodies which can be used for planar paths only.

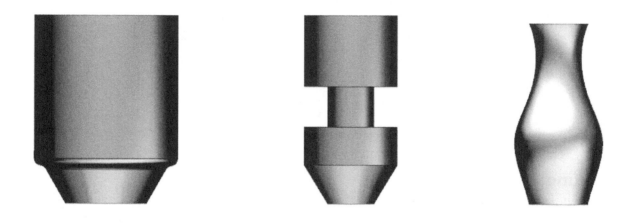

Sweeping Volume using Planar Tool Path

Activate the **Swept Volume** command (on the ribbon, click **Home > Feature > More > Sweep > Swept Volume**). Next, select the tool body and the planar tool path. On the **Swept Volume** dialog, expand the **Orientation** section, and specify the **Sweep Orientation**. Expand the **Boolean** section and select **Boolean > Subtract** to remove material from the target body. Click **OK** to create the swept volume.

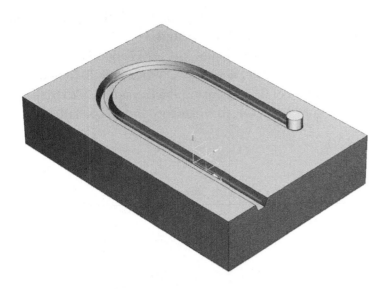

Sweeping Volume using Non-Planar Tool Path

Activate the **Swept Volume** command (on the ribbon, click **Home > Feature > More > Sweep > Swept Volume**). Next, select the tool body and the Non-planar tool path. On the **Swept Volume** dialog, expand the **Orientation** section, and select **Sweep Orientation > Normal To Path**. Click **Specify Lock Direction** and select the axis perpendicular to the tool body. Specify the **Boolean** type and click **OK**.

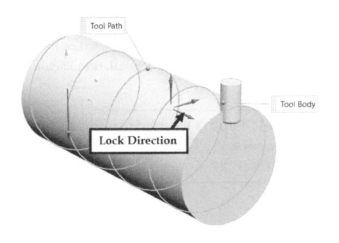

Creating Lattice

A lattice is a lightweight structural body created using the **Lattice** command. A lattice is created by tessellating (arranging) structural cells in two ways: **Unit graph** and **Conformal graph**.

Creating a Unit Graph Lattice

The Unit Graph lattice is created by arranging the structural cells within a closed volume defined by a solid body. Activate the **Lattice** command (on the ribbon, click **Home > Feature > More > Design Feature > Lattice**) and select **Type > Unit Graph** from the **Lattice** dialog. Next, click on the solid body that you want to use as the boundary of the lattice. On the **Lattice** dialog, under the **Unit Cell** section, select an option from the **Cell Type** drop-down (there are fifteen cell types to select from the drop-down). You can preview the cell type by placing the mouse pointer on the options available in the **Cell Type** drop-down. Check the **Uniform Cube** option, if you want the cell to be uniform in all the directions. Next, specify a value in the **Edge Length** box.

On the **Body Creation** section, specify the **Rod Diameter** and **Tessellation Factor**. The tessellation factor is multiplied with the rod diameter to get the tessellation tolerance (pattern tolerance). On the **Seed Placement** section, click **Specify Orientation**, and then specify the orientation of the cells using the Dynamic CSYS (refer to **Chapter 3: Extrude and Revolve Features, Datum CSYS** section). Click **OK** to create the Unit Graph lattice. Hide the solid body to view the lattice.

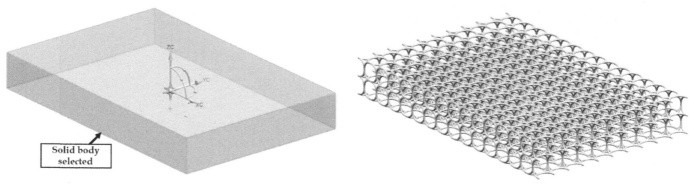

Creating a Conformal Lattice

The conformal lattice is created by arranging the cells in the boundary defined by a surface. You can also offset the lattice and create multiple layers of it. Activate the **Lattice** command (on the ribbon, click **Home > Feature > More > Design Feature > Lattice**) and select **Type > Conformal Graph** from the **Lattice** dialog. Click on a face to define the boundary of the lattice. Select a **Cell Type** from the **Unit Cell** section and check the **Uniform Cube** option. Type in a value in the **Edge Length** box to define the size of the cell. On the **Graph** section, specify the number of layers in the **Layer** box. Next, type in a value in the **Offset** box if you want to offset the lattice from the selected boundary surface. On the **Body Creation** section, specify the **Rod Diameter** and **Tessellation Factor**. Click **OK** to create the conformal lattice.

Cell Type: Octahedroid
Layers: 2
Offset: 20

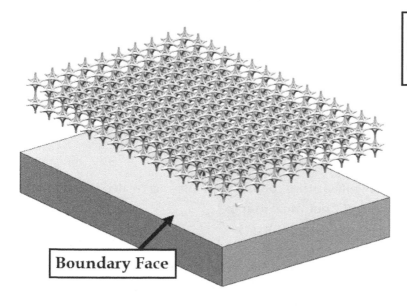

Examples

Example 1 (Millimetres)
In this example, you will create the part shown next.

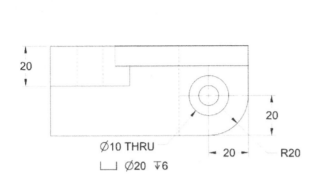

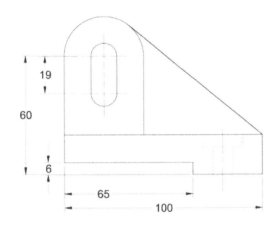

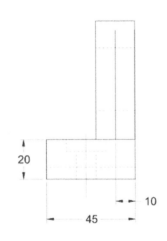

1. Start **NX 12** and open a part file using the **Model** template.
2. On the ribbon, click **Home > Feature > Extrude**. Next, select the XY Plane from the Datum Coordinate System.
3. On the ribbon click **Home > Curve > Rectangle**. Select the origin point of the sketch, move the pointer diagonally toward bottom right corner, and click create the rectangle.
4. Add dimensions to the sketch, as shown. Next, click **Finish** on the ribbon.
5. On the **Extrude** dialog, type 20 in the **Distance** box available under the **End** drop-down in the **Limits** section.

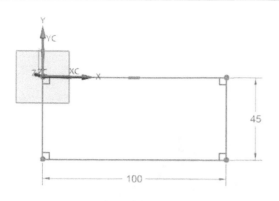

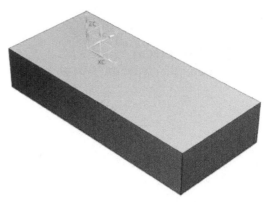

6. Activate the **Extrude** command (On the ribbon, click **Home > Feature > Extrude**). Select the XZ Plane from the Datum Coordinate System.

7. Activate the **Profile** command, if not already active. Create the sketch, as shown (Refer Chapter 2 for help). Next, click **Finish** on the ribbon.

8. On the Extrude dialog, type 20 in the **Distance** box available under the **End** drop-down in the **Limits** section. Expand the **Boolean** section and select **Boolean > Unite**.

9. .

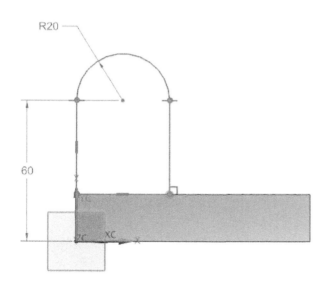

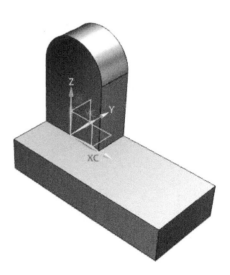

10. Activate the **Rib** command (On the ribbon, click **Home > Feature > More > Design Feature > Rib**). Click the **Select Curve** option and click on the XZ plane.

11. Draw a line, which is tangent to the curved face of the second feature and connected to the top right vertex of the first feature. Click **Finish** on the ribbon.

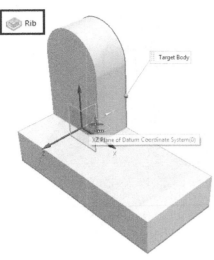

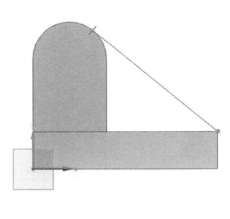

12. On the **Rib** dialog, under the **Walls** section, select **Parallel to Section Plane**.

13. Select **Dimension > Asymmetric,** and then type-in **10** in the **Thickness**.

14. Check the **Combine Rib with Target** option and click **OK** to create the rib.

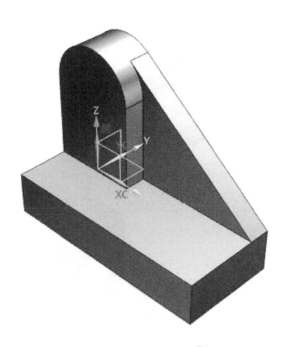

15. Activate the **Extrude** command (on the ribbon, click **Home > Feature > Extrude**).

16. Click the **Reset** icon on the **Extrude** dialog.

17. Click on the front face of the second feature.

18. Sketch a slot using the **Profile** command (refer to Chapter 2: Sketch Techniques to learn about the **Profile** command). Click **Finish** on the ribbon.

19. On the **Slot** dialog, select **Rectangular** and click **OK**.

20. On the **Extrude** dialog, under the **Limits** section, select **End > Through All**. Click the **Reverse Direction** icon in the **Direction** section, if the material is displayed outside the model.

21. Under the **Boolean** section, select **Boolean > Subtract**. Click **OK**.

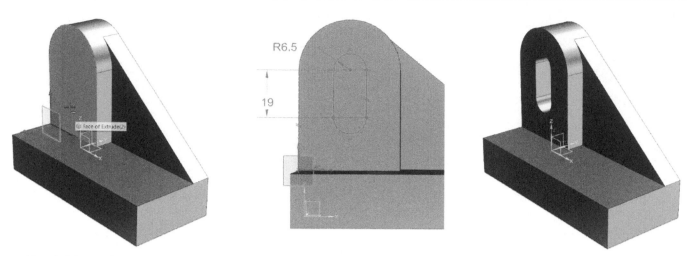

22. Add an edge blend of 20 mm radius to the right vertical edge of the rectangular base.

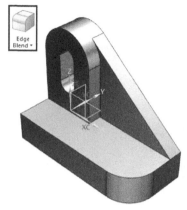

23. Activate the **Hole** command and create a counterbore hole concentric to the edge blend.

24. Construct an extruded cutout on the front face of the rectangular base.

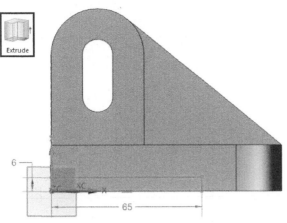

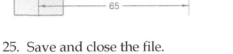

25. Save and close the file.

Example 2 (Inches)

In this example, you will create the part shown next.

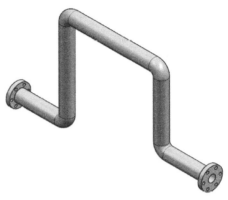

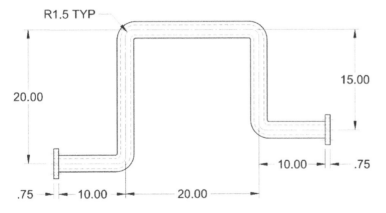

PIPE I.D. - 2
PIPE O.D. - 2.5

1. Start **NX 12**.
2. On the ribbon, click the **New** icon to open the **New** dialog.
3. On the **New** dialog, select **Units > Inches**.
4. Click the **Model** template, and then click **OK**.
5. Draw the sketch shown in figure on the XZ plane.

6. On the ribbon, click **Finish Sketch** to complete the sketch.

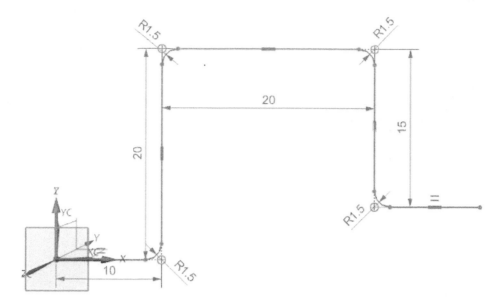

7. On the ribbon, click **Home > Feature > More > Sweep > Tube**.
8. On the **Tube** dialog, type-in **2.5** and **2** in the **Outer Diameter** and **Inner Diameter** boxes, respectively.
9. Click on the sketch, and then click **OK** to complete the *Tube* feature.

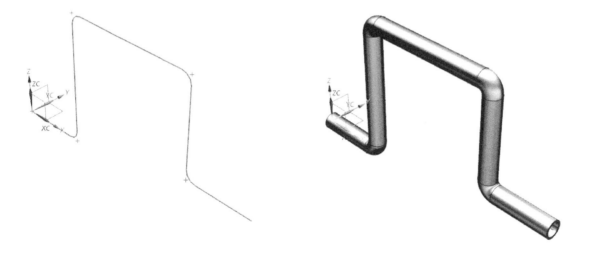

10. Activate the **Extrude** command and click on the front-end face of the *Tube* feature.

11. On ribbon, click **Home > Curve > Project Curve** and click on the inner circular edge.
12. On the **Project Curve** dialog, click **OK** to project the curve onto the sketch plane.
13. Draw a circle of 4.5 inches' diameter.

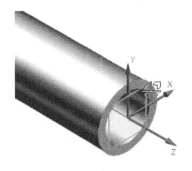
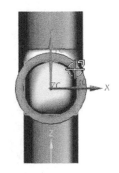
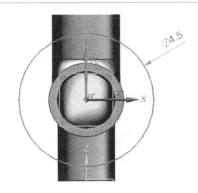

14. On the ribbon, click **Finish** to complete the sketch.
15. Type-in **0.75** in the **End** box attached to the preview. Click **OK** to complete the *Extrude* feature.

16. Create a hole of 0.50 diameter on the *Extrude* feature.

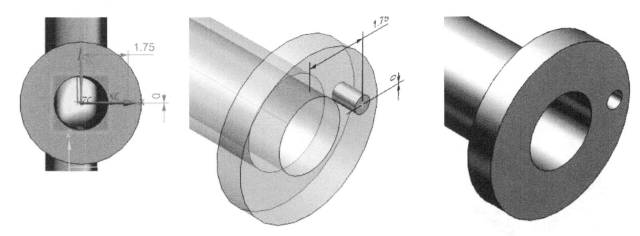

17. On the ribbon, click **Home > Feature > Pattern Feature**.
18. Click on the hole on the part geometry.
19. On the **Pattern Feature** dialog, select **Layout > Circular**.
20. Under the **Rotations Axis** section, click **Specify Vector** and select the X-axis.
21. Click on a circular edge of the flange to define the pattern axis.
22. Under the **Angular Direction** section, select **Spacing > Count and Span**.
23. Type-in **6** and **360** in the **Count** and **Span** boxes, respectively. Click **OK** to pattern the holes in a circular fashion.

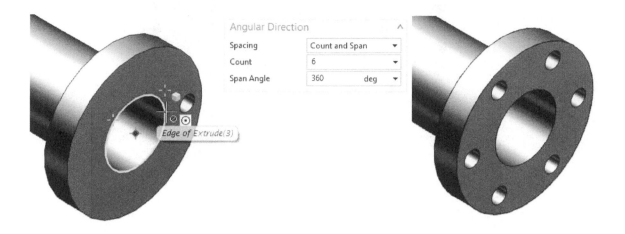

24. Change the model view orientation, as shown.

25. Create another flange and circular pattern.

26. Save and close the part file.

Questions

1. What is the use of the **Rib** command?

2. Why do we create multi body parts?
3. How do you split a single body into multiple bodies?
4. How do you add draft to a rib feature?

Exercises

Exercise 1

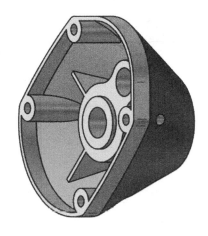

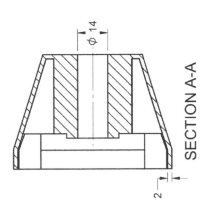

SECTION A-A

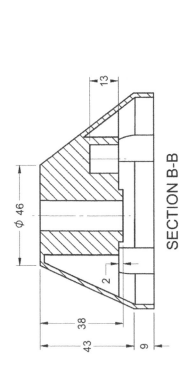

SECTION B-B

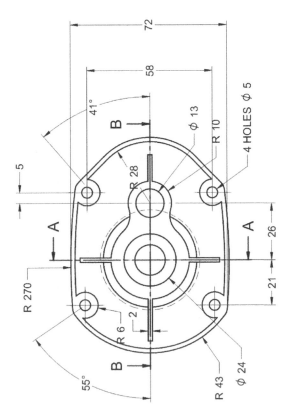

Exercise 2

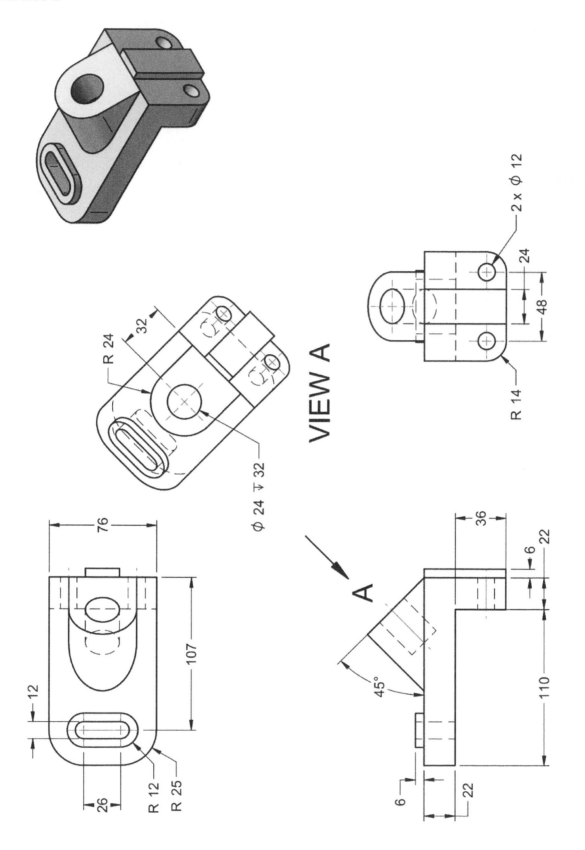

VIEW A

R 24
32

ϕ 24 ▽ 32

76

107

12

26

R 12
R 25

2 x ϕ 12

24

48

R 14

36

6
22

110

45°

6
22

Exercise 3 (Inches)

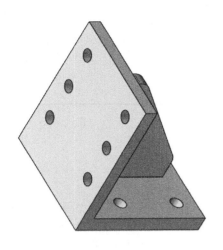

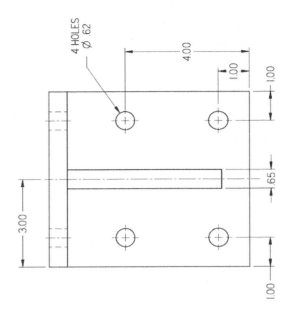

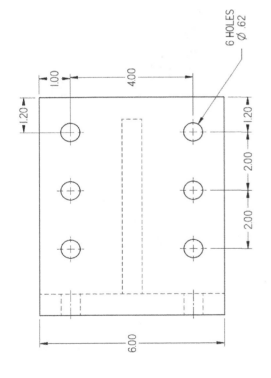

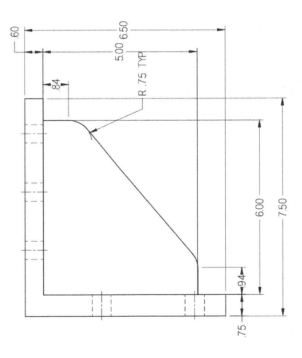

Chapter 7: Modifying Parts

In design process, it is not required to achieve the final model in the first attempt. There is always a need to modify the existing parts to get the desired part geometry. In this chapter, you will learn various commands and techniques to make changes to a part.

The topics covered in this chapter are:

- *Edit Sketches*
- *Edit Feature Parameters*
- *Synchronous Modeling commands*

Edit Sketches

Sketches form the base of a 3D geometry. They control the size and shape of the geometry. If you want to modify the 3D geometry, most of the times, you are required to edit sketches. To do this, click the right-mouse button on the feature to edit and select **Edit Sketch**. Now, modify the sketch and click **Finish** on the ribbon. You will notice that the part geometry updates immediately.

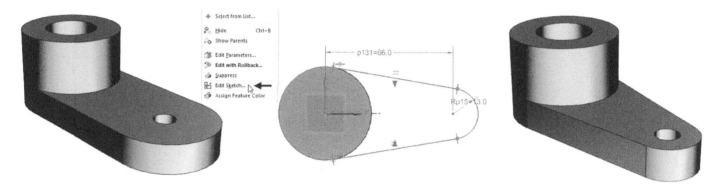

Edit Feature Parameters

Features are the building blocks of model geometry. To modify a feature, click the right mouse button on it and select **Edit Parameters**. The dialog related to the feature appears. On this dialog, modify the parameters of the feature and click **OK**. The changes take place instantaneously. You can also modify a feature by simply double-clicking on it and changing the parameters.

Suppress Features

Sometimes you may need to suppress the features of model geometry. To do this, click the right mouse button on

the feature and select **Suppress** .

Synchronous Modeling Commands

NX allows you to modify the part geometry instantaneously using the Synchronous Modeling commands. These commands help you to move, rotate, copy, replace, and offset faces. In addition, you can define relations and dimensions between the faces of the model geometry. The following sections explain various Synchronous Modeling commands.

Move Face

This command moves a set of faces and adjusts the side faces to accommodate changes. Activate the **Move Face** command (on the ribbon, click **Home > Synchronous Modeling > Move face**) and select a face. Drag the arrow that appears on the selected face, and then release the pointer to define the distance. You can also type-in a value in the **Distance** box.

To rotate a face, select **Transform > Motion > Angle** on the **Move Face** dialog, and then select a vector axis. Click on a vertex to define the origin of the vector axis. Select the face to rotate and drag the angle handle.

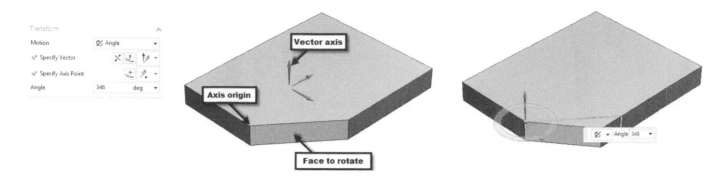

Use the **Cut and Paste** option to cut and paste a model face. To do this, activate the **Move Face** command, click on a model face, and then select **Settings > Move Behavior > Cut and Paste** on the **Move Face** dialog. Now, select **Transform > Motion > Distance**, and then select a vector axis to define the moving direction. Under the **Settings** section, check the **Heal** and **Paste** options, and then drag the arrow that appears on the selected face.

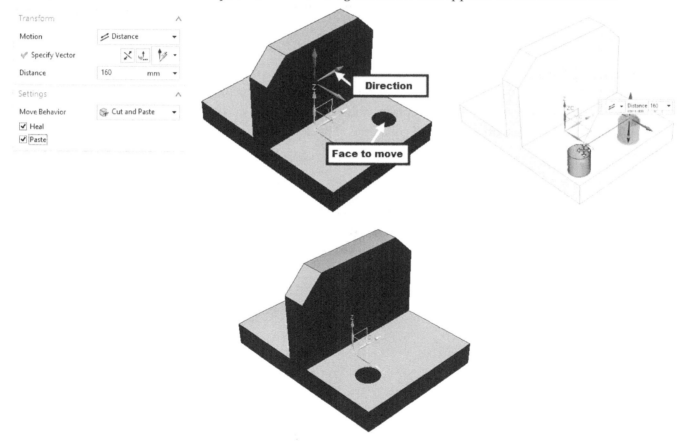

Pull Face

Use the **Pull Face** command (on the ribbon, click **Home > Synchronous Modeling > More > Pull Face**), if you want to pull the selected face and add new faces to the model. The new faces will be added perpendicular to the modified face.

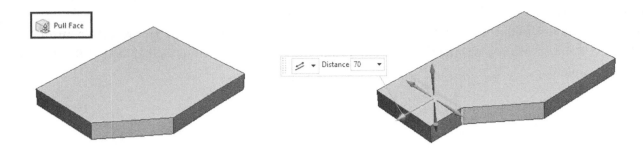

Offset Region

This command offsets a set of faces from the current position. Activate this command (click **Home > Synchronous Modeling > Offset Region** on the ribbon) and click on one or more faces. Drag the arrow that appears on the selected set or type-in a value in the **Distance** box.

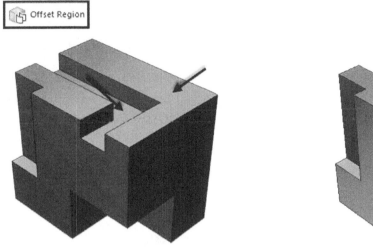
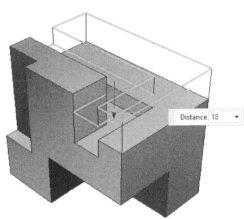

Replace Face

This command replaces a set of faces with another set of faces. Activate this command (click **Home > Synchronous Modeling > Replace Face** on the ribbon) and select the faces to replace. On the **Replace Face** dialog, under the **Replacement Face** section, click **Select Face** and select faces to replace with.

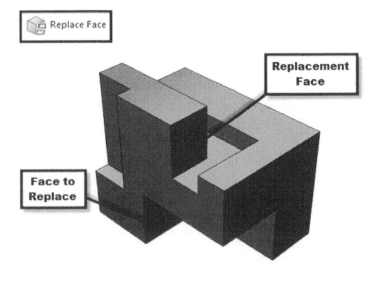
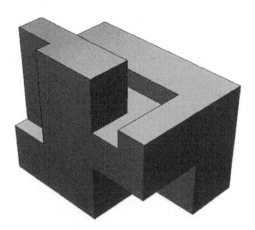

Make Coplanar

This command brings the selected faces onto one plane. Activate this command (click **Home > Synchronous Modeling > More > Relate > Make Coplanar** on the ribbon), and the select the first and second faces. Click **OK** to make the two faces coplanar.

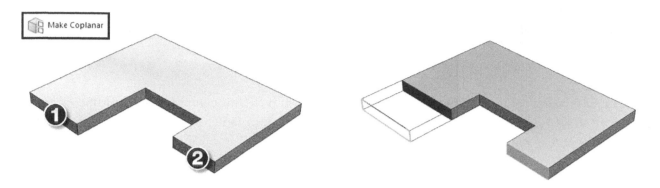

Make Coaxial

This command makes two cylindrical faces share same centerpoint. Activate this command (click **Home > Synchronous Modeling > More > Relate > Make Coaxial** on the ribbon) and select the first and second cylindrical face. On the **Make Coaxial** dialog, under the **Settings** section, select **Overflow Behavior > Extend Change Face**. Click **OK** to make the first face concentric to the second face.

Make Symmetric

This command makes two faces symmetric about a plane. Activate this command (click **Home > Synchronous Modeling > More > Relate > Make Symmetric** on the ribbon), and select the first face. Click on the symmetric plane, and then the face to remain stationary. Click **OK** to make the faces symmetric.

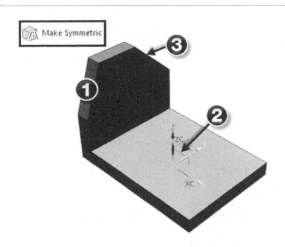

Make Offset

This command defines an offset distance between two faces. The selected faces should share a common face, which is perpendicular to both of them. Activate this command (click **Home > Synchronous Modeling > More > Relate > Make Offset** on the ribbon), select a face to define the motion face. Select a stationary face and type-in an offset value in the **Distance** box. Click **OK**; the first face will be offset from the second face by the value you specified.

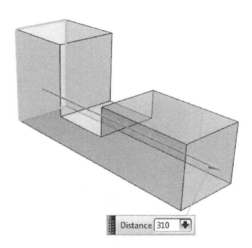

Linear Dimension

NX allows you to move a set of faces by adding a dimension and changing its value. To do this, activate the **Linear Dimension** command (click **Home > Synchronous Modeling > More > Relate > Linear Dimension** on the ribbon) and select the origin object. Click the on the object to move. Specify the measure direction by selecting a vector from the OrientXpress tool. Click to position the linear dimension. Now, type-in a value in the **Distance** box and click **OK**.

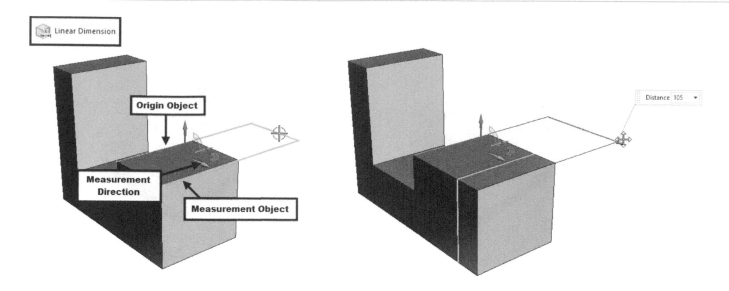

Angular Dimension

This command rotates a set of faces by adding a dimension and changing its value. Activate the **Angular Dimension** command (click **Home > Synchronous Modeling > More > Relate > Angular Dimension** on the ribbon) and select the origin object. Select the measurement object and click to specify the location of the angular dimension. Type a value in the **Angle** box or drag the handle to rotate the measurement object.

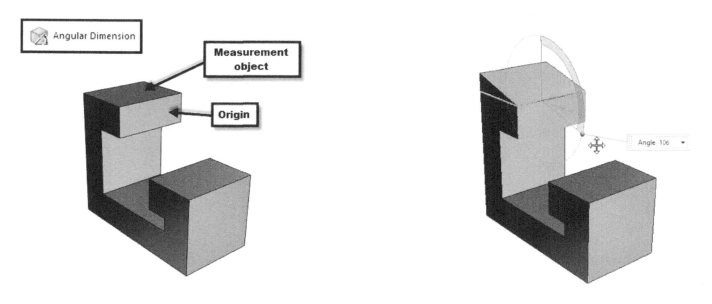

Make Parallel

This command makes two faces parallel to each other. The first face will be parallel to the second face.

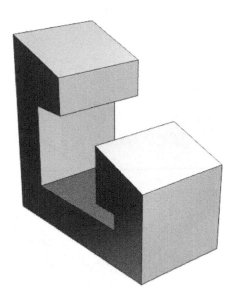

Make Perpendicular

This command makes two faces perpendicular to each other. The first face will be perpendicular to the second face.

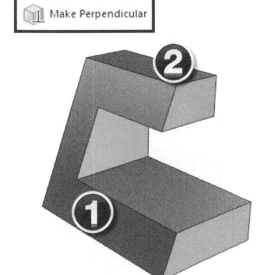

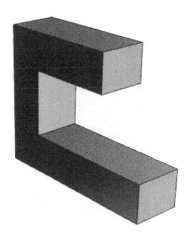

Label Notch Blend

This command recognises a curved face as a notch blend so that you can modify it using the synchronous modeling commands.

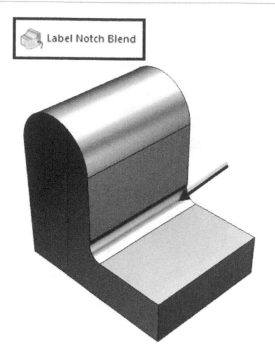

Resize Blend

This command increases or decreases the size of a blend.

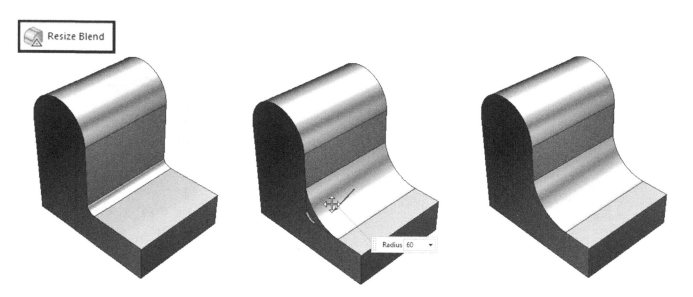

Replace Blend

This command converts a blend like face into an actual blend feature. For example, if you have created blends by adding sketch fillets, then you must edit the sketch in order to edit the blends. To solve this problem, activate the **Replace Blend** command (click **Home > Synchronous Modeling > More > Replace Blend** on the ribbon) and select the blend like faces. Click **OK** and now you can modify the blend using the Synchronous modeling commands.

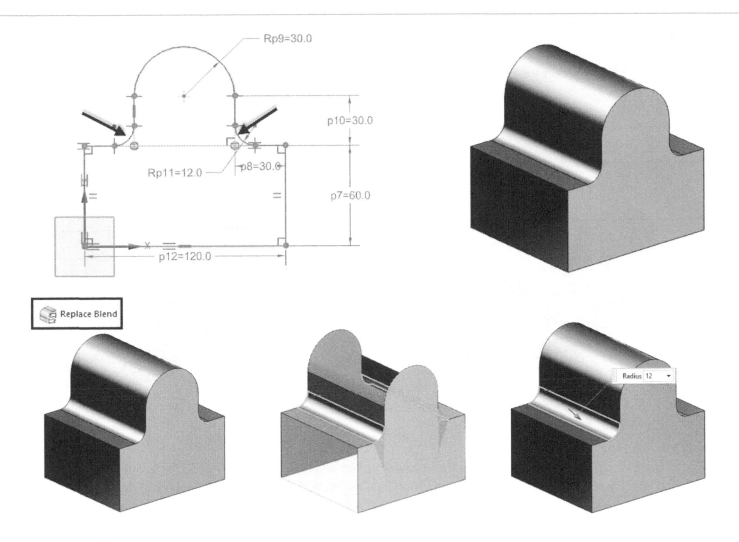

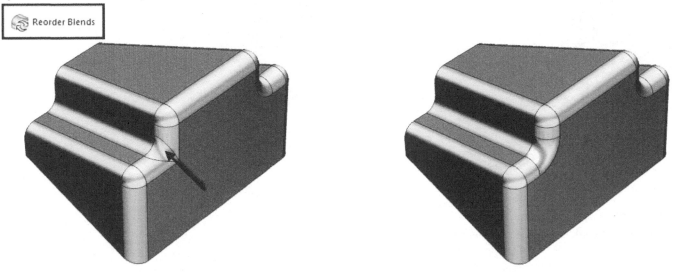

Reorder Blends

This command changes the order of intersecting blends. For example, if the blend 'B' overflows blend 'A', the **Reorder Blends** command results in blend 'A 'overflowing blend 'B'. Activate this command (click **Home > Synchronous Modeling > More > Reorder Blends** on the ribbon) and click on the intersecting portion of the blends.

Label Chamfer

This command recognises a bevel face as a chamfer. Activate this command (click **Home > Synchronous Modeling > More > Label Chamfer** on the ribbon), and then select a bevel face. Click **OK** to recognise the selected face as a chamfer.

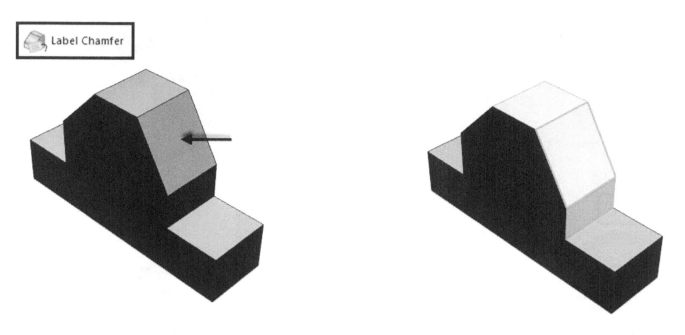

Resize Chamfer

This command changes the size of a chamfer. Activate this command (click **Home > Synchronous Modeling > More > Resize Chamfer** on the ribbon), and then select a chamfer. On the **Resize Chamfer** dialog, set the **Cross Section** type and specify the chamfer offset. For example, if you set the **Cross Section** to **Symmetric Offset**, then you have to specify only one offset. Click **OK** to make the changes.

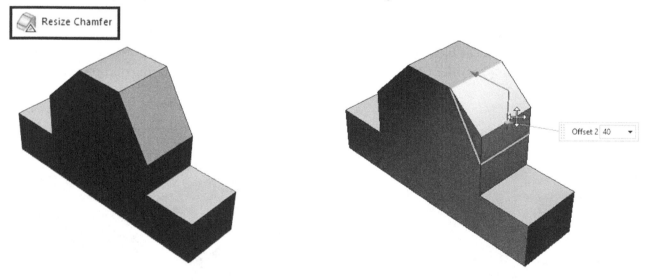

Make Tangent

This command makes two faces tangent to one another.

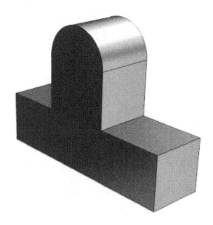

Radial Dimension

This command modifies a cylindrical face by adding a dimension and changing its value.

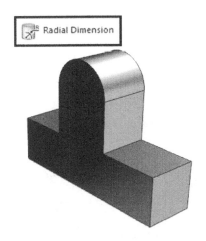

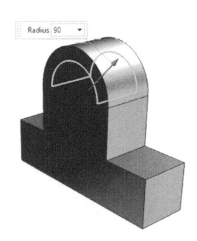

Resize Face

This command changes the diameter of a cylindrical face.

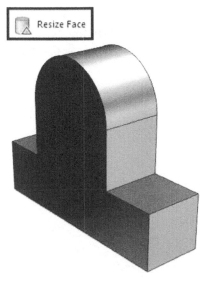

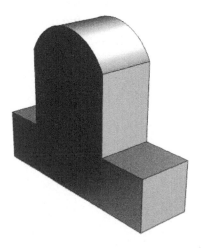

Edit Cross Section

If you want to create live sections and edit them, then activate the **Edit Cross Section** command (click **Home > Synchronous Modeling > More > Relate > Edit Cross Section**) and select the faces on the model. On the **Edit Cross Section** dialog, click **Select Plane** and click on a datum plane to create the cross section.

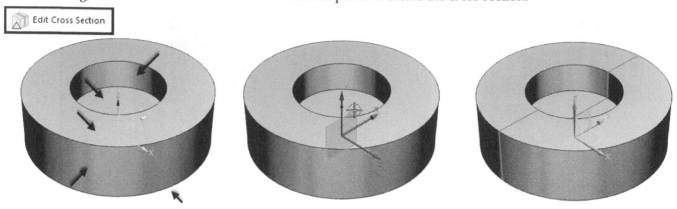

Now, click the **Edit Section Curve** button on the **Edit Cross Section** dialog to edit the cross section. You can now drag the sketch elements or apply relations and dimensions to the sketch. After editing the sketch, click **Finish** on the ribbon, and then click **OK**.

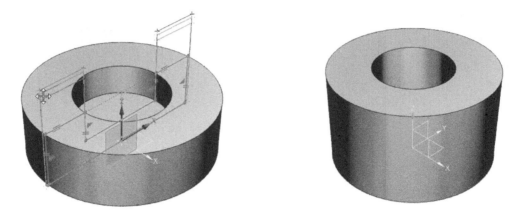

Delete Face

This command deletes the selected set of faces and adjusts the side faces. Activate this command (click **Home > Synchronous Modeling > Delete Face** on the ribbon) and select **Type > Face** on the **Delete Face** dialog. Next, select the faces to delete. If you want to replace the deleted face with another face, then click **Select Face** under the **Cap Face** section, and then select a face to use as a healing.

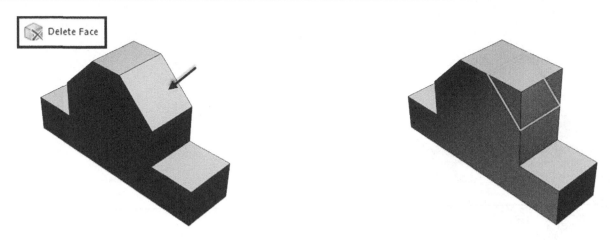

If you want to delete holes within a specific range of size, then select **Type > Hole** on the **Delete Face** dialog and type-in a value in the **Hole Size <=** box. Now, select a hole within the size range. You will notice the entire holes within the size range will be selected. Click **OK** to delete the holes.

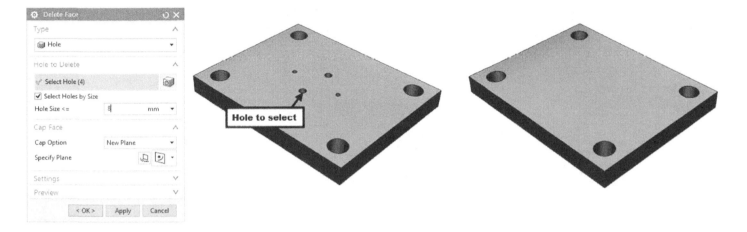

Likewise, you can delete blends using the **Blend Size** option.

Group Face

This command groups the selected set of faces. Activate this command (click **Home > Synchronous Modeling > More > Group Face** on the ribbon) and click on one or more faces. You can also drag a selection box to select multiple faces. Click **OK** to create a group. You can now copy and paste this group.

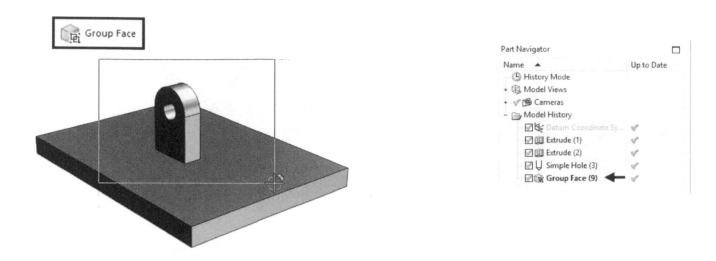

Copy Face

This command copies the selected set of faces or a group. Activate this command (click **Home > Synchronous Modeling > More > Copy Face** on the ribbon) and select a face or group of faces. Click on the origin of the OrientXpress Tool to display the axes. Select an axes to define the direction in which you want to move the copy. Drag the arrow that appears on the selected set and click **OK**.

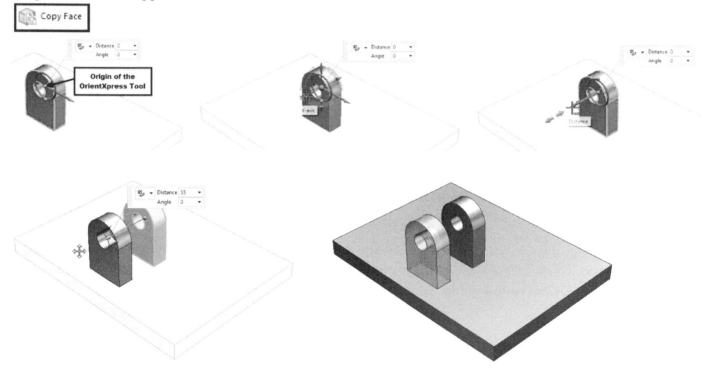

Paste Face

This command adds or subtracts a sheet body (surface body without any physical properties) to the model geometry. Activate this command (click **Home > Synchronous Modeling > More > Paste Face**) and select the target body (solid). Next, click on the sheet body, and then click **OK**.

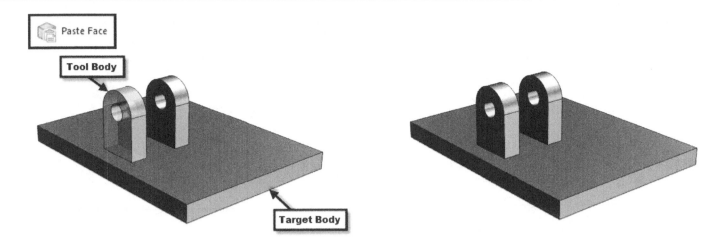

Mirror Face

This command copies and mirrors the selected set of faces across a plane. Activate this command (click **Home > Synchronous Modeling > More > Mirror Face** on the ribbon) and select the faces connected to each other. You can drag a selection box to select multiple faces at a time. Next, on the **Mirror Face** dialog, under the **Mirror Plane** section, click **Select Plane**, and then select a datum plane. Click **OK** to mirror the faces.

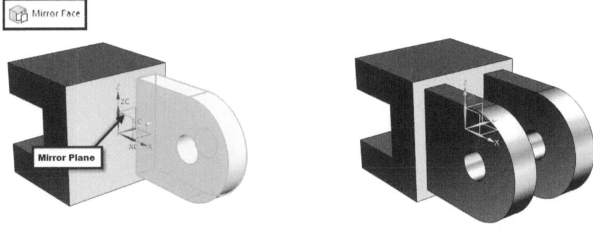

Examples

Example 1 (Millimetres)

In this example, you will create the part shown below, and then modify it using the Synchronous Modeling tools.

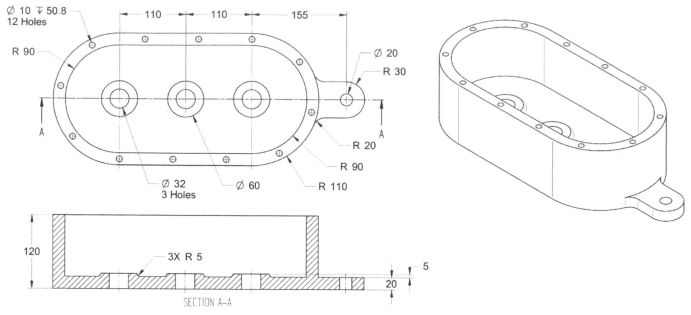

1. Start **NX 12** and open a part file using the **Model** template
2. Create the part using the tools and commands in NX. You can also download the part from the companion website.
3. Click on the 20 mm diameter hole. The context toolbar appears on the hole.
4. On the context toolbar, click **Edit Parameters** to open the **Hole** dialog.

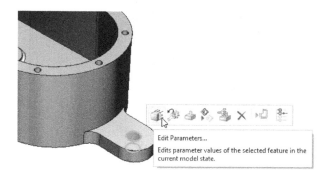

5. On the **Hole** dialog, set the hole **Form** to **Counterbored**. Set the **C-Bore Diameter** to 30 and **C-Bore Depth** to 10. Set the **Depth Limit** to **Through Body** and click **OK** to close the dialog.

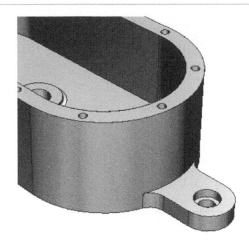

6. Activate the **Move Face** command (on the ribbon, click **Home > Synchronous Modeling > Move Face**) and click on the counterbore hole.

7. On the **Move Face** dialog, under the **Face Finder** section, select **Coaxial**.

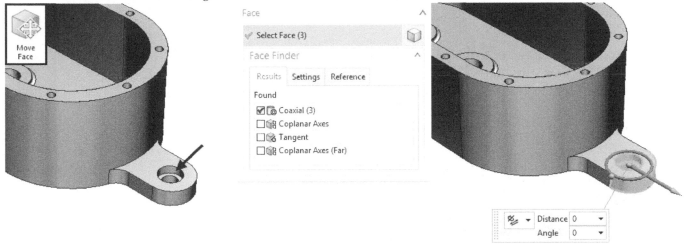

8. Drag the arrow that appears on the selected set, and then type-in 20 in the **Distance** box. Click **OK** on the dialog.

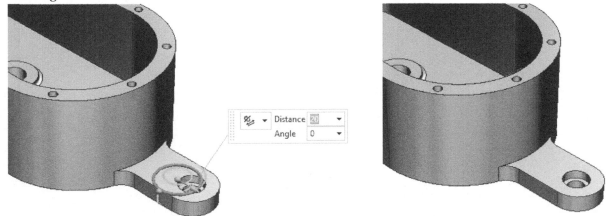

9. Activate the **Move Face** command and click on the side face of the bottom feature.

10. On the **Move Face** dialog, under the **Results** tab, check the **Symmetric** option.

11. Under the **Transform** section, select **Motion > Angle**.

12. Click on the Z-axis vector to define the rotation axis, and then click on the vertex shown in figure.

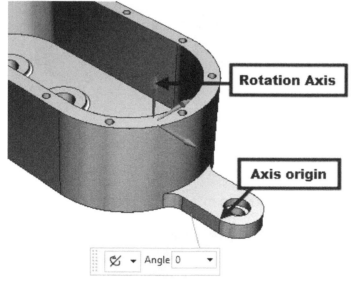

13. Click the spear handle and drag it.
14. Type-in 20 in the **Angle** box that appears on the geometry. Click **OK** to rotate the faces.

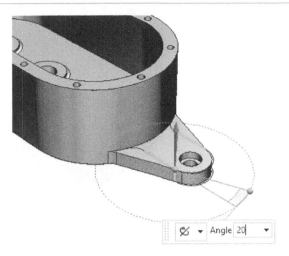

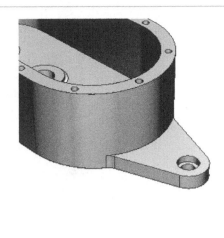

15. Select a hole from the **Pattern Feature (Along)** and select **Edit Parameters**.

16. On the **Pattern Feature** dialog, type-in 14 in the **Count** box and click **OK** to update the pattern.

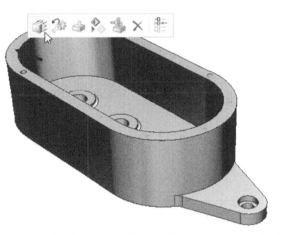

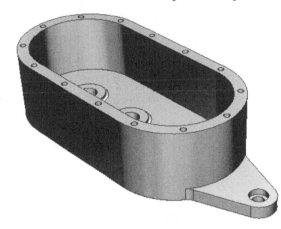

17. Activate the **Group Face** command (click **Home > Synchronous Modeling > More > Group Face**).

18. On the Part Navigator, select the **Pattern Feature** and **Simple Hole.**

19. Click on the top face of the geometry and click **OK**.

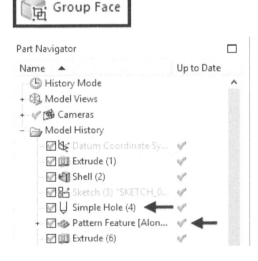

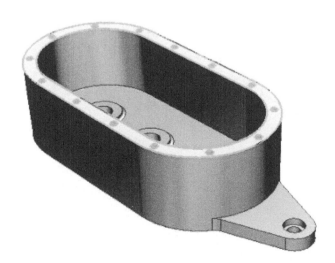

20. Activate the **Move Face** command and select **Group Face** on the **Part Navigator**.

21. On the **Move Face** dialog, select **Transform > Motion > Distance** and select the Z-axis vector.

22. Type-in -40 in **Distance** box and click **OK** to update the model.

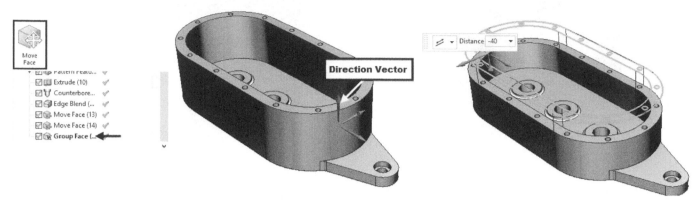

23. Save and close the file.

Questions

1. List any two face relationships.
2. List the uses of the **Move Face** command
3. How do you delete holes using the **Delete Face** command?
4. How do you modify revolved features using **Edit Cross Section** command?
5. What is the difference between the **Make Offset** and **Offset Region** command?

Exercises

Exercise 1

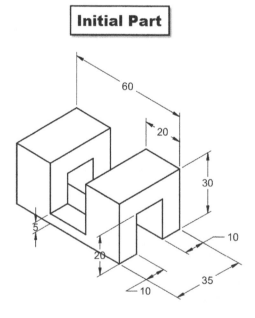

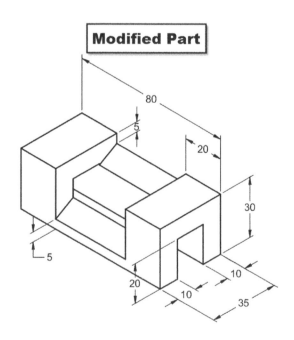

Chapter 8: Assemblies

After creating individual components, you can bring them together into an assembly. By doing so, it is possible to identify incorrect design problems that may not have been noticeable at the part level. In this chapter, you will learn how to bring components into the assembly environment and position them.

The topics covered in this chapter are:

- *Starting an assembly*
- *Inserting Components*
- *Adding Constraints*
- *Moving components*
- *Check Interference*
- *Remember Constraints*
- *Editing Assemblies*
- *Replace Components*
- *Pattern and Mirror Components*
- *Create Subassemblies*
- *Assembly Features*
- *Top-down Assembly Design*
- *Create Exploded Views*

Starting an Assembly

To begin an assembly file, you can use the **New** icon and select the **Assembly** template. Next, click **OK** to start the assembly file.

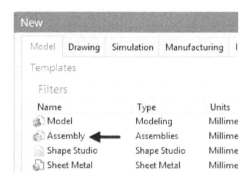

Now, you can insert components into the assembly by using the **Add Components** dialog. You can browse to the location of the components by using the **Open** icon available on the **Add Components** dialog.

Another way to start an assembly is to create it while a part is open. On the ribbon, click **Application > Assemblies**. This adds the **Assemblies** tab to the ribbon. Now, add components to the assembly using the **Add** command.

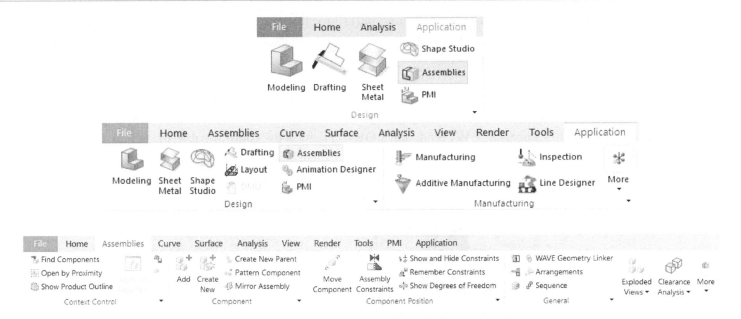

Inserting Components

There are two different methods to insert an existing part into an assembly. The first one is to insert using the **Add** command. The second way is to drag it directly from Windows Explorer. In the second method, you are not required to open the components in NX. You can simply drag-and-drop them into the assembly.

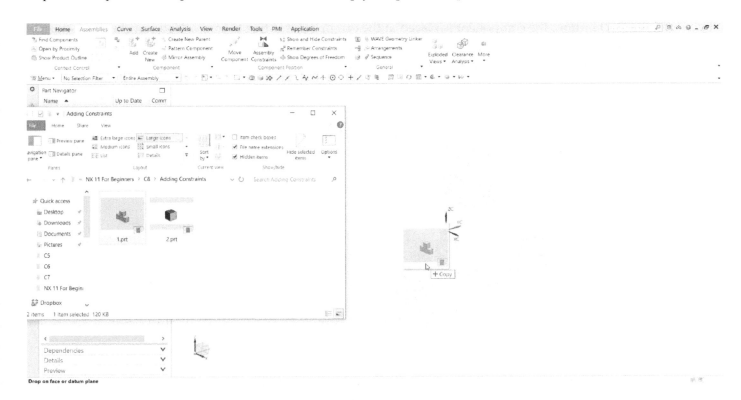

Adding Constraints

After inserting components into an assembly, you have to define constraints between them. By applying constraints, you can make components to flush with each other (or) two cylindrical faces concentric with each other, and so on. As you add constraints between components, the degrees of freedom will be removed from them. By default, there are six degrees of freedom for a part (three linear and three rotational). Eliminating degrees of freedom will make components attached and interact with each other as in real life. Now, you will learn to add constraints between components

Activate the **Add** command (on the ribbon, click **Assemblies > Component > Add**) and click **Open** on the **Add Component** dialog. Go to the location of the first component and double-click on it. On the **Add Component** dialog, select **Location > Assembly Location > WCS** and click **OK** to position the component at the origin; the **Create Fix Constraint** message box appears. Click **Yes** on the **Create Fix Constraint** dialog to fix the component at the origin.

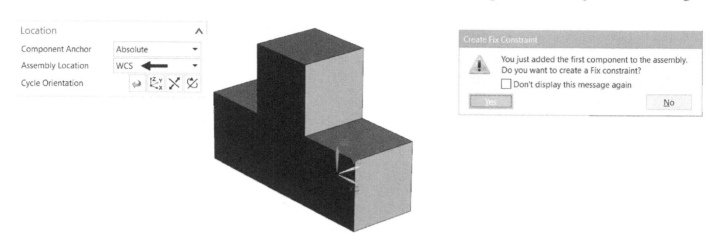

If you click the **NO** button, the component is placed at the origin but it is free to move. You can check the degrees of freedom by using the **Show Degrees of Freedom** command. Activate this command (On the ribbon, click **Assemblies > Component Position > Show Degrees of Freedom**) and select the component to display the degrees of freedom.

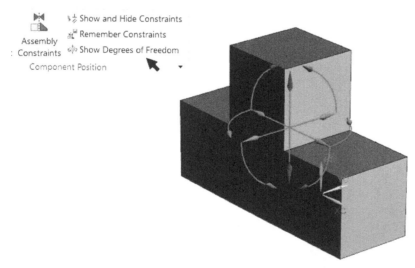

In order to remove the degrees of freedom, activate the **Assembly Constraints** command (on the ribbon, click **Assemblies > Component Position > Assembly Constraints**). On the **Assembly Constraints** dialog, select **Constraint Type > Fix** and click on the first component. Click **OK** on the **Assembly Constraints** dialog. Now, activate the **Show Degrees of Freedom** command and select the component. You can notice that the component is fixed at the origin.

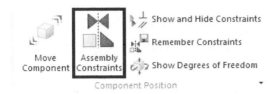

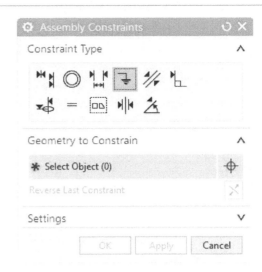

*Note: Click **Menu > View > Operation > Refresh** to update the view after applying the constraint.*

Now, activate the **Add** command and click the **Open** button on the **Add Component** dialog. Go to the location of the second component and select it. On the **Add Component** dialog, under the **Placement** section, select **Constrain** option. Next, click **Touch Align** button in the **Constrain Type** box. Select **Geometry to Constrain > Orientation > Prefer Touch**. Expand the **Settings** section, and then expand the **Interaction Options** subsection. Next, check the **Enable Preview Window** option; the **Component Preview** window is displayed. In the **Component Preview** window, click on the face to be constrained. Next, click on a face of the fixed part. Make sure that the **Preview** option is checked under the **Interaction Options** subsection. This shows the position of the component.

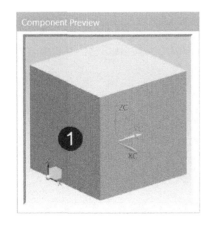

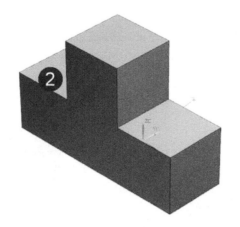

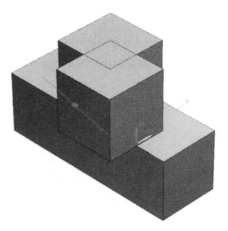

You can use the **Reverse Last Constraint** icon on the dialog to flip the part.

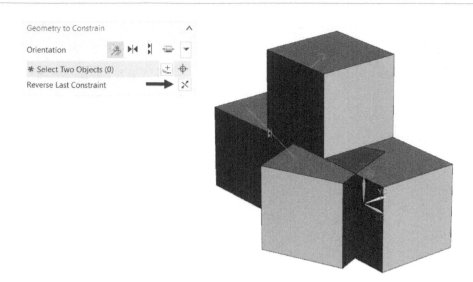

Select the second set of faces.

Select the third set of faces to constrain the part fully. Click **OK** to close the **Add Components** dialog. To confirm this, activate the **Show Degrees of Freedom** command and select the part.

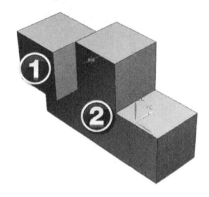

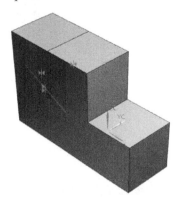

Move Component

While inserting a part into an assembly, you can choose to position it at the origin, add constraints, or move the component. To move the component, select **Placement > Move** option on the **Add Component** dialog, and then click **Specify Orientation** and click **Point** dialog button. On the **Point** dialog, select **Type > Cursor Location** and click in the graphics window. Click **OK** on the **Point** dialog. Now, use the Dynamic CSYS to move the part. For example, to move the part in the X-direction, select the **XC** handle and move the part (press and hold the left mouse button and drag the pointer).

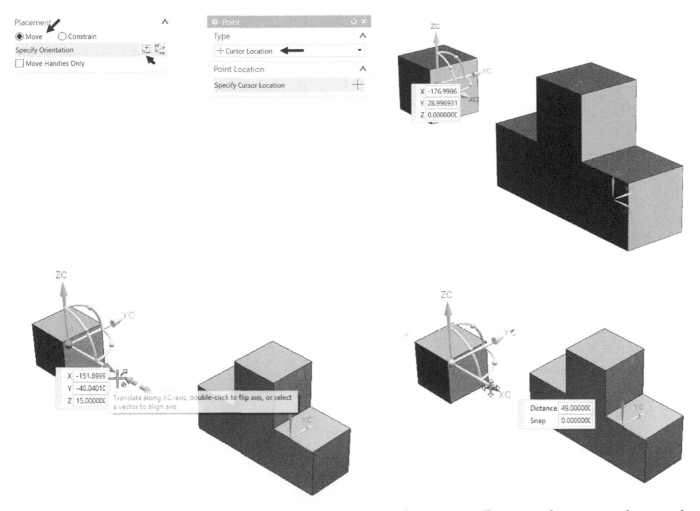

Use the rotate handles on the Dynamic CSYS to rotate the part about an axis. For example, to rotate the part about the X-axis, select the **Rotate about XC-axis** handle and rotate the part (press and hold the left mouse button and drag the pointer)

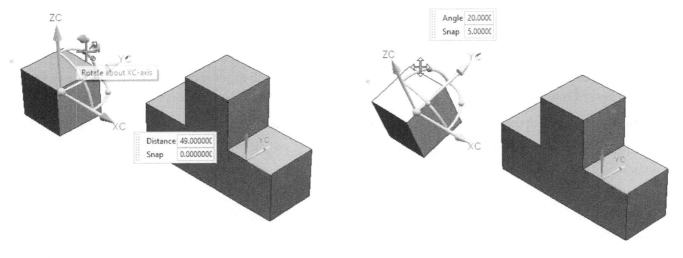

You can move the component using the **Move Component** command. Add the component to the assembly using the **Add** command. Next, click **Assemblies > Component Position > Move Component** on the ribbon. Select the component to be moved. On the **Move Component** dialog, select Transform > Motion > Dynamic. Next, click the Specify Orientation option and move the component using the Dynamic Coordinate System. On the **Move Component** dialog, select **Settings > Collision Detection > Collision Action > Highlight Collision**. Now, when the moving part collides with any other part, both the components will be highlighted.

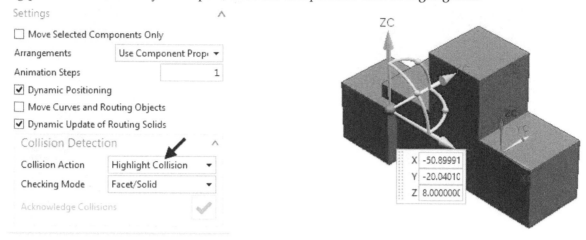

Use the **Stop Before Collision** option to stop the part when it collides with another part.

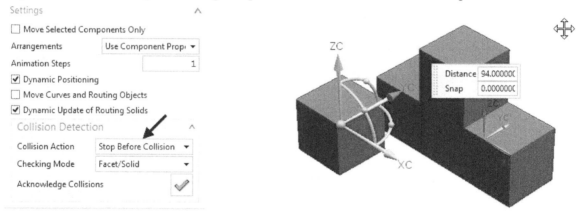

After completing the moving operation, click **OK** on the **Move Component** dialog to close it.

Touch Constraint

The **Touch** constraint makes two faces coincident and opposite to each other. You can define the **Touch** or any constraint between two components immediately after you insert them. On the **Add Component** dialog, under **Placement** section, select the **Constrain** option. Next, click the **Touch Align** icon in the Constraint Type section, and then select **Geometry to Constrain> Orientation > Touch** . Select a face of the inserted part, and then click on a face of the target part. The two selected faces will touch each other.

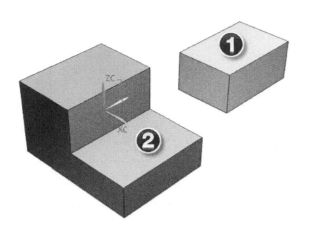

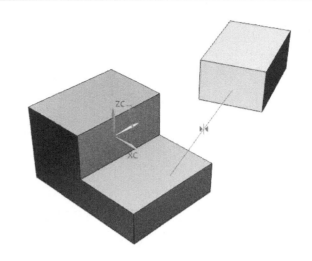

Similarly, select the second set of faces.

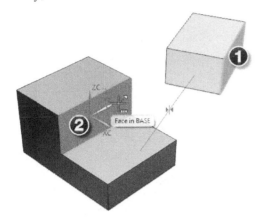

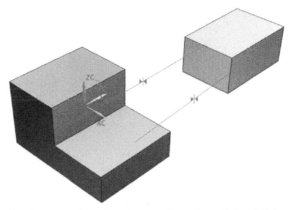

*Note: You need to check the **Preview** option in the **Settings** section under **Interaction Options** subsection of the **Add Constraints** dialog to view the placement component in the assembly window.*

You can also apply constraints using the **Assembly Constraints** command. You can activate this command after inserting the components and clicking **OK** on the **Add Components** dialog. The procedure to add different types of constraints is explained using the **Assembly Constraints** command. However, you can use the **Constraint Type** section on the **Add Components** dialog to apply constraints.

Align Constraint

The **Align** constraint makes two faces flush with each other. To add this constraint, insert the component into the assembly and click **OK** on the **Add Component** dialog. Next, click **Assemblies > Component Position >**

Assembly Constraints on the ribbon. On the **Assembly Constraints** dialog, click the **Touch Align** icon. Next, click the select **Geometry to Constrain > Orientation > Align** on the **Assembly Constraints** dialog. Select a face on the placement part, and then a face on the target part. This levels the two faces.

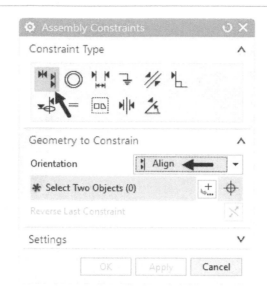

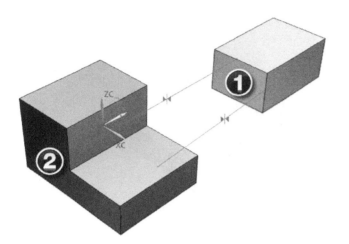
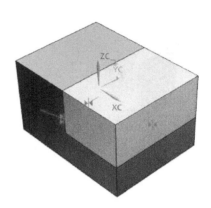

Infer Center/Axis

The **Infer Center/Axis** constraint makes the axes of two cylindrical faces coincide with each other. To do this, first activate the **Assembly Constraints** command, and select **Constraint Type > Touch Align**. Next, select **Orientation > Infer Center/Axis** and click on a cylindrical face, linear edge, or axis of the placement part. Click on an element on the target part. The two cylindrical axes will be aligned together.

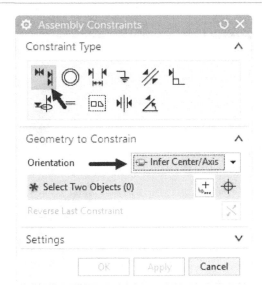

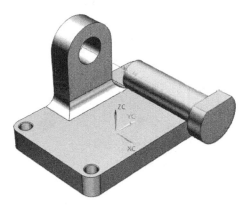

Align/Lock

If you want to align the axes of two cylindrical faces and lock the rotation, then the **Align/Lock** constraint will be useful. Activate the **Assembly Constraints** command and click the **Align/Lock** icon in the **Constraint Type** section. Next, select the axes of two cylindrical faces.

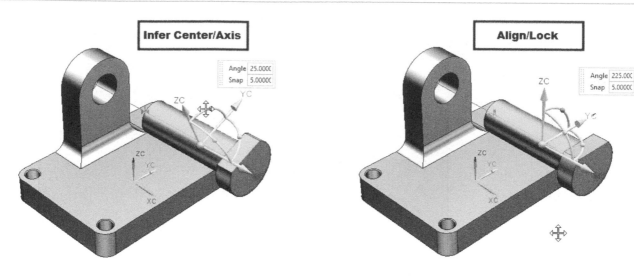

Concentric Constraint

The **Concentric** constraint helps you to make circular edges of two components concentric. To do this, activate the **Assembly Constraints** command and select **Constraint Type > Concentric**. Click on the circular edges of the two components.

Angle Constraint

The **Angle** constraint is used to position faces at a specified angle. On the **Assembly Constraints** dialog, select **Constraint Type > Angle** and set the **Subtype** to **3D Angle**. Click on a plane or linear element of the first part. Next, click on a plane or linear element of the second part and type-in a value in the **Angle** box on the **Assembly Constraints** dialog. Click **OK** to position the first part at the specified angle.

Parallel Constraint

The **Parallel** constraint makes an axis, face or edge of one-part parallel to that of another part. Activate the **Assembly Constraints** command and select **Constraint Type > Parallel** on the **Assembly Constraints** dialog. Select a planar face, cylindrical face, linear edge, or axis of the first part. Next, click on an element of the second part. Two selected elements will be parallel to each other.

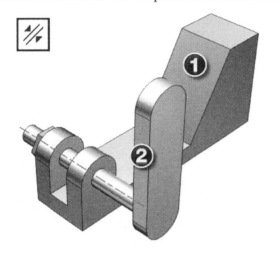

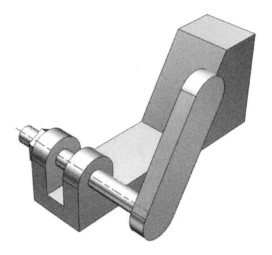

Perpendicular Constraint

The **Perpendicular** constraint makes an axis, face or edge of a part perpendicular to that of another part. Activate the **Assembly Constraints** command and select **Constraint Type > Perpendicular** on the **Assembly Constraints** dialog. Select a planar face, cylindrical face, linear edge, or axis of the first part. Next, click on an element of the second part. Two selected elements will be perpendicular to each other.

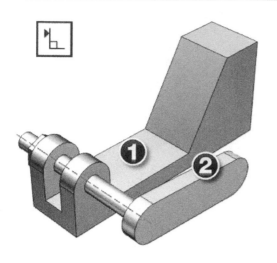

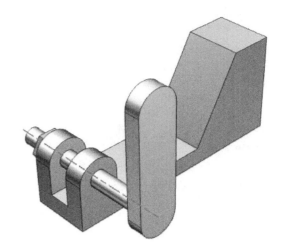

Distance Constraint

The **Distance** constraint offsets a component from another. To do this, select **Constraint Type > Distance** on the **Assembly Constraints** dialog and click planar faces of the two components. Next, type-in a value in the **Distance** box to define the distance between the selected faces. Next, expand the **Distance Limits** section and notice the **Upper Limit** and **Lower Limit** options. You can specify the maximum and minimum distance between the selected faces of the parts. Check the **Upper Limit** and **Lower Limit** checkboxes and specify the values in boxes located next to them. Next, click **OK** to apply the **Distance** constraint.

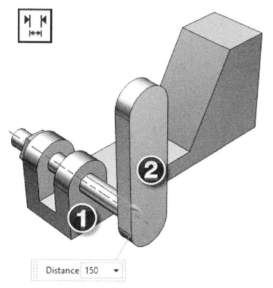

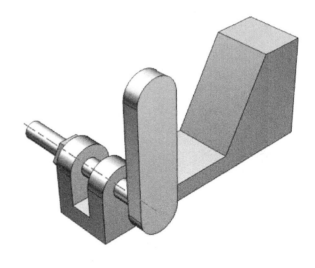

Next, click the **Constraint Navigator** tab on the **Resource Bar**. Next, right click on the **Distance** constraint and select **Make Driven**; the **Distance** constraint can be driven by another constraint or can be modified by the **Move Component** command. Activate the **Move Component** command (on the ribbon, click **Assemblies > Component Position > Move Component**). Select the component with the **Distance** constraint, and then click **Transform > Specify Orientation**. On the Dynamic Coordinated System, click on the axis which points in the direction of the **Distance** constraint. Next, drag the handle and notice that the selected part can be moved only between the upper and lower limit of the **Distance** constraint. Click **Cancel** on the **Move Component** dialog, and then **OK**.

Center Constraint

The **Center** constraint allows you to center a part between two faces. Select **Constraint Type > Center** ⫴ on the **Assembly Constraints** dialog and set the **Subtype** to **1 to 2** and **Axial Geometry** to **Use Geometry**. Select the first object to define the center, and then two references from the second component. Click **OK** to position the first part between the two references.

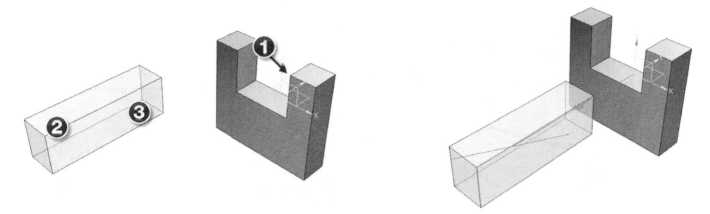

If you want to position a cylindrical part between two planar faces, then set **Axial Geometry** to **Infer Center/Axis**. Select the axis of the cylindrical object, and then click on two planar faces.

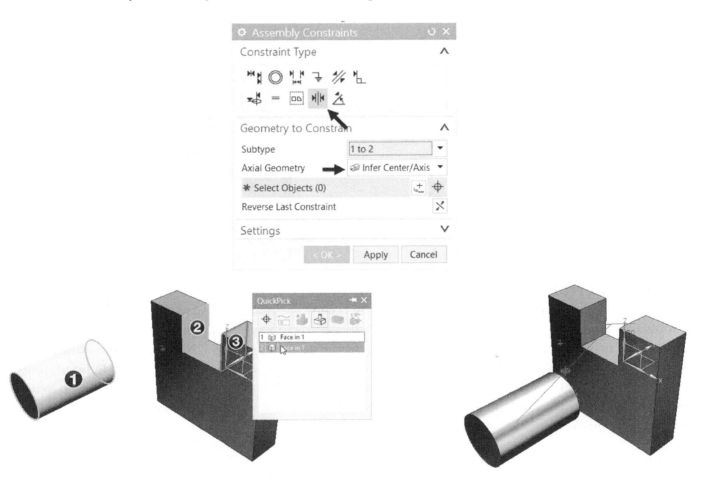

Bond Constraint

The **Bond** constraint makes components to form a rigid set. As you move a single part in a rigid set, all the other components will also be moved. To do this, activate the **Assembly Constraints** dialog and select **Constraint Type > Bond**. Next, select the components from the assembly window and click **Create Constraint** on the dialog. The selected components will form a rigid set. Click **OK** on the dialog. Now, if you change the position or orientation of one part, all the other components in the rigid set will also be affected.

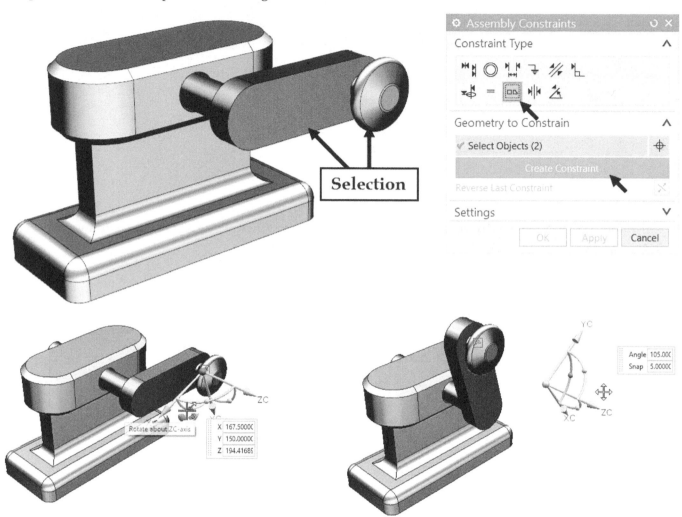

Simple Interference

In an assembly, two or more components can overlap or occupy the same space. However, this would be physically impossible in the real world. When you add relations between components, NX develops real-world contacts and movements between them. But, sometimes interferences can occur. To check such errors, NX provides you with a command called **Simple Interference**. Activate this command (click **Menu > Analysis > Simple Interference** on the Top Border Bar) and select the first body. Select the second body and set the **Resulting Object** option to **Interference Body**. Click **OK** to create a solid body at the intersection. Hide the two components to view the intersecting portion.

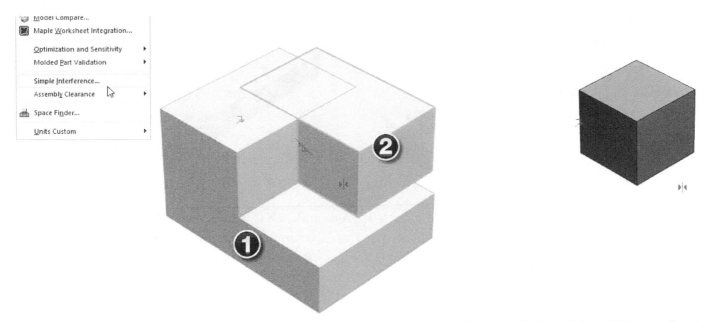

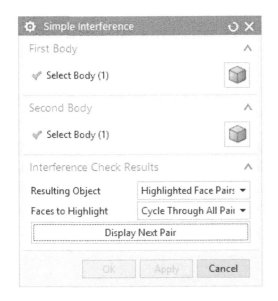

If you want to highlight the intersecting faces of the selected components, then set the **Resulting Object** option to **Highlighted Face Pairs** and select **Faces to Highlight > Cycle Through All Pairs**. Click the **Display Next Pair** button to view the next set of intersecting faces.

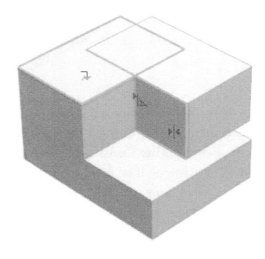

Remember Constraints

If you have an assembly in which you need to assemble the same part multiple times, it would be a tedious process. In such cases, the **Remember Constraints** command will drastically reduce the time used to assemble commonly used components. To use this command, first you need to define a constraint or set of constraints between two components. For example, define the **Concentric** constraint between the screw and the hole.

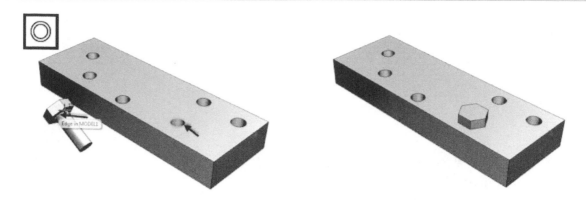

Activate the **Remember Constraints** command (click **Assemblies > Component Position > Remember Constraints** on the ribbon) and select the component (in this case, screw). On the **Assembly Navigator**, select the constraints associated with the selected component (in this case, the **Concentric** constraint) and click **OK** on the **Remember Constraints** dialog.

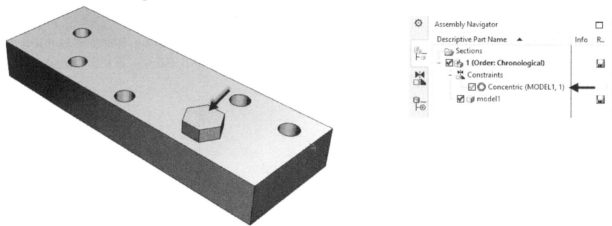

Now, activate the **Add** command and select the component (in this case, screw). On the **Add Component** dialog, select **Placement > Positioning > By Constraints**, and then select **Replication > Multiple Add > Repeat after Add**. Click **OK**; the **Redefine Constraints** dialog pops up on the screen. Now, select a circular edge on the block and click **OK**. The screw will be inserted in the hole and another instance of the screw appears. Select another circular edge on the block and click **OK**. Likewise, insert screws in rest of the holes and click **Cancel** to deactivate the **Redefine Constraints** dialog.

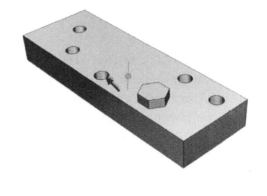

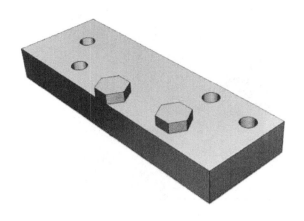
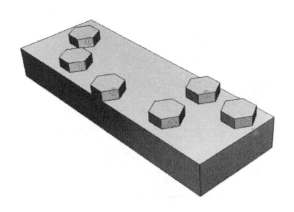

Editing and Updating Assemblies

During the design process, the correct design may not be achieved on the first attempt. There is always a need to go back and make modifications. NX, allows you to accomplish this process very easily. To modify a part in an assembly, left click on it and select **Make Work Part**, and then make changes to the part. Next, click **Assemblies > Context Control > Work on Assembly**. The part will be updated in the assembly, automatically.

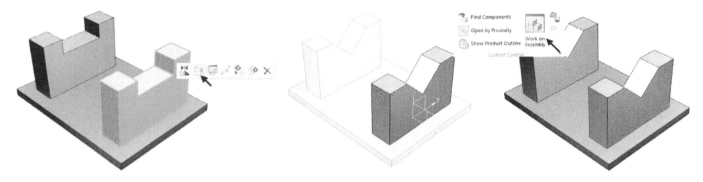

You can also redefine the existing constraints in an assembly. For example, if you want to change the faces that are aligned, then go to the **Assembly Navigator** and expand the **Constraints** section. Click the right mouse button on the **Align** constraint and select **Redefine**. The aligned faces will be highlighted. Press the Shift key and deselect the highlighted faces. Now, select another set of faces and click **OK** to align them.

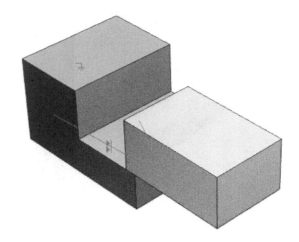

You can also convert an existing constraint into another type of constraint. For example, if you want to convert the **Align** constraint into **Distance** constraint, then click the right mouse button on it and select **Convert To > Distance**. Now, click the right mouse button on the **Distance** constraint and select **Edit** to change the distance value.

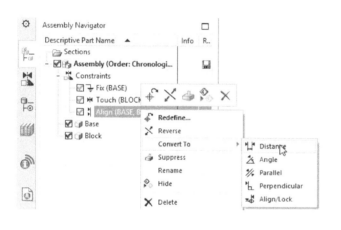
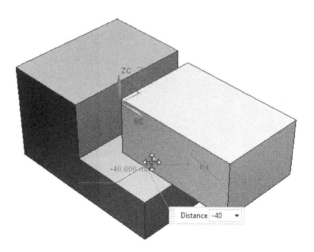

Likewise, you can delete, suppress, flip, or hide constraints.

Replace Component

NX allows you to replace any component in an assembly. To do this, go to the **Assembly Navigator** and click the right mouse button on the component to replace. Select **Replace Component** to open the **Replace Component** dialog. On this dialog, click the **Browse** button and go to the location of the replacement part. Select the component and click **OK**. If the new component is not similar to the old component, then a message appears showing that the component to replace is not a version of replacement part. Click **OK** to replace the component. Now, you can redefine the existing constraints or delete them and define new constraints. In this case, you can redefine the existing constraints.

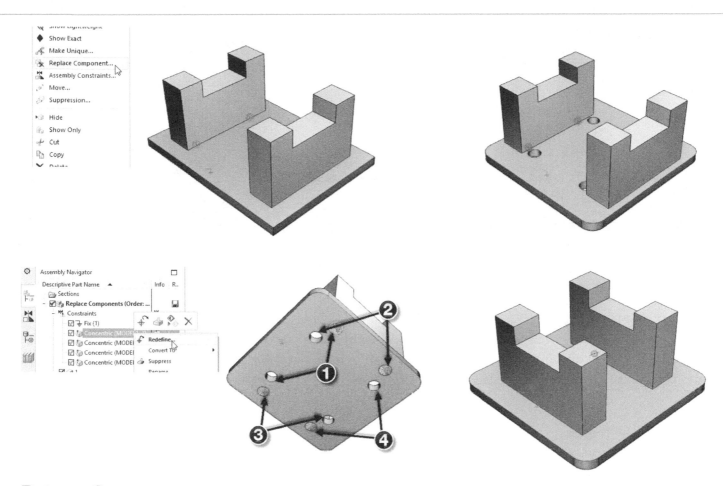

Pattern Component

The **Pattern Component** command allows you to replicate individual components in an assembly. However, instead of defining layouts of rectangular or circular patterns, you can select an existing pattern (**Pattern Feature**, **Pattern Face**, **Pattern Geometry**, or **Sketch Pattern Curve**) as a reference. For example, in the assembly shown in figure, you can position one screw using constraints, and then use the **Pattern Component** command to place screws in the remaining holes.

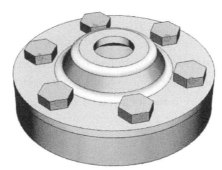

First, position the screw in one hole using the **Concentric** constraint. Next, activate the **Pattern Component** command (click **Assemblies > Component > Pattern Component** on the ribbon) and click on the part (In this case, screw) to include in the pattern. On the **Pattern Component** dialog, select **Layout > Reference**, and then click **OK**. The screw will be replicated using the existing pattern.

Mirror Assembly

When designing symmetric assemblies, the **Mirror Assembly** command will help you in saving time and capture design intent. To do this, first you must display the datum planes of the base component. Click the right mouse button on the base component and select **Replace Reference Set > Entire Part**.

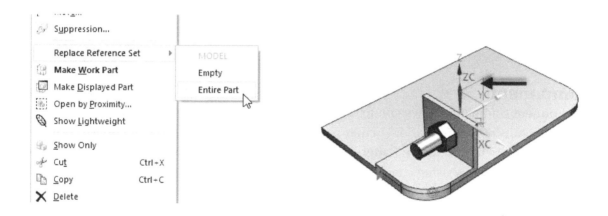

Now, activate the **Mirror Assembly** command (click **Assemblies > Component > Mirror Assembly** on the ribbon) and click **Next** on **Mirror Assemblies Wizard**. Select the components to mirror and click **Next**. Click on a datum plane to mirror about, and then click **Next**. Leave **Naming Rule** to default setting. Select **Add new parts to the specified directory** and click **Browse**. Go to the location of the current assembly folder and click **OK**. Click **Next** on the **Mirror Assemblies Wizard**.

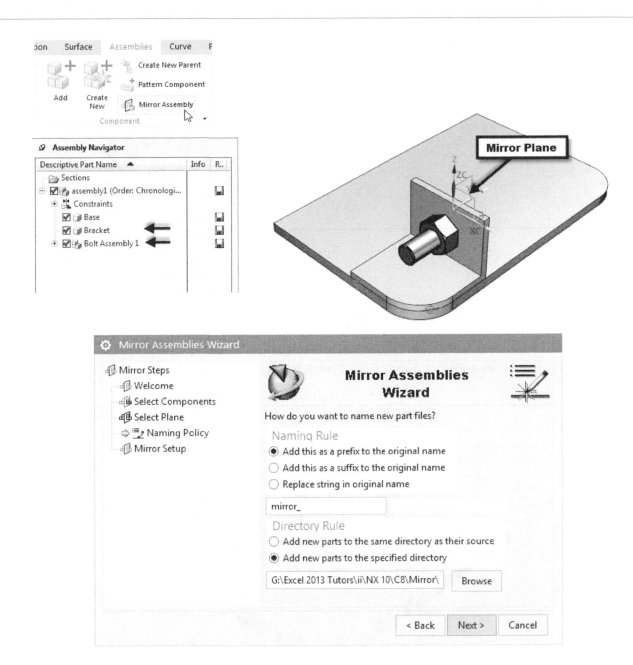

On the **Mirror Assemblies Wizard**, select the all the component to mirror, and then click the **Associative Mirror** icon. As you click **Next**, the **Mirror Components** message appears showing that this operation will create new part files and add them to the work part. Click **OK**.

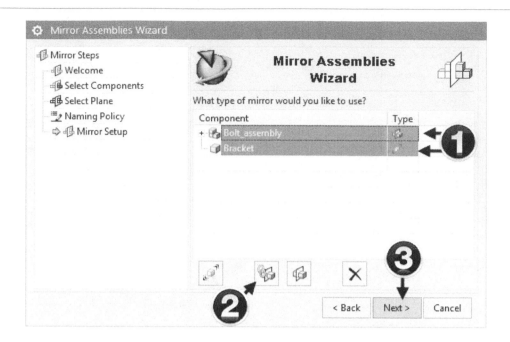

Review the mirror components and click **Next**. Click **Finish** to mirror the components.

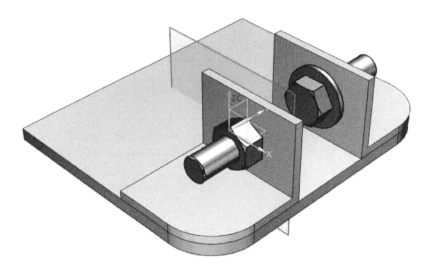

Sub-assemblies

The use of sub-assemblies has many advantages in NX. Sub-assemblies make large assemblies easier to manage. They make it easy for multiple users to collaborate on a single large assembly design. They can also affect the way you document a large assembly design in 2D drawings. For these reasons, it is important for you to create sub-assemblies in a variety of ways. The easiest way to create a sub-assembly is to insert an existing assembly into another assembly. You need to simply insert the assembly into an existing assembly using the **Add** command. Next, apply constraints to constrain the assembly. The process of applying constraints is also simplified. You are required to apply constraints between only one part of a sub-assembly and a part of the main assembly. In addition, you can convert a group of components into a sub-assembly and hide them. To do this, right-click on a sub-assembly and select **Hide**.

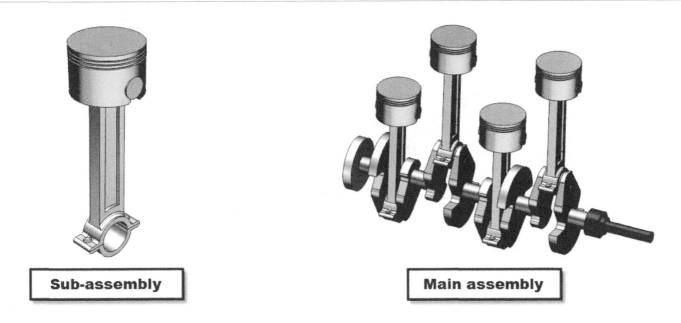

Assembly Cuts

Assembly cuts are the features that exist only in assemblies i.e. instead of creating them at the part level they are created at the assembly level. Most often the features created at the assembly level are cuts and holes. These features are commonly created at the assembly level to represent post assembly machining. For example, to add a cut feature to the assembly shown in figure, create a solid body in the assembly file, and then activate the **Assembly Cut** command (click **Home > Feature > More Gallery > Combine > Assembly Cut** ⊕ on the ribbon or click **Menu > Insert > Combine > Assembly Cut** on the Top Border Bar); the **Assembly Cut** dialog pops up on the screen. Select the target bodies, and then click the **Tool** button on the dialog. Select the solid body to define the tool, and then click **OK**.

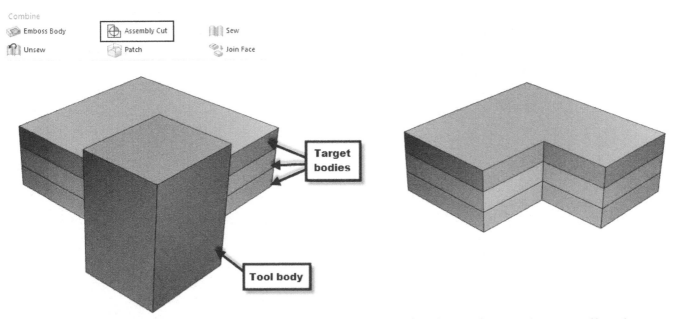

Now, open the individual part in another window. You will notice that the cut feature does not affect the part.

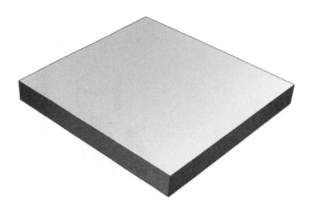

Top Down Assembly Design

In NX, there are two methods to create an assembly. The method you are probably familiar with is to create individual components, and then insert them into an assembly. This method is known as Bottom-Up Assembly Design. The second method is called Top Down Assembly Design. In this method, you will create individual components within the assembly environment. This allows you to design an individual part while taking into account how it will interact with other components in an assembly. There are several advantages in Top-Down Assembly Design. As you design a part within the assembly, you can be sure that it will fit properly. You can also use reference geometry from the other components.

Creating a New Component

Top-down assembly design can be used to add new components to an already existing assembly. You can also use it to create entirely new assemblies. To create a part at the assembly level using the Top Down Design, activate the **Create New** command (click **Assemblies > Component > Create New** on the ribbon). On the **New Component File** dialog, select the **Model** template from the **Template** section, and then type-in the name of the component in the **Name** box. Click **OK**. On the **Create New Component** dialog, define the required settings and click **OK**. You will notice that the component will be listed in the Assembly Navigator. Double-click on the component to activate the part mode. Now, create the features of the part, and then click **Assemblies > Context Control > Work on Assembly** to return to the assembly.

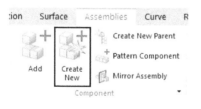
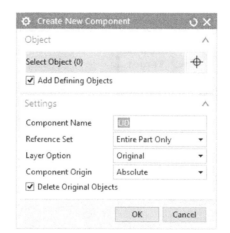
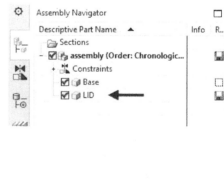

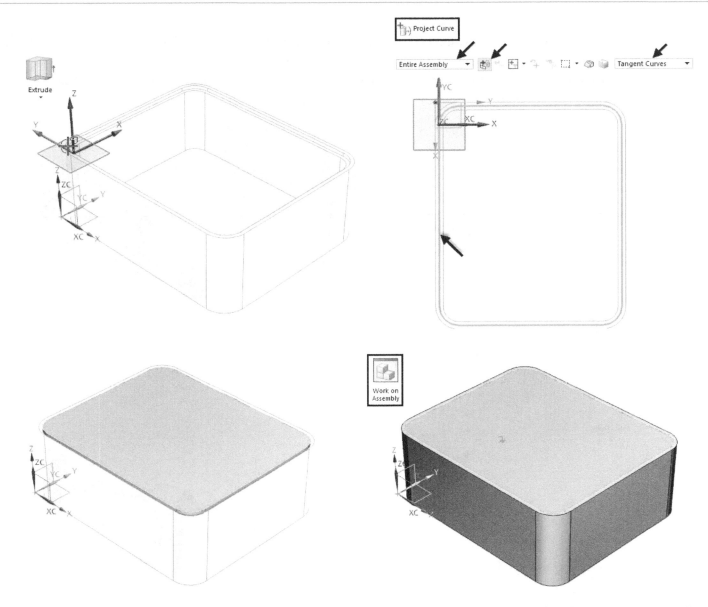

Now, if you change the parameters of the base component, the linked component will also change, automatically.

Exploding Assemblies

To document an assembly design properly, it is very common to create an exploded view. In an exploded view, the components of an assembly are pulled apart to show how they were assembled. To create an exploded view, activate the **New Explosion** command (click **Assemblies > Exploded Views > New Explosion** on the ribbon). Type-in the name of the explosion in the **Name** box and click **OK**.

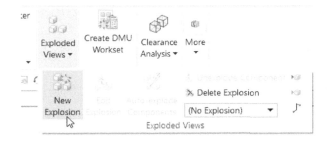

Use the **Auto Explode** command to explode the assembly, automatically. On activating this command, the **Class Selection** dialog pops up on the screen. Now, select all the components of the assembly by dragging a selection box, and then click **OK**. On the **Auto-explode Components** dialog, type-in the spread distance in the **Distance** box. Click **OK** to explode the assembly.

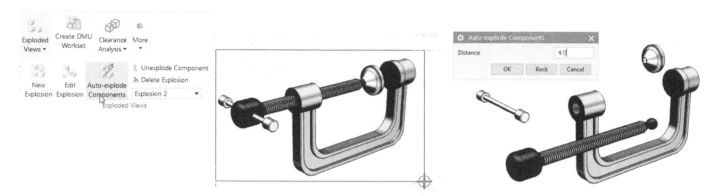

You will notice that the components are not exploded properly. To get a desired explosion, you need to use the **Edit Explode** command. First, unexplode this assembly using the **Unexplode Component** command. Click this button and select all the component of the assembly. Click **OK** to unexplode the assembly.

To explode an assembly manually, activate the **Edit Explosion** command; the **Edit Explosion** dialog pops up. Click on the components to be exploded, and then click the **Move Objects** option on the dialog. The Dynamic CSYS appears on the selected components. On the Dynamic CSYS, click on the X, Y, or Z handle to define the explosion direction. Type-in a value in the **Distance** box and click **OK** to explode the selected components.

Likewise, explode the other components.

If you want to draw a trace line, click **Tracelines** on the **Exploded Views** group and select the start and end points; a trace line appears between the selected points. Double-click on the arrow attached to the end-point to reverse the direction of the traceline.

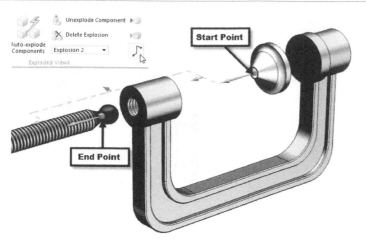
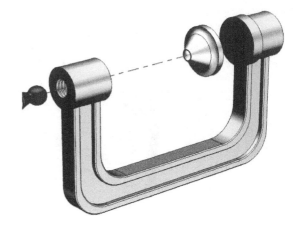

Likewise, create the other tracelines.

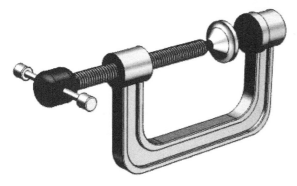

After the exploding the assembly, click **Exploded Views > Work View Explosion drop-down > No Explosion** on the ribbon to come back to the work view.

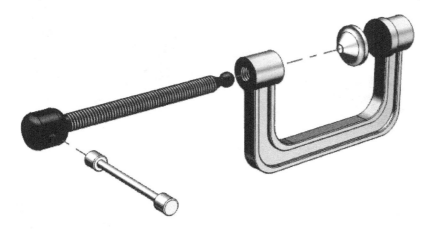

Examples

Example 1 (Bottom Up Assembly)

In this example, you will create the assembly shown next.

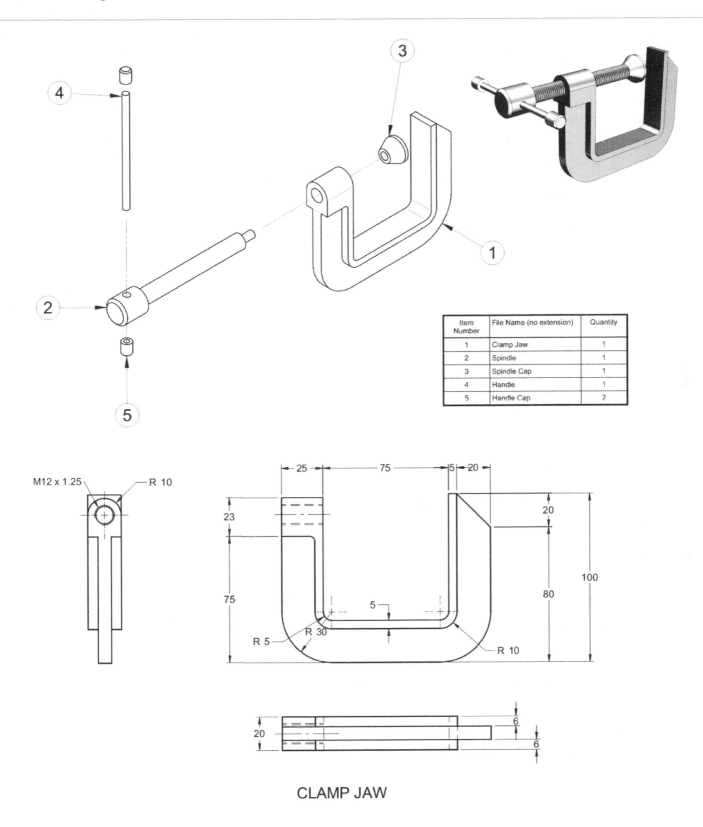

Item Number	File Name (no extension)	Quantity
1	Clamp Jaw	1
2	Spindle	1
3	Spindle Cap	1
4	Handle	1
5	Handle Cap	2

CLAMP JAW

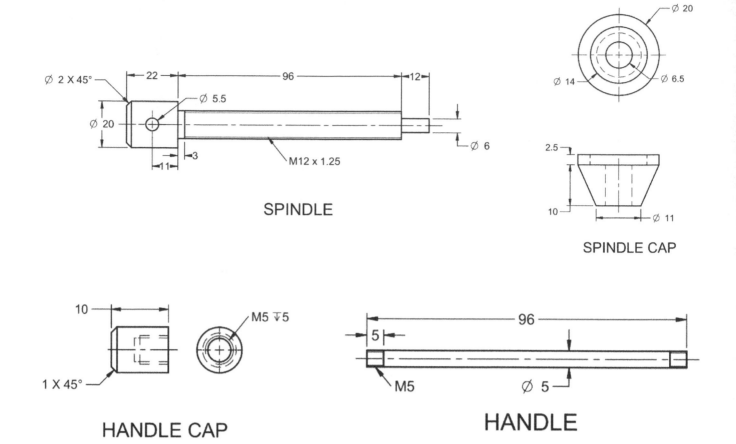

SPINDLE

SPINDLE CAP

HANDLE CAP

HANDLE

1. Start **NX 12**.
2. Create and save all the components of the assembly in a single folder. Name this folder as *G-Clamp*. Close all the files.
3. On the ribbon, click the **New** button to open the **New** dialog.
4. On the **New** dialog, select the **Assembly** template and click **OK**.
5. On the **Add Components** dialog, click the **Open** button and go to the *G-Clamp* folder. Select the *Clamp Jaw* and click **OK**.
6. On the **Add Component** dialog, click the **Reset** icon.
7. On the **Add Component** dialog, under the **Location** section, select **Assembly Location > WCS**. Next, select **Placement > Constrain**.
8. On the **Add Component** dialog, under the **Constraint Type** section, select the **Fix** icon and click on the *Clamp Jaw* displayed in the graphics window. Next, click the **OK** button.

9. Activate the **Add**  command (click **Assemblies > Component > Add** on the ribbon). On the **Add Component** dialog, click the **Open** button and go to the G-Clamp folder. Double-click on the *Spindle.prt* file.

10. On the **Add Component** dialog, select **Placement > Constrain**. Next, select **Constraint Type > Touch Align** and set the **Orientation** to **Infer Center/Axis** .

11. On the **Add Component** dialog, under the **Settings** section, uncheck the **Preview** option. Next, check the **Enable Preview Window** option.

12. Click on the cylindrical face of the *Spindle* and hole of the *Clamp Jaw*.

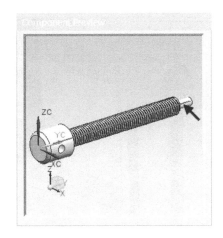

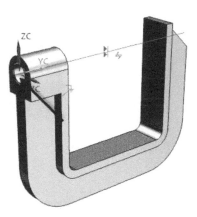

13. On the **Add Component** dialog, select **Constraint Type > Distance** and click on the back face of the *Spindle*.

14. Rotate the view and click on the flat face of the *Clamp Jaw*, as shown in figure.

15. Type-in **40** in the **Distance** box and click **OK**.

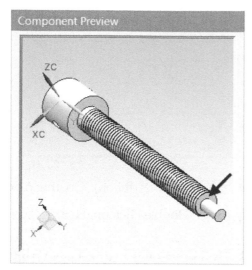

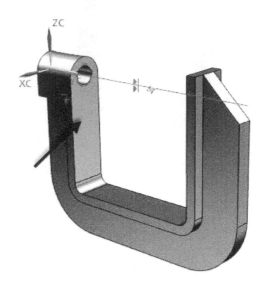

16. On the ribbon, click **Assemblies > Component Position > Show Degrees of Freedom** and select the *Spindle*. You can notice that the spindle is free to rotate.

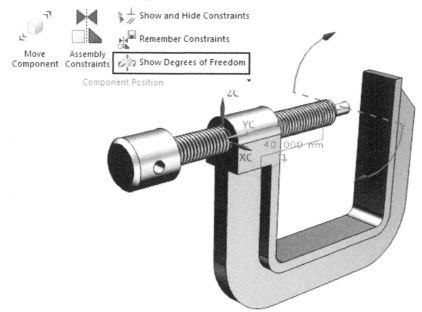

17. On the ribbon, click **Assemblies > More > Other > Replace Reference Set**, and then click on the spindle. Click **OK**.

18. On the **Replace Reference Set** dialog, select **Entire Part** and click **OK**. All the datum planes of the spindle appear.

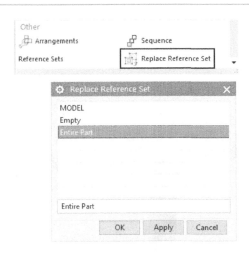

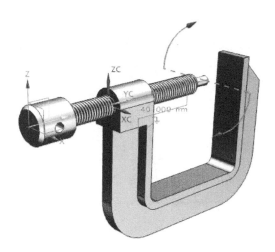

19. Activate the **Assembly Constraints** command (on the ribbon, click **Assemblies > Component Position > Assembly Constraints**) and select **Constraint Type > Parallel** .

20. Click on the XY plane of the *Spindle* and bottom flat face of the *Clamp Jaw*. Click **OK** to apply the parallel constraint.

21. On the Top Border Bar, click **Menu > View > Operations > Refresh**.

22. Now, activate the **Show Degrees of Freedom** command and select the spindle. You will notice that the spindle is fully constrained.

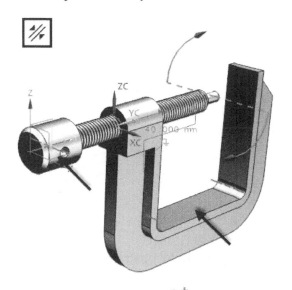

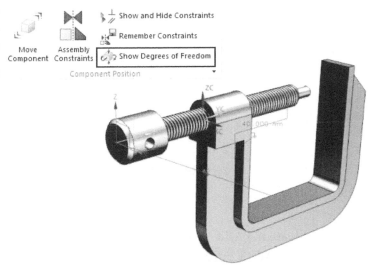

23. Activate the **Add** command(click **Assemblies > Component > Add** on the ribbon).

24. On the **Add Components** dialog, click the **Open** button and go to the *G-Clamp* folder. Select the *Spindle Cap.prt* file and click **OK**.

25. On the **Add Component** dialog, select **Settings > Reference Set > Entire Part**.

26. On the **Add Component** dialog, click **Placement > Constrain**. Next, select **Constraint Type > Concentric** and click on the inner circular edge of the *Spindle Cap* hole.

27. Rotate the assembly and select the circular edge of the spindle, as shown. Click **OK**.

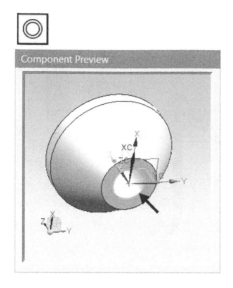

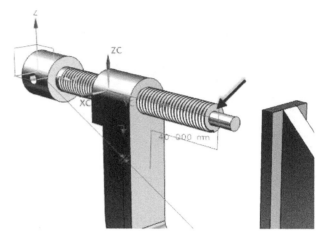

28. Activate the **Assembly Constraints** command. On the **Assembly Constraints** dialog, select **Type > Touch Align** and set the **Orientation** to **Align**.

29. Click on the YZ planes of the *Spindle Cap* and *Spindle*. Click **OK**.

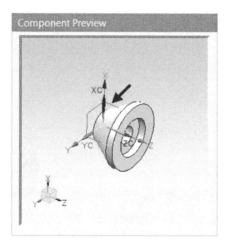

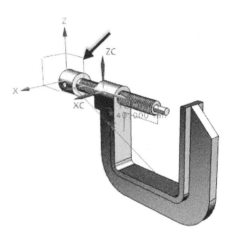

30. Activate the **Add** command and insert the *Handle*.

31. On the **Add Component** dialog, select **Placement > Constrain,** and then select **Constraint Type > Center** and set the **Subtype** to **1 to 2**.

32. Click on the YZ plane of the *Spindle*, and then the end faces of the *Handle*.

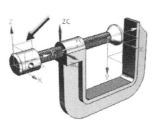

33. On the **Add Component** dialog, under the **Settings** section, check the **Preview** option to display the *Handle* in the graphics window.

34. Click the **Reverse Last Constraint** button, if the Datum Coordinate Planes of the *Handle* are displayed at the left side, as shown.

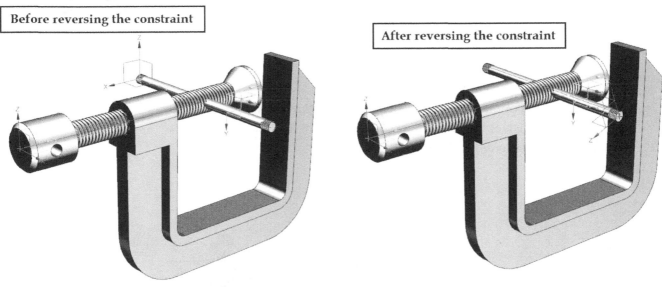

35. On the **Add Component** dialog, select **Constraint Type > Align/Lock** and click on the center line of the *Handle*.

36. Click on the center line of the hole on the *Spindle*, and then click **OK**.

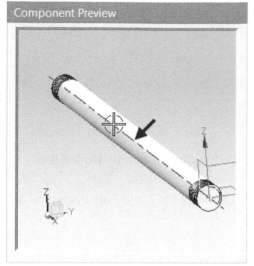

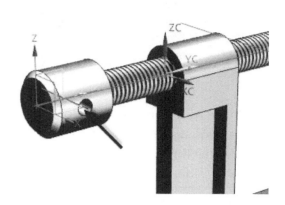

37. Activate the **Add** command and insert the *Handle Cap*.
38. On the **Add Component** dialog, select **Placement > Constrain,** and then select **Constraint Type > Concentric** and click on the innermost circular edge of the hole of the *Handle Cap*.
39. Click on the circular edge of the *Handle*.

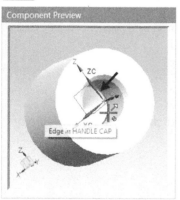

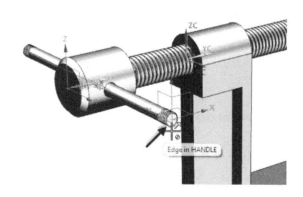

40. On the **Add Component** dialog, select **Constraint Type > Touch Align** and set the **Orientation** to **Align**.
41. Click on the YZ planes of the *Handle* and *Handle Cap*, and then click **OK**.

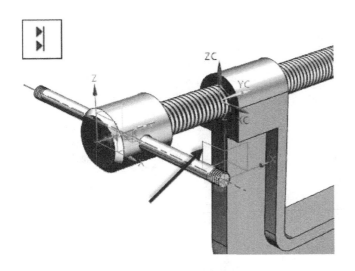

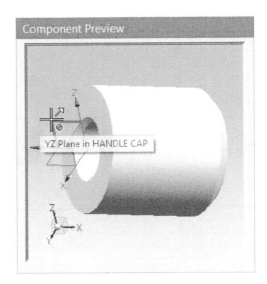

42. Activate the **Remember Constraints** command (on the ribbon, click **Assemblies > Component Position > Remember Constraints**) select the *Handle Cap*.

43. On the **Assembly Navigator**, expand the **Constraints** section, press the Ctrl key, and select the **Concentric** and **Align** constraints located at the bottom. Click **OK**.

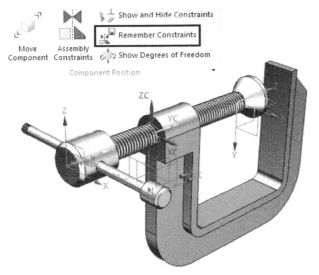

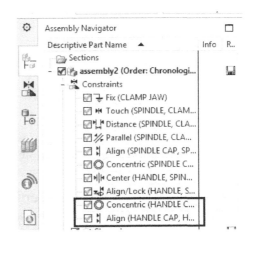

44. Activate the **Add** command and insert the *Handle Cap*. Next, click **OK** on the **Add Component** dialog; the **Redefine Constraints** dialog pops up on the screen. In addition, the **Align** constraint is active and the YZ plane of the *Handle Cap* is selected.

45. Click on the YZ plane of the *Handle*. The **Concentric** constraint is active and inner circular edge of the *Handle Cap* hole is selected.

46. Rotate the assembly view and click on the circular edge of the *Handle*. Expand the **Preview** section and check the **Preview Component in Main Window** option.

47. Click the **Reverse Constraint** button on the **Redefine Constraint** dialog, if the *Handle Cap* is displayed in reverse. Click **OK**.

48. Save and close the assembly.

Example 2 (Top Down Assembly)

In this example, you will create the assembly shown next.

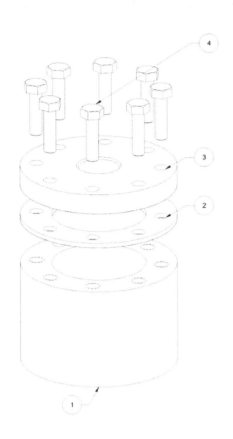

4	HEX BOLT AM.M8X1.25X30	8
3	COVER PLATE	1
2	GASKET	1
1	CYLINDER BASE	1
PC NO	PART NAME	QTY

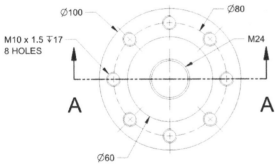

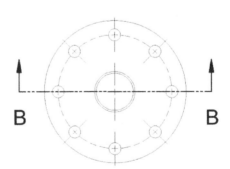

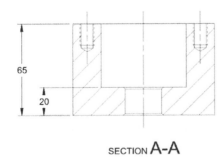

SECTION A-A

Cylinder Base

SECTION B-B

Cover Plate

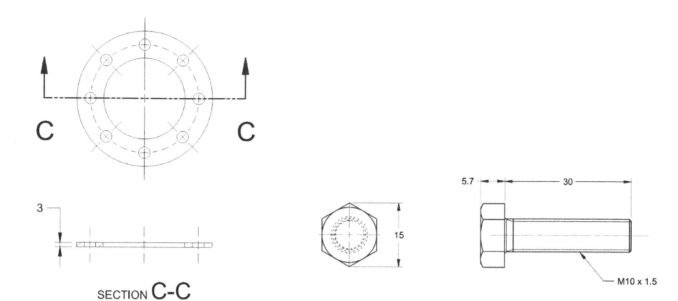

Gasket

Screw

1. Create a new folder with name the *Pressure Cylinder*.
2. Start **NX 12**.
3. On the ribbon, click the **New** button to open the **New** dialog.
4. On the **New** dialog, select the **Assembly** template and click **OK**.
5. Close the **Add Component** dialog.
6. On the ribbon, click **Assemblies > Component > Create New** to open the **New Component File** dialog.

7. On the **New Component File** dialog, click the **Browse** button next to the **Name** field and browse to the *Pressure Cylinder* folder.
8. Type-in Cylinder base in the **File name** box and click **OK**.
9. Select the **Model** template and click **OK**.
10. Click **OK** on the **Create New Component** dialog.

11. Click the **Assembly Navigator** tab on the Resource Bar.
12. On the **Assembly Navigator**, double-click on the **Cylinder base** to activate the part mode.

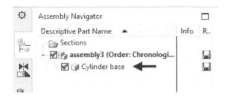

13. Create a sketch on the XZ coordinate plane, as shown.
14. Activate the **Revolve** command (on the ribbon, **Home > Feature > Revolve**). Select the sketch and create the revolved feature.

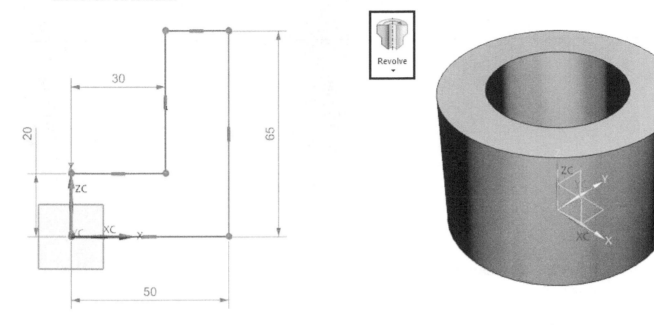

15. Activate the **Hole** command (on the ribbon, **Home > Feature > Hole**). On the **Hole** dialog, select **Type > Threaded Hole**.
16. Click on the top face of the model; a point is placed on the selected face. Add dimensions and constraints to the point, as shown.

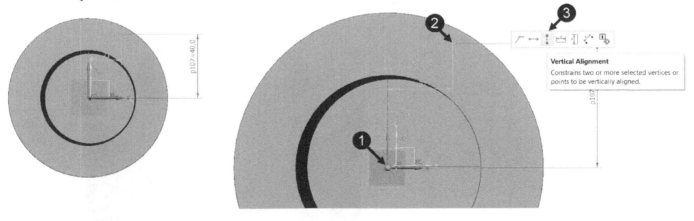

17. Click **Finish** on the **Sketch** group of the ribbon.
18. On the **Hole** dialog, set the options in the **Form and Directions** section, as shown. Click **OK** to complete the hole feature.

Form and Dimensions ∧

   Thread Dimensions ∧

Size	M10 x 1.5 ▼
Radial Engage	0.75 ▼
Tap Drill Diameter	8.5 mm ▼
Depth Type	Custom ▼
Thread Depth	15 mm ▼

   Handedness
   ◉ Right Handed   ○ Left Handed

   Dimensions ∧

Depth Limit	⬡ Value ▼
Depth	17 mm ▼
Depth To	⬚ Cylinder Bottom ▼
Tip Angle	118 deg ▼

Relief ∧

☐ Enable

Start Chamfer ∧

☐ Enable

End Chamfer ∧

☐ Enable

19. Activate the **Pattern Feature** command (on the ribbon, click **Home > Feature > Pattern Feature**).
20. On the Pattern Feature dialog, select **Layout > Circular**.
21. Select the hole feature from the model.
22. Click **Specify Vector** under the **Rotation Axis** section, and then select the cylindrical portion of the model.
23. Select **Spacing > Count and Span** under the **Angular Direction** section.
24. Set Count = 8 and Span = 360 degrees under the **Angular Direction** section, and then click **OK**.

Pattern Definition ∧

Layout	○ Circular ▼

  Boundary Definition ∨
  Rotation Axis ∧

✓ Specify Vector	⟲ ✕ ⌇ ⬦ ▼
Specify Point	± ⚡ ▼

  Angular Direction ∧

Spacing	Count and Span ▼
Count	8 ▼
Span Angle	360 deg ▼

  Radiate ∧

☐ Create Concentric Members

  Pattern Increment ∨
  Instance Points ∨
☐ Use Spreadsheet ▦
  Orientation ∨
  Pattern Settings ∨

25. On the ribbon, click **Assemblies > Context Control > Work on Assembly**.

26. Activate the **Create New** command (on the ribbon, click **Assemblies > Component > Create New**). The **New Component File** dialog pops up.

27. Type-in *Gasket* in the **Name** field and double-click on the **Model** template.

28. Click **OK** on the **Create New Component** dialog.

29. In the **Assembly Navigator**, double-click on Gasket to activate the part mode.

30. Activate the **Extrude** command (on the ribbon, click **Home > Feature > Extrude**).

31. On the Top Border Bar, set the **Selection Scope** to **Entire Assembly**, and then activate the **Create Interpart Link** button.

32. Click on the top face of the cylinder base. The **Interpart Copy** message pops up on the screen. Click **OK**; an interpart link is created between the **Gasket** and **Cylinder base**.

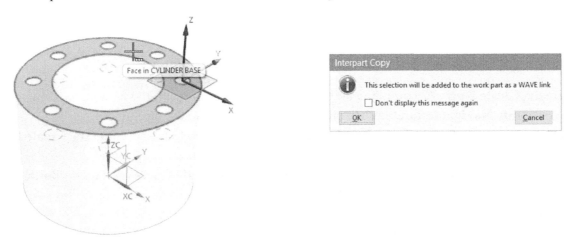

33. On the ribbon, click **Home > Curve > Project Curve**. Set the **Curve rule** to **Face Edges** and click on the top face of the cylinder base. Click **OK** on the **Project Curve** dialog to project all the edges of the top face.

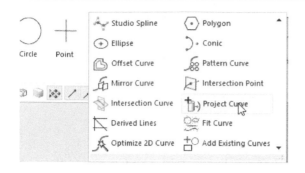

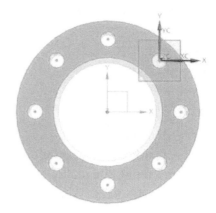

34. Click **Finish** on the ribbon and extrude the sketch up to 3 mm depth.

35. On the ribbon, click **Assemblies > Context Control > Work on Assembly**.

36. Activate the **Create New** command and create a component file with the name *Cover plate*.

37. In the **Assembly Navigator**, double-click on Cover plate to activate the part mode.

38. Activate the **Extrude** command and click the top face of the Gasket. Make sure that the **Create Interpart Link** icon is selected on the Top Border Bar.

39. Activate the **Project Curve** command and select **Curve Rule > Single Curve** on the Top Border Bar.

40. Select the outer edge and the edges of the hole pattern, and then click **OK**.

41. Click **Finish** on the ribbon.

42. Type 13 in the **End** box attached to the extrusion and click **OK**.

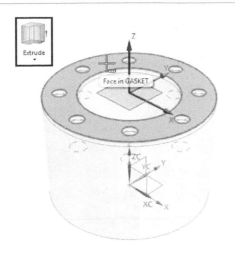

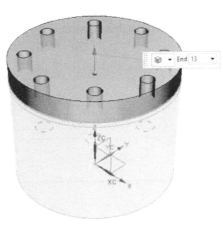

43. Activate the assembly mode, and then activate the **Hole** command.

44. On the **Hole** dialog, select **Type > Hole Series**. Set the **Screw Size** to M24 and create a hole on the top face.

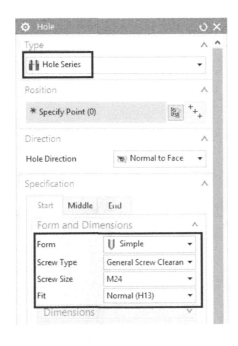

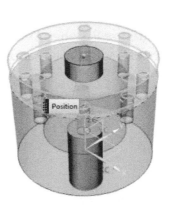

45. On the ribbon, click **Tools > Reuse Library > Fastener Assembly**.

46. On the **Fastener Assembly** dialog, check the **Find Coaxial Hole** option and click on the cylindrical face of anyone of the small holes.

47. You will notice a fastener assembly in the **Hole** section of the **Fastener Assembly** dialog. Click **OK**.

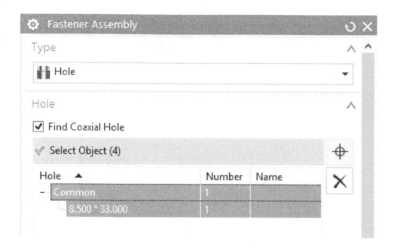

48. On the **Configure Fastener Assembly** dialog, set the **Standard** to **ANSI Metric**.

49. Under the **Fastener Configuration** section, delete **Top Stacks** and **Bottom Stacks** and click **OK**.

50. On the ribbon, click **Assemblies > Component > Pattern Component**.

51. On the **Assembly Navigator**, select the bolt assembly.

52. On the **Pattern Component** dialog, set the **Layout** type to **Circular**.
53. Set **Spacing** to **Count and Span** and type-in **8** and **360** in the **Count** and **Span Angle** boxes.
54. Under the **Rotation Axis** section, click **Specify Vector** and select Z-axis vector from the triad.
55. Select the center point of the cover plate and click **OK** to pattern the bolts.

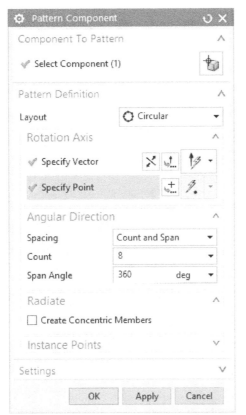

56. On the ribbon, click **Assemblies > Exploded Views > New Explosion**.

57. Click **OK** on the **New Explosion** dialog.
58. On the ribbon, click **Assemblies > Exploded Views > Edit Explosion** and select **AM-Hex Bolt Stacks 1x 8** from the **Assembly Navigator**.

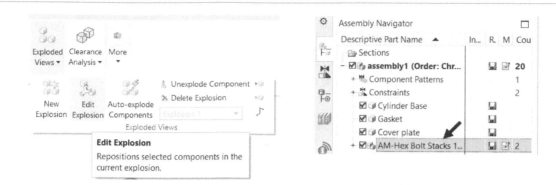

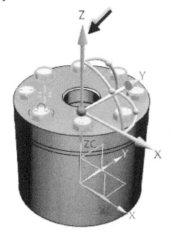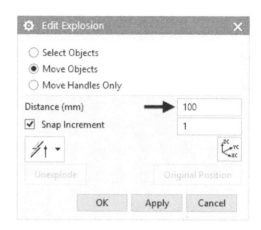

59. On the **Edit Explosion** dialog, select **Move Objects** and select the Z handle on the Dynamic CSYS.

60. Type-in 100 in the **Distance** box and click **OK**.

61. Activate the **Edit Explosion** command.

62. On the **Edit Explosion** dialog, click **Select Objects**, and then select the cover plate.

63. Click **Move Objects** and select the Z handle on the Dynamic CSYS.

64. Type-in 50 in the **Distance** box and click **OK**.

65. Likewise, explode the gasket up to 30 mm distance.

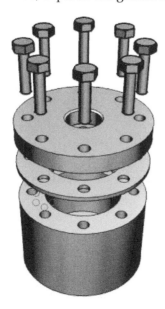

66. Save the assembly as Pressure Cylinder and close it.

Questions

1. How do you start an assembly from an already opened part?
2. What is the use of the **Remember Constraints** command?
3. List the advantages of Top-down assembly approach.
4. How do you create a sub-assembly in the assembly environment?
5. Briefly explain how to edit components in an assembly.
6. Why do we prefer the **Edit Explode** command to the **Auto Explode** command?
7. How to show or hide reference planes of a part?
8. How do you add fasteners to an assembly?
9. How do you redefine constraints in NX?
10. What is the use of **Align/Lock** constraint?

Exercise 1

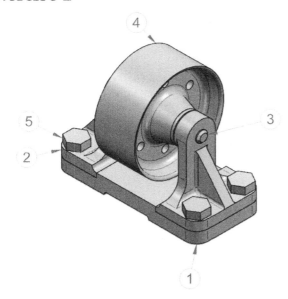

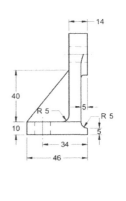

Item Number	File Name (no extension)	Quantity
1	Base	1
2	Bracket	2
3	Spindle	1
4	Roller-Bush assembly	1
5	Bolt	4

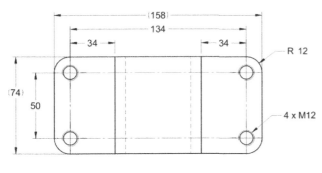

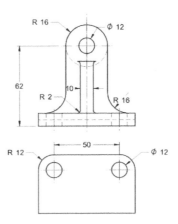

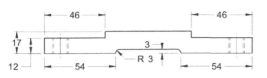

Base

Bracket

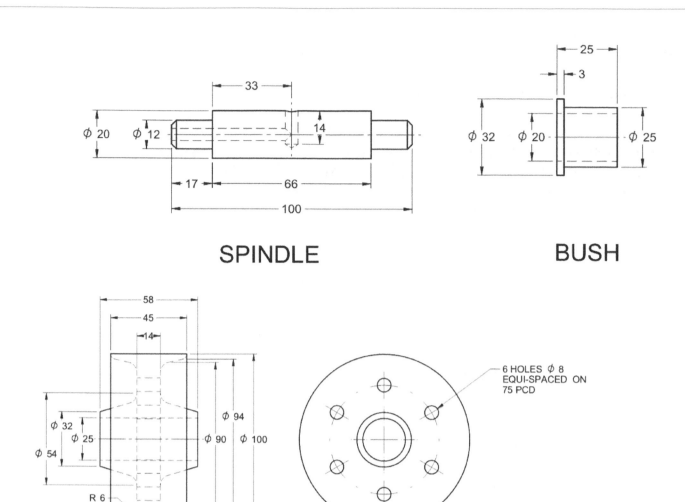

SPINDLE

BUSH

Roller

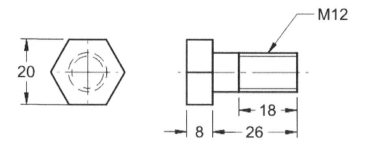

Bolt

Chapter 9: Drawings

Drawings are used to document your 3D models in the traditional 2D format including dimensions and other instructions useful for the manufacturing purpose. In NX, you first create 3D models and assemblies, and then use them to generate the drawing. There is a direct association between the 3D model and the drawing. When changes are made to the model, every view in the drawing will be updated. This relationship between 3D model and the drawing makes the drawing process fast and accurate. Because of the mainstream adoption of 2D drawings of the mechanical industry, drawings are one of the three main file types you can create in NX.

The topics covered in this chapter are:

- *Create model views*
- *Projected views*
- *Auxiliary views*
- *Sections views*
- *Detail views*
- *Break-out Section views*
- *View Breaks*
- *Display Options*
- *View Alignment*
- *Parts List and Balloons*
- *Retrieve Dimensions*
- *Maintain Alignment*
- *Remove Alignment*
- *Ordinate Dimensions*
- *Center Marks*
- *Centerlines*
- *Automatic Centerlines*
- *Bolt Circle Centerlines*
- *Callouts and Leaders*
- *Notes*

Starting a Drawing

To start a new drawing, click the **New** icon on the ribbon, and then click the **Drawing** tab on the **New** dialog. On the **Drawing** tab, set the **Units** value and click on a drawing sheet template. Click **OK** to start the drawing. Next, type-in values in the **Populate Title Block** dialog, and then click **Close**.

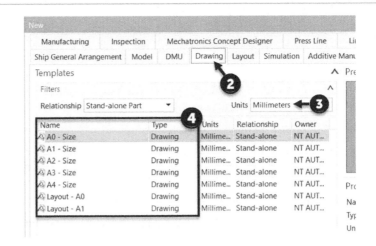

If you already have a part opened, you can click **Application > Design > Drafting** on the ribbon.

On the **Sheet** dialog, click **Use Template** to access different sheet templates. Select anyone of the sheet templates from the list. If the Sheet dialog does not appear, click **Home tab > Sheet drop-down > Edit Sheet.**

Click **Standard Size** to start a drawing by using standard sheet sizes. The drawing will start without a border and title block.

Click **Custom Size** to start a drawing using your own sheet size.

Under the **Settings** section, set the **Units** and **Projection** type. Check the **Always Start View Creation** option to start creating drawing views. If you uncheck this option, then you have to create the drawing views manually. Click **OK** to start a new drawing.

View Creation Wizard

There are different standard views of a 3D part such as front, right, top, and isometric. In NX, you can create these views using the **View Creation Wizard** command. This command is activated automatically, if you have created a drawing from an already opened part. If it is not active, click **Home > View > View Creation Wizard** on the ribbon. If there are no loaded parts in the current session, then a message pops up on the screen. Click **Yes** and browse to the location of the part or assembly, and then double-click on it. If the required part is not listed in the **Loaded Part** section, then collapse the **Loaded Parts** section. Next, select the **Open** button from the bottom of the dialog, browse to part location, and double-click on it. On the **View Creation Wizard** window, click **Next** to navigate to the **Options** page.

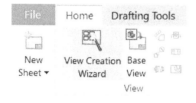

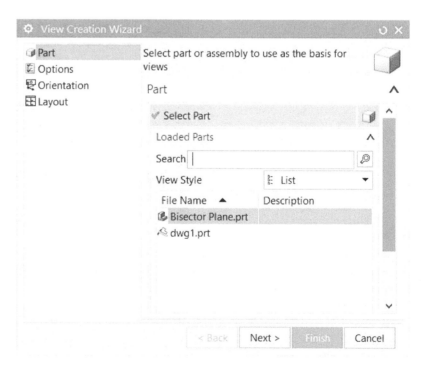

On the **Options** page, set the options related to view boundary, hidden lines, centerlines, silhouettes, view label and preview style. If you want to access additional settings related to the drawing views, then click **Settings** to open the **Settings** dialog. This dialog has various pages such as **Configuration**, **General**, **Angle**, **Visible Lines**, **Hidden Lines**, and so on. You can access the individual pages by select the corresponding options from the tree located at the left side on the dialog. Click **OK** after changing the settings on this dialog. On the **Options** page, click **Next** to navigate to the **Orientation** page.

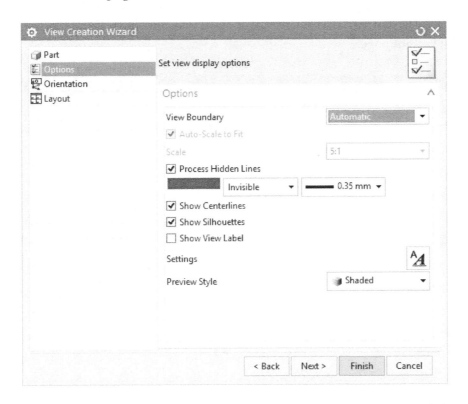

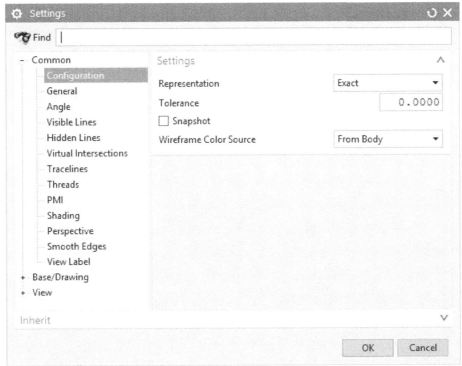

On the **Orientation** page, select the first view from the **Model Views** section. You can select from the standard orientations (Top, Front, Right, Back, Bottom, Left, Isometric, or Trimetric) of the model available in this section. If you want a different orientation, then click **Customized View** 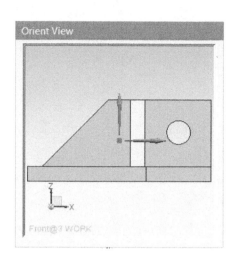 to open the **Orient View** window. In this window, use the vector axes to reorient the model view, and then click **OK**. On the **Orientation** page, click **Next** to navigate to the **Layout** page.

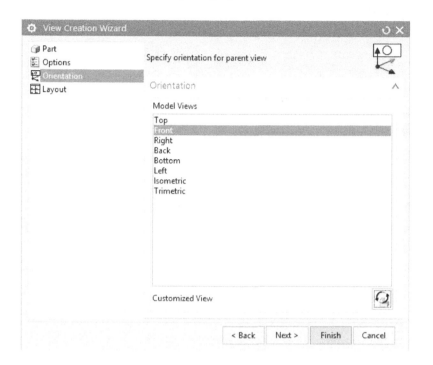

On the **Layout** page, click on the icons that represent the standard views that are to be created. After selecting the standard views, click **Finish** to create views. Click and drag the views to position them.

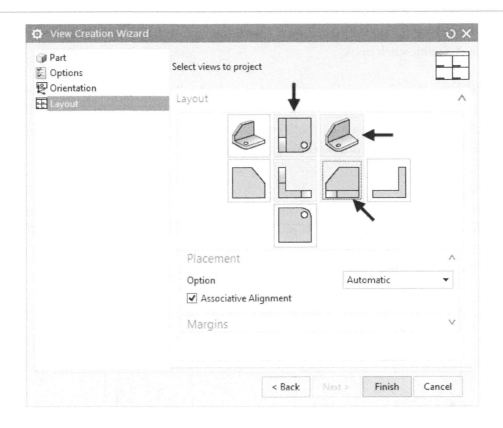

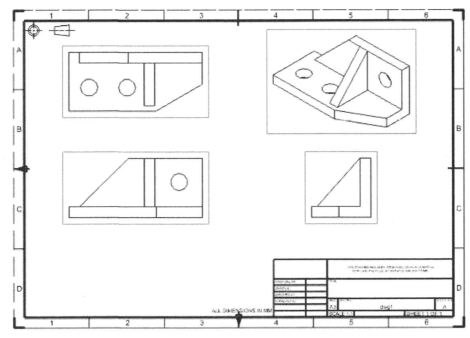

Base View

Unlike the **View Creation Wizard** command, the **Base View** command allows you create a single view of the drawing. You can later project this view to create other views. Activate this command (On the ribbon, click **Home >View > Base View**). If there are no loaded parts in the current session, then a message pops up on the screen. Click **Yes** and browse to the location of the part or assembly, and then double-click on it. If the required part is not loaded, then expand the **Part** section on the **Base View** dialog and click **Open**. Next, browse to the location of the part/assembly and double-click on it.

On the **Base View** dialog, select the model view (Top, Front, Right, Back, Bottom, Left, Isometric, or Trimetric) to use from the **Model View** section, and then set the **Scale** value in the **Scale** section. Click on the drawing sheet to position the first view. Now, you can create other views by projecting the base view. Close the dialog or create the projected views. The **Projected Views** are explained in the next section.

Projected View

After you have created the first view in your drawing, a projected view is one of the simplest views to create. Activate the **Projected View** command (click **Home > View > Projected View** on the ribbon). After activating the command, move the pointer in the direction you wish to have the view projected. Next, click on the sheet to specify the location. On the **Projected View** dialog, click **Close** to deactivate this command.

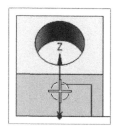
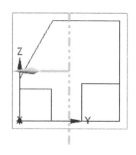
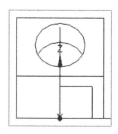
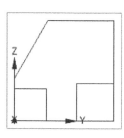

Auxiliary View

Most of the parts are represented by using orthographic views (front, top and/or side views). But many parts have features located on inclined faces. You cannot get the true shape and size for these features by using the orthographic views. To see an accurate size and shape of the inclined features, you need to create an auxiliary view. You can create an auxiliary view by projecting the part onto a plane other than horizontal, front or side planes. To create an auxiliary view, first activate the **Projected View** command. On the **Projected View** dialog, under **Hinge Line** section, select **Vector Option > Defined**. Now, click the angled edge of the model to establish the direction of the auxiliary view. Under the **View Origin** section, click **Specify Location** and drag the mouse to the desired location. Use the **Reverse Projected Direction** ✕ button in the **Hinge Line** section to reverse the projection direction, if needed. Click to locate the view and close the **Projected view** dialog.

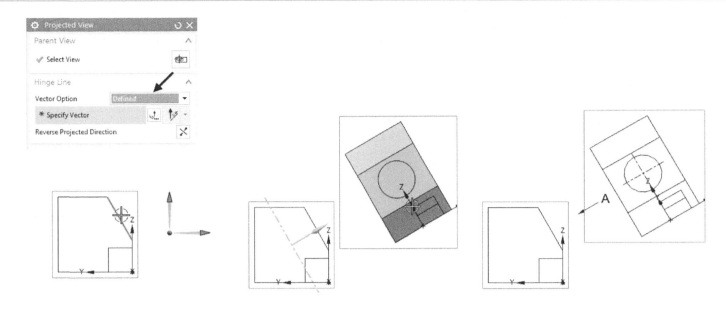

Section View

One of the common views used in 2D drawings is the section view. Creating a section view in NX is very simple. Activate the **Section View** command (On the ribbon, click **Home > View > Section View**) and select the view to section. Now, define the location of the section line by selecting a point on the view. Move the pointer on the either side of the view, and then click to position the section view.

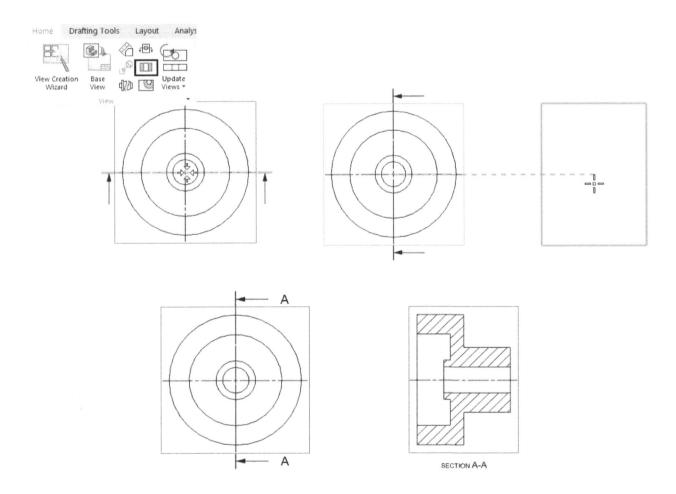

If you want to convert the single segment section line into multi-segment one, then click the right mouse button on the section line and select **Edit**. On the **Section Line** dialog, click the **Specify Location** option in the **Section Line Segments** section and select points on the parent view.

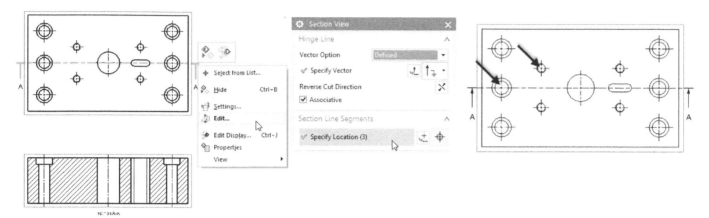

Click **Close** on the dialog. To update the section view, click the right mouse button on the section view and select **Update**.

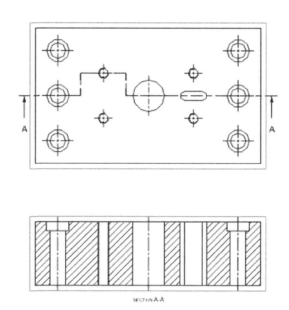

Half Section View

If you want to create a half section view, activate the **Section View** command (on the ribbon, click **Home > View > Section View**). On the **Section View** dialog, select **Method > Half**. Now, select a point on the view to define the cut position. Select another point to define the bend position of the half section line. Move the pointer and click to position the half section view.

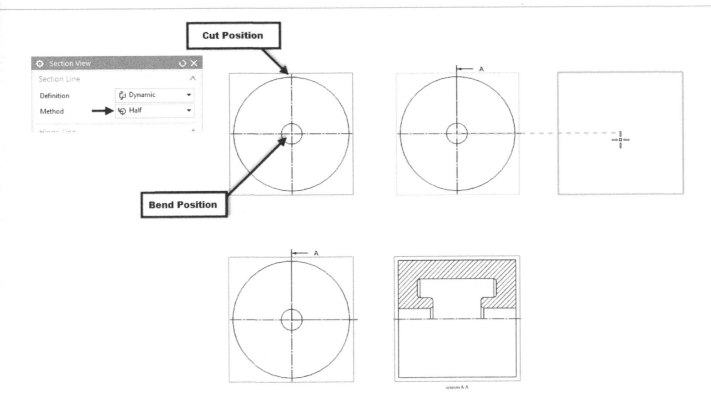

Revolved Section View

Use the **Section View** command to create a revolved section view. Activate this command (on the ribbon, click **Home > View > Section View**) and click the **Reset** icon on the **Section View** dialog. On the **Section View** dialog, under the **Section Line** section, select **Method > Revolved**. Select the view to section. On the selected view, define the rotation point and positions of the first and second line segments. Move the pointer and click to position the revolved section view.

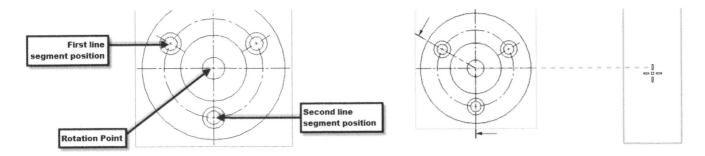

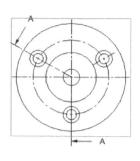

SECTION A-A

After creating a section view of an assembly, you can choose to exclude one or more components from the section cut. For example, to exclude the piston of a pneumatic cylinder, activate the **Section in View** command (on the ribbon, click **Home > View > Edit View** Drop-down **> Section in View** on the ribbon) and select the section view. On the **Section in View** dialog, under the **Body or Component** section, click **Select Object** and select the object from anyone of the views. Under the **Action** section, select **Make Non Sectioned** and click **OK**.

Note: If the Section in View command is not available in the Edit View drop-down, then click the down arrow located at the bottom right corner of the View group of the ribbon. Next, select Edit View Drop-down > Section in View from the drop-down; the Section in View command will be added to the Edit View Drop-down.

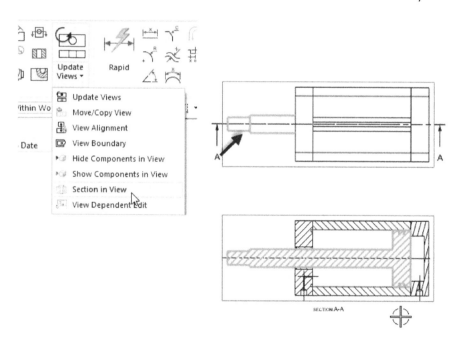

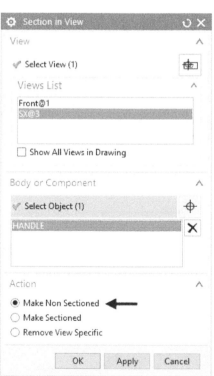

On the ribbon, click **Home > View > Update Views**. On the **Update Views** dialog, select the section view and click **OK**.

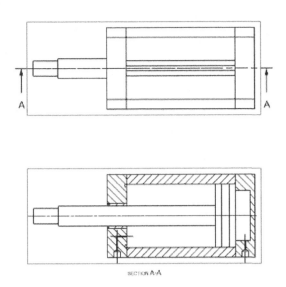

Detail View

If a drawing view contains small features that are difficult to see, a detailed view can be used to zoom in and make things clear. To create a detailed view, activate the **Detail View** command (click **Home > View > Detail View** on the ribbon); this automatically activates the circle tool. Draw a circle to identify the area that you wish to zoom in. Once the circle is drawn, set the **Scale** value on the **Detail View** dialog. Next, move the pointer and click to locate the view; the detail view will appear with a label.

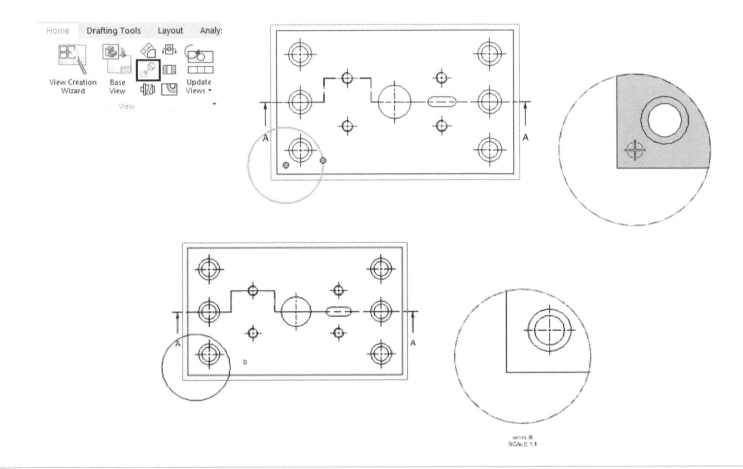

Add Break Lines

You can add break lines to a drawing view, which is too large to fit on the drawing sheet. They break the view so that only important details are shown. To add break lines, activate the **View Break** command (on the ribbon, click **Home > View > View Break**) and select the view. On the **View Break** dialog, select **Regular** or **Single-sided** from the **Type** drop-down. Click once on the drawing view to locate the beginning of the break. Next, select another point on the drawing view to locate the end of the break. On the **View Break** dialog, expand **Settings** section and type-in a value in the **Gap** box. Select the view break style that you need from the **Style** drop-down.

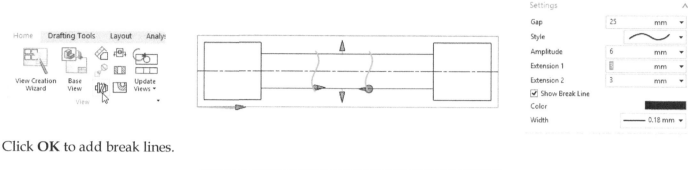

Click **OK** to add break lines.

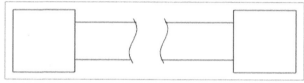

Break-out Section View

The **Break-out Section View** command alters an existing view to show the hidden portion of a part or assembly. This command is very useful to show the parts, which are hidden in an assembly view. You need to have a closed profile to breakout a view. For example, if you want to show the piston inside pneumatic cylinder, click on the right side view and select **Active Sketch View**.

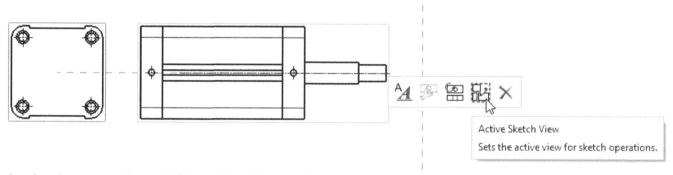

Use the sketch commands available on the ribbon and draw a closed profile on the view. Click **Finish Sketch** on the ribbon.

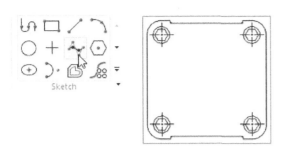
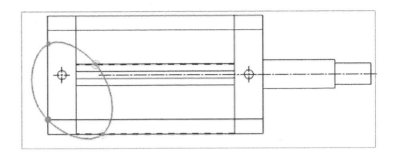

Activate the **Break-out Section View** command (click **Home > View > Break-out Section View** on the ribbon) and select the view. Define the base point on the other view. On the **Break-out Section** dialog, click **Reverse Vector** to reverse the extrusion direction.

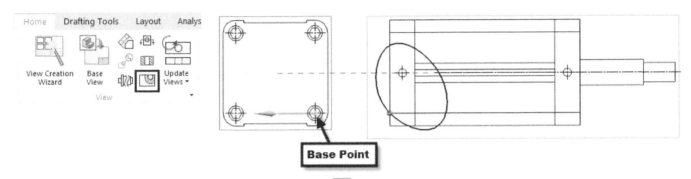

On the **Break-out section** dialog, click **Select Curves** and select the sketched profile. Click **Apply** to create the break-out section view.

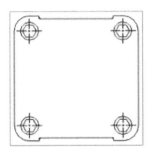
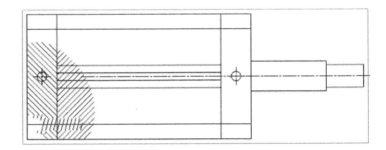

Exploded View

You can display an assembly in an exploded state as long as the assembly already has an exploded view defined (refer to **Chapter 8: Assemblies > Exploding Assemblies** section). If you want to add an exploded view to drawing, open the assembly file and switch to the **Drafting** application (Click **File > Application > Drafting**). Activate the **Base View** command and ensure that the assembly file is selected. On the **Base View** dialog, select **Model View > Model View to Use > Trimetric**. Under the **Scale** section, set the **Scale** value and click on the drawing sheet. Click **Close** on the **Projected View** dialog.

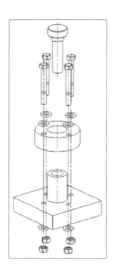

Display Options

When working with NX drawings, you can control the way a model view appears by using the display options. Select a view from the drawing sheet and click the **Settings** icon on the context toolbar. On the **Settings** dialog, select **Common > Shading**. Set the **Rendering Style** to **Fully Shaded** and click **OK**. The rendering style of the view will be changed.

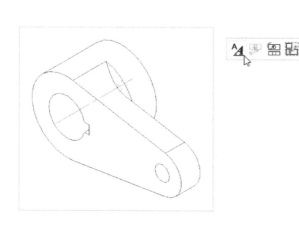

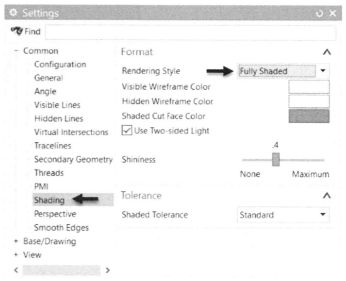

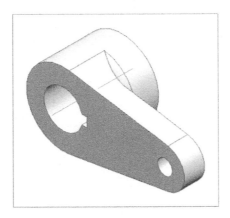

If you want to modify the display of hidden lines, then select the view and click **Settings**. On the **Settings** dialog, select **Common > Hidden Lines**. On the **Hidden Lines** page, check the **Process Hidden Lines** option. Set the line type to **Hidden** and click on the color swatch next to the line type drop-down. On the **Color** dialog, select the color and click **OK** twice.

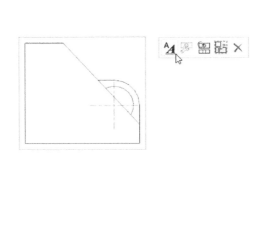

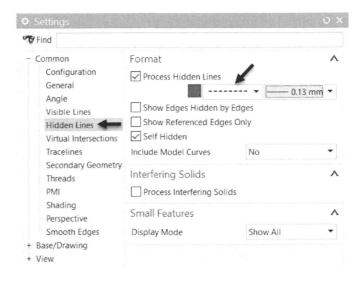

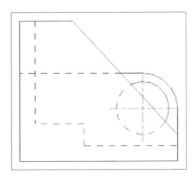

View Alignment

There are views that are automatically aligned to a parent view. These include auxiliary views and projected views. If you move down a view, the parent view associated with it will also move.

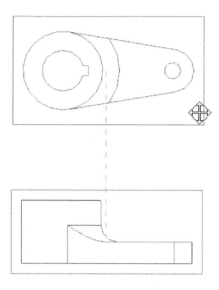

You need to break the alignment between them to move the view separately. Click the right mouse button on the view and select **View Alignment**. On the **View Alignment** dialog, under the **List** section, select the view and uncheck the **Associative Alignment** option. Click **OK**.

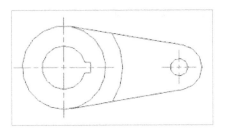

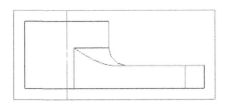

If you want to create an alignment between the views, click **Home > View > Edit View Drop-down > View Alignment** on the ribbon. Click on the view to align and select the alignment method from the **Placement** section. For example, select **Horizontal** from the **Method** drop-down available in the **Placement** section. Next, select the parent view and click **OK**; the both the views are aligned to each other, horizontally.

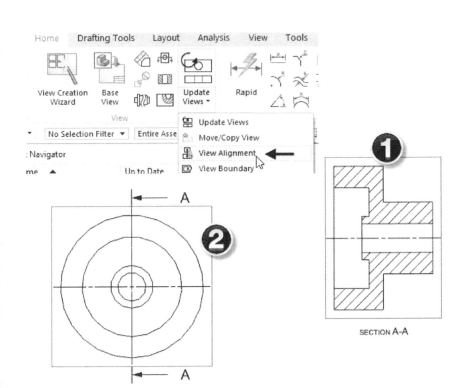

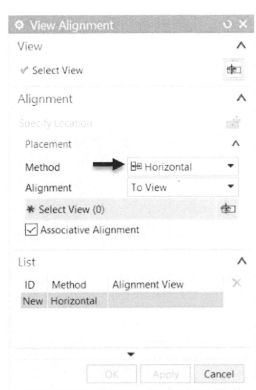

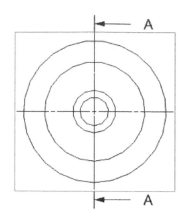

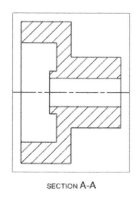

SECTION A-A

Parts List and Balloons in an Assembly Drawing

Creating an assembly drawing is very similar to creating a part drawing. However, there are few things unique in an assembly drawing. One of them is creating parts list. A parts list identifies the different components in an assembly. Generating a parts list is very easy in NX. First, you need to have an assembly view placed in the drawing. Next, you have to set your own preferences for the part list. To do this, click **File > Preferences > Drafting**. On the **Drafting Preferences** dialog, click **Table > Parts List** and set the preferences of the Parts list and balloons. Click **OK** to close the dialog.

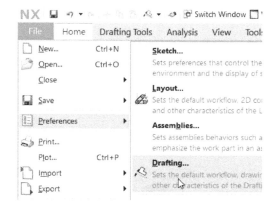

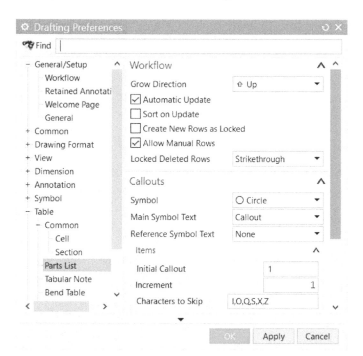

Now, click **Home > Table > Parts List** on the ribbon, and then click on the drawing sheet.

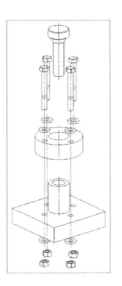

On the Top Border Bar, click **Menu > Format > Parts List Levels** and select the Part list. Click **OK** on the **Edit Levels** dialog. On the **Edit Levels** toolbar, click the **Top Level** button, and then click **OK**.

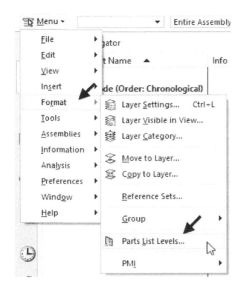

To add balloons to the assembly drawing, click **Home > Table > Auto Balloon** on the ribbon and select the parts list. Click **OK** on the **Parts List Auto Balloon** dialog.

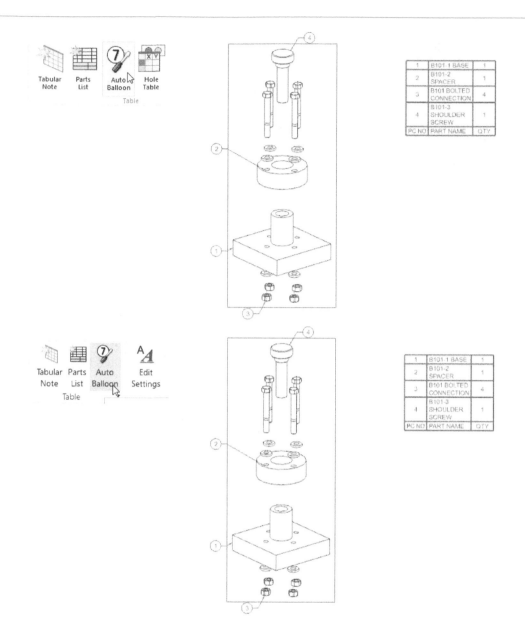

1	B101.1 BASE	1
2	B101-2 SPACER	1
3	B101 BOLTED CONNECTION	4
4	B101-3 SHOULDER SCREW	1
PC NO	PART NAME	QTY

1	B101.1 BASE	1
2	B101-2 SPACER	1
3	B101 BOLTED CONNECTION	4
4	B101-3 SHOULDER SCREW	1
PC NO	PART NAME	QTY

Dimensions

NX provides you with different types of commands to add dimensions to the drawing. However, before adding dimensions to a drawing, you must define some dimension preferences. These preferences control the display of the dimensions. To do this, click **File > Preferences > Drafting**. On the **Drafting Preferences** dialog, expand the **Dimension** section and modify the options that control the display of the dimensions. Expand the **Common** section and set the **Lettering** and **Line/Arrow** preferences. Click **OK** to apply the preferences.

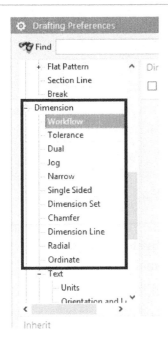

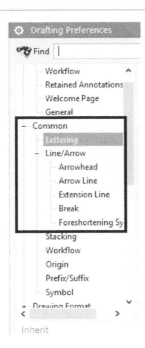

One of the methods is to retrieve the dimensions that are already contained in the 3D part file. The **Feature Dimensions** command helps you to do this. If you cannot find this command, then simply type **feature dimensions** in the Command Finder and press Enter. On the **Command Finder** dialog, click the right mouse button on the **Feature Parameters** command and select **Add to Ribbon Tab > Home**.

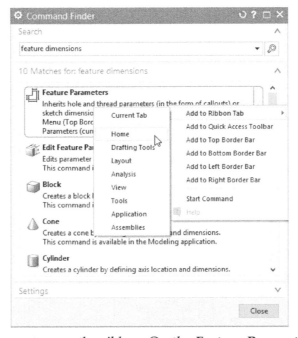

Now, click the **Home > Feature Parameters** on the ribbon. On the **Feature Parameters** dialog, select a **Template** and expand the **Features** section. Select the features and click the **Select Views** button. Click **OK** to retrieve the feature dimensions. You may notice that there are some unwanted dimensions. Simply select them and press **Delete** to remove them. In addition, the dimensions may not be positioned properly. Drag and position the dimensions properly.

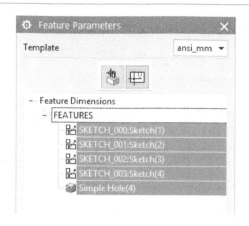

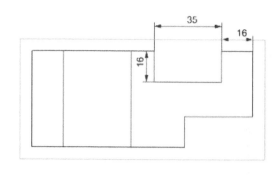

If you want to add some more dimensions, which are necessary to manufacture a part, activate the **Rapid Dimension** command and add them to the view (Learn about the **Rapid Dimension** command in **Chapter 2: Sketch Techniques**).

Ordinate Dimensions

Ordinate dimensions are another type of dimensions that you can add to the drawing. To create them, activate the **Ordinate** command (click **Home > Dimension > Ordinate** on the ribbon). On the **Ordinate Dimension** dialog, select **Type > Single Dimension** and then click on any end-point of the drawing view to define the ordinate or zero reference. Now, click on a point or edge of the drawing view. On the **Ordinate Dimension** dialog, under the **Baseline** section, check the **Activate Perpendicular** option to create ordinate dimensions in both the directions. Move the pointer and click to place the coordinate dimension. Likewise, add other ordinate dimensions.

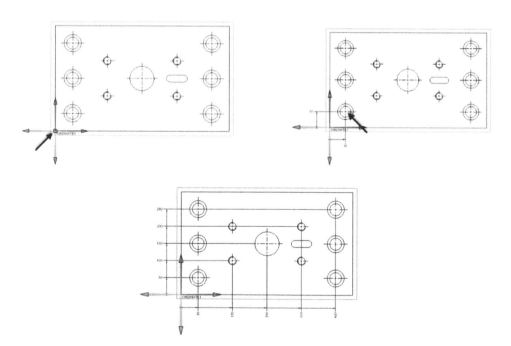

If you want to add multiple ordinate dimensions at a time, then select **Type > Multiple Dimensions** on the **Ordinate Dimensions** dialog and define the ordinate or zero reference. Now, click on multiple points or drag a rectangle selection box to select multiple points. If you want to select only the center points of holes, then check the **Select Only Arc Centers** option on the **Ordinate Dimension** dialog and drag a rectangular selection box. On the dialog, expand the **Margins** section and click the **Define Margins** button. Now, select the ordinate point to define the margin. On the **Define Margin** dialog, type-in values in the fields available under the **Settings** section. Click **OK** and **Close** to add ordinate dimensions to drawing.

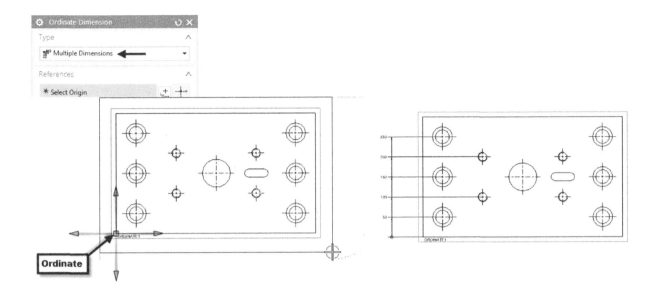

Adding Hole Callouts

If you want to add a hole callout, then activate the **Rapid Dimension** command (on the ribbon, click **Home >** **Dimension > Rapid**). On the **Rapid Dimension** dialog, under the **Measurement** section, select **Method >** **Diameteral** and create a diameter dimension. Close the **Rapid Dimension** dialog. Now, double-click on the diameter dimension to open a palette.

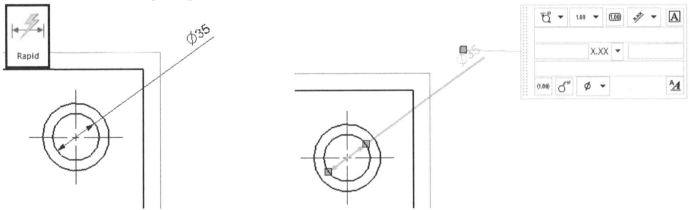

On the palette, click the **Edit Appended Text** button to open the **Appended Text** dialog. On this dialog, set the **Text Location** value and type-in the required text in the **Formatting** box. Use the **Text Location** drop-down to define the text location. Use the symbols buttons to insert symbols and click **Close**. (For example, select the **Text Location > After** and type **THRU** in the **Formatting** box. Next, select **Text Location > Below** and select the **Counterbore** symbol from the **Symbols** section. Type 50 and select the **Insert** symbol from the **Symbols** section. Next, type **20** and close the dialog).

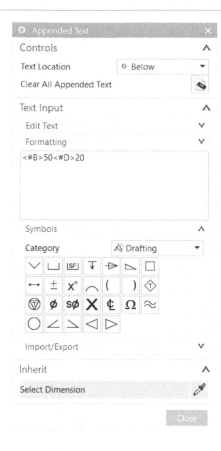

On palette, set the parameters such as tolerance, text orientation, precision, and so on. Click **Close** on the **Radial Dimension** dialog.

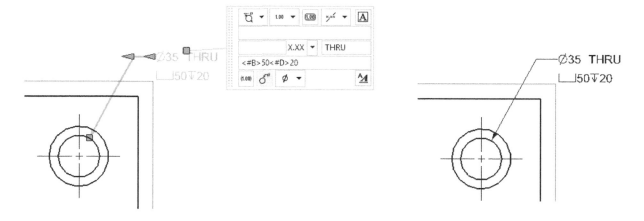

Center Marks and Centerlines

Centerlines and Centermarks are used in engineering drawings to denote hole centers and lines. Centerlines are automatically created while you create the drawing views. However, if you want to create centermarks and centerlines manually, then uncheck the **Show Centerlines** option on the **Options** page of the **View Creation Wizard**. If you create views individually, then open the **Settings** dialog (click the **Settings** icon on the **Base View** dialog) and uncheck the **Create with Centerlines** option on the **General** page.

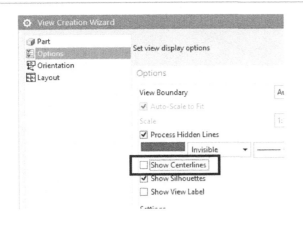

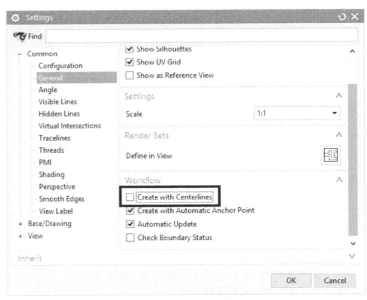

To add center marks to the drawing, activate the **Center Mark** command (click **Home > Annotation > Center Mark** on the ribbon) and click on the hole circles. Click **OK** on the **Center Marks** dialog to add center marks to the circles.

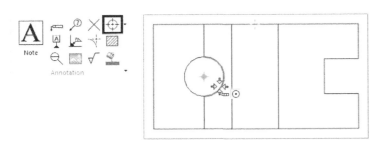

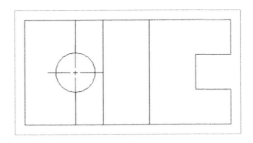

To add centerlines to a 2D view, activate the **2D Centerline** command (click **Home > Annotation > Centerline Drop-down > 2D Centerline** on the ribbon). Click on two parallel edges of the drawing view. Click **OK** to create a centerline between the two lines.

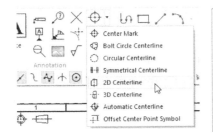

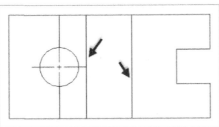

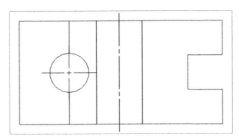

Likewise, you can add centerlines to an Isometric view by activating the **3D Centerline** ⌀ command (click **Home > Annotation > Centerline Drop-down > 3D Centerline** on the ribbon) and selecting the cylindrical face of the view. Click **OK** on the **3D Centerline** dialog after selecting the cylindrical face.

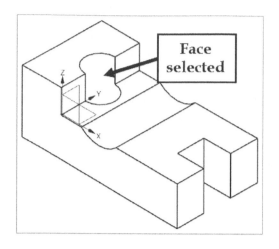
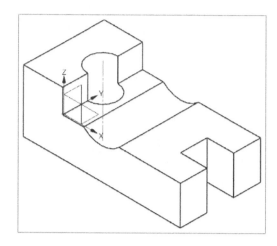

Bolt Circle Centerline

The **Bolt Circle Centerline** command (click **Home > Annotation > Bolt Circle Centerline** on the ribbon) allows you to add center marks to the holes arranged in a circular fashion. Activate this command and select **Type > Center Point** on the **Bolt Circle Centerline** dialog. Click for the center of the bolt circle. Drag the pointer and click for the radius point. Click on the center points of the circles located on bolt circle. Click **OK** on the **Bolt Circle Centerline** dialog.

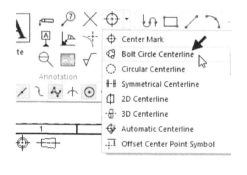

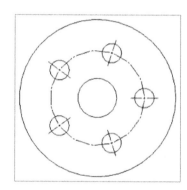

Notes

Notes are important part of a drawing. You add notes to provide additional details, which cannot be done using dimensions and annotations. To add a note or text, activate the **Note** command (click **Home > Annotation > Note** on the ribbon). On the **Note** dialog, under the **Formatting** section, select the font and font size. Type text in the **Formatting** section and then click in the drawing sheet to specify its location.

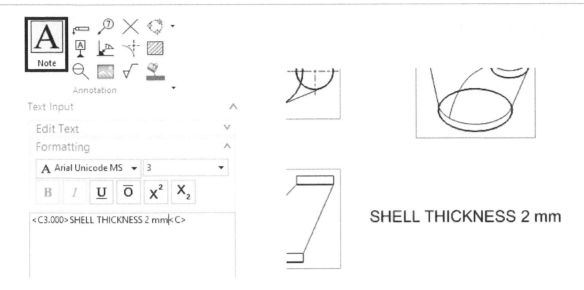

SHELL THICKNESS 2 mm

Examples

Example 1

In this example, you will create 2D drawing of the parts shown below.

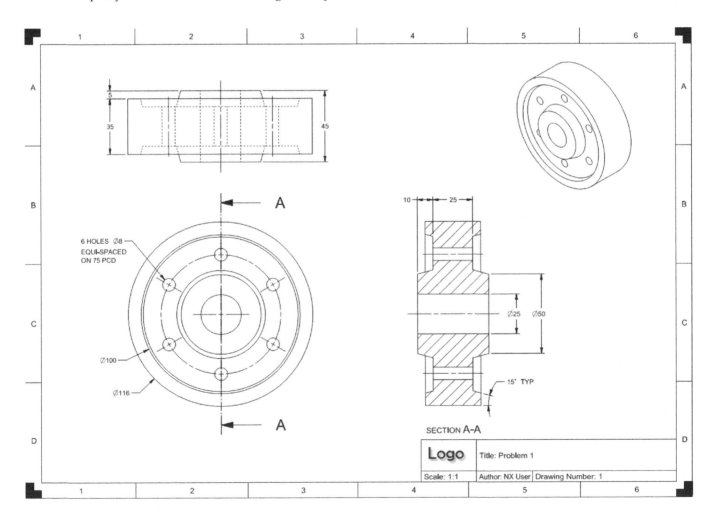

Start a New drawing and create a drawing template

1. Close the NX 12 application window, if it is opened.
2. Type NX 12 in the search bar located on the task bar; NX 12.0 appears in the search results.
3. Click the right mouse button on NX 12.0 and select **Run as administrator**.

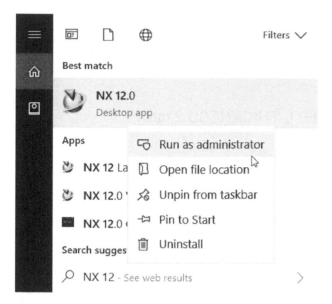

4. On the ribbon, click the **New** button.
5. Click the **Model** tab on the **New** dialog.
6. On the **New** dialog, double-click on the **Model** template.
7. Click **Application > Drafting** on the ribbon.

8. On the **Sheet** dialog, select **Standard Size**.
9. Set **Size** to **A3 – 297 x 420**.
10. Set **Scale** to **1:1**.
11. Under the **Settings** section, set **Units** to **Millimeters**.
12. Select 3ʳᵈ **Angle Projection** ⊕ ⊏ and uncheck **Always Start Drawing View** Creation Command.
13. Click **OK** to open a blank sheet.

Set Drafting Standard

1. On the Top Border Bar, click **Menu > Tools > Drafting Standard**.
2. On the **Load Drafting Standard** dialog, select **Standard > ASME**, and then click **OK**.

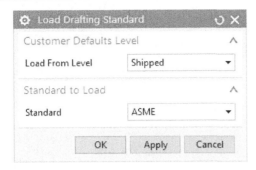

Adding Borders and Title Block

1. On the ribbon, click **Drafting Tools > Drawing Format > Borders and Zones**.

2. On the **Borders and Zones** dialog, leave the default settings and click **OK**.

3. On the ribbon, click **Home > Table > Tabular Note**.

4. Click the **Reset** icon on the **Tabular Note** dialog.
5. On the **Tabular Note** dialog, under the **Origin** section, expand the **Alignment** section and select **Anchor > Bottom Right**.
6. Under the **Table Size** section, set **Number of Columns** to 3 and **Number of Rows** to 2.
7. Type-in **50** in **Column Width** box.

8. Click on the bottom right corner of the sheet border. Click **Close** on the **Tabular Note** dialog.

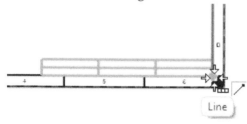

9. Click on the left vertical line of the tabular note.

10. Press the left mouse button and drag toward right. Release the left mouse button when column width is changed to 35.

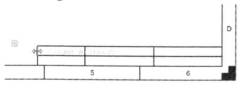

11. Likewise, change the width of the second and third columns.

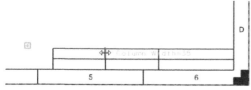

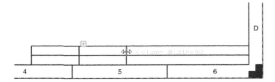

12. Change the height of the top row to 20.

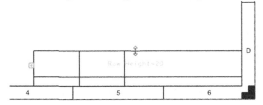

13. Click inside the second cell of the top row. Press the left mouse button and drag to the third cell.

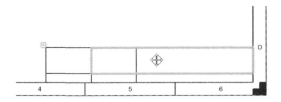

14. Click the right mouse button and select **Merge Cells**.

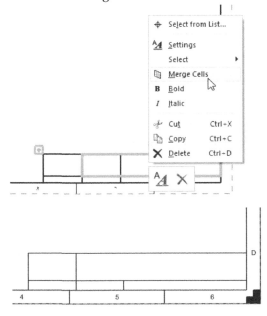

15. Click the right mouse button in the merged cell of the top row. Select **Settings**.

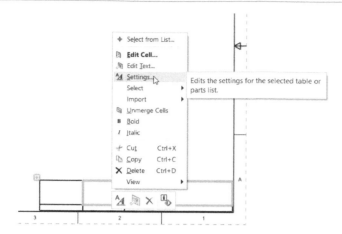

16. On the **Settings** dialog, select Prefix/Suffix from the left side. Next, type-in **Title:** in the **Prefix** box and press the Spacebar. Click **Close**.

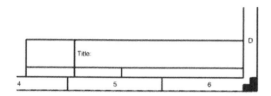

17. Likewise, add prefixes to other cells, as shown.

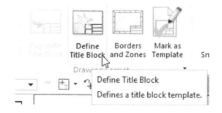

18. Click the right mouse button in the top left cell of the table, and then click **Import > Image**.

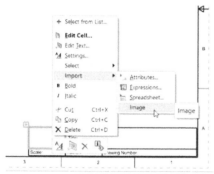

19. Select your company logo image and click **OK.**
20. On the ribbon, click **Drafting Tools > Drawing Format > Define Title Block**.

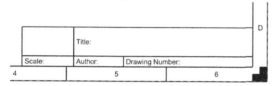

21. Click on the table, and then click **OK**.
22. On the ribbon, click **Drafting Tools > Drawing Format > Mark as Template**.

23. On the dialog, select **Mark as Template and Update PAX File**.
24. Under the **PAX File Settings** section, type-in **Sample Template** in the **Presentation Name** box.
25. Select **Template Type > Reference Existing Part**.
26. Click the **Browse** icon.
27. Go to
    C:\Program Files\Siemens\NX 12.0\LOCALIZATION\prc\english\startup
28. Click **ugs_drawing_templates**, and then click **OK**.
29. On the **Input Validation** box, click **Yes**.
30. Click **OK** twice.
31. Save and close the file.

Start a new drawing using the Sample Template

1. On the ribbon, click the **New** icon to open the **New** dialog. On this dialog, click **Drawing** tab and select **Relationship > Reference Existing Part**.
2. Under the **Templates** section, select **Sample Template**.
3. Under the **Part to create a drawing of** section, click the **Browse** button.
4. On the **Select master part** dialog, click **Open**. Go to the location of Exercise 1 of Chapter 5 and double-click on it.
5. Click **OK** twice.
6. On the **Populate Title Block** dialog, select **Label2** from the **List** and type-in Example 1.
7. Likewise, select the other labels and type in values, as shown.

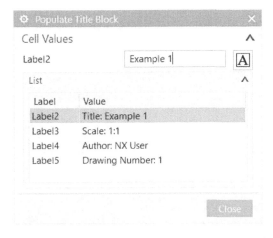

8. Click **Close**.

Generating Drawing Views

1. On the **View Creation Wizard** dialog, select **Loaded Parts > Exercise 1.prt**. Click **Next**.

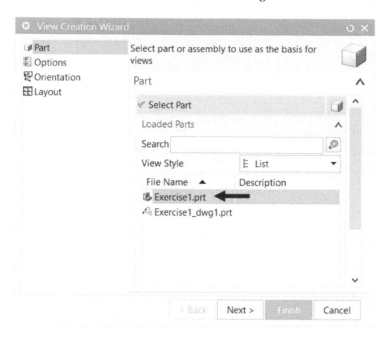

2. On the **Options** page, select **View Boundary > Manual**.
3. Uncheck the **Auto-Scale to Fit** option and select **Scale > 1:1**.
4. Check the **Process Hidden lines** option and select **Invisible**
5. Uncheck the **Show Centerlines** option and click **Next**.

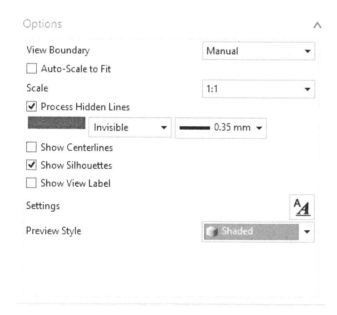

9. On the **Orientation** page, select **Model Views > Front**. Click **Next**.
10. On the **Layout** page, select the views, as shown.

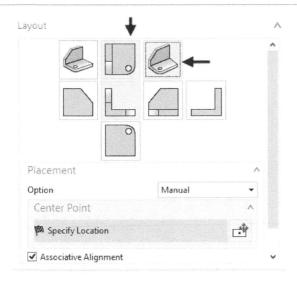

11. Select **Option > Manual**.
12. Click to define the center of the views, as shown next.

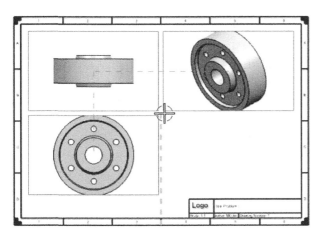

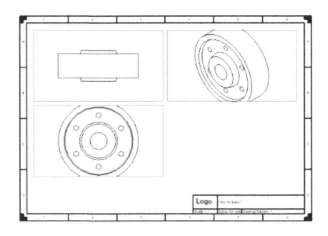

Editing the View Boundary

1. To edit a view boundary, click **Home > View > Edit View drop-down > View Boundary** on the ribbon. Select the front view.

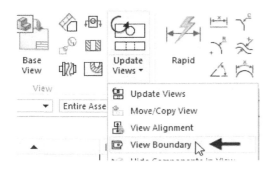

2. On the **View Boundary** dialog, select **Automatic Rectangle** from the drop-down and click **OK**.

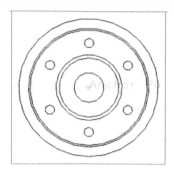

3. Click on the Isometric view and select **Edit**.

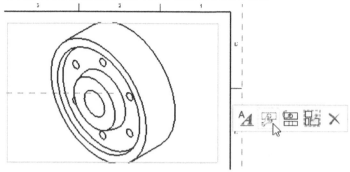

4. On the **Base View** dialog, under the **Scale** section, select **Scale > Ratio**.
5. Type-in **1** and **1.5** in the ratio boxes and click **Close**.
6. Change the view boundary of the Isometric view, as shown.

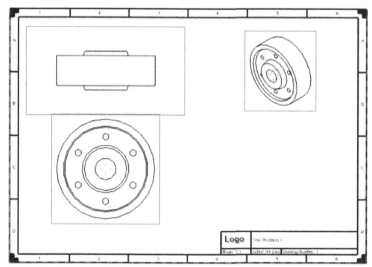

7. Likewise, change the view boundary of the top view by selecting the **Automatic Rectangle** option from the drop-down available on the **View Boundary** dialog.

Show the Hidden lines of the Top view

1. Click on the top view and select **Settings**.

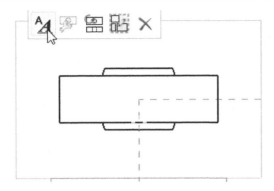

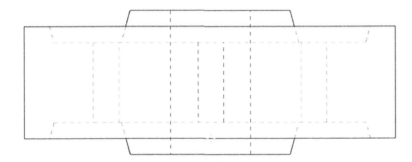

2. On the **Settings** dialog, select **Common > Hidden Lines**. Check the **Process Hidden Lines** option and set the hidden line type to **Dashed**. Change the hidden lines color to black and click **OK**.

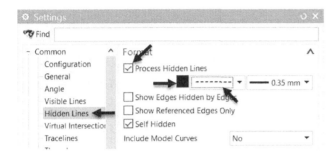

Create the Section view

1. On the ribbon, click **Home > View > Section View** .
2. On the **Section View** dialog, click the **Reset** icon.
3. Select the center point of front view and move the pointer toward right. Click to position the view. You will notice that the centerlines appear on the section view, automatically. Click **Close** on the **Section View** dialog.

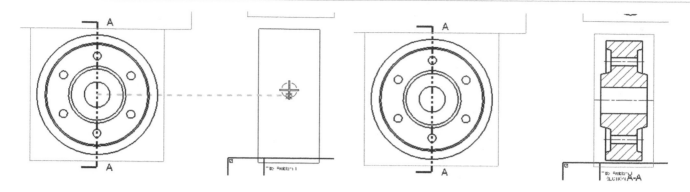

Add Centerlines, Centermarks, and Bolt Circle Centerlines

1. On the ribbon, click **Home > Annotation > Centerline Drop-down > Automatic Centerline**.
2. Click on the top view, and then click **OK**.

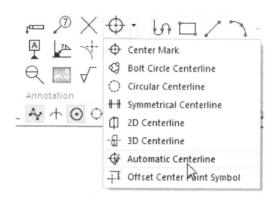

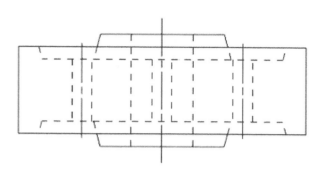

3. Activate the **Center Mark** ⊕ command (click **Home > Annotation > Center Mark** on the ribbon).
4. Click on the hole located at the center of the front view, and then click **OK**.

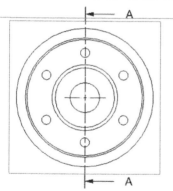

5. Activate the **Bolt Circle Centerline** ⟲ command (click **Home > Annotation > Centerline Drop-down > Bolt Circle Centerline** on the ribbon) and select **Type > Center Point** from the **Bolt Circle Centerline** dialog.
6. Click on the hole located at the center of the front view. Drag the pointer and click on anyone of the small holes.
7. Click on other circles located on the front view, and then click **OK**. This creates a bolt circle centerline.

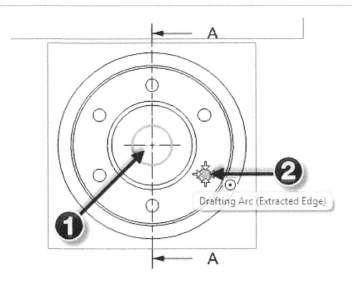

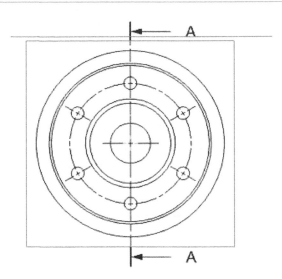

8. Activate the **Rapid Dimension** command and apply dimensions to the top view.

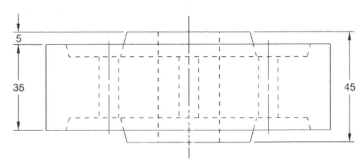

9. On the **Rapid Dimension** dialog, under the **Measurement** section, select **Method > Cylindrical** .
10. On the section view, select the end-points of the innermost horizontal edges. Drag the pointer and position the diameter dimension.

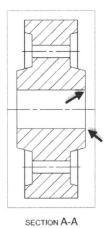

SECTION A-A

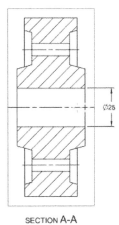

SECTION A-A

11. Likewise, create another diameter dimension.

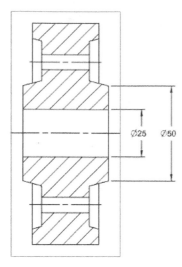

SECTION A-A

12. Activate the **Angular** ⟨△⟩ command (on the ribbon, click **Home > Dimension > Angular**) click on the inclined edge and lower horizontal edge of the section view. Drag the pointer and click to position the angle dimension. Press Esc to deactivate the **Angular** command.

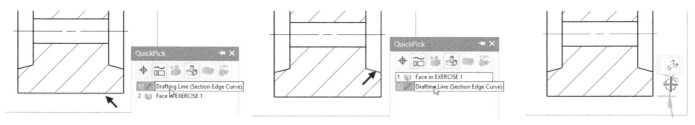

13. Click on the angle dimension and drag it upward.
14. Double-click on the angular dimension to open a palette.
15. On the palette, type-in **TYP** in suffix box. Click **Close** on the **Angular Dimension** dialog.

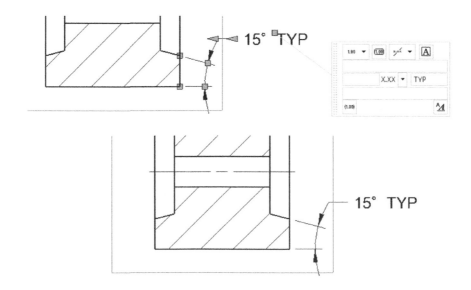

16. Activate the **Rapid Dimension** command and select **Measurement > Method > Diametral** on the **Rapid Dimension** dialog.

17. Click on the small hole of the front view and create diameter dimension. Close the dialog.

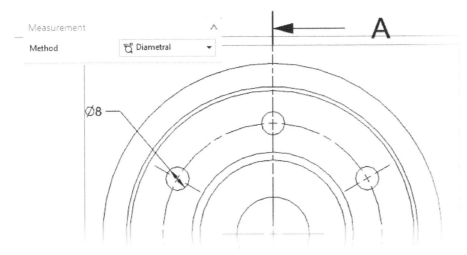

18. Double-click on the diameter dimension to open a palette.

19. On the palette, click the **Edit Appended Text** ⒶA button to open the **Appended Text** dialog.

20. On the **Edit Appended Text** dialog, select **Text Location > Before** and type-in **6 HOLES** in the **Formatting** box.

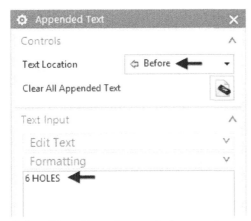

21. Select **Text Location > Below** and type-in **EQUI-SPACED ON 75 PCD** in the **Formatting** box. Click **Close** on the dialog.

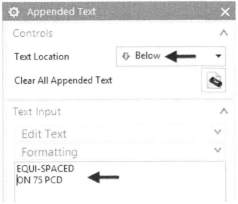

22. On the palette, click **Arrows Out Diameter**, and click **Close** on the **Radial Dimension** dialog.

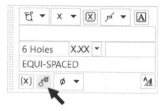

23. Create the other dimensions in the drawing.

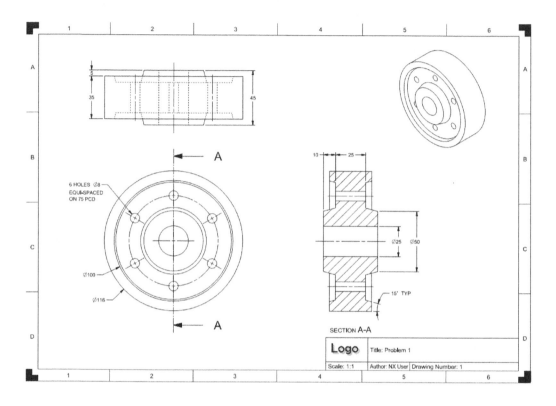

24. Save and close the drawing.

Example 2

In this example, you will create an assembly drawing shown below.

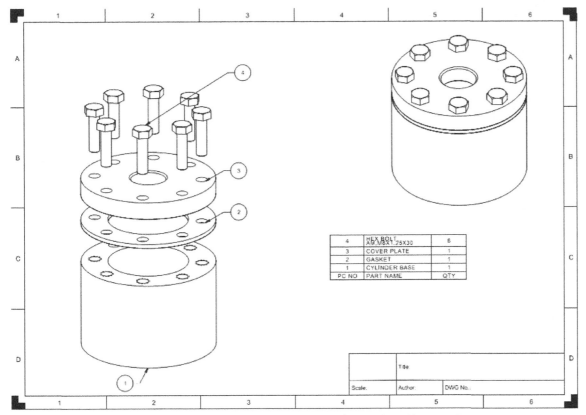

4	HEX BOLT AM.M8X1.25X30	6
3	COVER PLATE	1
2	GASKET	1
1	CYLINDER BASE	1
PC NO	PART NAME	QTY

	Title	
Scale:	Author:	DWG No.:

1. Open the Pressure Cylinder.prt file that you have created in Chapter 8.
2. Click **Application > Design > Drafting**.
3. On the **Sheet** dialog, select **Standard Size**.
4. Set **Size** to **A3 -297 x 420**.
5. Set **Scale** to **1:1**.
6. Under the **Settings** section, check the **Always Start View Creation** option, and then select the **Base View Command** option.
7. Click **OK**.
8. On the **Base View** dialog, under the **Model View** section, select **Model View to Use > Isometric**.
9. Under the **Scale** section, select **Scale > 1:1**.
10. Click on the top right side of the drawing sheet.
11. Click **Close** on the **Projected View** dialog.

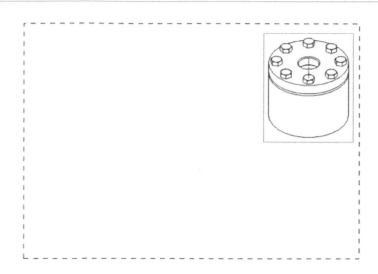

Generating the Exploded View

1. On the ribbon, click **Home > View > Base View**.
2. On the **Base View** dialog, select **Model View to Use >Trimetric**.
3. Click on the left side of the drawing sheet.
4. Click **Close**.

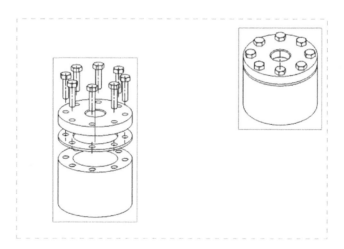

Generating the Part list

1. To generate a part list, click **Home > Table > Part List** on the ribbon.
2. Place the part list at the bottom-right corner.
3. On the Top Border Bar, click **Menu > Format > Part List Levels**.
4. Select the Parts list and click **OK**.
5. On the **Edit Levels** toolbar, select **Leaves Only** and click the green check. All the individual parts of the assembly are listed in the parts list.

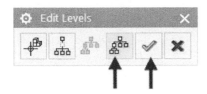

Generating Balloons

1. To generate balloons, click **Home > Table > Auto Balloon** 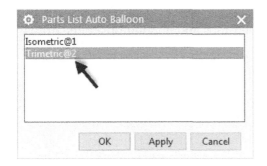 on ribbon.
2. Select the part list.
3. Click **OK**.
4. On the **Part List Auto-Balloon** dialog, select **Trimetric@2**.

5. Click **OK** to generate balloons.

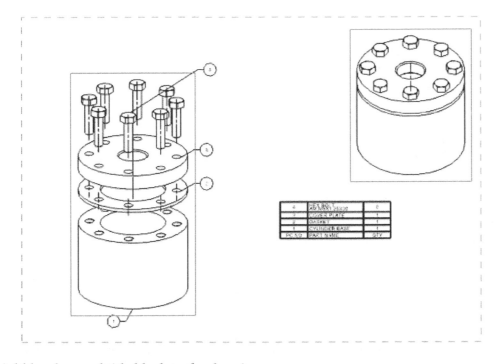

6. Add borders and title block to the drawing.
7. Save and close the file.

Questions

1. How to create drawing views using the **View Creation Wizard** command?

2. How do you show or hide hidden edges of a drawing view?
3. How do you change the display style of a drawing view?
4. How to update the drawing views when the part is edited?
5. How do you control the properties of dimensions and annotations?
6. List the commands used to create centerlines and center marks.
7. How do you add symbols and texts to a dimension?
8. How do you add break lines to a drawing view?
9. How do you create revolved section views?
10. How do you create exploded view of an assembly?

Exercises

Exercise 1

Create orthographic views of the part model shown next. Add dimensions and annotations to the drawing.

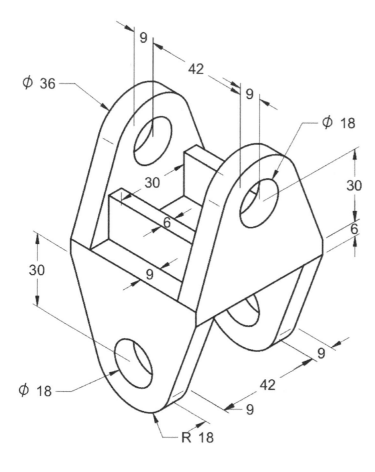

Exercise 2

Create orthographic views and an auxiliary view of the part model shown below. Add dimensions and annotations to the drawing.

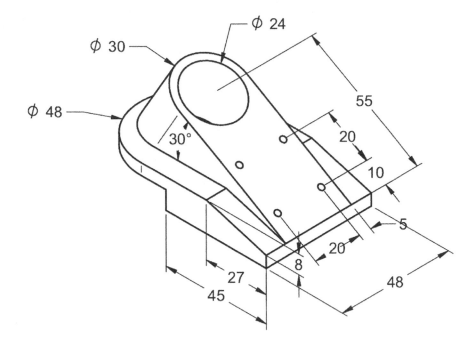

Chapter 10: Sheet Metal Design

You can make sheet metal parts by bending and forming flat sheets of metal. In NX, sheet-metal parts can be folded and unfolded enabling you to show them in the flat pattern as well as their bent-up state. There are two ways to design sheet-metal parts in NX. Either you can start the sheet-metal part from scratch using sheet-metal features throughout the design process (or) you can design it as a regular solid part and later convert it to a sheet-metal part. Most commonly, you design sheet-metal parts in Sheet Metal environment from the beginning. In this chapter, you will learn both the approaches.

The topics covered in this chapter are:

- *Tabs*
- *Flanges*
- *Bend Allowance*
- *Bend Tables*
- *Counter Flanges*
- *Hems*
- *Close 2-Bend Corners*
- *Bends*
- *Jogs*
- *Dimples*
- *Louvers*
- *Drawn Cutouts*
- *Beads*
- *Gussets*
- *Etches*
- *Embosses*
- *Cuts*
- *Convert to Sheet Metal*
- *Rip Corners*
- *Flat Pattern*
- *Export to DXF or DWG*

Starting a Sheet Metal part

To start a new sheet metal part, click **Home > Standard > New** on the ribbon. On the **New** dialog, click the **Model** tab, and then double-click on the **Sheet metal.psm** template.

Sheet Metal Part Properties

The most common Sheet Metal Part Properties are type of material and bend allowances. You can define these properties by clicking **File > Preferences > Sheet Metal.** On the **Sheet Metal Preferences** dialog, select **Parameter Entry > Value Entry** and type-in values in the **Material thickness, Bend radius, Relief depth,** and **Relief width** boxes. These parameters are illustrated in the following figure.

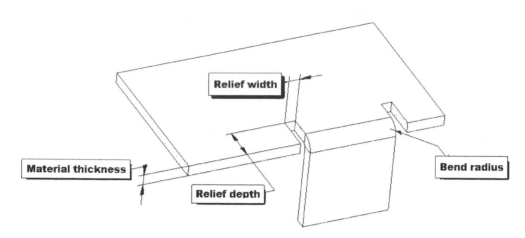

Next, type-in a value in **Neutral Factor Value** box. The **Neutral Factor** is the ratio that represents the location of neutral sheet measured from the inside face with respect to the thickness of the sheet metal part. The **Neutral Factor** defines the bend allowance of the sheet metal part. The standard formula that calculates the bend allowance is given below.

$$BA = \frac{\pi(R + KT)A}{180}$$

BA = Bend Allowance

R = Bend Radius

K = Neutral Factor = t/T

T = Material Thickness

t = Distance from inside face to the neutral sheet

A = Bend Angle

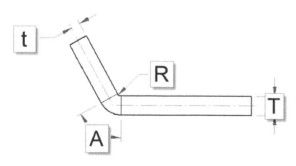

You can also define the bend allowance by using a bend table or your own bend allowance formula. To enter a bend allowance formula, select the **Bend Allowance Formula** option and type-in a value in the box. Click **OK** after specifying values on the **Sheet Metal Preferences** dialog.

Tab

The tab is a basic type of sheet metal feature. To create a tab, create a closed sketch on a plane. You can also create a sketch with internal loops. Next, activate the **Tab** command (On the ribbon, click **Home > Basic > Tab**). Click on the internal and external loops of the sketch, and then click **OK** on the **Tab** dialog.

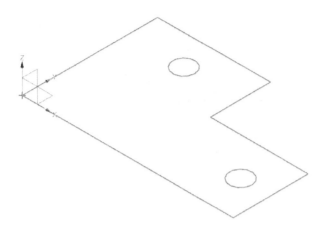

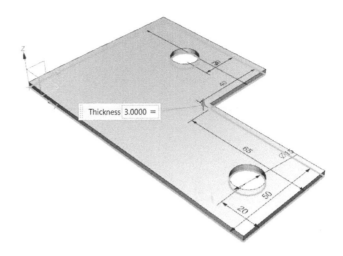

Flange

The second feature after creating a tab is flange. You can create this feature along an edge or multiple edges of a sheet metal part. In order to create a flange, all you need is to activate the **Flange** command (On the ribbon, click **Home > Bend > Flange**), and then click an edge of the tab feature. The flange preview appears on the selected face. Click the arrow attached to the preview and drag the pointer to change the length of the flange.

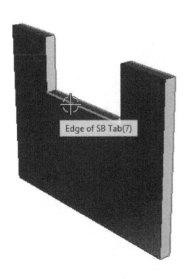

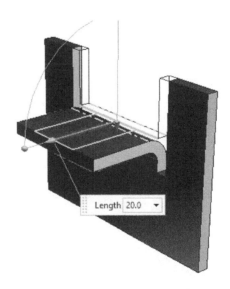

On the **Flange** dialog, select the required **Width Option** to define the flange width. The default width option is **Full**. The remaining width options are discussed next.

The **At Center** option creates a flange at the center of the selected edge.

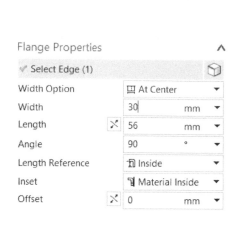

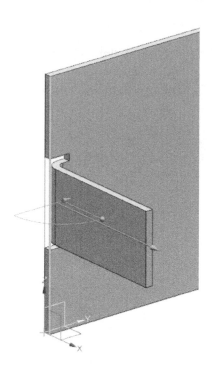

The **At End** option creates a flange at an end point of the selected edge. Select this option from the **Width Option** drop-down, and then click **Specify Point.** Next, select an endpoint to locate the flange.

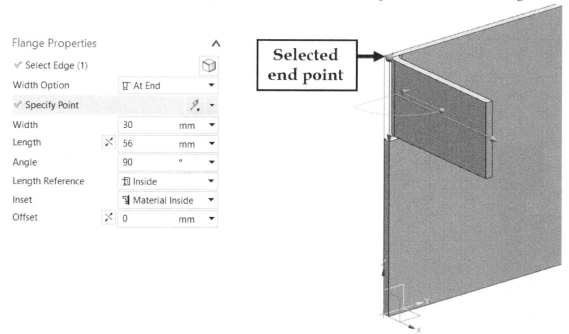

Selected end point

The **From End** option creates a flange at distance from the selected end point of the edge. You need to select an end point of the selected edge. Next, type in a value in the **Distance 1** box to define the start point of the flange.

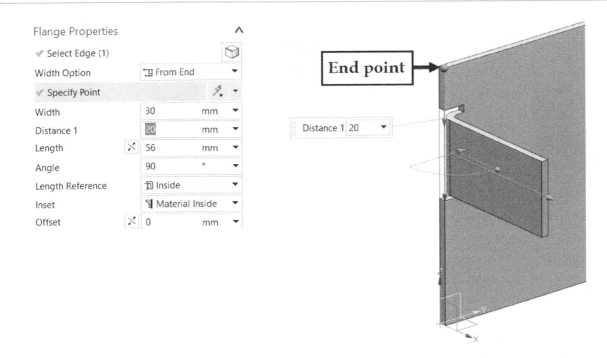

The **From Both Ends** option creates a flange by offsetting it from both the endpoints of the selected edge. You need to specify the values in the Distance 1 and Distance 2 boxes. The flange will be created between both the end of the selected.

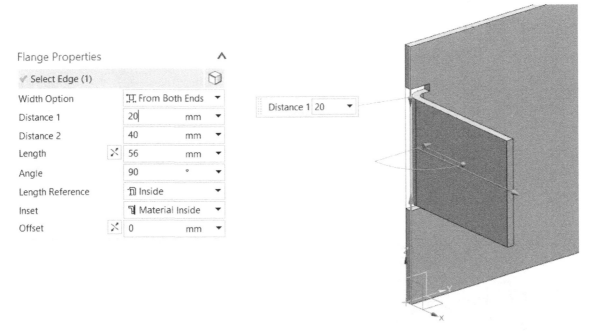

Type-in a value in the **Angle** box available in the **Flange Properties** section to create the flange at an angle.

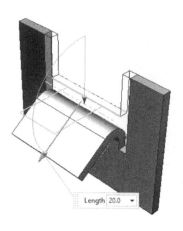

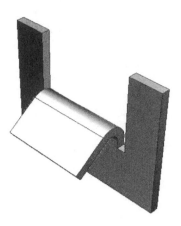

Under the **Flange Properties** section, select **Length Reference > Inside** to define the flange length from the inside face of the supporting tab. Select **Length Reference > Outside** to define the flange length from the outside face of the supporting tab. Select **Length Reference > Web** to exclude the bend from the flange length.

Define the material side using the **Inset** drop-down menu. The three types of material sides: **Material Inside**, **Material Outside**, and **Bend Outside** are shown below. The **Material Inside** option matches the outer face of the flange with the edge on which the flange is created. The **Material Outside** option matches the inner face of the flange with the edge on which the flange is created. The **Bend Outside** option starts the flange bend from the edge selected to create the flange.

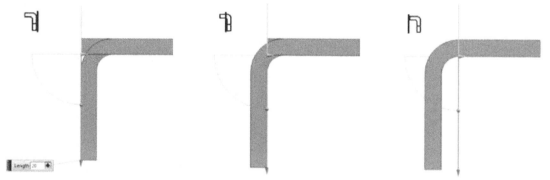

Type in a value in the **Offset** box, if you want to offset the flange from the selected edge.

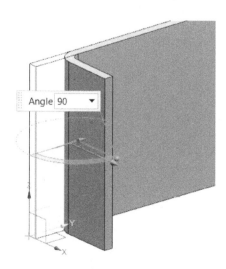

The **Geometry Properties** section has two options: **Enable Geometry Mirror and Pattern** and **Miter** options. The **Enable Geometry Mirror and Pattern** option helps you to mirror or pattern the flange geometry without considering the feature parameters. The **Miter** option avoids the intersection of two flanges by creating a miter at the corner at which two flanges meet.

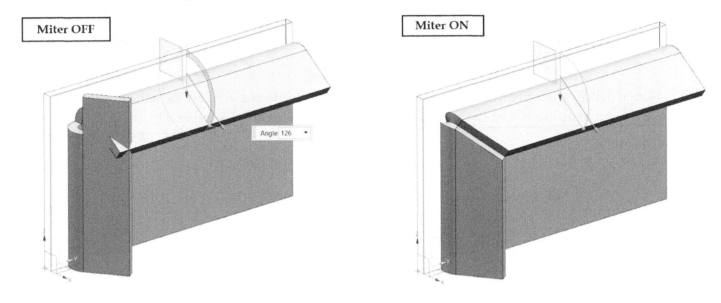

On the **Flange** dialog, you can override the sheet metal properties under the **Bend Parameters** and **Relief** sections. For example, to change the **Bend Radius** value, click **Launch Formula Editor** = > **Use Local Value**. Now, type-in a new bend radius value.

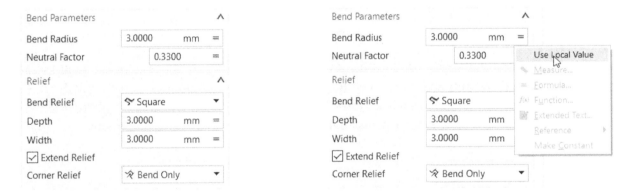

From the **Corner Relief** drop-down menu, select an option to define the type of corner relief. Corner relief is to be provided when two flanges meet at a corner. The following figure shows the three types of corner reliefs.

On the **Flange** dialog, select **Reference Plane > Match Face > Until Selected** to create the flange up to a selected face. Next, select a planar face from the graphics window; the outer face of the matches with the selected face.

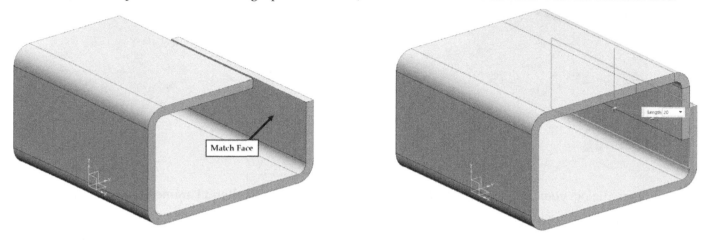

Click **OK** on the **Flange** dialog to complete the flange feature.

Closed Corner

The **Closed Corner** command allows you to control the appearance of sheet metal seams. For example, when two flanges meet at a corner, this command allows you to close the gap between them. In addition to that, it applies a corner treatment. Activate this command (click **Home > Corner > Closed Corner** on the ribbon) and click on two bends that meet at a corner. On the **Closed Corner** dialog, select the required corner treatment.

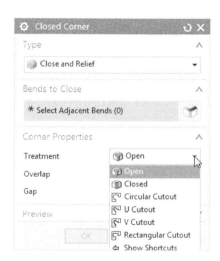

There are six types of corner treatments available in the **Treatment** drop-down menu, as shown below.

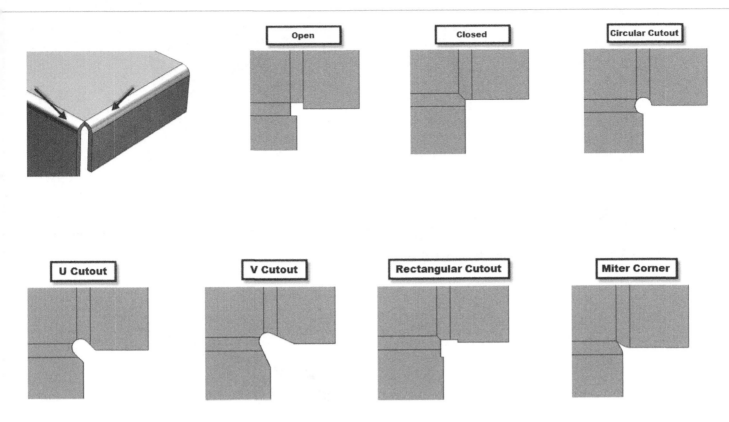

In the **Corner Properties** section, click **Overlap > Overlapping** to overlap one flange on the other. Next, type-in a value in the **Overlap ratio** box.

Contour Flange

The contour flange is another basic type of sheet metal feature. In order to create a contour flange, you need to have an open sketch. Activate the **Contour Flange** command (click **Home > Bend > Contour Flange** on the ribbon) and click on elements of an open sketch (*Tip: On the Top Border Bar, set the **Curve Rule** to **Connected Curves** if you want to select all the elements of the sketch with a single click*). Drag the arrow or type-in a value in the **Width** box to define the width of the contour flange. Press Enter to create the contour flange feature.

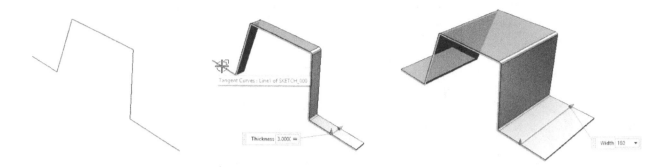

Creating a Rolled Sheet Metal part

You can use the **Contour Flange** command to create a rolled sheet metal part. To do this, create a sketch using The **Arc** command. Next, create contour flange using the sketch.

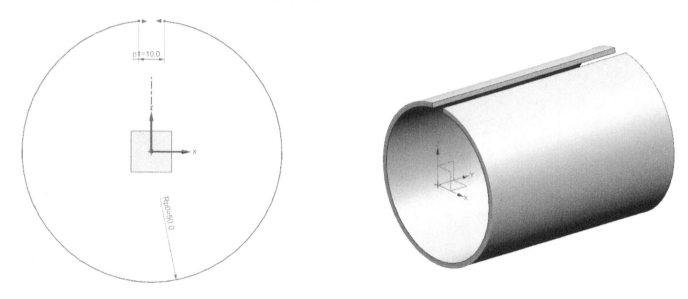

Creating a Secondary Contour Flange

You can also add contour flanges to a base tab. Activate the **Contour Flange** command and click an edge of the *Tab* feature. A plane appears normal to the selected edge. Type-in a value in the % **Arc Length** box to define the positon of the plane and click **OK**; a sketch will be started. Draw an open profile of the contour flange feature and click **Finish** on the ribbon. You will notice a contour flange preview. On the **Contour Flange** dialog, select **Width > Width Option > Finite** to define a finite distance of the contour flange.

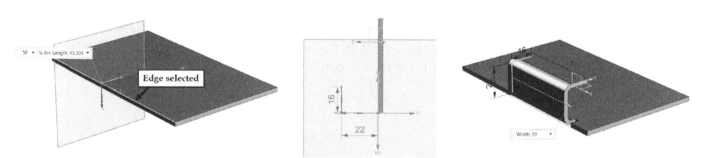

Select **Width Option > Symmetric** to create the contour flange on both sides of the profile. Select **Width Option > To End** to create the contour flange up to the end of the selected edge.

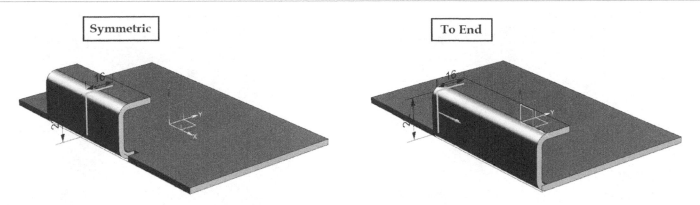

Select **Width Option > Chain** and select **Select edge** from the **Width** section. Next, click on the edges connected to the selected edge. The contour flange preview appears along the selected chain of edges.

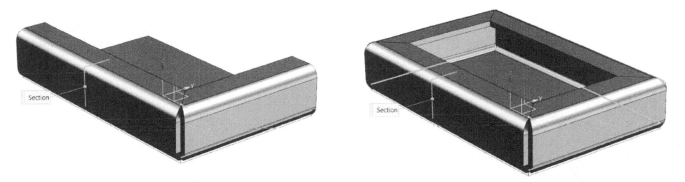

If you want to apply treatments at the corners of the contour flanges, then select **Corner > Close Corner**. The options in the **Treatment** drop-down are explained earlier in the **Closed Corner** command. Also, notice the **Miter Corner** option below the **Treatment** drop-down. Note that this option is available only when the **Treatment** type is set to **Closed, Circular Cutout, U Cutout,** or **V Cutout.** The **Miter Corner** option applies a miter to the closed corner. The following image displays a closed corner with and without miter.

The **Blend Miter** option blends the sharp corners of the miter. The following image shows a closed cutout with a blended miter.

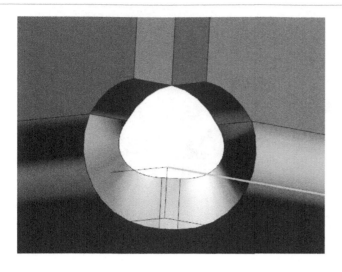

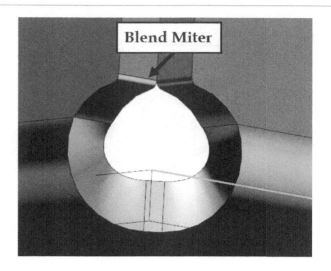

On the dialog, expand the **Miter** section and check the **Miter Corners** option to apply miter to the ends of the contour flange. Next, select an option from the **Cutout** drop-down: **Normal to Thickness Face** and **Normal to Source Face**. Type in a value in the **Angle** box.

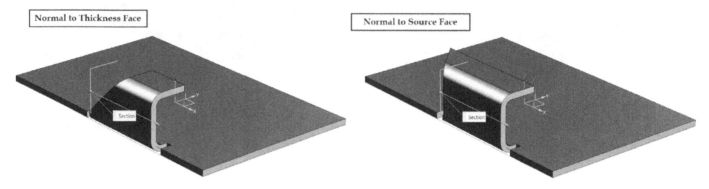

Hem Flange

The **Hem Flange** command folds an edge of a sheet metal part. To add a hem, activate the **Hem Flange** command (click **Home > Bend > More > Hem Flange** on the ribbon) and select the edge you need to fold over.

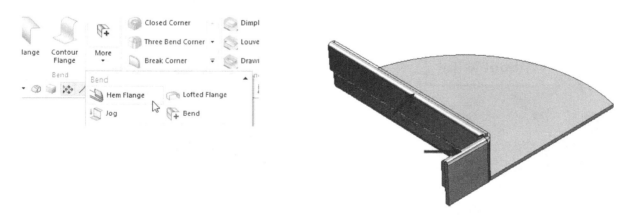

On the dialog, the **Inset** drop-down menu controls whether to add the material inside or outside of the existing edge.

On the Hem dialog, select a hem type from the **Type** drop-down menu and define its parameters. The following figure shows different hem types.

If you want to bevel the end faces of the hem, then expand the **Miter** section and check the **Miter Hem** option. Type-in a value in the **Miter Angle** box. Click the **OK** button to complete the hem feature.

Bend

In addition to adding flanges and contour flanges, you can also bend a flat sheet using the **Bend** command. Activate the **Bend** command (click **Home > Bend > More > Bend** on the ribbon) and click on the face to bend. Draw a sketch line on the flat sheet and click **Finish** on the ribbon. The flat sheet bends along the sketch line. On the **Bend** dialog, click the **Reverse Side** button to flip the bend side. Type-in a value in the **Angle** box to change the folding angle. Click the **Reverse Direction** to reverse the folding direction. Select an option from the **Inset** drop-down menu to define the material side of the bend feature. Click **OK** to complete the bend feature.

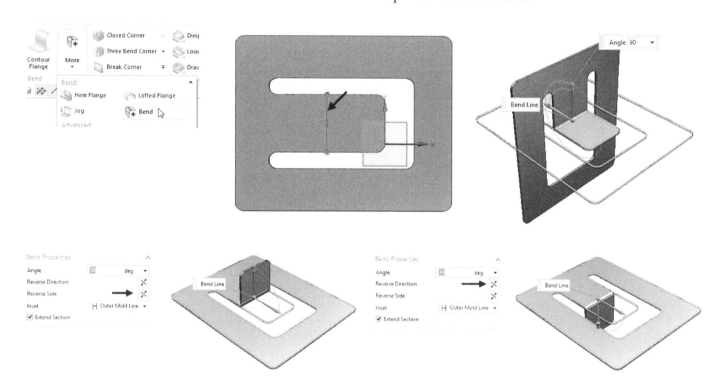

Jog

The **Jog** command adds a jog or offset to a flat sheet. Activate the **Jog** command (click **Home > Bend > More > Jog** on the ribbon) and click on a face to add the jog. Draw a line defining the location of the jog, and then click **Finish** on the ribbon. A preview of the jog feature appears. Type-in a value in the **Height** box to define the jog height. On the **Jog** dialog, click the **Reverse Side** button to flip the jog side. Click the **Reverse Direction** button to reverse the jog direction.

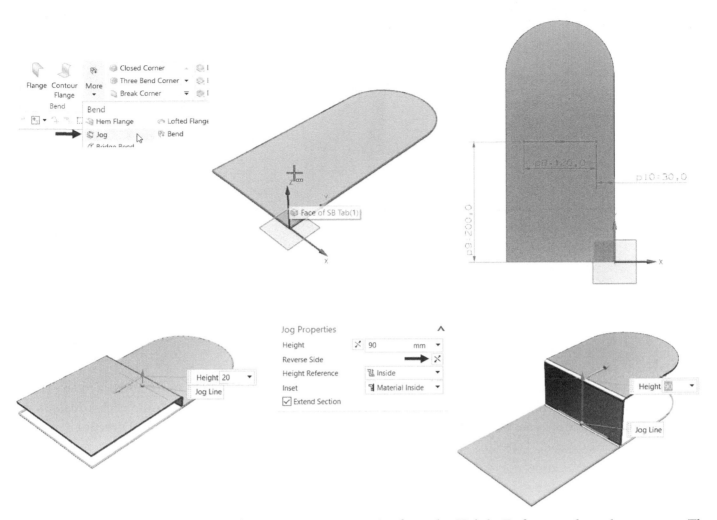

Under the **Jog Properties** section, select a measurement point from the **Height Reference** drop-down menu. The following figure illustrates both the measurement points.

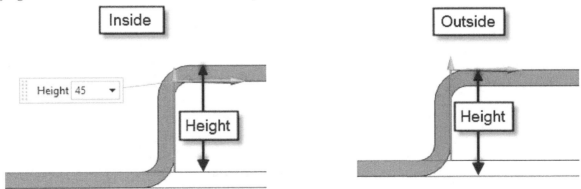

The **Extend Section** option extends the sketch profile up to the side edge of the sheet metal part. If you uncheck this option, it results in a jog, as shown in figure.

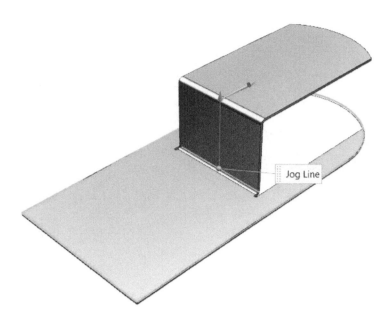

Click **OK** to create the Jog.

Dimple

The **Dimple** command adds a dimple to a flat sheet by deforming it. Activate the **Dimple** command (click **Home > Punch > Dimple** on the ribbon) and click on the face to add dimple. Draw a closed sketch and click **Finish** on the ribbon. A dimple shape appears on the sketch region. On the **Dimple** dialog, click the **Reverse Direction** button to change the dimple direction. Type-in a value in the **Depth** box to define the depth of the dimple feature.

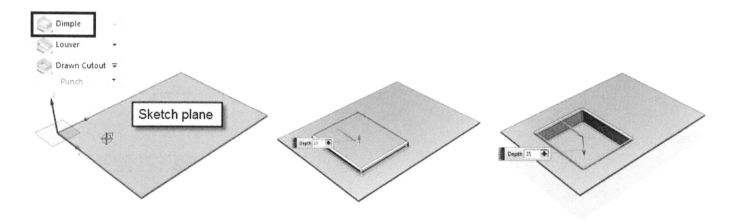

On the **Dimple** dialog, type-in the values of **Side Angle**, **Punch Radius**, **Die Radius**, and **Corner Radius**.

Use the **Side Walls** drop-down menu to define the material side of the dimple feature. You can select **Material Outside** or **Material Inside**.

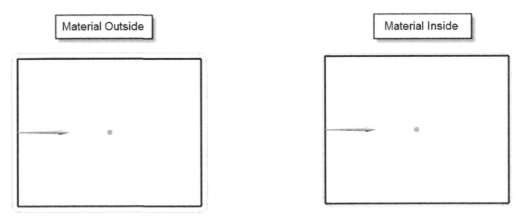

Drawn Cutout

The drawn cutout and dimple feature are almost alike, except that an opening is created in case of a drawn cut out. Activate the **Drawn Cutout** command (click **Home > Punch > Drawn Cutout** on the ribbon) and click on the face to add drawn cutout. Draw a closed sketch and click **Finish** on the ribbon. On the **Drawn Cutout** dialog, click the **Reverse Direction** button to change the cutout direction. Type-in a value in the **Depth** box to define the depth of the drawn cutout feature.

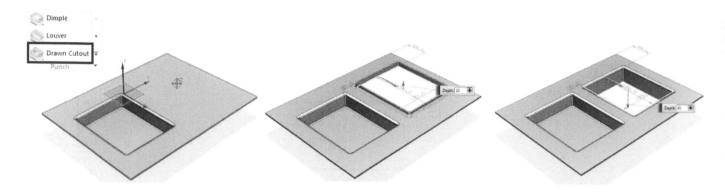

On the dialog, type-in values of **Side Angle**, **Die Radius**, and **Corner Radius**.

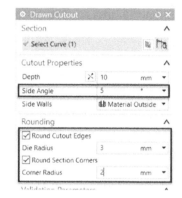

From the **Side Walls** drop-down menu, select **Material Outside** or **Material Inside**. This determines whether the sidewalls will appear inside or outside the sketch profile. Click **OK** on the dialog to complete the drawn cut out.

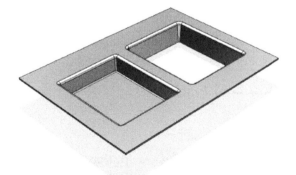

Bead

The **Bead** command creates a bead feature, which stiffens the sheet metal part. In order to create a bead feature, first you must have a sketch, which defines the bead size and shape. If the sketch is having curved edges, then ensure that they are tangent continuous. Activate the **Bead** command (click **Home > Punch > Bead** on the ribbon) and click on the sketch. On the **Bead** dialog, click the **Reverse Direction** button to flip the bead feature.

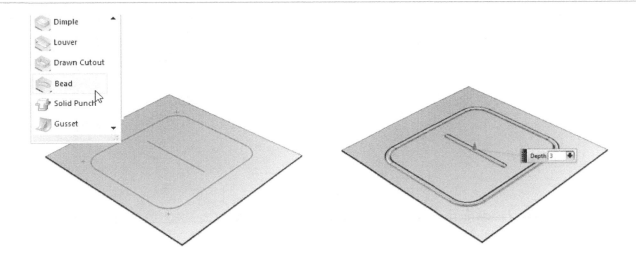

On this dialog, under **Bend Properties**, select the cross section type and define the size parameters. There are three different cross section types, as shown.

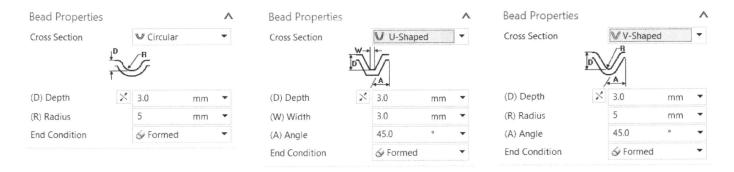

From the **End Condition** drop-down menu, select **Formed**, **Lanced**, **Punched** or **Tapered** (available only for the V-Shaped cross section). These end conditions are shown in the following figure.

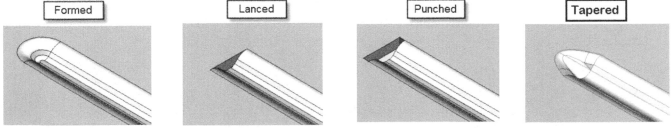

Under the **Rounding** section, check the **Round Bead Edges** option to apply rounds to the edges of the bead feature. Type-in values in the **Die Radius** and **Punch Radius** boxes. Note that the **Punch Radius** box is available only for the U-Shaped cross-section. Click **OK** to complete the bead feature.

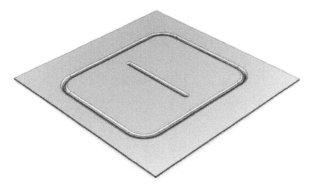

NX allows you to create beads across bends. First, you have to unbend the sheet metal part using the **Unbend** command. Activate the **Unbend** command (On the ribbon, click **Home > Form > Unbend**) and click on the face to remain stationary. Click on the bend and click **OK** to unbend the sheet metal part.

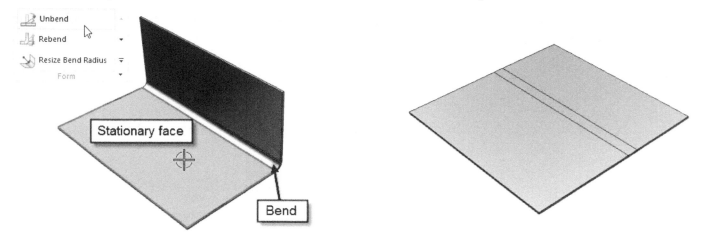

Activate the **Bead** command and click on the face to add beads. Draw bead profiles and click **Finish** on the ribbon. Define the bead parameters on the **Bead** dialog and click **OK**.

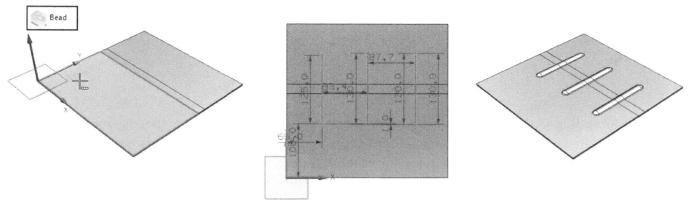

Now, activate the **Rebend** command (On the ribbon, click **Home > Form > Rebend**) and click on the bend. On the **Rebend** dialog, click **OK** to rebend the sheet metal part.

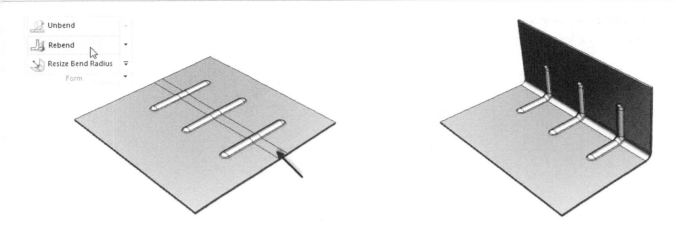

Louver

NX provides you with the **Louver** command, which makes it easy to create louvers. Activate this command (click **Home > Punch > Louver** on the ribbon) and click on a face. Draw a line on the selected face and click **Finish** on the ribbon. On the **Louver** dialog, type-in a value in the **Depth** box. Click **Reverse Direction** ⊠ next to the **Depth** box to reverse the depth direction. Type-in a value in the **Width** box to define the width of the louver. Click **Reverse Direction** ⊠ next to the **Width** box to reverse the width. You should ensure that the louver depth should be less than or equal to width minus the material thickness.

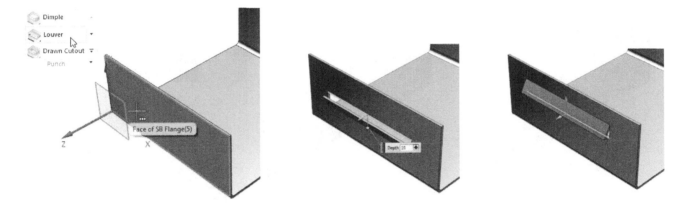

On the **Louver** dialog, define the end condition of the louver from the **Louver Shape** drop-down menu. The following figure shows the two end conditions.

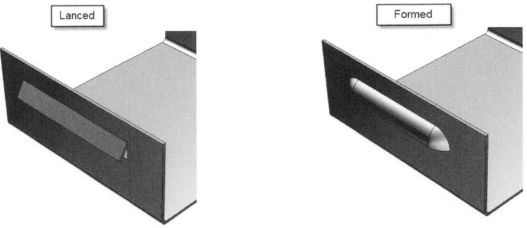

Under the **Rounding** section, check the **Round Louver Edges** option and type-in a value in the **Die Radius** box to round the edges of the louver. Click **OK** to complete the louver feature.

Gusset

Gussets are stiffening features created across a bend to reinforce the sheet metal part. Activate the **Gusset** command (click **Home > Punch > Gusset** on the ribbon) and click on a bend face. Select a point on the edge of the selected bend face; a gusset feature appears along with a plane. Drag the plane to define the location of the gusset.

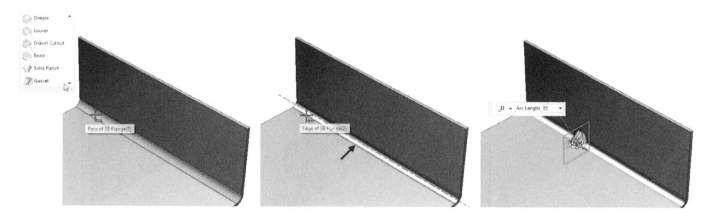

Under the **Shape** section, select the gusset form from the **Form** drop-down and type-in a value in the **Depth** box. Type-in values of **Width**, **Side Angle**, **Punch Radius** and **Die Radius**.

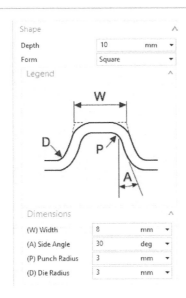

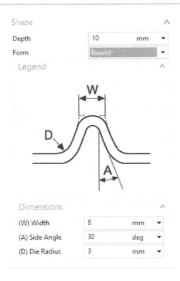

Click **OK** to complete the gusset feature.

In addition to creating a gusset with automatic profile, NX allows you to create a gusset with a user-defined profile. On the **Gusset** dialog, select **Type > User Defined Profile** and click on an edge of the bend. A plane appears normal to the edge. Click **OK** and draw a sketch. On the ribbon, click **Finish** to create the gusset with the custom profile. Under the **Section** section, use the **Width Side** drop-down menu to define the side of the gusset feature.

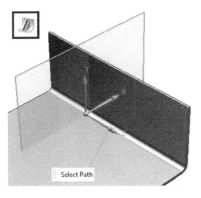

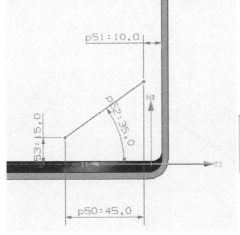

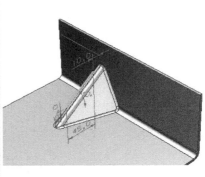

Normal Cutout

More often it is necessary to remove material from a sheet metal part. To do so, you must use the **Normal Cutout** command. First, draw a sketch, and then activate the **Normal Cutout** command (On the ribbon, click **Home > Feature > Normal Cutout**). Click on the sketch and select the extent type from **Cutout Properties > Limits**. Type-in a value in the **Depth** box in case the **Limits** is set to **Value**. You can also set the **Limits** to **Between**, **Until next**, or **Through All**. These options are explained in *Chapter 3: Extrude and Revolve Features*. On the dialog, click **OK** to create the cutout.

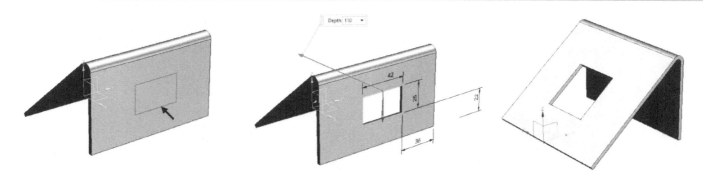

Cutting across Bends

If you want to create a cut across a bend, you must unbend the sheet metal part and draw a sketch.

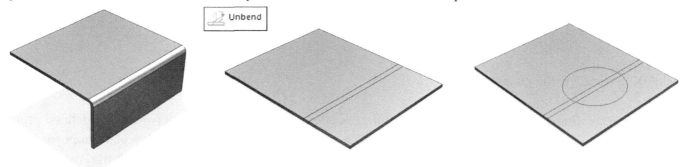

Activate the **Normal Cutout** command and create a cut across the bend. Use the **Rebend** command and fold the sheet metal part.

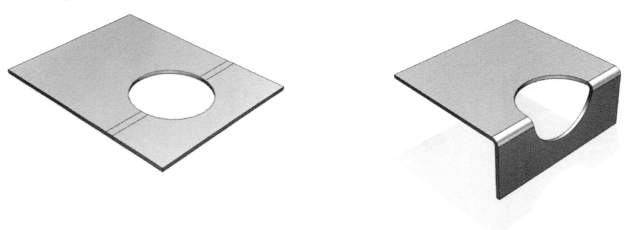

Break Corner

The **Break Corner** command rounds or chamfers the sharp corners of a sheet metal part. Activate this command (click **Home > Corner > Break Corner** on the ribbon) and click on the corner edges of the sheet metal part. If you want to break all the corners of the sheet metal part, then drag a selection window across the geometry. This will select all the corners of the sheet metal part.

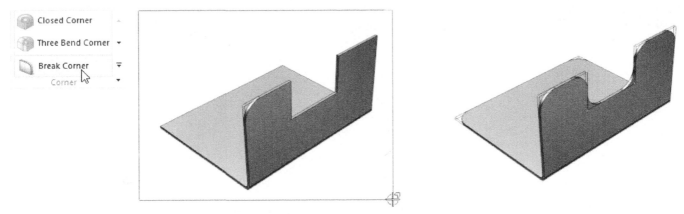

On the **Break Corner** dialog, select **Method > Chamfer** to apply a chamfer to the corner edges. Type-in a value in the **Radius** or **Distance** box. Click **OK** to complete the break corner feature.

Flat Pattern

The **Flat Pattern** command flattens the part so that you can easily display the manufacturing information. Activate the **Flat Pattern** command (click **Flat Pattern > Flat Pattern** on the ribbon) and click on a base sheet. On the **Flat Pattern** dialog, select **Orientation Method > Select Edge** in the **Orientation** section. Select an edge to define the x-axis of the flat pattern. Click **OK** to create the flat pattern.

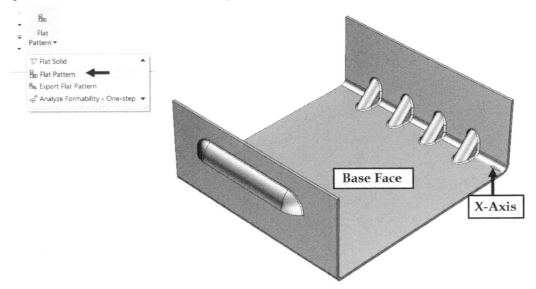

On the Top Border Bar, click **Menu > View > Layout > New** to open the **New Layout** dialog. On this dialog, select **FLAT-PATTERN** and click **OK**. The flat pattern appears. To switch back to the modeling mode, open the **New Layout** dialog, select **Isometric**, and click **OK**.

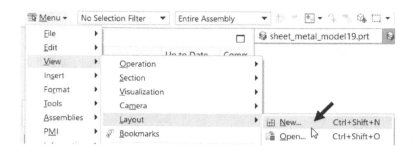

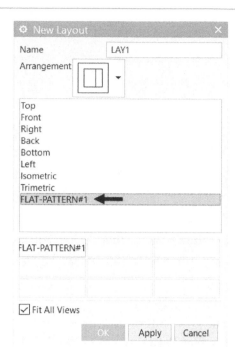

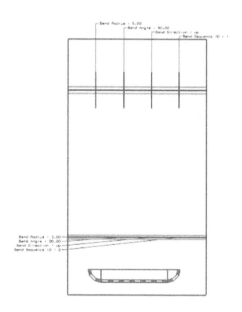

Flat Solid

Besides creating a flat pattern, NX allows you to create a flattened Solid of a sheet metal part. Activate the **Flat Solid** command (On the ribbon, click **Home > Flat Pattern > Flat Solid**) and click on the base face of the sheet metal part. Under the **Orientation** section, select **Orientation Method > Select Edge** and click on an edge to define the x-axis of the flat solid. Click **OK** to create the flat solid.

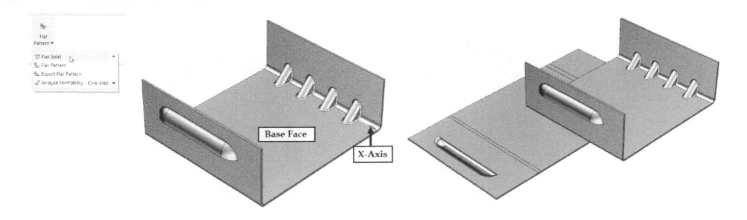

Lofted Flange

The **Lofted Flange** command creates a lofted flange that can be unfolded into a flat pattern. Create two sketches on planes parallel to each other. Ensure that the sketches are not closed. In addition, the openings should be in the same direction.

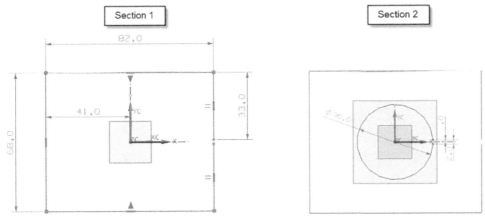

Activate the **Lofted Flange** command (click **Home > Bend > More > Lofted Flange** on the ribbon) click on the first cross section. On the **Lofted Flange** dialog, under **End Section**, click **Select Curve**. Click on the second cross section. Click **OK** to complete the lofted flange.

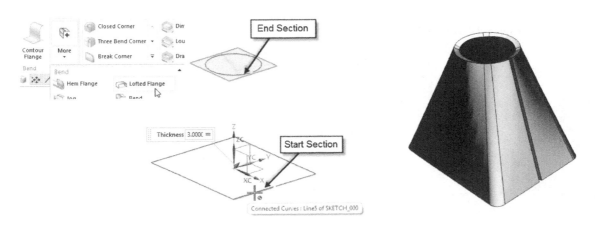

Create the flat pattern of the sheet metal part.

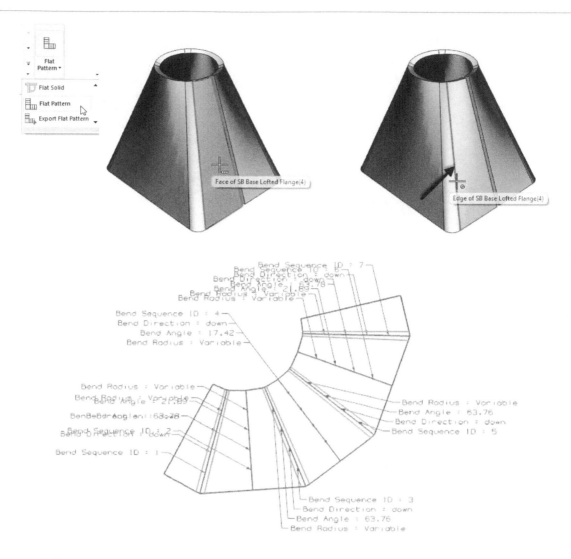

Sheet Metal from Solid

The **Sheet Metal from Solid** command creates a sheet metal part from a set of planar faces of a solid body. First, create a solid body using the **Extrude** command, and then activate the **Sheet Metal from Solid** command (On the ribbon, click **Home > Basic > Sheet Metal from Solid**). Click on the planar faces of the solid body, which connect each other. The **Sheet Metal from Solid** message appears. Click **OK** to preview the sheet metal.

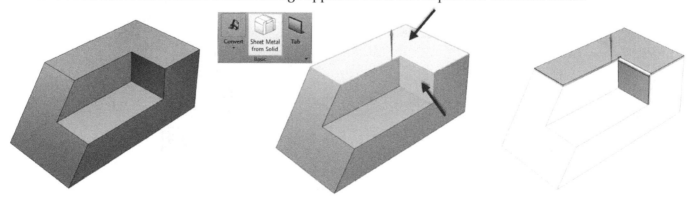

Click on the other faces connected to the previously selected faces. If an **Alert** message appears, then you have to select the bend edge manually. For example, if you click on the right-side face of the solid body, then an alert message appears asking you to select appropriate bend edges. On the **Sheet Metal from Solid** dialog, under the **Bend Edges** section, click **Select Bend Edge**. Click on the edge connecting the two faces.

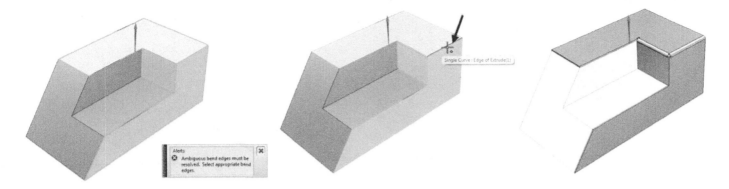

On the dialog, click **Select Web face** and start selecting the other planar faces. If any alert message appears, then select the bend edges manually. Hide the solid body to view the completed sheet metal part.

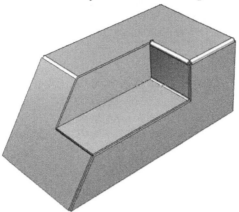

Convert to Sheet Metal Wizard

NX has a special command called **Convert to Sheet Metal Wizard**, which automates the process of converting an already existing part into a sheet metal part. First, create a part in the Modeling environment, and then shell it using the **Shell** command. Next, click **Application > Design > Sheet Metal** on the ribbon.

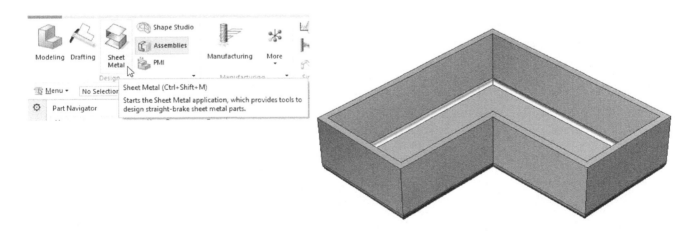

On the ribbon, click **Home > Basic > Convert > Convert to Sheet Metal Wizard**. Click on the edges to rip off. On the dialog, click the **Next** button and click on the horizontal face. Click **Next**. Expand the **Relief** section and define the **Bend Relief**. Click **Finish** to complete the conversion process.

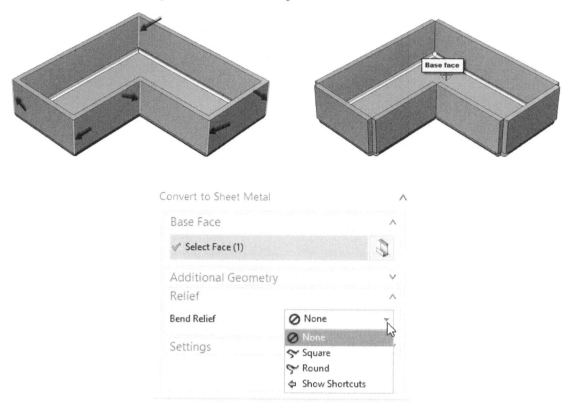

Resize Bend Radius

The **Resize Bend Radius** command changes the radius of a bend. Activate this command (On the ribbon, click **Home > Form > Resize Bend Radius**). On the **Resize Bend Radius** dialog, from the **Type** drop-down menu, select **Fixed Tab/Flange Position**. Click on a bend face and type-in a value in the **Bend Radius** box. If you select **Type > Unfolded Length,** then you must select a stationary face.

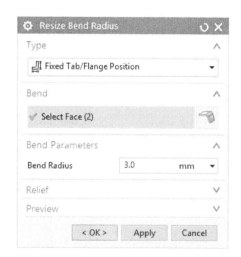

Resize Bend Angle

The **Resize Bend Angle** command changes the angle of a bend. Activate this command (On the ribbon, click **Home > Form > Resize Bend Angle**) and click on the face to remain stationary. Click on the bend face and type-in a new value in the **Angle** box. Check the **Keep Radius Fixed** option, if you do not want to change the bend radius value with the angler. Click **OK** to complete resizing the bend angle.

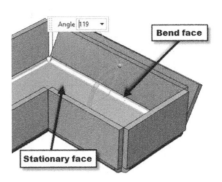

Resize Neutral Factor

The **Resize Neutral Factor** command changes the Neutral factor value of a sheet metal part. Neutral Factor defines the bend allowance of a sheet metal part. Activate this command (On the ribbon, click **Home > Form > Resize Neutral Factor**) and click on a bend face. Click the **Launch the formula editor** ＝ icon next to the **Neutral Factor** box, and then select **Use Local Value**. Type-in a value in the **Neutral Factor** box, and click **OK**.

Sheet Metal Drawings

Creating drawings of a sheet metal part is same as creating any other drawing. However, there are some options specific to sheet metal flat pattern. You can access these settings under **View > Flat Pattern** section of the **Drafting Preferences** dialog.

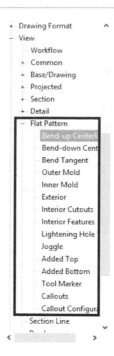

To insert a flat pattern view into the drawing, activate the **Base View** command (on the ribbon, click **Home > View > Base View**) and select the sheet metal part. On the **Base View** dialog, under the **Model View** section, select **Model View to Use > FLAT-PATTERN#1**.

On the dialog, set the **Scale** value and click to place the view. You will notice that lines represent the bends.

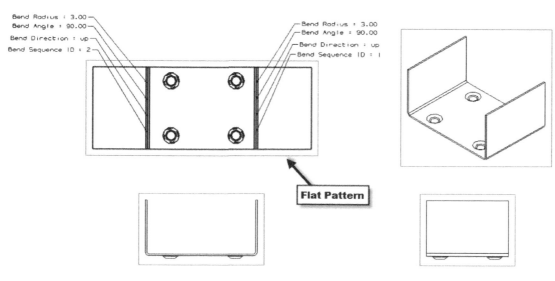

To add a bend table, click **Home > Table > Bend Table** ▦ on the ribbon, and then click on the flat pattern view. Click on the sheet to position the bend table.

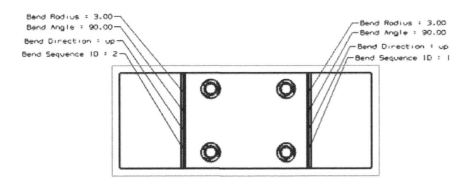

2	Bend 2	3.00	90.00	up	90.00
1	Bend 1	3.00	90.00	up	90.00
ID	Name	Radius	Angle	Direction	Included Angle

Export Flat Pattern

In addition to creating drawings, you can directly export a sheet metal to DWF or Trumpf GEO formats. All you have to do is click **Flat Pattern > Export Flat Pattern**. On the **Export Flat Pattern** dialog, select **Type > DWF** and specify the output file location. Under the **Flat Pattern Geometry Types** section, check the geometry types to export. Under the **Settings** section, select the **DWF Revision** type.

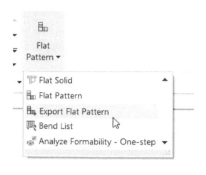

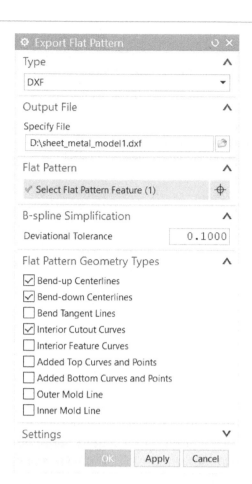

Under **Part Navigator**, click on the **Flat Pattern** feature to export, and the click **OK**.

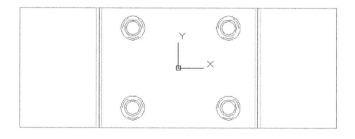

Examples

Example 1

In this example, you will construct the sheet metal part shown below.

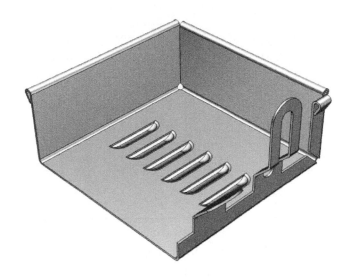

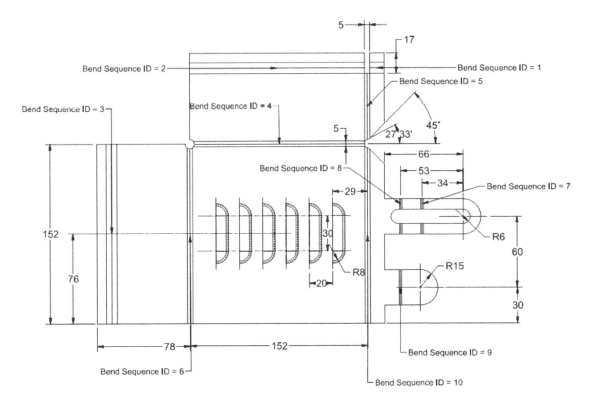

Bend Sequence ID = 2

Bend Sequence ID = 1

Bend Sequence ID = 5

Bend Sequence ID = 3

Bend Sequence ID = 4

5

17

45°

27°33'

5

66

53

34

Bend Sequence ID = 8

Bend Sequence ID = 7

29

R6

152

30

60

76

R8

R15

20

30

78

152

Bend Sequence ID = 9

Bend Sequence ID = 6

Bend Sequence ID = 10

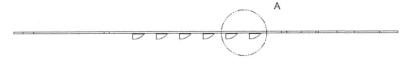

A

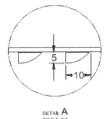

5

10

DETAIL A
SCALE 2:1

ID	Name	Radius	Angle	Direction	Included Angle
10	Bend 10	2.40	90.00	up	90.00
9	Bend 9	2.40	45.00	down	135.00
8	Bend 8	2.40	45.00	down	135.00
7	Bend 7	2.40	45.00	up	135.00
6	Bend 6	2.40	90.00	up	90.00
5	Bend 5	2.40	90.00	up	90.00
4	Bend 4	2.40	90.00	up	90.00
3	Bend 3	2.00	208.05	down	-28.05
2	Bend 2	2.00	208.05	down	-28.05
1	Bend 1	2.00	208.05	down	-28.05

1. Start **NX 12**.
2. On the ribbon, click the **New** button to open the **New** dialog.
3. On the **New** dialog, select **Units > Millimeters** and click **Sheet Metal**. Click **OK**.
4. On the **Top Border Bar**, click **Menu > Preferences > Sheet Metal**.
5. On the **Sheet Metal Preferences** dialog, under **Part Properties**, select **Parameter Entry > Type > Material Selection**. Click **Select Material**.
6. On the **Select Material** dialog, select **Aluminiun_6061** from the **Available Materials** section and click **OK**.

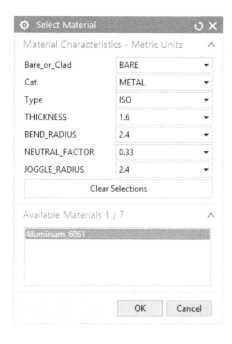

7. On the **Sheet Metal Preferences** dialog, under the **Parameter Entry** section, select **Type > Value Entry**.
8. On the **Sheet Metal Preferences** dialog, type-in **2.4** in the **Relief Depth** and **Relief Width** boxes. Click **OK**.
9. On the ribbon, click **Home > Basic > Tab** and click on the XY plane.
10. Create a sketch and click **Finish** on the ribbon. On the **Tab** dialog, click **OK** to create the tab feature.

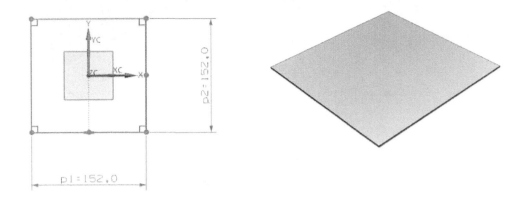

11. On the ribbon, click **Home > Bend > Flange** and click on the back edge.

12. On the **Flange** dialog, under **Flange Properties**, select **Length Reference > Outside**. Select **Inset > Material Outside**.

13. Type-in **65** in the **Length** box. Click **OK** to create the flange.

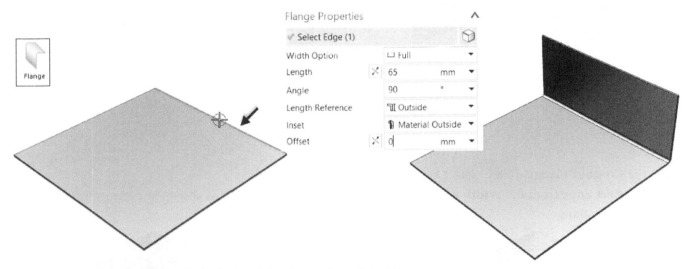

14. Create another flange on the left side. The flange length is 65 mm.

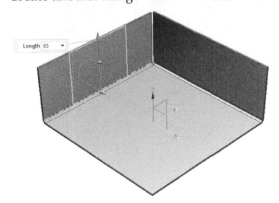

15. On the ribbon, click **Home > Bend > Contour Flange**.

16. On the **Contour Flange** dialog, select **Section > Sketch Section** and click on the right edge of the tab feature.

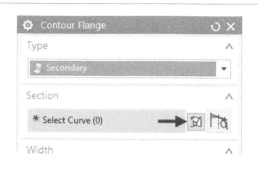

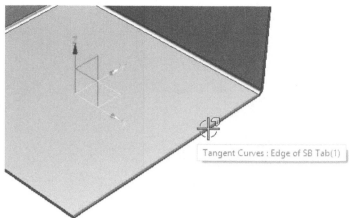

17. In the %**Arc Length** box, type-in **0** and click **OK**.
18. Draw a line of **15** mm length and click **Finish** on the ribbon.

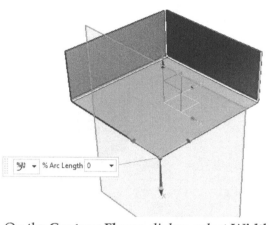

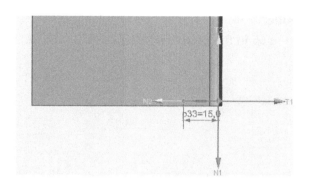

19. On the **Contour Flange** dialog, select **Width Option > Chain**.
20. Click **Select Edge** from the **Width** section and click on the edge of the tab, as shown in figure. Click **OK** to complete the flange.

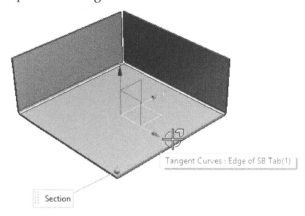

21. On the ribbon, click **Home > Basic > Tab**.
22. Click on the outer face of the contour flange and draw the sketch shown below.
23. Click **Finish** on the ribbon.
24. On the **Tab** dialog, select **Type > Secondary**, and then click **OK** to create a tab feature.

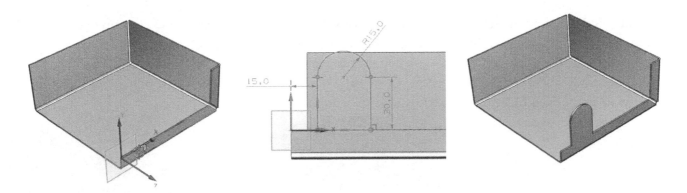

25. Activate the **Sketch** command, and then select **Sketch Type > On Plane**. Next, click on the outer face of the tab, and then click **OK**.

26. Draw a horizontal line at 12 mm distance from the top edge of the contour flange. Next, click **Finish Sketch**.

27. Activate the **Bend** command (On the ribbon, click **Home > Bend > More > Bend**) and click on the line.

28. On the **Bend** dialog, type-in **45** in the **Angle** box.

29. Use the **Reverse Side** button to make sure that the output matches that shown below. Next, click **OK** to bend the tab feature.

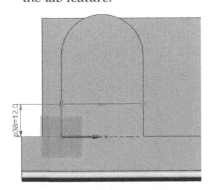
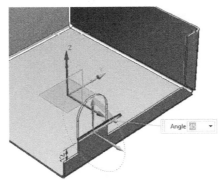
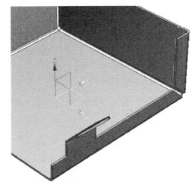

30. Draw another sketch on the outer face of the contour flange.

31. Activate the **Tab** command and create a tab feature using the sketch.

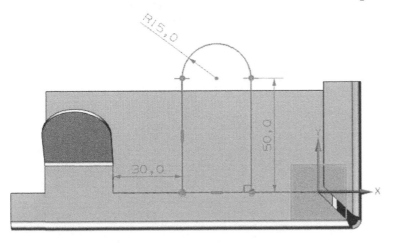
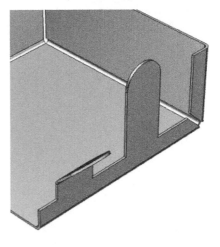

32. Draw a line on the outer face of the tab feature. Next, add 15mm dimension between the line and the top edge of the contour flange feature. Click **Finish Sketch** to exit the sketch.

33. Activate the **Jog** command (click **Home > Bend > More > Jog** on the ribbon) and click on the sketched line.
34. On the **Jog** dialog, select **Height Reference > Outside** and **Inset > Material Outside**.
35. Use the **Reverse Side** button to make sure that the output matches that shown below.
36. Make sure that the **Extend Section** option is selected.
37. Type-in **20** in the **Height** box and click **OK** to add jog to the tab feature.

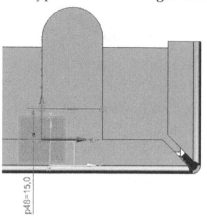
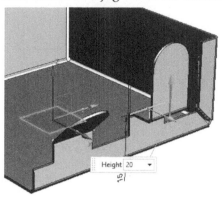
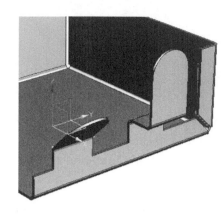

38. On the ribbon, click **Home > Form > Resize Bend Angle**.
39. Click on the outer face of the contour flange feature to define the stationary face.
40. Click on the lower bend of the jog feature and type-in **135** in the **Angle** box. Click **Apply**.

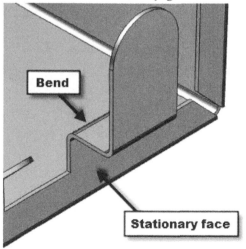
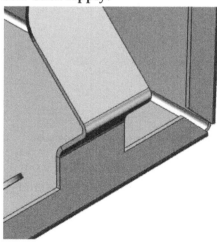

41. Click on the inclined face of the jog feature to define the stationary face.
42. Click on the upper bend of the jog and type-in 135 in the **Angle** box. Click **OK**.

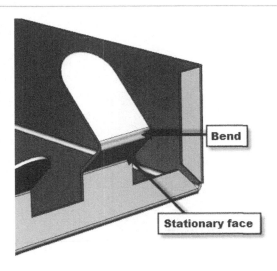

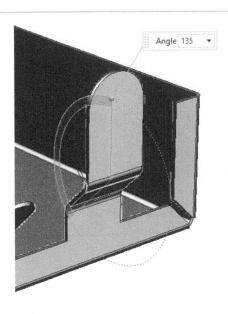

43. On the ribbon, click **Home > Form > Unbend** 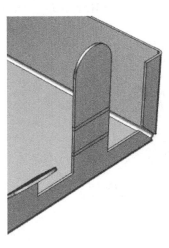.
44. Click on the outer face of the contour flange feature to define the stationary face.
45. Click on the lower bend of the jog feature. Click **Apply** to unbend the jog.

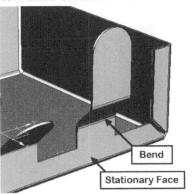

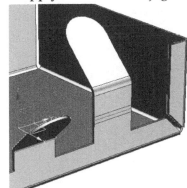

46. Click on the face located between two bends of the jog to define the stationary face.
47. Click on the upper bend and click **OK**.

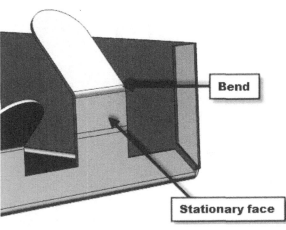

48. On ribbon, click **Home > Feature > Normal Cutout** .
49. Click on the outer face of the unbent jog feature. Create the sketch and click **Finish** on the ribbon.

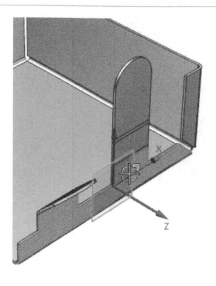

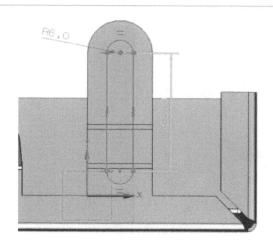

50. On the **Normal Cutout** dialog, select **Limits > Until Next**. Select Cut Method > Thickness, and then click **OK** to complete the normal cutout feature.

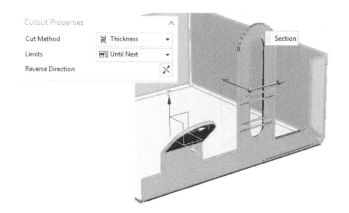

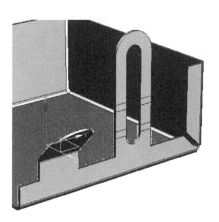

51. On the ribbon, click **Home > Form > Rebend** and click on the lower bend face of the jog feature. Click **Apply** to rebend the feature.

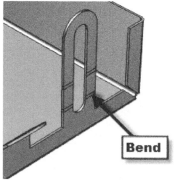

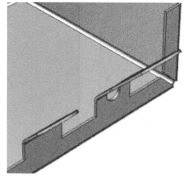

52. Click on the upper bend face, and click **OK**.

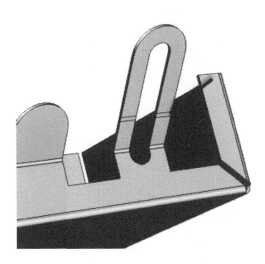

53. Activate the **Closed Corner** command (click **Home > Corner > Closed Corner** 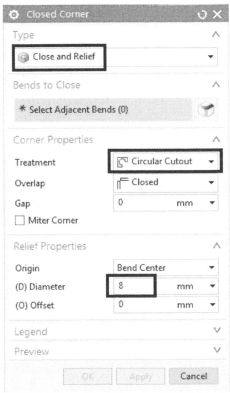 on the ribbon) and click on the bends of the flange features.
54. On the **Closed Corner** dialog, select **Type > Close and Relief**. Under **Corner Properties** section, select **Treatment > Circular Cutout**.
55. Under the **Relief Properties** section, set the **(D) Diameter** value to 8 mm. Click **OK** to close the bends.

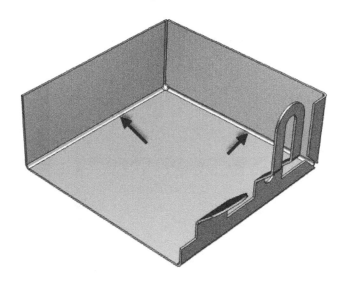

56. Activate the **Hem Flange** command (On the ribbon, click **Home > Bend > More > Hem Flange**)
57. On the **Hem Flange** dialog, select **Type > Closed Loop**.
58. Under **Inset Options**, select **Inset > Material Outside**.
59. Set **Bend Radius** to 2 and **Flange length** to 8.
60. Click on the outer edge of the left-side flange, and click **Apply**.

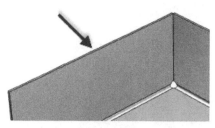
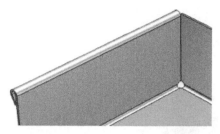

61. Click on the outer edge of the backside flange, and click Apply. Next, click on the outer edge of the contour flange, and then click **OK** to create the hem features.

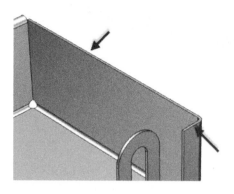
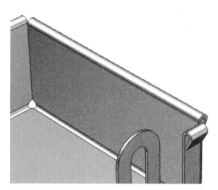

62. Activate the **Louver** command (click **Home > Punch > Louver** on the ribbon) and click the **Reset** icon on the **Louver** dialog.
63. Click on the top face of the tab feature.
64. Draw the sketch shown in figure and click **Finish** on the ribbon.

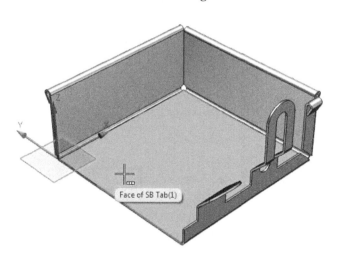
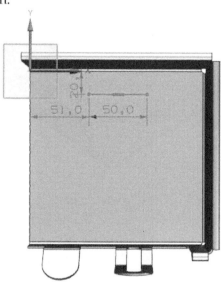

65. On the **Louver** dialog, type-in **5** in the **Depth** box and click the **Reverse Direction** button next to it.
66. Type-in **10** in the **Width** box.
67. Under the **Louver Properties** section, select **Louver Shape > Formed**.
68. Expand the **Louver** dialog and check the **Round Louver Edges** option under the **Rounding** section. Type-in **1** in the **Die Radius** box and click **OK** to create the louver.

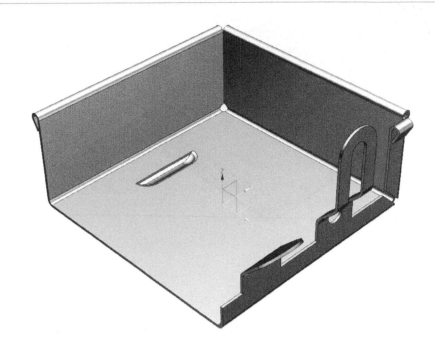

69. Activate the **Pattern Feature** command (On the ribbon, click **Home > Feature > Pattern Feature** 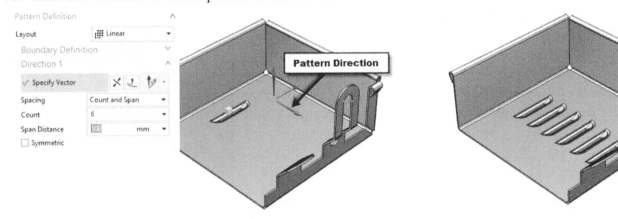) and click louver feature.

70. On the **Pattern Feature** dialog, select **Layout > Linear.**

71. Under the **Direction 1** section, click **Specify Vector** and click on the X-axis vector.

72. Under the **Direction 1** section, select **Spacing > Count and Span**. Type-in 6 and 100 in the **Count** and **Span Distance** boxes.

73. Click **OK** to create the linear pattern of the louver.

74. On the ribbon, click **Home > Flat Pattern > Flat Pattern**.

75. Click on the top face of the tab feature. On the **Flat Pattern** dialog, under the **Orientation** section, select **Orientation Method > Default**. Next, click **OK** on the **Flat Pattern** dialog to create the flat pattern. Next, click **OK** on the **Sheet Metal** message.

76. On the Top Border Bar, click **Menu > View > Layout > New**.

77. On the **New Layout** dialog, click FLAT-PATTERN#1 and click **OK** to view the flat pattern.

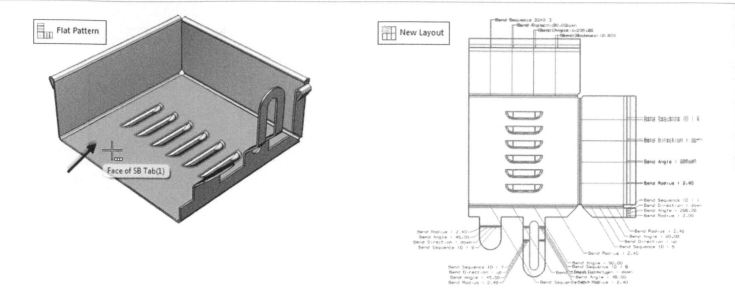

78. On the Top Border Bar, click Menu > **View > Layout > Replace View**. On the **Replace View with** dialog, click **Isometric**, and then click **OK**.
79. Save and close the sheet metal part.

Questions

1. How do you insert a flat pattern into a drawing?
2. Describe parameters that can be specified on the **Sheet Metal Preferences** dialog.
3. Define the term 'Neutral Factor'.
4. List any two sheet metal part preferences that can be overridden when creating a feature.
5. What is the use of the **Normal Cut** command?
6. Which command is used to apply rounds and chamfers to the corners of a sheet metal part?
7. List the types of hems that can be created in NX?
8. What does the **Close Corner** command do?
9. What are the corner treatment options available when closing a corner?
10. What is the difference between a dimple and drawn cutout?

Exercises
Exercise 1

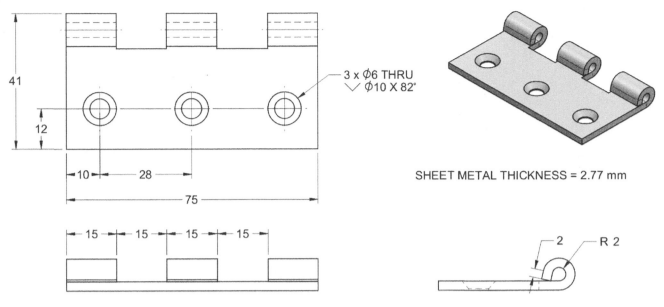

SHEET METAL THICKNESS = 2.77 mm

Exercise 2

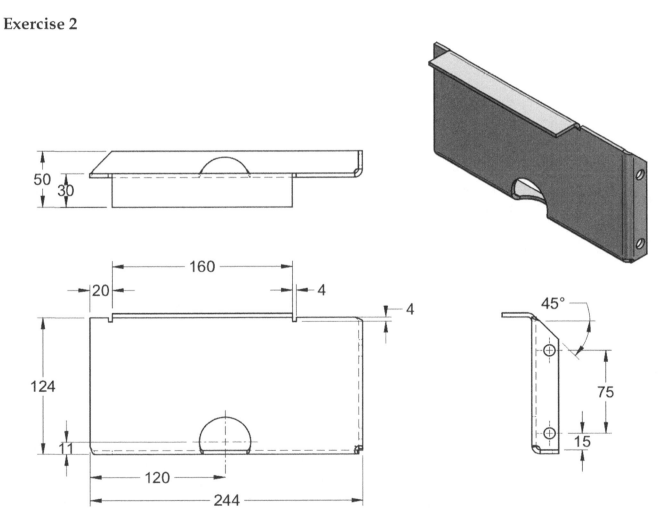

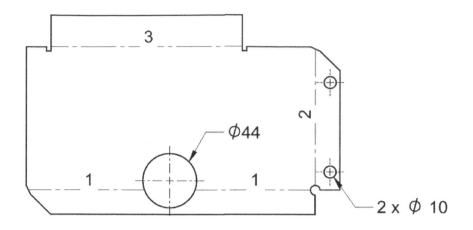

Sequence	Feature	Radius	Angle	Direction	Included Angle
1	Bend 1	3.58 mm	90.00 deg	Down	90.00 deg
2	Bend 2	3.58 mm	90.00 deg	Down	90.00 deg
3	Bend 3	3.58 mm	90.00 deg	Up	90.00 deg

Chapter 11: Surface Design

The topics covered in this chapter are:

- *Basic surfaces*
- *Swept command*
- *Sweep along Guide*
- *Styled Sweep*
- *Ruled*
- *Through Curves*
- *Through Curve Mesh*
- *Studio*
- *Bounded Plane*
- *Four Point Surface*
- *Swoop*
- *Transition*
- *Bridge Surface*
- *Face Blend*
- *Law Extension*
- *Offset Surface*
- *Variable Offset*
- *Offset Face*
- *Extract Geometry*
- *Trimmed Sheet*
- *Trim and Extend*
- *Extension Surface*
- *Untrim*
- *Delete Edges*
- *Patch Openings*
- *Sewing Surfaces*
- *Thicken*
- *Trim Body*
- *X-Form*

NX Surfacing commands can be used to create complex geometries that are very difficult to create using standard extruded features, revolve features, and so on. Surface modeling can also be used to edit and fix the broken imported parts. In this chapter, you learn the basics of surfacing command that are mostly used. The surfacing commands are available in the **Surface** tab.

If the **Surface** tab is not displayed by default, you can customize the Ribbon. Click the right mouse button on the empty area of the ribbon and select **Surface**.

In order to create a surface model, you must set the **Body Type** to **Sheet**. You can do this by clicking **Menu > Preferences > Modeling** on the Top Border Bar. On the **Modeling Preferences** dialog, set the **Body Type** to **Sheet** and click **OK**.

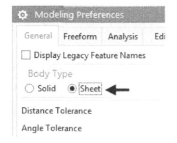

NX offers a rich set of surface design commands. A surface is an infinitely thin piece of geometry. For example, consider a cube shown in figure. It has six faces. Each of these faces is a surface, an infinitely thin piece of geometry that acts as a boundary in 3D space. Surfaces can be simple or complex shapes.

In solid modeling, when you have created solid features such as an Extruded feature or a Revolved feature, NX creates a set of features (surfaces) that enclose a volume. The airtight enclosure is considered as a solid body. The advantage of using the surfacing commands is that you can design a model with more flexibility.

Extruded Surface

To create an extruded surface, first create an open or closed sketch and activate the **Extrude** command. Select the sketch and type-in a value in the **Distance** box available below the **End** drop-down. Click **OK** to create the extruded surface. You will notice that the extrusion is not capped at the ends.

*Note: You need to make sure that the **Body Type** is set to **Sheet** in the **Modeling Preferences** dialog.*

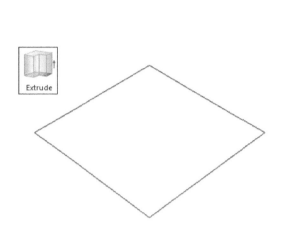

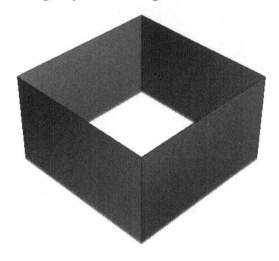

Revolved Surface

To create a revolved surface, first create an open or closed profile and the axis of revolution. Activate the **Revolve** command and select the sketch. On the **Revolve** dialog, under the **Axis** section, click **Specify Vector** and select the axis. Type-in the angle of revolution in the **End** box and click **OK**.

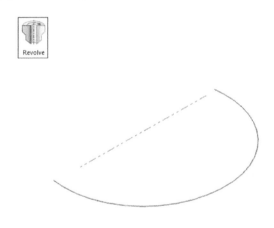

Even if you create an enclosed surface, NX will not recognize it as a solid body. You can examine this by activating the **Measure Body** command (on the ribbon, click **Analysis > Measure > More > Body > Measure Body**). You will notice that you are not able to select the surface body. This means that there exists no solid body. You will learn to convert a surface body into a solid later in this chapter.

Swept

This command creates a surface or a solid body by sweeping one or more cross-sections along guide curves. It also provides various options to control the shape along the guides. To create a swept surface or swept solid body, first create the cross-sections and guide curves. You must ensure that the guide curves and cross-sections are well connected. Activate the **Swept** command (on the ribbon, click **Surface > Surface > Swept**) and select the first cross-section. Click the middle mouse button and click on the second cross-section. Under the **Guides** section, click **Select Curve** and select the first guide curve. Click the middle mouse button and click on the second guide curve. Click **OK** to complete the swept body.

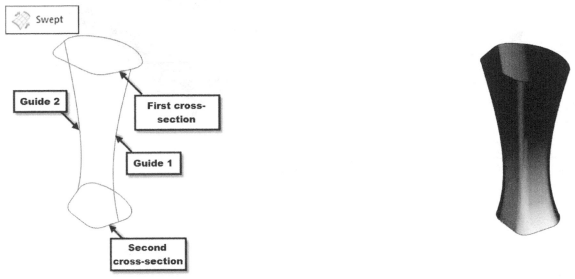

Sweep along Guide

This command creates a surface or solid body by sweeping a section along a guide curve. First create a sweep profile and a guide curve, and then activate the **Sweep along Guide** command (on the ribbon, click **Surface > Surface > More > Sweep > Sweep along Guide**). Click on the section curve, and then click **Guide > Select Curve** on the **Sweep along Guide** dialog. Click on the guide curve, and then click **OK**.

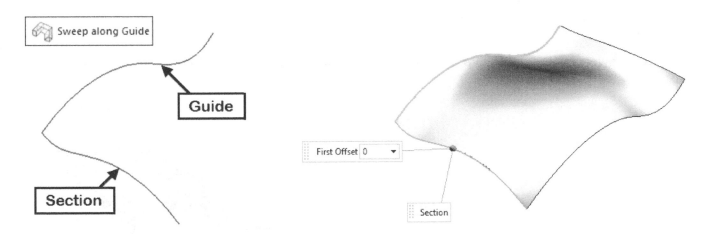

Styled Sweep

This command creates a smooth surface by sweeping section curves along the guide curves. You can use four different kinds of section and guide curve combinations to create a styled sweep surface. Activate this command (on the ribbon, click **Surface > Surface > More > Styled Sweep**) and select **Type > 1 Guide** on the **Styled Sweep** dialog. Click on the section curve, and then click **Guide Curves > Select Guide Curve**. Click on the guide curve and click **OK** to create the styled sweep surface.

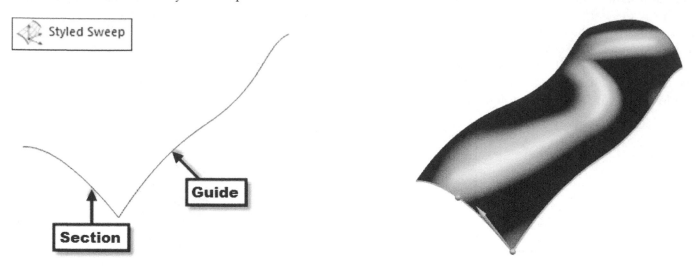

On the **Styled Sweep** dialog, select **Type > 1 Guide, 1 Touch** and click on the section curve. Click **Guide Curves > Select Guide Curve**, and then click on the guide curve. Click **Select Touch Curve**, and then click on the touch curve. Click **OK**.

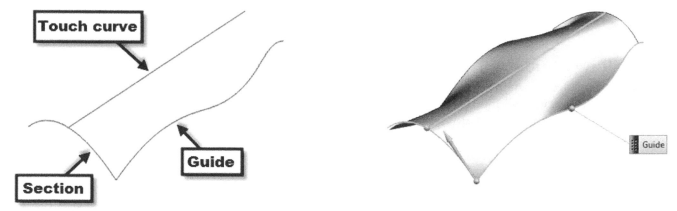

On the **Styled Sweep** dialog, select **Type > 1 Guide, 1 Orientation** and select the section, guide, and orientation curves.

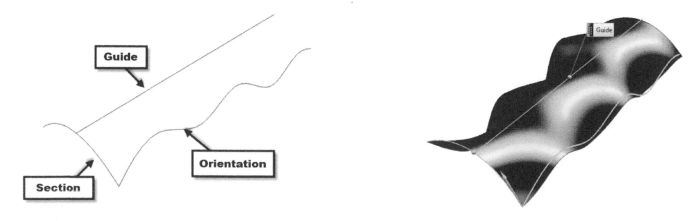

On the **Styled Sweep** dialog, select **Type > 2 Guides** and select the section and two guide curves.

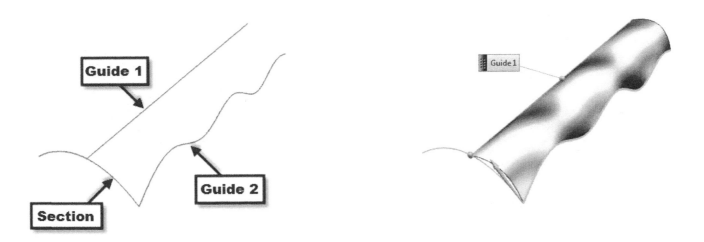

Ruled

The **Ruled** command creates a linear surface between two cross-sections. Activate this command (on the ribbon, click **Surface > Surface > More > Mesh Surface > Ruled**) and click on the first cross-section. If it has multiple segments, select **Curve Rule > Connected Curves** on the Top Border Bar, and then click on a segment. The whole cross section will be selected. On the **Ruled** dialog, under the **Select String 2** section, click **Select Curve**, and then select the second section.

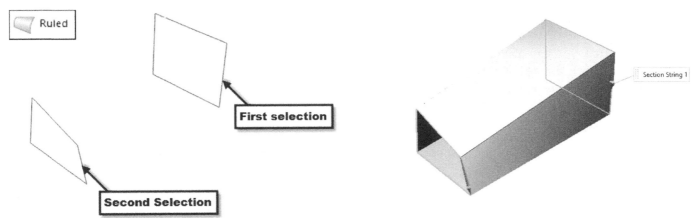

While selecting the cross-section, you must ensure that origin points are in same direction. Otherwise, a twisted result may appear, as shown.

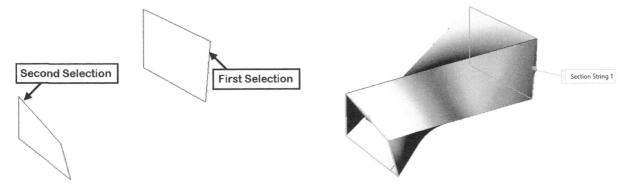

However, if you do happen to make a mistake, then select **Alignment > Alignment > By Points** on the **Ruled** dialog. Points appear on the vertices of the cross sections. Drag the points to fix any unwanted twisting.

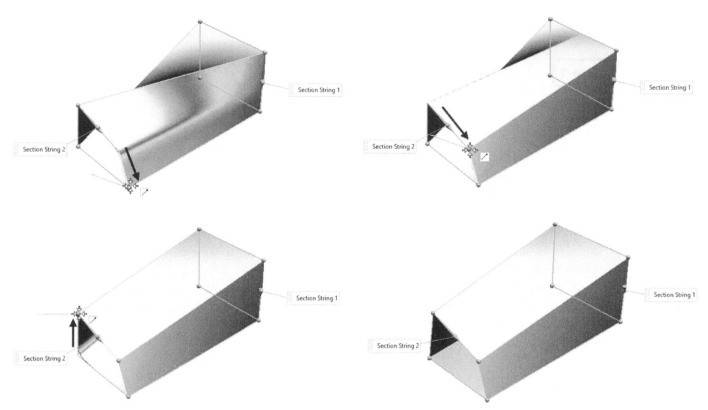

In addition to that, you can also reselect the origin curve of the second section matching that of the first one. To do this, click **Section String 2 > Specify Origin Curve** and select the curve from the second section. Make sure that the selected curve is on the same side of the origin curve of the first section.

Through Curves

This command creates a solid or surface body through multiple cross-sections. The shape of the geometry adjusts automatically to pass through the cross-sections. First, create cross-section on different planes. The cross-sections can be closed or open curves, or points, and they are not required to be on parallel planes. Next, activate the **Through Curves** command (on the ribbon, click **Surface > Surface > Through Curves**) and select the first cross section. Click the middle mouse button and select the second cross-section. Next, click the middle mouse button to accept the selection. Likewise, select the remaining cross-sections. While selecting the surfaces, ensure that arrows are pointing in the same direction. Next, click **OK**.

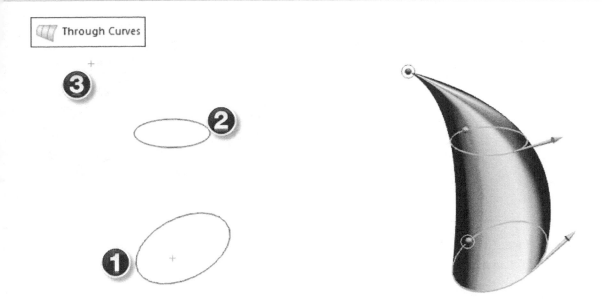

Through Curve Mesh

The **Through Curve Mesh** command creates a surface from a mesh of cross sections and guide curves. Create sections and guides curves, and ensure that they are well connected. Activate the **Through Curve Mesh** command (on the ribbon, click **Surface > Surface > Mesh Surface Drop-down > Through Curve Mesh**) and select the first primary curve. Click the middle mouse button and select the second primary curve. Ensure that the arrows point in the same direction. To do this, you must click on the same side of both the curves. Likewise, select the other primary curves. Likewise, use the **Cross Curves > Select Curve** option and select the cross curve. By mistake, if the primary and cross curves are not well connected, then a message appears showing that they do not intersect each other. In that case, expand the **Settings** section and increase the **Tolerance** values.

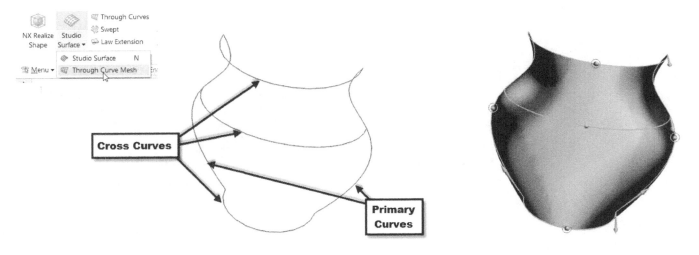

Studio

This command creates a surface, which sweeps through any number of sections and guide curves. The process to create this kind of surface is similar to that of through curve, through mesh, or swept surfaces. However, there would be a slight variation in the result obtained. First, create sections and guide curves and activate this command (on the ribbon, click **Surface > Surface > Mesh Surface Drop-down > Studio**). Select one or more section curves by clicking the middle mouse button after each selection. After selecting the section curves, click the **Guide (Cross) Curves** button and select the guide curves.

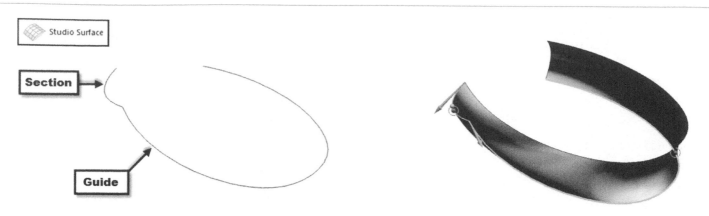

Bounded Plane

To create a bounded plane surface, Activate the **Bounded Plane** command (on the ribbon, click **Surface > Surface > More > Bounded Plane**) and select a closed sketch or closed loop of edges. Click **OK** to create the Bounded Plane surface.

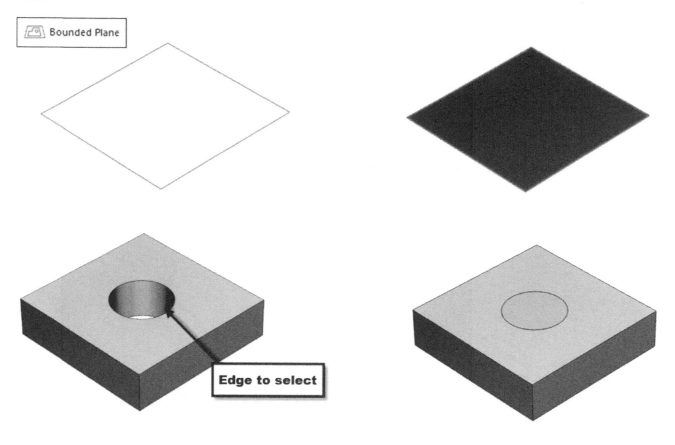

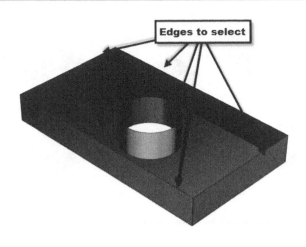

Four Point Surface

This command creates a surface by using four points that you specify. Activate this command (click **Surface >**

Surface > Four Point Surface ⬚ on the ribbon) and select four points. Click **OK** to create the four-point surface.

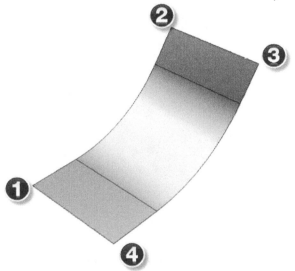

Transition

This command creates a transition surface connecting two or more curves. Activate this command (on the ribbon, click **Surface > Surface > More > Transition**) and select the first curve. If you want to select tangentially connected curves, then select **Curve Rule > Tangent Curves** on the **Top Border Bar**, and then select the curve. Click the middle mouse button and select the second curve string. Again, click the middle mouse button and select the third curve string. The wireframe preview of the transition surface appears. If the transition surface is self-intersecting, then click the **Reverse Direction** button. Click **OK** to complete the transition surface.

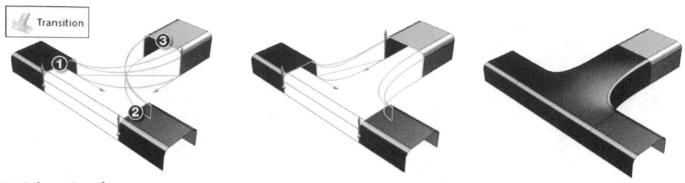

Bridge Surface

The **Bridge Surface** command creates a surface bridging the gap between two surfaces. This can be tangent, or curvature, continuous in both the directions. To create a bridge surface, activate the **Bridge Surface** command (On the ribbon, click **Surface > Surface > Blend Gallery > Bridge**) and select the first and second edges.

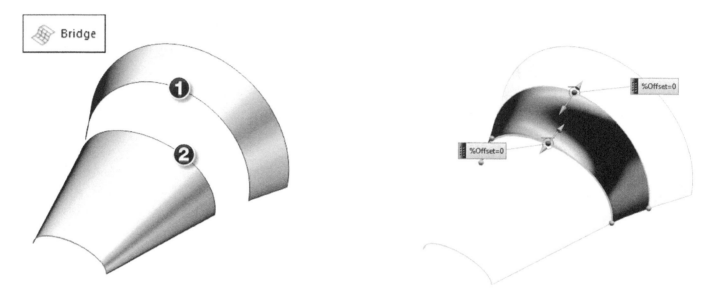

To avoid the twist, make sure that you click on the same side of the two curves. If a twist is created, then click the **Reverse Direction** button on the **Bridge Surface** dialog.

You can specify the way in which the boundary surface will be connected to the selected edges. To do this, expand the **Constraints** section on the **Bridge Surface** dialog. Select **Continuity > Edge 1 > G1 (Tangent)** to maintain tangency between the first edge and the bridge surface. Next, expand the **Tangent Magnitude** section and type-in a value in the **Edge 1** box to define the tangent length (or) simply drag the **Edge 1** slider. Likewise, set the continuity type of the second edge. You can also select **G0 (Position)** or **G2 (Curvature)**.

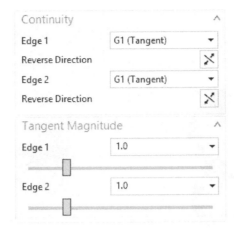

Next, set the **Flow Direction** of the first and second edges. You can select **Isoparametric** or **Perpendicular** or leave it **Not Specified**. If you want to create a partial bridge surface, then use the options in the **Edge Limit** section. You can drag the %**Start** and %**End** sliders in this section to position the start and end points of the bridge surface. If you want to offset the bridge surface, then drag the %**Offset** slider.

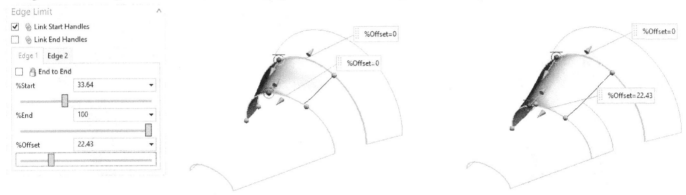

After you have the desired output, click **OK** to create the bridge surface.

Face Blend

Face blends have several uses. They can span across gaps between faces, they can be useful in blending complex surfaces, and they can be defined by a boundary curve instead of a radius. For example, you can create a face blend, which spans across a gap between two faces. To do this, activate the **Face Blend** command (on the ribbon, click **Surface > Surface > Face Blend**) and select **Type > Two-face**. Select the first face chain, and then click **Select Face 2**. Select the second face chain and type-in a value in the **Radius** box under the **Cross Section** section. Ensure that the arrows point in the same direction. Make sure that the radius is more than or equal to the distance between two surfaces;

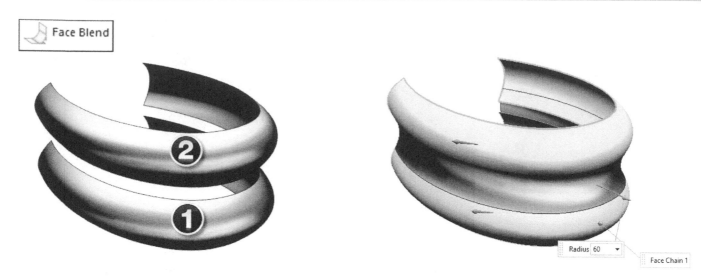

When you need to create a blend between two faces and a supporting face at the middle, select **Type > Three-face** on the **Face Blend** dialog. Use the options under the **Face Chains** section to select the three faces, and then click **OK**. Note that you need to select **Face rule > Single Face** on the Top Border Bar while selecting the faces.

Law Extension

The **Law Extension** command allows you to create surfaces attached to the edges of existing surfaces. Activate this command (on the ribbon, click **Surface > Surface > Law Extension**) and select an edge from the geometry. On the **Law Extension** dialog, click **Face > Select Face**, and then select the face attached to the selected edge. The preview of the extension surface appears.

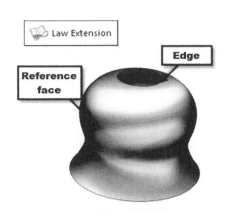

Now, type-in a value in the **Value** box under the **Length Law** section (or) simply drag the arrow handle that appears on the selected edge. You can also use the laws available in the **Law Type** drop-down to change the length of the extension surface. Go to NX help file to get more information about these law types. To manipulate the angle of the extension surface, type-in the **Value** box under the **Angle Law** section (or) simply drag the angle handle. Click **Apply**.

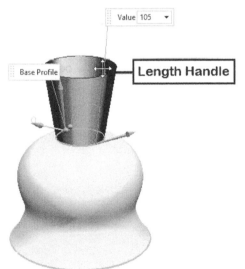

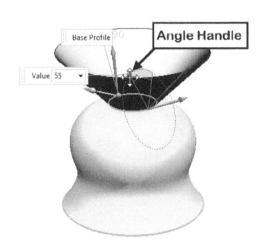

On the **Law Extension** dialog, select **Type > Vector**, and then click on the edge to extend. On the dialog, click **Reference Vector > Specify Vector** and select a vector axis. The extension surface appears perpendicular to the selected vector. You can change the length and angle of the extension surface. Next, click **OK** to create the law extension surface.

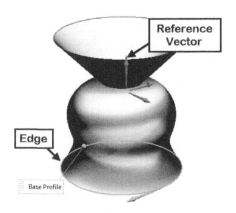

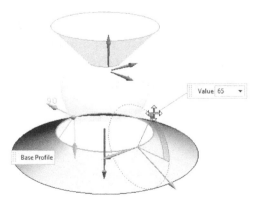

Offset Surface

To create an offset surface, activate the **Offset Surface** command (click **Surface > Surface Operations > Offset Surface** on the ribbon) and select the faces to offset. Note that you need to select **Face rule > Single Face** on the Top Border Bar while selecting the faces. Click the **Reset** icon on the **Offset Surface** dialog. Next, type-in a value in the **Offset 1** box.

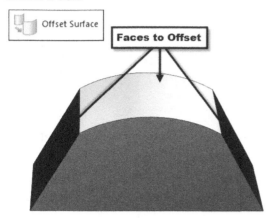
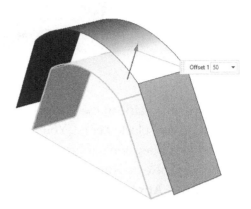

On the **Offset Surface** dialog, under the **Feature** section, select **Output > One Feature of Each Face** to offset faces. This results in offset surfaces, which are detached, from each other.

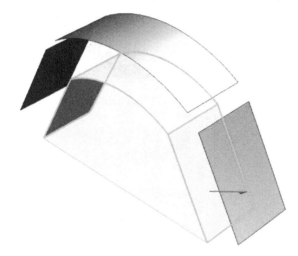

Click **OK** to create the offset surfaces.

Offset Face

The **Offset Face** command makes it easy to change to the geometry by offsetting a set of faces. For example, if you want to offset the front face of an imported solid, activate the **Offset Face** command (on the ribbon, click **Home > Feature > More > Offset/Scale > Offset Face**) select the face to move. Drag the arrow that appears on the selected face (or) type-in a value in the **Offset** box. You can click **Reverse direction** to reverse the direction of the offset. Click **OK** to offset the face.

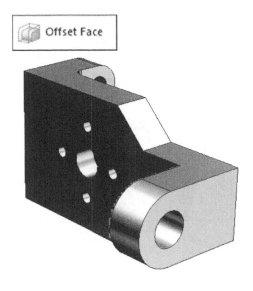

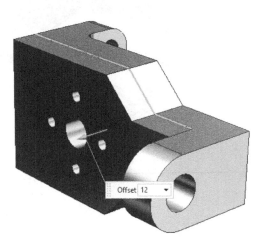

Extract Geometry

In some cases, you may need to extract the surfaces of the solid body. You can use the **Extract Geometry** command (click **Surface > Surface Operations > Extract Geometry** on the ribbon) to extract the surfaces of the solid body. Activate this command and select **Type > Face** on the **Extract Geometry** dialog. Click on the face of the solid body, and then click **OK**. Hide the solid body to see the extracted surfaces.

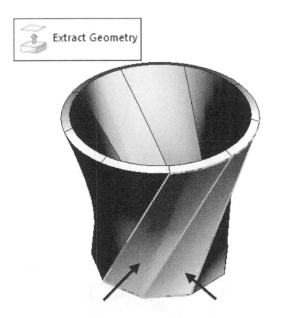

Trimmed Sheet

This command trims a portion of a surface using a trimming tool. The trimming tool can be a surface, plane or a sketched entity. Activate this command (click **Surface > Surface Operations > Trimmed Sheet** on the ribbon) and select the target body. You must select the target body by clicking on the portion to keep. On the **Trimmed Sheet** dialog, under the **Boundary** section, click **Select Object**, and then click on the trimming tool. Click **OK** to trim the surface.

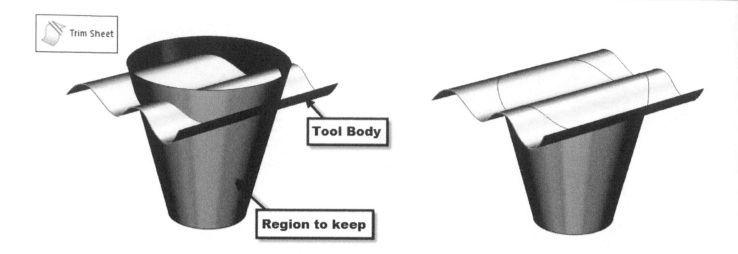

You can also trim a surface using a sketch. Activate the **Trimmed Sheet** command and select the target body. On the dialog, click **Boundary > Select Object**, and then click on the sketch. You will notice that the trimming boundary is created normal to the surface. If you want the trimming boundary to be normal to the curve plane, then select **Projection Direction > Normal to Curve Plane**.

You will notice that the trim boundary is created at the backside of the surface as well. If you want to trim only the front portion of the surface, click **Region > Select** region on the **Trimmed Sheet** dialog and click inside the trim boundary at the backside. Now, click **OK** to trim the surface.

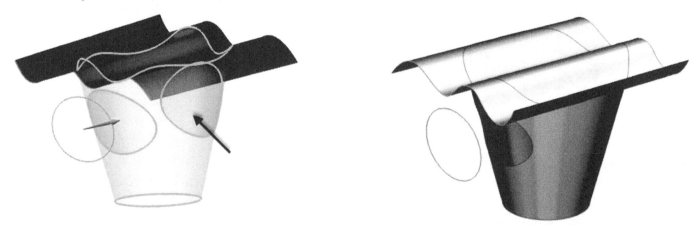

Trim and Extend

This command trims or extends a set of surfaces by the distance that you specify or up to another surface.

Activate this command (on the ribbon, click **Surface > Surface Operations > Trim and Extend**) and select **Type >**

Make Corner on the Trim and Extend dialog. Click on the edge to extend and click Tool > Select Face or Edge. Click on the surface to trim. Under the Desired Results section, select Arrow Side > Delete to trim the side in which the arrow is pointing. Click OK to create a corner.

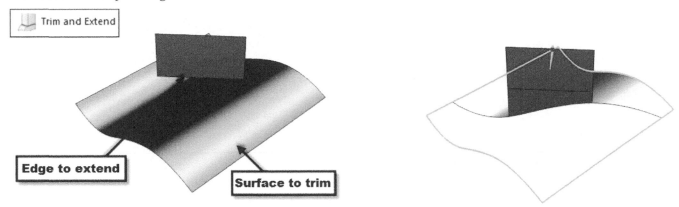

Combine

The Combine option is used to combine multiple surfaces into a single surface and trim the unwanted portions. You can also combine multiple surfaces to form a closed volume.

Combining surfaces

Activate the Combine command (On the ribbon, click Surface > Surface Operations > More > Combine > Combine) and click the Reset icon on the Combine dialog. On Combine dialog, under the Region section, select the Keep option. Next, click on the surfaces to combine, and then click OK.

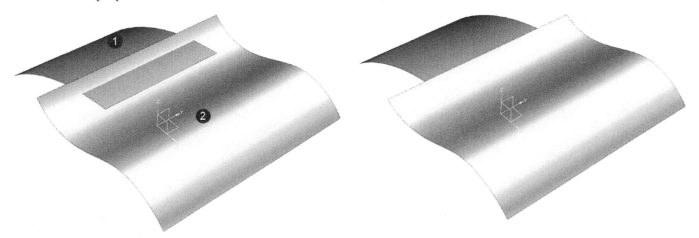

Combining Surfaces into a Closed Volume

Activate the Combine command (On the ribbon, click Surface > Surface Operations > More > Combine > Combine) and click on the surfaces that form a closed volume. On the Combine dialog, click the Find Volume button. Click OK to create a closed volume.

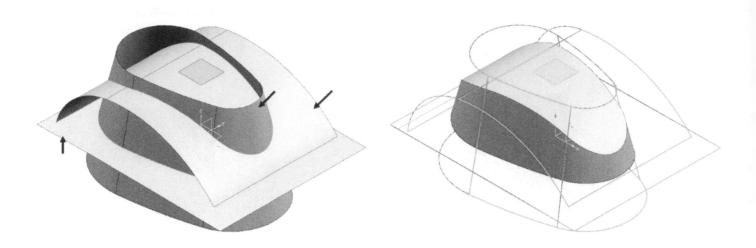

Extension Surface

During the design process, you may sometimes need to extend a surface. You can extend a surface using the **Extension Surface** command. Activate this command (On the ribbon, click **Surface > Surface > More > Flange Surface > Extension Surface**) and click the surface to extend. While selecting the surface, you must ensure that you click near the edge to be extended.

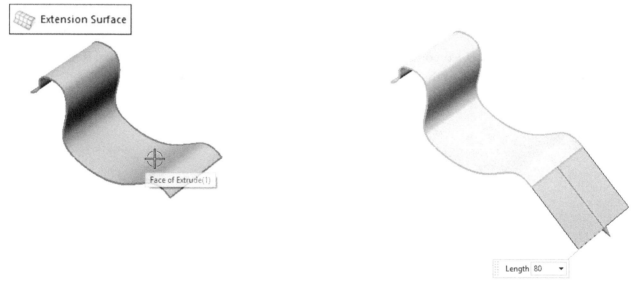

After selecting an edge, you can define the distance of the extension surface by using the options in the **Distance** drop-down (**By Length** and **By Percentage**). If you select the **By Length** option, you can define the distance by entering a value in the **Length** box. If you select the **By Percentage** option, you can define the distance by entering a value in the **% Length** box.

When the surface you have selected is not planar, you can decide the type of extension by using the **Method** options. Use the **Circular** option to extend the surface by maintaining the curvature of the original surface. If you select the **Tangential** option, the extended surface will be created tangent to the original surface.

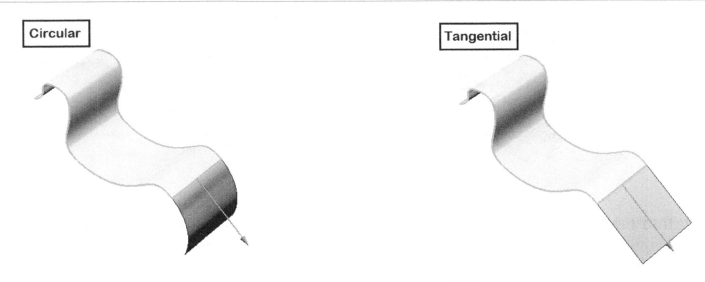

If you want to extend the corners of a surface, then select **Type > Corner** on the **Extension Surface** dialog and click near the corner to extend. Type-in values in the **%U Length** and **%V Length** boxes or simply drag the arrow handles to define the extension length in both the directions. Click **OK** after specifying the settings.

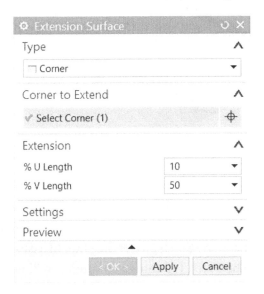

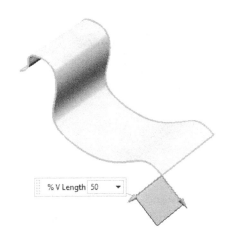

Untrim

You can untrim a trimmed surface using the **Untrim** command. Activate this command (on the ribbon, click **Surface > Surface Operations > More > Trim > Untrim**) and click on the trimmed surface. On the **Untrim** dialog, check the **Hide Original** option and click **OK**.

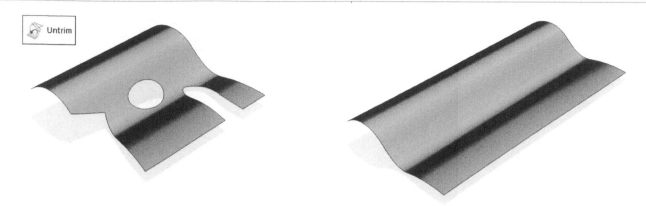

Delete Edge

You can also delete the individual edges of the surface using the **Delete Edge** command. Activate this command (on the ribbon, click **Surface > Surface Operations > More > Trim > Delete Edge**) and click on the edges of the surface body. Click **OK** to delete the edges.

Patch Openings

The **Patch Openings** command can be used to patch holes in models. As a patching tool, the **Patch Openings** command is more robust than deleting holes or untrimming. It provides more discrete control over the definition of the resultant patch. For example, consider the model shown in figure. You can see that a face is missing. In a case like this, both the **Delete Edge** and **Untrim** commands fail to fill this gap. The **Patch Openings** command will be used in this case.

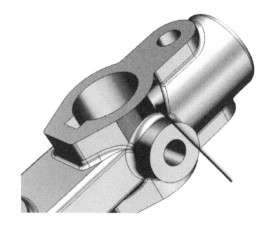

Activate the **Patch Openings** command (on the ribbon, click **Surface > Surface > More > Patch Openings**) and select **Type > N-sided Area Patch**. Select all the faces connected to the open face, and then click **Opening to Patch > Select Edge**. Select the edges of the opening and click **OK**.

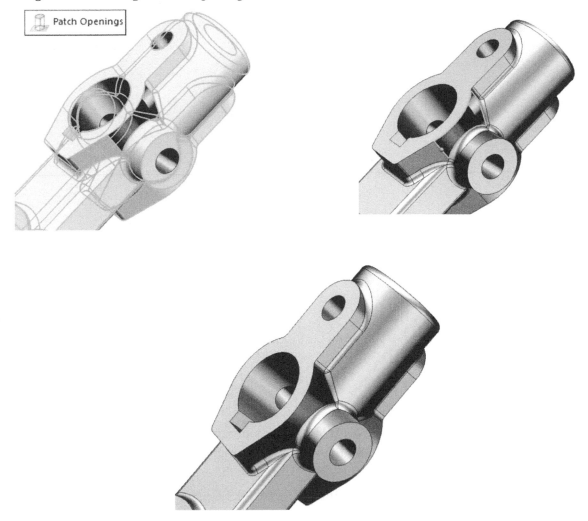

Fill Surface

The application of the **Fill Surface** command is similar to that of the **Patch Openings**, **Delete Edges**, and **Untrim** commands. In addition to filling the openings, this command has some additional options to control the shape of the fill surface. To fill the opening of a solid or surface body, activate the **Fill Surface** command (On the ribbon, click **Surface** tab > **Surface** panel > **Fill Surface**) and expand the **Settings** section on the **Fill Surface** dialog. In the **Settings** section, specify the **Default Edge Continuity** type (select **G0 (Position)** for this example). Select the edges of the opening and notice the preview of the fill surface.

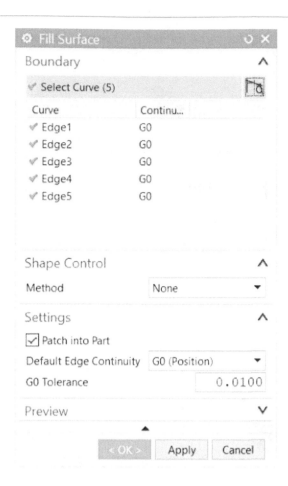

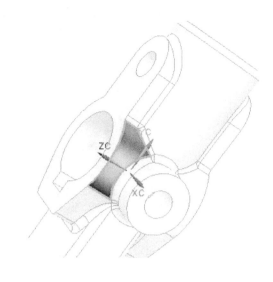

Under the **Shape Control** section, select **Method > Fullness** and notice that a dot appears on fill surface along with an arrow handle. This dot is called the control point. You can change the position of the control point by clicking and dragging it. You can offset the control point by dragging the arrow attached to it (or) dragging the **Control Point Offset** slider in the **Shape Control** section. After achieving the required shape, click **OK** to create the fill surface.

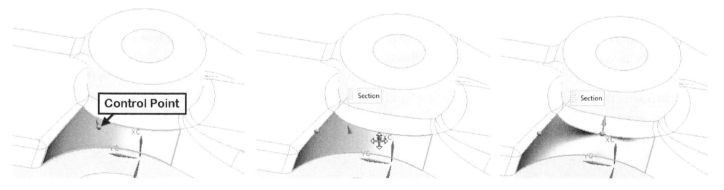

You can also use the curves to control the shape of the fill surface. To do this, select **Method > Fit to Curves** from the **Shape Control** section. Select the boundary and control curves. Click **OK**.

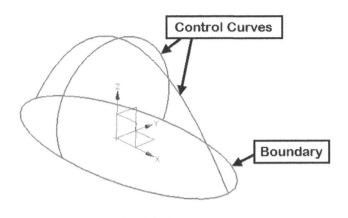 

Sewing Surfaces

The surfaces that are created act as individual surfaces unless they are sewed together. The **Sew** command lets you to combine two or more surfaces to form a single surface. To sew surfaces, activate the **Sew** command (click **Home > Feature > More > Combine > Sew** 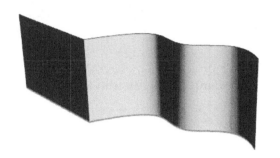 on the ribbon) and select the surfaces to sew.

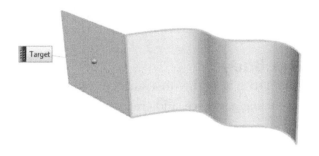

The value you type in the **Tolerance** box of the **Settings** section defines the tolerance gap. All the surfaces within the tolerance gap will be sewed. Click the **OK** button to knit the surfaces.

Thicken

Creating a solid from a surface can be accomplished by simply thickening a surface. To add thickness to a surface, activate the **Thicken** command (on the ribbon, click **Surface > Surface Operations > Thicken**) and click on a face of the surface geometry. Enter the thickness value in the **Offset 1** box.

If you want to keep a region of your surface body open, then click **Region Behavior > Region to Peirce > Select Boundary Curve** on the **Thicken** dialog. Click on the face to remain opened.

If you want a different thickness for a region, then click **Region of Different Thickness > Select Boundary Curve** on the dialog. Click on the region to have different thickness, and then drag the arrow handle to add different thickness to it.

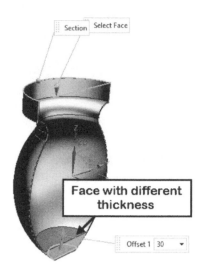

Trim Body

You can trim a solid with a surface using the **Trim Body** command. For example, you can trim the solid shown in figure using a surface, and create a complex face on the top.

To trim solid using a surface, activate the **Trim Body** command (on the ribbon, click **Surface > Surface Operations > Trim Body**) and select the target body. On the **Trim Body** dialog, click **Select Face or Plane** and select the tool body. If you want to reverse the trim direction, then click the **Reverse Direction** button. Click **OK**. Next, hide the tool body to view the result.

X-Form

The **X-Form** command is a powerful feature that is used to create ergonomic shapes. This command allows you push and pull on a surface to create complex shapes that are otherwise difficult to produce. An X-form can be applied to any face. It can be a surface or a face of a solid body.

To create an X-form surface, activate the **X-Form** command (on the ribbon, click **Surface > Edit Surface > X-Form**) and select a face. On the **X-Form** dialog, under the **Parameterization** section, specify the **Degree** and **Patches** values. A mesh appears on the selected surface. You will also notice the poles on the mesh.

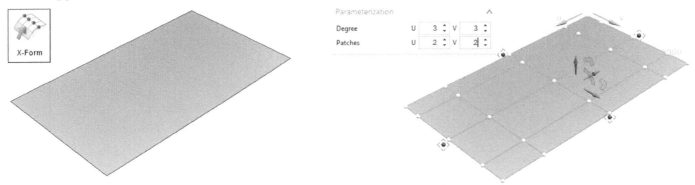

You can drag these poles to change the shape of the face.

You can use the triad to push and pull on the surface along the three directions (X, Y and Z). For example, if you want to pull the surface along the Z-direction, select the Z-axis vector and drag the poles. This pushes or pulls the surface along the Z-direction.

In addition, you can also select the rows to manipulate the surface. To do this, select **Pole Selection > Manipulate > Any** on the **X-Form** dialog, and the drag the rows.

Example

In this example, you will construct the model shown below.

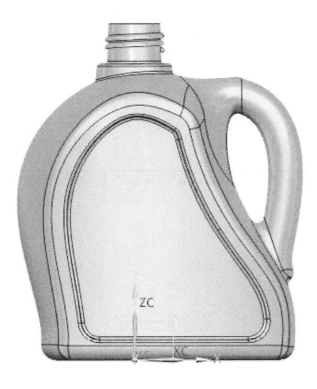

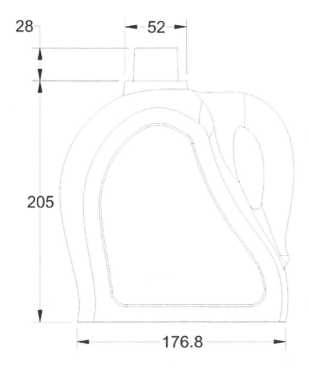

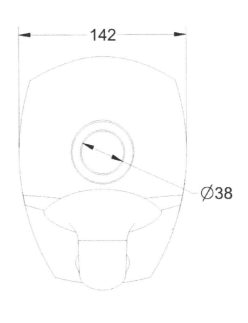

Drawing the Layout sketch

1. Start **NX 12**.
2. Start a new part file using the **Model** template.

3. Click **File > Preferences > Modeling.** On the **Modeling Preferences** dialog, set the **Body Type** to **Sheet** and click **OK**.

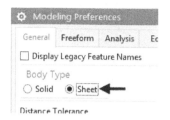

4. Start a sketch on the XZ plane.

5. Activate the **Line** ╱ command (on the ribbon, click **Home > Direct Sketch > Line**) and create the horizontal and vertical lines, as shown.

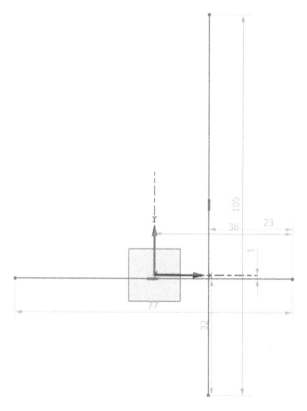

6. Make the horizontal and vertical lines collinear to the X-axis and Y-axis, respectively.

7. Select the vertical line and click the **Convert to Reference** ⫿ᵏ⫿ button on the contextual toolbar.

8. Activate the **Studio Spline** ⌁ (on the ribbon, click **Home > Direct Sketch > More Curve > Studio Spline**) command.

9. On the **Studio Spline** dialog, select **Type > Through Points** and specify the points, as shown.

10. Leave the default settings on the dialog, and then click **OK**.

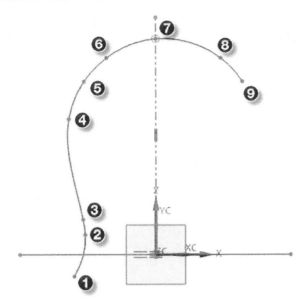

11. Activate the **Rapid Dimension** command and add dimensions to the sketch.

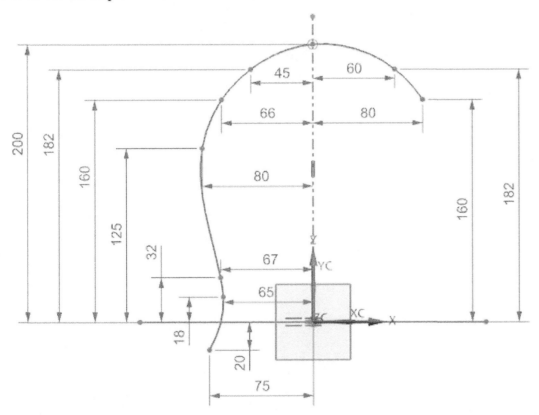

12. Click on the horizontal line and select **Convert to Reference** on the contextual toolbar.
13. Click **Home > Direct Sketch > Finish Sketch** on the ribbon.
14. Start a new sketch on the XZ-Plane.
15. Activate the **Studio Spline** command and draw another spline curve similar to the one shown in figure.

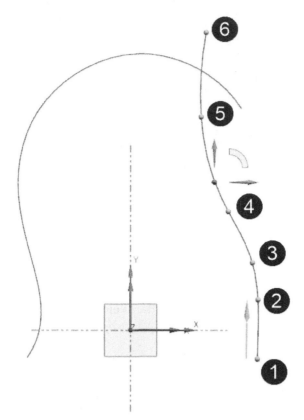

16. Add dimensions to the spline.

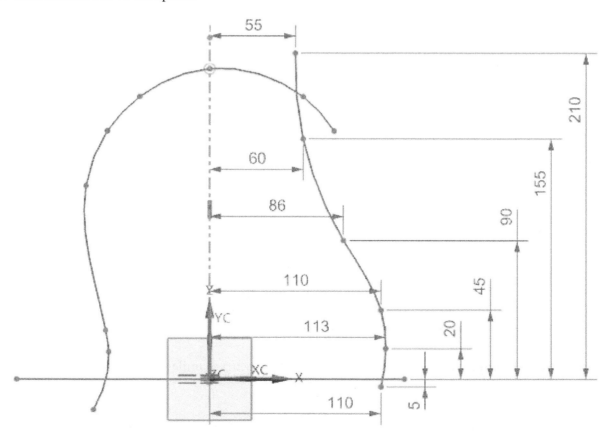

17. Click **Home > Direct Sketch > Finish Sketch** on the ribbon.
18. Start a new sketch on the XZ-Plane.
19. Create another spline similar to the one shown below.

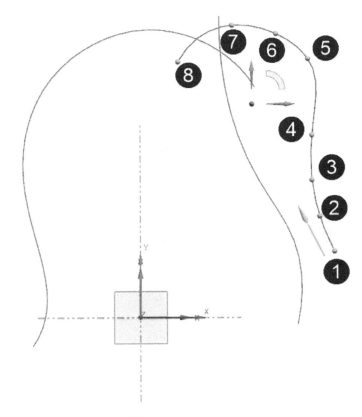

20. Add dimensions to the spline.

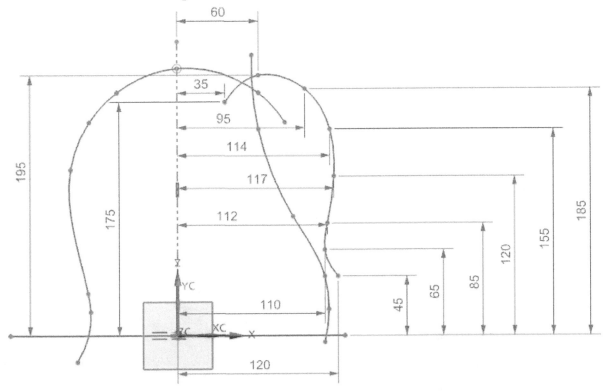

21. Finish the sketch.

If you find it difficult to create the layout sketch, then you can download it from our website.

Creating the Front Surface

1. Create an arc on the XY Plane and add dimensions to it. Note that you need to make the end points of the arc symmetric about the X-axis. Finish the sketch.

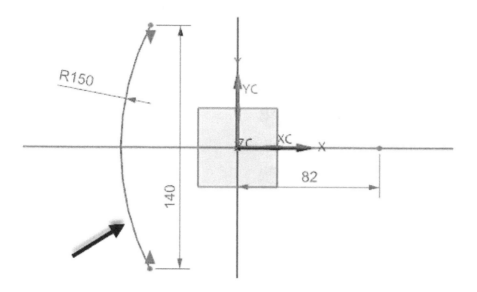

2. Create an arc on the YZ Plane and add dimensions to it. Note that you need to make the end points of the arc symmetric about the Y-axis. Finish the sketch.

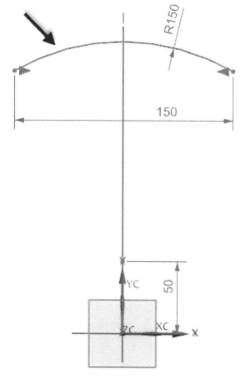

3. Create a datum plane normal to the front face spline.

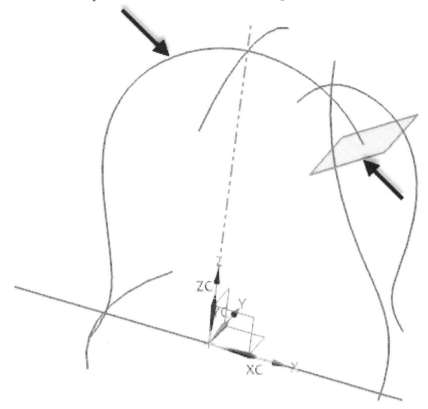

4. Create an arc on the plane normal to curve.

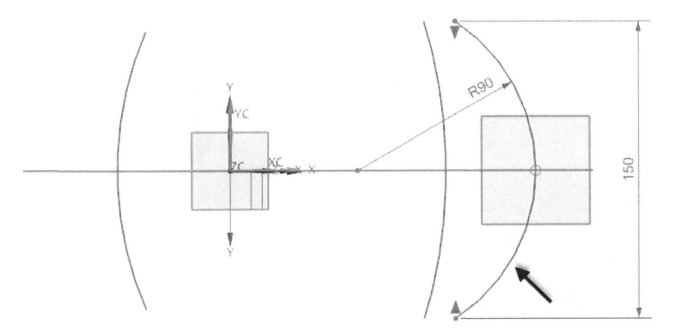

5. Change the orientation to Isometric, and then make sure that the quadrant point of the arc is coincident to the end point of the front face spline.

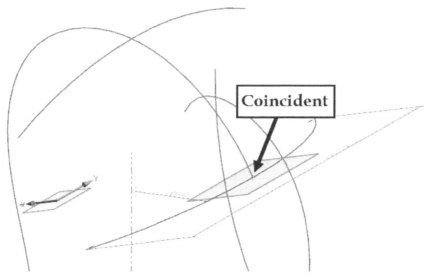

6. Click **Home > Direct Sketch > Finish Sketch**.
7. Activate the **Studio Surface** command (on the ribbon, click **Surface > Surface > Studio Surface**) and click on the spline to define the section curve.
8. On the dialog, click **Guide (Cross) Curves > Select Curve** and select the first guide curve.
9. Click the middle mouse button and select the second guide curve. Likewise, select the third guide curve. Click **OK** to create the studio surface.

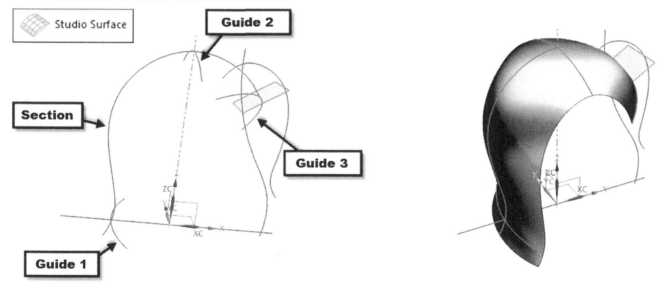

10. Save the file. As you are creating a complex geometry, it is advisable that you save the model after each operation.

Creating the Label surface

1. Start a sketch on the XY plane, and then draw a horizontal arc.
2. Draw a vertical line passing through the sketch origin. Next, convert it into a reference line.
3. Make the lower end point of the reference line coincident with the arc.
4. Make the end points of the arc symmetric about the reference line.
5. Make the end points of the reference lines symmetric about the X-axis.

6. Add dimensions to the sketch as shown below.
7. Click **Direct Sketch > Finish Sketch**.

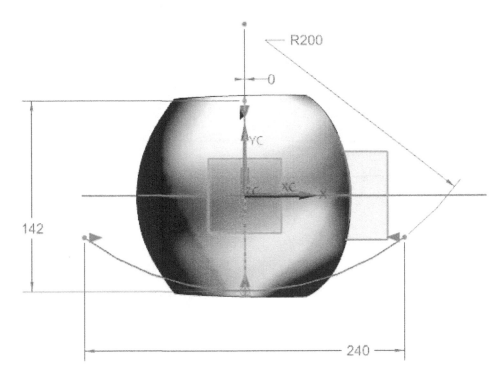

8. Activate the **Extrude** command (on the ribbon, click **Surface > Surface > More > Sweep > Extrude**) and extrude the arc up to 220 mm distance. Ensure that **Boolean** is set to **None**.
9. Activate the **Mirror Feature** command (on the ribbon, click **Home > Feature > More > Associate Copy > Mirror Feature**), and then mirror the extruded surface about the XZ plane.

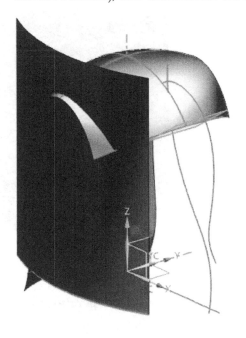 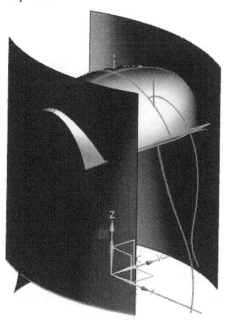

Creating the Back surface

1. Create an arc on the XY plane. Finish the sketch.

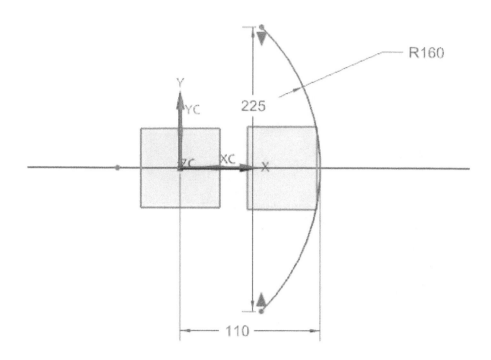

2. Activate the **Studio Surface** command.
3. Select the section from the graphics window, as shown.
4. On the **Studio Surface** dialog, click **Guide (Cross) Curves > Select Curve**, and then select the guide curve, as shown. Next, click **OK** to create the studio surface, as shown.

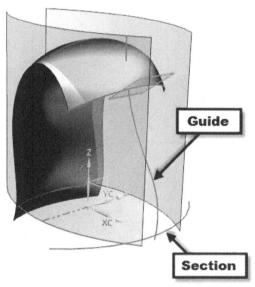

Guide

Section

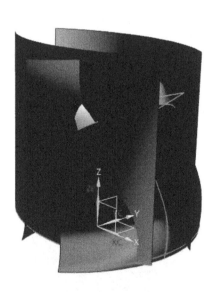

Trimming the Unwanted Portions

1. Activate the **Trim and Extend** command (on the ribbon, click **Surface > Surface Operations > Trim and Extend**) and select **Trim and Extend Type > Make Corner**.
2. Select the target body and click **Tool > Select Face or Edge**.
3. Click on the tool body and click the **Reverse Direction** buttons under the **Tool** and **Target** sections such that they are pointing inwards.

4. Click **Apply**; the two surfaces are trimmed and stitched together.

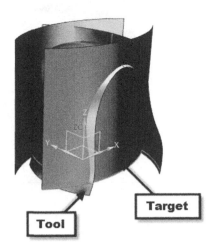 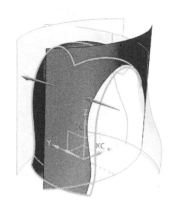 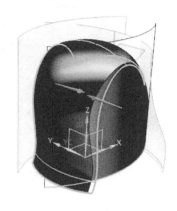

5. Likewise, trim the mirrored surface body by using the front face as a tool body. Click the **Apply** button selecting the target and tool bodies.

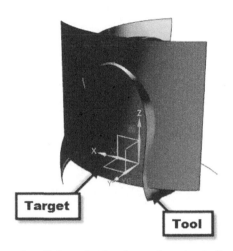 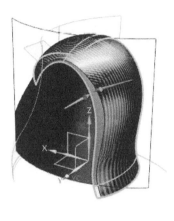 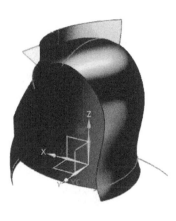

6. Select the back surface to define the target body.

7. On the **Trim and Extend** dialog, click **Tool > Select Face or Edge**, and then select the label surface.

8. Make sure that the arrows on the target and tool bodies point inward. You can change the arrow directions by double clicking on them or using the **Reverse Direction** buttons in the **Target** and **Tool** sections.

9. Click **OK** after the desired preview appears. Notice that the selected surfaces are trimmed and stitched together. This makes all the surfaces to act as a single surface body.

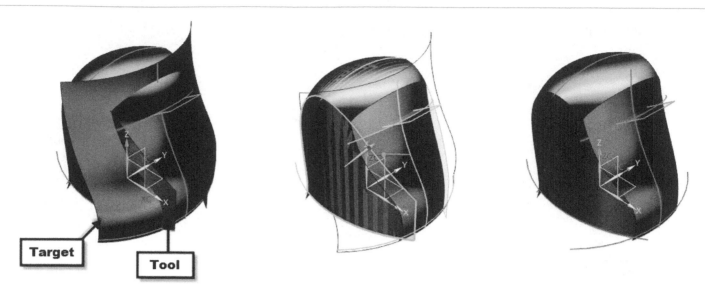

10. Activate the **Trim Sheet** command (on the ribbon, click **Surface > Surface Operations > Trim Sheet**) and click on the surface body.

11. On the **Trim Sheet** dialog, click **Boundary > Select Object**, and then select the XY Plane from the Datum Coordinate System.

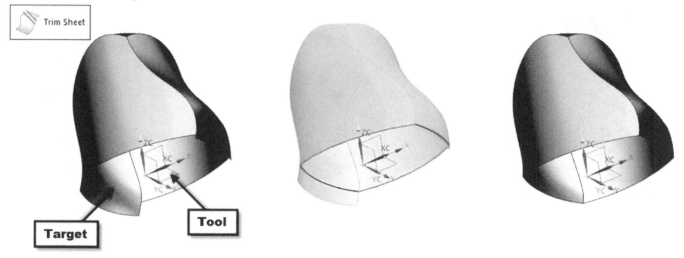

12. Click **OK** to trim the sheet.

Creating the Handle Surface

1. Activate the **Datum Plane** command and click on the lower end-point of the spline. Click **OK** to create the plane normal to the spline.

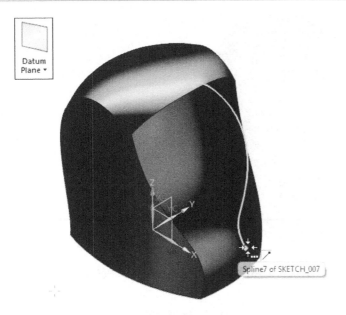

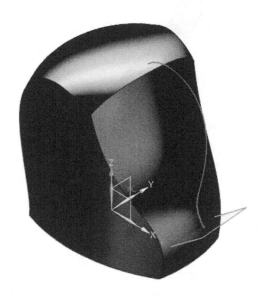

2. Start a sketch on the plane normal to the spline.
3. Activate the **Ellipse** command and create an ellipse on the sketch plane.
4. Create two lines between the ellipse and its center. Apply the **Horizontal** constraint to one line and the **Vertical** constraint to another.
5. Select the horizontal line and the ellipse. Click the **Parallel** icon on the **Context** toolbar. Next, select the two lines and click **Convert to Reference** on the Context toolbar.

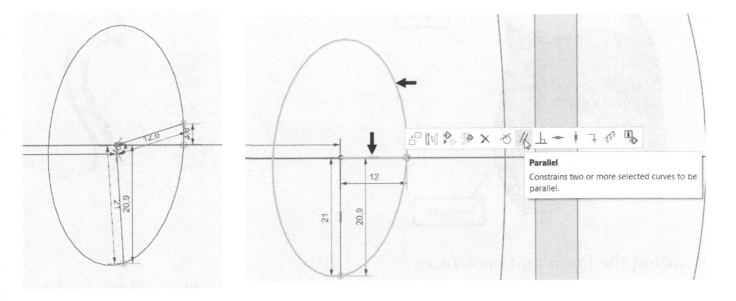

6. Apply 12 and 18 mm linear dimensions to the horizontal and vertical reference lines, respectively.
7. Make the upper quadrant point of the ellipse coincident with the end-point of the spline.
8. Add dimensions and relations to the sketch. Finish the sketch.

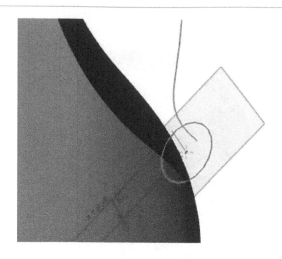

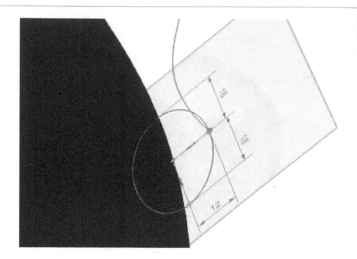

9. Activate the **Swept** command (on the ribbon, click **Surface > Surface > Swept**) and click on the section curve.

10. On the **Swept** dialog, click **Guides > Select Curve**, and then select the guide curve.

11. On the **Swept** dialog, expand the **Settings** section, and then select **Body Type > Sheet**. Click **OK** to create the handle surface.

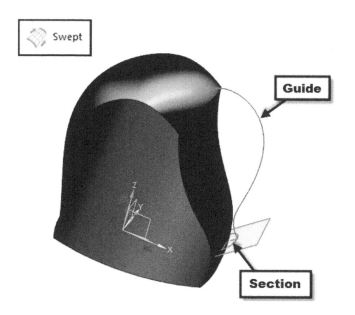

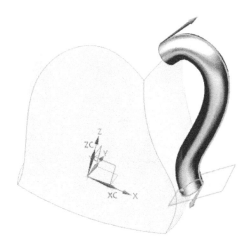

Blending the Front and back faces

1. Activate the **Face Blend** command (on the ribbon, click **Surface > Surface > Blend Gallery > Face Blend**) and select **Type > Two - face** on the **Face Blend** dialog.

2. On the Top Border Bar, select the **Face Rule > Single Face**.

3. Click on the front face, and then click **Select Face 2**.

4. Click on the back face and type-in 25 in the **Radius** box. Leave the default settings on the dialog and click **OK**.

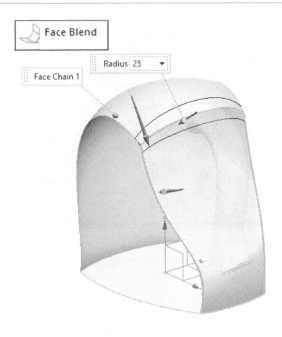

Trimming the Handle

1. Create a vertical line on the XZ Plane and finish the sketch.

2. Activate the **Trim Sheet** command and click on the Handle surface.

3. Click **Boundary > Select Object** and select the vertical line.

4. Select **Projection Direction > Normal to Curve Plane** and select the **Project Both Sides** option. Next, click **OK**.

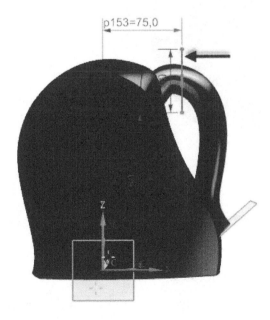

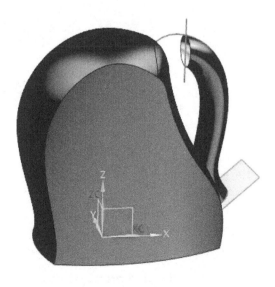

5. Create a datum plane, which is normal to the spline and located at the top end-point. Make sure that the arrow points downwards while creating the datum plane. Use the **Reverse Direction** icon in **Plane Orientation** section, if required.

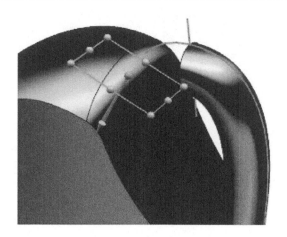

6. Start a sketch on the normal to the path and draw an ellipse. Next, fully constrain the ellipse using the steps given the *Creating Handle Surface* section of this example.

7. Add dimensions to an ellipse, as shown. Next, click **Direct Sketch1 > Finish Sketch**.

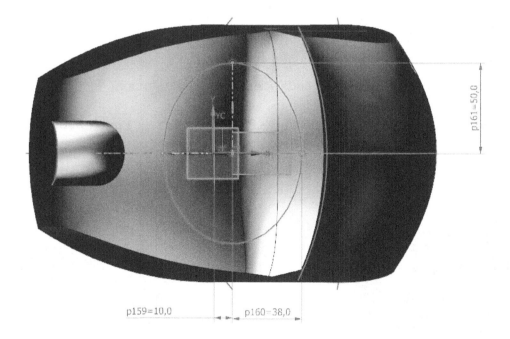

8. Activate the **Trim Sheet** command (on the ribbon, click **Surface > Surface Operations > Trim Sheet**) and click on the surface body.

9. Click **Boundary > Select Object** and select the elliptical sketch.

10. On the **Trimmed Sheet** dialog, select **Projection Direction > Normal to Curve Plane**.

11. On the **Trimmed Sheet** dialog, click   the **Region** icon. Rotate the model and click on the region, as shown. and click **OK**.

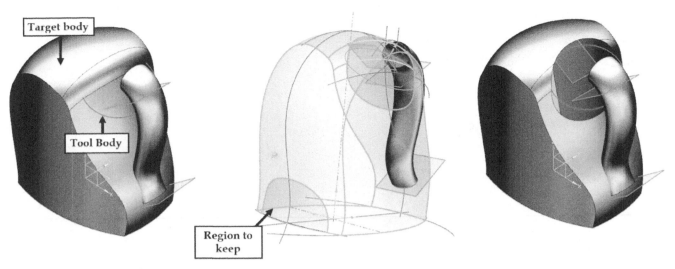

Blending the Top handle

1. Activate the **Through Curves** 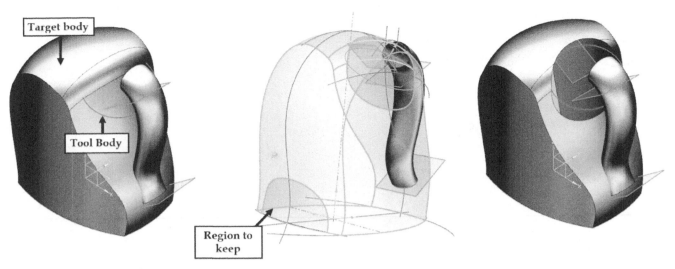 command (on the ribbon, click **Surface > Surface > Through Curves**) and click on the edges of the trimmed opening one-by-one in the clockwise direction.
2. On the **Through Curves** dialog, under the **Sections** section, click **Select Origin Curve** and click at the point, as shown.
3. Click the middle mouse button and select the top edge of the handle. Click the **Reverse Direction** button to ensure that both the arrows point in same direction.

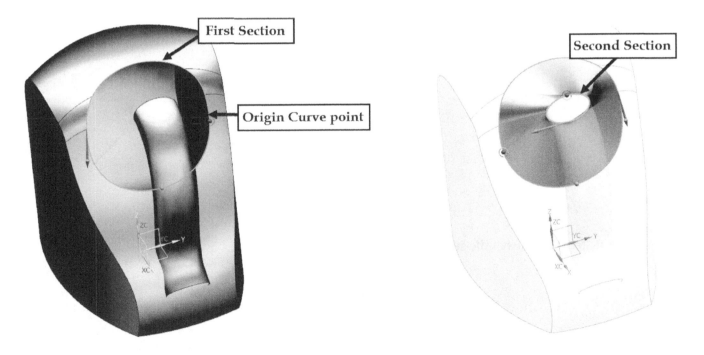

4. Under the **Continuity** section, select **First Section > G1 (Tangent)** and click on the surfaces connected to the first section.
5. Select the **Last Section > G1 (Tangent)** and click on the surface connected to the second section.

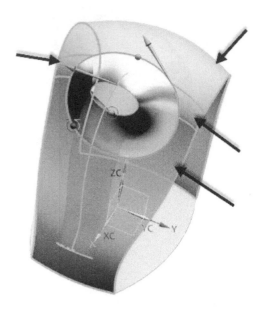
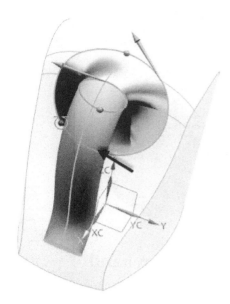

6. Select **Flow Direction > Perpendicular**.
7. Under the **Alignment** section, select **Alignment > By Points**.
8. Drag the first Point handle and position it, as shown.
9. Drag the second Point handle and position it, as shown.

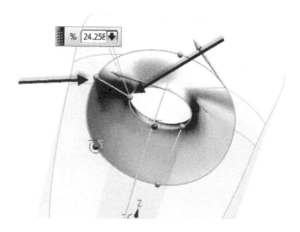
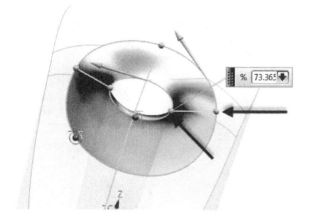

10. Click **OK** to blend the handle surface.

Blending the Bottom handle

1. Start a sketch on the XZ Plane and draw a line, a shown. Assume the dimension of the line.

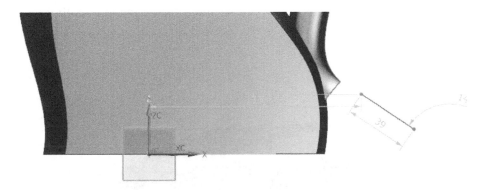

2. On the ribbon, click **Home > Sketch > More > Sketch Constraints > Geometric Constraints**. Next, click **OK** on the **Geometric Constraints** message box.

3. On the **Geometric Constraints** dialog, click the **Tangent** ⌀ icon, and then select the created line and the spline curve of the handle surface. Next, click **Close** on the **Geometric Constraints** dialog.

4. Click on the inclined line and select **Convert to Reference** from the contextual toolbar.

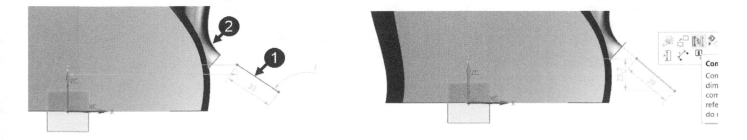

5. Click the **Finish Sketch** button on the ribbon.

6. Activate the **Datum Plane** command and select **Type > At Angle**.
7. Click on the XZ Plane and the reference line tangent to the spline. Click **OK** to create the datum plane.

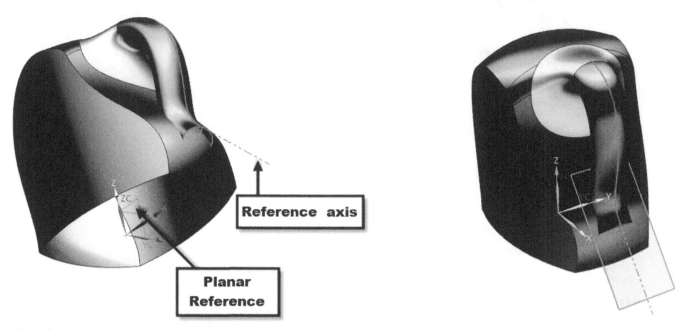

8. Create an ellipse on the new plane and fully constrain it using constraints and dimensions. Create a horizontal line passing through the center of the ellipse and intersecting it at both the ends. Activate the **Quick Trim** command, and then trim the ellipse using the horizontal line. Finish the sketch. Ensure that the sketch lies inside the handle surface.

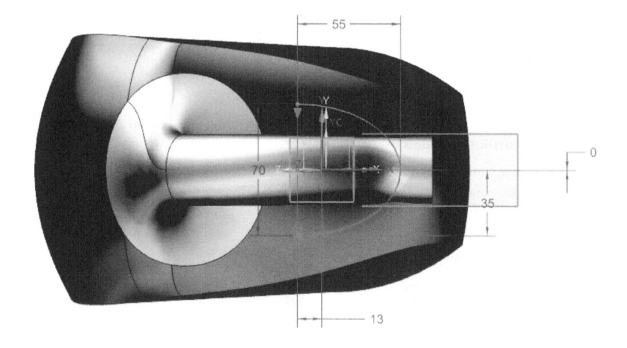

9. Extrude the sketch up to an arbitrary distance (approximately 60 mm) in both the directions.

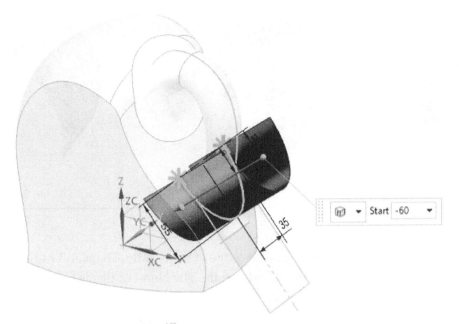

10. Activate the **Trim and Extend** command and select **Type > Make Corner**.
11. Click on the handle surface to define the target, and then click **Tool > Select Face or Edge**.
12. Click on the extruded surface to define the tool. Click the **Reverse Direction** button under the **Target** section. Also, make sure that the arrow on the tool body points upwards.

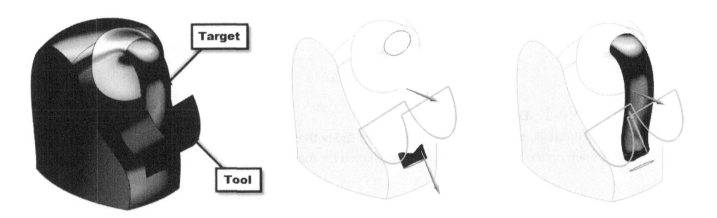

13. Click **Apply**.
14. Rotate the model and click on the inside portion of the handle.
15. Click **Tool > Select Face or Edge**, and then select the main surface body to define the tool.
16. Click the **Reverse Direction** buttons under the **Tool** section. Click **OK**.

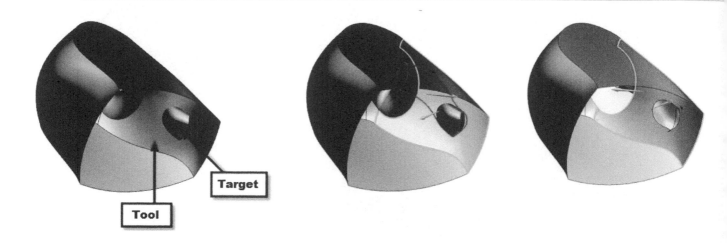

Tool

Target

17. Activate the **Edge Blend** ⬛command and blend the edge of the handle. The blend radius is 6 mm.

18. Blend the intersection between the main surface and handle. The blend radius is 5 mm.

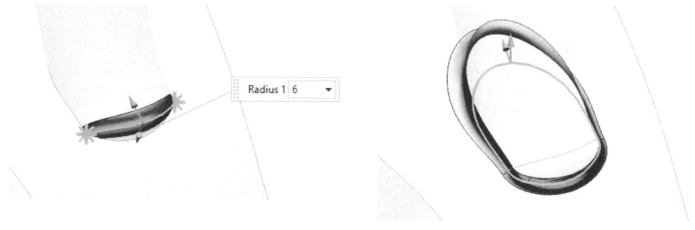

Radius 1 | 6

Creating the Neck and Spout

1. Show the layout sketch to view the centerline of the bottle.

2. Start a sketch on the XZ Plane and draw the sketch for the revolved surface.

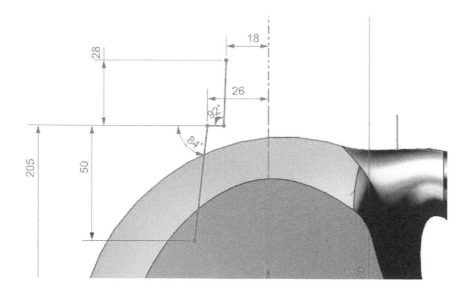

3. Finish the sketch and create a revolved surface. Make sure that the **Body Type** in the **Settings** section is set to **Sheet**.

4. Activate the **Trim and Extend** command and trim the unwanted portions of the revolved and main surface.

Creating the Bottom Face

1. Activate the **Bounded Plane** command (on the ribbon, click **Surface > Surface > More > Bounded Plane**) and click on the edges at the bottom of the surface model.

2. Click **OK** to create the bounded plane surface.

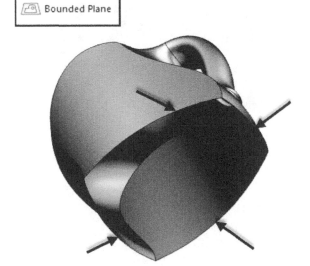

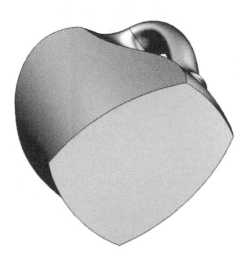

Creating the Emboss on the Label Face

1. Start a sketch on the XZ Plane.

2. Activate the **Offset Curve** command (on the ribbon, click **Home > Direct Sketch > Sketch Curve gallery > More Curve > Offset Curve**). Next, click the **Reset** button located at the top right corner of the **Offset Curve** dialog.1

3. On the Top Border Bar, set the **Curve Rule** to **Tangent Curves** and click on anyone of the boundary edges of the label face.

4. Type-in **15** in the **Distance** box. Click **Apply** to offset the curve. Ensure that the offset curve is created inside.

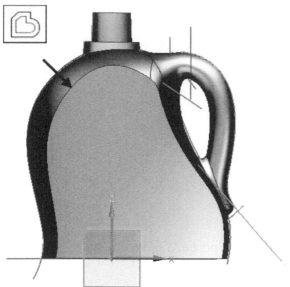
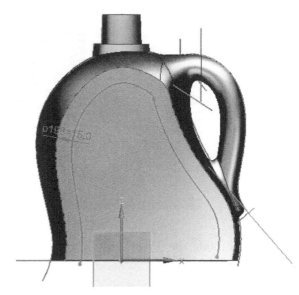

5. Click on the bottom edge of the label face. Click the **Reverse Direction** button on the **Offset Curve** dialog. Click **OK**.

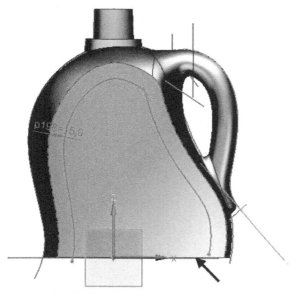
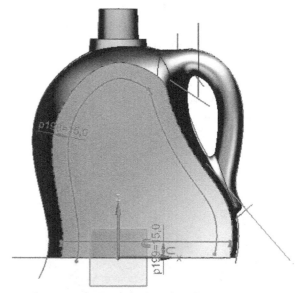

6. Add 12 radius fillets at the bottom, and then trim the unwanted portions. Finish the sketch.

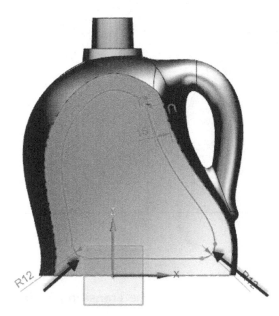

7. Activate the **Emboss** command (on the ribbon, click **Surface > Surface Operations > More > Combine > Emboss**) and select the sketch.

8. On the **Emboss** dialog, click **Face to Emboss > Select Face** and click on the label face.

9. Under the **End Cap** section, select **Geometry > Embossed Faces**.

10. Select **Location > Translate** and type-in 3 in the **Distance** box.

11. Under the **Draft** section, type-in 30 in the **Angle 1** box and click **OK**.

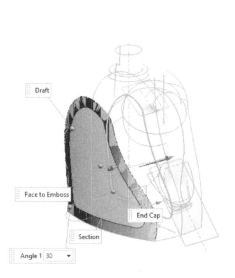

12. Likewise, create emboss on the label face on the opposite side (click the **Transitional Direction** ⌧ button in the **End Cap** section).

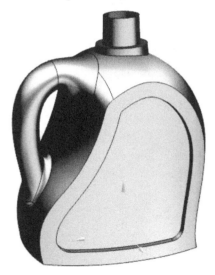

Blending the Label Faces

1. Activate the **Edge Blend** 🟦 command and select the edges of both the label faces
2. On the **Edge Blend** dialog, type-in **10** in the **Radius 1** box, and click **OK**.

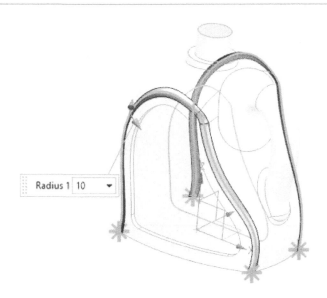

3. Activate **Face Blend** command (on the ribbon, click **Surface > Surface > Blend Gallery > Face Blend**) and select **Type > Two - Face** on the dialog.
4. Click on the bottom face, and then click **Select Face 2**.
5. Click on the label face and type-in 10 in the **Radius** box under the **Cross Section** section. Make sure that the arrows point inside the model. Click **OK**.

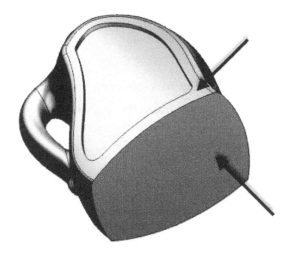

Embossing the bottom face

1. Construct a parallel datum plane at 5 mm distance below the bottom face.
2. Start a new sketch on the parallel datum plane.
3. Activate the **Offset Curve** command and set the **Curve Rule** on the Top Border Bar to **Connected Curves**.
4. Click on the inner boundary edges of the bottom face.
5. Type-in 10 in the **Distance** box and click the **Reverse Direction** button. Click **OK** to project and offset the edges.

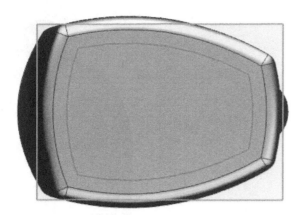

6. Add 12 mm fillets to the corners and trim the unwanted edge portions. Finish the sketch.

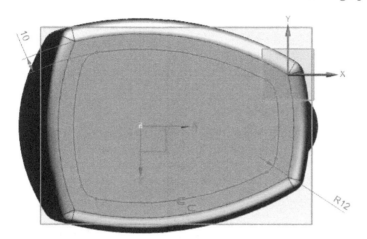

13. Activate the **Emboss** command (on the ribbon, click **Surface > Surface Operations > More > Combine > Emboss**) and click the **Reset** button located at the top right corner of the **Emboss** dialog. Next, click on the sketch.

7. On the **Emboss** dialog, click **Face to Emboss > Select Face** and click on the bottom face.

8. Under the **End Cap** section, select **Geometry > Embossed Faces**.

9. Select **Location > Offset** and type-in 2.5 in the **Distance** box.

10. Under the **Draft** section, type-in 50 in the **Angle 1** box. Click **OK** to add emboss.

11. Activate the **Edge Blend** command and blend the sharp edges of the emboss features. The blend radius is 2 mm.

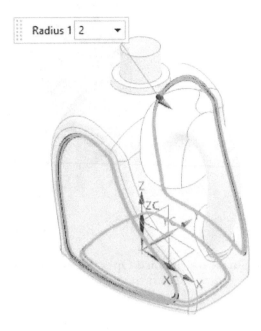

Sewing the Surfaces

1. Activate the **Sew** command (on the ribbon, click **Surface > Surface Operations > Sew**) and click on the main surface body.

2. Click on the Through Curves surface, and then click **OK**.

Adding thickness to the model

1. On the ribbon, click **View > Visibility > Edit Section** and select **Section Plane > Set Plane to Y** on the **View Section** dialog. Click **OK**.

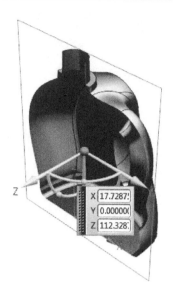

2. Activate the **Thicken** command (on the ribbon, click **Surface > Surface Operations > Thicken** ) and click on the surface body.

3. On the **Thicken** dialog, type-in 1.5 in the **Offset** box.

4. Under the **Region Behavior** section, click **Region of Different Thickness > Select Boundary Curve**, and select the neck and spout region.

5. Type-in 2.5 in the **Offset 1** box under the **Region of Different Thickness** section. Click **OK**.

6. Hide the Sew surface on the Part Navigator.

7. On the ribbon, click **View > Visibility > Clip Section**.

8. Activate the **Edge Blend** command, and then blend the sharp edges of the neck and spout.

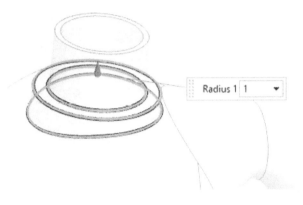

Creating threads

1. Activate the **Datum Plane** command, and then create a plane offset from the neck surface. The offset distance is 20 mm.

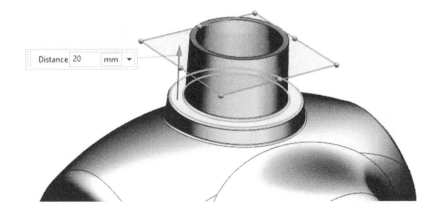

2. Create another offset plane at 10 mm distance.
3. Activate the **Intersection Curve** command (on the ribbon, click **Curve > Derived Curve > Intersection Curve**) and select the outer face of the spout.
4. Click the middle mouse button and select the two planes. Click **OK**.

5. Activate the **Helix** command (on the ribbon, click **Curve > Curve > Helix**) and select the center point of the lower intersection curve.

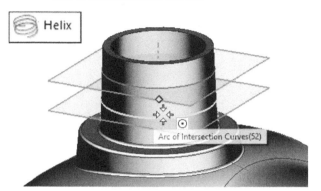

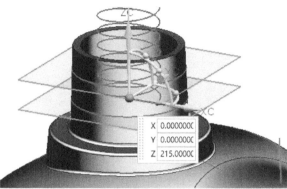

6. On the **Helix** dialog, under the **Size** section, select **Law Type > Linear**.
7. Click the down arrow next to the **Start Value** box and select **Measure**. On the **Measure** dialog, select **Type > Diameter** and click on the lower intersection curve. Click **OK**.
8. Click the down arrow next to the **End Value** box and select **Measure**. On the **Measure** dialog, select **Type > Diameter** and click on the upper intersection curve. Click **OK**.
9. Type-in 5 in the **Value** box under the **Pitch** section.
10. Under the **Length** section, select **Method > Turns**. Type-in 2 in the **Turns** box and click **OK**.
11. Hide the intersection curves and datum planes.

12. Create a datum plane normal to the helix.

13. Draw a sketch on the plane normal to the helix. Finish the sketch.

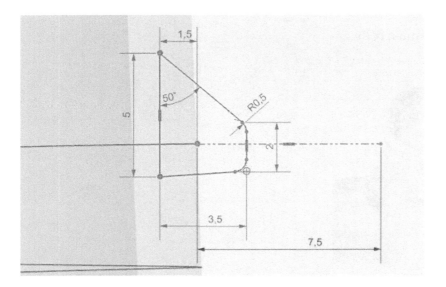

14. Activate the **Swept** command (on the ribbon, click **Surface > Surface > Swept**) and select the cross section.
15. Click **Guides > Select Curve** and select the helix.
16. Under the **Section Options** section, select **Orientation Method > Face Normals**. Select the outer face of the spout.
17. Under the **Settings** section, set the **Body Type** to **Solid**. Click **OK**.

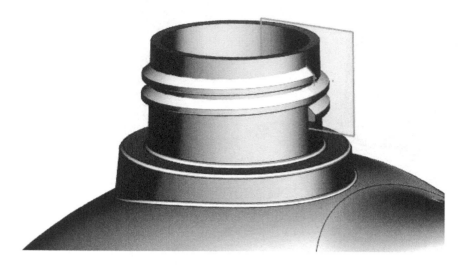

18. Unite the thread body with the main body.

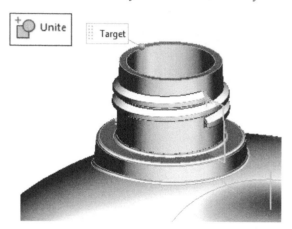

Measuring the Volume of the bottle

1. Activate the **Measure Body** command (on the ribbon, click **Analysis > Measure > More Gallery > Body > Measure Body**) and click on the geometry. The volume of the bottle appears. Next, click **OK** on the **Measure Body** dialog.

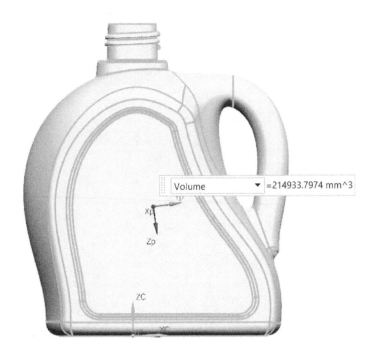

2. On the ribbon, click **View > True Shading** to activate the true shading.
3. Select the geometry and click **View >True Shading Setup > Object Materials > Yellow Glossy Plastic**

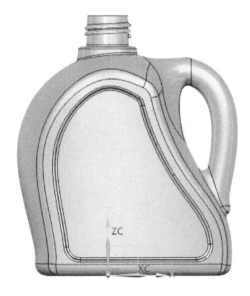

on the ribbon.

4. Save and close the file.

Questions

1. What is the use of the **Sew** command?
2. How many types of face blends can be created in NX?
3. Why do we use the **Patch Openings** command?
4. What are the commands that can be used to delete the openings on a surface?
5. Which commands can be used to bridge the gap between two surfaces?

6. Name the command that can be used to perform a variety of surface operations.
7. How do you add multiple thicknesses to a surface body?
8. List the commands used to extend surfaces from an edge.
9. Why do we use the **Face Blend** command?
10. List the commands used to offset faces.

Exercise 1

Create the model shown next.

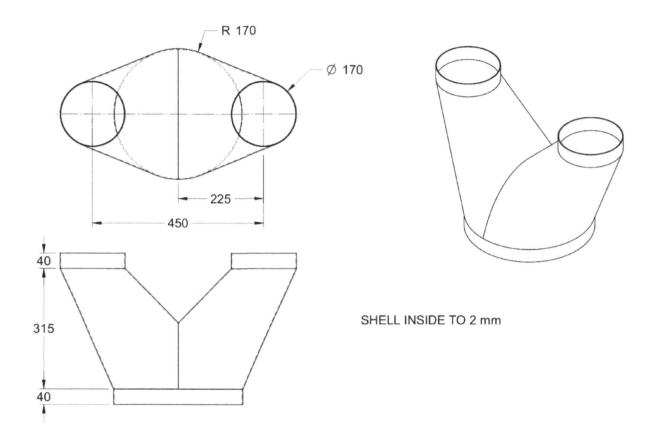

SHELL INSIDE TO 2 mm

Chapter 12: NX Realize Shape

NX Realize Shape environment allows you to create organic smooth solid or surface models by manipulating and subdividing the primitive shapes such as spheres, blocks, cylinders, and so on.

The topics covered in this chapter are:

- *Primitive Shapes*
- *Transform Cages*
- *Extrude Cages*
- *Revolve Cage*
- *Fill*
- *Tube Cage*
- *Loft Cage*
- *Sweep Cage*
- *Set Continuity*
- *Start Symmetric Modeling*
- *Mirror Cage*
- *Copy Cage*
- *Subdivide Face*
- *Bridge Face*
- *Split Face*
- *Merge Face*
- *Delete*
- *Sew Cage*
- *Project Cage*

Creating Primitive Shapes

In NX Realize Shape environment, first you create primitive shapes, and then refine them into finished models. The primitive shapes are simple geometric models such as sphere, cylinder, block, and so on. They are completely air tight closed surfaces. The **Primitive Shape** command helps you to create different primitive shapes. The procedures to create different primitive shapes are explained next.

Creating Sphere

To create a sphere, activate the **Primitive Shape** command (on the ribbon, click **Home > Create > Primitive Shape**), and then select **Type > Sphere** on the **Primitive Shape** dialog. The sphere appears at the origin of the Datum Coordinate System. You can also select a different point in the graphics window to define the location of the sphere (or) use the Dynamic CSYS to define the location of the sphere. Type-in a value in the **Size** box available on the **Primitive Shape** dialog to define the size of the sphere (or) click and drag the arrow handle that appears on the sphere in the graphics window.

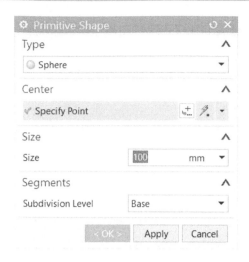

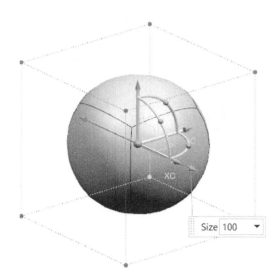

Next, you need to define the number of segments by selecting an option from the **Subdivision Level** drop-down (**Base, First**, and **Second**). The **Base** option creates a sphere with six segments. The **First** option creates a twenty-four segmented sphere. The **Second** option creates a ninety-six segmented sphere. Click **OK** to create the sphere.

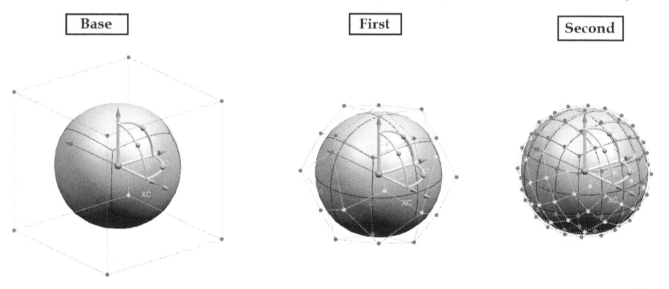

| Base | First | Second |

Creating Cylinder

To create a cylinder, activate the **Primitive Shape** command (on the ribbon, click **Home > Create > Primitive Shape**), and then select **Type > Cylinder** . Next, specify the location of the cylinder by using anyone of the options available in the **Specify Point** drop-down. Next, type in a value in the **Size** and **Height** boxes available on the **Primitive Shape** dialog (or) click and drag the horizontal and vertical arrows to define the diameter and height of the cylinder.

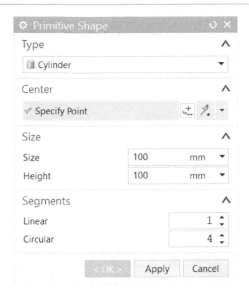

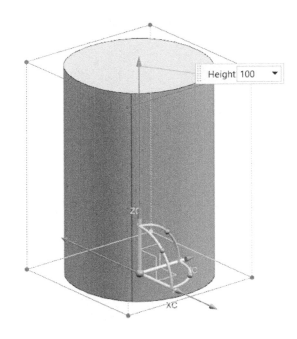

Next, specify the number of segments in the linear and circular direction by entering values in the **Linear** and **Circular** boxes available in the **Segments** section. Note that the number of segments in the circular direction should be between three and thirty-six. Click **OK** to complete the cylindrical shape.

| Linear: 3 |
| Circular : 4 |

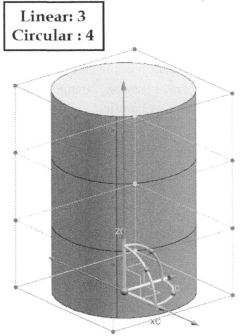

| Linear: 4 |
| Circular : 6 |

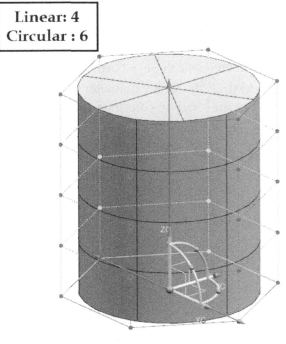

Creating Block

To create a block, activate the **Primitive Shape** command (on the ribbon, click **Home > Create > Primitive Shape**), and then select **Type > Block** . Specify the location of the block, and then type-in values in the **Length (XC)**, **Width (YC)**, and **Height (ZC)** boxes available on the **Primitive Shape** dialog (or) drag the arrows available on the edges of the block to the define the block size.

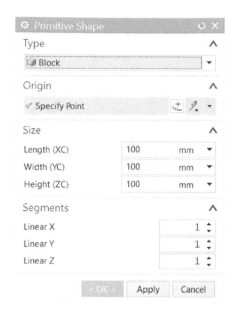

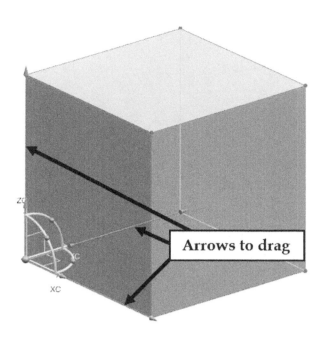

Arrows to drag

Next, type-in values in the **Linear X**, **Linear Y**, and **Linear Z** boxes to add segments along the X, Y, and Z directions, respectively. Click **OK** to complete the block.

Creating Torus

To create a torus, activate the **Primitive Shape** command (on the ribbon, click **Home > Create > Primitive Shape**), and then select **Type > Torus** ⊖. Type-in a value in the **Outer** box in the **Size** section of the **Primitive Shape** dialog (or) drag the **Outer** diameter handle to change the outer diameter of the torus. Likewise, change the inner diameter of the torus by entering a value in the Inner box or dragging the Inner diameter handle.

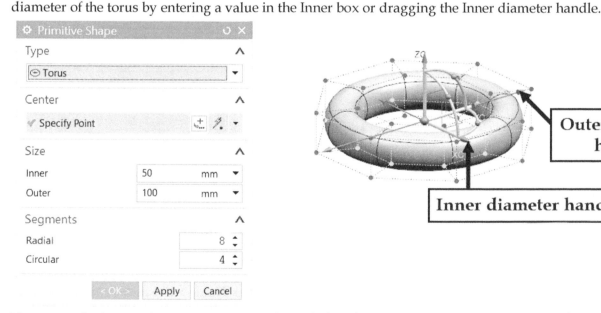

Outer diameter handle

Inner diameter handle

Next, specify the number of segments in the radial and circular direction by entering values in the **Radial** and **Circular** boxes, respectively. Next, click **OK** on the **Primitive Shape** dialog.

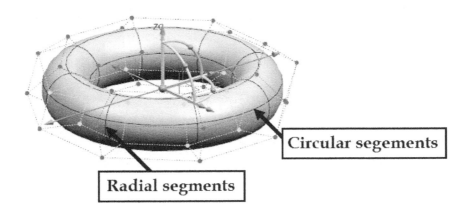

Circular segements

Radial segments

Creating Circle

To create a circle, activate the **Primitive Shape** command (on the ribbon, click **Home > Create > Primitive Shape**), and then select **Type > Circle** ○ . Next, specify the size of the circle and number of segments in the **Size** and **Circular** boxes, respectively. Use the Translate or Rotate handles of the Dynamic CSYS displayed on the circle to change its location and orientation. Click **OK** to create the circle.

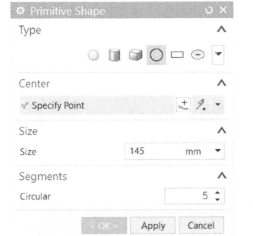

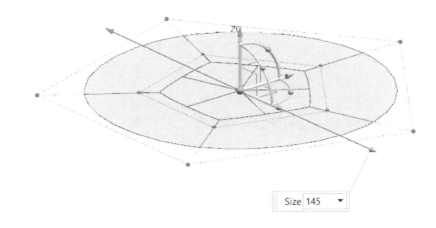

Creating Rectangle

To create a rectangle, activate the **Primitive Shape** command, and then select **Type > Rectangle** ⬜ . Next, specify the **Length (XC)** and **Width (YC)** values to define the size of the rectangle. Type in values in the Linear X and Linear Y boxes to divide the rectangle into number of segments along the X and Y directions.

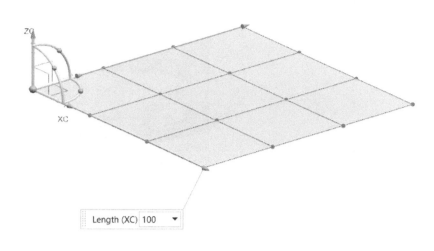

The Transform Cage command

After creating the freeform primitive shapes, you need to use the **Transform Cage** command to manipulate them. For example, create a block as shown below.

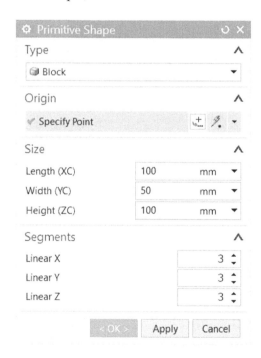

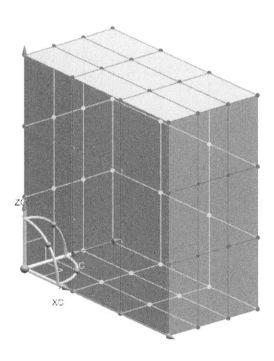

Next, activate the **Transform Cage** command (on the ribbon, click **Home > Modify > Transform Cage**). On the Top Border Bar, the **Selection Filter** drop-down has four filters: **Cage Edge**, **Cage Face**, **Cage Vertex**, and **Control Cage**. For example, if you set **Selection Filter** to **Cage Edge**, you will be able to select only the edges of the cage. The **Selection Rule** drop-down on the Top Border Bar has six options: **Single Object**, **Loop**, **Matrix**, **Region**, **Sharp Edges**, and **Weighted Edges**. You can also set the **Selection Rule** options in addition to the Selection Filters.

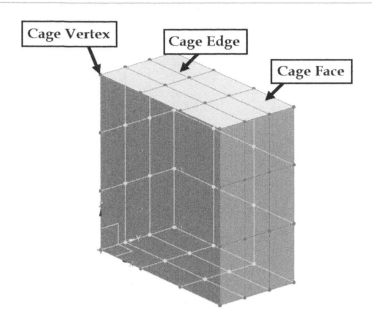

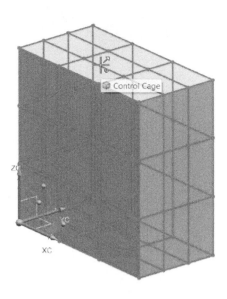

On the Top Border Bar, select **Selection Rule > Loop** and click on the cage edge, as shown; the entire loop is selected. Next, drag the selected loop by holding the left mouse button and release it, as shown. Click **Apply** on the **Transform Cage** dialog.

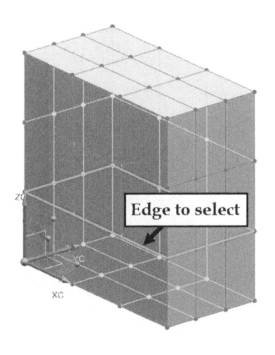

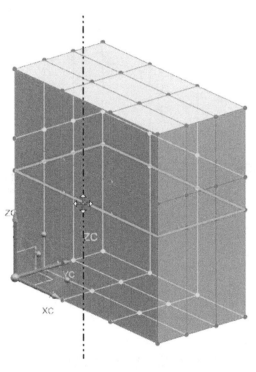

On the Top Border Bar, click **Selection Rule > Region**. Next, change the view orientation to **Right**. On the **Transform Cage** dialog, click the **Transform** tab and make sure that the **Relocate Tool to Selection** and **Reorient Tool to Selection** options are selected. Click and drag a selection window across the upper portion of the block, as shown; the entire region is selected. Also, notice that the transform handle is displayed in the selected region. Click on the YZ-Rotate handle and drag the pointer to rotate the region. Click **Apply** on the **Transform Cage** dialog.

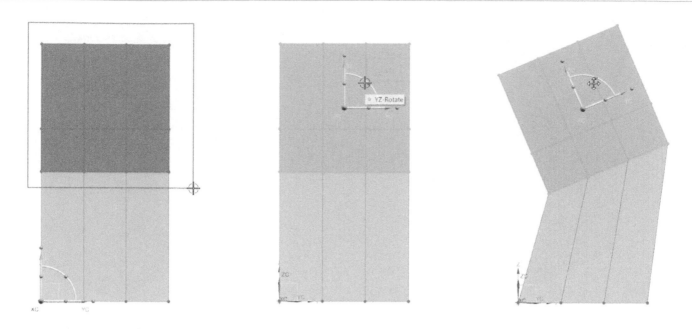

On the Top Border Bar, set **Selection Filter** to **Cage Face** and select **Selection Rule > Single Object**. Next, change the view orientation to **Isometric**. On the **Transform Cage** dialog, click the **Transform** tab and make sure that the **Relocate Tool to Selection** and **Reorient Tool to Selection** options are selected. Next, select **Scaling > Uniform** on the dialog. Click on the top face of the block, as shown. Click and drag the scale handle, as shown; the selected faces are scaled.

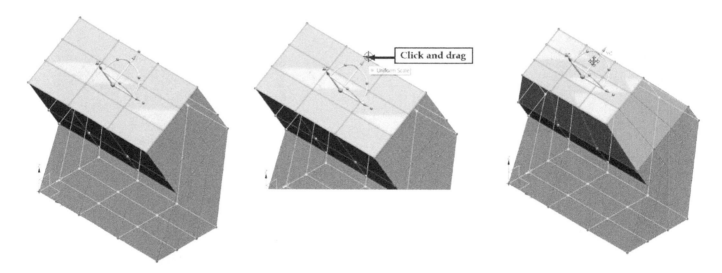

The Extrude Cage command

The **Extrude Cage** command is used to extrude the cage faces, cage edges, or curves. This command is practically illustrated in the following example. First, create a block using the **Primitive Shape** command, as shown. Next, activate the **Extrude Cage** command (on the ribbon, click **Home > Create > Extrude Cage**) and click the **Reset** icon. Click on the center face on the top face of the block, and then drag the Distance handle displayed on the selected face. Notice that there is a smooth transition at the bottom of the extrusion. On the **Extrude Cage** dialog, expand the **Settings** section, and select the **Sharp** option; the edges at the bottom are sharpened.

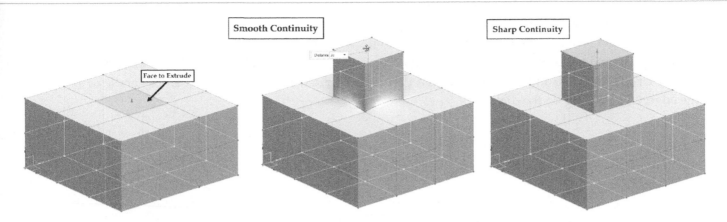

Click **Apply** on the dialog; notice that the Distance handle is displayed on the top face. Click and drag the Distance handle up to some distance, and then click **Apply**. On the **Extrude Cage** dialog, click the **Transform** tab and drag the Z-Translate handle up to some distance. Next, click and drag the YZ-Rotate handle to rotate the face, as shown. Again, click and drag the Z-Translate handle, and then click **OK**.

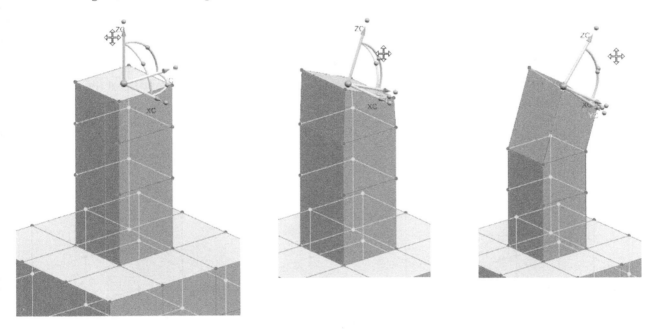

Extruding a Planar Face

Create a rectangle using the **Primitive Shape** command. Next, activate the **Extrude Cage** command and select all the faces of the planar face. Click and drag the Distance handle to add thickness to the face.

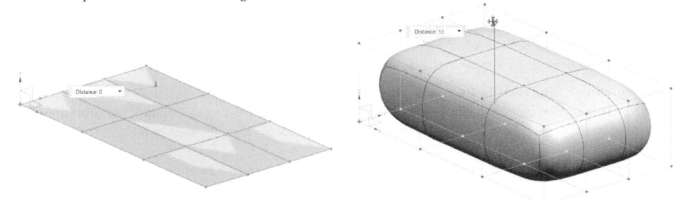

Extruding the Cage Edges

Create a rectangle using the **Primitive Shape** command. Next, activate the Extrude Cage command (on the ribbon, click **Home > Create > Extrude Cage**) and click on the cage edges, as shown. On the **Extrude Cage** dialog, click the **Drag Linear** tab and select **Direction > Perpendicular**. Click and drag the Distance handle to extrude the cage edge. Click **Apply** on the dialog.

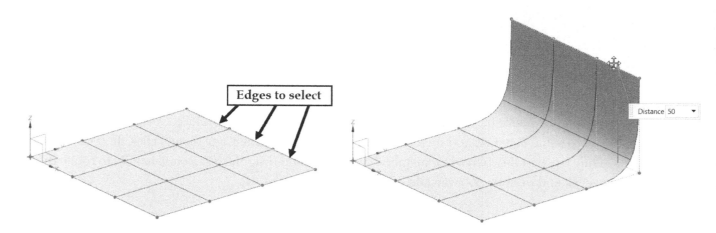

Click the **Transform** tab of the dialog and drag the Y-Translate handle of the Dynamic CSYS. Click the XZ – Rotate handle and drag to rotate the selected edges. Likewise, you can also use the scale handles of the Dynamic CSYS to modify the selected edges.

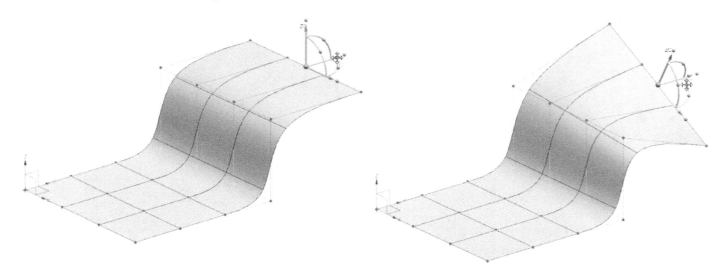

The Revolve Cage command

The **Revolve Cage** command revolves a polyline or cage edges to create cage faces. This command is practically illustrated in the following example. Activate the **Cage Polyline** command (on the ribbon, click **Home > Polyline > Cage Polyline**) and click the **Reset** icon on the **Cage Polyline** dialog. Next, click the **YC-ZC** icon in the **Drawing Plane** section of the **Cage Polyline** dialog. On the Top Border Bar, click **Orient View** drop-down > **Right**. Specify the points of the polyline, as shown. Next, click **OK** to create the cage polyline.

Activate the **Revolve Cage** command (on the ribbon, click **Home > Create > Extrude/Revolve** Drop-down > **Revolve Cage**) and click the **Reset** icon on the **Revolve Cage** dialog. Select the cage polyline from the graphics window. On the **Revolve Cage** dialog, click **Specify Vector** under the **Axis** section, and then select Z-axis from the vector triad displayed in the graphics window. Click on the origin point of the Datum Coordinate system to specify the location of the axis. Next, specify the **Start Angle** and **End Angle** of revolved cage. Expand the **Segmentation** section and type in a value in the **Number of Segments** box. Note that the number of segments should be three or more. Click **OK** to create the revolved cage.

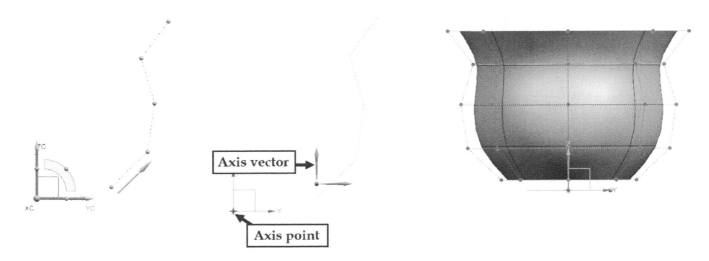

The Fill command

The **Fill** command adds a new face to the cage using two or more cage edges. Activate this command (on the ribbon, click **Home > Create > Fill**) and click on the open edges of a cage. On the **Fill** dialog, expand the Settings section and set **Continuity** to **Smooth**.

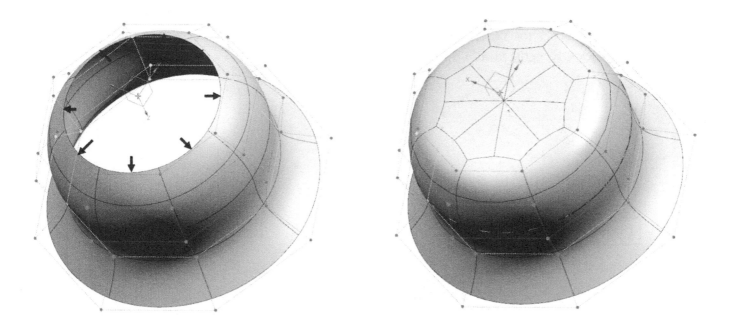

The Tube Cage command

The **Tube Cage** command creates a tube with a control cage using a polyline as its path. Activate this command (on the ribbon, click **Home > Create > Tube Cage**) and click on a polyline. On the **Tube Cage** dialog, under the **Cross Section** section, specify the **Size** and **Number of Segments**. Click **OK** to create the tube cage.

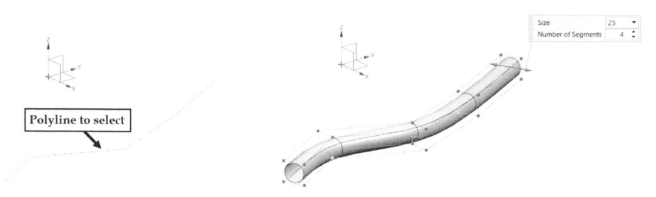

The Loft Cage command

The **Loft Cage** command creates a lofted surface with a control cage using two or more polylines. First, you need to create two or more polylines in the graphics window. You can use the **Cage Polyline** or **Extract Cage Polyline** commands to create polylines. In this example, the **Extract Cage Polyline** command is used to create cage polylines.

Activate the **Datum Plane** command and create two datum planes parallel to the YZ plane. The distance between each plane is 50. Next, activate the **Studio Spline** command (on the ribbon, click **Home > Construction Tools > Studio Spline**). Click the **Reset** icon on the **Studio Spline** dialog. On the **Studio Spline** dialog, under the **Drawing Plane** section click the **YC-ZC** plane icon and create the studio spline, as shown. Click **Apply** on the dialog, and then click **OK** on the **Studio Spline** message box.

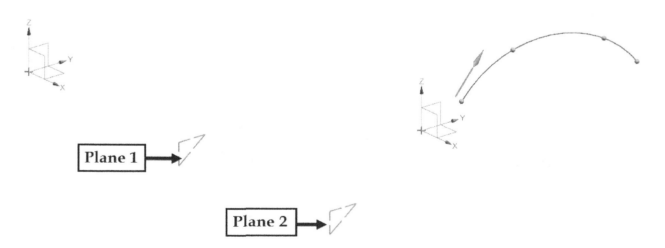

On the **Studio Spline** dialog, click the **General** icon in the **Drawing Plane** section. Click on the first plane in the graphics window. On the **Studio Spline** dialog, click **Specify Points** and create a studio spline, as shown. Click **OK** on the dialog.

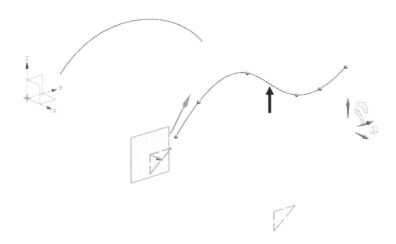

Activate the **Arc/Circle** command (on the ribbon, click **Home > Construction Tools > Arc/Circle**), and then click the **Reset** icon on the **Arc/Circle** dialog. Next, expand the **Support Plane** section and select **Plane Options > Select Plane** . Select the second plane from the graphics window. Specify the start, end and mid points of the arc, as shown. Click **OK** to complete the arc.

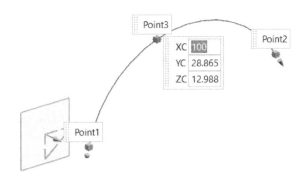

Activate the **Extract Cage Polyline** command (On the ribbon, click **Home > Polyline > Extract Cage Polyline**) and select the first spline curve from the graphics window. Next, set the **Number of Segments** value to **3**. Click Apply. Likewise, convert the remaining curves to polylines.

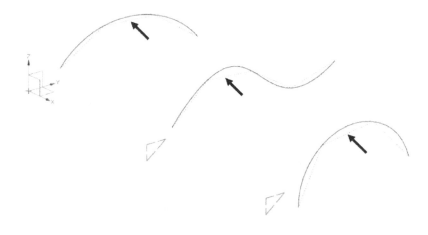

Activate the **Loft Cage** command (on the ribbon, click **Home > Create > Loft Cage**) and click on the first polyline. Next, click the **Add New Set** icon and click on the second polyline. Likewise, click the **Add New Set** icon and click on the third polyline. Make sure that the arrows on the selected polylines point in the same direction. Use the **Reverse Direction** icon, if they are in different directions. Next, expand the **Segmentation** section and set the **Number of Segments** value to 3. Click **OK** to create the loft cage.

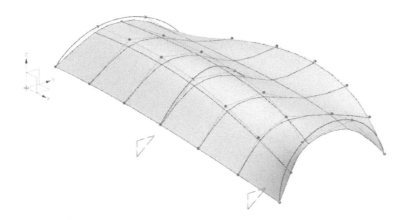

The Sweep Cage command

The **Sweep Cage** command is similar to the **Swept** command except that this command creates a surface along with a control cage. Activate this command (on the ribbon, click **Home > Create > Sweep Cage**) and click on the polyline to be swept. On the **Sweep Cage** dialog, under the **Guides (2 Maximum)** section, click **Select Face Edge or Polyline** click on the polyline to define the first guide polyline. Next, click the **Add New Set** icon and select another polyline to define the second guide. Make sure that the arrows on selected guides point in the same direction. Use the **Reverse Direction** icon in the **Guides** section to change their direction. Click **OK** to create the swept cage.

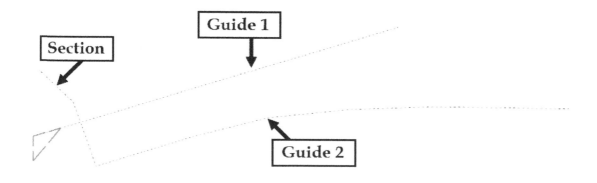

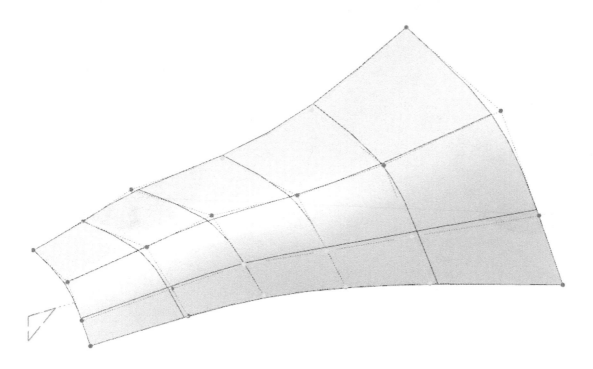

The Set Continuity command

The **Set Continuity** command helps you to smoothen or sharpen the edges of the cage. Activate this command (on the ribbon, click **Home > Modify > Set Continuity**) and select a cage edge to set the continuity. You can also drag the selection window across the entire model to select all its edges. Next, select the **Smooth** or **Sharp** option from the **Continuity** section of the **Set Continuity** dialog, and then click **OK**.

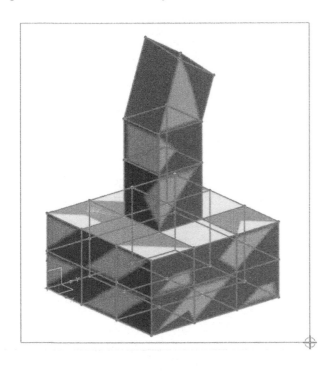

Smooth Continuity

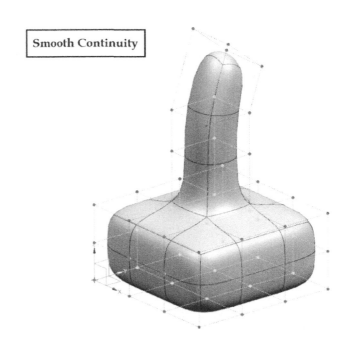

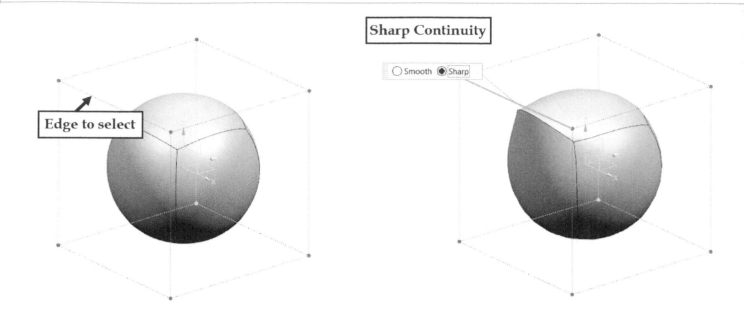

Start Symmetric Modeling

The **Start Symmetric Modeling** command helps you to create B-surface models that are symmetrical about a

plane. Activate this command (on the ribbon, click **Home > NX Realize Shape > Start Symmetric Modeling**)
and select a plane from the graphics window to define the symmetric plane. Click the **Switch Side** icon to change
the side to be manipulated. Next, click **OK** to start symmetric modeling.

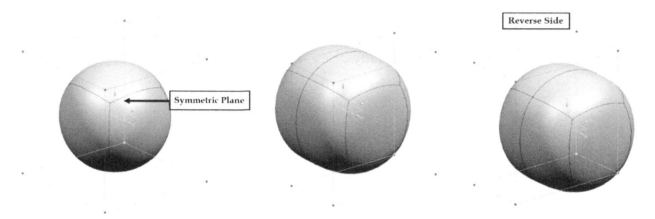

Now, activate the **Transform Cage** command and manipulate the cage edge, as shown; the cage is modified
symmetrically.

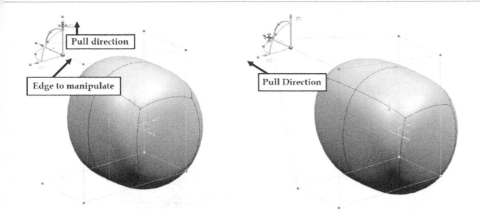

You can use the **Stop Symmetric Modeling** command to stop manipulating the model symmetrically. Activate this command (on the ribbon, click **Home > NX Realize Shape > Stop Symmetric Modeling**) and notice that the cage is displayed on both sides of the model. You can manipulate the model independently on both sides.

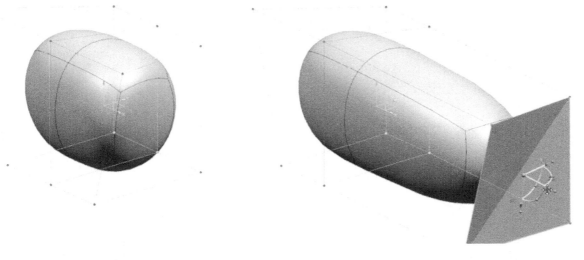

Select Projection Edge

The **Select Projection Edge** option is useful while creating a symmetrical body using an open surface. This option is practically illustrated in the following example. First, create a circle using the **Primitive Shape** command, as shown. Next, click on the inner cage face of the circle, as shown. On the Context toolbar, click the **Transform Cage** icon. Click on the Z-Translate handle of the Dynamic CSYS, press and hold the left mouse button, and drag the pointer toward right; the cage face is manipulated, as shown. Click **Apply** on the **Transform Cage** dialog.

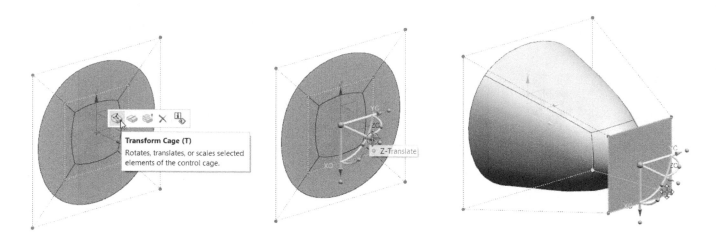

Click on the left top edge of the cage, and then drag the ZC handle of the Dynamic CSYS upward. Click **OK** on the **Transform Cage** dialog. On the ribbon, click **Home > Construction Tools > Datum Plane**, and then click on the YZ Plane of the Datum Coordinate System; a datum plane appears. Click and drag the datum plane toward left up to a random distance. Click **OK** on the **Plane** dialog.

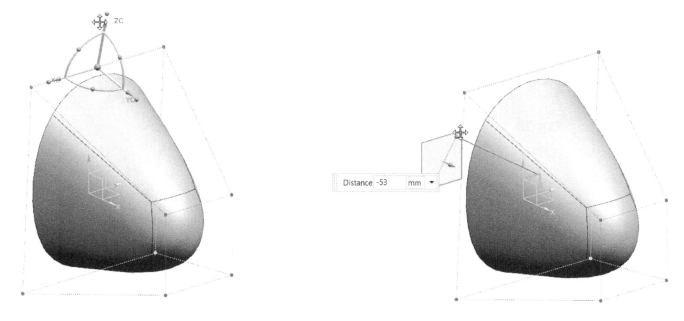

On the ribbon, click **Home > NX Realize Shape > Start Symmetric Modeling**, and then click on the newly created plane. Make sure that the arrow on the plane points towards the model (use the **Switch Side** ⊠ icon to change the arrow direction). Click **OK** and notice that the surface body is mirrored without any connected.

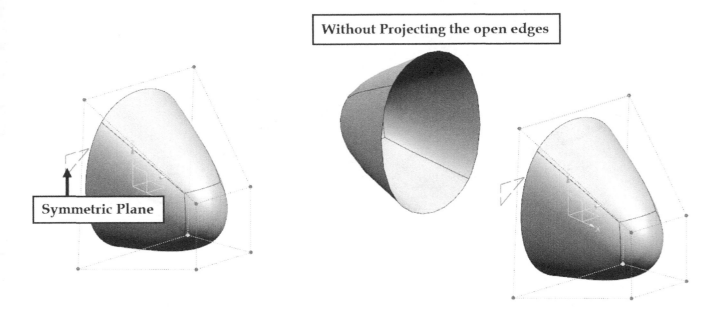

On the Quick Access Toolbar, click the **Undo** icon (or) press Ctrl+Z on your keyboard. Next, click the **Start Symmetric Modeling** icon on the **NX Realize Shape** panel. Select the datum plane from the graphics window to define the symmetric plane. On the **Start Symmetric Modeling** dialog, click **Select Projection Edge**, and then select the open edges of the cage, as shown. Click **OK** on the Start Symmetric Modeling dialog; the selected edges are projected on to the symmetric plane.

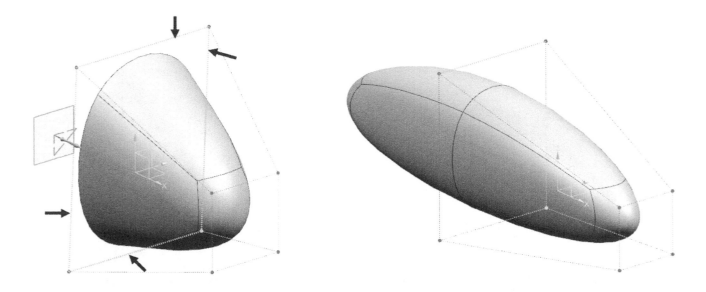

Click on a cage edge and transform it, as shown.

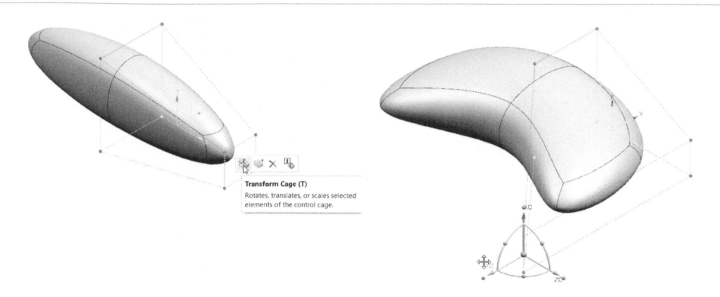

Mirror Cage

The **Mirror Cage** command helps you to create a mirror copy of the selected surface body. This command is similar to the **Start Symmetric Modeling** command except that there is no associative link between the original body and the mirrored copy. This command is practically illustrated in the following example. First, create a rectangle using the **Primitive Shape** command, as shown. Click on the cage vertex of the rectangle, and then select the **Transform Cage** icon from the Context toolbar. Press and hold the left mouse button on the selected vertex, and then drag it upwards. Release the mouse button, and then click **OK** on the **Transform Cage** dialog.

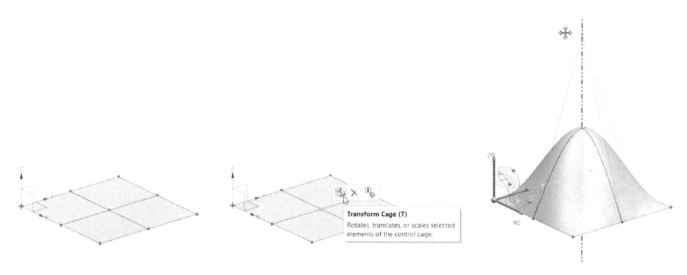

Activate this command (on the ribbon, click **Home > Create > Mirror Cage**) and select a cage face of the surface body to be mirrored. Next, select a plane from the graphics window to define the mirror plane. Click **OK** to mirror the cage.

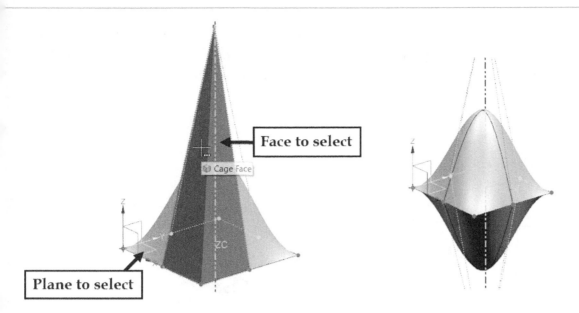

Face to select

Cage Face

Plane to select

Copy Cage

The **Copy Cage** command creates a copy of the select cage faces, edges or entire cage. The following example is one of many ways in which this command can be used. Activate the **Primitive Shape** command and create a rectangle, as shown.

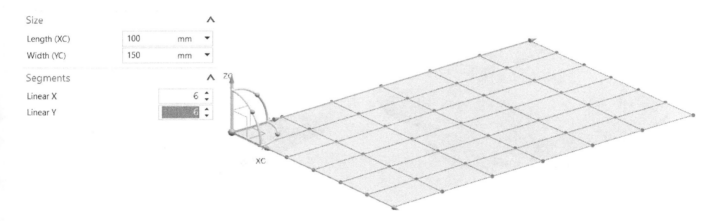

Activate the **Extrude Cage** command and drag a selection window across the rectangle. Next, click and drag the Distance handle up to 50 mm and click **OK**.

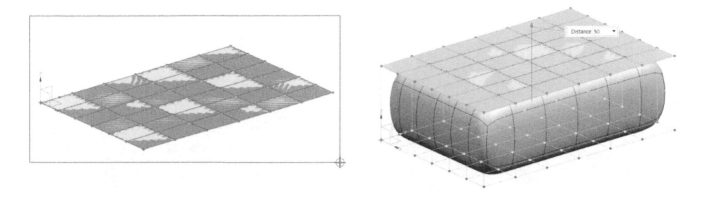

Activate the **Copy Cage** command (on the ribbon, click **Home > Create > Copy Cage**). On the Top Border Bar, set **Selection Rule** to **Loop**, and then click on the two faces of the cage, as shown; the loops associated with the selected faces are selected. On the **Copy Cage** dialog, under the **Result** section, set the **Number of Copies** to **1**. Click **OK** to copy the selected cage faces.

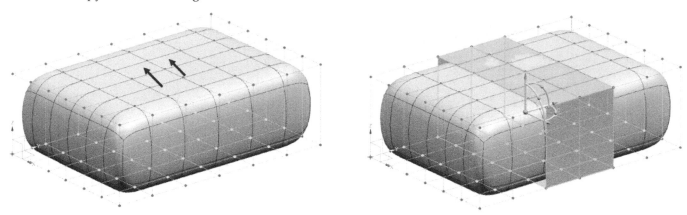

Activate the **Extrude Face** command and set the **Selection Rule** to **Loop**. Click on the two faces of the copied surface, as shown; the entire copied surface is selected. Click and drag the **Distance** handle up to 10 mm in the upward direction. Click **OK**.

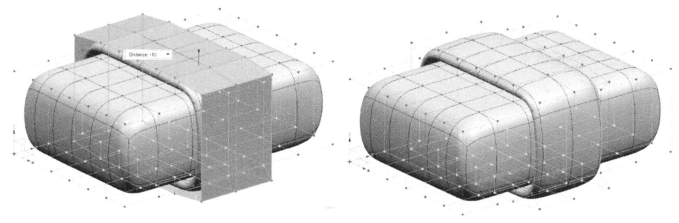

Subdivide Face

The **Subdivide Face** command subdivides the selected face by offsetting its edges. Activate this command (on the ribbon, click **Home > Modify > Subdivide Face**) and click on a face to subdivide. Drag the **Percentage** handle or enter value in the **Percentage** box in the **Offset** section of the **Subdivide** dialog; the edges of the face will be offset in the inward direction based on the **Percentage** value. Click OK and notice that the selected face is subdivided into five faces.

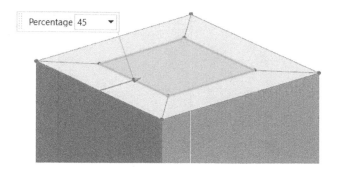
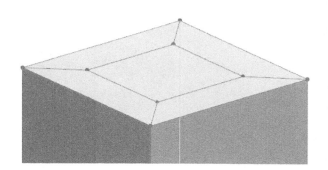

Subdividing Faces that are Perpendicular to each other

Subdividing two faces which are perpendicular to each other produces a different result. Activate the **Subdivide Face** command and select the two faces that are perpendicular to each other. Drag the **Percentage** handle to offset the edges of the faces. Notice that the common edge of the two perpendicular faces is not offset.

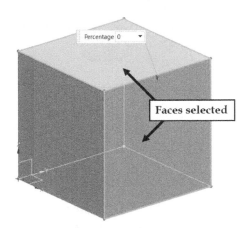
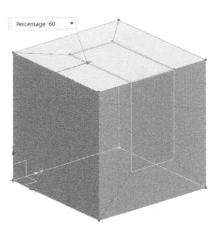

Likewise, select three faces that are perpendicular to each other and notice a different result.

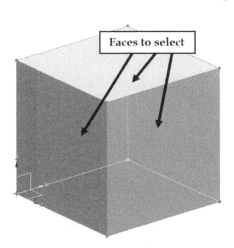
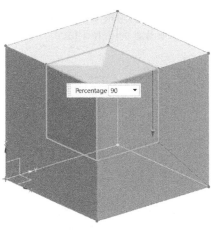

Bridge Face

The **Bridge Face** command creates a closed tunnel-like surface between two faces. The following example illustrates the use of this command. First, create a torus with the specifications, as shown. Next, create a sphere of 100 mm size at the center of the torus.

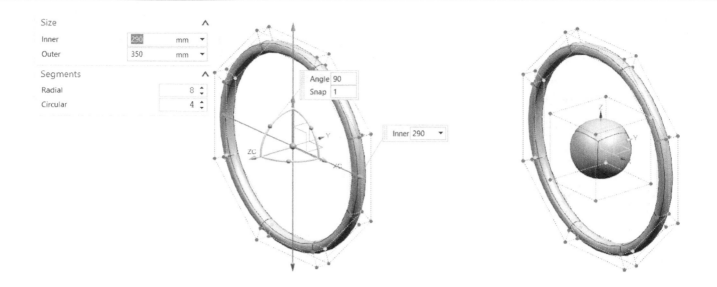

Activate the **Bridge Face** command (on the ribbon, click **Home > Create > Bridge Face**) and click on the right face of the sphere, as shown. On the **Bridge Face** dialog, click **Select Object** under the **Face Set 2** section. Rotate the model and click on the inner face of the torus, as shown. On the **Bridge Face** dialog, under the **Segmentation** section, change the **Number of Segments** value to **2**. Expand the **Settings** section and select **Smooth**. Click **Apply** to create bridge face between the selected face.

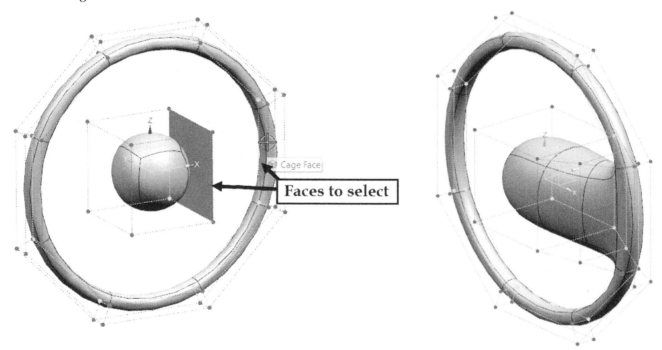

Likewise, bridge the left and bottom faces of the sphere with the torus.

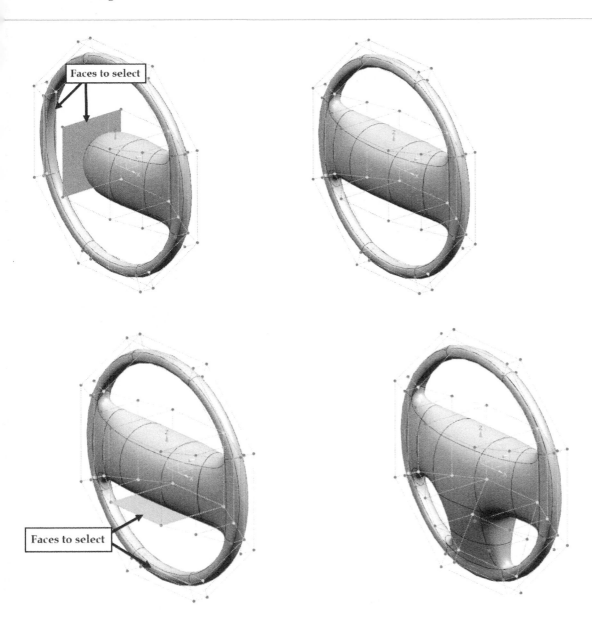

Subdivide the center faces on front and back side of the model, as shown.

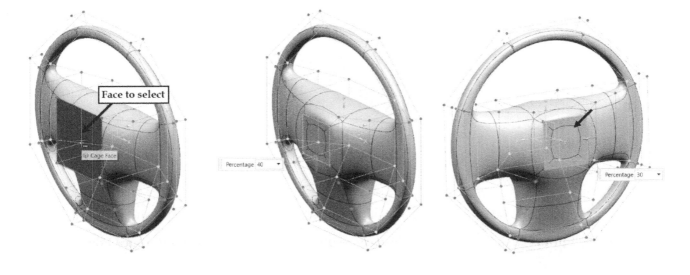

Activate the **Bridge Face** command and select the subdivided center face on the front side. Next, click **Select object** in the **Face Set 2** section of the **Bridge Face** dialog. Rotate the model and select the subdivided center face on the back side. Expand the **Segmentation** section and change the **Number of Segments** value to 1. Click **OK** to create a tunnel between the two selected faces.

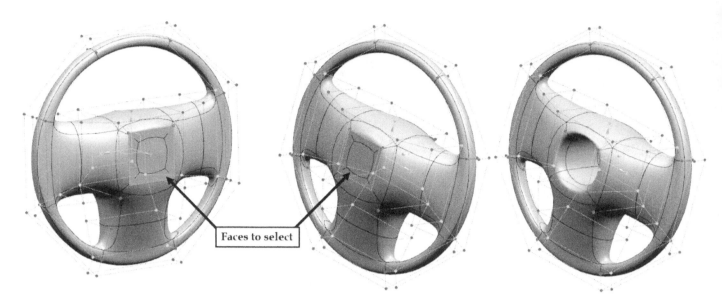

Faces to select

Split Face

The **Split Face** command splits a cage face into multiple faces uniformly or through selected points. The following example illustrates the use of this command. First, create a cylinder with the specifications, as shown.

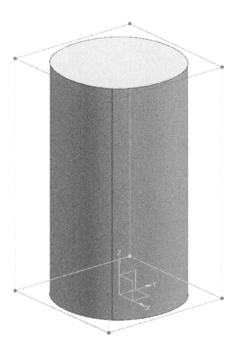

Activate the **Split Face** command (on the ribbon, click **Home > Modify > Split Face**), and then select **Type > Uniform** on the **Split Face** dialog. Click on the face to split, and then click **Select Reference Edge** from the

Split section. Select an edge of the selected cage face, and then specify the number of splitting edges in the **Number** box. Expand the **Preview** section and click the **Show Result** icon.

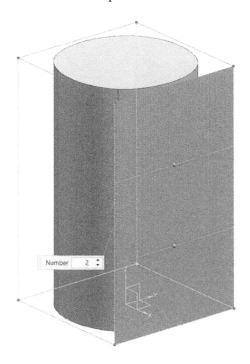

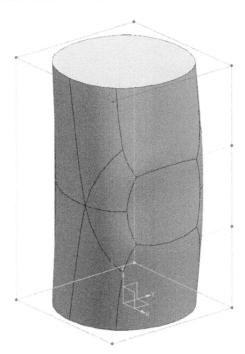

Notice that the adjacent faces of the split face are affected. Click the **Undo Result** icon in the **Preview** section. On Top Border Bar, set the **Selection Rule** to **Loop**. On the **Split Face** dialog, under the **Face** section, click **Select Face**. Click on the side face of the previously selected face; all the cylindrical faces of the cage are selected. Click **Apply** to split the selected cage faces.

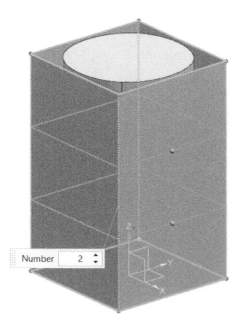

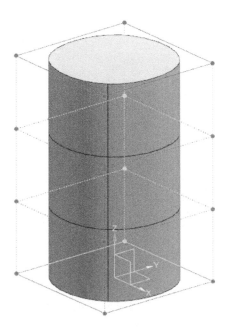

On the **Split Face** dialog, select **Type > Along Polyline**, and then select the midpoints of the cage edges, as shown.

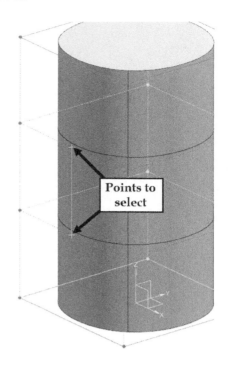 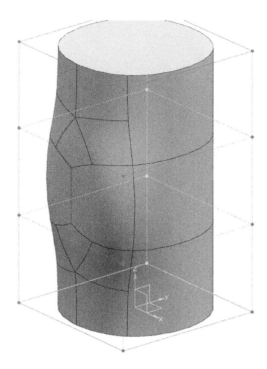

Merge Face

The **Merge Face** command merges two or more faces of the cage to simplify the design. Activate this command (on the ribbon, click **Home > Modify > Merge Face**) and click on the faces to merge. Next, click **OK**.

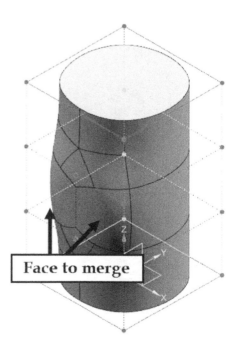 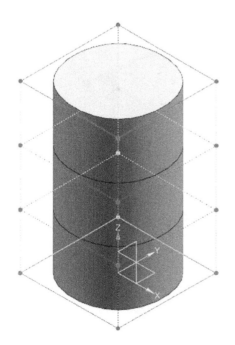

Delete

The **Delete** command deletes a cage point, edge, face, or the entire cage. Activate this command (on the ribbon, click **Home > Modify > Delete** ✕) and select the objects to delete.

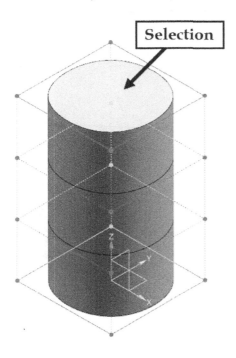

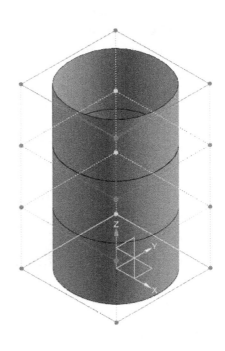

Sew Cage

The **Sew Cage** command connects the open edges of two control cages. Activate this command (on the ribbon, click **Home > Modify > Sew Cage** 📖) and click on the first set of the open edges. Next, click **Select Open Edges** in the **Side 2** section of the **Sew Cage** dialog. Select the open edges of the second side. Click **OK** to connect the selected open edges

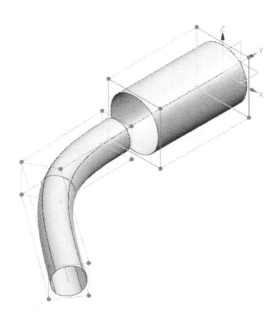

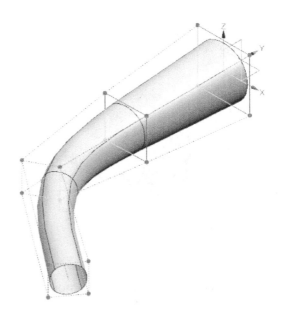

Set Weight

The **Set Weight** command sets weights on the selected edge or face. The edges are slightly sharpened by weight factor that you specify in the **Percentage** box. Activate this command (on the ribbon, click **Home > Modify > Set Weight**) select the edges to set weight. Next, click and drag the **Percentage** dragger to specify the weight factor. Click **OK** on the **Set Weight** dialog. On the ribbon, click **Home > Preferences > Show Weight** to display the weight factor on the edges.

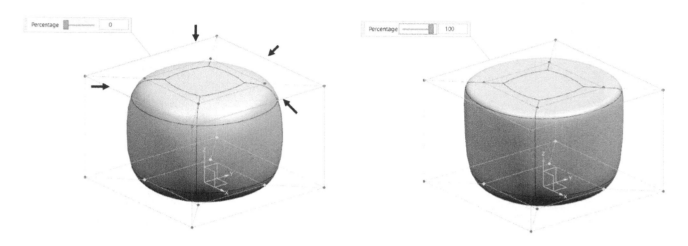

Project Cage

The **Project Cage** command projects the elements of the cage (edge, face, or vertex) up to a selected target element. The target element can be a planar face or a linear element. Activate this command (on the ribbon, click **Home > Modify > Project Cage**) and select **Type > To Target**. Next, select the **Target Type** (**Object** in this example) and click on the target element. Select the cage face to project.

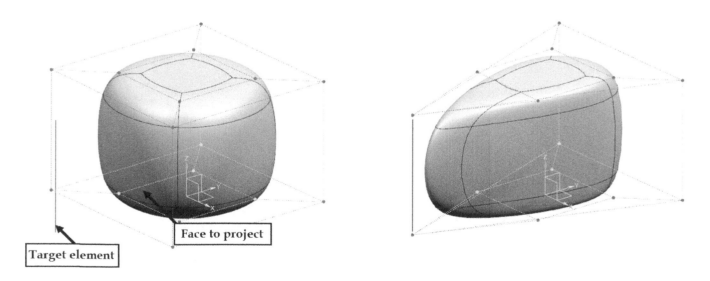

Example 1

In this example, you will construct the model shown below.

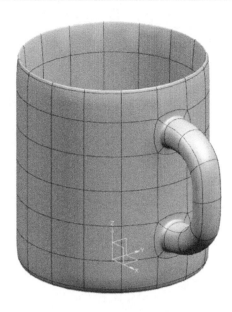

Activating the NX Realize Shape Environment

1. Start **NX 12**.
2. Start a new part file using the **Model** template.
3. On the ribbon, click **Home > Surface > Surface > NX Realize Shape** 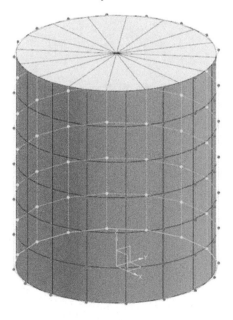.

Creating a Cylinder Shape

1. On the ribbon, click **Home > Create > Primitive Shape**.
2. Click the **Reset** icon on the **Primitive Shape** dialog. Next, select **Type > Cylinder**.
3. Under the **Size** section, type 80 and 90 in the **Size** and **Height** boxes, respectively. Next, type 6 and 16 in the **Linear** and **Circular** boxes of the **Segments** section. Click **OK** to create the cylinder.

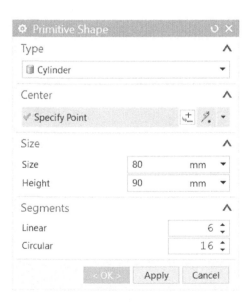

Adding Symmetry to the model

1. On the ribbon, click **Home > NX Realize Shape > Start Symmetric Modeling** 🦃 . Click the **Reset** 🔄 icon on the **Start Symmetric Modeling** dialog.

2. Click on the XY plane of the Datum Coordinate System. Type 45 in the **Distance** box, and then press Enter; a plane is created at the middle of the model. Leave the default options and click **OK** to make the model symmetric about the newly created plane.

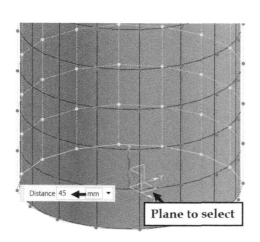
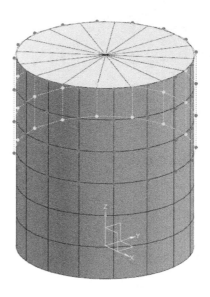

Subdividing Top Face

1. On the ribbon, click **Home > Modify > Subdivide Face** 🔲 . Click on the top face of the model. Type **8** in the **Percentage** box and click **Apply** to subdivide the face.

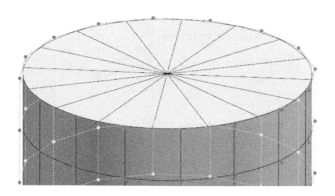
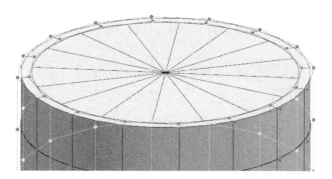

2. Likewise, subdivide the inner face of the top surface. The Percentage value is 15.

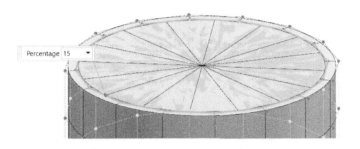

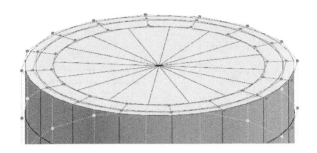

Creating the Handle

1. On the Top Border Bar, select **Orient** drop-down > **Right**. Next, activate the **Subdivide Face** command (on the ribbon, click **Home > Modify > Subdivide Face**). Click on the cage face, as shown. Type **10** in the **Percentage** box, and then click **OK**.

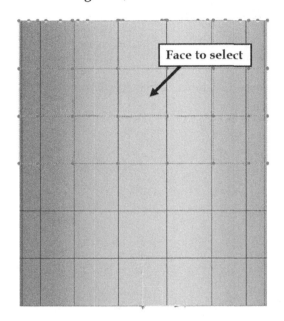

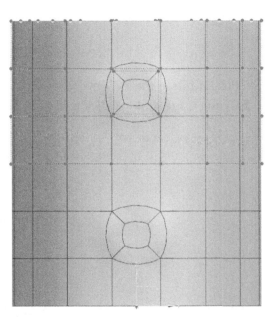

2. On the ribbon, click **Home > Create > Extrude Cage** . Click the **Reset** icon on the **Extrude Cage** dialog. Click the **Transform** tab on the **Extrude Cage** dialog. Click on the subdivided face, and then select **Orient** drop-down > **Front** on the Top Border Bar.

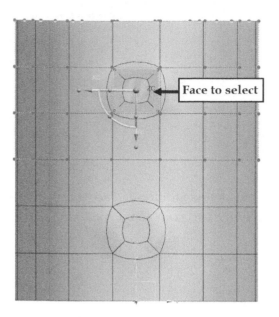

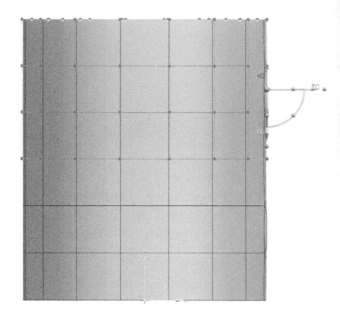

3. Click and drag the Z-Translate handle of the transform tool up to a small distance. Click **Apply** on the **Extrude Cage** dialog. Click and drag the YZ-Rotate handle, as shown.

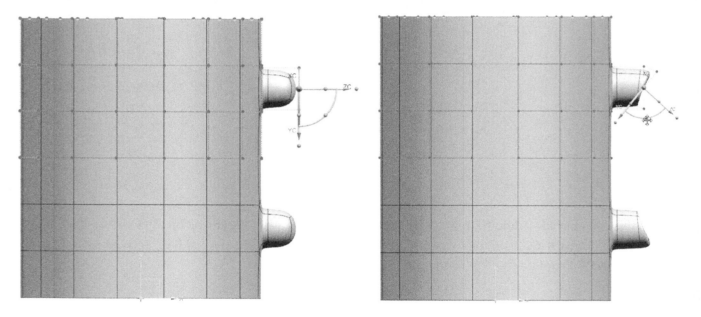

4. Click and drag the Z-Translate handle, as shown. Click **OK** to complete the extrude cage process.

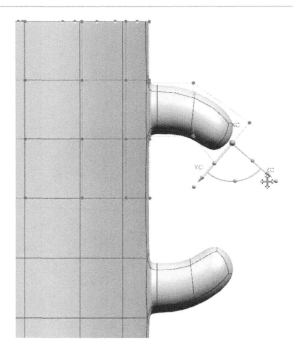

5. On the ribbon, click **Home > NX Realize Shape > Stop Symmetric Modeling**. Next, click **Orient View** drop-down > **Trimetric** on the Top Border Bar.

6. On the ribbon, click **Home > Create > Bridge Face** . Click the **Reset** icon on the **Bridge Face** dialog. Click on the end face of anyone of the extruded cages. Click **Select object** in the **Face Set 2** section, and then click on the end face of the remaining extruded cage. Expand the **Segmentation** section set the **Number of Segments** value to **2**. Click **OK** to bridge the end faces.

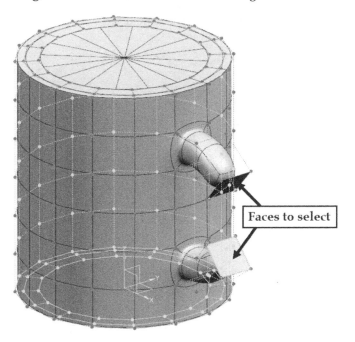

Faces to select

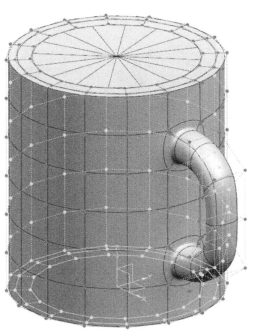

Shelling the Mug

1. On the ribbon, click **Home > Create > Extrude Cage** . Click on the center face and the faces surrounding it on the top surface. Next, select **Orient View** drop-down > **Front** on the Top Border Bar. Click and drag the **Z-Translate** handle of the transform tool downwards, as shown. Click **OK** to shell the model.

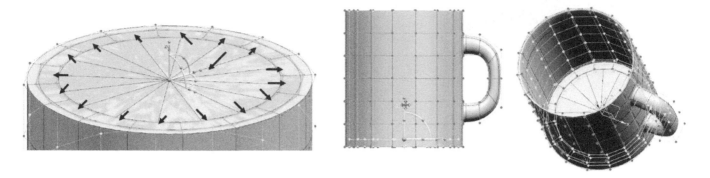

Creating a Bump at the bottom

1. On the ribbon, click **Home > Modify > Transform Cage** . Click the **Reset** icon on the **Transform Cage** dialog. Click the **Transform** tab on the dialog. Rotate the model such that the bottom face is visible. Next, click on the center face of the bottom.
2. Click on the Z-Translate handle of the transform handle. Type -2 in the **Distance** box, and then click **OK**.

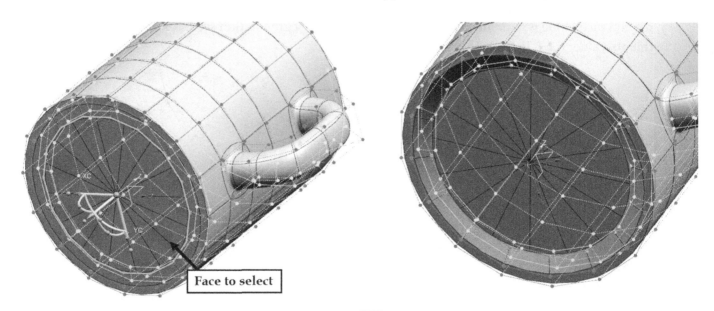

Face to select

3. On the ribbon, click **Home > Modify > Set Continuity** . Create a selection window across the entire model.
4. On the **Set Continuity** dialog, select **Continuity > Smooth**. Click **OK**.

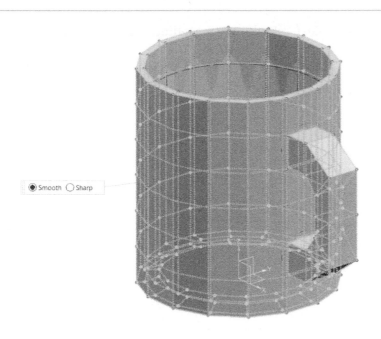

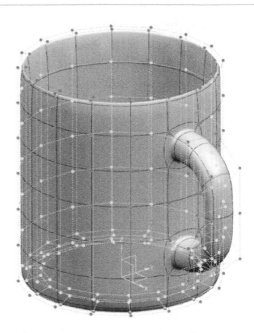

5. On the ribbon, click **Home > NX Realize Shape > Finish**.
6. Save and close the part file.

Example 2

In this example, you will construct the part shown below.

Importing the Raster Image

1. Download the image files related to *Example 2* of *Chapter 12:NX Realize Shape* from the companion website.
2. Start **NX 12**.
3. Start a new part file using the **Model** template.

4. On the ribbon, click **Home > Feature > Datum/Point drop-down > Raster Image** . Click the **Reset** icon on the **Raster Image** dialog. Click on the XY plane of the Datum Coordinate System.

5. Click the **Choose Image File** icon and select the Top_View.jpg file. Select **Orientation > Basepoint > Middle Center** . Check the **Preview** option, and then click the **Flip Horizontal** icon.

6. Check the **Lock Aspect Ratio** option in the **Size** section. Next, select **Scaling Method > User Defined** and then type **150** in the **Width** box.
7. Expand the **Image Settings** section, and then select **Transparency > Pixel Color**. Click in the white portion in the **Transparency** window. Next, click **OK** to insert the image file.

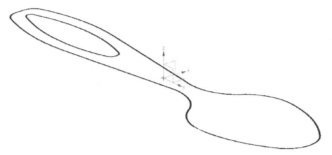

8. Likewise, insert the Front_view.jpg file on the XZ Plane.

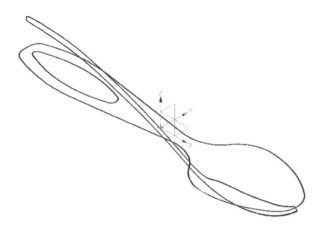

Creating and Manipulating the Circle

1. On the ribbon, click **Home > Surface > Surface > NX Realize Shape** .
2. On the Top Border Bar, select **Orient** drop-down > **Top**.
3. On the ribbon, click **Home > Create > Primitive Shape** . On the **Primitive Shape** dialog, select **Type > Circle**. Type-in 42 and 8 in the **Size** and **Circular** boxes, respectively.
4. Click and drag the move handle displayed on the circle to position it at the location, as shown. Click **OK** to create the circle.

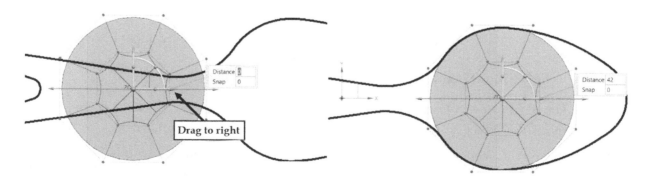

5. On the ribbon, click **Home > Modify > Transform Cage** . Click the **Reset** icon on the **Transform Cage** dialog. Click the **Transform** tab and select the right cage edge, as shown. Click and drag the Y-Translate up to the image outline, as shown. Click **OK**.

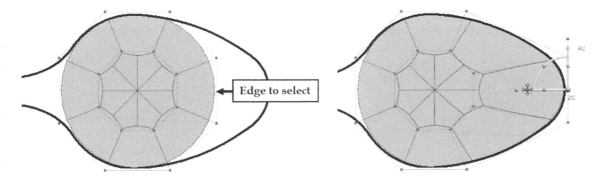

6. On the ribbon, click **Home > Create > Extrude Cage** , and then click the **Reset** icon on the **Extrude Cage** dialog. Click and drag the **Distance** handle up to the left end of the image. Click **OK**.

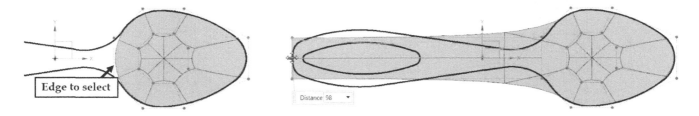

7. On the ribbon, click **Home > Modify > Split Face**. Click the **Reset** icon on the **Split Face** dialog. Select **Type > Uniform**.

8. Click on the extruded face to define the face to split. Next, click **Select Reference Edge** in the **Split** section of the dialog, and then select the horizontal cage edge, as shown. Type **3** in the **Number** box, and then click **OK**.

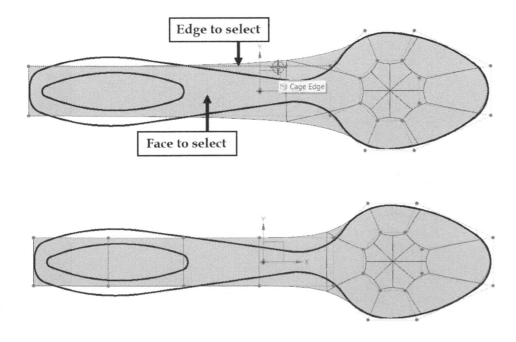

9. On the ribbon, click **Home > NX Realize Shape > Start Symmetric Modeling**. Click the **Reset** icon on the **Start Symmetric Modeling** dialog. Click on the XZ Plane of the Datum Coordinate System. Click **OK** to start symmetric modeling.

10. On the ribbon, click **Home > Modify > Transform Cage**. Click the **Reset** icon on the **Transform Cage** dialog. Click the **Transform** tab and select the cage edge, as shown. Click and drag the Y-Translate up to the position, as shown.

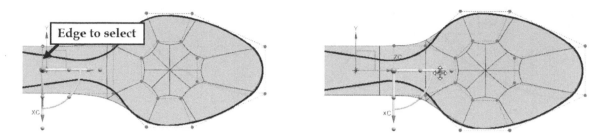

11. Click and drag the X-Scale handle downwards; the selected cage edge is scaled, as shown. Click **Apply**.

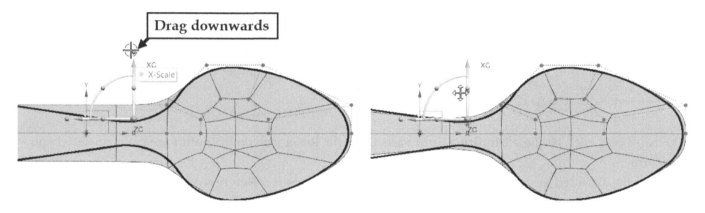

12. Select the cage edge and drag the X-Scale handle upwards, as shown. Click **Apply**.

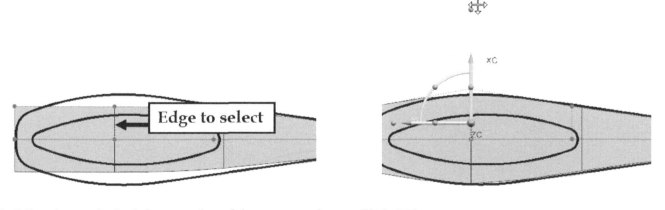

13. Likewise, scale the left most edge of the cage, as shown. Click **OK**.

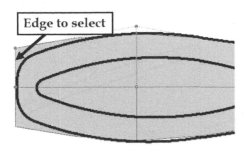

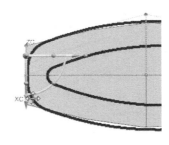

14. Change the view orientation the Trimetric. On the ribbon, click **Home > Modify > Transform Cage** . Click the **Transform** tab on the **Transform Cage** dialog. Next, select the cage face, as shown.

15. Change the view orientation to Front. Click and drag the Z-translate handle upward. Release the mouse button when the cage coincides with the lower edge of the image. Click **Apply**.

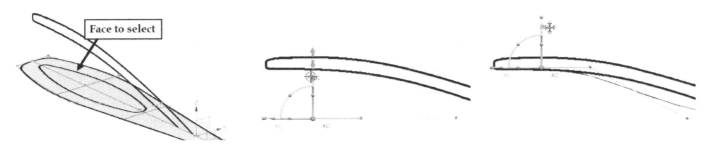

16. Change the view orientation to Trimetric. Click on the cage face, as shown.

17. Change the view orientation to Front. Click and drag the YZ-Rotate handle toward left to change the angle of the face.

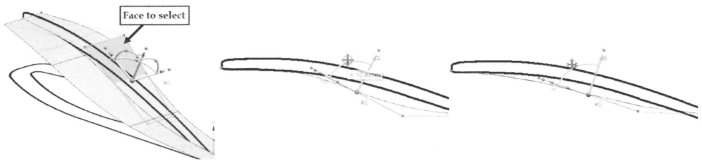

18. Click and drag the Z-Translate handle upward such that the face coincides with the lower edge in the image. Click **Apply**.

19. Change the view orientation to Trimetric. Click on the cage face, as shown. Next, change the view orientation to Front.

20. Click and drag the YZ-Rotate handle toward right. Next, drag the Z-Translate handle downward. Click **Apply**.

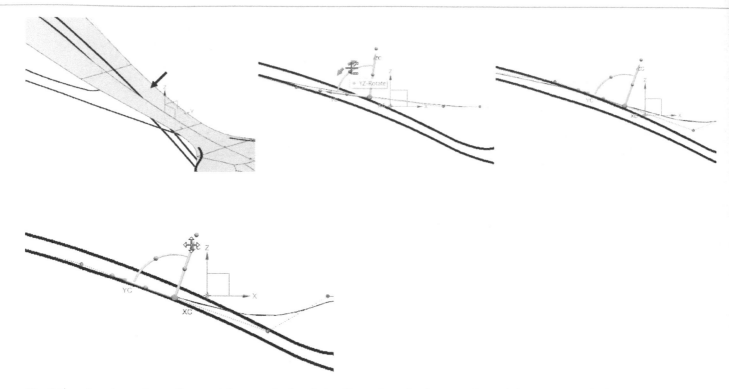

21. Likewise, transform the next face such that it is aligned to the lower edge of the image. Click **Apply**.

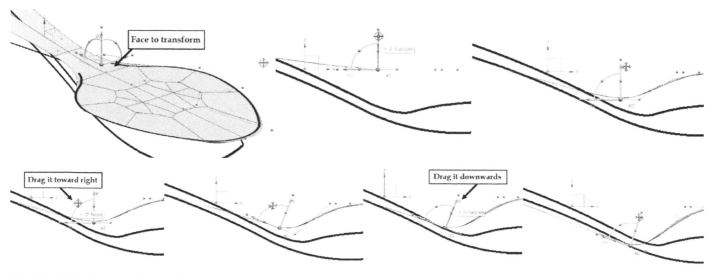

22. Modify the cage face adjacent to the previously modified face, as shown. Click **Apply**.

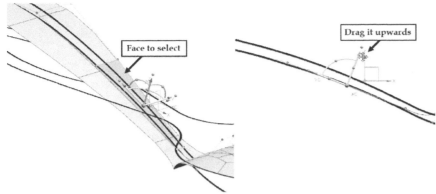

23. Transform the remaining faces to align them with the lower edge of the image. Click **OK**.

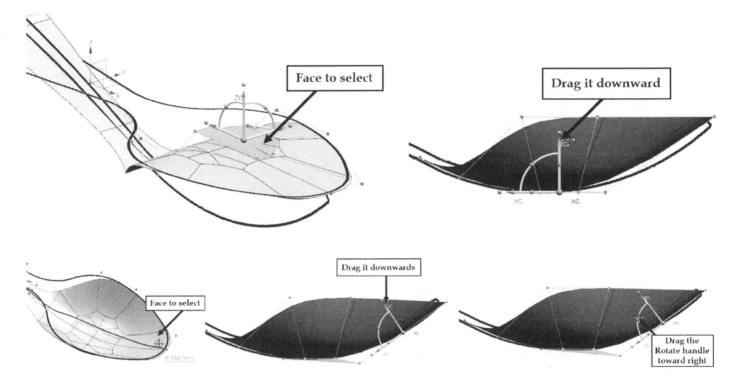

24. On the ribbon, click **Home > Create > Extrude Cage** . On the Top Border Bar, select **Selection Rule > Region**. Click anyone of the faces of the cage; all the faces are selected. Type 3 in the **Distance** box and click **OK**.

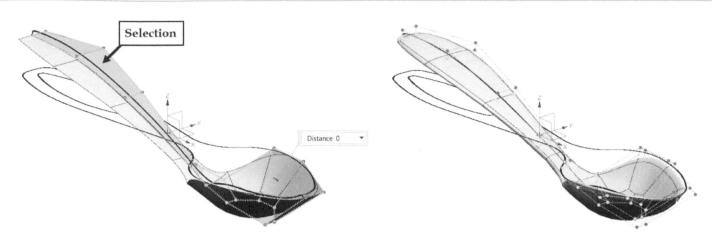

Creating a Cutout

1. On the ribbon, click **Home > Modify > Subdivide Face** . Select the faces of the cage, as shown. Type 40 in the **Percentage** box and click **Apply**.

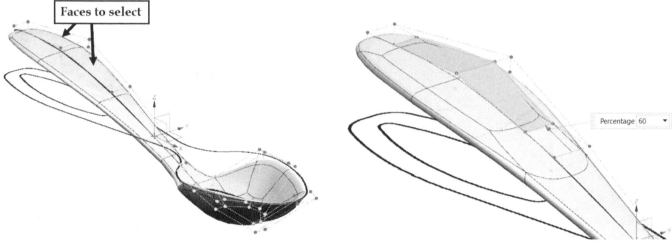

2. Rotate the model and click on the corresponding faces on the bottom side, as shown. Type **60** in the **Percentage** box and click **OK**.

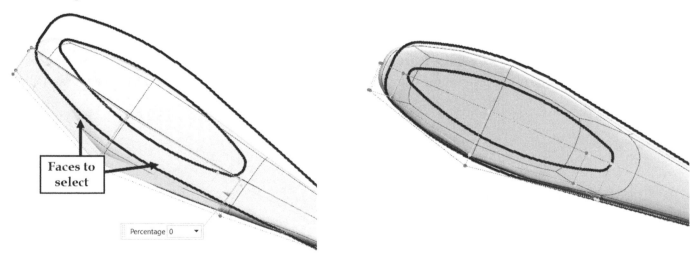

3. On the ribbon, click **Home > Create > Bridge Face** . Click the **Reset** icon on the **Bridge Face** dialog. Click on the cage faces on the top side of the model.

4. On the **Bridge Face** dialog, click **Select object** in the **Face Set 2** section. Rotate the model and select the two faces on the bottom side, as shown. Click **OK**.

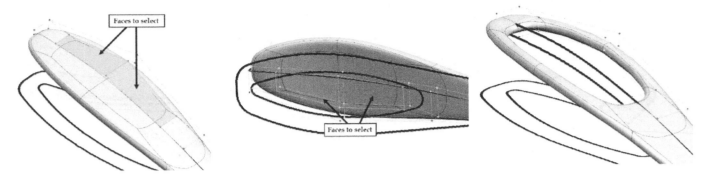

5. Click on the edge of the cage, as shown. Click the **Transform Cage** icon on the Context toolbar. Click the **Transform** tab on the **Transform Cage** dialog.

6. On the Top Border Bar, select **Orient** drop-down > **Top**. Drag the X-Translate handle toward left, as shown. Click **Apply**.

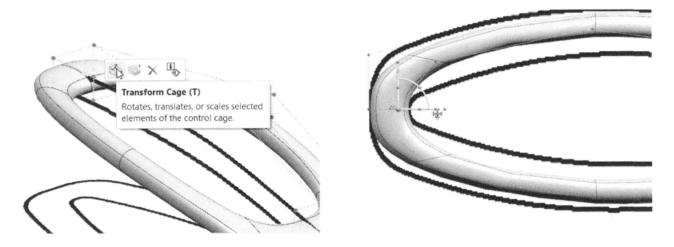

7. Likewise, transform the other edges of the bridged face.

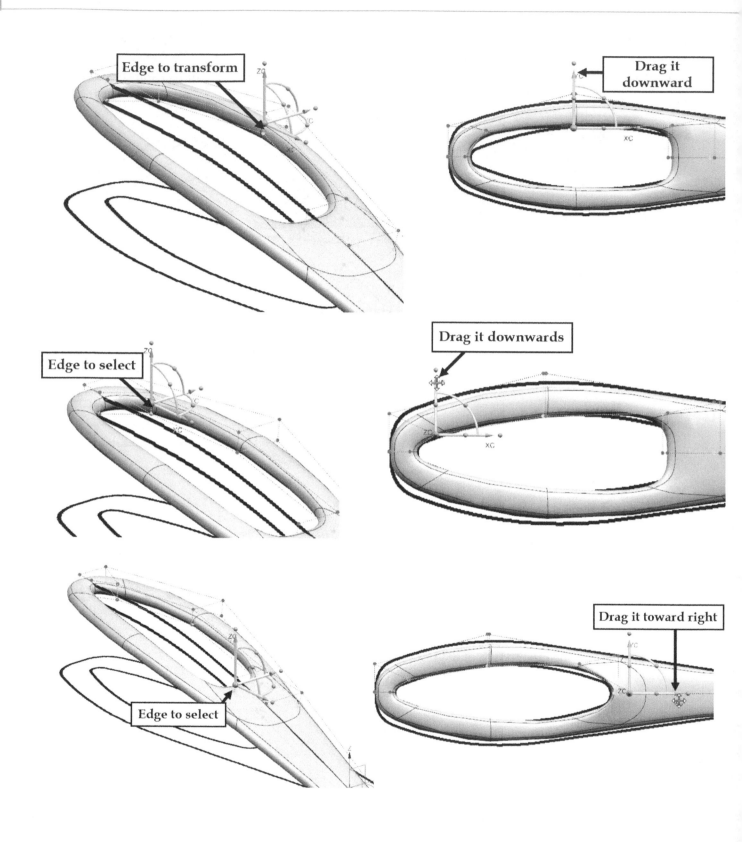

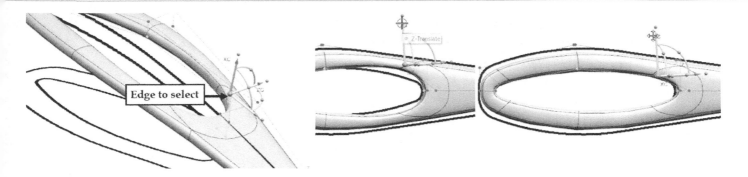

8. On the Top Border Bar, select **Orient** drop-down > **Front**. Activate the **Transform Cage** command and uncheck the **Reorient Tool to Selection** option in the **Transform** tab.

9. Select the cage edge, as shown. Click and drag the XZ-Rotate handle toward right.

10. Click and drag the Z-Translate handle downward, and then click **OK** on the **Transform Cage** dialog.

11. On the ribbon, click **Home > NZ Realize Shape > Finish**.

12. On the Top Border Bar, click **Show and Hide**. On the **Show and Hide** dialog, click the Hide icon next to the **Raster Images** option. Next, click the **Show and Hide** dialog.

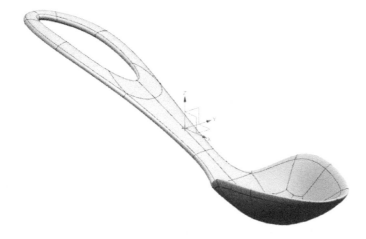

13. Save and close the file.

Questions

1. Explain how to bridge faces.
2. What are primitive shapes that you can create using the **Primitive Shapes** command?
3. Give one example of where you can use the **Bridge Face** command.
4. What is the difference between symmetric modeling and Mirror cage?
5. What are the two procedures to create cage polylines?

6. How can you change the size of a face using the **Transform Cage** command?
7. What is the difference between the **Subdivide Face** and **Split Face** command?

Index

Made in the USA
Monee, IL
17 November 2022

17970256R00254

CONTENTS

THE EXTRAORDINARY ADVENTURES OF ARSÈNE LUPIN, GENTLEMAN-BURGLAR

By Maurice Leblanc

I. The Arrest of Arsène Lupin

It was a strange ending to a voyage that had commenced in a most auspicious manner. The transatlantic steamship 'La Provence' was a swift and comfortable vessel, under the command of a most affable man. The passengers constituted a select and delightful society. The charm of new acquaintances and improvised amusements served to make the time pass agreeably. We enjoyed the pleasant sensation of being separated from the world, living, as it were, upon an unknown island, and consequently obliged to be sociable with each other.

Have you ever stopped to consider how much originality and spontaneity emanate from these various individuals who, on the preceding evening, did not even know each other, and who are now, for several days, condemned to lead a life of extreme intimacy, jointly defying the anger of the ocean, the terrible onslaught of the waves, the violence of the tempest and the agonizing monotony of the calm and sleepy water? Such a life becomes a sort of tragic existence, with its storms and its grandeurs, its monotony and its diversity; and that is why, perhaps, we embark upon that short voyage with mingled feelings of pleasure and fear.

But, during the past few years, a new sensation had been added to the life of the transatlantic traveler. The little floating island is now attached to the world from which it was once quite free. A bond united them, even in the very heart of the watery wastes of the Atlantic. That bond is the wireless telegraph, by means of which we receive news in the most mysterious manner. We know full well that the message is not transported by the medium of a hollow wire. No, the mystery is even more inexplicable, more romantic, and we must have recourse to the wings of the air in order to explain this new miracle. During the first day of the voyage, we felt that we were being followed, escorted, preceded even, by that distant voice, which, from time to time, whispered to one of us a few words from the receding world. Two friends spoke to me. Ten, twenty others sent gay or somber words of parting to other passengers.

On the second day, at a distance of five hundred miles from the French coast, in the midst of a violent storm, we received the following message by means of the wireless telegraph:

"Arsène Lupin is on your vessel, first cabin, blonde hair, wound right fore-arm, traveling alone under name of R........"

At that moment, a terrible flash of lightning rent the stormy skies. The electric waves were interrupted. The remainder of the dispatch never reached us. Of the name under which Arsène Lupin was concealing himself, we knew only the initial.

If the news had been of some other character, I have no doubt that the secret would have been carefully guarded by the telegraphic operator as well as by the officers of the vessel. But it was one of those events calculated to escape from the most rigorous discretion. The same day, no one knew how, the incident became a matter of current gossip and every passenger was aware that the famous Arsène Lupin was hiding in our midst.

Arsène Lupin in our midst! the irresponsible burglar whose exploits had been narrated in all the newspapers during the past few months! the mysterious individual with whom Ganimard, our shrewdest detective, had been engaged in an implacable conflict amidst interesting and picturesque surroundings. Arsène Lupin, the eccentric gentleman who operates only in the chateaux and salons, and who, one night, entered the residence of Baron Schormann, but emerged empty-handed, leaving, however, his card on which he had scribbled these words: "Arsène Lupin, gentleman-burglar, will return when the furniture is genuine." Arsène Lupin, the man of a thousand disguises: in turn a chauffer, detective, bookmaker, Russian physician, Spanish bull-fighter, commercial traveler, robust youth, or decrepit old man.

Then consider this startling situation: Arsène Lupin was wandering about within the limited bounds of a transatlantic steamer; in that very small corner of the world, in that dining saloon, in that smoking room, in that music room! Arsène Lupin was, perhaps, this gentleman.... or that one.... my neighbor at the table.... the sharer of my stateroom....

"And this condition of affairs will last for five days!" exclaimed Miss Nelly Underdown, next morning. "It is unbearable! I hope he will be arrested."

Then, addressing me, she added:

"And you, Monsieur d'Andrézy, you are on intimate terms with the captain; surely you know something?"

I should have been delighted had I possessed any information that would interest Miss Nelly. She was one of those magnificent creatures who inevitably attract attention in every assembly. Wealth and beauty form an irresistible combination, and Nelly possessed both.

Educated in Paris under the care of a French mother, she was now going to visit her father, the millionaire Underdown of Chicago. She was accompanied by one of her friends, Lady Jerland.

At first, I had decided to open a flirtation with her; but, in the rapidly growing intimacy of the voyage, I was soon impressed by her charming manner and my feelings became too deep and reverential for a mere flirtation. Moreover, she accepted my attentions with a certain degree of favor. She condescended to laugh at my witticisms and display an interest in my stories. Yet I felt that I had a rival in the person of a young man with quiet and refined tastes; and it struck me, at times, that she preferred his taciturn humor to my Parisian frivolity. He formed one in the circle of admirers that surrounded Miss Nelly at the time she addressed to me the foregoing question. We were all comfortably seated in our deck-chairs. The storm of the preceding evening had cleared the sky. The weather was now delightful.

"I have no definite knowledge, mademoiselle," I replied, "but can not we, ourselves, investigate the mystery quite as well as the detective Ganimard, the personal enemy of Arsène Lupin?"

"Oh! oh! you are progressing very fast, monsieur."

"Not at all, mademoiselle. In the first place, let me ask, do you find the problem a complicated one?"

"Very complicated."

"Have you forgotten the key we hold for the solution to the problem?"

"What key?"

"In the first place, Lupin calls himself Monsieur R————-."

"Rather vague information," she replied.

"Secondly, he is traveling alone."

"Does that help you?" she asked.

"Thirdly, he is blonde."

"Well?"

"Then we have only to peruse the passenger-list, and proceed by process of elimination."

I had that list in my pocket. I took it out and glanced through it. Then I remarked:

"I find that there are only thirteen men on the passenger-list whose names begin with the letter R."

"Only thirteen?"

"Yes, in the first cabin. And of those thirteen, I find that nine of them are accompanied by women, children or servants. That leaves only four who are traveling alone. First, the Marquis de Raverdan————"

"Secretary to the American Ambassador," interrupted Miss Nelly. "I know him."

"Major Rawson," I continued.

"He is my uncle," some one said.

"Mon. Rivolta."

"Here!" exclaimed an Italian, whose face was concealed beneath a heavy black beard.

Miss Nelly burst into laughter, and exclaimed: "That gentleman can scarcely be called a blonde."

"Very well, then," I said, "we are forced to the conclusion that the guilty party is the last one on the list."

"What is his name?"

"Mon. Rozaine. Does anyone know him?"

No one answered. But Miss Nelly turned to the taciturn young man, whose attentions to her had annoyed me, and said:

"Well, Monsieur Rozaine, why do you not answer?"

All eyes were now turned upon him. He was a blonde. I must confess that I myself felt a shock of surprise, and the profound silence that followed her question indicated that the others present also viewed the situation with a feeling of sudden alarm. However, the idea was an absurd one, because the gentleman in question presented an air of the most perfect innocence.

"Why do I not answer?" he said. "Because, considering my name, my position as a solitary traveler and the color of my hair, I have already reached the same conclusion, and now think that I should be arrested."

He presented a strange appearance as he uttered these words. His thin lips were drawn closer than usual and his face was ghastly pale, whilst his eyes were streaked with blood. Of course, he was joking, yet his appearance and attitude impressed us strangely.

"But you have not the wound?" said Miss Nelly, naively.

"That is true," he replied, "I lack the wound."

Then he pulled up his sleeve, removing his cuff, and showed us his arm. But that action did not deceive me. He had shown us his left arm, and I was on the point of calling his attention to the fact, when another incident diverted our attention. Lady Jerland, Miss Nelly's friend, came running towards us in a state of great excitement, exclaiming:

"My jewels, my pearls! Some one has stolen them all!"

No, they were not all gone, as we soon found out. The thief had taken only part of them; a very curious thing. Of the diamond sunbursts, jeweled pendants, bracelets and necklaces, the thief had taken, not the largest but the finest and most valuable stones. The mountings were lying upon the table. I saw them there, despoiled of their jewels, like flowers from which the beautiful colored petals had been ruthlessly plucked. And this theft must have been committed at the time Lady Jerland was taking her tea; in broad daylight, in a stateroom opening on a much frequented corridor; moreover, the thief had been obliged to force open the door of the stateroom, search for the jewel-case, which was hidden at the bottom of a hat-box, open it, select his booty and remove it from the mountings.

Of course, all the passengers instantly reached the same conclusion; it was the work of Arsène Lupin.

That day, at the dinner table, the seats to the right and left of Rozaine remained vacant; and, during the evening, it was rumored that the captain had placed him under arrest, which information produced a feeling of safety and relief. We breathed once more. That evening, we resumed our games and dances. Miss Nelly, especially, displayed a spirit of thoughtless gayety which convinced me that if Rozaine's attentions had been agreeable to her in the beginning, she had already forgotten them. Her charm and good-humor completed my conquest. At midnight, under a bright moon, I declared my devotion with an ardor that did not seem to displease her.

But, next day, to our general amazement, Rozaine was at liberty. We learned that the evidence against him was not sufficient. He had produced documents that were perfectly regular, which showed that he was the son of a wealthy merchant of Bordeaux. Besides, his arms did not bear the slightest trace of a wound.

"Documents! Certificates of birth!" exclaimed the enemies of Rozaine, "of course, Arsène Lupin will furnish you as many as you desire. And as to the wound, he never had it, or he has removed it."

Then it was proven that, at the time of the theft, Rozaine was promenading on the deck. To which fact, his enemies replied that a man like Arsène Lupin could commit a crime without being actually present. And then, apart from all other circumstances, there remained one point which even the most skeptical could not answer: Who except Rozaine, was traveling alone, was a blonde, and bore a name beginning with R? To whom did the telegram point, if it were not Rozaine?

And when Rozaine, a few minutes before breakfast, came boldly toward our group, Miss Nelly and Lady Jerland arose and walked away.

An hour later, a manuscript circular was passed from hand to hand amongst the sailors, the stewards, and the passengers of all classes. It announced that Mon. Louis Rozaine offered a reward of ten thousand francs for the discovery of Arsène Lupin or other person in possession of the stolen jewels.

"And if no one assists me, I will unmask the scoundrel myself," declared Rozaine.

Rozaine against Arsène Lupin, or rather, according to current opinion, Arsène Lupin himself against Arsène Lupin; the contest promised to be interesting.

Nothing developed during the next two days. We saw Rozaine wandering about, day and night, searching, questioning, investigating. The captain, also, displayed commendable activity. He caused the vessel to be searched from stern to stern; ransacked every stateroom under the plausible theory that the jewels might be concealed anywhere, except in the thief's own room.

"I suppose they will find out something soon," remarked Miss Nelly to me. "He may be a wizard, but he cannot make diamonds and pearls become invisible."

"Certainly not," I replied, "but he should examine the lining of our hats and vests and everything we carry with us."

Then, exhibiting my Kodak, a 9x12 with which I had been photographing her in various poses, I added: "In an apparatus no larger than that, a person could hide all of Lady Jerland's jewels. He could pretend to take pictures and no one would suspect the game."

"But I have heard it said that every thief leaves some clue behind him."

"That may be generally true," I replied, "but there is one exception: Arsène Lupin."

"Why?"

"Because he concentrates his thoughts not only on the theft, but on all the circumstances connected with it that could serve as a clue to his identity."

"A few days ago, you were more confident."

"Yes, but since I have seen him at work."

"And what do you think about it now?" she asked.

"Well, in my opinion, we are wasting our time."

And, as a matter of fact, the investigation had produced no result. But, in the meantime, the captain's watch had been stolen. He was furious. He quickened his efforts and watched Rozaine more closely than before. But, on the following day, the watch was found in the second officer's collar box.

This incident caused considerable astonishment, and displayed the humorous side of Arsène Lupin, burglar though he was, but dilettante as well. He combined business with pleasure. He reminded us of the author who almost died in a fit of laughter provoked by his own play. Certainly, he was an artist in his particular line of work, and whenever I saw Rozaine, gloomy and reserved, and thought of the double role that he was playing, I accorded him a certain measure of admiration.

On the following evening, the officer on deck duty heard groans emanating from the darkest corner of the ship. He approached and found a man lying there, his head enveloped in a thick gray scarf and his hands tied together with a heavy cord. It was Rozaine. He had been assaulted, thrown down and robbed. A card, pinned to his coat, bore these words: "Arsène Lupin accepts with pleasure the ten thousand francs offered by Mon. Rozaine." As a matter of fact, the stolen pocket-book contained twenty thousand francs.

Of course, some accused the unfortunate man of having simulated this attack on himself. But, apart from the fact that he could not have bound himself in that manner, it was established that the writing on the card was entirely different from that of Rozaine, but, on the contrary, resembled the handwriting of Arsène Lupin as it was reproduced in an old newspaper found on board.

Thus it appeared that Rozaine was not Arsène Lupin; but was Rozaine, the son of a Bordeaux merchant. And the presence of Arsène Lupin was once more affirmed, and that in a most alarming manner.

Such was the state of terror amongst the passengers that none would remain alone in a stateroom or wander singly in unfrequented parts of the vessel. We clung together as a matter of safety. And yet the most intimate acquaintances were estranged by a mutual feeling of distrust. Arsène Lupin was, now, anybody and everybody. Our excited imaginations attributed to him miraculous and unlimited power. We supposed him capable of assuming the most unexpected disguises; of being, by turns, the highly respectable Major Rawson or the noble Marquis de Raverdan, or even—for we no longer stopped with the accusing letter of R—or even such or such a person well known to all of us, and having wife, children and servants.

The first wireless dispatches from America brought no news; at least, the captain did not communicate any to us. The silence was not reassuring.

Our last day on the steamer seemed interminable. We lived in constant fear of some disaster. This time, it would not be a simple theft or a comparatively harmless assault; it would be a crime, a murder. No one imagined that Arsène Lupin would confine himself to those two trifling offenses. Absolute master of the ship, the authorities powerless, he could do whatever he pleased; our property and lives were at his mercy.

Yet those were delightful hours for me, since they secured to me the confidence of Miss Nelly. Deeply moved by those startling events and being of a highly nervous nature, she spontaneously sought at my side a protection and security that I was pleased to give her.

Inwardly, I blessed Arsène Lupin. Had he not been the means of bringing me and Miss Nelly closer to each other? Thanks to him, I could now indulge in delicious dreams of love and happiness—dreams that, I felt, were not unwelcome to Miss Nelly. Her smiling eyes authorized me to make them; the softness of her voice bade me hope.

As we approached the American shore, the active search for the thief was apparently abandoned, and we were anxiously awaiting the supreme moment in which the mysterious enigma would be explained. Who was Arsène Lupin? Under what name, under what disguise was the famous Arsène Lupin concealing himself? And, at last, that supreme moment arrived. If I live one hundred years, I shall not forget the slightest details of it.

"How pale you are, Miss Nelly," I said to my companion, as she leaned upon my arm, almost fainting.

"And you!" she replied, "ah! you are so changed."

"Just think! this is a most exciting moment, and I am delighted to spend it with you, Miss Nelly. I hope that your memory will sometimes revert—-"

But she was not listening. She was nervous and excited. The gangway was placed in position, but, before we could use it, the uniformed customs officers came on board. Miss Nelly murmured:

"I shouldn't be surprised to hear that Arsène Lupin escaped from the vessel during the voyage."

"Perhaps he preferred death to dishonor, and plunged into the Atlantic rather than be arrested."

"Oh, do not laugh," she said.

Suddenly I started, and, in answer to her question, I said:

"Do you see that little old man standing at the bottom of the gangway?"

"With an umbrella and an olive-green coat?"

"It is Ganimard."

"Ganimard?"

"Yes, the celebrated detective who has sworn to capture Arsène Lupin. Ah! I can understand now why we did not receive any news from this side of the Atlantic. Ganimard was here! and he always keeps his business secret."

"Then you think he will arrest Arsène Lupin?"

"Who can tell? The unexpected always happens when Arsène Lupin is concerned in the affair."

"Oh!" she exclaimed, with that morbid curiosity peculiar to women, "I should like to see him arrested."

"You will have to be patient. No doubt, Arsène Lupin has already seen his enemy and will not be in a hurry to leave the steamer."

The passengers were now leaving the steamer. Leaning on his umbrella, with an air of careless indifference, Ganimard appeared to be paying no attention to the crowd that was

10

hurrying down the gangway. The Marquis de Raverdan, Major Rawson, the Italian Rivolta, and many others had already left the vessel before Rozaine appeared. Poor Rozaine!

"Perhaps it is he, after all," said Miss Nelly to me. "What do you think?"

"I think it would be very interesting to have Ganimard and Rozaine in the same picture. You take the camera. I am loaded down."

I gave her the camera, but too late for her to use it. Rozaine was already passing the detective. An American officer, standing behind Ganimard, leaned forward and whispered in his ear. The French detective shrugged his shoulders and Rozaine passed on. Then, my God, who was Arsène Lupin?

"Yes," said Miss Nelly, aloud, "who can it be?"

Not more than twenty people now remained on board. She scrutinized them one by one, fearful that Arsène Lupin was not amongst them.

"We cannot wait much longer," I said to her.

She started toward the gangway. I followed. But we had not taken ten steps when Ganimard barred our passage.

"Well, what is it?" I exclaimed.

"One moment, monsieur. What's your hurry?"

"I am escorting mademoiselle."

"One moment," he repeated, in a tone of authority. Then, gazing into my eyes, he said:

"Arsène Lupin, is it not?"

I laughed, and replied: "No, simply Bernard d'Andrézy."

"Bernard d'Andrézy died in Macedonia three years ago."

"If Bernard d'Andrézy were dead, I should not be here. But you are mistaken. Here are my papers."

"They are his; and I can tell you exactly how they came into your possession."

"You are a fool!" I exclaimed. "Arsène Lupin sailed under the name of R——-"

"Yes, another of your tricks; a false scent that deceived them at Havre. You play a good game, my boy, but this time luck is against you."

I hesitated a moment. Then he hit me a sharp blow on the right arm, which caused me to utter a cry of pain. He had struck the wound, yet unhealed, referred to in the telegram.

I was obliged to surrender. There was no alternative. I turned to Miss Nelly, who had heard everything. Our eyes met; then she glanced at the Kodak I had placed in her hands, and made a gesture that conveyed to me the impression that she understood everything. Yes, there, between the narrow folds of black leather, in the hollow centre of the small object that I had taken the precaution to place in her hands before Ganimard arrested me, it was there I had deposited Rozaine's twenty thousand francs and Lady Jerland's pearls and diamonds.

Oh! I pledge my oath that, at that solemn moment, when I was in the grasp of Ganimard and his two assistants, I was perfectly indifferent to everything, to my arrest, the hostility of the people, everything except this one question: what will Miss Nelly do with the things I had confided to her?

In the absence of that material and conclusive proof, I had nothing to fear; but would Miss Nelly decide to furnish that proof? Would she betray me? Would she act the part of an enemy who cannot forgive, or that of a woman whose scorn is softened by feelings of indulgence and involuntary sympathy?

She passed in front of me. I said nothing, but bowed very low. Mingled with the other passengers, she advanced to the gangway with my Kodak in her hand. It occurred to me that she would not dare to expose me publicly, but she might do so when she reached a more private place. However, when she had passed only a few feet down the gangway, with a movement of simulated awkwardness, she let the camera fall into the water between the vessel and the pier. Then she walked down the gangway, and was quickly lost to sight in the crowd. She had passed out of my life forever.

For a moment, I stood motionless. Then, to Ganimard's great astonishment, I muttered:

"What a pity that I am not an honest man!"

Such was the story of his arrest as narrated to me by Arsène Lupin himself. The various incidents, which I shall record in writing at a later day, have established between us certain ties.... shall I say of friendship? Yes, I venture to believe that Arsène Lupin honors me with his friendship, and that it is through friendship that he occasionally calls on me, and brings, into the silence of my library, his youthful exuberance of spirits, the contagion of his enthusiasm, and the mirth of a man for whom destiny has naught but favors and smiles.

His portrait? How can I describe him? I have seen him twenty times and each time he was a different person; even he himself said to me on one occasion: "I no longer know who I am. I cannot recognize myself in the mirror." Certainly, he was a great actor, and possessed a marvelous faculty for disguising himself. Without the slightest effort, he could adopt the voice, gestures and mannerisms of another person.

"Why," said he, "why should I retain a definite form and feature? Why not avoid the danger of a personality that is ever the same? My actions will serve to identify me."

Then he added, with a touch of pride:

"So much the better if no one can ever say with absolute certainty: There is Arsène Lupin! The essential point is that the public may be able to refer to my work and say, without fear of mistake: Arsène Lupin did that!"

II. Arsène Lupin in Prison

There is no tourist worthy of the name who does not know the banks of the Seine, and has not noticed, in passing, the little feudal castle of the Malaquis, built upon a rock in the centre of the river. An arched bridge connects it with the shore. All around it, the calm waters of the great river play peacefully amongst the reeds, and the wagtails flutter over the moist crests of the stones.

The history of the Malaquis castle is stormy like its name, harsh like its outlines. It has passed through a long series of combats, sieges, assaults, rapines and massacres. A recital of the crimes that have been committed there would cause the stoutest heart to tremble. There are many mysterious legends connected with the castle, and they tell us of a famous subterranean tunnel that formerly led to the abbey of Jumieges and to the manor of Agnes Sorel, mistress of Charles VII.

In that ancient habitation of heroes and brigands, the Baron Nathan Cahorn now lived; or Baron Satan as he was formerly called on the Bourse, where he had acquired a fortune with incredible rapidity. The lords of Malaquis, absolutely ruined, had been obliged to sell the ancient castle at a great sacrifice. It contained an admirable collection of furniture, pictures, wood carvings, and faience. The Baron lived there alone, attended by three old servants. No one ever enters the place. No one had ever beheld the three Rubens that he possessed, his two Watteau, his Jean Goujon pulpit, and the many other treasures that he had acquired by a vast expenditure of money at public sales.

Baron Satan lived in constant fear, not for himself, but for the treasures that he had accumulated with such an earnest devotion and with so much perspicacity that the shrewdest merchant could not say that the Baron had ever erred in his taste or judgment. He loved them—his bibelots. He loved them intensely, like a miser; jealously, like a lover. Every day, at sunset, the iron gates at either end of the bridge and at the entrance to the court of honor are closed and barred. At the least touch on these gates, electric bells will ring throughout the castle.

One Thursday in September, a letter-carrier presented himself at the gate at the head of the bridge, and, as usual, it was the Baron himself who partially opened the heavy portal. He scrutinized the man as minutely as if he were a stranger, although the honest face and twinkling eyes of the postman had been familiar to the Baron for many years. The man laughed, as he said:

"It is only I, Monsieur le Baron. It is not another man wearing my cap and blouse."

"One can never tell," muttered the Baron.

The man handed him a number of newspapers, and then said:

"And now, Monsieur le Baron, here is something new."

"Something new?"

"Yes, a letter. A registered letter."

Living as a recluse, without friends or business relations, the baron never received any letters, and the one now presented to him immediately aroused within him a feeling of suspicion and distrust. It was like an evil omen. Who was this mysterious correspondent that dared to disturb the tranquility of his retreat?

"You must sign for it, Monsieur le Baron."

He signed; then took the letter, waited until the postman had disappeared beyond the bend in the road, and, after walking nervously to and fro for a few minutes, he leaned against the parapet of the bridge and opened the envelope. It contained a sheet of paper, bearing this heading: Prison de la Santé, Paris. He looked at the signature: Arsène Lupin. Then he read:

"*Monsieur le Baron:*

"*There is, in the gallery in your castle, a picture of Philippe*
de Champaigne, of exquisite finish, which pleases me beyond
measure. Your Rubens are also to my taste, as well as your
smallest Watteau. In the salon to the right, I have noticed the
Louis XIII cadence-table, the tapestries of Beauvais, the Empire
gueridon signed 'Jacob,' and the Renaissance chest. In the salon
to the left, all the cabinet full of jewels and miniatures.

"*For the present, I will content myself with those articles that*
can be conveniently removed. I will therefore ask you to pack
them carefully and ship them to me, charges prepaid, to the
station at Batignolles, within eight days, otherwise I shall be
obliged to remove them myself during the night of 27 September;
but, under those circumstances, I shall not content myself with
the articles above mentioned.

"*Accept my apologies for any inconvenience I may cause you, and*
believe me to be your humble servant,

"*Arsène Lupin.*"

14

> "P. S.—Please do not send the largest
> Watteau. Although you
>   paid thirty thousand francs for it, it
> is only a copy, the
>   original having been burned, under the
> Directoire by Barras,
>   during a night of debauchery. Consult
> the memoirs of Garat.

> "I do not care for the Louis XV
> chatelaine, as I doubt its
>   authenticity."

That letter completely upset the baron. Had it borne any other signature, he would have been greatly alarmed—but signed by Arsène Lupin!

As an habitual reader of the newspapers, he was versed in the history of recent crimes, and was therefore well acquainted with the exploits of the mysterious burglar. Of course, he knew that Lupin had been arrested in America by his enemy Ganimard and was at present incarcerated in the Prison de la Santé. But he knew also that any miracle might be expected from Arsène Lupin. Moreover, that exact knowledge of the castle, the location of the pictures and furniture, gave the affair an alarming aspect. How could he have acquired that information concerning things that no one had ever seen?

The baron raised his eyes and contemplated the stern outlines of the castle, its steep rocky pedestal, the depth of the surrounding water, and shrugged his shoulders. Certainly, there was no danger. No one in the world could force an entrance to the sanctuary that contained his priceless treasures.

No one, perhaps, but Arsène Lupin! For him, gates, walls and drawbridges did not exist. What use were the most formidable obstacles or the most careful precautions, if Arsène Lupin had decided to effect an entrance?

That evening, he wrote to the Procurer of the Republique at Rouen. He enclosed the threatening letter and solicited aid and protection.

The reply came at once to the effect that Arsène Lupin was in custody in the Prison de la Santé, under close surveillance, with no opportunity to write such a letter, which was, no doubt, the work of some imposter. But, as an act of precaution, the Procurer had submitted the letter to an expert in handwriting, who declared that, in spite of certain resemblances, the writing was not that of the prisoner.

But the words "in spite of certain resemblances" caught the attention of the baron; in them, he read the possibility of a doubt which appeared to him quite sufficient to warrant the intervention of the law. His fears increased. He read Lupin's letter over and over again. "I shall be obliged to remove them myself." And then there was the fixed date: the night of 27 September.

To confide in his servants was a proceeding repugnant to his nature; but now, for the first time in many years, he experienced the necessity of seeking counsel with some one. Abandoned by the legal official of his own district, and feeling unable to defend himself with his own resources, he was on the point of going to Paris to engage the services of a detective.

Two days passed; on the third day, he was filled with hope and joy as he read the following item in the 'Réveil de Caudebec', a newspaper published in a neighboring town:

"We have the pleasure of entertaining in our city, at the present time, the veteran detective Mon. Ganimard who acquired a world-wide reputation by his clever capture of Arsène Lupin. He has come here for rest and recreation, and, being an enthusiastic fisherman, he threatens to capture all the fish in our river."

Ganimard! Ah, here is the assistance desired by Baron Cahorn! Who could baffle the schemes of Arsène Lupin better than Ganimard, the patient and astute detective? He was the man for the place.

The baron did not hesitate. The town of Caudebec was only six kilometers from the castle, a short distance to a man whose step was accelerated by the hope of safety.

After several fruitless attempts to ascertain the detective's address, the baron visited the office of the 'Réveil,' situated on the quai. There he found the writer of the article who, approaching the window, exclaimed:

"Ganimard? Why, you are sure to see him somewhere on the quai with his fishing-pole. I met him there and chanced to read his name engraved on his rod. Ah, there he is now, under the trees."

"That little man, wearing a straw hat?"

"Exactly. He is a gruff fellow, with little to say."

Five minutes later, the baron approached the celebrated Ganimard, introduced himself, and sought to commence a conversation, but that was a failure. Then he broached the real object of his interview, and briefly stated his case. The other listened, motionless, with his attention riveted on his fishing-rod. When the baron had finished his story, the fisherman turned, with an air of profound pity, and said:

"Monsieur, it is not customary for thieves to warn people they are about to rob. Arsène Lupin, especially, would not commit such a folly."

"But——"

"Monsieur, if I had the least doubt, believe me, the pleasure of again capturing Arsène Lupin would place me at your disposal. But, unfortunately, that young man is already under lock and key."

"He may have escaped."

"No one ever escaped from the Santé."

"But, he——"

"He, no more than any other."

"Yet——"

"Well, if he escapes, so much the better. I will catch him again. Meanwhile, you go home and sleep soundly. That will do for the present. You frighten the fish."

The conversation was ended. The baron returned to the castle, reassured to some extent by Ganimard's indifference. He examined the bolts, watched the servants, and, during the next forty-eight hours, he became almost persuaded that his fears were groundless. Certainly, as Ganimard had said, thieves do not warn people they are about to rob.

The fateful day was close at hand. It was now the twenty-sixth of September and nothing had happened. But at three o'clock the bell rang. A boy brought this telegram:

"No goods at Batignolles station. Prepare everything for tomorrow night. Arsène."

This telegram threw the baron into such a state of excitement that he even considered the advisability of yielding to Lupin's demands.

However, he hastened to Caudebec. Ganimard was fishing at the same place, seated on a campstool. Without a word, he handed him the telegram.

"Well, what of it?" said the detective.

"What of it? But it is tomorrow."

"What is tomorrow?"

"The robbery! The pillage of my collections!"

Ganimard laid down his fishing-rod, turned to the baron, and exclaimed, in a tone of impatience:

"Ah! Do you think I am going to bother myself about such a silly story as that!"

"How much do you ask to pass tomorrow night in the castle?"

"Not a sou. Now, leave me alone."

"Name your own price. I am rich and can pay it."

This offer disconcerted Ganimard, who replied, calmly:

"I am here on a vacation. I have no right to undertake such work."

"No one will know. I promise to keep it secret."

"Oh! nothing will happen."

"Come! three thousand francs. Will that be enough?"

The detective, after a moment's reflection, said:

"Very well. But I must warn you that you are throwing your money out of the window."

"I do not care."

"In that case... but, after all, what do we know about this devil Lupin! He may have quite a numerous band of robbers with him. Are you sure of your servants?"

"My faith——"

"Better not count on them. I will telegraph for two of my men to help me. And now, go! It is better for us not to be seen together. Tomorrow evening about nine o'clock."

The following day—the date fixed by Arsène Lupin—Baron Cahorn arranged all his panoply of war, furbished his weapons, and, like a sentinel, paced to and fro in front of the castle. He saw nothing, heard nothing. At half-past eight o'clock in the evening, he dismissed his servants. They occupied rooms in a wing of the building, in a retired spot, well removed from the main portion of the castle. Shortly thereafter, the baron heard the sound of approaching footsteps. It was Ganimard and his two assistants—great, powerful fellows with immense hands, and necks like bulls. After asking a few questions relating to the location of the various entrances and rooms, Ganimard carefully closed and barricaded all the doors and windows through which one could gain access to the threatened rooms. He inspected the walls, raised the tapestries, and finally installed his assistants in the central gallery which was located between the two salons.

"No nonsense! We are not here to sleep. At the slightest sound, open the windows of the court and call me. Pay attention also to the water-side. Ten metres of perpendicular rock is no obstacle to those devils."

Ganimard locked his assistants in the gallery, carried away the keys, and said to the baron:

"And now, to our post."

He had chosen for himself a small room located in the thick outer wall, between the two principal doors, and which, in former years, had been the watchman's quarters. A peep-hole opened upon the bridge; another on the court. In one corner, there was an opening to a tunnel.

"I believe you told me, Monsieur le Baron, that this tunnel is the only subterranean entrance to the castle and that it has been closed up for time immemorial?"

"Yes."

"Then, unless there is some other entrance, known only to Arsène Lupin, we are quite safe."

He placed three chairs together, stretched himself upon them, lighted his pipe and sighed:

"Really, Monsieur le Baron, I feel ashamed to accept your money for such a sinecure as this. I will tell the story to my friend Lupin. He will enjoy it immensely."

The baron did not laugh. He was anxiously listening, but heard nothing save the beating of his own heart. From time to time, he leaned over the tunnel and cast a fearful eye into its depths. He heard the clock strike eleven, twelve, one.

Suddenly, he seized Ganimard's arm. The latter leaped up, awakened from his sleep.

"Do you hear?" asked the baron, in a whisper.

"Yes."

"What is it?"

"I was snoring, I suppose."

"No, no, listen."

"Ah! yes, it is the horn of an automobile."

"Well?"

"Well! it is very improbable that Lupin would use an automobile like a battering-ram to demolish your castle. Come, Monsieur le Baron, return to your post. I am going to sleep. Good-night."

That was the only alarm. Ganimard resumed his interrupted slumbers, and the baron heard nothing except the regular snoring of his companion. At break of day, they left the room. The castle was enveloped in a profound calm; it was a peaceful dawn on the bosom of a tranquil river. They mounted the stairs, Cahorn radiant with joy, Ganimard calm as usual. They heard no sound; they saw nothing to arouse suspicion.

"What did I tell you, Monsieur le Baron? Really, I should not have accepted your offer. I am ashamed."

He unlocked the door and entered the gallery. Upon two chairs, with drooping heads and pendent arms, the detective's two assistants were asleep.

"Tonnerre de nom d'un chien!" exclaimed Ganimard. At the same moment, the baron cried out:

"The pictures! The credence!"

He stammered, choked, with arms outstretched toward the empty places, toward the denuded walls where naught remained but the useless nails and cords. The Watteau, disappeared! The Rubens, carried away! The tapestries taken down! The cabinets, despoiled of their jewels!

"And my Louis XVI candelabra! And the Regent chandelier!...And my twelfth-century Virgin!"

He ran from one spot to another in wildest despair. He recalled the purchase price of each article, added up the figures, counted his losses, pell-mell, in confused words and unfinished phrases. He stamped with rage; he groaned with grief. He acted like a ruined man whose only hope is suicide.

If anything could have consoled him, it would have been the stupefaction displayed by Ganimard. The famous detective did not move. He appeared to be petrified; he examined the room in a listless manner. The windows?.... closed. The locks on the doors?.... intact. Not a break in the ceiling; not a hole in the floor. Everything was in perfect order. The theft had been carried out methodically, according to a logical and inexorable plan.

"Arsène Lupin....Arsène Lupin," he muttered.

Suddenly, as if moved by anger, he rushed upon his two assistants and shook them violently. They did not awaken.

"The devil!" he cried. "Can it be possible?"

He leaned over them and, in turn, examined them closely. They were asleep; but their response was unnatural.

"They have been drugged," he said to the baron.

"By whom?"

"By him, of course, or his men under his discretion. That work bears his stamp."

"In that case, I am lost—nothing can be done."

"Nothing," assented Ganimard.

"It is dreadful; it is monstrous."

"Lodge a complaint."

"What good will that do?"

"Oh; it is well to try it. The law has some resources."

"The law! Bah! it is useless. You represent the law, and, at this moment, when you should be looking for a clue and trying to discover something, you do not even stir."

"Discover something with Arsène Lupin! Why, my dear monsieur, Arsène Lupin never leaves any clue behind him. He leaves nothing to chance. Sometimes I think he put himself in my way and simply allowed me to arrest him in America."

"Then, I must renounce my pictures! He has taken the gems of my collection. I would give a fortune to recover them. If there is no other way, let him name his own price."

Ganimard regarded the baron attentively, as he said:

"Now, that is sensible. Will you stick to it?"

"Yes, yes. But why?"

"An idea that I have."

"What is it?"

"We will discuss it later—if the official examination does not succeed. But, not one word about me, if you wish my assistance."

He added, between his teeth:

"It is true I have nothing to boast of in this affair."

The assistants were gradually regaining consciousness with the bewildered air of people who come out of an hypnotic sleep. They opened their eyes and looked about them in astonishment. Ganimard questioned them; they remembered nothing.

"But you must have seen some one?"

"No."

"Can't you remember?"

"No, no."

"Did you drink anything?"

They considered a moment, and then one of them replied:

"Yes, I drank a little water."

"Out of that carafe?"

"Yes."

"So did I," declared the other.

Ganimard smelled and tasted it. It had no particular taste and no odor.

"Come," he said, "we are wasting our time here. One can't decide an Arsène Lupin problem in five minutes. But, morbleu! I swear I will catch him again."

The same day, a charge of burglary was duly performed by Baron Cahorn against Arsène Lupin, a prisoner in the Prison de la Santé.

The baron afterwards regretted making the charge against Lupin when he saw his castle delivered over to the gendarmes, the procureur, the judge d'instruction, the newspaper reporters and photographers, and a throng of idle curiosity-seekers.

The affair soon became a topic of general discussion, and the name of Arsène Lupin excited the public imagination to such an extent that the newspapers filled their columns with the most fantastic stories of his exploits which found ready credence amongst their readers.

But the letter of Arsène Lupin that was published in the 'Echo de France' (no once ever knew how the newspaper obtained it), that letter in which Baron Cahorn was impudently warned of the coming theft, caused considerable excitement. The most fabulous theories were advanced. Some recalled the existence of the famous subterranean tunnels, and that was the line of research pursued by the officers of the law, who searched the house from top to bottom, questioned every stone, studied the wainscoting and the chimneys, the window-frames and the girders in the ceilings. By the light of torches, they examined the immense cellars where the lords of Malaquis were wont to store their munitions and provisions. They sounded the rocky foundation to its very centre. But it was all in vain. They discovered no trace of a subterranean tunnel. No secret passage existed.

But the eager public declared that the pictures and furniture could not vanish like so many ghosts. They are substantial, material things and require doors and windows for their exits and their entrances, and so do the people that remove them. Who were those people? How did they gain access to the castle? And how did they leave it?

The police officers of Rouen, convinced of their own impotence, solicited the assistance of the Parisian detective force. Mon. Dudouis, chief of the Sûreté, sent the best sleuths of the iron brigade. He himself spent forty-eight hours at the castle, but met with no success. Then he sent for Ganimard, whose past services had proved so useful when all else failed.

Ganimard listened, in silence, to the instructions of his superior; then, shaking his head, he said:

"In my opinion, it is useless to ransack the castle. The solution of the problem lies elsewhere."

"Where, then?"

"With Arsène Lupin."

"With Arsène Lupin! To support that theory, we must admit his intervention."

"I do admit it. In fact, I consider it quite certain."

"Come, Ganimard, that is absurd. Arsène Lupin is in prison."

"I grant you that Arsène Lupin is in prison, closely guarded; but he must have fetters on his feet, manacles on his wrists, and gag in his mouth before I change my opinion."

"Why so obstinate, Ganimard?"

"Because Arsène Lupin is the only man in France of sufficient calibre to invent and carry out a scheme of that magnitude."

"Mere words, Ganimard."

"But true ones. Look! What are they doing? Searching for subterranean passages, stones swinging on pivots, and other nonsense of that kind. But Lupin doesn't employ such old-fashioned methods. He is a modern cracksman, right up to date."

"And how would you proceed?"

"I should ask your permission to spend an hour with him."

"In his cell?"

"Yes. During the return trip from America we became very friendly, and I venture to say that if he can give me any information without compromising himself he will not hesitate to save me from incurring useless trouble."

It was shortly after noon when Ganimard entered the cell of Arsène Lupin. The latter, who was lying on his bed, raised his head and uttered a cry of apparent joy.

"Ah! This is a real surprise. My dear Ganimard, here!"

"Ganimard himself."

"In my chosen retreat, I have felt a desire for many things, but my fondest wish was to receive you here."

"Very kind of you, I am sure."

"Not at all. You know I hold you in the highest regard."

"I am proud of it."

"I have always said: Ganimard is our best detective. He is almost,—you see how candid I am!—he is almost as clever as Sherlock Holmes. But I am sorry that I cannot offer you anything better than this hard stool. And no refreshments! Not even a glass of beer! Of course, you will excuse me, as I am here only temporarily."

Ganimard smiled, and accepted the proffered seat. Then the prisoner continued:

"Mon Dieu, how pleased I am to see the face of an honest man. I am so tired of those devils of spies who come here ten times a day to ransack my pockets and my cell to satisfy themselves that I am not preparing to escape. The government is very solicitous on my account."

"It is quite right."

"Why so? I should be quite contented if they would allow me to live in my own quiet way."

"On other people's money."

"Quite so. That would be so simple. But here, I am joking, and you are, no doubt, in a hurry. So let us come to business, Ganimard. To what do I owe the honor of this visit?

"The Cahorn affair," declared Ganimard, frankly.

"Ah! Wait, one moment. You see I have had so many affairs! First, let me fix in my mind the circumstances of this particular case....Ah! yes, now I have it. The Cahorn affair, Malaquis castle, Seine-Inférieure....Two Rubens, a Watteau, and a few trifling articles."

"Trifling!"

"Oh! ma foi, all that is of slight importance. But it suffices to know that the affair interests you. How can I serve you, Ganimard?"

"Must I explain to you what steps the authorities have taken in the matter?"

"Not at all. I have read the newspapers and I will frankly state that you have made very little progress."

"And that is the reason I have come to see you."

"I am entirely at your service."

"In the first place, the Cahorn affair was managed by you?"

"From A to Z."

"The letter of warning? the telegram?"

"All mine. I ought to have the receipts somewhere."

Arsène opened the drawer of a small table of plain white wood which, with the bed and stool, constituted all the furniture in his cell, and took therefrom two scraps of paper which he handed to Ganimard.

"Ah!" exclaimed the detective, in surprise, "I though you were closely guarded and searched, and I find that you read the newspapers and collect postal receipts."

"Bah! these people are so stupid! They open the lining of my vest, they examine the soles of my shoes, they sound the walls of my cell, but they never imagine that Arsène Lupin would be foolish enough to choose such a simple hiding place."

Ganimard laughed, as he said:

"What a droll fellow you are! Really, you bewilder me. But, come now, tell me about the Cahorn affair."

"Oh! oh! not quite so fast! You would rob me of all my secrets; expose all my little tricks. That is a very serious matter."

"Was I wrong to count on your complaisance?"

"No, Ganimard, and since you insist——-"

Arsène Lupin paced his cell two or three times, then, stopping before Ganimard, he asked:

"What do you think of my letter to the baron?"

"I think you were amusing yourself by playing to the gallery."

"Ah! playing to the gallery! Come, Ganimard, I thought you knew me better. Do I, Arsène Lupin, ever waste my time on such puerilities? Would I have written that letter if I could have robbed the baron without writing to him? I want you to understand that the letter was indispensable; it was the motor that set the whole machine in motion. Now, let us discuss together a scheme for the robbery of the Malaquis castle. Are you willing?"

"Yes, proceed."

"Well, let us suppose a castle carefully closed and barricaded like that of the Baron Cahorn. Am I to abandon my scheme and renounce the treasures that I covet, upon the pretext that the castle which holds them is inaccessible?"

"Evidently not."

"Should I make an assault upon the castle at the head of a band of adventurers as they did in ancient times?"

"That would be foolish."

"Can I gain admittance by stealth or cunning?"

"Impossible."

"Then there is only one way open to me. I must have the owner of the castle invite me to it."

"That is surely an original method."

"And how easy! Let us suppose that one day the owner receives a letter warning him that a notorious burglar known as Arsène Lupin is plotting to rob him. What will he do?"

"Send a letter to the Procureur."

"Who will laugh at him, because the said Arsène Lupin is actually in prison. Then, in his anxiety and fear, the simple man will ask the assistance of the first-comer, will he not?"

"Very likely."

"And if he happens to read in a country newspaper that a celebrated detective is spending his vacation in a neighboring town—-"

"He will seek that detective."

"Of course. But, on the other hand, let us presume that, having foreseen that state of affairs, the said Arsène Lupin has requested one of his friends to visit Caudebec, make the acquaintance of the editor of the 'Réveil,' a newspaper to which the baron is a subscriber, and let said editor understand that such person is the celebrated detective—then, what will happen?"

"The editor will announce in the 'Réveil' the presence in Caudebec of said detective."

"Exactly; and one of two things will happen: either the fish—I mean Cahorn—will not bite, and nothing will happen; or, what is more likely, he will run and greedily swallow the bait. Thus, behold my Baron Cahorn imploring the assistance of one of my friends against me."

"Original, indeed!"

"Of course, the pseudo-detective at first refuses to give any assistance. On top of that comes the telegram from Arsène Lupin. The frightened baron rushes once more to my friend and offers him a definite sum of money for his services. My friend accepts and summons two members of our band, who, during the night, whilst Cahorn is under the watchful eye of his protector, removes certain articles by way of the window and lowers them with ropes into a nice little launch chartered for the occasion. Simple, isn't it?"

"Marvelous! Marvelous!" exclaimed Ganimard. "The boldness of the scheme and the ingenuity of all its details are beyond criticism. But who is the detective whose name and fame served as a magnet to attract the baron and draw him into your net?"

"There is only one name could do it—only one."

"And that is?"

"Arsène Lupin's personal enemy—the most illustrious Ganimard."

"I?"

"Yourself, Ganimard. And, really, it is very funny. If you go there, and the baron decides to talk, you will find that it will be your duty to arrest yourself, just as you arrested me in America. Hein! the revenge is really amusing: I cause Ganimard to arrest Ganimard."

Arsène Lupin laughed heartily. The detective, greatly vexed, bit his lips; to him the joke was quite devoid of humor. The arrival of a prison guard gave Ganimard an opportunity to recover himself. The man brought Arsène Lupin's luncheon, furnished by a neighboring restaurant. After depositing the tray upon the table, the guard retired. Lupin broke his bread, ate a few morsels, and continued:

"But, rest easy, my dear Ganimard, you will not go to Malaquis. I can tell you something that will astonish you: the Cahorn affair is on the point of being settled."

"Excuse me; I have just seen the Chief of the Sureté."

"What of that? Does Mon. Dudouis know my business better than I do myself? You will learn that Ganimard—excuse me—that the pseudo-Ganimard still remains on very good terms with the baron. The latter has authorized him to negotiate a very delicate transaction with me, and, at the present moment, in consideration of a certain sum, it is probable that the baron has recovered possession of his pictures and other treasures. And on their return, he will withdraw his complaint. Thus, there is no longer any theft, and the law must abandon the case."

Ganimard regarded the prisoner with a bewildered air.

"And how do you know all that?"

"I have just received the telegram I was expecting."

"You have just received a telegram?"

"This very moment, my dear friend. Out of politeness, I did not wish to read it in your presence. But if you will permit me—-"

"You are joking, Lupin."

"My dear friend, if you will be so kind as to break that egg, you will learn for yourself that I am not joking."

Mechanically, Ganimard obeyed, and cracked the egg-shell with the blade of a knife. He uttered a cry of surprise. The shell contained nothing but a small piece of blue paper. At the request of Arsène he unfolded it. It was a telegram, or rather a portion of a telegram from which the post-marks had been removed. It read as follows:

"Contract closed. Hundred thousand balls delivered. All well."

"One hundred thousand balls?" said Ganimard.

"Yes, one hundred thousand francs. Very little, but then, you know, these are hard times....And I have some heavy bills to meet. If you only knew my budget.... living in the city comes very high."

Ganimard arose. His ill humor had disappeared. He reflected for a moment, glancing over the whole affair in an effort to discover a weak point; then, in a tone and manner that betrayed his admiration of the prisoner, he said:

"Fortunately, we do not have a dozen such as you to deal with; if we did, we would have to close up shop."

Arsène Lupin assumed a modest air, as he replied:

"Bah! a person must have some diversion to occupy his leisure hours, especially when he is in prison."

"What!" exclaimed Ganimard, "your trial, your defense, the examination—isn't that sufficient to occupy your mind?"

"No, because I have decided not to be present at my trial."

"Oh! oh!"

Arsène Lupin repeated, positively:

"I shall not be present at my trial."

"Really!"

"Ah! my dear monsieur, do you suppose I am going to rot upon the wet straw? You insult me. Arsène Lupin remains in prison just as long as it pleases him, and not one minute more."

"Perhaps it would have been more prudent if you had avoided getting there," said the detective, ironically.

"Ah! monsieur jests? Monsieur must remember that he had the honor to effect my arrest. Know then, my worthy friend, that no one, not even you, could have placed a hand upon me if a much more important event had not occupied my attention at that critical moment."

"You astonish me."

"A woman was looking at me, Ganimard, and I loved her. Do you fully understand what that means: to be under the eyes of a woman that one loves? I cared for nothing in the world but that. And that is why I am here."

"Permit me to say: you have been here a long time."

"In the first place, I wished to forget. Do not laugh; it was a delightful adventure and it is still a tender memory. Besides, I have been suffering from neurasthenia. Life is so feverish these days that it is necessary to take the 'rest cure' occasionally, and I find this spot a sovereign remedy for my tired nerves."

"Arsène Lupin, you are not a bad fellow, after all."

"Thank you," said Lupin. "Ganimard, this is Friday. On Wednesday next, at four o'clock in the afternoon, I will smoke my cigar at your house in the rue Pergolese."

"Arsène Lupin, I will expect you."

They shook hands like two old friends who valued each other at their true worth; then the detective stepped to the door.

"Ganimard!"

"What is it?" asked Ganimard, as he turned back.

"You have forgotten your watch."

"My watch?"

"Yes, it strayed into my pocket."

He returned the watch, excusing himself.

"Pardon me.... a bad habit. Because they have taken mine is no reason why I should take yours. Besides, I have a chronometer here that satisfies me fairly well."

He took from the drawer a large gold watch and heavy chain.

"From whose pocket did that come?" asked Ganimard.

Arsène Lupin gave a hasty glance at the initials engraved on the watch.

"J.B.....Who the devil can that be?....Ah! yes, I remember. Jules Bouvier, the judge who conducted my examination. A charming fellow!...."

III. The Escape of Arsène Lupin

Arsène Lupin had just finished his repast and taken from his pocket an excellent cigar, with a gold band, which he was examining with unusual care, when the door of his cell was opened. He had barely time to throw the cigar into the drawer and move away from the table. The guard entered. It was the hour for exercise.

"I was waiting for you, my dear boy," exclaimed Lupin, in his accustomed good humor.

They went out together. As soon as they had disappeared at a turn in the corridor, two men entered the cell and commenced a minute examination of it. One was Inspector Dieuzy; the other was Inspector Folenfant. They wished to verify their suspicion that Arsène Lupin was in communication with his accomplices outside of the prison. On the preceding evening, the 'Grand Journal' had published these lines addressed to its court reporter:

"Monsieur:

"In a recent article you referred to me in most unjustifiable terms. Some days before the opening of my trial I will call you to account. Arsène Lupin."

The handwriting was certainly that of Arsène Lupin. Consequently, he sent letters; and, no doubt, received letters. It was certain that he was preparing for that escape thus arrogantly announced by him.

The situation had become intolerable. Acting in conjunction with the examining judge, the chief of the Sûreté, Mon. Dudouis, had visited the prison and instructed the gaoler in regard to the precautions necessary to insure Lupin's safety. At the same time, he sent the two men to examine the prisoner's cell. They raised every stone, ransacked the bed, did everything customary in such a case, but they discovered nothing, and were about to abandon their investigation when the guard entered hastily and said:

"The drawer.... look in the table-drawer. When I entered just now he was closing it."

They opened the drawer, and Dieuzy exclaimed:

"Ah! we have him this time."

Folenfant stopped him.

"Wait a moment. The chief will want to make an inventory."

"This is a very choice cigar."

"Leave it there, and notify the chief."

Two minutes later Mon. Dudouis examined the contents of the drawer. First he discovered a bundle of newspaper clippings relating to Arsène Lupin taken from the 'Argus de la Presse,' then a tobacco-box, a pipe, some paper called "onion-peel," and two books. He read the titles of the books. One was an English edition of Carlyle's "Hero-worship"; the other was a charming elzevir, in modern binding, the "Manual of Epictetus," a German translation published at Leyden in 1634. On examining the books, he found that all the pages were underlined and annotated. Were they prepared as a code for correspondence, or did they simply express the studious character of the reader? Then he examined the tobacco-box and the pipe. Finally, he took up the famous cigar with its gold band.

"Fichtre!" he exclaimed. "Our friend smokes a good cigar. It's a Henry Clay."

With the mechanical action of an habitual smoker, he placed the cigar close to his ear and squeezed it to make it crack. Immediately he uttered a cry of surprise. The cigar had yielded under the pressure of his fingers. He examined it more closely, and quickly discovered something white between the leaves of tobacco. Delicately, with the aid of a pin, he withdrew a roll of very thin paper, scarcely larger than a toothpick. It was a letter. He unrolled it, and found these words, written in a feminine handwriting:

"The basket has taken the place of the others. Eight out of ten are ready. On pressing the outer foot the plate goes downward. From twelve to sixteen every day, H-P will wait. But where? Reply at once. Rest easy; your friend is watching over you."

Mon. Dudouis reflected a moment, then said:

"It is quite clear.... the basket.... the eight compartments.... From twelve to sixteen means from twelve to four o'clock."

"But this H-P, that will wait?"

"H-P must mean automobile. H-P, horsepower, is the way they indicate strength of the motor. A twenty-four H-P is an automobile of twenty-four horsepower."

Then he rose, and asked:

"Had the prisoner finished his breakfast?"

"Yes."

"And as he has not yet read the message, which is proved by the condition of the cigar, it is probable that he had just received it."

"How?"

"In his food. Concealed in his bread or in a potato, perhaps."

"Impossible. His food was allowed to be brought in simply to trap him, but we have never found anything in it."

"We will look for Lupin's reply this evening. Detain him outside for a few minutes. I shall take this to the examining judge, and, if he agrees with me, we will have the letter photographed at once, and in an hour you can replace the letter in the drawer in a cigar similar to this. The prisoner must have no cause for suspicion."

It was not without a certain curiosity that Mon. Dudouis returned to the prison in the evening, accompanied by Inspector Dieuzy. Three empty plates were sitting on the stove in the corner.

"He has eaten?"

"Yes," replied the guard.

"Dieuzy, please cut that macaroni into very small pieces, and open that bread-roll....Nothing?"

"No, chief."

Mon. Dudouis examined the plates, the fork, the spoon, and the knife—an ordinary knife with a rounded blade. He turned the handle to the left; then to the right. It yielded and unscrewed. The knife was hollow, and served as a hiding-place for a sheet of paper.

"Peuh!" he said, "that is not very clever for a man like Arsène. But we mustn't lose any time. You, Dieuzy, go and search the restaurant."

Then he read the note:

"I trust to you, H-P will follow at a distance every day. I will go ahead. Au revoir, dear friend."

"At last," cried Mon. Dudouis, rubbing his hands gleefully, "I think we have the affair in our own hands. A little strategy on our part, and the escape will be a success in so far as the arrest of his confederates are concerned."

"But if Arsène Lupin slips through your fingers?" suggested the guard.

"We will have a sufficient number of men to prevent that. If, however, he displays too much cleverness, ma foi, so much the worse for him! As to his band of robbers, since the chief refuses to speak, the others must."

_____

And, as a matter of fact, Arsène Lupin had very little to say. For several months, Mon. Jules Bouvier, the examining judge, had exerted himself in vain. The investigation had been reduced to a few uninteresting arguments between the judge and the advocate, Maître Danval, one of the leaders of the bar. From time to time, through courtesy, Arsène Lupin would speak. One day he said:

"Yes, monsieur, le judge, I quite agree with you: the robbery of the Crédit Lyonnais, the theft in the rue de Babylone, the issue of the counterfeit bank-notes, the burglaries at the various châteaux, Armesnil, Gouret, Imblevain, Groseillers, Malaquis, all my work, monsieur, I did it all."

"Then will you explain to me—-"

"It is useless. I confess everything in a lump, everything and even ten times more than you know nothing about."

Wearied by his fruitless task, the judge had suspended his examinations, but he resumed them after the two intercepted messages were brought to his attention; and regularly, at mid-day, Arsène Lupin was taken from the prison to the Dépôt in the prison-van with a certain number of other prisoners. They returned about three or four o'clock.

Now, one afternoon, this return trip was made under unusual conditions. The other prisoners not having been examined, it was decided to take back Arsène Lupin first, thus he found himself alone in the vehicle.

These prison-vans, vulgarly called "panniers à salade"—or salad-baskets—are divided lengthwise by a central corridor from which open ten compartments, five on either side. Each compartment is so arranged that the occupant must assume and retain a sitting posture, and, consequently, the five prisoners are seated one upon the other, and yet separated one from the other by partitions. A municipal guard, standing at one end, watches over the corridor.

Arsène was placed in the third cell on the right, and the heavy vehicle started. He carefully calculated when they left the quai de l'Horloge, and when they passed the Palais de Justice. Then, about the centre of the bridge Saint Michel, with his outer foot, that is to say, his right foot, he pressed upon the metal plate that closed his cell. Immediately something clicked, and the metal plate moved. He was able to ascertain that he was located between the two wheels.

He waited, keeping a sharp look-out. The vehicle was proceeding slowly along the boulevard Saint Michel. At the corner of Saint Germain it stopped. A truck horse had fallen. The traffic having been interrupted, a vast throng of fiacres and omnibuses had gathered there. Arsène Lupin looked out. Another prison-van had stopped close to the one he occupied. He moved the plate still farther, put his foot on one of the spokes of the wheel and leaped to the ground. A coachman saw him, roared with laughter, then tried to raise an outcry, but his voice was lost in the noise of the traffic that had commenced to move again. Moreover, Arsène Lupin was already far away.

He had run for a few steps; but, once upon the sidewalk, he turned and looked around; he seemed to scent the wind like a person who is uncertain which direction to take. Then, having decided, he put his hands in his pockets, and, with the careless air of an idle stroller, he proceeded up the boulevard. It was a warm, bright autumn day, and the cafés were full. He took a seat on the terrace of one of them. He ordered a bock and a package of cigarettes. He emptied his glass slowly, smoked one cigarette and lighted a second. Then he asked the waiter to send the proprietor to him. When the proprietor came, Arsène spoke to him in a voice loud enough to be heard by everyone:

"I regret to say, monsieur, I have forgotten my pocketbook. Perhaps, on the strength of my name, you will be pleased to give me credit for a few days. I am Arsène Lupin."

The proprietor looked at him, thinking he was joking. But Arsène repeated:

"Lupin, prisoner at the Santé, but now a fugitive. I venture to assume that the name inspires you with perfect confidence in me."

And he walked away, amidst shouts of laughter, whilst the proprietor stood amazed.

Lupin strolled along the rue Soufflot, and turned into the rue Saint Jacques. He pursued his way slowly, smoking his cigarettes and looking into the shop-windows. At the Boulevard de Port Royal he took his bearings, discovered where he was, and then walked in the direction of the rue de la Santé. The high forbidding walls of the prison were now before him. He pulled his hat forward to shade his face; then, approaching the sentinel, he asked:

"Is this the prison de la Santé?"

"Yes."

"I wish to regain my cell. The van left me on the way, and I would not abuse—"

"Now, young man, move along—quick!" growled the sentinel.

"Pardon me, but I must pass through that gate. And if you prevent Arsène Lupin from entering the prison it will cost you dear, my friend."

"Arsène Lupin! What are you talking about!"

"I am sorry I haven't a card with me," said Arsène, fumbling in his pockets.

The sentinel eyed him from head to foot, in astonishment. Then, without a word, he rang a bell. The iron gate was partly opened, and Arsène stepped inside. Almost immediately he encountered the keeper of the prison, gesticulating and feigning a violent anger. Arsène smiled and said:

"Come, monsieur, don't play that game with me. What! they take the precaution to carry me alone in the van, prepare a nice little obstruction, and imagine I am going to take to my heels and rejoin my friends. Well, and what about the twenty agents of the Sûreté who accompanied us on foot, in fiacres and on bicycles? No, the arrangement did not please me. I should not have got away alive. Tell me, monsieur, did they count on that?"

He shrugged his shoulders, and added:

"I beg of you, monsieur, not to worry about me. When I wish to escape I shall not require any assistance."

On the second day thereafter, the 'Echo de France,' which had apparently become the official reporter of the exploits of Arsène Lupin,—it was said that he was one of its principal shareholders—published a most complete account of this attempted escape. The exact wording of the messages exchanged between the prisoner and his mysterious friend, the means by which correspondence was constructed, the complicity of the police, the promenade on the Boulevard Saint Michel, the incident at the café Soufflot, everything was disclosed. It was known that the search of the restaurant and its waiters by Inspector Dieuzy had been fruitless. And the public also learned an extraordinary thing which demonstrated the infinite variety of resources that Lupin possessed: the prison-van, in which he was being carried, was prepared for the occasion and substituted by his accomplices for one of the six vans which did service at the prison.

The next escape of Arsène Lupin was not doubted by anyone. He announced it himself, in categorical terms, in a reply to Mon. Bouvier on the day following his attempted escape. The judge having made a jest about the affair, Arsène was annoyed, and, firmly eyeing the judge, he said, emphatically:

"Listen to me, monsieur! I give you my word of honor that this attempted flight was simply preliminary to my general plan of escape."

"I do not understand," said the judge.

"It is not necessary that you should understand."

And when the judge, in the course of that examination which was reported at length in the columns of the 'Echo de France,' when the judge sought to resume his investigation, Arsène Lupin exclaimed, with an assumed air of lassitude:

"Mon Dieu, Mon Dieu, what's the use! All these questions are of no importance!"

"What! No importance?" cried the judge.

"No; because I shall not be present at the trial."

"You will not be present?"

"No; I have fully decided on that, and nothing will change my mind."

Such assurance combined with the inexplicable indiscretions that Arsène committed every day served to annoy and mystify the officers of the law. There were secrets known only to

Arsène Lupin; secrets that he alone could divulge. But for what purpose did he reveal them? And how?

Arsène Lupin was changed to another cell. The judge closed his preliminary investigation. No further proceedings were taken in his case for a period of two months, during which time Arsène was seen almost constantly lying on his bed with his face turned toward the wall. The changing of his cell seemed to discourage him. He refused to see his advocate. He exchanged only a few necessary words with his keepers.

During the fortnight preceding his trial, he resumed his vigorous life. He complained of want of air. Consequently, early every morning he was allowed to exercise in the courtyard, guarded by two men.

Public curiosity had not died out; every day it expected to be regaled with news of his escape; and, it is true, he had gained a considerable amount of public sympathy by reason of his verve, his gayety, his diversity, his inventive genius and the mystery of his life. Arsène Lupin must escape. It was his inevitable fate. The public expected it, and was surprised that the event had been delayed so long. Every morning the Préfect of Police asked his secretary:

"Well, has he escaped yet?"

"No, Monsieur le Préfect."

"To-morrow, probably."

And, on the day before the trial, a gentleman called at the office of the 'Grand Journal,' asked to see the court reporter, threw his card in the reporter's face, and walked rapidly away. These words were written on the card: "Arsène Lupin always keeps his promises."

It was under these conditions that the trial commenced. An enormous crowd gathered at the court. Everybody wished to see the famous Arsène Lupin. They had a gleeful anticipation that the prisoner would play some audacious pranks upon the judge. Advocates and magistrates, reporters and men of the world, actresses and society women were crowded together on the benches provided for the public.

It was a dark, sombre day, with a steady downpour of rain. Only a dim light pervaded the courtroom, and the spectators caught a very indistinct view of the prisoner when the guards brought him in. But his heavy, shambling walk, the manner in which he dropped into his seat, and his passive, stupid appearance were not at all prepossessing. Several times his advocate— one of Mon. Danval's assistants—spoke to him, but he simply shook his head and said nothing.

The clerk read the indictment, then the judge spoke:

"Prisoner at the bar, stand up. Your name, age, and occupation?"

Not receiving any reply, the judge repeated:

"Your name? I ask you your name?"

A thick, slow voice muttered:

"Baudru, Désiré."

A murmur of surprise pervaded the courtroom. But the judge proceeded:

"Baudru, Désiré? Ah! a new alias! Well, as you have already assumed a dozen different names and this one is, no doubt, as imaginary as the others, we will adhere to the name of Arsène Lupin, by which you are more generally known."

The judge referred to his notes, and continued:

"For, despite the most diligent search, your past history remains unknown. Your case is unique in the annals of crime. We know not whom you are, whence you came, your birth and breeding—all is a mystery to us. Three years ago you appeared in our midst as Arsène Lupin, presenting to us a strange combination of intelligence and perversion, immorality and generosity. Our knowledge of your life prior to that date is vague and problematical. It may be that the man called Rostat who, eight years ago, worked with Dickson, the prestidigitator, was none other than Arsène Lupin. It is probable that the Russian student who, six years ago, attended the laboratory of Doctor Altier at the Saint Louis Hospital, and who often astonished the doctor by the ingenuity of his hypotheses on subjects of bacteriology and the boldness of his experiments in diseases of the skin, was none other than Arsène Lupin. It is probable, also, that Arsène Lupin was the professor who introduced the Japanese art of jiu-jitsu to the Parisian public. We have some reason to believe that Arsène Lupin was the bicyclist who won the Grand Prix de l'Exposition, received his ten thousand francs, and was never heard of again. Arsène Lupin may have been, also, the person who saved so many lives through the little dormer-window at the Charity Bazaar; and, at the same time, picked their pockets."

The judge paused for a moment, then continued:

"Such is that epoch which seems to have been utilized by you in a thorough preparation for the warfare you have since waged against society; a methodical apprenticeship in which you developed your strength, energy and skill to the highest point possible. Do you acknowledge the accuracy of these facts?"

During this discourse the prisoner had stood balancing himself, first on one foot, then on the other, with shoulders stooped and arms inert. Under the strongest light one could observe his extreme thinness, his hollow cheeks, his projecting cheek-bones, his earthen-colored face dotted with small red spots and framed in a rough, straggling beard. Prison life had caused him to age and wither. He had lost the youthful face and elegant figure we had seen portrayed so often in the newspapers.

It appeared as if he had not heard the question propounded by the judge. Twice it was repeated to him. Then he raised his eyes, seemed to reflect, then, making a desperate effort, he murmured:

"Baudru, Désiré."

The judge smiled, as he said:

"I do not understand the theory of your defense, Arsène Lupin. If you are seeking to avoid responsibility for your crimes on the ground of imbecility, such a line of defense is open to you. But I shall proceed with the trial and pay no heed to your vagaries."

He then narrated at length the various thefts, swindles and forgeries charged against Lupin. Sometimes he questioned the prisoner, but the latter simply grunted or remained silent. The examination of witnesses commenced. Some of the evidence given was immaterial; other portions of it seemed more important, but through all of it there ran a vein of contradictions and inconsistencies. A wearisome obscurity enveloped the proceedings, until Detective Ganimard was called as a witness; then interest was revived.

From the beginning the actions of the veteran detective appeared strange and unaccountable. He was nervous and ill at ease. Several times he looked at the prisoner, with obvious doubt and anxiety. Then, with his hands resting on the rail in front of him, he recounted the events in which he had participated, including his pursuit of the prisoner across Europe and his arrival in America. He was listened to with great avidity, as his capture of Arsène Lupin was well known to everyone through the medium of the press. Toward the close of his testimony, after referring to his conversations with Arsène Lupin, he stopped, twice, embarrassed and undecided. It was apparent that he was possessed of some thought which he feared to utter. The judge said to him, sympathetically:

"If you are ill, you may retire for the present."

"No, no, but——"

He stopped, looked sharply at the prisoner, and said:

"I ask permission to scrutinize the prisoner at closer range. There is some mystery about him that I must solve."

He approached the accused man, examined him attentively for several minutes, then returned to the witness-stand, and, in an almost solemn voice, he said:

"I declare, on oath, that the prisoner now before me is not Arsène Lupin."

A profound silence followed the statement. The judge, nonplused for a moment, exclaimed:

"Ah! What do you mean? That is absurd!"

The detective continued:

"At first sight there is a certain resemblance, but if you carefully consider the nose, the mouth, the hair, the color of skin, you will see that it is not Arsène Lupin. And the eyes! Did he ever have those alcoholic eyes!"

"Come, come, witness! What do you mean? Do you pretend to say that we are trying the wrong man?"

"In my opinion, yes. Arsène Lupin has, in some manner, contrived to put this poor devil in his place, unless this man is a willing accomplice."

This dramatic dénouement caused much laughter and excitement amongst the spectators. The judge adjourned the trial, and sent for Mon. Bouvier, the gaoler, and guards employed in the prison.

When the trial was resumed, Mon. Bouvier and the gaoler examined the accused and declared that there was only a very slight resemblance between the prisoner and Arsène Lupin.

"Well, then!" exclaimed the judge, "who is this man? Where does he come from? What is he in prison for?"

Two of the prison-guards were called and both of them declared that the prisoner was Arsène Lupin. The judged breathed once more.

But one of the guards then said:

"Yes, yes, I think it is he."

"What!" cried the judge, impatiently, "you *think* it is he! What do you mean by that?"

"Well, I saw very little of the prisoner. He was placed in my charge in the evening and, for two months, he seldom stirred, but laid on his bed with his face to the wall."

"What about the time prior to those two months?"

"Before that he occupied a cell in another part of the prison. He was not in cell 24."

Here the head gaoler interrupted, and said:

"We changed him to another cell after his attempted escape."

"But you, monsieur, you have seen him during those two months?"

"I had no occasion to see him. He was always quiet and orderly."

"And this prisoner is not Arsène Lupin?"

"No."

"Then who is he?" demanded the judge.

"I do not know."

"Then we have before us a man who was substituted for Arsène Lupin, two months ago. How do you explain that?"

"I cannot."

In absolute despair, the judge turned to the accused and addressed him in a conciliatory tone:

"Prisoner, can you tell me how, and since when, you became an inmate of the Prison de la Santé?"

The engaging manner of the judge was calculated to disarm the mistrust and awaken the understanding of the accused man. He tried to reply. Finally, under clever and gentle questioning, he succeeded in framing a few phrases from which the following story was gleaned: Two months ago he had been taken to the Dépôt, examined and released. As he was leaving the building, a free man, he was seized by two guards and placed in the prison-van. Since then he had occupied cell 24. He was contented there, plenty to eat, and he slept well— so he did not complain.

All that seemed probable; and, amidst the mirth and excitement of the spectators, the judge adjourned the trial until the story could be investigated and verified.

The following facts were at once established by an examination of the prison records: Eight weeks before a man named Baudru Désiré had slept at the Dépôt. He was released the next day, and left the Dépôt at two o'clock in the afternoon. On the same day at two o'clock, having been examined for the last time, Arsène Lupin left the Dépôt in a prison-van.

Had the guards made a mistake? Had they been deceived by the resemblance and carelessly substituted this man for their prisoner?

Another question suggested itself: Had the substitution been arranged in advance? In that event Baudru must have been an accomplice and must have caused his own arrest for the express purpose of taking Lupin's place. But then, by what miracle had such a plan, based on a series of improbable chances, been carried to success?

Baudru Désiré was turned over to the anthropological service; they had never seen anything like him. However, they easily traced his past history. He was known at Courbevois, at Asnières and at Levallois. He lived on alms and slept in one of those rag-picker's huts near the barrier de Ternes. He had disappeared from there a year ago.

Had he been enticed away by Arsène Lupin? There was no evidence to that effect. And even if that was so, it did not explain the flight of the prisoner. That still remained a mystery. Amongst twenty theories which sought to explain it, not one was satisfactory. Of the escape itself, there was no doubt; an escape that was incomprehensible, sensational, in which the public, as well as the officers of the law, could detect a carefully prepared plan, a combination of circumstances marvelously dove-tailed, whereof the dénouement fully justified the confident prediction of Arsène Lupin: "I shall not be present at my trial."

After a month of patient investigation, the problem remained unsolved. The poor devil of a Baudru could not be kept in prison indefinitely, and to place him on trial would be ridiculous. There was no charge against him. Consequently, he was released; but the chief of the Sûrété resolved to keep him under surveillance. This idea originated with Ganimard. From his point of view there was neither complicity nor chance. Baudru was an instrument upon which Arsène Lupin had played with his extraordinary skill. Baudru, when set at liberty, would lead them to Arsène Lupin or, at least, to some of his accomplices. The two inspectors, Folenfant and Dieuzy, were assigned to assist Ganimard.

One foggy morning in January the prison gates opened and Baudru Désiré stepped forth—a free man. At first he appeared to be quite embarrassed, and walked like a person who has no precise idea whither he is going. He followed the rue de la Santé and the rue Saint Jacques. He stopped in front of an old-clothes shop, removed his jacket and his vest, sold his vest on which he realized a few sous; then, replacing his jacket, he proceeded on his way. He crossed the Seine. At the Châtelet an omnibus passed him. He wished to enter it, but there was no place. The controller advised him to secure a number, so he entered the waiting-room.

Ganimard called to his two assistants, and, without removing his eyes from the waiting room, he said to them:

"Stop a carriage.... no, two. That will be better. I will go with one of you, and we will follow him."

The men obeyed. Yet Baudru did not appear. Ganimard entered the waiting-room. It was empty.

"Idiot that I am!" he muttered, "I forgot there was another exit."

There was an interior corridor extending from the waiting-room to the rue Saint Martin. Ganimard rushed through it and arrived just in time to observe Baudru upon the top of the Batignolles-Jardin de Plates omnibus as it was turning the corner of the rue de Rivoli. He ran and caught the omnibus. But he had lost his two assistants. He must continue the pursuit alone. In his anger he was inclined to seize the man by the collar without ceremony. Was it not with premeditation and by means of an ingenious ruse that his pretended imbecile had separated him from his assistants?

He looked at Baudru. The latter was asleep on the bench, his head rolling from side to side, his mouth half-opened, and an incredible expression of stupidity on his blotched face. No, such an adversary was incapable of deceiving old Ganimard. It was a stroke of luck—nothing more.

At the Galleries-Lafayette, the man leaped from the omnibus and took the La Muette tramway, following the boulevard Haussmann and the avenue Victor Hugo. Baudru alighted at La Muette station; and, with a nonchalant air, strolled into the Bois de Boulogne.

He wandered through one path after another, and sometimes retraced his steps. What was he seeking? Had he any definite object? At the end of an hour, he appeared to be faint from fatigue, and, noticing a bench, he sat down. The spot, not far from Auteuil, on the edge of a pond hidden amongst the trees, was absolutely deserted. After the lapse of another half-hour, Ganimard became impatient and resolved to speak to the man. He approached and took a seat beside Baudru, lighted a cigarette, traced some figures in the sand with the end of his cane, and said:

"It's a pleasant day."

No response. But, suddenly the man burst into laughter, a happy, mirthful laugh, spontaneous and irresistible. Ganimard felt his hair stand on end in horror and surprise. It was that laugh, that infernal laugh he knew so well!

With a sudden movement, he seized the man by the collar and looked at him with a keen, penetrating gaze; and found that he no longer saw the man Baudru. To be sure, he saw Baudru; but, at the same time, he saw the other, the real man, Lupin. He discovered the intense life in the eyes, he filled up the shrunken features, he perceived the real flesh beneath the flabby skin, the real mouth through the grimaces that deformed it. Those were the eyes and mouth of the other, and especially his keen, alert, mocking expression, so clear and youthful!

"Arsène Lupin, Arsène Lupin," he stammered.

Then, in a sudden fit of rage, he seized Lupin by the throat and tried to hold him down. In spite of his fifty years, he still possessed unusual strength, whilst his adversary was apparently in a weak condition. But the struggle was a brief one. Arsène Lupin made only a slight movement, and, as suddenly as he had made the attack, Ganimard released his hold. His right arm fell inert, useless.

"If you had taken lessons in jiu-jitsu at the quai des Orfèvres," said Lupin, "you would know that that blow is called udi-shi-ghi in Japanese. A second more, and I would have broken your arm and that would have been just what you deserve. I am surprised that you, an old friend whom I respect and before whom I voluntarily expose my incognito, should abuse my confidence in that violent manner. It is unworthy—Ah! What's the matter?"

Ganimard did not reply. That escape for which he deemed himself responsible—was it not he, Ganimard, who, by his sensational evidence, had led the court into serious error? That escape appeared to him like a dark cloud on his professional career. A tear rolled down his cheek to his gray moustache.

"Oh! mon Dieu, Ganimard, don't take it to heart. If you had not spoken, I would have arranged for some one else to do it. I couldn't allow poor Baudru Désiré to be convicted."

"Then," murmured Ganimard, "it was you that was there? And now you are here?"

"It is I, always I, only I."

"Can it be possible?"

"Oh, it is not the work of a sorcerer. Simply, as the judge remarked at the trial, the apprenticeship of a dozen years that equips a man to cope successfully with all the obstacles in life."

"But your face? Your eyes?"

"You can understand that if I worked eighteen months with Doctor Altier at the Saint-Louis hospital, it was not out of love for the work. I considered that he, who would one day have the honor of calling himself Arsène Lupin, ought to be exempt from the ordinary laws governing appearance and identity. Appearance? That can be modified at will. For instance, a hypodermic injection of paraffine will puff up the skin at the desired spot. Pyrogallic acid will change your skin to that of an Indian. The juice of the greater celandine will adorn you with the most beautiful eruptions and tumors. Another chemical affects the growth of your beard and hair; another changes the tone of your voice. Add to that two months of dieting in cell 24; exercises repeated a thousand times to enable me to hold my features in a certain grimace, to carry my head at a certain inclination, and adapt my back and shoulders to a stooping posture. Then five drops of atropine in the eyes to make them haggard and wild, and the trick is done."

"I do not understand how you deceived the guards."

"The change was progressive. The evolution was so gradual that they failed to notice it."

"But Baudru Désiré?"

"Baudru exists. He is a poor, harmless fellow whom I met last year; and, really, he bears a certain resemblance to me. Considering my arrest as a possible event, I took charge of Baudru and studied the points wherein we differed in appearance with a view to correct them in my own person. My friends caused him to remain at the Dépôt overnight, and to leave there next day about the same hour as I did—a coincidence easily arranged. Of course, it was necessary to have a record of his detention at the Dépôt in order to establish the fact that such a person was a reality; otherwise, the police would have sought elsewhere to find out my identity. But, in offering to them this excellent Baudru, it was inevitable, you understand, inevitable that they would seize upon him, and, despite the insurmountable difficulties of a substitution, they would prefer to believe in a substitution than confess their ignorance."

"Yes, yes, of course," said Ganimard.

"And then," exclaimed Arsène Lupin, "I held in my hands a trump-card: an anxious public watching and waiting for my escape. And that is the fatal error into which you fell, you and the others, in the course of that fascinating game pending between me and the officers of the law wherein the stake was my liberty. And you supposed that I was playing to the gallery; that I was intoxicated with my success. I, Arsène Lupin, guilty of such weakness! Oh, no! And, no longer ago than the Cahorn affair, you said: "When Arsène Lupin cries from the housetops that he will escape, he has some object in view." But, sapristi, you must understand that in

39

order to escape I must create, in advance, a public belief in that escape, a belief amounting to an article of faith, an absolute conviction, a reality as glittering as the sun. And I did create that belief that Arsène Lupin would escape, that Arsène Lupin would not be present at his trial. And when you gave your evidence and said: "That man is not Arsène Lupin," everybody was prepared to believe you. Had one person doubted it, had any one uttered this simple restriction: Suppose it is Arsène Lupin?—from that moment, I was lost. If anyone had scrutinized my face, not imbued with the idea that I was not Arsène Lupin, as you and the others did at my trial, but with the idea that I might be Arsène Lupin; then, despite all my precautions, I should have been recognized. But I had no fear. Logically, psychologically, no once could entertain the idea that I was Arsène Lupin."

He grasped Ganimard's hand.

"Come, Ganimard, confess that on the Wednesday after our conversation in the prison de la Santé, you expected me at your house at four o'clock, exactly as I said I would go."

"And your prison-van?" said Ganimard, evading the question.

"A bluff! Some of my friends secured that old unused van and wished to make the attempt. But I considered it impractical without the concurrence of a number of unusual circumstances. However, I found it useful to carry out that attempted escape and give it the widest publicity. An audaciously planned escape, though not completed, gave to the succeeding one the character of reality simply by anticipation."

"So that the cigar...."

"Hollowed by myself, as well as the knife."

"And the letters?"

"Written by me."

"And the mysterious correspondent?"

"Did not exist."

Ganimard reflected a moment, then said:

"When the anthropological service had Baudru's case under consideration, why did they not perceive that his measurements coincided with those of Arsène Lupin?"

"My measurements are not in existence."

"Indeed!"

"At least, they are false. I have given considerable attention to that question. In the first place, the Bertillon system of records the visible marks of identification—and you have seen that they are not infallible—and, after that, the measurements of the head, the fingers, the ears, etc. Of course, such measurements are more or less infallible."

"Absolutely."

"No; but it costs money to get around them. Before we left America, one of the employees of the service there accepted so much money to insert false figures in my measurements. Consequently, Baudru's measurements should not agree with those of Arsène Lupin."

After a short silence, Ganimard asked:

"What are you going to do now?"

"Now," replied Lupin, "I am going to take a rest, enjoy the best of food and drink and gradually recover my former healthy condition. It is all very well to become Baudru or some other person, on occasion, and to change your personality as you do your shirt, but you soon grow weary of the change. I feel exactly as I imagine the man who lost his shadow must have felt, and I shall be glad to be Arsène Lupin once more."

He walked to and fro for a few minutes, then, stopping in front of Ganimard, he said:

"You have nothing more to say, I suppose?"

"Yes. I should like to know if you intend to reveal the true state of facts connected with your escape. The mistake that I made—-"

"Oh! no one will ever know that it was Arsène Lupin who was discharged. It is to my own interest to surround myself with mystery, and therefore I shall permit my escape to retain its almost miraculous character. So, have no fear on that score, my dear friend. I shall say nothing. And now, good-bye. I am going out to dinner this evening, and have only sufficient time to dress."

"I though you wanted a rest."

"Ah! there are duties to society that one cannot avoid. To-morrow, I shall rest."

"Where do you dine to-night?"

"With the British Ambassador!"

IV. The Mysterious Traveller

The evening before, I had sent my automobile to Rouen by the highway. I was to travel to Rouen by rail, on my way to visit some friends that live on the banks of the Seine.

At Paris, a few minutes before the train started, seven gentlemen entered my compartment; five of them were smoking. No matter that the journey was a short one, the thought of traveling with such a company was not agreeable to me, especially as the car was built on the old model, without a corridor. I picked up my overcoat, my newspapers and my time-table, and sought refuge in a neighboring compartment.

It was occupied by a lady, who, at sight of me, made a gesture of annoyance that did not escape my notice, and she leaned toward a gentleman who was standing on the step and was, no doubt, her husband. The gentleman scrutinized me closely, and, apparently, my appearance did not displease him, for he smiled as he spoke to his wife with the air of one who reassures a frightened child. She smiled also, and gave me a friendly glance as if she now understood that I was one of those gallant men with whom a woman can remain shut up for two hours in a little box, six feet square, and have nothing to fear.

Her husband said to her:

"I have an important appointment, my dear, and cannot wait any longer. Adieu."

He kissed her affectionately and went away. His wife threw him a few kisses and waved her handkerchief. The whistle sounded, and the train started.

At that precise moment, and despite the protests of the guards, the door was opened, and a man rushed into our compartment. My companion, who was standing and arranging her luggage, uttered a cry of terror and fell upon the seat. I am not a coward—far from it—but I confess that such intrusions at the last minute are always disconcerting. They have a suspicious, unnatural aspect.

However, the appearance of the new arrival greatly modified the unfavorable impression produced by his precipitant action. He was correctly and elegantly dressed, wore a tasteful cravat, correct gloves, and his face was refined and intelligent. But, where the devil had I seen that face before? Because, beyond all possible doubt, I had seen it. And yet the memory of it was so vague and indistinct that I felt it would be useless to try to recall it at that time.

Then, directing my attention to the lady, I was amazed at the pallor and anxiety I saw in her face. She was looking at her neighbor—they occupied seats on the same side of the compartment—with an expression of intense alarm, and I perceived that one of her trembling hands was slowly gliding toward a little traveling bag that was lying on the seat about twenty inches from her. She finished by seizing it and nervously drawing it to her. Our eyes met, and I read in hers so much anxiety and fear that I could not refrain from speaking to her:

"Are you ill, madame? Shall I open the window?"

Her only reply was a gesture indicating that she was afraid of our companion. I smiled, as her husband had done, shrugged my shoulders, and explained to her, in pantomime, that she had nothing to fear, that I was there, and, besides, the gentleman appeared to be a very harmless individual. At that moment, he turned toward us, scrutinized both of us from head to foot, then settled down in his corner and paid us no more attention.

After a short silence, the lady, as if she had mustered all her energy to perform a desperate act, said to me, in an almost inaudible voice:

"Do you know who is on our train?"

"Who?"

"He.... he....I assure you...."

"Who is he?"

"Arsène Lupin!"

She had not taken her eyes off our companion, and it was to him rather than to me that she uttered the syllables of that disquieting name. He drew his hat over his face. Was that to conceal his agitation or, simply, to arrange himself for sleep? Then I said to her:

"Yesterday, through contumacy, Arsène Lupin was sentenced to twenty years' imprisonment at hard labor. Therefore it is improbable that he would be so imprudent, to-day, as to show himself in public. Moreover, the newspapers have announced his appearance in Turkey since his escape from the Santé."

"But he is on this train at the present moment," the lady proclaimed, with the obvious intention of being heard by our companion; "my husband is one of the directors in the penitentiary service, and it was the stationmaster himself who told us that a search was being made for Arsène Lupin."

"They may have been mistaken——"

"No; he was seen in the waiting-room. He bought a first-class ticket for Rouen."

"He has disappeared. The guard at the waiting-room door did not see him pass, and it is supposed that he had got into the express that leaves ten minutes after us."

"In that case, they will be sure to catch him."

"Unless, at the last moment, he leaped from that train to come here, into our train.... which is quite probable.... which is almost certain."

"If so, he will be arrested just the same; for the employees and guards would no doubt observe his passage from one train to the other, and, when we arrive at Rouen, they will arrest him there."

"Him—never! He will find some means of escape."

"In that case, I wish him 'bon voyage.'"

"But, in the meantime, think what he may do!"

"What?"

"I don't know. He may do anything."

She was greatly agitated, and, truly, the situation justified, to some extent, her nervous excitement. I was impelled to say to her:

"Of course, there are many strange coincidences, but you need have no fear. Admitting that Arsène Lupin is on this train, he will not commit any indiscretion; he will be only too happy to escape the peril that already threatens him."

My words did not reassure her, but she remained silent for a time. I unfolded my newspapers and read reports of Arsène Lupin's trial, but, as they contained nothing that was new to me, I was not greatly interested. Moreover, I was tired and sleepy. I felt my eyelids close and my head drop.

"But, monsieur, you are not going to sleep!"

She seized my newspaper, and looked at me with indignation.

"Certainly not," I said.

"That would be very imprudent."

"Of course," I assented.

I struggled to keep awake. I looked through the window at the landscape and the fleeting clouds, but in a short time all that became confused and indistinct; the image of the nervous lady and the drowsy gentleman were effaced from my memory, and I was buried in the soothing depths of a profound sleep. The tranquility of my response was soon disturbed by disquieting dreams, wherein a creature that had played the part and bore the name of Arsène Lupin held an important place. He appeared to me with his back laden with articles of value; he leaped over walls, and plundered castles. But the outlines of that creature, who was no longer Arsène Lupin, assumed a more definite form. He came toward me, growing larger and larger, leaped into the compartment with incredible agility, and landed squarely on my chest. With a cry of fright and pain, I awoke. The man, the traveller, our companion, with his knee on my breast, held me by the throat.

My sight was very indistinct, for my eyes were suffused with blood. I could see the lady, in a corner of the compartment, convulsed with fright. I tried even not to resist. Besides, I did not have the strength. My temples throbbed; I was almost strangled. One minute more, and I would have breathed my last. The man must have realized it, for he relaxed his grip, but did not remove his hand. Then he took a cord, in which he had prepared a slip-knot, and tied my wrists together. In an instant, I was bound, gagged, and helpless.

Certainly, he accomplished the trick with an ease and skill that revealed the hand of a master; he was, no doubt, a professional thief. Not a word, not a nervous movement; only coolness and audacity. And I was there, lying on the bench, bound like a mummy, I—Arsène Lupin!

It was anything but a laughing matter, and yet, despite the gravity of the situation, I keenly appreciated the humor and irony that it involved. Arsène Lupin seized and bound like a novice! robbed as if I were an unsophisticated rustic—for, you must understand, the scoundrel had deprived me of my purse and wallet! Arsène Lupin, a victim, duped, vanquished....What an adventure!

The lady did not move. He did not even notice her. He contented himself with picking up her traveling-bag that had fallen to the floor and taking from it the jewels, purse, and gold and silver trinkets that it contained. The lady opened her eyes, trembled with fear, drew the rings from her fingers and handed them to the man as if she wished to spare him unnecessary trouble. He took the rings and looked at her. She swooned.

Then, quite unruffled, he resumed his seat, lighted a cigarette, and proceeded to examine the treasure that he had acquired. The examination appeared to give him perfect satisfaction.

But I was not so well satisfied. I do not speak of the twelve thousand francs of which I had been unduly deprived: that was only a temporary loss, because I was certain that I would recover possession of that money after a very brief delay, together with the important papers contained in my wallet: plans, specifications, addresses, lists of correspondents, and compromising letters. But, for the moment, a more immediate and more serious question troubled me: How would this affair end? What would be the outcome of this adventure?

As you can imagine, the disturbance created by my passage through the Saint-Lazare station has not escaped my notice. Going to visit friends who knew me under the name of Guillaume Berlat, and amongst whom my resemblance to Arsène Lupin was a subject of many innocent jests, I could not assume a disguise, and my presence had been remarked. So, beyond question, the commissary of police at Rouen, notified by telegraph, and assisted by numerous agents, would be awaiting the train, would question all suspicious passengers, and proceed to search the cars.

Of course, I had foreseen all that, but it had not disturbed me, as I was certain that the police of Rouen would not be any shrewder than the police of Paris and that I could escape recognition; would it not be sufficient for me to carelessly display my card as "député," thanks to which I had inspired complete confidence in the gate-keeper at Saint-Lazare?—But the situation was greatly changed. I was no longer free. It was impossible to attempt one of my usual tricks. In one of the compartments, the commissary of police would find Mon. Arsène Lupin, bound hand and foot, as docile as a lamb, packed up, all ready to be dumped into a prison-van. He would have simply to accept delivery of the parcel, the same as if it were so much merchandise or a basket of fruit and vegetables. Yet, to avoid that shameful dénouement, what could I do?—bound and gagged, as I was? And the train was rushing on toward Rouen, the next and only station.

Another problem was presented, in which I was less interested, but the solution of which aroused my professional curiosity. What were the intentions of my rascally companion? Of course, if I had been alone, he could, on our arrival at Rouen, leave the car slowly and fearlessly. But the lady? As soon as the door of the compartment should be opened, the lady, now so quiet and humble, would scream and call for help. That was the dilemma that perplexed me! Why had he not reduced her to a helpless condition similar to mine? That would have given him ample time to disappear before his double crime was discovered.

He was still smoking, with his eyes fixed upon the window that was now being streaked with drops of rain. Once he turned, picked up my time-table, and consulted it.

The lady had to feign a continued lack of consciousness in order to deceive the enemy. But fits of coughing, provoked by the smoke, exposed her true condition. As to me, I was very uncomfortable, and very tired. And I meditated; I plotted.

The train was rushing on, joyously, intoxicated with its own speed.

Saint Etienne!....At that moment, the man arose and took two steps toward us, which caused the lady to utter a cry of alarm and fall into a genuine swoon. What was the man about to do? He lowered the window on our side. A heavy rain was now falling, and, by a gesture, the man expressed his annoyance at his not having an umbrella or an overcoat. He glanced at the rack. The lady's umbrella was there. He took it. He also took my overcoat and put it on.

We were now crossing the Seine. He turned up the bottoms of his trousers, then leaned over and raised the exterior latch of the door. Was he going to throw himself upon the track? At that speed, it would have been instant death. We now entered a tunnel. The man opened the door half-way and stood on the upper step. What folly! The darkness, the smoke, the noise, all gave a fantastic appearance to his actions. But suddenly, the train diminished its speed. A moment later it increased its speed, then slowed up again. Probably, some repairs were being made in that part of the tunnel which obliged the trains to diminish their speed, and the man was aware of the fact. He immediately stepped down to the lower step, closed the door behind him, and leaped to the ground. He was gone.

The lady immediately recovered her wits, and her first act was to lament the loss of her jewels. I gave her an imploring look. She understood, and quickly removed the gag that stifled me. She wished to untie the cords that bound me, but I prevented her.

"No, no, the police must see everything exactly as it stands. I want them to see what the rascal did to us."

"Suppose I pull the alarm-bell?"

"Too late. You should have done that when he made the attack on me."

"But he would have killed me. Ah! monsieur, didn't I tell you that he was on this train. I recognized him from his portrait. And now he has gone off with my jewels."

"Don't worry. The police will catch him."

"Catch Arsène Lupin! Never."

"That depends on you, madame. Listen. When we arrive at Rouen, be at the door and call. Make a noise. The police and the railway employees will come. Tell what you have seen: the assault made on me and the flight of Arsène Lupin. Give a description of him—soft hat, umbrella—yours—gray overcoat...."

"Yours," said she.

"What! mine? Not at all. It was his. I didn't have any."

"It seems to me he didn't have one when he came in."

"Yes, yes.... unless the coat was one that some one had forgotten and left in the rack. At all events, he had it when he went away, and that is the essential point. A gray overcoat—remember!....Ah! I forgot. You must tell your name, first thing you do. Your husband's official position will stimulate the zeal of the police."

We arrived at the station. I gave her some further instructions in a rather imperious tone:

"Tell them my name—Guillaume Berlat. If necessary, say that you know me. That will save time. We must expedite the preliminary investigation. The important thing is the pursuit of Arsène Lupin. Your jewels, remember! Let there be no mistake. Guillaume Berlat, a friend of your husband."

"I understand....Guillaume Berlat."

She was already calling and gesticulating. As soon as the train stopped, several men entered the compartment. The critical moment had come.

Panting for breath, the lady exclaimed:

"Arsène Lupin.... he attacked us.... he stole my jewels....I am Madame Renaud.... my husband is a director of the penitentiary service....Ah! here is my brother, Georges Ardelle, director of the Crédit Rouennais.... you must know...."

She embraced a young man who had just joined us, and whom the commissary saluted. Then she continued, weeping:

"Yes, Arsène Lupin.... while monsieur was sleeping, he seized him by the throat....Mon. Berlat, a friend of my husband."

The commissary asked:

"But where is Arsène Lupin?"

"He leaped from the train, when passing through the tunnel."

"Are you sure that it was he?"

"Am I sure! I recognized him perfectly. Besides, he was seen at the Saint-Lazare station. He wore a soft hat—-"

"No, a hard felt, like that," said the commissary, pointing to my hat.

"He had a soft hat, I am sure," repeated Madame Renaud, "and a gray overcoat."

"Yes, that is right," replied the commissary, "the telegram says he wore a gray overcoat with a black velvet collar."

"Exactly, a black velvet collar," exclaimed Madame Renaud, triumphantly.

I breathed freely. Ah! the excellent friend I had in that little woman.

The police agents had now released me. I bit my lips until they ran blood. Stooping over, with my handkerchief over my mouth, an attitude quite natural in a person who has remained for a long time in an uncomfortable position, and whose mouth shows the bloody marks of the gag, I addressed the commissary, in a weak voice:

"Monsieur, it was Arsène Lupin. There is no doubt about that. If we make haste, he can be caught yet. I think I may be of some service to you."

The railway car, in which the crime occurred, was detached from the train to serve as a mute witness at the official investigation. The train continued on its way to Havre. We were then conducted to the station-master's office through a crowd of curious spectators.

Then, I had a sudden access of doubt and discretion. Under some pretext or other, I must gain my automobile, and escape. To remain there was dangerous. Something might happen; for instance, a telegram from Paris, and I would be lost.

Yes, but what about my thief? Abandoned to my own resources, in an unfamiliar country, I could not hope to catch him.

"Bah! I must make the attempt," I said to myself. "It may be a difficult game, but an amusing one, and the stake is well worth the trouble."

And when the commissary asked us to repeat the story of the robbery, I exclaimed:

"Monsieur, really, Arsène Lupin is getting the start of us. My automobile is waiting in the courtyard. If you will be so kind as to use it, we can try...."

The commissary smiled, and replied:

"The idea is a good one; so good, indeed, that it is already being carried out. Two of my men have set out on bicycles. They have been gone for some time."

"Where did they go?"

"To the entrance of the tunnel. There, they will gather evidence, secure witnesses, and follow on the track of Arsène Lupin."

I could not refrain from shrugging my shoulders, as I replied:

"Your men will not secure any evidence or any witnesses."

"Really!"

"Arsène Lupin will not allow anyone to see him emerge from the tunnel. He will take the first road—-"

"To Rouen, where we will arrest him."

"He will not go to Rouen."

"Then he will remain in the vicinity, where his capture will be even more certain."

"He will not remain in the vicinity."

"Oh! oh! And where will he hide?"

I looked at my watch, and said:

"At the present moment, Arsène Lupin is prowling around the station at Darnétal. At ten fifty, that is, in twenty-two minutes from now, he will take the train that goes from Rouen to Amiens."

"Do you think so? How do you know it?"

"Oh! it is quite simple. While we were in the car, Arsène Lupin consulted my railway guide. Why did he do it? Was there, not far from the spot where he disappeared, another line of railway, a station upon that line, and a train stopping at that station? On consulting my railway guide, I found such to be the case."

"Really, monsieur," said the commissary, "that is a marvelous deduction. I congratulate you on your skill."

I was now convinced that I had made a mistake in displaying so much cleverness. The commissary regarded me with astonishment, and I thought a slight suspicion entered his official mind....Oh! scarcely that, for the photographs distributed broadcast by the police department were too imperfect; they presented an Arsène Lupin so different from the one he had before him, that he could not possibly recognize me by it. But, all the same, he was troubled, confused and ill-at-ease.

"Mon Dieu! nothing stimulates the comprehension so much as the loss of a pocketbook and the desire to recover it. And it seems to me that if you will give me two of your men, we may be able...."

"Oh! I beg of you, monsieur le commissaire," cried Madame Renaud, "listen to Mon. Berlat."

The intervention of my excellent friend was decisive. Pronounced by her, the wife of an influential official, the name of Berlat became really my own, and gave me an identity that no mere suspicion could affect. The commissary arose, and said:

"Believe me, Monsieur Berlat, I shall be delighted to see you succeed. I am as much interested as you are in the arrest of Arsène Lupin."

He accompanied me to the automobile, and introduced two of his men, Honoré Massol and Gaston Delivet, who were assigned to assist me. My chauffer cranked up the car and I took my place at the wheel. A few seconds later, we left the station. I was saved.

Ah! I must confess that in rolling over the boulevards that surrounded the old Norman city, in my swift thirty-five horse-power Moreau-Lepton, I experienced a deep feeling of pride, and the motor responded, sympathetically to my desires. At right and left, the trees flew past us with startling rapidity, and I, free, out of danger, had simply to arrange my little personal affairs with the two honest representatives of the Rouen police who were sitting behind me. Arsène Lupin was going in search of Arsène Lupin!

Modest guardians of social order—Gaston Delivet and Honoré Massol—how valuable was your assistance! What would I have done without you? Without you, many times, at the cross-roads, I might have taken the wrong route! Without you, Arsène Lupin would have made a mistake, and the other would have escaped!

But the end was not yet. Far from it. I had yet to capture the thief and recover the stolen papers. Under no circumstances must my two acolytes be permitted to see those papers, much less to seize them. That was a point that might give me some difficulty.

We arrived at Darnétal three minutes after the departure of the train. True, I had the consolation of learning that a man wearing a gray overcoat with a black velvet collar had taken the train at the station. He had bought a second-class ticket for Amiens. Certainly, my début as detective was a promising one.

Delivet said to me:

"The train is express, and the next stop is Montérolier-Buchy in nineteen minutes. If we do not reach there before Arsène Lupin, he can proceed to Amiens, or change for the train going to Clères, and, from that point, reach Dieppe or Paris."

"How far to Montérolier?"

"Twenty-three kilometres."

"Twenty-three kilometres in nineteen minutes....We will be there ahead of him."

We were off again! Never had my faithful Moreau-Repton responded to my impatience with such ardor and regularity. It participated in my anxiety. It indorsed my determination. It comprehended my animosity against that rascally Arsène Lupin. The knave! The traitor!

"Turn to the right," cried Delivet, "then to the left."

We fairly flew, scarcely touching the ground. The mile-stones looked like little timid beasts that vanished at our approach. Suddenly, at a turn of the road, we saw a vortex of smoke. It was the Northern Express. For a kilometre, it was a struggle, side by side, but an unequal struggle in which the issue was certain. We won the race by twenty lengths.

In three seconds we were on the platform standing before the second-class carriages. The doors were opened, and some passengers alighted, but not my thief. We made a search through the compartments. No sign of Arsène Lupin.

"Sapristi!" I cried, "he must have recognized me in the automobile as we were racing, side by side, and he leaped from the train."

"Ah! there he is now! crossing the track."

I started in pursuit of the man, followed by my two acolytes, or rather followed by one of them, for the other, Massol, proved himself to be a runner of exceptional speed and endurance. In a few moments, he had made an appreciable gain upon the fugitive. The man noticed it, leaped over a hedge, scampered across a meadow, and entered a thick grove. When we reached this grove, Massol was waiting for us. He went no farther, for fear of losing us.

"Quite right, my dear friend," I said. "After such a run, our victim must be out of wind. We will catch him now."

I examined the surroundings with the idea of proceeding alone in the arrest of the fugitive, in order to recover my papers, concerning which the authorities would doubtless ask many disagreeable questions. Then I returned to my companions, and said:

"It is all quite easy. You, Massol, take your place at the left; you, Delivet, at the right. From there, you can observe the entire posterior line of the bush, and he cannot escape without you seeing him, except by that ravine, and I shall watch it. If he does not come out voluntarily, I will enter and drive him out toward one or the other of you. You have simply to wait. Ah! I forgot: in case I need you, a pistol shot."

Massol and Delivet walked away to their respective posts. As soon as they had disappeared, I entered the grove with the greatest precaution so as to be neither seen nor heard. I encountered dense thickets, through which narrow paths had been cut, but the overhanging boughs compelled me to adopt a stooping posture. One of these paths led to a clearing in which I found footsteps upon the wet grass. I followed them; they led me to the foot of a mound which was surmounted by a deserted, dilapidated hovel.

"He must be there," I said to myself. "It is a well-chosen retreat."

I crept cautiously to the side of the building. A slight noise informed me that he was there; and, then, through an opening, I saw him. His back was turned toward me. In two bounds, I was upon him. He tried to fire a revolver that he held in his hand. But he had no time. I threw him to the ground, in such a manner that his arms were beneath him, twisted and helpless, whilst I held him down with my knee on his breast.

"Listen, my boy," I whispered in his ear. "I am Arsène Lupin. You are to deliver over to me, immediately and gracefully, my pocketbook and the lady's jewels, and, in return therefore, I will save you from the police and enroll you amongst my friends. One word: yes or no?"

"Yes," he murmured.

"Very good. Your escape, this morning, was well planned. I congratulate you."

I arose. He fumbled in his pocket, drew out a large knife and tried to strike me with it.

"Imbecile!" I exclaimed.

With one hand, I parried the attack; with the other, I gave him a sharp blow on the carotid artery. He fell—stunned!

In my pocketbook, I recovered my papers and bank-notes. Out of curiosity, I took his. Upon an envelope, addressed to him, I read his name: Pierre Onfrey. It startled me. Pierre Onfrey, the assassin of the rue Lafontaine at Auteuil! Pierre Onfrey, he who had cut the throats of Madame Delbois and her two daughters. I leaned over him. Yes, those were the features which, in the compartment, had evoked in me the memory of a face I could not then recall.

But time was passing. I placed in an envelope two bank-notes of one hundred francs each, with a card bearing these words: "Arsène Lupin to his worthy colleagues Honoré Massol and Gaston Delivet, as a slight token of his gratitude." I placed it in a prominent spot in the room, where they would be sure to find it. Beside it, I placed Madame Renaud's handbag. Why could I not return it to the lady who had befriended me? I must confess that I had taken from it everything that possessed any interest or value, leaving there only a shell comb, a stick of rouge Dorin for the lips, and an empty purse. But, you know, business is business. And then, really, her husband is engaged in such a dishonorable vocation!

The man was becoming conscious. What was I to do? I was unable to save him or condemn him. So I took his revolver and fired a shot in the air.

"My two acolytes will come and attend to his case," I said to myself, as I hastened away by the road through the ravine. Twenty minutes later, I was seated in my automobile.

At four o'clock, I telegraphed to my friends at Rouen that an unexpected event would prevent me from making my promised visit. Between ourselves, considering what my friends must now know, my visit is postponed indefinitely. A cruel disillusion for them!

At six o'clock I was in Paris. The evening newspapers informed me that Pierre Onfrey had been captured at last.

Next day,—let us not despise the advantages of judicious advertising,—the 'Echo de France' published this sensational item:

"Yesterday, near Buchy, after numerous exciting incidents, Arsène Lupin effected the arrest of Pierre Onfrey. The assassin of the rue Lafontaine had robbed Madame Renaud, wife of the director in the penitentiary service, in a railway carriage on the Paris-Havre line. Arsène Lupin restored to Madame Renaud the hand-bag that contained her jewels, and gave a generous recompense to the two detectives who had assisted him in making that dramatic arrest."

V. The Queen's Necklace

Two or three times each year, on occasions of unusual importance, such as the balls at the Austrian Embassy or the soirées of Lady Billingstone, the Countess de Dreux-Soubise wore upon her white shoulders "The Queen's Necklace."

It was, indeed, the famous necklace, the legendary necklace that Bohmer and Bassenge, court jewelers, had made for Madame Du Barry; the veritable necklace that the Cardinal de Rohan-Soubise intended to give to Marie-Antoinette, Queen of France; and the same that the adventuress Jeanne de Valois, Countess de la Motte, had pulled to pieces one evening in February, 1785, with the aid of her husband and their accomplice, Rétaux de Villette.

To tell the truth, the mounting alone was genuine. Rétaux de Villette had kept it, whilst the Count de la Motte and his wife scattered to the four winds of heaven the beautiful stones so carefully chosen by Bohmer. Later, he sold the mounting to Gaston de Dreux-Soubise, nephew and heir of the Cardinal, who re-purchased the few diamonds that remained in the possession of the English jeweler, Jeffreys; supplemented them with other stones of the same size but of much inferior quality, and thus restored the marvelous necklace to the form in which it had come from the hands of Bohmer and Bassenge.

For nearly a century, the house of Dreux-Soubise had prided itself upon the possession of this historic jewel. Although adverse circumstances had greatly reduced their fortune, they preferred to curtail their household expenses rather than part with this relic of royalty. More particularly, the present count clung to it as a man clings to the home of his ancestors. As a matter of prudence, he had rented a safety-deposit box at the Crédit Lyonnais in which to keep it. He went for it himself on the afternoon of the day on which his wife wished to wear it, and he, himself, carried it back next morning.

On this particular evening, at the reception given at the Palais de Castille, the Countess achieved a remarkable success; and King Christian, in whose honor the fête was given, commented on her grace and beauty. The thousand facets of the diamond sparkled and shone like flames of fire about her shapely neck and shoulders, and it is safe to say that none but she could have borne the weight of such an ornament with so much ease and grace.

This was a double triumph, and the Count de Dreux was highly elated when they returned to their chamber in the old house of the faubourg Saint-Germain. He was proud of his wife, and quite as proud, perhaps, of the necklace that had conferred added luster to his noble house for generations. His wife, also, regarded the necklace with an almost childish vanity, and it was not without regret that she removed it from her shoulders and handed it to her husband who admired it as passionately as if he had never seen it before. Then, having placed it in its case of red leather, stamped with the Cardinal's arms, he passed into an adjoining room which was simply an alcove or cabinet that had been cut off from their chamber, and which could be entered only by means of a door at the foot of their bed. As he had done on previous occasions, he hid it on a high shelf amongst hat-boxes and piles of linen. He closed the door, and retired.

Next morning, he arose about nine o'clock, intending to go to the Crédit Lyonnais before breakfast. He dressed, drank a cup of coffee, and went to the stables to give his orders. The condition of one of the horses worried him. He caused it to be exercised in his presence. Then

52

he returned to his wife, who had not yet left the chamber. Her maid was dressing her hair. When her husband entered, she asked:

"Are you going out?"

"Yes, as far as the bank."

"Of course. That is wise."

He entered the cabinet; but, after a few seconds, and without any sign of astonishment, he asked:

"Did you take it, my dear?"

"What?....No, I have not taken anything."

"You must have moved it."

"Not at all. I have not even opened that door."

He appeared at the door, disconcerted, and stammered, in a scarcely intelligible voice:

"You haven't....It wasn't you?....Then...."

She hastened to his assistance, and, together, they made a thorough search, throwing the boxes to the floor and overturning the piles of linen. Then the count said, quite discouraged:

"It is useless to look any more. I put it here, on this shelf."

"You must be mistaken."

"No, no, it was on this shelf—nowhere else."

They lighted a candle, as the room was quite dark, and then carried out all the linen and other articles that the room contained. And, when the room was emptied, they confessed, in despair, that the famous necklace had disappeared. Without losing time in vain lamentations, the countess notified the commissary of police, Mon. Valorbe, who came at once, and, after hearing their story, inquired of the count:

"Are you sure that no one passed through your chamber during the night?"

"Absolutely sure, as I am a very light sleeper. Besides, the chamber door was bolted, and I remember unbolting it this morning when my wife rang for her maid."

"And there is no other entrance to the cabinet?"

"None."

"No windows?"

"Yes, but it is closed up."

"I will look at it."

Candles were lighted, and Mon. Valorbe observed at once that the lower half of the window was covered by a large press which was, however, so narrow that it did not touch the casement on either side.

"On what does this window open?"

"A small inner court."

"And you have a floor above this?"

"Two; but, on a level with the servant's floor, there is a close grating over the court. That is why this room is so dark."

When the press was moved, they found that the window was fastened, which would not have been the case if anyone had entered that way.

"Unless," said the count, "they went out through our chamber."

"In that case, you would have found the door unbolted."

The commissary considered the situation for a moment, then asked the countess:

"Did any of your servants know that you wore the necklace last evening?"

"Certainly; I didn't conceal the fact. But nobody knew that it was hidden in that cabinet."

"No one?"

"No one.... unless...."

"Be quite sure, madam, as it is a very important point."

She turned to her husband, and said:

"I was thinking of Henriette."

"Henriette? She didn't know where we kept it."

"Are you sure?"

"Who is this woman Henriette?" asked Mon. Valorbe.

"A school-mate, who was disowned by her family for marrying beneath her. After her husband's death, I furnished an apartment in this house for her and her son. She is clever with her needle and has done some work for me."

"What floor is she on?"

"Same as ours.... at the end of the corridor.... and I think.... the window of her kitchen...."

"Opens on this little court, does it not?"

"Yes, just opposite ours."

Mon. Valorbe then asked to see Henriette. They went to her apartment; she was sewing, whilst her son Raoul, about six years old, was sitting beside her, reading. The commissary was surprised to see the wretched apartment that had been provided for the woman. It consisted of one room without a fireplace, and a very small room that served as a kitchen. The commissary proceeded to question her. She appeared to be overwhelmed on learning of the theft. Last evening she had herself dressed the countess and placed the necklace upon her shoulders.

"Good God!" she exclaimed, "it can't be possible!"

"And you have no idea? Not the least suspicion? Is it possible that the thief may have passed through your room?"

She laughed heartily, never supposing that she could be an object of suspicion.

"But I have not left my room. I never go out. And, perhaps, you have not seen?"

She opened the kitchen window, and said:

"See, it is at least three metres to the ledge of the opposite window."

"Who told you that we supposed the theft might have been committed in that way?"

"But.... the necklace was in the cabinet, wasn't it?"

"How do you know that?"

"Why, I have always known that it was kept there at night. It had been mentioned in my presence."

Her face, though still young, bore unmistakable traces of sorrow and resignation. And it now assumed an expression of anxiety as if some danger threatened her. She drew her son toward her. The child took her hand, and kissed it affectionately.

When they were alone again, the count said to the commissary:

"I do not suppose you suspect Henriette. I can answer for her. She is honesty itself."

"I quite agree with you," replied Mon. Valorbe. "At most, I thought there might have been an unconscious complicity. But I confess that even that theory must be abandoned, as it does not help solve the problem now before us."

The commissary of police abandoned the investigation, which was now taken up and completed by the examining judge. He questioned the servants, examined the condition of the bolt, experimented with the opening and closing of the cabinet window, and explored the little court from top to bottom. All was in vain. The bolt was intact. The window could not be opened or closed from the outside.

The inquiries especially concerned Henriette, for, in spite of everything, they always turned in her direction. They made a thorough investigation of her past life, and ascertained that, during the last three years, she had left the house only four times, and her business, on those occasions, was satisfactorily explained. As a matter of fact, she acted as chambermaid and seamstress to the countess, who treated her with great strictness and even severity.

At the end of a week, the examining judge had secured no more definite information than the commissary of police. The judge said:

"Admitting that we know the guilty party, which we do not, we are confronted by the fact that we do not know how the theft was committed. We are brought face to face with two obstacles: a door and a window—both closed and fastened. It is thus a double mystery. How could anyone enter, and, moreover, how could any one escape, leaving behind him a bolted door and a fastened window?"

At the end of four months, the secret opinion of the judge was that the count and countess, being hard pressed for money, which was their normal condition, had sold the Queen's Necklace. He closed the investigation.

The loss of the famous jewel was a severe blow to the Dreux-Soubise. Their credit being no longer propped up by the reserve fund that such a treasure constituted, they found themselves confronted by more exacting creditors and money-lenders. They were obliged to cut down to the quick, to sell or mortgage every article that possessed any commercial value. In brief, it would have been their ruin, if two large legacies from some distant relatives had not saved them.

Their pride also suffered a downfall, as if they had lost a quartering from their escutcheon. And, strange to relate, it was upon her former schoolmate, Henriette, that the countess vented her spleen. Toward her, the countess displayed the most spiteful feelings, and even openly accused her. First, Henriette was relegated to the servants' quarters, and, next day, discharged.

For some time, the count and countess passed an uneventful life. They traveled a great deal. Only one incident of record occurred during that period. Some months after the departure of Henriette, the countess was surprised when she received and read the following letter, signed by Henriette:

"Madame,"

"I do not know how to thank you; for it was you, was it not, who sent me that? It could not have been anyone else. No one but you knows where I live. If I am wrong, excuse me, and accept my sincere thanks for your past favors...."

What did the letter mean? The present or past favors of the countess consisted principally of injustice and neglect. Why, then, this letter of thanks?

When asked for an explanation, Henriette replied that she had received a letter, through the mails, enclosing two bank-notes of one thousand francs each. The envelope, which she enclosed with her reply, bore the Paris post-mark, and was addressed in a handwriting that was obviously disguised. Now, whence came those two thousand francs? Who had sent them? And why had they sent them?

Henriette received a similar letter and a like sum of money twelve months later. And a third time; and a fourth; and each year for a period of six years, with this difference, that in the fifth and sixth years the sum was doubled. There was another difference: the post-office authorities having seized one of the letters under the pretext that it was not registered, the last two letters were duly sent according to the postal regulations, the first dated from Saint-Germain, the other from Suresnes. The writer signed the first one, "Anquety"; and the other, "Péchard." The addresses that he gave were false.

At the end of six years, Henriette died, and the mystery remained unsolved.

All these events are known to the public. The case was one of those which excite public interest, and it was a strange coincidence that this necklace, which had caused such a great commotion in France at the close of the eighteenth century, should create a similar commotion a century later. But what I am about to relate is known only to the parties directly interested and a few others from whom the count exacted a promise of secrecy. As it is probable that some day or other that promise will be broken, I have no hesitation in rending the veil and thus disclosing the key to the mystery, the explanation of the letter published in the morning papers two days ago; an extraordinary letter which increased, if possible, the mists and shadows that envelope this inscrutable drama.

Five days ago, a number of guests were dining with the Count de Dreux-Soubise. There were several ladies present, including his two nieces and his cousin, and the following gentlemen: the president of Essaville, the deputy Bochas, the chevalier Floriani, whom the count had known in Sicily, and General Marquis de Rouzières, and old club friend.

After the repast, coffee was served by the ladies, who gave the gentlemen permission to smoke their cigarettes, provided they would not desert the salon. The conversation was general, and finally one of the guests chanced to speak of celebrated crimes. And that gave the Marquis de Rouzières, who delighted to tease the count, an opportunity to mention the affair of the Queen's Necklace, a subject that the count detested.

Each one expressed his own opinion of the affair; and, of course, their various theories were not only contradictory but impossible.

"And you, monsieur," said the countess to the chevalier Floriani, "what is your opinion?"

"Oh! I—I have no opinion, madame."

All the guests protested; for the chevalier had just related in an entertaining manner various adventures in which he had participated with his father, a magistrate at Palermo, and which established his judgment and taste in such manners.

"I confess," said he, "I have sometimes succeeded in unraveling mysteries that the cleverest detectives have renounced; yet I do not claim to be Sherlock Holmes. Moreover, I know very little about the affair of the Queen's Necklace."

Everybody now turned to the count, who was thus obliged, quite unwillingly, to narrate all the circumstances connected with the theft. The chevalier listened, reflected, asked a few questions, and said:

"It is very strange.... at first sight, the problem appears to be a very simple one."

The count shrugged his shoulders. The others drew closer to the chevalier, who continued, in a dogmatic tone:

"As a general rule, in order to find the author of a crime or a theft, it is necessary to determine how that crime or theft was committed, or, at least, how it could have been committed. In the present case, nothing is more simple, because we are face to face, not with several theories, but with one positive fact, that is to say: the thief could only enter by the chamber door or the window of the cabinet. Now, a person cannot open a bolted door from the outside. Therefore, he must have entered through the window."

"But it was closed and fastened, and we found it fastened afterward," declared the count.

"In order to do that," continued Floriani, without heeding the interruption, "he had simply to construct a bridge, a plank or a ladder, between the balcony of the kitchen and the ledge of the window, and as the jewel-case——"

"But I repeat that the window was fastened," exclaimed the count, impatiently.

This time, Floriani was obliged to reply. He did so with the greatest tranquility, as if the objection was the most insignificant affair in the world.

"I will admit that it was; but is there not a transom in the upper part of the window?"

"How do you know that?"

"In the first place, that was customary in houses of that date; and, in the second place, without such a transom, the theft cannot be explained."

"Yes, there is one, but it was closed, the same as the window. Consequently, we did not pay attention to it."

"That was a mistake; for, if you had examined it, you would have found that it had been opened."

"But how?"

"I presume that, like all others, it opens by means of a wire with a ring on the lower end."

"Yes, but I do not see——"

"Now, through a hole in the window, a person could, by the aid of some instrument, let us say a poker with a hook at the end, grip the ring, pull down, and open the transom."

The count laughed and said:

"Excellent! excellent! Your scheme is very cleverly constructed, but you overlook one thing, monsieur, there is no hole in the window."

"There was a hole."

"Nonsense, we would have seen it."

"In order to see it, you must look for it, and no one has looked. The hole is there; it must be there, at the side of the window, in the putty. In a vertical direction, of course."

The count arose. He was greatly excited. He paced up and down the room, two or three times, in a nervous manner; then, approaching Floriani, said:

"Nobody has been in that room since; nothing has been changed."

"Very well, monsieur, you can easily satisfy yourself that my explanation is correct."

"It does not agree with the facts established by the examining judge. You have seen nothing, and yet you contradict all that we have seen and all that we know."

Floriani paid no attention to the count's petulance. He simply smiled and said:

"Mon Dieu, monsieur, I submit my theory; that is all. If I am mistaken, you can easily prove it."

"I will do so at once....I confess that your assurance——"

The count muttered a few more words; then suddenly rushed to the door and passed out. Not a word was uttered in his absence; and this profound silence gave the situation an air of almost tragic importance. Finally, the count returned. He was pale and nervous. He said to his friends, in a trembling voice:

"I beg your pardon.... the revelations of the chevalier were so unexpected....I should never have thought...."

His wife questioned him, eagerly:

"Speak.... what is it?"

He stammered: "The hole is there, at the very spot, at the side of the window——"

He seized the chevalier's arm, and said to him in an imperious tone:

"Now, monsieur, proceed. I admit that you are right so far, but now.... that is not all.... go on.... tell us the rest of it."

Floriani disengaged his arm gently, and, after a moment, continued:

"Well, in my opinion, this is what happened. The thief, knowing that the countess was going to wear the necklace that evening, had prepared his gangway or bridge during your absence. He watched you through the window and saw you hide the necklace. Afterward, he cut the glass and pulled the ring."

"Ah! but the distance was so great that it would be impossible for him to reach the window-fastening through the transom."

"Well, then, if he could not open the window by reaching through the transom, he must have crawled through the transom."

"Impossible; it is too small. No man could crawl through it."

"Then it was not a man," declared Floriani.

"What!"

"If the transom is too small to admit a man, it must have been a child."

"A child!"

"Did you not say that your friend Henriette had a son?"

"Yes; a son named Raoul."

"Then, in all probability, it was Raoul who committed the theft."

"What proof have you of that?"

"What proof! Plenty of it....For instance—-"

He stopped, and reflected for a moment, then continued:

"For instance, that gangway or bridge. It is improbable that the child could have brought it in from outside the house and carried it away again without being observed. He must have used something close at hand. In the little room used by Henriette as a kitchen, were there not some shelves against the wall on which she placed her pans and dishes?"

"Two shelves, to the best of my memory."

"Are you sure that those shelves are really fastened to the wooden brackets that support them? For, if they are not, we could be justified in presuming that the child removed them, fastened them together, and thus formed his bridge. Perhaps, also, since there was a stove, we might find the bent poker that he used to open the transom."

Without saying a word, the count left the room; and, this time, those present did not feel the nervous anxiety they had experienced the first time. They were confident that Floriani was right, and no one was surprised when the count returned and declared:

"It was the child. Everything proves it."

"You have seen the shelves and the poker?"

"Yes. The shelves have been unnailed, and the poker is there yet."

But the countess exclaimed:

"You had better say it was his mother. Henriette is the guilty party. She must have compelled her son—-"

"No," declared the chevalier, "the mother had nothing to do with it."

"Nonsense! they occupied the same room. The child could not have done it without the mother's knowledge."

"True, they lived in the same room, but all this happened in the adjoining room, during the night, while the mother was asleep."

"And the necklace?" said the count. "It would have been found amongst the child's things."

"Pardon me! He had been out. That morning, on which you found him reading, he had just come from school, and perhaps the commissary of police, instead of wasting his time on the innocent mother, would have been better employed in searching the child's desk amongst his school-books."

"But how do you explain those two thousand francs that Henriette received each year? Are they not evidence of her complicity?"

"If she had been an accomplice, would she have thanked you for that money? And then, was she not closely watched? But the child, being free, could easily go to a neighboring city, negotiate with some dealer and sell him one diamond or two diamonds, as he might wish, upon condition that the money should be sent from Paris, and that proceeding could be repeated from year to year."

An indescribable anxiety oppressed the Dreux-Soubise and their guests. There was something in the tone and attitude of Floriani—something more than the chevalier's assurance which, from the beginning, had so annoyed the count. There was a touch of irony, that seemed rather hostile than sympathetic. But the count affected to laugh, as he said:

"All that is very ingenious and interesting, and I congratulate you upon your vivid imagination."

"No, not at all," replied Floriani, with the utmost gravity, "I imagine nothing. I simply describe the events as they must have occurred."

"But what do you know about them?"

"What you yourself have told me. I picture to myself the life of the mother and child down there in the country; the illness of the mother, the schemes of and inventions of the child sell the precious stones in order to save his mother's life, or, at least, soothe her dying moments. Her illness overcomes her. She dies. Years roll on. The child becomes a man; and then—and now I will give my imagination a free rein—let us suppose that the man feels a desire to return to the home of his childhood, that he does so, and that he meets there certain people who suspect and accuse his mother.... do you realize the sorrow and anguish of such an interview in the very house wherein the original drama was played?"

His words seemed to echo for a few seconds in the ensuing silence, and one could read upon the faces of the Count and Countess de Dreux a bewildered effort to comprehend his meaning and, at the same time, the fear and anguish of such a comprehension. The count spoke at last, and said:

"Who are you, monsieur?"

"I? The chevalier Floriani, whom you met at Palermo, and whom you have been gracious enough to invite to your house on several occasions."

"Then what does this story mean?"

"Oh! nothing at all! It is simply a pastime, so far as I am concerned. I endeavor to depict the pleasure that Henriette's son, if he still lives, would have in telling you that he was the guilty party, and that he did it because his mother was unhappy, as she was on the point of losing the place of a.... servant, by which she lived, and because the child suffered at sight of his mother's sorrow."

He spoke with suppressed emotion, rose partially and inclined toward the countess. There could be no doubt that the chevalier Floriani was Henriette's son. His attitude and words proclaimed it. Besides, was it not his obvious intention and desire to be recognized as such?

The count hesitated. What action would he take against the audacious guest? Ring? Provoke a scandal? Unmask the man who had once robbed him? But that was a long time ago! And who would believe that absurd story about the guilty child? No; better far to accept the situation, and pretend not to comprehend the true meaning of it. So the count, turning to Floriani, exclaimed:

"Your story is very curious, very entertaining; I enjoyed it much. But what do you think has become of this young man, this model son? I hope he has not abandoned the career in which he made such a brilliant début."

"Oh! certainly not."

"After such a début! To steal the Queen's Necklace at six years of age; the celebrated necklace that was coveted by Marie-Antoinette!"

"And to steal it," remarked Floriani, falling in with the count's mood, "without costing him the slightest trouble, without anyone thinking to examine the condition of the window, or to observe that the window-sill was too clean—that window-sill which he had wiped in order to efface the marks he had made in the thick dust. We must admit that it was sufficient to turn the head of a boy at that age. It was all so easy. He had simply to desire the thing, and reach out his hand to get it."

"And he reached out his hand."

"Both hands," replied the chevalier, laughing.

His companions received a shock. What mystery surrounded the life of the so-called Floriani? How wonderful must have been the life of that adventurer, a thief at six years of age, and who, to-day, in search of excitement or, at most, to gratify a feeling of resentment, had come to brave his victim in her own house, audaciously, foolishly, and yet with all the grace and delicacy of a courteous guest!

He arose and approached the countess to bid her adieu. She recoiled, unconsciously. He smiled.

"Oh! Madame, you are afraid of me! Did I pursue my role of parlor-magician a step too far?"

She controlled herself, and replied, with her accustomed ease:

"Not at all, monsieur. The legend of that dutiful son interested me very much, and I am pleased to know that my necklace had such a brilliant destiny. But do you not think that the son of that woman, that Henriette, was the victim of hereditary influence in the choice of his vocation?"

He shuddered, feeling the point, and replied:

"I am sure of it; and, moreover, his natural tendency to crime must have been very strong or he would have been discouraged."

"Why so?"

"Because, as you must know, the majority of the diamonds were false. The only genuine stones were the few purchased from the English jeweler, the others having been sold, one by one, to meet the cruel necessities of life."

"It was still the Queen's Necklace, monsieur," replied the countess, haughtily, "and that is something that he, Henriette's son, could not appreciate."

"He was able to appreciate, madame, that, whether true or false, the necklace was nothing more that an object of parade, an emblem of senseless pride."

The count made a threatening gesture, but his wife stopped him.

"Monsieur," she said, "if the man to whom you allude has the slightest sense of honor——-"

She stopped, intimidated by Floriani's cool manner.

"If that man has the slightest sense of honor," he repeated.

She felt that she would not gain anything by speaking to him in that manner, and in spite of her anger and indignation, trembling as she was from humiliated pride, she said to him, almost politely:

"Monsieur, the legend says that Rétaux de Villette, when in possession of the Queen's Necklace, did not disfigure the mounting. He understood that the diamonds were simply the ornament, the accessory, and that the mounting was the essential work, the creation of the artist, and he respected it accordingly. Do you think that this man had the same feeling?"

"I have no doubt that the mounting still exists. The child respected it."

"Well, monsieur, if you should happen to meet him, will you tell him that he unjustly keeps possession of a relic that is the property and pride of a certain family, and that, although the stones have been removed, the Queen's necklace still belongs to the house of Dreux-Soubise. It belongs to us as much as our name or our honor."

The chevalier replied, simply:

"I shall tell him, madame."

He bowed to her, saluted the count and the other guests, and departed.

Four days later, the countess de Dreux found upon the table in her chamber a red leather case bearing the cardinal's arms. She opened it, and found the Queen's Necklace.

But as all things must, in the life of a man who strives for unity and logic, converge toward the same goal—and as a little advertising never does any harm—on the following day, the 'Echo de France' published these sensational lines:

"The Queen's Necklace, the famous historical jewelry stolen from the family of Dreux-Soubise, has been recovered by Arsène Lupin, who hastened to restore it to its rightful owner. We cannot too highly commend such a delicate and chivalrous act."

VI. The Seven of Hearts

I am frequently asked this question: "How did you make the acquaintance of Arsène Lupin?"

My connection with Arsène Lupin was well known. The details that I gather concerning that mysterious man, the irrefutable facts that I present, the new evidence that I produce, the interpretation that I place on certain acts of which the public has seen only the exterior manifestations without being able to discover the secret reasons or the invisible mechanism, all establish, if not an intimacy, at least amicable relations and regular confidences.

But how did I make his acquaintance? Why was I selected to be his historiographer? Why I, and not some one else?

The answer is simple: chance alone presided over my choice; my merit was not considered. It was chance that put me in his way. It was by chance that I was participant in one of his strangest and most mysterious adventures; and by chance that I was an actor in a drama of which he was the marvelous stage director; an obscure and intricate drama, bristling with such thrilling events that I feel a certain embarrassment in undertaking to describe it.

The first act takes place during that memorable night of 22 June, of which so much has already been said. And, for my part, I attribute the anomalous conduct of which I was guilty on that occasion to the unusual frame of mind in which I found myself on my return home. I had dined with some friends at the Cascade restaurant, and, the entire evening, whilst we smoked and the orchestra played melancholy waltzes, we talked only of crimes and thefts, and dark and frightful intrigues. That is always a poor overture to a night's sleep.

The Saint-Martins went away in an automobile. Jean Daspry—that delightful, heedless Daspry who, six months later, was killed in such a tragic manner on the frontier of Morocco— Jean Daspry and I returned on foot through the dark, warm night. When we arrived in front of the little house in which I had lived for a year at Neuilly, on the boulevard Maillot, he said to me:

"Are you afraid?"

"What an idea!"

"But this house is so isolated.... no neighbors.... vacant lots....Really, I am not a coward, and yet—-"

"Well, you are very cheering, I must say."

"Oh! I say that as I would say anything else. The Saint-Martins have impressed me with their stories of brigands and thieves."

We shook hands and said good-night. I took out my key and opened the door.

"Well, that is good," I murmured, "Antoine has forgotten to light a candle."

Then I recalled the fact that Antoine was away; I had given him a short leave of absence. Forthwith, I was disagreeably oppressed by the darkness and silence of the night. I ascended the stairs on tiptoe, and reached my room as quickly as possible; then, contrary to my usual habit, I turned the key and pushed the bolt.

The light of my candle restored my courage. Yet I was careful to take my revolver from its case—a large, powerful weapon—and place it beside my bed. That precaution completed my reassurance. I laid down and, as usual, took a book from my night-table to read myself to sleep. Then I received a great surprise. Instead of the paper-knife with which I had marked my place on the preceding, I found an envelope, closed with five seals of red wax. I seized it eagerly. It was addressed to me, and marked: "Urgent."

A letter! A letter addressed to me! Who could have put it in that place? Nervously, I tore open the envelope, and read:

"From the moment you open this letter, whatever happens, whatever you may hear, do not move, do not utter one cry. Otherwise you are doomed."

I am not a coward, and, quite as well as another, I can face real danger, or smile at the visionary perils of imagination. But, let me repeat, I was in an anomalous condition of mind, with my nerves set on edge by the events of the evening. Besides, was there not, in my present situation, something startling and mysterious, calculated to disturb the most courageous spirit?

My feverish fingers clutched the sheet of paper, and I read and re-read those threatening words: "Do not move, do not utter one cry. Otherwise, you are doomed."

"Nonsense!" I thought. "It is a joke; the work of some cheerful idiot."

I was about to laugh—a good loud laugh. Who prevented me? What haunting fear compressed my throat?

At least, I would blow out the candle. No, I could not do it. "Do not move, or you are doomed," were the words he had written.

These auto-suggestions are frequently more imperious than the most positive realities; but why should I struggle against them? I had simply to close my eyes. I did so.

At that moment, I heard a slight noise, followed by crackling sounds, proceeding from a large room used by me as a library. A small room or antechamber was situated between the library and my bedchamber.

The approach of an actual danger greatly excited me, and I felt a desire to get up, seize my revolver, and rush into the library. I did not rise; I saw one of the curtains of the left window move. There was no doubt about it: the curtain had moved. It was still moving. And I saw—oh! I saw quite distinctly—in the narrow space between the curtains and the window, a human form; a bulky mass that prevented the curtains from hanging straight. And it is equally certain that the man saw me through the large meshes of the curtain. Then, I understood the situation. His mission was to guard me while the others carried away their booty. Should I rise and seize my revolver? Impossible! He was there! At the least movement, at the least cry, I was doomed.

Then came a terrific noise that shook the house; this was followed by lighter sounds, two or three together, like those of a hammer that rebounded. At least, that was the impression formed in my confused brain. These were mingled with other sounds, thus creating a veritable uproar which proved that the intruders were not only bold, but felt themselves secure from interruption.

They were right. I did not move. Was it cowardice? No, rather weakness, a total inability to move any portion of my body, combined with discretion; for why should I struggle? Behind that man, there were ten others who would come to his assistance. Should I risk my life to save a few tapestries and bibelots?

Throughout the night, my torture endured. Insufferable torture, terrible anguish! The noises had stopped, but I was in constant fear of their renewal. And the man! The man who was guarding me, weapon in hand. My fearful eyes remained cast in his direction. And my heart beat! And a profuse perspiration oozed from every pore of my body!

Suddenly, I experienced an immense relief; a milk-wagon, whose sound was familiar to me, passed along the boulevard; and, at the same time, I had an impression that the light of a new day was trying to steal through the closed window-blinds.

At last, daylight penetrated the room; other vehicles passed along the boulevard; and all the phantoms of the night vanished. Then I put one arm out of the bed, slowly and cautiously. My eyes were fixed upon the curtain, locating the exact spot at which I must fire; I made an exact calculation of the movements I must make; then, quickly, I seized my revolver and fired.

I leaped from my bed with a cry of deliverance, and rushed to the window. The bullet had passed through the curtain and the window-glass, but it had not touched the man—for the very good reason that there was none there. Nobody! Thus, during the entire night, I had been hypnotized by a fold of the curtain. And, during that time, the malefactors....Furiously, with an enthusiasm that nothing could have stopped, I turned the key, opened the door, crossed the antechamber, opened another door, and rushed into the library. But amazement stopped me on the threshold, panting, astounded, more astonished than I had been by the absence of the man. All the things that I supposed had been stolen, furniture, books, pictures, old tapestries, everything was in its proper place.

It was incredible. I could not believe my eyes. Notwithstanding that uproar, those noises of removal....I made a tour, I inspected the walls, I made a mental inventory of all the familiar objects. Nothing was missing. And, what was more disconcerting, there was no clue to the intruders, not a sign, not a chair disturbed, not the trace of a footstep.

"Well! Well!" I said to myself, pressing my hands on my bewildered head, "surely I am not crazy! I hear something!"

Inch by inch, I made a careful examination of the room. It was in vain. Unless I could consider this as a discovery: Under a small Persian rug, I found a card—an ordinary playing card. It was the seven of hearts; it was like any other seven of hearts in French playing-cards, with this slight but curious exception: The extreme point of each of the seven red spots or hearts was pierced by a hole, round and regular as if made with the point of an awl.

Nothing more. A card and a letter found in a book. But was not that sufficient to affirm that I had not been the plaything of a dream?

Throughout the day, I continued my searches in the library. It was a large room, much too large for the requirements of such a house, and the decoration of which attested the bizarre taste of its founder. The floor was a mosaic of multicolored stones, formed into large

65

symmetrical designs. The walls were covered with a similar mosaic, arranged in panels, Pompeiian allegories, Byzantine compositions, frescoes of the Middle Ages. A Bacchus bestriding a cask. An emperor wearing a gold crown, a flowing beard, and holding a sword in his right hand.

Quite high, after the style of an artist's studio, there was a large window—the only one in the room. That window being always open at night, it was probable that the men had entered through it, by the aid of a ladder. But, again, there was no evidence. The bottom of the ladder would have left some marks in the soft earth beneath the window; but there were none. Nor were there any traces of footsteps in any part of the yard.

I had no idea of informing the police, because the facts I had before me were so absurd and inconsistent. They would laugh at me. However, as I was then a reporter on the staff of the 'Gil Blas,' I wrote a lengthy account of my adventure and it was published in the paper on the second day thereafter. The article attracted some attention, but no one took it seriously. They regarded it as a work of fiction rather than a story of real life. The Saint-Martins rallied me. But Daspry, who took an interest in such matters, came to see me, made a study of the affair, but reached no conclusion.

A few mornings later, the door-bell rang, and Antoine came to inform me that a gentleman desired to see me. He would not give his name. I directed Antoine to show him up. He was a man of about forty years of age with a very dark complexion, lively features, and whose correct dress, slightly frayed, proclaimed a taste that contrasted strangely with his rather vulgar manners. Without any preamble, he said to me—in a rough voice that confirmed my suspicion as to his social position:

"Monsieur, whilst in a café, I picked up a copy of the 'Gil Blas,' and read your article. It interested me very much.

"Thank you."

"And here I am."

"Ah!"

"Yes, to talk to you. Are all the facts related by you quite correct?"

"Absolutely so."

"Well, in that case, I can, perhaps, give you some information."

"Very well; proceed."

"No, not yet. First, I must be sure that the facts are exactly as you have related them."

"I have given you my word. What further proof do you want?"

"I must remain alone in this room."

"I do not understand," I said, with surprise.

"It's an idea that occurred to me when reading your article. Certain details established an extraordinary coincidence with another case that came under my notice. If I am mistaken, I shall say nothing more. And the only means of ascertaining the truth is by my remaining in the room alone."

What was at the bottom of this proposition? Later, I recalled that the man was exceedingly nervous; but, at the same time, although somewhat astonished, I found nothing particularly abnormal about the man or the request he had made. Moreover, my curiosity was aroused; so I replied:

"Very well. How much time do you require?"

"Oh! three minutes—not longer. Three minutes from now, I will rejoin you."

I left the room, and went downstairs. I took out my watch. One minute passed. Two minutes. Why did I feel so depressed? Why did those moments seem so solemn and weird? Two minutes and a half....Two minutes and three quarters. Then I heard a pistol shot.

I bounded up the stairs and entered the room. A cry of horror escaped me. In the middle of the room, the man was lying on his left side, motionless. Blood was flowing from a wound in his forehead. Near his hand was a revolver, still smoking.

But, in addition to this frightful spectacle, my attention was attracted by another object. At two feet from the body, upon the floor, I saw a playing-card. It was the seven of hearts. I picked it up. The lower extremity of each of the seven spots was pierced with a small round hole.

A half-hour later, the commissary of police arrived, then the coroner and the chief of the Sûreté, Mon. Dudouis. I had been careful not to touch the corpse. The preliminary inquiry was very brief, and disclosed nothing. There were no papers in the pockets of the deceased; no name upon his clothes; no initial upon his linen; nothing to give any clue to his identity. The room was in the same perfect order as before. The furniture had not been disturbed. Yet this man had not come to my house solely for the purpose of killing himself, or because he considered my place the most convenient one for his suicide! There must have been a motive for his act of despair, and that motive was, no doubt, the result of some new fact ascertained by him during the three minutes he was alone.

What was that fact? What had he seen? What frightful secret had been revealed to him? There was no answer to these questions. But, at the last moment, an incident occurred that appeared to us of considerable importance. As two policemen were raising the body to place it on a stretcher, the left hand thus being disturbed, a crumpled card fell from it. The card bore these words: "Georges Andermatt, 37 Rue de Berry."

What did that mean? Georges Andermatt was a rich banker in Paris, the founder and president of the Metal Exchange which had given such an impulse to the metallic industries in France. He lived in princely style; was the possessor of numerous automobiles, coaches, and an expensive racing-stable. His social affairs were very select, and Madame Andermatt was noted for her grace and beauty.

"Can that be the man's name?" I asked. —

The chief of the Sûreté leaned over him.

"It is not he. Mon. Andermatt is a thin man, and slightly grey."

"But why this card?"

"Have you a telephone, monsieur?"

"Yes, in the vestibule. Come with me."

He looked in the directory, and then asked for number 415.21.

"Is Mon. Andermatt at home?....Please tell him that Mon. Dudouis wished him to come at once to 102 Boulevard Maillot. Very important."

Twenty minutes later, Mon. Andermatt arrived in his automobile. After the circumstances had been explained to him, he was taken in to see the corpse. He displayed considerable emotion, and spoke, in a low tone, and apparently unwillingly:

"Etienne Varin," he said.

"You know him?"

"No.... or, at least, yes.... by sight only. His brother...."

"Ah! he has a brother?"

"Yes, Alfred Varin. He came to see me once on some matter of business....I forget what it was."

"Where does he live?"

"The two brothers live together—rue de Provence, I think."

"Do you know any reason why he should commit suicide?"

"None."

"He held a card in his hand. It was your card with your address."

"I do not understand that. It must have been there by some chance that will be disclosed by the investigation."

A very strange chance, I thought; and I felt that the others entertained the same impression.

I discovered the same impression in the papers next day, and amongst all my friends with whom I discussed the affair. Amid the mysteries that enveloped it, after the double discovery of the seven of hearts pierced with seven holes, after the two inscrutable events that had happened in my house, that visiting card promised to throw some light on the affair. Through it, the truth may be revealed. But, contrary to our expectations, Mon. Andermatt furnished no explanation. He said:

"I have told you all I know. What more can I do? I am greatly surprised that my card should be found in such a place, and I sincerely hope the point will be cleared up."

It was not. The official investigation established that the Varin brothers were of Swiss origin, had led a shifting life under various names, frequenting gambling resorts, associating with a band of foreigners who had been dispersed by the police after a series of robberies in which their participation was established only by their flight. At number 24 rue de Provence, where the Varin brothers had lived six years before, no one knew what had become of them.

I confess that, for my part, the case seemed to me so complicated and so mysterious that I did not think the problem would ever be solved, so I concluded to waste no more time upon it. But Jean Daspry, whom I frequently met at that period, became more and more interested in it each day. It was he who pointed out to me that item from a foreign newspaper which was reproduced and commented upon by the entire press. It was as follows:

"The first trial of a new model of submarine boat, which is expected to revolutionize naval warfare, will be given in presence of the former Emperor at a place that will be kept secret until the last minute. An indiscretion has revealed its name; it is called 'The Seven-of-Hearts.'"

The Seven-of-Hearts! That presented a new problem. Could a connection be established between the name of the sub-marine and the incidents which we have related? But a connection of what nature? What had happened here could have no possible relation with the sub-marine.

"What do you know about it?" said Daspry to me. "The most diverse effects often proceed from the same cause."

Two days later, the following foreign news item was received and published:

"It is said that the plans of the new sub-marine 'Seven-of-Hearts' were prepared by French engineers, who, having sought, in vain, the support of their compatriots, subsequently entered into negotiations with the British Admiralty, without success."

I do not wish to give undue publicity to certain delicate matters which once provoked considerable excitement. Yet, since all danger of injury therefrom has now come to an end, I must speak of the article that appeared in the 'Echo de France,' which aroused so much comment at that time, and which threw considerable light upon the mystery of the Seven-of-Hearts. This is the article as it was published over the signature of Salvator:

"THE AFFAIR OF THE SEVEN-OF-HEARTS.

"A CORNER OF THE VEIL RAISED.

"We will be brief. Ten years ago, a young mining engineer, Louis Lacombe, wishing to devote his time and fortune to certain studies, resigned his position he then held, and rented number 102 boulevard Maillot, a small house that had been recently built and decorated for an Italian count. Through the agency of the Varin brothers of Lausanne, one of whom assisted in the preliminary experiments and the other acted as financial agent, the young engineer was introduced to Georges Andermatt, the founder of the Metal Exchange.

69

"After several interviews, he succeeded in interesting the banker in a sub-marine boat on which he was working, and it was agreed that as soon as the invention was perfected, Mon. Andermatt would use his influence with the Minister of Marine to obtain a series of trials under the direction of the government. For two years, Louis Lacombe was a frequent visitor at Andermatt's house, and he submitted to the banker the various improvements he made upon his original plans, until one day, being satisfied with the perfection of his work, he asked Mon. Andermatt to communicate with the Minister of Marine. That day, Louis Lacombe dined at Mon. Andermatt's house. He left there about half-past eleven at night. He has not been seen since.

"A perusal of the newspapers of that date will show that the young man's family caused every possible inquiry to be made, but without success; and it was the general opinion that Louis Lacombe— who was known as an original and visionary youth—had quietly left for parts unknown.

"Let us accept that theory—improbable, though it be,—and let us consider another question, which is a most important one for our country: What has become of the plans of the sub-marine? Did Louis Lacombe carry them away? Are they destroyed?

"After making a thorough investigation, we are able to assert, positively, that the plans are in existence, and are now in the possession of the two brothers Varin. How did they acquire such a possession? That is a question not yet determined; nor do we know why they have not tried to sell them at an earlier date. Did they fear that their title to them would be called in question? If so, they have lost that fear, and we can announce definitely, that the plans of Louis Lacombe are now the property of foreign power, and we are in a position to publish the correspondence that passed between the Varin brothers and the representative of that power. The 'Seven-of-Hearts' invented by Louis Lacombe has been actually constructed by our neighbor.

"Will the invention fulfill the optimistic expectations of those who were concerned in that treacherous act?"

And a post-script adds:

"LATER.—OUR SPECIAL CORRESPONDENT INFORMS US THAT THE PRELIMINARY TRIAL OF THE 'SEVEN-OF-HEARTS' HAS NOT BEEN SATISFACTORY. IT IS QUITE LIKELY THAT THE PLANS SOLD AND DELIVERED BY THE VARIN BROTHERS DID NOT INCLUDE THE FINAL DOCUMENT CARRIED BY LOUIS LACOMBE TO MON. ANDERMATT ON THE DAY OF HIS DISAPPEARANCE, A DOCUMENT THAT WAS INDISPENSABLE TO A THOROUGH UNDERSTANDING OF THE INVENTION. IT CONTAINED A SUMMARY OF THE FINAL CONCLUSIONS OF THE INVENTOR, AND ESTIMATES AND FIGURES NOT CONTAINED IN THE OTHER

PAPERS. WITHOUT THIS DOCUMENT, THE PLANS ARE INCOMPLETE; ON THE OTHER HAND, WITHOUT THE PLANS, THE DOCUMENT IS WORTHLESS.

"NOW IS THE TIME TO ACT AND RECOVER WHAT BELONGS TO US. IT MAY BE A DIFFICULT MATTER, BUT WE RELY UPON THE ASSISTANCE OF MON. ANDERMATT. IT WILL BE TO HIS INTEREST TO EXPLAIN HIS CONDUCT WHICH HAS HITHERTO BEEN SO STRANGE AND INSCRUTABLE. HE WILL EXPLAIN NOT ONLY WHY HE CONCEALED THESE FACTS AT THE TIME OF THE SUICIDE OF ETIENNE VARIN, BUT ALSO WHY HE HAS NEVER REVEALED THE DISAPPEARANCE OF THE PAPER—A FACT WELL KNOWN TO HIM. HE WILL TELL WHY, DURING THE LAST SIX YEARS, HE PAID SPIES TO WATCH THE MOVEMENTS OF THE VARIN BROTHERS. WE EXPECT FROM HIM, NOT ONLY WORDS, BUT ACTS. AND AT ONCE. OTHERWISE—-"

The threat was plainly expressed. But of what did it consist? What whip was Salvator, the anonymous writer of the article, holding over the head of Mon. Andermatt?

An army of reporters attacked the banker, and ten interviewers announced the scornful manner in which they were treated. Thereupon, the 'Echo de France' announced its position in these words:

"Whether Mon. Andermatt is willing or not, he will be, henceforth, our collaborator in the work we have undertaken."

Daspry and I were dining together on the day on which that announcement appeared. That evening, with the newspapers spread over my table, we discussed the affair and examined it from every point of view with that exasperation that a person feels when walking in the dark and finding himself constantly falling over the same obstacles. Suddenly, without any warning whatsoever, the door opened and a lady entered. Her face was hidden behind a thick veil. I rose at once and approached her.

"Is it you, monsieur, who lives here?" she asked.

"Yes, madame, but I do not understand—-"

"The gate was not locked," she explained.

"But the vestibule door?"

She did not reply, and it occurred to me that she had used the servants' entrance. How did she know the way? Then there was a silence that was quite embarrassing. She looked at Daspry, and I was obliged to introduce him. I asked her to be seated and explain the object of her visit. She raised her veil, and I saw that she was a brunette with regular features and, though not handsome, she was attractive—principally, on account of her sad, dark eyes.

"I am Madame Andermatt," she said.

"Madame Andermatt!" I repeated, with astonishment.

After a brief pause, she continued with a voice and manner that were quite easy and natural:

"I have come to see you about that affair—you know. I thought I might be able to obtain some information—-"

"Mon Dieu, madame, I know nothing but what has already appeared in the papers. But if you will point out in what way I can help you...."

"I do not know....I do not know."

Not until then did I suspect that her calm demeanor was assumed, and that some poignant grief was concealed beneath that air of tranquility. For a moment, we were silent and embarrassed. Then Daspry stepped forward, and said:

"Will you permit me to ask you a few questions?"

"Yes, yes," she cried. "I will answer."

"You will answer.... whatever those questions may be?"

"Yes."

"Did you know Louis Lacombe?" he asked.

"Yes, through my husband."

"When did you see him for the last time?"

"The evening he dined with us."

"At that time, was there anything to lead you to believe that you would never see him again?"

"No. But he had spoken of a trip to Russia—in a vague way."

"Then you expected to see him again?"

"Yes. He was to dine with us, two days later."

"How do you explain his disappearance?"

"I cannot explain it."

"And Mon. Andermatt?"

"I do not know."

"Yet the article published in the 'Echo de France' indicates—-"

"Yes, that the Varin brothers had something to do with his disappearance."

"Is that your opinion?"

"Yes."

"On what do you base your opinion?"

"When he left our house, Louis Lacombe carried a satchel containing all the papers relating to his invention. Two days later, my husband, in a conversation with one of the Varin brothers, learned that the papers were in their possession."

"And he did not denounce them?"

"No."

"Why not?"

"Because there was something else in the satchel—something besides the papers of Louis Lacombe."

"What was it?"

She hesitated; was on the point of speaking, but, finally, remained silent. Daspry continued:

"I presume that is why your husband has kept a close watch over their movements instead of informing the police. He hoped to recover the papers and, at the same time, that compromising article which has enabled the two brothers to hold over him threats of exposure and blackmail."

"Over him, and over me."

"Ah! over you, also?"

"Over me, in particular."

She uttered the last words in a hollow voice. Daspry observed it; he paced to and fro for a moment, then, turning to her, asked:

"Had you written to Louis Lacombe?"

"Of course. My husband had business with him—"

"Apart from those business letters, had you written to Louis Lacombe.... other letters? Excuse my insistence, but it is absolutely necessary that I should know the truth. Did you write other letters?"

"Yes," she replied, blushing.

"And those letters came into the possession of the Varin brothers?"

"Yes."

"Does Mon. Andermatt know it?"

"He has not seen them, but Alfred Varin has told him of their existence and threatened to publish them if my husband should take any steps against him. My husband was afraid.... of a scandal."

"But he has tried to recover the letters?"

"I think so; but I do not know. You see, after that last interview with Alfred Varin, and after some harsh words between me and my husband in which he called me to account—we live as strangers."

"In that case, as you have nothing to lose, what do you fear?"

"I may be indifferent to him now, but I am the woman that he has loved, the one he would still love—oh! I am quite sure of that," she murmured, in a fervent voice, "he would still love me if he had not got hold of those cursed letters——"

"What! Did he succeed?....But the two brothers still defied him?"

"Yes, and they boasted of having a secure hiding-place."

"Well?"

"I believe my husband discovered that hiding-place."

"Ah! where was it?"

"Here."

"Here!" I cried in alarm.

"Yes. I always had that suspicion. Louis Lacombe was very ingenious and amused himself in his leisure hours, by making safes and locks. No doubt, the Varin brothers were aware of that fact and utilized one of Lacombe's safes in which to conceal the letters.... and other things, perhaps."

"But they did not live here," I said.

"Before you came, four months ago, the house had been vacant for some time. And they may have thought that your presence here would not interfere with them when they wanted to get the papers. But they did not count on my husband, who came here on the night of 22 June, forced the safe, took what he was seeking, and left his card to inform the two brothers that he feared them no more, and that their positions were now reversed. Two days later, after reading the article in the 'Gil Blas,' Etienne Varin came here, remained alone in this room, found the safe empty, and.... killed himself."

After a moment, Daspry said:

"A very simple theory....Has Mon. Andermatt spoken to you since then?"

"No."

"Has his attitude toward you changed in any way? Does he appear more gloomy, more anxious?"

"No, I haven't noticed any change."

"And yet you think he has secured the letters. Now, in my opinion, he has not got those letters, and it was not he who came here on the night of 22 June."

"Who was it, then?"

"The mysterious individual who is managing this affair, who holds all the threads in his hands, and whose invisible but far-reaching power we have felt from the beginning. It was he and his friends who entered this house on 22 June; it was he who discovered the hiding-place of the papers; it was he who left Mon. Andermatt's card; it is he who now holds the correspondence and the evidence of the treachery of the Varin brothers."

"Who is he?" I asked, impatiently.

"The man who writes letters to the 'Echo de France'.... Salvator! Have we not convincing evidence of that fact? Does he not mention in his letters certain details that no one could know, except the man who had thus discovered the secrets of the two brothers?"

"Well, then," stammered Madame Andermatt, in great alarm, "he has my letters also, and it is he who now threatens my husband. Mon Dieu! What am I to do?"

"Write to him," declared Daspry. "Confide in him without reserve. Tell him all you know and all you may hereafter learn. Your interest and his interest are the same. He is not working against Mon. Andermatt, but against Alfred Varin. Help him."

"How?"

"Has your husband the document that completes the plans of Louis Lacombe?"

"Yes."

"Tell that to Salvator, and, if possible, procure the document for him. Write to him at once. You risk nothing."

The advice was bold, dangerous even at first sight, but Madame Andermatt had no choice. Besides, as Daspry had said, she ran no risk. If the unknown writer were an enemy, that step would not aggravate the situation. If he were a stranger seeking to accomplish a particular purpose, he would attach to those letters only a secondary importance. Whatever might happen, it was the only solution offered to her, and she, in her anxiety, was only too glad to act on it. She thanked us effusively, and promised to keep us informed.

In fact, two days later, she sent us the following letter that she had received from Salvator:

"Have not found the letters, but I will get them. Rest easy. I am watching everything. S."

I looked at the letter. It was in the same handwriting as the note I found in my book on the night of 22 June.

Daspry was right. Salvator was, indeed, the originator of that affair.

We were beginning to see a little light coming out of the darkness that surrounded us, and an unexpected light was thrown on certain points; but other points yet remained obscure—for instance, the finding of the two seven-of-hearts. Perhaps I was unnecessarily concerned about those two cards whose seven punctured spots had appeared to me under such startling circumstances! Yet I could not refrain from asking myself: What role will they play in the drama? What importance do they bear? What conclusion must be drawn from the fact that the submarine constructed from the plans of Louis Lacombe bore the name of 'Seven-of-Hearts'?

Daspry gave little thought to the other two cards; he devoted all his attention to another problem which he considered more urgent; he was seeking the famous hiding-place.

"And who knows," said he, "I may find the letters that Salvator did not find—by inadvertence, perhaps. It is improbable that the Varin brothers would have removed from a spot, which they deemed inaccessible, the weapon which was so valuable to them."

And he continued to search. In a short time, the large room held no more secrets for him, so he extended his investigations to the other rooms. He examined the interior and the exterior, the stones of the foundation, the bricks in the walls; he raised the slates of the roof.

One day, he came with a pickaxe and a spade, gave me the spade, kept the pickaxe, pointed to the adjacent vacant lots, and said: "Come."

I followed him, but I lacked his enthusiasm. He divided the vacant land into several sections which he examined in turn. At last, in a corner, at the angle formed by the walls of two neighboring proprietors, a small pile of earth and gravel, covered with briers and grass, attracted his attention. He attacked it. I was obliged to help him. For an hour, under a hot sun, we labored without success. I was discouraged, but Daspry urged me on. His ardor was as strong as ever.

At last, Daspry's pickaxe unearthed some bones—the remains of a skeleton to which some scraps of clothing still hung. Suddenly, I turned pale. I had discovered, sticking in the earth, a small piece of iron cut in the form of a rectangle, on which I thought I could see red spots. I stooped and picked it up. That little iron plate was the exact size of a playing-card, and the red spots, made with red lead, were arranged upon it in a manner similar to the seven-of-hearts, and each spot was pierced with a round hole similar to the perforations in the two playing cards.

"Listen, Daspry, I have had enough of this. You can stay if it interests you. But I am going."

Was that simply the expression of my excited nerves? Or was it the result of a laborious task executed under a burning sun? I know that I trembled as I walked away, and that I went to bed, where I remained forty-eight hours, restless and feverish, haunted by skeletons that danced around me and threw their bleeding hearts at my head.

Daspry was faithful to me. He came to my house every day, and remained three or four hours, which he spent in the large room, ferreting, thumping, tapping.

"The letters are here, in this room," he said, from time to time, "they are here. I will stake my life on it."

On the morning of the third day I arose—feeble yet, but cured. A substantial breakfast cheered me up. But a letter that I received that afternoon contributed, more than anything else, to my complete recovery, and aroused in me a lively curiosity. This was the letter:

"MONSIEUR,

"THE DRAMA, THE FIRST ACT OF WHICH TRANSPIRED ON THE NIGHT OF 22

JUNE, IS NOW DRAWING TO A CLOSE. FORCE OF CIRCUMSTANCES COMPEL ME

TO BRING THE TWO PRINCIPAL ACTORS IN THAT DRAMA FACE TO FACE, AND I

WISH THAT MEETING TO TAKE PLACE IN YOUR HOUSE, IF YOU WILL BE SO

KIND AS TO GIVE ME THE USE OF IT FOR THIS EVENING FROM NINE O'CLOCK

TO ELEVEN. IT WILL BE ADVISABLE TO GIVE YOUR SERVANT LEAVE OF

ABSENCE FOR THE EVENING, AND, PERHAPS, YOU WILL BE SO KIND AS TO

LEAVE THE FIELD OPEN TO THE TWO ADVERSARIES. YOU WILL REMEMBER

THAT WHEN I VISITED YOUR HOUSE ON THE NIGHT OF 22 JUNE, I TOOK

EXCELLENT CARE OF YOUR PROPERTY. I FEEL THAT I WOULD DO YOU AN

INJUSTICE IF I SHOULD DOUBT, FOR ONE MOMENT, YOUR ABSOLUTE

DISCRETION IN THIS AFFAIR. YOUR DEVOTED,

"SALVATOR."

I was amused at the facetious tone of his letter and also at the whimsical nature of his request. There was a charming display of confidence and candor in his language, and nothing in the world could have induced me to deceive him or repay his confidence with ingratitude.

I gave my servant a theatre ticket, and he left the house at eight o'clock. A few minutes later, Daspry arrived. I showed him the letter.

"Well?" said he.

"Well, I have left the garden gate unlocked, so anyone can enter."

"And you—are you going away?"

"Not at all. I intend to stay right here."

"But he asks you to go—-"

"But I am not going. I will be discreet, but I am resolved to see what takes place."

"Ma foi!" exclaimed Daspry, laughing, "you are right, and I shall stay with you. I shouldn't like to miss it."

We were interrupted by the sound of the door-bell.

"Here already?" said Daspry, "twenty minutes ahead of time! Incredible!"

I went to the door and ushered in the visitor. It was Madame Andermatt. She was faint and nervous, and in a stammering voice, she ejaculated:

"My husband.... is coming.... he has an appointment.... they intend to give him the letters...."

"How do you know?" I asked.

"By chance. A message came for my husband while we were at dinner. The servant gave it to me by mistake. My husband grabbed it quickly, but he was too late. I had read it."

"You read it?"

"Yes. It was something like this: 'At nine o'clock this evening, be at Boulevard Maillot with the papers connected with the affair. In exchange, the letters.' So, after dinner, I hastened here."

"Unknown to your husband?"

"Yes."

"What do you think about it?" asked Daspry, turning to me.

"I think as you do, that Mon. Andermatt is one of the invited guests."

"Yes, but for what purpose?"

"That is what we are going to find out."

I led the men to a large room. The three of us could hide comfortably behind the velvet chimney-mantle, and observe all that should happen in the room. We seated ourselves there, with Madame Andermatt in the centre.

The clock struck nine. A few minutes later, the garden gate creaked upon its hinges. I confess that I was greatly agitated. I was about to learn the key to the mystery. The startling events of the last few weeks were about to be explained, and, under my eyes, the last battle was going to be fought. Daspry seized the hand of Madame Andermatt, and said to her:

"Not a word, not a movement! Whatever you may see or hear, keep quiet!"

Some one entered. It was Alfred Varin. I recognized him at once, owing to the close resemblance he bore to his brother Etienne. There was the same slouching gait; the same cadaverous face covered with a black beard.

He entered with the nervous air of a man who is accustomed to fear the presence of traps and ambushes; who scents and avoids them. He glanced about the room, and I had the impression that the chimney, masked with a velvet portière, did not please him. He took three steps in our direction, when something caused him to turn and walk toward the old mosaic king, with the flowing beard and flamboyant sword, which he examined minutely, mounting on a chair and following with his fingers the outlines of the shoulders and head and feeling certain parts of the face. Suddenly, he leaped from the chair and walked away from it. He had heard the sound of approaching footsteps. Mon. Andermatt appeared at the door.

"You! You!" exclaimed the banker. "Was it you who brought me here?"

"I? By no means," protested Varin, in a rough, jerky voice that reminded me of his brother, "on the contrary, it was your letter that brought me here."

"My letter?"

"A letter signed by you, in which you offered—-"

"I never wrote to you," declared Mon. Andermatt.

"You did not write to me!"

Instinctively, Varin was put on his guard, not against the banker, but against the unknown enemy who had drawn him into this trap. A second time, he looked in our direction, then walked toward the door. But Mon. Andermatt barred his passage.

"Well, where are you going, Varin?"

"There is something about this affair I don't like. I am going home. Good evening."

"One moment!"

"No need of that, Mon. Andermatt. I have nothing to say to you."

"But I have something to say to you, and this is a good time to say it."

"Let me pass."

"No, you will not pass."

Varin recoiled before the resolute attitude of the banker, as he muttered:

"Well, then, be quick about it."

One thing astonished me; and I have no doubt my two companions experienced a similar feeling. Why was Salvator not there? Was he not a necessary party at this conference? Or was he satisfied to let these two adversaries fight it out between themselves? At all events, his absence was a great disappointment, although it did not detract from the dramatic strength of the situation.

After a moment, Mon. Andermatt approached Varin and, face to face, eye to eye, said:

"Now, after all these years and when you have nothing more to fear, you can answer me candidly: What have you done with Louis Lacombe?"

"What a question! As if I knew anything about him!"

"You do know! You and your brother were his constant companions, almost lived with him in this very house. You knew all about his plans and his work. And the last night I ever saw Louis Lacombe, when I parted with him at my door, I saw two men slinking away in the shadows of the trees. That, I am ready to swear to."

"Well, what has that to do with me?"

"The two men were you and your brother."

"Prove it."

"The best proof is that, two days later, you yourself showed me the papers and the plans that belonged to Lacombe and offered to sell them. How did these papers come into your possession?"

"I have already told you, Mon. Andermatt, that we found them on Louis Lacombe's table, the morning after his disappearance."

"That is a lie!"

"Prove it."

"The law will prove it."

"Why did you not appeal to the law?"

"Why? Ah! Why——," stammered the banker, with a slight display of emotion.

"You know very well, Mon. Andermatt, if you had the least certainty of our guilt, our little threat would not have stopped you."

"What threat? Those letters? Do you suppose I ever gave those letters a moment's thought?"

"If you did not care for the letters, why did you offer me thousands of francs for their return? And why did you have my brother and me tracked like wild beasts?"

"To recover the plans."

"Nonsense! You wanted the letters. You knew that as soon as you had the letters in your possession, you could denounce us. Oh! no, I couldn't part with them!"

He laughed heartily, but stopped suddenly, and said:

"But, enough of this! We are merely going over old ground. We make no headway. We had better let things stand as they are."

"We will not let them stand as they are," said the banker, "and since you have referred to the letters, let me tell you that you will not leave this house until you deliver up those letters."

"I shall go when I please."

"You will not."

"Be careful, Mon. Andermatt. I warn you——-"

"I say, you shall not go."

"We will see about that," cried Varin, in such a rage that Madame Andermatt could not suppress a cry of fear. Varin must have heard it, for he now tried to force his way out. Mon. Andermatt pushed him back. Then I saw him put his hand into his coat pocket.

"For the last time, let me pass," he cried.

"The letters, first!"

Varin drew a revolver and, pointing it at Mon. Andermatt, said:

"Yes or no?"

The banker stooped quickly. There was the sound of a pistol-shot. The weapon fell from Varin's hand. I was amazed. The shot was fired close to me. It was Daspry who had fired it at Varin, causing him to drop the revolver. In a moment, Daspry was standing between the two men, facing Varin; he said to him, with a sneer:

"You were lucky, my friend, very lucky. I fired at your hand and struck only the revolver."

Both of them looked at him, surprised. Then he turned to the banker, and said:

"I beg your pardon, monsieur, for meddling in your business; but, really, you play a very poor game. Let me hold the cards."

Turning again to Varin, Daspry said:

"It's between us two, comrade, and play fair, if you please. Hearts are trumps, and I play the seven."

Then Daspry held up, before Varin's bewildered eyes, the little iron plate, marked with the seven red spots. It was a terrible shock to Varin. With livid features, staring eyes, and an air of intense agony, the man seemed to be hypnotized at the sight of it.

"Who are you?" he gasped.

"One who meddles in other people's business, down to the very bottom."

"What do you want?"

"What you brought here tonight."

"I brought nothing."

"Yes, you did, or you wouldn't have come. This morning, you received an invitation to come here at nine o'clock, and bring with you all the papers held by you. You are here. Where are the papers?"

There was in Daspry's voice and manner a tone of authority that I did not understand; his manner was usually quite mild and conciliatory. Absolutely conquered, Varin placed his hand on one of his pockets, and said:

"The papers are here."

"All of them?"

"Yes."

"All that you took from Louis Lacombe and afterwards sold to Major von Lieben?"

"Yes."

"Are these the copies or the originals?"

"I have the originals."

"How much do you want for them?"

"One hundred thousand francs."

"You are crazy," said Daspry. "Why, the major gave you only twenty thousand, and that was like money thrown into the sea, as the boat was a failure at the preliminary trials."

"They didn't understand the plans."

"The plans are not complete."

"Then, why do you ask me for them?"

"Because I want them. I offer you five thousand francs—not a sou more."

"Ten thousand. Not a sou less."

"Agreed," said Daspry, who now turned to Mon. Andermatt, and said:

"Monsieur will kindly sign a check for the amount."

"But....I haven't got——"

"Your check-book? Here it is."

Astounded, Mon. Andermatt examined the check-book that Daspry handed to him.

"It is mine," he gasped. "How does that happen?"

"No idle words, monsieur, if you please. You have merely to sign."

The banker took out his fountain pen, filled out the check and signed it. Varin held out his hand for it.

"Put down your hand," said Daspry, "there is something more." Then, to the banker, he said: "You asked for some letters, did you not?"

"Yes, a package of letters."

"Where are they, Varin?"

"I haven't got them."

"Where are they, Varin?"

"I don't know. My brother had charge of them."

"They are hidden in this room."

"In that case, you know where they are."

"How should I know?"

"Was it not you who found the hiding-place? You appear to be as well informed.... as Salvator."

"The letters are not in the hiding-place."

"They are."

"Open it."

Varin looked at him, defiantly. Were not Daspry and Salvator the same person? Everything pointed to that conclusion. If so, Varin risked nothing in disclosing a hiding-place already known.

"Open it," repeated Daspry.

"I have not got the seven of hearts."

"Yes, here it is," said Daspry, handing him the iron plate. Varin recoiled in terror, and cried:

"No, no, I will not."

"Never mind," replied Daspry, as he walked toward the bearded king, climbed on a chair and applied the seven of hearts to the lower part of the sword in such a manner that the edges of the iron plate coincided exactly with the two edges of the sword. Then, with the assistance of an awl which he introduced alternately into each of the seven holes, he pressed upon seven of the little mosaic stones. As he pressed upon the seventh one, a clicking sound was heard, and the entire bust of the King turned upon a pivot, disclosing a large opening lined with steel. It was really a fire-proof safe.

"You can see, Varin, the safe is empty."

"So I see. Then, my brother has taken out the letters."

Daspry stepped down from the chair, approached Varin, and said:

"Now, no more nonsense with me. There is another hiding-place. Where is it?"

"There is none."

"Is it money you want? How much?"

"Ten thousand."

"Monsieur Andermatt, are those letters worth ten thousand francs to you?"

"Yes," said the banker, firmly.

Varin closed the safe, took the seven of hearts and placed it again on the sword at the same spot. He thrust the awl into each of the seven holes. There was the same clicking sound, but this time, strange to relate, it was only a portion of the safe that revolved on the pivot, disclosing quite a small safe that was built within the door of the larger one. The packet of letters was here, tied with a tape, and sealed. Varin handed the packet to Daspry. The latter turned to the banker, and asked:

"Is the check ready, Monsieur Andermatt?"

"Yes."

"And you have also the last document that you received from Louis Lacombe—the one that completes the plans of the sub-marine?"

"Yes."

The exchange was made. Daspry pocketed the document and the checks, and offered the packet of letters to Mon. Andermatt.

"This is what you wanted, Monsieur."

The banker hesitated a moment, as if he were afraid to touch those cursed letters that he had sought so eagerly. Then, with a nervous movement, he took them. Close to me, I heard a moan. I grasped Madame Andermatt's hand. It was cold.

"I believe, monsieur," said Daspry to the banker, "that our business is ended. Oh! no thanks. It was only by a mere chance that I have been able to do you a good turn. Good-night."

Mon. Andermatt retired. He carried with him the letters written by his wife to Louis Lacombe.

"Marvelous!" exclaimed Daspry, delighted. "Everything is coming our way. Now, we have only to close our little affair, comrade. You have the papers?"

"Here they are—all of them."

Daspry examined them carefully, and then placed them in his pocket.

"Quite right. You have kept your word," he said.

"But—-"

"But what?"

"The two checks? The money?" said Varin, eagerly.

"Well, you have a great deal of assurance, my man. How dare you ask such a thing?"

"I ask only what is due to me."

"Can you ask pay for returning papers that you stole? Well, I think not!"

Varin was beside himself. He trembled with rage; his eyes were bloodshot.

"The money.... the twenty thousand...." he stammered.

"Impossible! I need it myself."

"The money!"

"Come, be reasonable, and don't get excited. It won't do you any good."

Daspry seized his arm so forcibly, that Varin uttered a cry of pain. Daspry continued:

"Now, you can go. The air will do you good. Perhaps you want me to show you the way. Ah! yes, we will go together to the vacant lot near here, and I will show you a little mound of earth and stones and under it—-"

"That is false! That is false!"

"Oh! no, it is true. That little iron plate with the seven spots on it came from there. Louis Lacombe always carried it, and you buried it with the body—and with some other things that will prove very interesting to a judge and jury."

Varin covered his face with his hands, and muttered:

"All right, I am beaten. Say no more. But I want to ask you one question. I should like to know—-"

"What is it?"

"Was there a little casket in the large safe?"

"Yes."

"Was it there on the night of 22 June?"

"Yes."

"What did it contain?"

"Everything that the Varin brothers had put in it—a very pretty collection of diamonds and pearls picked up here and there by the said brothers."

"And did you take it?"

"Of course I did. Do you blame me?"

"I understand.... it was the disappearance of that casket that caused my brother to kill himself."

"Probably. The disappearance of your correspondence was not a sufficient motive. But the disappearance of the casket....Is that all you wish to ask me?"

"One thing more: your name?"

"You ask that with an idea of seeking revenge."

"Parbleu! The tables may be turned. Today, you are on top. To-morrow—-"

"It will be you."

"I hope so. Your name?"

"Arsène Lupin."

"Arsène Lupin!"

The man staggered, as though stunned by a heavy blow. Those two words had deprived him of all hope.

Daspry laughed, and said:

"Ah! did you imagine that a Monsieur Durand or Dupont could manage an affair like this? No, it required the skill and cunning of Arsène Lupin. And now that you have my name, go and prepare your revenge. Arsène Lupin will wait for you."

Then he pushed the bewildered Varin through the door.

"Daspry! Daspry!" I cried, pushing aside the curtain. He ran to me.

"What? What's the matter?"

"Madame Andermatt is ill."

He hastened to her, caused her to inhale some salts, and, while caring for her, questioned me:

"Well, what did it?"

"The letters of Louis Lacombe that you gave to her husband."

He struck his forehead and said:

"Did she think that I could do such a thing!...But, of course she would. Imbecile that I am!"

Madame Andermatt was now revived. Daspry took from his pocket a small package exactly similar to the one that Mon. Andermatt had carried away.

"Here are your letters, Madame. These are the genuine letters."

"But.... the others?"

"The others are the same, rewritten by me and carefully worded. Your husband will not find anything objectionable in them, and will never suspect the substitution since they were taken from the safe in his presence."

"But the handwriting—-"

"There is no handwriting that cannot be imitated."

She thanked him in the same words she might have used to a man in her own social circle, so I concluded that she had not witnessed the final scene between Varin and Arsène Lupin. But the surprising revelation caused me considerable embarrassment. Lupin! My club companion was none other than Arsène Lupin. I could not realize it. But he said, quite at his ease:

"You can say farewell to Jean Daspry."

"Ah!"

"Yes, Jean Daspry is going on a long journey. I shall send him to Morocco. There, he may find a death worthy of him. I may say that that is his expectation."

"But Arsène Lupin will remain?"

"Oh! Decidedly. Arsène Lupin is simply at the threshold of his career, and he expects—-"

I was impelled by curiosity to interrupt him, and, leading him away from the hearing of Madame Andermatt, I asked:

"Did you discover the smaller safe yourself—the one that held the letters?"

"Yes, after a great deal of trouble. I found it yesterday afternoon while you were asleep. And yet, God knows it was simple enough! But the simplest things are the ones that usually escape our notice." Then, showing me the seven-of-hearts, he added: "Of course I had guessed that, in order to open the larger safe, this card must be placed on the sword of the mosaic king."

"How did you guess that?"

"Quite easily. Through private information, I knew that fact when I came here on the evening of 22 June—-"

"After you left me—-"

"Yes, after turning the subject of our conversation to stories of crime and robbery which were sure to reduce you to such a nervous condition that you would not leave your bed, but would allow me to complete my search uninterrupted."

"The scheme worked perfectly."

"Well, I knew when I came here that there was a casket concealed in a safe with a secret lock, and that the seven-of-hearts was the key to that lock. I had merely to place the card upon the spot that was obviously intended for it. An hour's examination showed me where the spot was."

"One hour!"

"Observe the fellow in mosaic."

"The old emperor?"

"That old emperor is an exact representation of the king of hearts on all playing cards."

"That's right. But how does the seven of hearts open the larger safe at one time and the smaller safe at another time? And why did you open only the larger safe in the first instance? I mean on the night of 22 June."

"Why? Because I always placed the seven of hearts in the same way. I never changed the position. But, yesterday, I observed that by reversing the card, by turning it upside down, the arrangement of the seven spots on the mosaic was changed."

"Parbleu!"

"Of course, parbleu! But a person has to think of those things."

"There is something else: you did not know the history of those letters until Madame Andermatt—-"

"Spoke of them before me? No. Because I found in the safe, besides the casket, nothing but the correspondence of the two brothers which disclosed their treachery in regard to the plans."

"Then it was by chance that you were led, first, to investigate the history of the two brothers, and then to search for the plans and documents relating to the sub-marine?"

"Simply by chance."

"For what purpose did you make the search?"

"Mon Dieu!" exclaimed Daspry, laughing, "how deeply interested you are!"

"The subject fascinates me."

"Very well, presently, after I have escorted Madame Andermatt to a carriage, and dispatched a short story to the 'Echo de France,' I will return and tell you all about it."

He sat down and wrote one of those short, clear-cut articles which served to amuse and mystify the public. Who does not recall the sensation that followed that article produced throughout the entire world?

"Arsène Lupin has solved the problem recently submitted by Salvator. Having acquired possession of all the documents and original plans of the engineer Louis Lacombe, he has placed them in the hands of the Minister of Marine, and he has headed a subscription list for the purpose of presenting to the nation the first submarine constructed from those plans. His subscription is twenty thousand francs."

"Twenty thousand francs! The checks of Mon. Andermatt?" I exclaimed, when he had given me the paper to read.

"Exactly. It was quite right that Varin should redeem his treachery."

And that is how I made the acquaintance of Arsène Lupin. That is how I learned that Jean Daspry, a member of my club, was none other than Arsène Lupin, gentleman-thief. That is how I formed very agreeable ties of friendship with that famous man, and, thanks to the confidence with which he honored me, how I became his very humble and faithful historiographer.

VII. Madame Imbert's Safe

At three o'clock in the morning, there were still half a dozen carriages in front of one of those small houses which form only the side of the boulevard Berthier. The door of that house opened, and a number of guests, male and female, emerged. The majority of them entered their carriages and were quickly driven away, leaving behind only two men who walked down Courcelles, where they parted, as one of them lived in that street. The other decided to return on foot as far as the Porte-Maillot. It was a beautiful winter's night, clear and cold; a night on which a brisk walk is agreeable and refreshing.

But, at the end of a few minutes, he had the disagreeable impression that he was being followed. Turning around, he saw a man skulking amongst the trees. He was not a coward; yet he felt it advisable to increase his speed. Then his pursuer commenced to run; and he deemed it prudent to draw his revolver and face him. But he had no time. The man rushed at him and attacked him violently. Immediately, they were engaged in a desperate struggle, wherein he felt that his unknown assailant had the advantage. He called for help, struggled, and was thrown down on a pile of gravel, seized by the throat, and gagged with a handkerchief that his assailant forced into his mouth. His eyes closed, and the man who was smothering him with his weight arose to defend himself against an unexpected attack. A blow from a cane and a kick from a boot; the man uttered two cries of pain, and fled, limping and cursing. Without deigning to pursue the fugitive, the new arrival stooped over the prostrate man and inquired:

"Are you hurt, monsieur?"

He was not injured, but he was dazed and unable to stand. His rescuer procured a carriage, placed him in it, and accompanied him to his house on the avenue de la Grande-Armée. On his arrival there, quite recovered, he overwhelmed his saviour with thanks.

"I owe you my life, monsieur, and I shall not forget it. I do not wish to alarm my wife at this time of night, but, to-morrow, she will be pleased to thank you personally. Come and breakfast with us. My name is Ludovic Imbert. May I ask yours?"

"Certainly, monsieur."

And he handed Mon. Imbert a card bearing the name: "Arsène Lupin."

At that time, Arsène Lupin did not enjoy the celebrity which the Cahorn affair, his escape from the Prison de la Santé, and other brilliant exploits, afterwards gained for him. He had not even used the name of Arsène Lupin. The name was specially invented to designate the rescuer of Mon. Imbert; that is to say, it was in that affair that Arsène Lupin was baptized. Fully armed and ready for the fray, it is true, but lacking the resources and authority which command success, Arsène Lupin was then merely an apprentice in a profession wherein he soon became a master.

With what a thrill of joy he recalled the invitation he received that night! At last, he had reached his goal! At last, he had undertaken a task worthy of his strength and skill! The Imbert millions! What a magnificent feast for an appetite like his!

He prepared a special toilet for the occasion; a shabby frock-coat, baggy trousers, a frayed silk hat, well-worn collar and cuffs, all quite correct in form, but bearing the unmistakable stamp of poverty. His cravat was a black ribbon pinned with a false diamond. Thus accoutred, he descended the stairs of the house in which he lived at Montmartre. At the third floor, without stopping, he rapped on a closed door with the head of his cane. He walked to the exterior boulevards. A tram-car was passing. He boarded it, and some one who had been following him took a seat beside him. It was the lodger who occupied the room on the third floor. A moment later, this man said to Lupin:

"Well, governor?"

"Well, it is all fixed."

"How?"

"I am going there to breakfast."

"You breakfast—there!"

"Certainly. Why not? I rescued Mon. Ludovic Imbert from certain death at your hands. Mon. Imbert is not devoid of gratitude. He invited me to breakfast."

There was a brief silence. Then the other said:

"But you are not going to throw up the scheme?"

"My dear boy," said Lupin, "When I arranged that little case of assault and battery, when I took the trouble at three o'clock in the morning, to rap you with my cane and tap you with my boot at the risk of injuring my only friend, it was not my intention to forego the advantages to be gained from a rescue so well arranged and executed. Oh! no, not at all."

"But the strange rumors we hear about their fortune?"

"Never mind about that. For six months, I have worked on this affair, investigated it, studied it, questioned the servants, the money-lenders and men of straw; for six months, I have shadowed the husband and wife. Consequently, I know what I am talking about. Whether the fortune came to them from old Brawford, as they pretend, or from some other source, I do not care. I know that it is a reality; that it exists. And some day it will be mine."

"Bigre! One hundred millions!"

"Let us say ten, or even five—that is enough! They have a safe full of bonds, and there will be the devil to pay if I can't get my hands on them."

The tram-car stopped at the Place de l'Etoile. The man whispered to Lupin:

"What am I to do now?"

"Nothing, at present. You will hear from me. There is no hurry."

Five minutes later, Arsène Lupin was ascending the magnificent flight of stairs in the Imbert mansion, and Mon. Imbert introduced him to his wife. Madame Gervaise Imbert was a short plump woman, and very talkative. She gave Lupin a cordial welcome.

"I desired that we should be alone to entertain our saviour," she said.

From the outset, they treated "our saviour" as an old and valued friend. By the time dessert was served, their friendship was well cemented, and private confidences were being exchanged. Arsène related the story of his life, the life of his father as a magistrate, the sorrows of his childhood, and his present difficulties. Gervaise, in turn, spoke of her youth, her marriage, the kindness of the aged Brawford, the hundred millions that she had inherited, the obstacles that prevented her from obtaining the enjoyment of her inheritance, the moneys she had been obliged to borrow at an exorbitant rate of interest, her endless contentions with Brawford's nephews, and the litigation! the injunctions! in fact, everything!

"Just think of it, Monsieur Lupin, the bonds are there, in my husband's office, and if we detach a single coupon, we lose everything! They are there, in our safe, and we dare not touch them."

Monsieur Lupin shivered at the bare idea of his proximity to so much wealth. Yet he felt quite certain that Monsieur Lupin would never suffer from the same difficulty as his fair hostess who declared she dare not touch the money.

"Ah! they are there!" he repeated, to himself; "they are there!"

A friendship formed under such circumstances soon led to closer relations. When discreetly questioned, Arsène Lupin confessed his poverty and distress. Immediately, the unfortunate young man was appointed private secretary to the Imberts, husband and wife, at a salary of one hundred francs a month. He was to come to the house every day and receive orders for his work, and a room on the second floor was set apart as his office. This room was directly over Mon. Imbert's office.

Arsène soon realized that his position as secretary was essentially a sinecure. During the first two months, he had only four important letters to recopy, and was called only once to Mon. Imbert's office; consequently, he had only one opportunity to contemplate, officially, the Imbert safe. Moreover, he noticed that the secretary was not invited to the social functions of the employer. But he did not complain, as he preferred to remain, modestly, in the shade and maintain his peace and freedom.

However, he was not wasting any time. From the beginning, he made clandestine visits to Mon. Imbert's office, and paid his respects to the safe, which was hermetically closed. It was an immense block of iron and steel, cold and stern in appearance, which could not be forced open by the ordinary tools of the burglar's trade. But Arsène Lupin was not discouraged.

"Where force fails, cunning prevails," he said to himself. "The essential thing is to be on the spot when the opportunity occurs. In the meantime, I must watch and wait."

He made immediately some preliminary preparations. After careful soundings made upon the floor of his room, he introduced a lead pipe which penetrated the ceiling of Mon. Imbert's office at a point between the two screeds of the cornice. By means of this pipe, he hoped to see and hear what transpired in the room below.

Henceforth, he passed his days stretched at full length upon the floor. He frequently saw the Imberts holding a consultation in front of the safe, investigating books and papers. When they turned the combination lock, he tried to learn the figures and the number of turns they made to the right and left. He watched their movements; he sought to catch their words. There was also a key necessary to complete the opening of the safe. What did they do with it? Did they hide it?

One day, he saw them leave the room without locking the safe. He descended the stairs quickly, and boldly entered the room. But they had returned.

"Oh! excuse me," said, "I made a mistake in the door."

"Come in, Monsieur Lupin, come in," cried Madame Imbert, "are you not at home here? We want your advice. What bonds should we sell? The foreign securities or the government annuities?"

"But the injunction?" said Lupin, with surprise.

"Oh! it doesn't cover all the bonds."

She opened the door of the safe and withdrew a package of bonds. But her husband protested.

"No, no, Gervaise, it would be foolish to sell the foreign bonds. They are going up, whilst the annuities are as high as they ever will be. What do you think, my dear friend?"

The dear friend had no opinion; yet he advised the sacrifice of the annuities. Then she withdrew another package and, from it, she took a paper at random. It proved to be a three-per-cent annuity worth two thousand francs. Ludovic placed the package of bonds in his pocket. That afternoon, accompanied by his secretary, he sold the annuities to a stock-broker and realized forty-six thousand francs.

Whatever Madame Imbert might have said about it, Arsène Lupin did not feel at home in the Imbert house. On the contrary, his position there was a peculiar one. He learned that the servants did not even know his name. They called him "monsieur." Ludovic always spoke of him in the same way: "You will tell monsieur. Has monsieur arrived?" Why that mysterious appellation?

Moreover, after their first outburst of enthusiasm, the Imberts seldom spoke to him, and, although treating him with the consideration due to a benefactor, they gave him little or no attention. They appeared to regard him as an eccentric character who did not like to be disturbed, and they respected his isolation as if it were a stringent rule on his part. On one occasion, while passing through the vestibule, he heard Madame Imbert say to the two gentlemen:

"He is such a barbarian!"

"Very well," he said to himself, "I am a barbarian."

And, without seeking to solve the question of their strange conduct, he proceeded with the execution of his own plans. He had decided that he could not depend on chance, nor on the negligence of Madame Imbert, who carried the key of the safe, and who, on locking the safe, invariably scattered the letters forming the combination of the lock. Consequently, he must act for himself.

Finally, an incident precipitated matters; it was the vehement campaign instituted against the Imberts by certain newspapers that accused the Imberts of swindling. Arsène Lupin was present at certain family conferences when this new vicissitude was discussed. He decided that if he waited much longer, he would lose everything. During the next five days, instead of leaving the house about six o'clock, according to his usual habit, he locked himself in his room. It was supposed that he had gone out. But he was lying on the floor surveying the office of Mon. Imbert. During those five evenings, the favorable opportunity that he awaited did not take place. He left the house about midnight by a side door to which he held the key.

But on the sixth day, he learned that the Imberts, actuated by the malevolent insinuations of their enemies, proposed to make an inventory of the contents of the safe.

"They will do it to-night," thought Lupin.

And truly, after dinner, Imbert and his wife retired to the office and commenced to examine the books of account and the securities contained in the safe. Thus, one hour after another passed away. He heard the servants go upstairs to their rooms. No one now remained on the first floor. Midnight! The Imberts were still at work.

"I must get to work," murmured Lupin.

He opened his window. It opened on a court. Outside, everything was dark and quiet. He took from his desk a knotted rope, fastened it to the balcony in front of his window, and quietly descended as far as the window below, which was that of the of Imbert's office. He stood upon the balcony for a moment, motionless, with attentive ear and watchful eye, but the heavy curtains effectually concealed the interior of the room. He cautiously pushed on the double window. If no one had examined it, it ought to yield to the slightest pressure, for, during the afternoon, he had so fixed the bolt that it would not enter the staple.

The window yielded to his touch. Then, with infinite care, he pushed it open sufficiently to admit his head. He parted the curtains a few inches, looked in, and saw Mon. Imbert and his wife sitting in front of the safe, deeply absorbed in their work and speaking softly to each other at rare intervals.

He calculated the distance between him and them, considered the exact movements he would require to make in order to overcome them, one after the other, before they could call for help, and he was about to rush upon them, when Madame Imbert said:

"Ah! the room is getting quite cold. I am going to bed. And you, my dear?"

"I shall stay and finish."

"Finish! Why, that will take you all night."

"Not at all. An hour, at the most."

She retired. Twenty minutes, thirty minutes passed. Arsène pushed the window a little farther open. The curtains shook. He pushed once more. Mon. Imbert turned, and, seeing the curtains blown by the wind, he rose to close the window.

There was not a cry, not the trace of struggle. With a few precise moments, and without causing him the least injury, Arsène stunned him, wrapped the curtain about his head, bound him hand and foot, and did it all in such a manner that Mon. Imbert had no opportunity to recognize his assailant.

Quickly, he approached the safe, seized two packages that he placed under his arm, left the office, and opened the servants' gate. A carriage was stationed in the street.

"Take that, first—and follow me," he said to the coachman. He returned to the office, and, in two trips, they emptied the safe. Then Arsène went to his own room, removed the rope, and all other traces of his clandestine work.

A few hours later, Arsène Lupin and his assistant examined the stolen goods. Lupin was not disappointed, as he had foreseen that the wealth of the Imberts had been greatly exaggerated. It did not consist of hundreds of millions, nor even tens of millions. Yet it amounted to a very respectable sum, and Lupin expressed his satisfaction.

"Of course," he said, "there will be a considerable loss when we come to sell the bonds, as we will have to dispose of them surreptitiously at reduced prices. In the meantime, they will rest quietly in my desk awaiting a propitious moment."

Arsène saw no reason why he should not go to the Imbert house the next day. But a perusal of the morning papers revealed this startling fact: Ludovic and Gervaise Imbert had disappeared.

When the officers of the law seized the safe and opened it, they found there what Arsène Lupin had left—nothing.

Such are the facts; and I learned the sequel to them, one day, when Arsène Lupin was in a confidential mood. He was pacing to and fro in my room, with a nervous step and a feverish eye that were unusual to him.

"After all," I said to him, "it was your most successful venture."

Without making a direct reply, he said:

"There are some impenetrable secrets connected with that affair; some obscure points that escape my comprehension. For instance: What caused their flight? Why did they not take advantage of the help I unconsciously gave them? It would have been so simple to say: 'The hundred millions were in the safe. They are no longer there, because they have been stolen.'"

"They lost their nerve."

"Yes, that is it—they lost their nerve...On the other hand, it is true—-"

"What is true?"

"Oh! nothing."

What was the meaning of Lupin's reticence? It was quite obvious that he had not told me everything; there was something he was loath to tell. His conduct puzzled me. It must indeed be a very serious matter to cause such a man as Arsène Lupin even a momentary hesitation. I threw out a few questions at random.

"Have you seen them since?"

"No."

"And have you never experienced the slightest degree of pity for those unfortunate people?"

"I!" he exclaimed, with a start.

His sudden excitement astonished me. Had I touched him on a sore spot? I continued:

"Of course. If you had not left them alone, they might have been able to face the danger, or, at least, made their escape with full pockets."

"What do you mean?" he said, indignantly. "I suppose you have an idea that my soul should be filled with remorse?"

"Call it remorse or regrets—anything you like—-"

"They are not worth it."

"Have you no regrets or remorse for having stolen their fortune?"

"What fortune?"

"The packages of bonds you took from their safe."

"Oh! I stole their bonds, did I? I deprived them of a portion of their wealth? Is that my crime? Ah! my dear boy, you do not know the truth. You never imagined that those bonds were not worth the paper they were written on. Those bonds were false—they were counterfeit—every one of them—do you understand? THEY WERE COUNTERFEIT!"

I looked at him, astounded.

"Counterfeit! The four or five millions?"

"Yes, counterfeit!" he exclaimed, in a fit of rage. "Only so many scraps of paper! I couldn't raise a sou on the whole of them! And you ask me if I have any remorse. THEY are the ones who should have remorse and pity. They played me for a simpleton; and I fell into their trap. I was their latest victim, their most stupid gull!"

He was affected by genuine anger—the result of malice and wounded pride. He continued:

"From start to finish, I got the worst of it. Do you know the part I played in that affair, or rather the part they made me play? That of André Brawford! Yes, my boy, that is the truth, and I never suspected it. It was not until afterwards, on reading the newspapers, that the light finally dawned in my stupid brain. Whilst I was posing as his "saviour," as the gentleman who had risked his life to rescue Mon. Imbert from the clutches of an assassin, they were passing me off as Brawford. Wasn't that splendid? That eccentric individual who had a room on the second floor, that barbarian that was exhibited only at a distance, was Brawford, and Brawford was I! Thanks to me, and to the confidence that I inspired under the name of Brawford, they were enabled to borrow money from the bankers and other money-lenders. Ha! what an experience for a novice! And I swear to you that I shall profit by the lesson!"

He stopped, seized my arm, and said to me, in a tone of exasperation:

"My dear fellow, at this very moment, Gervaise Imbert owes me fifteen hundred francs."

I could not refrain from laughter, his rage was so grotesque. He was making a mountain out of a molehill. In a moment, he laughed himself, and said:

"Yes, my boy, fifteen hundred francs. You must know that I had not received one sou of my promised salary, and, more than that, she had borrowed from me the sum of fifteen hundred francs. All my youthful savings! And do you know why? To devote the money to charity! I am giving you a straight story. She wanted it for some poor people she was assisting—unknown to her husband. And my hard-earned money was wormed out of me by that silly pretense! Isn't it amusing, hein? Arsène Lupin done out of fifteen hundred francs by the fair lady from whom he stole four millions in counterfeit bonds! And what a vast amount of time and patience and cunning I expended to achieve that result! It was the first time in my life that I was played for a fool, and I frankly confess that I was fooled that time to the queen's taste!"

VIII. The Black Pearl

A violent ringing of the bell awakened the concierge of number nine, avenue Hoche. She pulled the doorstring, grumbling:

"I thought everybody was in. It must be three o'clock!"

"Perhaps it is some one for the doctor," muttered her husband.

"Third floor, left. But the doctor won't go out at night."

"He must go to-night."

The visitor entered the vestibule, ascended to the first floor, the second, the third, and, without stopping at the doctor's door, he continued to the fifth floor. There, he tried two keys. One of them fitted the lock.

"Ah! good!" he murmured, "that simplifies the business wonderfully. But before I commence work I had better arrange for my retreat. Let me see.... have I had sufficient time to rouse the doctor and be dismissed by him? Not yet.... a few minutes more."

At the end of ten minutes, he descended the stairs, grumbling noisily about the doctor. The concierge opened the door for him and heard it click behind him. But the door did not lock, as the man had quickly inserted a piece of iron in the lock in such a manner that the bolt could not enter. Then, quietly, he entered the house again, unknown to the concierge. In case of alarm, his retreat was assured. Noiselessly, he ascended to the fifth floor once more. In the antechamber, by the light of his electric lantern, he placed his hat and overcoat on one of the chairs, took a seat on another, and covered his heavy shoes with felt slippers.

"Ouf! Here I am—and how simple it was! I wonder why more people do not adopt the profitable and pleasant occupation of burglar. With a little care and reflection, it becomes a most delightful profession. Not too quiet and monotonous, of course, as it would then become wearisome."

He unfolded a detailed plan of the apartment.

"Let me commence by locating myself. Here, I see the vestibule in which I am sitting. On the street front, the drawing-room, the boudoir and dining-room. Useless to waste any time there, as it appears that the countess has a deplorable taste.... not a bibelot of any value!...Now, let's get down to business!... Ah! here is a corridor; it must lead to the bed chambers. At a distance of three metres, I should come to the door of the wardrobe-closet which connects with the chamber of the countess." He folded his plan, extinguished his lantern, and proceeded down the corridor, counting his distance, thus:

"One metre.... two metres.... three metres....Here is the door....Mon Dieu, how easy it is! Only a small, simple bolt now separates me from the chamber, and I know that the bolt is located exactly one metre, forty-three centimeters, from the floor. So that, thanks to a small incision I am about to make, I can soon get rid of the bolt."

He drew from his pocket the necessary instruments. Then the following idea occurred to him:

"Suppose, by chance, the door is not bolted. I will try it first."

He turned the knob, and the door opened.

"My brave Lupin, surely fortune favors you....What's to be done now? You know the situation of the rooms; you know the place in which the countess hides the black pearl. Therefore, in order to secure the black pearl, you have simply to be more silent than silence, more invisible than darkness itself."

Arsène Lupin was employed fully a half-hour in opening the second door—a glass door that led to the countess' bedchamber. But he accomplished it with so much skill and precaution, that even had had the countess been awake, she would not have heard the slightest sound. According to the plan of the rooms, that he holds, he has merely to pass around a reclining chair and, beyond that, a small table close to the bed. On the table, there was a box of letter-paper, and the black pearl was concealed in that box. He stooped and crept cautiously over the carpet, following the outlines of the reclining-chair. When he reached the extremity of it, he stopped in order to repress the throbbing of his heart. Although he was not moved by any sense of fear, he found it impossible to overcome the nervous anxiety that one usually feels in the midst of profound silence. That circumstance astonished him, because he had passed through many more solemn moments without the slightest trace of emotion. No danger threatened him. Then why did his heart throb like an alarm-bell? Was it that sleeping woman who affected him? Was it the proximity of another pulsating heart?

He listened, and thought he could discern the rhythmical breathing of a person asleep. It gave him confidence, like the presence of a friend. He sought and found the armchair; then, by slow, cautious movements, advanced toward the table, feeling ahead of him with outstretched arm. His right had touched one of the feet of the table. Ah! now, he had simply to rise, take the pearl, and escape. That was fortunate, as his heart was leaping in his breast like a wild beast, and made so much noise that he feared it would waken the countess. By a powerful effort of the will, he subdued the wild throbbing of his heart, and was about to rise from the floor when his left hand encountered, lying on the floor, an object which he recognized as a candlestick—an overturned candlestick. A moment later, his hand encountered another object: a clock—one of those small traveling clocks, covered with leather. ———-

Well! What had happened? He could not understand. That candlestick, that clock; why were those articles not in their accustomed places? Ah! what had happened in the dread silence of the night?

Suddenly a cry escaped him. He had touched—oh! some strange, unutterable thing! "No! no!" he thought, "it cannot be. It is some fantasy of my excited brain." For twenty seconds, thirty seconds, he remained motionless, terrified, his forehead bathed with perspiration, and his fingers still retained the sensation of that dreadful contact.

Making a desperate effort, he ventured to extend his arm again. Once more, his hand encountered that strange, unutterable thing. He felt it. He must feel it and find out what it is. He found that it was hair, human hair, and a human face; and that face was cold, almost icy.

However frightful the circumstances may be, a man like Arsène Lupin controls himself and commands the situation as soon as he learns what it is. So, Arsène Lupin quickly brought his lantern into use. A woman was lying before him, covered with blood. Her neck and shoulders were covered with gaping wounds. He leaned over her and made a closer examination. She was dead.

"Dead! Dead!" he repeated, with a bewildered air.

He stared at those fixed eyes, that grim mouth, that livid flesh, and that blood—all that blood which had flowed over the carpet and congealed there in thick, black spots. He arose and turned on the electric lights. Then he beheld all the marks of a desperate struggle. The bed was in a state of great disorder. On the floor, the candlestick, and the clock, with the hands pointing to twenty minutes after eleven; then, further away, an overturned chair; and, everywhere, there was blood, spots of blood and pools of blood.

"And the black pearl?" he murmured.

The box of letter-paper was in its place. He opened it, eagerly. The jewel-case was there, but it was empty.

"Fichtre!" he muttered. "You boasted of your good fortune much too soon, my friend Lupin. With the countess lying cold and dead, and the black pearl vanished, the situation is anything but pleasant. Get out of here as soon as you can, or you may get into serious trouble."

Yet, he did not move.

"Get out of here? Yes, of course. Any person would, except Arsène Lupin. He has something better to do. Now, to proceed in an orderly way. At all events, you have a clear conscience. Let us suppose that you are the commissary of police and that you are proceeding to make an inquiry concerning this affair——Yes, but in order to do that, I require a clearer brain. Mine is muddled like a ragout."

He tumbled into an armchair, with his clenched hands pressed against his burning forehead.

The murder of the avenue Hoche is one of those which have recently surprised and puzzled the Parisian public, and, certainly, I should never have mentioned the affair if the veil of mystery had not been removed by Arsène Lupin himself. No one knew the exact truth of the case.

Who did not know—from having met her in the Bois—the fair Léotine Zalti, the once-famous cantatrice, wife and widow of the Count d'Andillot; the Zalti, whose luxury dazzled all Paris some twenty years ago; the Zalti who acquired an European reputation for the magnificence of her diamonds and pearls? It was said that she wore upon her shoulders the capital of several banking houses and the gold mines of numerous Australian companies. Skilful jewelers worked for Zalti as they had formerly wrought for kings and queens. And who does not remember the catastrophe in which all that wealth was swallowed up? Of all that marvelous collection, nothing remained except the famous black pearl. The black pearl! That is to say a fortune, if she had wished to part with it.

But she preferred to keep it, to live in a commonplace apartment with her companion, her cook, and a man-servant, rather than sell that inestimable jewel. There was a reason for it; a reason she was not afraid to disclose: the black pearl was the gift of an emperor! Almost ruined, and reduced to the most mediocre existence, she remained faithful to the companion of her happy and brilliant youth. The black pearl never left her possession. She wore it during the day, and, at night, concealed it in a place known to her alone.

All these facts, being republished in the columns of the public press, served to stimulate curiosity; and, strange to say, but quite obvious to those who have the key to the mystery, the arrest of the presumed assassin only complicated the question and prolonged the excitement. Two days later, the newspapers published the following item:

"Information has reached us of the arrest of Victor Danègre, the servant of the Countess d'Andillot. The evidence against him is clear and convincing. On the silken sleeve of his liveried waistcoat, which chief detective Dudouis found in his garret between the mattresses of his bed, several spots of blood were discovered. In addition, a cloth-covered button was missing from that garment, and this button was found beneath the bed of the victim.

"It is supposed that, after dinner, in place of going to his own room, Danègre slipped into the wardrobe-closet, and, through the glass door, had seen the countess hide the precious black pearl. This is simply a theory, as yet unverified by any evidence. There is, also, another obscure point. At seven o'clock in the morning, Danègre went to the tobacco-shop on the Boulevard de Courcelles; the concierge and the shop-keeper both affirm this fact. On the other hand, the countess' companion and cook, who sleep at the end of the hall, both declare that, when they arose at eight o'clock, the door of the antechamber and the door of the kitchen were locked. These two persons have been in the service of the countess for twenty years, and are above suspicion. The question is: How did Danègre leave the apartment? Did he have another key? These are matters that the police will investigate."

As a matter of fact, the police investigation threw no light on the mystery. It was learned that Victor Danègre was a dangerous criminal, a drunkard and a debauchee. But, as they proceeded with the investigation, the mystery deepened and new complications arose. In the first place, a young woman, Mlle. De Sinclèves, the cousin and sole heiress of the countess, declared that the countess, a month before her death, had written a letter to her and in it described the manner in which the black pearl was concealed. The letter disappeared the day after she received it. Who had stolen it?

Again, the concierge related how she had opened the door for a person who had inquired for Doctor Harel. On being questioned, the doctor testified that no one had rung his bell. Then who was that person? And accomplice?

The theory of an accomplice was thereupon adopted by the press and public, and also by Ganimard, the famous detective.

"Lupin is at the bottom of this affair," he said to the judge.

"Bah!" exclaimed the judge, "you have Lupin on the brain. You see him everywhere."

"I see him everywhere, because he is everywhere."

"Say rather that you see him every time you encounter something you cannot explain. Besides, you overlook the fact that the crime was committed at twenty minutes past eleven in the evening, as is shown by the clock, while the nocturnal visit, mentioned by the concierge, occurred at three o'clock in the morning."

Officers of the law frequently form a hasty conviction as to the guilt of a suspected person, and then distort all subsequent discoveries to conform to their established theory. The deplorable antecedents of Victor Danègre, habitual criminal, drunkard and rake, influenced the judge, and despite the fact that nothing new was discovered in corroboration of the early clues, his official opinion remained firm and unshaken. He closed his investigation, and, a few weeks later, the trial commenced. It proved to be slow and tedious. The judge was listless, and the public prosecutor presented the case in a careless manner. Under those circumstances, Danègre's counsel had an easy task. He pointed out the defects and inconsistencies of the case for the prosecution, and argued that the evidence was quite insufficient to convict the accused. Who had made the key, the indispensable key without which Danègre, on leaving the apartment, could not have locked the door behind him? Who had ever seen such a key, and what had become of it? Who had seen the assassin's knife, and where is it now?

"In any event," argued the prisoner's counsel, "the prosecution must prove, beyond any reasonable doubt, that the prisoner committed the murder. The prosecution must show that the mysterious individual who entered the house at three o'clock in the morning is not the guilty party. To be sure, the clock indicated eleven o'clock. But what of that? I contend, that proves nothing. The assassin could turn the hands of the clock to any hour he pleased, and thus deceive us in regard to the exact hour of the crime."

Victor Danègre was acquitted.

He left the prison on Friday about dusk in the evening, weak and depressed by his six months' imprisonment. The inquisition, the solitude, the trial, the deliberations of the jury, combined to fill him with a nervous fear. At night, he had been afflicted with terrible nightmares and haunted by weird visions of the scaffold. He was a mental and physical wreck.

Under the assumed name of Anatole Dufour, he rented a small room on the heights of Montmartre, and lived by doing odd jobs wherever he could find them. He led a pitiful existence. Three times, he obtained regular employment, only to be recognized and then discharged. Sometimes, he had an idea that men were following him—detectives, no doubt, who were seeking to trap and denounce him. He could almost feel the strong hand of the law clutching him by the collar.

One evening, as he was eating his dinner at a neighboring restaurant, a man entered and took a seat at the same table. He was a person about forty years of age, and wore a frock-coat of doubtful cleanliness. He ordered soup, vegetables, and a bottle of wine. After he had finished his soup, he turned his eyes on Danègre, and gazed at him intently. Danègre winced. He was certain that this was one of the men who had been following him for several weeks. What did he want? Danègre tried to rise, but failed. His limbs refused to support him. The man poured himself a glass of wine, and then filled Danègre's glass. The man raised his glass, and said:

"To your health, Victor Danègre."

Victor started in alarm, and stammered:

"I!....I!.... no, no....I swear to you...."

"You will swear what? That you are not yourself? The servant of the countess?"

"What servant? My name is Dufour. Ask the proprietor."

"Yes, Anatole Dufour to the proprietor of this restaurant, but Victor Danègre to the officers of the law."

"That's not true! Some one has lied to you."

The new-comer took a card from his pocket and handed it to Victor, who read on it: "Grimaudan, ex-inspector of the detective force. Private business transacted." Victor shuddered as he said:

"You are connected with the police?"

"No, not now, but I have a liking for the business and I continue to work at it in a manner more—profitable. From time to time I strike upon a golden opportunity—such as your case presents."

"My case?"

"Yes, yours. I assure you it is a most promising affair, provided you are inclined to be reasonable."

"But if I am not reasonable?"

"Oh! my good fellow, you are not in a position to refuse me anything I may ask."

"What is it.... you want?" stammered Victor, fearfully.

"Well, I will inform you in a few words. I am sent by Mademoiselle de Sinclèves, the heiress of the Countess d'Andillot."

"What for?"

"To recover the black pearl."

"Black pearl?"

"That you stole."

"But I haven't got it."

"You have it."

"If I had, then I would be the assassin."

"You are the assassin."

Danègre showed a forced smile.

"Fortunately for me, monsieur, the Assizecourt was not of your opinion. The jury returned an unanimous verdict of acquittal. And when a man has a clear conscience and twelve good men in his favor—"

The ex-inspector seized him by the arm and said:

"No fine phrases, my boy. Now, listen to me and weigh my words carefully. You will find they are worthy of your consideration. Now, Danègre, three weeks before the murder, you abstracted the cook's key to the servants' door, and had a duplicate key made by a locksmith named Outard, 244 rue Oberkampf."

"It's a lie—it's a lie!" growled Victor. "No person has seen that key. There is no such key."

"Here it is."

After a silence, Grimaudan continued:

"You killed the countess with a knife purchased by you at the Bazar de la Republique on the same day as you ordered the duplicate key. It has a triangular blade with a groove running from end to end."

"That is all nonsense. You are simply guessing at something you don't know. No one ever saw the knife."

"Here it is."

Victor Danègre recoiled. The ex-inspector continued:

"There are some spots of rust upon it. Shall I tell you how they came there?"

"Well!.... you have a key and a knife. Who can prove that they belong to me?"

"The locksmith, and the clerk from whom you bought the knife. I have already refreshed their memories, and, when you confront them, they cannot fail to recognize you."

His speech was dry and hard, with a tone of firmness and precision. Danègre was trembling with fear, and yet he struggled desperately to maintain an air of indifference.

"Is that all the evidence you have?"

"Oh! no, not at all. I have plenty more. For instance, after the crime, you went out the same way you had entered. But, in the centre of the wardrobe-room, being seized by some sudden fear, you leaned against the wall for support."

"How do you know that? No one could know such a thing," argued the desperate man.

"The police know nothing about it, of course. They never think of lighting a candle and examining the walls. But if they had done so, they would have found on the white plaster a faint red spot, quite distinct, however, to trace in it the imprint of your thumb which you had pressed against the wall while it was wet with blood. Now, as you are well aware, under the Bertillon system, thumb-marks are one of the principal means of identification."

Victor Danègre was livid; great drops of perspiration rolled down his face and fell upon the table. He gazed, with a wild look, at the strange man who had narrated the story of his crime as faithfully as if he had been an invisible witness to it. Overcome and powerless, Victor bowed his head. He felt that it was useless to struggle against this marvelous man. So he said:

"How much will you give me, if I give you the pearl?"

"Nothing."

"Oh! you are joking! Or do you mean that I should give you an article worth thousands and hundreds of thousands and get nothing in return?"

"You will get your life. Is that nothing?"

The unfortunate man shuddered. Then Grimaudan added, in a milder tone:

"Come, Danègre, that pearl has no value in your hands. It is quite impossible for you to sell it; so what is the use of your keeping it?"

"There are pawnbrokers.... and, some day, I will be able to get something for it."

"But that day may be too late."

"Why?"

"Because by that time you may be in the hands of the police, and, with the evidence that I can furnish—the knife, the key, the thumb-mark—what will become of you?"

Victor rested his head on his hands and reflected. He felt that he was lost, irremediably lost, and, at the same time, a sense of weariness and depression overcame him. He murmured, faintly:

"When must I give it to you?"

"To-night—-within an hour."

"If I refuse?"

"If you refuse, I shall post this letter to the Procureur of the Republic; in which letter Mademoiselle de Sinclèves denounces you as the assassin."

Danègre poured out two glasses of wine which he drank in rapid succession, then, rising, said:

"Pay the bill, and let us go. I have had enough of the cursed affair."

Night had fallen. The two men walked down the rue Lepic and followed the exterior boulevards in the direction of the Place de l'Etoile. They pursued their way in silence; Victor had a stooping carriage and a dejected face. When they reached the Parc Monceau, he said:

"We are near the house."

"Parbleu! You only left the house once, before your arrest, and that was to go to the tobacco-shop."

"Here it is," said Danègre, in a dull voice.

They passed along the garden wall of the countess' house, and crossed a street on a corner of which stood the tobacco-shop. A few steps further on, Danègre stopped; his limbs shook beneath him, and he sank to a bench.

"Well! what now?" demanded his companion.

"It is there."

"Where? Come, now, no nonsense!"

"There—in front of us."

"Where?"

"Between two paving-stones."

"Which?"

"Look for it."

"Which stones?"

Victor made no reply.

"Ah; I see!" exclaimed Grimaudan, "you want me to pay for the information."

"No.... but....I am afraid I will starve to death."

"So! that is why you hesitate. Well, I'll not be hard on you. How much do you want?"

"Enough to buy a steerage pass to America."

"All right."

"And a hundred francs to keep me until I get work there."

"You shall have two hundred. Now, speak."

"Count the paving-stones to the right from the sewer-hole. The pearl is between the twelfth and thirteenth."

"In the gutter?"

"Yes, close to the sidewalk."

Grimaudan glanced around to see if anyone were looking. Some tram-cars and pedestrians were passing. But, bah, they will not suspect anything. He opened his pocketknife and thrust it between the twelfth and thirteenth stones.

"And if it is not there?" he said to Victor.

"It must be there, unless someone saw me stoop down and hide it."

Could it be possible that the back pearl had been cast into the mud and filth of the gutter to be picked up by the first comer? The black pearl—a fortune!

"How far down?" he asked.

"About ten centimetres."

He dug up the wet earth. The point of his knife struck something. He enlarged the hole with his finger. Then he abstracted the black pearl from its filthy hiding-place.

"Good! Here are your two hundred francs. I will send you the ticket for America."

On the following day, this article was published in the 'Echo de France,' and was copied by the leading newspapers throughout the world:

"Yesterday, the famous black pearl came into the possession of

Arsène Lupin, who recovered it from the murderer of the Countess

d'Andillot. In a short time, fac-similes of that precious jewel

will be exhibited in London, St. Petersburg, Calcutta, Buenos Ayres

and New York.

"Arsène Lupin will be pleased to consider all propositions

submitted to him through his agents."

"And that is how crime is always punished and virtue rewarded," said Arsène Lupin, after he had told me the foregoing history of the black pearl.

"And that is how you, under the assumed name of Grimaudan, ex-inspector of detectives, were chosen by fate to deprive the criminal of the benefit of his crime."

"Exactly. And I confess that the affair gives me infinite satisfaction and pride. The forty minutes that I passed in the apartment of the Countess d'Andillot, after learning of her death, were the most thrilling and absorbing moments of my life. In those forty minutes, involved as I was in a most dangerous plight, I calmly studied the scene of the murder and reached the conclusion that the crime must have been committed by one of the house servants. I also decided that, in order to get the pearl, that servant must be arrested, and so I left the wainscoat button; it was necessary, also, for me to hold some convincing evidence of his guilt, so I carried away the knife which I found upon the floor, and the key which I found in the lock. I closed and locked the door, and erased the finger-marks from the plaster in the wardrobe-closet. In my opinion, that was one of those flashes—"

"Of genius," I said, interrupting.

"Of genius, if you wish. But, I flatter myself, it would not have occurred to the average mortal. To frame, instantly, the two elements of the problem—an arrest and an acquittal; to make use of the formidable machinery of the law to crush and humble my victim, and reduce him to a condition in which, when free, he would be certain to fall into the trap I was laying for him!"

"Poor devil—"

"Poor devil, do you say? Victor Danègre, the assassin! He might have descended to the lowest depths of vice and crime, if he had retained the black pearl. Now, he lives! Think of that: Victor Danègre is alive!"

"And you have the black pearl."

He took it out of one of the secret pockets of his wallet, examined it, gazed at it tenderly, and caressed it with loving fingers, and sighed, as he said:

"What cold Russian prince, what vain and foolish rajah may some day possess this priceless treasure! Or, perhaps, some American millionaire is destined to become the owner of this morsel of exquisite beauty that once adorned the fair bosom of Leontine Zalti, the Countess d'Andillot."

IX. Sherlock Holmes Arrives Too Late

"It is really remarkable, Velmont, what a close resemblance you bear to Arsène Lupin!"

"How do you know?"

"Oh! like everyone else, from photographs, no two of which are alike, but each of them leaves the impression of a face.... something like yours."

Horace Velmont displayed some vexation.

"Quite so, my dear Devanne. And, believe me, you are not the first one who has noticed it."

"It is so striking," persisted Devanne, "that if you had not been recommended to me by my cousin d'Estevan, and if you were not the celebrated artist whose beautiful marine views I so admire, I have no doubt I should have warned the police of your presence in Dieppe."

This sally was greeted with an outburst of laughter. The large dining-hall of the Château de Thibermesnil contained on this occasion, besides Velmont, the following guests: Father Gélis, the parish priest, and a dozen officers whose regiments were quartered in the vicinity and who had accepted the invitation of the banker Georges Devanne and his mother. One of the officers then remarked:

"I understand that an exact description of Arsène Lupin has been furnished to all the police along this coast since his daring exploit on the Paris-Havre express."

"I suppose so," said Devanne. "That was three months ago; and a week later, I made the acquaintance of our friend Velmont at the casino, and, since then, he has honored me with several visits—an agreeable preamble to a more serious visit that he will pay me one of these days—or, rather, one of these nights."

This speech evoked another round of laughter, and the guests then passed into the ancient "Hall of the Guards," a vast room with a high ceiling, which occupied the entire lower part of the Tour Guillaume—William's Tower—and wherein Georges Devanne had collected the incomparable treasures which the lords of Thibermesnil had accumulated through many centuries. It contained ancient chests, credences, andirons and chandeliers. The stone walls were overhung with magnificent tapestries. The deep embrasures of the four windows were furnished with benches, and the Gothic windows were composed of small panes of colored glass set in a leaden frame. Between the door and the window to the left stood an immense bookcase of Renaissance style, on the pediment of which, in letters of gold, was the word "Thibermesnil," and, below it, the proud family device: "Fais ce que veulx" (Do what thou wishest). When the guests had lighted their cigars, Devanne resumed the conversation.

"And remember, Velmont, you have no time to lose; in fact, to-night is the last chance you will have."

"How so?" asked the painter, who appeared to regard the affair as a joke. Devanne was about to reply, when his mother mentioned to him to keep silent, but the excitement of the occasion and a desire to interest his guests urged him to speak.

"Bah!" he murmured. "I can tell it now. It won't do any harm."

The guests drew closer, and he commenced to speak with the satisfied air of a man who has an important announcement to make.

"To-morrow afternoon at four o'clock, Sherlock Holmes, the famous English detective, for whom such a thing as mystery does not exist; Sherlock Holmes, the most remarkable solver of enigmas the world has ever known, that marvelous man who would seem to be the creation of a romantic novelist—Sherlock Holmes will be my guest!"

Immediately, Devanne was the target of numerous eager questions. "Is Sherlock Holmes really coming?" "Is it so serious as that?" "Is Arsène Lupin really in this neighborhood?"

"Arsène Lupin and his band are not far away. Besides the robbery of the Baron Cahorn, he is credited with the thefts at Montigny, Gruchet and Crasville."

"Has he sent you a warning, as he did to Baron Cahorn?"

"No," replied Devanne, "he can't work the same trick twice."

"What then?"

"I will show you."

He rose, and pointing to a small empty space between the two enormous folios on one of the shelves of the bookcase, he said:

"There used to be a book there—a book of the sixteenth century entitled 'Chronique de Thibermesnil,' which contained the history of the castle since its construction by Duke Rollo on the site of a former feudal fortress. There were three engraved plates in the book; one of which was a general view of the whole estate; another, the plan of the buildings; and the third—I call your attention to it, particularly—the third was the sketch of a subterranean passage, an entrance to which is outside the first line of ramparts, while the other end of the passage is here, in this very room. Well, that book disappeared a month ago."

"The deuce!" said Velmont, "that looks bad. But it doesn't seem to be a sufficient reason for sending for Sherlock Holmes."

"Certainly, that was not sufficient in itself, but another incident happened that gives the disappearance of the book a special significance. There was another copy of this book in the National Library at Paris, and the two books differed in certain details relating to the subterranean passage; for instance, each of them contained drawings and annotations, not printed, but written in ink and more or less effaced. I knew those facts, and I knew that the exact location of the passage could be determined only by a comparison of the two books. Now, the day after my book disappeared, the book was called for in the National Library by a reader who carried it away, and no one knows how the theft was effected."

The guests uttered many exclamations of surprise.

"Certainly, the affair looks serious," said one.

"Well, the police investigated the matter, and, as usual, discovered no clue whatever."

"They never do, when Arsène Lupin is concerned in it."

"Exactly; and so I decided to ask the assistance of Sherlock Holmes, who replied that he was ready and anxious to enter the lists with Arsène Lupin."

"What glory for Arsène Lupin!" said Velmont. "But if our national thief, as they call him, has no evil designs on your castle, Sherlock Holmes will have his trip in vain."

"There are other things that will interest him, such as the discovery of the subterranean passage."

"But you told us that one end of the passage was outside the ramparts and the other was in this very room!"

"Yes, but in what part of the room? The line which represents the passage on the charts ends here, with a small circle marked with the letters 'T.G.,' which no doubt stand for 'Tour Guillaume.' But the tower is round, and who can tell the exact spot at which the passage touches the tower?"

Devanne lighted a second cigar and poured himself a glass of Benedictine. His guests pressed him with questions and he was pleased to observe the interest that his remarks had created. The he continued:

"The secret is lost. No one knows it. The legend is to the effect that the former lords of the castle transmitted the secret from father to son on their deathbeds, until Geoffroy, the last of the race, was beheaded during the Revolution in his nineteenth year."

"That is over a century ago. Surely, someone has looked for it since that time?"

"Yes, but they failed to find it. After I purchased the castle, I made a diligent search for it, but without success. You must remember that this tower is surrounded by water and connected with the castle only by a bridge; consequently, the passage must be underneath the old moat. The plan that was in the book in the National Library showed a series of stairs with a total of forty-eight steps, which indicates a depth of more than ten meters. You see, the mystery lies within the walls of this room, and yet I dislike to tear them down."

"Is there nothing to show where it is?"

"Nothing."

"Mon. Devanne, we should turn our attention to the two quotations," suggested Father Gélis.

"Oh!" exclaimed Mon. Devanne, laughing, "our worthy father is fond of reading memoirs and delving into the musty archives of the castle. Everything relating to Thibermesnil interests him greatly. But the quotations that he mentions only serve to complicate the mystery. He has read somewhere that two kings of France have known the key to the puzzle."

"Two kings of France! Who were they?"

"Henry the Fourth and Louis the Sixteenth. And the legend runs like this: On the eve of the battle of Arques, Henry the Fourth spent the night in this castle. At eleven o'clock in the evening, Louise de Tancarville, the prettiest woman in Normandy, was brought into the castle through the subterranean passage by Duke Edgard, who, at the same time, informed the king of the secret passage. Afterward, the king confided the secret to his minister Sully, who, in turn, relates the story in his book, "Royales Economies d'Etat," without making any comment upon it, but linking with it this incomprehensible sentence: 'Turn one eye on the bee that shakes, the other eye will lead to God!'"

After a brief silence, Velmont laughed and said:

"Certainly, it doesn't throw a dazzling light upon the subject."

"No; but Father Gélis claims that Sully concealed the key to the mystery in this strange sentence in order to keep the secret from the secretaries to whom he dictated his memoirs."

"That is an ingenious theory," said Velmont.

"Yes, and it may be nothing more; I cannot see that it throws any light on the mysterious riddle."

"And was it also to receive the visit of a lady that Louis the Sixteenth caused the passage to be opened?"

"I don't know," said Mon. Devanne. "All I can say is that the king stopped here one night in 1784, and that the famous Iron Casket found in the Louvre contained a paper bearing these words in the king's own writing: 'Thibermesnil 3-4-11.'"

Horace Velmont laughed heartily, and exclaimed:

"At last! And now that we have the magic key, where is the man who can fit it to the invisible lock?"

"Laugh as much as you please, monsieur," said Father Gèlis, "but I am confident the solution is contained in those two sentences, and some day we will find a man able to interpret them."

"Sherlock Holmes is the man," said Mon. Devanne, "unless Arsène Lupin gets ahead of him. What is your opinion, Velmont?"

Velmont arose, placed his hand on Devanne's shoulder, and declared:

"I think that the information furnished by your book and the book of the National Library was deficient in a very important detail which you have now supplied. I thank you for it."

"What is it?"

"The missing key. Now that I have it, I can go to work at once," said Velmont.

"Of course; without losing a minute," said Devanne, smiling.

"Not even a second!" replied Velmont. "To-night, before the arrival of Sherlock Holmes, I must plunder your castle."

"You have no time to lose. Oh! by the way, I can drive you over this evening."

"To Dieppe?"

"Yes. I am going to meet Monsieur and Madame d'Androl and a young lady of their acquaintance who are to arrive by the midnight train."

Then addressing the officers, Devanne added:

"Gentlemen, I shall expect to see all of you at breakfast to-morrow."

The invitation was accepted. The company dispersed, and a few moments later Devanne and Velmont were speeding toward Dieppe in an automobile. Devanne dropped the artist in front of the Casino, and proceeded to the railway station. At twelve o'clock his friends alighted from the train. A half hour later the automobile was at the entrance to the castle. At one o'clock, after a light supper, they retired. The lights were extinguished, and the castle was enveloped in the darkness and silence of the night.

The moon appeared through a rift in the clouds, and filled the drawing-room with its bright white light. But only for a moment. Then the moon again retired behind its ethereal draperies, and darkness and silence reigned supreme. No sound could be heard, save the monotonous ticking of the clock. It struck two, and then continued its endless repetitions of the seconds. Then, three o'clock.

Suddenly, something clicked, like the opening and closing of a signal-disc that warns the passing train. A thin stream of light flashed to every corner of the room, like an arrow that leaves behind it a trail of light. It shot forth from the central fluting of a column that supported the pediment of the bookcase. It rested for a moment on the panel opposite like a glittering circle of burnished silver, then flashed in all directions like a guilty eye that scrutinizes every shadow. It disappeared for a short time, but burst forth again as a whole section of the bookcase revolved on a pivot and disclosed a large opening like a vault.

A man entered, carrying an electric lantern. He was followed by a second man, who carried a coil of rope and various tools. The leader inspected the room, listened a moment, and said:

"Call the others."

Then eight men, stout fellows with resolute faces, entered the room, and immediately commenced to remove the furnishings. Arsène Lupin passed quickly from one piece of furniture to another, examined each, and, according to its size or artistic value, he directed his men to take it or leave it. If ordered to be taken, it was carried to the gaping mouth of the tunnel, and ruthlessly thrust into the bowels of the earth. Such was the fate of six armchairs, six small Louis XV chairs, a quantity of Aubusson tapestries, some candelabra, paintings by Fragonard and Nattier, a bust by Houdon, and some statuettes. Sometimes, Lupin would linger before a beautiful chest or a superb picture, and sigh:

"That is too heavy.... too large.... what a pity!"

In forty minutes the room was dismantled; and it had been accomplished in such an orderly manner and with as little noise as if the various articles had been packed and wadded for the occasion.

Lupin said to the last man who departed by way of the tunnel:

"You need not come back. You understand, that as soon as the auto-van is loaded, you are to proceed to the grange at Roquefort."

"But you, patron?"

"Leave me the motor-cycle."

When the man had disappeared, Arsène Lupin pushed the section of the bookcase back into its place, carefully effaced the traces of the men's footsteps, raised a portière, and entered a gallery, which was the only means of communication between the tower and the castle. In the center of this gallery there was a glass cabinet which had attracted Lupin's attentions. It contained a valuable collection of watches, snuff-boxes, rings, chatelaines and miniatures of rare and beautiful workmanship. He forced the lock with a small jimmy, and experienced a great pleasure in handling those gold and silver ornaments, those exquisite and delicate works of art.

He carried a large linen bag, specially prepared for the removal of such knick-knacks. He filled it. Then he filled the pockets of his coat, waistcoat and trousers. And he was just placing over his left arm a number of pearl reticules when he heard a slight sound. He listened. No, he was not deceived. The noise continued. Then he remembered that, at one end of the gallery, there was a stairway leading to an unoccupied apartment, but which was probably occupied that night by the young lady whom Mon. Devanne had brought from Dieppe with his other visitors.

Immediately he extinguished his lantern, and had scarcely gained the friendly shelter of a window-embrasure, when the door at the top of the stairway was opened and a feeble light illuminated the gallery. He could feel—for, concealed by a curtain, he could not see—that a woman was cautiously descending the upper steps of the stairs. He hoped she would come no closer. Yet, she continued to descend, and even advanced some distance into the room. Then she uttered a faint cry. No doubt she had discovered the broken and dismantled cabinet.

She advanced again. Now he could smell the perfume, and hear the throbbing of her heart as she drew closer to the window where he was concealed. She passed so close that her skirt brushed against the window-curtain, and Lupin felt that she suspected the presence of another, behind her, in the shadow, within reach of her hand. He thought: "She is afraid. She will go away." But she did not go. The candle, that she carried in her trembling hand, grew brighter. She turned, hesitated a moment, appeared to listen, then suddenly drew aside the curtain.

They stood face to face. Arsène was astounded. He murmured, involuntarily:

"You—you—mademoiselle."

It was Miss Nelly. Miss Nelly! his fellow passenger on the transatlantic steamer, who had been the subject of his dreams on that memorable voyage, who had been a witness to his arrest, and who, rather than betray him, had dropped into the water the Kodak in which he had concealed the bank-notes and diamonds. Miss Nelly! that charming creature, the memory of whose face had sometimes cheered, sometimes saddened the long hours of imprisonment.

It was such an unexpected encounter that brought them face to face in that castle at that hour of the night, that they could not move, nor utter a word; they were amazed, hypnotized, each at the sudden apparition of the other. Trembling with emotion, Miss Nelly staggered to a seat. He remained standing in front of her.

Gradually, he realized the situation and conceived the impression he must have produced at that moment with his arms laden with knick-knacks, and his pockets and a linen sack overflowing with plunder. He was overcome with confusion, and he actually blushed to find himself in the position of a thief caught in the act. To her, henceforth, he was a thief, a man who puts his hand in another's pocket, who steals into houses and robs people while they sleep.

A watch fell upon the floor; then another. These were followed by other articles which slipped from his grasp one by one. Then, actuated by a sudden decision, he dropped the other articles into an armchair, emptied his pockets and unpacked his sack. He felt very uncomfortable in Nelly's presence, and stepped toward her with the intention of speaking to her, but she shuddered, rose quickly and fled toward the salon. The portière closed behind her.

He followed her. She was standing trembling and amazed at the sight of the devastated room. He said to her, at once:

"To-morrow, at three o'clock, everything will be returned. The furniture will be brought back."

She made no reply, so he repeated:

"I promise it. To-morrow, at three o'clock. Nothing in the world could induce me to break that promise....To-morrow, at three o'clock."

Then followed a long silence that he dared not break, whilst the agitation of the young girl caused him a feeling of genuine regret. Quietly, without a word, he turned away, thinking: "I hope she will go away. I can't endure her presence." But the young girl suddenly spoke, and stammered:

"Listen.... footsteps....I hear someone...."

He looked at her with astonishment. She seemed to be overwhelmed by the thought of approaching peril.

"I don't hear anything," he said.

"But you must go—you must escape!"

"Why should I go?"

"Because—you must. Oh! do not remain here another minute. Go!"

She ran, quickly, to the door leading to the gallery and listened. No, there was no one there. Perhaps the noise was outside. She waited a moment, then returned reassured.

But Arsène Lupin had disappeared.

As soon as Mon. Devanne was informed of the pillage of his castle, he said to himself: It was Velmont who did it, and Velmont is Arsène Lupin. That theory explained everything, and there was no other plausible explanation. And yet the idea seemed preposterous. It was ridiculous to suppose that Velmont was anyone else than Velmont, the famous artist, and club-fellow of his cousin d'Estevan. So, when the captain of the gendarmes arrived to investigate the affair, Devanne did not even think of mentioning his absurd theory.

Throughout the forenoon there was a lively commotion at the castle. The gendarmes, the local police, the chief of police from Dieppe, the villagers, all circulated to and fro in the halls, examining every nook and corner that was open to their inspection. The approach of the maneuvering troops, the rattling fire of the musketry, added to the picturesque character of the scene.

The preliminary search furnished no clue. Neither the doors nor windows showed any signs of having been disturbed. Consequently, the removal of the goods must have been effected by means of the secret passage. Yet, there were no indications of footsteps on the floor, nor any unusual marks upon the walls.

Their investigations revealed, however, one curious fact that denoted the whimsical character of Arsène Lupin: the famous Chronique of the sixteenth century had been restored to its accustomed place in the library and, beside it, there was a similar book, which was none other than the volume stolen from the National Library.

At eleven o'clock the military officers arrived. Devanne welcomed them with his usual gayety; for, no matter how much chagrin he might suffer from the loss of his artistic treasures, his great wealth enabled him to bear his loss philosophically. His guests, Monsieur and Madame d'Androl and Miss Nelly, were introduced; and it was then noticed that one of the expected guests had not arrived. It was Horace Velmont. Would he come? His absence had awakened the suspicions of Mon. Devanne. But at twelve o'clock he arrived. Devanne exclaimed:

"Ah! here you are!"

"Why, am I not punctual?" asked Velmont.

"Yes, and I am surprised that you are.... after such a busy night! I suppose you know the news?"

"What news?"

"You have robbed the castle."

"Nonsense!" exclaimed Velmont, smiling.

"Exactly as I predicted. But, first escort Miss Underdown to the dining-room. Mademoiselle, allow me—"

He stopped, as he remarked the extreme agitation of the young girl. Then, recalling the incident, he said:

"Ah! of course, you met Arsène Lupin on the steamer, before his arrest, and you are astonished at the resemblance. Is that it?"

She did not reply. Velmont stood before her, smiling. He bowed. She took his proffered arm. He escorted her to her place, and took his seat opposite her. During the breakfast, the conversation related exclusively to Arsène Lupin, the stolen goods, the secret passage, and Sherlock Holmes. It was only at the close of the repast, when the conversation had drifted to other subjects, that Velmont took any part in it. Then he was, by turns, amusing and grave, talkative and pensive. And all his remarks seemed to be directed to the young girl. But she, quite absorbed, did not appear to hear them.

Coffee was served on the terrace overlooking the court of honor and the flower garden in front of the principal façade. The regimental band played on the lawn, and scores of soldiers and peasants wandered through the park.

Miss Nelly had not forgotten, for one moment, Lupin's solemn promise: "To-morrow, at three o'clock, everything will be returned."

At three o'clock! And the hands of the great clock in the right wing of the castle now marked twenty minutes to three. In spite of herself, her eyes wandered to the clock every minute. She also watched Velmont, who was calmly swinging to and fro in a comfortable rocking chair.

Ten minutes to three!....Five minutes to three!....Nelly was impatient and anxious. Was it possible that Arsène Lupin would carry out his promise at the appointed hour, when the castle, the courtyard, and the park were filled with people, and at the very moment when the officers of the law were pursuing their investigations? And yet....Arsène Lupin had given her his solemn promise. "It will be exactly as he said," thought she, so deeply was she impressed with the authority, energy and assurance of that remarkable man. To her, it no longer assumed the form of a miracle, but, on the contrary, a natural incident that must occur in the ordinary course of events. She blushed, and turned her head.

Three o'clock! The great clock struck slowly: one.... two.... three....Horace Velmont took out his watch, glanced at the clock, then returned the watch to his pocket. A few seconds passed in silence; and then the crowd in the courtyard parted to give passage to two wagons, that had just entered the park-gate, each drawn by two horses. They were army-wagons, such as are used for the transportation of provisions, tents, and other necessary military stores. They stopped in front of the main entrance, and a commissary-sergeant leaped from one of the wagons and inquired for Mon. Devanne. A moment later, that gentleman emerged from the house, descended the steps, and, under the canvas covers of the wagons, beheld his furniture, pictures and ornaments carefully packaged and arranged.

When questioned, the sergeant produced an order that he had received from the officer of the day. By that order, the second company of the fourth battalion were commanded to proceed to the crossroads of Halleux in the forest of Arques, gather up the furniture and other articles deposited there, and deliver same to Monsieur Georges Devanne, owner of the Thibermesnil castle, at three o'clock. Signed: Col. Beauvel.

"At the crossroads," explained the sergeant, "we found everything ready, lying on the grass, guarded by some passers-by. It seemed very strange, but the order was imperative."

One of the officers examined the signature. He declared it a forgery; but a clever imitation. The wagons were unloaded, and the goods restored to their proper places in the castle.

During this commotion, Nelly had remained alone at the extreme end of the terrace, absorbed by confused and distracted thoughts. Suddenly, she observed Velmont approaching her. She would have avoided him, but the balustrade that surrounded the terrace cut off her retreat. She was cornered. She could not move. A gleam of sunshine, passing through the scant foliage of a bamboo, lighted up her beautiful golden hair. Some one spoke to her in a low voice:

"Have I not kept my promise?"

Arsène Lupin stood close to her. No one else was near. He repeated, in a calm, soft voice:

"Have I not kept my promise?"

He expected a word of thanks, or at least some slight movement that would betray her interest in the fulfillment of his promise. But she remained silent.

Her scornful attitude annoyed Arsène Lupin; and he realized the vast distance that separated him from Miss Nelly, now that she had learned the truth. He would gladly have justified himself in her eyes, or at least pleaded extenuating circumstances, but he perceived the absurdity and futility of such an attempt. Finally, dominated by a surging flood of memories, he murmured:

"Ah! how long ago that was! You remember the long hours on the deck of the 'Provence.' Then, you carried a rose in your hand, a white rose like the one you carry to-day. I asked you for it. You pretended you did not hear me. After you had gone away, I found the rose—forgotten, no doubt—and I kept it."

She made no reply. She seemed to be far away. He continued:

"In memory of those happy hours, forget what you have learned since. Separate the past from the present. Do not regard me as the man you saw last night, but look at me, if only for a moment, as you did in those far-off days when I was Bernard d'Andrezy, for a short time. Will you, please?"

She raised her eyes and looked at him as he had requested. Then, without saying a word, she pointed to a ring he was wearing on his forefinger. Only the ring was visible; but the setting, which was turned toward the palm of his hand, consisted of a magnificent ruby. Arsène Lupin blushed. The ring belonged to Georges Devanne. He smiled bitterly, and said:

"You are right. Nothing can be changed. Arsène Lupin is now and always will be Arsène Lupin. To you, he cannot be even so much as a memory. Pardon me....I should have known that any attention I may now offer you is simply an insult. Forgive me."

He stepped aside, hat in hand. Nelly passed before him. He was inclined to detain her and beseech her forgiveness. But his courage failed, and he contented himself by following her with his eyes, as he had done when she descended the gangway to the pier at New York. She mounted the steps leading to the door, and disappeared within the house. He saw her no more.

A cloud obscured the sun. Arsène Lupin stood watching the imprints of her tiny feet in the sand. Suddenly, he gave a start. Upon the box which contained the bamboo, beside which Nelly had been standing, he saw the rose, the white rose which he had desired but dared not ask for. Forgotten, no doubt—it, also! But how—designedly or through distraction? He seized it eagerly. Some of its petals fell to the ground. He picked them up, one by one, like precious relics.

"Come!" he said to himself, "I have nothing more to do here. I must think of my safety, before Sherlock Holmes arrives."

The park was deserted, but some gendarmes were stationed at the park-gate. He entered a grove of pine trees, leaped over the wall, and, as a short cut to the railroad station, followed a path across the fields. After walking about ten minutes, he arrived at a spot where the road grew narrower and ran between two steep banks. In this ravine, he met a man traveling in the opposite direction. It was a man about fifty years of age, tall, smooth-shaven, and wearing clothes of a foreign cut. He carried a heavy cane, and a small satchel was strapped across his shoulder. When they met, the stranger spoke, with a slight English accent:

"Excuse me, monsieur, is this the way to the castle?"

"Yes, monsieur, straight ahead, and turn to the left when you come to the wall. They are expecting you."

"Ah!"

"Yes, my friend Devanne told us last night that you were coming, and I am delighted to be the first to welcome you. Sherlock Holmes has no more ardent admirer than.... myself."

There was a touch of irony in his voice that he quickly regretted, for Sherlock Holmes scrutinized him from head to foot with such a keen, penetrating eye that Arsène Lupin experienced the sensation of being seized, imprisoned and registered by that look more thoroughly and precisely than he had ever been by a camera.

"My negative is taken now," he thought, "and it will be useless to use a disguise with that man. He would look right through it. But, I wonder, has he recognized me?"

They bowed to each other as if about to part. But, at that moment, they heard a sound of horses' feet, accompanied by a clinking of steel. It was the gendarmes. The two men were obliged to draw back against the embankment, amongst the brushes, to avoid the horses. The gendarmes passed by, but, as they followed each other at a considerable distance, they were several minutes in doing so. And Lupin was thinking:

"It all depends on that question: has he recognized me? If so, he will probably take advantage of the opportunity. It is a trying situation."

When the last horseman had passed, Sherlock Holmes stepped forth and brushed the dust from his clothes. Then, for a moment, he and Arsène Lupin gazed at each other; and, if a person could have seen them at that moment, it would have been an interesting sight, and memorable as the first meeting of two remarkable men, so strange, so powerfully equipped, both of superior quality, and destined by fate, through their peculiar attributes, to hurl themselves one at the other like two equal forces that nature opposes, one against the other, in the realms of space.

Then the Englishman said: "Thank you, monsieur."

They parted. Lupin went toward the railway station, and Sherlock Holmes continued on his way to the castle.

The local officers had given up the investigation after several hours of fruitless efforts, and the people at the castle were awaiting the arrival of the English detective with a lively curiosity. At first sight, they were a little disappointed on account of his commonplace appearance, which differed so greatly from the pictures they had formed of him in their own minds. He did not in any way resemble the romantic hero, the mysterious and diabolical personage that the name of Sherlock Holmes had evoked in their imaginations. However, Mon. Devanne exclaimed with much gusto:

"Ah! monsieur, you are here! I am delighted to see you. It is a long-deferred pleasure. Really, I scarcely regret what has happened, since it affords me the opportunity to meet you. But, how did you come?"

"By the train."

"But I sent my automobile to meet you at the station."

"An official reception, eh? with music and fireworks! Oh! no, not for me. That is not the way I do business," grumbled the Englishman.

This speech disconcerted Devanne, who replied, with a forced smile:

"Fortunately, the business has been greatly simplified since I wrote to you."

"In what way?"

"The robbery took place last night."

"If you had not announced my intended visit, it is probable the robbery would not have been committed last night."

"When, then?"

"To-morrow, or some other day."

"And in that case?"

"Lupin would have been trapped," said the detective.

"And my furniture?"

"Would not have been carried away."

"Ah! but my goods are here. They were brought back at three o'clock."

"By Lupin."

"By two army-wagons."

Sherlock Holmes put on his cap and adjusted his satchel. Devanne exclaimed, anxiously:

"But, monsieur, what are you going to do?"

"I am going home."

"Why?"

"Your goods have been returned; Arsène Lupin is far away—there is nothing for me to do."

"Yes, there is. I need your assistance. What happened yesterday, may happen again to-morrow, as we do not know how he entered, or how he escaped, or why, a few hours later, he returned the goods."

"Ah! you don't know—"

The idea of a problem to be solved quickened the interest of Sherlock Holmes.

"Very well, let us make a search—at once—and alone, if possible."

Devanne understood, and conducted the Englishman to the salon. In a dry, crisp voice, in sentences that seemed to have been prepared in advance, Holmes asked a number of questions about the events of the preceding evening, and enquired also concerning the guests and the members of the household. Then he examined the two volumes of the "Chronique," compared the plans of the subterranean passage, requested a repetition of the sentences discovered by Father Gélis, and then asked:

"Was yesterday the first time you have spoken those two sentences to any one?"

"Yes."

"You had never communicated then to Horace Velmont?"

"No."

"Well, order the automobile. I must leave in an hour."

"In an hour?"

"Yes; within that time, Arsène Lupin solved the problem that you placed before him."

"I.... placed before him—"

"Yes, Arsène Lupin or Horace Velmont—same thing."

"I thought so. Ah! the scoundrel!"

"Now, let us see," said Holmes, "last night at ten o'clock, you furnished Lupin with the information that he lacked, and that he had been seeking for many weeks. During the night, he found time to solve the problem, collect his men, and rob the castle. I shall be quite as expeditious."

He walked from end to end of the room, in deep thought, then sat down, crossed his long legs and closed his eyes.

Devanne waited, quite embarrassed. Thought he: "Is the man asleep? Or is he only meditating?" However, he left the room to give some orders, and when he returned he found the detective on his knees scrutinizing the carpet at the foot of the stairs in the gallery.

"What is it?" he enquired.

"Look.... there.... spots from a candle."

"You are right—and quite fresh."

"And you will also find them at the top of the stairs, and around the cabinet that Arsène Lupin broke into, and from which he took the bibelots that he afterward placed in this armchair."

"What do you conclude from that?"

"Nothing. These facts would doubtless explain the cause for the restitution, but that is a side issue that I cannot wait to investigate. The main question is the secret passage. First, tell me, is there a chapel some two or three hundred metres from the castle?"

"Yes, a ruined chapel, containing the tomb of Duke Rollo."

"Tell your chauffer to wait for us near that chapel."

"My chauffer hasn't returned. If he had, they would have informed me. Do you think the secret passage runs to the chapel? What reason have—"

"I would ask you, monsieur," interrupted the detective, "to furnish me with a ladder and a lantern."

"What! do you require a ladder and a lantern?"

"Certainly, or I shouldn't have asked for them."

Devanne, somewhat disconcerted by this crude logic, rang the bell. The two articles were given with the sternness and precision of military commands.

"Place the ladder against the bookcase, to the left of the word Thibermesnil."

Devanne placed the ladder as directed, and the Englishman continued:

"More to the left.... to the right....There!....Now, climb up.... All the letters are in relief, aren't they?"

"Yes."

"First, turn the letter I one way or the other."

"Which one? There are two of them."

"The first one."

Devanne took hold of the letter, and exclaimed:

"Ah! yes, it turns toward the right. Who told you that?"

Sherlock Holmes did not reply to the question, but continued his directions:

"Now, take the letter B. Move it back and forth as you would a bolt."

Devanne did so, and, to his great surprise, it produced a clicking sound.

"Quite right," said Holmes. "Now, we will go to the other end of the word Thibermesnil, try the letter I, and see if it will open like a wicket."

With a certain degree of solemnity, Devanne seized the letter. It opened, but Devanne fell from the ladder, for the entire section of the bookcase, lying between the first and last letters of the words, turned on a pivot and disclosed the subterranean passage.

Sherlock Holmes said, coolly:

"You are not hurt?"

"No, no," said Devanne, as he rose to his feet, "not hurt, only bewildered. I can't understand now.... those letters turn.... the secret passage opens...."

"Certainly. Doesn't that agree exactly with the formula given by Sully? Turn one eye on the bee that shakes, the other eye will lead to God."

"But Louis the sixteenth?" asked Devanne.

"Louis the sixteenth was a clever locksmith. I have read a book he wrote about combination locks. It was a good idea on the part of the owner of Thibermesnil to show His Majesty a clever bit of mechanism. As an aid to his memory, the king wrote: 3-4-11, that is to say, the third, fourth and eleventh letters of the word."

"Exactly. I understand that. It explains how Lupin got out of the room, but it does not explain how he entered. And it is certain he came from the outside."

Sherlock Holmes lighted his lantern, and stepped into the passage.

"Look! All the mechanism is exposed here, like the works of a clock, and the reverse side of the letters can be reached. Lupin worked the combination from this side—that is all."

"What proof is there of that?"

"Proof? Why, look at that puddle of oil. Lupin foresaw that the wheels would require oiling."

"Did he know about the other entrance?"

"As well as I know it," said Holmes. "Follow me."

"Into that dark passage?"

"Are you afraid?"

"No, but are you sure you can find the way out?"

"With my eyes closed."

At first, they descended twelve steps, then twelve more, and, farther on, two other flights of twelve steps each. Then they walked through a long passageway, the brick walls of which showed the marks of successive restorations, and, in spots, were dripping with water. The earth, also, was very damp.

"We are passing under the pond," said Devanne, somewhat nervously.

At last, they came to a stairway of twelve steps, followed by three others of twelve steps each, which they mounted with difficulty, and then found themselves in a small cavity cut in the rock. They could go no further.

"The deuce!" muttered Holmes, "nothing but bare walls. This is provoking."

"Let us go back," said Devanne. "I have seen enough to satisfy me."

But the Englishman raised his eye and uttered a sigh of relief. There, he saw the same mechanism and the same word as before. He had merely to work the three letters. He did so, and a block of granite swung out of place. On the other side, this granite block formed the tombstone of Duke Rollo, and the word "Thibermesnil" was engraved on it in relief. Now, they were in the little ruined chapel, and the detective said:

"The other eye leads to God; that means, to the chapel."

"It is marvelous!" exclaimed Devanne, amazed at the clairvoyance and vivacity of the Englishman. "Can it be possible that those few words were sufficient for you?"

"Bah!" declared Holmes, "they weren't even necessary. In the chart in the book of the National Library, the drawing terminates at the left, as you know, in a circle, and at the right, as you do not know, in a cross. Now, that cross must refer to the chapel in which we now stand."

Poor Devanne could not believe his ears. It was all so new, so novel to him. He exclaimed:

"It is incredible, miraculous, and yet of a childish simplicity! How is it that no one has ever solved the mystery?"

"Because no one has ever united the essential elements, that is to say, the two books and the two sentences. No one, but Arsène Lupin and myself."

"But, Father Gélis and I knew all about those things, and, likewise—"

Holmes smiled, and said:

"Monsieur Devanne, everybody cannot solve riddles."

"I have been trying for ten years to accomplish what you did in ten minutes."

"Bah! I am used to it."

They emerged from the chapel, and found an automobile.

"Ah! there's an auto waiting for us."

"Yes, it is mine," said Devanne.

"Yours? You said your chauffeur hadn't returned."

They approached the machine, and Mon. Devanne questioned the chauffer:

"Edouard, who gave you orders to come here?"

"Why, it was Monsieur Velmont."

"Mon. Velmont? Did you meet him?"

"Near the railway station, and he told me to come to the chapel."

"To come to the chapel! What for?"

"To wait for you, monsieur, and your friend."

Devanne and Holmes exchanged looks, and Mon. Devanne said:

"He knew the mystery would be a simple one for you. It is a delicate compliment."

A smile of satisfaction lighted up the detective's serious features for a moment. The compliment pleased him. He shook his head, as he said:

"A clever man! I knew that when I saw him."

"Have you seen him?"

"I met him a short time ago—on my way from the station."

"And you knew it was Horace Velmont—I mean, Arsène Lupin?"

"That is right. I wonder how it came—"

"No, but I supposed it was—from a certain ironical speech he made."

"And you allowed him to escape?"

"Of course I did. And yet I had everything on my side, such as five gendarmes who passed us."

"Sacrableu!" cried Devanne. "You should have taken advantage of the opportunity."

"Really, monsieur," said the Englishman, haughtily, "when I encounter an adversary like Arsène Lupin, I do not take advantage of chance opportunities, I create them."

But time pressed, and since Lupin had been so kind as to send the automobile, they resolved to profit by it. They seated themselves in the comfortable limousine; Edouard took his place at the wheel, and away they went toward the railway station. Suddenly, Devanne's eyes fell upon a small package in one of the pockets of the carriage.

"Ah! what is that? A package! Whose is it? Why, it is for you."

"For me?"

"Yes, it is addressed: Sherlock Holmes, from Arsène Lupin."

The Englishman took the package, opened it, and found that it contained a watch.

"Ah!" he exclaimed, with an angry gesture.

"A watch," said Devanne. "How did it come there?"

The detective did not reply.

"Oh! it is your watch! Arsène Lupin returns your watch! But, in order to return it, he must have taken it. Ah! I see! He took your watch! That is a good one! Sherlock Holmes' watch stolen by Arsène Lupin! Mon Dieu! that is funny! Really.... you must excuse me....I can't help it."

He roared with laughter, unable to control himself. After which, he said, in a tone of earnest conviction:

"A clever man, indeed!"

The Englishman never moved a muscle. On the way to Dieppe, he never spoke a word, but fixed his gaze on the flying landscape. His silence was terrible, unfathomable, more violent than the wildest rage. At the railway station, he spoke calmly, but in a voice that impressed one with the vast energy and will power of that famous man. He said:

"Yes, he is a clever man, but some day I shall have the pleasure of

placing on his shoulder the hand I now offer to you, Monsieur Devanne.

And I believe that Arsène Lupin and Sherlock Holmes will meet again

some day. Yes, the world is too small—we will meet—we must meet—and

then—"

"—The further startling and thrilling adventures of Arsène Lupin will be

found in the book entitled "Arsène Lupin versus Herlock Sholmes."—

ARSÈNE LUPIN VERSUS HERLOCK SHOLMES

BY

MAURICE LEBLANC

Translated from the French

By GEORGE MOREHEAD

M.A. DONOHUE & CO.

CHICAGO

1910

CHAPTER I.

LOTTERY TICKET NO. 514.

On the eighth day of last December, Mon. Gerbois, professor of mathematics at the College of Versailles, while rummaging in an old curiosity-shop, unearthed a small mahogany writing-desk which pleased him very much on account of the multiplicity of its drawers.

"Just the thing for Suzanne's birthday present," thought he. And as he always tried to furnish some simple pleasures for his daughter, consistent with his modest income, he enquired the price, and, after some keen bargaining, purchased it for sixty-five francs. As he was giving his address to the shopkeeper, a young man, dressed with elegance and taste, who had been exploring the stock of antiques, caught sight of the writing-desk, and immediately enquired its price.

"It is sold," replied the shopkeeper.

"Ah! to this gentleman, I presume?"

Monsieur Gerbois bowed, and left the store, quite proud to be the possessor of an article which had attracted the attention of a gentleman of quality. But he had not taken a dozen steps in the street, when he was overtaken by the young man who, hat in hand and in a tone of perfect courtesy, thus addressed him:

"I beg your pardon, monsieur; I am going to ask you a question that you may deem impertinent. It is this: Did you have any special object in view when you bought that writing-desk?"

"No, I came across it by chance and it struck my fancy."

"But you do not care for it particularly?"

"Oh! I shall keep it—that is all."

"Because it is an antique, perhaps?"

"No; because it is convenient," declared Mon. Gerbois.

"In that case, you would consent to exchange it for another desk that would be quite as convenient and in better condition?"

"Oh! this one is in good condition, and I see no object in making an exchange."

"But——"

Mon. Gerbois is a man of irritable disposition and hasty temper. So he replied, testily:

"I beg of you, monsieur, do not insist."

But the young man firmly held his ground.

"I don't know how much you paid for it, monsieur, but I offer you double."

"No."

"Three times the amount."

"Oh! that will do," exclaimed the professor, impatiently; "I don't wish to sell it."

The young man stared at him for a moment in a manner that Mon. Gerbois would not readily forget, then turned and walked rapidly away.

An hour later, the desk was delivered at the professor's house on the Viroflay road. He called his daughter, and said:

"Here is something for you, Suzanne, provided you like it."

Suzanne was a pretty girl, with a gay and affectionate nature. She threw her arms around her father's neck and kissed him rapturously. To her, the desk had all the semblance of a royal gift. That evening, assisted by Hortense, the servant, she placed the desk in her room; then she dusted it, cleaned the drawers and pigeon-holes, and carefully arranged within it her papers, writing material, correspondence, a collection of post-cards, and some souvenirs of her cousin Philippe that she kept in secret.

Next morning, at half past seven, Mon. Gerbois went to the college. At ten o'clock, in pursuance of her usual custom, Suzanne went to meet him, and it was a great pleasure for him to see her slender figure and childish smile waiting for him at the college gate. They returned home together.

"And your writing desk—how is it this morning?"

"Marvellous! Hortense and I have polished the brass mountings until they look like gold."

"So you are pleased with it?"

"Pleased with it! Why, I don't see how I managed to get on without it for such a long time."

As they were walking up the pathway to the house, Mon. Gerbois said:

"Shall we go and take a look at it before breakfast?"

"Oh! yes, that's a splendid idea!"

She ascended the stairs ahead of her father, but, on arriving at the door of her room, she uttered a cry of surprise and dismay.

"What's the matter?" stammered Mon. Gerbois.

"The writing-desk is gone!"

When the police were called in, they were astonished at the admirable simplicity of the means employed by the thief. During Suzanne's absence, the servant had gone to market, and while the house was thus left unguarded, a drayman, wearing a badge—some of the neighbors saw it—stopped his cart in front of the house and rang twice. Not knowing that Hortense was absent, the neighbors were not suspicious; consequently, the man carried on his work in peace and tranquility.

Apart from the desk, not a thing in the house had been disturbed. Even Suzanne's purse, which she had left upon the writing-desk, was found upon an adjacent table with its contents untouched. It was obvious that the thief had come with a set purpose, which rendered the crime even more mysterious; because, why did he assume so great a risk for such a trifling object?

The only clue the professor could furnish was the strange incident of the preceding evening. He declared:

"The young man was greatly provoked at my refusal, and I had an idea that he threatened me as he went away."

But the clue was a vague one. The shopkeeper could not throw any light on the affair. He did not know either of the gentlemen. As to the desk itself, he had purchased it for forty francs at an executor's sale at Chevreuse, and believed he had resold it at its fair value. The police investigation disclosed nothing more.

But Mon. Gerbois entertained the idea that he had suffered an enormous loss. There must have been a fortune concealed in a secret drawer, and that was the reason the young man had resorted to crime.

"My poor father, what would we have done with that fortune?" asked Suzanne.

"My child! with such a fortune, you could make a most advantageous marriage."

Suzanne sighed bitterly. Her aspirations soared no higher than her cousin Philippe, who was indeed a most deplorable object. And life, in the little house at Versailles, was not so happy and contented as of yore.

Two months passed away. Then came a succession of startling events, a strange blending of good luck and dire misfortune!

On the first day of February, at half-past five, Mon. Gerbois entered the house, carrying an evening paper, took a seat, put on his spectacles, and commenced to read. As politics did not interest him, he turned to the inside of the paper. Immediately his attention was attracted by an article entitled:

"Third Drawing of the Press Association Lottery.

"No. 514, series 23, draws a million."

The newspaper slipped from his fingers. The walls swam before his eyes, and his heart ceased to beat. He held No. 514, series 23. He had purchased it from a friend, to oblige him, without any thought of success, and behold, it was the lucky number!

Quickly, he took out his memorandum-book. Yes, he was quite right. The No. 514, series 23, was written there, on the inside of the cover. But the ticket?

He rushed to his desk to find the envelope-box in which he had placed the precious ticket; but the box was not there, and it suddenly occurred to him that it had not been there for several weeks. He heard footsteps on the gravel walk leading from the street.

He called:

"Suzanne! Suzanne!"

She was returning from a walk. She entered hastily. He stammered, in a choking voice:

"Suzanne ... the box ... the box of envelopes?"

"What box?"

"The one I bought at the Louvre ... one Saturday ... it was at the end of that table."

"Don't you remember, father, we put all those things away together."

"When?"

"The evening ... you know ... the same evening...."

"But where?... Tell me, quick!... Where?"

"Where? Why, in the writing-desk."

"In the writing-desk that was stolen?"

"Yes."

"Oh, mon Dieu!... In the stolen desk!"

He uttered the last sentence in a low voice, in a sort of stupor. Then he seized her hand, and in a still lower voice, he said:

"It contained a million, my child."

"Ah! father, why didn't you tell me?" she murmured, naively.

"A million!" he repeated. "It contained the ticket that drew the grand prize in the Press Lottery."

The colossal proportions of the disaster overwhelmed them, and for a long time they maintained a silence that they feared to break. At last, Suzanne said:

"But, father, they will pay you just the same."

"How? On what proof?"

"Must you have proof?"

"Of course."

"And you haven't any?"

"It was in the box."

"In the box that has disappeared."

"Yes; and now the thief will get the money."

"Oh! that would be terrible, father. You must prevent it."

For a moment he was silent; then, in an outburst of energy, he leaped up, stamped on the floor, and exclaimed:

"No, no, he shall not have that million; he shall not have it! Why should he have it? Ah! clever as he is, he can do nothing. If he goes to claim the money, they will arrest him. Ah! now, we will see, my fine fellow!"

"What will you do, father?"

"Defend our just rights, whatever happens! And we will succeed. The million francs belong to me, and I intend to have them."

A few minutes later, he sent this telegram:

"Governor Crédit Foncier

"rue Capucines, Paris.

"Am holder of No. 514, series 23. Oppose by all legal means any other claimant.

"GERBOIS."

Almost at the same moment, the Crédit Foncier received the following telegram:

"No. 514, series 23, is in my possession.

"ARSÈNE LUPIN."

Every time I undertake to relate one of the many extraordinary adventures that mark the life of Arsène Lupin, I experience a feeling of embarrassment, as it seems to me that the most commonplace of those adventures is already well known to my readers. In fact, there is not a movement of our "national thief," as he has been so aptly described, that has not been given the widest publicity, not an exploit that has not been studied in all its phases, not an action that has not been discussed with that particularity usually reserved for the recital of heroic deeds.

For instance, who does not know the strange history of "The Blonde Lady," with those curious episodes which were proclaimed by the newspapers with heavy black headlines, as follows: "Lottery Ticket No. 514!" ... "The Crime on the Avenue Henri-Martin!" ... "The Blue Diamond!" ... The interest created by the intervention of the celebrated English detective, Herlock Sholmes! The excitement aroused by the various vicissitudes which marked the struggle between those famous artists! And what a commotion on the boulevards, the day on which the newsboys announced: "Arrest of Arsène Lupin!"

My excuse for repeating these stories at this time is the fact that I produce the key to the enigma. Those adventures have always been enveloped in a certain degree of obscurity, which I now remove. I reproduce old newspaper articles, I relate old-time interviews, I present ancient letters; but I have arranged and classified all that material and reduced it to the exact truth. My collaborators in this work have been Arsène Lupin himself, and also the ineffable Wilson, the friend and confidant of Herlock Sholmes.

Every one will recall the tremendous burst of laughter which greeted the publication of those two telegrams. The name "Arsène Lupin" was in itself a stimulus to curiosity, a promise of amusement for the gallery. And, in this case, the gallery means the entire world.

An investigation was immediately commenced by the Crédit Foncier, which established these facts: That ticket No. 514, series 23, had been sold by the Versailles branch office of the Lottery to an artillery officer named Bessy, who was afterward killed by a fall from his horse. Some time before his death, he informed some of his comrades that he had transferred his ticket to a friend.

"And I am that friend," affirmed Mon. Gerbois.

"Prove it," replied the governor of the Crédit Foncier.

"Of course I can prove it. Twenty people can tell you that I was an intimate friend of Monsieur Bessy, and that we frequently met at the Café de la Place-d'Armes. It was there, one day, I purchased the ticket from him for twenty francs—simply as an accommodation to him.

"Have you any witnesses to that transaction?"

"No."

"Well, how do you expect to prove it?"

"By a letter he wrote to me."

"What letter?"

"A letter that was pinned to the ticket."

"Produce it."

"It was stolen at the same time as the ticket."

"Well, you must find it."

It was soon learned that Arsène Lupin had the letter. A short paragraph appeared in the *Echo de France*—which has the honor to be his official organ, and of which, it is said, he is one of the principal shareholders—the paragraph announced that Arsène Lupin had placed in the hands of Monsieur Detinan, his advocate and legal adviser, the letter that Monsieur Bessy had written to him—to him personally.

This announcement provoked an outburst of laughter. Arsène Lupin had engaged a lawyer! Arsène Lupin, conforming to the rules and customs of modern society, had appointed a legal representative in the person of a well-known member of the Parisian bar!

Mon. Detinan had never enjoyed the pleasure of meeting Arsène Lupin—a fact he deeply regretted—but he had actually been retained by that mysterious gentleman and felt greatly honored by the choice. He was prepared to defend the interests of his client to the best of his ability. He was pleased, even proud, to exhibit the letter of Mon. Bessy, but, although it proved the transfer of the ticket, it did not mention the name of the purchaser. It was simply addressed to "My Dear Friend."

"My Dear Friend! that is I," added Arsène Lupin, in a note attached to Mon. Bessy's letter. "And the best proof of that fact is that I hold the letter."

The swarm of reporters immediately rushed to see Mon. Gerbois, who could only repeat:

"My Dear Friend! that is I.... Arsène Lupin stole the letter with the lottery ticket."

"Let him prove it!" retorted Lupin to the reporters.

"He must have done it, because he stole the writing-desk!" exclaimed Mon. Gerbois before the same reporters.

"Let him prove it!" replied Lupin.

Such was the entertaining comedy enacted by the two claimants of ticket No. 514; and the calm demeanor of Arsène Lupin contrasted strangely with the nervous perturbation of poor Mon. Gerbois. The newspapers were filled with the lamentations of that unhappy man. He announced his misfortune with pathetic candor.

"Understand, gentlemen, it was Suzanne's dowry that the rascal stole! Personally, I don't care a straw for it,... but for Suzanne! Just think of it, a whole million! Ten times one hundred thousand francs! Ah! I knew very well that the desk contained a treasure!"

It was in vain to tell him that his adversary, when stealing the desk, was unaware that the lottery ticket was in it, and that, in any event, he could not foresee that the ticket would draw the grand prize. He would reply;

"Nonsense! of course, he knew it ... else why would he take the trouble to steal a poor, miserable desk?"

"For some unknown reason; but certainly not for a small scrap of paper which was then worth only twenty francs."

"A million francs! He knew it;... he knows everything! Ah! you do not know him—the scoundrel!... He hasn't robbed you of a million francs!"

The controversy would have lasted for a much longer time, but, on the twelfth day, Mon. Gerbois received from Arsène Lupin a letter, marked "confidential," which read as follows:

"Monsieur, the gallery is being amused at our expense. Do you not think it is time for us to be serious? The situation is this: I possess a ticket to which I have no legal right, and you have the legal right to a ticket you do not possess. Neither of us can do anything. You will not relinquish your rights to me; I will not deliver the ticket to you. Now, what is to be done?

"I see only one way out of the difficulty: Let us divide the spoils. A half-million for you; a half-million for me. Is not that a fair division? In my opinion, it is an equitable solution, and an immediate one. I will give you three days' time to consider the proposition. On Thursday morning I shall expect to read in the personal column of the Echo de France a discreet message addressed to *M. Ars. Lup*, expressing in veiled terms your consent to my offer. By so doing you will recover immediate possession of the ticket; then you can collect the money and send me half a million in a manner that I will describe to you later.

"In case of your refusal, I shall resort to other measures to accomplish the same result. But, apart from the very serious annoyances that such obstinacy on your part will cause you, it will cost you twenty-five thousand francs for supplementary expenses.

"Believe me, monsieur, I remain your devoted servant, ARSÈNE LUPIN."

In a fit of exasperation Mon. Gerbois committed the grave mistake of showing that letter and allowing a copy of it to be taken. His indignation overcame his discretion.

"Nothing! He shall have nothing!" he exclaimed, before a crowd of reporters. "To divide my property with him? Never! Let him tear up the ticket if he wishes!"

"Yet five hundred thousand francs is better than nothing."

"That is not the question. It is a question of my just right, and that right I will establish before the courts."

"What! attack Arsène Lupin? That would be amusing."

"No; but the Crédit Foncier. They must pay me the million francs."

"Without producing the ticket, or, at least, without proving that you bought it?"

"That proof exists, since Arsène Lupin admits that he stole the writing-desk."

"But would the word of Arsène Lupin carry any weight with the court?"

"No matter; I will fight it out."

The gallery shouted with glee; and wagers were freely made upon the result with the odds in favor of Lupin. On the following Thursday the personal column in the *Echo de France* was eagerly perused by the expectant public, but it contained nothing addressed to *M. Ars. Lup.* Mon. Gerbois had not replied to Arsène Lupin's letter. That was the declaration of war.

That evening the newspapers announced the abduction of Mlle. Suzanne Gerbois.

The most entertaining feature in what might be called the Arsène Lupin dramas is the comic attitude displayed by the Parisian police. Arsène Lupin talks, plans, writes, commands, threatens and executes as if the police did not exist. They never figure in his calculations.

And yet the police do their utmost. But what can they do against such a foe—a foe that scorns and ignores them?

Suzanne had left the house at twenty minutes to ten; such was the testimony of the servant. On leaving the college, at five minutes past ten, her father did not find her at the place she was accustomed to wait for him. Consequently, whatever had happened must have occurred during the course of Suzanne's walk from the house to the college. Two neighbors had met her about three hundred yards from the house. A lady had seen, on the avenue, a young girl corresponding to Suzanne's description. No one else had seen her.

Inquiries were made in all directions; the employees of the railways and street-car lines were questioned, but none of them had seen anything of the missing girl. However, at Ville-d'Avray, they found a shopkeeper who had furnished gasoline to an automobile that had come from Paris on the day of the abduction. It was occupied by a blonde woman—extremely blonde, said the witness. An hour later, the automobile again passed through Ville-d'Avray on its way from Versailles to Paris. The shopkeeper declared that the automobile now contained a second woman who was heavily veiled. No doubt, it was Suzanne Gerbois.

The abduction must have taken place in broad daylight, on a frequented street, in the very heart of the town. How? And at what spot? Not a cry was heard; not a suspicious action had been seen. The shopkeeper described the automobile as a royal-blue limousine of twenty-four horse-power made by the firm of Peugeot & Co. Inquiries were then made at the Grand-Garage, managed by Madame Bob-Walthour, who made a specialty of abductions by automobile. It was learned that she had rented a Peugeot limousine on that day to a blonde woman whom she had never seen before nor since.

"Who was the chauffeur?"

"A young man named Ernest, whom I had engaged only the day before. He came well recommended."

"Is he here now?"

133

"No. He brought back the machine, but I haven't seen him since," said Madame Bob-Walthour.

"Do you know where we can find him?"

"You might see the people who recommended him to me. Here are the names."

Upon inquiry, it was learned that none of these people knew the man called Ernest. The recommendations were forged.

Such was the fate of every clue followed by the police. It ended nowhere. The mystery remained unsolved.

Mon. Gerbois had not the strength or courage to wage such an unequal battle. The disappearance of his daughter crushed him; he capitulated to the enemy. A short announcement in the *Echo de France* proclaimed his unconditional surrender.

Two days later, Mon. Gerbois visited the office of the Crédit Foncier and handed lottery ticket number 514, series 23, to the governor, who exclaimed, with surprise:

"Ah! you have it! He has returned it to you!"

"It was mislaid. That was all," replied Mon. Gerbois.

"But you pretended that it had been stolen."

"At first, I thought it had ... but here it is."

"We will require some evidence to establish your right to the ticket."

"Will the letter of the purchaser, Monsieur Bessy, be sufficient!"

"Yes, that will do."

"Here it is," said Mon. Gerbois, producing the letter.

"Very well. Leave these papers with us. The rules of the lottery allow us fifteen days' time to investigate your claim. I will let you know when to call for your money. I presume you desire, as much as I do, that this affair should be closed without further publicity."

"Quite so."

Mon. Gerbois and the governor henceforth maintained a discreet silence. But the secret was revealed in some way, for it was soon commonly known that Arsène Lupin had returned the lottery ticket to Mon. Gerbois. The public received the news with astonishment and admiration. Certainly, he was a bold gamester who thus threw upon the table a trump card of such importance as the precious ticket. But, it was true, he still retained a trump card of equal importance. However, if the young girl should escape? If the hostage held by Arsène Lupin should be rescued?

The police thought they had discovered the weak spot of the enemy, and now redoubled their efforts. Arsène Lupin disarmed by his own act, crushed by the wheels of his own machination, deprived of every sou of the coveted million ... public interest now centered in the camp of his adversary.

But it was necessary to find Suzanne. And they did not find her, nor did she escape. Consequently, it must be admitted, Arsène Lupin had won the first hand. But the game was not yet decided. The most difficult point remained. Mlle. Gerbois is in his possession, and he will hold her until he receives five hundred thousand francs. But how and where will such an exchange be made? For that purpose, a meeting must be arranged, and then what will prevent Mon. Gerbois from warning the police and, in that way, effecting the rescue of his daughter and, at the same time, keeping his money? The professor was interviewed, but he was extremely reticent. His answer was:

"I have nothing to say."

"And Mlle. Gerbois?"

"The search is being continued."

"But Arsène Lupin has written to you?"

"No."

"Do you swear to that?"

"No."

"Then it is true. What are his instructions?"

"I have nothing to say."

Then the interviewers attacked Mon. Detinan, and found him equally discreet.

"Monsieur Lupin is my client, and I cannot discuss his affairs," he replied, with an affected air of gravity.

These mysteries served to irritate the gallery. Obviously, some secret negotiations were in progress. Arsène Lupin had arranged and tightened the meshes of his net, while the police maintained a close watch, day and night, over Mon. Gerbois. And the three and only possible dénouements—the arrest, the triumph, or the ridiculous and pitiful abortion—were freely discussed; but the curiosity of the public was only partially satisfied, and it was reserved for these pages to reveal the exact truth of the affair.

On Monday, March 12th, Mon. Gerbois received a notice from the Crédit Foncier. On Wednesday, he took the one o'clock train for Paris. At two o'clock, a thousand bank-notes of one thousand francs each were delivered to him. Whilst he was counting them, one by one, in a state of nervous agitation—that money, which represented Suzanne's ransom—a carriage containing two men stopped at the curb a short distance from the bank. One of the men had grey hair and an unusually shrewd expression which formed a striking contrast to his shabby make-up. It was Detective Ganimard, the relentless enemy of Arsène Lupin. Ganimard said to his companion, Folenfant:

"In five minutes, we will see our clever friend Lupin. Is everything ready?"

"Yes."

"How many men have we?"

"Eight—two of them on bicycles."

"Enough, but not too many. On no account, must Gerbois escape us; if he does, it is all up. He will meet Lupin at the appointed place, give half a million in exchange for the girl, and the game will be over."

"But why doesn't Gerbois work with us? That would be the better way, and he could keep all the money himself."

"Yes, but he is afraid that if he deceives the other, he will not get his daughter."

"What other?"

"Lupin."

Ganimard pronounced the word in a solemn tone, somewhat timidly, as if he were speaking of some supernatural creature whose claws he already felt.

"It is very strange," remarked Folenfant, judiciously, "that we are obliged to protect this gentleman contrary to his own wishes."

"Yes, but Lupin always turns the world upside down," said Ganimard, mournfully.

A moment later, Mon. Gerbois appeared, and started up the street. At the end of the rue des Capucines, he turned into the boulevards, walking slowly, and stopping frequently to gaze at the shop-windows.

"Much too calm, too self-possessed," said Ganimard. "A man with a million in his pocket would not have that air of tranquillity."

"What is he doing?"

"Oh! nothing, evidently.... But I have a suspicion that it is Lupin—yes, Lupin!"

At that moment, Mon. Gerbois stopped at a news-stand, purchased a paper, unfolded it and commenced to read it as he walked slowly away. A moment later, he gave a sudden bound into an automobile that was standing at the curb. Apparently, the machine had been waiting for him, as it started away rapidly, turned at the Madeleine and disappeared.

"Nom de nom!" cried Ganimard, "that's one of his old tricks!"

Ganimard hastened after the automobile around the Madeleine. Then, he burst into laughter. At the entrance to the Boulevard Malesherbes, the automobile had stopped and Mon. Gerbois had alighted.

"Quick, Folenfant, the chauffeur! It may be the man Ernest."

Folenfant interviewed the chauffeur. His name was Gaston; he was an employee of the automobile cab company; ten minutes ago, a gentleman had engaged him and told him to wait near the news-stand for another gentleman.

"And the second man—what address did he give?" asked Folenfant.

"No address. 'Boulevard Malesherbes ... avenue de Messine ... double pourboire.' That is all."

But, during this time, Mon. Gerbois had leaped into the first passing carriage.

"To the Concorde station, Metropolitan," he said to the driver.

He left the underground at the Place du Palais-Royal, ran to another carriage and ordered it to go to the Place de la Bourse. Then a second journey by the underground to the Avenue de Villiers, followed by a third carriage drive to number 25 rue Clapeyron.

Number 25 rue Clapeyron is separated from the Boulevard des Batignolles by the house which occupies the angle formed by the two streets. He ascended to the first floor and rang. A gentleman opened the door.

"Does Monsieur Detinan live here?"

"Yes, that is my name. Are you Monsieur Gerbois?"

"Yes."

"I was expecting you. Step in."

As Mon. Gerbois entered the lawyer's office, the clock struck three. He said:

"I am prompt to the minute. Is he here?"

"Not yet."

Mon. Gerbois took a seat, wiped his forehead, looked at his watch as if he did not know the time, and inquired, anxiously:

"Will he come?"

"Well, monsieur," replied the lawyer, "that I do not know, but I am quite as anxious and impatient as you are to find out. If he comes, he will run a great risk, as this house has been closely watched for the last two weeks. They distrust me."

"They suspect me, too. I am not sure whether the detectives lost sight of me or not on my way here."

"But you were—"

"It wouldn't be my fault," cried the professor, quickly. "You cannot reproach me. I promised to obey his orders, and I followed them to the very letter. I drew the money at the time fixed by him, and I came here in the manner directed by him. I have faithfully performed my part of the agreement—let him do his!"

After a short silence, he asked, anxiously:

"He will bring my daughter, won't he?"

"I expect so."

"But ... you have seen him?"

"I? No, not yet. He made the appointment by letter, saying both of you would be here, and asking me to dismiss my servants before three o'clock and admit no one while you were here. If I would not consent to that arrangement, I was to notify him by a few words in *the Echo de France*. But I am only too happy to oblige Mon. Lupin, and so I consented."

"Ah! how will this end?" moaned Mon. Gerbois.

He took the bank-notes from his pocket, placed them on the table and divided them into two equal parts. Then the two men sat there in silence. From time to time, Mon. Gerbois would listen. Did someone ring?... His nervousness increased every minute, and Monsieur Detinan also displayed considerable anxiety. At last, the lawyer lost his patience. He rose abruptly, and said:

"He will not come.... We shouldn't expect it. It would be folly on his part. He would run too great a risk."

And Mon. Gerbois, despondent, his hands resting on the bank-notes, stammered:

"Oh! Mon Dieu! I hope he will come. I would give the whole of that money to see my daughter again."

The door opened.

"Half of it will be sufficient, Monsieur Gerbois."

These words were spoken by a well-dressed young man who now entered the room and was immediately recognized by Mon. Gerbois as the person who had wished to buy the desk from him at Versailles. He rushed toward him.

"Where is my daughter—my Suzanne?"

Arsène Lupin carefully closed the door, and, while slowly removing his gloves, said to the lawyer:

"My dear maître, I am indebted to you very much for your kindness in consenting to defend my interests. I shall not forget it."

Mon. Detinan murmured:

"But you did not ring. I did not hear the door—"

"Doors and bells are things that should work without being heard. I am here, and that is the important point."

"My daughter! Suzanne! Where is she!" repeated the professor.

"Mon Dieu, monsieur," said Lupin, "what's your hurry? Your daughter will be here in a moment."

Lupin walked to and fro for a minute, then, with the pompous air of an orator, he said:

"Monsieur Gerbois, I congratulate you on the clever way in which you made the journey to this place."

Then, perceiving the two piles of bank-notes, he exclaimed:

"Ah! I see! the million is here. We will not lose any time. Permit me."

"One moment," said the lawyer, placing himself before the table. "Mlle. Gerbois has not yet arrived."

"Well?"

"Is not her presence indispensable?"

"I understand! I understand! Arsène Lupin inspires only a limited confidence. He might pocket the half-million and not restore the hostage. Ah! monsieur, people do not understand me. Because I have been obliged, by force of circumstances, to commit certain actions a little ... out of the ordinary, my good faith is impugned ... I, who have always observed the utmost scrupulosity and delicacy in business affairs. Besides, my dear monsieur if you have any fear, open the window and call. There are at least a dozen detectives in the street."

"Do you think so?"

Arsène Lupin raised the curtain.

"I think that Monsieur Gerbois could not throw Ganimard off the scent.... What did I tell you? There he is now."

"Is it possible!" exclaimed the professor. "But I swear to you—"

"That you have not betrayed me?... I do not doubt you, but those fellows are clever—sometimes. Ah! I can see Folenfant, and Greaume, and Dieuzy—all good friends of mine!"

Mon. Detinan looked at Lupin in amazement. What assurance! He laughed as merrily as if engaged in some childish sport, as if no danger threatened him. This unconcern reassured the lawyer more than the presence of the detectives. He left the table on which the bank-notes were lying. Arsène Lupin picked up one pile of bills after the other, took from each of them twenty-five bank-notes which he offered to Mon. Detinan, saying:

"The reward of your services to Monsieur Gerbois and Arsène Lupin. You well deserve it."

"You owe me nothing," replied the lawyer.

"What! After all the trouble we have caused you!"

"And all the pleasure you have given me!"

"That means, my dear monsieur, that you do not wish to accept anything from Arsène Lupin. See what it is to have a bad reputation."

He then offered the fifty thousand francs to Mon. Gerbois, saying:

"Monsieur, in memory of our pleasant interview, permit me to return you this as a wedding-gift to Mlle. Gerbois."

Mon. Gerbois took the money, but said:

"My daughter will not marry."

"She will not marry if you refuse your consent; but she wishes to marry."

"What do you know about it?"

"I know that young girls often dream of such things unknown to their parents. Fortunately, there are sometimes good genii like Arsène Lupin who discover their little secrets in the drawers of their writing desks."

"Did you find anything else?" asked the lawyer. "I confess I am curious to know why you took so much trouble to get possession of that desk."

"On account of its historic interest, my friend. Although despite the opinion of Monsieur Gerbois, the desk contained no treasure except the lottery ticket—and that was unknown to me—I had been seeking it for a long time. That writing-desk of yew and mahogany was discovered in the little house in which Marie Walêwska once lived in Boulogne, and, on one of the drawers there is this inscription: '*Dedicated to Napoleon I, Emperor of the French, by his very faithful servant, Mancion.*' And above it, these words, engraved with the point of a knife: 'To you, Marie.' Afterwards, Napoleon had a similar desk made for the Empress Josephine; so that the secretary that was so much admired at the Malmaison was only an imperfect copy of the one that will henceforth form part of my collection."

"Ah! if I had known, when in the shop, I would gladly have given it up to you," said the professor.

Arsène Lupin smiled, as he replied:

"And you would have had the advantage of keeping for your own use lottery ticket number 514."

"And you would not have found it necessary to abduct my daughter."

"Abduct your daughter?"

"Yes."

"My dear monsieur, you are mistaken. Mlle. Gerbois was not abducted."

"No?"

"Certainly not. Abduction means force or violence. And I assure you that she served as hostage of her own free will."

"Of her own free will!" repeated Mon. Gerbois, in amazement.

"In fact, she almost asked to be taken. Why, do you suppose that an intelligent young girl like Mlle. Gerbois, and who, moreover, nourishes an unacknowledged passion, would hesitate to do what was necessary to secure her dowry. Ah! I swear to you it was not difficult to make her understand that it was the only way to overcome your obstinacy."

Mon. Detinan was greatly amused. He replied to Lupin:

"But I should think it was more difficult to get her to listen to you. How did you approach her?"

"Oh! I didn't approach her myself. I have not the honor of her acquaintance. A friend of mine, a lady, carried on the negotiations."

"The blonde woman in the automobile, no doubt."

"Precisely. All arrangements were made at the first interview near the college. Since then, Mlle. Gerbois and her new friend have been travelling in Belgium and Holland in a manner that should prove most pleasing and instructive to a young girl. She will tell you all about it herself—"

The bell of the vestibule door rang, three rings in quick succession, followed by two isolated rings.

"It is she," said Lupin. "Monsieur Detinan, if you will be so kind—"

The lawyer hastened to the door.

Two young women entered. One of them threw herself into the arms of Mon. Gerbois. The other approached Lupin. The latter was a tall woman of a good figure, very pale complexion, and with blond hair, parted over her forehead in undulating waves, that glistened and shone like the setting sun. She was dressed in black, with no display of jewelled ornaments; but, on the contrary, her appearance indicated good taste and refined elegance. Arsène Lupin spoke a few words to her; then, bowing to Mlle. Gerbois, he said:

"I owe you an apology, mademoiselle, for all your troubles, but I hope you have not been too unhappy—"

"Unhappy! Why, I should have been very happy, indeed, if it hadn't been for leaving my poor father."

"Then all is for the best. Kiss him again, and take advantage of the opportunity—it is an excellent one—to speak to him about your cousin."

"My cousin! What do you mean? I don't understand."

"Of course, you understand. Your cousin Philippe. The young man whose letters you kept so carefully."

Suzanne blushed; but, following Lupin's advice, she again threw herself into her father's arms. Lupin gazed upon them with a tender look.

"Ah! Such is my reward for a virtuous act! What a touching picture! A happy father and a happy daughter! And to know that their joy is your work, Lupin! Hereafter these people will bless you, and reverently transmit your name unto their descendants, even unto the fourth generation. What a glorious reward, Lupin, for one act of kindness!"

He walked to the window.

"Is dear old Ganimard still waiting?... He would like very much to be present at this charming domestic scene!... Ah! he is not there.... Nor any of the others.... I don't see anyone. The deuce! The situation is becoming serious. I dare say they are already under the porte-cochere ... talking to the concierge, perhaps ... or, even, ascending the stairs!"

Mon. Gerbois made a sudden movement. Now, that his daughter had been restored to him, he saw the situation in a different light. To him, the arrest of his adversary meant half-a-million francs. Instinctively, he made a step forward. As if by chance, Lupin stood in his way.

"Where are you going, Monsieur Gerbois? To defend me against them! That is very kind of you, but I assure you it is not necessary. They are more worried than I."

Then he continued to speak, with calm deliberation:

"But, really, what do they know? That you are here, and, perhaps, that Mlle. Gerbois is here, for they may have seen her arrive with an unknown lady. But they do not imagine that I am here. How is it possible that I could be in a house that they ran-sacked from cellar to garret this morning? They suppose that the unknown lady was sent by me to make the exchange, and they will be ready to arrest her when she goes out—"

At that moment, the bell rang. With a brusque movement, Lupin seized Mon. Gerbois, and said to him, in an imperious tone:

"Do not move! Remember your daughter, and be prudent—otherwise—As to you, Monsieur Detinan, I have your promise."

Mon. Gerbois was rooted to the spot. The lawyer did not stir. Without the least sign of haste, Lupin picked up his hat and brushed the dust from off it with his sleeve.

"My dear Monsieur Detinan, if I can ever be of service to you.... My best wishes, Mademoiselle Suzanne, and my kind regards to Monsieur Philippe."

He drew a heavy gold watch from his pocket.

"Monsieur Gerbois, it is now forty-two minutes past three. At forty-six minutes past three, I give you permission to leave this room. Not one minute sooner than forty-six minutes past three."

"But they will force an entrance," suggested Mon. Detinan.

"You forget the law, my dear monsieur! Ganimard would never venture to violate the privacy of a French citizen. But, pardon me, time flies, and you are all slightly nervous."

He placed his watch on the table, opened the door of the room and addressing the blonde lady he said:

"Are you ready my dear?"

He drew back to let her pass, bowed respectfully to Mlle. Gerbois, and went out, closing the door behind him. Then they heard him in the vestibule, speaking, in a loud voice: "Good-day,

Ganimard, how goes it? Remember me to Madame Ganimard. One of these days, I shall invite her to breakfast. Au revoir, Ganimard."

The bell rang violently, followed by repeated rings, and voices on the landing.

"Forty-five minutes," muttered Mon. Gerbois.

After a few seconds, he left the room and stepped into the vestibule. Arsène Lupin and the blonde lady had gone.

"Papa!... you mustn't! Wait!" cried Suzanne.

"Wait! you are foolish!... No quarter for that rascal!... And the half-million?"

He opened the outer door. Ganimard rushed in.

"That woman—where is she? And Lupin?"

"He was here ... he is here."

Ganimard uttered a cry of triumph.

"We have him. The house is surrounded."

"But the servant's stairway?" suggested Mon. Detinan.

"It leads to the court," said Ganimard. "There is only one exit—the street-door. Ten men are guarding it."

"But he didn't come in by the street-door, and he will not go out that way."

"What way, then?" asked Ganimard. "Through the air?"

He drew aside a curtain and exposed a long corridor leading to the kitchen. Ganimard ran along it and tried the door of the servants' stairway. It was locked. From the window he called to one of his assistants:

"Seen anyone?"

"No."

"Then they are still in the house!" he exclaimed. "They are hiding in one of the rooms! They cannot have escaped. Ah! Lupin, you fooled me before, but, this time, I get my revenge."

At seven o'clock in the evening, Mon. Dudonis, chief of the detective service, astonished at not receiving any news, visited the rue Clapeyron. He questioned the detectives who were guarding the house, then ascended to Mon. Detinan's apartment. The lawyer led him into his room. There, Mon. Dudonis beheld a man, or rather two legs kicking in the air, while the body to which they belonged was hidden in the depths of the chimney.

"Ohé!... Ohé!" gasped a stifled voice. And a more distant voice, from on high, replied:

"Ohé!... Ohé!"

Mon. Dudonis laughed, and exclaimed:

"Here! Ganimard, have you turned chimney-sweep?"

The detective crawled out of the chimney. With his blackened face, his sooty clothes, and his feverish eyes, he was quite unrecognizable.

"I am looking for *him*," he growled.

"Who?"

"Arsène Lupin ... and his friend."

"Well, do you suppose they are hiding in the chimney?"

Ganimard arose, laid his sooty hand on the sleeve of his superior officer's coat, and exclaimed, angrily:

"Where do you think they are, chief? They must be somewhere! They are flesh and blood like you and me, and can't fade away like smoke."

"No, but they have faded away just the same."

"But how? How? The house is surrounded by our men—even on the roof."

"What about the adjoining house?"

"There's no communication with it."

"And the apartments on the other floors?"

"I know all the tenants. They have not seen anyone."

"Are you sure you know all of them?"

"Yes. The concierge answers for them. Besides, as an extra precaution, I have placed a man in each apartment. They can't escape. If I don't get them to-night, I will get them to-morrow. I shall sleep here."

He slept there that night and the two following nights. Three days and nights passed away without the discovery of the irrepressible Lupin or his female companion; more than that, Ganimard did not unearth the slightest clue on which to base a theory to explain their escape. For that reason, he adhered to his first opinion.

"There is no trace of their escape; therefore, they are here."

It may be that, at the bottom of his heart, his conviction was less firmly established, but he would not confess it. No, a thousand times, no! A man and a woman could not vanish like the evil spirits in a fairy tale. And, without losing his courage, he continued his searches, as if he expected to find the fugitives concealed in some impenetrable retreat, or embodied in the stone walls of the house.

CHAPTER II.

THE BLUE DIAMOND.

On the evening of March 27, at number 134 avenue Henri-Martin, in the house that he had inherited from his brother six months before, the old general Baron d'Hautrec, ambassador at Berlin under the second Empire, was asleep in a comfortable armchair, while his secretary was reading to him, and the Sister Auguste was warming his bed and preparing the night-lamp. At eleven o'clock, the Sister, who was obliged to return to the convent of her order at that hour, said to the secretary:

"Mademoiselle Antoinette, my work is finished; I am going."

"Very well, Sister."

"Do not forget that the cook is away, and that you are alone in the house with the servant."

"Have no fear for the Baron. I sleep in the adjoining room and always leave the door open."

The Sister left the house. A few moments later, Charles, the servant, came to receive his orders. The Baron was now awake, and spoke for himself.

"The usual orders, Charles: see that the electric bell rings in your room, and, at the first alarm, run for the doctor. Now, Mademoiselle Antoinette, how far did we get in our reading?"

"Is Monsieur not going to bed now?"

"No, no, I will go later. Besides, I don't need anyone."

Twenty minutes later, he was sleeping again, and Antoinette crept away on tiptoe. At that moment, Charles was closing the shutters on the lower floor. In the kitchen, he bolted the door leading to the garden, and, in the vestibule, he not only locked the door but hooked the chain as well. Then he ascended to his room on the third floor, went to bed, and was soon asleep.

Probably an hour had passed, when he leaped from his bed in alarm. The bell was ringing. It rang for some time, seven or eight seconds perhaps, without intermission.

"Well?" muttered Charles, recovering his wits, "another of the Baron's whims."

He dressed himself quickly, descended the stairs, stopped in front of the door, and rapped, according to his custom. He received no reply. He opened the door and entered.

"Ah! no light," he murmured. "What is that for?"

Then, in a low voice, he called:

"Mademoiselle?"

No reply.

"Are you there, mademoiselle? What's the matter? Is Monsieur le Baron ill?"

No reply. Nothing but a profound silence that soon became depressing. He took two steps forward; his foot struck a chair, and, having touched it, he noticed that it was overturned. Then, with his hand, he discovered other objects on the floor—a small table and a screen. Anxiously, he approached the wall, felt for the electric button, and turned on the light.

In the centre of the room, between the table and dressing-case, lay the body of his master, the Baron d'Hautrec.

"What!... It can't be possible!" he stammered.

He could not move. He stood there, with bulging eyes, gazing stupidly at the terrible disorder, the overturned chairs, a large crystal candelabra shattered in a thousand pieces, the clock lying on the marble hearthstone, all evidence of a fearful and desperate struggle. The handle of a stiletto glittered, not far from the corpse; the blade was stained with blood. A handkerchief, marked with red spots, was lying on the edge of the bed.

Charles recoiled with horror: the body lying at his feet extended itself for a moment, then shrunk up again; two or three tremors, and that was the end.

He stooped over the body. There was a clean-cut wound on the neck from which the blood was flowing and then congealing in a black pool on the carpet. The face retained an expression of extreme terror.

"Some one has killed him!" he muttered, "some one has killed him!"

Then he shuddered at the thought that there might be another dreadful crime. Did not the baron's secretary sleep in the adjoining room! Had not the assassin killed her also! He opened the door; the room was empty. He concluded that Antoinette had been abducted, or else she had gone away before the crime. He returned to the baron's chamber, his glance falling on the secretary, he noticed that that article of furniture remained intact. Then, he saw upon a table, beside a bunch of keys and a pocketbook that the baron placed there every night, a handful of golden louis. Charles seized the pocketbook, opened it, and found some bank-notes. He counted them; there were thirteen notes of one hundred francs each.

Instinctively, mechanically, he put the bank-notes in his pocket, rushed down the stairs, drew the bolt, unhooked the chain, closed the door behind him, and fled to the street.

***

Charles was an honest man. He had scarcely left the gate, when, cooled by the night air and the rain, he came to a sudden halt. Now, he saw his action in its true light, and it filled him with horror. He hailed a passing cab, and said to the driver:

"Go to the police-office, and bring the commissary. Hurry! There has been a murder in that house."

The cab-driver whipped his horse. Charles wished to return to the house, but found the gate locked. He had closed it himself when he came out, and it could not be opened from the outside. On the other hand, it was useless to ring, as there was no one in the house.

It was almost an hour before the arrival of the police. When they came, Charles told his story and handed the bank-notes to the commissary. A locksmith was summoned, and, after considerable difficulty, he succeeded in forcing open the garden gate and the vestibule door. The commissary of police entered the room first, but, immediately, turned to Charles and said:

"You told me that the room was in the greatest disorder."

Charles stood at the door, amazed, bewildered; all the furniture had been restored to its accustomed place. The small table was standing between the two windows, the chairs were upright, and the clock was on the centre of the mantel. The debris of the candelabra had been removed.

"Where is.... Monsieur le Baron?" stammered Charles.

"That's so!" exclaimed the officer, "where is the victim?"

He approached the bed, and drew aside a large sheet, under which reposed the Baron d'Hautrec, formerly French Ambassador at Berlin. Over him, lay his military coat, adorned with the Cross of Honor. His features were calm. His eyes were closed.

"Some one has been here," said Charles.

"How did they get in?"

"I don't know, but some one has been here during my absence. There was a stiletto on the floor—there! And a handkerchief, stained with blood, on the bed. They are not here now. They have been carried away. And some one has put the room in order."

"Who would do that?"

"The assassin."

"But we found all the doors locked."

"He must have remained in the house."

"Then he must be here yet, as you were in front of the house all the time."

Charles reflected a moment, then said, slowly:

"Yes ... of course.... I didn't go away from the gate."

"Who was the last person you saw with the baron?"

"Mademoiselle Antoinette, his secretary."

"What has become of her?"

"I don't know. Her bed wasn't occupied, so she must have gone out. I am not surprised at that, as she is young and pretty."

"But how could she leave the house?"

"By the door," said Charles.

"But you had bolted and chained it."

"Yes, but she must have left before that."

"And the crime was committed after her departure?"

"Of course," said the servant.

The house was searched from cellar to garret, but the assassin had fled. How? And when? Was it he or an accomplice who had returned to the scene of the crime and removed everything that might furnish a clue to his identity? Such were the questions the police were called upon to solve.

The coroner came at seven o'clock; and, at eight o'clock, Mon. Dudouis, the head of the detective service, arrived on the scene. They were followed by the Procureur of the Republic and the investigating magistrate. In addition to these officials, the house was overrun with policemen, detectives, newspaper reporters, photographers, and relatives and acquaintances of the murdered man.

A thorough search was made; they studied out the position of the corpse according to the information furnished by Charles; they questioned Sister Auguste when she arrived; but they discovered nothing new. Sister Auguste was astonished to learn of the disappearance of Antoinette Bréhat. She had engaged the young girl twelve days before, on excellent recommendations, and refused to believe that she would neglect her duty by leaving the house during the night.

"But, you see, she hasn't returned yet," said the magistrate, "and we are still confronted with the question: What has become of her?"

"I think she was abducted by the assassin," said Charles.

The theory was plausible, and was borne out by certain facts. Mon. Dudouis agreed with it. He said:

"Abducted? ma foi! that is not improbable."

"Not only improbable," said a voice, "but absolutely opposed to the facts. There is not a particle of evidence to support such a theory."

The voice was harsh, the accent sharp, and no one was surprised to learn that the speaker was Ganimard. In no one else, would they tolerate such a domineering tone.

"Ah! it is you, Ganimard!" exclaimed Mon. Dudouis. "I had not seen you before."

"I have been here since two o'clock."

"So you are interested in some things outside of lottery ticket number 514, the affair of the rue Clapeyron, the blonde lady and Arsène Lupin?"

"Ha-ha!" laughed the veteran detective. "I would not say that Lupin is a stranger to the present case. But let us forget the affair of the lottery ticket for a few moments, and try to unravel this new mystery."

Ganimard is not one of those celebrated detectives whose methods will create a school, or whose name will be immortalized in the criminal annals of his country. He is devoid of those flashes of genius which characterize the work of Dupin, Lecoq and Sherlock Holmes. Yet, it must be admitted, he possesses superior qualities of observation, sagacity, perseverance and even intuition. His merit lies in his absolute independence. Nothing troubles or influences him, except, perhaps, a sort of fascination that Arsène Lupin holds over him. However that may be, there is no doubt that his position on that morning, in the house of the late Baron d'Hautrec, was one of undoubted superiority, and his collaboration in the case was appreciated and desired by the investigating magistrate.

"In the first place," said Ganimard, "I will ask Monsieur Charles to be very particular on one point: He says that, on the occasion of his first visit to the room, various articles of furniture were overturned and strewn about the place; now, I ask him whether, on his second visit to the room, he found all those articles restored to their accustomed places—I mean, of course, correctly placed."

"Yes, all in their proper places," replied Charles.

"It is obvious, then, that the person who replaced them must have been familiar with the location of those articles."

The logic of this remark was apparent to his hearers. Ganimard continued:

"One more question, Monsieur Charles. You were awakened by the ringing of your bell. Now, who, do you think, rang it?"

"Monsieur le baron, of course."

"When could he ring it?"

"After the struggle ... when he was dying."

"Impossible; because you found him lying, unconscious, at a point more than four metres from the bell-button."

"Then he must have rung during the struggle."

"Impossible," declared Ganimard, "since the ringing, as you have said, was continuous and uninterrupted, and lasted seven or eight seconds. Do you think his antagonist would have permitted him to ring the bell in that leisurely manner?"

"Well, then, it was before the attack."

"Also, quite impossible, since you have told us that the lapse of time between the ringing of the bell and your entrance to the room was not more than three minutes. Therefore, if the baron rang before the attack, we are forced to the conclusion that the struggle, the murder and the flight of the assassin, all occurred within the short space of three minutes. I repeat: that is impossible."

"And yet," said the magistrate, "some one rang. If it were not the baron, who was it?"

"The murderer."

"For what purpose?"

"I do not know. But the fact that he did ring proves that he knew that the bell communicated with the servant's room. Now, who would know that, except an inmate of the house?"

Ganimard was drawing the meshes of his net closer and tighter. In a few clear and logical sentences, he had unfolded and defined his theory of the crime, so that it seemed quite natural when the magistrate said:

"As I understand it, Ganimard, you suspect the girl Antoinette Bréhat?"

"I do not suspect her; I accuse her."

"You accuse her of being an accomplice?"

"I accuse her of having killed Baron d'Hautrec."

"Nonsense! What proof have you?"

"The handful of hair I found in the right hand of the victim."

He produced the hair; it was of a beautiful blond color, and glittered like threads of gold. Charles looked at it, and said:

"That is Mademoiselle Antoinette's hair. There can be no doubt of it. And, then, there is another thing. I believe that the knife, which I saw on my first visit to the room, belonged to her. She used it to cut the leaves of books."

A long, dreadful silence followed, as if the crime had acquired an additional horror by reason of having been committed by a woman. At last, the magistrate said:

"Let us assume, until we are better informed, that the baron was killed by Antoinette Bréhat. We have yet to learn where she concealed herself after the crime, how she managed to return after Charles left the house, and how she made her escape after the arrival of the police. Have you formed any opinion on those points Ganimard?"

"None."

"Well, then, where do we stand?"

Ganimard was embarrassed. Finally, with a visible effort, he said:

"All I can say is that I find in this case the same method of procedure as we found in the affair of the lottery ticket number 514; the same phenomena, which might be termed the faculty of disappearing. Antoinette Bréhat has appeared and disappeared in this house as mysteriously as Arsène Lupin entered the house of Monsieur Detinan and escaped therefrom in the company of the blonde lady.

"Does that signify anything?"

"It does to me. I can see a probable connection between those two strange incidents. Antoinette Bréhat was hired by Sister Auguste twelve days ago, that is to say, on the day after the blonde Lady so cleverly slipped through my fingers. In the second place, the hair of the blonde Lady was exactly of the same brilliant golden hue as the hair found in this case."

"So that, in your opinion, Antoinette Bréhat—"

"Is the blonde Lady—precisely."

"And that Lupin had a hand in both cases?"

"Yes, that is my opinion."

This statement was greeted with an outburst of laughter. It came from Mon. Dudouis.

"Lupin! always Lupin! Lupin is into everything; Lupin is everywhere!"

"Yes, Lupin is into everything of any consequence," replied Ganimard, vexed at the ridicule of his superior.

"Well, so far as I see," observed Mon. Dudouis, "you have not discovered any motive for this crime. The secretary was not broken into, nor the pocketbook carried away. Even, a pile of gold was left upon the table."

"Yes, that is so," exclaimed Ganimard, "but the famous diamond?"

"What diamond?"

"The blue diamond! The celebrated diamond which formed part of the royal crown of France, and which was given by the Duke d'Aumale to Leonide Lebrun, and, at the death of Leonide Lebrun, was purchased by the Baron d'Hautrec as a souvenir of the charming comedienne that he had loved so well. That is one of those things that an old Parisian, like I, does not forget."

"It is obvious that if the blue diamond is not found, the motive for the crime is disclosed," said the magistrate. "But where should we search for it?"

"On the baron's finger," replied Charles. "He always wore the blue diamond on his left hand."

"I saw that hand, and there was only a plain gold ring on it," said Ganimard, as he approached the corpse.

"Look in the palm of the hand," replied the servant.

Ganimard opened the stiffened hand. The bezel was turned inward, and, in the centre of that bezel, the blue diamond shone with all its glorious splendor.

"The deuce!" muttered Ganimard, absolutely amazed, "I don't understand it."

"You will now apologize to Lupin for having suspected him, eh?" said Mon. Dudouis, laughing.

Ganimard paused for a moment's reflection, and then replied, sententiously:

"It is only when I do not understand things that I suspect Arsène Lupin."

Such were the facts established by the police on the day after the commission of that mysterious crime. Facts that were vague and incoherent in themselves, and which were not explained by any subsequent discoveries. The movements of Antoinette Bréhat remained as inexplicable as those of the blonde Lady, and the police discovered no trace of that mysterious creature with the golden hair who had killed Baron d'Hautrec and had failed to take from his finger the famous diamond that had once shone in the royal crown of France.

The heirs of the Baron d'Hautrec could not fail to benefit by such notoriety. They established in the house an exhibition of the furniture and other objects which were to be sold at the auction rooms of Drouot & Co. Modern furniture of indifferent taste, various objects of no artistic value ... but, in the centre of the room, in a case of purple velvet, protected by a glass globe, and guarded by two officers, was the famous blue diamond ring.

A large magnificent diamond of incomparable purity, and of that indefinite blue which the clear water receives from an unclouded sky, of that blue which can be detected in the whiteness of linen. Some admired, some enthused ... and some looked with horror on the chamber of the victim, on the spot where the corpse had lain, on the floor divested of its blood-stained carpet, and especially the walls, the unsurmountable walls over which the criminal must have passed. Some assured themselves that the marble mantel did not move, others imagined gaping holes, mouths of tunnels, secret connections with the sewers, and the catacombs—

The sale of the blue diamond took place at the salesroom of Drouot & Co. The place was crowded to suffocation, and the bidding was carried to the verge of folly. The sale was attended by all those who usually appear at similar events in Paris; those who buy, and those who make a pretense of being able to buy; bankers, brokers, artists, women of all classes, two cabinet ministers, an Italian tenor, an exiled king who, in order to maintain his credit, bid, with much ostentation, and in a loud voice, as high as one hundred thousand francs. One hundred thousand francs! He could offer that sum without any danger of his bid being accepted. The Italian tenor risked one hundred and fifty thousand, and a member of the Comédie-Française bid one hundred and seventy-five thousand francs.

When the bidding reached two hundred thousand francs, the smaller competitors fell out of the race. At two hundred and fifty thousand, only two bidders remained in the field: Herschmann, the well-known capitalist, the king of gold mines; and the Countess de Crozon, the wealthy American, whose collection of diamonds and precious stones is famed throughout the world.

"Two hundred and sixty thousand ... two hundred and seventy thousand ... seventy-five ... eighty...." exclaimed the auctioneer, as he glanced at the two competitors in succession. "Two hundred and eighty thousand for madame.... Do I hear any more?"

"Three hundred thousand," said Herschmann.

There was a short silence. The countess was standing, smiling, but pale from excitement. She was leaning against the back of the chair in front of her. She knew, and so did everyone present, that the issue of the duel was certain; logically, inevitably, it must terminate to the advantage of the capitalist, who had untold millions with which to indulge his caprices. However, the countess made another bid:

"Three hundred and five thousand."

Another silence. All eyes were now directed to the capitalist in the expectation that he would raise the bidding. But Herschmann was not paying any attention to the sale; his eyes were fixed on a sheet of paper which he held in his right hand, while the other hand held a torn envelope.

"Three hundred and five thousand," repeated the auctioneer. "Once!... Twice!... For the last time.... Do I hear any more?... Once!... Twice!... Am I offered any more? Last chance!..."

Herschmann did not move.

"Third and last time!... Sold!" exclaimed the auctioneer, as his hammer fell.

"Four hundred thousand," cried Herschman, starting up, as if the sound of the hammer had roused him from his stupor.

Too late; the auctioneer's decision was irrevocable. Some of Herschmann's acquaintances pressed around him. What was the matter? Why did he not speak sooner? He laughed, and said:

"Ma foi! I simply forgot—in a moment of abstraction."

"That is strange."

"You see, I just received a letter."

"And that letter was sufficient—"

"To distract my attention? Yes, for a moment."

Ganimard was there. He had come to witness the sale of the ring. He stopped one of the attendants of the auction room, and said:

"Was it you who carried the letter to Monsieur Herschmann?"

"Yes."

"Who gave it to you?"

"A lady."

"Where is she?"

"Where is she?... She was sitting down there ... the lady who wore a thick veil."

"She has gone?"

"Yes, just this moment."

Ganimard hastened to the door, and saw the lady descending the stairs. He ran after her. A crush of people delayed him at the entrance. When he reached the sidewalk, she had disappeared. He returned to the auction room, accosted Herschmann, introduced himself, and enquired about the letter. Herschmann handed it to him. It was carelessly scribbled in pencil, in a handwriting unknown to the capitalist, and contained these few words:

"The blue diamond brings misfortune. Remember the Baron d'Hautrec."

The vicissitudes of the blue diamond were not yet at an end. Although it had become well-known through the murder of the Baron d'Hautrec and the incidents at the auction-rooms, it was six months later that it attained even greater celebrity. During the following summer, the Countess de Crozon was robbed of the famous jewel she had taken so much trouble to acquire.

Let me recall that strange affair, of which the exciting and dramatic incidents sent a thrill through all of us, and over which I am now permitted to throw some light.

On the evening of August 10, the guests of the Count and Countess de Crozon were assembled in the drawing-room of the magnificent château which overlooks the Bay de Somme. To entertain her friends, the countess seated herself at the piano to play for them, after first placing her jewels on a small table near the piano, and, amongst them, was the ring of the Baron d'Hautrec.

An hour later, the count and the majority of the guests retired, including his two cousins and Madame de Réal, an intimate friend of the countess. The latter remained in the drawing-room with Herr Bleichen, the Austrian consul, and his wife.

They conversed for a time, and then the countess extinguished the large lamp that stood on a table in the centre of the room. At the same moment, Herr Bleichen extinguished the two piano lamps. There was a momentary darkness; then the consul lighted a candle, and the three of them retired to their rooms. But, as soon as she reached her apartment, the countess remembered her jewels and sent her maid to get them. When the maid returned with the jewels, she placed them on the mantel without the countess looking at them. Next day, Madame de Crozon found that one of her rings was missing; it was the blue diamond ring.

She informed her husband, and, after talking it over, they reached the conclusion that the maid was above suspicion, and that the guilty party must be Herr Bleichen.

The count notified the commissary of police at Amiens, who commenced an investigation and, discreetly, exercised a strict surveillance over the Austrian consul to prevent his disposing of the ring.

The château was surrounded by detectives day and night. Two weeks passed without incident. Then Herr Bleichen announced his intended departure. That day, a formal complaint was entered against him. The police made an official examination of his luggage. In a small satchel, the key to which was always carried by the consul himself, they found a bottle of dentifrice, and in that bottle they found the ring.

Madame Bleichen fainted. Her husband was placed under arrest.

Everyone will remember the line of defense adopted by the accused man. He declared that the ring must have been placed there by the Count de Crozen as an act of revenge. He said:

"The count is brutal and makes his wife very unhappy. She consulted me, and I advised her to get a divorce. The count heard of it in some way, and, to be revenged on me, he took the ring and placed it in my satchel."

The count and countess persisted in pressing the charge. Between the explanation which they gave and that of the consul, both equally possible and equally probable, the public had to choose. No new fact was discovered to turn the scale in either direction. A month of gossip, conjectures and investigations failed to produce a single ray of light.

Wearied of the excitement and notoriety, and incapable of securing the evidence necessary to sustain their charge against the consul, the count and countess at last sent to Paris for a detective competent to unravel the tangled threads of this mysterious skein. This brought Ganimard into the case.

For four days, the veteran detective searched the house from top to bottom, examined every foot of the ground, had long conferences with the maid, the chauffeur, the gardeners, the employees in the neighboring post-offices, visited the rooms that had been occupied by the various guests. Then, one morning, he disappeared without taking leave of his host or hostess. But a week later, they received this telegram:

"Please come to the Japanese Tea-room, rue Boissy d'Anglas, to-morrow, Friday, evening at five o'clock. Ganimard."

At five o'clock, Friday evening, their automobile stopped in front of number nine rue Boissy-d'Anglas. The old detective was standing on the sidewalk, waiting for them. Without a word, he conducted them to the first floor of the Japanese Tea-room. In one of the rooms, they met two men, whom Ganimard introduced in these words:

"Monsieur Gerbois, professor in the College of Versailles, from whom, you will remember, Arsène Lupin stole half a million; Monsieur Léonce d'Hautrec, nephew and sole legatee of the Baron d'Hautrec."

A few minutes later, another man arrived. It was Mon. Dudouis, head of the detective service, and he appeared to be in a particularly bad temper. He bowed, and then said:

"What's the trouble now, Ganimard? I received your telephone message asking me to come here. Is it anything of consequence?"

"Yes, chief, it is a very important matter. Within an hour, the last two cases to which I was assigned will have their dénouement here. It seemed to me that your presence was indispensable."

"And also the presence of Dieuzy and Folenfant, whom I noticed standing near the door as I came in?"

"Yes, chief."

"For what? Are you going to make an arrest, and you wish to do it with a flourish? Come, Ganimard, I am anxious to hear about it."

Ganimard hesitated a moment, then spoke with the obvious intention of making an impression on his hearers:

"In the first place, I wish to state that Herr Bleichen had nothing to do with the theft of the ring."

"Oh! oh!" exclaimed Mon. Dudouis, "that is a bold statement and a very serious one."

"And is that all you have discovered?" asked the Count de Crozon.

"Not at all. On the second day after the theft, three of your guests went on an automobile trip as far as Crécy. Two of them visited the famous battlefield; and, while they were there, the third party paid a hasty visit to the post-office, and mailed a small box, tied and sealed according to the regulations, and declared its value to be one hundred francs."

"I see nothing strange in that," said the count.

"Perhaps you will see something strange in it when I tell you that this person, in place of giving her true name, sent the box under the name of Rousseau, and the person to whom it was addressed, a certain Monsieur Beloux of Paris, moved his place of residence immediately after receiving the box, in other words, the ring."

"I presume you refer to one of my cousins d'Andelle?"

"No," replied Ganimard.

"Madame de Réal, then?"

"Yes."

"You accuse my friend, Madam de Réal?" cried the countess, shocked and amazed.

"I wish to ask you one question, madame," said Ganimard. "Was Madam de Réal present when you purchased the ring?"

"Yes, but we did not go there together."

"Did she advise you to buy the ring?"

The countess considered for a moment, then said:

"Yes, I think she mentioned it first—"

"Thank you, madame. Your answer establishes the fact that it was Madame de Réal who was the first to mention the ring, and it was she who advised you to buy it."

"But, I consider my friend is quite incapable—"

"Pardon me, countess, when I remind you that Madame de Réal is only a casual acquaintance and not your intimate friend, as the newspapers have announced. It was only last winter that you met her for the first time. Now, I can prove that everything she has told you about herself, her past life, and her relatives, is absolutely false; that Madame Blanche de Réal had no actual existence before she met you, and she has now ceased to exist."

"Well?"

"Well?" replied Ganimard.

"Your story is a very strange one," said the countess, "but it has no application to our case. If Madame de Réal had taken the ring, how do you explain the fact that it was found in Herr Bleichen's tooth-powder? Anyone who would take the risk and trouble of stealing the blue diamond would certainly keep it. What do you say to that?"

"I—nothing—but Madame de Réal will answer it."

"Oh! she does exist, then?"

"She does—and does not. I will explain in a few words. Three days ago, while reading a newspaper, I glanced over the list of hotel arrivals at Trouville, and there I read: 'Hôtel Beaurivage—Madame de Réal, etc.'

"I went to Trouville immediately, and interviewed the proprietor of the hotel. From the description and other information I received from him, I concluded that she was the very Madame de Réal that I was seeking; but she had left the hotel, giving her address in Paris as number three rue de Colisée. The day before yesterday I went to that address, and learned that there was no person there called Madame de Réal, but there was a Madame Réal, living on the second floor, who acted as a diamond broker and was frequently away from home. She had returned from a journey on the preceding evening. Yesterday, I called on her and, under an assumed name, I offered to act as an intermedium in the sale of some diamonds to certain wealthy friends of mine. She is to meet me here to-day to carry out that arrangement."

"What! You expect her to come here?"

"Yes, at half-past five."

"Are you sure it is she?"

"Madame de Réal of the Château de Crozon? Certainly. I have convincing evidence of that fact. But ... listen!... I hear Folenfant's signal."

It was a whistle. Ganimard arose quickly.

"There is no time to lose. Monsieur and Madame de Crozon, will you be kind enough to go into the next room. You also, Monsieur d'Hautrec, and you, Monsieur Gerbois. The door will remain open, and when I give the signal, you will come out. Of course, Chief, you will remain here."

"We may be disturbed by other people," said Mon. Dudouis.

"No. This is a new establishment, and the proprietor is one of my friends. He will not let anyone disturb us—except the blonde Lady."

"The blonde Lady! What do you mean?"

"Yes, the blonde Lady herself, chief; the friend and accomplice of Arsène Lupin, the mysterious blonde Lady against whom I hold convincing evidence; but, in addition to that, I wish to confront her with all the people she has robbed."

He looked through the window.

"I see her. She is coming in the door now. She can't escape: Folenfant and Dieuzy are guarding the door.... The blonde Lady is captured at last, Chief!"

A moment later a woman appeared at the door; she was tall and slender, with a very pale complexion and bright golden hair. Ganimard trembled with excitement; he could not move, nor utter a word. She was there, in front of him, at his mercy! What a victory over Arsène Lupin! And what a revenge! And, at the same time, the victory was such an easy one that he asked himself if the blonde Lady would not yet slip through his fingers by one of those miracles that usually terminated the exploits of Arsène Lupin. She remained standing near the door, surprised at the silence, and looked about her without any display of suspicion or fear.

"She will get away! She will disappear!" thought Ganimard.

Then he managed to get between her and the door. She turned to go out.

"No, no!" he said. "Why are you going away?"

"Really, monsieur, I do not understand what this means. Allow me—"

"There is no reason why you should go, madame, and very good reasons why you should remain."

"But—"

"It is useless, madame. You cannot go."

Trembling, she sat on a chair, and stammered:

"What is it you want?"

Ganimard had won the battle and captured the blonde Lady. He said to her:

"Allow me to present the friend I mentioned, who desires to purchase some diamonds. Have you procured the stones you promised to bring?"

"No—no—I don't know. I don't remember."

"Come! Jog your memory! A person of your acquaintance intended to send you a tinted stone.... 'Something like the blue diamond,' I said, laughing; and you replied: 'Exactly, I expect to have just what you want.' Do you remember?"

She made no reply. A small satchel fell from her hand. She picked it up quickly, and held it securely. Her hands trembled slightly.

"Come!" said Ganimard, "I see you have no confidence in us, Madame de Réal. I shall set you a good example by showing you what I have."

He took from his pocketbook a paper which he unfolded, and disclosed a lock of hair.

"These are a few hairs torn from the head of Antoinette Bréhat by the Baron d'Hautrec, which I found clasped in his dead hand. I have shown them to Mlle. Gerbois, who declares they are of the exact color of the hair of the blonde Lady. Besides, they are exactly the color of your hair—the identical color."

Madame Réal looked at him in bewilderment, as if she did not understand his meaning. He continued:

"And here are two perfume bottles, without labels, it is true, and empty, but still sufficiently impregnated with their odor to enable Mlle. Gerbois to recognize in them the perfume used by that blonde Lady who was her traveling companion for two weeks. Now, one of these bottles was found in the room that Madame de Réal occupied at the Château de Crozon, and the other in the room that you occupied at the Hôtel Beaurivage."

"What do you say?... The blonde Lady ... the Château de Crozon...."

The detective did not reply. He took from his pocket and placed on the table, side by side, four small sheets of paper. Then he said:

"I have, on these four pieces of paper, various specimens of handwriting; the first is the writing of Antoinette Bréhat; the second was written by the woman who sent the note to Baron Herschmann at the auction sale of the blue diamond; the third is that of Madame de Réal, written while she was stopping at the Château de Crozon; and the fourth is your handwriting, madame ... it is your name and address, which you gave to the porter of the Hôtel Beaurivage at Trouville. Now, compare the four handwritings. They are identical."

"What absurdity is this? really, monsieur, I do not understand. What does it mean?"

"It means, madame," exclaimed Ganimard, "that the blonde Lady, the friend and accomplice of Arsène Lupin, is none other than you, Madame Réal."

Ganimard went to the adjoining room and returned with Mon. Gerbois, whom he placed in front of Madame Réal, as he said:

"Monsieur Gerbois, is this the person who abducted your daughter, the woman you saw at the house of Monsieur Detinan?"

"No."

Ganimard was so surprised that he could not speak for a moment; finally, he said: "No?... You must be mistaken...."

"I am not mistaken. Madame is blonde, it is true, and in that respect resembles the blonde Lady; but, in all other respects, she is totally different."

"I can't believe it. You must be mistaken."

Ganimard called in his other witnesses.

"Monsieur d'Hautrec," he said, "do you recognize Antoinette Bréhat?"

"No, this is not the person I saw at my uncle's house."

"This woman is not Madame de Réal," declared the Count de Crozon.

That was the finishing touch. Ganimard was crushed. He was buried beneath the ruins of the structure he had erected with so much care and assurance. His pride was humbled, his spirit was broken, by the force of this unexpected blow.

Mon. Dudouis arose, and said:

"We owe you an apology, madame, for this unfortunate mistake. But, since your arrival here, I have noticed your nervous agitation. Something troubles you; may I ask what it is?"

"Mon Dieu, monsieur, I was afraid. My satchel contains diamonds to the value of a hundred thousand francs, and the conduct of your friend was rather suspicious."

"But you were frequently absent from Paris. How do you explain that?"

"I make frequent journeys to other cities in the course of my business. That is all."

Mon. Dudouis had nothing more to ask. He turned to his subordinate, and said:

"Your investigation has been very superficial, Ganimard, and your conduct toward this lady is really deplorable. You will come to my office to-morrow and explain it."

The interview was at an end, and Mon. Dudouis was about to leave the room when a most annoying incident occurred. Madame Réal turned to Ganimard, and said:

"I understand that you are Monsieur Ganimard. Am I right?"

"Yes."

"Then, this letter must be for you. I received it this morning. It was addressed to 'Mon. Justin Ganimard, care of Madame Réal.' I thought it was a joke, because I did not know you under that name, but it appears that your unknown correspondent knew of our rendezvous."

Ganimard was inclined to put the letter in his pocket unread, but he dared not do so in the presence of his superior, so he opened the envelope and read the letter aloud, in an almost inaudible tone:

"Once upon a time, there were a blonde Lady, a Lupin, and a Ganimard. Now, the wicked Ganimard had evil designs on the pretty blonde Lady, and the good Lupin was her friend and protector. When the good Lupin wished the blonde Lady to become the friend of the Countess de Crozon, he caused her to assume the name of Madame de Réal, which is a close resemblance to the name of a certain diamond broker, a woman with a pale complexion and golden hair. And the good Lupin said to himself: If ever the wicked Ganimard gets upon the track of the blonde Lady, how useful it will be to me if he should be diverted to the track of the honest diamond broker. A wise precaution that has borne good fruit. A little note sent to the newspaper read by the wicked Ganimard, a perfume bottle intentionally forgotten by the genuine blonde Lady at the Hôtel Beaurivage, the name and address of Madame Réal written on the hotel register by the genuine blonde Lady, and the trick is played. What do you think of it, Ganimard! I wished to tell you the true story of this affair, knowing that you would be the first to laugh over it. Really, it is quite amusing, and I have enjoyed it very much.

"Accept my best wishes, dear friend, and give my kind regards to the worthy Mon. Dudouis.

"ARSÈNE LUPIN."

"He knows everything," muttered Ganimard, but he did not see the humor of the situation as Lupin had predicted. "He knows some things I have never mentioned to any one. How could he find out that I was going to invite you here, chief? How could he know that I had found the first perfume bottle? How could he find out those things?"

He stamped his feet and tore his hair—a prey to the most tragic despair. Mon. Dudouis felt sorry for him, and said:

"Come, Ganimard, never mind; try to do better next time."

And Mon. Dudouis left the room, accompanied by Madame Réal.

During the next ten minutes, Ganimard read and re-read the letter of Arsène Lupin. Monsieur and Madame de Crozon, Monsieur d'Hautrec and Monsieur Gerbois were holding an animated discussion in a corner of the room. At last, the count approached the detective, and said:

"My dear monsieur, after your investigation, we are no nearer the truth than we were before."

"Pardon me, but my investigation has established these facts: that the blonde Lady is the mysterious heroine of these exploits, and that Arsène Lupin directed them."

"Those facts do not solve the mystery; in fact, they render it more obscure. The blonde Lady commits a murder in order to steal the blue diamond, and yet she does not steal it. Afterward she steals it and gets rid of it by secretly giving it to another person. How do you explain her strange conduct?"

"I cannot explain it."

"Of course; but, perhaps, someone else can."

"Who?"

The Count hesitated, so the Countess replied, frankly:

"There is only one man besides yourself who is competent to enter the arena with Arsène Lupin and overcome him. Have you any objection to our engaging the services of Herlock Sholmes in this case?"

Ganimard was vexed at the question, but stammered a reply:

"No ... but ... I do not understand what——"

"Let me explain. All this mystery annoys me. I wish to have it cleared up. Monsieur Gerbois and Monsieur d'Hautrec have the same desire, and we have agreed to send for the celebrated English detective."

"You are right, madame," replied the detective, with a loyalty that did him credit, "you are right. Old Ganimard is not able to overcome Arsène Lupin. But will Herlock Sholmes succeed? I hope so, as I have the greatest admiration for him. But ... it is improbable."

"Do you mean to say that he will not succeed?"

"That is my opinion. I can foresee the result of a duel between Herlock Sholmes and Arsène Lupin. The Englishman will be defeated."

"But, in any event, can we count on your assistance?"

"Quite so, madame. I shall be pleased to render Monsieur Sholmes all possible assistance."

"Do you know his address?"

"Yes; 219 Parker street."

That evening Monsieur and Madame de Crozon withdrew the charge they had made against Herr Bleichen, and a joint letter was addressed to Herlock Sholmes.

CHAPTER III.

HERLOCK SHOLMES OPENS HOSTILITIES.

"What does monsieur wish?"

"Anything," replied Arsène Lupin, like a man who never worries over the details of a meal; "anything you like, but no meat or alcohol."

The waiter walked away, disdainfully.

"What! still a vegetarian?" I exclaimed.

"More so than ever," replied Lupin.

"Through taste, faith, or habit?"

"Hygiene."

"And do you never fall from grace?"

"Oh! yes ... when I am dining out ... and wish to avoid being considered eccentric."

We were dining near the Northern Railway station, in a little restaurant to which Arsène Lupin had invited me. Frequently he would send me a telegram asking me to meet him in some obscure restaurant, where we could enjoy a quiet dinner, well served, and which was always made interesting to me by his recital of some startling adventure theretofore unknown to me.

On that particular evening he appeared to be in a more lively mood than usual. He laughed and joked with careless animation, and with that delicate sarcasm that was habitual with him—a light and spontaneous sarcasm that was quite free from any tinge of malice. It was a pleasure to find him in that jovial mood, and I could not resist the desire to tell him so.

"Ah! yes," he exclaimed, "there are days in which I find life as bright and gay as a spring morning; then life seems to be an infinite treasure which I can never exhaust. And yet God knows I lead a careless existence!"

"Too much so, perhaps."

"Ah! but I tell you, the treasure is infinite. I can spend it with a lavish hand. I can cast my youth and strength to the four winds of Heaven, and it is replaced by a still younger and greater force. Besides, my life is so pleasant!... If I wished to do so, I might become—what shall I say?... An orator, a manufacturer, a politician.... But, I assure you, I shall never have such a desire. Arsène Lupin, I am; Arsène Lupin, I shall remain. I have made a vain search in history to find a career comparable to mine; a life better filled or more intense.... Napoleon? Yes, perhaps.... But Napoleon, toward the close of his career, when all Europe was trying to crush him, asked himself on the eve of each battle if it would not be his last."

Was he serious? Or was he joking? He became more animated as he proceeded:

"That is everything, do you understand, the danger! The continuous feeling of danger! To breathe it as you breathe the air, to scent it in every breath of wind, to detect it in every unusual sound.... And, in the midst of the tempest, to remain calm ... and not to stumble! Otherwise, you are lost. There is only one sensation equal to it: that of the chauffeur in an automobile race. But that race lasts only a few hours; my race continues until death!"

"What fantasy!" I exclaimed. "And you wish me to believe that you have no particular motive for your adoption of that exciting life?"

"Come," he said, with a smile, "you are a clever psychologist. Work it out for yourself."

He poured himself a glass of water, drank it, and said:

"Did you read *'Le Temps'* to-day?"

"No."

"Herlock Sholmes crossed the Channel this afternoon, and arrived in Paris about six o'clock."

"The deuce! What is he coming for?"

"A little journey he has undertaken at the request of the Count and Countess of Crozon, Monsieur Gerbois, and the nephew of Baron d'Hautrec. They met him at the Northern Railway station, took him to meet Ganimard, and, at this moment, the six of them are holding a consultation."

Despite a strong temptation to do so, I had never ventured to question Arsène Lupin concerning any action of his private life, unless he had first mentioned the subject to me. Up to that moment his name had not been mentioned, at least officially, in connection with the blue diamond. Consequently, I consumed my curiosity in patience. He continued:

"There is also in *'Le Temps'* an interview with my old friend Ganimard, according to whom a certain blonde lady, who should be my friend, must have murdered the Baron d'Hautrec and tried to rob Madame de Crozon of her famous ring. And—what do you think?—he accuses me of being the instigator of those crimes."

I could not suppress a slight shudder. Was this true? Must I believe that his career of theft, his mode of existence, the logical result of such a life, had drawn that man into more serious crimes, including murder? I looked at him. He was so calm, and his eyes had such a frank expression! I observed his hands: they had been formed from a model of exceeding delicacy, long and slender; inoffensive, truly; and the hands of an artist....

"Ganimard has pipe-dreams," I said.

"No, no!" protested Lupin. "Ganimard has some cleverness; and, at times, almost inspiration."

"Inspiration!"

"Yes. For instance, that interview is a master-stroke. In the first place, he announces the coming of his English rival in order to put me on my guard, and make his task more difficult. In the second place, he indicates the exact point to which he has conducted the affair in order that Sholmes will not get credit for the work already done by Ganimard. That is good warfare."

"Whatever it may be, you have two adversaries to deal with, and such adversaries!"

"Oh! one of them doesn't count."

"And the other?"

"Sholmes? Oh! I confess he is a worthy foe; and that explains my present good humor. In the first place, it is a question of self-esteem; I am pleased to know that they consider me a subject worthy the attention of the celebrated English detective. In the next place, just imagine the pleasure a man, such as I, must experience in the thought of a duel with Herlock Sholmes. But I shall be obliged to strain every muscle; he is a clever fellow, and will contest every inch of the ground."

"Then you consider him a strong opponent?"

"I do. As a detective, I believe, he has never had an equal. But I have one advantage over him; he is making the attack and I am simply defending myself. My rôle is the easier one. Besides, I am familiar with his method of warfare, and he does not know mine. I am prepared to show him a few new tricks that will give him something to think about."

He tapped the table with his fingers as he uttered the following sentences, with an air of keen delight:

"Arsène Lupin against Herlock Sholmes.... France against England.... Trafalgar will be revenged at last.... Ah! the rascal ... he doesn't suspect that I am prepared ... and a Lupin warned—"

He stopped suddenly, seized with a fit of coughing, and hid his face in his napkin, as if something had stuck in his throat.

"A bit of bread?" I inquired. "Drink some water."

"No, it isn't that," he replied, in a stifled voice.

"Then, what is it?"

"The want of air."

"Do you wish a window opened?"

"No, I shall go out. Give me my hat and overcoat, quick! I must go."

"What's the matter?"

"The two gentlemen who came in just now.... Look at the taller one ... now, when we go out, keep to my left, so he will not see me."

"The one who is sitting behind you?"

"Yes. I will explain it to you, outside."

"Who is it?"

"Herlock Sholmes."

He made a desperate effort to control himself, as if he were ashamed of his emotion, replaced his napkin, drank a glass of water, and, quite recovered, said to me, smiling:

165

"It is strange, hein, that I should be affected so easily, but that unexpected sight—"

"What have you to fear, since no one can recognize you, on account of your many transformations? Every time I see you it seems to me your face is changed; it's not at all familiar. I don't know why."

"But *he* would recognize me," said Lupin. "He has seen me only once; but, at that time, he made a mental photograph of me—not of my external appearance but of my very soul—not what I appear to be but just what I am. Do you understand? And then ... and then.... I did not expect to meet him here.... Such a strange encounter!... in this little restaurant...."

"Well, shall we go out?"

"No, not now," said Lupin.

"What are you going to do?"

"The better way is to act frankly ... to have confidence in him—trust him...."

"You will not speak to him?"

"Why not! It will be to my advantage to do so, and find out what he knows, and, perhaps, what he thinks. At present I have the feeling that his gaze is on my neck and shoulders, and that he is trying to remember where he has seen them before."

He reflected a moment. I observed a malicious smile at the corner of his mouth; then, obedient, I think, to a whim of his impulsive nature, and not to the necessities of the situation, he arose, turned around, and, with a bow and a joyous air, he said:

"By what lucky chance? Ah! I am delighted to see you. Permit me to introduce a friend of mine."

For a moment the Englishman was disconcerted; then he made a movement as if he would seize Arsène Lupin. The latter shook his head, and said:

"That would not be fair; besides, the movement would be an awkward one and ... quite useless."

The Englishman looked about him, as if in search of assistance.

"No use," said Lupin. "Besides, are you quite sure you can place your hand on me? Come, now, show me that you are a real Englishman and, therefore, a good sport."

This advice seemed to commend itself to the detective, for he partially rose and said, very formally:

"Monsieur Wilson, my friend and assistant—Monsieur Arsène Lupin."

Wilson's amazement evoked a laugh. With bulging eyes and gaping mouth, he looked from one to the other, as if unable to comprehend the situation. Herlock Sholmes laughed and said:

"Wilson, you should conceal your astonishment at an incident which is one of the most natural in the world."

"Why do you not arrest him?" stammered Wilson.

"Have you not observed, Wilson, that the gentleman is between me and the door, and only a few steps from the door. By the time I could move my little finger he would be outside."

"Don't let that make any difference," said Lupin, who now walked around the table and seated himself so that the Englishman was between him and the door—thus placing himself at the mercy of the foreigner.

Wilson looked at Sholmes to find out if he had the right to admire this act of wanton courage. The Englishman's face was impenetrable; but, a moment later, he called:

"Waiter!"

When the waiter came he ordered soda, beer and whisky. The treaty of peace was signed—until further orders. In a few moments the four men were conversing in an apparently friendly manner.

Herlock Sholmes is a man such as you might meet every day in the business world. He is about fifty years of age, and looks as if he might have passed his life in an office, adding up columns of dull figures or writing out formal statements of business accounts. There was nothing to distinguish him from the average citizen of London, except the appearance of his eyes, his terribly keen and penetrating eyes.

But then he is Herlock Sholmes—which means that he is a wonderful combination of intuition, observation, clairvoyance and ingenuity. One could readily believe that nature had been pleased to take the two most extraordinary detectives that the imagination of man has hitherto conceived, the Dupin of Edgar Allen Poe and the Lecoq of Emile Gaboriau, and, out of that material, constructed a new detective, more extraordinary and supernatural than either of them. And when a person reads the history of his exploits, which have made him famous throughout the entire world, he asks himself whether Herlock Sholmes is not a mythical personage, a fictitious hero born in the brain of a great novelist—Conan Doyle, for instance.

When Arsène Lupin questioned him in regard to the length of his sojourn in France he turned the conversation into its proper channel by saying:

"That depends on you, monsieur."

"Oh!" exclaimed Lupin, laughing, "if it depends on me you can return to England to-night."

"That is a little too soon, but I expect to return in the course of eight or nine days—ten at the outside."

"Are you in such a hurry?"

"I have many cases to attend to; such as the robbery of the Anglo-Chinese Bank, the abduction of Lady Eccleston.... But, don't you think, Monsieur Lupin, that I can finish my business in Paris within a week?"

"Certainly, if you confine your efforts to the case of the blue diamond. It is, moreover, the length of time that I require to make preparations for my safety in case the solution of that affair should give you certain dangerous advantages over me."

"And yet," said the Englishman, "I expect to close the business in eight or ten days."

"And arrest me on the eleventh, perhaps?"

"No, the tenth is my limit."

Lupin shook his head thoughtfully, as he said:

"That will be difficult—very difficult."

"Difficult, perhaps, but possible, therefore certain—"

"Absolutely certain," said Wilson, as if he had clearly worked out the long series of operations which would conduct his collaborator to the desired result.

"Of course," said Herlock Sholmes, "I do not hold all the trump cards, as these cases are already several months old, and I lack certain information and clues upon which I am accustomed to base my investigations."

"Such as spots of mud and cigarette ashes," said Wilson, with an air of importance.

"In addition to the remarkable conclusions formed by Monsieur Ganimard, I have obtained all the articles written on the subject, and have formed a few deductions of my own."

"Some ideas which were suggested to us by analysis or hypothesis," added Wilson, sententiously.

"I wish to enquire," said Arsène Lupin, in that deferential tone which he employed in speaking to Sholmes, "would I be indiscreet if I were to ask you what opinion you have formed about the case?"

Really, it was a most exciting situation to see those two men facing each other across the table, engaged in an earnest discussion as if they were obliged to solve some abstruse problem or come to an agreement upon some controverted fact. Wilson was in the seventh heaven of delight. Herlock Sholmes filled his pipe slowly, lighted it, and said:

"This affair is much simpler than it appeared to be at first sight."

"Much simpler," said Wilson, as a faithful echo.

"I say 'this affair,' for, in my opinion, there is only one," said Sholmes. "The death of the Baron d'Hautrec, the story of the ring, and, let us not forget, the mystery of lottery ticket number 514, are only different phases of what one might call the mystery of the blonde Lady. Now, according to my view, it is simply a question of discovering the bond that unites those three episodes in the same story—the fact which proves the unity of the three events.

Ganimard, whose judgment is rather superficial, finds that unity in the faculty of disappearance; that is, in the power of coming and going unseen and unheard. That theory does not satisfy me."

"Well, what is your idea?" asked Lupin.

"In my opinion," said Sholmes, "the characteristic feature of the three episodes is your design and purpose of leading the affair into a certain channel previously chosen by you. It is, on your part, more than a plan; it is a necessity, an indispensable condition of success."

"Can you furnish any details of your theory?"

"Certainly. For example, from the beginning of your conflict with Monsieur Gerbois, is it not evident that the apartment of Monsieur Detinan is the place selected by you, the inevitable spot where all the parties must meet? In your opinion, it was the only safe place, and you arranged a rendezvous there, publicly, one might say, for the blonde Lady and Mademoiselle Gerbois."

"The professor's daughter," added Wilson. "Now, let us consider the case of the blue diamond. Did you try to appropriate it while the Baron d'Hautrec possessed it! No. But the baron takes his brother's house. Six months later we have the intervention of Antoinette Bréhat and the first attempt. The diamond escapes you, and the sale is widely advertised to take place at the Drouot auction-rooms. Will it be a free and open sale? Is the richest amateur sure to carry off the jewel! No. Just as the banker Herschmann is on the point of buying the ring, a lady sends him a letter of warning, and it is the Countess de Crozon, prepared and influenced by the same lady, who becomes the purchaser of the diamond. Will the ring disappear at once? No; you lack the opportunity. Therefore, you must wait. At last the Countess goes to her château. That is what you were waiting for. The ring disappears."

"To reappear again in the tooth-powder of Herr Bleichen," remarked Lupin.

"Oh! such nonsense!" exclaimed Sholmes, striking the table with his fist, "don't tell me such a fairy tale. I am too old a fox to be led away by a false scent."

"What do you mean?"

"What do I mean?" said Sholmes, then paused a moment as if he wished to arrange his effect. At last he said:

"The blue diamond that was found in the tooth-powder was false. You kept the genuine stone."

Arsène Lupin remained silent for a moment; then, with his eyes fixed on the Englishman, he replied, calmly:

"You are impertinent, monsieur."

"Impertinent, indeed!" repeated Wilson, beaming with admiration.

"Yes," said Lupin, "and, yet, to do you credit, you have thrown a strong light on a very mysterious subject. Not a magistrate, not a special reporter, who has been engaged on this case, has come so near the truth. It is a marvellous display of intuition and logic."

"Oh! a person has simply to use his brains," said Herlock Sholmes, nattered at the homage of the expert criminal.

"And so few have any brains to use," replied Lupin. "And, now, that the field of conjectures has been narrowed down, and the rubbish cleared away——"

"Well, now, I have simply to discover why the three episodes were enacted at 25 rue Clapeyron, 134 avenue Henri-Martin, and within the walls of the Château de Crozon and my work will be finished. What remains will be child's play. Don't you think so?"

"Yes, I think you are right."

"In that case, Monsieur Lupin, am I wrong in saying that my business will be finished in ten days?"

"In ten days you will know the whole truth," said Lupin.

"And you will be arrested."

"No."

"No?"

"In order that I may be arrested there must occur such a series of improbable and unexpected misfortunes that I cannot admit the possibility of such an event."

"We have a saying in England that 'the unexpected always happens.'"

They looked at each other for a moment calmly and fearlessly, without any display of bravado or malice. They met as equals in a contest of wit and skill. And this meeting was the formal crossing of swords, preliminary to the duel.

"Ah!" exclaimed Lupin, "at last I shall have an adversary worthy of the name—one whose defeat will be the proudest achievement in my career."

"Are you not afraid!" asked Wilson.

"Almost, Monsieur Wilson," replied Lupin, rising from his chair, "and the proof is that I am about to make a hasty retreat. Then, we will say ten days, Monsieur Sholmes?"

"Yes, ten days. This is Sunday. A week from next Wednesday, at eight o'clock in the evening, it will be all over."

"And I shall be in prison?"

"No doubt of it."

"Ha! not a pleasant outlook for a man who gets so much enjoyment out of life as I do. No cares, a lively interest in the affairs of the world, a justifiable contempt for the police, and the consoling sympathy of numerous friends and admirers. And now, behold, all that is about to be changed! It is the reverse side of the medal. After sunshine comes the rain. It is no longer a laughing matter. Adieu!"

"Hurry up!" said Wilson, full of solicitude for a person in whom Herlock Sholmes had inspired so much respect, "do not lose a minute."

"Not a minute, Monsieur Wilson; but I wish to express my pleasure at having met you, and to tell you how much I envy the master in having such a valuable assistant as you seem to be."

Then, after they had courteously saluted each other, like adversaries in a duel who entertain no feeling of malice but are obliged to fight by force of circumstances, Lupin seized me by the arm and drew me outside.

"What do you think of it, dear boy? The strange events of this evening will form an interesting chapter in the memoirs you are now preparing for me."

He closed the door of the restaurant behind us, and, after taking a few steps, he stopped and said:

"Do you smoke?"

"No. Nor do you, it seems to me."

"You are right, I don't."

He lighted a cigarette with a wax-match, which he shook several times in an effort to extinguish it. But he threw away the cigarette immediately, ran across the street, and joined two men who emerged from the shadows as if called by a signal. He conversed with them for a few minutes on the opposite sidewalk, and then returned to me.

"I beg your pardon, but I fear that cursed Sholmes is going to give me trouble. But, I assure you, he is not yet through with Arsène Lupin. He will find out what kind of fuel I use to warm my blood. And now—au revoir! The genial Wilson is right; there is not a moment to lose."

He walked away rapidly.

Thus ended the events of that exciting evening, or, at least, that part of them in which I was a participant. Subsequently, during the course of the evening, other stirring incidents occurred which have come to my knowledge through the courtesy of other members of that unique dinner-party.

At the very moment in which Lupin left me, Herlock Sholmes rose from the table, and looked at his watch.

"Twenty minutes to nine. At nine o'clock I am to meet the Count and Countess at the railway station."

"Then, we must be off!" exclaimed Wilson, between two drinks of whisky.

They left the restaurant.

"Wilson, don't look behind. We may be followed, and, in that case, let us act as if we did not care. Wilson, I want your opinion: why was Lupin in that restaurant?"

"To get something to eat," replied Wilson, quickly.

"Wilson, I must congratulate you on the accuracy of your deduction. I couldn't have done better myself."

Wilson blushed with pleasure, and Sholmes continued:

"To get something to eat. Very well, and, after that, probably, to assure himself whether I am going to the Château de Crozon, as announced by Ganimard in his interview. I must go in order not to disappoint him. But, in order to gain time on him, I shall not go."

"Ah!" said Wilson, nonplused.

"You, my friend, will walk down this street, take a carriage, two, three carriages. Return later and get the valises that we left at the station, and make for the Elysée-Palace at a galop."

"And when I reach the Elysée-Palace?"

"Engage a room, go to sleep, and await my orders."

Quite proud of the important rôle assigned to him, Wilson set out to perform his task. Herlock Sholmes proceeded to the railway station, bought a ticket, and repaired to the Amiens' express in which the Count and Countess de Crozon were already installed. He bowed to them, lighted his pipe, and had a quiet smoke in the corridor. The train started. Ten minutes later he took a seat beside the Countess, and said to her:

"Have you the ring here, madame?"

"Yes."

"Will you kindly let me see it?"

He took it, and examined it closely.

"Just as I suspected: it is a manufactured diamond."

"A manufactured diamond?"

"Yes; a new process which consists in submitting diamond dust to a tremendous heat until it melts and is then molded into a single stone."

"But my diamond is genuine."

"Yes, *your* diamond is; but this is not yours."

"Where is mine?"

"It is held by Arsène Lupin."

"And this stone?"

"Was substituted for yours, and slipped into Herr Bleichen's tooth-powder, where it was afterwards found."

"Then you think this is false?"

"Absolutely false."

The Countess was overwhelmed with surprise and grief, while her husband scrutinized the diamond with an incredulous air. Finally she stammered:

"Is it possible? And why did they not merely steal it and be done with it? And how did they steal it?"

"That is exactly what I am going to find out."

"At the Château de Crozon?"

"No. I shall leave the train at Creil and return to Paris. It is there the game between me and Arsène Lupin must be played. In fact, the game has commenced already, and Lupin thinks I am on my way to the château."

"But—"

"What does it matter to you, madame? The essential thing is your diamond, is it not?"

"Yes."

"Well, don't worry. I have just undertaken a much more difficult task than that. You have my promise that I will restore the true diamond to you within ten days."

The train slackened its speed. He put the false diamond in his pocket and opened the door. The Count cried out:

"That is the wrong side of the train. You are getting out on the tracks."

"That is my intention. If Lupin has anyone on my track, he will lose sight of me now. Adieu."

An employee protested in vain. After the departure of the train, the Englishman sought the station-master's office. Forty minutes later he leaped into a train that landed him in Paris shortly before midnight. He ran across the platform, entered the lunch-room, made his exit at another door, and jumped into a cab.

"Driver—rue Clapeyron."

Having reached the conclusion that he was not followed, he stopped the carriage at the end of the street, and proceeded to make a careful examination of Monsieur Detinan's house and the two adjoining houses. He made measurements of certain distances and entered the figures in his notebook.

"Driver—avenue Henri-Martin."

At the corner of the avenue and the rue de la Pompe, he dismissed the carriage, walked down the street to number 134, and performed the same operations in front of the house of the late

Baron d'Hautrec and the two adjoining houses, measuring the width of the respective façades and calculating the depth of the little gardens that stood in front of them.

The avenue was deserted, and was very dark under its four rows of trees, between which, at considerable intervals, a few gas-lamps struggled in vain to light the deep shadows. One of them threw a dim light over a portion of the house, and Sholmes perceived the "To-let" sign posted on the gate, the neglected walks which encircled the small lawn, and the large bare windows of the vacant house.

"I suppose," he said to himself, "the house has been unoccupied since the death of the baron.... Ah! if I could only get in and view the scene of the murder!"

No sooner did the idea occur to him than he sought to put it in execution. But how could he manage it? He could not climb over the gate; it was too high. So he took from his pocket an electric lantern and a skeleton key which he always carried. Then, to his great surprise, he discovered that the gate was not locked; in fact, it was open about three or four inches. He entered the garden, and was careful to leave the gate as he had found it—partly open. But he had not taken many steps from the gate when he stopped. He had seen a light pass one of the windows on the second floor.

He saw the light pass a second window and a third, but he saw nothing else, except a silhouette outlined on the walls of the rooms. The light descended to the first floor, and, for a long time, wandered from room to room.

"Who the deuce is walking, at one o'clock in the morning, through the house in which the Baron d'Hautrec was killed?" Herlock Sholmes asked himself, deeply interested.

There was only one way to find out, and that was to enter the house himself. He did not hesitate, but started for the door of the house. However, at the moment when he crossed the streak of gaslight that came from the street-lamp, the man must have seen him, for the light in the house was suddenly extinguished and Herlock Sholmes did not see it again. Softly, he tried the door. It was open, also. Hearing no sound, he advanced through the hallway, encountered the foot of the stairs, and ascended to the first floor. Here there was the same silence, the same darkness.

He entered, one of the rooms and approached a window through which came a feeble light from the outside. On looking through the window he saw the man, who had no doubt descended by another stairway and escaped by another door. The man was threading his way through the shrubbery which bordered the wall that separated the two gardens.

"The deuce!" exclaimed Sholmes, "he is going to escape."

He hastened down the stairs and leaped over the steps in his eagerness to cut off the man's retreat. But he did not see anyone, and, owing to the darkness, it was several seconds before he was able to distinguish a bulky form moving through the shrubbery. This gave the Englishman food for reflection. Why had the man not made his escape, which he could have done so easily? Had he remained in order to watch the movements of the intruder who had disturbed him in his mysterious work?

"At all events," concluded Sholmes, "it is not Lupin; he would be more adroit. It may be one of his men."

For several minutes Herlock Sholmes remained motionless, with his gaze fixed on the adversary who, in his turn was watching the detective. But as that adversary had become passive, and as the Englishman was not one to consume his time in idle waiting, he examined his revolver to see if it was in good working order, remove his knife from its sheath, and walked toward the enemy with that cool effrontery and scorn of danger for which he had become famous.

He heard a clicking sound; it was his adversary preparing his revolver. Herlock Sholmes dashed boldly into the thicket, and grappled with his foe. There was a sharp, desperate struggle, in the course of which Sholmes suspected that the man was trying to draw a knife. But the Englishman, believing his antagonist to be an accomplice of Arsène Lupin and anxious to win the first trick in the game with that redoubtable foe, fought with unusual strength and determination. He hurled his adversary to the ground, held him there with the weight of his body, and, gripping him by the throat with one hand, he used his free hand to take out his electric lantern, press the button, and throw the light over the face of his prisoner.

"Wilson!" he exclaimed, in amazement.

"Herlock Sholmes!" stammered a weak, stifled voice.

For a long time they remained silent, astounded, foolish. The shriek of an automobile rent the air. A slight breeze stirred the leaves. Suddenly, Herlock Sholmes seized his friend by the shoulders and shook him violently, as he cried:

"What are you doing here? Tell me.... What?... Did I tell you to hide in the bushes and spy on me?"

"Spy on you!" muttered Wilson, "why, I didn't know it was you."

"But what are you doing here? You ought to be in bed."

"I was in bed."

"You ought to be asleep."

"I was asleep."

"Well, what brought you here?" asked Sholmes.

"Your letter."

"My letter? I don't understand."

"Yes, a messenger brought it to me at the hotel."

"From me? Are you crazy?"

"It is true—I swear it."

"Where is the letter?"

Wilson handed him a sheet of paper, which he read by the light of his lantern. It was as follows:

"Wilson, come at once to avenue Henri-Martin. The house is empty. Inspect the whole place and make an exact plan. Then return to hotel.—Herlock Sholmes."

"I was measuring the rooms," said Wilson, "when I saw a shadow in the garden. I had only one idea——"

"That was to seize the shadow.... The idea was excellent.... But remember this, Wilson, whenever you receive a letter from me, be sure it is my handwriting and not a forgery."

"Ah!" exclaimed Wilson, as the truth dawned on him, "then the letter wasn't from you?"

"No."

"Who sent it, then?"

"Arsène Lupin."

"Why? For what purpose?" asked Wilson.

"I don't know, and that's what worries me. I don't understand why he took the trouble to disturb you. Of course, if he had sent me on such a foolish errand I wouldn't be surprised; but what was his object in disturbing you?"

"I must hurry back to the hotel."

"So must I, Wilson."

They arrived at the gate. Wilson, who was ahead, took hold of it and pulled.

"Ah! you closed it?" he said.

"No, I left it partly open."

Sholmes tried the gate; then, alarmed, he examined the lock. An oath escaped him:

"Good God! it is locked! locked with a key!"

He shook the gate with all his strength; then, realizing the futility of his efforts, he dropped his arms, discouraged, and muttered, in a jerky manner:

"I can see it all now—it is Lupin. He fore-saw that I would leave the train at Creil, and he prepared this neat little trap for me in case I should commence my investigation this evening. Moreover, he was kind enough to send me a companion to share my captivity. All done to make me lose a day, and, perhaps, also, to teach me to mind my own business."

"Do you mean to say we are prisoners?"

"Exactly. Herlock Sholmes and Wilson are the prisoners of Arsène Lupin. It's a bad beginning; but he laughs best who laughs last."

Wilson seized Sholmes' arm, and exclaimed:

"Look!... Look up there!... A light...."

A light shone through one of the windows of the first floor. Both of them ran to the house, and each ascended by the stairs he had used on coming out a short time before, and they met again at the entrance to the lighted chamber. A small piece of a candle was burning in the center of the room. Beside it there was a basket containing a bottle, a roasted chicken, and a loaf of bread.

Sholmes was greatly amused, and laughed heartily.

"Wonderful! we are invited to supper. It is really an enchanted place, a genuine fairy-land. Come, Wilson, cheer up! this is not a funeral. It's all very funny."

"Are you quite sure it is so very funny?" asked Wilson, in a lugubrious tone.

"Am I sure?" exclaimed Sholmes, with a gaiety that was too boisterous to be natural, "why, to tell the truth, it's the funniest thing I ever saw. It's a jolly good comedy! What a master of sarcasm this Arsène Lupin is! He makes a fool of you with the utmost grace and delicacy. I wouldn't miss this feast for all the money in the Bank of England. Come, Wilson, you grieve me. You should display that nobility of character which rises superior to misfortune. I don't see that you have any cause for complaint, really, I don't."

After a time, by dint of good humor and sarcasm, he managed to restore Wilson to his normal mood, and make him swallow a morsel of chicken and a glass of wine. But when the candle went out and they prepared to spend the night there, with the bare floor for a mattress and the hard wall for a pillow, the harsh and ridiculous side of the situation was impressed upon them. That particular incident will not form a pleasant page in the memoirs of the famous detective.

Next morning Wilson awoke, stiff and cold. A slight noise attracted his attention: Herlock Sholmes was kneeling on the floor, critically examining some grains of sand and studying some chalk-marks, now almost effaced, which formed certain figures and numbers, which figures he entered in his notebook.

Accompanied by Wilson, who was deeply interested in the work, he examined each room, and found similar chalk-marks in two other apartments. He noticed, also, two circles on the oaken panels, an arrow on a wainscot, and four figures on four steps of the stairs. At the end of an hour Wilson said:

"The figures are correct, aren't they?"

"I don't know; but, at all events, they mean something," replied Sholmes, who had forgotten the discomforts of the night in the joy created by his new discoveries.

"It is quite obvious," said Wilson, "they represent the number of pieces in the floor."

"Ah!"

"Yes. And the two circles indicate that the panels are false, as you can readily ascertain, and the arrow points in the direction in which the panels move."

Herlock Sholmes looked at Wilson, in astonishment.

"Ah! my dear friend, how do you know all that? Your clairvoyance makes my poor ability in that direction look quite insignificant."

"Oh! it is very simple," said Wilson, inflated with pride; "I examined those marks last night, according to your instructions, or, rather, according to the instructions of Arsène Lupin, since he wrote the letter you sent to me."

At that moment Wilson faced a greater danger than he had during his struggle in the garden with Herlock Sholmes. The latter now felt a furious desire to strangle him. But, dominating his feelings, Sholmes made a grimace which was intended for a smile, and said:

"Quite so, Wilson, you have done well, and your work shows commendable progress. But, tell me, have you exercised your powers of observation and analysis on any other points? I might profit by your deductions."

"Oh! no, I went no farther."

"That's a pity. Your début was such a promising one. But, since that is all, we may as well go."

"Go! but how can we get out?"

"The way all honest people go out: through the gate."

"But it is locked."

"It will be opened."

"By whom?"

"Please call the two policemen who are strolling down the avenue."

"But——"

"But what?"

"It is very humiliating. What will be said when it becomes known that Herlock Sholmes and Wilson were the prisoners of Arsène Lupin?"

"Of course, I understand they will roar with laughter," replied Herlock Sholmes, in a dry voice and with frowning features, "but we can't set up housekeeping in this place."

"And you will not try to find another way out?"

"No."

"But the man who brought us the basket of provisions did not cross the garden, coming or going. There is some other way out. Let us look for it, and not bother with the police."

"Your argument is sound, but you forget that all the detectives in Paris have been trying to find it for the last six months, and that I searched the house from top to bottom while you were asleep. Ah! my dear Wilson, we have not been accustomed to pursue such game as Arsène Lupin. He leaves no trail behind him."

At eleven o'clock, Herlock Sholmes and Wilson were liberated, and conducted to the nearest police station, where the commissary, after subjecting them to a severe examination, released them with an affectation of good-will that was quite exasperating.

"I am very sorry, messieurs, that this unfortunate incident has occurred. You will have a very poor opinion of French hospitality. Mon Dieu! what a night you must have passed! Ah! that rascally Lupin is no respecter of persons."

They took a carriage to their hotel. At the office Wilson asked for the key of his room.

After some search the clerk replied, much astonished:

"But, monsieur, you have given up the room."

"I gave it up? When?"

"This morning, by the letter your friend brought here."

"What friend?"

"The gentleman who brought your letter.... Ah! your card is still attached to the letter. Here they are."

Wilson looked at them. Certainly, it was one of his cards, and the letter was in his handwriting.

"Good Lord!" he muttered, "this is another of his tricks," and he added, aloud: "Where is my luggage?"

"Your friend took it."

"Ah!... and you gave it to him?"

"Certainly; on the strength of your letter and card."

"Of course ... of course."

They left the hotel and walked, slowly and thoughtfully, through the Champs-Elysées. The avenue was bright and cheerful beneath a clear autumn sun; the air was mild and pleasant.

At Rond-Point, Herlock Sholmes lighted his pipe. Then Wilson spoke:

"I can't understand you, Sholmes. You are so calm and unruffled. They play with you as a cat plays with a mouse, and yet you do not say a word."

Sholmes stopped, as he replied:

"Wilson, I was thinking of your card."

"Well?"

"The point is this: here is a man who, in view of a possible struggle with us, procures specimens of our handwriting, and who holds, in his possession, one or more of your cards. Now, have you considered how much precaution and skill those facts represent?"

"Well?"

"Well, Wilson, to overcome an enemy so well prepared and so thoroughly equipped requires the infinite shrewdness of ... of a Herlock Sholmes. And yet, as you have seen, Wilson, I have lost the first round."

At six o'clock the *Echo de France* published the following article in its evening edition:

"This morning Mon. Thenard, commissary of police in the sixteenth district, released Herlock Sholmes and his friend Wilson, both of whom had been locked in the house of the late Baron d'Hautrec, where they spent a very pleasant night—thanks to the thoughtful care and attention of Arsène Lupin."

"In addition to their other troubles, these gentlemen have been robbed of their valises, and, in consequence thereof, they have entered a formal complaint against Arsène Lupin."

"Arsène Lupin, satisfied that he has given them a mild reproof, hopes these gentlemen will not force him to resort to more stringent measures."

"Bah!" exclaimed Herlock Sholmes, crushing the paper in his hands, "that is only child's play! And that is the only criticism I have to make of Arsène Lupin: he plays to the gallery. There is that much of the fakir in him."

"Ah! Sholmes, you are a wonderful man! You have such a command over your temper. Nothing ever disturbs you."

"No, nothing disturbs me," replied Sholmes, in a voice that trembled from rage; "besides, what's the use of losing my temper?... I am quite confident of the final result; I shall have the last word."

CHAPTER IV.

LIGHT IN THE DARKNESS.

However well-tempered a man's character may be—and Herlock Sholmes is one of those men over whom ill-fortune has little or no hold—there are circumstances wherein the most courageous combatant feels the necessity of marshaling his forces before risking the chances of a battle.

"I shall take a vacation to-day," said Sholmes.

"And what shall I do?" asked Wilson.

"You, Wilson—let me see! You can buy some underwear and linen to replenish our wardrobe, while I take a rest."

"Very well, Sholmes, I will watch while you sleep."

Wilson uttered these words with all the importance of a sentinel on guard at the outpost, and therefore exposed to the greatest danger. His chest was expanded; his muscles were tense. Assuming a shrewd look, he scrutinized, officially, the little room in which they had fixed their abode.

"Very well, Wilson, you can watch. I shall occupy myself in the preparation of a line of attack more appropriate to the methods of the enemy we are called upon to meet. Do you see, Wilson, we have been deceived in this fellow Lupin. My opinion is that we must commence at the very beginning of this affair."

"And even before that, if possible. But have we sufficient time?"

"Nine days, dear boy. That is five too many."

The Englishman spent the entire afternoon in smoking and sleeping. He did not enter upon his new plan of attack until the following day. Then he said:

"Wilson, I am ready. Let us attack the enemy."

"Lead on, Macduff!" exclaimed Wilson, full of martial ardor. "I wish to fight in the front rank. Oh! have no fear. I shall do credit to my King and country, for I am an Englishman."

In the first place, Sholmes had three long and important interviews: With Monsieur Detinan, whose rooms he examined with the greatest care and precision; with Suzanne Gerbois, whom he questioned in regard to the blonde Lady; and with Sister Auguste, who had retired to the convent of the Visitandines since the murder of Baron d'Hautrec.

At each of these interviews Wilson had remained outside; and each time he asked:

"Satisfactory?"

"Quite so."

"I was sure we were on the right track."

They paid a visit to the two houses adjoining that of the late Baron d'Hautrec in the avenue Henri-Martin; then they visited the rue Clapeyron, and, while he was examining the front of number 25, Sholmes said:

"All these houses must be connected by secret passages, but I can't find them."

For the first time in his life, Wilson doubted the omnipotence of his famous associate. Why did he now talk so much and accomplish so little?

"Why?" exclaimed Sholmes, in answer to Wilson's secret thought, "because, with this fellow Lupin, a person has to work in the dark, and, instead of deducting the truth from established facts, a man must extract it from his own brain, and afterward learn if it is supported by the facts in the case."

"But what about the secret passages?"

"They must exist. But even though I should discover them, and thus learn how Arsène Lupin made his entrance to the lawyer's house and how the blonde Lady escaped from the house of Baron d'Hautrec after the murder, what good would it do? How would it help me? Would it furnish me with a weapon of attack?"

"Let us attack him just the same," exclaimed Wilson, who had scarcely uttered these words when he jumped back with a cry of alarm. Something had fallen at their feet; it was a bag filled with sand which might have caused them serious injury if it had struck them.

Sholmes looked up. Some men were working on a scaffolding attached to the balcony at the fifth floor of the house. He said:

"We were lucky; one step more, and that heavy bag would have fallen on our heads. I wonder if—"

Moved by a sudden impulse, he rushed into the house, up the five flights of stairs, rang the bell, pushed his way into the apartment to the great surprise and alarm of the servant who came to the door, and made his way to the balcony in front of the house. But there was no one there.

"Where are the workmen who were here a moment ago?" he asked the servant.

"They have just gone."

"Which way did they go?"

"By the servants' stairs."

Sholmes leaned out of the window. He saw two men leaving the house, carrying bicycles. They mounted them and quickly disappeared around the corner.

"How long have they been working on this scaffolding?"

"Those men?... only since this morning. It's their first day."

Sholmes returned to the street, and joined Wilson. Together they returned to the hotel, and thus the second day ended in a mournful silence.

182

On the following day their programme was almost similar. They sat together on a bench in the avenue Henri-Martin, much to Wilson's disgust, who did not find it amusing to spend long hours watching the house in which the tragedy had occurred.

"What do you expect, Sholmes? That Arsène Lupin will walk out of the house?"

"No."

"That the blonde Lady will make her appearance?"

"No."

"What then?"

"I am looking for something to occur; some slight incident that will furnish me with a clue to work on."

"And if it does not occur!"

"Then I must, myself, create the spark that will set fire to the powder."

A solitary incident—and that of a disagreeable nature— broke the monotony of the forenoon.

A gentleman was riding along the avenue when his horse suddenly turned aside in such a manner that it ran against the bench on which they were sitting, and struck Sholmes a slight blow on the shoulder.

"Ha!" exclaimed Sholmes, "a little more and I would have had a broken shoulder."

The gentleman struggled with his horse. The Englishman drew his revolver and pointed it; but Wilson seized his arm, and said:

"Don't be foolish! What are you going to do! Kill the man!"

"Leave me alone, Wilson! Let go!"

During the brief struggle between Sholmes and Wilson the stranger rode away.

"Now, you can shoot," said Wilson, triumphantly, when the horseman was at some distance.

"Wilson, you're an idiot! Don't you understand that the man is an accomplice of Arsène Lupin?"

Sholmes was trembling from rage. Wilson stammered pitifully:

"What!... that man ... an accomplice?"

"Yes, the same as the workmen who tried to drop the bag of sand on us yesterday."

"It can't be possible!"

"Possible or not, there was only one way to prove it."

"By killing the man?"

"No—by killing the horse. If you hadn't grabbed my arm, I should have captured one of Lupin's accomplices. Now, do you understand the folly of your act?"

Throughout the afternoon both men were morose. They did not speak a word to each other. At five o'clock they visited the rue Clapeyron, but were careful to keep at a safe distance from the houses. However, three young men who were passing through the street, arm in arm, singing, ran against Sholmes and Wilson and refused to let them pass. Sholmes, who was in an ill humor, contested the right of way with them. After a brief struggle, Sholmes resorted to his fists. He struck one of the men a hard blow on the chest, another a blow in the face, and thus subdued two of his adversaries. Thereupon the three of them took to their heels and disappeared.

"Ah!" exclaimed Sholmes, "that does me good. I needed a little exercise."

But Wilson was leaning against the wall. Sholmes said:

"What's the matter, old chap? You're quite pale."

Wilson pointed to his left arm, which hung inert, and stammered:

"I don't know what it is. My arm pains me."

"Very much?... Is it serious?"

"Yes, I am afraid so."

He tried to raise his arm, but it was helpless. Sholmes felt it, gently at first, then in a rougher way, "to see how badly it was hurt," he said. He concluded that Wilson was really hurt, so he led him to a neighboring pharmacy, where a closer examination revealed the fact that the arm was broken and that Wilson was a candidate for the hospital. In the meantime they bared his arm and applied some remedies to ease his suffering.

"Come, come, old chap, cheer up!" said Sholmes, who was holding Wilson's arm, "in five or six weeks you will be all right again. But I will pay them back ... the rascals! Especially Lupin, for this is his work ... no doubt of that. I swear to you if ever——"

He stopped suddenly, dropped the arm—which caused Wilson such an access of pain that he almost fainted—and, striking his forehead, Sholmes said:

"Wilson, I have an idea. You know, I have one occasionally."

He stood for a moment, silent, with staring eyes, and then muttered, in short, sharp phrases:

"Yes, that's it ... that will explain all ... right at my feet ... and I didn't see it ... ah, parbleu! I should have thought of it before.... Wilson, I shall have good news for you."

Abruptly leaving his old friend, Sholmes ran into the street and went directly to the house known as number 25. On one of the stones, to the right of the door, he read this inscription: "Destange, architect, 1875."

There was a similar inscription on the house numbered 23.

Of course, there was nothing unusual in that. But what might be read on the houses in the avenue Henri-Martin?

A carriage was passing. He engaged it and directed the driver to take him to No. 134 avenue Henri-Martin. He was roused to a high pitch of excitement. He stood up in the carriage and urged the horse to greater speed. He offered extra pourboires to the driver. Quicker! Quicker!

How great was his anxiety as they turned from the rue de la Pompe! Had he caught a glimpse of the truth at last?

On one of the stones of the late Baron's house he read the words: "Destange, architect, 1874." And a similar inscription appeared on the two adjoining houses.

The reaction was such that he settled down in the seat of the carriage, trembling from joy. At last, a tiny ray of light had penetrated the dark shadows which encompassed these mysterious crimes! In the vast sombre forest wherein a thousand pathways crossed and re-crossed, he had discovered the first clue to the track followed by the enemy!

He entered a branch postoffice and obtained telephonic connection with the château de Crozon. The Countess answered the telephone call.

"Hello!... Is that you, madame?"

"Monsieur Sholmes, isn't it? Everything going all right?"

"Quite well, but I wish to ask you one question.... Hello!"

"Yes, I hear you."

"Tell me, when was the château de Crozon built?"

"It was destroyed by fire and rebuilt about thirty years ago."

"Who built it, and in what year?"

"There is an inscription on the front of the house which reads: 'Lucien Destange, architect, 1877.'"

"Thank you, madame, that is all. Good-bye."

He went away, murmuring: "Destange ... Lucien Destange ... that name has a familiar sound."

He noticed a public reading-room, entered, consulted a dictionary of modern biography, and copied the following information: "Lucien Destange, born 1840, Grand-Prix de Rome, officer of the Legion of Honor, author of several valuable books on architecture, etc...."

Then he returned to the pharmacy and found that Wilson had been taken to the hospital. There Sholmes found him with his arm in splints, and shivering with fever.

"Victory! Victory!" cried Sholmes. "I hold one end of the thread."

"Of what thread?"

"The one that leads to victory. I shall now be walking on solid ground, where there will be footprints, clues...."

"Cigarette ashes?" asked Wilson, whose curiosity had overcome his pain.

"And many other things! Just think, Wilson, I have found the mysterious link which unites the different adventures in which the blonde Lady played a part. Why did Lupin select those three houses for the scenes of his exploits?"

"Yes, why?"

"Because those three houses were built by the same architect. That was an easy problem, eh? Of course ... but who would have thought of it?"

"No one but you."

"And who, except I, knows that the same architect, by the use of analogous plans, has rendered it possible for a person to execute three distinct acts which, though miraculous in appearance, are, in reality, quite simple and easy?"

"That was a stroke of good luck."

"And it was time, dear boy, as I was becoming very impatient. You know, this is our fourth day."

"Out of ten."

"Oh! after this——"

Sholmes was excited, delighted, and gayer than usual.

"And when I think that these rascals might have attacked me in the street and broken my arm just as they did yours! Isn't that so, Wilson?"

Wilson simply shivered at the horrible thought. Sholmes continued:

"We must profit by the lesson. I can see, Wilson, that we were wrong to try and fight Lupin in the open, and leave ourselves exposed to his attacks."

"I can see it, and feel it, too, in my broken arm," said Wilson.

"You have one consolation, Wilson; that is, that I escaped. Now, I must be doubly cautious. In an open fight he will defeat me; but if I can work in the dark, unseen by him, I have the advantage, no matter how strong his forces may be."

"Ganimard might be of some assistance."

"Never! On the day that I can truly say: Arsène Lupin is there; I show you the quarry, and how to catch it; I shall go and see Ganimard at one of the two addresses that he gave me—his residence in the rue Pergolese, or at the Suisse tavern in the Place du Châtelet. But, until that time, I shall work alone."

He approached the bed, placed his hand on Wilson's shoulder—on the sore one, of course—and said to him:

"Take care of yourself, old fellow. Henceforth your rôle will be to keep two or three of Arsène Lupin's men busy watching here in vain for my return to enquire about your health. It is a secret mission for you, eh?"

"Yes, and I shall do my best to fulfil it conscientiously. Then you do not expect to come here any more?"

"What for?" asked Sholmes.

"I don't know ... of course.... I am getting on as well as possible. But, Herlock, do me a last service: give me a drink."

"A drink?"

"Yes, I am dying of thirst; and with my fever——"

"To be sure—directly——"

He made a pretense of getting some water, perceived a package of tobacco, lighted his pipe, and then, as if he had not heard his friend's request, he went away, whilst Wilson uttered a mute prayer for the inaccessible water.

"Monsieur Destange!"

The servant eyed from head to foot the person to whom he had opened the door of the house—the magnificent house that stood at the corner of the Place Malcsherbes and the rue Montchanin—and at the sight of the man with gray hairs, badly shaved, dressed in a shabby black coat, with a body as ill-formed and ungracious as his face, he replied with the disdain which he thought the occasion warranted:

"Monsieur Destange may or may not be at home. That depends. Has monsieur a card?"

Monsieur did not have a card, but he had a letter of introduction and, after the servant had taken the letter to Mon. Destange, he was conducted into the presence of that gentleman who was sitting in a large circular room or rotunda which occupied one of the wings of the house. It was a library, and contained a profusion of books and architectural drawings. When the stranger entered, the architect said to him:

"You are Monsieur Stickmann?"

"Yes, monsieur."

"My secretary tells me that he is ill, and has sent you to continue the general catalogue of the books which he commenced under my direction, and, more particularly, the catalogue of German books. Are you familiar with that kind of work?"

"Yes, monsieur, quite so," he replied, with a strong German accent.

Under those circumstances the bargain was soon concluded, and Mon. Destange commenced work with his new secretary.

Herlock Sholmes had gained access to the house.

In order to escape the vigilance of Arsène Lupin and gain admittance to the house occupied by Lucien Destange and his daughter Clotilde, the famous detective had been compelled to resort to a number of stratagems, and, under a variety of names, to ingratiate himself into the good graces and confidence of a number of persons—in short, to live, during forty-eight hours, a most complicated life. During that time he had acquired the following information: Mon. Destange, having retired from active business on account of his failing health, now lived amongst the many books he had accumulated on the subject of architecture. He derived infinite pleasure in viewing and handling those dusty old volumes.

His daughter Clotilde was considered eccentric. She passed her time in another part of the house, and never went out.

"Of course," Sholmes said to himself, as he wrote in a register the titles of the books which Mon. Destange dictated to him, "all that is vague and incomplete, but it is quite a long step in advance. I shall surely solve one of these absorbing problems: Is Mon. Destange associated with Arsène Lupin? Does he continue to see him? Are the papers relating to the construction of the three houses still in existence? Will those papers not furnish me with the location of other houses of similar construction which Arsène Lupin and his associates will plunder in the future?

"Monsieur Destange, an accomplice of Arsène Lupin! That venerable man, an officer of the Legion of Honor, working in league with a burglar—such an idea was absurd! Besides, if we concede that such a complicity exists, how could Mon. Destange, thirty years ago, have possibly foreseen the thefts of Arsène Lupin, who was then an infant?"

No matter! The Englishman was implacable. With his marvellous scent, and that instinct which never fails him, he felt that he was in the heart of some strange mystery. Ever since he first entered the house, he had been under the influence of that impression, and yet he could not define the grounds on which he based his suspicions.

Up to the morning of the second day he had not made any significant discovery. At two o'clock of that day he saw Clotilde Destange for the first time; she came to the library in search of a book. She was about thirty years of age, a brunette, slow and silent in her movements, with features imbued with that expression of indifference which is characteristic of people who live a secluded life. She exchanged a few words with her father, and then retired, without even looking at Sholmes.

The afternoon dragged along monotonously. At five o'clock Mon. Destange announced his intention to go out. Sholmes was alone on the circular gallery that was constructed about ten feet above the floor of the rotunda. It was almost dark. He was on the point of going out, when he heard a slight sound and, at the same time, experienced the feeling that there was someone in the room. Several minutes passed before he saw or heard anything more. Then he shuddered; a shadowy form emerged from the gloom, quite close to him, upon the balcony. It seemed incredible. How long had this mysterious visitor been there? Whence did he come?

The strange man descended the steps and went directly to a large oaken cupboard. Sholmes was a keen observer of the man's movements. He watched him searching amongst the papers with which the cupboard was filled. What was he looking for?

Then the door opened and Mlle. Destange entered, speaking to someone who was following her:

"So you have decided not to go out, father?... Then I will make a light ... one second ... do not move...."

The strange man closed the cupboard and hid in the embrasure of a large window, drawing the curtains together. Did Mlle. Destange not see him? Did she not hear him? Calmly she turned on the electric lights; she and her father sat down close to each other. She opened a book she had brought with her, and commenced to read. After the lapse of a few minutes she said:

"Your secretary has gone."

"Yes, I don't see him."

"Do you like him as well as you did at first?" she asked, as if she were not aware of the illness of the real secretary and his replacement by Stickmann.

"Oh! yes."

Monsieur Destange's head bobbed from one side to the other. He was asleep. The girl resumed her reading. A moment later one of the window curtains was pushed back, and the strange man emerged and glided along the wall toward the door, which obliged him to pass behind Mon. Destange but in front of Clotilde, and brought him into the light so that Herlock Sholmes obtained a good view of the man's face. It was Arsène Lupin.

The Englishman was delighted. His forecast was verified; he had penetrated to the very heart of the mystery, and found Arsène Lupin to be the moving spirit in it.

Clotilde had not yet displayed any knowledge of his presence, although it was quite improbable that any movement of the intruder had escaped her notice. Lupin had almost reached the door and, in fact, his hand was already seeking the door-knob, when his coat brushed against a small table and knocked something to the floor. Monsieur Destange awoke with a start. Arsène Lupin was already standing in front of him, hat in hand, smiling.

"Maxime Bermond," exclaimed Mon. Destange, joyfully. "My dear Maxime, what lucky chance brings you here?"

"The wish to see you and Mademoiselle Destange."

"When did you return from your journey?"

"Yesterday."

"You must stay to dinner."

"No, thank you, I am sorry, but I have an appointment to dine with some friends at a restaurant."

"Come, to-morrow, then, Clotilde, you must urge him to come to-morrow. Ah! my dear Maxime.... I thought of you many times during your absence."

"Really?"

"Yes, I went through all my old papers in that cupboard, and found our last statement of account."

"What account?"

"Relating to the avenue Henri-Martin."

"Ah! do you keep such papers? What for?"

Then the three of them left the room, and continued their conversation in a small parlor which adjoined the library.

"Is it Lupin?" Sholmes asked himself, in a sudden access of doubt. Certainly, from all appearances, it was he; and yet it was also someone else who resembled Arsène Lupin in certain respects, and who still maintained his own individuality, features, and color of hair. Sholmes could hear Lupin's voice in the adjoining room. He was relating some stories at which Mon. Destange laughed heartily, and which even brought a smile to the lips of the melancholy Clotilde. And each of those smiles appeared to be the reward which Arsène Lupin was seeking, and which he was delighted to have secured. His success caused him to redouble his efforts and, insensibly, at the sound of that clear and happy voice, Clotilde's face brightened and lost that cold and listless expression which usually pervaded it.

"They love each other," thought Sholmes, "but what the deuce can there be in common between Clotilde Destange and Maxime Bermond? Does she know that Maxime is none other than Arsène Lupin?"

Until seven o'clock Sholmes was an anxious listener, seeking to profit by the conversation. Then, with infinite precaution, he descended from the gallery, crept along the side of the room to the door in such a manner that the people in the adjoining room did not see him.

When he reached the street Sholmes satisfied himself that there was neither an automobile nor a cab waiting there; then he slowly limped along the boulevard Malesherbes. He turned into an adjacent street, donned the overcoat which he had carried on his arm, altered the shape of his hat, assumed an upright carriage, and, thus transformed, returned to a place whence he could watch the door of Mon. Destange's house.

In a few minutes Arsène Lupin came out, and proceeded to walk toward the center of Paris by way of the rues de Constantinople and London. Herlock Sholmes followed at a distance of a hundred paces.

Exciting moments for the Englishman! He sniffed the air, eagerly, like a hound following a fresh scent. It seemed to him a delightful thing thus to follow his adversary. It was no longer Herlock Sholmes who was being watched, but Arsène Lupin, the invisible Arsène Lupin. He held him, so to speak, within the grasp of his eye, by an imperceptible bond that nothing could break. And he was pleased to think that the quarry belonged to him.

But he soon observed a suspicious circumstance. In the intervening space between him and Arsène Lupin he noticed several people traveling in the same direction, particularly two husky fellows in slouch hats on the left side of the street, and two others on the right wearing caps and smoking cigarettes. Of course, their presence in that vicinity may have been the result of chance, but Sholmes was more astonished when he observed that the four men stopped when Lupin entered a tobacco shop; and still more surprised when the four men started again after Lupin emerged from the shop, each keeping to his own side of the street.

"Curse it!" muttered Sholmes; "he is being followed."

He was annoyed at the idea that others were on the trail of Arsène Lupin; that someone might deprive him, not of the glory—he cared little for that—but of the immense pleasure of capturing, single-handed, the most formidable enemy he had ever met. And he felt that he was not mistaken; the men presented to Sholmes' experienced eye the appearance and manner of those who, while regulating their gait to that of another, wish to present a careless and natural air.

"Is this some of Ganimard's work?" muttered Sholmes. "Is he playing me false?"

He felt inclined to speak to one of the men with a view of acting in concert with him; but as they were now approaching the boulevard the crowd was becoming denser, and he was afraid he might lose sight of Lupin. So he quickened his pace and turned into the boulevard just in time to see Lupin ascending the steps of the Hungarian restaurant at the corner of the rue du Helder. The door of the restaurant was open, so that Sholmes, while sitting on a bench on the other side of the boulevard, could see Lupin take a seat at a table, luxuriously appointed and decorated with flowers, at which three gentlemen and two ladies of elegant appearance were already seated and who extended to Lupin a hearty greeting.

Sholmes now looked about for the four men and perceived them amongst a crowd of people who were listening to a gipsy orchestra that was playing in a neighboring café. It was a curious thing that they were paying no attention to Arsène Lupin, but seemed to be friendly with the people around them. One of them took a cigarette from his pocket and approached a gentleman who wore a frock coat and silk hat. The gentleman offered the other his cigar for a light, and Sholmes had the impression that they talked to each other much longer than the occasion demanded. Finally the gentleman approached the Hungarian restaurant, entered and looked around. When he caught sight of Lupin he advanced and spoke to him for a moment, then took a seat at an adjoining table. Sholmes now recognized this gentleman as the horseman who had tried to run him down in the avenue Henri-Martin.

Then Sholmes understood that these men were not tracking Arsène Lupin; they were a part of his band. They were watching over his safety. They were his bodyguard, his satellites, his vigilant escort. Wherever danger threatened Lupin, these confederates were at hand to avert it, ready to defend him. The four men were accomplices. The gentleman in the frock coat was an accomplice. These facts furnished the Englishman with food for reflection. Would he ever succeed in capturing that inaccessible individual? What unlimited power was possessed by such an organization, directed by such a chief!

He tore a leaf from his notebook, wrote a few lines in pencil, which he placed in an envelope, and said to a boy about fifteen years of age who was sitting on the bench beside him:

"Here, my boy; take a carriage and deliver this letter to the cashier of the Suisse tavern, Place du Châtelet. Be quick!"

He gave him a five-franc piece. The boy disappeared.

A half hour passed away. The crowd had grown larger, and Sholmes perceived only at intervals the accomplices of Arsène Lupin. Then someone brushed against him and whispered in his ear:

"Well? what is it, Monsieur Sholmes?"

"Ah! it is you, Ganimard?"

"Yes; I received your note at the tavern. What's the matter?"

"He is there."

"What do you mean?"

"There ... in the restaurant. Lean to the right.... Do you see him now?"

"No."

"He is pouring a glass of champagne for the lady."

"That is not Lupin."

"Yes, it is."

"But I tell you.... Ah! yet, it may be. It looks a great deal like him," said Ganimard, naively. "And the others—accomplices?"

"No; the lady sitting beside him is Lady Cliveden; the other is the Duchess de Cleath. The gentleman sitting opposite Lupin is the Spanish Ambassador to London."

Ganimard took a step forward. Sholmes retained him.

"Be prudent. You are alone."

"So is he."

"No, he has a number of men on the boulevard mounting guard. And inside the restaurant that gentleman——"

"And I, when I take Arsène Lupin by the collar and announce his name, I shall have the entire room on my side and all the waiters."

"I should prefer to have a few policemen."

"But, Monsieur Sholmes, we have no choice. We must catch him when we can."

He was right; Sholmes knew it. It was better to take advantage of the opportunity and make the attempt. Sholmes simply gave this advice to Ganimard:

"Conceal your identity as long as possible."

Sholmes glided behind a newspaper kiosk, whence he could still watch Lupin, who was leaning toward Lady Cliveden, talking and smiling.

Ganimard crossed the street, hands in his pockets, as if he were going down the boulevard, but when he reached the opposite sidewalk he turned quickly and bounded up the steps of the restaurant. There was a shrill whistle. Ganimard ran against the head waiter, who had suddenly planted himself in the doorway and now pushed Ganimard back with a show of indignation, as if he were an intruder whose presence would bring disgrace upon the restaurant. Ganimard was surprised. At the same moment the gentleman in the frock coat came out. He took the part of the detective and entered into an exciting argument with the waiter; both of them hung on to Ganimard, one pushing him in, the other pushing him out in such a manner that, despite all his efforts and despite his furious protestations, the unfortunate detective soon found himself on the sidewalk.

The struggling men were surrounded by a crowd. Two policemen, attracted by the noise, tried to force their way through the crowd, but encountered a mysterious resistance and could make no headway through the opposing backs and pressing shoulders of the mob.

But suddenly, as if by magic, the crowd parted and the passage to the restaurant was clear. The head waiter, recognizing his mistake, was profuse in his apologies; the gentleman in the frock coat ceased his efforts on behalf of the detective, the crowd dispersed, the policemen passed on, and Ganimard hastened to the table at which the six guests were sitting. But now there were only five! He looked around.... The only exit was the door.

"The person who was sitting here!" he cried to the five astonished guests. "Where is he?"

"Monsieur Destro?"

"No; Arsène Lupin!"

A waiter approached and said:

"The gentleman went upstairs."

Ganimard rushed up in the hope of finding him. The upper floor of the restaurant contained private dining-rooms and had a private stairway leading to the boulevard.

"No use looking for him now," muttered Ganimard. "He is far away by this time."

He was not far away—two hundred yards at most—in the Madeleine-Bastille omnibus, which was rolling along very peacefully with its three horses across the Place de l'Opéra toward the

Boulevard des Capucines. Two sturdy fellows were talking together on the platform. On the roof of the omnibus near the stairs an old fellow was sleeping; it was Herlock Sholmes.

With bobbing head, rocked by the movement of the vehicle, the Englishman said to himself:

"If Wilson could see me now, how proud he would be of his collaborator!... Bah! It was easy to foresee that the game was lost, as soon as the man whistled; nothing could be done but watch the exits and see that our man did not escape. Really, Lupin makes life exciting and interesting."

At the terminal point Herlock Sholmes, by leaning over, saw Arsène Lupin leaving the omnibus, and as he passed in front of the men who formed his bodyguard Sholmes heard him say: "A l'Etoile."

"A l'Etoile, exactly, a rendezvous. I shall be there," thought Sholmes. "I will follow the two men."

Lupin took an automobile; but the men walked the entire distance, followed by Sholmes. They stopped at a narrow house, No. 40 rue Chalgrin, and rang the bell. Sholmes took his position in the shadow of a doorway, whence he could watch the house in question. A man opened one of the windows of the ground floor and closed the shutters. But the shutters did not reach to the top of the window. The impost was clear.

At the end of ten minutes a gentleman rang at the same door and a few minutes later another man came. A short time afterward an automobile stopped in front of the house, bringing two passengers: Arsène Lupin and a lady concealed beneath a large cloak and a thick veil.

"The blonde Lady, no doubt," said Sholmes to himself, as the automobile drove away.

Herlock Sholmes now approached the house, climbed to the window-ledge and, by standing on tiptoe, he was able to see through the window above the shutters. What did he see?

Arsène Lupin, leaning against the mantel, was speaking with considerable animation. The others were grouped around him, listening to him attentively. Amongst them Sholmes easily recognized the gentleman in the frock coat and he thought one of the other men resembled the head-waiter of the restaurant. As to the blonde Lady, she was seated in an armchair with her back to the window.

"They are holding a consultation," thought Sholmes. "They are worried over the incident at the restaurant and are holding a council of war. Ah! what a master stroke it would be to capture all of them at one fell stroke!"

One of them, having moved toward the door, Sholmes leaped to the ground and concealed himself in the shadow. The gentleman in the frock coat and the head-waiter left the house. A moment later a light appeared at the windows of the first floor, but the shutters were closed immediately and the upper part of the house was dark as well as the lower.

"Lupin and the woman are on the ground floor; the two confederates live on the upper floor," said Sholmes.

Sholmes remained there the greater part of the night, fearing that if he went away Arsène Lupin might leave during his absence. At four o'clock, seeing two policemen at the end of the street, he approached them, explained the situation and left them to watch the house. He went to Ganimard's residence in the rue Pergolese and wakened him.

"I have him yet," said Sholmes.

"Arsène Lupin?"

"Yes."

"If you haven't got any better hold on him than you had a while ago, I might as well go back to bed. But we may as well go to the station-house."

They went to the police station in the rue Mesnil and from there to the residence of the commissary, Mon. Decointre. Then, accompanied by half a dozen policemen, they went to the rue Chalgrin.

"Anything new?" asked Sholmes, addressing the two policemen.

"Nothing."

It was just breaking day when, after taking necessary measures to prevent escape, the commissary rang the bell and commenced to question the concierge. The woman was greatly frightened at this early morning invasion, and she trembled as she replied that there were no tenants on the ground floor.

"What! not a tenant?" exclaimed Ganimard.

"No; but on the first floor there are two men named Leroux. They have furnished the apartment on the ground floor for some country relations."

"A gentleman and lady."

"Yes."

"Who came here last night."

"Perhaps ... but I don't know ... I was asleep. But I don't think so, for the key is here. They did not ask for it."

With that key the commissary opened the door of the ground-floor apartment. It comprised only two rooms and they were empty.

"Impossible!" exclaimed Sholmes. "I saw both of them in this room."

"I don't doubt your word," said the commissary; "but they are not here now."

"Let us go to the first floor. They must be there."

"The first floor is occupied by two men named Leroux."

"We will examine the Messieurs Leroux."

They all ascended the stairs and the commissary rang. At the second ring a man opened the door; he was in his shirt-sleeves. Sholmes recognized him as one of Lupin's bodyguard. The man assumed a furious air:

"What do you mean by making such a row at this hour of the morning ... waking people up...."

But he stopped suddenly, astounded.

"God forgive me!... really, gentlemen, I didn't notice who it was. Why, it is Monsieur Decointre!... and you, Monsieur Ganimard. What can I do for you!"

Ganimard burst into an uncontrollable fit of laughter, which caused him to bend double and turn black in the face.

"Ah! it is you, Leroux," he stammered. "Oh! this is too funny! Leroux, an accomplice of Arsène Lupin! Oh, I shall die! and your brother, Leroux, where is he?"

"Edmond!" called the man. "It is Ganimard, who has come to visit us."

Another man appeared and at sight of him Ganimard's mirth redoubled.

"Oh! oh! we had no idea of this! Ah! my friends, you are in a bad fix now. Who would have ever suspected it?"

Turning to Sholmes, Ganimard introduced the man:

"Victor Leroux, a detective from our office, one of the best men in the iron brigade ... Edmond Leroux, chief clerk in the anthropometric service."

CHAPTER V.

AN ABDUCTION.

Herlock Sholmes said nothing. To protest? To accuse the two men? That would be useless. In the absence of evidence which he did not possess and had no time to seek, no one would believe him. Moreover, he was stifled with rage, but would not display his feelings before the triumphant Ganimard. So he bowed respectfully to the brothers Leroux, guardians of society, and retired.

In the vestibule he turned toward a low door which looked like the entrance to a cellar, and picked up a small red stone; it was a garnet. When he reached the street he turned and read on the front of the house this inscription: "Lucien Destange, architect, 1877."

The adjoining house, No. 42, bore the same inscription.

"Always the double passage—numbers 40 and 42 have a secret means of communication. Why didn't I think of that? I should have remained with the two policemen."

He met the policemen near the corner and said to them:

"Two people came out of house No. 42 during my absence, didn't they?"

"Yes; a gentleman and lady."

Ganimard approached. Sholmes took his arm, and as they walked down the street he said:

"Monsieur Ganimard, you have had a good laugh and will no doubt forgive me for the trouble I have caused you."

"Oh! there's no harm done; but it was a good joke."

"I admit that; but the best jokes have only a short life, and this one can't last much longer."

"I hope not."

"This is now the seventh day, and I can remain only three days more. Then I must return to London."

"Oh!"

"I wish to ask you to be in readiness, as I may call on you at any hour on Tuesday or Wednesday night."

"For an expedition of the same kind as we had to-night?"

"Yes, monsieur, the very same."

"With what result?"

"The capture of Arsène Lupin," replied Sholmes.

"Do you think so?"

"I swear it, on my honor, monsieur."

Sholmes bade Ganimard good-bye and went to the nearest hotel for a few hours' sleep; after which, refreshed and with renewed confidence in himself, he returned to the rue Chalgrin, slipped two louis into the hand of the concierge, assured himself that the brothers Leroux had gone out, learned that the house belonged to a Monsieur Harmingeat, and, provided with a candle, descended to the cellar through the low door near which he had found the garnet. At the bottom of the stairs he found another exactly like it.

"I am not mistaken," he thought; "this is the means of communication. Let me see if my skeleton-key will open the cellar reserved for the tenant of the ground floor. Yes; it will. Now, I will examine those cases of wine... oh! oh! here are some places where the dust has been cleared away ... and some footprints on the ground...."

A slight noise caused him to listen attentively. Quickly he pushed the door shut, blew out his candle and hid behind a pile of empty wine cases. After a few seconds he noticed that a portion of the wall swung on a pivot, the light of a lantern was thrown into the cellar, an arm appeared, then a man entered.

He was bent over, as if he were searching for something. He felt in the dust with his fingers and several times he threw something into a cardboard box that he carried in his left hand. Afterward he obliterated the traces of his footsteps, as well as the footprints left by Lupin and the blonde lady, and he was about to leave the cellar by the same way as he had entered, when he uttered a harsh cry and fell to the ground. Sholmes had leaped upon him. It was the work of a moment, and in the simplest manner in the world the man found himself stretched on the ground, bound and handcuffed. The Englishman leaned over him and said:

"Have you anything to say?... To tell what you know?"

The man replied by such an ironical smile that Sholmes realized the futility of questioning him. So he contented himself by exploring the pockets of his captive, but he found only a bunch of keys, a handkerchief and the small cardboard box which contained a dozen garnets similar to those which Sholmes had found.

Then what was he to do with the man? Wait until his friends came to his help and deliver all of them to the police? What good would that do? What advantage would that give him over Lupin?

He hesitated; but an examination of the box decided the question. The box bore this name and address: "Leonard, jeweler, rue de la Paix."

He resolved to abandon the man to his fate. He locked the cellar and left the house. At a branch postoffice he sent a telegram to Monsieur Destange, saying that he could not come that day. Then he went to see the jeweler and, handing him the garnets, said:

"Madame sent me with these stones. She wishes to have them reset."

Sholmes had struck the right key. The jeweler replied:

"Certainly; the lady telephoned to me. She said she would be here to-day."

Sholmes established himself on the sidewalk to wait for the lady, but it was five o'clock when he saw a heavily-veiled lady approach and enter the store. Through the window he saw her place on the counter a piece of antique jewelry set with garnets.

She went away almost immediately, walking quickly and passed through streets that were unknown to the Englishman. As it was now almost dark, he walked close behind her and followed her into a five-story house of double flats and, therefore, occupied by numerous tenants. At the second floor she stopped and entered. Two minutes later the Englishman commenced to try the keys on the bunch he had taken from the man in the rue Chalgrin. The fourth key fitted the lock.

Notwithstanding the darkness of the rooms, he perceived that they were absolutely empty, as if unoccupied, and the various doors were standing open so that he could see all the apartments. At the end of a corridor he perceived a ray of light and, by approaching on tiptoe and looking through the glass door, he saw the veiled lady who had removed her hat and dress and was now wearing a velvet dressing-gown. The discarded garments were lying on the only chair in the room and a lighted lamp stood on the mantel.

Then he saw her approach the fireplace and press what appeared to be the button of an electric bell. Immediately the panel to the right of the fireplace moved and slowly glided behind the adjoining panel, thus disclosing an opening large enough for a person to pass through. The lady disappeared through this opening, taking the lamp with her.

The operation was a very simple one. Sholmes adopted it and followed the lady. He found himself in total darkness and immediately he felt his face brushed by some soft articles. He lighted a match and found that he was in a very small room completely filled with cloaks and dresses suspended on hangers. He picked his way through until he reached a door that was draped with a portiere. He peeped through and, behold, the blonde lady was there, under his eyes, and almost within reach of his hand.

She extinguished the lamp and turned on the electric lights. Then for the first time Herlock Sholmes obtained a good look at her face. He was amazed. The woman, whom he had overtaken after so much trouble and after so many tricks and manoeuvres, was none other than Clotilde Destange.

Clotilde Destange, the assassin of the Baron d'Hautrec and the thief who stole the blue diamond! Clotilde Destange, the mysterious friend of Arsène Lupin! And the blonde lady!

"Yes, I am only a stupid ass," thought Herlock Sholmes at that moment. "Because Lupin's friend was a blonde and Clotilde is a brunette, I never dreamed that they were the same person. But how could the blonde lady remain a blonde after the murder of the baron and the theft of the diamond?"

Sholmes could see a portion of the room; it was a boudoir, furnished with the most delightful luxury and exquisite taste, and adorned with beautiful tapestries and costly ornaments. A mahogany couch, upholstered in silk, was located on the side of the room opposite the door at which Sholmes was standing. Clotilde was sitting on this couch, motionless, her face covered by her hands. Then he perceived that she was weeping. Great tears rolled down her pale cheeks and fell, drop by drop, on the velvet corsage. The tears came thick and fast, as if their source were inexhaustible.

A door silently opened behind her and Arsène Lupin entered. He looked at her for a long time without making his presence known; then he approached her, knelt at her feet, pressed her head to his breast, folded her in his arms, and his actions indicated an infinite measure of love and sympathy. For a time not a word was uttered, but her tears became less abundant.

"I was so anxious to make you happy," he murmured.

"I am happy."

"No; you are crying.... Your tears break my heart, Clotilde."

The caressing and sympathetic tone of his voice soothed her, and she listened to him with an eager desire for hope and happiness. Her features were softened by a smile, and yet how sad a smile! He continued to speak in a tone of tender entreaty:

"You should not be unhappy, Clotilde; you have no cause to be."

She displayed her delicate white hands and said, solemnly:

"Yes, Maxime; so long as I see those hands I shall be sad."

"Why?"

"They are stained with blood."

"Hush! Do not think of that!" exclaimed Lupin. "The dead is past and gone. Do not resurrect it."

And he kissed the long, delicate hand, while she regarded him with a brighter smile as if each kiss effaced a portion of that dreadful memory.

"You must love me, Maxime; you must—because no woman will ever love you as I do. For your sake, I have done many things, not at your order or request, but in obedience to your secret desires. I have done things at which my will and conscience revolted, but there was some unknown power that I could not resist. What I did I did involuntarily, mechanically, because it helped you, because you wished it ... and I am ready to do it again to-morrow ... and always."

"Ah, Clotilde," he said, bitterly, "why did I draw you into my adventurous life? I should have remained the Maxime Bermond that you loved five years ago, and not have let you know the ... other man that I am."

She replied in a low voice:

"I love the other man, also, and I have nothing to regret."

"Yes, you regret your past life—the free and happy life you once enjoyed."

"I have no regrets when you are here," she said, passionately. "All faults and crimes disappear when I see you. When you are away I may suffer, and weep, and be horrified at what I have done; but when you come it is all forgotten. Your love wipes it all away. And I am happy again.... But you must love me!"

"I do not love you on compulsion, Clotilde. I love you simply because ... I love you."

"Are you sure of it?"

"I am just as sure of my own love as I am of yours. Only my life is a very active and exciting one, and I cannot spend as much time with you as I would like—just now."

"What is it? Some new danger? Tell me!"

"Oh! nothing serious. Only...."

"Only what?" she asked.

"Well, he is on our track."

"Who? Herlock Sholmes?"

"Yes; it was he who dragged Ganimard into that affair at the Hungarian restaurant. It was he who instructed the two policemen to watch the house in the rue Chalgrin. I have proof of it. Ganimard searched the house this morning and Sholmes was with him. Besides——"

"Besides? What?"

"Well, there is another thing. One of our men is missing."

"Who?"

"Jeanniot."

"The concierge?"

"Yes."

"Why, I sent him to the rue Chalgrin this morning to pick up the garnets that fell out of my brooch."

"There is no doubt, then, that Sholmes caught him."

"No; the garnets were delivered to the jeweler in the rue de la Paix."

"Then, what has become of him!"

"Oh! Maxime, I am afraid."

"There is nothing to be afraid of, but I confess the situation is very serious. What does he know? Where does he hide himself? His isolation is his strong card. I cannot reach him."

"What are you going to do?"

"Act with extreme prudence, Clotilde. Some time ago I decided to change my residence to a safer place, and Sholmes' appearance on the scene has prompted me to do so at once. When a man like that is on your track, you must be prepared for the worst. Well, I am making my preparations. Day after to-morrow, Wednesday, I shall move. At noon it will be finished. At two o'clock I shall leave the place, after removing the last trace of our residence there, which will be no small matter. Until then——"

"Well?"

"Until then we must not see each other and no one must see you, Clotilde. Do not go out. I have no fear for myself, but I have for you."

"That Englishman cannot possibly reach me."

"I am not so sure of that. He is a dangerous man. Yesterday I came here to search the cupboard that contains all of Monsieur Destange's old papers and records. There is danger there. There is danger everywhere. I feel that he is watching us—that he is drawing his net around us closer and closer. It is one of those intuitions which never deceive me."

"In that case, Maxime, go, and think no more of my tears. I shall be brave, and wait patiently until the danger is past. Adieu, Maxime."

They held one another for some time in a last fond embrace. And it was she that gently pushed him outside. Sholmes could hear the sound of their voices in the distance.

Emboldened by the necessities of the situation and the urgent need of bringing his investigation to a speedy termination, Sholmes proceeded to make an examination of the house in which he now found himself. He passed through Clotilde's boudoir into a corridor, at the end of which there was a stairway leading to the lower floor; he was about to descend this stairway when he heard voices below, which caused him to change his route. He followed the corridor, which was a circular one, and discovered another stairway, which he descended and found himself amidst surroundings that bore a familiar appearance. He passed through a door that stood partly open and entered a large circular room. It was Monsieur Destange's library.

"Ah! splendid!" he exclaimed. "Now I understand everything. The boudoir of Mademoiselle Clotilde—the blonde Lady—communicates with a room in the adjoining house, and that house does not front on the Place Malesherbes, but upon an adjacent street, the rue Montchanin, if I remember the name correctly.... And I now understand how Clotilde Destange can meet her lover and at the same time create the impression that she never leaves the house; and I understand also how Arsène Lupin was enabled to make his mysterious entrance to the gallery last night. Ah! there must be another connection between the library and the adjoining room. One more house full of ways that are dark! And no doubt Lucien Destange was the architect, as usual!... I should take advantage of this opportunity to examine the contents of the cupboard and perhaps learn the location of other houses with secret passages constructed by Monsieur Destange."

Sholmes ascended to the gallery and concealed himself behind some draperies, where he remained until late in the evening. At last a servant came and turned off the electric lights. An hour later the Englishman, by the light of his lantern, made his way to the cupboard. As he had surmised, it contained the architect's old papers, plans, specifications and books of account. It also contained a series of registers, arranged according to date, and Sholmes, having selected those of the most recent dates, searched in the indexes for the name "Harmingeat." He found it in one of the registers with a reference to page 63. Turning to that page, he read:

"Harmingeat, 40 rue Chalgrin."

This was followed by a detailed account of the work done in and about the installation of a furnace in the house. And in the margin of the book someone had written these words: "See account M.B."

"Ah! I thought so!" said Sholmes; "the account M.B. is the one I want. I shall learn from it the actual residence of Monsieur Lupin."

It was morning before he found that important account. It comprised sixteen pages, one of which was a copy of the page on which was described the work done for Mon. Harmingeat of the rue Chalgrin. Another page described the work performed for Mon. Vatinel as owner of the house at No. 25 rue Clapeyron. Another page was reserved for the Baron d'Hautrec, 134 avenue Henri-Martin; another was devoted to the Château de Crozon, and the eleven other pages to various owners of houses in Paris.

Sholmes made a list of those eleven names and addresses; after which he returned the books to their proper places, opened a window, jumped out onto the deserted street and closed the shutters behind him.

When he reached his room at the hotel he lighted his pipe with all the solemnity with which he was wont to characterize that act, and amidst clouds of smoke he studied the deductions that might be drawn from the account of M.B., or rather, from the account of Maxime Bermond alias Arsène Lupin.

At eight o'clock he sent the following message to Ganimard:

"I expect to pass through the rue Pergolese this forenoon and will inform you of a person whose arrest is of the highest importance. In any event, be at home to-night and to-morrow until noon and have at least thirty men at your service."

Then he engaged an automobile at the stand on the boulevard, choosing one whose chauffeur looked good-natured but dull-witted, and instructed him to drive to the Place Malesherbes, where he stopped him about one hundred feet from Monsieur Destange's house.

"My boy, close your carriage," he said to the chauffeur; "turn up the collar of your coat, for the wind is cold, and wait patiently. At the end of an hour and a half, crank up your machine. When I return we will go to the rue Pergolese."

As he was ascending the steps leading to the door a doubt entered his mind. Was it not a mistake on his part to be spending his time on the affairs of the blonde Lady, while Arsène Lupin was preparing to move? Would he not be better engaged in trying to find the abode of his adversary amongst the eleven houses on his list?

"Ah!" he exclaimed, "when the blonde Lady becomes my prisoner, I shall be master of the situation."

And he rang the bell.

Monsieur Destange was already in the library. They had been working only a few minutes, when Clotilde entered, bade her father good morning, entered the adjoining parlor and sat down to write. From his place Sholmes could see her leaning over the table and from time to time absorbed in deep meditation. After a short time he picked up a book and said to Monsieur Destange:

"Here is a book that Mademoiselle Destange asked me to bring to her when I found it."

He went into the little parlor, stood before Clotilde in such a manner that her father could not see her, and said:

"I am Monsieur Stickmann, your father's new secretary."

"Ah!" said Clotilde, without moving, "my father has changed his secretary? I didn't know it."

"Yes, mademoiselle, and I desire to speak with you."

"Kindly take a seat, monsieur; I have finished."

She added a few words to her letter, signed it, enclosed it in the envelope, sealed it, pushed her writing material away, rang the telephone, got in communication with her dressmaker, asked the latter to hasten the completion of a traveling dress, as she required it at once, and then, turning to Sholmes, she said:

"I am at your service, monsieur. But do you wish to speak before my father? Would not that be better?"

"No, mademoiselle; and I beg of you, do not raise your voice. It is better that Monsieur Destange should not hear us."

"For whose sake is it better?"

"Yours, mademoiselle."

"I cannot agree to hold any conversation with you that my father may not hear."

"But you must agree to this. It is imperative."

Both of them arose, eye to eye. She said:

"Speak, monsieur."

Still standing, he commenced:

204

"You will be so good as to pardon me if I am mistaken on certain points of secondary importance. I will guarantee, however, the general accuracy of my statements."

"Can we not dispense with these preliminaries, monsieur? Or are they necessary?"

Sholmes felt the young woman was on her guard, so he replied:

"Very well; I will come to the point. Five years ago your father made the acquaintance of a certain young man called Maxime Bermond, who was introduced as a contractor or an architect, I am not sure which it was; but it was one or the other. Monsieur Destange took a liking to the young man, and as the state of his health compelled him to retire from active business, he entrusted to Monsieur Bermond the execution of certain orders he had received from some of his old customers and which seemed to come within the scope of Monsieur Bermond's ability."

Herlock Sholmes stopped. It seemed to him that the girl's pallor had increased. Yet there was not the slightest tremor in her voice when she said:

"I know nothing about the circumstances to which you refer, monsieur, and I do not see in what way they can interest me."

"In this way, mademoiselle: You know, as well as I, that Maxime Bermond is also known by the name of Arsène Lupin."

She laughed, and said:

"Nonsense! Arsène Lupin? Maxime Bermond is Arsène Lupin? Oh! no! It isn't possible!"

"I have the honor to inform you of that fact, and since you refuse to understand my meaning, I will add that Arsène Lupin has found in this house a friend—more than a friend—and accomplice, blindly and passionately devoted to him."

Without emotion, or at least with so little emotion that Sholmes was astonished at her self-control, she declared:

"I do not understand your object, monsieur, and I do not care to; but I command you to say no more and leave this house."

"I have no intention of forcing my presence on you," replied Sholmes, with equal sang-froid, "but I shall not leave this house alone."

"And who will accompany you, monsieur?"

"You will."

"I?"

"Yes, mademoiselle, we will leave this house together, and you will follow me without one word of protest."

The strange feature of the foregoing interview was the absolute coolness of the two adversaries. It bore no resemblance to an implacable duel between two powerful wills; but, judging solely from their attitude and the tone of their voices, an onlooker would have supposed their conversation to be nothing more serious than a courteous argument over some impersonal subject.

Clotilde resumed her seat without deigning to reply to the last remark of Herlock Sholmes, except by a shrug of her shoulders. Sholmes looked at his watch and said:

"It is half-past ten. We will leave here in five minutes."

"Perhaps."

"If not, I shall go to Monsieur Destange, and tell him——"

"What?"

"The truth. I will tell him of the vicious life of Maxime Bermond, and I will tell him of the double life of his accomplice."

"Of his accomplice?"

"Yes, of the woman known as the blonde Lady, of the woman who was blonde."

"What proofs will you give him?"

"I will take him to the rue Chalgrin, and show him the secret passage made by Arsène Lupin's workmen,—while doing the work of which he had the control—between the houses numbered 40 and 42; the passage which you and he used two nights ago."

"Well?"

"I will then take Monsieur Destange to the house of Monsieur Detinan; we will descend the servant's stairway which was used by you and Arsène Lupin when you escaped from Ganimard, and we will search together the means of communication with the adjoining house, which fronts on the Boulevard des Batignolles, and not upon the rue Clapeyron."

"Well?"

"I will take Monsieur Destange to the château de Crozon, and it will be easy for him, who knows the nature of the work performed by Arsène Lupin in the restoration of the Château, to discover the secret passages constructed there by his workmen. It will thus be established that those passages allowed the blonde Lady to make a nocturnal visit to the Countess' room and take the blue diamond from the mantel; and, two weeks later, by similar means, to enter the room of Herr Bleichen and conceal the blue diamond in his tooth-powder—a strange action, I confess; a woman's revenge, perhaps; but I don't know, and I don't care."

"Well?"

"After that," said Herlock Sholmes, in a more serious tone, "I will take Monsieur Destange to 134 avenue Henri-Martin, and we will learn how the Baron d'Hautrec——"

"No, no, keep quiet," stammered the girl, struck with a sudden terror, "I forbid you!... you dare to say that it was I ... you accuse me?..."

"I accuse you of having killed the Baron d'Hautrec."

"No, no, it is a lie."

"You killed the Baron d'Hautrec, mademoiselle. You entered his service under the name of Antoinette Bréhat, for the purpose of stealing the blue diamond and you killed him."

"Keep quiet, monsieur," she implored him. "Since you know so much, you must know that I did not murder the baron."

"I did not say that you murdered him, mademoiselle. Baron d'Hautrec was subject to fits of insanity that only Sister Auguste could control. She told me so herself. In her absence, he must have attacked you, and in the course of the struggle you struck him in order to save your own life. Frightened at your awful situation, you rang the bell, and fled without even taking the blue diamond from the finger of your victim. A few minutes later you returned with one of Arsène Lupin's accomplices, who was a servant in the adjoining house, you placed the baron on the bed, you put the room in order, but you were afraid to take the blue diamond. Now, I have told you what happened on that night. I repeat, you did not murder the baron, and yet it was your hand that struck the blow."

She had crossed them over her forehead—those long delicate white hands—and kept them thus for a long time. At last, loosening her fingers, she said, in a voice rent by anguish:

"And do you intend to tell all that to my father?"

"Yes; and I will tell him that I have secured as witnesses: Mademoiselle Gerbois, who will recognize the blonde Lady; Sister Auguste, who will recognize Antoinette Bréhat; and the Countess de Crozon, who will recognize Madame de Réal. That is what I shall tell him."

"You will not dare," she said, recovering her self-possession in the face of an immediate peril.

He arose, and made a step toward the library. Clotilde stopped him:

"One moment, monsieur."

She paused, reflected a moment, and then, perfect mistress of herself, said:

"You are Herlock Sholmes?"

"Yes."

"What do you want of me?"

"What do I want? I am fighting a duel with Arsène Lupin, and I must win. The contest is now drawing to a climax, and I have an idea that a hostage as precious as you will give me an important advantage over my adversary. Therefore, you will follow me, mademoiselle; I will entrust you to one of my friends. As soon as the duel is ended, you will be set at liberty."

"Is that all?"

"That is all. I do not belong to the police service of this country, and, consequently, I do not consider that I am under any obligation ... to cause your arrest."

She appeared to have come to a decision ... yet she required a momentary respite. She closed her eyes, the better to concentrate her thoughts. Sholmes looked at her in surprise; she was now so tranquil and, apparently, indifferent to the dangers which threatened her. Sholmes thought: Does she believe that she is in danger? Probably not—since Lupin protects her. She has confidence in him. She believes that Lupin is omnipotent, and infallible.

"Mademoiselle," he said, "I told you that we would leave here in five minutes. That time has almost expired."

"Will you permit me to go to my room, monsieur, to get some necessary articles?"

"Certainly, mademoiselle; and I will wait for you in the rue Montchanin. Jeanniot, the concierge, is a friend of mine."

"Ah! you know...." she said, visibly alarmed.

"I know many things."

"Very well. I will ring for the maid."

The maid brought her hat and jacket. Then Sholmes said:

"You must give Monsieur Destange some reason for our departure, and, if possible, let your excuse serve for an absence of several days."

"That shall not be necessary. I shall be back very soon."

"They exchanged defiant glances and an ironic smile.

"What faith you have in him!" said Sholmes.

"Absolute."

"He does everything well, doesn't he? He succeeds in everything he undertakes. And whatever he does receives your approval and cooperation."

"I love him," she said, with a touch of passion in her voice.

"And you think that he will save you?"

She shrugged her shoulders, and, approaching her father, she said:

"I am going to deprive you of Monsieur Stickmann. We are going to the National Library."

"You will return for luncheon?"

"Perhaps ... no, I think not ... but don't be uneasy."

Then she said to Sholmes, in a firm voice:

"I am at your service, monsieur."

"Absolutely?"

"Quite so."

"I warn you that if you attempt to escape, I shall call the police and have you arrested. Do not forget that the blonde Lady is on parole."

"I give you my word of honor that I shall not attempt to escape."

"I believe you. Now, let us go."

They left the house together, as he had predicted.

The automobile was standing where Sholmes had left it. As they approached it, Sholmes could hear the rumbling of the motor. He opened the door, asked Clotilde to enter, and took a seat beside her. The machine started at once, gained the exterior boulevards, the avenue Hoche and the avenue de la Grande-Armée. Sholmes was considering his plans. He thought:

"Ganimard is at home. I will leave the girl in his care. Shall I tell him who she is? No, he would take her to prison at once, and that would spoil everything. When I am alone, I can consult my list of addresses taken from the 'account M.B.,' and run them down. To-night, or to-morrow morning at the latest, I shall go to Ganimard, as I agreed, and deliver into his hands Arsène Lupin and all his band."

He rubbed his hand, gleefully, at the thought that his duel with Lupin was drawing to a close, and he could not see any serious obstacle in the way of his success. And, yielding to an irrepressible desire to give vent to his feelings—an unusual desire on his part—he exclaimed:

"Excuse me, mademoiselle, if I am unable to conceal my satisfaction and delight. The battle has been a difficult one, and my success is, therefore, more enjoyable."

"A legitimate success, monsieur, of which you have a just right to be proud."

"Thank you. But where are we going? The chauffeur must have misunderstood my directions."

At that moment they were leaving Paris by the gate de Neuilly. That was strange, as the rue Pergolese is not outside the fortifications. Sholmes lowered the glass, and said:

"Chauffeur, you have made a mistake.... Rue Pergolese!"

The man made no reply. Sholmes repeated, in a louder voice:

"I told you to go to the rue Pergolese."

Still the man did not reply.

"Ah! but you are deaf, my friend. Or is he doing it on purpose? We are very much out of our way.... Rue Pergolese!... Turn back at once!... Rue Pergolese!"

The chauffeur made no sign of having heard the order. The Englishman fretted with impatience. He looked at Clotilde; a mysterious smile played upon her lips.

"Why do you laugh?" he said. "It is an awkward mistake, but it won't help you."

"Of course not," she replied.

Then an idea occurred to him. He rose and made a careful scrutiny of the chauffeur. His shoulders were not so broad; his bearing was not so stiff and mechanical. A cold perspiration covered his forehead and his hands clenched with sudden fear, as his mind was seized with the conviction that the chauffeur was Arsène Lupin.

"Well, Monsieur Sholmes, what do you think of our little ride?"

"Delightful, monsieur, really delightful," replied Sholmes.

Never in his life had he experienced so much difficulty in uttering a few simple words without a tremor, or without betraying his feelings in his voice. But quickly, by a sort of reaction, a flood of hatred and rage burst its bounds, overcame his self-control, and, brusquely drawing his revolver, he pointed it at Mademoiselle Destange.

"Lupin, stop, this minute, this second, or I fire at mademoiselle."

"I advise you to aim at the cheek if you wish to hit the temple," replied Lupin, without turning his head.

"Maxime, don't go so fast," said Clotilde, "the pavement is slippery and I am very timid."

She was smiling; her eyes were fixed on the pavement, over which the carriage was traveling at enormous speed.

"Let him stop! Let him stop!" said Sholmes to her, wild with rage, "I warn you that I am desperate."

The barrel of the revolver brushed the waving locks of her hair. She replied, calmly:

"Maxime is so imprudent. He is going so fast, I am really afraid of some accident."

Sholmes returned the weapon to his pocket and seized the handle of the door, as if to alight, despite the absurdity of such an act. Clotilde said to him:

"Be careful, monsieur, there is an automobile behind us."

He leaned over. There was an automobile close behind; a large machine of formidable aspect with its sharp prow and blood-red body, and holding four men clad in fur coats.

"Ah! I am well guarded," thought Sholmes. "I may as well be patient."

He folded his arms across his chest with that proud air of submission so frequently assumed by heroes when fate has turned against them. And while they crossed the river Seine and rushed through Suresnes, Rueil and Chatou, motionless and resigned, controlling his actions and his passions, he tried to explain to his own satisfaction by what miracle Arsène Lupin had substituted himself for the chauffeur. It was quite improbable that the honest-looking fellow he had selected on the boulevard that morning was an accomplice placed there in advance. And yet Arsène Lupin had received a warning in some way, and it must have been after he, Sholmes, had approached Clotilde in the house, because no one could have suspected his project prior to that time. Since then, Sholmes had not allowed Clotilde out of his sight.

Then an idea struck him: the telephone communication desired by Clotilde and her conversation with the dressmaker. Now, it was all quite clear to him. Even before he had spoken to her, simply upon his request to speak to her as the new secretary of Monsieur Destange, she had scented the danger, surmised the name and purpose of the visitor, and, calmly, naturally, as if she were performing a commonplace action of her every-day life, she had called Arsène Lupin to her assistance by some preconcerted signal.

How Arsène Lupin had come and caused himself to be substituted for the chauffeur were matters of trifling importance. That which affected Sholmes, even to the point of appeasing his fury, was the recollection of that incident whereby an ordinary woman, a sweetheart it is true, mastering her nerves, controlling her features, and subjugating the expression of her eyes, had completely deceived the astute detective Herlock Sholmes. How difficult to overcome an adversary who is aided by such confederates, and who, by the mere force of his authority, inspires in a woman so much courage and strength!

They crossed the Seine and climbed the hill at Saint-Germain; but, some five hundred metres beyond that town, the automobile slackened its speed. The other automobile advanced, and the two stopped, side by side. There was no one else in the neighborhood.

"Monsieur Sholmes," said Lupin, "kindly exchange to the other machine. Ours is really a very slow one."

"Indeed!" said Sholmes, calmly, convinced that he had no choice.

"Also, permit me to loan you a fur coat, as we will travel quite fast and the air is cool. And accept a couple of sandwiches, as we cannot tell when we will dine."

The four men alighted from the other automobile. One of them approached, and, as he raised his goggles, Sholmes recognized in him the gentleman in the frock coat that he had seen at the Hungarian restaurant. Lupin said to him:

"You will return this machine to the chauffeur from whom I hired it. He is waiting in the first wine-shop to the right as you go up the rue Legendre. You will give him the balance of the thousand francs I promised him.... Ah! yes, kindly give your goggles to Monsieur Sholmes."

He talked to Mlle. Destange for a moment, then took his place at the wheel and started, with Sholmes at his side and one of his men behind him. Lupin had not exaggerated when he said "we will travel quite fast." From the beginning he set a breakneck pace. The horizon rushed to meet them, as if attracted by some mysterious force, and disappeared instantly as though swallowed up in an abyss, into which many other things, such as trees, houses, fields and forests, were hurled with the tumultuous fury and haste of a torrent as it approached the cataract.

Sholmes and Lupin did not exchange a word. Above their heads the leaves of the poplars made a great noise like the waves of the sea, rhythmically arranged by the regular spacing of the trees. And the towns swept by like spectres: Manteo, Vernon, Gaillon. From one hill to the other, from Bon-Secours to Canteleu, Rouen, its suburbs, its harbor, its miles of wharves, Rouen seemed like the straggling street of a country village. And this was Duclair, Caudebec, the country of Caux which they skimmed over in their terrific flight, and Lillebonne, and Quillebeuf. Then, suddenly, they found themselves on the banks of the Seine, at the extremity of a little wharf, beside which lay a staunch sea-going yacht that emitted great volumes of black smoke from its funnel.

The automobile stopped. In two hours they had traveled over forty leagues.

A man, wearing a blue uniform and a goldlaced cap, came forward and saluted. Lupin said to him:

"All ready, captain? Did you receive my telegram?"

"Yes, I got it."

"Is *The Swallow* ready?"

"Yes, monsieur."

"Come, Monsieur Sholmes."

The Englishman looked around, saw a group of people on the terrace in front of a café, hesitated a moment, then, realizing that before he could secure any assistance he would be seized, carried aboard and placed in the bottom of the hold, he crossed the gang-plank and followed Lupin into the captain's cabin. It was quite a large room, scrupulously clean, and presented a cheerful appearance with its varnished woodwork and polished brass. Lupin closed the door and addressed Sholmes abruptly, and almost rudely, as he said:

"Well, what do you know?"

"Everything."

"Everything? Come, be precise."

His voice contained no longer that polite, if ironical, tone, which he had affected when speaking to the Englishman. Now, his voice had the imperious tone of a master accustomed to command and accustomed to be obeyed—even by a Herlock Sholmes. They measured each other by their looks, enemies now—open and implacable foes. Lupin spoke again, but in a milder tone:

"I have grown weary of your pursuit, and do not intend to waste any more time in avoiding the traps you lay for me. I warn you that my treatment of you will depend on your reply. Now, what do you know?"

"Everything, monsieur."

Arsène Lupin controlled his temper and said, in a jerky manner:

"I will tell you what you know. You know that, under the name of Maxime Bermond, I have ... *improved* fifteen houses that were originally constructed by Monsieur Destange."

"Yes."

"Of those fifteen houses, you have seen four."

"Yes."

"And you have a list of the other eleven."

"Yes."

"You made that list at Monsieur Destange's house on that night, no doubt."

"Yes."

"And you have an idea that, amongst those eleven houses, there is one that I have kept for the use of myself and my friends, and you have intrusted to Ganimard the task of finding my retreat."

"No."

"What does that signify?"

"It signifies that I choose to act alone, and do not want his help."

"Then I have nothing to fear, since you are in my hands."

"You have nothing to fear as long as I remain in your hands."

"You mean that you will not remain?"

"Yes."

Arsène Lupin approached the Englishman and, placing his hand on the latter's shoulder, said:

"Listen, monsieur; I am not in a humor to argue with you, and, unfortunately for you, you are not in a position to choose. So let us finish our business."

"Very well."

"You are going to give me your word of honor that you will not try to escape from this boat until you arrive in English waters."

"I give you my word of honor that I shall escape if I have an opportunity," replied the indomitable Sholmes.

"But, sapristi! you know quite well that at a word from me you would soon be rendered helpless. All these men will obey me blindly. At a sign from me they would place you in irons——"

"Irons can be broken."

"And throw you overboard ten miles from shore."

"I can swim."

"I hadn't thought of that," said Lupin, with a laugh. "Excuse me, master ... and let us finish. You will agree that I must take the measures necessary to protect myself and my friends."

"Certainly; but they will be useless."

"And yet you do not wish me to take them."

"It is your duty."

"Very well, then."

Lupin opened the door and called the captain and two sailors. The latter seized the Englishman, bound him hand and foot, and tied him to the captain's bunk.

"That will do," said Lupin. "It was only on account of your obstinacy and the unusual gravity of the situation, that I ventured to offer you this indignity."

The sailors retired. Lupin said to the captain:

"Let one of the crew remain here to look after Monsieur Sholmes, and you can give him as much of your own company as possible. Treat him with all due respect and consideration. He is not a prisoner, but a guest. What time have you, captain?"

"Five minutes after two."

Lupin consulted his watch, then looked at the clock that was attached to the wall of the cabin.

"Five minutes past two is right. How long will it take you to reach Southampton?"

"Nine hours, easy going."

"Make it eleven. You must not land there until after the departure of the midnight boat, which reaches Havre at eight o'clock in the morning. Do you understand, captain? Let me repeat: As it would be very dangerous for all of us to permit Monsieur to return to France by that boat, you must not reach Southampton before one o'clock in the morning."

"I understand."

"Au revoir, master; next year, in this world or in the next."

"Until to-morrow," replied Sholmes.

A few minutes later Sholmes heard the automobile going away, and at the same time the steam puffed violently in the depths of *The Swallow*. The boat had started for England. About three o'clock the vessel left the mouth of the river and plunged into the open sea. At that moment Sholmes was lying on the captain's bunk, sound asleep.

Next morning—it being the tenth and last day of the duel between Sholmes and Lupin— the *Echo de France* published this interesting bit of news:

"Yesterday a judgment of ejectment was entered in the case of Arsène Lupin against Herlock Sholmes, the English detective. Although signed at noon, the judgment was executed the same day. At one o'clock this morning Sholmes was landed at Southampton."

CHAPTER VI.

SECOND ARREST OF ARSÈNE LUPIN.

Since eight o'clock a dozen moving-vans had encumbered the rue Crevaux between the avenue du Bois-de-Boulogne and the avenue Bugeaud. Mon. Felix Davey was leaving the apartment in which he lived on the fourth floor of No. 8; and Mon. Dubreuil, who had united into a single apartment the fifth floor of the same house and the fifth floor of the two adjoining houses, was moving on the same day—a mere coincidence, since the gentlemen were unknown to each other—the vast collection of furniture regarding which so many foreign agents visited him every day.

A circumstance which had been noticed by some of the neighbors, but was not spoken of until later, was this: None of the twelve vans bore the name and address of the owner, and none of the men accompanying them visited the neighboring wine shops. They worked so diligently that the furniture was all out by eleven o'clock. Nothing remained but those scraps of papers and rags that are always left behind in the corners of the empty rooms.

Mon. Felix Davey, an elegant young man, dressed in the latest fashion, carried in his hand a walking-stick, the weight of which indicated that its owner possessed extraordinary biceps— Mon. Felix Davey walked calmly away and took a seat on a bench in the avenue du Bois-de-Boulogne facing the rue Pergolese. Close to him a woman, dressed in a neat but inexpensive costume, was reading a newspaper, whilst a child was playing with a shovel in a heap of sand.

After a few minutes Felix Davey spoke to the woman, without turning his head:

"Ganimard!"

"Went out at nine o'clock this morning."

"Where?"

"To police headquarters."

"Alone?"

"Yes."

"No telegram during the night?"

"No."

"Do they suspect you in the house?"

"No; I do some little things for Madame Ganimard, and she tells me everything her husband does. I have been with her all morning."

"Very well. Until further orders come here every day at eleven o'clock."

He rose and walked away in the direction of the Dauphine gate, stopping at the Chinese pavilion, where he partook of a frugal repast consisting of two eggs, with some fruit and vegetables. Then he returned to the rue Crevaux and said to the concierge:

"I will just glance through the rooms and then give you the keys."

He finished his inspection of the room that he had used as a library; then he seized the end of a gas-pipe, which hung down the side of the chimney. The pipe was bent and a hole made in the elbow. To this hole he fitted a small instrument in the form of an ear-trumpet and blew into it. A slight whistling sound came by way of reply. Placing the trumpet to his mouth, he said:

"Anyone around, Dubreuil?"

"No."

"May I come up!"

"Yes."

He returned the pipe to its place, saying to himself:

"How progressive we are! Our century abounds with little inventions which render life really charming and picturesque. And so amusing!... especially when a person knows how to enjoy life as I do."

He turned one of the marble mouldings of the mantel, and the entire half of the mantel moved, and the mirror above it glided in invisible grooves, disclosing an opening and the lower steps of a stairs built in the very body of the chimney; all very clean and complete—the stairs were constructed of polished metal and the walls of white tiles. He ascended the steps, and at the fifth floor there was the same opening in the chimney. Mon. Dubreuil was waiting for him.

"Have you finished in your rooms?"

"Yes."

"Everything cleared out?"

"Yes."

"And the people?"

"Only the three men on guard."

"Very well; come on."

They ascended to the upper floor by the same means, one after the other, and there found three men, one of whom was looking through the window.

"Anything new?"

"Nothing, governor."

"All quiet in the street?"

"Yes."

"In ten minutes I will be ready to leave. You will go also. But in the meantime if you see the least suspicious movement in the street, warn me."

"I have my finger on the alarm-bell all the time."

"Dubreuil, did you tell the moving men not to touch the wire of that bell?"

"Certainly; it is working all right."

"That is all I want to know."

The two gentlemen then descended to the apartment of Felix Davey and the latter, after adjusting the marble mantel, exclaimed, joyfully:

"Dubreuil, I should like to see the man who is able to discover all the ingenious devices, warning bells, net-works of electric wires and acoustic tubes, invisible passages, moving floors and hidden stairways. A real fairy-land!"

"What fame for Arsène Lupin!"

"Fame I could well dispense with. It's a pity to be compelled to leave a place so well equipped, and commence all over again, Dubreuil ... and on a new model, of course, for it would never do to duplicate this. Curse Herlock Sholmes!"

"Has he returned to Paris?"

"How could he? There has been only one boat come from Southampton and it left there at midnight; only one train from Havre, leaving there at eight o'clock this morning and due in Paris at eleven fifteen. As he could not catch the midnight boat at Southampton—and the instructions to the captain on that point were explicit—he cannot reach France until this evening via Newhaven and Dieppe."

"Do you think he will come back?"

"Yes; he never gives up. He will return to Paris; but it will be too late. We will be far away."

"And Mademoiselle Destange?"

"I am to see her in an hour."

"At her house?"

"Oh! no; she will not return there for several days. But you, Dubreuil, you must hurry. The loading of our goods will take a long time and you should be there to look after them."

"Are you sure that we are not being watched?"

"By whom? I am not afraid of anyone but Sholmes."

Dubreuil retired. Felix Davey made a last tour of the apartment, picked up two or three torn letters, then, noticing a piece of chalk, he took it and, on the dark paper of the drawing-room, drew a large frame and wrote within it the following:

"*Arsène Lupin, gentleman-burglar, lived here for five years at the beginning of the twentieth century.*"

This little pleasantry seemed to please him very much. He looked at it for a moment, whistling a lively air, then said to himself:

"Now that I have placed myself in touch with the historians of future generations, I can go. You must hurry, Herlock Sholmes, as I shall leave my present abode in three minutes, and your defeat will be an accomplished fact.... Two minutes more! you are keeping me waiting, Monsieur Sholmes.... One minute more! Are you not coming? Well, then, I proclaim your downfall and my apotheosis. And now I make my escape. Farewell, kingdom of Arsène Lupin! I shall never see you again. Farewell to the fifty-five rooms of the six apartments over which I reigned! Farewell, my own royal bed chamber!"

His outburst of joy was interrupted by the sharp ringing of a bell, which stopped twice, started again and then ceased. It was the alarm bell.

What was wrong? What unforeseen danger? Ganimard? No; that wasn't possible!

He was on the point of returning to his library and making his escape. But, first, he went to the window. There was no one in the street. Was the enemy already in the house? He listened and thought he could discern certain confused sounds. He hesitated no longer. He ran to his library, and as he crossed the threshold he heard the noise of a key being inserted in the lock of the vestibule door.

"The deuce!" he murmured; "I have no time to lose. The house may be surrounded. The servants' stairway—impossible! Fortunately, there is the chimney."

He pushed the moulding; it did not move. He made a greater effort—still it refused to move. At the same time he had the impression that the door below opened and that he could hear footsteps.

"Good God!" he cried; "I am lost if this cursed mechanism—"

He pushed with all his strength. Nothing moved—nothing! By some incredible accident, by some evil stroke of fortune, the mechanism, which had worked only a few moments ago, would not work now.

He was furious. The block of marble remained immovable. He uttered frightful imprecations on the senseless stone. Was his escape to be prevented by that stupid obstacle? He struck the marble wildly, madly; he hammered it, he cursed it.

"Ah! what's the matter, Monsieur Lupin? You seem to be displeased about something."

Lupin turned around. Herlock Sholmes stood before him!

Herlock Sholmes!... Lupin gazed at him with squinting eyes as if his sight were defective and misleading. Herlock Sholmes in Paris! Herlock Sholmes, whom he had shipped to England only the day before as a dangerous person, now stood before him free and victorious!... Ah! such a thing was nothing less than a miracle; it was contrary to all natural laws; it was the culmination of all that is illogical and abnormal.... Herlock Sholmes here—before his face!

And when the Englishman spoke his words were tinged with that keen sarcasm and mocking politeness with which his adversary had so often lashed him. He said:

"Monsieur Lupin, in, the first place I have the honor to inform you that at this time and place I blot from my memory forever all thoughts of the miserable night that you forced me to endure in the house of Baron d'Hautrec, of the injury done to my friend Wilson, of my abduction in the automobile, and of the voyage I took yesterday under your orders, bound to a very uncomfortable couch. But the joy of this moment effaces all those bitter memories. I forgive everything. I forget everything—I wipe out the debt. I am paid—and royally paid."

Lupin made no reply. So the Englishman continued:

"Don't you think so yourself?"

He appeared to insist as if demanding an acquiescence, as a sort of receipt in regard to the part.

After a moment's reflection, during which the Englishman felt that he was scrutinized to the very depth of his soul, Lupin declared:

"I presume, monsieur, that your conduct is based upon serious motives?"

"Very serious."

"The fact that you have escaped from my captain and his crew is only a secondary incident of our struggle. But the fact that you are here before me alone—understand, alone—face to face with Arsène Lupin, leads me to think that your revenge is as complete as possible."

"As complete as possible."

"This house?"

"Surrounded."

"The two adjoining houses?"

"Surrounded."

"The apartment above this?"

"The *three* apartments on the fifth floor that were formerly occupied by Monsieur Dubreuil are surrounded."

"So that——"

"So that you are captured, Monsieur Lupin—absolutely captured."

The feelings that Sholmes had experienced during his trip in the automobile were now suffered by Lupin, the same concentrated fury, the same revolt, and also, let us admit, the same loyalty of submission to force of circumstances. Equally brave in victory or defeat.

"Our accounts are squared, monsieur," said Lupin, frankly.

The Englishman was pleased with that confession. After a short silence Lupin, now quite self-possessed, said smiling:

219

"And I am not sorry! It becomes monotonous to win all the time. Yesterday I had only to stretch out my hand to finish you forever. Today I belong to you. The game is yours." Lupin laughed heartily and then continued: "At last the gallery will be entertained! Lupin in prison! How will he get out? In prison!... What an adventure!... Ah! Sholmes, life is just one damn thing after another!"

He pressed his closed hands to his temples as if to suppress the tumultuous joy that surged within him, and his actions indicated that he was moved by an uncontrollable mirth. At last, when he had recovered his self-possession, he approached the detective and said:

"And now what are you waiting for?"

"What am I waiting for?"

"Yes; Ganimard is here with his men—why don't they come in?"

"I asked him not to."

"And he consented?"

"I accepted his services on condition that he would be guided by me. Besides, he thinks that Felix Davey is only an accomplice of Arsène Lupin."

"Then I will repeat my question in another form. Why did you come in alone?"

"Because I wished to speak to you alone."

"Ah! ah! you have something to say to me."

That idea seemed to please Lupin immensely. There are certain circumstances in which words are preferable to deeds.

"Monsieur Sholmes, I am sorry I cannot offer you an easy chair. How would you like that broken box? Or perhaps you would prefer the window ledge? I am sure a glass of beer would be welcome ... light or dark?... But sit down, please."

"Thank you; we can talk as well standing up."

"Very well—proceed."

"I will be brief. The object of my sojourn in France was not to accomplish your arrest. If I have been led to pursue you, it was because I saw no other way to achieve my real object."

"Which was?"

"To recover the blue diamond."

"The blue diamond!"

"Certainly; since the one found in Herr Bleichen's tooth-powder was only an imitation."

"Quite right; the genuine diamond was taken by the blonde Lady. I made an exact duplicate of it and then, as I had designs on other jewels belonging to the Countess and as the Consul Herr Bleichen was already under suspicion, the aforesaid blonde Lady, in order to avert suspicion, slipped the false stone into the aforesaid Consul's luggage."

"While you kept the genuine diamond?"

"Of course."

"That diamond—I want it."

"I am very sorry, but it is impossible."

"I have promised it to the Countess de Crozon. I must have it."

"How will you get it, since it is in my possession?"

"That is precisely the reason—because it is in your possession."

"Oh! I am to give it to you?"

"Yes."

"Voluntarily?"

"I will buy it."

"Ah!" exclaimed Lupin, in an access of mirth, "you are certainly an Englishman. You treat this as a matter of business."

"It is a matter of business."

"Well? what is your offer?"

"The liberty of Mademoiselle Destange."

"Her liberty?... I didn't know she was under arrest."

"I will give Monsieur Ganimard the necessary information. When deprived of your protection, she can readily be taken."

Lupin laughed again, and said:

"My dear monsieur, you are offering me something you do not possess. Mademoiselle Destange is in a place of safety, and has nothing to fear. You must make me another offer."

The Englishman hesitated, visibly embarrassed and vexed. Then, placing his hand on the shoulder of his adversary, he said:

"And if I should propose to you-"

"My liberty?"

"No ... but I can leave the room to consult with Ganimard."

"And leave me alone!"

"Yes."

"Ah! mon dieu, what good would that be? The cursed mechanism will not work," said Lupin, at the same time savagely pushing the moulding of the mantel. He stifled a cry of surprise; this time fortune favored him—the block of marble moved. It was his salvation; his hope of escape. In that event, why submit to the conditions imposed by Sholmes? He paced up and

221

down the room, as if he were considering his reply. Then, in his turn, he placed his hand on the shoulder of his adversary, and said:

"All things considered, Monsieur Sholmes, I prefer to do my own business in my own way."

"But—"

"No, I don't require anyone's assistance."

"When Ganimard gets his hand on you, it will be all over. You can't escape from them."

"Who knows?"

"Come, that is foolish. Every door and window is guarded."

"Except one."

"Which?"

"*The one I will choose.*"

"Mere words! Your arrest is as good as made."

"Oh! no—not at all."

"Well?"

"I shall keep the blue diamond."

Sholmes looked at his watch, and said:

"It is now ten minutes to three. At three o'clock I shall call Ganimard."

"Well, then, we have ten minutes to chat. And to satisfy my curiosity, Monsieur Sholmes, I should like to know how you procured my address and my name of Felix Davey?"

Although his adversary's easy manner caused Sholmes some anxiety, he was willing to give Lupin the desired information since it reflected credit on his professional astuteness; so he replied:

"Your address? I got it from the blonde Lady."

"Clotilde!"

"Herself. Do you remember, yesterday morning, when I wished to take her away in the automobile, she telephoned to her dressmaker."

"Well?"

"Well, I understood, later, that you were the dressmaker. And last night, on the boat, by exercising my memory—and my memory is something I have good reason to be proud of—I was able to recollect the last two figures of your telephone number—73. Then, as I possessed a list of the houses you had 'improved,' it was an easy matter, on my arrival in Paris at eleven o'clock this morning, to search in the telephone directory and find there the name and address of Felix Davey. Having obtained that information, I asked the aid of Monsieur Ganimard."

"Admirable! I congratulate you. But bow did you manage to catch the eight o'clock train at Havre! How did you escape from *The Swallow*?"

"I did not escape."

"But——"

"You ordered the captain not to reach Southampton before one o'clock. He landed me there at midnight. I was able to catch the twelve o'clock boat for Havre."

"Did the captain betray me? I can't believe it."

"No, he did not betray you."

"Well, what then?"

"It was his watch."

"His watch?"

"Yes, I put it ahead one hour."

"How?"

"In the usual way, by turning the hands. We were sitting side by side, talking, and I was telling him some funny stories.... Why! he never saw mc do it."

"Bravo! a very clever trick. I shall not forget it. But the clock that was hanging on the wall of the cabin?"

"Ah! the clock was a more difficult matter, as my feet were tied, but the sailor, who guarded me during the captain's absence, was kind enough to turn the hands for me."

"He? Nonsense! He wouldn't do it."

"Oh! but he didn't know the importance of his act. I told him I must catch the first train for London, at any price, and ... he allowed himself to be persuaded——"

"By means of——"

"By means of a slight gift, which the excellent fellow, loyal and true to his master, intends to send to you."

"What was it!"

"A mere trifle."

"But what?"

"The blue diamond."

"The blue diamond!"

"Yes, the false stone that you substituted for the Countess' diamond. She gave it to me."

There was a sudden explosion of violent laughter. Lupin laughed until the tears started in his eyes.

"Mon dieu, but it is funny! My false diamond palmed off on my innocent sailor! And the captain's watch! And the hands of the clock!"

Sholmes felt that the duel between him and Lupin was keener than ever. His marvellous instinct warned him that, behind his adversary's display of mirth, there was a shrewd intellect debating the ways and means to escape. Gradually Lupin approached the Englishman, who recoiled, and, unconsciously, slipped his hand into his watch-pocket.

"It is three o'clock, Monsieur Lupin."

"Three o'clock, already! What a pity! We were enjoying our chat so much."

"I am waiting for your answer."

"My answer? Mon dieu! but you are particular!... And so this is the last move in our little game—and the stake is my liberty!"

"Or the blue diamond."

"Very well. It's your play. What are you going to do!"

"I play the king," said Sholmes, as he fired his revolver.

"And I the ace," replied Lupin, as he struck at Sholmes with his fist.

Sholmes had fired into the air, as a signal to Ganimard, whose assistance he required. But Lupin's fist had caught Sholmes in the stomach, and caused him to double up with pain. Lupin rushed to the fireplace and set the marble slab in motion.... Too late! The door opened.

"Surrender, Lupin, or I fire!"

Ganimard, doubtless stationed closer than Lupin had thought, Ganimard was there, with his revolver turned on Lupin. And behind Ganimard there were twenty men, strong and ruthless fellows, who would beat him like a dog at the least sign of resistance.

"Hands down! I surrender!" said Lupin, calmly; and he folded his arms across his breast.

Everyone was amazed. In the room, divested of its furniture and hangings, Arsène Lupin's words sounded like an echo.... "I surrender!" ... It seemed incredible. No one would have been astonished if he had suddenly vanished through a trap, or if a section of the wall had rolled away and allowed him to escape. But he surrendered!

Ganimard advanced, nervously, and with all the gravity that the importance of the occasion demanded, he placed his hand on the shoulder of his adversary, and had the infinite pleasure of saying:

"I arrest you, Arsène Lupin."

"Brrr!" said Lupin, "you make me shiver, my dear Ganimard. What a lugubrious face! One would imagine you were speaking over the grave of a friend. For Heaven's sakc, don't assume such a funereal air."

"I arrest you."

"Don't let that worry you! In the name of the law, of which he is a well-deserving pillar, Ganimard, the celebrated Parisian detective, arrests the wicked Arsène Lupin. An historic event, of which you will appreciate the true importance.... And it is the second time that it has happened. Bravo, Ganimard, you are sure of advancement in your chosen profession!"

And he held out his wrists for the hand-cuffs. Ganimard adjusted them in a most solemn manner. The numerous policemen, despite their customary presumption and the bitterness of their feelings toward Lupin, conducted themselves with becoming modesty, astonished at being permitted to gaze upon that mysterious and intangible creature.

"My poor Lupin," sighed our hero, "what would your aristocratic friends say if they should see you in this humiliating position?"

He pulled his wrists apart with all his strength. The veins in his forehead expanded. The links of the chain cut into his flesh. The chain fell off—broken.

"Another, comrades, that one was useless."

They placed two on him this time.

"Quite right," he said. "You cannot be too careful."

Then, counting the detectives and policemen, he said:

"How many are you, my friends? Twenty-five? Thirty? That's too many. I can't do anything. Ah! if there had been only fifteen!"

There was something fascinating about Lupin; it was the fascination of the great actor who plays his rôle with spirit and understanding, combined with assurance and ease. Sholmes regarded him as one might regard a beautiful painting with a due appreciation of all its perfection in coloring and technique. And he really thought that it was an equal struggle between those thirty men on one side, armed as they were with all the strength and majesty of the law, and, on the other side, that solitary individual, unarmed and handcuffed. Yes, the two sides were well-matched.

"Well, master," said Lupin to the Englishman, "this is your work. Thanks to you, Lupin is going to rot on the damp straw of a dungeon. Confess that your conscience pricks you a little, and that your soul is filled with remorse."

In spite of himself, Sholmes shrugged his shoulders, as if to say: "It's your own fault."

"Never! never!" exclaimed Lupin. "Give you the blue diamond? Oh! no, it has cost me too much trouble. I intend to keep it. On my occasion of my first visit to you in London—which will probably be next month—I will tell you my reasons. But will you be in London next month? Or do you prefer Vienna? Or Saint Petersburg?"

Then Lupin received a surprise. A bell commenced to ring. It was not the alarm-bell, but the bell of the telephone which was located between the two windows of the room and had not yet been removed.

The telephone! Ah! Who could it be? Who was about to fall into this unfortunate trap? Arsène Lupin exhibited an access of rage against the unlucky instrument as if he would like to break it into a thousand pieces and thus stifle the mysterious voice that was calling for him. But it was Ganimard who took down the receiver, and said:

"Hello!... Hello!... number 648.73 ... yes, this is it."

Then Sholmes stepped up, and, with an air of authority, pushed Ganimard aside, took the receiver, and covered the transmitter with his handkerchief in order to obscure the tone of his voice. At that moment he glanced toward Lupin, and the look which they exchanged indicated that the same idea had occurred to each of them, and that they fore-saw the ultimate result of that theory: it was the blonde Lady who was telephoning. She wished to telephone to Felix Davey, or rather to Maxime Bermond, and it was to Sholmes she was about to speak. The Englishman said:

"Hello ... Hello!"

Then, after a silence, he said:

"Yes, it is I, Maxime."

The drama had commenced and was progressing with tragic precision. Lupin, the irrepressible and nonchalant Lupin, did not attempt to conceal his anxiety, and he strained every nerve in a desire to hear or, at least, to divine the purport of the conversation. And Sholmes continued, in reply to the mysterious voice:

"Hello!... Hello!... Yes, everything has been moved, and I am just ready to leave here and meet you as we agreed.... Where?... Where you are now.... Don't believe that he is here yet!..."

Sholmes stopped, seeking for words. It was clear that he was trying to question the girl without betraying himself, and that he was ignorant of her whereabouts. Moreover, Ganimard's presence seemed to embarrass him.... Ah! if some miracle would only interrupt that cursed conversation! Lupin prayed for it with all his strength, with all the intensity of his incited nerves! After a momentary pause, Sholmes continued:

"Hello!... Hello!... Do you hear me?... I can't hear you very well.... Can scarcely make out what you say.... Are you listening? Well, I think you had better return home.... No danger now.... But he is in England! I have received a telegram from Southampton announcing his arrival."

The sarcasm of those words! Sholmes uttered them with an inexpressible comfort. And he added:

"Very well, don't lose any time. I will meet you there."

He hung up the receiver.

"Monsieur Ganimard, can you furnish me with three men?"

"For the blonde Lady, eh?"

"Yes."

"You know who she is, and where she is?"

"Yes."

"Good! That settles Monsieur Lupin.... Folenfant, take two men, and go with Monsieur Sholmes."

The Englishman departed, accompanied by the three men.

The game was ended. The blonde Lady was, also, about to fall into the hands of the Englishman. Thanks to his commendable persistence and to a combination of fortuitous circumstances, the battle had resulted in a victory for the detective, and in irreparable disaster for Lupin.

"Monsieur Sholmes!"

The Englishman stopped.

"Monsieur Lupin?"

Lupin was clearly shattered by this final blow. His forehead was marked by deep wrinkles. He was sullen and dejected. However, he pulled himself together, and, notwithstanding his defeat, he exclaimed, in a cheerful tone:

"You will concede that fate has been against me. A few minutes ago, it prevented my escape through that chimney, and delivered me into your hands. Now, by means of the telephone, it presents you with the blonde Lady. I submit to its decrees."

"What do you mean?"

"I mean that I am ready to re-open our negotiation."

Sholmes took Ganimard aside and asked, in a manner that did not permit a reply, the authority to exchange a few words with the prisoner. Then he approached Lupin, and said, in a sharp, nervous tone:

"What do you want?"

"Mademoiselle Destange's liberty."

"You know the price."

"Yes."

"And you accept?"

"Yes; I accept your terms."

"Ah!" said the Englishman, in surprise, "but ... you refused ... for yourself——"

"Yes, I can look out for myself, Monsieur Sholmes, but now the question concerns a young woman ... and a woman I love. In France, understand, we have very decided ideas about such things. And Lupin has the same feelings as other people."

He spoke with simplicity and candor. Sholmes replied by an almost imperceptible inclination of his head, and murmured:

"Very well, the blue diamond."

"Take my cane, there, at the end of the mantel. Press on the head of the cane with one hand, and, with the other, turn the iron ferrule at the bottom."

Holmes took the cane and followed the directions. As he did so, the head of the cane divided and disclosed a cavity which contained a small ball of wax which, in turn, enclosed a diamond. He examined it. It was the blue diamond.

"Monsieur Lupin, Mademoiselle Destange is free."

"Is her future safety assured? Has she nothing to fear from you?"

"Neither from me, nor anyone else."

"How can you manage it?"

"Quite easily. I have forgotten her name and address."

"Thank you. And au revoir—for I will see you again, sometime, Monsieur Sholmes?"

"I have no doubt of it."

Then followed an animated conversation between Sholmes and Ganimard, which was abruptly terminated by the Englishman, who said:

"I am very sorry, Monsieur Ganimard, that we cannot agree on that point, but I have no time to waste trying to convince you. I leave for England within an hour."

"But ... the blonde Lady?"

"I do not know such a person."

"And yet, a moment ago——"

"You must take the affair as it stands. I have delivered Arsène Lupin into your hands. Here is the blue diamond, which you will have the pleasure of returning to the Countess de Crozon. What more do you want?"

"The blonde Lady."

"Find her."

Sholmes pulled his cap down over his forehead and walked rapidly away, like a man who is accustomed to go as soon as his business is finished.

"Bon voyage, monsieur," cried Lupin, "and, believe me, I shall never forget the friendly way in which our little business affairs have been arranged. My regards to Monsieur Wilson."

Not receiving any reply, Lupin added, sneeringly:

"That is what is called 'taking British leave.' Ah! their insular dignity lacks the flower of courtesy by which we are distinguished. Consider for a moment, Ganimard, what a charming exit a Frenchman would have made under similar circumstances! With what exquisite courtesy he would have masked his triumph!... But, God bless me, Ganimard, what are you doing? Making a search? Come, what's the use? There is nothing left—not even a scrap of paper. I assure you my archives are in a safe place."

"I am not so sure of that," replied Ganimard. "I must search everything."

Lupin submitted to the operation. Held by two detectives and surrounded by the others, he patiently endured the proceedings for twenty minutes, then he said:

"Hurry up, Ganimard, and finish!"

"You are in a hurry."

"Of course I am. An important appointment."

"At the police station?"

"No; in the city."

"Ah! at what time?"

"Two o'clock."

"It is three o'clock now."

"Just so; I will be late. And punctuality is one of my virtues."

"Well, give me five minutes."

"Not a second more," said Lupin.

"I am doing my best to expedite——"

"Oh! don't talk so much.... Still searching that cupboard? It is empty."

"Here are some letters."

"Old invoices, I presume!"

"No; a packet tied with a ribbon."

"A red ribbon? Oh! Ganimard, for God's sake, don't untie it!"

"From a woman?"

"Yes."

"A woman of the world?"

"The best in the world."

"Her name?"

"Madame Ganimard."

"Very funny! very funny!" exclaimed the detective.

At that moment the men, who had been sent to search the other rooms, returned and announced their failure to find anything. Lupin laughed and said:

"Parbleu! Did you expect to find my visiting list, or evidence of my business relations with the Emperor of Germany? But I can tell you what you should investigate, Ganimard: All the little mysteries of this apartment. For instance, that gas-pipe is a speaking tube. That chimney contains a stairway. That wall is hollow. And the marvellous system of bells! Ah! Ganimard, just press that button!"

Ganimard obeyed.

"Did you hear anything?" asked Lupin.

"No."

"Neither did I. And yet you notified my aeronaut to prepare the dirigible balloon which will soon carry us into the clouds.

"Come!" said Ganimard, who had completed his search; "we've had enough nonsense—let's be off."

He started away, followed by his men. Lupin did not move. His guardians pushed him in vain.

"Well," said Ganimard, "do you refuse to go?"

"Not at all. But it depends."

"On what?"

"Where you want to take me."

"To the station-house, of course."

"Then I refuse to go. I have no business there."

"Are you crazy?"

"Did I not tell you that I had an important appointment?"

"Lupin!"

"Why, Ganimard, I have an appointment with the blonde Lady, and do you suppose I would be so discourteous as to cause her a moment's anxiety? That would be very ungentlemanly."

"Listen, Lupin," said the detective, who was becoming annoyed by this persiflage; "I have been very patient with you, but I will endure no more. Follow me."

"Impossible; I have an appointment and I shall keep it."

"For the last time—follow me!"

"Im-pos-sible!"

At a sign from Ganimard two men seized Lupin by the arms; but they released him at once, uttering cries of pain. Lupin had thrust two long needles into them. The other men now rushed at Lupin with cries of rage and hatred, eager to avenge their comrades and to avenge themselves for the many affronts he had heaped upon them; and now they struck and beat him to their heart's desire. A violent blow on the temple felled Lupin to the floor.

"If you hurt him you will answer to me," growled Ganimard, in a rage.

He leaned over Lupin to ascertain his condition. Then, learning that he was breathing freely, Ganimard ordered his men to carry the prisoner by the head and feet, while he himself supported the body.

"Go gently, now!... Don't jolt him. Ah! the brutes would have killed him.... Well, Lupin, how goes it?"

"None too well, Ganimard ... you let them knock me out."

"It was your own fault; you were so obstinate," replied Ganimard. "But I hope they didn't hurt you."

They had left the apartment and were now on the landing. Lupin groaned and stammered:

"Ganimard ... the elevator ... they are breaking my bones."

"A good idea, an excellent idea," replied Ganimard. "Besides, the stairway is too narrow."

He summoned the elevator. They placed Lupin on the seat with the greatest care. Ganimard took his place beside him and said to his men:

"Go down the stairs and wait for me below. Understand?"

Ganimard closed the door of the elevator. Suddenly the elevator shot upward like a balloon released from its cable. Lupin burst into a fit of sardonic laughter.

"Good God!" cried Ganimard, as he made a frantic search in the dark for the button of descent. Having found it, he cried:

"The fifth floor! Watch the door of the fifth floor."

His assistants clambered up the stairs, two and three steps at a time. But this strange circumstance happened: The elevator seemed to break through the ceiling of the last floor, disappeared from the sight of Ganimard's assistants, suddenly made its appearance on the upper floor—the servants' floor—and stopped. Three men were there waiting for it. They opened the door. Two of them seized Ganimard, who, astonished at the sudden attack, scarcely made any defence. The other man carried off Lupin.

"I warned you, Ganimard ... about the dirigible balloon. Another time, don't be so tender-hearted. And, moreover, remember that Arsène Lupin doesn't allow himself to be struck and knocked down without sufficient reason. Adieu."

The door of the elevator was already closed on Ganimard, and the machine began to descend; and it all happened so quickly that the old detective reached the ground floor as soon as his assistants. Without exchanging a word they crossed the court and ascended the servants' stairway, which was the only way to reach the servants' floor through which the escape had been made.

A long corridor with several turns and bordered with little numbered rooms led to a door that was not locked. On the other side of this door and, therefore, in another house there was another corridor with similar turns and similar rooms, and at the end of it a servants' stairway. Ganimard descended it, crossed a court and a vestibule and found himself in the rue Picot. Then he understood the situation: the two houses, built the entire depth of the lots, touched at the rear, while the fronts of the houses faced upon two streets that ran parallel to each other at a distance of more than sixty metres apart.

He found the concierge and, showing his card, enquired:

"Did four men pass here just now?"

"Yes; the two servants from the fourth and fifth floors, with two friends."

"Who lives on the fourth and fifth floors?"

"Two men named Fauvel and their cousins, whose name is Provost. They moved to-day, leaving the two servants, who went away just now."

"Ah!" thought Ganimard; "what a grand opportunity we have missed! The entire band lived in these houses."

And he sank down on a chair in despair.

Forty minutes later two gentlemen were driven up to the station of the Northern Railway and hurried to the Calais express, followed by a porter who carried their valises. One of them had his arm in a sling, and the pallor of his face denoted some illness. The other man was in a jovial mood.

"We must hurry, Wilson, or we will miss the train.... Ah! Wilson, I shall never forget these ten days."

"Neither will I."

"Ah! it was a great struggle!"

"Superb!"

"A few repulses, here and there—"

"Of no consequence."

"And, at last, victory all along the line. Lupin arrested! The blue diamond recovered!"

"My arm broken!"

"What does a broken arm count for in such a victory as that?"

"Especially when it is my arm."

"Ah! yes, don't you remember, Wilson, that it was at the very time you were in the pharmacy, suffering like a hero, that I discovered the clue to the whole mystery?"

"How lucky!"

The doors of the carriages were being closed.

"All aboard. Hurry up, gentlemen!"

The porter climbed into an empty compartment and placed their valises in the rack, whilst Sholmes assisted the unfortunate Wilson.

"What's the matter, Wilson? You're not done up, are you? Come, pull your nerves together."

"My nerves are all right."

"Well, what is it, then?"

"I have only one hand."

"What of it?" exclaimed Sholmes, cheerfully. "You are not the only one who has had a broken arm. Cheer up!"

Sholmes handed the porter a piece of fifty centimes.

"Thank you, Monsieur Sholmes," said the porter.

The Englishman looked at him; it was Arsène Lupin.

"You!... you!" he stammered, absolutely astounded.

And Wilson brandished his sound arm in the manner of a man who demonstrates a fact as he said:

"You! you! but you were arrested! Sholmes told me so. When he left you Ganimard and thirty men had you in charge."

Lupin folded his arms and said, with an air of indignation:

"Did you suppose I would let you go away without bidding you adieu? After the very friendly relations that have always existed between us! That would be discourteous and ungrateful on my part."

The train whistled. Lupin continued:

"I beg your pardon, but have you everything you need? Tobacco and matches ... yes ... and the evening papers? You will find in them an account of my arrest—your last exploit, Monsieur Sholmes. And now, au revoir. Am delighted to have made your acquaintance. And if ever I can be of any service to you, I shall be only too happy...." He leaped to the platform and closed the door.

"Adieu," he repeated, waving his handkerchief. "Adieu.... I shall write to you.... You will write also, eh? And your arm broken, Wilson.... I am truly sorry.... I shall expect to hear from both of you. A postal card, now and then, simply address: Lupin, Paris. That is sufficient.... Adieu.... See you soon."

CHAPTER VII.

THE JEWISH LAMP.

Herlock Sholmes and Wilson were sitting in front of the fireplace, in comfortable armchairs, with the feet extended toward the grateful warmth of a glowing coke fire.

Sholmes' pipe, a short brier with a silver band, had gone out. He knocked out the ashes, filled it, lighted it, pulled the skirts of his dressing-gown over his knees, and drew from his pipe great puffs of smoke, which ascended toward the ceiling in scores of shadow rings.

Wilson gazed at him, as a dog lying curled up on a rug before the fire might look at his master, with great round eyes which have no hope other than to obey the least gesture of his owner. Was the master going to break the silence? Would he reveal to Wilson the subject of his reverie and admit his satellite into the charmed realm of his thoughts? When Sholmes had maintained his silent attitude for some time. Wilson ventured to speak:

"Everything seems quiet now. Not the shadow of a case to occupy our leisure moments."

Sholmes did not reply, but the rings of smoke emitted by Sholmes were better formed, and Wilson observed that his companion drew considerable pleasure from that trifling fact—an indication that the great man was not absorbed in any serious meditation. Wilson, discouraged, arose and went to the window.

The lonely street extended between the gloomy façades of grimy houses, unusually gloomy this morning by reason of a heavy downfall of rain. A cab passed; then another. Wilson made an entry of their numbers in his memorandum-book. One never knows!

"Ah!" he exclaimed, "the postman."

The man entered, shown in by the servant.

"Two registered letters, sir ... if you will sign, please?"

Sholmes signed the receipts, accompanied the man to the door, and was opening one of the letters as he returned.

"It seems to please you," remarked Wilson, after a moment's silence.

"This letter contains a very interesting proposition. You are anxious for a case—here's one. Read——"

Wilson read:

"Monsieur,

"I desire the benefit of your services and experience. I have been the victim of a serious theft, and the investigation has as yet been unsuccessful. I am sending to you by this mail a number of newspapers which will inform you of the affair, and if you will undertake the case, I will

234

place my house at your disposal and ask you to fill in the enclosed check, signed by me, for whatever sum you require for your expenses.

"Kindly reply by telegraph, and much oblige,

"Your humble servant,

"Baron Victor d'Imblevalle,

"18 rue Murillo, Paris."

"Ah!" exclaimed Sholmes, "that sounds good ... a little trip to Paris ... and why not, Wilson? Since my famous duel with Arsène Lupin, I have not had an excuse to go there. I should be pleased to visit the capital of the world under less strenuous conditions."

He tore the check into four pieces and, while Wilson, whose arm had not yet regained its former strength, uttered bitter words against Paris and the Parisians, Sholmes opened the second envelope. Immediately, he made a gesture of annoyance, and a wrinkle appeared on his forehead during the reading of the letter; then, crushing the paper into a ball, he threw it, angrily, on the floor.

"Well? What's the matter?" asked Wilson, anxiously.

He picked up the ball of paper, unfolded it, and read, with increasing amazement:

"My Dear Monsieur:

"You know full well the admiration I have for you and the interest I take in your renown. Well, believe me, when I warn you to have nothing whatever to do with the case on which you have just now been called to Paris. Your intervention will cause much harm; your efforts will produce a most lamentable result; and you will be obliged to make a public confession of your defeat.

"Having a sincere desire to spare you such humiliation, I implore you, in the name of the friendship that unites us, to remain peacefully reposing at your own fireside.

"My best wishes to Monsieur Wilson, and, for yourself, the sincere regards of your devoted ARSÈNE LUPIN."

"Arsène Lupin!" repeated Wilson, astounded.

Sholmes struck the table with his fist, and exclaimed:

"Ah! he is pestering me already, the fool! He laughs at me as if I were a schoolboy! The public confession of my defeat! Didn't I force him to disgorge the blue diamond?"

"I tell you—he's afraid," suggested Wilson.

"Nonsense! Arsène Lupin is not afraid, and this taunting letter proves it."

"But how did he know that the Baron d'Imblevalle had written to you?"

"What do I know about it? You do ask some stupid questions, my boy."

"I thought ... I supposed——"

"What? That I am a clairvoyant? Or a sorcerer?"

"No, but I have seen you do some marvellous things."

"No person can perform *marvellous* things. I no more than you. I reflect, I deduct, I conclude—that is all; but I do not divine. Only fools divine."

Wilson assumed the attitude of a whipped cur, and resolved not to make a fool of himself by trying to divine why Sholmes paced the room with quick, nervous strides. But when Sholmes rang for the servant and ordered his valise, Wilson thought that he was in possession of a material fact which gave him the right to reflect, deduct and conclude that his associate was about to take a journey. The same mental operation permitted him to assert, with almost mathematical exactness:

"Sholmes, you are going to Paris."

"Possibly."

"And Lupin's affront impels you to go, rather than the desire to assist the Baron d'Imblevalle."

"Possibly."

"Sholmes, I shall go with you."

"Ah; ah! my old friend," exclaimed Sholmes, interrupting his walking, "you are not afraid that your right arm will meet the same fate as your left?"

"What can happen to me? You will be there."

"That's the way to talk, Wilson. We will show that clever Frenchman that he made a mistake when he threw his glove in our faces. Be quick, Wilson, we must catch the first train."

"Without waiting for the papers the baron has sent you?"

"What good are they?"

"I will send a telegram."

"No; if you do that, Arsène Lupin will know of my arrival. I wish to avoid that. This time, Wilson, we must fight under cover."

That afternoon, the two friends embarked at Dover. The passage was a delightful one. In the train from Calais to Paris, Sholmes had three hours sound sleep, while Wilson guarded the door of the compartment.

Sholmes awoke in good spirits. He was delighted at the idea of another duel with Arsène Lupin, and he rubbed his hands with the satisfied air of a man who looks forward to a pleasant vacation.

"At last!" exclaimed Wilson, "we are getting to work again."

And he rubbed his hands with the same satisfied air.

At the station, Sholmes took the wraps and, followed by Wilson, who carried the valises, he gave up his tickets and started off briskly.

"Fine weather, Wilson.... Blue sky and sunshine! Paris is giving us a royal reception."

"Yes, but what a crowd!"

"So much the better, Wilson, we will pass unnoticed. No one will recognize us in such a crowd."

"Is this Monsieur Sholmes?"

He stopped, somewhat puzzled. Who the deuce could thus address him by his name? A woman stood beside him; a young girl whose simple dress outlined her slender form and whose pretty face had a sad and anxious expression. She repeated her enquiry:

"You are Monsieur Sholmes?"

As he still remained silent, as much from confusion as from a habit of prudence, the girl asked a third time:

"Have I the honor of addressing Monsieur Sholmes?"

"What do you want?" he replied, testily, considering the incident a suspicious one.

"You must listen to me, Monsieur Sholmes, as it is a serious matter. I know that you are going to the rue Murillo."

"What do you say?"

"I know ... I know ... rue Murillo ... number 18. Well, you must not go ... no, you must not. I assure you that you will regret it. Do not think that I have any interest in the matter. I do it because it is right ... because my conscience tells me to do it."

Sholmes tried to get away, but she persisted:

"Oh! I beg of you, don't neglect my advice.... Ah! if I only knew how to convince you! Look at me! Look into my eyes! They are sincere ... they speak the truth."

She gazed at Sholmes, fearlessly but innocently, with those beautiful eyes, serious and clear, in which her very soul seemed to be reflected.

Wilson nodded his head, as he said:

"Mademoiselle looks honest."

"Yes," she implored, "and you must have confidence——"

"I have confidence in you, mademoiselle," replied Wilson.

"Oh, how happy you make me! And so has your friend? I feel it ... I am sure of it! What happiness! Everything will be all right now!... What a good idea of mine!... Ah! yes, there is a train for Calais in twenty minutes. You will take it.... Quick, follow me ... you must come this way ... there is just time."

She tried to drag them along. Sholmes seized her arm, and in as gentle a voice as he could assume, said to her:

"Excuse me, mademoiselle, if I cannot yield to your wishes, but I never abandon a task that I have once undertaken."

"I beseech you ... I implore you.... Ah if you could only understand!"

Sholmes passed outside and walked away at a quick pace. Wilson said to the girl:

"Have no fear ... he will be in at the finish. He never failed yet."

And he ran to overtake Sholmes.

HERLOCK SHOLMES—ARSÈNE LUPIN.

These words, in great black letters, met their gaze as soon as they left the railway station. A number of sandwich-men were parading through the street, one behind the other, carrying heavy canes with iron ferrules with which they struck the pavement in harmony, and, on their backs, they carried large posters, on which one could read the following notice:

THE   MATCH   BETWEEN   HERLOCK   SHOLMES AND   ARSÈNE   LUPIN.   ARRIVAL   OF   THE   ENGLISH CHAMPION.   THE   GREAT   DETECTIVE   ATTACKS THE   MYSTERY   OF   THE   RUE   MURILLO.   READ   THE DETAILS IN THE "ECHO DE FRANCE".

Wilson shook his head, and said:

"Look at that, Sholmes, and we thought we were traveling incognito! I shouldn't be surprised to find the republican guard waiting for us at the rue Murillo to give us an official reception with toasts and champagne."

"Wilson, when you get funny, you get beastly funny," growled Sholmes.

Then he approached one of the sandwich-men with the obvious intention of seizing him in his powerful grip and crushing him, together with his infernal sign-board. There was quite a crowd gathered about the men, reading the notices, and joking and laughing.

Repressing a furious access of rage, Sholmes said to the man:

"When did they hire you?"

"This morning."

"How long have you been parading?"

"About an hour."

"But the boards were ready before that?"

"Oh, yes, they were ready when we went to the agency this morning."

So then it appears that Arsène Lupin had foreseen that he, Sholmes, would accept the challenge. More than that, the letter written by Lupin showed that he was eager for the fray and that he was prepared to measure swords once more with his formidable rival. Why? What motive could Arsène Lupin have in renewing the struggle?

Sholmes hesitated for a moment. Lupin must be very confident of his success to show so much insolence in advance; and was not he, Sholmes, falling into a trap by rushing into the battle at the first call for help?

However, he called a carriage.

"Come, Wilson!... Driver, 18 rue Murillo!" he exclaimed, with an outburst of his accustomed energy. With distended veins and clenched fists, as if he were about to engage in a boxing bout, he jumped into the carriage.

The rue Murillo is bordered with magnificent private residences, the rear of which overlook the Parc Monceau. One of the most pretentious of these houses is number 18, owned and occupied by the Baron d'Imblevalle and furnished in a luxurious manner consistent with the owner's taste and wealth. There was a courtyard in front of the house, and, in the rear, a garden well filled with trees whose branches mingle with those of the park.

After ringing the bell, the two Englishmen were admitted, crossed the courtyard, and were received at the door by a footman who showed them into a small parlor facing the garden in the rear of the house. They sat down and, glancing about, made a rapid inspection of the many valuable objects with which the room was filled.

"Everything very choice," murmured Wilson, "and in the best of taste. It is a safe deduction to make that those who had the leisure to collect these articles must now be at least fifty years of age."

The door opened, and the Baron d'Imblevalle entered, followed by his wife. Contrary to the deduction made by Wilson, they were both quite young, of elegant appearance, and vivacious in speech and action. They were profuse in their expressions of gratitude.

"So kind of you to come! Sorry to have caused you so much trouble! The theft now seems of little consequence, since it has procured us this pleasure."

"How charming these French people are!" thought Wilson, evolving one of his commonplace deductions.

"But time is money," exclaimed the baron, "especially your time, Monsieur Sholmes. So I will come to the point. Now, what do you think of the affair? Do you think you can succeed in it?"

"Before I can answer that I must know what it is about."

"I thought you knew."

"No; so I must ask you for full particulars, even to the smallest detail. First, what is the nature of the case?"

"A theft."

"When did it take place?"

"Last Saturday," replied the baron, "or, at least, some time during Saturday night or Sunday morning."

"That was six days ago. Now, you can tell me all about it."

"In the first place, monsieur, I must tell you that my wife and I, conforming to the manner of life that our position demands, go out very little. The education of our children, a few receptions, and the care and decoration of our house—such constitutes our life; and nearly all our evenings are spent in this little room, which is my wife's boudoir, and in which we have gathered a few artistic objects. Last Saturday night, about eleven o'clock, I turned off the electric lights, and my wife and I retired, as usual, to our room."

"Where is your room?"

"It adjoins this. That is the door. Next morning, that is to say, Sunday morning, I arose quite early. As Suzanne, my wife, was still asleep, I passed into the boudoir as quietly as possible so as not to wake her. What was my astonishment when I found that window open—as we had left it closed the evening before!"

"A servant——"

"No one enters here in the morning until we ring. Besides, I always take the precaution to bolt the second door which communicates with the ante-chamber. Therefore, the window must have been opened from the outside. Besides, I have some evidence of that: the second pane of glass from the right—close to the fastening—had been cut."

"And what does that window overlook?"

"As you can see for yourself, it opens on a little balcony, surrounded by a stone railing. Here, we are on the first floor, and you can see the garden behind the house and the iron fence which separates it from the Parc Monceau. It is quite certain that the thief came through the park, climbed the fence by the aid of a ladder, and thus reached the terrace below the window."

"That is quite certain, you say!"

"Well, in the soft earth on either side of the fence, they found the two holes made by the bottom of the ladder, and two similar holes can be seen below the window. And the stone railing of the balcony shows two scratches which were doubtless made by the contact of the ladder."

"Is the Parc Monceau closed at night?"

"No; but if it were, there is a house in course of erection at number 14, and a person could enter that way."

Herlock Sholmes reflected for a few minutes, and then said:

"Let us come down to the theft. It must have been committed in this room?"

"Yes; there was here, between that twelfth century Virgin and that tabernacle of chased silver, a small Jewish lamp. It has disappeared."

"And is that all?"

"That is all."

"Ah!... And what is a Jewish lamp?"

"One of those copper lamps used by the ancient Jews, consisting of a standard which supported a bowl containing the oil, and from this bowl projected several burners intended for the wicks."

"Upon the whole, an object of small value."

"No great value, of course. But this one contained a secret hiding-place in which we were accustomed to place a magnificent jewel, a chimera in gold, set with rubies and emeralds, which was of great value."

"Why did you hide it there?"

"Oh! I can't give any reason, monsieur, unless it was an odd fancy to utilize a hiding-place of that kind."

"Did anyone know it?"

"No."

"No one—except the thief," said Sholmes. "Otherwise he would not have taken the trouble to steal the lamp."

"Of course. But how could he know it, as it was only by accident that the secret mechanism of the lamp was revealed to us."

"A similar accident has revealed it to some one else ... a servant ... or an acquaintance. But let us proceed: I suppose the police have been notified?"

"Yes. The examining magistrate has completed his investigation. The reporter-detectives attached to the leading newspapers have also made their investigations. But, as I wrote to you, it seems to me the mystery will never be solved."

Sholmes arose, went to the window, examined the casement, the balcony, the terrace, studied the scratches on the stone railing with his magnifying-glass, and then requested Mon. d'Imblevalle to show him the garden.

Outside, Sholmes sat down in a rattan chair and gazed at the roof of the house in a dreamy way. Then he walked over to the two little wooden boxes with which they had covered the holes made in the ground by the bottom of the ladder with a view of preserving them intact. He raised the boxes, kneeled on the ground, scrutinized the holes and made some measurements. After making a similar examination of the holes near the fence, he and the baron returned to the boudoir where Madame d'Imblevalle was waiting for them. After a short silence Sholmes said:

"At the very outset of your story, baron, I was surprised at the very simple methods employed by the thief. To raise a ladder, cut a window-pane, select a valuable article, and walk out again—no, that is not the way such things are done. All that is too plain, too simple."

"Well, what do you think?"

"That the Jewish lamp was stolen under the direction of Arsène Lupin."

"Arsène Lupin!" exclaimed the baron.

"Yes, but he did not do it himself, as no one came from the outside. Perhaps a servant descended from the upper floor by means of a waterspout that I noticed when I was in the garden."

"What makes you think so?"

"Arsène Lupin would not leave this room empty-handed."

"Empty-handed! But he had the lamp."

"But that would not have prevented his taking that snuff-box, set with diamonds, or that opal necklace. When he leaves anything, it is because he can't carry it away."

"But the marks of the ladder outside?"

"A false scent. Placed there simply to avert suspicion."

"And the scratches on the balustrade?"

"A farce! They were made with a piece of sandpaper. See, here are scraps of the paper that I picked up in the garden."

"And what about the marks made by the bottom of the ladder?"

"Counterfeit! Examine the two rectangular holes below the window, and the two holes near the fence. They are of a similar form, but I find that the two holes near the house are closer to each other than the two holes near the fence. What does that fact suggest? To me, it suggested that the four holes were made by a piece of wood prepared for the purpose."

"The better proof would be the piece of wood itself."

"Here it is," said Sholmes, "I found it in the garden, under the box of a laurel tree."

The baron bowed to Sholmes in recognition of his skill. Only forty minutes had elapsed since the Englishman had entered the house, and he had already exploded all the theories theretofore formed, and which had been based on what appeared to be obvious and undeniable facts. But what now appeared to be the real facts of the case rested upon a more solid foundation, to-wit, the astute reasoning of a Herlock Sholmes.

"The accusation which you make against one of our household is a very serious matter," said the baroness. "Our servants have been with us a long time and none of them would betray our trust."

"If none of them has betrayed you, how can you explain the fact that I received this letter on the same day and by the same mail as the letter you wrote to me?"

He handed to the baroness the letter that he had received from Arsène Lupin. She exclaimed, in amazement:

"Arsène Lupin! How could he know?"

"Did you tell anyone that you had written to me?"

"No one," replied the baron. "The idea occurred to us the other evening at the dinner-table."

"Before the servants?"

"No, only our two children. Oh, no ... Sophie and Henriette had left the table, hadn't they, Suzanne?"

Madame d'Imblevalle, after a moment's reflection, replied:

"Yes, they had gone to Mademoiselle."

"Mademoiselle?" queried Sholmes.

"The governess, Mademoiselle Alice Demun."

"Does she take her meals with you?"

"No. Her meals are served in her room."

Wilson had an idea. He said:

"The letter written to my friend Herlock Sholmes was posted?"

"Of course."

"Who posted it?"

"Dominique, who has been my valet for twenty years," replied the baron. "Any search in that direction would be a waste of time."

"One never wastes his time when engaged in a search," said Wilson, sententiously.

This preliminary investigation now ended, and Sholmes asked permission to retire.

At dinner, an hour later, he saw Sophie and Henriette, the two children of the family, one was six and the other eight years of age. There was very little conversation at the table. Sholmes responded to the friendly advances of his hosts in such a curt manner that they were soon reduced to silence. When the coffee was served, Sholmes swallowed the contents of his cup, and rose to take his leave.

At that moment, a servant entered with a telephone message addressed to Sholmes. He opened it, and read:

"You have my enthusiastic admiration. The results attained by you in so short a time are simply marvellous. I am dismayed.

"ARSÈNE LUPIN."

Sholmes made a gesture of indignation and handed the message to the baron, saying:

"What do you think now, monsieur? Are the walls of your house furnished with eyes and ears?"

"I don't understand it," said the baron, in amazement.

"Nor do I; but I do understand that Lupin has knowledge of everything that occurs in this house. He knows every movement, every word. There is no doubt of it. But how does he get his information? That is the first mystery I have to solve, and when I know that I will know everything."

That night, Wilson retired with the clear conscience of a man who has performed his whole duty and thus acquired an undoubted right to sleep and repose. So he fell asleep very quickly, and was soon enjoying the most delightful dreams in which he pursued Lupin and captured him single-handed; and the sensation was so vivid and exciting that it woke him from his sleep. Someone was standing at his bedside. He seized his revolver, and cried:

"Don't move, Lupin, or I'll fire."

"The deuce! Wilson, what do you mean?"

"Oh! it is you, Sholmes. Do you want me?"

"I want to show you something. Get up."

Sholmes led him to the window, and said:

"Look!... on the other side of the fence...."

"In the park?"

"Yes. What do you see?"

"I don't see anything."

"Yes, you do see something."

"Ah! of course, a shadow ... two of them."

"Yes, close to the fence. See, they are moving. Come, quick!"

Quickly they descended the stairs, and reached a room which opened into the garden. Through the glass door they could see the two shadowy forms in the same place.

"It is very strange," said Sholmes, "but it seems to me I can hear a noise inside the house."

"Inside the house? Impossible! Everybody is asleep."

"Well, listen——"

At that moment a low whistle came from the other side of the fence, and they perceived a dim light which appeared to come from the house.

"The baron must have turned on the light in his room. It is just above us."

"That must have been the noise you heard," said Wilson. "Perhaps they are watching the fence also."

Then there was a second whistle, softer than before.

"I don't understand it; I don't understand," said Sholmes, irritably.

"No more do I," confessed Wilson.

Sholmes turned the key, drew the bolt, and quietly opened the door. A third whistle, louder than before, and modulated to another form. And the noise above their heads became more pronounced. Sholmes said:

"It seems to be on the balcony outside the boudoir window."

He put his head through the half-opened door, but immediately recoiled, with a stifled oath. Then Wilson looked. Quite close to them there was a ladder, the upper end of which was resting on the balcony.

"The deuce!" said Sholmes, "there is someone in the boudoir. That is what we heard. Quick, let us remove the ladder."

But at that instant a man slid down the ladder and ran toward the spot where his accomplices were waiting for him outside the fence. He carried the ladder with him. Sholmes and Wilson pursued the man and overtook him just as he was placing the ladder against the fence. From the other side of the fence two shots were fired.

"Wounded?" cried Sholmes.

"No," replied Wilson.

Wilson seized the man by the body and tried to hold him, but the man turned and plunged a knife into Wilson's breast. He uttered a groan, staggered and fell.

"Damnation!" muttered Sholmes, "if they have killed him I will kill them."

He laid Wilson on the grass and rushed toward the ladder. Too late—the man had climbed the fence and, accompanied by his confederates, had fled through the bushes.

"Wilson, Wilson, it is not serious, hein? Merely a scratch."

The house door opened, and Monsieur d'Imblevalle appeared, followed by the servants, carrying candles.

"What's the matter?" asked the baron. "Is Monsieur Wilson wounded?"

"Oh! it's nothing—a mere scratch," repeated Sholmes, trying to deceive himself.

The blood was flowing profusely, and Wilson's face was livid. Twenty minutes later the doctor ascertained that the point of the knife had penetrated to within an inch and a half of the heart.

"An inch and a half of the heart! Wilson always was lucky!" said Sholmes, in an envious tone.

"Lucky ... lucky...." muttered the doctor.

"Of course! Why, with his robust constitution he will soon be out again."

"Six weeks in bed and two months of convalescence."

"Not more?"

"No, unless complications set in."

"Oh! the devil! what does he want complications for?"

Fully reassured, Sholmes joined the baron in the boudoir. This time the mysterious visitor had not exercised the same restraint. Ruthlessly, he had laid his vicious hand upon the diamond snuff-box, upon the opal necklace, and, in a general way, upon everything that could find a place in the greedy pockets of an enterprising burglar.

The window was still open; one of the window-panes had been neatly cut; and, in the morning, a summary investigation showed that the ladder belonged to the house then in course of construction.

"Now, you can see," said Mon. d'Imblevalle, with a touch of irony, "it is an exact repetition of the affair of the Jewish lamp."

"Yes, if we accept the first theory adopted by the police."

"Haven't you adopted it yet? Doesn't this second theft shatter your theory in regard to the first?"

"It only confirms it, monsieur."

"That is incredible! You have positive evidence that last night's theft was committed by an outsider, and yet you adhere to your theory that the Jewish lamp was stolen by someone in the house."

"Yes, I am sure of it."

"How do you explain it?"

"I do not explain anything, monsieur; I have established two facts which do not appear to have any relation to each other, and yet I am seeking the missing link that connects them."

His conviction seemed to be so earnest and positive that the baron submitted to it, and said:

"Very well, we will notify the police——"

"Not at all!" exclaimed the Englishman, quickly, "not at all! I intend to ask for their assistance when I need it—but not before."

"But the attack on your friend?"

"That's of no consequence. He is only wounded. Secure the license of the doctor. I shall be responsible for the legal side of the affair."

The next two days proved uneventful. Yet Sholmes was investigating the case with a minute care, and with a sense of wounded pride resulting from that audacious theft, committed under his nose, in spite of his presence and beyond his power to prevent it. He made a thorough investigation of the house and garden, interviewed the servants, and paid lengthy visits to the kitchen and stables. And, although his efforts were fruitless, he did not despair.

"I will succeed," he thought, "and the solution must be sought within the walls of this house. This affair is quite different from that of the blonde Lady, where I had to work in the dark, on unknown ground. This time I am on the battlefield itself. The enemy is not the elusive and invisible Lupin, but the accomplice, in flesh and blood, who lives and moves within the confines of this house. Let me secure the slightest clue and the game is mine!"

That clue was furnished to him by accident.

On the afternoon of the third day, when he entered a room located above the boudoir, which served as a study for the children, he found Henriette, the younger of the two sisters. She was looking for her scissors.

"You know," she said to Sholmes, "I make papers like that you received the other evening."

"The other evening?"

"Yes, just as dinner was over, you received a paper with marks on it ... you know, a telegram.... Well, I make them, too."

She left the room. To anyone else these words would seem to be nothing more than the insignificant remark of a child, and Sholmes himself listened to them with a distracted air and continued his investigation. But, suddenly, he ran after the child, and overtook her at the head of the stairs. He said to her:

"So you paste stamps and marks on papers?"

Henriette, very proudly, replied:

"Yes, I cut them out and paste them on."

"Who taught you that little game?"

"Mademoiselle ... my governess ... I have seen her do it often. She takes words out of the newspapers and pastes them——"

"What does she make out of them?"

"Telegrams and letters that she sends away."

Herlock Sholmes returned to the study, greatly puzzled by the information and seeking to draw from it a logical deduction. There was a pile of newspapers on the mantel. He opened them and found that many words and, in some places, entire lines had been cut out. But, after reading a few of the word's which preceded or followed, he decided that the missing words had been cut out at random—probably by the child. It was possible that one of the newspapers had been cut by mademoiselle; but how could he assure himself that such was the case?

Mechanically, Sholmes turned over the school-books on the table; then others which were lying on the shelf of a bookcase. Suddenly he uttered a cry of joy. In a corner of the bookcase, under a pile of old exercise books, he found a child's alphabet-book, in which the letters were ornamented with pictures, and on one of the pages of that book he discovered a place where a word had been removed. He examined it. It was a list of the days of the week. Monday, Tuesday, Wednesday, etc. The word "Saturday" was missing. Now, the theft of the Jewish lamp had occurred on a Saturday night.

Sholmes experienced that slight fluttering of the heart which always announced to him, in the clearest manner, that he had discovered the road which leads to victory. That ray of truth, that feeling of certainty, never deceived him.

With nervous fingers he hastened to examine the balance of the book. Very soon he made another discovery. It was a page composed of capital letters, followed by a line of figures. Nine of those letters and three of those figures had been carefully cut out. Sholmes made a list of the missing letters and figures in his memorandum book, in alphabetical and numerical order, and obtained the following result:

CDEHNOPEZ—237.

"Well? at first sight, it is a rather formidable puzzle," he murmured, "but, by transposing the letters and using all of them, is it possible to form one, two or three complete words?"

Sholmes tried it, in vain.

Only one solution seemed possible; it constantly appeared before him, no matter which way he tried to juggle the letters, until, at length, he was satisfied it was the true solution, since it harmonized with the logic of the facts and the general circumstances of the case.

As that page of the book did not contain any duplicate letters it was probable, in fact quite certain, that the words he could form from those letters would be incomplete, and that the original words had been completed with letters taken from other pages. Under those conditions he obtained the following solution, errors and omissions excepted:

REPOND Z—CH—237.

The first word was quite clear: répondez , a letter E is missing because it occurs twice in the word, and the book furnished only one letter of each kind.

As to the second incomplete word, no doubt it formed, with the aid of the number 237, an address to which the reply was to be sent. They appointed Saturday as the time, and requested a reply to be sent to the address CH. 237.

Or, perhaps, CH. 237 was an address for a letter to be sent to the "general delivery" of some postoffice, or, again, they might form a part of some incomplete word. Sholmes searched the book once more, but did not discover that any other letters had been removed. Therefore, until further orders, he decided to adhere to the foregoing interpretation.

Henriette returned and observed what he was doing.

"Amusing, isn't it?"

"Yes, very amusing," he replied. "But, have you any other papers?... Or, rather, words already cut out that I can paste?"

"Papers?... No.... And Mademoiselle wouldn't like it."

"Mademoiselle?"

"Yes, she has scolded me already."

"Why?"

"Because I have told you some things ... and she says that a person should never tell things about those they love."

"You are quite right."

Henriette was delighted to receive his approbation, in fact so highly pleased that she took from a little silk bag that was pinned to her dress some scraps of cloth, three buttons, two cubes of sugar and, lastly, a piece of paper which she handed to Sholmes.

"See, I give it to you just the same."

It was the number of a cab—8,279.

"Where did this number come from?"

"It fell out of her pocketbook."

"When?"

"Sunday, at mass, when she was taking out some sous for the collection."

"Exactly! And now I shall tell you how to keep from being scolded again. Do not tell Mademoiselle that you saw me."

Sholmes then went to Mon. d'Imblevalle and questioned him in regard to Mademoiselle. The baron replied, indignantly:

"Alice Demun! How can you imagine such a thing? It is utterly impossible!"

"How long has she been in your service?"

"Only a year, but there is no one in the house in whom I have greater confidence."

"Why have I not seen her yet?"

"She has been away for a few days."

"But she is here now."

"Yes; since her return she has been watching at the bedside of your friend. She has all the qualities of a nurse ... gentle ... thoughtful ... Monsieur Wilson seems much pleased...."

"Ah!" said Sholmes, who had completely neglected to inquire about his friend. After a moment's reflection he asked:

"Did she go out on Sunday morning?"

"The day after the theft?"

"Yes."

The baron called his wife and asked her. She replied:

"Mademoiselle went to the eleven o'clock mass with the children, as usual."

"But before that?"

"Before that? No.... Let me see!... I was so upset by the theft ... but I remember now that, on the evening before, she asked permission to go out on Sunday morning ... to see a cousin who was passing through Paris, I think. But, surely, you don't suspect her?"

"Of course not ... but I would like to see her."

He went to Wilson's room. A woman dressed in a gray cloth dress, as in the hospitals, was bending over the invalid, giving him a drink. When she turned her face Sholmes recognized her as the young girl who had accosted him at the railway station.

Alice Demun smiled sweetly; her great serious, innocent eyes showed no sign of embarrassment. The Englishman tried to speak, muttered a few syllables, and stopped. Then she resumed her work, acting quite naturally under Sholmes' astonished gaze, moved the bottles, unrolled and rolled cotton bandages, and again regarded Sholmes with her charming smile of pure innocence.

He turned on his heels, descended the stairs, noticed Mon. d'Imblevalle's automobile in the courtyard, jumped into it, and went to Levallois, to the office of the cab company whose address was printed on the paper he had received from Henriette. The man who had driven carriage number 8,279 on Sunday morning not being there, Sholmes dismissed the automobile and waited for the man's return. He told Sholmes that he had picked up a woman in the vicinity of the Parc Monceau, a young woman dressed in black, wearing a heavy veil, and, apparently, quite nervous.

"Did she have a package?"

"Yes, quite a long package."

"Where did you take her?"

"Avenue des Ternes, corner of the Place Saint-Ferdinand. She remained there about ten minutes, and then returned to the Parc Monceau."

"Could you recognize the house in the avenue des Ternes?"

"Parbleu! Shall I take you there?"

"Presently. First take me to 36 quai des Orfèvres."

At the police office he saw Detective Ganimard.

"Monsieur Ganimard, are you at liberty?"

"If it has anything to do with Lupin—no!"

"It has something to do with Lupin."

"Then I do not go."

"What! you surrender——"

"I bow to the inevitable. I am tired of the unequal struggle, in which we are sure to be defeated. Lupin is stronger than I am—stronger than the two of us; therefore, we must surrender."

"I will not surrender."

"He will make you, as he has all others."

"And you would be pleased to see it—eh, Ganimard?"

"At all events, it is true," said Ganimard, frankly. "And since you are determined to pursue the game, I will go with you."

Together they entered the carriage and were driven to the avenue des Ternes. Upon their order the carriage stopped on the other side of the street, at some distance from the house, in front of a little café, on the terrace of which the two men took seats amongst the shrubbery. It was commencing to grow dark.

"Waiter," said Sholmes, "some writing material."

He wrote a note, recalled the waiter and gave him the letter with instructions to deliver it to the concierge of the house which he pointed out.

In a few minutes the concierge stood before them. Sholmes asked him if, on the Sunday morning, he had seen a young woman dressed in black.

"In black? Yes, about nine o'clock. She went to the second floor."

"Have you seen her often?"

"No, but for some time—well, during the last few weeks, I have seen her almost every day."

"And since Sunday?"

"Only once ... until to-day."

"What! Did she come to-day?"

"She is here now."

"Here now?"

"Yes, she came about ten minutes ago. Her carriage is standing in the Place Saint-Ferdinand, as usual. I met her at the door."

"Who is the occupant of the second floor?"

"There are two: a modiste, Mademoiselle Langeais, and a gentleman who rented two furnished rooms a month ago under the name of Bresson."

"Why do you say 'under the name'?"

"Because I have an idea that it is an assumed name. My wife takes care of his rooms, and ... well, there are not two shirts there with the same initials."

"Is he there much of the time?"

"No; he is nearly always out. He has not been here for three days."

"Was he here on Saturday night?"

"Saturday night?... Let me think.... Yes, Saturday night, he came in and stayed all night."

"What sort of a man is he?"

"Well, I can scarcely answer that. He is so changeable. He is, by turns, big, little, fat, thin ... dark and light. I do not always recognize him."

Ganimard and Sholmes exchanged looks.

"That is he, all right," said Ganimard.

"Ah!" said the concierge, "there is the girl now."

Mademoiselle had just emerged from the house and was walking toward her carriage in the Place Saint-Ferdinand.

"And there is Monsieur Bresson."

"Monsieur Bresson? Which is he?"

"The man with the parcel under his arm."

"But he is not looking after the girl. She is going to her carriage alone."

"Yes, I have never seen them together."

The two detectives had arisen. By the light of the street-lamps they recognized the form of Arsène Lupin, who had started off in a direction opposite to that taken by the girl.

"Which will you follow?" asked Ganimard.

"I will follow him, of course. He's the biggest game."

"Then I will follow the girl," proposed Ganimard.

"No, no," said Sholmes, quickly, who did not wish to disclose the girl's identity to Ganimard, "I know where to find her. Come with me."

They followed Lupin at a safe distance, taking care to conceal themselves as well as possible amongst the moving throng and behind the newspaper kiosks. They found the pursuit an easy one, as he walked steadily forward without turning to the right or left, but with a slight limp in the right leg, so slight as to require the keen eye of a professional observer to detect it. Ganimard observed it, and said:

"He is pretending to be lame. Ah! if we could only collect two or three policemen and pounce on our man! We run a chance to lose him."

But they did not meet any policemen before they reached the Porte des Ternes, and, having passed the fortifications, there was no prospect of receiving any assistance.

"We had better separate," said Sholmes, "as there are so few people on the street."

They were now on the Boulevard Victor-Hugo. They walked one on each side of the street, and kept well in the shadow of the trees. They continued thus for twenty minutes, when Lupin turned to the left and followed the Seine. Very soon they saw him descend to the edge of the river. He remained there only a few seconds, but they could not observe his movements. Then Lupin retraced his steps. His pursuers concealed themselves in the shadow of a gateway. Lupin passed in front of them. His parcel had disappeared. And as he walked away another man emerged from the shelter of a house and glided amongst the trees.

"He seems to be following him also," said Sholmes, in a low voice.

The pursuit continued, but was now embarrassed by the presence of the third man. Lupin returned the same way, passed through the Porte des Ternes, and re-entered the house in the avenue des Ternes.

The concierge was closing the house for the night when Ganimard presented himself.

"Did you see him?"

"Yes," replied the concierge, "I was putting out the gas on the landing when he closed and bolted his door."

"Is there any person with him?"

"No; he has no servant. He never eats here."

"Is there a servants' stairway?"

"No."

Ganimard said to Sholmes:

"I had better stand at the door of his room while you go for the commissary of police in the rue Demours."

"And if he should escape during that time?" said Sholmes.

"While I am here! He can't escape."

"One to one, with Lupin, is not an even chance for you."

"Well, I can't force the door. I have no right to do that, especially at night."

Sholmes shrugged his shoulders and said:

"When you arrest Lupin no one will question the methods by which you made the arrest. However, let us go up and ring, and see what happens then."

They ascended to the second floor. There was a double door at the left of the landing. Ganimard rang the bell. No reply. He rang again. Still no reply.

"Let us go in," said Sholmes.

"All right, come on," replied Ganimard.

Yet, they stood still, irresolute. Like people who hesitate when they ought to accomplish a decisive action they feared to move, and it seemed to them impossible that Arsène Lupin was there, so close to them, on the other side of that fragile door that could be broken down by one blow of the fist. But they knew Lupin too well to suppose that he would allow himself to be trapped in that stupid manner. No, no—a thousand times, no—Lupin was no longer there. Through the adjoining houses, over the roofs, by some conveniently prepared exit, he must have already made his escape, and, once more, it would only be Lupin's shadow that they would seize.

They shuddered as a slight noise, coming from the other side of the door, reached their ears. Then they had the impression, amounting almost to a certainty, that he was there, separated from them by that frail wooden door, and that he was listening to them, that he could hear them.

What was to be done? The situation was a serious one. In spite of their vast experience as detectives, they were so nervous and excited that they thought they could hear the beating of their own hearts. Ganimard questioned Sholmes by a look. Then he struck the door a violent blow with his fist. Immediately they heard the sound of footsteps, concerning which there was no attempt at concealment.

Ganimard shook the door. Then he and Sholmes, uniting their efforts, rushed at the door, and burst it open with their shoulders. Then they stood still, in surprise. A shot had been fired in the adjoining room. Another shot, and the sound of a falling body.

When they entered they saw the man lying on the floor with his face toward the marble mantel. His revolver had fallen from his hand. Ganimard stooped and turned the man's head. The face was covered with blood, which was flowing from two wounds, one in the cheek, the other in the temple.

"You can't recognize him for blood."

"No matter!" said Sholmes. "It is not Lupin."

"How do you know? You haven't even looked at him."

"Do you think that Arsène Lupin is the kind of a man that would kill himself?" asked Sholmes, with a sneer.

"But we thought we recognized him outside."

"We thought so, because the wish was father to the thought. That man has us bewitched."

"Then it must be one of his accomplices."

"The accomplices of Arsène Lupin do not kill themselves."

"Well, then, who is it?"

They searched the corpse. In one pocket Herlock Sholmes found an empty pocketbook; in another Ganimard found several louis. There were no marks of identification on any part of his clothing. In a trunk and two valises they found nothing but wearing apparel. On the mantel there was a pile of newspapers. Ganimard opened them. All of them contained articles referring to the theft of the Jewish lamp.

An hour later, when Ganimard and Sholmes left the house, they had acquired no further knowledge of the strange individual who had been driven to suicide by their untimely visit.

Who was he? Why had he killed himself? What was his connection with the affair of the Jewish lamp? Who had followed him on his return from the river? The situation involved many complex questions—many mysteries——

Herlock Sholmes went to bed in a very bad humor. Early next morning he received the following telephonic message:

"Arsène Lupin has the honor to inform you of his tragic death in the person of Monsieur Bresson, and requests the honor of your presence at the funeral service and burial, which will be held at the public expense on Thursday, 25 June."

CHAPTER VIII

THE SHIPWRECK.

"That's what I don't like, Wilson," said Herlock Sholmes, after he had read Arsène Lupin's message; "that is what exasperates me in this affair—to feel that the cunning, mocking eye of that fellow follows me everywhere. He sees everything; he knows everything; he reads my inmost thoughts; he even foresees my slightest movement. Ah! he is possessed of a marvellous intuition, far surpassing that of the most instinctive woman, yes, surpassing even that of Herlock Sholmes himself. Nothing escapes him. I resemble an actor whose every step and movement are directed by a stage-manager; who says this and does that in obedience to a superior will. That is my position. Do you understand, Wilson?"

Certainly Wilson would have understood if his faculties had not been deadened by the profound slumber of a man whose temperature varies between one hundred and one hundred and three degrees. But whether he heard or not was a matter of no consequence to Herlock Sholmes, who continued:

"I have to concentrate all my energy and bring all my resources into action in order to make the slightest progress. And, fortunately for me, those petty annoyances are like so many pricks from a needle and serve only to stimulate me. As soon as the heat of the wound is appeased and the shock to my vanity has subsided I say to myself: 'Amuse yourself, my dear fellow, but remember that he who laughs last laughs best. Sooner or later you will betray yourself.' For you know, Wilson, it was Lupin himself, who, by his first dispatch and the observation that it suggested to little Henriette, disclosed to me the secret of his correspondence with Alice Hemun. Have you forgotten that circumstance, dear boy?"

But Wilson was asleep; and Sholmes, pacing to and fro, resumed his speech:

"And, now, things are not in a bad shape; a little obscure, perhaps, but the light is creeping in. In the first place, I must learn all about Monsieur Bresson. Ganimard and I will visit the bank of the river, at the spot where Bresson threw away the package, and the particular rôle of that gentleman will be known to me. After that the game will be played between me and Alice Demun. Rather a light-weight opponent, hein, Wilson? And do you not think that I will soon know the phrase represented by the letters clipped from the alphabet-book, and what the isolated letters—the 'C' and the 'H'—mean? That is all I want to know, Wilson."

Mademoiselle entered at that moment, and, observing Sholmes gesticulating, she said, in her sweetest manner:

"Monsieur Sholmes, I must scold you if you waken my patient. It isn't nice of you to disturb him. The doctor has ordered absolute rest."

He looked at her in silence, astonished, as on their first meeting, at her wonderful self-possession.

"Why do you look at me so, Monsieur Sholmes?... You seem to be trying to read my thoughts.... No?... Then what is it?"

She questioned him with the most innocent expression on her pretty face and in her frank blue eyes. A smile played upon her lips; and she displayed so much unaffected candor that the Englishman almost lost his temper. He approached her and said, in a low voice:

"Bresson killed himself last night."

She affected not to understand him; so he repeated:

"Bresson killed himself yesterday...."

She did not show the slightest emotion; she acted as if the matter did not concern or interest her in any way.

"You have been informed," said Sholmes, displaying his annoyance. "Otherwise, the news would have caused you to start, at least. Ah! you are stronger than I expected. But what's the use of your trying to conceal anything from me?"

He picked up the alphabet-book, which he had placed on a convenient table, and, opening it at the mutilated page, said:

"Will you tell me the order in which the missing letters should be arranged in order to express the exact wording of the message you sent to Bresson four days before the theft of the Jewish lamp?"

"The order?... Bresson?... the theft of the Jewish lamp?"

She repeated the words slowly, as if trying to grasp their meaning. He continued:

"Yes. Here are the letters employed ... on this bit of paper.... What did you say to Bresson?"

"The letters employed ... what did I say...."

Suddenly she burst into laughter:

"Ah! that is it! I understand! I am an accomplice in the crime! There is a Monsieur Bresson who stole the Jewish lamp and who has now committed suicide. And I am the friend of that gentleman. Oh! how absurd you are!"

"Whom did you go to see last night on the second floor of a house in the avenue des Ternes?"

"Who? My modiste, Mademoiselle Langeais. Do you suppose that my modiste and my friend Monsieur Bresson are the same person?"

Despite all he knew, Sholmes was now in doubt. A person can feign terror, joy, anxiety, in fact all emotions; but a person cannot feign absolute indifference or light, careless laughter. Yet he continued to question her:

"Why did you accost me the other evening at the Northern Railway station? And why did you entreat me to leave Paris immediately without investigating this theft?"

"Ah! you are too inquisitive, Monsieur Sholmes," she replied, still laughing in the most natural manner. "To punish you I will tell you nothing, and, besides, you must watch the patient while I go to the pharmacy on an urgent message. Au revoir."

257

She left the room.

"I am beaten ... by a girl," muttered Sholmes. "Not only did I get nothing out of her but I exposed my hand and put her on her guard."

And he recalled the affair of the blue diamond and his first interview with Clotilde Destange. Had not the blonde Lady met his question with the same unruffled serenity, and was he not once more face to face with one of those creatures who, under the protection and influence of Arsène Lupin, maintain the utmost coolness in the face of a terrible danger?

"Sholmes ... Sholmes...."

It was Wilson who called him. Sholmes approached the bed, and, leaning over, said:

"What's the matter, Wilson? Does your wound pain you?"

Wilson's lips moved, but he could not speak. At last, with a great effort, he stammered:

"No ... Sholmes ... it is not she ... that is impossible——"

"Come, Wilson, what do you know about it? I tell you that it is she! It is only when I meet one of Lupin's creatures, prepared and instructed by him, that I lose my head and make a fool of myself.... I bet you that within an hour Lupin will know all about our interview. Within an hour? What am I saying?... Why, he may know already. The visit to the pharmacy ... urgent message. All nonsense!... She has gone to telephone to Lupin."

Sholmes left the house hurriedly, went down the avenue de Messine, and was just in time to see Mademoiselle enter a pharmacy. Ten minutes later she emerged from the shop carrying some small packages and a bottle wrapped in white paper. But she had not proceeded far, when she was accosted by a man who, with hat in hand and an obsequious air, appeared to be asking for charity. She stopped, gave him something, and proceeded on her way.

"She spoke to him," said the Englishman to himself.

If not a certainty, it was at least an intuition, and quite sufficient to cause him to change his tactics. Leaving the girl to pursue her own course, he followed the suspected mendicant, who walked slowly to the avenue des Ternes and lingered for a long time around the house in which Bresson had lived, sometimes raising his eyes to the windows of the second floor and watching the people who entered the house.

At the end of an hour he climbed to the top of a tramcar going in the direction of Neuilly. Sholmes followed and took a seat behind the man, and beside a gentleman who was concealed behind the pages of a newspaper. At the fortifications the gentleman lowered the paper, and Sholmes recognized Ganimard, who thereupon whispered, as he pointed to the man in front:

"It is the man who followed Bresson last night. He has been watching the house for an hour."

"Anything new in regard to Bresson?" asked Sholmes.

"Yes, a letter came to his address this morning."

"This morning? Then it was posted yesterday before the sender could know of Bresson's death."

"Exactly. It is now in the possession of the examining magistrate. But I read it. It says: *He will not accept any compromise. He wants everything—the first thing as well as those of the second affair. Otherwise he will proceed.*"

"There is no signature," added Ganimard. "It seems to me those few lines won't help us much."

"I don't agree with you, Monsieur Ganimard. To me those few lines are very interesting."

"Why so? I can't see it."

"For reasons that are personal to me," replied Sholmes, with the indifference that he frequently displayed toward his colleague.

The tramcar stopped at the rue de Château, which was the terminus. The man descended and walked away quietly. Sholmes followed at so short a distance that Ganimard protested, saying:

"If he should turn around he will suspect us."

"He will not turn around."

"How do you know?"

"He is an accomplice of Arsène Lupin, and the fact that he walks in that manner, with his hands in his pockets, proves, in the first place, that he knows he is being followed and, in the second place, that he is not afraid."

"But I think we are keeping too close to him."

"Not too close to prevent his slipping through our fingers. He is too sure of himself."

"Ah! Look there! In front of that café there are two of the bicycle police. If I summon them to our assistance, how can the man slip through our fingers?"

"Well, our friend doesn't seem to be worried about it. In fact, he is asking for their assistance himself."

"Mon Dieu!" exclaimed Ganimard, "he has a nerve."

The man approached the two policemen just as they were mounting their bicycles. After a few words with them he leaped on a third bicycle, which was leaning against the wall of the café, and rode away at a fast pace, accompanied by the two policemen.

"Hein! one, two, three and away!" growled Sholmes. "And through, whose agency, Monsieur Ganimard? Two of your colleagues.... Ah! but Arsène Lupin has a wonderful organization! Bicycle policemen in his service!... I told you our man was too calm, too sure of himself."

"Well, then," said Ganimard, quite vexed, "what are we to do now? It is easy enough to laugh! Anyone can do that."

"Come, come, don't lose your temper! We will get our revenge. But, in the meantime, we need reinforcements."

"Folenfant is waiting for me at the end of the avenue de Neuilly."

"Well, go and get him and join me later. I will follow our fugitive."

Sholmes followed the bicycle tracks, which were plainly visible in the dust of the road as two of the machines were furnished with striated tires. Very soon he ascertained that the tracks were leading him to the edge of the Seine, and that the three men had turned in the direction taken by Bresson on the preceding evening. Thus he arrived at the gateway where he and Ganimard had concealed themselves, and, a little farther on, he discovered a mingling of the bicycle tracks which showed that the men had halted at that spot. Directly opposite there was a little point of land which projected into the river and, at the extremity thereof, an old boat was moored.

It was there that Bresson had thrown away the package, or, rather, had dropped it. Sholmes descended the bank and saw that the declivity was not steep and the water quite shallow, so it would be quite easy to recover the package, provided the three men had not forestalled him.

"No, that can't be," he thought, "they have not had time. A quarter of an hour at the most. And yet, why did they come this way?"

A fisherman was seated on the old boat. Sholmes asked him:

"Did you see three men on bicycles a few minutes ago?"

The fisherman made a negative gesture. But Sholmes insisted:

"Three men who stopped on the road just on top of the bank?"

The fisherman rested his pole under his arm, took a memorandum book from his pocket, wrote on one of the pages, tore it out, and handed it to Sholmes. The Englishman gave a start of surprise. In the middle of the paper which he held in his hand he saw the series of letters cut from the alphabet-book:

CDEHNOPRZEO—237.

The man resumed his fishing, sheltered from the sun by a large straw hat, with his coat and vest lying beside him. He was intently watching the cork attached to his line as it floated on the surface of the water.

There was a moment of silence—solemn and terrible.

"Is it he?" conjectured Sholmes, with an anxiety that was almost pitiful. Then the truth burst upon him:

"It is he! It is he! No one else could remain there so calmly, without the slightest display of anxiety, without the least fear of what might happen. And who else would know the story of those mysterious letters? Alice had warned him by means of her messenger."

Suddenly the Englishman felt that his hand—that his own hand had involuntarily seized the handle of his revolver, and that his eyes were fixed on the man's back, a little below the neck. One movement, and the drama would be finished; the life of the strange adventurer would come to a miserable end.

The fisherman did not stir.

Sholmes nervously toyed with his revolver, and experienced a wild desire to fire it and end everything; but the horror of such an act was repugnant to his nature. Death would be certain and would end all.

"Ah!" he thought, "let him get up and defend himself. If he doesn't, so much the worse for him. One second more ... and I fire...."

But a sound of footsteps behind him caused him to turn his head. It was Ganimard coming with some assistants.

Then, quickly changing his plans, Sholmes leaped into the boat, which was broken from its moorings by his sudden action; he pounced upon the man and seized him around the body. They rolled to the bottom of the boat together.

"Well, now!" exclaimed Lupin, struggling to free himself, "what does this mean? When one of us has conquered the other, what good will it do? You will not know what to do with me, nor I with you. We will remain here like two idiots."

The two oars slipped into the water. The boat drifted into the stream.

"Good Lord, what a fuss you make! A man of your age ought to know better! You act like a child."

Lupin succeeded in freeing himself from the grasp of the detective, who, thoroughly exasperated and ready to kill, put his hand in his pocket. He uttered an oath: Lupin had taken his revolver. Then he knelt down and tried to capture one of the lost oars in order to regain the shore, while Lupin was trying to capture the other oar in order to drive the boat down the river.

"It's gone! I can't reach it," said Lupin. "But it's of no consequence. If you get your oar I can prevent your using it. And you could do the same to me. But, you see, that is the way in this world, we act without any purpose or reason, as our efforts are in vain since Fate decides everything. Now, don't you see, Fate is on the side of his friend Lupin. The game is mine! The current favors me!"

The boat was slowly drifting down the river.

"Look out!" cried Lupin, quickly.

Someone on the bank was pointing a revolver. Lupin stooped, a shot was fired; it struck the water beyond the boat. Lupin burst into laughter.

"God bless me! It's my friend Ganimard! But it was very wrong of you to do that, Ganimard. You have no right to shoot except in self-defense. Does poor Lupin worry you so much that you forget yourself?... Now, be good, and don't shoot again!... If you do you will hit our English friend."

He stood behind Sholmes, facing Ganimard, and said:

"Now, Ganimard, I am ready! Aim for his heart!... Higher!... A little to the left.... Ah! you missed that time ... deuced bad shot.... Try again.... Your hand shakes, Ganimard.... Now, once more ... one, two, three, fire!... Missed!... Parbleu! the authorities furnish you with toy-pistols."

Lupin drew a long revolver and fired without taking aim. Ganimard put his hand to his hat: the bullet had passed through it.

"What do you think of that, Ganimard! Ah! that's a real revolver! A genuine English bulldog. It belongs to my friend, Herlock Sholmes."

And, with a laugh, he threw the revolver to the shore, where it landed at Ganimard's feet.

Sholmes could not withhold a smile of admiration. What a torrent of youthful spirits! And how he seemed to enjoy himself! It appeared as if the sensation of peril caused him a physical pleasure; and this extraordinary man had no other purpose in life than to seek for dangers simply for the amusement it afforded him in avoiding them.

Many people had now gathered on the banks of the river, and Ganimard and his men followed the boat as it slowly floated down the stream. Lupin's capture was a mathematical certainty.

"Confess, old fellow," said Lupin, turning to the Englishman, "that you would not exchange your present position for all the gold in the Transvaal! You are now in the first row of the orchestra chairs! But, in the first place, we must have the prologue ... after which we can leap, at one bound, to the fifth act of the drama, which will represent the capture or escape of Arsène Lupin. Therefore, I am going to ask you a plain question, to which I request a plain answer—a simple yes or no. Will you renounce this affair? At present I can repair the damage you have done; later it will be beyond my power. Is it a bargain?"

"No."

Lupin's face showed his disappointment and annoyance. He continued:

"I insist. More for your sake than my own, I insist, because I am certain you will be the first to regret your intervention. For the last time, yes or no?"

"No."

Lupin stooped down, removed one of the boards in the bottom of the boat, and, for some minutes, was engaged in a work the nature of which Sholmes could not discern. Then he arose, seated himself beside the Englishman, and said:

"I believe, monsieur, that we came to the river to-day for the same purpose: to recover the object which Bresson threw away. For my part I had invited a few friends to join me here, and I was on the point of making an examination of the bed of the river when my friends announced your approach. I confess that the news did not surprise me, as I have been notified every hour concerning the progress of your investigation. That was an easy matter. Whenever anything occurred in the rue Murillo that might interest me, simply a ring on the telephone and I was informed."

He stopped. The board that he had displaced in the bottom of the boat was rising and water was working into the boat all around it.

"The deuce! I didn't know how to fix it. I was afraid this old boat would leak. You are not afraid, monsieur?"

Sholmes shrugged his shoulders. Lupin continued:

"You will understand then, in those circumstances, and knowing in advance that you would be more eager to seek a battle than I would be to avoid it, I assure you I was not entirely displeased to enter into a contest of which the issue is quite certain, since I hold all the trump cards in my hand. And I desired that our meeting should be given the widest publicity in order that your defeat may be universally known, so that another Countess de Crozon or another Baron d'Imblevalle may not be tempted to solicit your aid against me. Besides, my dear monsieur—"

He stopped again and, using his half-closed hands as a lorgnette, he scanned the banks of the river.

"Mon Dieu! they have chartered a superb boat, a real war-vessel, and see how they are rowing. In five minutes they will be along-side, and I am lost. Monsieur Sholmes, a word of advice; you seize me, bind me and deliver me to the officers of the law. Does that programme please you?... Unless, in the meantime, we are shipwrecked, in which event we can do nothing but prepare our wills. What do you think?"

They exchanged looks. Sholmes now understood Lupin's scheme: he had scuttled the boat. And the water was rising. It had reached the soles of their boots. Then it covered their feet; but they did not move. It was half-way to their knees. The Englishman took out his tobacco, rolled a cigarette, and lighted it. Lupin continued to talk:

"But do not regard that offer as a confession of my weakness. I surrender to you in a battle in which I can achieve a victory in order to avoid a struggle upon a field not of my own choosing. In so doing I recognize the fact that Sholmes is the only enemy I fear, and announce my anxiety that Sholmes will not be diverted from my track. I take this opportunity to tell you these things since fate has accorded me the honor of a conversation with you. I have only one regret; it is that our conversation should have occurred while we are taking a foot-bath ... a situation that is lacking in dignity, I must confess.... What did I say? A foot-bath? It is worse than that."

The water had reached the board on which they were sitting, and the boat was gradually sinking.

Sholmes, smoking his cigarette, appeared to be calmly admiring the scenery. For nothing in the world, while face to face with that man who, while threatened by dangers, surrounded by a crowd, followed by a posse of police, maintained his equanimity and good humor, for nothing in the world would he, Sholmes, display the slightest sign of nervousness.

Each of them looked as if he might say: Should a person be disturbed by such trifles? Are not people drowned in a river every day? Is it such an unusual event as to deserve special attention? One chatted, whilst the other dreamed; both concealing their wounded pride beneath a mask of indifference.

One minute more and the boat will sink. Lupin continued his chatter:

"The important thing to know is whether we will sink before or after the arrival of the champions of the law. That is the main question. As to our shipwreck, that is a fore-gone conclusion. Now, monsieur, the hour has come in which we must make our wills. I give, devise and bequeath all my property to Herlock Sholmes, a citizen of England, for his own use and benefit. But, mon Dieu, how quickly the champions of the law are approaching! Ah! the brave fellows! It is a pleasure to watch them. Observe the precision of the oars! Ah! is it you, Brigadier Folenfant? Bravo! The idea of a war-vessel is an excellent one. I commend you to your superiors, Brigadier Folenfant.... Do you wish a medal? You shall have it. And your comrade Dieuzy, where is he?... Ah! yes, I think I see him on the left bank of the river at the head of a hundred natives. So that, if I escape shipwreck, I shall be captured on the left by Dieuzy and his natives, or, on the right, by Ganimard and the populace of Neuilly. An embarrassing dilemma!"

The boat entered an eddy; it swung around and Sholmes caught hold of the oarlocks. Lupin said to him:

"Monsieur, you should remove your coat. You will find it easier to swim without a coat. No? You refuse? Then I shall put on my own."

He donned his coat, buttoned it closely, the same as Sholmes, and said:

"What a discourteous man you are! And what a pity that you should be so stubborn in this affair, in which, of course, you display your strength, but, oh! so vainly! really, you mar your genius——"

"Monsieur Lupin," interrupted Sholmes, emerging from his silence, "you talk too much, and you frequently err through excess of confidence and through your frivolity."

"That is a severe reproach."

"Thus, without knowing it, you furnished me, only a moment ago, with the information I required."

"What! you required some information and you didn't tell me?"

"I had no occasion to ask you for it—you volunteered it. Within three hours I can deliver the key of the mystery to Monsieur d'Imblevalle. That is the only reply——"

He did not finish the sentence. The boat suddenly sank, taking both of the men down with it. It emerged immediately, with its keel in the air. Shouts were heard on either bank, succeeded by an anxious moment of silence. Then the shouts were renewed: one of the shipwrecked party had come to the surface.

It was Herlock Sholmes. He was an excellent swimmer, and struck out, with powerful strokes, for Folenfant's boat.

"Courage, Monsieur Sholmes," shouted Folenfant; "we are here. Keep it up ... we will get you ... a little more, Monsieur Sholmes ... catch the rope."

The Englishman seized the rope they had thrown to him. But, while they were hauling him into the boat, he heard a voice behind him, saying:

"The key of the mystery, monsieur, yes, you shall have it. I am astonished that you haven't got it already. What then? What good will it do you? By that time you will have lost the battle...."

Now comfortably installed astride the keel of the boat, Lupin continued his speech with solemn gestures, as if he hoped to convince his adversary.

"You must understand, my dear Sholmes, there is nothing to be done, absolutely nothing. You find yourself in the deplorable position of a gentleman——"

"Surrender, Lupin!" shouted Folenfant.

"You are an ill-bred fellow, Folenfant, to interrupt me in the middle of a sentence. I was saying——"

"Surrender, Lupin!"

"Oh! parbleu! Brigadier Folenfant, a man surrenders only when he is in danger. Surely, you do not pretend to say that I am in any danger."

"For the last time, Lupin, I call on you to surrender."

"Brigadier Folenfant, you have no intention of killing me; you may wish to wound me since you are afraid I may escape. But if by chance the wound prove mortal! Just think of your remorse! It would embitter your old age."

The shot was fired.

Lupin staggered, clutched at the keel of the boat for a moment, then let go and disappeared.

It was exactly three o'clock when the foregoing events transpired. Precisely at six o'clock, as he had foretold, Herlock Sholmes, dressed in trousers that were too short and a coat that was too small, which he had borrowed from an innkeeper at Neuilly, wearing a cap and a flannel shirt, entered the boudoir in the Rue Murillo, after having sent word to Monsieur and Madame d'Imblevalle that he desired an interview.

They found him walking up and down the room. And he looked so ludicrous in his strange costume that they could scarcely suppress their mirth. With pensive air and stooped shoulders, he walked like an automaton from the window to the door and from the door to the window, taking each time the same number of steps, and turning each time in the same manner.

He stopped, picked up a small ornament, examined it mechanically, and resumed his walk. At last, planting himself before them, he asked:

"Is Mademoiselle here?"

"Yes, she is in the garden with the children.'"

"I wish Mademoiselle to be present at this interview."

"Is it necessary——"

"Have a little patience, monsieur. From the facts I am going to present to you, you will see the necessity for her presence here."

"Very well. Suzanne, will you call her?"

Madame d'Imblevalle arose, went out, and returned almost immediately, accompanied by Alice Demun. Mademoiselle, who was a trifle paler than usual, remained standing, leaning against a table, and without even asking why she had been called. Sholmes did not look at her, but, suddenly turning toward Monsieur d'Imblevalle, he said, in a tone which did not admit of a reply:

"After several days' investigation, monsieur, I must repeat what I told you when I first came here: the Jewish lamp was stolen by some one living in the house."

"The name of the guilty party?"

"I know it."

"Your proof?"

"I have sufficient to establish that fact."

"But we require more than that. We desire the restoration of the stolen goods."

"The Jewish lamp? It is in my possession."

"The opal necklace? The snuff-box?"

"The opal necklace, the snuff-box, and all the goods stolen on the second occasion are in my possession."

Sholmes delighted in these dramatic dialogues, and it pleased him to announce his victories in that curt manner. The baron and his wife were amazed, and looked at Sholmes with a silent curiosity, which was the highest praise.

He related to them, very minutely, what he had done during those three days. He told of his discovery of the alphabet book, wrote upon a sheet of paper the sentence formed by the missing letters, then related the journey of Bresson to the bank of the river and the suicide of the adventurer, and, finally, his struggle with Lupin, the shipwreck, and the disappearance of Lupin. When he had finished, the baron said, in a low voice:

"Now, you have told us everything except the name of the guilty party. Whom do you accuse?"

"I accuse the person who cut the letters from the alphabet book, and communicated with Arsène Lupin by means of those letters."

266

"How do you know that such correspondence was carried on with Arsène Lupin?"

"My information comes from Lupin himself."

He produced a piece of paper that was wet and crumpled. It was the page which Lupin had torn from his memorandum-book, and upon which he had written the phrase.

"And you will notice," said Sholmes, with satisfaction, "that he was not obliged to give me that sheet of paper, and, in that way, disclose his identity. Simple childishness on his part, and yet it gave me exactly the information I desired."

"What was it?" asked the baron. "I don't understand."

Sholmes took a pencil and made a fresh copy of the letters and figures.

"CDEHNOPRZEO—237."

"Well?" said the baron; "it is the formula you showed me yourself."

"No. If you had turned and returned that formula in every way, as I have done, you would have seen at first glance that this formula is not like the first one."

"In what respect do they differ?"

"This one has two more letters—an E and an O."

"Really; I hadn't noticed that."

"Join those two letters to the C and the H which remained after forming the word 'respondez,' and you will agree with me that the only possible word is ECHO."

"What does that mean?"

"It refers to the *Echo de France*, Lupin's newspaper, his official organ, the one in which he publishes his communications. Reply in the *Echo de France*, in the personal advertisements, under number 237. That is the key to the mystery, and Arsène Lupin was kind enough to furnish it to me. I went to the newspaper office."

"What did you find there?"

"I found the entire story of the relations between Arsène Lupin and his accomplice."

Sholmes produced seven newspapers which he opened at the fourth page and pointed to the following lines:

1. Ars. Lup. Lady implores protection. 540.

2. 540. Awaiting particulars. A.L.

3. A.L. Under domin. enemy. Lost.

4. 540. Write address. Will make investigation.

5. A.L. Murillo.

6. 540. Park three o'clock. Violets.

7. 237. Understand. Sat. Will be Sun. morn. park.

"And you call that the whole story!" exclaimed the baron.

"Yes, and if you will listen to me for a few minutes, I think I can convince you. In the first place, a lady who signs herself 540 implores the protection of Arsène Lupin, who replies by asking for particulars. The lady replies that she is under the domination of an enemy—who is Bresson, no doubt—and that she is lost if some one does not come to her assistance. Lupin is suspicious and does not yet venture to appoint an interview with the unknown woman, demands the address and proposes to make an investigation. The lady hesitates for four days—look at the dates—finally, under stress of circumstances and influenced by Bresson's threats, she gives the name of the street—Murillo. Next day, Arsène Lupin announces that he will be in the Park Monceau at three o'clock, and asks his unknown correspondent to wear a bouquet of violets as a means of identification. Then there is a lapse of eight days in the correspondence. Arsène Lupin and the lady do not require to correspond through the newspaper now, as they see each other or write directly. The scheme is arranged in this way: in order to satisfy Bresson's demands, the lady is to carry off the Jewish lamp. The date is not yet fixed. The lady who, as a matter of prudence, corresponds by means of letters cut out of a book, decides on Saturday and adds: *Reply Echo 237*. Lupin replies that it is understood and that he will be in the park on Sunday morning. Sunday morning, the theft takes place."

"Really, that is an excellent chain of circumstantial evidence and every link is complete," said the baron.

"The theft has taken place," continued Sholmes. "The lady goes out on Sunday morning, tells Lupin what she has done, and carries the Jewish lamp to Bresson. Everything occurs then exactly as Lupin had foreseen. The officers of the law, deceived by an open window, four holes in the ground and two scratches on the balcony railing, immediately advance the theory that the theft was committed by a burglar. The lady is safe."

"Yes, I confess the theory was a logical one," said the baron. "But the second theft—"

"The second theft was provoked by the first. The newspapers having related how the Jewish lamp had disappeared, some one conceived the idea of repeating the crime and carrying away what had been left. This time, it was not a simulated theft, but a real one, a genuine burglary, with ladders and other paraphernalia—"

"Lupin, of course—"

"No. Lupin does not act so stupidly. He doesn't fire at people for trifling reasons."

"Then, who was it?"

"Bresson, no doubt, and unknown to the lady whom he had menaced. It was Bresson who entered here; it was Bresson that I pursued; it was Bresson who wounded poor Wilson."

"Are you sure of it?"

"Absolutely. One of Bresson's accomplices wrote to him yesterday, before his suicide, a letter which proves that negotiations were pending between this accomplice and Lupin for the restitution of all the articles stolen from your house. Lupin demanded everything, '*the first thing* (that is, the Jewish lamp) *as well as those of the second affair.*' Moreover, he was watching Bresson. When the latter returned from the river last night, one of Lupin's men followed him as well as we."

"What was Bresson doing at the river?"

"Having been warned of the progress of my investigations——"

"Warned! by whom?"

"By the same lady, who justly feared that the discovery of the Jewish lamp would lead to the discovery of her own adventure. Thereupon, Bresson, having been warned, made into a package all the things that could compromise him and threw them into a place where he thought he could get them again when the danger was past. It was after his return, tracked by Ganimard and myself, having, no doubt, other sins on his conscience, that he lost his head and killed himself."

"But what did the package contain?"

"The Jewish lamp and your other ornaments."

"Then, they are not in your possession?"

"Immediately after Lupin's disappearance, I profited by the bath he had forced upon me, went to the spot selected by Bresson, where I found the stolen articles wrapped in some soiled linen. They are there, on the table."

Without a word, the baron cut the cord, tore open the wet linen, picked out the lamp, turned a screw in the foot, then divided the bowl of the lamp which opened in two equal parts and there he found the golden chimera, set with rubies and emeralds.

It was intact.

There was in that scene, so natural in appearance and which consisted of a simple exposition of facts, something which rendered it frightfully tragic—it was the formal, direct, irrefutable accusation that Sholmes launched in each of his words against Mademoiselle. And it was also the impressive silence of Alice Demun.

During that long, cruel accumulation of accusing circumstances heaped one upon another, not a muscle of her face had moved, not a trace of revolt or fear had marred the serenity of her limpid eyes. What were her thoughts. And, especially, what was she going to say at the solemn moment when it would become necessary for her to speak and defend herself in order to break the chain of evidence that Herlock Sholmes had so cleverly woven around her?

That moment had come, but the girl was silent.

"Speak! Speak!" cried Mon. d'Imblevalle.

She did not speak. So he insisted:

"One word will clear you. One word of denial, and I will believe you."

That word, she would not utter.

The baron paced to and fro in his excitement; then, addressing Sholmes, he said:

"No, monsieur, I cannot believe it, I do not believe it. There are impossible crimes! and this is opposed to all I know and to all that I have seen during the past year. No, I cannot believe it."

He placed his hand on the Englishman's shoulder, and said:

"But you yourself, monsieur, are you absolutely certain that you are right?"

Sholmes hesitated, like a man on whom a sudden demand is made and cannot frame an immediate reply. Then he smiled, and said:

"Only the person whom I accuse, by reason of her situation in your house, could know that the Jewish lamp contained that magnificent jewel."

"I cannot believe it," repeated the baron.

"Ask her."

It was, really, the very thing he would not have done, blinded by the confidence the girl had inspired in him. But he could no longer refrain from doing it. He approached her and, looking into her eyes, said:

"Was it you, mademoiselle? Was it you who took the jewel? Was it you who corresponded with Arsène Lupin and committed the theft?"

"It was I, monsieur," she replied.

She did not drop her head. Her face displayed no sign of shame or fear.

"Is it possible?" murmured Mon. d'Imblevalle. "I would never have believed it.... You are the last person in the world that I would have suspected. How did you do it?"

"I did it exactly as Monsieur Sholmes has told it. On Saturday night I came to the boudoir, took the lamp, and, in the morning I carried it ... to that man."

"No," said the baron; "what you pretend to have done is impossible."

"Impossible—why?"

"Because, in the morning I found the door of the boudoir bolted."

She blushed, and looked at Sholmes as if seeking his counsel. Sholmes was astonished at her embarrassment. Had she nothing to say? Did the confessions, which had corroborated the report that he, Sholmes, had made concerning the theft of the Jewish lamp, merely serve to mask a lie? Was she misleading them by a false confession?

The baron continued:

"That door was locked. I found the door exactly as I had left it the night before. If you entered by that door, as you pretend, some one must have opened it from the interior—that is to say, from the boudoir or from our chamber. Now, there was no one inside these two rooms ... there was no one except my wife and myself."

Sholmes bowed his head and covered his face with his hands in order to conceal his emotion. A sudden light had entered his mind, that startled him and made him exceedingly uncomfortable. Everything was revealed to him, like the sudden lifting of a fog from the morning landscape. He was annoyed as well as ashamed, because his deductions were fallacious and his entire theory was wrong.

Alice Demun was innocent!

Alice Demun was innocent. That proposition explained the embarrassment he had experienced from the beginning in directing the terrible accusation against that young girl. Now, he saw the truth; he knew it. After a few seconds, he raised his head, and looked at Madame d'Imblevalle as naturally as he could. She was pale—with that unusual pallor which invades us in the relentless moments of our lives. Her hands, which she endeavored to conceal, were trembling as if stricken with palsy.

"One minute more," thought Sholmes, "and she will betray herself."

He placed himself between her and her husband in the desire to avert the awful danger which, *through his fault*, now threatened that man and woman. But, at sight of the baron, he was shocked to the very centre of his soul. The same dreadful idea had entered the mind of Monsieur d'Imblevalle. The same thought was at work in the brain of the husband. He understood, also! He saw the truth!

In desperation, Alice Demun hurled herself against the implacable truth, saying:

"You are right, monsieur. I made a mistake. I did not enter by this door. I came through the garden and the vestibule ... by aid of a ladder—"

It was a supreme effort of true devotion. But a useless effort! The words rang false. The voice did not carry conviction, and the poor girl no longer displayed those clear, fearless eyes and that natural air of innocence which had served her so well. Now, she bowed her head—vanquished.

The silence became painful. Madame d'Imblevalle was waiting for her husband's next move, overwhelmed with anxiety and fear. The baron appeared to be struggling against the dreadful suspicion, as if he would not submit to the overthrow of his happiness. Finally, he said to his wife:

"Speak! Explain!"

"I have nothing to tell you," she replied, in a very low voice, and with features drawn by anguish.

"So, then ... Mademoiselle...."

"Mademoiselle saved me ... through devotion ... through affection ... and accused herself...."

"Saved you from what? From whom?"

"From that man."

"Bresson?"

"Yes; it was I whom he held in fear by threats.... I met him at one of my friends'.... and I was foolish enough to listen to him. Oh! there was nothing that you cannot pardon. But I wrote him two letters ... letters which you will see.... I had to buy them back ... you know how.... Oh! have pity on me?... I have suffered so much!"

"You! You! Suzanne!"

He raised his clenched fists, ready to strike her, ready to kill her. But he dropped his arms, and murmured:

"You, Suzanne.... You!... Is it possible?"

By short detached sentences, she related the heartrending story, her dreadful awakening to the infamy of the man, her remorse, her fear, and she also told of Alice's devotion; how the young girl divined the sorrow of her mistress, wormed a confession out of her, wrote to Lupin, and devised the scheme of the theft in order to save her from Bresson.

"You, Suzanne, you," repeated Monsieur d'Imblevalle, bowed with grief and shame.... "How could you?"

*****

On the same evening, the steamer "City of London," which plies between Calais and Dover, was gliding slowly over the smooth sea. The night was dark; the wind was fainter than a zephyr. The majority of the passengers had retired to their cabins; but a few, more intrepid, were promenading on the deck or sleeping in large rocking-chairs, wrapped in their travelling-rugs. One could see, here and there, the light of a cigar, and one could hear, mingled with the soft murmur of the breeze, the faint sound of voices which were carefully subdued to harmonize with the deep silence of the night.

One of the passengers, who had been pacing to and fro upon the deck, stopped before a woman who was lying on a bench, scrutinized her, and, when she moved a little, he said:

"I thought you were asleep, Mademoiselle Alice."

"No, Monsieur Sholmes, I am not sleepy. I was thinking."

"Of what? If I may be so bold as to inquire?"

"I was thinking of Madame d'Imblevalle. She must be very unhappy. Her life is ruined."

"Oh! no, no," he replied quickly. "Her mistake was not a serious one. Monsieur d'Imblevalle will forgive and forget it. Why, even before we left, his manner toward her had softened."

"Perhaps ... but he will remember it for a long time ... and she will suffer a great deal."

"You love her?"

"Very much. It was my love for her that gave me strength to smile when I was trembling from fear, that gave me courage to look in your face when I desired to hide from your sight."

"And you are sorry to leave her?"

"Yes, very sorry. I have no relatives, no friends—but her."

"You will have friends," said the Englishman, who was affected by her sorrow. "I have promised that. I have relatives ... and some influence. I assure you that you will have no cause to regret coming to England."

"That may be, monsieur, but Madame d'Imblevalle will not be there."

Herlock Sholmes resumed his promenade upon the deck. After a few minutes, he took a seat near his travelling companion, filled his pipe, and struck four matches in a vain effort to light it. Then, as he had no more matches, he arose and said to a gentleman who was sitting near him:

"May I trouble you for a match?"

The gentleman opened a box of matches and struck one. The flame lighted up his face. Sholmes recognized him—it was Arsène Lupin.

If the Englishman had not given an almost imperceptible movement of surprise, Lupin would have supposed that his presence on board had been known to Sholmes, so well did he control his feelings and so natural was the easy manner in which he extended his hand to his adversary.

"How's the good health, Monsieur Lupin?"

"Bravo!" exclaimed Lupin, who could not repress a cry of admiration at the Englishman's sang-froid.

"Bravo? and why?"

"Why? Because I appear before you like a ghost, only a few hours after you saw me drowned in the Seine; and through pride—a quality that is essentially English—you evince not the slightest surprise. You greet me as a matter of course. Ah! I repeat: Bravo! Admirable!"

"There is nothing remarkable about it. From the manner in which you fell from the boat, I knew very well that you fell voluntarily, and that the bullet had not touched you."

"And you went away without knowing what had become of me?"

"What had become of you? Why, I knew that. There were at least five hundred people on the two banks of the river within a space of half-a-mile. If you escaped death, your capture was certain."

"And yet I am here."

"Monsieur Lupin, there are two men in the world at whom I am never astonished: in the first place, myself—and then, Arsène Lupin."

The treaty of peace was concluded.

If Sholmes had not been successful in his contests with Arsène Lupin; if Lupin remained the only enemy whose capture he must never hope to accomplish; if, in the course of their struggles, he had not always displayed a superiority, the Englishman had, none the less, by means of his extraordinary intuition and tenacity, succeeded in recovering the Jewish lamp as well as the blue diamond.

This time, perhaps, the finish had not been so brilliant, especially from the stand-point of the public spectators, since Sholmes was obliged to maintain a discreet silence in regard to the circumstances in which the Jewish lamp had been recovered, and to announce that he did not know the name of the thief. But as man to man, Arsène Lupin against Herlock Sholmes, detective against burglar, there was neither victor nor vanquished. Each of them had won corresponding victories.

Therefore they could now converse as courteous adversaries who had lain down their arms and held each other in high regard.

At Sholmes' request, Arsène Lupin related the strange story of his escape.

"If I may dignify it by calling it an escape," he said. "It was so simple! My friends were watching for me, as I had asked them to meet me there to recover the Jewish lamp. So, after remaining a good half-hour under the overturned boat, I took advantage of an occasion when Folenfant and his men were searching for my dead body along the bank of the river, to climb on top of the boat. Then my friends simply picked me up as they passed by in their motor-boat, and we sailed away under the staring eyes of an astonished multitude, including Ganimard and Folenfant."

"Very good," exclaimed Sholmes, "very neatly played. And now you have some business in England?"

"Yes, some accounts to square up.... But I forgot ... what about Monsieur d'Imblevalle?"

"He knows everything."

"All! my dear Sholmes, what did I tell you? The wrong is now irreparable. Would it not have been better to have allowed me to carry out the affair in my own way? In a day or two more, I should have recovered the stolen goods from Bresson, restored them to Monsieur d'Imblevalle, and those two honest citizens would have lived together in peace and happiness ever after. Instead of that—"

"Instead of that," said Sholmes, sneeringly, "I have mixed the cards and sown the seeds of discord in the bosom of a family that was under your protection."

"Mon Dieu! of course, I was protecting them. Must a person steal, cheat and wrong all the time?"

"Then you do good, also?"

"When I have the time. Besides, I find it amusing. Now, for instance, in our last adventure, I found it extremely diverting that I should be the good genius seeking to help and save unfortunate mortals, while you were the evil genius who dispensed only despair and tears."

"Tears! Tears!" protested Sholmes.

"Certainly! The d'Imblevalle household is demolished, and Alice Demun weeps."

"She could not remain any longer. Ganimard would have discovered her some day, and, through her, reached Madame d'Imblevalle."

"Quite right, monsieur; but whose fault is it?"

Two men passed by. Sholmes said to Lupin, in a friendly tone:

"Do you know those gentlemen?"

"I thought I recognized one of them as the captain of the steamer."

"And the other?"

"I don't know."

"It is Austin Gilett, who occupies in London a position similar to that of Monsieur Dudouis in Paris."

"Ah! how fortunate! Will you be so kind as to introduce me? Monsieur Dudouis is one of my best friends, and I shall be delighted to say as much of Monsieur Austin Gilett."

The two gentlemen passed again.

"And if I should take you at your word, Monsieur Lupin?" said Sholmes, rising, and seizing Lupin's wrist with a hand of iron.

"Why do you grasp me so tightly, monsieur? I am quite willing to follow you."

In fact, he allowed himself to be dragged along without the least resistance. The two gentlemen were disappearing from sight. Sholmes quickened his pace. His finger-nails even sank into Lupin's flesh.

"Come! Come!" he exclaimed, with a sort of feverish haste, in harmony with his action. "Come! quicker than that."

But he stopped suddenly. Alice Demun was following them.

"What are you doing, Mademoiselle? You need not come. You must not come!"

It was Lupin who replied:

"You will notice, monsieur, that she is not coming of her own free will. I am holding her wrist in the same tight grasp that you have on mine."

"Why!"

"Because I wish to present her also. Her part in the affair of the Jewish lamp is much more important than mine. Accomplice of Arsène Lupin, accomplice of Bresson, she has a right to tell her adventure with the Baroness d'Imblevalle—which will deeply interest Monsieur Gilett as an officer of the law. And by introducing her also, you will have carried your gracious intervention to the very limit, my dear Sholmes."

The Englishman released his hold on his prisoner's wrist. Lupin liberated Mademoiselle.

They stood looking at each other for a few seconds, silently and motionless. Then Sholmes returned to the bench and sat down, followed by Lupin and the girl. After a long silence, Lupin said: "You see, monsieur, whatever we may do, we will never be on the same side. You are on one side of the fence; I am on the other. We can exchange greetings, shake hands, converse a moment, but the fence is always there. You will remain Herlock Sholmes, detective, and I, Arsène Lupin, gentleman-burglar. And Herlock Sholmes will ever obey, more or less spontaneously, with more or less propriety, his instinct as a detective, which is to pursue the burglar and run him down, if possible. And Arsène Lupin, in obedience to his burglarious instinct, will always be occupied in avoiding the reach of the detective, and making sport of the detective, if he can do it. And, this time, he can do it. Ha-ha-ha!"

He burst into a loud laugh, cunning, cruel and odious.

Then, suddenly becoming serious, he addressed Alice Demun:

"You may be sure, mademoiselle, even when reduced to the last extremity, I shall not betray you. Arsène Lupin never betrays anyone—especially those whom he loves and admires. And, may I be permitted to say, I love and admire the brave, dear woman you have proved yourself to be."

He took from his pocket a visiting card, tore it in two, gave one-half of it to the girl, as he said, in a voice shaken with emotion:

"If Monsieur Sholmes' plans for you do not succeed, mademoiselle, go to Lady Strongborough—you can easily find her address—and give her that half of the card, and, at the same time, say to her: *Faithful friend.* Lady Strongborough will show you the true devotion of a sister."

"Thank you," said the girl; "I shall see her to-morrow."

"And now, Monsieur Sholmes," exclaimed Lupin, with the satisfied air of a gentleman who has fulfilled his duty, "I will say good-night. We will not land for an hour yet, so I will get that much rest."

He lay down on the bench, with his hands beneath his head.

In a short time the high cliffs of the English coast loomed up in the increasing light of a new-born day. The passengers emerged from the cabins and crowded the deck, eagerly gazing on the approaching shore. Austin Gilette passed by, accompanied by two men whom Sholmes recognized as sleuths from Scotland Yard.

Lupin was asleep, on his bench.

THE END.

ARSENE LUPIN

BY

EDGAR JEPSON AND MAURICE LEBLANC

CHAPTER I THE MILLIONAIRE'S DAUGHTER

The rays of the September sun flooded the great halls of the old chateau of the Dukes of Charmerace, lighting up with their mellow glow the spoils of so many ages and many lands, jumbled together with the execrable taste which so often afflicts those whose only standard of value is money. The golden light warmed the panelled walls and old furniture to a dull lustre, and gave back to the fading gilt of the First Empire chairs and couches something of its old brightness. It illumined the long line of pictures on the walls, pictures of dead and gone Charmeraces, the stern or debonair faces of the men, soldiers, statesmen, dandies, the gentle or imperious faces of beautiful women. It flashed back from armour of brightly polished steel, and drew dull gleams from armour of bronze. The hues of rare porcelain, of the rich inlays of Oriental or Renaissance cabinets, mingled with the hues of the pictures, the tapestry, the Persian rugs about the polished floor to fill the hall with a rich glow of colour.

But of all the beautiful and precious things which the sun-rays warmed to a clearer beauty, the face of the girl who sat writing at a table in front of the long windows, which opened on to the centuries-old turf of the broad terrace, was the most beautiful and the most precious.

It was a delicate, almost frail, beauty. Her skin was clear with the transparent lustre of old porcelain, and her pale cheeks were only tinted with the pink of the faintest roses. Her straight nose was delicately cut, her rounded chin admirably moulded. A lover of beauty would have been at a loss whether more to admire her clear, germander eyes, so melting and so adorable, or the sensitive mouth, with its rather full lips, inviting all the kisses. But assuredly he would have been grieved by the perpetual air of sadness which rested on the beautiful face—the wistful melancholy of the Slav, deepened by something of personal misfortune and suffering.

Her face was framed by a mass of soft fair hair, shot with strands of gold where the sunlight fell on it; and little curls, rebellious to the comb, strayed over her white forehead, tiny feathers of gold.

She was addressing envelopes, and a long list of names lay on her left hand. When she had addressed an envelope, she slipped into it a wedding-card. On each was printed:

"M. Gournay-Martin has the honour to
inform
you of the marriage of his daughter
Germaine to the Duke of Charmerace."

She wrote steadily on, adding envelope after envelope to the pile ready for the post, which rose in front of her. But now and again, when the flushed and laughing girls who were playing lawn-tennis on the terrace, raised their voices higher than usual as they called the score, and distracted her attention from her work, her gaze strayed through the open window and lingered on them wistfully; and as her eyes came back to her task she sighed with so faint a wistfulness that she hardly knew she sighed. Then a voice from the terrace cried, "Sonia! Sonia!"

"Yes. Mlle. Germaine?" answered the writing girl.

"Tea! Order tea, will you?" cried the voice, a petulant voice, rather harsh to the ear.

"Very well, Mlle. Germaine," said Sonia; and having finished addressing the envelope under her pen, she laid it on the pile ready to be posted, and, crossing the room to the old, wide fireplace, she rang the bell.

She stood by the fireplace a moment, restoring to its place a rose which had fallen from a vase on the mantelpiece; and her attitude, as with arms upraised she arranged the flowers, displayed the delightful line of a slender figure. As she let fall her arms to her side, a footman entered the room.

"Will you please bring the tea, Alfred," she said in a charming voice of that pure, bell-like tone which has been Nature's most precious gift to but a few of the greatest actresses.

"For how many, miss?" said Alfred.

"For four—unless your master has come back."

"Oh, no; he's not back yet, miss. He went in the car to Rennes to lunch; and it's a good many miles away. He won't be back for another hour."

"And the Duke—he's not back from his ride yet, is he?"

"Not yet, miss," said Alfred, turning to go.

"One moment," said Sonia. "Have all of you got your things packed for the journey to Paris? You will have to start soon, you know. Are all the maids ready?"

"Well, all the men are ready, I know, miss. But about the maids, miss, I can't say. They've been bustling about all day; but it takes them longer than it does us."

"Tell them to hurry up; and be as quick as you can with the tea, please," said Sonia.

Alfred went out of the room; Sonia went back to the writing-table. She did not take up her pen; she took up one of the wedding-cards; and her lips moved slowly as she read it in a pondering depression.

The petulant, imperious voice broke in upon her musing.

"Whatever are you doing, Sonia? Aren't you getting on with those letters?" it cried angrily; and Germaine Gournay-Martin came through the long window into the hall.

The heiress to the Gournay-Martin millions carried her tennis racquet in her hand; and her rosy cheeks were flushed redder than ever by the game. She was a pretty girl in a striking, high-coloured, rather obvious way—the very foil to Sonia's delicate beauty. Her lips were a little too thin, her eyes too shallow; and together they gave her a rather hard air, in strongest contrast to the gentle, sympathetic face of Sonia.

The two friends with whom Germaine had been playing tennis followed her into the hall: Jeanne Gautier, tall, sallow, dark, with a somewhat malicious air; Marie Bullier, short, round, commonplace, and sentimental.

They came to the table at which Sonia was at work; and pointing to the pile of envelopes, Marie said, "Are these all wedding-cards?"

"Yes; and we've only got to the letter V," said Germaine, frowning at Sonia.

"Princesse de Vernan—Duchesse de Vauvieuse—Marquess—Marchioness? You've invited the whole Faubourg Saint-Germain," said Marie, shuffling the pile of envelopes with an envious air.

"You'll know very few people at your wedding," said Jeanne, with a spiteful little giggle.

"I beg your pardon, my dear," said Germaine boastfully. "Madame de Relzieres, my fiance's cousin, gave an At Home the other day in my honour. At it she introduced half Paris to me—the Paris I'm destined to know, the Paris you'll see in my drawing-rooms."

"But we shall no longer be fit friends for you when you're the Duchess of Charmerace," said Jeanne.

"Why?" said Germaine; and then she added quickly, "Above everything, Sonia, don't forget Veauleglise, 33, University Street—33, University Street."

"Veauleglise—33, University Street," said Sonia, taking a fresh envelope, and beginning to address it.

"Wait—wait! don't close the envelope. I'm wondering whether Veauleglise ought to have a cross, a double cross, or a triple cross," said Germaine, with an air of extreme importance.

"What's that?" cried Marie and Jeanne together.

"A single cross means an invitation to the church, a double cross an invitation to the marriage and the wedding-breakfast, and the triple cross means an invitation to the marriage, the breakfast, and the signing of the marriage-contract. What do you think the Duchess of Veauleglise ought to have?"

"Don't ask me. I haven't the honour of knowing that great lady," cried Jeanne.

"Nor I," said Marie.

"Nor I," said Germaine. "But I have here the visiting-list of the late Duchess of Charmerace, Jacques' mother. The two duchesses were on excellent terms. Besides the Duchess of Veauleglise is rather worn-out, but greatly admired for her piety. She goes to early service three times a week."

"Then put three crosses," said Jeanne.

"I shouldn't," said Marie quickly. "In your place, my dear, I shouldn't risk a slip. I should ask my fiance's advice. He knows this world."

"Oh, goodness—my fiance! He doesn't care a rap about this kind of thing. He has changed so in the last seven years. Seven years ago he took nothing seriously. Why, he set off on an expedition to the South Pole—just to show off. Oh, in those days he was truly a duke."

"And to-day?" said Jeanne.

"Oh, to-day he's a regular slow-coach. Society gets on his nerves. He's as sober as a judge," said Germaine.

"He's as gay as a lark," said Sonia, in sudden protest.

Germaine pouted at her, and said: "Oh, he's gay enough when he's making fun of people. But apart from that he's as sober as a judge."

"Your father must be delighted with the change," said Jeanne.

"Naturally he's delighted. Why, he's lunching at Rennes to-day with the Minister, with the sole object of getting Jacques decorated."

"Well; the Legion of Honour is a fine thing to have," said Marie.

"My dear! The Legion of Honour is all very well for middle-class people, but it's quite out of place for a duke!" cried Germaine.

Alfred came in, bearing the tea-tray, and set it on a little table near that at which Sonia was sitting.

Germaine, who was feeling too important to sit still, was walking up and down the room. Suddenly she stopped short, and pointing to a silver statuette which stood on the piano, she said, "What's this? Why is this statuette here?"

"Why, when we came in, it was on the cabinet, in its usual place," said Sonia in some astonishment.

"Did you come into the hall while we were out in the garden, Alfred?" said Germaine to the footman.

"No, miss," said Alfred.

"But some one must have come into it," Germaine persisted.

"I've not heard any one. I was in my pantry," said Alfred.

"It's very odd," said Germaine.

"It is odd," said Sonia. "Statuettes don't move about of themselves."

All of them stared at the statuette as if they expected it to move again forthwith, under their very eyes. Then Alfred put it back in its usual place on one of the cabinets, and went out of the room.

Sonia poured out the tea; and over it they babbled about the coming marriage, the frocks they would wear at it, and the presents Germaine had already received. That reminded her to ask Sonia if any one had yet telephoned from her father's house in Paris; and Sonia said that no one had.

"That's very annoying," said Germaine. "It shows that nobody has sent me a present to-day."

282

Pouting, she shrugged her shoulders with an air of a spoiled child, which sat but poorly on a well-developed young woman of twenty-three.

"It's Sunday. The shops don't deliver things on Sunday," said Sonia gently.

But Germaine still pouted like a spoiled child.

"Isn't your beautiful Duke coming to have tea with us?" said Jeanne a little anxiously.

"Oh, yes; I'm expecting him at half-past four. He had to go for a ride with the two Du Buits. They're coming to tea here, too," said Germaine.

"Gone for a ride with the two Du Buits? But when?" cried Marie quickly.

"This afternoon."

"He can't be," said Marie. "My brother went to the Du Buits' house after lunch, to see Andre and Georges. They went for a drive this morning, and won't be back till late to-night."

"Well, but—but why did the Duke tell me so?" said Germaine, knitting her brow with a puzzled air.

"If I were you, I should inquire into this thoroughly. Dukes—well, we know what dukes are—it will be just as well to keep an eye on him," said Jeanne maliciously.

Germaine flushed quickly; and her eyes flashed. "Thank you. I have every confidence in Jacques. I am absolutely sure of him," she said angrily.

"Oh, well—if you're sure, it's all right," said Jeanne.

The ringing of the telephone-bell made a fortunate diversion.

Germaine rushed to it, clapped the receiver to her ear, and cried: "Hello, is that you, Pierre? ... Oh, it's Victoire, is it? ... Ah, some presents have come, have they? ... Well, well, what are they? ... What! a paper-knife—another paper-knife! ... Another Louis XVI. inkstand—oh, bother! ... Who are they from? ... Oh, from the Countess Rudolph and the Baron de Valery." Her voice rose high, thrilling with pride.

Then she turned her face to her friends, with the receiver still at her ear, and cried: "Oh, girls, a pearl necklace too! A large one! The pearls are big ones!"

"How jolly!" said Marie.

"Who sent it?" said Germaine, turning to the telephone again. "Oh, a friend of papa's," she added in a tone of disappointment. "Never mind, after all it's a pearl necklace. You'll be sure and lock the doors carefully, Victoire, won't you? And lock up the necklace in the secret cupboard.... Yes; thanks very much, Victoire. I shall see you to-morrow."

She hung up the receiver, and came away from the telephone frowning.

"It's preposterous!" she said pettishly. "Papa's friends and relations give me marvellous presents, and all the swells send me paper-knives. It's all Jacques' fault. He's above all this kind of thing. The Faubourg Saint-Germain hardly knows that we're engaged."

"He doesn't go about advertising it," said Jeanne, smiling.

"You're joking, but all the same what you say is true," said Germaine. "That's exactly what his cousin Madame de Relzieres said to me the other day at the At Home she gave in my honour—wasn't it, Sonia?" And she walked to the window, and, turning her back on them, stared out of it.

"She HAS got her mouth full of that At Home," said Jeanne to Marie in a low voice.

There was an awkward silence. Marie broke it:

"Speaking of Madame de Relzieres, do you know that she is on pins and needles with anxiety? Her son is fighting a duel to-day," she said.

"With whom?" said Sonia.

"No one knows. She got hold of a letter from the seconds," said Marie.

"My mind is quite at rest about Relzieres," said Germaine. "He's a first-class swordsman. No one could beat him."

Sonia did not seem to share her freedom from anxiety. Her forehead was puckered in little lines of perplexity, as if she were puzzling out some problem; and there was a look of something very like fear in her gentle eyes.

"Wasn't Relzieres a great friend of your fiance at one time?" said Jeanne.

"A great friend? I should think he was," said Germaine. "Why, it was through Relzieres that we got to know Jacques."

"Where was that?" said Marie.

"Here—in this very chateau," said Germaine.

"Actually in his own house?" said Marie, in some surprise.

"Yes; actually here. Isn't life funny?" said Germaine. "If, a few months after his father's death, Jacques had not found himself hard-up, and obliged to dispose of this chateau, to raise the money for his expedition to the South Pole; and if papa and I had not wanted an historic chateau; and lastly, if papa had not suffered from rheumatism, I should not be calling myself in a month from now the Duchess of Charmerace."

"Now what on earth has your father's rheumatism got to do with your being Duchess of Charmerace?" cried Jeanne.

"Everything," said Germaine. "Papa was afraid that this chateau was damp. To prove to papa that he had nothing to fear, Jacques, en grand seigneur, offered him his hospitality, here, at Charmerace, for three weeks."

"That was truly ducal," said Marie.

"But he is always like that," said Sonia.

"Oh, he's all right in that way, little as he cares about society," said Germaine. "Well, by a miracle my father got cured of his rheumatism here. Jacques fell in love with me; papa made up his mind to buy the chateau; and I demanded the hand of Jacques in marriage."

"You did? But you were only sixteen then," said Marie, with some surprise.

"Yes; but even at sixteen a girl ought to know that a duke is a duke. I did," said Germaine. "Then since Jacques was setting out for the South Pole, and papa considered me much too young to get married, I promised Jacques to wait for his return."

"Why, it was everything that's romantic!" cried Marie.

"Romantic? Oh, yes," said Germaine; and she pouted. "But between ourselves, if I'd known that he was going to stay all that time at the South Pole—"

"That's true," broke in Marie. "To go away for three years and stay away seven—at the end of the world."

"All Germaine's beautiful youth," said Jeanne, with her malicious smile.

"Thanks!" said Germaine tartly.

"Well, you ARE twenty-three. It's the flower of one's age," said Jeanne.

285

"Not quite twenty-three," said Germaine hastily. "And look at the wretched luck I've had. The Duke falls ill and is treated at Montevideo. As soon as he recovers, since he's the most obstinate person in the world, he resolves to go on with the expedition. He sets out; and for an age, without a word of warning, there's no more news of him—no news of any kind. For six months, you know, we believed him dead."

"Dead? Oh, how unhappy you must have been!" said Sonia.

"Oh, don't speak of it! For six months I daren't put on a light frock," said Germaine, turning to her.

"A lot she must have cared for him," whispered Jeanne to Marie.

"Fortunately, one fine day, the letters began again. Three months ago a telegram informed us that he was coming back; and at last the Duke returned," said Germaine, with a theatrical air.

"The Duke returned," cried Jeanne, mimicking her.

"Never mind. Fancy waiting nearly seven years for one's fiance. That was constancy," said Sonia.

"Oh, you're a sentimentalist, Mlle. Kritchnoff," said Jeanne, in a tone of mockery. "It was the influence of the castle."

"What do you mean?" said Germaine.

"Oh, to own the castle of Charmerace and call oneself Mlle. Gournay-Martin—it's not worth doing. One MUST become a duchess," said Jeanne.

"Yes, yes; and for all this wonderful constancy, seven years of it, Germaine was on the point of becoming engaged to another man," said Marie, smiling.

"And he a mere baron," said Jeanne, laughing.

"What? Is that true?" said Sonia.

"Didn't you know, Mlle. Kritchnoff? She nearly became engaged to the Duke's cousin, the Baron de Relzieres. It was not nearly so grand."

"Oh, it's all very well to laugh at me; but being the cousin and heir of the Duke, Relzieres would have assumed the title, and I should have been Duchess just the same," said Germaine triumphantly.

"Evidently that was all that mattered," said Jeanne. "Well, dear, I must be off. We've promised to run in to see the Comtesse de Grosjean. You know the Comtesse de Grosjean?"

She spoke with an air of careless pride, and rose to go.

"Only by name. Papa used to know her husband on the Stock Exchange when he was still called simply M. Grosjean. For his part, papa preferred to keep his name intact," said Germaine, with quiet pride.

"Intact? That's one way of looking at it. Well, then, I'll see you in Paris. You still intend to start to-morrow?" said Jeanne.

"Yes; to-morrow morning," said Germaine.

Jeanne and Marie slipped on their dust-coats to the accompaniment of chattering and kissing, and went out of the room.

As she closed the door on them, Germaine turned to Sonia, and said: "I do hate those two girls! They're such horrible snobs."

"Oh, they're good-natured enough," said Sonia.

"Good-natured? Why, you idiot, they're just bursting with envy of me—bursting!" said Germaine. "Well, they've every reason to be," she added confidently, surveying herself in a Venetian mirror with a petted child's self-content.

CHAPTER II THE COMING OF THE CHAROLAIS

Sonia went back to her table, and once more began putting wedding-cards in their envelopes and addressing them. Germaine moved restlessly about the room, fidgeting with the bric-a-brac on the cabinets, shifting the pieces about, interrupting Sonia to ask whether she preferred this arrangement or that, throwing herself into a chair to read a magazine, getting up in a couple of minutes to straighten a picture on the wall, throwing out all the while idle questions not worth answering. Ninety-nine human beings would have been irritated to exasperation by her fidgeting; Sonia endured it with a perfect patience. Five times Germaine asked her whether she should wear her heliotrope or her pink gown at a forthcoming dinner at Madame de Relzieres'. Five times Sonia said, without the slightest variation in her tone, "I think you look better in the pink." And all the while the pile of addressed envelopes rose steadily.

Presently the door opened, and Alfred stood on the threshold.

"Two gentlemen have called to see you, miss," he said.

"Ah, the two Du Buits," cried Germaine.

"They didn't give their names, miss."

"A gentleman in the prime of life and a younger one?" said Germaine.

"Yes, miss."

"I thought so. Show them in."

"Yes, miss. And have you any orders for me to give Victoire when we get to Paris?" said Alfred.

"No. Are you starting soon?"

"Yes, miss. We're all going by the seven o'clock train. It's a long way from here to Paris; we shall only reach it at nine in the morning. That will give us just time to get the house ready for you by the time you get there to-morrow evening," said Alfred.

"Is everything packed?"

"Yes, miss—everything. The cart has already taken the heavy luggage to the station. All you'll have to do is to see after your bags."

"That's all right. Show M. du Buit and his brother in," said Germaine.

She moved to a chair near the window, and disposed herself in an attitude of studied, and obviously studied, grace.

As she leant her head at a charming angle back against the tall back of the chair, her eyes fell on the window, and they opened wide.

"Why, whatever's this?" she cried, pointing to it.

"Whatever's what?" said Sonia, without raising her eyes from the envelope she was addressing.

"Why, the window. Look! one of the panes has been taken out. It looks as if it had been cut."

"So it has—just at the level of the fastening," said Sonia. And the two girls stared at the gap.

"Haven't you noticed it before?" said Germaine.

"No; the broken glass must have fallen outside," said Sonia.

The noise of the opening of the door drew their attention from the window. Two figures were advancing towards them—a short, round, tubby man of fifty-five, red-faced, bald, with bright grey eyes, which seemed to be continually dancing away from meeting the eyes of any other human being. Behind him came a slim young man, dark and grave. For all the difference in their colouring, it was clear that they were father and son: their eyes were set so close together. The son seemed to have inherited, along with her black eyes, his mother's nose, thin and aquiline; the nose of the father started thin from the brow, but ended in a scarlet bulb eloquent of an exhaustive acquaintance with the vintages of the world.

Germaine rose, looking at them with an air of some surprise and uncertainty: these were not her friends, the Du Buits.

The elder man, advancing with a smiling bonhomie, bowed, and said in an adenoid voice, ingratiating of tone: "I'm M. Charolais, young ladies—M. Charolais—retired brewer—chevalier of the Legion of Honour—landowner at Rennes. Let me introduce my son." The young man bowed awkwardly. "We came from Rennes this morning, and we lunched at Kerlor's farm."

"Shall I order tea for them?" whispered Sonia.

"Gracious, no!" said Germaine sharply under her breath; then, louder, she said to M. Charolais, "And what is your object in calling?"

"We asked to see your father," said M. Charolais, smiling with broad amiability, while his eyes danced across her face, avoiding any meeting with hers. "The footman told us that M. Gournay-Martin was out, but that his daughter was at home. And we were unable, quite unable, to deny ourselves the pleasure of meeting you." With that he sat down; and his son followed his example.

Sonia and Germaine, taken aback, looked at one another in some perplexity.

"What a fine chateau, papa!" said the young man.

"Yes, my boy; it's a very fine chateau," said M. Charolais, looking round the hall with appreciative but greedy eyes.

There was a pause.

"It's a very fine chateau, young ladies," said M. Charolais.

"Yes; but excuse me, what is it you have called about?" said Germaine.

M. Charolais crossed his legs, leant back in his chair, thrust his thumbs into the arm-holes of his waistcoat, and said: "Well, we've come about the advertisement we saw in the RENNES ADVERTISER, that M. Gournay-Martin wanted to get rid of a motor-car; and my son is always saying to me, 'I should like a motor-car which rushes the hills, papa.' He means a sixty horse-power."

"We've got a sixty horse-power; but it's not for sale. My father is even using it himself to-day," said Germaine.

"Perhaps it's the car we saw in the stable-yard," said M. Charolais.

"No; that's a thirty to forty horse-power. It belongs to me. But if your son really loves rushing hills, as you say, we have a hundred horse-power car which my father wants to get rid of. Wait; where's the photograph of it, Sonia? It ought to be here somewhere."

The two girls rose, went to a table set against the wall beyond the window, and began turning over the papers with which it was loaded in the search for the photograph. They had barely turned their backs, when the hand of young Charolais shot out as swiftly as the tongue of a lizard catching a fly, closed round the silver statuette on the top of the cabinet beside him, and flashed it into his jacket pocket.

Charolais was watching the two girls; one would have said that he had eyes for nothing else, yet, without moving a muscle of his face, set in its perpetual beaming smile, he hissed in an angry whisper, "Drop it, you idiot! Put it back!"

The young man scowled askance at him.

"Curse you! Put it back!" hissed Charolais.

The young man's arm shot out with the same quickness, and the statuette stood in its place.

There was just the faintest sigh of relief from Charolais, as Germaine turned and came to him with the photograph in her hand. She gave it to him.

"Ah, here we are," he said, putting on a pair of gold-rimmed pince-nez. "A hundred horse-power car. Well, well, this is something to talk over. What's the least you'll take for it?"

"*I* have nothing to do with this kind of thing," cried Germaine. "You must see my father. He will be back from Rennes soon. Then you can settle the matter with him."

M. Charolais rose, and said: "Very good. We will go now, and come back presently. I'm sorry to have intruded on you, young ladies—taking up your time like this—"

"Not at all—not at all," murmured Germaine politely.

"Good-bye—good-bye," said M. Charolais; and he and his son went to the door, and bowed themselves out.

"What creatures!" said Germaine, going to the window, as the door closed behind the two visitors. "All the same, if they do buy the hundred horse-power, papa will be awfully pleased. It is odd about that pane. I wonder how it happened. It's odd too that Jacques hasn't come back yet. He told me that he would be here between half-past four and five."

"And the Du Buits have not come either," said Sonia. "But it's hardly five yet."

"Yes; that's so. The Du Buits have not come either. What on earth are you wasting your time for?" she added sharply, raising her voice. "Just finish addressing those letters while you're waiting."

"They're nearly finished," said Sonia.

"Nearly isn't quite. Get on with them, can't you!" snapped Germaine.

Sonia went back to the writing-table; just the slightest deepening of the faint pink roses in her cheeks marked her sense of Germaine's rudeness. After three years as companion to Germaine Gournay-Martin, she was well inured to millionaire manners; they had almost lost the power to move her.

Germaine dropped into a chair for twenty seconds; then flung out of it.

"Ten minutes to five!" she cried. "Jacques is late. It's the first time I've ever known him late."

She went to the window, and looked across the wide stretch of meadow-land and woodland on which the chateau, set on the very crown of the ridge, looked down. The road, running with the irritating straightness of so many of the roads of France, was visible for a full three miles. It was empty.

"Perhaps the Duke went to the Chateau de Relzieres to see his cousin—though I fancy that at bottom the Duke does not care very much for the Baron de Relzieres. They always look as though they detested one another," said Sonia, without raising her eyes from the letter she was addressing.

"You've noticed that, have you?" said Germaine. "Now, as far as Jacques is concerned—he's—he's so indifferent. None the less, when we were at the Relzieres on Thursday, I caught him quarrelling with Paul de Relzieres."

"Quarrelling?" said Sonia sharply, with a sudden uneasiness in air and eyes and voice.

"Yes; quarrelling. And they said good-bye to one another in the oddest way."

"But surely they shook hands?" said Sonia.

"Not a bit of it. They bowed as if each of them had swallowed a poker."

"Why—then—then—" said Sonia, starting up with a frightened air; and her voice stuck in her throat.

"Then what?" said Germaine, a little startled by her panic-stricken face.

"The duel! Monsieur de Relzieres' duel!" cried Sonia.

"What? You don't think it was with Jacques?"

"I don't know—but this quarrel—the Duke's manner this morning—the Du Buits' drive—" said Sonia.

"Of course—of course! It's quite possible—in fact it's certain!" cried Germaine.

"It's horrible!" gasped Sonia. "Consider—just consider! Suppose something happened to him. Suppose the Duke—"

"It's me the Duke's fighting about!" cried Germaine proudly, with a little skipping jump of triumphant joy.

Sonia stared through her without seeing her. Her face was a dead white—fear had chilled the lustre from her skin; her breath panted through her parted lips; and her dilated eyes seemed to look on some dreadful picture.

Germaine pirouetted about the hall at the very height of triumph. To have a Duke fighting a duel about her was far beyond the wildest dreams of snobbishness. She chuckled again and again, and once she clapped her hands and laughed aloud.

"He's fighting a swordsman of the first class—an invincible swordsman—you said so yourself," Sonia muttered in a tone of anguish. "And there's nothing to be done—nothing."

She pressed her hands to her eyes as if to shut out a hideous vision.

Germaine did not hear her; she was staring at herself in a mirror, and bridling to her own image.

Sonia tottered to the window and stared down at the road along which must come the tidings of weal or irremediable woe. She kept passing her hand over her eyes as if to clear their vision.

Suddenly she started, and bent forward, rigid, all her being concentrated in the effort to see.

Then she cried: "Mademoiselle Germaine! Look! Look!"

"What is it?" said Germaine, coming to her side.

"A horseman! Look! There!" said Sonia, waving a hand towards the road.

"Yes; and isn't he galloping!" said Germaine.

"It's he! It's the Duke!" cried Sonia.

"Do you think so?" said Germaine doubtfully.

"I'm sure of it—sure!"

"Well, he gets here just in time for tea," said Germaine in a tone of extreme satisfaction. "He knows that I hate to be kept waiting. He said to me, 'I shall be back by five at the latest.' And here he is."

"It's impossible," said Sonia. "He has to go all the way round the park. There's no direct road; the brook is between us."

"All the same, he's coming in a straight line," said Germaine.

It was true. The horseman had left the road and was galloping across the meadows straight for the brook. In twenty seconds he reached its treacherous bank, and as he set his horse at it, Sonia covered her eyes.

"He's over!" said Germaine. "My father gave three hundred guineas for that horse."

CHAPTER III LUPIN'S WAY

Sonia, in a sudden revulsion of feeling, in a reaction from her fears, slipped back and sat down at the tea-table, panting quickly, struggling to keep back the tears of relief. She did not see the Duke gallop up the slope, dismount, and hand over his horse to the groom who came running to him. There was still a mist in her eyes to blur his figure as he came through the window.

"If it's for me, plenty of tea, very little cream, and three lumps of sugar," he cried in a gay, ringing voice, and pulled out his watch. "Five to the minute—that's all right." And he bent down, took Germaine's hand, and kissed it with an air of gallant devotion.

If he had indeed just fought a duel, there were no signs of it in his bearing. His air, his voice, were entirely careless. He was a man whose whole thought at the moment was fixed on his tea and his punctuality.

He drew a chair near the tea-table for Germaine; sat down himself; and Sonia handed him a cup of tea with so shaky a hand that the spoon clinked in the saucer.

"You've been fighting a duel?" said Germaine.

"What! You've heard already?" said the Duke in some surprise.

"I've heard," said Germaine. "Why did you fight it?"

"You're not wounded, your Grace?" said Sonia anxiously.

"Not a scratch," said the Duke, smiling at her.

"Will you be so good as to get on with those wedding-cards, Sonia," said Germaine sharply; and Sonia went back to the writing-table.

Turning to the Duke, Germaine said, "Did you fight on my account?"

"Would you be pleased to know that I had fought on your account?" said the Duke; and there was a faint mocking light in his eyes, far too faint for the self-satisfied Germaine to perceive.

"Yes. But it isn't true. You've been fighting about some woman," said Germaine petulantly.

"If I had been fighting about a woman, it could only be you," said the Duke.

"Yes, that is so. Of course. It could hardly be about Sonia, or my maid," said Germaine. "But what was the reason of the duel?"

"Oh, the reason of it was entirely childish," said the Duke. "I was in a bad temper; and De Relzieres said something that annoyed me."

"Then it wasn't about me; and if it wasn't about me, it wasn't really worth while fighting," said Germaine in a tone of acute disappointment.

The mocking light deepened a little in the Duke's eyes.

"Yes. But if I had been killed, everybody would have said, 'The Duke of Charmerace has been killed in a duel about Mademoiselle Gournay-Martin.' That would have sounded very fine indeed," said the Duke; and a touch of mockery had crept into his voice.

"Now, don't begin trying to annoy me again," said Germaine pettishly.

"The last thing I should dream of, my dear girl," said the Duke, smiling.

"And De Relzieres? Is he wounded?" said Germaine.

"Poor dear De Relzieres: he won't be out of bed for the next six months," said the Duke; and he laughed lightly and gaily.

"Good gracious!" cried Germaine.

"It will do poor dear De Relzieres a world of good. He has a touch of enteritis; and for enteritis there is nothing like rest," said the Duke.

Sonia was not getting on very quickly with the wedding-cards. Germaine was sitting with her back to her; and over her shoulder Sonia could watch the face of the Duke—an extraordinarily mobile face, changing with every passing mood. Sometimes his eyes met hers; and hers fell before them. But as soon as they turned away from her she was watching him again, almost greedily, as if she could not see enough of his face in which strength of will and purpose was mingled with a faint, ironic scepticism, and tempered by a fine air of race.

He finished his tea; then he took a morocco case from his pocket, and said to Germaine, "It must be quite three days since I gave you anything."

He opcned the case, disclosed a pearl pendant, and handed it to her.

"Oh, how nice!" she cried, taking it.

She took it from the case, saying that it was a beauty. She showed it to Sonia; then she put it on and stood before a mirror admiring the effect. To tell the truth, the effect was not entirely desirable. The pearls did not improve the look of her rather coarse brown skin; and her skin added nothing to the beauty of the pearls. Sonia saw this, and so did the Duke. He looked at Sonia's white throat. She met his eyes and blushed. She knew that the same thought was in both their minds; the pearls would have looked infinitely better there.

Germaine finished admiring herself; she was incapable even of suspecting that so expensive a pendant could not suit her perfectly.

The Duke said idly: "Goodness! Are all those invitations to the wedding?"

"That's only down to the letter V," said Germaine proudly.

"And there are twenty-five letters in the alphabet! You must be inviting the whole world. You'll have to have the Madeleine enlarged. It won't hold them all. There isn't a church in Paris that will," said the Duke.

"Won't it be a splendid marriage!" said Germaine. "There'll be something like a crush. There are sure to be accidents."

"If I were you, I should have careful arrangements made," said the Duke.

"Oh, let people look after themselves. They'll remember it better if they're crushed a little," said Germaine.

There was a flicker of contemptuous wonder in the Duke's eyes. But he only shrugged his shoulders, and turning to Sonia, said, "Will you be an angel and play me a little Grieg, Mademoiselle Kritchnoff? I heard you playing yesterday. No one plays Grieg like you."

"Excuse me, Jacques, but Mademoiselle Kritchnoff has her work to do," said Germaine tartly.

"Five minutes' interval—just a morsel of Grieg, I beg," said the Duke, with an irresistible smile.

"All right," said Germaine grudgingly. "But I've something important to talk to you about."

"By Jove! So have I. I was forgetting. I've the last photograph I took of you and Mademoiselle Sonia." Germaine frowned and shrugged her shoulders. "With your light frocks in the open air, you look like two big flowers," said the Duke.

"You call that important!" cried Germaine.

297

"It's very important—like all trifles," said the Duke, smiling. "Look! isn't it nice?" And he took a photograph from his pocket, and held it out to her.

"Nice? It's shocking! We're making the most appalling faces," said Germaine, looking at the photograph in his hand.

"Well, perhaps you ARE making faces," said the Duke seriously, considering the photograph with grave earnestness. "But they're not appalling faces—not by any means. You shall be judge, Mademoiselle Sonia. The faces—well, we won't talk about the faces—but the outlines. Look at the movement of your scarf." And he handed the photograph to Sonia.

"Jacques!" said Germaine impatiently.

"Oh, yes, you've something important to tell me. What is it?" said the Duke, with an air of resignation; and he took the photograph from Sonia and put it carefully back in his pocket.

"Victoire has telephoned from Paris to say that we've had a paper-knife and a Louis Seize inkstand given us," said Germaine.

"Hurrah!" cried the Duke in a sudden shout that made them both jump.

"And a pearl necklace," said Germaine.

"Hurrah!" cried the Duke.

"You're perfectly childish," said Germaine pettishly. "I tell you we've been given a paper-knife, and you shout 'hurrah!' I say we've been given a pearl necklace, and you shout 'hurrah!' You can't have the slightest sense of values."

"I beg your pardon. This pearl necklace is from one of your father's friends, isn't it?" said the Duke.

"Yes; why?" said Germaine.

"But the inkstand and the paper-knife must be from the Faubourg Saint-Germain, and well on the shabby side?" said the Duke.

"Yes; well?"

"Well then, my dear girl, what are you complaining about? They balance; the equilibrium is restored. You can't have everything," said the Duke; and he laughed mischievously.

Germaine flushed, and bit her lip; her eyes sparkled.

"You don't care a rap about me," she said stormily.

"But I find you adorable," said the Duke.

"You keep annoying me," said Germaine pettishly. "And you do it on purpose. I think it's in very bad taste. I shall end by taking a dislike to you—I know I shall."

"Wait till we're married for that, my dear girl," said the Duke; and he laughed again, with a blithe, boyish cheerfulness, which deepened the angry flush in Germaine's cheeks.

"Can't you be serious about anything?" she cried.

"I am the most serious man in Europe," said the Duke.

Germaine went to the window and stared out of it sulkily.

The Duke walked up and down the hall, looking at the pictures of some of his ancestors—somewhat grotesque persons—with humorous appreciation. Between addressing the envelopes Sonia kept glancing at him. Once he caught her eye, and smiled at her. Germaine's back was eloquent of her displeasure. The Duke stopped at a gap in the line of pictures in which there hung a strip of old tapestry.

"I can never understand why you have left all these ancestors of mine staring from the walls and have taken away the quite admirable and interesting portrait of myself," he said carelessly.

Germaine turned sharply from the window; Sonia stopped in the middle of addressing an envelope; and both the girls stared at him in astonishment.

"There certainly was a portrait of me where that tapestry hangs. What have you done with it?" said the Duke.

"You're making fun of us again," said Germaine.

"Surely your Grace knows what happened," said Sonia.

"We wrote all the details to you and sent you all the papers three years ago. Didn't you get them?" said Germaine.

"Not a detail or a newspaper. Three years ago I was in the neighbourhood of the South Pole, and lost at that," said the Duke.

"But it was most dramatic, my dear Jacques. All Paris was talking of it," said Germaine. "Your portrait was stolen."

"Stolen? Who stole it?" said the Duke.

Germaine crossed the hall quickly to the gap in the line of pictures.

"I'll show you," she said.

She drew aside the piece of tapestry, and in the middle of the panel over which the portrait of the Duke had hung he saw written in chalk the words:

ARSENE LUPIN

"What do you think of that autograph?" said Germaine.

"'Arsene Lupin?'" said the Duke in a tone of some bewilderment.

"He left his signature. It seems that he always does so," said Sonia in an explanatory tone.

"But who is he?" said the Duke.

"Arsene Lupin? Surely you know who Arsene Lupin is?" said Germaine impatiently.

"I haven't the slightest notion," said the Duke.

"Oh, come! No one is as South-Pole as all that!" cried Germaine. "You don't know who Lupin is? The most whimsical, the most audacious, and the most genial thief in France. For the last ten years he has kept the police at bay. He has baffled Ganimard, Holmlock Shears, the great English detective, and even Guerchard, whom everybody says is the greatest detective we've had in France since Vidocq. In fact, he's our national robber. Do you mean to say you don't know him?"

"Not even enough to ask him to lunch at a restaurant," said the Duke flippantly. "What's he like?"

"Like? Nobody has the slightest idea. He has a thousand disguises. He has dined two evenings running at the English Embassy."

"But if nobody knows him, how did they learn that?" said the Duke, with a puzzled air.

"Because the second evening, about ten o'clock, they noticed that one of the guests had disappeared, and with him all the jewels of the ambassadress."

"All of them?" said the Duke.

"Yes; and Lupin left his card behind him with these words scribbled on it:"

"'This is not a robbery; it is a restitution. You took the Wallace collection from us.'"

"But it was a hoax, wasn't it?" said the Duke.

"No, your Grace; and he has done better than that. You remember the affair of the Daray Bank—the savings bank for poor people?" said Sonia, her gentle face glowing with a sudden enthusiastic animation.

"Let's see," said the Duke. "Wasn't that the financier who doubled his fortune at the expense of a heap of poor wretches and ruined two thousand people?"

"Yes; that's the man," said Sonia. "And Lupin stripped Daray's house and took from him everything he had in his strong-box. He didn't leave him a sou of the money. And then, when he'd taken it from him, he distributed it among all the poor wretches whom Daray had ruined."

"But this isn't a thief you're talking about—it's a philanthropist," said the Duke.

"A fine sort of philanthropist!" broke in Germaine in a peevish tone. "There was a lot of philanthropy about his robbing papa, wasn't there?"

"Well," said the Duke, with an air of profound reflection, "if you come to think of it, that robbery was not worthy of this national hero. My portrait, if you except the charm and beauty of the face itself, is not worth much."

"If you think he was satisfied with your portrait, you're very much mistaken. All my father's collections were robbed," said Germaine.

"Your father's collections?" said the Duke. "But they're better guarded than the Bank of France. Your father is as careful of them as the apple of his eye."

"That's exactly it—he was too careful of them. That's why Lupin succeeded."

"This is very interesting," said the Duke; and he sat down on a couch before the gap in the pictures, to go into the matter more at his ease. "I suppose he had accomplices in the house itself?"

"Yes, one accomplice," said Germaine.

"Who was that?" asked the Duke.

"Papa!" said Germaine.

"Oh, come! what on earth do you mean?" said the Duke. "You're getting quite incomprehensible, my dear girl."

"Well, I'll make it clear to you. One morning papa received a letter—but wait. Sonia, get me the Lupin papers out of the bureau."

Sonia rose from the writing-table, and went to a bureau, an admirable example of the work of the great English maker, Chippendale. It stood on the other side of the hall between an Oriental cabinet and a sixteenth-century Italian cabinet—for all the world as if it were standing in a crowded curiosity shop—with the natural effect that the three pieces, by their mere incongruity, took something each from the beauty of the other. Sonia raised the flap of the bureau, and taking from one of the drawers a small portfolio, turned over the papers in it and handed a letter to the Duke.

"This is the envelope," she said. "It's addressed to M. Gournay-Martin, Collector, at the Chateau de Charmerace, Ile-et-Vilaine."

The Duke opened the envelope and took out a letter.

"It's an odd handwriting," he said.

"Read it—carefully," said Germaine.

It was an uncommon handwriting. The letters of it were small, but perfectly formed. It looked the handwriting of a man who knew exactly what he wanted to say, and liked to say it with extreme precision. The letter ran:

"DEAR SIR,"

"Please forgive my writing to you without our having been introduced to one another; but I flatter myself that you know me, at any rate, by name."

"There is in the drawing-room next your hall a Gainsborough of admirable quality which affords me infinite pleasure. Your Goyas in the same drawing-room are also to my liking, as well as your Van Dyck. In the further drawing-room I note the Renaissance cabinets—a marvellous pair—the Flemish tapestry, the Fragonard, the clock signed Boulle, and various other objects of less importance. But above all I have set my heart on that coronet which you bought at the sale of the Marquise de Ferronaye, and which was formerly worn by the unfortunate Princesse de Lamballe. I take the greatest interest in this coronet: in the first place, on account of the charming and tragic memories which it calls up in the mind of a poet passionately fond of history, and in the second place— though it is hardly worth while talking about that kind of thing—on account of its intrinsic value. I reckon indeed that the stones in your coronet are, at the very lowest, worth half a million francs."

"I beg you, my dear sir, to have these different objects properly packed up, and to forward them, addressed to me, carriage paid, to the Batignolles Station. Failing this, I shall Proceed to remove them myself on the night of Thursday, August 7th."

"Please pardon the slight trouble to which I am putting you, and believe me,"

"Yours very sincerely," "ARSENE LUPIN."

"P.S.—It occurs to me that the pictures have not glass before them. It would be as well to repair this omission before forwarding them to me, and I am sure that you will take this extra trouble cheerfully. I am aware, of course, that some of the best judges declare that a picture loses some of its quality when seen through glass. But it preserves them, and we should always be ready and willing to sacrifice a portion of our own pleasure for the benefit of posterity. France demands it of us.—A. L."

The Duke laughed, and said, "Really, this is extraordinarily funny. It must have made your father laugh."

"Laugh?" said Germaine. "You should have seen his face. He took it seriously enough, I can tell you."

"Not to the point of forwarding the things to Batignolles, I hope," said the Duke.

"No, but to the point of being driven wild," said Germaine. "And since the police had always been baffled by Lupin, he had the brilliant idea of trying what soldiers could do. The Commandant at Rennes is a great friend of papa's; and papa went to him, and told him about Lupin's letter and what he feared. The colonel laughed at him; but he offered him a corporal and six soldiers to guard his collection, on the night of the seventh. It was arranged that they should come from Rennes by the last train so that the burglars should have no warning of their coming. Well, they came, seven picked men—men who had seen service in Tonquin. We gave them supper; and then the corporal posted them in the hall and the two drawing-rooms where the pictures and things were. At eleven we all went to bed, after promising the corporal that, in the event of any fight with the burglars, we would not stir from our rooms. I can tell you I felt awfully nervous. I couldn't get to sleep for ages and ages. Then, when I did, I did not wake till morning. The night had passed absolutely quietly. Nothing out of the common had happened. There had not been the slightest noise. I awoke Sonia and my father. We dressed as quickly as we could, and rushed down to the drawing-room."

She paused dramatically.

"Well?" said the Duke.

"Well, it was done."

"What was done?" said the Duke.

"Everything," said Germaine. "Pictures had gone, tapestries had gone, cabinets had gone, and the clock had gone."

"And the coronet too?" said the Duke.

"Oh, no. That was at the Bank of France. And it was doubtless to make up for not getting it that Lupin stole your portrait. At any rate he didn't say that he was going to steal it in his letter."

"But, come! this is incredible. Had he hypnotized the corporal and the six soldiers? Or had he murdered them all?" said the Duke.

"Corporal? There wasn't any corporal, and there weren't any soldiers. The corporal was Lupin, and the soldiers were part of his gang," said Germaine.

"I don't understand," said the Duke. "The colonel promised your father a corporal and six men. Didn't they come?"

"They came to the railway station all right," said Germaine. "But you know the little inn half-way between the railway station and the chateau? They stopped to drink there, and at eleven o'clock next morning one of the villagers found all seven of them, along with the footman who was guiding them to the chateau, sleeping like logs in the little wood half a mile from the inn. Of course the innkeeper could not explain when their wine was drugged. He could only tell us that a motorist, who had stopped at the inn to get some supper, had called the soldiers in and insisted on standing them drinks. They had seemed a little fuddled before they left the inn, and the motorist had insisted on driving them to the chateau in his car. When the drug took effect he simply carried them out of it one by one, and laid them in the wood to sleep it off."

"Lupin seems to have made a thorough job of it, anyhow," said the Duke.

"I should think so," said Germaine. "Guerchard was sent down from Paris; but he could not find a single clue. It was not for want of trying, for he hates Lupin. It's a regular fight between them, and so far Lupin has scored every point."

"He must be as clever as they make 'em," said the Duke.

"He is," said Germaine. "And do you know, I shouldn't be at all surprised if he's in the neighbourhood now."

"What on earth do you mean?" said the Duke.

"I'm not joking," said Germaine. "Odd things are happening. Some one has been changing the place of things. That silver statuette now—it was on the cabinet, and we found it moved to the piano. Yet nobody had touched it. And look at this window. Some one has broken a pane in it just at the height of the fastening."

"The deuce they have!" said the Duke.

CHAPTER IV THE DUKE INTERVENES

The Duke rose, came to the window, and looked at the broken pane. He stepped out on to the terrace and looked at the turf; then he came back into the room.

"This looks serious," he said. "That pane has not been broken at all. If it had been broken, the pieces of glass would be lying on the turf. It has been cut out. We must warn your father to look to his treasures."

"I told you so," said Germaine. "I said that Arsene Lupin was in the neighbourhood."

"Arsene Lupin is a very capable man," said the Duke, smiling. "But there's no reason to suppose that he's the only burglar in France or even in Ile-et-Vilaine."

"I'm sure that he's in the neighbourhood. I have a feeling that he is," said Germaine stubbornly.

The Duke shrugged his shoulders, and said a smile: "Far be it from me to contradict you. A woman's intuition is always—well, it's always a woman's intuition."

He came back into the hall, and as he did so the door opened and a shock-headed man in the dress of a gamekeeper stood on the threshold.

"There are visitors to see you, Mademoiselle Germaine," he said, in a very deep bass voice.

"What! Are you answering the door, Firmin?" said Germaine.

"Yes, Mademoiselle Germaine: there's only me to do it. All the servants have started for the station, and my wife and I are going to see after the family to-night and to-morrow morning. Shall I show these gentlemen in?"

"Who are they?" said Germaine.

"Two gentlemen who say they have an appointment."

"What are their names?" said Germaine.

"They are two gentlemen. I don't know what their names are. I've no memory for names."

"That's an advantage to any one who answers doors," said the Duke, smiling at the stolid Firmin.

"Well, it can't be the two Charolais again. It's not time for them to come back. I told them papa would not be back yet," said Germaine.

"No, it can't be them, Mademoiselle Germaine," said Firmin, with decision.

"Very well; show them in," she said.

Firmin went out, leaving the door open behind him; and they heard his hob-nailed boots clatter and squeak on the stone floor of the outer hall.

"Charolais?" said the Duke idly. "I don't know the name. Who are they?"

"A little while ago Alfred announced two gentlemen. I thought they were Georges and Andre du Buit, for they promised to come to tea. I told Alfred to show them in, and to my surprise there appeared two horrible provincials. I never—Oh!"

She stopped short, for there, coming through the door, were the two Charolais, father and son.

M. Charolais pressed his motor-cap to his bosom, and bowed low. "Once more I salute you, mademoiselle," he said.

His son bowed, and revealed behind him another young man.

"My second son. He has a chemist's shop," said M. Charolais, waving a large red hand at the young man.

The young man, also blessed with the family eyes, set close together, entered the hall and bowed to the two girls. The Duke raised his eyebrows ever so slightly.

"I'm very sorry, gentlemen," said Germaine, "but my father has not yet returned."

"Please don't apologize. There is not the slightest need," said M. Charolais; and he and his two sons settled themselves down on three chairs, with the air of people who had come to make a considerable stay.

For a moment, Germaine, taken aback by their coolness, was speechless; then she said hastily: "Very likely he won't be back for another hour. I shouldn't like you to waste your time."

"Oh, it doesn't matter," said M. Charolais, with an indulgent air; and turning to the Duke, he added, "However, while we're waiting, if you're a member of the family, sir, we might perhaps discuss the least you will take for the motor-car."

"I'm sorry," said the Duke, "but I have nothing to do with it."

Before M. Charolais could reply the door opened, and Firmin's deep voice said:

"Will you please come in here, sir?"

A third young man came into the hall.

"What, you here, Bernard?" said M. Charolais. "I told you to wait at the park gates."

"I wanted to see the car too," said Bernard.

"My third son. He is destined for the Bar," said M. Charolais, with a great air of paternal pride.

"But how many are there?" said Germaine faintly.

Before M. Charolais could answer, Firmin once more appeared on the threshold.

"The master's just come back, miss," he said.

"Thank goodness for that!" said Germaine; and turning to M. Charolais, she added, "If you will come with me, gentlemen, I will take you to my father, and you can discuss the price of the car at once."

As she spoke she moved towards the door. M. Charolais and his sons rose and made way for her. The father and the two eldest sons made haste to follow her out of the room. But Bernard lingered behind, apparently to admire the bric-a-brac on the cabinets. With infinite quickness he grabbed two objects off the nearest, and followed his brothers. The Duke sprang across the hall in three strides, caught him by the arm on the very threshold, jerked him back into the hall, and shut the door.

"No you don't, my young friend," he said sharply.

"Don't what?" said Bernard, trying to shake off his grip.

"You've taken a cigarette-case," said the Duke.

"No, no, I haven't—nothing of the kind!" stammered Bernard.

The Duke grasped the young man's left wrist, plunged his hand into the motor-cap which he was carrying, drew out of it a silver cigarette-case, and held it before his eyes.

Bernard turned pale to the lips. His frightened eyes seemed about to leap from their sockets.

"It—it—was a m-m-m-mistake," he stammered.

The Duke shifted his grip to his collar, and thrust his hand into the breast-pocket of his coat. Bernard, helpless in his grip, and utterly taken aback by his quickness, made no resistance.

The Duke drew out a morocco case, and said: "Is this a mistake too?"

"Heavens! The pendant!" cried Sonia, who was watching the scene with parted lips and amazed eyes.

Bernard dropped on his knees and clasped his hands.

"Forgive me!" he cried, in a choking voice. "Forgive me! Don't tell any one! For God's sake, don't tell any one!"

And the tears came streaming from his eyes.

"You young rogue!" said the Duke quietly.

"I'll never do it again—never! Oh, have pity on me! If my father knew! Oh, let me off!" cried Bernard.

The Duke hesitated, and looked down on him, frowning and pulling at his moustache. Then, more quickly than one would have expected from so careless a trifler, his mind was made up.

"All right," he said slowly. "Just for this once ... be off with you." And he jerked him to his feet and almost threw him into the outer hall.

"Thanks! ... oh, thanks!" said Bernard.

The Duke shut the door and looked at Sonia, breathing quickly.

"Well? Did you ever see anything like that? That young fellow will go a long way. The cheek of the thing! Right under our very eyes! And this pendant, too: it would have been a pity to lose it. Upon my word, I ought to have handed him over to the police."

"No, no!" cried Sonia. "You did quite right to let him off—quite right."

The Duke set the pendant on the ledge of the bureau, and came down the hall to Sonia.

"What's the matter?" he said gently. "You're quite pale."

"It has upset me ... that unfortunate boy," said Sonia; and her eyes were swimming with tears.

"Do you pity the young rogue?" said the Duke.

"Yes; it's dreadful. His eyes were so terrified, and so boyish. And, to be caught like that ... stealing ... in the act. Oh, it's hateful!"

"Come, come, how sensitive you are!" said the Duke, in a soothing, almost caressing tone. His eyes, resting on her charming, troubled face, were glowing with a warm admiration.

"Yes; it's silly," said Sonia; "but you noticed his eyes—the hunted look in them? You pitied him, didn't you? For you are kind at bottom."

"Why at bottom?" said the Duke.

"Oh, I said at bottom because you look sarcastic, and at first sight you're so cold. But often that's only the mask of those who have suffered the most.... They are the most indulgent," said Sonia slowly, hesitating, picking her words.

"Yes, I suppose they are," said the Duke thoughtfully.

"It's because when one has suffered one understands.... Yes: one understands," said Sonia.

There was a pause. The Duke's eyes still rested on her face. The admiration in them was mingled with compassion.

"You're very unhappy here, aren't you?" he said gently.

"Me? Why?" said Sonia quickly.

"Your smile is so sad, and your eyes so timid," said the Duke slowly. "You're just like a little child one longs to protect. Are you quite alone in the world?"

His eyes and tones were full of pity; and a faint flush mantled Sonia's cheeks.

"Yes, I'm alone," she said.

"But have you no relations—no friends?" said the Duke.

"No," said Sonia.

"I don't mean here in France, but in your own country.... Surely you have some in Russia?"

"No, not a soul. You see, my father was a Revolutionist. He died in Siberia when I was a baby. And my mother, she died too—in Paris. She had fled from Russia. I was two years old when she died."

"It must be hard to be alone like that," said the Duke.

"No," said Sonia, with a faint smile, "I don't mind having no relations. I grew used to that so young ... so very young. But what is hard—but you'll laugh at me—"

"Heaven forbid!" said the Duke gravely.

"Well, what is hard is, never to get a letter ... an envelope that one opens ... from some one who thinks about one—"

She paused, and then added gravely: "But I tell myself that it's nonsense. I have a certain amount of philosophy."

She smiled at him—an adorable child's smile.

The Duke smiled too. "A certain amount of philosophy," he said softly. "You look like a philosopher!"

As they stood looking at one another with serious eyes, almost with eyes that probed one another's souls, the drawing-room door flung open, and Germaine's harsh voice broke on their ears.

"You're getting quite impossible, Sonia!" she cried. "It's absolutely useless telling you anything. I told you particularly to pack my leather writing-case in my bag with your own hand. I happen to open a drawer, and what do I see? My leather writing-case."

"I'm sorry," said Sonia. "I was going—"

"Oh, there's no need to bother about it. I'll see after it myself," said Germaine. "But upon my word, you might be one of our guests, seeing how easily you take things. You're negligence personified."

"Come, Germaine ... a mere oversight," said the Duke, in a coaxing tone.

"Now, excuse me, Jacques; but you've got an unfortunate habit of interfering in household matters. You did it only the other day. I can no longer say a word to a servant—"

"Germaine!" said the Duke, in sharp protest.

Germaine turned from him to Sonia, and pointed to a packet of envelopes and some letters, which Bernard Charolais had knocked off the table, and said, "Pick up those envelopes and letters, and bring everything to my room, and be quick about it!"

She flung out of the room, and slammed the door behind her.

Sonia seemed entirely unmoved by the outburst: no flush of mortification stained her cheeks, her lips did not quiver. She stooped to pick up the fallen papers.

"No, no; let me, I beg you," said the Duke, in a tone of distress. And dropping on one knee, he began to gather together the fallen papers. He set them on the table, and then he said: "You mustn't mind what Germaine says. She's—she's—she's all right at heart. It's her manner. She's always been happy, and had everything she wanted. She's been spoiled, don't you know. Those kind of people never have any consideration for any one else. You mustn't let her outburst hurt you."

"Oh, but I don't. I don't really," protested Sonia.

"I'm glad of that," said the Duke. "It isn't really worth noticing."

He drew the envelopes and unused cards into a packet, and handed them to her.

"There!" he said, with a smile. "That won't be too heavy for you."

"Thank you," said Sonia, taking it from him.

"Shall I carry them for you?" said the Duke.

"No, thank you, your Grace," said Sonia.

With a quick, careless, almost irresponsible movement, he caught her hand, bent down, and kissed it. A great wave of rosy colour flowed over her face, flooding its whiteness to her hair and throat. She stood for a moment turned to stone; she put her hand to her heart. Then on

312

hasty, faltering feet she went to the door, opened it, paused on the threshold, turned and looked back at him, and vanished.

CHAPTER V A LETTER FROM LUPIN

The Duke stood for a while staring thoughtfully at the door through which Sonia had passed, a faint smile playing round his lips. He crossed the hall to the Chippendale bureau, took a cigarette from a box which stood on the ledge of it, beside the morocco case which held the pendant, lighted it, and went slowly out on to the terrace. He crossed it slowly, paused for a moment on the edge of it, and looked across the stretch of country with musing eyes, which saw nothing of its beauty. Then he turned to the right, went down a flight of steps to the lower terrace, crossed the lawn, and took a narrow path which led into the heart of a shrubbery of tall deodoras. In the middle of it he came to one of those old stone benches, moss-covered and weather-stained, which adorn the gardens of so many French chateaux. It faced a marble basin from which rose the slender column of a pattering fountain. The figure of a Cupid danced joyously on a tall pedestal to the right of the basin. The Duke sat down on the bench, and was still, with that rare stillness which only comes of nerves in perfect harmony, his brow knitted in careful thought. Now and again the frown cleared from his face, and his intent features relaxed into a faint smile, a smile of pleasant memory. Once he rose, walked round the fountains frowning, came back to the bench, and sat down again. The early September dusk was upon him when at last he rose and with quick steps took his way through the shrubbery, with the air of a man whose mind, for good or ill, was at last made up.

When he came on to the upper terrace his eyes fell on a group which stood at the further corner, near the entrance of the chateau, and he sauntered slowly up to it.

In the middle of it stood M. Gournay-Martin, a big, round, flabby hulk of a man. He was nearly as red in the face as M. Charolais; and he looked a great deal redder owing to the extreme whiteness of the whiskers which stuck out on either side of his vast expanse of cheek. As he came up, it struck the Duke as rather odd that he should have the Charolais eyes, set close together; any one who did not know that they were strangers to one another might have thought it a family likeness.

The millionaire was waving his hands and roaring after the manner of a man who has cultivated the art of brow-beating those with whom he does business; and as the Duke neared the group, he caught the words:

"No; that's the lowest I'll take. Take it or leave it. You can say Yes, or you can say Good-bye; and I don't care a hang which."

"It's very dear," said M. Charolais, in a mournful tone.

"Dear!" roared M. Gournay-Martin. "I should like to see any one else sell a hundred horse-power car for eight hundred pounds. Why, my good sir, you're having me!"

"No, no," protested M. Charolais feebly.

"I tell you you're having me," roared M. Gournay-Martin. "I'm letting you have a magnificent car for which I paid thirteen hundred pounds for eight hundred! It's scandalous the way you've beaten me down!"

"No, no," protested M. Charolais.

He seemed frightened out of his life by the vehemence of the big man.

"You wait till you've seen how it goes," said M. Gournay-Martin.

"Eight hundred is very dear," said M. Charolais.

"Come, come! You're too sharp, that's what you are. But don't say any more till you've tried the car."

He turned to his chauffeur, who stood by watching the struggle with an appreciative grin on his brown face, and said: "Now, Jean, take these gentlemen to the garage, and run them down to the station. Show them what the car can do. Do whatever they ask you—everything."

He winked at Jean, turned again to M. Charolais, and said: "You know, M. Charolais, you're too good a man of business for me. You're hot stuff, that's what you are—hot stuff. You go along and try the car. Good-bye—good-bye."

The four Charolais murmured good-bye in deep depression, and went off with Jean, wearing something of the air of whipped dogs. When they had gone round the corner the millionaire turned to the Duke and said, with a chuckle: "He'll buy the car all right—had him fine!"

"No business success of yours could surprise me," said the Duke blandly, with a faint, ironical smile.

M. Gournay-Martin's little pig's eyes danced and sparkled; and the smiles flowed over the distended skin of his face like little ripples over a stagnant pool, reluctantly. It seemed to be too tightly stretched for smiles.

"The car's four years old," he said joyfully. "He'll give me eight hundred for it, and it's not worth a pipe of tobacco. And eight hundred pounds is just the price of a little Watteau I've had my eye on for some time—a first-class investment."

They strolled down the terrace, and through one of the windows into the hall. Firmin had lighted the lamps, two of them. They made but a small oasis of light in a desert of dim hall. The millionaire let himself down very gingerly into an Empire chair, as if he feared, with excellent reason, that it might collapse under his weight.

"Well, my dear Duke," he said, "you don't ask me the result of my official lunch or what the minister said."

"Is there any news?" said the Duke carelessly.

"Yes. The decree will be signed to-morrow. You can consider yourself decorated. I hope you feel a happy man," said the millionaire, rubbing his fat hands together with prodigious satisfaction.

"Oh, charmed—charmed," said the Duke, with entire indifference.

"As for me, I'm delighted—delighted," said the millionaire. "I was extremely keen on your being decorated. After that, and after a volume or two of travels, and after you've published your grandfather's letters with a good introduction, you can begin to think of the Academy."

"The Academy!" said the Duke, startled from his usual coolness. "But I've no title to become an Academician."

"How, no title?" said the millionaire solemnly; and his little eyes opened wide. "You're a duke."

"There's no doubt about that," said the Duke, watching him with admiring curiosity.

"I mean to marry my daughter to a worker—a worker, my dear Duke," said the millionaire, slapping his big left hand with his bigger right. "I've no prejudices—not I. I wish to have for son-in-law a duke who wears the Order of the Legion of Honour, and belongs to the Academie Francaise, because that is personal merit. I'm no snob."

A gentle, irrepressible laugh broke from the Duke.

"What are you laughing at?" said the millionaire, and a sudden lowering gloom overspread his beaming face.

"Nothing—nothing," said the Duke quietly. "Only you're so full of surprises."

"I've startled you, have I? I thought I should. It's true that I'm full of surprises. It's my knowledge. I understand so much. I understand business, and I love art, pictures, a good bargain, bric-a-brac, fine tapestry. They're first-class investments. Yes, certainly I do love the beautiful. And I don't want to boast, but I understand it. I have taste, and I've something better than taste; I have a flair, the dealer's flair."

"Yes, your collections, especially your collection in Paris, prove it," said the Duke, stifling a yawn.

"And yet you haven't seen the finest thing I have—the coronet of the Princesse de Lamballe. It's worth half a million francs."

"So I've heard," said the Duke, a little wearily. "I don't wonder that Arsene Lupin envied you it."

The Empire chair creaked as the millionaire jumped.

"Don't speak of the swine!" he roared. "Don't mention his name before me."

"Germaine showed me his letter," said the Duke. "It is amusing."

"His letter! The blackguard! I just missed a fit of apoplexy from it," roared the millionaire. "I was in this very hall where we are now, chatting quietly, when all at once in comes Firmin, and hands me a letter."

He was interrupted by the opening of the door. Firmin came clumping down the room, and said in his deep voice, "A letter for you, sir."

"Thank you," said the millionaire, taking the letter, and, as he fitted his eye-glass into his eye, he went on, "Yes, Firmin brought me a letter of which the handwriting,"—he raised the envelope he was holding to his eyes, and bellowed, "Good heavens!"

"What's the matter?" said the Duke, jumping in his chair at the sudden, startling burst of sound.

"The handwriting!—the handwriting!—it's THE SAME HANDWRITING!" gasped the millionaire. And he let himself fall heavily backwards against the back of his chair.

There was a crash. The Duke had a vision of huge arms and legs waving in the air as the chair-back gave. There was another crash. The chair collapsed. The huge bulk banged to the floor.

The laughter of the Duke rang out uncontrollably. He caught one of the waving arms, and jerked the flabby giant to his feet with an ease which seemed to show that his muscles were of steel.

"Come," he said, laughing still. "This is nonsense! What do you mean by the same handwriting? It can't be."

"It is the same handwriting. Am I likely to make a mistake about it?" spluttered the millionaire. And he tore open the envelope with an air of frenzy.

He ran his eyes over it, and they grew larger and larger—they grew almost of an average size.

"Listen," he said "listen:"

"DEAR SIR,"

"My collection of pictures, which I had the pleasure of starting three years ago with some of your own, only contains, as far as Old Masters go, one Velasquez, one Rembrandt, and three paltry Rubens. You have a great many more. Since it is a shame such masterpieces should be in your hands, I propose to appropriate them; and I shall set about a respectful acquisition of them in your Paris house tomorrow morning."

"Yours very sincerely,"
"ARSENE LUPIN."

"He's humbugging," said the Duke.

"Wait! wait!" gasped the millionaire. "There's a postscript. Listen:"

"P.S.—You must understand that since you have been keeping the coronet of the Princesse de Lamballe during these three years, I shall avail myself of the same occasion to compel you to restore that piece of jewellery to me.—
A. L."

"The thicf! The scoundrel! I'm choking!" gasped the millionaire, clutching at his collar.

To judge from the blackness of his face, and the way he staggered and dropped on to a couch, which was fortunately stronger than the chair, he was speaking the truth.

"Firmin! Firmin!" shouted the Duke. "A glass of water! Quick! Your master's ill."

He rushed to the side of the millionaire, who gasped: "Telephone! Telephone to the Prefecture of Police! Be quick!"

318

The Duke loosened his collar with deft fingers; tore a Van Loo fan from its case hanging on the wall, and fanned him furiously. Firmin came clumping into the room with a glass of water in his hand.

The drawing-room door opened, and Germaine and Sonia, alarmed by the Duke's shout, hurried in.

"Quick! Your smelling-salts!" said the Duke.

Sonia ran across the hall, opened one of the drawers in the Oriental cabinet, and ran to the millionaire with a large bottle of smelling-salts in her hand. The Duke took it from her, and applied it to the millionaire's nose. The millionaire sneezed thrice with terrific violence. The Duke snatched the glass from Firmin and dashed the water into his host's purple face. The millionaire gasped and spluttered.

Germaine stood staring helplessly at her gasping sire.

"Whatever's the matter?" she said.

"It's this letter," said the Duke. "A letter from Lupin."

"I told you so—I said that Lupin was in the neighbourhood," cried Germaine triumphantly.

"Firmin—where's Firmin?" said the millionaire, dragging himself upright. He seemed to have recovered a great deal of his voice. "Oh, there you are!"

He jumped up, caught the gamekeeper by the shoulder, and shook him furiously.

"This letter. Where did it come from? Who brought it?" he roared.

"It was in the letter-box—the letter-box of the lodge at the bottom of the park. My wife found it there," said Firmin, and he twisted out of the millionaire's grasp.

"Just as it was three years ago," roared the millionaire, with an air of desperation. "It's exactly the same coup. Oh, what a catastrophe! What a catastrophe!"

He made as if to tear out his hair; then, remembering its scantiness, refrained.

"Now, come, it's no use losing your head," said the Duke, with quiet firmness. "If this letter isn't a hoax—"

"Hoax?" bellowed the millionaire. "Was it a hoax three years ago?"

319

"Very good," said the Duke. "But if this robbery with which you're threatened is genuine, it's just childish."

"How?" said the millionaire.

"Look at the date of the letter—Sunday, September the third. This letter was written to-day."

"Yes. Well, what of it?" said the millionaire.

"Look at the letter: 'I shall set about a respectful acquisition of them in your Paris house to-morrow morning'—to-morrow morning."

"Yes, yes; 'to-morrow morning'—what of it?" said the millionaire.

"One of two things," said the Duke. "Either it's a hoax, and we needn't bother about it; or the threat is genuine, and we have the time to stop the robbery."

"Of course we have. Whatever was I thinking of?" said the millionaire. And his anguish cleared from his face.

"For once in a way our dear Lupin's fondness for warning people will have given him a painful jar," said the Duke.

"Come on! let me get at the telephone," cried the millionaire.

"But the telephone's no good," said Sonia quickly.

"No good! Why?" roared the millionaire, dashing heavily across the room to it.

"Look at the time," said Sonia; "the telephone doesn't work as late as this. It's Sunday."

The millionaire stopped dead.

"It's true. It's appalling," he groaned.

"But that doesn't matter. You can always telegraph," said Germaine.

"But you can't. It's impossible," said Sonia. "You can't get a message through. It's Sunday; and the telegraph offices shut at twelve o'clock."

"Oh, what a Government!" groaned the millionaire. And he sank down gently on a chair beside the telephone, and mopped the beads of anguish from his brow. They looked at him, and they looked at one another, cudgelling their brains for yet another way of communicating with the Paris police.

"Hang it all!" said the Duke. "There must be some way out of the difficulty."

"What way?" said the millionaire.

The Duke did not answer. He put his hands in his pockets and walked impatiently up and down the hall. Germaine sat down on a chair. Sonia put her hands on the back of a couch, and leaned forward, watching him. Firmin stood by the door, whither he had retired to be out of the reach of his excited master, with a look of perplexity on his stolid face. They all watched the Duke with the air of people waiting for an oracle to deliver its message. The millionaire kept mopping the beads of anguish from his brow. The more he thought of his impending loss, the more freely he perspired. Germaine's maid, Irma, came to the door leading into the outer hall, which Firmin, according to his usual custom, had left open, and peered in wonder at the silent group.

"I have it!" cried the Duke at last. "There is a way out."

"What is it?" said the millionaire, rising and coming to the middle of the hall.

"What time is it?" said the Duke, pulling out his watch.

The millionaire pulled out his watch. Germaine pulled out hers. Firmin, after a struggle, produced from some pocket difficult of access an object not unlike a silver turnip. There was a brisk dispute between Germaine and the millionaire about which of their watches was right. Firmin, whose watch apparently did not agree with the watch of either of them, made his deep voice heard above theirs. The Duke came to the conclusion that it must be a few minutes past seven.

"It's seven or a few minutes past," he said sharply. "Well, I'm going to take a car and hurry off to Paris. I ought to get there, bar accidents, between two and three in the morning, just in time to inform the police and catch the burglars in the very midst of their burglary. I'll just get a few things together."

So saying, he rushed out of the hall.

"Excellent! excellent!" said the millionaire. "Your young man is a man of resource, Germaine. It seems almost a pity that he's a duke. He'd do wonders in the building trade. But I'm going to Paris too, and you're coming with me. I couldn't wait idly here, to save my life. And I can't leave you here, either. This scoundrel may be going to make a simultaneous attempt on the chateau—not that there's much here that I really value. There's that statuette that moved, and the pane cut out of the window. I can't leave you two girls with burglars in the house. After all, there's the sixty horse-power and the thirty horse-power car—there'll be lots of room for all of us."

"Oh, but it's nonsense, papa; we shall get there before the servants," said Germaine pettishly. "Think of arriving at an empty house in the dead of night."

"Nonsense!" said the millionaire. "Hurry off and get ready. Your bag ought to be packed. Where are my keys? Sonia, where are my keys—the keys of the Paris house?"

"They're in the bureau," said Sonia.

"Well, see that I don't go without them. Now hurry up. Firmin, go and tell Jean that we shall want both cars. I will drive one, the Duke the other. Jean must stay with you and help guard the chateau."

So saying he bustled out of the hall, driving the two girls before him.

CHAPTER VI AGAIN THE CHAROLAIS

Hardly had the door closed behind the millionaire when the head of M. Charolais appeared at one of the windows opening on to the terrace. He looked round the empty hall, whistled softly, and stepped inside. Inside of ten seconds his three sons came in through the windows, and with them came Jean, the millionaire's chauffeur.

"Take the door into the outer hall, Jean," said M. Charolais, in a low voice. "Bernard, take that door into the drawing-room. Pierre and Louis, help me go through the drawers. The whole family is going to Paris, and if we're not quick we shan't get the cars."

"That comes of this silly fondness for warning people of a coup," growled Jean, as he hurried to the door of the outer hall. "It would have been so simple to rob the Paris house without sending that infernal letter. It was sure to knock them all silly."

"What harm can the letter do, you fool?" said M. Charolais. "It's Sunday. We want them knocked silly for to-morrow, to get hold of the coronet. Oh, to get hold of that coronet! It must be in Paris. I've been ransacking this chateau for hours."

Jean opened the door of the outer hall half an inch, and glued his eyes to it. Bernard had done the same with the door opening into the drawing-room. M. Charolais, Pierre, and Louis were opening drawers, ransacking them, and shutting them with infinite quickness and noiselessly.

"Bureau! Which is the bureau? The place is stuffed with bureaux!" growled M. Charolais. "I must have those keys."

"That plain thing with the brass handles in the middle on the left—that's a bureau," said Bernard softly.

"Why didn't you say so?" growled M. Charolais.

He dashed to it, and tried it. It was locked.

"Locked, of course! Just my luck! Come and get it open, Pierre. Be smart!"

The son he had described as an engineer came quickly to the bureau, fitting together as he came the two halves of a small jemmy. He fitted it into the top of the flap. There was a crunch, and the old lock gave. He opened the flap, and he and M. Charolais pulled open drawer after drawer.

"Quick! Here's that fat old fool!" said Jean, in a hoarse, hissing whisper.

He moved down the hall, blowing out one of the lamps as he passed it. In the seventh drawer lay a bunch of keys. M. Charolais snatched it up, glanced at it, took a bunch of keys from his own pocket, put it in the drawer, closed it, closed the flap, and rushed to the window. Jean and his sons were already out on the terrace.

M. Charolais was still a yard from the window when the door into the outer hall opened and in came M. Gournay-Martin.

He caught a glimpse of a back vanishing through the window, and bellowed: "Hi! A man! A burglar! Firmin! Firmin!"

He ran blundering down the hall, tangled his feet in the fragments of the broken chair, and came sprawling a thundering cropper, which knocked every breath of wind out of his capacious body. He lay flat on his face for a couple of minutes, his broad back wriggling convulsively—a pathetic sight!—in the painful effort to get his breath back. Then he sat up, and with perfect frankness burst into tears. He sobbed and blubbered, like a small child that has hurt itself, for three or four minutes. Then, having recovered his magnificent voice, he bellowed furiously: "Firmin! Firmin! Charmerace! Charmerace!"

Then he rose painfully to his feet, and stood staring at the open windows.

Presently he roared again: "Firmin! Firmin! Charmerace! Charmerace!"

He kept looking at the window with terrified eyes, as though he expected somebody to step in and cut his throat from ear to ear.

"Firmin! Firmin! Charmerace! Charmerace!" he bellowed again.

The Duke came quietly into the hall, dressed in a heavy motor-coat, his motor-cap on his head, and carrying a kit-bag in his hand.

"Did I hear you call?" he said.

"Call?" said the millionaire. "I shouted. The burglars are here already. I've just seen one of them. He was bolting through the middle window."

The Duke raised his eyebrows.

"Nerves," he said gently—"nerves."

"Nerves be hanged!" said the millionaire. "I tell you I saw him as plainly as I see you."

"Well, you can't see me at all, seeing that you're lighting an acre and a half of hall with a single lamp," said the Duke, still in a tone of utter incredulity.

"It's that fool Firmin! He ought to have lighted six. Firmin! Firmin!" bellowed the millionaire.

They listened for the sonorous clumping of the promoted gamekeeper's boots, but they did not hear it. Evidently Firmin was still giving his master's instructions about the cars to Jean.

"Well, we may as well shut the windows, anyhow," said the Duke, proceeding to do so. "If you think Firmin would be any good, you might post him in this hall with a gun to-night. There could be no harm in putting a charge of small shot into the legs of these ruffians. He has only to get one of them, and the others will go for their lives. Yet I don't like leaving you and Germaine in this big house with only Firmin to look after you."

"I shouldn't like it myself, and I'm not going to chance it," growled the millionaire. "We're going to motor to Paris along with you, and leave Jean to help Firmin fight these burglars. Firmin's all right—he's an old soldier. He fought in '70. Not that I've much belief in soldiers against this cursed Lupin, after the way he dealt with that corporal and his men three years ago."

"I'm glad you're coming to Paris," said the Duke. "It'll be a weight off my mind. I'd better drive the limousine, and you take the landaulet."

"That won't do," said the millionaire. "Germaine won't go in the limousine. You know she has taken a dislike to it."

"Nevertheless, I'd better bucket on to Paris, and let you follow slowly with Germaine. The sooner I get to Paris the better for your collection. I'll take Mademoiselle Kritchnoff with me, and, if you like, Irma, though the lighter I travel the sooner I shall get there."

"No, I'll take Irma and Germaine," said the millionaire. "Germaine would prefer to have Irma with her, in case you had an accident. She wouldn't like to get to Paris and have to find a fresh maid."

The drawing-room door opened, and in came Germaine, followed by Sonia and Irma. They wore motor-cloaks and hoods and veils. Sonia and Irma were carrying hand-bags.

"I think it's extremely tiresome your dragging us off to Paris like this in the middle of the night," said Germaine pettishly.

"Do you?" said the millionaire. "Well, then, you'll be interested to hear that I've just seen a burglar here in this very room. I frightened him, and he bolted through the window on to the terrace."

"He was greenish-pink, slightly tinged with yellow," said the Duke softly.

"Greenish-pink? Oh, do stop your jesting, Jacques! Is this a time for idiocy?" cried Germaine, in a tone of acute exasperation.

"It was the dim light which made your father see him in those colours. In a bright light, I think he would have been an Alsatian blue," said the Duke suavely.

"You'll have to break yourself of this silly habit of trifling, my dear Duke, if ever you expect to be a member of the Academie Francaise," said the millionaire with some acrimony. "I tell you I did see a burglar."

"Yes, yes. I admitted it frankly. It was his colour I was talking about," said the Duke, with an ironical smile.

"Oh, stop your idiotic jokes! We're all sick to death of them!" said Germaine, with something of the fine fury which so often distinguished her father.

"There are times for all things," said the millionaire solemnly. "And I must say that, with the fate of my collection and of the coronet trembling in the balance, this does not seem to me a season for idle jests."

"I stand reproved," said the Duke; and he smiled at Sonia.

"My keys, Sonia—the keys of the Paris house," said the millionaire.

Sonia took her own keys from her pocket and went to the bureau. She slipped a key into the lock and tried to turn it. It would not turn; and she bent down to look at it.

"Why—why, some one's been tampering with the lock! It's broken!" she cried.

"I told you I'd seen a burglar!" cried the millionaire triumphantly. "He was after the keys."

Sonia drew back the flap of the bureau and hastily pulled open the drawer in which the keys had been.

"They're here!" she cried, taking them out of the drawer and holding them up.

"Then I was just in time," said the millionaire. "I startled him in the very act of stealing the keys."

"I withdraw! I withdraw!" said the Duke. "You did see a burglar, evidently. But still I believe he was greenish-pink. They often are. However, you'd better give me those keys, Mademoiselle Sonia, since I'm to get to Paris first. I should look rather silly if, when I got there, I had to break into the house to catch the burglars."

Sonia handed the keys to the Duke. He contrived to take her little hand, keys and all, into his own, as he received them, and squeezed it. The light was too dim for the others to see the flush which flamed in her face. She went back and stood beside the bureau.

"Now, papa, are you going to motor to Paris in a thin coat and linen waistcoat? If we're going, we'd better go. You always do keep us waiting half an hour whenever we start to go anywhere," said Germaine firmly.

The millionaire bustled out of the room. With a gesture of impatience Germaine dropped into a chair. Irma stood waiting by the drawing-room door. Sonia sat down by the bureau.

There came a sharp patter of rain against the windows.

"Rain! It only wanted that! It's going to be perfectly beastly!" cried Germaine.

"Oh, well, you must make the best of it. At any rate you're well wrapped up, and the night is warm enough, though it is raining," said the Duke. "Still, I could have wished that Lupin confined his operations to fine weather." He paused, and added cheerfully, "But, after all, it will lay the dust."

They sat for three or four minutes in a dull silence, listening to the pattering of the rain against the panes. The Duke took his cigarette-case from his pocket and lighted a cigarette.

Suddenly he lost his bored air; his face lighted up; and he said joyfully: "Of course, why didn't I think of it? Why should we start from a pit of gloom like this? Let us have the proper illumination which our enterprise deserves."

With that he set about lighting all the lamps in the hall. There were lamps on stands, lamps on brackets, lamps on tables, and lamps which hung from the roof—old-fashioned lamps with new reservoirs, new lamps of what is called chaste design, brass lamps, silver lamps, and lamps in porcelain. The Duke lighted them one after another, patiently, missing none, with a cold perseverance. The operation was punctuated by exclamations from Germaine. They were all to the effect that she could not understand how he could be such a fool. The Duke paid no attention whatever to her. His face illumined with boyish glee, he lighted lamp after lamp.

Sonia watched him with a smiling admiration of the childlike enthusiasm with which he performed the task. Even the stolid face of the ox-eyed Irma relaxed into grins, which she smoothed quickly out with a respectful hand.

The Duke had just lighted the twenty-second lamp when in bustled the millionaire.

"What's this? What's this?" he cried, stopping short, blinking.

"Just some more of Jacques' foolery!" cried Germaine in tones of the last exasperation.

"But, my dear Duke!—my dear Duke! The oil!—the oil!" cried the millionaire, in a tone of bitter distress. "Do you think it's my object in life to swell the Rockefeller millions? We never have more than six lamps burning unless we are holding a reception."

"I think it looks so cheerful," said the Duke, looking round on his handiwork with a beaming smile of satisfaction. "But where are the cars? Jean seems a deuce of a time bringing them round. Does he expect us to go to the garage through this rain? We'd better hurry him up. Come on; you've got a good carrying voice."

He caught the millionaire by the arm, hurried him through the outer hall, opened the big door of the chateau, and said: "Now shout!"

The millionaire looked at him, shrugged his shoulders, and said: "You don't beat about the bush when you want anything."

"Why should I?" said the Duke simply. "Shout, my good chap—shout!"

The millionaire raised his voice in a terrific bellow of "Jean! Jean! Firmin! Firmin!"

There was no answer.

CHAPTER VII THE THEFT OF THE MOTOR-CARS

The night was very black; the rain pattered in their faces.

Again the millionaire bellowed: "Jean! Firmin! Firmin! Jean!"

No answer came out of the darkness, though his bellow echoed and re-echoed among the out-buildings and stables away on the left.

He turned and looked at the Duke and said uneasily, "What on earth can they be doing?"

"I can't conceive," said the Duke. "I suppose we must go and hunt them out."

"What! in this darkness, with these burglars about?" said the millionaire, starting back.

"If we don't, nobody else will," said the Duke. "And all the time that rascal Lupin is stealing nearer and nearer your pictures. So buck up, and come along!"

He seized the reluctant millionaire by the arm and drew him down the steps. They took their way to the stables. A dim light shone from the open door of the motor-house. The Duke went into it first, and stopped short.

"Well, I'll be hanged!" he cried,

Instead of three cars the motor-house held but one—the hundred horse-power Mercrac. It was a racing car, with only two seats. On them sat two figures, Jean and Firmin.

"What are you sitting there for? You idle dogs!" bellowed the millionaire.

Neither of the men answered, nor did they stir. The light from the lamp gleamed on their fixed eyes, which stared at their infuriated master.

"What on earth is this?" said the Duke; and seizing the lamp which stood beside the car, he raised it so that its light fell on the two figures. Then it was clear what had happened: they were trussed like two fowls, and gagged.

The Duke pulled a penknife from his pocket, opened the blade, stepped into the car and set Firmin free. Firmin coughed and spat and swore. The Duke cut the bonds of Jean.

"Well," said the Duke, in a tone of cutting irony, "what new game is this? What have you been playing at?"

"It was those Charolais—those cursed Charolais!" growled Firmin.

"They came on us unawares from behind," said Jean.

"They tied us up, and gagged us—the swine!" said Firmin.

"And then—they went off in the two cars," said Jean.

"Went off in the two cars?" cried the millionaire, in blank stupefaction.

The Duke burst into a shout of laughter.

"Well, your dear friend Lupin doesn't do things by halves," he cried. "This is the funniest thing I ever heard of."

"Funny!" howled the millionaire. "Funny! Where does the fun come in? What about my pictures and the coronet?"

The Duke laughed his laugh out; then changed on the instant to a man of action.

"Well, this means a change in our plans," he said. "I must get to Paris in this car here."

"It's such a rotten old thing," said the millionaire. "You'll never do it."

"Never mind," said the Duke. "I've got to do it somehow. I daresay it's better than you think. And after all, it's only a matter of two hundred miles." He paused, and then said in an anxious tone: "All the same I don't like leaving you and Germaine in the chateau. These rogues have probably only taken the cars out of reach just to prevent your getting to Paris. They'll leave them in some field and come back."

"You're not going to leave us behind. I wouldn't spend the night in the chateau for a million francs. There's always the train," said the millionaire.

"The train! Twelve hours in the train—with all those changes! You don't mean that you will actually go to Paris by train?" said the Duke.

"I do," said the millionaire. "Come along—I must go and tell Germaine; there's no time to waste," and he hurried off to the chateau.

"Get the lamps lighted, Jean, and make sure that the tank's full. As for the engine, I must humour it and trust to luck. I'll get her to Paris somehow," said the Duke.

He went back to the chateau, and Firmin followed him.

When the Duke came into the great hall he found Germaine and her father indulging in recriminations. She was declaring that nothing would induce her to make the journey by train;

her father was declaring that she should. He bore down her opposition by the mere force of his magnificent voice.

When at last there came a silence, Sonia said quietly: "But is there a train? I know there's a train at midnight; but is there one before?"

"A time-table—where's a time-table?" said the millionaire.

"Now, where did I see a time-table?" said the Duke. "Oh, I know; there's one in the drawer of that Oriental cabinet." Crossing to the cabinet, he opened the drawer, took out the time-table, and handed it to M. Gournay-Martin.

The millionaire took it and turned over the leaves quickly, ran his eye down a page, and said, "Yes, thank goodness, there is a train. There's one at a quarter to nine."

"And what good is it to us? How are we to get to the station?" said Germaine.

They looked at one another blankly. Firmin, who had followed the Duke into the hall, came to the rescue.

"There's the luggage-cart," he said.

"The luggage-cart!" cried Germaine contemptuously.

"The very thing!" said the millionaire. "I'll drive it myself. Off you go, Firmin; harness a horse to it."

Firmin went clumping out of the hall.

It was perhaps as well that he went, for the Duke asked what time it was; and since the watches of Germaine and her father differed still, there ensued an altercation in which, had Firmin been there, he would doubtless have taken part.

The Duke cut it short by saying: "Well, I don't think I'll wait to see you start for the station. It won't take you more than half an hour. The cart is light. You needn't start yet. I'd better get off as soon as the car is ready. It isn't as though I could trust it."

"One moment," said Germaine. "Is there a dining-car on the train? I'm not going to be starved as well as have my night's rest cut to pieces."

"Of course there isn't a dining-car," snapped her father. "We must eat something now, and take something with us."

"Sonia, Irma, quick! Be off to the larder and see what you can find. Tell Mother Firmin to make an omelette. Be quick!"

Sonia went towards the door of the hall, followed by Irma.

"Good-night, and bon voyage, Mademoiselle Sonia," said the Duke.

"Good-night, and bon voyage, your Grace," said Sonia.

The Duke opened the door of the hall for her; and as she went out, she said anxiously, in a low voice: "Oh, do—do be careful. I hate to think of your hurrying to Paris on a night like this. Please be careful."

"I will be careful," said the Duke.

The honk of the motor-horn told him that Jean had brought the car to the door of the chateau. He came down the room, kissed Germaine's hands, shook hands with the millionaire, and bade them good-night. Then he went out to the car. They heard it start; the rattle of it grew fainter and fainter down the long avenue and died away.

M. Gournay-Martin arose, and began putting out lamps. As he did so, he kept casting fearful glances at the window, as if he feared lest, now that the Duke had gone, the burglars should dash in upon him.

There came a knock at the door, and Jean appeared on the threshold.

"His Grace told me that I was to come into the house, and help Firmin look after it," he said.

The millionaire gave him instructions about the guarding of the house. Firmin, since he was an old soldier, was to occupy the post of honour, and guard the hall, armed with his gun. Jean was to guard the two drawing-rooms, as being less likely points of attack. He also was to have a gun; and the millionaire went with him to the gun-room and gave him one and a dozen cartridges. When they came back to the hall, Sonia called them into the dining-room; and there, to the accompaniment of an unsubdued grumbling from Germaine at having to eat cold food at eight at night, they made a hasty but excellent meal, since the chef had left an elaborate cold supper ready to be served.

They had nearly finished it when Jean came in, his gun on his arm, to say that Firmin had harnessed the horse to the luggage-cart, and it was awaiting them at the door of the chateau.

"Send him in to me, and stand by the horse till we come out," said the millionaire.

Firmin came clumping in.

The millionaire gazed at him solemnly, and said: "Firmin, I am relying on you. I am leaving you in a position of honour and danger—a position which an old soldier of France loves."

Firmin did his best to look like an old soldier of France. He pulled himself up out of the slouch which long years of loafing through woods with a gun on his arm had given him. He lacked also the old soldier of France's fiery gaze. His eyes were lack-lustre.

"I look for anything, Firmin—burglary, violence, an armed assault," said the millionaire.

"Don't be afraid, sir. I saw the war of '70," said Firmin boldly, rising to the occasion.

"Good!" said the millionaire. "I confide the chateau to you. I trust you with my treasures."

He rose, and saying "Come along, we must be getting to the station," he led the way to the door of the chateau.

The luggage-cart stood rather high, and they had to bring a chair out of the hall to enable the girls to climb into it. Germaine did not forget to give her real opinion of the advantages of a seat formed by a plank resting on the sides of the cart. The millionaire climbed heavily up in front, and took the reins.

"Never again will I trust only to motor-cars. The first thing I'll do after I've made sure that my collections are safe will be to buy carriages—something roomy," he said gloomily, as he realized the discomfort of his seat.

He turned to Jean and Firmin, who stood on the steps of the chateau watching the departure of their master, and said: "Sons of France, be brave—be brave!"

The cart bumped off into the damp, dark night.

Jean and Firmin watched it disappear into the darkness. Then they came into the chateau and shut the door.

Firmin looked at Jean, and said gloomily: "I don't like this. These burglars stick at nothing. They'd as soon cut your throat as look at you."

"It can't be helped," said Jean. "Besides, you've got the post of honour. You guard the hall. I'm to look after the drawing-rooms. They're not likely to break in through the drawing-rooms. And I shall lock the door between them and the hall."

"No, no; you won't lock that door!" cried Firmin.

"But I certainly will," said Jean. "You'd better come and get a gun."

They went to the gun-room, Firmin still protesting against the locking of the door between the drawing-rooms and the hall. He chose his gun; and they went into the kitchen. Jean took two bottles of wine, a rich-looking pie, a sweet, and carried them to the drawing-room. He came back into the hall, gathered together an armful of papers and magazines, and went back to the drawing-room. Firmin kept trotting after him, like a little dog with a somewhat heavy footfall.

On the threshold of the drawing-room Jean paused and said: "The important thing with burglars is to fire first, old cock. Good-night. Pleasant dreams."

He shut the door and turned the key. Firmin stared at the decorated panels blankly. The beauty of the scheme of decoration did not, at the moment, move him to admiration.

He looked fearfully round the empty hall and at the windows, black against the night. Under the patter of the rain he heard footsteps—distinctly. He went hastily clumping down the hall, and along the passage to the kitchen.

His wife was setting his supper on the table.

"My God!" he said. "I haven't been so frightened since '70." And he mopped his glistening forehead with a dish-cloth. It was not a clean dish-cloth; but he did not care.

"Frightened? What of?" said his wife.

"Burglars! Cut-throats!" said Firmin.

He told her of the fears of M. Gournay-Martin, and of his own appointment to the honourable and dangerous post of guard of the chateau.

"God save us!" said his wife. "You lock the door of that beastly hall, and come into the kitchen. Burglars won't bother about the kitchen."

"But the master's treasures!" protested Firmin. "He confided them to me. He said so distinctly."

"Let the master look after his treasures himself," said Madame Firmin, with decision. "You've only one throat; and I'm not going to have it cut. You sit down and eat your supper. Go and lock that door first, though."

Firmin locked the door of the hall; then he locked the door of the kitchen; then he sat down, and began to eat his supper. His appetite was hearty, but none the less he derived little pleasure from the meal. He kept stopping with the food poised on his fork, midway between the plate and his mouth, for several seconds at a time, while he listened with straining ears for the sound of burglars breaking in the windows of the hall. He was much too far from those windows to hear anything that happened to them, but that did not prevent him from straining his ears. Madame Firmin ate her supper with an air of perfect ease. She felt sure that burglars would not bother with the kitchen.

Firmin's anxiety made him terribly thirsty. Tumbler after tumbler of wine flowed down the throat for which he feared. When he had finished his supper he went on satisfying his thirst. Madame Firmin lighted his pipe for him, and went and washed up the supper-dishes in the scullery. Then she came back, and sat down on the other side of the hearth, facing him. About the middle of his third bottle of wine, Firmin's cold, relentless courage was suddenly restored to him. He began to talk firmly about his duty to his master, his resolve to die, if need were, in defence of his interests, of his utter contempt for burglars—probably Parisians. But he did not go into the hall. Doubtless the pleasant warmth of the kitchen fire held him in his chair.

He had described to his wife, with some ferocity, the cruel manner in which he would annihilate the first three burglars who entered the hall, and was proceeding to describe his method of dealing with the fourth, when there came a loud knocking on the front door of the chateau.

Stricken silent, turned to stone, Firmin sat with his mouth open, in the midst of an unfinished word. Madame Firmin scuttled to the kitchen door she had left unlocked on her return from the scullery, and locked it. She turned, and they stared at one another.

The heavy knocker fell again and again and again. Between the knocking there was a sound like the roaring of lions. Husband and wife stared at one another with white faces. Firmin picked up his gun with trembling hands, and the movement seemed to set his teeth chattering. They chattered like castanets.

The knocking still went on, and so did the roaring.

It had gone on at least for five minutes, when a slow gleam of comprehension lightened Madame Firmin's face.

"I believe it's the master's voice," she said.

"The master's voice!" said Firmin, in a hoarse, terrified whisper.

"Yes," said Madame Firmin. And she unlocked the thick door and opened it a few inches.

The barrier removed, the well-known bellow of the millionaire came distinctly to their ears. Firmin's courage rushed upon him in full flood. He clumped across the room, brushed his wife aside, and trotted to the door of the chateau. He unlocked it, drew the bolts, and threw it open. On the steps stood the millionaire, Germaine, and Sonia. Irma stood at the horse's head.

"What the devil have you been doing?" bellowed the millionaire. "What do you keep me standing in the rain for? Why didn't you let me in?"

"B-b-b-burglars—I thought you were b-b-b-burglars," stammered Firmin.

"Burglars!" howled the millionaire. "Do I sound like a burglar?"

At the moment he did not; he sounded more like a bull of Bashan. He bustled past Firmin to the door of the hall.

"Here! What's this locked for?" he bellowed.

"I—I—locked it in case burglars should get in while I was opening the front door," stammered Firmin.

The millionaire turned the key, opened the door, and went into the hall. Germaine followed him. She threw off her dripping coat, and said with some heat: "I can't conceive why you didn't make sure that there was a train at a quarter to nine. I will not go to Paris to-night. Nothing shall induce me to take that midnight train!"

"Nonsense!" said the millionaire. "Nonsense—you'll have to go! Where's that infernal time-table?" He rushed to the table on to which he had thrown the time-table after looking up the train, snatched it up, and looked at the cover. "Why, hang it!" he cried. "It's for June—June, 1903!"

"Oh!" cried Germaine, almost in a scream. "It's incredible! It's one of Jacques' jokes!"

CHAPTER VIII THE DUKE ARRIVES

The morning was gloomy, and the police-station with its bare, white-washed walls—their white expanse was only broken by notice-boards to which were pinned portraits of criminals with details of their appearance, their crime, and the reward offered for their apprehension—with its shabby furniture, and its dingy fireplace, presented a dismal and sordid appearance entirely in keeping with the September grey. The inspector sat at his desk, yawning after a night which had passed without an arrest. He was waiting to be relieved. The policeman at the door and the two policemen sitting on a bench by the wall yawned in sympathy.

The silence of the street was broken by the rattle of an uncommonly noisy motor-car. It stopped before the door of the police-station, and the eyes of the inspector and his men turned, idly expectant, to the door of the office.

It opened, and a young man in motor-coat and cap stood on the threshold.

He looked round the office with alert eyes, which took in everything, and said, in a brisk, incisive voice: "I am the Duke of Charmerace. I am here on behalf of M. Gournay-Martin. Last evening he received a letter from Arsene Lupin saying he was going to break into his Paris house this very morning."

At the name of Arsene Lupin the inspector sprang from his chair, the policemen from their bench. On the instant they were wide awake, attentive, full of zeal.

"The letter, your Grace!" said the inspector briskly.

The Duke pulled off his glove, drew the letter from the breast-pocket of his under-coat, and handed it to the inspector.

The inspector glanced through it, and said. "Yes, I know the handwriting well." Then he read it carefully, and added, "Yes, yes: it's his usual letter."

"There's no time to be lost," said the Duke quickly. "I ought to have been here hours ago—hours. I had a break-down. I'm afraid I'm too late as it is."

"Come along, your Grace—come along, you," said the inspector briskly.

The four of them hurried out of the office and down the steps of the police-station. In the roadway stood a long grey racing-car, caked with muds—grey mud, brown mud, red mud—from end to end. It looked as if it had brought samples of the soil of France from many districts.

"Come along; I'll take you in the car. Your men can trot along beside us," said the Duke to the inspector.

He slipped into the car, the inspector jumped in and took the seat beside him, and they started. They went slowly, to allow the two policemen to keep up with them. Indeed, the car could not have made any great pace, for the tyre of the off hind-wheel was punctured and deflated.

In three minutes they came to the Gournay-Martin house, a wide-fronted mass of undistinguished masonry, in an undistinguished row of exactly the same pattern. There were no signs that any one was living in it. Blinds were drawn, shutters were up over all the windows, upper and lower. No smoke came from any of its chimneys, though indeed it was full early for that.

Pulling a bunch of keys from his pocket, the Duke ran up the steps. The inspector followed him. The Duke looked at the bunch, picked out the latch-key, and fitted it into the lock. It did not open it. He drew it out and tried another key and another. The door remained locked.

"Let me, your Grace," said the inspector. "I'm more used to it. I shall be quicker."

The Duke handed the keys to him, and, one after another, the inspector fitted them into the lock. It was useless. None of them opened the door.

"They've given me the wrong keys," said the Duke, with some vexation. "Or no—stay— I see what's happened. The keys have been changed."

"Changed?" said the inspector. "When? Where?"

"Last night at Charmerace," said the Duke. "M. Gournay-Martin declared that he saw a burglar slip out of one of the windows of the hall of the chateau, and we found the lock of the bureau in which the keys were kept broken."

The inspector seized the knocker, and hammered on the door.

"Try that door there," he cried to his men, pointing to a side-door on the right, the tradesmen's entrance, giving access to the back of the house. It was locked. There came no sound of movement in the house in answer to the inspector's knocking.

"Where's the concierge?" he said.

The Duke shrugged his shoulders. "There's a housekeeper, too—a woman named Victoire," he said. "Let's hope we don't find them with their throats cut."

"That isn't Lupin's way," said the inspector. "They won't have come to much harm."

"It's not very likely that they'll be in a position to open doors," said the Duke drily.

"Hadn't we better have it broken open and be done with it?"

The inspector hesitated.

"People don't like their doors broken open," he said. "And M. Gournay-Martin—"

"Oh, I'll take the responsibility of that," said the Duke.

"Oh, if you say so, your Grace," said the inspector, with a brisk relief. "Henri, go to Ragoneau, the locksmith in the Rue Theobald. Bring him here as quickly as ever you can get him."

"Tell him it's a couple of louis if he's here inside of ten minutes," said the Duke.

The policeman hurried off. The inspector bent down and searched the steps carefully. He searched the roadway. The Duke lighted a cigarette and watched him. The house of the millionaire stood next but one to the corner of a street which ran at right angles to the one in which it stood, and the corner house was empty. The inspector searched the road, then he went round the corner. The other policeman went along the road, searching in the opposite direction. The Duke leant against the door and smoked on patiently. He showed none of the weariness of a man who has spent the night in a long and anxious drive in a rickety motor-car. His eyes were bright and clear; he looked as fresh as if he had come from his bed after a long night's rest. If he had not found the South Pole, he had at any rate brought back fine powers of endurance from his expedition in search of it.

The inspector came back, wearing a disappointed air.

"Have you found anything?" said the Duke.

"Nothing," said the inspector.

He came up the steps and hammered again on the door. No one answered his knock. There was a clatter of footsteps, and Henri and the locksmith, a burly, bearded man, his bag of tools slung over his shoulder, came hurrying up. He was not long getting to work, but it was not an easy job. The lock was strong. At the end of five minutes he said that he might spend an hour struggling with the lock itself; should he cut away a piece of the door round it?

"Cut away," said the Duke.

The locksmith changed his tools, and in less than three minutes he had cut away a square piece from the door, a square in which the lock was fixed, and taken it bodily away.

The door opened. The inspector drew his revolver, and entered the house. The Duke followed him. The policemen drew their revolvers, and followed the Duke. The big hall was but dimly lighted. One of the policemen quickly threw back the shutters of the windows and let in the light. The hall was empty, the furniture in perfect order; there were no signs of burglary there.

"The concierge?" said the inspector, and his men hurried through the little door on the right which opened into the concierge's rooms. In half a minute one of them came out and said: "Gagged and bound, and his wife too."

"But the rooms which were to be plundered are upstairs," said the Duke—"the big drawing-rooms on the first floor. Come on; we may be just in time. The scoundrels may not yet have got away."

He ran quickly up the stairs, followed by the inspector, and hurried along the corridor to the door of the big drawing-room. He threw it open, and stopped dead on the threshold. He had arrived too late.

The room was in disorder. Chairs were overturned, there were empty spaces on the wall where the finest pictures of the millionaire had been hung. The window facing the door was wide open. The shutters were broken; one of them was hanging crookedly from only its bottom hinge. The top of a ladder rose above the window-sill, and beside it, astraddle the sill, was an Empire card-table, half inside the room, half out. On the hearth-rug, before a large tapestry fire-screen, which masked the wide fireplace, built in imitation of the big, wide fireplaces of our ancestors, and rose to the level of the chimney-piece—a magnificent chimney-piece in carved oak-were some chairs tied together ready to be removed.

The Duke and the inspector ran to the window, and looked down into the garden. It was empty. At the further end of it, on the other side of its wall, rose the scaffolding of a house a-building. The burglars had found every convenience to their hand—a strong ladder, an egress through the door in the garden wall, and then through the gap formed by the house in process of erection, which had rendered them independent of the narrow passage between the walls of the gardens, which debouched into a side-street on the right.

The Duke turned from the window, glanced at the wall opposite, then, as if something had caught his eye, went quickly to it.

"Look here," he said, and he pointed to the middle of one of the empty spaces in which a picture had hung.

There, written neatly in blue chalk, were the words:

"This is a job for Guerchard," said the inspector. "But I had better get an examining magistrate to take the matter in hand first." And he ran to the telephone.

The Duke opened the folding doors which led into the second drawing-room. The shutters of the windows were open, and it was plain that Arsene Lupin had plundered it also of everything that had struck his fancy. In the gaps between the pictures on the walls was again the signature "Arsene Lupin."

The inspector was shouting impatiently into the telephone, bidding a servant wake her master instantly. He did not leave the telephone till he was sure that she had done so, that her master was actually awake, and had been informed of the crime. The Duke sat down in an easy chair and waited for him.

When he had finished telephoning, the inspector began to search the two rooms for traces of the burglars. He found nothing, not even a finger-mark.

When he had gone through the two rooms he said, "The next thing to do is to find the house-keeper. She may be sleeping still—she may not even have heard the noise of the burglars."

"I find all this extremely interesting," said the Duke; and he followed the inspector out of the room.

The inspector called up the two policemen, who had been freeing the concierge and going through the rooms on the ground-floor. They did not then examine any more of the rooms on the first floor to discover if they also had been plundered. They went straight up to the top of the house, the servants' quarters.

The inspector called, "Victoire! Victoire!" two or three times; but there was no answer.

They opened the door of room after room and looked in, the inspector taking the rooms on the right, the policemen the rooms on the left.

"Here we are," said one of the policemen. "This room's been recently occupied." They looked in, and saw that the bed was unmade. Plainly Victoire had slept in it.

"Where can she be?" said the Duke.

"Be?" said the inspector. "I expect she's with the burglars—an accomplice."

"I gather that M. Gournay-Martin had the greatest confidence in her," said the Duke.

"He'll have less now," said the inspector drily. "It's generally the confidential ones who let their masters down."

The inspector and his men set about a thorough search of the house. They found the other rooms undisturbed. In half an hour they had established the fact that the burglars had confined their attention to the two drawing-rooms. They found no traces of them; and they did not find Victoire. The concierge could throw no light on her disappearance. He and his wife had been taken by surprise in their sleep and in the dark.

They had been gagged and bound, they declared, without so much as having set eyes on their assailants. The Duke and the inspector came back to the plundered drawing-room.

The inspector looked at his watch and went to the telephone.

"I must let the Prefecture know," he said.

"Be sure you ask them to send Guerchard," said the Duke.

"Guerchard?" said the inspector doubtfully.

"M. Formery, the examining magistrate, does not get on very well with Guerchard."

"What sort of a man is M. Formery? Is he capable?" said the Duke.

"Oh, yes—yes. He's very capable," said the inspector quickly. "But he doesn't have very good luck."

"M. Gournay-Martin particularly asked me to send for Guerchard if I arrived too late, and found the burglary already committed," said the Duke. "It seems that there is war to the knife between Guerchard and this Arsene Lupin. In that case Guerchard will leave no stone unturned to catch the rascal and recover the stolen treasures. M. Gournay-Martin felt that Guerchard was the man for this piece of work very strongly indeed."

"Very good, your Grace," said the inspector. And he rang up the Prefecture of Police.

The Duke heard him report the crime and ask that Guerchard should be sent. The official in charge at the moment seemed to make some demur.

The Duke sprang to his feet, and said in an anxious tone, "Perhaps I'd better speak to him myself."

He took his place at the telephone and said, "I am the Duke of Charmerace. M. Gournay-Martin begged me to secure the services of M. Guerchard. He laid the greatest stress on my securing them, if on reaching Paris I found that the crime had already been committed."

The official at the other end of the line hesitated. He did not refuse on the instant as he had refused the inspector. It may be that he reflected that M. Gournay-Martin was a millionaire and a man of influence; that the Duke of Charmerace was a Duke; that he, at any rate, had nothing whatever to gain by running counter to their wishes. He said that Chief-Inspector Guerchard was not at the Prefecture, that he was off duty; that he would send down two detectives, who were on duty, at once, and summon Chief-Inspector Guerchard with all speed. The Duke thanked him and rang off.

"That's all right," he said cheerfully, turning to the inspector. "What time will M. Formery be here?"

"Well, I don't expect him for another hour," said the inspector. "He won't come till he's had his breakfast. He always makes a good breakfast before setting out to start an inquiry, lest he shouldn't find time to make one after he's begun it."

"Breakfast—breakfast—that's a great idea," said the Duke. "Now you come to remind me, I'm absolutely famished. I got some supper on my way late last night; but I've had nothing since. I suppose nothing interesting will happen till M. Formery comes; and I may as well get some food. But I don't want to leave the house. I think I'll see what the concierge can do for me."

So saying, he went downstairs and interviewed the concierge. The concierge seemed to be still doubtful whether he was standing on his head or his heels, but he undertook to supply the needs of the Duke. The Duke gave him a louis, and he hurried off to get food from a restaurant.

The Duke went upstairs to the bathroom and refreshed himself with a cold bath. By the time he had bathed and dressed the concierge had a meal ready for him in the dining-room. He ate it with the heartiest appetite. Then he sent out for a barber and was shaved.

He then repaired to the pillaged drawing-room, disposed himself in the most restful attitude on a sofa, and lighted an excellent cigar. In the middle of it the inspector came to him. He was not wearing a very cheerful air; and he told the Duke that he had found no clue to the perpetrators of the crime, though M. Dieusy and M. Bonavent, the detectives from the Prefecture of Police, had joined him in the search.

The Duke was condoling with him on this failure when they heard a knocking at the front door, and then voices on the stairs.

"Ah! Here is M. Formery!" said the inspector cheerfully. "Now we can get on."

CHAPTER IX M. FORMERY OPENS THE INQUIRY

The examining magistrate came into the room. He was a plump and pink little man, with very bright eyes. His bristly hair stood up straight all over his head, giving it the appearance of a broad, dapple-grey clothes-brush. He appeared to be of the opinion that Nature had given the world the toothbrush as a model of what a moustache should be; and his own was clipped to that pattern.

"The Duke of Charmerace, M. Formery," said the inspector.

The little man bowed and said, "Charmed, charmed to make your acquaintance, your Grace—though the occasion—the occasion is somewhat painful. The treasures of M. Gournay-Martin are known to all the world. France will deplore his losses." He paused, and added hastily, "But we shall recover them—we shall recover them."

The Duke rose, bowed, and protested his pleasure at making the acquaintance of M. Formery.

"Is this the scene of the robbery, inspector?" said M. Formery; and he rubbed his hands together with a very cheerful air.

"Yes, sir," said the inspector. "These two rooms seem to be the only ones touched, though of course we can't tell till M. Gournay-Martin arrives. Jewels may have been stolen from the bedrooms."

"I fear that M. Gournay-Martin won't be of much help for some days," said the Duke. "When I left him he was nearly distracted; and he won't be any better after a night journey to Paris from Charmerace. But probably these are the only two rooms touched, for in them M. Gournay-Martin had gathered together the gems of his collection. Over the doors hung some pieces of Flemish tapestry—marvels—the composition admirable—the colouring delightful."

"It is easy to see that your Grace was very fond of them," said M. Formery.

"I should think so," said the Duke. "I looked on them as already belonging to me, for my father-in-law was going to give them to me as a wedding present."

"A great loss—a great loss. But we will recover them, sooner or later, you can rest assured of it. I hope you have touched nothing in this room. If anything has been moved it may put me off the scent altogether. Let me have the details, inspector."

The inspector reported the arrival of the Duke at the police-station with Arsene Lupin's letter to M. Gournay-Martin; the discovery that the keys had been changed and would not open the door of the house; the opening of it by the locksmith; the discovery of the concierge and his wife gagged and bound.

"Probably accomplices," said M. Formery.

"Does Lupin always work with accomplices?" said the Duke. "Pardon my ignorance—but I've been out of France for so long—before he attained to this height of notoriety."

"Lupin—why Lupin?" said M. Formery sharply.

"Why, there is the letter from Lupin which my future father-in-law received last night; its arrival was followed by the theft of his two swiftest motor-cars; and then, these signatures on the wall here," said the Duke in some surprise at the question.

"Lupin! Lupin! Everybody has Lupin on the brain!" said M. Formery impatiently. "I'm sick of hearing his name. This letter and these signatures are just as likely to be forgeries as not."

"I wonder if Guerchard will take that view," said the Duke.

"Guerchard? Surely we're not going to be cluttered up with Guerchard. He has Lupin on the brain worse than any one else."

"But M. Gournay-Martin particularly asked me to send for Guerchard if I arrived too late to prevent the burglary. He would never forgive me if I had neglected his request: so I telephoned for him—to the Prefecture of Police," said the Duke.

"Oh, well, if you've already telephoned for him. But it was unnecessary—absolutely unnecessary," said M. Formery sharply.

"I didn't know," said the Duke politely.

"Oh, there was no harm in it—it doesn't matter," said M. Formery in a discontented tone with a discontented air.

He walked slowly round the room, paused by the windows, looked at the ladder, and scanned the garden:

"Arsene Lupin," he said scornfully. "Arsene Lupin doesn't leave traces all over the placc. There's nothing but traces. Are we going to have that silly Lupin joke all over again?"

"I think, sir, that this time joke is the word, for this is a burglary pure and simple," said the inspector.

"Yes, it's plain as daylight," said M. Formery "The burglars came in by this window, and they went out by it."

He crossed the room to a tall safe which stood before the unused door. The safe was covered with velvet, and velvet curtains hung before its door. He drew the curtains, and tried the handle of the door of the safe. It did not turn; the safe was locked.

"As far as I can see, they haven't touched this," said M. Formery.

"Thank goodness for that," said the Duke. "I believe, or at least my fiancee does, that M. Gournay-Martin keeps the most precious thing in his collection in that safe—the coronet."

"What! the famous coronet of the Princesse de Lamballe?" said M. Formery.

"Yes," said the Duke.

"But according to your report, inspector, the letter signed 'Lupin' announced that he was going to steal the coronet also."

"It did—in so many words," said the Duke.

"Well, here is a further proof that we're not dealing with Lupin. That rascal would certainly have put his threat into execution, M. Formery," said the inspector.

"Who's in charge of the house?" said M. Formery.

"The concierge, his wife, and a housekeeper—a woman named Victoire," said the inspector.

"I'll see to the concierge and his wife presently. I've sent one of your men round for their dossier. When I get it I'll question them. You found them gagged and bound in their bedroom?"

"Yes, M. Formery; and always this imitation of Lupin—a yellow gag, blue cords, and the motto, 'I take, therefore I am,' on a scrap of cardboard—his usual bag of tricks."

"Then once again they're going to touch us up in the papers. It's any odds on it," said M. Formery gloomily. "Where's the housekeeper? I should like to see her."

"The fact is, we don't know where she is," said the inspector.

"You don't know where she is?" said M. Formery.

"We can't find her anywhere," said the inspector.

"That's excellent, excellent. We've found the accomplice," said M. Formery with lively delight; and he rubbed his hands together. "At least, we haven't found her, but we know her."

"I don't think that's the case," said the Duke. "At least, my future father-in-law and my fiancee had both of them the greatest confidence in her. Yesterday she telephoned to us at the Chateau de Charmerace. All the jewels were left in her charge, and the wedding presents as they were sent in."

"And these jewels and wedding presents—have they been stolen too?" said M. Formery.

"They don't seem to have been touched," said the Duke, "though of course we can't tell till M. Gournay-Martin arrives. As far as I can see, the burglars have only touched these two drawing-rooms."

"That's very annoying," said M. Formery.

"I don't find it so," said the Duke, smiling.

"I was looking at it from the professional point of view," said M. Formery. He turned to the inspector and added, "You can't have searched thoroughly. This housekeeper must be somewhere about—if she's really trustworthy. Have you looked in every room in the house?"

"In every room—under every bed—in every corner and every cupboard," said the inspector.

"Bother!" said M. Formery. "Are there no scraps of torn clothes, no blood-stains, no traces of murder, nothing of interest?"

"Nothing!" said the inspector.

"But this is very regrettable," said M. Formery. "Where did she sleep? Was her bed unmade?"

"Her room is at the top of the house," said the inspector. "The bed had been slept in, but she does not appear to have taken away any of her clothes."

"Extraordinary! This is beginning to look a very complicated business," said M. Formery gravely.

"Perhaps Guerchard will be able to throw a little more light on it," said the Duke.

M. Formery frowned and said, "Yes, yes. Guerchard is a good assistant in a business like this. A little visionary, a little fanciful—wrong-headed, in fact; but, after all, he IS Guerchard. Only, since Lupin is his bugbear, he's bound to find some means of muddling us up with that wretched animal. You're going to see Lupin mixed up with all this to a dead certainty, your Grace."

The Duke looked at the signatures on the wall. "It seems to me that he is pretty well mixed up with it already," he said quietly.

"Believe me, your Grace, in a criminal affair it is, above all things, necessary to distrust appearances. I am growing more and more confident that some ordinary burglars have committed this crime and are trying to put us off the scent by diverting our attention to Lupin."

The Duke stooped down carelessly and picked up a book which had fallen from a table.

"Excuse me, but please—please—do not touch anything," said M. Formery quickly.

"Why, this is odd," said the Duke, staring at the floor.

"What is odd?" said M. Formery.

"Well, this book looks as if it had been knocked off the table by one of the burglars. And look here; here's a footprint under it—a footprint on the carpet," said the Duke.

M. Formery and the inspector came quickly to the spot. There, where the book had fallen, plainly imprinted on the carpet, was a white footprint. M. Formery and the inspector stared at it.

"It looks like plaster. How did plaster get here?" said M. Formery, frowning at it.

"Well, suppose the robbers came from the garden," said the Duke.

"Of course they came from the garden, your Grace. Where else should they come from?" said M. Formery, with a touch of impatience in his tone.

"Well, at the end of the garden they're building a house," said the Duke.

"Of course, of course," said M. Formery, taking him up quickly. "The burglars came here with their boots covered with plaster. They've swept away all the other marks of their feet from the carpet; but whoever did the sweeping was too slack to lift up that book and sweep under it. This footprint, however, is not of great importance, though it is corroborative of all the other evidence we have that they came and went by the garden. There's the ladder, and that table half out of the window. Still, this footprint may turn out useful, after all. You had better take the measurements of it, inspector. Here's a foot-rule for you. I make a point of carrying this foot-rule about with me, your Grace. You would be surprised to learn how often it has come in useful."

He took a little ivory foot-rule from his waist-coat pocket, and gave it to the inspector, who fell on his knees and measured the footprint with the greatest care.

"I must take a careful look at that house they're building. I shall find a good many traces there, to a dead certainty," said M. Formery.

The inspector entered the measurements of the footprint in his note-book. There came the sound of a knocking at the front door.

"I shall find footprints of exactly the same dimensions as this one at the foot of some heap of plaster beside that house," said M. Formery; with an air of profound conviction, pointing through the window to the house building beyond the garden.

A policeman opened the door of the drawing-room and saluted.

"If you please, sir, the servants have arrived from Charmerace," he said.

"Let them wait in the kitchen and the servants' offices," said M. Formery. He stood silent, buried in profound meditation, for a couple of minutes. Then he turned to the Duke and said, "What was that you said about a theft of motor-cars at Charmerace?"

"When he received the letter from Arsene Lupin, M. Gournay-Martin decided to start for Paris at once," said the Duke. "But when we sent for the cars we found that they had just been stolen. M. Gournay-Martin's chauffeur and another servant were in the garage gagged and bound. Only an old car, a hundred horse-power Mercrac, was left. I drove it to Paris, leaving M. Gournay-Martin and his family to come on by train."

"Very important—very important indeed," said M. Formery. He thought for a moment, and then added. "Were the motor-cars the only things stolen? Were there no other thefts?"

"Well, as a matter of fact, there was another theft, or rather an attempt at theft," said the Duke with some hesitation. "The rogues who stole the motor-cars presented themselves at the chateau under the name of Charolais—a father and three sons—on the pretext of buying the hundred-horse-power Mercrac. M. Gournay-Martin had advertised it for sale in the Rennes Advertiser. They were waiting in the big hall of the chateau, which the family uses as the chief living-room, for the return of M. Gournay-Martin. He came; and as they left the hall one of them attempted to steal a pendant set with pearls which I had given to Mademoiselle Gournay-Martin half an hour before. I caught him in the act and saved the pendant."

"Good! good! Wait—we have one of the gang--wait till I question him," said M. Formery, rubbing his hands; and his eyes sparkled with joy.

"Well, no; I'm afraid we haven't," said the Duke in an apologetic tone.

"What! We haven't? Has he escaped from the police? Oh, those country police!" cried M. Formery.

"No; I didn't charge him with the theft," said the Duke.

"You didn't charge him with the theft?" cried M. Formery, astounded.

"No; he was very young and he begged so hard. I had the pendant. I let him go," said the Duke.

"Oh, your Grace, your Grace! Your duty to society!" cried M. Formery.

"Yes, it does seem to have been rather weak," said the Duke; "but there you are. It's no good crying over spilt milk."

M. Formery folded his arms and walked, frowning, backwards and forwards across the room.

He stopped, raised his hand with a gesture commanding attention, and said, "I have no hesitation in saying that there is a connection—an intimate connection—between the thefts at Charmerace and this burglary!"

The Duke and the inspector gazed at him with respectful eyes—at least, the eyes of the inspector were respectful; the Duke's eyes twinkled.

"I am gathering up the threads," said M. Formery. "Inspector, bring up the concierge and his wife. I will question them on the scene of the crime. Their dossier should be here. If it is, bring it up with them; if not, no matter; bring them up without it."

The inspector left the drawing-room. M. Formery plunged at once into frowning meditation.

"I find all this extremely interesting," said the Duke.

"Charmed! Charmed!" said M. Formery, waving his hand with an absent-minded air.

The inspector entered the drawing-room followed by the concierge and his wife. He handed a paper to M. Formery. The concierge, a bearded man of about sixty, and his wife, a somewhat bearded woman of about fifty-five, stared at M. Formery with fascinated, terrified eyes. He sat down in a chair, crossed his legs, read the paper through, and then scrutinized them keenly.

"Well, have you recovered from your adventure?" he said.

"Oh, yes, sir," said the concierge. "They hustled us a bit, but they did not really hurt us."

"Nothing to speak of, that is," said his wife. "But all the same, it's a disgraceful thing that an honest woman can't sleep in peace in her bed of a night without being disturbed by rascals like that. And if the police did their duty things like this wouldn't happen. And I don't care who hears me say it."

"You say that you were taken by surprise in your sleep?" said M. Formery. "You say you saw nothing, and heard nothing?"

"There was no time to see anything or hear anything. They trussed us up like greased lightning," said the concierge.

"But the gag was the worst," said the wife. "To lie there and not be able to tell the rascals what I thought about them!"

"Didn't you hear the noise of footsteps in the garden?" said M. Formery.

"One can't hear anything that happens in the garden from our bedroom," said the concierge.

"Even the night when Mlle. Germaine's great Dane barked from twelve o'clock till seven in the morning, all the household was kept awake except us; but bless you, sir, we slept like tops," said his wife proudly.

"If they sleep like that it seems rather a waste of time to have gagged them," whispered the Duke to the inspector.

The inspector grinned, and whispered scornfully, "Oh, them common folks; they do sleep like that, your Grace."

"Didn't you hear any noise at the front door?" said M. Formery.

"No, we heard no noise at the door," said the concierge.

"Then you heard no noise at all the whole night?" said M. Formery.

"Oh, yes, sir, we heard noise enough after we'd been gagged," said the concierge.

"Now, this is important," said M. Formery. "What kind of a noise was it?"

"Well, it was a bumping kind of noise," said the concierge. "And there was a noise of footsteps, walking about the room."

"What room? Where did these noises come from?" said M. Formery.

"From the room over our heads—the big drawing-room," said the concierge.

"Didn't you hear any noise of a struggle, as if somebody was being dragged about—no screaming or crying?" said M. Formery.

The concierge and his wife looked at one another with inquiring eyes.

"No, I didn't," said the concierge.

"Neither did I," said his wife.

M. Formery paused. Then he said, "How long have you been in the service of M. Gournay-Martin?"

"A little more than a year," said the concierge.

M. Formery looked at the paper in his hand, frowned, and said severely, "I see you've been convicted twice, my man."

"Yes, sir, but—"

"My husband's an honest man, sir—perfectly honest," broke in his wife. "You've only to ask M. Gournay-Martin; he'll—"

"Be so good as to keep quiet, my good woman," said M. Formery; and, turning to her husband, he went on: "At your first conviction you were sentenced to a day's imprisonment with costs; at your second conviction you got three days' imprisonment."

"I'm not going to deny it, sir," said the concierge; "but it was an honourable imprisonment."

"Honourable?" said M. Formery.

"The first time, I was a gentleman's servant, and I got a day's imprisonment for crying, 'Hurrah for the General Strike!'—on the first of May."

"You were a valet? In whose service?" said M. Formery.

"In the service of M. Genlis, the Socialist leader."

"And your second conviction?" said M. Formery.

"It was for having cried in the porch of Ste. Clotilde, 'Down with the cows!'—meaning the police, sir," said the concierge.

"And were you in the service of M. Genlis then?" said M. Formery.

"No, sir; I was in the service of M. Bussy-Rabutin, the Royalist deputy."

"You don't seem to have very well-defined political convictions," said M. Formery.

"Oh, yes, sir, I have," the concierge protested. "I'm always devoted to my masters; and I have the same opinions that they have—always."

"Very good; you can go," said M. Formery.

The concierge and his wife left the room, looking as if they did not quite know whether to feel relieved or not.

"Those two fools are telling the exact truth, unless I'm very much mistaken," said M. Formery.

"They look honest enough people," said the Duke.

"Well, now to examine the rest of the house," said M. Formery.

"I'll come with you, if I may," said the Duke.

"By all means, by all means," said M. Formery.

"I find it all so interesting," said the Duke,

CHAPTER X GUERCHARD ASSISTS

Leaving a policeman on guard at the door of the drawing-room M. Formery, the Duke, and the inspector set out on their tour of inspection. It was a long business, for M. Formery examined every room with the most scrupulous care—with more care, indeed, than he had displayed in his examination of the drawing-rooms. In particular he lingered long in the bedroom of Victoire, discussing the possibilities of her having been murdered and carried away by the burglars along with their booty. He seemed, if anything, disappointed at finding no blood-stains, but to find real consolation in the thought that she might have been strangled. He found the inspector in entire agreement with every theory he enunciated, and he grew more and more disposed to regard him as a zealous and trustworthy officer. Also he was not at all displeased at enjoying this opportunity of impressing the Duke with his powers of analysis and synthesis. He was unaware that, as a rule, the Duke's eyes did not usually twinkle as they twinkled during this solemn and deliberate progress through the house of M. Gournay-Martin. M. Formery had so exactly the air of a sleuthhound; and he was even noisier.

Having made this thorough examination of the house, M. Formery went out into the garden and set about examining that. There were footprints on the turf about the foot of the ladder, for the grass was close-clipped, and the rain had penetrated and softened the soil; but there were hardly as many footprints as might have been expected, seeing that the burglars must have made many journeys in the course of robbing the drawing-rooms of so many objects of art, some of them of considerable weight. The footprints led to a path of hard gravel; and M. Formery led the way down it, out of the door in the wall at the bottom of the garden, and into the space round the house which was being built.

As M. Formery had divined, there was a heap, or, to be exact, there were several heaps of plaster about the bottom of the scaffolding. Unfortunately, there were also hundreds of footprints. M. Formery looked at them with longing eyes; but he did not suggest that the inspector should hunt about for a set of footprints of the size of the one he had so carefully measured on the drawing-room carpet.

While they were examining the ground round the half-built house a man came briskly down the stairs from the second floor of the house of M. Gournay-Martin. He was an ordinary-looking man, almost insignificant, of between forty and fifty, and of rather more than middle height. He had an ordinary, rather shapeless mouth, an ordinary nose, an ordinary chin, an ordinary forehead, rather low, and ordinary ears. He was wearing an ordinary top-hat, by no means new. His clothes were the ordinary clothes of a fairly well-to-do citizen; and his boots had been chosen less to set off any slenderness his feet might possess than for their comfortable roominess. Only his eyes relieved his face from insignificance. They were extraordinarily alert eyes, producing in those on whom they rested the somewhat uncomfortable impression that the depths of their souls were being penetrated. He was the famous Chief-Inspector Guerchard, head of the Detective Department of the Prefecture of Police, and sworn foe of Arsene Lupin.

The policeman at the door of the drawing-room saluted him briskly. He was a fine, upstanding, red-faced young fellow, adorned by a rich black moustache of extraordinary fierceness.

"Shall I go and inform M. Formery that you have come, M. Guerchard?" he said.

"No, no; there's no need to take the trouble," said Guerchard in a gentle, rather husky voice. "Don't bother any one about me—I'm of no importance."

"Oh, come, M. Guerchard," protested the policeman.

"Of no importance," said M. Guerchard decisively. "For the present, M. Formery is everything. I'm only an assistant."

He stepped into the drawing-room and stood looking about it, curiously still. It was almost as if the whole of his being was concentrated in the act of seeing—as if all the other functions of his mind and body were in suspension.

"M. Formery and the inspector have just been up to examine the housekeeper's room. It's right at the top of the house—on the second floor. You take the servants' staircase. Then it's right at the end of the passage on the left. Would you like me to take you up to it, sir?" said the policeman eagerly. His heart was in his work.

"Thank you, I know where it is—I've just come from it," said Guerchard gently.

A grin of admiration widened the already wide mouth of the policeman, and showed a row of very white, able-looking teeth.

"Ah, M. Guerchard!" he said, "you're cleverer than all the examining magistrates in Paris put together!"

"You ought not to say that, my good fellow. I can't prevent you thinking it, of course; but you ought not to say it," said Guerchard with husky gentleness; and the faintest smile played round the corners of his mouth.

He walked slowly to the window, and the policeman walked with him.

"Have you noticed this, sir?" said the policeman, taking hold of the top of the ladder with a powerful hand. "It's probable that the burglars came in and went away by this ladder."

"Thank you," said Guerchard.

"They have even left this card-table on the window-sill," said the policeman; and he patted the card-table with his other powerful hand.

"Thank you, thank you," said Guerchard.

"They don't think it's Lupin's work at all," said the policeman. "They think that Lupin's letter announcing the burglary and these signatures on the walls are only a ruse."

"Is that so?" said Guerchard.

"Is there any way I can help you, sir?" said policeman.

"Yes," said Guerchard. "Take up your post outside that door and admit no one but M. Formery, the inspector, Bonavent, or Dieusy, without consulting me." And he pointed to the drawing-room door.

"Shan't I admit the Duke of Charmerace? He's taking a great interest in this affair," said the policeman.

"The Duke of Charmerace? Oh, yes—admit the Duke of Charmerace," said Guerchard.

The policeman went to his post of responsibility, a proud man.

Hardly had the door closed behind him when Guerchard was all activity—activity and eyes. He examined the ladder, the gaps on the wall from which the pictures had been taken, the signatures of Arsene Lupin. The very next thing he did was to pick up the book which the Duke had set on the top of the footprint again, to preserve it; and he measured, pacing it, the distance between the footprint and the window.

The result of this measuring did not appear to cause him any satisfaction, for he frowned, measured the distance again, and then stared out of the window with a perplexed air, thinking hard. It was curious that, when he concentrated himself on a process of reasoning, his eyes seemed to lose something of their sharp brightness and grew a little dim.

At last he seemed to come to some conclusion. He turned away from the window, drew a small magnifying-glass from his pocket, dropped on his hands and knees, and began to examine the surface of the carpet with the most minute care.

He examined a space of it nearly six feet square, stopped, and gazed round the room. His eyes rested on the fireplace, which he could see under the bottom of the big tapestried fire-screen which was raised on legs about a foot high, fitted with big casters. His eyes filled with interest; without rising, he crawled quickly across the room, peeped round the edge of the screen and rose, smiling.

He went on to the further drawing-room and made the same careful examination of it, again examining a part of the surface of the carpet with his magnifying-glass. He came back to the window to which the ladder had been raised and examined very carefully the broken shutter. He whistled softly to himself, lighted a cigarette, and leant against the side of the window. He looked out of it, with dull eyes which saw nothing, the while his mind worked upon the facts he had discovered.

He had stood there plunged in reflection for perhaps ten minutes, when there came a sound of voices and footsteps on the stairs. He awoke from his absorption, seemed to prick his ears, then slipped a leg over the window-ledge, and disappeared from sight down the ladder.

The door opened, and in came M. Formery, the Duke, and the inspector. M. Formery looked round the room with eyes which seemed to expect to meet a familiar sight, then walked to the other drawing-room and looked round that. He turned to the policeman, who had stepped inside the drawing-room, and said sharply, "M. Guerchard is not here."

"I left him here," said the policeman. "He must have disappeared. He's a wonder."

"Of course," said M. Formery. "He has gone down the ladder to examine that house they're building. He's just following in our tracks and doing all over again the work we've already done. He might have saved himself the trouble. We could have told him all he wants to know. But there! He very likely would not be satisfied till he had seen everything for himself."

"He may see something which we have missed," said the Duke.

M. Formery frowned, and said sharply "That's hardly likely. I don't think that your Grace realizes to what a perfection constant practice brings one's power of observation. The inspector and I will cheerfully eat anything we've missed—won't we, inspector?" And he laughed heartily at his joke.

"It might always prove a large mouthful," said the Duke with an ironical smile.

M. Formery assumed his air of profound reflection, and walked a few steps up and down the room, frowning:

"The more I think about it," he said, "the clearer it grows that we have disposed of the Lupin theory. This is the work of far less expert rogues than Lupin. What do you think, inspector?"

"Yes; I think you have disposed of that theory, sir," said the inspector with ready acquiescence.

"All the same, I'd wager anything that we haven't disposed of it to the satisfaction of Guerchard," said M. Formery.

"Then he must be very hard to satisfy," said the Duke.

"Oh, in any other matter he's open to reason," said M. Formery; "but Lupin is his fixed idea; it's an obsession—almost a mania."

"But yet he never catches him," said the Duke.

"No; and he never will. His very obsession by Lupin hampers him. It cramps his mind and hinders its working," said M. Formery.

He resumed his meditative pacing, stopped again, and said:

"But considering everything, especially the absence of any traces of violence, combined with her entire disappearance, I have come to another conclusion. Victoire is the key to the mystery. She is the accomplice. She never slept in her bed. She unmade it to put us off the scent. That, at any rate, is something gained, to have found the accomplice. We shall have this good news, at least, to tell M, Gournay-Martin on his arrival."

"Do you really think that she's the accomplice?" said the Duke.

"I'm dead sure of it," said M. Formery. "We will go up to her room and make another thorough examination of it."

Guerchard's head popped up above the window-sill:

"My dear M. Formery," he said, "I beg that you will not take the trouble."

M. Formery's mouth opened: "What! You, Guerchard?" he stammered.

"Myself," said Guerchard; and he came to the top of the ladder and slipped lightly over the window-sill into the room.

He shook hands with M. Formery and nodded to the inspector. Then he looked at the Duke with an air of inquiry.

"Let me introduce you," said M. Formery. "Chief-Inspector Guerchard, head of the Detective Department—the Duke of Charmerace."

The Duke shook hands with Guerchard, saying, "I'm delighted to make your acquaintance, M. Guerchard. I've been expecting your coming with the greatest interest. Indeed it was I who begged the officials at the Prefecture of Police to put this case in your hands. I insisted on it."

"What were you doing on that ladder?" said M. Formery, giving Guerchard no time to reply to the Duke.

"I was listening," said Guerchard simply—"listening. I like to hear people talk when I'm engaged on a case. It's a distraction—and it helps. I really must congratulate you, my dear M. Formery, on the admirable manner in which you have conducted this inquiry."

M. Formery bowed, and regarded him with a touch of suspicion.

"There are one or two minor points on which we do not agree, but on the whole your method has been admirable," said Guerchard.

"Well, about Victoire," said M. Formery. "You're quite sure that an examination, a more thorough examination, of her room, is unnecessary?"

"Yes, I think so," said Guerchard. "I have just looked at it myself."

The door opened, and in came Bonavent, one of the detectives who had come earlier from the Prefecture. In his hand he carried a scrap of cloth.

He saluted Guerchard, and said to M. Formery, "I have just found this scrap of cloth on the edge of the well at the bottom of the garden. The concierge's wife tells me that it has been torn from Victoire's dress."

"I feared it," said M. Formery, taking the scrap of cloth from him. "I feared foul play. We must go to the well at once, send some one down it, or have it dragged."

He was moving hastily to the door, when Guerchard said, in his husky, gentle voice, "I don't think there is any need to look for Victoire in the well."

"But this scrap of cloth," said M. Formery, holding it out to him.

"Yes, yes, that scrap of cloth," said Guerchard. And, turning to the Duke, he added, "Do you know if there's a dog or cat in the house, your Grace? I suppose that, as the fiance of Mademoiselle Gournay-Martin, you are familiar with the house?"

"What on earth—" said M. Formery.

"Excuse me," interrupted Guerchard. "But this is important—very important."

"Yes, there is a cat," said the Duke. "I've seen a cat at the door of the concierge's rooms."

"It must have been that cat which took this scrap of cloth to the edge of the well," said Guerchard gravely.

"This is ridiculous—preposterous!" cried M. Formery, beginning to flush. "Here we're dealing with a most serious crime—a murder—the murder of Victoire—and you talk about cats!"

"Victoire has not been murdered," said Guerchard; and his husky voice was gentler than ever, only just audible.

"But we don't know that—we know nothing of the kind," said M. Formery.

"I do," said Guerchard.

"You?" said M. Formery.

"Yes," said Guerchard.

"Then how do you explain her disappearance?"

"If she had disappeared I shouldn't explain it," said Guerchard.

"But since she has disappeared?" cried M. Formery, in a tone of exasperation.

"She hasn't," said Guerchard.

"You know nothing about it!" cried M. Formery, losing his temper.

"Yes, I do," said Guerchard, with the same gentleness.

"Come, do you mean to say that you know where she is?" cried M. Formery.

"Certainly," said Guerchard.

"Do you mean to tell us straight out that you've seen her?" cried M. Formery.

"Oh, yes; I've seen her," said Guerchard.

"You've seen her—when?" cried M. Formery.

Guerchard paused to consider. Then he said gently:

"It must have been between four and five minutes ago."

"But hang it all, you haven't been out of this room!" cried M. Formery.

"No, I haven't," said Guerchard.

"And you've seen her?" cried M. Formery.

"Yes," said Guerchard, raising his voice a little.

"Well, why the devil don't you tell us where she is? Tell us!" cried M. Formery, purple with exasperation.

"But you won't let me get a word out of my mouth," protested Guerchard with aggravating gentleness.

"Well, speak!" cried M. Formery; and he sank gasping on to a chair.

"Ah, well, she's here," said Guerchard.

"Here! How did she GET here?" said M. Formery.

"On a mattress," said Guerchard.

M. Formery sat upright, almost beside himself, glaring furiously at Guerchard:

"What do you stand there pulling all our legs for?" he almost howled.

"Look here," said Guerchard.

He walked across the room to the fireplace, pushed the chairs which stood bound together on the hearth-rug to one side of the fireplace, and ran the heavy fire-screen on its casters to the other side of it, revealing to their gaze the wide, old-fashioned fireplace itself. The iron brazier which held the coals had been moved into the corner, and a mattress lay on the floor of the fireplace. On the mattress lay the figure of a big, middle-aged woman, half-dressed. There was a yellow gag in her mouth; and her hands and feet were bound together with blue cords.

"She is sleeping soundly," said Guerchard. He stooped and picked up a handkerchief, and smelt it. "There's the handkerchief they chloroformed her with. It still smells of chloroform."

They stared at him and the sleeping woman.

"Lend a hand, inspector," he said. "And you too, Bonavent. She looks a good weight."

The three of them raised the mattress, and carried it and the sleeping woman to a broad couch, and laid them on it. They staggered under their burden, for truly Victoire was a good weight.

M. Formery rose, with recovered breath, but with his face an even richer purple. His eyes were rolling in his head, as if they were not under proper control.

He turned on the inspector and cried savagely, "You never examined the fireplace, inspector!"

"No, sir," said the downcast inspector.

"It was unpardonable—absolutely unpardonable!" cried M. Formery. "How is one to work with subordinates like this?"

"It was an oversight," said Guerchard.

M. Formery turned to him and said, "You must admit that it was materially impossible for me to see her."

"It was possible if you went down on all fours," said Guerchard.

"On all fours?" said M. Formery.

"Yes; on all fours you could see her heels sticking out beyond the mattress," said Guerchard simply.

M. Formery shrugged his shoulders: "That screen looked as if it had stood there since the beginning of the summer," he said.

"The first thing, when you're dealing with Lupin, is to distrust appearances," said Guerchard.

"Lupin!" cried M. Formery hotly. Then he bit his lip and was silent.

He walked to the side of the couch and looked down on the sleeping Victoire, frowning: "This upsets everything," he said. "With these new conditions, I've got to begin all over again, to find a new explanation of the affair. For the moment—for the moment, I'm thrown completely off the track. And you, Guerchard?"

"Oh, well," said Guerchard, "I have an idea or two about the matter still."

"Do you really mean to say that it hasn't thrown you off the track too?" said M. Formery, with a touch of incredulity in his tone.

363

"Well, no—not exactly," said Guerchard. "I wasn't on that track, you see."

"No, of course not—of course not. You were on the track of Lupin," said M. Formery; and his contemptuous smile was tinged with malice.

The Duke looked from one to the other of them with curious, searching eyes: "I find all this so interesting," he said.

"We do not take much notice of these checks; they do not depress us for a moment," said M. Formery, with some return of his old grandiloquence. "We pause hardly for an instant; then we begin to reconstruct—to reconstruct."

"It's perfectly splendid of you," said the Duke, and his limpid eyes rested on M. Formery's self-satisfied face in a really affectionate gaze; they might almost be said to caress it.

Guerchard looked out of the window at a man who was carrying a hod-full of bricks up one of the ladders set against the scaffolding of the building house. Something in this honest workman's simple task seemed to amuse him, for he smiled.

Only the inspector, thinking of the unexamined fireplace, looked really depressed.

"We shan't get anything out of this woman till she wakes," said M. Formery, "When she does, I shall question her closely and fully. In the meantime, she may as well be carried up to her bedroom to sleep off the effects of the chloroform."

Guerchard turned quickly: "Not her own bedroom, I think," he said gently.

"Certainly not—of course, not her own bedroom," said M. Formery quickly.

"And I think an officer at the door of whatever bedroom she does sleep in," said Guerchard.

"Undoubtedly—most necessary," said M. Formery gravely. "See to it, inspector. You can take her away."

The inspector called in a couple of policemen, and with their aid he and Bonavent raised the sleeping woman, a man at each corner of the mattress, and bore her from the room.

"And now to reconstruct," said M. Formery; and he folded his arms and plunged into profound reflection.

The Duke and Guerchard watched him in silence.

CHAPTER XI THE FAMILY ARRIVES

In carrying out Victoire, the inspector had left the door of the drawing-room open. After he had watched M. Formery reflect for two minutes, Guerchard faded—to use an expressive Americanism—through it. The Duke felt in the breast-pocket of his coat, murmured softly, "My cigarettes," and followed him.

He caught up Guerchard on the stairs and said, "I will come with you, if I may, M. Guerchard. I find all these investigations extraordinarily interesting. I have been observing M. Formery's methods—I should like to watch yours, for a change."

"By all means," said Guerchard. "And there are several things I want to hear about from your Grace. Of course it might be an advantage to discuss them together with M. Formery, but—" and he hesitated.

"It would be a pity to disturb M. Formery in the middle of the process of reconstruction," said the Duke; and a faint, ironical smile played round the corners of his sensitive lips.

Guerchard looked at him quickly: "Perhaps it would," he said.

They went through the house, out of the back door, and into the garden. Guerchard moved about twenty yards from the house, then he stopped and questioned the Duke at great length. He questioned him first about the Charolais, their appearance, their actions, especially about Bernard's attempt to steal the pendant, and the theft of the motor-cars.

"I have been wondering whether M. Charolais might not have been Arsene Lupin himself," said the Duke.

"It's quite possible," said Guerchard. "There seem to be no limits whatever to Lupin's powers of disguising himself. My colleague, Ganimard, has come across him at least three times that he knows of, as a different person. And no single time could he be sure that it was the same man. Of course, he had a feeling that he was in contact with some one he had met before, but that was all. He had no certainty. He may have met him half a dozen times besides without knowing him. And the photographs of him—they're all different. Ganimard declares that Lupin is so extraordinarily successful in his disguises because he is a great actor. He actually becomes for the time being the person he pretends to be. He thinks and feels absolutely like that person. Do you follow me?"

"Oh, yes; but he must be rather fluid, this Lupin," said the Duke; and then he added thoughtfully, "It must be awfully risky to come so often into actual contact with men like Ganimard and you."

"Lupin has never let any consideration of danger prevent him doing anything that caught his fancy. He has odd fancies, too. He's a humourist of the most varied kind—grim, ironic, farcical, as the mood takes him. He must be awfully trying to live with," said Guerchard.

"Do you think humourists are trying to live with?" said the Duke, in a meditative tone. "I think they brighten life a good deal; but of course there are people who do not like them—the middle-classes."

"Yes, yes, they're all very well in their place; but to live with they must be trying," said Guerchard quickly.

He went on to question the Duke closely and at length about the household of M. Gournay-Martin, saying that Arsene Lupin worked with the largest gang a burglar had ever captained, and it was any odds that he had introduced one, if not more, of that gang into it. Moreover, in the case of a big affair like this, Lupin himself often played two or three parts under as many disguises.

"If he was Charolais, I don't see how he could be one of M. Gournay-Martin's household, too," said the Duke in some perplexity.

"I don't say that he WAS Charolais," said Guerchard. "It is quite a moot point. On the whole, I'm inclined to think that he was not. The theft of the motor-cars was a job for a subordinate. He would hardly bother himself with it."

The Duke told him all that he could remember about the millionaire's servants—and, under the clever questioning of the detective, he was surprised to find how much he did remember—all kinds of odd details about them which he had scarcely been aware of observing.

The two of them, as they talked, afforded an interesting contrast: the Duke, with his air of distinction and race, his ironic expression, his mobile features, his clear enunciation and well-modulated voice, his easy carriage of an accomplished fencer—a fencer with muscles of steel—seemed to be a man of another kind from the slow-moving detective, with his husky voice, his common, slurring enunciation, his clumsily moulded features, so ill adapted to the expression of emotion and intelligence. It was a contrast almost between the hawk and the mole, the warrior and the workman. Only in their eyes were they alike; both of them had the keen, alert eyes of observers. Perhaps the most curious thing of all was that, in spite of the fact that he had for so much of his life been an idler, trifling away his time in the pursuit of pleasure, except when he had made his expedition to the South Pole, the Duke gave one the impression of being a cleverer man, of a far finer brain, than the detective who had spent so much of his life sharpening his wits on the more intricate problems of crime.

When Guerchard came to the end of his questions, the Duke said: "You have given me a very strong feeling that it is going to be a deuce of a job to catch Lupin. I don't wonder that, so far, you have none of you laid hands on him."

"But we have!" cried Guerchard quickly. "Twice Ganimard has caught him. Once he had him in prison, and actually brought him to trial. Lupin became another man, and was let go from the very dock."

"Really? It sounds absolutely amazing," said the Duke.

"And then, in the affair of the Blue Diamond, Ganimard caught him again. He has his weakness, Lupin—it's women. It's a very common weakness in these masters of crime. Ganimard and Holmlock Shears, in that affair, got the better of him by using his love for a woman—'the fair-haired lady,' she was called—to nab him."

"A shabby trick," said the Duke.

"Shabby?" said Guerchard in a tone of utter wonder. "How can anything be shabby in the case of a rogue like this?"

"Perhaps not—perhaps not—still—" said the Duke, and stopped.

The expression of wonder faded from Guerchard's face, and he went on, "Well, Holmlock Shears recovered the Blue Diamond, and Ganimard nabbed Lupin. He held him for ten minutes, then Lupin escaped."

"What became of the fair-haired lady?" said the Duke.

"I don't know. I have heard that she is dead," said Guerchard. "Now I come to think of it, I heard quite definitely that she died."

"It must be awful for a woman to love a man like Lupin—the constant, wearing anxiety," said the Duke thoughtfully.

"I dare say. Yet he can have his pick of sweethearts. I've been offered thousands of francs by women—women of your Grace's world and wealthy Viennese—to make them acquainted with Lupin," said Guerchard.

"You don't surprise me," said the Duke with his ironic smile. "Women never do stop to think—where one of their heroes is concerned. And did you do it?"

"How could I? If I only could! If I could find Lupin entangled with a woman like Ganimard did—well—" said Guerchard between his teeth.

"He'd never get out of YOUR clutches," said the Duke with conviction.

"I think not—I think not," said Guerchard grimly. "But come, I may as well get on."

He walked across the turf to the foot of the ladder and looked at the footprints round it. He made but a cursory examination of them, and took his way down the garden-path, out of the door in the wall into the space about the house that was building. He was not long examining it, and he went right through it out into the street on which the house would face when it was finished. He looked up and down it, and began to retrace his footsteps.

"I've seen all I want to see out here. We may as well go back to the house," he said to the Duke.

"I hope you've seen what you expected to see," said the Duke.

"Exactly what I expected to see—exactly," said Guerchard.

"That's as it should be," said the Duke.

They went back to the house and found M. Formery in the drawing-room, still engaged in the process of reconstruction.

"The thing to do now is to hunt the neighbourhood for witnesses of the departure of the burglars with their booty. Loaded as they were with such bulky objects, they must have had a big conveyance. Somebody must have noticed it. They must have wondered why it was standing in front of a half-built house. Somebody may have actually seen the burglars loading it, though it was so early in the morning. Bonavent had better inquire at every house in the street on which that half-built house faces. Did you happen to notice the name of it?" said M. Formery.

"It's Sureau Street," said Guerchard. "But Dieusy has been hunting the neighbourhood for some one who saw the burglars loading their conveyance, or saw it waiting to be loaded, for the last hour."

"Good," said M. Formery. "We are getting on."

M. Formery was silent. Guerchard and the Duke sat down and lighted cigarettes.

"You found plenty of traces," said M. Formery, waving his hand towards the window.

"Yes; I've found plenty of traces," said Guerchard.

"Of Lupin?" said M. Formery, with a faint sneer.

"No; not of Lupin," said Guerchard.

A smile of warm satisfaction illumined M. Formery's face:

"What did I tell you?" he said. "I'm glad that you've changed your mind about that."

"I have hardly changed my mind," said Guerchard, in his husky, gentle voice.

There came a loud knocking on the front door, the sound of excited voices on the stairs. The door opened, and in burst M. Gournay-Martin. He took one glance round the devastated room, raised his clenched hands towards the ceiling, and bellowed, "The scoundrels! the dirty scoundrels!" And his voice stuck in his throat. He tottered across the room to a couch, dropped heavily to it, gazed round the scene of desolation, and burst into tears.

Germaine and Sonia came into the room. The Duke stepped forward to greet them.

"Do stop crying, papa. You're as hoarse as a crow as it is," said Germaine impatiently. Then, turning on the Duke with a frown, she said: "I think that joke of yours about the train was simply disgraceful, Jacques. A joke's a joke, but to send us out to the station on a night like last night, through all that heavy rain, when you knew all the time that there was no quarter-to-nine train—it was simply disgraceful."

"I really don't know what you're talking about," said the Duke quietly. "Wasn't there a quarter-to-nine train?"

"Of course there wasn't," said Germaine. "The time-table was years old. I think it was the most senseless attempt at a joke I ever heard of."

"It doesn't seem to me to be a joke at all," said the Duke quietly. "At any rate, it isn't the kind of a joke I make—it would be detestable. I never thought to look at the date of the time-table. I keep a box of cigarettes in that drawer, and I have noticed the time-table there. Of course, it may have been lying there for years. It was stupid of me not to look at the date."

"I said it was a mistake. I was sure that his Grace would not do anything so unkind as that," said Sonia.

The Duke smiled at her.

"Well, all I can say is, it was very stupid of you not to look at the date," said Germaine.

M. Gournay-Martin rose to his feet and wailed, in the most heartrending fashion: "My pictures! My wonderful pictures! Such investments! And my cabinets! My Renaissance cabinets! They can't be replaced! They were unique! They were worth a hundred and fifty thousand francs."

370

M. Formery stepped forward with an air and said, "I am distressed, M. Gournay-Martin—truly distressed by your loss. I am M. Formery, examining magistrate."

"It is a tragedy, M. Formery—a tragedy!" groaned the millionaire.

"Do not let it upset you too much. We shall find your masterpieces—we shall find them. Only give us time," said M. Formery in a tone of warm encouragement.

The face of the millionaire brightened a little.

"And, after all, you have the consolation, that the burglars did not get hold of the gem of your collection. They have not stolen the coronet of the Princesse de Lamballe," said M. Formery.

"No," said the Duke. "They have not touched this safe. It is unopened."

"What has that got to do with it?" growled the millionaire quickly. "That safe is empty."

"Empty ... but your coronet?" cried the Duke.

"Good heavens! Then they HAVE stolen it," cried the millionaire hoarsely, in a panic-stricken voice.

"But they can't have—this safe hasn't been touched," said the Duke.

"But the coronet never was in that safe. It was—have they entered my bedroom?" said the millionaire.

"No," said M. Formery.

"They don't seem to have gone through any of the rooms except these two," said the Duke.

"Ah, then my mind is at rest about that. The safe in my bedroom has only two keys. Here is one." He took a key from his waistcoat pocket and held it out to them. "And the other is in this safe."

The face of M. Formery was lighted up with a splendid satisfaction. He might have rescued the coronet with his own hands. He cried triumphantly, "There, you see!"

"See? See?" cried the millionaire in a sudden bellow. "I see that they have robbed me—plundered me. Oh, my pictures! My wonderful pictures! Such investments!"

CHAPTER XII THE THEFT OF THE PENDANT

They stood round the millionaire observing his anguish, with eyes in which shone various degrees of sympathy. As if no longer able to bear the sight of such woe, Sonia slipped out of the room.

The millionaire lamented his loss and abused the thieves by turns, but always at the top of his magnificent voice.

Suddenly a fresh idea struck him. He clapped his hand to his brow and cried: "That eight hundred pounds! Charolais will never buy the Mercrac now! He was not a bona fide purchaser!"

The Duke's lips parted slightly and his eyes opened a trifle wider than their wont. He turned sharply on his heel, and almost sprang into the other drawing-room. There he laughed at his ease.

M. Formery kept saying to the millionaire: "Be calm, M. Gournay-Martin. Be calm! We shall recover your masterpieces. I pledge you my word. All we need is time. Have patience. Be calm!"

His soothing remonstrances at last had their effect. The millionaire grew calm:

"Guerchard?" he said. "Where is Guerchard?"

M. Formery presented Guerchard to him.

"Are you on their track? Have you a clue?" said the millionaire.

"I think," said M. Formery in an impressive tone, "that we may now proceed with the inquiry in the ordinary way."

He was a little piqued by the millionaire's so readily turning from him to the detective. He went to a writing-table, set some sheets of paper before him, and prepared to make notes on the answers to his questions. The Duke came back into the drawing-room; the inspector was summoned. M. Gournay-Martin sat down on a couch with his hands on his knees and gazed gloomily at M. Formery. Germaine, who was sitting on a couch near the door, waiting with an air of resignation for her father to cease his lamentations, rose and moved to a chair nearer the writing-table. Guerchard kept moving restlessly about the room, but noiselessly. At last he came to a standstill, leaning against the wall behind M. Formery.

M. Formery went over all the matters about which he had already questioned the Duke. He questioned the millionaire and his daughter about the Charolais, the theft of the motor-cars, and the attempted theft of the pendant. He questioned them at less length about the composition of their household—the servants and their characters. He elicited no new fact.

He paused, and then he said, carelessly as a mere matter of routine: "I should like to know, M. Gournay-Martin, if there has ever been any other robbery committed at your house?"

"Three years ago this scoundrel Lupin—" the millionaire began violently.

"Yes, yes; I know all about that earlier burglary. But have you been robbed since?" said M. Formery, interrupting him.

"No, I haven't been robbed since that burglary; but my daughter has," said the millionaire.

"Your daughter?" said M. Formery.

"Yes; I have been robbed two or three times during the last three years," said Germaine.

"Dear me! But you ought to have told us about this before. This is extremely interesting, and most important," said M. Formery, rubbing his hands, "I suppose you suspect Victoire?"

"No, I don't," said Germaine quickly. "It couldn't have been Victoire. The last two thefts were committed at the chateau when Victoire was in Paris in charge of this house."

M. Formery seemed taken aback, and he hesitated, consulting his notes. Then he said: "Good—good. That confirms my hypothesis."

"What hypothesis?" said M. Gournay-Martin quickly.

"Never mind—never mind," said M. Formery solemnly. And, turning to Germaine, he went on: "You say, Mademoiselle, that these thefts began about three years ago?"

"Yes, I think they began about three years ago in August."

"Let me see. It was in the month of August, three years ago, that your father, after receiving a threatening letter like the one he received last night, was the victim of a burglary?" said M. Formery.

"Yes, it was —the scoundrels!" cried the millionaire fiercely.

"Well, it would be interesting to know which of your servants entered your service three years ago," said M. Formery.

"Victoire has only been with us a year at the outside," said Germaine.

"Only a year?" said M. Formery quickly, with an air of some vexation. He paused and added, "Exactly—exactly. And what was the nature of the last theft of which you were the victim?"

"It was a pearl brooch—not unlike the pendant which his Grace gave me yesterday," said Germaine.

"Would you mind showing me that pendant? I should like to see it," said M. Formery.

"Certainly—show it to him, Jacques. You have it, haven't you?" said Germaine, turning to the Duke.

"Me? No. How should I have it?" said the Duke in some surprise. "Haven't you got it?"

"I've only got the case—the empty case," said Germaine, with a startled air.

"The empty case?" said the Duke, with growing surprise.

"Yes," said Germaine. "It was after we came back from our useless journey to the station. I remembered suddenly that I had started without the pendant. I went to the bureau and picked up the case; and it was empty."

"One moment—one moment," said M. Formery. "Didn't you catch this young Bernard Charolais with this case in his hands, your Grace?"

"Yes," said the Duke. "I caught him with it in his pocket."

"Then you may depend upon it that the young rascal had slipped the pendant out of its case and you only recovered the empty case from him," said M. Formery triumphantly.

"No," said the Duke. "That is not so. Nor could the thief have been the burglar who broke open the bureau to get at the keys. For long after both of them were out of the house I took a cigarette from the box which stood on the bureau beside the case which held the pendant. And it occurred to me that the young rascal might have played that very trick on me. I opened the case and the pendant was there."

"It has been stolen!" cried the millionaire; "of course it has been stolen."

"Oh, no, no," said the Duke. "It hasn't been stolen. Irma, or perhaps Mademoiselle Kritchnoff, has brought it to Paris for Germaine."

"Sonia certainly hasn't brought it. It was she who suggested to me that you had seen it lying on the bureau, and slipped it into your pocket," said Germaine quickly.

"Then it must be Irma," said the Duke.

"We had better send for her and make sure," said M. Formery. "Inspector, go and fetch her."

The inspector went out of the room and the Duke questioned Germaine and her father about the journey, whether it had been very uncomfortable, and if they were very tired by it. He learned that they had been so fortunate as to find sleeping compartments on the train, so that they had suffered as little as might be from their night of travel.

M. Formery looked through his notes; Guerchard seemed to be going to sleep where he stood against the wall.

The inspector came back with Irma. She wore the frightened, half-defensive, half-defiant air which people of her class wear when confronted by the authorities. Her big, cow's eyes rolled uneasily.

"Oh, Irma—" Germaine began.

M. Formery cut her short, somewhat brusquely. "Excuse me, excuse me. I am conducting this inquiry," he said. And then, turning to Irma, he added, "Now, don't be frightened, Mademoiselle Irma; I want to ask you a question or two. Have you brought up to Paris the pendant which the Duke of Charmerace gave your mistress yesterday?"

"Me, sir? No, sir. I haven't brought the pendant," said Irma.

"You're quite sure?" said M. Formery.

"Yes, sir; I haven't seen the pendant. Didn't Mademoiselle Germaine leave it on the bureau?" said Irma.

"How do you know that?" said M. Formery.

"I heard Mademoiselle Germaine say that it had been on the bureau. I thought that perhaps Mademoiselle Kritchnoff had put it in her bag."

"Why should Mademoiselle Kritchnoff put it in her bag?" said the Duke quickly.

"To bring it up to Paris for Mademoiselle Germaine," said Irma.

"But what made you think that?" said Guerchard, suddenly intervening.

"Oh, I thought Mademoiselle Kritchnoff might have put it in her bag because I saw her standing by the bureau," said Irma.

"Ah, and the pendant was on the bureau?" said M. Formery.

"Yes, sir," said Irma.

There was a silence. Suddenly the atmosphere of the room seemed to have become charged with an oppression—a vague menace. Guerchard seemed to have become wide awake again. Germaine and the Duke looked at one another uneasily.

"Have you been long in the service of Mademoiselle Gournay-Martin?" said M. Formery.

"Six months, sir," said Irma.

"Very good, thank you. You can go," said M. Formery. "I may want you again presently."

Irma went quickly out of the room with an air of relief.

M. Formery scribbled a few words on the paper before him and then said: "Well, I will proceed to question Mademoiselle Kritchnoff."

"Mademoiselle Kritchnoff is quite above suspicion," said the Duke quickly.

"Oh, yes, quite," said Germaine.

"How long has Mademoiselle Kritchnoff been in your service, Mademoiselle?" said Guerchard.

"Let me think," said Germaine, knitting her brow.

"Can't you remember?" said M. Formery.

"Just about three years," said Germaine.

"That's exactly the time at which the thefts began," said M. Formery.

"Yes," said Germaine, reluctantly.

"Ask Mademoiselle Kritchnoff to come here, inspector," said M. Formery.

"Yes, sir," said the inspector.

"I'll go and fetch her—I know where to find her," said the Duke quickly, moving toward the door.

"Please, please, your Grace," protested Guerchard. "The inspector will fetch her."

The Duke turned sharply and looked at him: "I beg your pardon, but do you—" he said.

"Please don't be annoyed, your Grace," Guerchard interrupted. "But M. Formery agrees with me—it would be quite irregular."

"Yes, yes, your Grace," said M. Formery. "We have our method of procedure. It is best to adhere to it—much the best. It is the result of years of experience of the best way of getting the truth."

"Just as you please," said the Duke, shrugging his shoulders.

The inspector came into the room: "Mademoiselle Kritchnoff will be here in a moment. She was just going out."

"She was going out?" said M. Formery. "You don't mean to say you're letting members of the household go out?"

"No, sir," said the inspector. "I mean that she was just asking if she might go out."

M. Formery beckoned the inspector to him, and said to him in a voice too low for the others to hear:

"Just slip up to her room and search her trunks."

"There is no need to take the trouble," said Guerchard, in the same low voice, but with sufficient emphasis.

"No, of course not. There's no need to take the trouble," M. Formery repeated after him.

The door opened, and Sonia came in. She was still wearing her travelling costume, and she carried her cloak on her arm. She stood looking round her with an air of some surprise; perhaps there was even a touch of fear in it. The long journey of the night before did not seem to have dimmed at all her delicate beauty. The Duke's eyes rested on her in an inquiring, wondering, even searching gaze. She looked at him, and her own eyes fell.

"Will you come a little nearer, Mademoiselle?" said M. Formery. "There are one or two questions—"

"Will you allow me?" said Guerchard, in a tone of such deference that it left M. Formery no grounds for refusal.

M. Formery flushed and ground his teeth. "Have it your own way!" he said ungraciously.

"Mademoiselle Kritchnoff," said Guerchard, in a tone of the most good-natured courtesy, "there is a matter on which M. Formery needs some information. The pendant which the Duke of Charmerace gave Mademoiselle Gournay-Martin yesterday has been stolen."

"Stolen? Are you sure?" said Sonia in a tone of mingled surprise and anxiety.

"Quite sure," said Guerchard. "We have exactly determined the conditions under which the theft was committed. But we have every reason to believe that the culprit, to avoid detection, has hidden the pendant in the travelling-bag or trunk of somebody else in order to—"

"My bag is upstairs in my bedroom, sir," Sonia interrupted quickly. "Here is the key of it."

In order to free her hands to take the key from her wrist-bag, she set her cloak on the back of a couch. It slipped off it, and fell to the ground at the feet of the Duke, who had not returned to his place beside Germaine. While she was groping in her bag for the key, and all eyes were on her, the Duke, who had watched her with a curious intentness ever since her entry into the room, stooped quietly down and picked up the cloak. His hand slipped into the pocket of it; his fingers touched a hard object wrapped in tissue-paper. They closed round it, drew it from the pocket, and, sheltered by the cloak, transferred it to his own. He set the cloak on the back of the sofa, and very softly moved back to his place by Germaine's side. No one in the room observed the movement, not even Guerchard: he was watching Sonia too intently.

Sonia found the key, and held it out to Guerchard.

He shook his head and said: "There is no reason to search your bag—none whatever. Have you any other luggage?"

She shrank back a little from his piercing eyes, almost as if their gaze scared her.

"Yes, my trunk ... it's upstairs in my bedroom too ... open."

She spoke in a faltering voice, and her troubled eyes could not meet those of the detective.

"You were going out, I think," said Guerchard gently.

379

"I was asking leave to go out. There is some shopping that must be done," said Sonia.

"You do not see any reason why Mademoiselle Kritchnoff should not go out, M. Formery, do you?" said Guerchard.

"Oh, no, none whatever; of course she can go out," said M. Formery.

Sonia turned round to go.

"One moment," said Guerchard, coming forward. "You've only got that wrist-bag with you?"

"Yes," said Sonia. "I have my money and my handkerchief in it." And she held it out to him.

Guerchard's keen eyes darted into it; and he muttered, "No point in looking in that. I don't suppose any one would have had the audacity—" and he stopped.

Sonia made a couple of steps toward the door, turned, hesitated, came back to the couch, and picked up her cloak.

There was a sudden gleam in Guerchard's eyes—a gleam of understanding, expectation, and triumph. He stepped forward, and holding out his hands, said: "Allow me."

"No, thank you," said Sonia. "I'm not going to put it on."

"No ... but it's possible ... some one may have ... have you felt in the pockets of it? That one, now? It seems as if that one—"

He pointed to the pocket which had held the packet.

Sonia started back with an air of utter dismay; her eyes glanced wildly round the room as if seeking an avenue of escape; her fingers closed convulsively on the pocket.

"But this is abominable!" she cried. "You look as if—"

"I beg you, mademoiselle," interrupted Guerchard. "We are sometimes obliged—"

"Really, Mademoiselle Sonia," broke in the Duke, in a singularly clear and piercing tone, "I cannot see why you should object to this mere formality."

"Oh, but—but—" gasped Sonia, raising her terror-stricken eyes to his.

The Duke seemed to hold them with his own; and he said in the same clear, piercing voice, "There isn't the slightest reason for you to be frightened."

Sonia let go of the cloak, and Guerchard, his face all alight with triumph, plunged his hand into the pocket. He drew it out empty, and stared at it, while his face fell to an utter, amazed blankness.

"Nothing? nothing?" he muttered under his breath. And he stared at his empty hand as if he could not believe his eyes.

By a violent effort he forced an apologetic smile on his face, and said to Sonia: "A thousand apologies, mademoiselle."

He handed the cloak to her. Sonia took it and turned to go. She took a step towards the door, and tottered.

The Duke sprang forward and caught her as she was falling.

"Do you feel faint?" he said in an anxious voice.

"Thank you, you just saved me in time," muttered Sonia.

"I'm really very sorry," said Guerchard.

"Thank you, it was nothing. I'm all right now," said Sonia, releasing herself from the Duke's supporting arm.

She drew herself up, and walked quietly out of the room.

Guerchard went back to M. Formery at the writing-table.

"You made a clumsy mistake there, Guerchard," said M. Formery, with a touch of gratified malice in his tone.

Guerchard took no notice of it: "I want you to give orders that nobody leaves the house without my permission," he said, in a low voice.

"No one except Mademoiselle Kritchnoff, I suppose," said M. Formery, smiling.

"She less than any one," said Guerchard quickly.

"I don't understand what you're driving at a bit," said M. Formery. "Unless you suppose that Mademoiselle Kritchnoff is Lupin in disguise."

Guerchard laughed softly: "You will have your joke, M. Formery," he said.

"Well, well, I'll give the order," said M. Formery, somewhat mollified by the tribute to his humour.

He called the inspector to him and whispered a word in his ear. Then he rose and said: "I think, gentlemen, we ought to go and examine the bedrooms, and, above all, make sure that the safe in M. Gournay-Martin's bedroom has not been tampered with."

"I was wondering how much longer we were going to waste time here talking about that stupid pendant," grumbled the millionaire; and he rose and led the way.

"There may also be some jewel-cases in the bedrooms," said M. Formery. "There are all the wedding presents. They were in charge of Victoire." said Germaine quickly. "It would be dreadful if they had been stolen. Some of them are from the first families in France."

"They would replace them ... those paper-knives," said the Duke, smiling.

Germaine and her father led the way. M. Formery, Guerchard, and the inspector followed them. At the door the Duke paused, stopped, closed it on them softly. He came back to the window, put his hand in his pocket, and drew out the packet wrapped in tissue-paper.

He unfolded the paper with slow, reluctant fingers, and revealed the pendant.

CHAPTER XIII LUPIN WIRES

The Duke stared at the pendant, his eyes full of wonder and pity.

"Poor little girl!" he said softly under his breath.

He put the pendant carefully away in his waistcoat-pocket and stood staring thoughtfully out of the window.

The door opened softly, and Sonia came quickly into the room, closed the door, and leaned back against it. Her face was a dead white; her skin had lost its lustre of fine porcelain, and she stared at him with eyes dim with anguish.

In a hoarse, broken voice, she muttered: "Forgive me! Oh, forgive me!"

"A thief—you?" said the Duke, in a tone of pitying wonder.

Sonia groaned.

"You mustn't stop here," said the Duke in an uneasy tone, and he looked uneasily at the door.

"Ah, you don't want to speak to me any more," said Sonia, in a heartrending tone, wringing her hands.

"Guerchard is suspicious of everything. It is dangerous for us to be talking here. I assure you that it's dangerous," said the Duke.

"What an opinion must you have of me! It's dreadful—cruel!" wailed Sonia.

"For goodness' sake don't speak so loud," said the Duke, with even greater uneasiness. "You MUST think of Guerchard."

"What do I care?" cried Sonia. "I've lost the liking of the only creature whose liking I wanted. What does anything else matter? What DOES it matter?"

"We'll talk somewhere else presently. That'll be far safer," said the Duke.

"No, no, we must talk now!" cried Sonia. "You must know.... I must tell ... Oh, dear! ... Oh, dear! ... I don't know how to tell you.... And then it is so unfair.... she ... Germaine ... she has everything," she panted. "Yesterday, before me, you gave her that pendant, ... she smiled ... she was proud of it.... I saw her pleasure.... Then I took it—I took it—I took it! And if I could, I'd take her fortune, too.... I hate her! Oh, how I hate her!"

"What!" said the Duke.

"Yes, I do ... I hate her!" said Sonia; and her eyes, no longer gentle, glowed with the sombre resentment, the dull rage of the weak who turn on Fortune. Her gentle voice was harsh with rebellious wrath.

"You hate her?" said the Duke quickly.

"I should never have told you that.... But now I dare.... I dare speak out.... It's you! ... It's you—" The avowal died on her lips. A burning flush crimsoned her cheeks and faded as quickly as it came: "I hate her!" she muttered.

"Sonia—" said the Duke gently.

"Oh! I know that it's no excuse.... I know that you're thinking 'This is a very pretty story, but it's not her first theft'; ... and it's true—it's the tenth, ... perhaps it's the twentieth.... It's true—I am a thief." She paused, and the glow deepened in her eyes. "But there's one thing you must believe—you shall believe; since you came, since I've known you, since the first day you set eyes on me, I have stolen no more ... till yesterday when you gave her the pendant before me. I could not bear it ... I could not." She paused and looked at him with eyes that demanded an assent.

"I believe you," said the Duke gravely.

She heaved a deep sigh of relief, and went on more quietly—some of its golden tone had returned to her voice: "And then, if you knew how it began ... the horror of it," she said.

"Poor child!" said the Duke softly.

"Yes, you pity me, but you despise me—you despise me beyond words. You shall not! I will not have it!" she cried fiercely.

"Believe me, no," said the Duke, in a soothing tone.

"Listen," said Sonia. "Have you ever been alone—alone in the world? ... Have you ever been hungry? Think of it ... in this big city where I was starving in sight of bread ... bread in the shops .... One only had to stretch out one's hand to touch it ... a penny loaf. Oh, it's commonplace!" she broke off: "quite commonplace!"

"Go on: tell me," said the Duke curtly.

"There was one way I could make money and I would not do it: no, I would not," she went on. "But that day I was dying ... understand, I was dying ....I went to the rooms of a man

I knew a little. It was my last resource. At first I was glad ... he gave me food and wine ... and then, he talked to me ... he offered me money."

"What!" cried the Duke; and a sudden flame of anger flared up in his eyes.

"No; I could not ... and then I robbed him.... I preferred to ... it was more decent. Ah, I had excuses then. I began to steal to remain an honest woman ... and I've gone on stealing to keep up appearances. You see ... I joke about it." And she laughed, the faint, dreadful, mocking laugh of a damned soul. "Oh, dear! Oh, dear!" she cried; and, burying her face in her hands, she burst into a storm of weeping.

"Poor child," said the Duke softly. And he stared gloomily on the ground, overcome by this revelation of the tortures of the feeble in the underworld beneath the Paris he knew.

"Oh, you do pity me ... you do understand ... and feel," said Sonia, between her sobs.

The Duke raised his head and gazed at her with eyes full of an infinite sympathy and compassion.

"Poor little Sonia," he said gently. "I understand."

She gazed at him with incredulous eyes, in which joy and despair mingled, struggling.

He came slowly towards her, and stopped short. His quick ear had caught the sound of a footstep outside the door.

"Quick! Dry your eyes! You must look composed. The other room!" he cried, in an imperative tone.

He caught her hand and drew her swiftly into the further drawing-room.

With the quickness which came of long practice in hiding her feelings Sonia composed her face to something of its usual gentle calm. There was even a faint tinge of colour in her cheeks; they had lost their dead whiteness. A faint light shone in her eyes; the anguish had cleared from them. They rested on the Duke with a look of ineffable gratitude. She sat down on a couch. The Duke went to the window and lighted a cigarette. They heard the door of the outer drawing-room open, and there was a pause. Quick footsteps crossed the room, and Guerchard stood in the doorway. He looked from one to the other with keen and eager eyes. Sonia sat staring rather listlessly at the carpet. The Duke turned, and smiled at him.

"Well, M. Guerchard," he said. "I hope the burglars have not stolen the coronet."

"The coronet is safe, your Grace," said Guerchard.

"And the paper-knives?" said the Duke.

"The paper-knives?" said Guerchard with an inquiring air.

"The wedding presents," said the Duke.

"Yes, your Grace, the wedding presents are safe," said Guerchard.

"I breathe again," said the Duke languidly.

Guerchard turned to Sonia and said, "I was looking for you, Mademoiselle, to tell you that M. Formery has changed his mind. It is impossible for you to go out. No one will be allowed to go out."

"Yes?" said Sonia, in an indifferent tone.

"We should be very much obliged if you would go to your room," said Guerchard. "Your meals will be sent up to you."

"What?" said Sonia, rising quickly; and she looked from Guerchard to the Duke. The Duke gave her the faintest nod.

"Very well, I will go to my room," she said coldly.

They accompanied her to the door of the outer drawing-room. Guerchard opened it for her and closed it after her.

"Really, M. Guerchard," said the Duke, shrugging his shoulders. "This last measure—a child like that!"

"Really, I'm very sorry, your Grace; but it's my trade, or, if you prefer it, my duty. As long as things are taking place here which I am still the only one to perceive, and which are not yet clear to me, I must neglect no precaution."

"Of course, you know best," said the Duke. "But still, a child like that—you're frightening her out of her life."

Guerchard shrugged his shoulders, and went quietly out of the room.

The Duke sat down in an easy chair, frowning and thoughtful. Suddenly there struck on his ears the sound of a loud roaring and heavy bumping on the stairs, the door flew open, and M. Gournay-Martin stood on the threshold waving a telegram in his hand.

M. Formery and the inspector came hurrying down the stairs behind him, and watched his emotion with astonished and wondering eyes.

"Here!" bellowed the millionaire. "A telegram! A telegram from the scoundrel himself! Listen! Just listen:"

"A thousand apologies for not having been able to keep my promise about the coronet. Had an appointment at the Acacias. Please have coronet ready in your room to-night. Will come without fail to fetch it, between a quarter to twelve and twelve o'clock."

"Yours affectionately,"
"ARSENE LUPIN."

"There! What do you think of that?"

"If you ask me, I think he's humbug," said the Duke with conviction.

"Humbug! You always think it's humbug! You thought the letter was humbug; and look what has happened!" cried the millionaire.

"Give me the telegram, please," said M. Formery quickly.

The millionaire gave it to him; and he read it through.

"Find out who brought it, inspector," he said.

The inspector hurried to the top of the staircase and called to the policeman in charge of the front door. He came back to the drawing-room and said: "It was brought by an ordinary post-office messenger, sir."

"Where is he?" said M. Formery. "Why did you let him go?"

"Shall I send for him, sir?" said the inspector.

"No, no, it doesn't matter," said M. Formery; and, turning to M. Gournay-Martin and the Duke, he said, "Now we're really going to have trouble with Guerchard. He is going to muddle up everything. This telegram will be the last straw. Nothing will persuade him now that this is not Lupin's work. And just consider, gentlemen: if Lupin had come last night, and if he had really set his heart on the coronet, he would have stolen it then, or at any rate he would have tried to open the safe in M. Gournay-Martin's bedroom, in which the coronet actually is, or

387

this safe here"—he went to the safe and rapped on the door of it—"in which is the second key."

"That's quite clear," said the inspector.

"If, then, he did not make the attempt last night, when he had a clear field—when the house was empty—he certainly will not make the attempt now when we are warned, when the police are on the spot, and the house is surrounded. The idea is childish, gentlemen"—he leaned against the door of the safe—"absolutely childish, but Guerchard is mad on this point; and I foresee that his madness is going to hamper us in the most idiotic way."

He suddenly pitched forward into the middle of the room, as the door of the safe opened with a jerk, and Guerchard shot out of it.

"What the devil!" cried M. Formery, gaping at him.

"You'd be surprised how clearly you hear everything in these safes—you'd think they were too thick," said Guerchard, in his gentle, husky voice.

"How on earth did you get into it?" cried M. Formery.

"Getting in was easy enough. It's the getting out that was awkward. These jokers had fixed up some kind of a spring so that I nearly shot out with the door," said Guerchard, rubbing his elbow.

"But how did you get into it? How the deuce DID you get into it?" cried M. Formery.

"Through the little cabinet into which that door behind the safe opens. There's no longer any back to the safe; they've cut it clean out of it—a very neat piece of work. Safes like this should always be fixed against a wall, not stuck in front of a door. The backs of them are always the weak point."

"And the key? The key of the safe upstairs, in my bedroom, where the coronet is—is the key there?" cried M. Gournay-Martin.

Guerchard went back into the empty safe, and groped about in it. He came out smiling.

"Well, have you found the key?" cried the millionaire.

"No. I haven't; but I've found something better," said Guerchard.

"What is it?" said M. Formery sharply.

"I'll give you a hundred guesses," said Guerchard with a tantalizing smile.

"What is it?" said M. Formery.

"A little present for you," said Guerchard.

"What do you mean?" cried M. Formery angrily.

Guerchard held up a card between his thumb and forefinger and said quietly:

"The card of Arsene Lupin."

CHAPTER XIV GUERCHARD PICKS UP THE TRUE SCENT

The millionaire gazed at the card with stupefied eyes, the inspector gazed at it with extreme intelligence, the Duke gazed at it with interest, and M. Formery gazed at it with extreme disgust.

"It's part of the same ruse—it was put there to throw us off the scent. It proves nothing—absolutely nothing," he said scornfully.

"No; it proves nothing at all," said Guerchard quietly.

"The telegram is the important thing—this telegram," said M. Gournay-Martin feverishly. "It concerns the coronet. Is it going to be disregarded?"

"Oh, no, no," said M. Formery in a soothing tone. "It will be taken into account. It will certainly be taken into account."

M. Gournay-Martin's butler appeared in the doorway of the drawing-room: "If you please, sir, lunch is served," he said.

At the tidings some of his weight of woe appeared to be lifted from the head of the millionaire. "Good!" he said, "good! Gentlemen, you will lunch with me, I hope."

"Thank you," said M. Formery. "There is nothing else for us to do, at any rate at present, and in the house. I am not quite satisfied about Mademoiselle Kritchnoff—at least Guerchard is not. I propose to question her again—about those earlier thefts."

"I'm sure there's nothing in that," said the Duke quickly.

"No, no; I don't think there is," said M. Formery. "But still one never knows from what quarter light may come in an affair like this. Accident often gives us our best clues."

"It seems rather a shame to frighten her—she's such a child," said the Duke.

"Oh, I shall be gentle, your Grace—as gentle as possible, that is. But I look to get more from the examination of Victoire. She was on the scene. She has actually seen the rogues at work; but till she recovers there is nothing more to be done, except to wait the discoveries of the detectives who are working outside; and they will report here. So in the meantime we shall be charmed to lunch with you, M. Gournay-Martin."

They went downstairs to the dining-room and found an elaborate and luxurious lunch, worthy of the hospitality of a millionaire, awaiting them. The skill of the cook seemed to have been quite unaffected by the losses of his master. M. Formery, an ardent lover of good things, enjoyed himself immensely. He was in the highest spirits. Germaine, a little upset by the night-journey, was rather querulous. Her father was plunged in a gloom which lifted for but a brief space at the appearance of a fresh delicacy. Guerchard ate and drank seriously, answering the questions of the Duke in a somewhat absent-minded fashion. The Duke himself seemed to have lost his usual flow of good spirits, and at times his brow was knitted in an anxious frown. His questions to Guerchard showed a far less keen interest in the affair.

To him the lunch seemed very long and very tedious; but at last it came to an end. M. Gournay-Martin seemed to have been much cheered by the wine he had drunk. He was almost hopeful. M. Formery, who had not by any means trifled with the champagne, was raised to the very height of sanguine certainty. Their coffee and liqueurs were served in the smoking-room. Guerchard lighted a cigar, refused a liqueur, drank his coffee quickly, and slipped out of the room.

The Duke followed him, and in the hall said: "I will continue to watch you unravel the threads of this mystery, if I may, M. Guerchard."

Good Republican as Guerchard was, he could not help feeling flattered by the interest of a Duke; and the excellent lunch he had eaten disposed him to feel the honour even more deeply.

"I shall be charmed," he said. "To tell the truth, I find the company of your Grace really quite stimulating."

"It must be because I find it all so extremely interesting," said the Duke.

They went up to the drawing-room and found the red-faced young policeman seated on a chair by the door eating a lunch, which had been sent up to him from the millionaire's kitchen, with a very hearty appetite.

They went into the drawing-room. Guerchard shut the door and turned the key: "Now," he said, "I think that M. Formery will give me half an hour to myself. His cigar ought to last him at least half an hour. In that time I shall know what the burglars really did with their plunder—at least I shall know for certain how they got it out of the house."

"Please explain," said the Duke. "I thought we knew how they got it out of the house." And he waved his hand towards the window.

"Oh, that!—that's childish," said Guerchard contemptuously. "Those are traces for an examining magistrate. The ladder, the table on the window-sill, they lead nowhere. The only people who came up that ladder were the two men who brought it from the scaffolding. You can see their footsteps. Nobody went down it at all. It was mere waste of time to bother with those traces."

"But the footprint under the book?" said the Duke.

"Oh, that," said Guerchard. "One of the burglars sat on the couch there, rubbed plaster on the sole of his boot, and set his foot down on the carpet. Then he dusted the rest of the plaster off his boot and put the book on the top of the footprint."

"Now, how do you know that?" said the astonished Duke.

"It's as plain as a pike-staff," said Guerchard. "There must have been several burglars to move such pieces of furniture. If the soles of all of them had been covered with plaster, all the sweeping in the world would not have cleared the carpet of the tiny fragments of it. I've been over the carpet between the footprint and the window with a magnifying glass. There are no fragments of plaster on it. We dismiss the footprint. It is a mere blind, and a very fair blind too—for an examining magistrate."

"I understand," said the Duke.

"That narrows the problem, the quite simple problem, how was the furniture taken out of the room. It did not go through that window down the ladder. Again, it was not taken down the stairs, and out of the front door, or the back. If it had been, the concierge and his wife would have heard the noise. Besides that, it would have been carried down into a main street, in which there are people at all hours. Somebody would have been sure to tell a policeman that this house was being emptied. Moreover, the police were continually patrolling the main streets, and, quickly as a man like Lupin would do the job, he could not do it so quickly that a policeman would not have seen it. No; the furniture was not taken down the stairs or out of the front door. That narrows the problem still more. In fact, there is only one mode of egress left."

"The chimney!" cried the Duke.

"You've hit it," said Guerchard, with a husky laugh. "By that well-known logical process, the process of elimination, we've excluded all methods of egress except the chimney."

He paused, frowning, in some perplexity; and then he said uneasily: "What I don't like about it is that Victoire was set in the fireplace. I asked myself at once what was she doing there. It was unnecessary that she should be drugged and set in the fireplace—quite unnecessary."

"It might have been to put off an examining magistrate," said the Duke. "Having found Victoire in the fireplace, M. Formery did not look for anything else."

"Yes, it might have been that," said Guerchard slowly. "On the other hand, she might have been put there to make sure that I did not miss the road the burglars took. That's the worst of having to do with Lupin. He knows me to the bottom of my mind. He has something up his sleeve—some surprise for me. Even now, I'm nowhere near the bottom of the mystery.

But come along, we'll take the road the burglars took. The inspector has put my lantern ready for me."

As he spoke he went to the fireplace, picked up a lantern which had been set on the top of the iron fire-basket, and lighted it. The Duke stepped into the great fireplace beside him. It was four feet deep, and between eight and nine feet broad. Guerchard threw the light from the lantern on to the back wall of it. Six feet from the floor the soot from the fire stopped abruptly, and there was a dappled patch of bricks, half of them clean and red, half of them blackened by soot, five feet broad, and four feet high.

"The opening is higher up than I thought," said Guerchard. "I must get a pair of steps."

He went to the door of the drawing-room and bade the young policeman fetch him a pair of steps. They were brought quickly. He took them from the policeman, shut the door, and locked it again. He set the steps in the fireplace and mounted them.

"Be careful," he said to the Duke, who had followed him into the fireplace, and stood at the foot of the steps. "Some of these bricks may drop inside, and they'll sting you up if they fall on your toes."

The Duke stepped back out of reach of any bricks that might fall.

Guerchard set his left hand against the wall of the chimney-piece between him and the drawing-room, and pressed hard with his right against the top of the dappled patch of bricks. At the first push, half a dozen of them fell with a bang on to the floor of the next house. The light came flooding in through the hole, and shone on Guerchard's face and its smile of satisfaction. Quickly he pushed row after row of bricks into the next house until he had cleared an opening four feet square.

"Come along," he said to the Duke, and disappeared feet foremost through the opening.

The Duke mounted the steps, and found himself looking into a large empty room of the exact size and shape of the drawing-room of M. Gournay-Martin, save that it had an ordinary modern fireplace instead of one of the antique pattern of that in which he stood. Its chimney-piece was a few inches below the opening. He stepped out on to the chimney-piece and dropped lightly to the floor.

"Well," he said, looking back at the opening through which he had come. "That's an ingenious dodge."

"Oh, it's common enough," said Guerchard. "Robberies at the big jewellers' are sometimes worked by these means. But what is uncommon about it, and what at first sight put me off the track, is that these burglars had the cheek to pierce the wall with an opening large enough to enable them to remove the furniture of a house."

393

"It's true," said the Duke. "The opening's as large as a good-sized window. Those burglars seem capable of everything—even of a first-class piece of mason's work."

"Oh, this has all been prepared a long while ago. But now I'm really on their track. And after all, I haven't really lost any time. Dieusy wasted no time in making inquiries in Sureau Street; he's been working all this side of the house."

Guerchard drew up the blinds, opened the shutters, and let the daylight flood the dim room. He came back to the fireplace and looked down at the heap of bricks, frowning:

"I made a mistake there," he said. "I ought to have taken those bricks down carefully, one by one."

Quickly he took brick after brick from the pile, and began to range them neatly against the wall on the left. The Duke watched him for two or three minutes, then began to help him. It did not take them long, and under one of the last few bricks Guerchard found a fragment of a gilded picture-frame.

"Here's where they ought to have done their sweeping," he said, holding it up to the Duke.

"I tell you what," said the Duke, "I shouldn't wonder if we found the furniture in this house still."

"Oh, no, no!" said Guerchard. "I tell you that Lupin would allow for myself or Ganimard being put in charge of the case; and he would know that we should find the opening in the chimney. The furniture was taken straight out into the side-street on to which this house opens." He led the way out of the room on to the landing and went down the dark staircase into the hall. He opened the shutters of the hall windows, and let in the light. Then he examined the hall. The dust lay thick on the tiled floor. Down the middle of it was a lane formed by many feet. The footprints were faint, but still plain in the layer of dust. Guerchard came back to the stairs and began to examine them. Half-way up the flight he stooped, and picked up a little spray of flowers: "Fresh!" he said. "These have not been long plucked."

"Salvias," said the Duke.

"Salvias they are," said Guerchard. "Pink salvias; and there is only one gardener in France who has ever succeeded in getting this shade—M. Gournay-Martin's gardener at Charmerace. I'm a gardener myself."

"Well, then, last night's burglars came from Charmerace. They must have," said the Duke.

"It looks like it," said Guerchard.

"The Charolais," said the Duke.

"It looks like it," said Guerchard.

"It must be," said the Duke. "This IS interesting—if only we could get an absolute proof."

"We shall get one presently," said Guerchard confidently.

"It is interesting," said the Duke in a tone of lively enthusiasm. "These clues—these tracks which cross one another—each fact by degrees falling into its proper place—extraordinarily interesting." He paused and took out his cigarette-case: "Will you have a cigarette?" he said.

"Are they caporal?" said Guerchard.

"No, Egyptians—Mercedes."

"Thank you," said Guerchard; and he took one.

The Duke struck a match, lighted Guerchard's cigarette, and then his own:

"Yes, it's very interesting," he said. "In the last quarter of an hour you've practically discovered that the burglars came from Charmerace—that they were the Charolais—that they came in by the front door of this house, and carried the furniture out of it."

"I don't know about their coming in by it," said Guerchard. "Unless I'm very much mistaken, they came in by the front door of M. Gournay-Martin's house."

"Of course," said the Duke. "I was forgetting. They brought the keys from Charmerace."

"Yes, but who drew the bolts for them?" said Guerchard. "The concierge bolted them before he went to bed. He told me so. He was telling the truth—I know when that kind of man is telling the truth."

"By Jove!" said the Duke softly. "You mean that they had an accomplice?"

"I think we shall find that they had an accomplice. But your Grace is beginning to draw inferences with uncommon quickness. I believe that you would make a first-class detective yourself—with practice, of course—with practice."

"Can I have missed my true career?" said the Duke, smiling. "It's certainly a very interesting game."

"Well, I'm not going to search this barracks myself," said Guerchard. "I'll send in a couple of men to do it; but I'll just take a look at the steps myself."

So saying, he opened the front door and went out and examined the steps carefully.

"We shall have to go back the way we came," he said, when he had finished his examination. "The drawing-room door is locked. We ought to find M. Formery hammering on it." And he smiled as if he found the thought pleasing.

They went back up the stairs, through the opening, into the drawing-room of M. Gournay-Martin's house. Sure enough, from the other side of the locked door came the excited voice of M. Formery, crying:

"Guerchard! Guerchard! What are you doing? Let me in! Why don't you let me in?"

Guerchard unlocked the door; and in bounced M. Formery, very excited, very red in the face.

"Hang it all, Guerchard! What on earth have you been doing?" he cried. "Why didn't you open the door when I knocked?"

"I didn't hear you," said Guerchard. "I wasn't in the room."

"Then where on earth have you been?" cried M. Formery.

Guerchard looked at him with a faint, ironical smile, and said in his gentle voice, "I was following the real track of the burglars."

CHAPTER XV THE EXAMINATION OF SONIA

M. Formery gasped: "The real track?" he muttered.

"Let me show you," said Guerchard. And he led him to the fireplace, and showed him the opening between the two houses.

"I must go into this myself!" cried M. Formery in wild excitement.

Without more ado he began to mount the steps. Guerchard followed him. The Duke saw their heels disappear up the steps. Then he came out of the drawing-room and inquired for M. Gournay-Martin. He was told that the millionaire was up in his bedroom; and he went upstairs, and knocked at the door of it.

M. Gournay-Martin bade him enter in a very faint voice, and the Duke found him lying on the bed. He was looking depressed, even exhausted, the shadow of the blusterous Gournay-Martin of the day before. The rich rosiness of his cheeks had faded to a moderate rose-pink.

"That telegram," moaned the millionaire. "It was the last straw. It has overwhelmed me. The coronet is lost."

"What, already?" said the Duke, in a tone of the liveliest surprise.

"No, no; it's still in the safe," said the millionaire. "But it's as good as lost—before midnight it will be lost. That fiend will get it."

"If it's in this safe now, it won't be lost before midnight," said the Duke. "But are you sure it's there now?"

"Look for yourself," said the millionaire, taking the key of the safe from his waistcoat pocket, and handing it to the Duke.

The Duke opened the safe. The morocco case which held the coronet lay on the middle shelf in front of him. He glanced at the millionaire, and saw that he had closed his eyes in the exhaustion of despair. Whistling softly, the Duke opened the case, took out the diadem, and examined it carefully, admiring its admirable workmanship. He put it back in the case, turned to the millionaire, and said thoughtfully:

"I can never make up my mind, in the case of one of these old diadems, whether one ought not to take out the stones and have them re-cut. Look at this emerald now. It's a very fine stone, but this old-fashioned cutting does not really do it justice."

"Oh, no, no: you should never interfere with an antique, historic piece of jewellery. Any alteration decreases its value—its value as an historic relic," cried the millionaire, in a shocked tone.

"I know that," said the Duke, "but the question for me is, whether one ought not to sacrifice some of its value to increasing its beauty."

"You do have such mad ideas," said the millionaire, in a tone of peevish exasperation.

"Ah, well, it's a nice question," said the Duke.

He snapped the case briskly, put it back on the shelf, locked the safe, and handed the key to the millionaire. Then he strolled across the room and looked down into the street, whistling softly.

"I think—I think—I'll go home and get out of these motoring clothes. And I should like to have on a pair of boots that were a trifle less muddy," he said slowly.

M. Gournay-Martin sat up with a jerk and cried, "For Heaven's sake, don't you go and desert me, my dear chap! You don't know what my nerves are like!"

"Oh, you've got that sleuth-hound, Guerchard, and the splendid Formery, and four other detectives, and half a dozen ordinary policemen guarding you. You can do without my feeble arm. Besides, I shan't be gone more than half an hour—three-quarters at the outside. I'll bring back my evening clothes with me, and dress for dinner here. I don't suppose that anything fresh will happen between now and midnight; but I want to be on the spot, and hear the information as it comes in fresh. Besides, there's Guerchard. I positively cling to Guerchard. It's an education, though perhaps not a liberal education, to go about with him," said the Duke; and there was a sub-acid irony in his voice.

"Well, if you must, you must," said M. Gournay-Martin grumpily.

"Good-bye for the present, then," said the Duke. And he went out of the room and down the stairs. He took his motor-cap from the hall-table, and had his hand on the latch of the door, when the policeman in charge of it said, "I beg your pardon, sir, but have you M. Guerchard's permission to leave the house?"

"M. Guerchard's permission?" said the Duke haughtily. "What has M. Guerchard to do with me? I am the Duke of Charmerace." And he opened the door.

"It was M. Formery's orders, your Grace," stammered the policeman doubtfully.

"M. Formery's orders?" said the Duke, standing on the top step. "Call me a taxi-cab, please."

The concierge, who stood beside the policeman, ran down the steps and blew his whistle. The policeman gazed uneasily at the Duke, shifting his weight from one foot to the other; but he said no more.

A taxi-cab came up to the door, the Duke went down the steps, stepped into it, and drove away.

Three-quarters of an hour later he came back, having changed into clothes more suited to a Paris drawing-room. He went up to the drawing-room, and there he found Guerchard, M. Formery, and the inspector, who had just completed their tour of inspection of the house next door and had satisfied themselves that the stolen treasures were not in it. The inspector and his men had searched it thoroughly just to make sure; but, as Guerchard had foretold, the burglars had not taken the chance of the failure of the police to discover the opening between the two houses. M. Formery told the Duke about their tour of inspection at length. Guerchard went to the telephone and told the exchange to put him through to Charmerace. He was informed that the trunk line was very busy and that he might have to wait half an hour.

The Duke inquired if any trace of the burglars, after they had left with their booty, had yet been found. M. Formery told him that, so far, the detectives had failed to find a single trace. Guerchard said that he had three men at work on the search, and that he was hopeful of getting some news before long.

"The layman is impatient in these matters," said M. Formery, with an indulgent smile. "But we have learnt to be patient, after long experience."

He proceeded to discuss with Guerchard the new theories with which the discovery of the afternoon had filled his mind. None of them struck the Duke as being of great value, and he listened to them with a somewhat absent-minded air. The coming examination of Sonia weighed heavily on his spirit. Guerchard answered only in monosyllables to the questions and suggestions thrown out by M. Formery. It seemed to the Duke that he paid very little attention to him, that his mind was still working hard on the solution of the mystery, seeking the missing facts which would bring him to the bottom of it. In the middle of one of M. Formery's more elaborate dissertations the telephone bell rang.

Guerchard rose hastily and went to it. They heard him say: "Is that Charmerace? ... I want the gardener.... Out? When will he be back? ... Tell him to ring me up at M. Gournay-Martin's house in Paris the moment he gets back.... Detective-Inspector Guerchard ... Guerchard ... Detective-Inspector."

He turned to them with a frown, and said, "Of course, since I want him, the confounded gardener has gone out for the day. Still, it's of very little importance—a mere corroboration I wanted." And he went back to his seat and lighted another cigarette.

M. Formery continued his dissertation. Presently Guerchard said, "You might go and see how Victoire is, inspector—whether she shows any signs of waking. What did the doctor say?"

"The doctor said that she would not really be sensible and have her full wits about her much before ten o'clock to-night," said the inspector; but he went to examine her present condition.

M. Formery proceeded to discuss the effects of different anesthetics. The others heard him with very little attention.

The inspector came back and reported that Victoire showed no signs of awaking.

"Well, then, M. Formery, I think we might get on with the examination of Mademoiselle Kritchnoff," said Guerchard. "Will you go and fetch her, inspector?"

"Really, I cannot conceive why you should worry that poor child," the Duke protested, in a tone of some indignation.

"It seems to me hardly necessary," said M. Formery.

"Excuse me," said Guerchard suavely, "but I attach considerable importance to it. It seems to me to be our bounden duty to question her fully. One never knows from what quarter light may come."

"Oh, well, since you make such a point of it," said M. Formery. "Inspector, ask Mademoiselle Kritchnoff to come here. Fetch her."

The inspector left the room.

Guerchard looked at the Duke with a faint air of uneasiness: "I think that we had better question Mademoiselle Kritchnoff by ourselves," he said.

M. Formery looked at him and hesitated. Then he said: "Oh, yes, of course, by ourselves."

"Certainly," said the Duke, a trifle haughtily. And he rose and opened the door. He was just going through it when Guerchard said sharply:

"Your Grace—"

The Duke paid no attention to him. He shut the door quickly behind him and sprang swiftly up the stairs. He met the inspector coming down with Sonia. Barring their way for a moment he said, in his kindliest voice: "Now you mustn't be frightened, Mademoiselle Sonia.

All you have to do is to try to remember as clearly as you can the circumstances of the earlier thefts at Charmerace. You mustn't let them confuse you."

"Thank you, your Grace, I will try and be as clear as I can," said Sonia; and she gave him an eloquent glance, full of gratitude for the warning; and went down the stairs with firm steps.

The Duke went on up the stairs, and knocked softly at the door of M. Gournay-Martin's bedroom. There was no answer to his knock, and he quietly opened the door and looked in. Overcome by his misfortunes, the millionaire had sunk into a profound sleep and was snoring softly. The Duke stepped inside the room, left the door open a couple of inches, drew a chair to it, and sat down watching the staircase through the opening of the door.

He sat frowning, with a look of profound pity on his face. Once the suspense grew too much for him. He rose and walked up and down the room. His well-bred calm seemed to have deserted him. He muttered curses on Guerchard, M. Formery, and the whole French criminal system, very softly, under his breath. His face was distorted to a mask of fury; and once he wiped the little beads of sweat from his forehead with his handkerchief. Then he recovered himself, sat down in the chair, and resumed his watch on the stairs.

At last, at the end of half an hour, which had seemed to him months long, he heard voices. The drawing-room door shut, and there were footsteps on the stairs. The inspector and Sonia came into view.

He waited till they were at the top of the stairs: then he came out of the room, with his most careless air, and said: "Well, Mademoiselle Sonia, I hope you did not find it so very dreadful, after all."

She was very pale, and there were undried tears on her cheeks. "It was horrible," she said faintly. "Horrible. M. Formery was all right—he believed me; but that horrible detective would not believe a word I said. He confused me. I hardly knew what I was saying."

The Duke ground his teeth softly. "Never mind, it's over now. You had better lie down and rest. I will tell one of the servants to bring you up a glass of wine."

He walked with her to the door of her room, and said: "Try to sleep—sleep away the unpleasant memory."

She went into her room, and the Duke went downstairs and told the butler to take a glass of champagne up to her. Then he went upstairs to the drawing-room. M. Formery was at the table writing. Guerchard stood beside him. He handed what he had written to Guerchard, and, with a smile of satisfaction, Guerchard folded the paper and put it in his pocket.

"Well, M. Formery, did Mademoiselle Kritchnoff throw any fresh light on this mystery?" said the Duke, in a tone of faint contempt.

"No—in fact she convinced ME that she knew nothing whatever about it. M. Guerchard seems to entertain a different opinion. But I think that even he is convinced that Mademoiselle Kritchnoff is not a friend of Arsene Lupin."

"Oh, well, perhaps she isn't. But there's no telling," said Guerchard slowly.

"Arsene Lupin?" cried the Duke. "Surely you never thought that Mademoiselle Kritchnoff had anything to do with Arsene Lupin?"

"I never thought so," said M. Formery. "But when one has a fixed idea ... well, one has a fixed idea." He shrugged his shoulders, and looked at Guerchard with contemptuous eyes.

The Duke laughed, an unaffected ringing laugh, but not a pleasant one: "It's absurd!" he cried.

"There are always those thefts," said Guerchard, with a nettled air.

"You have nothing to go upon," said M. Formery. "What if she did enter the service of Mademoiselle Gournay-Martin just before the thefts began? Besides, after this lapse of time, if she had committed the thefts, you'd find it a job to bring them home to her. It's not a job worth your doing, anyhow—it's a job for an ordinary detective, Guerchard."

"There's always the pendant," said Guerchard. "I am convinced that that pendant is in the house."

"Oh, that stupid pendant! I wish I'd never given it to Mademoiselle Gournay-Martin," said the Duke lightly.

"I have a feeling that if I could lay my hand on that pendant—if I could find who has it, I should have the key to this mystery."

"The devil you would!" said the Duke softly. "That is odd. It is the oddest thing about this business I've heard yet."

"I have that feeling—I have that feeling," said Guerchard quietly.

The Duke smiled.

CHAPTER XVI VICTOIRE'S SLIP

They were silent. The Duke walked to the fireplace, stepped into it, and studied the opening. He came out again and said: "Oh, by the way, M. Formery, the policeman at the front door wanted to stop me going out of the house when I went home to change. I take it that M. Guerchard's prohibition does not apply to me?"

"Of course not—of course not, your Grace," said M. Formery quickly.

"I saw that you had changed your clothes, your Grace," said Guerchard. "I thought that you had done it here."

"No," said the Duke, "I went home. The policeman protested; but he went no further, so I did not throw him into the middle of the street."

"Whatever our station, we should respect the law," said M. Formery solemnly.

"The Republican Law, M. Formery? I am a Royalist," said the Duke, smiling at him.

M. Formery shook his head sadly.

"I was wondering," said the Duke, "about M. Guerchard's theory that the burglars were let in the front door of this house by an accomplice. Why, when they had this beautiful large opening, did they want a front door, too?"

"I did not know that that was Guerchard's theory?" said M. Formery, a trifle contemptuously. "Of course they had no need to use the front door."

"Perhaps they had no need to use the front door," said Guerchard; "but, after all, the front door was unbolted, and they did not draw the bolts to put us off the scent. Their false scent was already prepared"—he waved his hand towards the window—"moreover, you must bear in mind that that opening might not have been made when they entered the house. Suppose that, while they were on the other side of the wall, a brick had fallen on to the hearth, and alarmed the concierge. We don't know how skilful they are; they might not have cared to risk it. I'm inclined to think, on the whole, that they did come in through the front door."

M. Formery sniffed contemptuously.

"Perhaps you're right," said the Duke. "But the accomplice?"

"I think we shall know more about the accomplice when Victoire awakes," said Guerchard.

"The family have such confidence in Victoire," said the Duke.

"Perhaps Lupin has, too," said Guerchard grimly.

"Always Lupin!" said M. Formery contemptuously.

There came a knock at the door, and a footman appeared on the threshold. He informed the Duke that Germaine had returned from her shopping expedition, and was awaiting him in her boudoir. He went to her, and tried to persuade her to put in a word for Sonia, and endeavour to soften Guerchard's rigour.

She refused to do anything of the kind, declaring that, in view of the value of the stolen property, no stone must be left unturned to recover it. The police knew what they were doing; they must have a free hand. The Duke did not press her with any great vigour; he realized the futility of an appeal to a nature so shallow, so self-centred, and so lacking in sympathy. He took his revenge by teasing her about the wedding presents which were still flowing in. Her father's business friends were still striving to outdo one another in the costliness of the jewelry they were giving her. The great houses of the Faubourg Saint-Germain were still refraining firmly from anything that savoured of extravagance or ostentation. While he was with her the eleventh paper-knife came—from his mother's friend, the Duchess of Veauleglise. The Duke was overwhelmed with joy at the sight of it, and his delighted comments drove Germaine to the last extremity of exasperation. The result was that she begged him, with petulant asperity, to get out of her sight.

He complied with her request, almost with alacrity, and returned to M. Formery and Guerchard. He found them at a standstill, waiting for reports from the detectives who were hunting outside the house for information about the movements of the burglars with the stolen booty, and apparently finding none. The police were also hunting for the stolen motor-cars, not only in Paris and its environs, but also all along the road between Paris and Charmerace.

At about five o'clock Guerchard grew tired of the inaction, and went out himself to assist his subordinates, leaving M. Formery in charge of the house itself. He promised to be back by half-past seven, to let the examining magistrate, who had an engagement for the evening, get away. The Duke spent his time between the drawing-room, where M. Formery entertained him with anecdotes of his professional skill, and the boudoir, where Germaine was entertaining envious young friends who came to see her wedding presents. The friends of Germaine were always a little ill at ease in the society of the Duke, belonging as they did to that wealthy middle class which has made France what she is. His indifference to the doings of the old friends of his family saddened them; and they were unable to understand his airy and persistent trifling. It seemed to them a discord in the cosmic tune.

The afternoon wore away, and at half-past seven Guerchard had not returned. M. Formery waited for him, fuming, for ten minutes, then left the house in charge of the inspector, and went off to his engagement. M. Gournay-Martin was entertaining two financiers and their wives, two of their daughters, and two friends of the Duke, the Baron de Vernan and the Comte de Vauvineuse, at dinner that night. Thanks to the Duke, the party was of a liveliness to which the gorgeous dining-room had been very little used since it had been so fortunate as to become the property of M. Gournay-Martin.

The millionaire had been looking forward to an evening of luxurious woe, deploring the loss of his treasures—giving their prices—to his sympathetic friends. The Duke had other views; and they prevailed. After dinner the guests went to the smoking-room, since the drawing-rooms were in possession of Guerchard. Soon after ten the Duke slipped away from them, and went to the detective. Guerchard's was not a face at any time full of expression, and all that the Duke saw on it was a subdued dulness.

"Well, M. Guerchard," he said cheerfully, "what luck? Have any of your men come across any traces of the passage of the burglars with their booty?"

"No, your Grace; so far, all the luck has been with the burglars. For all that any one seems to have seen them, they might have vanished into the bowels of the earth through the floor of the cellars in the empty house next door. That means that they were very quick loading whatever vehicle they used with their plunder. I should think, myself, that they first carried everything from this house down into the hall of the house next door; and then, of course, they could be very quick getting them from hall to their van, or whatever it was. But still, some one saw that van—saw it drive up to the house, or waiting at the house, or driving away from it."

"Is M. Formery coming back?" said the Duke.

"Not to-night," said Guerchard. "The affair is in my hands now; and I have my own men on it—men of some intelligence, or, at any rate, men who know my ways, and how I want things done."   ·

"It must be a relief," said the Duke.

"Oh, no, I'm used to M. Formery—to all the examining magistrates in Paris, and in most of the big provincial towns. They do not really hamper me; and often I get an idea from them; for some of them are men of real intelligence."

"And others are not: I understand," said the Duke.

The door opened and Bonavent, the detective, came in.

"The housekeeper's awake, M. Guerchard," he said.

"Good, bring her down here," said Guerchard.

"Perhaps you'd like me to go," said the Duke.

"Oh, no," said Guerchard. "If it would interest you to hear me question her, please stay."

Bonavent left the room. The Duke sat down in an easy chair, and Guerchard stood before the fireplace.

"M. Formery told me, when you were out this afternoon, that he believed this housekeeper to be quite innocent," said the Duke idly.

"There is certainly one innocent in this affair," said Guerchard, grinning.

"Who is that?" said the Duke.

"The examining magistrate," said Guerchard.

The door opened, and Bonavent brought Victoire in. She was a big, middle-aged woman, with a pleasant, cheerful, ruddy face, black-haired, with sparkling brown eyes, which did not seem to have been at all dimmed by her long, drugged sleep. She looked like a well-to-do farmer's wife, a buxom, good-natured, managing woman.

As soon as she came into the room, she said quickly:

"I wish, Mr. Inspector, your man would have given me time to put on a decent dress. I must have been sleeping in this one ever since those rascals tied me up and put that smelly handkerchief over my face. I never saw such a nasty-looking crew as they were in my life."

"How many were there, Madame Victoire?" said Guerchard.

"Dozens! The house was just swarming with them. I heard the noise; I came downstairs; and on the landing outside the door here, one of them jumped on me from behind and nearly choked me—to prevent me from screaming, I suppose."

"And they were a nasty-looking crew, were they?" said Guerchard. "Did you see their faces?"

"No, I wish I had! I should know them again if I had; but they were all masked," said Victoire.

"Sit down, Madame Victoire. There's no need to tire you," said Guerchard. And she sat down on a chair facing him.

"Let's see, you sleep in one of the top rooms, Madame Victoire. It has a dormer window, set in the roof, hasn't it?" said Guerchard, in the same polite, pleasant voice.

"Yes; yes. But what has that got to do with it?" said Victoire.

"Please answer my questions," said Guerchard sharply. "You went to sleep in your room. Did you hear any noise on the roof?"

"On the roof? How should I hear it on the roof? There wouldn't be any noise on the roof," said Victoire.

"You heard nothing on the roof?" said Guerchard.

"No; the noise I heard was down here," said Victoire.

"Yes, and you came down to see what was making it. And you were seized from behind on the landing, and brought in here," said Guerchard.

"Yes, that's right," said Madame Victoire.

"And were you tied up and gagged on the landing, or in here?" said Guerchard.

"Oh, I was caught on the landing, and pushed in here, and then tied up," said Victoire.

"I'm sure that wasn't one man's job," said Guerchard, looking at her vigorous figure with admiring eyes.

"You may be sure of that," said Victoire. "It took four of them; and at least two of them have some nice bruises on their shins to show for it."

"I'm sure they have. And it serves them jolly well right," said Guerchard, in a tone of warm approval. "And, I suppose, while those four were tying you up the others stood round and looked on."

"Oh, no, they were far too busy for that," said Victoire.

"What were they doing?" said Guerchard.

"They were taking the pictures off the walls and carrying them out of the window down the ladder," said Victoire.

Guerchard's eyes flickered towards the Duke, but the expression of earnest inquiry on his face never changed.

"Now, tell me, did the man who took a picture from the walls carry it down the ladder himself, or did he hand it through the window to a man who was standing on the top of a ladder ready to receive it?" he said.

Victoire paused as if to recall their action; then she said, "Oh, he got through the window, and carried it down the ladder himself."

"You're sure of that?" said Guerchard.

"Oh, yes, I am quite sure of it—why should I deceive you, Mr. Inspector?" said Victoire quickly; and the Duke saw the first shadow of uneasiness on her face.

"Of course not," said Guerchard. "And where were you?"

"Oh, they put me behind the screen."

"No, no, where were you when you came into the room?"

"I was against the door," said Victoire.

"And where was the screen?" said Guerchard. "Was it before the fireplace?"

"No; it was on one side—the left-hand side," said Victoire.

"Oh, will you show me exactly where it stood?" said Guerchard.

Victoire rose, and, Guerchard aiding her, set the screen on the left-hand side of the fireplace.

Guerchard stepped back and looked at it.

"Now, this is very important," he said. "I must have the exact position of the four feet of that screen. Let's see ... some chalk ... of course.... You do some dressmaking, don't you, Madame Victoire?"

"Oh, yes, I sometimes make a dress for one of the maids in my spare time," said Victoire.

"Then you've got a piece of chalk on you," said Guerchard.

"Oh, yes," said Victoire, putting her hand to the pocket of her dress.

She paused, took a step backwards, and looked wildly round the room, while the colour slowly faded in her ruddy cheeks.

"What am I talking about?" she said in an uncertain, shaky voice. "I haven't any chalk—I—ran out of chalk the day before yesterday."

"I think you have, Madame Victoire. Feel in your pocket and see," said Guerchard sternly. His voice had lost its suavity; his face its smile: his eyes had grown dangerous.

"No, no; I have no chalk," cried Victoire.

With a sudden leap Guerchard sprang upon her, caught her in a firm grip with his right arm, and his left hand plunged into her pocket.

"Let me go! Let me go! You're hurting," she cried.

Guerchard loosed her and stepped back.

"What's this?" he said; and he held up between his thumb and forefinger a piece of blue chalk.

Victoire drew herself up and faced him gallantly: "Well, what of it?—it is chalk. Mayn't an honest woman carry chalk in her pockets without being insulted and pulled about by every policeman she comes across?" she cried.

"That will be for the examining magistrate to decide," said Guerchard; and he went to the door and called Bonavent. Bonavent came in, and Guerchard said: "When the prison van comes, put this woman in it; and send her down to the station."

"But what have I done?" cried Victoire. "I'm innocent! I declare I'm innocent. I've done nothing at all. It's not a crime to carry a piece of chalk in one's pocket."

"Now, that's a matter for the examining magistrate. You can explain it to him," said Guerchard. "I've got nothing to do with it: so it's no good making a fuss now. Do go quietly, there's a good woman."

He spoke in a quiet, business-like tone. Victoire looked him in the eyes, then drew herself up, and went quietly out of the room.

CHAPTER XVII SONIA'S ESCAPE

"One of M. Formery's innocents," said Guerchard, turning to the Duke.

"The chalk?" said the Duke. "Is it the same chalk?"

"It's blue," said Guerchard, holding it out. "The same as that of the signatures on the walls. Add that fact to the woman's sudden realization of what she was doing, and you'll see that they were written with it."

"It is rather a surprise," said the Duke. "To look at her you would think that she was the most honest woman in the world."

"Ah, you don't know Lupin, your Grace," said Guerchard. "He can do anything with women; and they'll do anything for him. And, what's more, as far as I can see, it doesn't make a scrap of difference whether they're honest or not. The fair-haired lady I was telling you about was probably an honest woman; Ganimard is sure of it. We should have found out long ago who she was if she had been a wrong 'un. And Ganimard also swears that when he arrested Lupin on board the Provence some woman, some ordinary, honest woman among the passengers, carried away Lady Garland's jewels, which he had stolen and was bringing to America, and along with them a matter of eight hundred pounds which he had stolen from a fellow-passenger on the voyage."

"That power of fascination which some men exercise on women is one of those mysteries which science should investigate before it does anything else," said the Duke, in a reflective tone. "Now I come to think of it, I had much better have spent my time on that investigation than on that tedious journey to the South Pole. All the same, I'm deucedly sorry for that woman, Victoire. She looks such a good soul."

Guerchard shrugged his shoulders: "The prisons are full of good souls," he said, with cynical wisdom born of experience. "They get caught so much more often than the bad."

"It seems rather mean of Lupin to make use of women like this, and get them into trouble," said the Duke.

"But he doesn't," said Guerchard quickly. "At least he hasn't up to now. This Victoire is the first we've caught. I look on it as a good omen."

He walked across the room, picked up his cloak, and took a card-case from the inner pocket of it. "If you don't mind, your Grace, I want you to show this permit to my men who are keeping the door, whenever you go out of the house. It's just a formality; but I attach considerable importance to it, for I really ought not to make exceptions in favour of any one. I have two men at the door, and they have orders to let nobody out without my written permission. Of course M. Gournay-Martin's guests are different. Bonavent has orders to pass them out. And, if your Grace doesn't mind, it will help me. If you carry a permit, no one else will dream of complaining of having to do so."

"Oh, I don't mind, if it's of any help to you," said the Duke cheerfully.

"Thank you," said Guerchard. And he wrote on his card and handed it to the Duke.

The Duke took it and looked at it. On it was written:

> "Pass the Duke of Charmerace."
> "J. GUERCHARD."

"It's quite military," said the Duke, putting the card into his waistcoat pocket.

There came a knock at the door, and a tall, thin, bearded man came into the room.

"Ah, Dieusy! At last! What news?" cried Guerchard.

Dieusy saluted: "I've learnt that a motor-van was waiting outside the next house—in the side street," he said.

"At what time?" said Guerchard.

"Between four and five in the morning," said Dieusy.

"Who saw it?" said Guerchard.

"A scavenger. He thinks that it was nearly five o'clock when the van drove off."

"Between four and five—nearly five. Then they filled up the opening before they loaded the van. I thought they would," said Guerchard, thoughtfully. "Anything else?"

"A few minutes after the van had gone a man in motoring dress came out of the house," said Dieusy.

"In motoring dress?" said Guerchard quickly.

"Yes. And a little way from the house he threw away his cigarette. The scavenger thought the whole business a little queer, and he picked up the cigarette and kept it. Here it is."

He handed it to Guerchard, whose eyes scanned it carelessly and then glued themselves to it.

"A gold-tipped cigarette ... marked Mercedes ... Why, your Grace, this is one of your cigarettes!"

"But this is incredible!" cried the Duke.

"Not at all," said Guerchard. "It's merely another link in the chain. I've no doubt you have some of these cigarettes at Charmerace."

"Oh, yes, I've had a box on most of the tables," said the Duke.

"Well, there you are," said Guerchard.

"Oh, I see what you're driving at," said the Duke. "You mean that one of the Charolais must have taken a box."

"Well, we know that they'd hardly stick at a box of cigarettes," said Guerchard.

"Yes ... but I thought ..." said the Duke; and he paused.

"You thought what?" said Guerchard.

"Then Lupin ... since it was Lupin who managed the business last night—since you found those salvias in the house next door ... then Lupin came from Charmerace."

"Evidently," said Guerchard.

"And Lupin is one of the Charolais."

"Oh, that's another matter," said Guerchard.

"But it's certain, absolutely certain," said the Duke. "We have the connecting links ... the salvias ... this cigarette."

"It looks very like it. You're pretty quick on a scent, I must say," said Guerchard. "What a detective you would have made! Only ... nothing is certain."

"But it IS. Whatever more do you want? Was he at Charmerace yesterday, or was he not? Did he, or did he not, arrange the theft of the motor-cars?"

"Certainly he did. But he himself might have remained in the background all the while," said Guerchard.

"In what shape? ... Under what mask? ... By Jove, I should like to see this fellow!" said the Duke.

413

"We shall see him to-night," said Guerchard.

"To-night?" said the Duke.

"Of course we shall; for he will come to steal the coronet between a quarter to twelve and midnight," said Guerchard.

"Never!" said the Duke. "You don't really believe that he'll have the cheek to attempt such a mad act?"

"Ah, you don't know this man, your Grace ... his extraordinary mixture of coolness and audacity. It's the danger that attracts him. He throws himself into the fire, and he doesn't get burnt. For the last ten years I've been saying to myself, 'Here we are: this time I've got him! ... At last I'm going to nab him.' But I've said that day after day," said Guerchard; and he paused.

"Well?" said the Duke.

"Well, the days pass; and I never nab him. Oh, he is thick, I tell you.... He's a joker, he is ... a regular artist"—he ground his teeth—"The damned thief!"

The Duke looked at him, and said slowly, "Then you think that to-night Lupin—"

"You've followed the scent with me, your Grace," Guerchard interrupted quickly and vehemently. "We've picked up each clue together. You've almost seen this man at work.... You've understood him. Isn't a man like this, I ask you, capable of anything?"

"He is," said the Duke, with conviction.

"Well, then," said Guerchard.

"Perhaps you're right," said the Duke.

Guerchard turned to Dieusy and said, in a quieter voice, "And when the scavenger had picked up the cigarette, did he follow the motorist?"

"Yes, he followed him for about a hundred yards. He went down into Sureau Street, and turned westwards. Then a motor-car came along; he got into it, and went off."

"What kind of a motor-car?" said Guerchard.

"A big car, and dark red in colour," said Dieusy.

"The Limousine!" cried the Duke.

"That's all I've got so far, sir," said Dieusy.

"Well, off you go," said Guerchard. "Now that you've got started, you'll probably get something else before very long."

Dieusy saluted and went.

"Things are beginning to move," said Guerchard cheerfully. "First Victoire, and now this motor-van."

"They are indeed," said the Duke.

"After all, it ought not to be very difficult to trace that motor-van," said Guerchard, in a musing tone. "At any rate, its movements ought to be easy enough to follow up till about six. Then, of course, there would be a good many others about, delivering goods."

"You seem to have all the possible information you can want at your finger-ends," said the Duke, in an admiring tone.

"I suppose I know the life of Paris as well as anybody," said Guerchard.

They were silent for a while. Then Germaine's maid, Irma, came into the room and said:

"If you please, your Grace, Mademoiselle Kritchnoff would like to speak to you for a moment."

"Oh? Where is she?" said the Duke.

"She's in her room, your Grace."

"Oh, very well, I'll go up to her," said the Duke. "I can speak to her in the library."

He rose and was going towards the door when Guerchard stepped forward, barring his way, and said, "No, your Grace."

"No? Why?" said the Duke haughtily.

"I beg you will wait a minute or two till I've had a word with you," said Guerchard; and he drew a folded sheet of paper from his pocket and held it up.

The Duke looked at Guerchard's face, and he looked at the paper in his hand; then he said: "Oh, very well." And, turning to Irma, he added quietly, "Tell Mademoiselle Kritchnoff that I'm in the drawing-room."

"Yes, your Grace, in the drawing-room," said Irma; and she turned to go.

"Yes; and say that I shall be engaged for the next five minutes—the next five minutes, do you understand?" said the Duke.

"Yes, your Grace," said Irma; and she went out of the door.

"Ask Mademoiselle Kritchnoff to put on her hat and cloak," said Guerchard.

"Yes, sir," said Irma; and she went.

The Duke turned sharply on Guerchard, and said: "Now, why on earth? ... I don't understand."

"I got this from M. Formery," said Guerchard, holding up the paper.

"Well," said the Duke. "What is it?"

"It's a warrant, your Grace," said Guerchard.

"What! ... A warrant! ... Not for the arrest of Mademoiselle Kritchnoff?"

"Yes," said Guerchard.

"Oh, come, it's impossible," said the Duke. "You're never going to arrest that child?"

"I am, indeed," said Guerchard. "Her examination this afternoon was in the highest degree unsatisfactory. Her answers were embarrassed, contradictory, and in every way suspicious."

"And you've made up your mind to arrest her?" said the Duke slowly, knitting his brow in anxious thought.

"I have, indeed," said Guerchard. "And I'm going to do it now. The prison van ought to be waiting at the door." He looked at his watch. "She and Victoire can go together."

"So ... you're going to arrest her ... you're going to arrest her?" said the Duke thoughtfully: and he took a step or two up and down the room, still thinking hard.

"Well, you understand the position, don't you, your Grace?" said Guerchard, in a tone of apology. "Believe me that, personally, I've no animosity against Mademoiselle Kritchnoff. In fact, the child attracts me."

"Yes," said the Duke softly, in a musing tone. "She has the air of a child who has lost its way ... lost its way in life.... And that poor little hiding-place she found ... that rolled-up handkerchief ... thrown down in the corner of the little room in the house next door ... it was absolutely absurd."

"What! A handkerchief!" cried Guerchard, with an air of sudden, utter surprise.

"The child's clumsiness is positively pitiful," said the Duke.

"What was in the handkerchief? ... The pearls of the pendant?" cried Guerchard.

"Yes: I supposed you knew all about it. Of course M. Formery left word for you," said the Duke, with an air of surprise at the ignorance of the detective.

"No: I've heard nothing about it," cried Guerchard.

"He didn't leave word for you?" said the Duke, in a tone of greater surprise. "Oh, well, I dare say that he thought to-morrow would do. Of course you were out of the house when he found it. She must have slipped out of her room soon after you went."

"He found a handkerchief belonging to Mademoiselle Kritchnoff. Where is it?" cried Guerchard.

"M. Formery took the pearls, but he left the handkerchief. I suppose it's in the corner where he found it," said the Duke.

"He left the handkerchief?" cried Guerchard. "If that isn't just like the fool! He ought to keep hens; it's all he's fit for!"

He ran to the fireplace, seized the lantern, and began lighting it: "Where is the handkerchief?" he cried.

"In the left-hand corner of the little room on the right on the second floor. But if you're going to arrest Mademoiselle Kritchnoff, why are you bothering about the handkerchief? It can't be of any importance," said the Duke.

"I beg your pardon," said Guerchard. "But it is."

"But why?" said the Duke.

"I was arresting Mademoiselle Kritchnoff all right because I had a very strong presumption of her guilt. But I hadn't the slightest proof of it," said Guerchard.

"What?" cried the Duke, in a horrified tone.

"No, you've just given me the proof; and since she was able to hide the pearls in the house next door, she knew the road which led to it. Therefore she's an accomplice," said Guerchard, in a triumphant tone.

"What? Do you think that, too?" cried the Duke. "Good Heavens! And it's me! ... It's my senselessness! ... It's my fault that you've got your proof!" He spoke in a tone of acute distress.

"It was your duty to give it me," said Guerchard sternly; and he began to mount the steps.

"Shall I come with you? I know where the handkerchief is," said the Duke quickly.

"No, thank you, your Grace," said Guerchard. "I prefer to go alone."

"You'd better let me help you," said the Duke.

"No, your Grace," said Guerchard firmly.

"I must really insist," said the Duke.

"No—no—no," said Guerchard vehemently, with stern decision. "It's no use your insisting, your Grace; I prefer to go alone. I shall only be gone a minute or two."

"Just as you like," said the Duke stiffly.

The legs of Guerchard disappeared up the steps. The Duke stood listening with all his ears. Directly he heard the sound of Guerchard's heels on the floor, when he dropped from the chimney-piece of the next room, he went swiftly to the door, opened it, and went out. Bonavent was sitting on the chair on which the young policeman had sat during the afternoon. Sonia, in her hat and cloak, was half-way down the stairs.

The Duke put his head inside the drawing-room door, and said to the empty room: "Here is Mademoiselle Kritchnoff, M. Guerchard." He held open the door, Sonia came down the stairs, and went through it. The Duke followed her into the drawing-room, and shut the door.

"There's not a moment to lose," he said in a low voice.

"Oh, what is it, your Grace?" said Sonia anxiously.

"Guerchard has a warrant for your arrest."

"Then I'm lost!" cried Sonia, in a panic-stricken voice.

"No, you're not. You must go—at once," said the Duke.

"But how can I go? No one can get out of the house. M. Guerchard won't let them," cried Sonia, panic-stricken.

"We can get over that," said the Duke.

He ran to Guerchard's cloak, took the card-case from the inner pocket, went to the writing-table, and sat down. He took from his waist-coat pocket the permit which Guerchard had given him, and a pencil. Then he took a card from the card-case, set the permit on the table before him, and began to imitate Guerchard's handwriting with an amazing exactness. He wrote on the card:

"Pass   Mademoiselle   Kritchnoff."
"J. GUERCHARD."

Sonia stood by his side, panting quickly with fear, and watched him do it. He had scarcely finished the last stroke, when they heard a noise on the other side of the opening into the empty house. The Duke looked at the fireplace, and his teeth bared in an expression of cold ferocity. He rose with clenched fists, and took a step towards the fireplace.

"Your Grace? Your Grace?" called the voice of Guerchard.

"What is it?" answered the Duke quietly.

"I can't see any handkerchief," said Guerchard. "Didn't you say it was in the left-hand corner of the little room on the right?"

"I told you you'd better let me come with you, and find it," said the Duke, in a tone of triumph. "It's in the right-hand corner of the little room on the left."

"I could have sworn you said the little room on the right," said Guerchard.

They heard his footfalls die away.

"Now, you must get out of the house quickly." said the Duke. "Show this card to the detectives at the door, and they'll pass you without a word."

He pressed the card into her hand.

"But—but—this card?" stammered Sonia.

"There's no time to lose," said the Duke.

"But this is madness," said Sonia. "When Guerchard finds out about this card—that you—you—"

"There's no need to bother about that," interrupted the Duke quickly. "Where are you going to?"

"A little hotel near the Star. I've forgotten the name of it," said Sonia. "But this card—"

"Has it a telephone?" said the Duke.

"Yes—No. 555, Central," said Sonia.

"If I haven't telephoned to you before half-past eight to-morrow morning, come straight to my house," said the Duke, scribbling the telephone number on his shirt-cuff.

"Yes, yes," said Sonia. "But this card.... When Guerchard knows ... when he discovers.... Oh, I can't let you get into trouble for me."

"I shan't. But go—go," said the Duke, and he slipped his right arm round her and drew her to the door.

"Oh, how good you are to me," said Sonia softly.

The Duke's other arm went round her; he drew her to him, and their lips met.

He loosed her, and opened the door, saying loudly: "You're sure you won't have a cab, Mademoiselle Kritchnoff?"

"No; no, thank you, your Grace. Goodnight," said Sonia. And she went through the door with a transfigured face.

CHAPTER XVIII THE DUKE STAYS

The Duke shut the door and leant against it, listening anxiously, breathing quickly. There came the bang of the front door. With a deep sigh of relief he left the door, came briskly, smiling, across the room, and put the card-case back into the pocket of Guerchard's cloak. He lighted a cigarette, dropped into an easy chair, and sat waiting with an entirely careless air for the detective's return. Presently he heard quick footsteps on the bare boards of the empty room beyond the opening. Then Guerchard came down the steps and out of the fireplace.

His face wore an expression of extreme perplexity:

"I can't understand it," he said. "I found nothing."

"Nothing?" said the Duke.

"No. Are you sure you saw the handkerchief in one of those little rooms on the second floor—quite sure?" said Guerchard.

"Of course I did," said the Duke. "Isn't it there?"

"No," said Guerchard.

"You can't have looked properly," said the Duke, with a touch of irony in his voice. "If I were you, I should go back and look again."

"No. If I've looked for a thing, I've looked for it. There's no need for me to look a second time. But, all the same, it's rather funny. Doesn't it strike you as being rather funny, your Grace?" said Guerchard, with a worried air.

"It strikes me as being uncommonly funny," said the Duke, with an ambiguous smile.

Guerchard looked at him with a sudden uneasiness; then he rang the bell.

Bonavent came into the room.

"Mademoiselle Kritchnoff, Bonavent. It's quite time," said Guerchard.

"Mademoiselle Kritchnoff?" said Bonavent, with an air of surprise.

"Yes, it's time that she was taken to the police-station."

"Mademoiselle Kritchnoff has gone, sir," said Bonavent, in a tone of quiet remonstrance.

"Gone? What do you mean by gone?" said Guerchard.

"Gone, sir, gone!" said Bonavent patiently.

"But you're mad.... Mad!" cried Guerchard.

"No, I'm not mad," said Bonavent. "Gone! But who let her go?" cried Guerchard.

"The men at the door," said Bonavent.

"The men at the door," said Guerchard, in a tone of stupefaction. "But she had to have my permit ... my permit on my card! Send the fools up to me!"

Bonavent went to the top of the staircase, and called down it. Guerchard followed him. Two detectives came hurrying up the stairs and into the drawing-room.

"What the devil do you mean by letting Mademoiselle Kritchnoff leave the house without my permit, written on my card?" cried Guerchard violently.

"But she had your permit, sir, and it WAS written on your card," stammered one of the detectives.

"It was? ... it was?" said Guerchard. "Then, by Jove, it was a forgery!"

He stood thoughtful for a moment. Then quietly he told his two men to go back to their post. He did not stir for a minute or two, puzzling it out, seeking light.

Then he came back slowly into the drawing-room and looked uneasily at the Duke. The Duke was sitting in his easy chair, smoking a cigarette with a listless air. Guerchard looked at him, and looked at him, almost as if he now saw him for the first time.

"Well?" said the Duke, "have you sent that poor child off to prison? If I'd done a thing like that I don't think I should sleep very well, M. Guerchard."

"That poor child has just escaped, by means of a forged permit," said Guerchard very glumly.

"By Jove, I AM glad to hear that!" cried the Duke. "You'll forgive my lack of sympathy, M. Guerchard; but she was such a child."

"Not too young to be Lupin's accomplice," said Guerchard drily.

"You really think she is?" said the Duke, in a tone of doubt.

"I'm sure of it," said Guerchard, with decision; then he added slowly, with a perplexed air:

422

"But how—how—could she get that forged permit?"

The Duke shook his head, and looked as solemn as an owl. Guerchard looked at him uneasily, went out of the drawing-room, and shut the door.

"How long has Mademoiselle Kritchnoff been gone?" he said to Bonavent.

"Not much more than five minutes," said Bonavent. "She came out from talking to you in the drawing-room—"

"Talking to me in the drawing-room!" exclaimed Guerchard.

"Yes," said Bonavent. "She came out and went straight down the stairs and out of the house."

A faint, sighing gasp came from Guerchard's lips. He dashed into the drawing-room, crossed the room quickly to his cloak, picked it up, took the card-case out of the pocket, and counted the cards in it. Then he looked at the Duke.

The Duke smiled at him, a charming smile, almost caressing.

There seemed to be a lump in Guerchard's throat; he swallowed it loudly.

He put the card-case into the breast-pocket of the coat he was wearing. Then he cried sharply, "Bonavent! Bonavent!"

Bonavent opened the door, and stood in the doorway.

"You sent off Victoire in the prison-van, I suppose," said Guerchard.

"Oh, a long while ago, sir," said Bonavent.

"The van had been waiting at the door since half-past nine."

"Since half-past nine? ... But I told them I shouldn't want it till a quarter to eleven. I suppose they were making an effort to be in time for once. Well, it doesn't matter," said Guerchard.

"Then I suppose I'd better send the other prison-van away?" said Bonavent.

"What other van?" said Guerchard.

"The van which has just arrived," said Bonavent.

"What! What on earth are you talking about?" cried Guerchard, with a sudden anxiety in his voice and on his face.

"Didn't you order two prison-vans?" said Bonavent.

Guerchard jumped; and his face went purple with fury and dismay. "You don't mean to tell me that two prison-vans have been here?" he cried.

"Yes, sir," said Bonavent.

"Damnation!" cried Guerchard. "In which of them did you put Victoire? In which of them?"

"Why, in the first, sir," said Bonavent.

"Did you see the police in charge of it? The coachman?"

"Yes, sir," said Bonavent.

"Did you recognize them?" said Guerchard.

"No," said Bonavent; "they must have been new men. They told me they came from the Sante."

"You silly fool!" said Guerchard through his teeth. "A fine lot of sense you've got."

"Why, what's the matter?" said Bonavent.

"We're done, done in the eye!" roared Guerchard. "It's a stroke—a stroke—"

"Of Lupin's!" interposed the Duke softly.

"But I don't understand," said Bonavent.

"You don't understand, you idiot!" cried Guerchard. "You've sent Victoire away in a sham prison-van—a prison-van belonging to Lupin. Oh, that scoundrel! He always has something up his sleeve."

"He certainly shows foresight," said the Duke. "It was very clever of him to foresee the arrest of Victoire and provide against it."

"Yes, but where is the leakage? Where is the leakage?" cried Guerchard, fuming. "How did he learn that the doctor said that she would recover her wits at ten o'clock? Here I've had a guard at the door all day; I've imprisoned the household; all the provisions have been received directly by a man of mine; and here he is, ready to pick up Victoire the very moment she gives herself away! Where is the leakage?"

He turned on Bonavent, and went on: "It's no use your standing there with your mouth open, looking like a fool. Go upstairs to the servants' quarters and search Victoire's room again. That fool of an inspector may have missed something, just as he missed Victoire herself. Get on! Be smart!"

Bonavent went off briskly. Guerchard paced up and down the room, scowling.

"Really, I'm beginning to agree with you, M. Guerchard, that this Lupin is a remarkable man," said the Duke. "That prison-van is extraordinarily neat."

"I'll prison-van him!" cried Guerchard. "But what fools I have to work with. If I could get hold of people of ordinary intelligence it would be impossible to play such a trick as that."

"I don't know about that," said the Duke thoughtfully. "I think it would have required an uncommon fool to discover that trick."

"What on earth do you mean? Why?" said Guerchard.

"Because it's so wonderfully simple," said the Duke. "And at the same time it's such infernal cheek."

"There's something in that," said Guerchard grumpily. "But then, I'm always saying to my men, 'Suspect everything; suspect everybody; suspect, suspect, suspect.' I tell you, your Grace, that there is only one motto for the successful detective, and that is that one word, 'suspect.'"

"It can't be a very comfortable business, then," said the Duke. "But I suppose it has its charms."

"Oh, one gets used to the disagreeable part," said Guerchard.

The telephone bell rang; and he rose and went to it. He put the receiver to his ear and said, "Yes; it's I—Chief-Inspector Guerchard."

He turned and said to the Duke, "It's the gardener at Charmerace, your Grace."

"Is it?" said the Duke indifferently.

Guerchard turned to the telephone. "Are you there?" he said. "Can you hear me clearly? ... I want to know who was in your hot-house yesterday ... who could have gathered some of your pink salvias?"

"I told you that it was I," said the Duke.

"Yes, yes, I know," said Guerchard. And he turned again to the telephone. "Yes, yesterday," he said. "Nobody else? ... No one but the Duke of Charmerace? ... Are you sure?... quite sure?... absolutely sure? ... Yes, that's all I wanted to know ... thank you."

He turned to the Duke and said, "Did you hear that, your Grace? The gardener says that you were the only person in his hot-houses yesterday, the only person who could have plucked any pink salvias."

"Does he?" said the Duke carelessly.

Guerchard looked at him, his brow knitted in a faint, pondering frown. Then the door opened, and Bonavent came in: "I've been through Victoire's room," he said, "and all I could find that might be of any use is this—a prayer-book. It was on her dressing-table just as she left it. The inspector hadn't touched it."

"What about it?" said Guerchard, taking the prayer-book.

"There's a photograph in it," said Bonavent. "It may come in useful when we circulate her description; for I suppose we shall try to get hold of Victoire."

Guerchard took the photograph from the prayer-book and looked at it: "It looks about ten years old," he said. "It's a good deal faded for reproduction. Hullo! What have we here?"

The photograph showed Victoire in her Sunday best, and with her a boy of seventeen or eighteen. Guerchard's eyes glued themselves to the face of the boy. He stared at it, holding the portrait now nearer, now further off. His eyes kept stealing covertly from the photograph to the face of the Duke.

The Duke caught one of those covert glances, and a vague uneasiness flickered in his eyes. Guerchard saw it. He came nearer to the Duke and looked at him earnestly, as if he couldn't believe his eyes.

"What's the matter?" said the Duke. "What are you looking at so curiously? Isn't my tie straight?" And he put up his hand and felt it.

"Oh, nothing, nothing," said Guerchard. And he studied the photograph again with a frowning face.

There was a noise of voices and laughter in the hall.

"Those people are going," said the Duke. "I must go down and say good-bye to them." And he rose and went out of the room.

426

Guerchard stood staring, staring at the photograph.

The Duke ran down the stairs, and said goodbye to the millionaire's guests. After they had gone, M. Gournay-Martin went quickly up the stairs; Germaine and the Duke followed more slowly.

"My father is going to the Ritz to sleep," said Germaine, "and I'm going with him. He doesn't like the idea of my sleeping in this house to-night. I suppose he's afraid that Lupin will make an attack in force with all his gang. Still, if he did, I think that Guerchard could give a good account of himself—he's got men enough in the house, at any rate. Irma tells me it's swarming with them. It would never do for me to be in the house if there were a fight."

"Oh, come, you don't really believe that Lupin is coming to-night?" said the Duke, with a sceptical laugh. "The whole thing is sheer bluff—he has no more intention of coming tonight to steal that coronet than—than I have."

"Oh, well, there's no harm in being on the safe side," said Germaine. "Everybody's agreed that he's a very terrible person. I'll just run up to my room and get a wrap; Irma has my things all packed. She can come round tomorrow morning to the Ritz and dress me."

She ran up the stairs, and the Duke went into the drawing-room. He found Guerchard standing where he had left him, still frowning, still thinking hard.

"The family are off to the Ritz. It's rather a reflection on your powers of protecting them, isn't it?" said the Duke.

"Oh, well, I expect they'd be happier out of the house," said Guerchard. He looked at the Duke again with inquiring, searching eyes.

"What's the matter?" said the Duke. "IS my tie crooked?"

"Oh, no, no; it's quite straight, your Grace," said Guerchard, but he did not take his eyes from the Duke's face.

The door opened, and in came M. Gournay-Martin, holding a bag in his hand. "It seems to be settled that I'm never to sleep in my own house again," he said in a grumbling tone.

"There's no reason to go," said the Duke. "Why ARE you going?"

"Danger," said M. Gournay-Martin. "You read Lupin's telegram: 'I shall come to-night between a quarter to twelve and midnight to take the coronet.' He knows that it was in my bedroom. Do you think I'm going to sleep in that room with the chance of that scoundrel turning up and cutting my throat?"

"Oh, you can have a dozen policemen in the room if you like," said the Duke. "Can't he, M. Guerchard?"

"Certainly," said Guerchard. "I can answer for it that you will be in no danger, M. Gournay-Martin."

"Thank you," said the millionaire. "But all the same, outside is good enough for me."

Germaine came into the room, cloaked and ready to start.

"For once in a way you are ready first, papa," she said. "Are you coming, Jacques?"

"No; I think I'll stay here, on the chance that Lupin is not bluffing," said the Duke. "I don't think, myself, that I'm going to be gladdened by the sight of him—in fact, I'm ready to bet against it. But you're all so certain about it that I really must stay on the chance. And, after all, there's no doubt that he's a man of immense audacity and ready to take any risk."

"Well, at any rate, if he does come he won't find the diadem," said M. Gournay-Martin, in a tone of triumph. "I'm taking it with me—I've got it here." And he held up his bag.

"You are?" said the Duke.

"Yes, I am," said M. Gournay-Martin firmly.

"Do you think it's wise?" said the Duke.

"Why not?" said M. Gournay-Martin.

"If Lupin's really made up his mind to collar that coronet, and if you're so sure that, in spite of all these safeguards, he's going to make the attempt, it seems to me that you're taking a considerable risk. He asked you to have it ready for him in your bedroom. He didn't say which bedroom."

"Good Lord! I never thought of that!" said M. Gournay-Martin, with an air of sudden and very lively alarm.

"His Grace is right," said Guerchard. "It would be exactly like Lupin to send that telegram to drive you out of the house with the coronet to some place where you would be less protected. That is exactly one of his tricks."

"Good Heavens!" said the millionaire, pulling out his keys and unlocking the bag. He opened it, paused hesitatingly, and snapped it to again.

"Half a minute," he said. "I want a word with you, Duke."

He led the way out of the drawing-room door and the Duke followed him. He shut the door and said in a whisper:

"In a case like this, I suspect everybody."

"Everybody suspects everybody, apparently," said the Duke. "Are you sure you don't suspect me?"

"Now, now, this is no time for joking," said the millionaire impatiently. "What do you think about Guerchard?"

"About Guerchard?" said the Duke. "What do you mean?"

"Do you think I can put full confidence in Guerchard?" said M. Gournay-Martin.

"Oh, I think so," said the Duke. "Besides, I shall be here to look after Guerchard. And, though I wouldn't undertake to answer for Lupin, I think I can answer for Guerchard. If he tries to escape with the coronet, I will wring his neck for you with pleasure. It would do me good. And it would do Guerchard good, too."

The millionaire stood reflecting for a minute or two. Then he said, "Very good; I'll trust him."

Hardly had the door closed behind the millionaire and the Duke, when Guerchard crossed the room quickly to Germaine and drew from his pocket the photograph of Victoire and the young man.

"Do you know this photograph of his Grace, mademoiselle?" he said quickly.

Germaine took the photograph and looked at it.

"It's rather faded," she said.

"Yes; it's about ten years old," said Guerchard.

"I seem to know the face of the woman," said Germaine. "But if it's ten years old it certainly isn't the photograph of the Duke."

"But it's like him?" said Guerchard.

"Oh, yes, it's like the Duke as he is now—at least, it's a little like him. But it's not like the Duke as he was ten years ago. He has changed so," said Germaine.

"Oh, has he?" said Guerchard.

"Yes; there was that exhausting journey of his—and then his illness. The doctors gave up all hope of him, you know."

"Oh, did they?" said Guerchard.

"Yes; at Montevideo. But his health is quite restored now."

The door opened and the millionaire and the Duke came into the room. M. Gournay-Martin set his bag upon the table, unlocked it, and with a solemn air took out the case which held the coronet. He opened it; and they looked at it.

"Isn't it beautiful?" he said with a sigh.

"Marvellous!" said the Duke.

M. Gournay-Martin closed the case, and said solemnly:

"There is danger, M. Guerchard, so I am going to trust the coronet to you. You are the defender of my hearth and home—you are the proper person to guard the coronet. I take it that you have no objection?"

"Not the slightest, M. Gournay-Martin," said Guerchard. "It's exactly what I wanted you to ask me to do."

M. Gournay-Martin hesitated. Then he handed the coronet to Guerchard, saying with a frank and noble air, "I have every confidence in you, M. Guerchard."

"Thank you," said Guerchard.

"Good-night," said M. Gournay-Martin.

"Good-night, M. Guerchard," said Germaine.

"I think, after all, I'll change my mind and go with you. I'm very short of sleep," said the Duke. "Good-night, M. Guerchard."

"You're never going too, your Grace!" cried Guerchard.

"Why, you don't want me to stay, do you?" said the Duke.

"Yes," said Guerchard slowly.

"I think I would rather go to bed," said the Duke gaily.

"Are you afraid?" said Guerchard, and there was challenge, almost an insolent challenge, in his tone.

There was a pause. The Duke frowned slightly with a reflective air. Then he drew himself up; and said a little haughtily:

"You've certainly found the way to make me stay, M. Guerchard."

"Yes, yes; stay, stay," said M. Gournay-Martin hastily. "It's an excellent idea, excellent. You're the very man to help M. Guerchard, Duke. You're an intrepid explorer, used to danger and resourceful, absolutely fearless."

"Do you really mean to say you're not going home to bed, Jacques?" said Germaine, disregarding her father's wish with her usual frankness.

"No; I'm going to stay with M. Guerchard," said the Duke slowly.

"Well, you will be fresh to go to the Princess's to-morrow night." said Germaine petulantly. "You didn't get any sleep at all last night, you couldn't have. You left Charmerace at eight o'clock; you were motoring all the night, and only got to Paris at six o'clock this morning."

"Motoring all night, from eight o'clock to six!" muttered Guerchard under his breath.

"Oh, that will be all right," said the Duke carelessly. "This interesting affair is to be over by midnight, isn't it?"

"Well, I warn you that, tired or fresh, you will have to come with me to the Princess's to-morrow night. All Paris will be there—all Paris, that is, who are in Paris."

"Oh, I shall be fresh enough," said the Duke.

They went out of the drawing-room and down the stairs, all four of them. There was an alert readiness about Guerchard, as if he were ready to spring. He kept within a foot of the Duke right to the front door. The detective in charge opened it; and they went down the steps to the taxi-cab which was awaiting them. The Duke kissed Germaine's fingers and handed her into the taxi-cab.

M. Gournay-Martin paused at the cab-door, and turned and said, with a pathetic air, "Am I never to sleep in my own house again?" He got into the cab and drove off.

The Duke turned and came up the steps, followed by Guerchard. In the hall he took his opera-hat and coat from the stand, and went upstairs. Half-way up the flight he paused and said:

"Where shall we wait for Lupin, M. Guerchard? In the drawing-room, or in M. Gournay-Martin's bedroom?"

"Oh, the drawing-room," said Guerchard. "I think it very unlikely that Lupin will look for the coronet in M. Gournay-Martin's bedroom. He would know very well that that is the last place to find it now."

The Duke went on into the drawing-room. At the door Guerchard stopped and said: "I will just go and post my men, your Grace."

"Very good," said the Duke; and he went into the drawing-room.

He sat down, lighted a cigarette, and yawned. Then he took out his watch and looked at it.

"Another twenty minutes," he said.

CHAPTER XIX THE DUKE GOES

When Guerchard joined the Duke in the drawing-room, he had lost his calm air and was looking more than a little nervous. He moved about the room uneasily, fingering the bric-a-brac, glancing at the Duke and looking quickly away from him again. Then he came to a standstill on the hearth-rug with his back to the fireplace.

"Do you think it's quite safe to stand there, at least with your back to the hearth? If Lupin dropped through that opening suddenly, he'd catch you from behind before you could wink twice," said the Duke, in a tone of remonstrance.

"There would always be your Grace to come to my rescue," said Guerchard; and there was an ambiguous note in his voice, while his piercing eyes now rested fixed on the Duke's face. They seemed never to leave it; they explored, and explored it.

"It's only a suggestion," said the Duke.

"This is rather nervous work, don't you know."

"Yes; and of course you're hardly fit for it," said Guerchard. "If I'd known about your break-down in your car last night, I should have hesitated about asking you—"

"A break-down?" interrupted the Duke.

"Yes, you left Charmerace at eight o'clock last night. And you only reached Paris at six this morning. You couldn't have had a very high-power car?" said Guerchard.

"I had a 100 h.-p. car," said the Duke.

"Then you must have had a devil of a break-down," said Guerchard.

"Yes, it was pretty bad, but I've known worse," said the Duke carelessly. "It lost me about three hours: oh, at least three hours. I'm not a first-class repairer, though I know as much about an engine as most motorists."

"And there was nobody there to help you repair it?" said Guerchard.

"No; M. Gournay-Martin could not let me have his chauffeur to drive me to Paris, because he was keeping him to help guard the chateau. And of course there was nobody on the road, because it was two o'clock in the morning."

"Yes, there was no one," said Guerchard slowly.

"Not a soul," said the Duke.

"It was unfortunate," said Guerchard; and there was a note of incredulity in his voice.

"My having to repair the car myself?" said the Duke.

"Yes, of course," said Guerchard, hesitating a little over the assent.

The Duke dropped the end of his cigarette into a tray, and took out his case. He held it out towards Guerchard, and said, "A cigarette? or perhaps you prefer your caporal?"

"Yes, I do, but all the same I'll have one," said Guerchard, coming quickly across the room. And he took a cigarette from the case, and looked at it.

"All the same, all this is very curious," he said in a new tone, a challenging, menacing, accusing tone.

"What?" said the Duke, looking at him curiously.

"Everything: your cigarettes ... the salvias ... the photograph that Bonavent found in Victoire's prayer-book ... that man in motoring dress ... and finally, your break-down," said Guerchard; and the accusation and the threat rang clearer.

The Duke rose from his chair quickly and said haughtily, in icy tones: "M. Guerchard, you've been drinking!"

He went to the chair on which he had set his overcoat and his hat, and picked them up. Guerchard sprang in front of him, barring his way, and cried in a shaky voice: "No; don't go! You mustn't go!"

"What do you mean?" said the Duke, and paused. "What DO you mean?"

Guerchard stepped back, and ran his hand over his forehead. He was very pale, and his forehead was clammy to his touch:

"No ... I beg your pardon ... I beg your pardon, your Grace ... I must be going mad," he stammered.

"It looks very like it," said the Duke coldly.

"What I mean to say is," said Guerchard in a halting, uncertain voice, "what I mean to say is: help me ... I want you to stay here, to help me against Lupin, you understand. Will you, your Grace?"

"Yes, certainly; of course I will, if you want me to," said the Duke, in a more gentle voice. "But you seem awfully upset, and you're upsetting me too. We shan't have a nerve between us soon, if you don't pull yourself together."

"Yes, yes, please excuse me," muttered Guerchard.

"Very good," said the Duke. "But what is it we're going to do?"

Guerchard hesitated. He pulled out his handkerchief, and mopped his forehead: "Well ... the coronet ... is it in this case?" he said in a shaky voice, and set the case on the table.

"Of course it is," said the Duke impatiently.

Guerchard opened the case, and the coronet sparkled and gleamed brightly in the electric light: "Yes, it is there; you see it?" said Guerchard.

"Yes, I see it; well?" said the Duke, looking at him in some bewilderment, so unlike himself did he seem.

"We're going to wait," said Guerchard.

"What for?" said the Duke.

"Lupin," said Guerchard.

"Lupin? And you actually do believe that, just as in a fairy tale, when that clock strikes twelve, Lupin will enter and take the coronet?"

"Yes, I do; I do," said Guerchard with stubborn conviction. And he snapped the case to.

"This is most exciting," said the Duke.

"You're sure it doesn't bore you?" said Guerchard huskily.

"Not a bit of it," said the Duke, with cheerful derision. "To make the acquaintance of this scoundrel who has fooled you for ten years is as charming a way of spending the evening as I can think of."

"You say that to me?" said Guerchard with a touch of temper.

"Yes," said the Duke, with a challenging smile. "To you."

He sat down in an easy chair by the table. Guerchard sat down in a chair on the other side of it, and set his elbows on it. They were silent.

435

Suddenly the Duke said, "Somebody's coming."

Guerchard started, and said: "No, I don't hear any one."

Then there came distinctly the sound of a footstep and a knock at the door.

"You've got keener ears than I," said Guerchard grudgingly. "In all this business you've shown the qualities of a very promising detective." He rose, went to the door, and unlocked it.

Bonavent came in: "I've brought you the handcuffs, sir," he said, holding them out. "Shall I stay with you?"

"No," said Guerchard. "You've two men at the back door, and two at the front, and a man in every room on the ground-floor?"

"Yes, and I've got three men on every other floor," said Bonavent, in a tone of satisfaction.

"And the house next door?" said Guerchard.

"There are a dozen men in it," said Bonavent. "No communication between the two houses is possible any longer."

Guerchard watched the Duke's face with intent eyes. Not a shadow flickered its careless serenity.

"If any one tries to enter the house, collar him. If need be, fire on him," said Guerchard firmly. "That is my order; go and tell the others."

"Very good, sir," said Bonavent; and he went out of the room.

"By Jove, we are in a regular fortress," said the Duke.

"It's even more of a fortress than you think, your Grace. I've four men on that landing," said Guerchard, nodding towards the door.

"Oh, have you?" said the Duke, with a sudden air of annoyance.

"You don't like that?" said Guerchard quickly.

"I should jolly well think not," said the Duke. "With these precautions, Lupin will never be able to get into this room at all."

436

"He'll find it a pretty hard job," said Guerchard, smiling. "Unless he falls from the ceiling, or unless—"

"Unless you're Arsene Lupin," interrupted the Duke.

"In that case, you'd be another, your Grace," said Guerchard.

They both laughed. The Duke rose, yawned, picked up his coat and hat, and said, "Ah, well, I'm off to bed."

"What?" said Guerchard.

"Well," said the Duke, yawning again, "I was staying to see Lupin. As there's no longer any chance of seeing him—"

"But there is ... there is ... so stay," cried Guerchard.

"Do you still cling to that notion?" said the Duke wearily.

"We SHALL see him," said Guerchard.

"Nonsense!" said the Duke.

Guerchard lowered his voice and said with an air of the deepest secrecy: "He's already here, your Grace."

"Lupin? Here?" cried the Duke.

"Yes; Lupin," said Guerchard.

"Where?" cried the astonished Duke.

"He is," said Guerchard.

"As one of your men?" said the Duke eagerly.

"I don't think so," said Guerchard, watching him closely.

"Well, but, well, but—if he's here we've got him.... He is going to turn up," said the Duke triumphantly; and he set down his hat on the table beside the coronet.

"I hope so," said Guerchard. "But will he dare to?"

"How do you mean?" said the Duke, with a puzzled air.

"Well, you have said yourself that this is a fortress. An hour ago, perhaps, Lupin was resolved to enter this room, but is he now?"

"I see what you mean," said the Duke, in a tone of disappointment.

"Yes; you see that now it needs the devil's own courage. He must risk everything to gain everything, and throw off the mask. Is Lupin going to throw himself into the wolf's jaws? I dare not think it. What do you think about it?"

Guerchard's husky voice had hardened to a rough harshness; there was a ring of acute anxiety in it, and under the anxiety a faint note of challenge, of a challenge that dare not make itself too distinct. His anxious, challenging eyes burned on the face of the Duke, as if they strove with all intensity to pierce a mask.

The Duke looked at him curiously, as if he were trying to divine what he would be at, but with a careless curiosity, as if it were a matter of indifference to him what the detective's object was; then he said carelessly: "Well, you ought to know better than I. You have known him for ten years ...." He paused, and added with just the faintest stress in his tone, "At least, by reputation."

The anxiety in the detective's face grew plainer, it almost gave him the air of being unnerved; and he said quickly, in a jerky voice: "Yes, and I know his way of acting too. During the last ten years I have learnt to unravel his intrigues—to understand and anticipate his manoeuvres.... Oh, his is a clever system! ... Instead of lying low, as you'd expect, he attacks his opponent ... openly.... He confuses him—at least, he tries to." He smiled a half-confident, a half-doubtful smile, "It is a mass of entangled, mysterious combinations. I've been caught in them myself again and again. You smile?"

"It interests me so," said the Duke, in a tone of apology.

"Oh, it interests me," said Guerchard, with a snarl. "But this time I see my way clearly. No more tricks—no more secret paths ... We're fighting in the light of day." He paused, and said in a clear, sneering voice, "Lupin has pluck, perhaps, but it's only thief's pluck."

"Oh, is it?" said the Duke sharply, and there was a sudden faint glitter in his eyes.

"Yes; rogues have very poor qualities," sneered Guerchard.

"One can't have everything," said the Duke quietly; but his languid air had fallen from him.

"Their ambushes, their attacks, their fine tactics aren't up to much," said Guerchard, smiling contemptuously.

"You go a trifle too far, I think," said the Duke, smiling with equal contempt.

They looked one another in the eyes with a long, lingering look. They had suddenly the air of fencers who have lost their tempers, and are twisting the buttons off their foils.

"Not a bit of it, your Grace," said Guerchard; and his voice lingered on the words "your Grace" with a contemptuous stress. "This famous Lupin is immensely overrated."

"However, he has done some things which aren't half bad," said the Duke, with his old charming smile.

He had the air of a duelist drawing his blade lovingly through his fingers before he falls to.

"Oh, has he?" said Guerchard scornfully.

"Yes; one must be fair. Last night's burglary, for instance: it is not unheard of, but it wasn't half bad. And that theft of the motorcars: it was a neat piece of work," said the Duke in a gentle, insolent voice, infinitely aggravating.

Guerchard snorted scornfully.

"And a robbery at the British Embassy, another at the Treasury, and a third at M. Lepine's—all in the same week—it wasn't half bad, don't you know?" said the Duke, in the same gentle, irritating voice.

"Oh, no, it wasn't. But—"

"And the time when he contrived to pass as Guerchard—the Great Guerchard—do you remember that?" the Duke interrupted. "Come, come—to give the devil his due—between ourselves—it wasn't half bad."

"No," snarled Guerchard. "But he has done better than that lately.... Why don't you speak of that?"

"Of what?" said the Duke.

"Of the time when he passed as the Duke of Charmerace," snapped Guerchard.

"What! Did he do that?" cried the Duke; and then he added slowly, "But, you know, I'm like you—I'm so easy to imitate."

"What would have been amusing, your Grace, would have been to get as far as actual marriage," said Guerchard more calmly.

"Oh, if he had wanted to," said the Duke; and he threw out his hands. "But you know—married life—for Lupin."

"A large fortune ... a pretty girl," said Guerchard, in a mocking tone.

"He must be in love with some one else," said the Duke.

"A thief, perhaps," sneered Guerchard.

"Like himself.... And then, if you wish to know what I think, he must have found his fiancee rather trying," said the Duke, with his charming smile.

"After all, it's pitiful—heartrending, you must admit it, that, on the very eve of his marriage, he was such a fool as to throw off the mask. And yet at bottom it's quite logical; it's Lupin coming out through Charmerace. He had to grab at the dowry at the risk of losing the girl," said Guerchard, in a reflective tone; but his eyes were intent on the face of the Duke.

"Perhaps that's what one should call a marriage of reason," said the Duke, with a faint smile.

"What a fall!" said Guerchard, in a taunting voice. "To be expected, eagerly, at the Princess's to-morrow evening, and to pass the evening in a police-station ... to have intended in a month's time, as the Duke of Charmerace, to mount the steps of the Madeleine with all pomp and to fall down the father-in-law's staircase this evening—this very evening"—his voice rose suddenly on a note of savage triumph—"with the handcuffs on! What? Is that a good enough revenge for Guerchard—for that poor old idiot, Guerchard? The rogues' Brummel in a convict's cap! The gentleman-burglar in a gaol! For Lupin it's only a trifling annoyance, but for a duke it's a disaster! Come, in your turn, be frank: don't you find that amusing?"

The Duke rose quietly, and said coldly, "Have you finished?"

"DO you?" cried Guerchard; and he rose and faced him.

"Oh, yes; I find it quite amusing," said the Duke lightly.

"And so do I," cried Guerchard.

"No; you're frightened," said the Duke calmly.

"Frightened!" cried Guerchard, with a savage laugh.

"Yes, you're frightened," said the Duke. "And don't think, policeman, that because I'm familiar with you, I throw off a mask. I don't wear one. I've none to throw off. I AM the Duke of Charmerace."

"You lie! You escaped from the Sante four years ago. You are Lupin! I recognize you now."

"Prove it," said the Duke scornfully.

"I will!" cried Guerchard.

"You won't. I AM the Duke of Charmerace."

Guerchard laughed wildly.

"Don't laugh. You know nothing— nothing, dear boy," said the Duke tauntingly.

"Dear boy?" cried Guerchard triumphantly, as if the word had been a confession.

"What do I risk?" said the Duke, with scathing contempt. "Can you arrest me? ... You can arrest Lupin ... but arrest the Duke of Charmerace, an honourable gentleman, member of the Jockey Club, and of the Union, residing at his house, 34 B, University Street ... arrest the Duke of Charmerace, the fiance of Mademoiselle Gournay-Martin?"

"Scoundrel!" cried Guerchard, pale with sudden, helpless fury.

"Well, do it," taunted the Duke. "Be an ass.... Make yourself the laughing-stock of Paris ... call your coppers in. Have you a proof—one single proof? Not one."

"Oh, I shall get them," howled Guerchard, beside himself.

"I think you may," said the Duke coolly. "And you might be able to arrest me next week ... the day after to-morrow perhaps ... perhaps never ... but not to-night, that's certain."

"Oh, if only somebody could hear you!" gasped Guerchard.

"Now, don't excite yourself," said the Duke. "That won't produce any proofs for you.... The fact is, M. Formery told you the truth when he said that, when it is a case of Lupin, you lose your head. Ah, that Formery—there is an intelligent man if you like."

"At all events, the coronet is safe ... to-night—"

"Wait, my good chap ... wait," said the Duke slowly; and then he snapped out: "Do you know what's behind that door?" and he flung out his hand towards the door of the inner drawing-room, with a mysterious, sinister air.

"What?" cried Guerchard; and he whipped round and faced the door, with his eyes starting out of his head.

"Get out, you funk!" said the Duke, with a great laugh.

"Hang you!" said Guerchard shrilly.

"I said that you were going to be absolutely pitiable," said the Duke, and he laughed again cruelly.

"Oh, go on talking, do!" cried Guerchard, mopping his forehead.

"Absolutely pitiable," said the Duke, with a cold, disquieting certainty. "As the hand of that clock moves nearer and nearer midnight, you will grow more and more terrified." He paused, and then shouted violently, "Attention!"

Guerchard jumped; and then he swore.

"Your nerves are on edge," said the Duke, laughing.

"Joker!" snarled Guerchard.

"Oh, you're as brave as the next man. But who can stand the anguish of the unknown thing which is bound to happen? ... I'm right. You feel it, you're sure of it. At the end of these few fixed minutes an inevitable, fated event must happen. Don't shrug your shoulders, man; you're green with fear."

The Duke was no longer a smiling, cynical dandy. There emanated from him an impression of vivid, terrible force. His voice had deepened. It thrilled with a consciousness of irresistible power; it was overwhelming, paralyzing. His eyes were terrible.

"My men are outside ... I'm armed," stammered Guerchard.

"Child! Bear in mind ... bear in mind that it is always when you have foreseen everything, arranged everything, made every combination ... bear in mind that it is always then that some accident dashes your whole structure to the ground," said the Duke, in the same deep, thrilling voice. "Remember that it is always at the very moment at which you are going to triumph that he beats you, that he only lets you reach the top of the ladder to throw you more easily to the ground."

"Confess, then, that you are Lupin," muttered Guerchard.

"I thought you were sure of it," said the Duke in a jeering tone.

Guerchard dragged the handcuffs out of his pocket, and said between his teeth, "I don't know what prevents me, my boy."

The Duke drew himself up, and said haughtily, "That's enough."

"What?" cried Guerchard.

"I say that that's enough," said the Duke sternly. "It's all very well for me to play at being familiar with you, but don't you call me 'my boy.'"

"Oh, you won't impose on me much longer," muttered Guerchard; and his bloodshot, haggard eyes scanned the Duke's face in an agony, an anguish of doubting impotence.

"If I'm Lupin, arrest me," said the Duke.

"I'll arrest you in three minutes from now, or the coronet will be untouched," cried Guerchard in a firmer tone.

"In three minutes from now the coronet will have been stolen; and you will not arrest me," said the Duke, in a tone of chilling certainty.

"But I will! I swear I will!" cried Guerchard.

"Don't swear any foolish oaths! ... THERE ARE ONLY TWO MINUTES LEFT," said the Duke; and he drew a revolver from his pocket.

"No, you don't!" cried Guerchard, drawing a revolver in his turn.

"What's the matter?" said the Duke, with an air of surprise. "You haven't forbidden me to shoot Lupin. I have my revolver ready, since he's going to come.... THERE'S ONLY A MINUTE LEFT."

"There are plenty of us," said Guerchard; and he went towards the door.

"Funk!" said the Duke scornfully.

Guerchard turned sharply. "Very well," he said, "I'll stick it out alone."

"How rash!" sneered the Duke.

Guerchard ground his teeth. He was panting; his bloodshot eyes rolled in their sockets; the beads of cold sweat stood out on his forehead. He came back towards the table on unsteady feet, trembling from head to foot in the last excitation of the nerves. He kept jerking his head to shake away the mist which kept dimming his eyes.

"At your slightest gesture, at your slightest movement, I'll fire," he said jerkily, and covered the Duke with his revolver.

"I call myself the Duke of Charmerace. You will be arrested to-morrow!" said the Duke, in a compelling, thrilling voice.

"I don't care a curse!" cried Guerchard.

"Only FIFTY SECONDS!" said the Duke.

"Yes, yes," muttered Guerchard huskily. And his eyes shot from the coronet to the Duke, from the Duke to the coronet.

"In fifty seconds the coronet will be stolen," said the Duke.

"No!" cried Guerchard furiously.

"Yes," said the Duke coldly.

"No! no! no!" cried Guerchard.

Their eyes turned to the clock.

To Guerchard the hands seemed to be standing still. He could have sworn at them for their slowness.

Then the first stroke rang out; and the eyes of the two men met like crossing blades. Twice the Duke made the slightest movement. Twice Guerchard started forward to meet it.

At the last stroke both their hands shot out. Guerchard's fell heavily on the case which held the coronet. The Duke's fell on the brim of his hat; and he picked it up.

Guerchard gasped and choked. Then he cried triumphantly:

"I HAVE it; now then, have I won? Have I been fooled this time? Has Lupin got the coronet?"

"It doesn't look like it. But are you quite sure?" said the Duke gaily.

"Sure?" cried Guerchard.

"It's only the weight of it," said the Duke, repressing a laugh. "Doesn't it strike you that it's just a trifle light?"

"What?" cried Guerchard.

"This is merely an imitation." said the Duke, with a gentle laugh.

"Hell and damnation!" howled Guerchard. "Bonavent! Dieusy!"

The door flew open, and half a dozen detectives rushed in.

Guerchard sank into a chair, stupefied, paralyzed; this blow, on the top of the strain of the struggle with the Duke, had broken him.

"Gentlemen," said the Duke sadly, "the coronet has been stolen."

They broke into cries of surprise and bewilderment, surrounding the gasping Guerchard with excited questions.

The Duke walked quietly out of the room.

Guerchard sobbed twice; his eyes opened, and in a dazed fashion wandered from face to face; he said faintly: "Where is he?"

"Where's who?" said Bonavent.

"The Duke—the Duke!" gasped Guerchard.

"Why, he's gone!" said Bonavent.

Guerchard staggered to his feet and cried hoarsely, frantically: "Stop him from leaving the house! Follow him! Arrest him! Catch him before he gets home!"

CHAPTER XX LUPIN COMES HOME

The cold light of the early September morning illumined but dimly the charming smoking-room of the Duke of Charmerace in his house at 34 B, University Street, though it stole in through two large windows. The smoking-room was on the first floor; and the Duke's bedroom opened into it. It was furnished in the most luxurious fashion, but with a taste which nowadays infrequently accompanies luxury. The chairs were of the most comfortable, but their lines were excellent; the couch against the wall, between the two windows, was the last word in the matter of comfort. The colour scheme, of a light greyish-blue, was almost too bright for a man's room; it would have better suited a boudoir. It suggested that the owner of the room enjoyed an uncommon lightness and cheerfulness of temperament. On the walls, with wide gaps between them so that they did not clash, hung three or four excellent pictures. Two ballet-girls by Degas, a group of shepherdesses and shepherds, in pink and blue and white beribboned silk, by Fragonard, a portrait of a woman by Bastien-Lepage, a charming Corot, and two Conder fans showed that the taste of their fortunate owner was at any rate eclectic. At the end of the room was, of all curious things, the opening into the well of a lift. The doors of it were open, though the lift itself was on some other floor. To the left of the opening stood a book-case, its shelves loaded with books of a kind rather suited to a cultivated, thoughtful man than to an idle dandy.

Beside the window, half-hidden, and peering through the side of the curtain into the street, stood M. Charolais. But it was hardly the M. Charolais who had paid M. Gournay-Martin that visit at the Chateau de Charmerace, and departed so firmly in the millionaire's favourite motor-car. This was a paler M. Charolais; he lacked altogether the rich, ruddy complexion of the millionaire's visitor. His nose, too, was thinner, and showed none of the ripe acquaintance with the vintages of the world which had been so plainly displayed on it during its owner's visit to the country. Again, hair and eyebrows were no longer black, but fair; and his hair was no longer curly and luxuriant, but thin and lank. His moustache had vanished, and along with it the dress of a well-to-do provincial man of business. He wore a livery of the Charmeraces, and at that early morning hour had not yet assumed the blue waistcoat which is an integral part of it. Indeed it would have required an acute and experienced observer to recognize in him the bogus purchaser of the Mercrac. Only his eyes, his close-set eyes, were unchanged.

Walking restlessly up and down the middle of the room, keeping out of sight of the windows, was Victoire. She wore a very anxious air, as did Charolais too. By the door stood Bernard Charolais; and his natural, boyish timidity, to judge from his frightened eyes, had assumed an acute phase.

"By the Lord, we're done!" cried Charolais, starting back from the window. "That was the front-door bell."

"No, it was only the hall clock," said Bernard.

"That's seven o'clock! Oh, where can he be?" said Victoire, wringing her hands. "The coup was fixed for midnight.... Where can he be?"

"They must be after him," said Charolais. "And he daren't come home." Gingerly he drew back the curtain and resumed his watch.

"I've sent down the lift to the bottom, in case he should come back by the secret entrance," said Victoire; and she went to the opening into the well of the lift and stood looking down it, listening with all her ears.

"Then why, in the devil's name, have you left the doors open?" cried Charolais irritably. "How do you expect the lift to come up if the doors are open?"

"I must be off my head!" cried Victoire.

She stepped to the side of the lift and pressed a button. The doors closed, and there was a grunting click of heavy machinery settling into a new position.

"Suppose we telephone to Justin at the Passy house?" said Victoire.

"What on earth's the good of that?" said Charolais impatiently. "Justin knows no more than we do. How can he know any more?"

"The best thing we can do is to get out," said Bernard, in a shaky voice.

"No, no; he will come. I haven't given up hope," Victoire protested. "He's sure to come; and he may need us."

"But, hang it all! Suppose the police come! Suppose they ransack his papers.... He hasn't told us what to do ... we are not ready for them.... What are we to do?" cried Charolais, in a tone of despair.

"Well, I'm worse off than you are; and I'm not making a fuss. If the police come they'll arrest me," said Victoire.

"Perhaps they've arrested him," said Bernard, in his shaky voice.

"Don't talk like that," said Victoire fretfully. "Isn't it bad enough to wait and wait, without your croaking like a scared crow?"

She started again her pacing up and down the room, twisting her hands, and now and again moistening her dry lips with the tip of her tongue.

Presently she said: "Are those two plain-clothes men still there watching?" And in her anxiety she came a step nearer the window.

"Keep away from the window!" snapped Charolais. "Do you want to be recognized, you great idiot?" Then he added, more quietly, "They're still there all right, curse them, in front of the cafe.... Hullo!"

"What is it, now?" cried Victoire, starting.

"A copper and a detective running," said Charolais. "They are running for all they're worth."

"Are they coming this way?" said Victoire; and she ran to the door and caught hold of the handle.

"No," said Charolais.

"Thank goodness!" said Victoire.

"They're running to the two men watching the house ... they're telling them something. Oh, hang it, they're all running down the street."

"This way? ... Are they coming this way?" cried Victoire faintly; and she pressed her hand to her side.

"They are!" cried Charolais. "They are!" And he dropped the curtain with an oath.

"And he isn't here! Suppose they come.... Suppose he comes to the front door! They'll catch him!" cried Victoire.

There came a startling peal at the front-door bell. They stood frozen to stone, their eyes fixed on one another, staring.

The bell had hardly stopped ringing, when there was a slow, whirring noise. The doors of the lift flew open, and the Duke stepped out of it. But what a changed figure from the admirably dressed dandy who had walked through the startled detectives and out of the house of M. Gournay-Martin at midnight! He was pale, exhausted, almost fainting. His eyes were dim in a livid face; his lips were grey. He was panting heavily. He was splashed with mud from head to foot: one sleeve of his coat was torn along half its length. The sole of his left-hand pump was half off; and his cut foot showed white and red through the torn sock.

"The master! The master!" cried Charolais in a tone of extravagant relief; and he danced round the room snapping his fingers.

"You're wounded?" cried Victoire.

"No," said Arsene Lupin.

The front-door bell rang out again, startling, threatening, terrifying.

The note of danger seemed to brace Lupin, to spur him to a last effort.

He pulled himself together, and said in a hoarse but steady voice: "Your waistcoat, Charolais.... Go and open the door ... not too quickly ... fumble the bolts.... Bernard, shut the book-case. Victoire, get out of sight, do you want to ruin us all? Be smart now, all of you. Be smart!"

He staggered past them into his bedroom, and slammed the door. Victoire and Charolais hurried out of the room, through the anteroom, on to the landing. Victoire ran upstairs, Charolais went slowly down. Bernard pressed the button. The doors of the lift shut and there was a slow whirring as it went down. He pressed another button, and the book-case slid slowly across and hid the opening into the lift-well. Bernard ran out of the room and up the stairs.

Charolais went to the front door and fumbled with the bolts. He bawled through the door to the visitors not to be in such a hurry at that hour in the morning; and they bawled furiously at him to be quick, and knocked and rang again and again. He was fully three minutes fumbling with the bolts, which were already drawn. At last he opened the door an inch or two, and looked out.

On the instant the door was dashed open, flinging him back against the wall; and Bonavent and Dieusy rushed past him, up the stairs, as hard as they could pelt. A brown-faced, nervous, active policeman followed them in and stopped to guard the door.

On the landing the detectives paused, and looked at one another, hesitating.

"Which way did he go?" said Bonavent. "We were on his very heels."

"I don't know; but we've jolly well stopped his getting into his own house; and that's the main thing," said Dieusy triumphantly.

"But are you sure it was him?" said Bonavent, stepping into the anteroom.

"I can swear to it," said Dieusy confidently; and he followed him.

Charolais came rushing up the stairs and caught them up as they were entering the smoking-room:

"Here! What's all this?" he cried. "You mustn't come in here! His Grace isn't awake yet."

"Awake? Awake? Your precious Duke has been galloping all night," cried Dieusy. "And he runs devilish well, too."

The door of the bedroom opened; and Lupin stood on the threshold in slippers and pyjamas.

"What's all this?" he snapped, with the irritation of a man whose sleep has been disturbed; and his tousled hair and eyes dim with exhaustion gave him every appearance of being still heavy with sleep.

The eyes and mouths of Bonavent and Dieusy opened wide; and they stared at him blankly, in utter bewilderment and wonder.

"Is it you who are making all this noise?" said Lupin, frowning at them. "Why, I know you two; you're in the service of M. Guerchard."

"Yes, your Grace," stammered Bonavent.

"Well, what are you doing here? What is it you want?" said Lupin.

"Oh, nothing, your Grace ... nothing ... there's been a mistake," stammered Bonavent.

"A mistake?" said Lupin haughtily. "I should think there had been a mistake. But I take it that this is Guerchard's doing. I'd better deal with him directly. You two can go." He turned to Charolais and added curtly, "Show them out."

Charolais opened the door, and the two detectives went out of the room with the slinking air of whipped dogs. They went down the stairs in silence, slowly, reflectively; and Charolais let them out of the front door.

As they went down the steps Dieusy said: "What a howler! Guerchard risks getting the sack for this!"

"I told you so," said Bonavent. "A duke's a duke."

When the door closed behind the two detectives Lupin tottered across the room, dropped on to the couch with a groan of exhaustion, and closed his eyes. Presently the door opened, Victoire came in, saw his attitude of exhaustion, and with a startled cry ran to his side.

"Oh, dearie! dearie!" she cried. "Pull yourself together! Oh, do try to pull yourself together." She caught his cold hands and began to rub them, murmuring words of endearment like a mother over a young child. Lupin did not open his eyes; Charolais came in.

"Some breakfast!" she cried. "Bring his breakfast ... he's faint ... he's had nothing to eat this morning. Can you eat some breakfast, dearie?"

"Yes," said Lupin faintly.

"Hurry up with it," said Victoire in urgent, imperative tones; and Charolais left the room at a run.

"Oh, what a life you lead!" said Victoire, or, to be exact, she wailed it. "Are you never going to change? You're as white as a sheet.... Can't you speak, dearie?"

She stooped and lifted his legs on to the couch.

He stretched himself, and, without opening his eyes, said in a faint voice: "Oh, Victoire, what a fright I've had!"

"You? You've been frightened?" cried Victoire, amazed.

"Yes. You needn't tell the others, though. But I've had a night of it ... I did play the fool so ... I must have been absolutely mad. Once I had changed the coronet under that fat old fool Gournay-Martin's very eyes ... once you and Sonia were out of their clutches, all I had to do was to slip away. Did I? Not a bit of it! I stayed there out of sheer bravado, just to score off Guerchard.... And then I ... I, who pride myself on being as cool as a cucumber ... I did the one thing I ought not to have done.... Instead of going quietly away as the Duke of Charmerace ... what do you think I did? ... I bolted ... I started running ... running like a thief.... In about two seconds I saw the slip I had made. It did not take me longer; but that was too long— Guerchard's men were on my track ... I was done for."

"Then Guerchard understood—he recognized you?" said Victoire anxiously.

"As soon as the first paralysis had passed, Guerchard dared to see clearly ... to see the truth," said Lupin. "And then it was a chase. There were ten—fifteen of them on my heels. Out of breath—grunting, furious—a mob—a regular mob. I had passed the night before in a motor-car. I was dead beat. In fact, I was done for before I started ... and they were gaining ground all the time."

"Why didn't you hide?" said Victoire.

"For a long while they were too close. They must have been within five feet of me. I was done. Then I was crossing one of the bridges. ... There was the Seine ... handy ... I made up my mind that, rather than be taken, I'd make an end of it ... I'd throw myself over."

"Good Lord!—and then?" cried Victoire.

"Then I had a revulsion of feeling. At any rate, I'd stick it out to the end. I gave myself another minute... one more minute—the last, and I had my revolver on me... but during that minute I put forth every ounce of strength I had left ... I began to gain ground ... I had them pretty well strung out already ... they were blown too. The knowledge gave me back my courage, and I plugged on ... my feet did not feel so much as though they were made of lead. I began to run away from them ... they were dropping behind ... all of them but one ... he stuck to me. We went at a jog-trot, a slow jog-trot, for I don't know how long. Then we dropped to a walk—we could run no more; and on we went. My strength and wind began to come back. I suppose my pursuer's did too; for exactly what I expected happened. He gave a yell and dashed for me. I was ready for him. I pretended to start running, and when he was within three yards of me I dropped on one knee, caught his ankles, and chucked him over my head. I don't know whether he broke his neck or not. I hope he did."

"Splendid!" said Victoire. "Splendid!"

"Well, there I was, outside Paris, and I'm hanged if I know where. I went on half a mile, and then I rested. Oh, how sleepy I was! I would have given a hundred thousand francs for an hour's sleep—cheerfully. But I dared not let myself sleep. I had to get back here unseen. There were you and Sonia."

"Sonia? Another woman?" cried Victoire. "Oh, it's then that I'm frightened ... when you get a woman mixed up in your game. Always, when you come to grief ... when you really get into danger, there's a woman in it."

"Oh, but she's charming!" protested Lupin.

"They always are," said Victoire drily. "But go on. Tell me how you got here."

"Well, I knew it was going to be a tough job, so I took a good rest—an hour, I should think. And then I started to walk back. I found that I had come a devil of a way—I must have gone at Marathon pace. I walked and walked, and at last I got into Paris, and found myself with still a couple of miles to go. It was all right now; I should soon find a cab. But the luck was dead against me. I heard a man come round the corner of a side-street into a long street I was walking down. He gave a yell, and came bucketing after me. It was that hound Dieusy. He had recognized my figure. Off I went; and the chase began again. I led him a dance, but I couldn't shake him off. All the while I was working my way towards home. Then, just at last, I spurted for all I was worth, got out of his sight, bolted round the corner of the street into the secret entrance, and here I am." He smiled weakly, and added, "Oh, my dear Victoire, what a profession it is!"

CHAPTER XXI THE CUTTING OF THE TELEPHONE WIRES

The door opened, and in came Charolais, bearing a tray.

"Here's your breakfast, master," he said.

"Don't call me master—that's how his men address Guerchard. It's a disgusting practice," said Lupin severely.

Victoire and Charolais were quick laying the table. Charolais kept up a running fire of questions as he did it; but Lupin did not trouble to answer them. He lay back, relaxed, drawing deep breaths. Already his lips had lost their greyness, and were pink; there was a suggestion of blood under the skin of his pale face. They soon had the table laid; and he walked to it on fairly steady feet. He sat down; Charolais whipped off a cover, and said:

"Anyhow, you've got out of the mess neatly. It was a jolly smart escape."

"Oh, yes. So far it's all right," said Lupin. "But there's going to be trouble presently—lots of it. I shall want all my wits. We all shall."

He fell upon his breakfast with the appetite but not the manners of a wolf. Charolais went out of the room. Victoire hovered about him, pouring out his coffee and putting sugar into it.

"By Jove, how good these eggs are!" he said. "I think that, of all the thousand ways of cooking eggs, en cocotte is the best."

"Heavens! how empty I was!" he said presently. "What a meal I'm making! It's really a very healthy life, this of mine, Victoire. I feel much better already."

"Oh, yes; it's all very well to talk," said Victoire, in a scolding tone; for since he was better, she felt, as a good woman should, that the time had come to put in a word out of season. "But, all the same, you're trying to kill yourself—that's what you're doing. Just because you're young you abuse your youth. It won't last for ever; and you'll be sorry you used it up before it's time. And this life of lies and thefts and of all kinds of improper things—I suppose it's going to begin all over again. It's no good your getting a lesson. It's just thrown away upon you."

"What I want next is a bath," said Lupin.

"It's all very well your pretending not to listen to me, when you know very well that I'm speaking for your good," she went on, raising her voice a little. "But I tell you that all this is going to end badly. To be a thief gives you no position in the world—no position at all—and when I think of what you made me do the night before last, I'm just horrified at myself."

"We'd better not talk about that—the mess you made of it! It was positively excruciating!" said Lupin.

"And what did you expect? I'm an honest woman, I am!" said Victoire sharply. "I wasn't brought up to do things like that, thank goodness! And to begin at my time of life!"

"It's true, and I often ask myself how you bring yourself to stick to me," said Lupin, in a reflective, quite impersonal tone. "Please pour me out another cup of coffee."

"That's what I'm always asking myself," said Victoire, pouring out the coffee. "I don't know—I give it up. I suppose it is because I'm fond of you."

"Yes, and I'm very fond of you, my dear Victoire," said Lupin, in a coaxing tone.

"And then, look you, there are things that there's no understanding. I often talked to your poor mother about them. Oh, your poor mother! Whatever would she have said to these goings-on?"

Lupin helped himself to another cutlet; his eyes twinkled and he said, "I'm not sure that she would have been very much surprised. I always told her that I was going to punish society for the way it had treated her. Do you think she would have been surprised?"

"Oh, nothing you did would have surprised her," said Victoire. "When you were quite a little boy you were always making us wonder. You gave yourself such airs, and you had such nice manners of your own—altogether different from the other boys. And you were already a bad boy, when you were only seven years old, full of all kinds of tricks; and already you had begun to steal."

"Oh, only sugar," protested Lupin.

"Yes, you began by stealing sugar," said Victoire, in the severe tones of a moralist. "And then it was jam, and then it was pennies. Oh, it was all very well at that age—a little thief is pretty enough. But now—when you're twenty-eight years old."

"Really, Victoire, you're absolutely depressing," said Lupin, yawning; and he helped himself to jam.

"I know very well that you're all right at heart," said Victoire. "Of course you only rob the rich, and you've always been kind to the poor.... Yes; there's no doubt about it: you have a good heart."

"I can't help it—what about it?" said Lupin, smiling.

"Well, you ought to have different ideas in your head. Why are you a burglar?"

"You ought to try it yourself, my dear Victoire," said Lupin gently; and he watched her with a humorous eye.

"Goodness, what a thing to say!" cried Victoire.

"I assure you, you ought," said Lupin, in a tone of thoughtful conviction. "I've tried everything. I've taken my degree in medicine and in law. I have been an actor, and a professor of Jiu-jitsu. I have even been a member of the detective force, like that wretched Guerchard. Oh, what a dirty world that is! Then I launched out into society. I have been a duke. Well, I give you my word that not one of these professions equals that of burglar—not even the profession of Duke. There is so much of the unexpected in it, Victoire—the splendid unexpected.... And then, it's full of variety, so terrible, so fascinating." His voice sank a little, and he added, "And what fun it is!"

"Fun!" cried Victoire.

"Yes ... these rich men, these swells in their luxury—when one relieves them of a bank-note, how they do howl! ... You should have seen that fat old Gournay-Martin when I relieved him of his treasures—what an agony! You almost heard the death-rattle in his throat. And then the coronet! In the derangement of their minds—and it was sheer derangement, mind you— already prepared at Charmerace, in the derangement of Guerchard, I had only to put out my hand and pluck the coronet. And the joy, the ineffable joy of enraging the police! To see Guerchard's furious eyes when I downed him.... And look round you!" He waved his hand round the luxurious room. "Duke of Charmerace! This trade leads to everything ... to everything on condition that one sticks to it ....I tell you, Victoire, that when one cannot be a great artist or a great soldier, the only thing to be is a great thief!"

"Oh, be quiet!" cried Victoire. "Don't talk like that. You're working yourself up; you're intoxicating yourself! And all that, it is not Catholic. Come, at your age, you ought to have one idea in your head which should drive out all these others, which should make you forget all these thefts.... Love ... that would change you, I'm sure of it. That would make another man of you. You ought to marry."

"Yes ... perhaps ... that would make another man of me. That's what I've been thinking. I believe you're right," said Lupin thoughtfully.

"Is that true? Have you really been thinking of it?" cried Victoire joyfully.

"Yes," said Lupin, smiling at her eagerness. "I have been thinking about it—seriously."

"No more messing about—no more intrigues. But a real woman ... a woman for life?" cried Victoire.

"Yes," said Lupin softly; and his eyes were shining in a very grave face.

"Is it serious—is it real love, dearie?" said Victoire. "What's she like?"

"She's beautiful," said Lupin.

"Oh, trust you for that. Is she a blonde or a brunette?"

"She's very fair and delicate—like a princess in a fairy tale," said Lupin softly.

"What is she? What does she do?" said Victoire.

"Well, since you ask me, she's a thief," said Lupin with a mischievous smile.

"Good Heavens!" cried Victoire.

"But she's a very charming thief," said Lupin; and he rose smiling.

He lighted a cigar, stretched himself and yawned: "She had ever so much more reason for stealing than ever I had," he said. "And she has always hated it like poison."

"Well, that's something," said Victoire; and her blank and fallen face brightened a little.

Lupin walked up and down the room, breathing out long luxurious puffs of smoke from his excellent cigar, and watching Victoire with a humorous eye. He walked across to his bookshelf, and scanned the titles of his books with an appreciative, almost affectionate smile.

"This is a very pleasant interlude," he said languidly. "But I don't suppose it's going to last very long. As soon as Guerchard recovers from the shock of learning that I spent a quiet night in my ducal bed as an honest duke should, he'll be getting to work with positively furious energy, confound him! I could do with a whole day's sleep—twenty-four solid hours of it."

"I'm sure you could, dearie," said Victoire sympathetically.

"The girl I'm going to marry is Sonia Kritchnoff," he said.

"Sonia? That dear child! But I love her already!" cried Victoire. "Sonia, but why did you say she was a thief? That was a silly thing to say."

"It's my extraordinary sense of humour," said Lupin.

The door opened and Charolais bustled in: "Shall I clear away the breakfast?" he said.

Lupin nodded; and then the telephone bell rang. He put his finger on his lips and went to it.

"Are you there?" he said. "Oh, it's you, Germaine.... Good morning.... Oh, yes, I had a good night—excellent, thank you.... You want to speak to me presently? ... You're waiting for me at the Ritz?"

"Don't go—don't go—it isn't safe," said Victoire, in a whisper.

"All right, I'll be with you in about half an hour, or perhaps three-quarters. I'm not dressed yet ... but I'm ever so much more impatient than you ... good-bye for the present." He put the receiver on the stand.

"It's a trap," said Charolais.

"Never mind, what if it is? Is it so very serious?" said Lupin. "There'll be nothing but traps now; and if I can find the time I shall certainly go and take a look at that one."

"And if she knows everything? If she's taking her revenge ... if she's getting you there to have you arrested?" said Victoire.

"Yes, M. Formery is probably at the Ritz with Gournay-Martin. They're probably all of them there, weighing the coronet," said Lupin, with a chuckle.

He hesitated a moment, reflecting; then he said, "How silly you are! If they wanted to arrest me, if they had the material proof which they haven't got, Guerchard would be here already!"

"Then why did they chase you last night?" said Charolais.

"The coronet," said Lupin. "Wasn't that reason enough? But, as it turned out, they didn't catch me: and when the detectives did come here, they disturbed me in my sleep. And that me was ever so much more me than the man they followed. And then the proofs ... they must have proofs. There aren't any—or rather, what there are, I've got!" He pointed to a small safe let into the wall. "In that safe are the coronet, and, above all, the death certificate of the Duke of Charmerace ... everything that Guerchard must have to induce M. Formery to proceed. But still, there is a risk—I think I'd better have those things handy in case I have to bolt."

He went into his bedroom and came back with the key of the safe and a kit-bag. He opened the safe and took out the coronet, the real coronet of the Princesse de Lamballe, and along with it a pocket-book with a few papers in it. He set the pocket-book on the table, ready to put in his coat-pocket when he should have dressed, and dropped the coronet into the kit-bag.

"I'm glad I have that death certificate; it makes it much safer," he said. "If ever they do nab me, I don't wish that rascal Guerchard to accuse me of having murdered the Duke. It might prejudice me badly. I've not murdered anybody yet."

"That comes of having a good heart," said Victoire proudly.

"Not even the Duke of Charmerace," said Charolais sadly. "And it would have been so easy when he was ill—just one little draught. And he was in such a perfect place—so out of the way—no doctors."

"You do have such disgusting ideas, Charolais," said Lupin, in a tone of severe reproof.

"Instead of which you went and saved his life," said Charolais, in a tone of deep discontent; and he went on clearing the table.

"I did, I did: I had grown quite fond of him," said Lupin, with a meditative air. "For one thing, he was so very like one. I'm not sure that he wasn't even better-looking."

"No; he was just like you," said Victoire, with decision. "Any one would have said you were twin brothers."

"It gave me quite a shock the first time I saw his portrait," said Lupin. "You remember, Charolais? It was three years ago, the day, or rather the night, of the first Gournay-Martin burglary at Charmerace. Do you remember?"

"Do I remember?" said Charolais. "It was I who pointed out the likeness to you. I said, 'He's the very spit of you, master.' And you said, 'There's something to be done with that, Charolais.' And then off you started for the ice and snow and found the Duke, and became his friend; and then he went and died, not that you'd have helped him to, if he hadn't."

"Poor Charmerace. He was indeed grand seigneur. With him a great name was about to be extinguished.... Did I hesitate? ... No.... I continued it," said Lupin.

He paused and looked at the clock. "A quarter to eight," he said, hesitating. "Shall I telephone to Sonia, or shall I not? Oh, there's no hurry; let the poor child sleep on. She must be worn out after that night-journey and that cursed Guerchard's persecution yesterday. I'll dress first, and telephone to her afterwards. I'd better be getting dressed, by the way. The work I've got to do can't be done in pyjamas. I wish it could; for bed's the place for me. My wits aren't quite as clear as I could wish them to deal with an awkward business like this. Well, I must do the best I can with them."

He yawned and went to the bedroom, leaving the pocket-book on the table.

"Bring my shaving-water, Charolais, and shave me," he said, pausing; and he went into the bedroom and shut the door.

"Ah," said Victoire sadly, "what a pity it is! A few years ago he would have gone to the Crusades; and to-day he steals coronets. What a pity it is!"

459

"I think myself that the best thing we can do is to pack up our belongings," said Charolais. "And I don't think we've much time to do it either. This particular game is at an end, you may take it from me."

"I hope to goodness it is: I want to get back to the country," said Victoire.

He took up the tray; and they went out of the room. On the landing they separated; she went upstairs and he went down. Presently he came up with the shaving water and shaved his master; for in the house in University Street he discharged the double functions of valet and butler. He had just finished his task when there came a ring at the front-door bell.

"You'd better go and see who it is," said Lupin.

"Bernard is answering the door," said Charolais. "But perhaps I'd better keep an eye on it myself; one never knows."

He put away the razor leisurely, and went. On the stairs he found Bonavent, mounting— Bonavent, disguised in the livery and fierce moustache of a porter from the Ritz.

"Why didn't you come to the servants' entrance?" said Charolais, with the truculent air of the servant of a duke and a stickler for his master's dignity.

"I didn't know that there was one," said Bonavent humbly. "Well, you ought to have known that there was; and it's plain enough to see. What is it you want?" said Charolais.

"I've brought a letter—a letter for the Duke of Charmerace," said Bonavent.

"Give it to me," said Charolais. "I'll take it to him."

"No, no; I'm to give it into the hands of the Duke himself and to nobody else," said Bonavent.

"Well, in that case, you'll have to wait till he's finished dressing," said Charolais.

They went on up to the stairs into the ante-room. Bonavent was walking straight into the smoking-room.

"Here! where are you going to? Wait here," said Charolais quickly. "Take a chair; sit down."

Bonavent sat down with a very stolid air, and Charolais looked at him doubtfully, in two minds whether to leave him there alone or not. Before he had decided there came a thundering knock on the front door, not only loud but protracted. Charolais looked round with a scared air; and then ran out of the room and down the stairs.

460

On the instant Bonavent was on his feet, and very far from stolid. He opened the door of the smoking-room very gently and peered in. It was empty. He slipped noiselessly across the room, a pair of clippers ready in his hand, and cut the wires of the telephone. His quick eye glanced round the room and fell on the pocket-book on the table. He snatched it up, and slipped it into the breast of his tunic. He had scarcely done it—one button of his tunic was still to fasten—when the bedroom door opened, and Lupin came out:

"What do you want?" he said sharply; and his keen eyes scanned the porter with a disquieting penetration.

"I've brought a letter to the Duke of Charmerace, to be given into his own hands," said Bonavent, in a disguised voice.

"Give it to me," said Lupin, holding out his hand.

"But the Duke?" said Bonavent, hesitating.

"I am the Duke," said Lupin.

Bonavent gave him the letter, and turned to go.

"Don't go," said Lupin quietly. "Wait, there may be an answer."

There was a faint glitter in his eyes; but Bonavent missed it.

Charolais came into the room, and said, in a grumbling tone, "A run-away knock. I wish I could catch the brats; I'd warm them. They wouldn't go fetching me away from my work again, in a hurry, I can tell you."

Lupin opened the letter, and read it. As he read it, at first he frowned; then he smiled; and then he laughed joyously. It ran:

"SIR,"

"M. Guerchard has told me everything. With regard to Sonia I have judged you: a man who loves a thief can be nothing but a rogue. I have two pieces of news to announce to you: the death of the Duke of Charmerace, who died three years ago, and my intention of becoming engaged to his cousin and heir, M. de Relzieres, who will assume the title and the arms."

461

"For Mademoiselle Gournay-Martin,"
"Her maid, IRMA."

"She does write in shocking bad taste," said Lupin, shaking his head sadly. "Charolais, sit down and write a letter for me."

"Me?" said Charolais.

"Yes; you. It seems to be the fashion in financial circles; and I am bound to follow it when a lady sets it. Write me a letter," said Lupin.

Charolais went to the writing-table reluctantly, sat down, set a sheet of paper on the blotter, took a pen in his hand, and sighed painfully.

"Ready?" said Lupin; and he dictated:

"MADEMOISELLE,"

"I have a very robust constitution, and my indisposition will very soon be over. I shall have the honour of sending, this afternoon, my humble wedding present to the future Madame de Relzieres."

"For Jacques de Bartut, Marquis de Relzieres, Prince of Virieux, Duke of Charmerace."

"His butler, ARSENE."

"Shall I write Arsene?" said Charolais, in a horrified tone.

"Why not?" said Lupin. "It's your charming name, isn't it?"

Bonavent pricked up his ears, and looked at Charolais with a new interest.

Charolais shrugged his shoulders, finished the letter, blotted it, put it in an envelope, addressed it, and handed it to Lupin.

"Take this to Mademoiselle Gournay-Martin," said Lupin, handing it to Bonavent.

Bonavent took the letter, turned, and had taken one step towards the door when Lupin sprang. His arm went round the detective's neck; he jerked him backwards off his feet, scragging him.

"Stir, and I'll break your neck!" he cried in a terrible voice; and then he said quietly to Charolais, "Just take my pocket-book out of this fellow's tunic."

Charolais, with deft fingers, ripped open the detective's tunic, and took out the pocket-book.

"This is what they call Jiu-jitsu, old chap! You'll be able to teach it to your colleagues," said Lupin. He loosed his grip on Bonavent, and knocked him straight with a thump in the back, and sent him flying across the room. Then he took the pocket-book from Charolais and made sure that its contents were untouched.

"Tell your master from me that if he wants to bring me down he'd better fire the gun himself," said Lupin contemptuously. "Show the gentleman out, Charolais."

Bonavent staggered to the door, paused, and turned on Lupin a face livid with fury.

"He will be here himself in ten minutes," he said.

"Many thanks for the information," said Lupin quietly.

CHAPTER XXII THE BARGAIN

Charolais conducted the detective down the stairs and let him out of the front door, cursing and threatening vengeance as he went. Charolais took no notice of his words—he was the well-trained servant. He came back upstairs, and on the landing called to Victoire and Bernard. They came hurrying down; and the three of them went into the smoking-room.

"Now we know where we are," said Lupin, with cheerful briskness. "Guerchard will be here in ten minutes with a warrant for my arrest. All of you clear out."

"It won't be so precious easy. The house is watched," said Charolais. "And I'll bet it's watched back and front."

"Well, slip out by the secret entrance. They haven't found that yet," said Lupin. "And meet me at the house at Passy."

Charolais and Bernard wanted no more telling; they ran to the book-case and pressed the buttons; the book-case slid aside; the doors opened and disclosed the lift. They stepped into it. Victoire had followed them. She paused and said: "And you? Are you coming?"

"In an instant I shall slip out the same way," he said.

"I'll wait for him. You go on," said Victoire; and the lift went down.

Lupin went to the telephone, rang the bell, and put the receiver to his ear.

"You've no time to waste telephoning. They may be here at any moment!" cried Victoire anxiously.

"I must. If I don't telephone Sonia will come here. She will run right into Guerchard's arms. Why the devil don't they answer? They must be deaf!" And he rang the bell again.

"Let's go to her! Let's get out of here!" cried Victoire, more anxiously. "There really isn't any time to waste."

"Go to her? But I don't know where she is. I lost my head last night," cried Lupin, suddenly anxious himself. "Are you there?" he shouted into the telephone. "She's at a little hotel near the Star. ... Are you there? ... But there are twenty hotels near the Star.... Are you there? ... Oh, I did lose my head last night. ... Are you there? Oh, hang this telephone! Here I'm fighting with a piece of furniture. And every second is important!"

He picked up the machine, shook it, saw that the wires were cut, and cried furiously: "Ha! They've played the telephone trick on me! That's Guerchard.... The swine!"

"And now you can come along!" cried Victoire.

"But that's just what I can't do!" he cried.

"But there's nothing more for you to do here, since you can no longer telephone," said Victoire, bewildered.

Lupin caught her arm and shook her, staring into her face with panic-stricken eyes. "But don't you understand that, since I haven't telephoned, she'll come here?" he cried hoarsely. "Five-and-twenty minutes past eight! At half-past eight she will start—start to come here."

His face had suddenly grown haggard; this new fear had brought back all the exhaustion of the night; his eyes were panic-stricken.

"But what about you?" said Victoire, wringing her hands.

"What about her?" said Lupin; and his voice thrilled with anguished dread.

"But you'll gain nothing by destroying both of you—nothing at all."

"I prefer it," said Lupin slowly, with a suddenly stubborn air.

"But they're coming to take you," cried Victoire, gripping his arm.

"Take me?" cried Lupin, freeing himself quietly from her grip. And he stood frowning, plunged in deep thought, weighing the chances, the risks, seeking a plan, saving devices.

He crossed the room to the writing-table, opened a drawer, and took out a cardboard box about eight inches square and set it on the table.

"They shall never take me alive," he said gloomily.

"Oh, hush, hush!" said Victoire. "I know very well that you're capable of anything ... and they too—they'll destroy you. No, look you, you must go. They won't do anything to her—a child like that—so frail. She'll get off quite easily. You're coming, aren't you?"

"No, I'm not," said Lupin stubbornly.

"Oh, well, if you won't," said Victoire; and with an air of resolution she went to the side of the lift-well, and pressed the buttons. The doors closed; the book-case slid across. She sat down and folded her arms.

"What, you're not going to stop here?" cried Lupin.

465

"Make me stir if you can. I'm as fond of you as she is—you know I am," said Victoire, and her face set stonily obstinate.

Lupin begged her to go; ordered her to go; he seized her by the shoulder, shook her, and abused her like a pickpocket. She would not stir. He abandoned the effort, sat down, and knitted his brow again in profound and painful thought, working out his plan. Now and again his eyes flashed, once or twice they twinkled. Victoire watched his face with just the faintest hope on her own.

It was past five-and-twenty minutes to nine when the front-door bell rang. They gazed at one another with an unspoken question on their lips. The eyes of Victoire were scared, but in the eyes of Lupin the light of battle was gathering.

"It's her," said Victoire under her breath.

"No," said Lupin. "It's Guerchard."

He sprang to his feet with shining eyes. His lips were curved in a fighting smile. "The game isn't lost yet," he said in a tense, quiet voice. "I'm going to play it to the end. I've a card or two left still—good cards. I'm still the Duke of Charmerace." He turned to her.

"Now listen to me," he said. "Go down and open the door for him."

"What, you want me to?" said Victoire, in a shaky voice.

"Yes, I do. Listen to me carefully. When you have opened the door, slip out of it and watch the house. Don't go too far from it. Look out for Sonia. You'll see her coming. Stop her from entering, Victoire—stop her from entering." He spoke coolly, but his voice shook on the last words.

"But if Guerchard arrests me?" said Victoire.

"He won't. When he comes in, stand behind the door. He will be too eager to get to me to stop for you. Besides, for him you don't count in the game. Once you're out of the house, I'll hold him here for—for half an hour. That will leave a margin. Sonia will hurry here. She should be here in twelve minutes. Get her away to the house at Passy. If I don't come keep her there; she's to live with you. But I shall come."

As he spoke he was pushing her towards the door.

The bell rang again. They were at the top of the stairs.

"And suppose he does arrest me?" said Victoire breathlessly.

"Never mind, you must go all the same," said Lupin. "Don't give up hope—trust to me. Go—go—for my sake."

"I'm going, dearie," said Victoire; and she went down the stairs steadily, with a brave air.

He watched her half-way down the flight; then he muttered:

"If only she gets to Sonia in time."

He turned, went into the smoking-room, and shut the door. He sat quietly down in an easy chair, lighted a cigarette, and took up a paper. He heard the noise of the traffic in the street grow louder as the front door was opened. There was a pause; then he heard the door bang. There was the sound of a hasty footstep on the stairs; the door flew open, and Guerchard bounced into the room.

He stopped short in front of the door at the sight of Lupin, quietly reading, smoking at his ease. He had expected to find the bird flown. He stood still, hesitating, shuffling his feet— all his doubts had returned; and Lupin smiled at him over the lowered paper.

Guerchard pulled himself together by a violent effort, and said jerkily, "Good-morning, Lupin."

"Good-morning, M. Guerchard," said Lupin, with an ambiguous smile and all the air of the Duke of Charmerace.

"You were expecting me? ... I hope I haven't kept you waiting," said Guerchard, with an air of bravado.

"No, thank you: the time has passed quite quickly. I have so much to do in the morning always," said Lupin. "I hope you had a good night after that unfortunate business of the coronet. That was a disaster; and so unexpected too."

Guerchard came a few steps into the room, still hesitating:

"You've a very charming house here," he said, with a sneer.

"It's central," said Lupin carelessly. "You must please excuse me, if I cannot receive you as I should like; but all my servants have bolted. Those confounded detectives of yours have frightened them away."

"You needn't bother about that. I shall catch them," said Guerchard.

"If you do, I'm sure I wish you joy of them. Do, please, keep your hat on," said Lupin with ironic politeness.

Guerchard came slowly to the middle of the room, raising his hand to his hat, letting it fall again without taking it off. He sat down slowly facing him, and they gazed at one another with the wary eyes of duellists crossing swords at the beginning of a duel.

"Did you get M. Formery to sign a little warrant?" said Lupin, in a caressing tone full of quiet mockery.

"I did," said Guerchard through his teeth.

"And have you got it on you?" said Lupin.

"I have," said Guerchard.

"Against Lupin, or against the Duke of Charmerace?" said Lupin.

"Against Lupin, called Charmerace," said Guerchard.

"Well, that ought to cover me pretty well. Why don't you arrest me? What are you waiting for?" said Lupin. His face was entirely serene, his eyes were careless, his tone indifferent.

"I'm not waiting for anything," said Guerchard thickly; "but it gives me such pleasure that I wish to enjoy this minute to the utmost, Lupin," said Guerchard; and his eyes gloated on him.

"Lupin, himself," said Lupin, smiling.

"I hardly dare believe it," said Guerchard.

"You're quite right not to," said Lupin.

"Yes, I hardly dare believe it. You alive, here at my mercy?"

"Oh, dear no, not yet," said Lupin.

"Yes," said Guerchard, in a decisive tone. "And ever so much more than you think." He bent forwards towards him, with his hands on his knees, and said, "Do you know where Sonia Kritchnoff is at this moment?"

"What?" said Lupin sharply.

"I ask if you know where Sonia Kritchnoff is?" said Guerchard slowly, lingering over the words.

"Do you?" said Lupin.

"I do," said Guerchard triumphantly.

"Where is she?" said Lupin, in a tone of utter incredulity.

"In a small hotel near the Star. The hotel has a telephone; and you can make sure," said Guerchard.

"Indeed? That's very interesting. What's the number of it?" said Lupin, in a mocking tone.

"555 Central: would you like to telephone to her?" said Guerchard; and he smiled triumphantly at the disabled instrument.

Lupin shock his head with a careless smile, and said, "Why should I telephone to her? What are you driving at?"

"Nothing ... that's all," said Guerchard. And he leant back in his chair with an ugly smile on his face.

"Evidently nothing. For, after all, what has that child got to do with you? You're not interested in her, plainly. She's not big enough game for you. It's me you are hunting ... it's me you hate ... it's me you want. I've played you tricks enough for that, you old scoundrel. So you're going to leave that child in peace? ... You're not going to revenge yourself on her? ... It's all very well for you to be a policeman; it's all very well for you to hate me; but there are things one does not do." There was a ring of menace and appeal in the deep, ringing tones of his voice. "You're not going to do that, Guerchard.... You will not do it.... Me—yes—anything you like. But her—her you must not touch." He gazed at the detective with fierce, appealing eyes.

"That depends on you," said Guerchard curtly.

"On me?" cried Lupin, in genuine surprise.

"Yes, I've a little bargain to propose to you," said Guerchard.

"Have you?" said Lupin; and his watchful face was serene again, his smile almost pleasant.

"Yes," said Guerchard. And he paused, hesitating.

"Well, what is it you want?" said Lupin. "Out with it! Don't be shy about it."

"I offer you—"

"You offer me?" cried Lupin. "Then it isn't true. You're fooling me."

"Reassure yourself," said Guerchard coldly. "To you personally I offer nothing."

"Then you are sincere," said Lupin. "And putting me out of the question?"

"I offer you liberty."

"Who for? For my concierge?" said Lupin.

"Don't play the fool. You care only for a single person in the world. I hold you through her: Sonia Kritchnoff."

Lupin burst into a ringing, irrepressible laugh:

"Why, you're trying to blackmail me, you old sweep!" he cried.

"If you like to call it so," said Guerchard coldly.

Lupin rose and walked backwards and forwards across the room, frowning, calculating, glancing keenly at Guerchard, weighing him. Twice he looked at the clock.

He stopped and said coldly: "So be it. For the moment you're the stronger.... That won't last.... But you offer me this child's liberty."

"That's my offer," said Guerchard; and his eyes brightened at the prospect of success.

"Her complete liberty? ... on your word of honour?" said Lupin; and he had something of the air of a cat playing with a mouse.

"On my word of honour," said Guerchard.

"Can you do it?" said Lupin, with a sudden air of doubt; and he looked sharply from Guerchard to the clock.

"I undertake to do it," said Guerchard confidently.

"But how?" said Lupin, looking at him with an expression of the gravest doubt.

"Oh, I'll put the thefts on your shoulders. That will let her out all right," said Guerchard.

"I've certainly good broad shoulders," said Lupin, with a bitter smile. He walked slowly up and down with an air that grew more and more depressed: it was almost the air of a beaten man. Then he stopped and faced Guerchard, and said: "And what is it you want in exchange?"

"Everything," said Guerchard, with the air of a man who is winning. "You must give me back the pictures, tapestry, Renaissance cabinets, the coronet, and all the information about the death of the Duke of Charmerace. Did you kill him?"

"If ever I commit suicide, you'll know all about it, my good Guerchard. You'll be there. You may even join me," said Lupin grimly; he resumed his pacing up and down the room.

"Done for, yes; I shall be done for," he said presently. "The fact is, you want my skin."

"Yes, I want your skin," said Guerchard, in a low, savage, vindictive tone.

"My skin," said Lupin thoughtfully.

"Are you going to do it? Think of that girl," said Guerchard, in a fresh access of uneasy anxiety.

Lupin laughed: "I can give you a glass of port," he said, "but I'm afraid that's all I can do for you."

"I'll throw Victoire in," said Guerchard.

"What?" cried Lupin. "You've arrested Victoire?" There was a ring of utter dismay, almost despair, in his tone.

"Yes; and I'll throw her in. She shall go scot-free. I won't bother with her," said Guerchard eagerly.

The front-door bell rang.

"Wait, wait. Let me think," said Lupin hoarsely; and he strove to adjust his jostling ideas, to meet with a fresh plan this fresh disaster.

He stood listening with all his ears. There were footsteps on the stairs, and the door opened. Dieusy stood on the threshold.

"Who is it?" said Guerchard.

"I accept—I accept everything," cried Lupin in a frantic tone.

"It's a tradesman; am I to detain him?" said Dieusy. "You told me to let you know who came and take instructions."

"A tradesman? Then I refuse!" cried Lupin, in an ecstasy of relief.

"No, you needn't keep him," said Guerchard, to Dieusy.

Dieusy went out and shut the door.

"You refuse?" said Guerchard.

"I refuse," said Lupin.

"I'm going to gaol that girl," said Guerchard savagely; and he took a step towards the door.

"Not for long," said Lupin quietly. "You have no proof."

"She'll furnish the proof all right herself—plenty of proofs," said Guerchard brutally. "What chance has a silly child like that got, when we really start questioning her? A delicate creature like that will crumple up before the end of the third day's cross-examination."

"You swine!" said Lupin. "You know well enough that I can do it—on my head—with a feeble child like that; and you know your Code; five years is the minimum," said Guerchard, in a tone of relentless brutality, watching him carefully, sticking to his hope.

"By Jove, I could wring your neck!" said Lupin, trembling with fury. By a violent effort he controlled himself, and said thoughtfully, "After all, if I give up everything to you, I shall be free to take it back one of these days."

"Oh, no doubt, when you come out of prison," said Guerchard ironically; and he laughed a grim, jeering laugh.

"I've got to go to prison first," said Lupin quietly.

"Pardon me—if you accept, I mean to arrest you," said Guerchard.

"Manifestly you'll arrest me if you can," said Lupin.

"Do you accept?" said Guerchard. And again his voice quivered with anxiety.

"Well," said Lupin. And he paused as if finally weighing the matter.

"Well?" said Guerchard, and his voice shook.

"Well—no!" said Lupin; and he laughed a mocking laugh.

"You won't?" said Guerchard between his teeth.

"No; you wish to catch me. This is just a ruse," said Lupin, in quiet, measured tones. "At bottom you don't care a hang about Sonia, Mademoiselle Kritchnoff. You will not arrest her. And then, if you did you have no proofs. There ARE no proofs. As for the pendant, you'd have to prove it. You can't prove it. You can't prove that it was in her possession one moment. Where is the pendant?" He paused, and then went on in the same quiet tone: "No, Guerchard; after having kept out of your clutches for the last ten years, I'm not going to be caught to save this child, who is not even in danger. She has a very useful friend in the Duke of Charmerace. I refuse."

Guerchard stared at him, scowling, biting his lips, seeking a fresh point of attack. For the moment he knew himself baffled, but he still clung tenaciously to the struggle in which victory would be so precious.

The front-door bell rang again.

"There's a lot of ringing at your bell this morning," said Guerchard, under his breath; and hope sprang afresh in him.

Again they stood silent, waiting.

Dieusy opened the door, put in his head, and said, "It's Mademoiselle Kritchnoff."

"Collar her! ... Here's the warrant! ... collar her!" shouted Guerchard, with savage, triumphant joy.

"Never! You shan't touch her! By Heaven, you shan't touch her!" cried Lupin frantically; and he sprang like a tiger at Guerchard.

Guerchard jumped to the other side of the table. "Will you accept, then?" he cried.

Lupin gripped the edge of the table with both hands, and stood panting, grinding his teeth, pale with fury. He stood silent and motionless for perhaps half a minute, gazing at Guerchard with burning, murderous eyes. Then he nodded his head.

"Let Mademoiselle Kritchnoff wait," said Guerchard, with a sigh of deep relief. Dieusy went out of the room.

"Now let us settle exactly how we stand," said Lupin, in a clear, incisive voice. "The bargain is this: If I give you the pictures, the tapestry, the cabinets, the coronet, and the death-certificate of the Duke of Charmerace, you give me your word of honour that Mademoiselle Kritchnoff shall not be touched."

"That's it!" said Guerchard eagerly.

"Once I deliver these things to you, Mademoiselle Kritchnoff passes out of the game."

"Yes," said Guerchard.

"Whatever happens afterwards. If I get back anything—if I escape—she goes scot-free," said Lupin.

"Yes," said Guerchard; and his eyes were shining.

"On your word of honour?" said Lupin.

"On my word of honour," said Guerchard.

"Very well," said Lupin, in a quiet, businesslike voice. "To begin with, here in this pocket-book you'll find all the documents relating to the death of the Duke of Charmerace. In it you will also find the receipt of the Plantin furniture repository at Batignolles for the objects of art which I collected at Gournay-Martin's. I sent them to Batignolles because, in my letters asking the owners of valuables to forward them to me, I always make Batignolles the place to which they are to be sent; therefore I knew that you would never look there. They are all in cases; for, while you were making those valuable inquiries yesterday, my men were putting them into cases. You'll not find the receipt in the name of either the Duke of Charmerace or my own. It is in the name of a respected proprietor of Batignolles, a M. Pierre Servien. But he has lately left that charming suburb, and I do not think he will return to it."

Guerchard almost snatched the pocket-book out of his hand. He verified the documents in it with greedy eyes; and then he put them back in it, and stuffed it into the breast-pocket of his coat.

"And where's the coronet?" he said, in an excited voice.

"You're nearly standing on it," said Lupin.

"It's in that kit-bag at your feet, on the top of the change of clothes in it."

Guerchard snatched up the kit-bag, opened it, and took out the coronet.

"I'm afraid I haven't the case," said Lupin, in a tone of regret. "If you remember, I left it at Gournay-Martin's—in your charge."

Guerchard examined the coronet carefully. He looked at the stones in it; he weighed it in his right hand, and he weighed it in his left.

"Are you sure it's the real one?" said Lupin, in a tone of acute but affected anxiety. "Do not—oh, do not let us have any more of these painful mistakes about it. They are so wearing."

"Yes—yes—this is the real one," said Guerchard, with another deep sigh of relief.

"Well, have you done bleeding me?" said Lupin contemptuously.

"Your arms," said Guerchard quickly.

"They weren't in the bond," said Lupin. "But here you are." And he threw his revolver on the table.

Guerchard picked it up and put it into his pocket. He looked at Lupin as if he could not believe his eyes, gloating over him. Then he said in a deep, triumphant tone:

"And now for the handcuffs!"

CHAPTER XXIII THE END OF THE DUEL

"The handcuffs?" said Lupin; and his face fell. Then it cleared; and he added lightly, "After all, there's nothing like being careful; and, by Jove, with me you need to be. I might get away yet. What luck it is for you that I'm so soft, so little of a Charmerace, so human! Truly, I can't be much of a man of the world, to be in love like this!"

"Come, come, hold out your hands!" said Guerchard, jingling the handcuffs impatiently.

"I should like to see that child for the last time," said Lupin gently.

"All right," said Guerchard.

"Arsene Lupin—and nabbed by you! If you aren't in luck! Here you are!" said Lupin bitterly; and he held out his wrists.

Guerchard snapped the handcuffs on them with a grunt of satisfaction.

Lupin gazed down at them with a bitter face, and said: "Oh, you are in luck! You're not married by any chance?"

"Yes, yes; I am," said Guerchard hastily; and he went quickly to the door and opened it: "Dieusy!" he called. "Dieusy! Mademoiselle Kritchnoff is at liberty. Tell her so, and bring her in here."

Lupin started back, flushed and scowling; he cried: "With these things on my hands! ... No! ... I can't see her!"

Guerchard stood still, looking at him. Lupin's scowl slowly softened, and he said, half to himself, "But I should have liked to see her ... very much ... for if she goes like that ... I shall not know when or where—" He stopped short, raised his eyes, and said in a decided tone: "Ah, well, yes; I should like to see her."

"If you've quite made up your mind," said Guerchard impatiently, and he went into the anteroom.

Lupin stood very still, frowning thoughtfully. He heard footsteps on the stairs, and then the voice of Guerchard in the anteroom, saying, in a jeering tone, "You're free, mademoiselle; and you can thank the Duke for it. You owe your liberty to him."

"Free! And I owe it to him?" cried the voice of Sonia, ringing and golden with extravagant joy.

"Yes, mademoiselle," said Guerchard. "You owe it to him."

She came through the open door, flushed deliciously and smiling, her eyes brimming with tears of joy. Lupin had never seen her look half so adorable.

"Is it to you I owe it? Then I shall owe everything to you. Oh, thank you—thank you!" she cried, holding out her hands to him.

Lupin half turned away from her to hide his handcuffs.

She misunderstood the movement. Her face fell suddenly like that of a child rebuked: "Oh, I was wrong. I was wrong to come here!" she cried quickly, in changed, dolorous tones. "I thought yesterday ... I made a mistake ... pardon me. I'm going. I'm going."

Lupin was looking at her over his shoulder, standing sideways to hide the handcuffs. He said sadly. "Sonia—"

"No, no, I understand! It was impossible!" she cried quickly, cutting him short. "And yet if you only knew—if you knew how I have changed—with what a changed spirit I came here.... Ah, I swear that now I hate all my past. I loathe it. I swear that now the mere presence of a thief would overwhelm me with disgust."

"Hush!" said Lupin, flushing deeply, and wincing. "Hush!"

"But, after all, you're right," she said, in a gentler voice. "One can't wipe out what one has done. If I were to give back everything I've taken—if I were to spend years in remorse and repentance, it would be no use. In your eyes I should always be Sonia Kritchnoff, the thief!" The great tears welled slowly out of her eyes and rolled down her cheeks; she let them stream unheeded.

"Sonia!" cried Lupin, protesting.

But she would not hear him. She broke out with fresh vehemence, a feverish passion: "And yet, if I'd been a thief, like so many others... but you know why I stole. I'm not trying to defend myself, but, after all, I did it to keep honest; and when I loved you it was not the heart of a thief that thrilled, it was the heart of a poor girl who loved...that's all...who loved."

"You don't know what you're doing! You're torturing me! Be quiet!" cried Lupin hoarsely, beside himself.

"Never mind...I'm going...we shall never see one another any more," she sobbed. "But will you...will you shake hands just for the last time?"

"No!" cried Lupin.

"You won't?" wailed Sonia in a heartrending tone.

"I can't!" cried Lupin.

"You ought not to be like this.... Last night ... if you were going to let me go like this ... last night ... it was wrong," she wailed, and turned to go.

"Wait, Sonia! Wait!" cried Lupin hoarsely. "A moment ago you said something.... You said that the mere presence of a thief would overwhelm you with disgust. Is that true?"

"Yes, I swear it is," cried Sonia.

Guerchard appeared in the doorway.

"And if I were not the man you believe?" said Lupin sombrely.

"What?" said Sonia; and a faint bewilderment mingled with her grief. "If I were not the Duke of Charmerace?"

"Not the Duke?"

"If I were not an honest man?" said Lupin.

"You?" cried Sonia.

"If I were a thief? If I were—"

"Arsene Lupin," jeered Guerchard from the door.

Lupin turned and held out his manacled wrists for her to see.

"Arsene Lupin! ... it's ... it's true!" stammered Sonia. "But then, but then ... it must be for my sake that you've given yourself up. And it's for me you're going to prison. Oh, Heavens! How happy I am!"

She sprang to him, threw her arms round his neck, and pressed her lips to his.

"And that's what women call repenting," said Guerchard.

He shrugged his shoulders, went out on to the landing, and called to the policeman in the hall to bid the driver of the prison-van, which was waiting, bring it up to the door.

"Oh, this is incredible!" cried Lupin, in a trembling voice; and he kissed Sonia's lips and eyes and hair. "To think that you love me enough to go on loving me in spite of this—in spite of the fact that I'm Arsene Lupin. Oh, after this, I'll become an honest man! It's the least I can do. I'll retire."

"You will?" cried Sonia.

"Upon my soul, I will!" cried Lupin; and he kissed her again and again.

Guerchard came back into the room. He looked at them with a cynical grin, and said, "Time's up."

"Oh, Guerchard, after so many others, I owe you the best minute of my life!" cried Lupin.

Bonavent, still in his porter's livery, came hurrying through the anteroom: "Master," he cried, "I've found it."

"Found what?" said Guerchard.

"The secret entrance. It opens into that little side street. We haven't got the door open yet; but we soon shall."

"The last link in the chain," said Guerchard, with warm satisfaction. "Come along, Lupin."

"But he's going to take you away! We're going to be separated!" cried Sonia, in a sudden anguish of realization.

"It's all the same to me now!" cried Lupin, in the voice of a conqueror.

"Yes, but not to me!" cried Sonia, wringing her hands.

"Now you must keep calm and go. I'm not going to prison," said Lupin, in a low voice. "Wait in the hall, if you can. Stop and talk to Victoire; condole with her. If they turn you out of the house, wait close to the front door."

"Come, mademoiselle," said Guerchard. "You must go."

"Go, Sonia, go—good-bye—good-bye," said Lupin; and he kissed her.

She went quietly out of the room, her handkerchief to her eyes. Guerchard held open the door for her, and kept it open, with his hand still on the handle; he said to Lupin: "Come along."

Lupin yawned, stretched himself, and said coolly, "My dear Guerchard, what I want after the last two nights is rest—rest." He walked quickly across the room and stretched himself comfortably at full length on the couch.

"Come, get up," said Guerchard roughly. "The prison-van is waiting for you. That ought to fetch you out of your dream."

"Really, you do say the most unlucky things," said Lupin gaily.

He had resumed his flippant, light-hearted air; his voice rang as lightly and pleasantly as if he had not a care in the world.

"Do you mean that you refuse to come?" cried Guerchard in a rough, threatening tone.

"Oh, no," said Lupin quickly: and he rose.

"Then come along!" said Guerchard.

"No," said Lupin, "after all, it's too early." Once more he stretched himself out on the couch, and added languidly, "I'm lunching at the English Embassy."

"Now, you be careful!" cried Guerchard angrily. "Our parts are changed. If you're snatching at a last straw, it's waste of time. All your tricks—I know them. Understand, you rogue, I know them."

"You know them?" said Lupin with a smile, rising. "It's fatality!"

He stood before Guerchard, twisting his hands and wrists curiously. Half a dozen swift movements; and he held out his handcuffs in one hand and threw them on the floor.

"Did you know that trick, Guerchard? One of these days I shall teach you to invite me to lunch," he said slowly, in a mocking tone; and he gazed at the detective with menacing, dangerous eyes.

"Come, come, we've had enough of this!" cried Guerchard, in mingled astonishment, anger, and alarm. "Bonavent! Boursin! Dieusy! Here! Help! Help!" he shouted.

"Now listen, Guerchard, and understand that I'm not humbugging," said Lupin quickly, in clear, compelling tones. "If Sonia, just now, had had one word, one gesture of contempt for me, I'd have given way—yielded ... half-yielded, at any rate; for, rather than fall into your triumphant clutches, I'd have blown my brains out. I've now to choose between happiness, life with Sonia, or prison. Well, I've chosen. I will live happy with her, or else, my dear Guerchard, I'll die with you. Now let your men come—I'm ready for them."

Guerchard ran to the door and shouted again.

"I think the fat's in the fire now," said Lupin, laughing.

He sprang to the table, opened the cardboard box, whipped off the top layer of cotton-wool, and took out a shining bomb.

He sprang to the wall, pressed the button, the bookshelf glided slowly to one side, the lift rose to the level of the floor and its doors flew open just as the detectives rushed in.

"Collar him!" yelled Guerchard.

"Stand back—hands up!" cried Lupin, in a terrible voice, raising his right hand high above his head. "You know what this is ... a bomb.... Come and collar me now, you swine! ... Hands up, you ... Guerchard!"

"You silly funks!" roared Guerchard. "Do you think he'd dare?"

"Come and see!" cried Lupin.

"I will!" cried Guerchard. And he took a step forward.

As one man his detectives threw themselves upon him. Three of them gripped his arms, a fourth gripped him round the waist; and they all shouted at him together, not to be a madman! ... To look at Lupin's eyes! ... That Lupin was off his head!

"What miserable swine you are!" cried Lupin scornfully. He sprang forward, caught up the kit-bag in his left hand, and tossed it behind him into the lift. "You dirty crew!" he cried again. "Oh, why isn't there a photographer here? And now, Guerchard, you thief, give me back my pocket-book."

"Never!" screamed Guerchard, struggling with his men, purple with fury.

"Oh, Lord, master! Do be careful! Don't rile him!" cried Bonavent in an agony.

"What? Do you want me to smash up the whole lot?" roared Lupin, in a furious, terrible voice. "Do I look as if I were bluffing, you fools?"

"Let him have his way, master!" cried Dieusy.

"Yes, yes!" cried Bonavent.

"Let him have his way!" cried another.

"Give him his pocket-book!" cried a third.

"Never!" howled Guerchard.

"It's in his pocket—his breast-pocket! Be smart!" roared Lupin.

"Come, come, it's got to be given to him," cried Bonavent. "Hold the master tight!" And he thrust his hand into the breast of Guerchard's coat, and tore out the pocket-book.

"Throw it on the table!" cried Lupin.

Bonavent threw it on to the table; and it slid along it right to Lupin. He caught it in his left hand, and slipped it into his pocket. "Good!" he said. And then he yelled ferociously, "Look out for the bomb!" and made a feint of throwing it.

The whole group fell back with an odd, unanimous, sighing groan.

Lupin sprang into the lift, and the doors closed over the opening. There was a great sigh of relief from the frightened detectives, and then the chunking of machinery as the lift sank.

Their grip on Guerchard loosened. He shook himself free, and shouted, "After him! You've got to make up for this! Down into the cellars, some of you! Others go to the secret entrance! Others to the servants' entrance! Get into the street! Be smart! Dieusy, take the lift with me!"

The others ran out of the room and down the stairs, but with no great heartiness, since their minds were still quite full of the bomb, and Lupin still had it with him. Guerchard and Dieusy dashed at the doors of the opening of the lift-well, pulling and wrenching at them. Suddenly there was a click; and they heard the grunting of the machinery. There was a little bump and a jerk, the doors flew open of themselves; and there was the lift, empty, ready for them. They jumped into it; Guerchard's quick eye caught the button, and he pressed it. The doors banged to, and, to his horror, the lift shot upwards about eight feet, and stuck between the floors.

As the lift stuck, a second compartment, exactly like the one Guerchard and Dieusy were in, came up to the level of the floor of the smoking-room; the doors opened, and there was Lupin. But again how changed! The clothes of the Duke of Charmerace littered the floor; the kit-bag was open; and he was wearing the very clothes of Chief-Inspector Guerchard, his seedy top-hat, his cloak. He wore also Guerchard's sparse, lank, black hair, his little, bristling, black moustache. His figure, hidden by the cloak, seemed to have shrunk to the size of Guerchard's.

He sat before a mirror in the wall of the lift, a make-up box on the seat beside him. He darkened his eyebrows, and put a line or two about his eyes. That done he looked at himself earnestly for two or three minutes; and, as he looked, a truly marvellous transformation took place: the features of Arsene Lupin, of the Duke of Charmerace, decomposed, actually decomposed, into the features of Jean Guerchard. He looked at himself and laughed, the gentle, husky laugh of Guerchard.

He rose, transferred the pocket-book to the coat he was wearing, picked up the bomb, came out into the smoking-room, and listened. A muffled roaring thumping came from the well of the lift. It almost sounded as if, in their exasperation, Guerchard and Dieusy were engaged in a struggle to the death. Smiling pleasantly, he stole to the window and looked out. His eyes brightened at the sight of the motor-car, Guerchard's car, waiting just before the front door and in charge of a policeman. He stole to the head of the stairs, and looked down into the hall. Victoire was sitting huddled together on a chair; Sonia stood beside her, talking to her in a low voice; and, keeping guard on Victoire, stood a brown-faced, active, nervous policeman, all alertness, briskness, keenness.

"Hi! officer! come up here! Be smart," cried Lupin over the bannisters, in the husky, gentle voice of Chief-Inspector Guerchard.

The policeman looked up, recognized the great detective, and came bounding zealously up the stairs.

Lupin led the way through the anteroom into the sitting-room. Then he said sharply: "You have your revolver?"

"Yes," said the young policeman. And he drew it with a flourish.

"Put it away! Put it away at once!" said Lupin very smartly. "You're not to use it. You're not to use it on any account! You understand?"

"Yes," said the policeman firmly; and with a slightly bewildered air he put the revolver away.

"Here! Stand here!" cried Lupin, raising his voice. And he caught the policeman's arm, and hustled him roughly to the front of the doors of the lift-well. "Do you see these doors? Do you see them?" he snapped.

"Yes, yes," said the policeman, glaring at them.

"They're the doors of a lift," said Lupin. "In that lift are Dieusy and Lupin. You know Dieusy?"

"Yes, yes," said the policeman.

"There are only Dieusy and Lupin in the lift. They are struggling together. You can hear them," shouted Lupin in the policeman's ear. "Lupin is disguised. You understand—Dieusy and a disguised man are in the lift. The disguised man is Lupin. Directly the lift descends and the doors open, throw yourself on him! Hold him! Shout for assistance!" He almost bellowed the last words into the policeman's ear.

"Yes, yes," said the policeman. And he braced himself before the doors of the lift-well, gazing at them with harried eyes, as if he expected them to bite him.

"Be brave! Be ready to die in the discharge of your duty!" bellowed Lupin; and he walked out of the room, shut the door, and turned the key.

The policeman stood listening to the noise of the struggle in the lift, himself strung up to fighting point; he was panting. Lupin's instructions were whirling and dancing in his head.

Lupin went quietly down the stairs. Victoire and Sonia saw him coming. Victoire rose; and as he came to the bottom of the stairs Sonia stepped forward and said in an anxious, pleading voice:

"Oh, M. Guerchard, where is he?"

"He's here," said Lupin, in his natural voice.

Sonia sprang to him with outstretched arms.

"It's you! It IS you!" she cried.

"Just look how like him I am!" said Lupin, laughing triumphantly. "But do I look quite ruffian enough?"

"Oh, NO! You couldn't!" cried Sonia.

"Isn't he a wonder?" said Victoire.

"This time the Duke of Charmerace is dead, for good and all," said Lupin.

"No; it's Lupin that's dead," said Sonia softly.

"Lupin?" he said, surprised.

"Yes," said Sonia firmly.

"It would be a terrible loss, you know—a loss for France," said Lupin gravely.

"Never mind," said Sonia.

"Oh, I must be in love with you!" said Lupin, in a wondering tone; and he put his arm round her and kissed her violently.

"And you won't steal any more?" said Sonia, holding him back with both hands on his shoulders, looking into his eyes.

"I shouldn't dream of such a thing," said Lupin. "You are here. Guerchard is in the lift. What more could I possibly desire?" His voice softened and grew infinitely caressing as he went on: "Yet when you are at my side I shall always have the soul of a lover and the soul of a thief. I long to steal your kisses, your thoughts, the whole of your heart. Ah, Sonia, if you want me to steal nothing else, you have only to stay by my side."

Their lips met in a long kiss.

Sonia drew herself out of his arms and cried, "But we're wasting time! We must make haste! We must fly!"

"Fly?" said Lupin sharply. "No, thank you; never again. I did flying enough last night to last me a lifetime. For the rest of my life I'm going to crawl—crawl like a snail. But come along, you two, I must take you to the police-station."

He opened the front door, and they came out on the steps. The policeman in charge of the car saluted.

Lupin paused and said softly: "Hark! I hear the sound of wedding bells."

They went down the steps.

Even as they were getting into the car some chance blow of Guerchard or Dieusy struck a hidden spring and released the lift. It sank to the level of Lupin's smoking-room and stopped. The doors flew open, Dieusy and Guerchard sprang out of it; and on the instant the brown-faced, nervous policeman sprang actively on Guerchard and pinned him. Taken by surprise, Guerchard yelled loudly, "You stupid idiot!" somehow entangled his legs in those of his captor, and they rolled on the floor. Dieusy surveyed them for a moment with blank astonishment. Then, with swift intelligence, grasped the fact that the policeman was Lupin in disguise. He sprang upon them, tore them asunder, fell heavily on the policeman, and pinned him to the floor with a strangling hand on his throat.

Guerchard dashed to the door, tried it, and found it locked, dashed for the window, threw it open, and thrust out his head. Forty yards down the street a motor-car was rolling smoothly away—rolling to a honeymoon.

"Oh, hang it!" he screamed. "He's doing a bunk in my motor-car!"

THE CONFESSIONS OF ARSÈNE LUPIN

I. TWO HUNDRED THOUSAND FRANCS REWARD!

"Lupin," I said, "tell me something about yourself."

"Why, what would you have me tell you? Everybody knows my life!" replied Lupin, who lay drowsing on the sofa in my study.

"Nobody knows it!" I protested. "People know from your letters in the newspapers that you were mixed up in this case, that you started that case. But the part which you played in it all, the plain facts of the story, the upshot of the mystery: these are things of which they know nothing."

"Pooh! A heap of uninteresting twaddle!"

"What! Your present of fifty thousand francs to Nicolas Dugrival's wife! Do you call that uninteresting? And what about the way in which you solved the puzzle of the three pictures?"

Lupin laughed:

"Yes, that was a queer puzzle, certainly. I can suggest a title for you if you like: what do you say to *The Sign of the Shadow*?"

"And your successes in society and with the fair sex?" I continued. "The dashing Arsène's love-affairs!... And the clue to your good actions? Those chapters in your life to which you have so often alluded under the names of *The Wedding-ring*, *Shadowed by Death*, and so on!... Why delay these confidences and confessions, my dear Lupin?... Come, do what I ask you!..."

It was at the time when Lupin, though already famous, had not yet fought his biggest battles; the time that preceded the great adventures of *The Hollow Needle* and *813*. He had not yet dreamt of annexing the accumulated treasures of the French Royal House nor of changing the map of Europe under the Kaiser's nose: he contented himself with milder surprises and humbler profits, making his daily effort, doing evil from day to day and doing a little good as well, naturally and for the love of the thing, like a whimsical and compassionate Don Quixote.

He was silent; and I insisted:

"Lupin, I wish you would!"

To my astonishment, he replied:

"Take a sheet of paper, old fellow, and a pencil."

I obeyed with alacrity, delighted at the thought that he at last meant to dictate to me some of those pages which he knows how to clothe with such vigour and fancy, pages which I, unfortunately, am obliged to spoil with tedious explanations and boring developments.

"Are you ready?" he asked.

"Quite."

"Write down, 20, 1, 11, 5, 14, 15."

"What?"

"Write it down, I tell you."

He was now sitting up, with his eyes turned to the open window and his fingers rolling a Turkish cigarette. He continued:

"Write down, 21, 14, 14, 5...."

He stopped. Then he went on:

"3, 5, 19, 19 ..."

And, after a pause:

"5, 18, 25 ..."

Was he mad? I looked at him hard and, presently, I saw that his eyes were no longer listless, as they had been a little before, but keen and attentive and that they seemed to be watching, somewhere, in space, a sight that apparently captivated them.

Meanwhile, he dictated, with intervals between each number:

"18, 9, 19, 11, 19 ..."

There was hardly anything to be seen through the window but a patch of blue sky on the right and the front of the building opposite, an old private house, whose shutters were closed as usual. There was nothing particular about all this, no detail that struck me as new among those which I had had before my eyes for years....

"1, 2...."

And suddenly I understood ... or rather I thought I understood, for how could I admit that Lupin, a man so essentially level-headed under his mask of frivolity, could waste his time upon such childish nonsense? What he was counting was the intermittent flashes of a ray of sunlight playing on the dingy front of the opposite house, at the height of the second floor!

"15, 22 ..." said Lupin.

The flash disappeared for a few seconds and then struck the house again, successively, at regular intervals, and disappeared once more.

I had instinctively counted the flashes and I said, aloud:

"5...."

"Caught the idea? I congratulate you!" he replied, sarcastically.

He went to the window and leant out, as though to discover the exact direction followed by the ray of light. Then he came and lay on the sofa again, saying:

"It's your turn now. Count away!"

The fellow seemed so positive that I did as he told me. Besides, I could not help confessing that there was something rather curious about the ordered frequency of those gleams on the front of the house opposite, those appearances and disappearances, turn and turn about, like so many flash signals.

They obviously came from a house on our side of the street, for the sun was entering my windows slantwise. It was as though some one were alternately opening and shutting a casement, or, more likely, amusing himself by making sunlight flashes with a pocket-mirror.

"It's a child having a game!" I cried, after a moment or two, feeling a little irritated by the trivial occupation that had been thrust upon me.

"Never mind, go on!"

And I counted away.... And I put down rows of figures.... And the sun continued to play in front of me, with mathematical precision.

"Well?" said Lupin, after a longer pause than usual.

"Why, it seems finished.... There has been nothing for some minutes...."

We waited and, as no more light flashed through space, I said, jestingly:

"My idea is that we have been wasting our time. A few figures on paper: a poor result!"

Lupin, without stirring from his sofa, rejoined:

"Oblige me, old chap, by putting in the place of each of those numbers the corresponding letter of the alphabet. Count A as 1, B as 2 and so on. Do you follow me?"

"But it's idiotic!"

"Absolutely idiotic, but we do such a lot of idiotic things in this life.... One more or less, you know!..."

I sat down to this silly work and wrote out the first letters:

"*Take no....*"

I broke off in surprise:

"Words!" I exclaimed. "Two English words meaning...."

"Go on, old chap."

And I went on and the next letters formed two more words, which I separated as they appeared. And, to my great amazement, a complete English sentence lay before my eyes.

"Done?" asked Lupin, after a time.

"Done!... By the way, there are mistakes in the spelling...."

"Never mind those and read it out, please.... Read slowly."

Thereupon I read out the following unfinished communication, which I will set down as it appeared on the paper in front of me:

"*Take no unnecessery risks. Above all, avoid atacks, approach ennemy with great prudance and....*"

I began to laugh:

"And there you are! *Fiat lux!* We're simply dazed with light! But, after all, Lupin, confess that this advice, dribbled out by a kitchen-maid, doesn't help you much!"

Lupin rose, without breaking his contemptuous silence, and took the sheet of paper.

I remembered soon after that, at this moment, I happened to look at the clock. It was eighteen minutes past five.

Lupin was standing with the paper in his hand; and I was able at my ease to watch, on his youthful features, that extraordinary mobility of expression which baffles all observers and constitutes his great strength and his chief safeguard. By what signs can one hope to identify a face which changes at pleasure, even without the help of make-up, and whose every transient expression seems to be the final, definite expression?... By what signs? There was one which I knew well, an invariable sign: Two little crossed wrinkles that marked his forehead whenever he made a powerful effort of concentration. And I saw it at that moment, saw the tiny tell-tale cross, plainly and deeply scored.

He put down the sheet of paper and muttered:

"Child's play!"

The clock struck half-past five.

"What!" I cried. "Have you succeeded?... In twelve minutes?..."

He took a few steps up and down the room, lit a cigarette and said:

"You might ring up Baron Repstein, if you don't mind, and tell him I shall be with him at ten o'clock this evening."

"Baron Repstein?" I asked. "The husband of the famous baroness?"

"Yes."

"Are you serious?"

"Quite serious."

Feeling absolutely at a loss, but incapable of resisting him, I opened the telephone-directory and unhooked the receiver. But, at that moment, Lupin stopped me with a peremptory gesture and said, with his eyes on the paper, which he had taken up again:

"No, don't say anything.... It's no use letting him know.... There's something more urgent ... a queer thing that puzzles me.... Why on earth wasn't the last sentence finished? Why is the sentence...."

He snatched up his hat and stick:

"Let's be off. If I'm not mistaken, this is a business that requires immediate solution; and I don't believe I *am* mistaken."

He put his arm through mine, as we went down the stairs, and said:

"I know what everybody knows. Baron Repstein, the company-promoter and racing-man, whose colt Etna won the Derby and the Grand Prix this year, has been victimized by his wife. The wife, who was well known for her fair hair, her dress and her extravagance, ran away a fortnight ago, taking with her a sum of three million francs, stolen from her husband, and quite a collection of diamonds, pearls and jewellery which the Princesse de Berny had placed in her hands and which she was supposed to buy. For two weeks the police have been pursuing the baroness across France and the continent: an easy job, as she scatters gold and jewels wherever she goes. They think they have her every moment. Two days ago, our champion detective, the egregious Ganimard, arrested a visitor at a big hotel in Belgium, a woman against whom the most positive evidence seemed to be heaped up. On enquiry, the lady turned out to be a notorious chorus-girl called Nelly Darbal. As for the baroness, she has vanished. The baron, on his side, has offered a reward of two hundred thousand francs to whosoever finds his wife. The money is in the hands of a solicitor. Moreover, he has sold his racing-stud, his house on the Boulevard Haussmann and his country-seat of Roquencourt in one lump, so that he may indemnify the Princesse de Berny for her loss."

"And the proceeds of the sale," I added, "are to be paid over at once. The papers say that the princess will have her money to-morrow. Only, frankly, I fail to see the connection between this story, which you have told very well, and the puzzling sentence...."

Lupin did not condescend to reply.

We had been walking down the street in which I live and had passed some four or five houses, when he stepped off the pavement and began to examine a block of flats, not of the latest construction, which looked as if it contained a large number of tenants:

"According to my calculations," he said, "this is where the signals came from, probably from that open window."

"On the third floor?"

"Yes."

He went to the portress and asked her:

"Does one of your tenants happen to be acquainted with Baron Repstein?"

"Why, of course!" replied the woman. "We have M. Lavernoux here, such a nice gentleman; he is the baron's secretary and agent. I look after his flat."

"And can we see him?"

"See him?... The poor gentleman is very ill."

"Ill?"

"He's been ill a fortnight ... ever since the trouble with the baroness.... He came home the next day with a temperature and took to his bed."

"But he gets up, surely?"

"Ah, that I can't say!"

"How do you mean, you can't say?"

"No, his doctor won't let any one into his room. He took my key from me."

"Who did?"

"The doctor. He comes and sees to his wants, two or three times a day. He left the house only twenty minutes ago ... an old gentleman with a grey beard and spectacles.... Walks quite bent.... But where are you going sir?"

"I'm going up, show me the way," said Lupin, with his foot on the stairs. "It's the third floor, isn't it, on the left?"

"But I mustn't!" moaned the portress, running after him. "Besides, I haven't the key ... the doctor...."

They climbed the three flights, one behind the other. On the landing, Lupin took a tool from his pocket and, disregarding the woman's protests, inserted it in the lock. The door yielded almost immediately. We went in.

At the back of a small dark room we saw a streak of light filtering through a door that had been left ajar. Lupin ran across the room and, on reaching the threshold, gave a cry:

"Too late! Oh, hang it all!"

The portress fell on her knees, as though fainting.

I entered the bedroom, in my turn, and saw a man lying half-dressed on the carpet, with his legs drawn up under him, his arms contorted and his face quite white, an emaciated, fleshless face, with the eyes still staring in terror and the mouth twisted into a hideous grin.

"He's dead," said Lupin, after a rapid examination.

"But why?" I exclaimed. "There's not a trace of blood!"

"Yes, yes, there is," replied Lupin, pointing to two or three drops that showed on the chest, through the open shirt. "Look, they must have taken him by the throat with one hand and pricked him to the heart with the other. I say, 'pricked,' because really the wound can't be seen. It suggests a hole made by a very long needle."

"Lupin took a tool from his pocket ... and inserted it in the lock"

He looked on the floor, all round the corpse. There was nothing to attract his attention, except a little pocket-mirror, the little mirror with which M. Lavernoux had amused himself by making the sunbeams dance through space.

But, suddenly, as the portress was breaking into lamentations and calling for help, Lupin flung himself on her and shook her:

"Stop that!... Listen to me ... you can call out later.... Listen to me and answer me. It is most important. M. Lavernoux had a friend living in this street, had he not? On the same side, to the right? An intimate friend?"

"Yes."

"A friend whom he used to meet at the café in the evening and with whom he exchanged the illustrated papers?"

"Yes."

"Was the friend an Englishman?"

"Yes."

"What's his name?"

"Mr. Hargrove."

"Where does he live?"

"At No. 92 in this street."

"One word more: had that old doctor been attending him long?"

"No. I did not know him. He came on the evening when M. Lavernoux was taken ill."

Without another word, Lupin dragged me away once more, ran down the stairs and, once in the street, turned to the right, which took us past my flat again. Four doors further, he stopped at No. 92, a small, low-storied house, of which the ground-floor was occupied by the proprietor of a dram-shop, who stood smoking in his doorway, next to the entrance-passage. Lupin asked if Mr. Hargrove was at home.

"Mr. Hargrove went out about half-an-hour ago," said the publican. "He seemed very much excited and took a taxi-cab, a thing he doesn't often do."

"And you don't know...."

"Where he was going? Well, there's no secret about it He shouted it loud enough! 'Prefecture of Police' is what he said to the driver...."

Lupin was himself just hailing a taxi, when he changed his mind; and I heard him mutter:

"What's the good? He's got too much start of us...."

He asked if any one called after Mr. Hargrove had gone.

"Yes, an old gentleman with a grey beard and spectacles. He went up to Mr. Hargrove's, rang the bell, and went away again."

"I am much obliged," said Lupin, touching his hat.

He walked away slowly without speaking to me, wearing a thoughtful air. There was no doubt that the problem struck him as very difficult, and that he saw none too clearly in the darkness through which he seemed to be moving with such certainty.

He himself, for that matter, confessed to me:

"These are cases that require much more intuition than reflection. But this one, I may tell you, is well worth taking pains about."

We had now reached the boulevards. Lupin entered a public reading-room and spent a long time consulting the last fortnight's newspapers. Now and again, he mumbled:

"Yes ... yes ... of course ... it's only a guess, but it explains everything.... Well, a guess that answers every question is not far from being the truth...."

494

It was now dark. We dined at a little restaurant and I noticed that Lupin's face became gradually more animated. His gestures were more decided. He recovered his spirits, his liveliness. When we left, during the walk which he made me take along the Boulevard Haussmann, towards Baron Repstein's house, he was the real Lupin of the great occasions, the Lupin who had made up his mind to go in and win.

We slackened our pace just short of the Rue de Courcelles. Baron Repstein lived on the left-hand side, between this street and the Faubourg Saint-Honoré, in a three-storied private house of which we could see the front, decorated with columns and caryatides.

"Stop!" said Lupin, suddenly.

"What is it?"

"Another proof to confirm my supposition...."

"What proof? I see nothing."

"I do.... That's enough...."

He turned up the collar of his coat, lowered the brim of his soft hat and said:

"By Jove, it'll be a stiff fight! Go to bed, my friend. I'll tell you about my expedition to-morrow ... if it doesn't cost me my life."

"What are you talking about?"

"Oh, I know what I'm saying! I'm risking a lot. First of all, getting arrested, which isn't much. Next, getting killed, which is worse. But...." He gripped my shoulder. "But there's a third thing I'm risking, which is getting hold of two millions.... And, once I possess a capital of two millions, I'll show people what I can do! Good-night, old chap, and, if you never see me again...." He spouted Musset's lines:

"Plant a willow by my grave,
The weeping willow that I love...."

I walked away. Three minutes later—I am continuing the narrative as he told it to me next day—three minutes later, Lupin rang at the door of the Hôtel Repstein.

"Is monsieur le baron at home?"

"Yes," replied the butler, examining the intruder with an air of surprise, "but monsieur le baron does not see people as late as this."

"Does monsieur le baron know of the murder of M. Lavernoux, his land-agent?"

"Certainly."

"Well, please tell monsieur le baron that I have come about the murder and that there is not a moment to lose."

A voice called from above:

"Show the gentleman up, Antoine."

In obedience to this peremptory order, the butler led the way to the first floor. In an open doorway stood a gentleman whom Lupin recognized from his photograph in the papers as Baron Repstein, husband of the famous baroness and owner of Etna, the horse of the year.

He was an exceedingly tall, square-shouldered man. His clean-shaven face wore a pleasant, almost smiling expression, which was not affected by the sadness of his eyes. He was dressed in a well-cut morning-coat, with a tan waistcoat and a dark tie fastened with a pearl pin, the value of which struck Lupin as considerable.

He took Lupin into his study, a large, three-windowed room, lined with book-cases, sets of pigeonholes, an American desk and a safe. And he at once asked, with ill-concealed eagerness:

"Do you know anything?"

"Yes, monsieur le baron."

"About the murder of that poor Lavernoux?"

"Yes, monsieur le baron, and about madame le baronne also."

"Do you really mean it? Quick, I entreat you...."

He pushed forward a chair. Lupin sat down and began:

"Monsieur le baron, the circumstances are very serious. I will be brief."

"Yes, do, please."

"Well, monsieur le baron, in a few words, it amounts to this: five or six hours ago, Lavernoux, who, for the last fortnight, had been kept in a sort of enforced confinement by his doctor, Lavernoux—how shall I put it?—telegraphed certain revelations by means of signals which were partly taken down by me and which put me on the track of this case. He himself was surprised in the act of making this communication and was murdered."

"But by whom? By whom?"

"By his doctor."

"Who is this doctor?"

"I don't know. But one of M. Lavernoux's friends, an Englishman called Hargrove, the friend, in fact, with whom he was communicating, is bound to know and is also bound to know the exact and complete meaning of the communication, because, without waiting for the end, he jumped into a motor-cab and drove to the Prefecture of Police."

"Why? Why?... And what is the result of that step?"

"The result, monsieur le baron, is that your house is surrounded. There are twelve detectives under your windows. The moment the sun rises, they will enter in the name of the law and arrest the criminal."

"Then is Lavernoux's murderer concealed in my house? Who is he? One of the servants? But no, for you were speaking of a doctor!..."

"I would remark, monsieur le baron, that when this Mr. Hargrove went to the police to tell them of the revelations made by his friend Lavernoux, he was not aware that his friend Lavernoux was going to be murdered. The step taken by Mr Hargrove had to do with something else...."

"With what?"

"With the disappearance of madame la baronne, of which he knew the secret, thanks to the communication made by Lavernoux."

"What! They know at last! They have found the baroness! Where is she? And the jewels? And the money she robbed me of?"

Baron Repstein was talking in a great state of excitement. He rose and, almost shouting at Lupin, cried:

"Finish your story, sir! I can't endure this suspense!"

Lupin continued, in a slow and hesitating voice:

"The fact is ... you see ... it is rather difficult to explain ... for you and I are looking at the thing from a totally different point of view."

"I don't understand."

"And yet you ought to understand, monsieur le baron.... We begin by saying—I am quoting the newspapers—by saying, do we not, that Baroness Repstein knew all the secrets of your business and that she was able to open not only that safe over there, but also the one at the Crédit Lyonnais in which you kept your securities locked up?"

"Yes."

"Well, one evening, a fortnight ago, while you were at your club, Baroness Repstein, who, unknown to yourself, had converted all those securities into cash, left this house with a travelling-bag, containing your money and all the Princesse de Berny's jewels?"

"Yes."

"And, since then, she has not been seen?"

"No."

"Well, there is an excellent reason why she has not been seen."

"What reason?"

"This, that Baroness Repstein has been murdered...."

"Murdered!... The baroness!... But you're mad!"

"Murdered ... and probably that same evening."

"I tell you again, you are mad! How can the baroness have been murdered, when the police are following her tracks, so to speak, step by step?"

"They are following the tracks of another woman."

"What woman?"

"The murderer's accomplice."

"And who is the murderer?"

"The same man who, for the last fortnight, knowing that Lavernoux, through the situation which he occupied in this house, had discovered the truth, kept him imprisoned, forced him to silence, threatened him, terrorized him; the same man who, finding Lavernoux in the act of communicating with a friend, made away with him in cold blood by stabbing him to the heart."

"The doctor, therefore?"

"Yes."

"But who is this doctor? Who is this malevolent genius, this infernal being who appears and disappears, who slays in the dark and whom nobody suspects?"

"Can't you guess?"

"No."

"And do you want to know?"

"Do I want to know?... Why, speak, man, speak!... You know where he is hiding?"

"Yes."

"In this house?"

"Yes."

"And it is he whom the police are after?"

"Yes."

"And I know him?"

"Yes."

"Who is it?"

"You!"

"I!..."

Lupin had not been more than ten minutes with the baron; and the duel was commencing. The accusation was hurled, definitely, violently, implacably.

Lupin repeated:

"You yourself, got up in a false beard and a pair of spectacles, bent in two, like an old man. In short, you, Baron Repstein; and it is you for a very good reason, of which nobody has thought, which is that, if it was not you who contrived the whole plot, the case becomes inexplicable. Whereas, taking you as the criminal, you as murdering the baroness in order to get rid of her and run through those millions with another woman, you as murdering Lavernoux, your agent, in order to suppress an unimpeachable witness, oh, then the whole case is explained! Well, is it pretty clear? And are not you yourself convinced?"

The baron, who, throughout this conversation, had stood bending over his visitor, waiting for each of his words with feverish avidity, now drew himself up and looked at Lupin as though he undoubtedly had to do with a madman. When Lupin had finished speaking, the baron stepped back two or three paces, seemed on the point of uttering words which he ended by not saying, and then, without taking his eyes from his strange visitor, went to the fireplace and rang the bell.

Lupin did not make a movement. He waited smiling.

The butler entered. His master said:

"You can go to bed, Antoine. I will let this gentleman out."

"Shall I put out the lights, sir?"

"Leave a light in the hall."

Antoine left the room and the baron, after taking a revolver from his desk, at once came back to Lupin, put the weapon in his pocket and said, very calmly:

"You must excuse this little precaution, sir. I am obliged to take it in case you should be mad, though that does not seem likely. No, you are not mad. But you have come here with an object which I fail to grasp; and you have sprung upon me an accusation of so astounding a character that I am curious to know the reason. I have experienced so much disappointment and undergone so much suffering that an outrage of this kind leaves me indifferent. Continue, please."

His voice shook with emotion and his sad eyes seemed moist with tears.

Lupin shuddered. Had he made a mistake? Was the surmise which his intuition had suggested to him and which was based upon a frail groundwork of slight facts, was this surmise wrong?

His attention was caught by a detail: through the opening in the baron's waistcoat he saw the point of the pin fixed in the tie and was thus able to realize the unusual length of the pin. Moreover, the gold stem was triangular and formed a sort of miniature dagger, very thin and very delicate, yet formidable in an expert hand.

And Lupin had no doubt but that the pin attached to that magnificent pearl was the weapon which had pierced the heart of the unfortunate M. Lavernoux.

He muttered:

"You're jolly clever, monsieur le baron!"

The other, maintaining a rather scornful gravity, kept silence, as though he did not understand and as though waiting for the explanation to which he felt himself entitled. And, in spite of everything, this impassive attitude worried Arsène Lupin. Nevertheless, his conviction was so profound and, besides, he had staked so much on the adventure that he repeated:

"Yes, jolly clever, for it is evident that the baroness only obeyed your orders in realizing your securities and also in borrowing the princess's jewels on the pretence of buying them. And it is evident that the person who walked out of your house with a bag was not your wife, but an accomplice, that chorus-girl probably, and that it is your chorus-girl who is deliberately allowing herself to be chased across the continent by our worthy Ganimard. And I look upon the trick as marvellous. What does the woman risk, seeing that it is the baroness who is being looked for? And how could they look for any other woman than the baroness, seeing that you have promised a reward of two hundred thousand francs to the person who finds the baroness?... Oh, that two hundred thousand francs lodged with a solicitor: what a stroke of genius! It has dazzled the police! It has thrown dust in the eyes of the most clear-sighted! A gentleman who lodges two hundred thousand francs with a solicitor is a gentleman who speaks the truth.... So they go on hunting the baroness! And they leave you quietly to settle your affairs, to sell your stud and your two houses to the highest bidder and to prepare your flight! Heavens, what a joke!"

The baron did not wince. He walked up to Lupin and asked, without abandoning his imperturbable coolness:

"Who are you?"

Lupin burst out laughing.

"What can it matter who I am? Take it that I am an emissary of fate, looming out of the darkness for your destruction!"

He sprang from his chair, seized the baron by the shoulder and jerked out:

"Yes, for your destruction, my bold baron! Listen to me! Your wife's three millions, almost all the princess's jewels, the money you received to-day from the sale of your stud and your real estate: it's all there, in your pocket, or in that safe. Your flight is prepared. Look, I can see the leather of your portmanteau behind that hanging. The papers on your desk are in order. This very night, you would have done a guy. This very night, disguised beyond recognition, after taking all your precautions, you would have joined your chorus-girl, the creature for whose sake you have committed murder, that same Nelly Darbal, no doubt, whom Ganimard arrested in Belgium. But for one sudden, unforeseen obstacle: the police, the twelve detectives who, thanks to Lavernoux's revelations, have been posted under your windows. They've cooked your goose, old chap!... Well, I'll save you. A word through the telephone; and, by three or four o'clock in the morning, twenty of my friends will have removed the obstacle, polished off the twelve detectives, and you and I will slip away quietly. My conditions? Almost nothing; a trifle to you: we share the millions and the jewels. Is it a bargain?"

He was leaning over the baron, thundering at him with irresistible energy. The baron whispered:

"I'm beginning to understand. It's blackmail...."

"Blackmail or not, call it what you please, my boy, but you've got to go through with it and do as I say. And don't imagine that I shall give way at the last moment. Don't say to yourself, 'Here's a gentleman whom the fear of the police will cause to think twice. If I run a big risk in refusing, he also will be risking the handcuffs, the cells and the rest of it, seeing that we are both being hunted down like wild beasts.' That would be a mistake, monsieur le baron. I can always get out of it. It's a question of yourself, of yourself alone.... Your money or your life, my lord! Share and share alike ... if not, the scaffold! Is it a bargain?"

A quick movement. The baron released himself, grasped his revolver and fired.

But Lupin was prepared for the attack, the more so as the baron's face had lost its assurance and gradually, under the slow impulse of rage and fear, acquired an expression of almost bestial ferocity that heralded the rebellion so long kept under control.

He fired twice. Lupin first flung himself to one side and then dived at the baron's knees, seized him by both legs and brought him to the ground. The baron freed himself with an effort. The two enemies rolled over in each other's grip; and a stubborn, crafty, brutal, savage struggle followed.

Suddenly, Lupin felt a pain at his chest:

"You villain!" he yelled. "That's your Lavernoux trick; the tie-pin!"

Stiffening his muscles with a desperate effort, he overpowered the baron and clutched him by the throat victorious at last and omnipotent.

"You ass!" he cried. "If you hadn't shown your cards, I might have thrown up the game! You have such a look of the honest man about you! But what a biceps, my lord!... I thought for a moment.... But it's all over, now!... Come, my friend, hand us the pin and look cheerful.... No, that's what I call pulling a face.... I'm holding you too tight, perhaps? My lord's at his last gasp?... Come, be good!... That's it, just a wee bit of string round the wrists; do you allow me?... Why, you and I are agreeing like two brothers! It's touching!... At heart, you know, I'm rather fond of you.... And now, my bonnie lad, mind yourself! And a thousand apologies!..."

Half raising himself, with all his strength he caught the other a terrible blow in the pit of the stomach. The baron gave a gurgle and lay stunned and unconscious.

"That comes of having a deficient sense of logic, my friend," said Lupin. "I offered you half your money. Now I'll give you none at all ... provided I know where to find any of it. For that's the main thing. Where has the beggar hidden his dust? In the safe? By George, it'll be a tough job! Luckily, I have all the night before me...."

He began to feel in the baron's pockets, came upon a bunch of keys, first made sure that the portmanteau behind the curtain held no papers or jewels, and then went to the safe.

But, at that moment, he stopped short: he heard a noise somewhere. The servants? Impossible. Their attics were on the top floor. He listened. The noise came from below. And, suddenly, he understood: the detectives, who had heard the two shots, were banging at the front door, as was their duty, without waiting for daybreak. Then an electric bell rang, which Lupin recognized as that in the hall:

"By Jupiter!" he said. "Pretty work! Here are these jokers coming ... and just as we were about to gather the fruits of our laborious efforts! Tut, tut, Lupin, keep cool! What's expected of you? To open a safe, of which you don't know the secret, in thirty seconds. That's a mere trifle to lose your head about! Come, all you have to do is to discover the secret! How many letters are there in the word? Four?"

He went on thinking, while talking and listening to the noise outside. He double-locked the door of the outer room and then came back to the safe:

"Four ciphers.... Four letters ... four letters.... Who can lend me a hand?... Who can give me just a tiny hint?... Who? Why, Lavernoux, of course! That good Lavernoux, seeing that he took the trouble to indulge in optical telegraphy at the risk of his life.... Lord, what a fool I am!... Why, of course, why, of course, that's it!... By Jove, this is too exciting!... Lupin, you must count ten and suppress that distracted beating of your heart. If not, it means bad work."

He counted ten and, now quite calm, knelt in front of the safe. He turned the four knobs with careful attention. Next, he examined the bunch of keys, selected one of them, then another, and attempted, in vain, to insert them in the lock:

"There's luck in odd numbers," he muttered, trying a third key. "Victory! This is the right one! Open Sesame, good old Sesame, open!"

The lock turned. The door moved on its hinges. Lupin pulled it to him, after taking out the bunch of keys:

"The millions are ours," he said. "Baron, I forgive you!"

And then he gave a single bound backward, hiccoughing with fright. His legs staggered beneath him. The keys jingled together in his fevered hand with a sinister sound. And, for twenty, for thirty seconds, despite the din that was being raised and the electric bells that kept ringing through the house, he stood there, wild-eyed, gazing at the most horrible, the most abominable sight: a woman's body, half-dressed, bent in two in the safe, crammed in, like an over-large parcel ... and fair hair hanging down ... and blood ... clots of blood ... and livid flesh, blue in places, decomposing, flaccid.

"The baroness!" he gasped. "The baroness!... Oh, the monster!..."

He roused himself from his torpor, suddenly, to spit in the murderer's face and pound him with his heels:

"Take that, you wretch!... Take that, you villain!... And, with it, the scaffold, the bran-basket!..."

Meanwhile, shouts came from the upper floors in reply to the detectives' ringing. Lupin heard footsteps scurrying down the stairs. It was time to think of beating a retreat.

In reality, this did not trouble him greatly. During his conversation with the baron, the enemy's extraordinary coolness had given him the feeling that there must be a private outlet. Besides, how could the baron have begun the fight, if he were not sure of escaping the police?

Lupin went into the next room. It looked out on the garden. At the moment when the detectives were entering the house, he flung his legs over the balcony and let himself down by a rain-pipe. He walked round the building. On the opposite side was a wall lined with shrubs. He slipped in between the shrubs and the wall and at once found a little door which he easily opened with one of the keys on the bunch. All that remained for him to do was to walk across a yard and pass through the empty rooms of a lodge; and in a few moments he found himself in the Rue du Faubourg Saint-Honoré. Of course—and this he had reckoned on—the police had not provided for this secret outlet.

"Well, what do you think of Baron Repstein?" cried Lupin, after giving me all the details of that tragic night. "What a dirty scoundrel! And how it teaches one to distrust appearances! I swear to you, the fellow looked a thoroughly honest man!"

"But what about the millions?" I asked. "The princess's jewels?"

"They were in the safe. I remember seeing the parcel."

"Well?"

"They are there still."

"Impossible!"

"They are, upon my word! I might tell you that I was afraid of the detectives, or else plead a sudden attack of delicacy. But the truth is simpler ... and more prosaic: the smell was too awful!..."

"What?"

"Yes, my dear fellow, the smell that came from that safe ... from that coffin.... No, I couldn't do it ... my head swam.... Another second and I should have been ill.... Isn't it silly?... Look, this is all I got from my expedition: the tie-pin.... The bed-rock value of the pearl is thirty thousand francs.... But all the same, I feel jolly well annoyed. What a sell!"

"One more question," I said. "The word that opened the safe!"

"Well?"

"How did you guess it?"

"Oh, quite easily! In fact, I am surprised that I didn't think of it sooner."

"Well, tell me."

"It was contained in the revelations telegraphed by that poor Lavernoux."

"What?"

"Just think, my dear chap, the mistakes in spelling...."

"The mistakes in spelling?"

"Why, of course! They were deliberate. Surely, you don't imagine that the agent, the private secretary of the baron—who was a company-promoter, mind you, and a racing-man—did not know English better than to spell 'necessery' with an 'e,' 'atack' with one 't,' 'ennemy' with two 'n's' and 'prudance' with an 'a'! The thing struck me at once. I put the four letters together and got 'Etna,' the name of the famous horse."

"And was that one word enough?"

"Of course! It was enough to start with, to put me on the scent of the Repstein case, of which all the papers were full, and, next, to make me guess that it was the key-word of the safe, because, on the one hand, Lavernoux knew the gruesome contents of the safe and, on the other, he was denouncing the baron. And it was in the same way that I was led to suppose that Lavernoux had a friend in the street, that they both frequented the same café, that they amused themselves by working out the problems and cryptograms in the illustrated papers and that they had contrived a way of exchanging telegrams from window to window."

"That makes it all quite simple!" I exclaimed.

"Very simple. And the incident once more shows that, in the discovery of crimes, there is something much more valuable than the examination of facts, than observations, deductions, inferences and all that stuff and nonsense. What I mean is, as I said before, intuition ... intuition and intelligence.... And Arsène Lupin, without boasting, is deficient in neither one nor the other!..."

II. THE WEDDING-RING

Yvonne d'Origny kissed her son and told him to be good:

"You know your grandmother d'Origny is not very fond of children. Now that she has sent for you to come and see her, you must show her what a sensible little boy you are." And, turning to the governess, "Don't forget, Fräulein, to bring him home immediately after dinner.... Is monsieur still in the house?"

"Yes, madame, monsieur le comte is in his study."

As soon as she was alone, Yvonne d'Origny walked to the window to catch a glimpse of her son as he left the house. He was out in the street in a moment, raised his head and blew her a kiss, as was his custom every day. Then the governess took his hand with, as Yvonne remarked to her surprise, a movement of unusual violence. Yvonne leant further out of the window and, when the boy reached the corner of the boulevard, she suddenly saw a man step out of a motor-car and go up to him. The man, in whom she recognized Bernard, her husband's confidential servant, took the child by the arm, made both him and the governess get into the car, and ordered the chauffeur to drive off.

The whole incident did not take ten seconds.

Yvonne, in her trepidation, ran to her bedroom, seized a wrap and went to the door. The door was locked; and there was no key in the lock.

She hurried back to the boudoir. The door of the boudoir also was locked.

Then, suddenly, the image of her husband appeared before her, that gloomy face which no smile ever lit up, those pitiless eyes in which, for years, she had felt so much hatred and malice.

"It's he ... it's he!" she said to herself. "He has taken the child.... Oh, it's horrible!"

She beat against the door with her fists, with her feet, then flew to the mantelpiece and pressed the bell fiercely.

The shrill sound rang through the house from top to bottom. The servants would be sure to come. Perhaps a crowd would gather in the street. And, impelled by a sort of despairing hope, she kept her finger on the button.

A key turned in the lock.... The door was flung wide open. The count appeared on the threshold of the boudoir. And the expression of his face was so terrible that Yvonne began to tremble.

He entered the room. Five or six steps separated him from her. With a supreme effort, she tried to stir, but all movement was impossible; and, when she attempted to speak, she could only flutter her lips and emit incoherent sounds. She felt herself lost. The thought of death unhinged her. Her knees gave way beneath her and she sank into a huddled heap, with a moan.

The count rushed at her and seized her by the throat:

"Hold your tongue ... don't call out!" he said, in a low voice. "That will be best for you!..."

Seeing that she was not attempting to defend herself, he loosened his hold of her and took from his pocket some strips of canvas ready rolled and of different lengths. In a few minutes, Yvonne was lying on a sofa, with her wrists and ankles bound and her arms fastened close to her body.

It was now dark in the boudoir. The count switched on the electric light and went to a little writing-desk where Yvonne was accustomed to keep her letters. Not succeeding in opening it, he picked the lock with a bent wire, emptied the drawers and collected all the contents into a bundle, which he carried off in a cardboard file:

"Waste of time, eh?" he grinned. "Nothing but bills and letters of no importance.... No proof against you.... Tah! I'll keep my son for all that; and I swear before Heaven that I will not let him go!"

As he was leaving the room, he was joined, near the door, by his man Bernard. The two stopped and talked, in a low voice; but Yvonne heard these words spoken by the servant:

"I have had an answer from the working jeweller. He says he holds himself at my disposal."

And the count replied:

"The thing is put off until twelve o'clock midday, to-morrow. My mother has just telephoned to say that she could not come before."

Then Yvonne heard the key turn in the lock and the sound of steps going down to the ground-floor, where her husband's study was.

She long lay inert, her brain reeling with vague, swift ideas that burnt her in passing, like flames. She remembered her husband's infamous behaviour, his humiliating conduct to her, his threats, his plans for a divorce; and she gradually came to understand that she was the victim of a regular conspiracy, that the servants had been sent away until the following evening by their master's orders, that the governess had carried off her son by the count's instructions and with Bernard's assistance, that her son would not come back and that she would never see him again.

"My son!" she cried. "My son!..."

Exasperated by her grief, she stiffened herself, with every nerve, with every muscle tense, to make a violent effort. And she was astonished to find that her right hand, which the count had fastened too hurriedly, still retained a certain freedom.

Then a mad hope invaded her; and, slowly, patiently, she began the work of self-deliverance.

It was long in the doing. She needed a deal of time to widen the knot sufficiently and a deal of time afterward, when the hand was released, to undo those other bonds which tied her arms to her body and those which fastened her ankles.

Still, the thought of her son sustained her; and the last shackle fell as the clock struck eight. She was free!

She was no sooner on her feet than she flew to the window and flung back the latch, with the intention of calling the first passer-by. At that moment a policeman came walking along the pavement. She leant out. But the brisk evening air, striking her face, calmed her. She thought of the scandal, of the judicial investigation, of the cross-examination, of her son. O Heaven! What could she do to get him back? How could she escape? The count might appear at the least sound. And who knew but that, in a moment of fury ...?

She shivered from head to foot, seized with a sudden terror. The horror of death mingled, in her poor brain, with the thought of her son; and she stammered, with a choking throat:

"Help!... Help!..."

She stopped and said to herself, several times over, in a low voice, "Help!... Help!..." as though the word awakened an idea, a memory within her, and as though the hope of assistance no longer seemed to her impossible. For some minutes she remained absorbed in deep meditation, broken by fears and starts. Then, with an almost mechanical series of movements, she put out her arm to a little set of shelves hanging over the writing-desk, took down four books, one after the other, turned the pages with a distraught air, replaced them and ended by finding, between the pages of the fifth, a visiting-card on which her eyes spelt the name:

HORACE VELMONT,

followed by an address written in pencil:

CERCLE DE LA RUE ROYALE.

And her memory conjured up the strange thing which that man had said to her, a few years before, in that same house, on a day when she was at home to her friends:

"If ever a danger threatens you, if you need help, do not hesitate; post this card, which you see me put into this book; and, whatever the hour, whatever the obstacles, I will come."

With what a curious air he had spoken these words and how well he had conveyed the impression of certainty, of strength, of unlimited power, of indomitable daring!

Abruptly, unconsciously, acting under the impulse of an irresistible determination, the consequences of which she refused to anticipate, Yvonne, with the same automatic gestures, took a pneumatic-delivery envelope, slipped in the card, sealed it, directed it to "Horace Velmont, Cercle de la Rue Royale" and went to the open window. The policeman was walking up and down outside. She flung out the envelope, trusting to fate. Perhaps it would be picked up, treated as a lost letter and posted.

She had hardly completed this act when she realized its absurdity. It was mad to suppose that the message would reach the address and madder still to hope that the man to whom she was sending could come to her assistance, "whatever the hour, whatever the obstacles."

A reaction followed which was all the greater inasmuch as the effort had been swift and violent. Yvonne staggered, leant against a chair and, losing all energy, let herself fall.

The hours passed by, the dreary hours of winter evenings when nothing but the sound of carriages interrupts the silence of the street. The clock struck, pitilessly. In the half-sleep that numbed her limbs, Yvonne counted the strokes. She also heard certain noises, on different floors of the house, which told her that her husband had dined, that he was going up to his room, that he was going down again to his study. But all this seemed very shadowy to her; and her torpor was such that she did not even think of lying down on the sofa, in case he should come in....

The twelve strokes of midnight.... Then half-past twelve ... then one.... Yvonne thought of nothing, awaiting the events which were preparing and against which rebellion was useless. She pictured her son and herself as one pictures those beings who have suffered much and who suffer no more and who take each other in their loving arms. But a nightmare shattered this dream. For now those two beings were to be torn asunder; and she had the awful feeling, in her delirium, that she was crying and choking....

She leapt from her seat. The key had turned in the lock. The count was coming, attracted by her cries. Yvonne glanced round for a weapon with which to defend herself. But the door was pushed back quickly and, astounded, as though the sight that presented itself before her eyes seemed to her the most inexplicable prodigy, she stammered:

"You!... You!..."

A man was walking up to her, in dress-clothes, with his opera-hat and cape under his arm, and this man, young, slender and elegant, she had recognized as Horace Velmont.

"You!" she repeated.

He said, with a bow:

"I beg your pardon, madame, but I did not receive your letter until very late."

"Is it possible? Is it possible that this is you ... that you were able to ...?"

He seemed greatly surprised:

"Did I not promise to come in answer to your call?"

"Yes ... but ..."

"Well, here I am," he said, with a smile.

He examined the strips of canvas from which Yvonne had succeeded in freeing herself and nodded his head, while continuing his inspection:

"So those are the means employed? The Comte d'Origny, I presume?... I also saw that he locked you in.... But then the pneumatic letter?... Ah, through the window!... How careless of you not to close it!"

He pushed both sides to. Yvonne took fright:

"Suppose they hear!"

"There is no one in the house. I have been over it."

"Still ..."

"Your husband went out ten minutes ago."

"Where is he?"

"With his mother, the Comtesse d'Origny."

"How do you know?"

"Oh, it's very simple! He was rung up by telephone and I awaited the result at the corner of this street and the boulevard. As I expected, the count came out hurriedly, followed by his man. I at once entered, with the aid of special keys."

He told this in the most natural way, just as one tells a meaningless anecdote in a drawing-room. But Yvonne, suddenly seized with fresh alarm, asked:

"Then it's not true?... His mother is not ill?... In that case, my husband will be coming back...."

"Certainly, the count will see that a trick has been played on him and in three quarters of an hour at the latest...."

"Let us go.... I don't want him to find me here.... I must go to my son...."

"One moment...."

"One moment!... But don't you know that they have taken him from me?... That they are hurting him, perhaps?..."

With set face and feverish gestures, she tried to push Velmont back. He, with great gentleness, compelled her to sit down and, leaning over her in a respectful attitude, said, in a serious voice:

"Listen, madame, and let us not waste time, when every minute is valuable. First of all, remember this: we met four times, six years ago,.... And, on the fourth occasion, when I was speaking to you, in the drawing-room of this house, with too much—what shall I say?—with too much feeling, you gave me to understand that my visits were no longer welcome. Since that day I have not seen you. And, nevertheless, in spite of all, your faith in me was such that you kept the card which I put between the pages of that book and, six years later, you send for me and none other. That faith in me I ask you to continue. You must obey me blindly. Just as I surmounted every obstacle to come to you, so I will save you, whatever the position may be."

Horace Velmont's calmness, his masterful voice, with the friendly intonation, gradually quieted the countess. Though still very weak, she gained a fresh sense of ease and security in that man's presence.

"Have no fear," he went on. "The Comtesse d'Origny lives at the other end of the Bois de Vincennes. Allowing that your husband finds a motor-cab, it is impossible for him to be back before a quarter-past three. Well, it is twenty-five to three now. I swear to take you away at three o'clock exactly and to take you to your son. But I will not go before I know everything."

"What am I to do?" she asked.

"Answer me and very plainly. We have twenty minutes. It is enough. But it is not too much."

"Ask me what you want to know."

"Do you think that the count had any ... any murderous intentions?"

"No."

"Then it concerns your son?"

"Yes."

"He is taking him away, I suppose, because he wants to divorce you and marry another woman, a former friend of yours, whom you have turned out of your house. Is that it? Oh, I entreat you, answer me frankly! These are facts of public notoriety; and your hesitation, your scruples, must all cease, now that the matter concerns your son. So your husband wished to marry another woman?

"Yes."

"The woman has no money. Your husband, on his side, has gambled away all his property and has no means beyond the allowance which he receives from his mother, the Comtesse d'Origny, and the income of a large fortune which your son inherited from two of your uncles. It is this fortune which your husband covets and which he would appropriate more easily if the child were placed in his hands. There is only one way: divorce. Am I right?"

"Yes."

"And what has prevented him until now is your refusal?"

"Yes, mine and that of my mother-in-law, whose religious feelings are opposed to divorce. The Comtesse d'Origny would only yield in case ..."

"In case ...?"

"In case they could prove me guilty of shameful conduct."

Velmont shrugged his shoulders:

"Therefore he is powerless to do anything against you or against your son. Both from the legal point of view and from that of his own interests, he stumbles against an obstacle which is the most insurmountable of all: the virtue of an honest woman. And yet, in spite of everything, he suddenly shows fight."

"What do you mean?"

"I mean that, if a man like the count, after so many hesitations and in the face of so many difficulties, risks so doubtful an adventure, it must be because he thinks he has command of weapons ..."

"What weapons?"

"I don't know. But they exist ... or else he would not have begun by taking away your son."

Yvonne gave way to her despair:

"Oh, this is horrible!... How do I know what he may have done, what he may have invented?"

"Try and think.... Recall your memories.... Tell me, in this desk which he has broken open, was there any sort of letter which he could possibly turn against you?"

"No ... only bills and addresses...."

"And, in the words he used to you, in his threats, is there nothing that allows you to guess?"

"Nothing."

"Still ... still," Velmont insisted, "there must be something." And he continued, "Has the count a particularly intimate friend ... in whom he confides?"

"No."

"Did anybody come to see him yesterday?"

"No, nobody."

"Was he alone when he bound you and locked you in?"

"At that moment, yes."

"But afterward?"

"His man, Bernard, joined him near the door and I heard them talking about a working jeweller...."

"Is that all?"

"And about something that was to happen the next day, that is, to-day, at twelve o'clock, because the Comtesse d'Origny could not come earlier."

Velmont reflected:

"Has that conversation any meaning that throws a light upon your husband's plans?"

"I don't see any."

"Where are your jewels?"

"My husband has sold them all."

"You have nothing at all left?"

"No."

"Not even a ring?"

"No," she said, showing her hands, "none except this."

"Which is your wedding-ring?"

"Which is my ... wedding—..."

She stopped, nonplussed. Velmont saw her flush as she stammered:

"Could it be possible?... But no ... no ... he doesn't know...."

Velmont at once pressed her with questions and Yvonne stood silent, motionless, anxious-faced. At last, she replied, in a low voice:

"This is not my wedding-ring. One day, long ago, it dropped from the mantelpiece in my bedroom, where I had put it a minute before and, hunt for it as I might, I could not find it again. So I ordered another, without saying anything about it ... and this is the one, on my hand...."

"Did the real ring bear the date of your wedding?"

"Yes ... the 23rd of October."

"And the second?"

"This one has no date."

He perceived a slight hesitation in her and a confusion which, in point of fact, she did not try to conceal.

"I implore you," he exclaimed, "don't hide anything from me.... You see how far we have gone in a few minutes, with a little logic and calmness.... Let us go on, I ask you as a favour."

"Are you sure," she said, "that it is necessary?"

"I am sure that the least detail is of importance and that we are nearly attaining our object. But we must hurry. This is a crucial moment."

"I have nothing to conceal," she said, proudly raising her head. "It was the most wretched and the most dangerous period of my life. While suffering humiliation at home, outside I was surrounded with attentions, with temptations, with pitfalls, like any woman who is seen to be neglected by her husband. Then I remembered: before my marriage, a man had been in love with me. I had guessed his unspoken love; and he has died since. I had the name of that man engraved inside the ring; and I wore it as a talisman. There was no love in me, because I was the wife of another. But, in my secret heart, there was a memory, a sad dream, something sweet and gentle that protected me...."

She had spoken slowly, without embarrassment, and Velmont did not doubt for a second that she was telling the absolute truth. He kept silent; and she, becoming anxious again, asked:

"Do you suppose ... that my husband ...?"

He took her hand and, while examining the plain gold ring, said:

"The puzzle lies here. Your husband, I don't know how, knows of the substitution of one ring for the other. His mother will be here at twelve o'clock. In the presence of witnesses, he will compel you to take off your ring; and, in this way, he will obtain the approval of his mother and, at the same time, will be able to obtain his divorce, because he will have the proof for which he was seeking."

"I am lost!" she moaned. "I am lost!"

"On the contrary, you are saved! Give me that ring ... and presently he will find another there, another which I will send you, to reach you before twelve, and which will bear the date of the 23rd of October. So...."

He suddenly broke off. While he was speaking, Yvonne's hand had turned ice-cold in his; and, raising his eyes, he saw that the young woman was pale, terribly pale:

"What's the matter? I beseech you ..."

She yielded to a fit of mad despair:

"This is the matter, that I am lost!... This is the matter, that I can't get the ring off! It has grown too small for me!... Do you understand?... It made no difference and I did not give it a thought.... But to-day ... this proof ... this accusation.... Oh, what torture!... Look ... it forms part of my finger ... it has grown into my flesh ... and I can't ... I can't...."

She pulled at the ring, vainly, with all her might, at the risk of injuring herself. But the flesh swelled up around the ring; and the ring did not budge.

"Oh!" she cried, seized with an idea that terrified her. "I remember ... the other night ... a nightmare I had.... It seemed to me that some one entered my room and caught hold of my hand.... And I could not wake up.... It was he! It was he! He had put me to sleep, I was sure of it ... and he was looking at the ring.... And presently he will pull it off before his mother's eyes.... Ah, I understand everything: that working jeweller!... He will cut it from my hand to-morrow.... You see, you see.... I am lost!..."

She hid her face in her hands and began to weep. But, amid the silence, the clock struck once ... and twice ... and yet once more. And Yvonne drew herself up with a jerk:

"There he is!" she cried. "He is coming!... It is three o'clock!... Let us go!..."

She grabbed at her cloak and ran to the door ... Velmont barred the way and, in a masterful tone:

"You shall not go!"

"My son.... I want to see him, to take him back...."

"You don't even know where he is!"

"I want to go."

"You shall not go!... It would be madness...."

He took her by the wrists. She tried to release herself; and Velmont had to employ a little force to overcome her resistance. In the end, he succeeded in getting her back to the sofa, then in laying her at full length and, at once, without heeding her lamentations, he took the canvas strips and fastened her wrists and ankles:

"Yes," he said, "It would be madness! Who would have set you free? Who would have opened that door for you? An accomplice? What an argument against you and what a pretty use your husband would make of it with his mother!... And, besides, what's the good? To run away means accepting divorce ... and what might that not lead to?... You must stay here...."

She sobbed:

"I'm frightened.... I'm frightened ... this ring burns me.... Break it.... Take it away.... Don't let him find it!"

"And if it is not found on your finger, who will have broken it? Again an accomplice.... No, you must face the music ... and face it boldly, for I answer for everything.... Believe me ... I answer for everything.... If I have to tackle the Comtesse d'Origny bodily and thus delay the interview.... If I had to come myself before noon ... it is the real wedding-ring that shall be taken from your finger—that I swear!—and your son shall be restored to you."

Swayed and subdued, Yvonne instinctively held out her hands to the bonds. When he stood up, she was bound as she had been before.

He looked round the room to make sure that no trace of his visit remained. Then he stooped over the countess again and whispered:

"Think of your son and, whatever happens, fear nothing.... I am watching over you."

She heard him open and shut the door of the boudoir and, a few minutes later, the hall-door.

At half-past three, a motor-cab drew up. The door downstairs was slammed again; and, almost immediately after, Yvonne saw her husband hurry in, with a furious look in his eyes. He ran up to her, felt to see if she was still fastened and, snatching her hand, examined the ring. Yvonne fainted....

———————————

She could not tell, when she woke, how long she had slept. But the broad light of day was filling the boudoir; and she perceived, at the first movement which she made, that her bonds were cut. Then she turned her head and saw her husband standing beside her, looking at her:

"My son ... my son ..." she moaned. "I want my son...."

He replied, in a voice of which she felt the jeering insolence:

"Our son is in a safe place. And, for the moment, it's a question not of him, but of you. We are face to face with each other, probably for the last time, and the explanation between us will be a very serious one. I must warn you that it will take place before my mother. Have you any objection?"

Yvonne tried to hide her agitation and answered:

"None at all."

"Can I send for her?"

"Yes. Leave me, in the meantime. I shall be ready when she comes."

"My mother is here."

"Your mother is here?" cried Yvonne, in dismay, remembering Horace Velmont's promise.

"What is there to astonish you in that?"

"And is it now ... is it at once that you want to ...?

"Yes."

"Why?... Why not this evening?... Why not to-morrow?"

"To-day and now," declared the count. "A rather curious incident happened in the course of last night, an incident which I cannot account for and which decided me to hasten the explanation. Don't you want something to eat first?"

"No ... no...."

"Then I will go and fetch my mother."

He turned to Yvonne's bedroom. Yvonne glanced at the clock. It marked twenty-five minutes to eleven!

"Ah!" she said, with a shiver of fright.

Twenty-five minutes to eleven! Horace Velmont would not save her and nobody in the world and nothing in the world would save her, for there was no miracle that could place the wedding-ring upon her finger.

The count, returning with the Comtesse d'Origny, asked her to sit down. She was a tall, lank, angular woman, who had always displayed a hostile feeling to Yvonne. She did not even bid her daughter-in-law good-morning, showing that her mind was made up as regards the accusation:

"I don't think," she said, "that we need speak at length. In two words, my son maintains...."

"I don't maintain, mother," said the count, "I declare. I declare on my oath that, three months ago, during the holidays, the upholsterer, when laying the carpet in this room and the boudoir, found the wedding-ring which I gave my wife lying in a crack in the floor. Here is the ring. The date of the 23rd of October is engraved inside."

"Then," said the countess, "the ring which your wife carries...."

"That is another ring, which she ordered in exchange for the real one. Acting on my instructions, Bernard, my man, after long searching, ended by discovering in the outskirts of Paris, where he now lives, the little jeweller to whom she went. This man remembers perfectly and is willing to bear witness that his customer did not tell him to engrave a date, but a name. He has forgotten the name, but the man who used to work with him in his shop may be able to remember it. This working jeweller has been informed by letter that I required his services and he replied yesterday, placing himself at my disposal. Bernard went to fetch him at nine o'clock this morning. They are both waiting in my study."

He turned to his wife:

"Will you give me that ring of your own free will?"

"You know," she said, "from the other night, that it won't come off my finger."

"In that case, can I have the man up? He has the necessary implements with him."

"Yes," she said, in a voice faint as a whisper.

She was resigned. She conjured up the future as in a vision: the scandal, the decree of divorce pronounced against herself, the custody of the child awarded to the father; and she accepted this, thinking that she would carry off her son, that she would go with him to the ends of the earth and that the two of them would live alone together and happy....

Her mother-in-law said:

"You have been very thoughtless, Yvonne."

Yvonne was on the point of confessing to her and asking for her protection. But what was the good? How could the Comtesse d'Origny possibly believe her innocent? She made no reply.

Besides, the count at once returned, followed by his servant and by a man carrying a bag of tools under his arm.

And the count said to the man:

"You know what you have to do?"

515

"Yes," said the workman. "It's to cut a ring that's grown too small.... That's easily done.... A touch of the nippers...."

"And then you will see," said the count, "if the inscription inside the ring was the one you engraved."

Yvonne looked at the clock. It was ten minutes to eleven. She seemed to hear, somewhere in the house, a sound of voices raised in argument; and, in spite of herself, she felt a thrill of hope. Perhaps Velmont has succeeded.... But the sound was renewed; and she perceived that it was produced by some costermongers passing under her window and moving farther on.

It was all over. Horace Velmont had been unable to assist her. And she understood that, to recover her child, she must rely upon her own strength, for the promises of others are vain.

She made a movement of recoil. She had felt the workman's heavy hand on her hand; and that hateful touch revolted her.

The man apologized, awkwardly. The count said to his wife:

"You must make up your mind, you know."

Then she put out her slim and trembling hand to the workman, who took it, turned it over and rested it on the table, with the palm upward. Yvonne felt the cold steel. She longed to die, then and there; and, at once attracted by that idea of death, she thought of the poisons which she would buy and which would send her to sleep almost without her knowing it.

The operation did not take long. Inserted on the slant, the little steel pliers pushed back the flesh, made room for themselves and bit the ring. A strong effort ... and the ring broke. The two ends had only to be separated to remove the ring from the finger. The workman did so.

The count exclaimed, in triumph:

"At last! Now we shall see!... The proof is there! And we are all witnesses...."

He snatched up the ring and looked at the inscription. A cry of amazement escaped him. The ring bore the date of his marriage to Yvonne: "23rd of October"!...

We were sitting on the terrace at Monte Carlo. Lupin finished his story, lit a cigarette and calmly puffed the smoke into the blue air.

I said:

"Well?"

"Well what?"

"Why, the end of the story...."

"The end of the story? But what other end could there be?"

"Come ... you're joking ..."

"Not at all. Isn't that enough for you? The countess is saved. The count, not possessing the least proof against her, is compelled by his mother to forego the divorce and to give up the child. That is all. Since then, he has left his wife, who is living happily with her son, a fine lad of sixteen."

"Yes ... yes ... but the way in which the countess was saved?"

Lupin burst out laughing:

"My dear old chap"—Lupin sometimes condescends to address me in this affectionate manner—"my dear old chap, you may be rather smart at relating my exploits, but, by Jove, you do want to have the i's dotted for you! I assure you, the countess did not ask for explanations!"

"Very likely. But there's no pride about me," I added, laughing. "Dot those i's for me, will you?"

He took out a five-franc piece and closed his hand over it.

"What's in my hand?"

"A five-franc piece."

He opened his hand. The five-franc piece was gone.

"You see how easy it is! A working jeweller, with his nippers, cuts a ring with a date engraved upon it: 23rd of October. It's a simple little trick of sleight-of-hand, one of many which I have in my bag. By Jove, I didn't spend six months with Dickson, the conjurer, for nothing!"

"But then ...?"

"Out with it!"

"The working jeweller?"

"Was Horace Velmont! Was good old Lupin! Leaving the countess at three o'clock in the morning, I employed the few remaining minutes before the husband's return to have a look round his study. On the table I found the letter from the working jeweller. The letter gave me the address. A bribe of a few louis enabled me to take the workman's place; and I arrived with a wedding-ring ready cut and engraved. Hocus-pocus! Pass!... The count couldn't make head or tail of it."

"Splendid!" I cried. And I added, a little chaffingly, in my turn, "But don't you think that you were humbugged a bit yourself, on this occasion?"

"Oh! And by whom, pray?"

"By the countess?"

"In what way?"

"Hang it all, that name engraved as a talisman!... The mysterious Adonis who loved her and suffered for her sake!... All that story seems very unlikely; and I wonder whether, Lupin though you be, you did not just drop upon a pretty love-story, absolutely genuine and ... none too innocent."

Lupin looked at me out of the corner of his eye:

"No," he said.

"How do you know?"

"If the countess made a misstatement in telling me that she knew that man before her marriage—and that he was dead—and if she really did love him in her secret heart, I, at least, have a positive proof that it was an ideal love and that he did not suspect it."

"And where is the proof?"

"It is inscribed inside the ring which I myself broke on the countess's finger ... and which I carry on me. Here it is. You can read the name she had engraved on it."

He handed me the ring. I read:

"Horace Velmont."

There was a moment of silence between Lupin and myself; and, noticing it, I also observed on his face a certain emotion, a tinge of melancholy.

I resumed:

"What made you tell me this story ... to which you have often alluded in my presence?"

"What made me ...?"

He drew my attention to a woman, still exceedingly handsome, who was passing on a young man's arm. She saw Lupin and bowed.

"It's she," he whispered. "She and her son."

"Then she recognized you?"

"She always recognizes me, whatever my disguise."

"But since the burglary at the Château de Thibermesnil, the police have identified the two names of Arsène Lupin and Horace Velmont."

"Yes."

"Therefore she knows who you are."

"Yes."

"And she bows to you?" I exclaimed, in spite of myself.

He caught me by the arm and, fiercely:

"Do you think that I am Lupin to her? Do you think that I am a burglar in her eyes, a rogue, a cheat?... Why, I might be the lowest of miscreants, I might be a murderer even ... and still she would bow to me!"

"Why? Because she loved you once?"

"Rot! That would be an additional reason, on the contrary, why she should now despise me."

518

"What then?"

"I am the man who gave her back her son!"

III. THE SIGN OF THE SHADOW

"I received your telegram and here I am," said a gentleman with a grey moustache, who entered my study, dressed in a dark-brown frock-coat and a wide-brimmed hat, with a red ribbon in his buttonhole. "What's the matter?"

Had I not been expecting Arsène Lupin, I should certainly never have recognized him in the person of this old half-pay officer:

"What's the matter?" I echoed. "Oh, nothing much: a rather curious coincidence, that's all. And, as I know that you would just as soon clear up a mystery as plan one...."

"Well?"

"You seem in a great hurry!"

"I am ... unless the mystery in question is worth putting myself out for. So let us get to the point."

"Very well. Just begin by casting your eye on this little picture, which I picked up, a week or two ago, in a grimy old shop on the other side of the river. I bought it for the sake of its Empire frame, with the palm-leaf ornaments on the mouldings ... for the painting is execrable."

"Execrable, as you say," said Lupin, after he had examined it, "but the subject itself is rather nice. That corner of an old courtyard, with its rotunda of Greek columns, its sun-dial and its fish-pond and that ruined well with the Renascence roof and those stone steps and stone benches: all very picturesque."

"And genuine," I added. "The picture, good or bad, has never been taken out of its Empire frame. Besides, it is dated.... There, in the left-hand bottom corner: those red figures, 15. 4. 2, which obviously stand for 15 April, 1802."

"I dare say ... I dare say.... But you were speaking of a coincidence and, so far, I fail to see...."

I went to a corner of my study, took a telescope, fixed it on its stand and pointed it, through the open window, at the open window of a little room facing my flat, on the other side of the street. And I asked Lupin to look through it.

He stooped forward. The slanting rays of the morning sun lit up the room opposite, revealing a set of mahogany furniture, all very simple, a large bed and a child's bed hung with cretonne curtains.

"Ah!" cried Lupin, suddenly. "The same picture!"

"Exactly the same!" I said. "And the date: do you see the date, in red? 15. 4. 2."

"Yes, I see.... And who lives in that room?"

"A lady ... or, rather, a workwoman, for she has to work for her living ... needlework, hardly enough to keep herself and her child."

"What is her name?"

"Louise d'Ernemont.... From what I hear, she is the great-granddaughter of a farmer-general who was guillotined during the Terror."

"Yes, on the same day as André Chénier," said Lupin. "According to the memoirs of the time, this d'Ernemont was supposed to be a very rich man." He raised his head and said, "It's an interesting story.... Why did you wait before telling me?"

"Because this is the 15th of April."

"Well?"

"Well, I discovered yesterday—I heard them talking about it in the porter's box—that the 15th of April plays an important part in the life of Louise d'Ernemont."

"Nonsense!"

"Contrary to her usual habits, this woman who works every day of her life, who keeps her two rooms tidy, who cooks the lunch which her little girl eats when she comes home from the parish school ... this woman, on the 15th of April, goes out with the child at ten o'clock in the morning and does not return until nightfall. And this has happened for years and in all weathers. You must admit that there is something queer about this date which I find on an old picture, which is inscribed on another, similar picture and which controls the annual movements of the descendant of d'Ernemont the farmer-general."

"Yes, it's curious ... you're quite right," said Lupin, slowly. "And don't you know where she goes to?"

"Nobody knows. She does not confide in a soul. As a matter of fact, she talks very little."

"Are you sure of your information?"

"Absolutely. And the best proof of its accuracy is that here she comes."

A door had opened at the back of the room opposite, admitting a little girl of seven or eight, who came and looked out of the window. A lady appeared behind her, tall, good-looking still and wearing a sad and gentle air. Both of them were ready and dressed, in clothes which were simple in themselves, but which pointed to a love of neatness and a certain elegance on the part of the mother.

"You see," I whispered, "they are going out."

And presently the mother took the child by the hand and they left the room together.

Lupin caught up his hat:

"Are you coming?"

My curiosity was too great for me to raise the least objection. I went downstairs with Lupin.

As we stepped into the street, we saw my neighbour enter a baker's shop. She bought two rolls and placed them in a little basket which her daughter was carrying and which seemed already to contain some other provisions. Then they went in the direction of the outer boulevards and followed them as far as the Place de l'Étoile, where they turned down the Avenue Kléber to walk toward Passy.

Lupin strolled silently along, evidently obsessed by a train of thought which I was glad to have provoked. From time to time, he uttered a sentence which showed me the thread of his reflections; and I was able to see that the riddle remained as much a mystery to him as to myself.

Louise d'Ernemont, meanwhile, had branched off to the left, along the Rue Raynouard, a quiet old street in which Franklin and Balzac once lived, one of those streets which, lined with old-fashioned houses and walled gardens, give you the impression of being in a country-town. The Seine flows at the foot of the slope which the street crowns; and a number of lanes run down to the river.

My neighbour took one of these narrow, winding, deserted lanes. The first building, on the right, was a house the front of which faced the Rue Raynouard. Next came a moss-grown wall, of a height above the ordinary, supported by buttresses and bristling with broken glass.

Half-way along the wall was a low, arched door. Louise d'Ernemont stopped in front of this door and opened it with a key which seemed to us enormous. Mother and child entered and closed the door.

"In any case," said Lupin, "she has nothing to conceal, for she has not looked round once...."

He had hardly finished his sentence when we heard the sound of footsteps behind us. It was two old beggars, a man and a woman, tattered, dirty, squalid, covered in rags. They passed us without paying the least attention to our presence. The man took from his wallet a key similar to my neighbour's and put it into the lock. The door closed behind them.

And, suddenly, at the top of the lane, came the noise of a motor-car stopping.... Lupin dragged me fifty yards lower down, to a corner in which we were able to hide. And we saw coming down the lane, carrying a little dog under her arm, a young and very much over-dressed woman, wearing a quantity of jewellery, a young woman whose eyes were too dark, her lips too red, her hair too fair. In front of the door, the same performance, with the same key.... The lady and the dog disappeared from view.

"This promises to be most amusing," said Lupin, chuckling. "What earthly connection can there be between those different people?"

There hove in sight successively two elderly ladies, lean and rather poverty-stricken in appearance, very much alike, evidently sisters; a footman in livery; an infantry corporal; a fat gentleman in a soiled and patched jacket-suit; and, lastly, a workman's family, father, mother, and four children, all six of them pale and sickly, looking like people who never eat their fill. And each of the newcomers carried a basket or string-bag filled with provisions.

"It's a picnic!" I cried.

"It grows more and more surprising," said Lupin, "and I sha'n't be satisfied till I know what is happening behind that wall."

To climb it was out of the question. We also saw that it finished, at the lower as well as at the upper end, at a house none of whose windows overlooked the enclosure which the wall contained.

During the next hour, no one else came along. We vainly cast about for a stratagem; and Lupin, whose fertile brain had exhausted every possible expedient, was about to go in search of a ladder, when, suddenly, the little door opened and one of the workman's children came out.

The boy ran up the lane to the Rue Raynouard. A few minutes later he returned, carrying two bottles of water, which he set down on the pavement to take the big key from his pocket.

By that time Lupin had left me and was strolling slowly along the wall. When the child, after entering the enclosure, pushed back the door Lupin sprang forward and stuck the point of his knife into the staple of the lock. The bolt failed to catch; and it became an easy matter to push the door ajar.

"That's done the trick!" said Lupin.

He cautiously put his hand through the doorway and then, to my great surprise, entered boldly. But, on following his example, I saw that, ten yards behind the wall, a clump of laurels formed a sort of curtain which allowed us to come up unobserved.

Lupin took his stand right in the middle of the clump. I joined him and, like him, pushed aside the branches of one of the shrubs. And the sight which presented itself to my eyes was so unexpected that I was unable to suppress an exclamation, while Lupin, on his side, muttered, between his teeth:

"By Jupiter! This is a funny job!"

We saw before us, within the confined space that lay between the two windowless houses, the identical scene represented in the old picture which I had bought at a second-hand dealer's!

The identical scene! At the back, against the opposite wall, the same Greek rotunda displayed its slender columns. In the middle, the same stone benches topped a circle of four steps that ran down to a fish-pond with moss-grown flags. On the left, the same well raised its wrought-iron roof; and, close at hand, the same sun-dial showed its slanting gnomon and its marble face.

The identical scene! And what added to the strangeness of the sight was the memory, obsessing Lupin and myself, of that date of the 15th of April, inscribed in a corner of the picture, and the thought that this very day was the 15th of April and that sixteen or seventeen people, so different in age, condition and manners, had chosen the 15th of April to come together in this forgotten corner of Paris!

All of them, at the moment when we caught sight of them, were sitting in separate groups on the benches and steps; and all were eating. Not very far from my neighbour and her daughter, the workman's family and the beggar couple were sharing their provisions; while the footman, the gentleman in the soiled suit, the infantry corporal and the two lean sisters were making a common stock of their sliced ham, their tins of sardines and their gruyère cheese.

The lady with the little dog alone, who had brought no food with her, sat apart from the others, who made a show of turning their backs upon her. But Louise d'Ernemont offered her a sandwich, whereupon her example was followed by the two sisters; and the corporal at once began to make himself as agreeable to the young person as he could.

It was now half-past one. The beggar-man took out his pipe, as did the fat gentleman; and, when they found that one had no tobacco and the other no matches, their needs soon brought them together. The men went and smoked by the rotunda and the women joined them. For that matter, all these people seemed to know one another quite well.

They were at some distance from where we were standing, so that we could not hear what they said. However, we gradually perceived that the conversation was becoming animated. The young person with the dog, in particular, who by this time appeared to be in great request, indulged in much voluble talk, accompanying her words with many gestures, which set the little dog barking furiously.

But, suddenly, there was an outcry, promptly followed by shouts of rage; and one and all, men and women alike, rushed in disorder toward the well. One of the workman's brats was at that moment coming out of it, fastened by his belt to the hook at the end of the rope; and the three other urchins were drawing him up by turning the handle. More active than the rest, the corporal flung himself upon him;

and forthwith the footman and the fat gentleman seized hold of him also, while the beggars and the lean sisters came to blows with the workman and his family.

In a few seconds the little boy had not a stitch left on him beyond his shirt. The footman, who had taken possession of the rest of the clothes, ran away, pursued by the corporal, who snatched away the boy's breeches, which were next torn from the corporal by one of the lean sisters.

"They are mad!" I muttered, feeling absolutely at sea.

"Not at all, not at all," said Lupin.

"What! Do you mean to say that you can make head or tail of what is going on?"

He did not reply. The young lady with the little dog, tucking her pet under her arm, had started running after the child in the shirt, who uttered loud yells. The two of them raced round the laurel-clump in which we stood hidden; and the brat flung himself into his mother's arms.

At long last, Louise d'Ernemont, who had played a conciliatory part from the beginning, succeeded in allaying the tumult. Everybody sat down again; but there was a reaction in all those exasperated people and they remained motionless and silent, as though worn out with their exertions.

And time went by. Losing patience and beginning to feel the pangs of hunger, I went to the Rue Raynouard to fetch something to eat, which we divided while watching the actors in the incomprehensible comedy that was being performed before our eyes. They hardly stirred. Each minute that passed seemed to load them with increasing melancholy; and they sank into attitudes of discouragement, bent their backs more and more and sat absorbed in their meditations.

The afternoon wore on in this way, under a grey sky that shed a dreary light over the enclosure.

"Are they going to spend the night here?" I asked, in a bored voice.

But, at five o'clock or so, the fat gentleman in the soiled jacket-suit took out his watch. The others did the same and all, watch in hand, seemed to be anxiously awaiting an event of no little importance to themselves. The event did not take place, for, in fifteen or twenty minutes, the fat gentleman gave a gesture of despair, stood up and put on his hat.

Then lamentations broke forth. The two lean sisters and the workman's wife fell upon their knees and made the sign of the cross. The lady with the little dog and the beggar-woman kissed each other and sobbed; and we saw Louise d'Ernemont pressing her daughter sadly to her.

"Let's go," said Lupin.

"You think it's over?"

"Yes; and we have only just time to make ourselves scarce."

We went out unmolested. At the top of the lane, Lupin turned to the left and, leaving me outside, entered the first house in the Rue Raynouard, the one that backed on to the enclosure.

After talking for a few seconds to the porter, he joined me and we stopped a passing taxi-cab:

"No. 34 Rue de Turin," he said to the driver.

The ground-floor of No. 34 was occupied by a notary's office; and we were shown in, almost without waiting, to Maître Valandier, a smiling, pleasant-spoken man of a certain age.

Lupin introduced himself by the name of Captain Jeanniot, retired from the army. He said that he wanted to build a house to his own liking and that some one had suggested to him a plot of ground situated near the Rue Raynouard.

"But that plot is not for sale," said Maître Valandier.

"Oh, I was told...."

"You have been misinformed, I fear."

The lawyer rose, went to a cupboard and returned with a picture which he showed us. I was petrified. It was the same picture which I had bought, the same picture that hung in Louise d'Ernemont's room.

"This is a painting," he said, "of the plot of ground to which you refer. It is known as the Clos d'Ernemont."

"Precisely."

"Well, this close," continued the notary, "once formed part of a large garden belonging to d'Ernemont, the farmer-general, who was executed during the Terror. All that could be sold has been sold, piecemeal, by the heirs. But this last plot has remained and will remain in their joint possession ... unless...."

The notary began to laugh.

"Unless what?" asked Lupin.

"Well, it's quite a romance, a rather curious romance, in fact. I often amuse myself by looking through the voluminous documents of the case."

"Would it be indiscreet, if I asked ...?"

"Not at all, not at all," declared Maître Valandier, who seemed delighted, on the contrary, to have found a listener for his story. And, without waiting to be pressed, he began: "At the outbreak of the Revolution, Louis Agrippa d'Ernemont, on the pretence of joining his wife, who was staying at Geneva with their daughter Pauline, shut up his mansion in the Faubourg Saint-Germain, dismissed his servants and, with his son Charles, came and took up his abode in his pleasure-house at Passy, where he was known to nobody except an old and devoted serving-woman. He remained there in hiding for three years and he had every reason to hope that his retreat would not be discovered, when, one day, after luncheon, as he was having a nap, the old servant burst into his room. She had seen, at the end of the street, a patrol of armed men who seemed to be making for the house. Louis d'Ernemont got ready quickly and, at the moment when the men were knocking at the front door, disappeared through the door that led to the garden, shouting to his son, in a scared voice, to keep them talking, if only for five minutes. He may have intended to escape and found the outlets through the garden watched. In any case, he returned in six or seven minutes, replied very calmly to the questions put to him and raised no difficulty about accompanying the men. His son Charles, although only eighteen years of age, was arrested also."

"When did this happen?" asked Lupin.

"It happened on the 26th day of Germinal, Year II, that is to say, on the...."

Maître Valandier stopped, with his eyes fixed on a calendar that hung on the wall, and exclaimed:

"Why, it was on this very day! This is the 15th of April, the anniversary of the farmer-general's arrest."

"What an odd coincidence!" said Lupin. "And considering the period at which it took place, the arrest, no doubt, had serious consequences?"

"Oh, most serious!" said the notary, laughing. "Three months later, at the beginning of Thermidor, the farmer-general mounted the scaffold. His son Charles was forgotten in prison and their property was confiscated."

"The property was immense, I suppose?" said Lupin.

"Well, there you are! That's just where the thing becomes complicated. The property, which was, in fact, immense, could never be traced. It was discovered that the Faubourg Saint-Germain mansion had been sold, before the Revolution, to an Englishman, together with all the country-seats and estates and all the jewels, securities and collections belonging to the farmer-general. The Convention instituted minute inquiries, as did the Directory afterward. But the inquiries led to no result."

"There remained, at any rate, the Passy house," said Lupin.

"The house at Passy was bought, for a mere song, by a delegate of the Commune, the very man who had arrested d'Ernemont, one Citizen Broquet. Citizen Broquet shut himself up in the house, barricaded the doors, fortified the walls and, when Charles d'Ernemont was at last set free and appeared outside, received him by firing a musket at him. Charles instituted one law-suit after another, lost them all and then proceeded to offer large sums of money. But Citizen Broquet proved intractable. He had bought the house and he stuck to the house; and he would have stuck to it until his death, if Charles had not obtained the support of Bonaparte. Citizen Broquet cleared out on the 12th of February, 1803; but Charles d'Ernemont's joy was so great and his brain, no doubt, had been so violently unhinged by all that he had gone through, that, on reaching the threshold of the house of which he had at last recovered the ownership, even before opening the door he began to dance and sing in the street. He had gone clean off his head."

"By Jove!" said Lupin. "And what became of him?"

"His mother and his sister Pauline, who had ended by marrying a cousin of the same name at Geneva, were both dead. The old servant-woman took care of him and they lived together in the Passy house. Years passed without any notable event; but, suddenly, in 1812, an unexpected incident happened. The old servant made a series of strange revelations on her death-bed, in the presence of two witnesses whom she sent for. She declared that the farmer-general had carried to his house at Passy a number of bags filled with gold and silver and that those bags had disappeared a few days before the arrest. According to earlier confidences made by Charles d'Ernemont, who had them from his father, the treasures were hidden in the garden, between the rotunda, the sun-dial and the well. In proof of her statement, she produced three pictures, or rather, for they were not yet framed, three canvases, which the farmer-general had painted during his captivity and which he had succeeded in conveying to her, with instructions to hand them to his wife, his son and his daughter. Tempted by the lure of wealth, Charles and the old servant had kept silence. Then came the law-suits, the recovery of the house, Charles's madness, the servant's own useless searches; and the treasures were still there."

"And they are there now," chuckled Lupin.

"And they will be there always," exclaimed Maître Valandier. "Unless ... unless Citizen Broquet, who no doubt smelt a rat, succeeded in ferreting them out. But this is an unlikely supposition, for Citizen Broquet died in extreme poverty."

"So then ...?"

"So then everybody began to hunt. The children of Pauline, the sister, hastened from Geneva. It was discovered that Charles had been secretly married and that he had sons. All these heirs set to work."

"But Charles himself?"

"Charles lived in the most absolute retirement. He did not leave his room."

"Never?"

"Well, that is the most extraordinary, the most astounding part of the story. Once a year, Charles d'Ernemont, impelled by a sort of subconscious will-power, came downstairs, took the exact road which his father had taken, walked across the garden and sat down either on the steps of the rotunda, which you see here, in the picture, or on the kerb of the well. At twenty-seven minutes past five, he rose and went indoors again; and until his death, which occurred in 1820, he never once failed to perform this incomprehensible pilgrimage. Well, the day on which this happened was invariably the 15th of April, the anniversary of the arrest."

Maître Valandier was no longer smiling and himself seemed impressed by the amazing story which he was telling us.

"And, since Charles's death?" asked Lupin, after a moment's reflection.

"Since that time," replied the lawyer, with a certain solemnity of manner, "for nearly a hundred years, the heirs of Charles and Pauline d'Ernemont have kept up the pilgrimage of the 15th of April. During the first few years they made the most thorough excavations. Every inch of the garden was searched, every clod of ground dug up. All this is now over. They take hardly any pains. All they do is, from time to time, for no particular reason, to turn over a stone or explore the well. For the most part, they are content to sit down on the steps of the rotunda, like the poor madman; and, like him, they wait. And that, you see, is the sad part of their destiny. In those hundred years, all these people who have succeeded one another, from father to son, have lost—what shall I say?—the energy of life. They have no courage left, no initiative. They wait. They wait for the 15th of April; and, when the 15th of April comes, they wait for a miracle to take place. Poverty has ended by overtaking every one of them. My predecessors and I have sold first the house, in order to build another which yields a better rent, followed by bits of the garden and further bits. But, as to that corner over there," pointing to the picture, "they would rather die than sell it. On this they are all agreed: Louise d'Ernemont, who is the direct heiress of Pauline, as well as the beggars, the workman, the footman, the circus-rider and so on, who represent the unfortunate Charles."

There was a fresh pause; and Lupin asked:

"What is your own opinion, Maître Valandier?"

"My private opinion is that there's nothing in it. What credit can we give to the statements of an old servant enfeebled by age? What importance can we attach to the crotchets of a madman? Besides, if the farmer-general had realized his fortune, don't you think that that fortune would have been found? One could manage to hide a paper, a document, in a confined space like that, but not treasures."

"Still, the pictures?..."

"Yes, of course. But, after all, are they a sufficient proof?"

Lupin bent over the copy which the solicitor had taken from the cupboard and, after examining it at length, said:

"You spoke of three pictures."

"Yes, the one which you see was handed to my predecessor by the heirs of Charles. Louise d'Ernemont possesses another. As for the third, no one knows what became of it."

Lupin looked at me and continued:

"And do they all bear the same date?"

"Yes, the date inscribed by Charles d'Ernemont when he had them framed, not long before his death.... The same date, that is to say the 15th of April, Year II, according to the revolutionary calendar, as the arrest took place in April, 1794."

"Oh, yes, of course," said Lupin. "The figure 2 means...."

He thought for a few moments and resumed:

"One more question, if I may. Did no one ever come forward to solve the problem?"

Maître Valandier threw up his arms:

"Goodness gracious me!" he cried. "Why, it was the plague of the office! One of my predecessors, Maître Turbon, was summoned to Passy no fewer than eighteen times, between 1820 and 1843, by the groups of heirs, whom fortune-tellers, clairvoyants, visionaries, impostors of all sorts had promised that they would discover the farmer-general's treasures. At last, we laid down a rule: any outsider applying to institute a search was to begin by depositing a certain sum."

"What sum?"

"A thousand francs."

"And did this have the effect of frightening them off?"

"No. Four years ago, an Hungarian hypnotist tried the experiment and made me waste a whole day. After that, we fixed the deposit at five thousand francs. In case of success, a third of the treasure goes to the finder. In case of failure, the deposit is forfeited to the heirs. Since then, I have been left in peace."

"Here are your five thousand francs."

The lawyer gave a start:

"Eh? What do you say?"

"I say," repeated Lupin, taking five bank-notes from his pocket and calmly spreading them on the table, "I say that here is the deposit of five thousand francs. Please give me a receipt and invite all the d'Ernemont heirs to meet me at Passy on the 15th of April next year."

The notary could not believe his senses. I myself, although Lupin had accustomed me to these surprises, was utterly taken back.

"Are you serious?" asked Maître Valandier.

"Perfectly serious."

"But, you know, I told you my opinion. All these improbable stories rest upon no evidence of any kind."

"I don't agree with you," said Lupin.

The notary gave him the look which we give to a person who is not quite right in his head. Then, accepting the situation, he took his pen and drew up a contract on stamped paper, acknowledging the payment of the deposit by Captain Jeanniot and promising him a third of such moneys as he should discover:

"If you change your mind," he added, "you might let me know a week before the time comes. I shall not inform the d'Ernemont family until the last moment, so as not to give those poor people too long a spell of hope."

"You can inform them this very day, Maître Valandier. It will make them spend a happier year."

We said good-bye. Outside, in the street, I cried:

"So you have hit upon something?"

"I?" replied Lupin. "Not a bit of it! And that's just what amuses me."

"But they have been searching for a hundred years!"

"It is not so much a matter of searching as of thinking. Now I have three hundred and sixty-five days to think in. It is a great deal more than I want; and I am afraid that I shall forget all about the business, interesting though it may be. Oblige me by reminding me, will you?"

I reminded him of it several times during the following months, though he never seemed to attach much importance to the matter. Then came a long period during which I had no opportunity of seeing him. It was the period, as I afterward learnt, of his visit to Armenia and of the terrible struggle on which he embarked against Abdul the Damned, a struggle which ended in the tyrant's downfall.

I used to write to him, however, at the address which he gave me and I was thus able to send him certain particulars which I had succeeded in gathering, here and there, about my neighbour Louise d'Ernemont, such as the love which she had conceived, a few years earlier, for a very rich young man, who still loved her, but who had been compelled by his family to throw her over; the young widow's despair, and the plucky life which she led with her little daughter.

Lupin replied to none of my letters. I did not know whether they reached him; and, meantime, the date was drawing near and I could not help wondering whether his numerous undertakings would not prevent him from keeping the appointment which he himself had fixed.

As a matter of fact, the morning of the 15th of April arrived and Lupin was not with me by the time I had finished lunch. It was a quarter-past twelve. I left my flat and took a cab to Passy.

I had no sooner entered the lane than I saw the workman's four brats standing outside the door in the wall. Maître Valandier, informed by them of my arrival, hastened in my direction:

"Well?" he cried. "Where's Captain Jeanniot?"

"Hasn't he come?"

"No; and I can assure you that everybody is very impatient to see him."

The different groups began to crowd round the lawyer; and I noticed that all those faces which I recognized had thrown off the gloomy and despondent expression which they wore a year ago.

"They are full of hope," said Maître Valandier, "and it is my fault. But what could I do? Your friend made such an impression upon me that I spoke to these good people with a confidence ... which I cannot say I feel. However, he seems a queer sort of fellow, this Captain Jeanniot of yours...."

He asked me many questions and I gave him a number of more or less fanciful details about the captain, to which the heirs listened, nodding their heads in appreciation of my remarks.

"Of course, the truth was bound to be discovered sooner or later," said the fat gentleman, in a tone of conviction.

The infantry corporal, dazzled by the captain's rank, did not entertain a doubt in his mind.

The lady with the little dog wanted to know if Captain Jeanniot was young.

But Louise d'Ernemont said:

"And suppose he does not come?"

"We shall still have the five thousand francs to divide," said the beggar-man.

For all that, Louise d'Ernemont's words had damped their enthusiasm. Their faces began to look sullen and I felt an atmosphere as of anguish weighing upon us.

At half-past one, the two lean sisters felt faint and sat down. Then the fat gentleman in the soiled suit suddenly rounded on the notary:

"It's you, Maître Valandier, who are to blame.... You ought to have brought the captain here by main force.... He's a humbug, that's quite clear."

He gave me a savage look, and the footman, in his turn, flung muttered curses at me.

I confess that their reproaches seemed to me well-founded and that Lupin's absence annoyed me greatly:

"He won't come now," I whispered to the lawyer.

And I was thinking of beating a retreat, when the eldest of the brats appeared at the door, yelling:

"There's some one coming!... A motor-cycle!..."

A motor was throbbing on the other side of the wall. A man on a motor-bicycle came tearing down the lane at the risk of breaking his neck. Suddenly, he put on his brakes, outside the door, and sprang from his machine.

Under the layer of dust which covered him from head to foot, we could see that his navy-blue reefer-suit, his carefully creased trousers, his black felt hat and patent-leather boots were not the clothes in which a man usually goes cycling.

"But that's not Captain Jeanniot!" shouted the notary, who failed to recognize him.

"Yes, it is," said Lupin, shaking hands with us. "I'm Captain Jeanniot right enough ... only I've shaved off my moustache.... Besides, Maître Valandier, here's your receipt."

He caught one of the workman's children by the arm and said:

"Run to the cab-rank and fetch a taxi to the corner of the Rue Raynouard. Look sharp! I have an urgent appointment to keep at two o'clock, or a quarter-past at the latest."

There was a murmur of protest. Captain Jeanniot took out his watch:

"Well! It's only twelve minutes to two! I have a good quarter of an hour before me. But, by Jingo, how tired I feel! And how hungry into the bargain!"

The corporal thrust his ammunition-bread into Lupin's hand; and he munched away at it as he sat down and said:

"You must forgive me. I was in the Marseilles express, which left the rails between Dijon and Laroche. There were twelve people killed and any number injured, whom I had to help. Then I found this motor-cycle in the luggage-van.... Maître Valandier, you must be good enough to restore it to the owner. You will find the label fastened to the handle-bar. Ah, you're back, my boy! Is the taxi there? At the corner of the Rue Raynouard? Capital!"

He looked at his watch again:

"Hullo! No time to lose!"

I stared at him with eager curiosity. But how great must the excitement of the d'Ernemont heirs have been! True, they had not the same faith in Captain Jeanniot that I had in Lupin. Nevertheless, their faces were pale and drawn. Captain Jeanniot turned slowly to the left and walked up to the sun-dial. The pedestal represented the figure of a man with a powerful torso, who bore on his shoulders a marble slab the surface of which had been so much worn by time that we could hardly distinguish the engraved lines that marked the hours. Above the slab, a Cupid, with outspread wings, held an arrow that served as a gnomon.

The captain stood leaning forward for a minute, with attentive eyes.

Then he said:

"Somebody lend me a knife, please."

A clock in the neighbourhood struck two. At that exact moment, the shadow of the arrow was thrown upon the sunlit dial along the line of a crack in the marble which divided the slab very nearly in half.

The captain took the knife handed to him. And with the point, very gently, he began to scratch the mixture of earth and moss that filled the narrow cleft.

Almost immediately, at a couple of inches from the edge, he stopped, as though his knife had encountered an obstacle, inserted his thumb and forefinger and withdrew a small object which he rubbed between the palms of his hands and gave to the lawyer:

"Here, Maître Valandier. Something to go on with."

It was an enormous diamond, the size of a hazelnut and beautifully cut.

The captain resumed his work. The next moment, a fresh stop. A second diamond, magnificent and brilliant as the first, appeared in sight.

And then came a third and a fourth.

In a minute's time, following the crack from one edge to the other and certainly without digging deeper than half an inch, the captain had taken out eighteen diamonds of the same size.

During this minute, there was not a cry, not a movement around the sun-dial. The heirs seemed paralyzed with a sort of stupor. Then the fat gentleman muttered:

"Geminy!"

And the corporal moaned:

"Oh, captain!... Oh, captain!..."

The two sisters fell in a dead faint. The lady with the little dog dropped on her knees and prayed, while the footman, staggering like a drunken man, held his head in his two hands, and Louise d'Ernemont wept.

When calm was restored and all became eager to thank Captain Jeanniot, they saw that he was gone.

Some years passed before I had an opportunity of talking to Lupin about this business. He was in a confidential vein and answered:

"The business of the eighteen diamonds? By Jove, when I think that three or four generations of my fellow-men had been hunting for the solution! And the eighteen diamonds were there all the time, under a little mud and dust!"

"But how did you guess?..."

"I did not guess. I reflected. I doubt if I need even have reflected. I was struck, from the beginning, by the fact that the whole circumstance was governed by one primary question: the question of time. When Charles d'Ernemont was still in possession of his wits, he wrote a date upon the three pictures. Later, in the gloom in which he was struggling, a faint glimmer of intelligence led him every year to the centre of the old garden; and the same faint glimmer led him away from it every year at the same moment, that is to say, at twenty-seven minutes past five. Something must have acted on the disordered machinery of his brain in this way. What was the superior force that controlled the poor madman's movements? Obviously, the instinctive notion of time represented by the sun-dial in the farmer-general's pictures. It was the annual revolution of the earth around the sun that brought Charles d'Ernemont back to the garden at a fixed date. And it was the earth's daily revolution upon its own axis that took him from it at a fixed hour, that is to say, at the hour, most likely, when the sun, concealed by objects different from those of to-day, ceased to light the Passy garden. Now of all this the sun-dial was the symbol. And that is why I at once knew where to look."

"But how did you settle the hour at which to begin looking?"

"Simply by the pictures. A man living at that time, such as Charles d'Ernemont, would have written either 26 Germinal, Year II, or else 15 April, 1794, but not 15 April, Year II. I was astounded that no one had thought of that."

"Then the figure 2 stood for two o'clock?"

"Evidently. And what must have happened was this: the farmer-general began by turning his fortune into solid gold and silver money. Then, by way of additional precaution, with this gold and silver he bought eighteen wonderful diamonds. When he was surprised by the arrival of the patrol, he fled into his garden. Which was the best place to hide the diamonds? Chance caused his eyes to light upon the sun-dial. It was two o'clock. The shadow of the arrow was then falling along the crack in the marble. He obeyed this sign of the shadow, rammed his eighteen diamonds into the dust and calmly went back and surrendered to the soldiers."

"But the shadow of the arrow coincides with the crack in the marble every day of the year and not only on the 15th of April."

"You forget, my dear chap, that we are dealing with a lunatic and that he remembered only this date of the 15th of April."

"Very well; but you, once you had solved the riddle, could easily have made your way into the enclosure and taken the diamonds."

"Quite true; and I should not have hesitated, if I had had to do with people of another description. But I really felt sorry for those poor wretches. And then you know the sort of idiot that Lupin is. The idea of appearing suddenly as a benevolent genius and amazing his kind would be enough to make him commit any sort of folly."

"Tah!" I cried. "The folly was not so great as all that. Six magnificent diamonds! How delighted the d'Ernemont heirs must have been to fulfil their part of the contract!"

Lupin looked at me and burst into uncontrollable laughter:

"So you haven't heard? Oh, what a joke! The delight of the d'Ernemont heirs!.... Why, my dear fellow, on the next day, that worthy Captain Jeanniot had so many mortal enemies! On the very next day, the two lean sisters and the fat gentleman organized an opposition. A contract? Not worth the paper it was written on, because, as could easily be proved, there was no such person as Captain Jeanniot. Where did that adventurer spring from? Just let him sue them and they'd soon show him what was what!"

"Louise d'Ernemont too?"

"No, Louise d'Ernemont protested against that piece of rascality. But what could she do against so many? Besides, now that she was rich, she got back her young man. I haven't heard of her since."

"So ...?"

"So, my dear fellow, I was caught in a trap, with not a leg to stand on, and I had to compromise and accept one modest diamond as my share, the smallest and the least handsome of the lot. That comes of doing one's best to help people!"

And Lupin grumbled between his teeth:

"Oh, gratitude!... All humbug!... Where should we honest men be if we had not our conscience and the satisfaction of duty performed to reward us?"

IV. THE INFERNAL TRAP

When the race was over, a crowd of people, streaming toward the exit from the grand stand, pushed against Nicolas Dugrival. He brought his hand smartly to the inside pocket of his jacket.

"What's the matter?" asked his wife.

"I still feel nervous ... with that money on me! I'm afraid of some nasty accident."

She muttered:

"And I can't understand you. How can you think of carrying such a sum about with you? Every farthing we possess! Lord knows, it cost us trouble enough to earn!"

"Pooh!" he said. "No one would guess that it is here, in my pocket-book."

"Yes, yes," she grumbled. "That young man-servant whom we discharged last week knew all about it, didn't he, Gabriel?"

"Yes, aunt," said a youth standing beside her.

Nicolas Dugrival, his wife and his nephew Gabriel were well-known figures at the race-meetings, where the regular frequenters saw them almost every day: Dugrival, a big, fat, red-faced man, who looked as if he knew how to enjoy life; his wife, also built on heavy lines, with a coarse, vulgar face, and always dressed in a plum-coloured silk much the worse for wear; the nephew, quite young, slender, with pale features, dark eyes and fair and rather curly hair.

As a rule, the couple remained seated throughout the afternoon. It was Gabriel who betted for his uncle, watching the horses in the paddock, picking up tips to right and left among the jockeys and stable-lads, running backward and forward between the stands and the *pari-mutuel*.

Luck had favoured them that day, for, three times, Dugrival's neighbours saw the young man come back and hand him money.

The fifth race was just finishing. Dugrival lit a cigar. At that moment, a gentleman in a tight-fitting brown suit, with a face ending in a peaked grey beard, came up to him and asked, in a confidential whisper:

"Does this happen to belong to you, sir?"

And he displayed a gold watch and chain.

Dugrival gave a start:

"Why, yes ... it's mine.... Look, here are my initials, N. G.: Nicolas Dugrival!"

And he at once, with a movement of terror, clapped his hand to his jacket-pocket. The note-case was still there.

"Ah," he said, greatly relieved, "that's a piece of luck!... But, all the same, how on earth was it done?... Do you know the scoundrel?"

"Yes, we've got him locked up. Pray come with me and we'll soon look into the matter."

"Whom have I the honour ...?"

"M. Delangle, detective-inspector. I have sent to let M. Marquenne, the magistrate, know."

Nicolas Dugrival went out with the inspector; and the two of them started for the commissary's office, some distance behind the grand stand. They were within fifty yards of it, when the inspector was accosted by a man who said to him, hurriedly:

"The fellow with the watch has blabbed; we are on the tracks of a whole gang. M. Marquenne wants you to wait for him at the *pari-mutuel* and to keep a look-out near the fourth booth."

There was a crowd outside the betting-booths and Inspector Delangle muttered:

"It's an absurd arrangement.... Whom am I to look out for?... That's just like M. Marquenne!..."

He pushed aside a group of people who were crowding too close upon him:

"By Jove, one has to use one's elbows here and keep a tight hold on one's purse. That's the way you got your watch pinched, M. Dugrival!"

"I can't understand...."

"Oh, if you knew how those gentry go to work! One never guesses what they're up to next. One of them treads on your foot, another gives you a poke in the eye with his stick and the third picks your pocket before you know where you are.... I've been had that way myself." He stopped and then continued, angrily. "But, bother it, what's the use of hanging about here! What a mob! It's unbearable!... Ah, there's M. Marquenne making signs to us!... One moment, please ... and be sure and wait for me here."

He shouldered his way through the crowd. Nicolas Dugrival followed him for a moment with his eyes. Once the inspector was out of sight, he stood a little to one side, to avoid being hustled.

A few minutes passed. The sixth race was about to start, when Dugrival saw his wife and nephew looking for him. He explained to them that Inspector Delangle was arranging matters with the magistrate.

"Have you your money still?" asked his wife.

"Why, of course I have!" he replied. "The inspector and I took good care, I assure you, not to let the crowd jostle us."

He felt his jacket, gave a stifled cry, thrust his hand into his pocket and began to stammer inarticulate syllables, while Mme. Dugrival gasped, in dismay:

"What is it? What's the matter?"

"Stolen!" he moaned. "The pocket-book ... the fifty notes!..."

"It's not true!" she screamed. "It's not true!"

"Yes, the inspector ... a common sharper ... he's the man...."

She uttered absolute yells:

"Thief! Thief! Stop thief!... My husband's been robbed!... Fifty thousand francs!... We are ruined!... Thief! Thief ..."

In a moment they were surrounded by policemen and taken to the commissary's office. Dugrival went like a lamb, absolutely bewildered. His wife continued to shriek at the top of her voice, piling up explanations, railing against the inspector:

"Have him looked for!... Have him found!... A brown suit.... A pointed beard.... Oh, the villain, to think what he's robbed us of!... Fifty thousand francs!... Why ... why, Dugrival, what are you doing?"

With one bound, she flung herself upon her husband. Too late! He had pressed the barrel of a revolver against his temple. A shot rang out. Dugrival fell. He was dead.

The reader cannot have forgotten the commotion made by the newspapers in connection with this case, nor how they jumped at the opportunity once more to accuse the police of carclessness and blundering. Was it conceivable that a pick-pocket could play the part of an inspector like that, in broad daylight and in a public place, and rob a respectable man with impunity?

Nicolas Dugrival's widow kept the controversy alive, thanks to her jeremiads and to the interviews which she granted on every hand. A reporter had secured a snapshot of her in front of her husband's body, holding up her hand and swearing to revenge his death. Her nephew Gabriel was standing beside her, with hatred pictured in his face. He, too, it appeared, in a few words uttered in a whisper, but in a tone of fierce determination, had taken an oath to pursue and catch the murderer.

The accounts described the humble apartment which they occupied at the Batignolles; and, as they had been robbed of all their means, a sporting-paper opened a subscription on their behalf.

As for the mysterious Delangle, he remained undiscovered. Two men were arrested, but had to be released forthwith. The police took up a number of clues, which were at once abandoned; more than one name was mentioned; and, lastly, they accused Arsène Lupin, an action which provoked the famous burglar's celebrated cable, dispatched from New York six days after the incident:

"Protest indignantly against calumny invented by baffled police. Send my condolences to unhappy victims. Instructing my bankers to remit them fifty thousand francs.

True enough, on the day after the publication of the cable, a stranger rang at Mme. Dugrival's door and handed her an envelope. The envelope contained fifty thousand-franc notes.

This theatrical stroke was not at all calculated to allay the universal comment. But an event soon occurred which provided any amount of additional excitement. Two days later, the people living in the same house as Mme. Dugrival and her nephew were awakened, at four o'clock in the morning, by horrible cries and shrill calls for help. They rushed to the flat. The porter succeeded in opening the door. By the light of a lantern carried by one of the neighbours, he found Gabriel stretched at full-length in his bedroom, with his wrists and ankles bound and a gag forced into his mouth, while, in the next room, Mme. Dugrival lay with her life's blood ebbing away through a great gash in her breast.

She whispered:

"The money.... I've been robbed.... All the notes gone...."

And she fainted away.

What had happened? Gabriel said—and, as soon as she was able to speak, Mme. Dugrival completed her nephew's story—that he was startled from his sleep by finding himself attacked by two men, one of whom gagged him, while the other fastened him down. He was unable to see the men in the dark, but he heard the noise of the struggle between them and his aunt. It was a terrible struggle, Mme. Dugrival declared. The ruffians, who obviously knew their way about, guided by some intuition, made straight for the little cupboard containing the money and, in spite of her resistance and outcries, laid hands upon the bundle of bank-notes. As they left, one of them, whom she had bitten in the arm, stabbed her with a knife, whereupon the men had both fled.

"Which way?" she was asked.

"Through the door of my bedroom and afterward, I suppose, through the hall-door."

"Impossible! The porter would have noticed them."

For the whole mystery lay in this: how had the ruffians entered the house and how did they manage to leave it? There was no outlet open to them. Was it one of the tenants? A careful inquiry proved the absurdity of such a supposition.

What then?

Chief-inspector Ganimard, who was placed in special charge of the case, confessed that he had never known anything more bewildering:

"It's very like Lupin," he said, "and yet it's not Lupin.... No, there's more in it than meets the eye, something very doubtful and suspicious.... Besides, if it were Lupin, why should he take back the fifty thousand francs which he sent? There's another question that puzzles me: what is the connection between the second robbery and the first, the one on the race-course? The whole thing is incomprehensible and I have a sort of feeling—which is very rare with me—that it is no use hunting. For my part, I give it up."

The examining-magistrate threw himself into the case with heart and soul. The reporters united their efforts with those of the police. A famous English sleuth-hound crossed the Channel. A wealthy American, whose head had been turned by detective-stories, offered a big reward to whosoever should supply the first information leading to the discovery of the truth. Six weeks later, no one was any the wiser. The public adopted Ganimard's view; and the examining-magistrate himself grew tired of struggling in a darkness which only became denser as time went on.

And life continued as usual with Dugrival's widow. Nursed by her nephew, she soon recovered from her wound. In the mornings, Gabriel settled her in an easy-chair at the dining-room window, did the rooms and then went out marketing. He cooked their lunch without even accepting the proffered assistance of the porter's wife.

Worried by the police investigations and especially by the requests for interviews, the aunt and nephew refused to see anybody. Not even the portress, whose chatter disturbed and wearied Mme. Dugrival, was admitted. She fell back upon Gabriel, whom she accosted each time that he passed her room:

"Take care, M. Gabriel, you're both of you being spied upon. There are men watching you. Why, only last night, my husband caught a fellow staring up at your windows."

"Nonsense!" said Gabriel. "It's all right. That's the police, protecting us."

One afternoon, at about four o'clock, there was a violent altercation between two costermongers at the bottom of the street. The porter's wife at once left her room to listen to the invectives which the adversaries were hurling at each other's heads. Her back was no sooner turned than a man, young, of medium height and dressed in a grey suit of irreproachable cut, slipped into the house and ran up the staircase.

When he came to the third floor, he rang the bell. Receiving no answer, he rang again. At the third summons, the door opened.

"Mme. Dugrival?" he asked, taking off his hat.

"Mme. Dugrival is still an invalid and unable to see any one," said Gabriel, who stood in the hall.

"It's most important that I should speak to her."

"I am her nephew and perhaps I could take her a message...."

"Very well," said the man. "Please tell Mme. Dugrival that an accident has supplied me with valuable information concerning the robbery from which she has suffered and that I should like to go over the flat and ascertain certain particulars for myself. I am accustomed to this sort of inquiry; and my call is sure to be of use to her."

Gabriel examined the visitor for a moment, reflected and said:

"In that case, I suppose my aunt will consent ... Pray come in."

He opened the door of the dining-room and stepped back to allow the other to pass. The stranger walked to the threshold, but, at the moment when he was crossing it, Gabriel raised his arm and, with a swift movement, struck him with a dagger over the right shoulder.

A burst of laughter rang through the room:

"Got him!" cried Mme. Dugrival, darting up from her chair. "Well done, Gabriel! But, I say, you haven't killed the scoundrel, have you?"

"I don't think so, aunt. It's a small blade and I didn't strike him too hard."

The man was staggering, with his hands stretched in front of him and his face deathly pale.

"You fool!" sneered the widow. "So you've fallen into the trap ... and a good job too! We've been looking out for you a long time. Come, my fine fellow, down with you! You don't care about it, do you? But you can't help yourself, you see. That's right: one knee on the ground, before the missus ... now the other knee.... How well we've been brought up!... Crash, there we go on the floor! Lord, if my poor Dugrival could only see him like that!... And now, Gabriel, to work!"

She went to her bedroom and opened one of the doors of a hanging wardrobe filled with dresses. Pulling these aside, she pushed open another door which formed the back of the wardrobe and led to a room in the next house:

"Help me carry him, Gabriel. And you'll nurse him as well as you can, won't you? For the present, he's worth his weight in gold to us, the artist!..."

The hours succeeded one another. Days passed.

One morning, the wounded man regained a moment's consciousness. He raised his eyelids and looked around him.

He was lying in a room larger than that in which he had been stabbed, a room sparsely furnished, with thick curtains hanging before the windows from top to bottom. There was light enough, however, to enable him to see young Gabriel Dugrival seated on a chair beside him and watching him.

"Ah, it's you, youngster!" he murmured. "I congratulate you, my lad. You have a sure and pretty touch with the dagger."

And he fell asleep again.

That day and the following days, he woke up several times and, each time, he saw the stripling's pale face, his thin lips and his dark eyes, with the hard look in them:

"You frighten me," he said. "If you have sworn to do for me, don't stand on ceremony. But cheer up, for goodness' sake. The thought of death has always struck me as the most humorous thing in the world. Whereas, with you, old chap, it simply becomes lugubrious. I prefer to go to sleep. Good-night!"

Still, Gabriel, in obedience to Mme. Dugrival's orders, continued to nurse him with the utmost care and attention. The patient was almost free from fever and was beginning to take beef-tea and milk. He gained a little strength and jested:

"When will the convalescent be allowed his first drive? Is the bath-chair there? Why, cheer up, stupid! You look like a weeping-willow contemplating a crime. Come, just one little smile for daddy!"

One day, on waking, he had a very unpleasant feeling of constraint. After a few efforts, he perceived that, during his sleep, his legs, chest and arms had been fastened to the bedstead with thin wire strands that cut into his flesh at the least movements.

"Ah," he said to his keeper, "this time it's the great performance! The chicken's going to be bled. Are you operating, Angel Gabriel? If so, see that your razor's nice and clean, old chap! The antiseptic treatment, *if* you please!"

But he was interrupted by the sound of a key grating in the lock. The door opposite opened and Mme. Dugrival appeared.

She approached slowly, took a chair and, producing a revolver from her pocket, cocked it and laid it on the table by the bedside.

"Brrrrr!" said the prisoner. "We might be at the Ambigu!... Fourth act: the Traitor's Doom. And the fair sex to do the deed.... The hand of the Graces.... What an honour!... Mme. Dugrival, I rely on you not to disfigure me."

"Hold your tongue, Lupin."

"Ah, so you know?... By Jove, how clever we are!"

"Hold your tongue, Lupin."

There was a solemn note in her voice that impressed the captive and compelled him to silence. He watched his two gaolers in turns. The bloated features and red complexion of Mme. Dugrival formed a striking contrast with her nephew's refined face; but they both wore the same air of implacable resolve.

The widow leant forward and said:

"Are you prepared to answer my questions?"

"Why not?"

"Then listen to me. How did you know that Dugrival carried all his money in his pocket?"

"Servants' gossip...."

"A young man-servant whom we had in our employ: was that it?"

"Yes."

"And did you steal Dugrival's watch in order to give it back to him and inspire him with confidence?"

"Yes."

She suppressed a movement of fury:

"You fool! You fool!... What! You rob my man, you drive him to kill himself and, instead of making tracks to the uttermost ends of the earth and hiding yourself, you go on playing Lupin in the heart of Paris!... Did you forget that I swore, on my dead husband's head, to find his murderer?"

"That's what staggers me," said Lupin. "How did you come to suspect me?"

"How? Why, you gave yourself away!"

"I did?..."

"Of course.... The fifty thousand francs...."

"Well, what about it? A present...."

"Yes, a present which you gave cabled instructions to have sent to me, so as to make believe that you were in America on the day of the races. A present, indeed! What humbug! The fact is, you didn't like to think of the poor fellow whom you had murdered. So you restored the money to the widow, publicly, of course, because you love playing to the gallery and ranting and posing, like the mountebank that you are. That was all very nicely thought out. Only, my fine fellow, you ought not to have sent me the selfsame notes that were stolen from Dugrival! Yes, you silly fool, the selfsame notes and no others! We knew the numbers, Dugrival and I did. And you were stupid enough to send the bundle to me. Now do you understand your folly?"

Lupin began to laugh:

"It was a pretty blunder, I confess. I'm not responsible; I gave different orders. But, all the same I can't blame any one except myself."

"Ah, so you admit it! You signed your theft and you signed your ruin at the same time. There was nothing left to be done but to find you. Find you? No, better than that. Sensible people don't find Lupin: they make him come to them! That was a masterly notion. It belongs to my young nephew, who loathes you as much as I do, if possible, and who knows you thoroughly, through reading all the books that have been written about you. He knows your prying nature, your need to be always plotting, your mania for hunting in the dark and unravelling what others have failed to unravel. He also knows that sort of sham kindness of yours, the drivelling sentimentality that makes you shed crocodile tears over the people you victimize; And he planned the whole farce! He invented the story of the two burglars, the second theft of fifty thousand francs! Oh, I swear to you, before Heaven, that the stab which I gave myself with my own hands never hurt me! And I swear to you, before Heaven, that we spent a glorious time waiting for you, the boy and I, peeping out at your confederates who prowled under our windows, taking their bearings! And there was no mistake about it: you were bound to come! Seeing that you had restored the Widow Dugrival's fifty thousand francs, it was out of the question that you should allow the Widow Dugrival to be robbed of her fifty thousand francs! You were bound to come, attracted by the scent of the mystery. You were bound to come, for swagger, out of vanity! And you come!"

The widow gave a strident laugh:

"Well played, wasn't it? The Lupin of Lupins, the master of masters, inaccessible and invisible, caught in a trap by a woman and a boy!... Here he is in flesh and bone ... here he is with hands and feet tied, no more dangerous than a sparrow ... here is he ... here he is!..."

She shook with joy and began to pace the room, throwing sidelong glances at the bed, like a wild beast that does not for a moment take its eyes from its victim. And never had Lupin beheld greater hatred and savagery in any human being.

"Enough of this prattle," she said.

Suddenly restraining herself, she stalked back to him and, in a quite different tone, in a hollow voice, laying stress on every syllable:

"Thanks to the papers in your pocket, Lupin, I have made good use of the last twelve days. I know all your affairs, all your schemes, all your assumed names, all the organization of your band, all the lodgings which you possess in Paris and elsewhere. I have even visited one of them, the most secret, the one where you hide your papers, your ledgers and the whole story of your financial operations. The result of my investigations is very satisfactory. Here are four cheques, taken from four cheque-books and corresponding with four accounts which you keep at four different banks under four different names. I have filled in each of them for ten thousand francs. A larger figure would have been too risky. And, now, sign."

"By Jove!" said Lupin, sarcastically. "This is blackmail, my worthy Mme. Dugrival."

"That takes your breath away, what?"

"It takes my breath away, as you say."

"And you find an adversary who is a match for you?"

"The adversary is far beyond me. So the trap—let us call it infernal—the infernal trap into which I have fallen was laid not merely by a widow thirsting for revenge, but also by a first-rate business woman anxious to increase her capital?"

"Just so."

"My congratulations. And, while I think of it, used M. Dugrival perhaps to ...?"

"You have hit it, Lupin. After all, why conceal the fact? It will relieve your conscience. Yes, Lupin, Dugrival used to work on the same lines as yourself. Oh, not on the same scale!... We were modest people: a louis here, a louis there ... a purse or two which we trained Gabriel to pick up at the races.... And, in this way, we had made our little pile ... just enough to buy a small place in the country."

"I prefer it that way," said Lupin.

"That's all right! I'm only telling you, so that you may know that I am not a beginner and that you have nothing to hope for. A rescue? No. The room in which we now are communicates with my bedroom. It has a private outlet of which nobody knows. It was Dugrival's special apartment. He used to see his friends here. He kept his implements and tools here, his disguises ... his telephone even, as you perceive. So there's no hope, you see. Your accomplices have given up looking for you here. I have sent them off on another track. Your goose is cooked. Do you begin to realize the position?"

"Yes."

"Then sign the cheques."

"And, when I have signed them, shall I be free?"

"I must cash them first."

"And after that?"

"After that, on my soul, as I hope to be saved, you will be free."

"I don't trust you."

"Have you any choice?"

"That's true. Hand me the cheques."

She unfastened Lupin's right hand, gave him a pen and said:

"Don't forget that the four cheques require four different signatures and that the handwriting has to be altered in each case."

"Never fear."

He signed the cheques.

"Gabriel," said the widow, "it is ten o'clock. If I am not back by twelve, it will mean that this scoundrel has played me one of his tricks. At twelve o'clock, blow out his brains. I am leaving you the revolver with which your uncle shot himself. There are five bullets left out of the six. That will be ample."

She left the room, humming a tune as she went.

Lupin mumbled:

"I wouldn't give twopence for my life."

He shut his eyes for an instant and then, suddenly, said to Gabriel:

"How much?"

And, when the other did not appear to understand, he grew irritated:

"I mean what I say. How much? Answer me, can't you? We drive the same trade, you and I. I steal, thou stealest, we steal. So we ought to come to terms: that's what we are here for. Well? Is it a bargain? Shall we clear out together. I will give you a post in my gang, an easy, well-paid post. How much do you want for yourself? Ten thousand? Twenty thousand? Fix your own price; don't be shy. There's plenty to be had for the asking."

An angry shiver passed through his frame as he saw the impassive face of his keeper:

"Oh, the beggar won't even answer! Why, you can't have been so fond of old Dugrival as all that! Listen to me: if you consent to release me...."

But he interrupted himself. The young man's eyes wore the cruel expression which he knew so well. What was the use of trying to move him?

"Hang it all!" he snarled. "I'm not going to croak here, like a dog! Oh, if I could only...."

Stiffening all his muscles, he tried to burst his bonds, making a violent effort that drew a cry of pain from him; and he fell back upon his bed, exhausted.

"Well, well," he muttered, after a moment, "it's as the widow said: my goose is cooked. Nothing to be done. *De profundis*, Lupin."

A quarter of an hour passed, half an hour....

Gabriel, moving closer to Lupin, saw that his eyes were shut and that his breath came evenly, like that of a man sleeping. But Lupin said:

"Don't imagine that I'm asleep, youngster. No, people don't sleep at a moment like this. Only I am consoling myself. Needs must, eh?... And then I am thinking of what is to come after.... Exactly. I have a little theory of my own about that. You wouldn't think it, to look at me, but I believe in metempsychosis, in the transmigration of souls. It would take too long to explain, however.... I say, boy ... suppose we shook hands before we part? You won't? Then good-bye. Good health and a long life to you, Gabriel!..."

He closed his eyelids and did not stir again before Mme. Dugrival's return.

The widow entered with a lively step, at a few minutes before twelve. She seemed greatly excited:

"I have the money," she said to her nephew. "Run away. I'll join you in the motor down below."

"But...."

"I don't want your help to finish him off. I can do that alone. Still, if you feel like seeing the sort of a face a rogue can pull.... Pass me the weapon."

Gabriel handed her the revolver and the widow continued:

"Have you burnt our papers?"

"Yes."

"Then to work. And, as soon as he's done for, be off. The shots may bring the neighbours. They must find both the flats empty."

She went up to the bed:

"Are you ready, Lupin?"

"Ready's not the word: I'm burning with impatience."

"Have you any request to make of me?"

"None."

"Then...."

"One word, though."

"What is it?"

"If I meet Dugrival in the next world, what message am I to give him from you?"

She shrugged her shoulders and put the barrel of the revolver to Lupin's temple.

"That's it," he said, "and be sure your hand doesn't shake, my dear lady. It won't hurt you, I swear. Are you ready? At the word of command, eh? One ... two ... three...."

The widow pulled the trigger. A shot rang out.

"Is this death?" said Lupin. "That's funny! I should have thought it was something much more different from life!"

There was a second shot. Gabriel snatched the weapon from his aunt's hands and examined it:

"Ah," he exclaimed, "the bullets have been removed!... There are only the percussion-caps left!..."

His aunt and he stood motionless, for a moment, and confused:

"Impossible!" she blurted out. "Who could have done it?... An inspector?... The examining-magistrate?..."

She stopped and, in a low voice:

"Hark.... I hear a noise...."

They listened and the widow went into the hall. She returned, furious, exasperated by her failure and by the scare which she had received:

"There's nobody there.... It must have been the neighbours going out.... We have plenty of time.... Ah, Lupin, you were beginning to make merry!... The knife, Gabriel."

"It's in my room."

"Go and fetch it."

Gabriel hurried away. The widow stamped with rage:

"I've sworn to do it!... You've got to suffer, my fine fellow!... I swore to Dugrival that I would do it and I have repeated my oath every morning and evening since.... I have taken it on my knees, yes, on my knees, before Heaven that listens to me! It's my duty and my right to revenge my dead husband!... By the way, Lupin, you don't look quite as merry as you did!... Lord, one would almost think you were afraid!... He's afraid! He's afraid! I can see it in his eyes!... Come along, Gabriel, my boy!... Look at his eyes!... Look at his lips!... He's trembling!... Give me the knife, so that I may dig it into his heart while he's shivering.... Oh, you coward!... Quick, quick, Gabriel, the knife!..."

"I can't find it anywhere," said the young man, running back in dismay. "It has gone from my room! I can't make it out!"

"Never mind!" cried the Widow Dugrival, half demented. "All the better! I will do the business myself."

She seized Lupin by the throat, clutched him with her ten fingers, digging her nails into his flesh, and began to squeeze with all her might. Lupin uttered a hoarse rattle and gave himself up for lost.

Suddenly, there was a crash at the window. One of the panes was smashed to pieces.

"What's that? What is it?" stammered the widow, drawing herself erect, in alarm.

Gabriel, who had turned even paler than usual, murmured:

"I don't know.... I can't think...."

"Who can have done it?" said the widow.

She dared not move, waiting for what would come next. And one thing above all terrified her, the fact that there was no missile on the floor around them, although the pane of glass, as was clearly visible, had given way before the crash of a heavy and fairly large object, a stone, probably.

After a while, she looked under the bed, under the chest of drawers:

"Nothing," she said.

"No," said her nephew, who was also looking. And, resuming her seat, she said:

"I feel frightened ... my arms fail me ... you finish him off...."

Gabriel confessed:

"I'm frightened also."

"Still ... still," she stammered, "it's got to be done.... I swore it...."

Making one last effort, she returned to Lupin and gasped his neck with her stiff fingers. But Lupin, who was watching her pallid face, received a very clear sensation that she would not have the courage to kill him. To her he was becoming something sacred, invulnerable. A mysterious power was protecting him against every attack, a power which had already saved him three times by inexplicable means and which would find other means to protect him against the wiles of death.

She said to him, in a hoarse voice:

"How you must be laughing at me!"

"Not at all, upon my word. I should feel frightened myself, in your place."

"Nonsense, you scum of the earth! You imagine that you will be rescued ... that your friends are waiting outside? It's out of the question, my fine fellow."

"I know. It's not they defending me ... nobody's defending me...."

"Well, then?..."

"Well, all the same, there's something strange at the bottom of it, something fantastic and miraculous that makes your flesh creep, my fine lady."

"You villain!... You'll be laughing on the other side of your mouth before long."

"I doubt it."

"You wait and see."

She reflected once more and said to her nephew:

"What would you do?"

"Fasten his arm again and let's be off," he replied.

A hideous suggestion! It meant condemning Lupin to the most horrible of all deaths, death by starvation.

"No," said the widow. "He might still find a means of escape. I know something better than that."

She took down the receiver of the telephone, waited and asked:

"Number 82248, please."

And, after a second or two:

"Hullo!... Is that the Criminal Investigation Department?... Is Chief-inspector Ganimard there?... In twenty minutes, you say?... I'm sorry!... However!... When he comes, give him this message from Mme. Dugrival.... Yes, Mme. Nicolas Dugrival.... Ask him to come to my flat. Tell him to open the looking-glass door of my wardrobe; and, when he has done so, he will see that the wardrobe hides an outlet which makes my bedroom communicate with two other rooms. In one of these, he will find a man bound hand and foot. It is the thief, Dugrival's murderer.... You don't believe me?... Tell M. Ganimard; he'll believe me right enough.... Oh, I was almost forgetting to give you the man's name: Arsène Lupin!"

And, without another word, she replaced the receiver.

"There, Lupin, that's done. After all, I would just as soon have my revenge this way. How I shall hold my sides when I read the reports of the Lupin trial!... Are you coming, Gabriel?"

"Yes, aunt."

"Good-bye, Lupin. You and I sha'n't see each other again, I expect, for we are going abroad. But I promise to send you some sweets while you're in prison."

"Chocolates, mother! We'll eat them together!"

"Good-bye."

"*Au revoir.*"

The widow went out with her nephew, leaving Lupin fastened down to the bed.

He at once moved his free arm and tried to release himself; but he realized, at the first attempt, that he would never have the strength to break the wire strands that bound him. Exhausted with fever and pain, what could he do in the twenty minutes or so that were left to him before Ganimard's arrival?

Nor did he count upon his friends. True, he had been thrice saved from death; but this was evidently due to an astounding series of accidents and not to any interference on the part of his allies. Otherwise they would not have contented themselves with these extraordinary manifestations, but would have rescued him for good and all.

No, he must abandon all hope. Ganimard was coming. Ganimard would find him there. It was inevitable. There was no getting away from the fact.

And the prospect of what was coming irritated him singularly. He already heard his old enemy's gibes ringing in his ears. He foresaw the roars of laughter with which the incredible news would be greeted on the morrow. To be arrested in action, so to speak, on the battlefield, by an imposing detachment of adversaries, was one thing: but to be arrested, or rather picked up, scraped up, gathered up, in such condition, was really too silly. And Lupin, who had so often scoffed at others, felt all the ridicule that was falling to his share in this ending of the Dugrival business, all the bathos of allowing himself to be caught in the widow's infernal trap and finally of being "served up" to the police like a dish of game, roasted to a turn and nicely seasoned.

"Blow the widow!" he growled. "I had rather she had cut my throat and done with it."

He pricked up his ears. Some one was moving in the next room. Ganimard! No. Great as his eagerness would be, he could not be there yet. Besides, Ganimard would not have acted like that, would not have opened the door as gently as that other person was doing. What other person? Lupin remembered the three miraculous interventions to which he owed his life. Was it possible that there was really somebody who had protected him against the widow, and that that somebody was now attempting to rescue him? But, if so, who?

Unseen by Lupin, the stranger stooped behind the bed. Lupin heard the sound of the pliers attacking the wire strands and releasing him little by little. First his chest was freed, then his arms, then his legs.

And a voice said to him:

"You must get up and dress."

Feeling very weak, he half-raised himself in bed at the moment when the stranger rose from her stooping posture.

"Who are you?" he whispered. "Who are you?"

And a great surprise over came him.

By his side stood a woman, a woman dressed in black, with a lace shawl over her head, covering part of her face. And the woman, as far as he could judge, was young and of a graceful and slender stature.

"Who are you?" he repeated.

"You must come now," said the woman. "There's no time to lose."

"Can I?" asked Lupin, making a desperate effort. "I doubt if I have the strength."

"Drink this."

She poured some milk into a cup; and, as she handed it to him, her lace opened, leaving the face uncovered.

"You!" he stammered. "It's you!... It's you who ... it was you who were...."

He stared in amazement at this woman whose features presented so striking a resemblance to Gabriel's, whose delicate, regular face had the same pallor, whose mouth wore the same hard and forbidding expression. No sister could have borne so great a likeness to her brother. There was not a doubt possible: it was the identical person. And, without believing for a moment that Gabriel had concealed himself in a woman's clothes, Lupin, on the contrary, received the distinct impression that it was a woman standing beside him and that the stripling who had pursued him with his hatred and struck him with the dagger was in very deed a woman. In order to follow their trade with greater ease, the Dugrival pair had accustomed her to disguise herself as a boy.

"You ... you ...!" he repeated. "Who would have suspected ...?"

She emptied the contents of a phial into the cup:

"Drink this cordial," she said.

He hesitated, thinking of poison.

She added:

"It was I who saved you."

"Of course, of course," he said. "It was you who removed the bullets from the revolver?"

"Yes."

"And you who hid the knife?"

"Here it is, in my pocket."

"And you who smashed the window-pane while your aunt was throttling me?"

"Yes, it was I, with the paper-weight on the table: I threw it into the street."

"But why? Why?" he asked, in utter amazement.

"Drink the cordial."

"Didn't you want me to die? But then why did you stab me to begin with?"

"Drink the cordial."

He emptied the cup at a draught, without quite knowing the reason of his sudden confidence.

"Dress yourself ... quickly," she commanded, retiring to the window.

He obeyed and she came back to him, for he had dropped into a chair, exhausted.

"We must go now, we must, we have only just time.... Collect your strength."

She bent forward a little, so that he might lean on her shoulder, and turned toward the door and the staircase.

And Lupin walked as one walks in a dream, one of those queer dreams in which the most inconsequent things occur, a dream that was the happy sequel of the terrible nightmare in which he had lived for the past fortnight.

A thought struck him, however. He began to laugh:

"Poor Ganimard! Upon my word, the fellow has no luck, I would give twopence to see him coming to arrest me."

After descending the staircase with the aid of his companion, who supported him with incredible vigour, he found himself in the street, opposite a motor-car into which she helped him to mount.

"Right away," she said to the driver.

Lupin, dazed by the open air and the speed at which they were travelling, hardly took stock of the drive and of the incidents on the road. He recovered all his consciousness when he found himself at home in one of the flats which he occupied, looked after by his servant, to whom the girl gave a few rapid instructions.

"You can go," he said to the man.

But, when the girl turned to go as well, he held her back by a fold of her dress.

"No ... no ... you must first explain.... Why did you save me? Did you return unknown to your aunt? But why did you save me? Was it from pity?"

She did not answer. With her figure drawn up and her head flung back a little, she retained her hard and impenetrable air. Nevertheless, he thought he noticed that the lines of her mouth showed not so much cruelty as bitterness. Her eyes, her beautiful dark eyes, revealed melancholy. And Lupin, without as yet understanding, received a vague intuition of what was passing within her. He seized her hand. She pushed him away, with a start of revolt in which he felt hatred, almost repulsion. And, when he insisted, she cried:

"Let me be, will you?... Let me be!... Can't you see that I detest you?"

They looked at each other for a moment, Lupin disconcerted, she quivering and full of uneasiness, her pale face all flushed with unwonted colour.

He said to her, gently:

"If you detested me, you should have let me die.... It was simple enough.... Why didn't you?"

"Why?... Why?... How do I know?..."

Her face contracted. With a sudden movement, she hid it in her two hands; and he saw tears trickle between her fingers.

Greatly touched, he thought of addressing her in fond words, such as one would use to a little girl whom one wished to console, and of giving her good advice and saving her, in his turn, and snatching her from the bad life which she was leading, perhaps against her better nature.

But such words would have sounded ridiculous, coming from his lips, and he did not know what to say, now that he understood the whole story and was able to picture the young woman sitting beside his sick-bed, nursing the man whom she had wounded, admiring his pluck and gaiety, becoming attached to him, falling in love with him and thrice over, probably in spite of herself, under a sort of instinctive impulse, amid fits of spite and rage, saving him from death.

And all this was so strange, so unforeseen; Lupin was so much unmanned by his astonishment, that, this time, he did not try to retain her when she made for the door, backward, without taking her eyes from him.

She lowered her head, smiled for an instant and disappeared.

He rang the bell, quickly:

"Follow that woman," he said to his man. "Or no, stay where you are.... After all, it is better so...."

He sat brooding for a while, possessed by the girl's image. Then he revolved in his mind all that curious, stirring and tragic adventure, in which he had been so very near succumbing; and, taking a hand-glass from the table, he gazed for a long time and with a certain self-complacency at his features, which illness and pain had not succeeded in impairing to any great extent:

"Good looks count for something, after all!" he muttered.

V. THE RED SILK SCARF

On leaving his house one morning, at his usual early hour for going to the Law Courts, Chief-inspector Ganimard noticed the curious behaviour of an individual who was walking along the Rue Pergolèse in front of him. Shabbily dressed and wearing a straw hat, though the day was the first of December, the man stooped at every thirty or forty yards to fasten his boot-lace, or pick up his stick, or for some other reason. And, each time, he took a little piece of orange-peel from his pocket and laid it stealthily on the kerb of the pavement. It was probably a mere display of eccentricity, a childish amusement to which no one else would have paid attention; but Ganimard was one of those shrewd observers who are indifferent to nothing that strikes their eyes and who are never satisfied until they know the secret cause of things. He therefore began to follow the man.

Now, at the moment when the fellow was turning to the right, into the Avenue de la Grande-Armée, the inspector caught him exchanging signals with a boy of twelve or thirteen, who was walking along the houses on the left-hand side. Twenty yards farther, the man stooped and turned up the bottom of his trousers legs. A bit of orange-peel marked the place. At the same moment, the boy stopped and, with a piece of chalk, drew a white cross, surrounded by a circle, on the wall of the house next to him.

The two continued on their way. A minute later, a fresh halt. The strange individual picked up a pin and dropped a piece of orange-peel; and the boy at once made a second cross on the wall and again drew a white circle round it.

"By Jove!" thought the chief-inspector, with a grunt of satisfaction. "This is rather promising.... What on earth can those two merchants be plotting?"

The two "merchants" went down the Avenue Friedland and the Rue du Faubourg-Saint-Honoré, but nothing occurred that was worthy of special mention. The double performance was repeated at almost regular intervals and, so to speak, mechanically. Nevertheless, it was obvious, on the one hand, that the man with the orange-peel did not do his part of the business until after he had picked out with a glance the house that was to be marked and, on the other hand, that the boy did not mark that particular house until after he had observed his companion's signal. It was certain, therefore, that there was an agreement between the two; and the proceedings presented no small interest in the chief-inspector's eyes.

At the Place Beauveau the man hesitated. Then, apparently making up his mind, he twice turned up and twice turned down the bottom of his trousers legs. Hereupon, the boy sat down on the kerb, opposite the sentry who was mounting guard outside the Ministry of the Interior, and marked the flagstone with two little crosses contained within two circles. The same ceremony was gone through a little further on, when they reached the Elysée. Only, on the pavement where the President's sentry was marching up and down, there were three signs instead of two.

"Hang it all!" muttered Ganimard, pale with excitement and thinking, in spite of himself, of his inveterate enemy, Lupin, whose name came to his mind whenever a mysterious circumstance presented itself. "Hang it all, what does it mean?"

He was nearly collaring and questioning the two "merchants." But he was too clever to commit so gross a blunder. The man with the orange-peel had now lit a cigarette; and the boy, also placing a cigarette-end between his lips, had gone up to him, apparently with the object of asking for a light.

They exchanged a few words. Quick as thought, the boy handed his companion an object which looked—at least, so the inspector believed—like a revolver. They both bent over this object; and the man, standing with his face to the wall, put his hand six times in his pocket and made a movement as though he were loading a weapon.

As soon as this was done, they walked briskly to the Rue de Surène; and the inspector, who followed them as closely as he was able to do without attracting their attention, saw them enter the gateway of an old house of which all the shutters were closed, with the exception of those on the third or top floor.

He hurried in after them. At the end of the carriage-entrance he saw a large courtyard, with a house-painter's sign at the back and a staircase on the left.

He went up the stairs and, as soon as he reached the first floor, ran still faster, because he heard, right up at the top, a din as of a free-fight.

When he came to the last landing he found the door open. He entered, listened for a second, caught the sound of a struggle, rushed to the room from which the sound appeared to proceed and remained standing on the threshold, very much out of breath and greatly surprised to see the man of the orange-peel and the boy banging the floor with chairs.

At that moment a third person walked out of an adjoining room. It was a young man of twenty-eight or thirty, wearing a pair of short whiskers in addition to his moustache, spectacles, and a smoking-jacket with an astrakhan collar and looking like a foreigner, a Russian.

"Good morning, Ganimard," he said. And turning to the two companions, "Thank you, my friends, and all my congratulations on the successful result. Here's the reward I promised you."

He gave them a hundred-franc note, pushed them outside and shut both doors.

"I am sorry, old chap," he said to Ganimard. "I wanted to talk to you ... wanted to talk to you badly."

He offered him his hand and, seeing that the inspector remained flabbergasted and that his face was still distorted with anger, he exclaimed:

"Why, you don't seem to understand!... And yet it's clear enough.... I wanted to see you particularly.... So what could I do?" And, pretending to reply to an objection, "No, no, old chap," he continued. "You're quite wrong. If I had written or telephoned, you would not have come ... or else you would have come with a regiment. Now I wanted to see you all alone; and I thought the best thing was to send those two decent fellows to meet you, with orders to scatter bits of orange-peel and draw crosses and circles, in short, to mark out your road to this place.... Why, you look quite bewildered! What is it? Perhaps you don't recognize me? Lupin.... Arsène Lupin.... Ransack your memory.... Doesn't the name remind you of anything?"

"You dirty scoundrel!" Ganimard snarled between his teeth.

Lupin seemed greatly distressed and, in an affectionate voice:

"Are you vexed? Yes, I can see it in your eyes.... The Dugrival business, I suppose? I ought to have waited for you to come and take me in charge?... There now, the thought never occurred to me! I promise you, next time...."

"You scum of the earth!" growled Ganimard.

"And I thinking I was giving you a treat! Upon my word, I did. I said to myself, 'That dear old Ganimard! We haven't met for an age. He'll simply rush at me when he sees me!'"

Ganimard, who had not yet stirred a limb, seemed to be waking from his stupor. He looked around him, looked at Lupin, visibly asked himself whether he would not do well to rush at him in reality and then, controlling himself, took hold of a chair and settled himself in it, as though he had suddenly made up his mind to listen to his enemy:

"Speak," he said. "And don't waste my time with any nonsense. I'm in a hurry."

"That's it," said Lupin, "let's talk. You can't imagine a quieter place than this. It's an old manor-house, which once stood in the open country, and it belongs to the Duc de Rochelaure. The duke, who has never lived in it, lets this floor to me and the outhouses to a painter and decorator. I always keep up a few establishments of this kind: it's a sound, practical plan. Here, in spite of my looking like a Russian nobleman, I am M. Daubreuil, an ex-cabinet-minister.... You understand, I had to select a rather overstocked profession, so as not to attract attention...."

"Do you think I care a hang about all this?" said Ganimard, interrupting him.

"Quite right, I'm wasting words and you're in a hurry. Forgive me. I sha'n't be long now.... Five minutes, that's all.... I'll start at once.... Have a cigar? No? Very well, no more will I."

He sat down also, drummed his fingers on the table, while thinking, and began in this fashion:

"On the 17th of October, 1599, on a warm and sunny autumn day ... Do you follow me?... But, now that I come to think of it, is it really necessary to go back to the reign of Henry IV, and tell you all about the building of the Pont-Neuf? No, I don't suppose you are very well up in French history; and I should only end by muddling you. Suffice it, then, for you to know that, last night, at one o'clock in the morning, a boatman passing under the last arch of the Pont-Neuf aforesaid, along the left bank of the river, heard something drop into the front part of his barge. The thing had been flung from the bridge and its evident destination was the bottom of the Seine. The bargee's dog rushed forward, barking, and, when the man reached the end of his craft, he saw the animal worrying a piece of newspaper that had served to wrap up a number of objects. He took from the dog such of the contents as had not fallen into the water, went to his cabin and examined them carefully. The result struck him as interesting; and, as the man is connected with one of my friends, he sent to let me know. This morning I was waked up and placed in possession of the facts and of the objects which the man had collected. Here they are."

He pointed to them, spread out on a table. There were, first of all, the torn pieces of a newspaper. Next came a large cut-glass inkstand, with a long piece of string fastened to the lid. There was a bit of broken glass and a sort of flexible cardboard, reduced to shreds. Lastly, there was a piece of bright scarlet silk, ending in a tassel of the same material and colour.

"You see our exhibits, friend of my youth," said Lupin. "No doubt, the problem would be more easily solved if we had the other objects which went overboard owing to the stupidity of the dog. But it seems to me, all the same, that we ought to be able to manage, with a little reflection and intelligence. And those are just your great qualities. How does the business strike you?"

Ganimard did not move a muscle. He was willing to stand Lupin's chaff, but his dignity commanded him not to speak a single word in answer nor even to give a nod or shake of the head that might have been taken to express approval or or criticism.

"I see that we are entirely of one mind," continued Lupin, without appearing to remark the chief-inspector's silence. "And I can sum up the matter briefly, as told us by these exhibits. Yesterday evening, between nine and twelve o'clock, a showily dressed young woman was wounded with a knife and then caught round the throat and choked to death by a well-dressed gentleman, wearing a single eyeglass and interested in racing, with whom the aforesaid showily dressed young lady had been eating three meringues and a coffee éclair."

Lupin lit a cigarette and, taking Ganimard by the sleeve:

"Aha, that's up against you, chief-inspector! You thought that, in the domain of police deductions, such feats as those were prohibited to outsiders! Wrong, sir! Lupin juggles with inferences and deductions for all the world like a detective in a novel. My proofs are dazzling and absolutely simple."

And, pointing to the objects one by one, as he demonstrated his statement, he resumed:

"I said, after nine o'clock yesterday evening. This scrap of newspaper bears yesterday's date, with the words, 'Evening edition.' Also, you will see here, pasted to the paper, a bit of one of those yellow wrappers in which the subscribers' copies are sent out. These copies are always delivered by the nine o'clock post. Therefore, it was after nine o'clock. I said, a well-dressed man. Please observe that this tiny piece of glass has the round hole of a single eyeglass at one of the edges and that the single eyeglass is an essentially aristocratic article of wear. This well-dressed man walked into a pastry-cook's shop. Here is the very thin cardboard, shaped like a box, and still showing a little of the cream of the meringues and éclairs which were packed in it in the usual way. Having got his parcel, the gentleman with the eyeglass joined a young person whose eccentricity in the matter of dress is pretty clearly indicated by this bright-red silk scarf. Having joined her, for some reason as yet unknown he first stabbed her with a knife and then strangled her with the help of this same scarf. Take your magnifying glass, chief-inspector, and you will see, on the silk, stains of a darker red which are, here, the marks of a knife wiped on the scarf and, there, the marks of a hand, covered with blood, clutching the material. Having committed the murder, his next business is to leave no trace behind him. So he takes from his pocket, first, the newspaper to which he subscribes—a racing-paper, as you will see by glancing at the contents of this scrap; and you will have no difficulty in discovering the title—and, secondly, a cord, which, on inspection, turns out to be a length of whip-cord. These two details prove—do they not?—that our man is interested in racing and that he himself rides. Next, he picks up the fragments of his eyeglass, the cord of which has been broken in the struggle. He takes a pair of scissors—observe the hacking of the scissors—and cuts off the stained part of the scarf, leaving the other end, no doubt, in his victim's clenched hands. He makes a ball of the confectioner's cardboard box. He also puts in certain things that would have betrayed him, such as the knife, which must have slipped into the Seine. He wraps everything in the newspaper, ties it with the cord and fastens this cut-glass inkstand to it, as a make-weight. Then he makes himself scarce. A little later, the parcel falls into the waterman's barge. And there you are. Oof, it's hot work!... What do you say to the story?"

He looked at Ganimard to see what impression his speech had produced on the inspector. Ganimard did not depart from his attitude of silence.

Lupin began to laugh:

"As a matter of fact, you're annoyed and surprised. But you're suspicious as well: 'Why should that confounded Lupin hand the business over to me,' say you, 'instead of keeping it for himself, hunting down the murderer and rifling his pockets, if there was a robbery?' The question is quite logical, of course. But—there is a 'but'—I have no time, you see. I am full up with work at the present moment: a burglary in London, another at Lausanne, an exchange of children at Marseilles, to say nothing of having to save a young girl who is at this moment shadowed by death. That's always the way: it never rains but it pours. So I said to myself, 'Suppose I handed the business over to my dear old Ganimard? Now that it is half-solved for him, he is quite capable of succeeding. And what a service I shall be doing him! How magnificently he will be able to distinguish himself!' No sooner said than done. At eight o'clock in the morning, I sent the joker with the orange-peel to meet you. You swallowed the bait; and you were here by nine, all on edge and eager for the fray."

Lupin rose from his chair. He went over to the inspector and, with his eyes in Ganimard's, said:

"That's all. You now know the whole story. Presently, you will know the victim: some ballet-dancer, probably, some singer at a music-hall. On the other hand, the chances are that the criminal lives near the Pont-Neuf, most likely on the left bank. Lastly, here are all the exhibits. I make you a present of them. Set to work. I shall only keep this end of the scarf. If ever you want to piece the scarf together, bring me the other end, the one which the police will find round the victim's neck. Bring it me in four weeks from now to the day, that is to say, on the 29th of December, at ten o'clock in the morning. You can be sure of finding me here. And don't be afraid: this is all perfectly serious, friend of my youth; I swear it is. No humbug, honour bright. You can go straight ahead. Oh, by the way, when you arrest the fellow with the eyeglass, be a bit careful: he is left-handed! Good-bye, old dear, and good luck to you!"

Lupin spun round on his heel, went to the door, opened it and disappeared before Ganimard had even thought of taking a decision. The inspector rushed after him, but at once found that the handle of the door, by some trick of mechanism which he did not know, refused to turn. It took him ten minutes to unscrew the lock and ten minutes more to unscrew the lock of the hall-door. By the time that he had scrambled down the three flights of stairs, Ganimard had given up all hope of catching Arsène Lupin.

Besides, he was not thinking of it. Lupin inspired him with a queer, complex feeling, made up of fear, hatred, involuntary admiration and also the vague instinct that he, Ganimard, in spite of all his efforts, in spite of the persistency of his endeavours, would never get the better of this particular adversary. He pursued him from a sense of duty and pride, but with the continual dread of being taken in by that formidable hoaxer and scouted and fooled in the face of a public that was always only too willing to laugh at the chief-inspector's mishaps.

This business of the red scarf, in particular, struck him as most suspicious. It was interesting, certainly, in more ways than one, but so very improbable! And Lupin's explanation, apparently so logical, would never stand the test of a severe examination!

"No," said Ganimard, "this is all swank: a parcel of suppositions and guesswork based upon nothing at all. I'm not to be caught with chaff."

When he reached the headquarters of police, at 36 Quai des Orfèvres, he had quite made up his mind to treat the incident as though it had never happened.

He went up to the Criminal Investigation Department. Here, one of his fellow-inspectors said:

"Seen the chief?"

"No."

"He was asking for you just now."

"Oh, was he?"

"Yes, you had better go after him."

"Where?"

"To the Rue de Berne ... there was a murder there last night."

"Oh! Who's the victim?"

"I don't know exactly ... a music-hall singer, I believe."

Ganimard simply muttered:

"By Jove!"

Twenty minutes later he stepped out of the underground railway-station and made for the Rue de Berne.

The victim, who was known in the theatrical world by her stage-name of Jenny Saphir, occupied a small flat on the second floor of one of the houses. A policeman took the chief-inspector upstairs and showed him the way, through two sitting-rooms, to a bedroom, where he found the magistrates in charge of the inquiry, together with the divisional surgeon and M. Dudouis, the head of the detective-service.

Ganimard started at the first glance which he gave into the room. He saw, lying on a sofa, the corpse of a young woman whose hands clutched a strip of red silk! One of the shoulders, which appeared above the low-cut bodice, bore the marks of two wounds surrounded with clotted blood. The distorted and almost blackened features still bore an expression of frenzied terror.

The divisional surgeon, who had just finished his examination, said:

"My first conclusions are very clear. The victim was twice stabbed with a dagger and afterward strangled. The immediate cause of death was asphyxia."

"By Jove!" thought Ganimard again, remembering Lupin's words and the picture which he had drawn of the crime.

The examining-magistrate objected:

"But the neck shows no discoloration."

"She may have been strangled with a napkin or a handkerchief," said the doctor.

"Most probably," said the chief detective, "with this silk scarf, which the victim was wearing and a piece of which remains, as though she had clung to it with her two hands to protect herself."

"But why does only that piece remain?" asked the magistrate. "What has become of the other?"

"The other may have been stained with blood and carried off by the murderer. You can plainly distinguish the hurried slashing of the scissors."

558

"By Jove!" said Ganimard, between his teeth, for the third time. "That brute of a Lupin saw everything without seeing a thing!"

"And what about the motive of the murder?" asked the magistrate. "The locks have been forced, the cupboards turned upside down. Have you anything to tell me, M. Dudouis?"

The chief of the detective-service replied:

"I can at least suggest a supposition, derived from the statements made by the servant. The victim, who enjoyed a greater reputation on account of her looks than through her talent as a singer, went to Russia, two years ago, and brought back with her a magnificent sapphire, which she appears to have received from some person of importance at the court. Since then, she went by the name of Jenny Saphir and seems generally to have been very proud of that present, although, for prudence sake, she never wore it. I daresay that we shall not be far out if we presume the theft of the sapphire to have been the cause of the crime."

"But did the maid know where the stone was?"

"No, nobody did. And the disorder of the room would tend to prove that the murderer did not know either."

"We will question the maid," said the examining-magistrate.

M. Dudouis took the chief-inspector aside and said:

"You're looking very old-fashioned, Ganimard. What's the matter? Do you suspect anything?"

"Nothing at all, chief."

"That's a pity. We could do with a bit of showy work in the department. This is one of a number of crimes, all of the same class, of which we have failed to discover the perpetrator. This time we want the criminal ... and quickly!"

"A difficult job, chief."

"It's got to be done. Listen to me, Ganimard. According to what the maid says, Jenny Saphir led a very regular life. For a month past she was in the habit of frequently receiving visits, on her return from the music-hall, that is to say, at about half-past ten, from a man who would stay until midnight or so. 'He's a society man,' Jenny Saphir used to say, 'and he wants to marry me.' This society man took every precaution to avoid being seen, such as turning up his coat-collar and lowering the brim of his hat when he passed the porter's box. And Jenny Saphir always made a point of sending away her maid, even before he came. This is the man whom we have to find."

"Has he left no traces?"

"None at all. It is obvious that we have to deal with a very clever scoundrel, who prepared his crime beforehand and committed it with every possible chance of escaping unpunished. His arrest would be a great feather in our cap. I rely on you, Ganimard."

"Ah, you rely on me, chief?" replied the inspector. "Well, we shall see ... we shall see.... I don't say no.... Only...."

He seemed in a very nervous condition, and his agitation struck M. Dudouis.

"Only," continued Ganimard, "only I swear ... do you hear, chief? I swear...."

"What do you swear?"

"Nothing.... We shall see, chief ... we shall see...."

Ganimard did not finish his sentence until he was outside, alone. And he finished it aloud, stamping his foot, in a tone of the most violent anger:

"Only, I swear to Heaven that the arrest shall be effected by my own means, without my employing a single one of the clues with which that villain has supplied me. Ah, no! Ah, no!..."

Railing against Lupin, furious at being mixed up in this business and resolved, nevertheless, to get to the bottom of it, he wandered aimlessly about the streets. His brain was seething with irritation; and he tried to adjust his ideas a little and to discover, among the chaotic facts, some trifling detail, unperceived by all, unsuspected by Lupin himself, that might lead him to success.

He lunched hurriedly at a bar, resumed his stroll and suddenly stopped, petrified, astounded and confused. He was walking under the gateway of the very house in the Rue de Surène to which Lupin had enticed him a few hours earlier! A force stronger than his own will was drawing him there once more. The solution of the problem lay there. There and there alone were all the elements of the truth. Do and say what he would, Lupin's assertions were so precise, his calculations so accurate, that, worried to the innermost recesses of his being by so prodigious a display of perspicacity, he could not do other than take up the work at the point where his enemy had left it.

Abandoning all further resistance, he climbed the three flights of stairs. The door of the flat was open. No one had touched the exhibits. He put them in his pocket and walked away.

From that moment, he reasoned and acted, so to speak, mechanically, under the influence of the master whom he could not choose but obey.

Admitting that the unknown person whom he was seeking lived in the neighbourhood of the Pont-Neuf, it became necessary to discover, somewhere between that bridge and the Rue de Berne, the first-class confectioner's shop, open in the evenings, at which the cakes were bought. This did not take long to find. A pastry-cook near the Gare Saint-Lazare showed him some little cardboard boxes, identical in material and shape with the one in Ganimard's possession. Moreover, one of the shop-girls remembered having served, on the previous evening, a gentleman whose face was almost concealed in the collar of his fur coat, but whose eyeglass she had happened to notice.

"That's one clue checked," thought the inspector. "Our man wears an eyeglass."

He next collected the pieces of the racing-paper and showed them to a newsvendor, who easily recognized the *Turf Illustré*. Ganimard at once went to the offices of the *Turf* and asked to see the list of subscribers. Going through the list, he jotted down the names and addresses of all those who lived anywhere near the Pont-Neuf and principally—because Lupin had said so—those on the left bank of the river.

He then went back to the Criminal Investigation Department, took half a dozen men and packed them off with the necessary instructions.

At seven o'clock in the evening, the last of these men returned and brought good news with him. A certain M. Prévailles, a subscriber to the *Turf*, occupied an entresol flat on the Quai des Augustins. On the previous evening, he left his place, wearing a fur coat, took his letters and his paper, the *Turf Illustré*, from the porter's wife, walked away and returned home at midnight. This M. Prévailles wore a single eyeglass. He was a regular race-goer and himself owned several hacks which he either rode himself or jobbed out.

The inquiry had taken so short a time and the results obtained were so exactly in accordance with Lupin's predictions that Ganimard felt quite overcome on hearing the detective's report. Once more he was measuring the prodigious extent of the resources at Lupin's disposal. Never in the course of his life—and Ganimard was already well-advanced in years—had he come across such perspicacity, such a quick and far-seeing mind.

He went in search of M. Dudouis.

"Everything's ready, chief. Have you a warrant?"

"Eh?"

"I said, everything is ready for the arrest, chief."

"You know the name of Jenny Saphir's murderer?"

"Yes."

"But how? Explain yourself."

Ganimard had a sort of scruple of conscience, blushed a little and nevertheless replied:

"An accident, chief. The murderer threw everything that was likely to compromise him into the Seine. Part of the parcel was picked up and handed to me."

"By whom?"

"A boatman who refused to give his name, for fear of getting into trouble. But I had all the clues I wanted. It was not so difficult as I expected."

And the inspector described how he had gone to work.

"And you call that an accident!" cried M. Dudouis. "And you say that it was not difficult! Why, it's one of your finest performances! Finish it yourself, Ganimard, and be prudent."

Ganimard was eager to get the business done. He went to the Quai des Augustins with his men and distributed them around the house. He questioned the portress, who said that her tenant took his meals out of doors, but made a point of looking in after dinner.

A little before nine o'clock, in fact, leaning out of her window, she warned Ganimard, who at once gave a low whistle. A gentleman in a tall hat and a fur coat was coming along the pavement beside the Seine. He crossed the road and walked up to the house.

Ganimard stepped forward:

"M. Prévailles, I believe?"

"Yes, but who are you?"

"I have a commission to...."

He had not time to finish his sentence. At the sight of the men appearing out of the shadow, Prévailles quickly retreated to the wall and faced his adversaries, with his back to the door of a shop on the ground-floor, the shutters of which were closed.

"Stand back!" he cried. "I don't know you!"

His right hand brandished a heavy stick, while his left was slipped behind him and seemed to be trying to open the door.

Ganimard had an impression that the man might escape through this way and through some secret outlet:

"None of this nonsense," he said, moving closer to him. "You're caught.... You had better come quietly."

But, just as he was laying hold of Prévailles' stick, Ganimard remembered the warning which Lupin gave him: Prévailles was left-handed; and it was his revolver for which he was feeling behind his back.

The inspector ducked his head. He had noticed the man's sudden movement. Two reports rang out. No one was hit.

A second later, Prévailles received a blow under the chin from the butt-end of a revolver, which brought him down where he stood. He was entered at the Dépôt soon after nine o'clock.

Ganimard enjoyed a great reputation even at that time. But this capture, so quickly effected, by such very simple means, and at once made public by the police, won him a sudden celebrity. Prévailles was forthwith saddled with all the murders that had remained unpunished; and the newspapers vied with one another in extolling Ganimard's prowess.

The case was conducted briskly at the start. It was first of all ascertained that Prévailles, whose real name was Thomas Derocq, had already been in trouble. Moreover, the search instituted in his rooms, while not supplying any fresh proofs, at least led to the discovery of a ball of whip-cord similar to the cord used for doing up the parcel and also to the discovery of daggers which would have produced a wound similar to the wounds on the victim.

But, on the eighth day, everything was changed. Until then Prévailles had refused to reply to the questions put to him; but now, assisted by his counsel, he pleaded a circumstantial alibi and maintained that he was at the Folies-Bergère on the night of the murder.

As a matter of fact, the pockets of his dinner-jacket contained the counterfoil of a stall-ticket and a programme of the performance, both bearing the date of that evening.

"An alibi prepared in advance," objected the examining-magistrate.

"Prove it," said Prévailles.

The prisoner was confronted with the witnesses for the prosecution. The young lady from the confectioner's "thought she knew" the gentleman with the eyeglass. The hall-porter in the Rue de Berne "thought he knew" the gentleman who used to come to see Jenny Saphir. But nobody dared to make a more definite statement.

The examination, therefore, led to nothing of a precise character, provided no solid basis whereon to found a serious accusation.

The judge sent for Ganimard and told him of his difficulty.

"I can't possibly persist, at this rate. There is no evidence to support the charge."

"But surely you are convinced in your own mind, monsieur le juge d'instruction! Prévailles would never have resisted his arrest unless he was guilty."

"He says that he thought he was being assaulted. He also says that he never set eyes on Jenny Saphir; and, as a matter of fact, we can find no one to contradict his assertion. Then again, admitting that the sapphire has been stolen, we have not been able to find it at his flat."

"Nor anywhere else," suggested Ganimard.

"Quite true, but that is no evidence against him. I'll tell you what we shall want, M. Ganimard, and that very soon: the other end of this red scarf."

"The other end?"

"Yes, for it is obvious that, if the murderer took it away with him, the reason was that the stuff is stained with the marks of the blood on his fingers."

Ganimard made no reply. For several days he had felt that the whole business was tending to this conclusion. There was no other proof possible. Given the silk scarf—and in no other circumstances—Prévailles' guilt was certain. Now Ganimard's position required that Prévailles' guilt should be established. He was responsible for the arrest, it had cast a glamour around him, he had been praised to the skies as the most formidable adversary of criminals; and he would look absolutely ridiculous if Prévailles were released.

Unfortunately, the one and only indispensable proof was in Lupin's pocket. How was he to get hold of it?

Ganimard cast about, exhausted himself with fresh investigations, went over the inquiry from start to finish, spent sleepless nights in turning over the mystery of the Rue de Berne, studied the records of Prévailles' life, sent ten men hunting after the invisible sapphire. Everything was useless.

On the 28th of December, the examining-magistrate stopped him in one of the passages of the Law Courts:

"Well, M. Ganimard, any news?"

"No, monsieur le juge d'instruction."

"Then I shall dismiss the case."

"Wait one day longer."

"What's the use? We want the other end of the scarf; have you got it?"

"I shall have it to-morrow."

"To-morrow!"

"Yes, but please lend me the piece in your possession."

"What if I do?"

"If you do, I promise to let you have the whole scarf complete."

"Very well, that's understood."

Ganimard followed the examining-magistrate to his room and came out with the piece of silk:

"Hang it all!" he growled. "Yes, I will go and fetch the proof and I shall have it too ... always presuming that Master Lupin has the courage to keep the appointment."

In point of fact, he did not doubt for a moment that Master Lupin would have this courage, and that was just what exasperated him. Why had Lupin insisted on this meeting? What was his object, in the circumstances?

Anxious, furious and full of hatred, he resolved to take every precaution necessary not only to prevent his falling into a trap himself, but to make his enemy fall into one, now that the opportunity offered. And, on the next day, which was the 29th of December, the date fixed by Lupin, after spending the night in studying the old manor-house in the Rue de Surène and convincing himself that there was no other outlet than the front door, he warned his men that he was going on a dangerous expedition and arrived with them on the field of battle.

He posted them in a café and gave them formal instructions: if he showed himself at one of the third-floor windows, or if he failed to return within an hour, the detectives were to enter the house and arrest any one who tried to leave it.

The chief-inspector made sure that his revolver was in working order and that he could take it from his pocket easily. Then he went upstairs.

He was surprised to find things as he had left them, the doors open and the locks broken. After ascertaining that the windows of the principal room looked out on the street, he visited the three other rooms that made up the flat. There was no one there.

"Master Lupin was afraid," he muttered, not without a certain satisfaction.

"Don't be silly," said a voice behind him.

Turning round, he saw an old workman, wearing a house-painter's long smock, standing in the doorway.

"You needn't bother your head," said the man. "It's I, Lupin. I have been working in the painter's shop since early morning. This is when we knock off for breakfast. So I came upstairs."

He looked at Ganimard with a quizzing smile and cried:

"'Pon my word, this is a gorgeous moment I owe you, old chap! I wouldn't sell it for ten years of your life; and yet you know how I love you! What do you think of it, artist? Wasn't it well thought out and well foreseen? Foreseen from alpha to omega? Did I understand the business? Did I penetrate the mystery of the scarf? I'm not saying that there were no holes in my argument, no links missing in the chain.... But what a masterpiece of intelligence! Ganimard, what a reconstruction of events! What an intuition of everything that had taken place and of everything that was going to take place, from the discovery of the crime to your arrival here in search of a proof! What really marvellous divination! Have you the scarf?"

"Yes, half of it. Have you the other?"

"Here it is. Let's compare."

They spread the two pieces of silk on the table. The cuts made by the scissors corresponded exactly. Moreover, the colours were identical.

"But I presume," said Lupin, "that this was not the only thing you came for. What you are interested in seeing is the marks of the blood. Come with me, Ganimard: it's rather dark in here."

They moved into the next room, which, though it overlooked the courtyard, was lighter; and Lupin held his piece of silk against the window-pane:

"Look," he said, making room for Ganimard.

The inspector gave a start of delight. The marks of the five fingers and the print of the palm were distinctly visible. The evidence was undeniable. The murderer had seized the stuff in his bloodstained hand, in the same hand that had stabbed Jenny Saphir, and tied the scarf round her neck.

"And it is the print of a left hand," observed Lupin. "Hence my warning, which had nothing miraculous about it, you see. For, though I admit, friend of my youth, that you may look upon me as a superior intelligence, I won't have you treat me as a wizard."

Ganimard had quickly pocketed the piece of silk. Lupin nodded his head in approval:

"Quite right, old boy, it's for you. I'm so glad you're glad! And, you see, there was no trap about all this ... only the wish to oblige ... a service between friends, between pals.... And also, I confess, a little curiosity.... Yes, I wanted to examine this other piece of silk, the one the police had.... Don't be afraid: I'll give it back to you.... Just a second...."

Lupin, with a careless movement, played with the tassel at the end of this half of the scarf, while Ganimard listened to him in spite of himself:

"How ingenious these little bits of women's work are! Did you notice one detail in the maid's evidence? Jenny Saphir was very handy with her needle and used to make all her own hats and frocks. It is obvious that she made this scarf herself.... Besides, I noticed that from the first. I am naturally curious, as I have already told you, and I made a thorough examination of the piece of silk which you have just put in your pocket. Inside the tassel, I found a little sacred medal, which the poor girl had stitched into it to bring her luck. Touching, isn't it, Ganimard? A little medal of Our Lady of Good Succour."

The inspector felt greatly puzzled and did not take his eyes off the other. And Lupin continued:

"Then I said to myself, 'How interesting it would be to explore the other half of the scarf, the one which the police will find round the victim's neck!' For this other half, which I hold in my hands at last, is finished off in the same way ... so I shall be able to see if it has a hiding-place too and what's inside it.... But look, my friend, isn't it cleverly made? And so simple! All you have to do is to take a skein of red cord and braid it round a wooden cup, leaving a little recess, a little empty space in the middle, very small, of course, but large enough to hold a medal of a saint ... or anything.... A precious stone, for instance.... Such as a sapphire...."

At that moment he finished pushing back the silk cord and, from the hollow of a cup he took between his thumb and forefinger a wonderful blue stone, perfect in respect of size and purity.

"Ha! What did I tell you, friend of my youth?"

He raised his head. The inspector had turned livid and was staring wild-eyed, as though fascinated by the stone that sparkled before him. He at last realized the whole plot:

"You dirty scoundrel!" he muttered, repeating the insults which he had used at the first interview. "You scum of the earth!"

The two men were standing one against the other.

"Give me back that," said the inspector.

Lupin held out the piece of silk.

"And the sapphire," said Ganimard, in a peremptory tone.

"Don't be silly."

"Give it back, or...."

"Or what, you idiot!" cried Lupin. "Look here, do you think I put you on to this soft thing for nothing?"

"Give it back!"

"You haven't noticed what I've been about, that's plain! What! For four weeks I've kept you on the move like a deer; and you want to ...! Come, Ganimard, old chap, pull yourself together!... Don't you see that you've been playing the good dog for four weeks on end?... Fetch it, Rover!... There's a nice blue pebble over there, which master can't get at. Hunt it, Ganimard, fetch it ... bring it to master.... Ah, he's his master's own good little dog!... Sit up! Beg!... Does'ms want a bit of sugar, then?..."

Ganimard, containing the anger that seethed within him, thought only of one thing, summoning his detectives. And, as the room in which he now was looked out on the courtyard, he tried gradually to work his way round to the communicating door. He would then run to the window and break one of the panes.

"All the same," continued Lupin, "what a pack of dunderheads you and the rest must be! You've had the silk all this time and not one of you ever thought of feeling it, not one of you ever asked himself the reason why the poor girl hung on to her scarf. Not one of you! You just acted at haphazard, without reflecting, without foreseeing anything...."

The inspector had attained his object. Taking advantage of a second when Lupin had turned away from him, he suddenly wheeled round and grasped the door-handle. But an oath escaped him: the handle did not budge.

Lupin burst into a fit of laughing:

"Not even that! You did not even foresee that! You lay a trap for me and you won't admit that I may perhaps smell the thing out beforehand.... And you allow yourself to be brought into this room without asking whether I am not bringing you here for a particular reason and without remembering that the locks are fitted with a special mechanism. Come now, speaking frankly, what do you think of it yourself?"

"What do I think of it?" roared Ganimard, beside himself with rage.

He had drawn his revolver and was pointing it straight at Lupin's face.

"Hands up!" he cried. "That's what I think of it!"

Lupin placed himself in front of him and shrugged his shoulders:

"Sold again!" he said.

"Hands up, I say, once more!"

"And sold again, say I. Your deadly weapon won't go off."

"What?"

"Old Catherine, your housekeeper, is in my service. She damped the charges this morning while you were having your breakfast coffee."

Ganimard made a furious gesture, pocketed the revolver and rushed at Lupin.

"Well?" said Lupin, stopping him short with a well-aimed kick on the shin.

Their clothes were almost touching. They exchanged defiant glances, the glances of two adversaries who mean to come to blows. Nevertheless, there was no fight. The recollection of the earlier struggles made any present struggle useless. And Ganimard, who remembered all his past failures, his vain attacks, Lupin's crushing reprisals, did not lift a limb. There was nothing to be done. He felt it. Lupin had forces at his command against which any individual force simply broke to pieces. So what was the good?

"I agree," said Lupin, in a friendly voice, as though answering Ganimard's unspoken thought, "you would do better to let things be as they are. Besides, friend of my youth, think of all that this incident has brought you: fame, the certainty of quick promotion and, thanks to that, the prospect of a happy and comfortable old age! Surely, you don't want the discovery of the sapphire and the head of poor Arsène Lupin in addition! It wouldn't be fair. To say nothing of the fact that poor Arsène Lupin saved your life.... Yes, sir! Who warned you, at this very spot, that Prévailles was left-handed?... And is this the way you thank me? It's not pretty of you, Ganimard. Upon my word, you make me blush for you!"

While chattering, Lupin had gone through the same performance as Ganimard and was now near the door. Ganimard saw that his foe was about to escape him. Forgetting all prudence, he tried to block his way and received a tremendous butt in the stomach, which sent him rolling to the opposite wall.

Lupin dexterously touched a spring, turned the handle, opened the door and slipped away, roaring with laughter as he went.

Twenty minutes later, when Ganimard at last succeeded in joining his men, one of them said to him:

"A house-painter left the house, as his mates were coming back from breakfast, and put a letter in my hand. 'Give that to your governor,' he said. 'Which governor?' I asked; but he was gone. I suppose it's meant for you."

"Let's have it."

Ganimard opened the letter. It was hurriedly scribbled in pencil and contained these words:

"This is to warn you, friend of my youth, against excessive credulity. When a fellow tells you that the cartridges in your revolver are damp, however great your confidence in that fellow may be, even though his name be Arsène Lupin, never allow yourself to be taken in. Fire first; and, if the fellow hops the twig, you will have acquired the proof (1) that the cartridges are not damp; and (2) that old Catherine is the most honest and respectable of housekeepers.

"One of these days, I hope to have the pleasure of making her acquaintance.

"Meanwhile, friend of my youth, believe me always affectionately and sincerely yours,

"Arsène Lupin."

VI. SHADOWED BY DEATH

After he had been round the walls of the property, Arsène Lupin returned to the spot from which he started. It was perfectly clear to him that there was no breach in the walls; and the only way of entering the extensive grounds of the Château de Maupertuis was through a little low door, firmly bolted on the inside, or through the principal gate, which was overlooked by the lodge.

"Very well," he said. "We must employ heroic methods."

Pushing his way into the copsewood where he had hidden his motor-bicycle, he unwound a length of twine from under the saddle and went to a place which he had noticed in the course of his exploration. At this place, which was situated far from the road, on the edge of a wood, a number of large trees, standing inside the park, overlapped the wall.

Lupin fastened a stone to the end of the string, threw it up and caught a thick branch, which he drew down to him and bestraddled. The branch, in recovering its position, raised him from the ground. He climbed over the wall, slipped down the tree, and sprang lightly on the grass.

It was winter; and, through the leafless boughs, across the undulating lawns, he could see the little Château de Maupertuis in the distance. Fearing lest he should be perceived, he concealed himself behind a clump of fir-trees. From there, with the aid of a field-glass, he studied the dark and melancholy front of the manor-house. All the windows were closed and, as it were, barricaded with solid shutters. The house might easily have been uninhabited.

"By Jove!" muttered Lupin. "It's not the liveliest of residences. I shall certainly not come here to end my days!"

But the clock struck three; one of the doors on the ground-floor opened; and the figure of a woman appeared, a very slender figure wrapped in a brown cloak.

The woman walked up and down for a few minutes and was at once surrounded by birds, to which she scattered crumbs of bread. Then she went down the stone steps that led to the middle lawn and skirted it, taking the path on the right.

With his field-glass, Lupin could distinctly see her coming in his direction. She was tall, fair-haired, graceful in appearance, and seemed to be quite a young girl. She walked with a sprightly step, looking at the pale December sun and amusing herself by breaking the little dead twigs on the shrubs along the road.

She had gone nearly two thirds of the distance that separated her from Lupin when there came a furious sound of barking and a huge dog, a colossal Danish boarhound, sprang from a neighbouring kennel and stood erect at the end of the chain by which it was fastened.

The girl moved a little to one side, without paying further attention to what was doubtless a daily incident. The dog grew angrier than ever, standing on its legs and dragging at its collar, at the risk of strangling itself.

Thirty or forty steps farther, yielding probably to an impulse of impatience, the girl turned round and made a gesture with her hand. The great Dane gave a start of rage, retreated to the back of its kennel and rushed out again, this time unfettered. The girl uttered a cry of mad terror. The dog was covering the space between them, trailing its broken chain behind it.

569

She began to run, to run with all her might, and screamed out desperately for help. But the dog came up with her in a few bounds.

She fell, at once exhausted, giving herself up for lost. The animal was already upon her, almost touching her.

At that exact moment a shot rang out. The dog turned a complete somersault, recovered its feet, tore the ground and then lay down, giving a number of hoarse, breathless howls, which ended in a dull moan and an indistinct gurgling. And that was all.

"Dead," said Lupin, who had hastened up at once, prepared, if necessary, to fire his revolver a second time.

The girl had risen and stood pale, still staggering. She looked in great surprise at this man whom she did not know and who had saved her life; and she whispered:

"Thank you.... I have had a great fright.... You were in the nick of time.... I thank you, monsieur."

Lupin took off his hat:

"Allow me to introduce myself, mademoiselle.... My name is Paul Daubreuil.... But before entering into any explanations, I must ask for one moment...."

He stooped over the dog's dead body and examined the chain at the part where the brute's effort had snapped it:

"That's it," he said, between his teeth. "It's just as I suspected. By Jupiter, things are moving rapidly!... I ought to have come earlier."

Returning to the girl's side, he said to her, speaking very quickly:

"Mademoiselle, we have not a minute to lose. My presence in these grounds is quite irregular. I do not wish to be surprised here; and this for reasons that concern yourself alone. Do you think that the report can have been heard at the house?"

The girl seemed already to have recovered from her emotion; and she replied, with a calmness that revealed all her pluck:

"I don't think so."

"Is your father in the house to-day?"

"My father is ill and has been in bed for months. Besides, his room looks out on the other front."

"And the servants?"

"Their quarters and the kitchen are also on the other side. No one ever comes to this part. I walk here myself, but nobody else does."

"It is probable, therefore, that I have not been seen either, especially as the trees hide us?"

"It is most probable."

"Then I can speak to you freely?"

"Certainly, but I don't understand...."

"You will, presently. Permit me to be brief. The point is this: four days ago, Mlle. Jeanne Darcieux...."

"That is my name," she said, smiling.

"Mlle. Jeanne Darcieux," continued Lupin, "wrote a letter to one of her friends, called Marceline, who lives at Versailles...."

"How do you know all that?" asked the girl, in astonishment. "I tore up the letter before I had finished it."

"And you flung the pieces on the edge of the road that runs from the house to Vendôme."

"That's true.... I had gone out walking...."

"The pieces were picked up and they came into my hands next day."

"Then ... you must have read them," said Jeanne Darcieux, betraying a certain annoyance by her manner.

"Yes, I committed that indiscretion; and I do not regret it, because I can save you."

"Save me? From what?"

"From death."

Lupin spoke this little sentence in a very distinct voice. The girl gave a shudder. Then she said:

"I am not threatened with death."

"Yes, you are, mademoiselle. At the end of October, you were reading on a bench on the terrace where you were accustomed to sit at the same hour every day, when a block of stone fell from the cornice above your head and you were within a few inches of being crushed."

"An accident...."

"One fine evening in November, you were walking in the kitchen-garden, by moonlight. A shot was fired, The bullet whizzed past your ear."

"At least, I thought so."

"Lastly, less than a week ago, the little wooden bridge that crosses the river in the park, two yards from the waterfall, gave way while you were on it. You were just able, by a miracle, to catch hold of the root of a tree."

Jeanne Darcieux tried to smile.

"Very well. But, as I wrote to Marceline, these are only a series of coincidences, of accidents...."

"No, mademoiselle, no. One accident of this sort is allowable.... So are two ... and even then!... But we have no right to suppose that the chapter of accidents, repeating the same act three times in such different and extraordinary circumstances, is a mere amusing coincidence. That is why I thought that I might presume to come to your assistance. And, as my intervention can be of no use unless it remains

571

secret, I did not hesitate to make my way in here ... without walking through the gate. I came in the nick of time, as you said. Your enemy was attacking you once more."

"What!... Do you think?... No, it is impossible.... I refuse to believe...."

Lupin picked up the chain and, showing it to her:

"Look at the last link. There is no question but that it has been filed. Otherwise, so powerful a chain as this would never have yielded. Besides, you can see the mark of the file here."

Jeanne turned pale and her pretty features were distorted with terror:

"But who can bear me such a grudge?" she gasped. "It is terrible.... I have never done any one harm.... And yet you are certainly right.... Worse still...."

She finished her sentence in a lower voice:

"Worse still, I am wondering whether the same danger does not threaten my father."

"Has he been attacked also?"

"No, for he never stirs from his room. But his is such a mysterious illness!... He has no strength ... he cannot walk at all.... In addition to that, he is subject to fits of suffocation, as though his heart stopped beating.... Oh, what an awful thing!"

Lupin realized all the authority which he was able to assert at such a moment, and he said:

"Have no fear, mademoiselle. If you obey me blindly, I shall be sure to succeed."

"Yes ... yes ... I am quite willing ... but all this is so terrible...."

"Trust me, I beg of you. And please listen to me, I shall want a few particulars."

He rapped out a number of questions, which Jeanne Darcieux answered hurriedly:

"That animal was never let loose, was he?"

"Never."

"Who used to feed him?"

"The lodge-keeper. He brought him his food every evening."

"Consequently, he could go near him without being bitten?"

"Yes; and he only, for the dog was very savage."

"You don't suspect the man?"

"Oh, no!... Baptiste?... Never!"

"And you can't think of anybody?"

"No. Our servants are quite devoted to us. They are very fond of me."

"You have no friends staying in the house?"

"No."

"No brother?"

"No."

"Then your father is your only protector?"

"Yes; and I have told you the condition he is in."

"Have you told him of the different attempts?"

"Yes; and it was wrong of me to do so. Our doctor, old Dr. Guéroult, forbade me to cause him the least excitement."

"Your mother?..."

"I don't remember her. She died sixteen years ago ... just sixteen years ago."

"How old were you then?"

"I was not quite five years old."

"And were you living here?"

"We were living in Paris. My father only bought this place the year after."

Lupin was silent for a few moments. Then he concluded:

"Very well, mademoiselle, I am obliged to you. Those particulars are all I need for the present. Besides, it would not be wise for us to remain together longer."

"But," she said, "the lodge-keeper will find the dog soon.... Who will have killed him?"

"You, mademoiselle, to defend yourself against an attack."

"I never carry firearms."

"I am afraid you do," said Lupin, smiling, "because you killed the dog and there is no one but you who could have killed him. For that matter, let them think what they please. The great thing is that I shall not be suspected when I come to the house."

"To the house? Do you intend to?"

"Yes. I don't yet know how ... But I shall come.... This very evening.... So, once more, be easy in your mind. I will answer for everything."

Jeanne looked at him and, dominated by him, conquered by his air of assurance and good faith, she said, simply:

"I am quite easy."

"Then all will go well. Till this evening, mademoiselle."

"Till this evening."

She walked away; and Lupin, following her with his eyes until the moment when she disappeared round the corner of the house, murmured:

"What a pretty creature! It would be a pity if any harm were to come to her. Luckily, Arsène Lupin is keeping his weather-eye open."

Taking care not to be seen, with eyes and ears attentive to the least sight or sound, he inspected every nook and corner of the grounds, looked for the little low door which he had noticed outside and which was the door of the kitchen garden, drew the bolt, took the key and then skirted the walls and found himself once more near the tree which he had climbed. Two minutes later, he was mounting his motor-cycle.

The village of Maupertuis lay quite close to the estate. Lupin inquired and learnt that Dr. Guéroult lived next door to the church.

He rang, was shown into the consulting-room and introduced himself by his name of Paul Daubreuil, of the Rue de Surène, Paris, adding that he had official relations with the detective-service, a fact which he requested might be kept secret. He had become acquainted, by means of a torn letter, with the incidents that had endangered Mlle. Darcieux's life; and he had come to that young lady's assistance.

Dr. Guéroult, an old country practitioner, who idolized Jeanne, on hearing Lupin's explanations at once admitted that those incidents constituted undeniable proofs of a plot. He showed great concern, offered his visitor hospitality and kept him to dinner.

The two men talked at length. In the evening, they walked round to the manor-house together.

The doctor went to the sick man's room, which was on the first floor, and asked leave to bring up a young colleague, to whom he intended soon to make over his practice, when he retired.

Lupin, on entering, saw Jeanne Darcieux seated by her father's bedside. She suppressed a movement of surprise and, at a sign from the doctor, left the room.

The consultation thereupon took place in Lupin's presence. M. Darcieux's face was worn, with much suffering and his eyes were bright with fever. He complained particularly, that day, of his heart. After the auscultation, he questioned the doctor with obvious anxiety; and each reply seemed to give him relief. He also spoke of Jeanne and expressed his conviction that they were deceiving him and that his daughter had escaped yet more accidents. He continued perturbed, in spite of the doctor's denials. He wanted to have the police informed and inquiries set on foot.

But his excitement tired him and he gradually dropped off to sleep.

Lupin stopped the doctor in the passage:

"Come, doctor, give me your exact opinion. Do you think that M. Darcieux's illness can be attributed to an outside cause?"

"How do you mean?"

"Well, suppose that the same enemy should be interested in removing both father and daughter."

The doctor seemed struck by the suggestion.

"Upon my word, there is something in what you say.... The father's illness at times adopts such a very unusual character!... For instance, the paralysis of the legs, which is almost complete, ought to be accompanied by...."

The doctor reflected for a moment and then said in a low voice:

"You think it's poison, of course ... but what poison?... Besides, I see no toxic symptoms.... It would have to be.... But what are you doing? What's the matter?..."

The two men were talking outside a little sitting-room on the first floor, where Jeanne, seizing the opportunity while the doctor was with her father, had begun her evening meal. Lupin, who was watching her through the open door, saw her lift a cup to her lips and take a few sups.

Suddenly, he rushed at her and caught her by the arm:

"What are you drinking there?"

"Why," she said, taken aback, "only tea!"

"You pulled a face of disgust ... what made you do that?"

"I don't know ... I thought...."

"You thought what?"

"That ... that it tasted rather bitter.... But I expect that comes from the medicine I mixed with it."

"What medicine?"

"Some drops which I take at dinner ... the drops which you prescribed for me, you know, doctor."

"Yes," said Dr. Guéroult, "but that medicine has no taste of any kind.... You know it hasn't, Jeanne, for you have been taking it for a fortnight and this is the first time...."

"Quite right," said the girl, "and this does have a taste.... There—oh!—my mouth is still burning."

Dr. Guéroult now took a sip from the cup;

"Faugh!" he exclaimed, spitting it out again. "There's no mistake about it...."

Lupin, on his side, was examining the bottle containing the medicine; and he asked:

"Where is this bottle kept in the daytime?"

But Jeanne was unable to answer. She had put her hand to her heart and, wan-faced, with staring eyes, seemed to be suffering great pain:

"It hurts ... it hurts," she stammered.

The two men quickly carried her to her room and laid her on the bed:

"She ought to have an emetic," said Lupin.

"Open the cupboard," said the doctor. "You'll see a medicine-case.... Have you got it?... Take out one of those little tubes.... Yes, that one.... And now some hot water.... You'll find some on the tea-tray in the other room."

Jeanne's own maid came running up in answer to the bell. Lupin told her that Mlle. Darcieux had been taken unwell, for some unknown reason.

He next returned to the little dining-room, inspected the sideboard and the cupboards, went down to the kitchen and pretended that the doctor had sent him to ask about M. Darcieux's diet. Without appearing to do so, he catechized the cook, the butler, and Baptiste, the lodge-keeper, who had his meals at the manor-house with the servants. Then he went back to the doctor:

"Well?"

"She's asleep."

"Any danger?"

"No. Fortunately, she had only taken two or three sips. But this is the second time to-day that you have saved her life, as the analysis of this bottle will show."

"Quite superfluous to make an analysis, doctor. There is no doubt about the fact that there has been an attempt at poisoning."

"By whom?"

"I can't say. But the demon who is engineering all this business clearly knows the ways of the house. He comes and goes as he pleases, walks about in the park, files the dog's chain, mixes poison with the food and, in short, moves and acts precisely as though he were living the very life of her—or rather of those—whom he wants to put away."

"Ah! You really believe that M. Darcieux is threatened with the same danger?"

"I have not a doubt of it."

"Then it must be one of the servants? But that is most unlikely! Do you think ...?"

"I think nothing, doctor. I know nothing. All I can say is that the situation is most tragic and that we must be prepared for the worst. Death is here, doctor, shadowing the people in this house; and it will soon strike at those whom it is pursuing."

"What's to be done?"

"Watch, doctor. Let us pretend that we are alarmed about M. Darcieux's health and spend the night in here. The bedrooms of both the father and daughter are close by. If anything happens, we are sure to hear."

There was an easy-chair in the room. They arranged to sleep in it turn and turn about.

In reality, Lupin slept for only two or three hours. In the middle of the night he left the room, without disturbing his companion, carefully looked round the whole of the house and walked out through the principal gate.

He reached Paris on his motor-cycle at nine o'clock in the morning. Two of his friends, to whom he telephoned on the road, met him there. They all three spent the day in making searches which Lupin had planned out beforehand.

He set out again hurriedly at six o'clock; and never, perhaps, as he told me subsequently, did he risk his life with greater temerity than in his breakneck ride, at a mad rate of speed, on a foggy December evening, with the light of his lamp hardly able to pierce through the darkness.

He sprang from his bicycle outside the gate, which was still open, ran to the house and reached the first floor in a few bounds.

There was no one in the little dining-room.

Without hesitating, without knocking, he walked into Jeanne's bedroom:

"Ah, here you are!" he said, with a sigh of relief, seeing Jeanne and the doctor sitting side by side, talking.

"What? Any news?" asked the doctor, alarmed at seeing such a state of agitation in a man whose coolness he had had occasion to observe.

"No," said Lupin. "No news. And here?"

"None here, either. We have just left M. Darcieux. He has had an excellent day and he ate his dinner with a good appetite. As for Jeanne, you can see for yourself, she has all her pretty colour back again."

"Then she must go."

"Go? But it's out of the question!" protested the girl.

"You must go, you must!" cried Lupin, with real violence, stamping his foot on the floor.

He at once mastered himself, spoke a few words of apology and then, for three or four minutes, preserved a complete silence, which the doctor and Jeanne were careful not to disturb.

At last, he said to the young girl:

"You shall go to-morrow morning, mademoiselle. It will be only for one or two weeks. I will take you to your friend at Versailles, the one to whom you were writing. I entreat you to get everything ready to-night ... without concealment of any kind. Let the servants know that you are going.... On the other hand, the doctor will be good enough to tell M. Darcieux and give him to understand, with every possible precaution, that this journey is essential to your safety. Besides, he can join you as soon as his strength permits.... That's settled, is it not?"

"Yes," she said, absolutely dominated by Lupin's gentle and imperious voice.

"In that case," he said, "be as quick as you can ... and do not stir from your room...."

"But," said the girl, with a shudder, "am I to stay alone to-night?"

"Fear nothing. Should there be the least danger, the doctor and I will come back. Do not open your door unless you hear three very light taps."

Jeanne at once rang for her maid. The doctor went to M. Darcieux, while Lupin had some supper brought to him in the little dining-room.

"That's done," said the doctor, returning to him in twenty minutes' time. "M. Darcieux did not raise any great difficulty. As a matter of fact, he himself thinks it just as well that we should send Jeanne away."

They then went downstairs together and left the house.

On reaching the lodge, Lupin called the keeper.

"You can shut the gate, my man. If M. Darcieux should want us, send for us at once."

The clock of Maupertuis church struck ten. The sky was overcast with black clouds, through which the moon broke at moments.

The two men walked on for sixty or seventy yards.

They were nearing the village, when Lupin gripped his companion by the arm:

"Stop!"

"What on earth's the matter?" exclaimed the doctor.

"The matter is this," Lupin jerked out, "that, if my calculations turn out right, if I have not misjudged the business from start to finish, Mlle. Darcieux will be murdered before the night is out."

"Eh? What's that?" gasped the doctor, in dismay. "But then why did we go?"

"With the precise object that the miscreant, who is watching all our movements in the dark, may not postpone his crime and may perpetrate it, not at the hour chosen by himself, but at the hour which I have decided upon."

"Then we are returning to the manor-house?"

"Yes, of course we are, but separately."

"In that case, let us go at once."

"Listen to me, doctor," said Lupin, in a steady voice, "and let us waste no time in useless words. Above all, we must defeat any attempt to watch us. You will therefore go straight home and not come out again until you are quite certain that you have not been followed. You will then make for the walls of the property, keeping to the left, till you come to the little door of the kitchen-garden. Here is the key. When the church clock strikes eleven, open the door very gently and walk right up to the terrace at the back of the house. The fifth window is badly fastened. You have only to climb over the balcony. As soon as you are inside Mlle. Darcieux's room, bolt the door and don't budge. You quite understand, don't budge, either of you, whatever happens. I have noticed that Mlle. Darcieux leaves her dressing-room window ajar, isn't that so?"

"Yes, it's a habit which I taught her."

"That's the way they'll come."

"And you?"

"That's the way I shall come also."

"And do you know who the villain is?"

Lupin hesitated and then replied:

"No, I don't know.... And that is just how we shall find out. But, I implore you, keep cool. Not a word, not a movement, *whatever happens*!"

"I promise you."

"I want more than that, doctor. You must give me your word of honour."

"I give you my word of honour."

The doctor went away. Lupin at once climbed a neighbouring mound from which he could see the windows of the first and second floor. Several of them were lighted.

He waited for some little time. The lights went out one by one. Then, taking a direction opposite to that in which the doctor had gone, he branched off to the right and skirted the wall until he came to the clump of trees near which he had hidden his motor-cycle on the day before.

Eleven o'clock struck. He calculated the time which it would take the doctor to cross the kitchen-garden and make his way into the house.

"That's one point scored!" he muttered. "Everything's all right on that side. And now, Lupin to the rescue? The enemy won't be long before he plays his last trump ... and, by all the gods, I must be there!..."

He went through the same performance as on the first occasion, pulled down the branch and hoisted himself to the top of the wall, from which he was able to reach the bigger boughs of the tree.

Just then he pricked up his ears. He seemed to hear a rustling of dead leaves. And he actually perceived a dark form moving on the level thirty yards away:

"Hang it all!" he said to himself. "I'm done: the scoundrel has smelt a rat."

A moonbeam pierced through the clouds. Lupin distinctly saw the man take aim. He tried to jump to the ground and turned his head. But he felt something hit him in the chest, heard the sound of a report, uttered an angry oath and came crashing down from branch to branch, like a corpse.

Meanwhile, Doctor Guéroult, following Arsène Lupin's instructions, had climbed the ledge of the fifth window and groped his way to the first floor. On reaching Jeanne's room, he tapped lightly, three times, at the door and, immediately on entering, pushed the bolt:

"Lie down at once," he whispered to the girl, who had not taken off her things. "You must appear to have gone to bed. Brrrr, it's cold in here! Is the window open in your dressing-room?"

"Yes ... would you like me to ...?"

"No, leave it as it is. They are coming."

"They are coming!" spluttered Jeanne, in affright.

"Yes, beyond a doubt."

"But who? Do you suspect any one?"

"I don't know who.... I expect that there is some one hidden in the house ... or in the park."

"Oh, I feel so frightened!"

"Don't be frightened. The sportsman who's looking after you seems jolly clever and makes a point of playing a safe game. I expect he's on the look-out in the court."

The doctor put out the night-light, went to the window and raised the blind. A narrow cornice, running along the first story, prevented him from seeing more than a distant part of the courtyard; and he came back and sat down by the bed.

Some very painful minutes passed, minutes that appeared to them interminably long. The clock in the village struck; but, taken up as they were with all the little noises of the night, they hardly noticed the sound. They listened, listened, with all their nerves on edge:

"Did you hear?" whispered the doctor.

"Yes ... yes," said Jeanne, sitting up in bed.

"Lie down ... lie down," he said, presently. "There's some one coming."

There was a little tapping sound outside, against the cornice. Next came a series of indistinct noises, the nature of which they could not make out for certain. But they had a feeling that the window in the dressing-room was being opened wider, for they were buffeted by gusts of cold air.

Suddenly, it became quite clear: there was some one next door.

The doctor, whose hand was trembling a little, seized his revolver. Nevertheless, he did not move, remembering the formal orders which he had received and fearing to act against them.

The room was in absolute darkness; and they were unable to see where the adversary was. But they felt his presence.

They followed his invisible movements, the sound of his footsteps deadened by the carpet; and they did not doubt but that he had already crossed the threshold of the room.

And the adversary stopped. Of that they were certain. He was standing six steps away from the bed, motionless, undecided perhaps, seeking to pierce the darkness with his keen eyes.

Jeanne's hand, icy-cold and clammy, trembled in the doctor's grasp.

With his other hand, the doctor clutched his revolver, with his finger on the trigger. In spite of his pledged word, he did not hesitate. If the adversary touched the end of the bed, the shot would be fired at a venture.

The adversary took another step and then stopped again. And there was something awful about that silence, that impassive silence, that darkness in which those human beings were peering at one another, wildly.

Who was it looming in the murky darkness? Who was the man? What horrible enmity was it that turned his hand against the girl and what abominable aim was he pursuing?

Terrified though they were, Jeanne and the doctor thought only of that one thing: to see, to learn the truth, to gaze upon the adversary's face.

He took one more step and did not move again. It seemed to them that his figure stood out, darker, against the dark space and that his arm rose slowly, slowly....

A minute passed and then another minute....

And, suddenly, beyond the man, on the right a sharp click.... A bright light flashed, was flung upon the man, lit him full in the face, remorselessly.

Jeanne gave a cry of affright. She had seen—standing over her, with a dagger in his hand—she had seen ... her father!

Almost at the same time, though the light was already turned off, there came a report: the doctor had fired.

"Dash it all, don't shoot!" roared Lupin.

He threw his arms round the doctor, who choked out:

"Didn't you see?... Didn't you see?... Listen!... He's escaping!..."

"Let him escape: it's the best thing that could happen."

He pressed the spring of his electric lantern again, ran to the dressing-room, made certain that the man had disappeared and, returning quietly to the table, lit the lamp.

Jeanne lay on her bed, pallid, in a dead faint.

The doctor, huddled in his chair, emitted inarticulate sounds.

"Come," said Lupin, laughing, "pull yourself together. There is nothing to excite ourselves about: it's all over."

"Her father!... Her father!" moaned the old doctor.

"If you please, doctor, Mlle. Darcieux is ill. Look after her."

Without more words, Lupin went back to the dressing-room and stepped out on the window-ledge. A ladder stood against the ledge. He ran down it. Skirting the wall of the house, twenty steps farther, he tripped over the rungs of a rope-ladder, which he climbed and found himself in M. Darcieux's bedroom. The room was empty.

"Just so," he said. "My gentleman did not like the position and has cleared out. Here's wishing him a good journey.... And, of course, the door is bolted?... Exactly!... That is how our sick man, tricking his worthy medical attendant, used to get up at night in full security, fasten his rope-ladder to the balcony and prepare his little games. He's no fool, is friend Darcieux!"

He drew the bolts and returned to Jeanne's room. The doctor, who was just coming out of the doorway, drew him to the little dining-room:

"She's asleep, don't let us disturb her. She has had a bad shock and will take some time to recover."

Lupin poured himself out a glass of water and drank it down. Then he took a chair and, calmly:

"Pooh! She'll be all right by to-morrow."

"What do you say?"

"I say that she'll be all right by to-morrow."

"Why?"

"In the first place, because it did not strike me that Mlle. Darcieux felt any very great affection for her father."

"Never mind! Think of it: a father who tries to kill his daughter! A father who, for months on end, repeats his monstrous attempt four, five, six times over again!... Well, isn't that enough to blight a less sensitive soul than Jeanne's for good and all? What a hateful memory!"

"She will forget."

"One does not forget such a thing as that."

"She will forget, doctor, and for a very simple reason...."

"Explain yourself!"

"She is not M. Darcieux's daughter!"

"Eh?"

"I repeat, she is not that villain's daughter."

"What do you mean? M. Darcieux...."

"M. Darcieux is only her step-father. She had just been born when her father, her real father, died. Jeanne's mother then married a cousin of her husband's, a man bearing the same name, and she died within a year of her second wedding. She left Jeanne in M. Darcieux's charge. He first took her abroad and then bought this country-house; and, as nobody knew him in the neighbourhood, he represented the child as being his daughter. She herself did not know the truth about her birth."

The doctor sat confounded. He asked:

"Are you sure of your facts?"

"I spent my day in the town-halls of the Paris municipalities. I searched the registers, I interviewed two solicitors, I have seen all the documents. There is no doubt possible."

"But that does not explain the crime, or rather the series of crimes."

"Yes, it does," declared Lupin. "And, from the start, from the first hour when I meddled in this business, some words which Mlle. Darcieux used made me suspect that direction which my investigations must take. 'I was not quite five years old when my mother died,' she said. 'That was sixteen years ago.' Mlle. Darcieux, therefore, was nearly twenty-one, that is to say, she was on the verge of attaining her majority. I at once saw that this was an important detail. The day on which you reach your majority is the day on which your accounts are rendered. What was the financial position of Mlle. Darcieux, who was her mother's natural heiress? Of course, I did not think of the father for a second. To begin with, one can't imagine a thing like that; and then the farce which M. Darcieux was playing ... helpless, bedridden, ill...."

"Really ill," interrupted the doctor.

"All this diverted suspicion from him ... the more so as I believe that he himself was exposed to criminal attacks. But was there not in the family some person who would be interested in their removal? My journey to Paris revealed the truth to me: Mlle. Darcieux inherits a large fortune from her mother, of which her step-father draws the income. The solicitor was to have called a meeting of the family in Paris next month. The truth would have been out. It meant ruin to M. Darcieux."

"Then he had put no money by?"

"Yes, but he had lost a great deal as the result of unfortunate speculations."

"But, after all, Jeanne would not have taken the management of her fortune out of his hands!"

"There is one detail which you do not know, doctor, and which I learnt from reading the torn letter. Mlle. Darcieux is in love with the brother of Marceline, her Versailles friend; M. Darcieux was opposed to the marriage; and—you now see the reason—she was waiting until she came of age to be married."

"You're right," said the doctor, "you're right.... It meant his ruin."

"His absolute ruin. One chance of saving himself remained, the death of his step-daughter, of whom he is the next heir."

"Certainly, but on condition that no one suspected him."

"Of course; and that is why he contrived the series of accidents, so that the death might appear to be due to misadventure. And that is why I, on my side, wishing to bring things to a head, asked you to tell him of Mlle. Darcieux's impending departure. From that moment, it was no longer enough for the would-be sick man to wander about the grounds and the passages, in the dark, and execute some leisurely thought-out plan. No, he had to act, to act at once, without preparation, violently, dagger in hand. I had no doubt that he would decide to do it. And he did."

"Then he had no suspicions?"

"Of me, yes. He felt that I would return to-night, and he kept a watch at the place where I had already climbed the wall."

"Well?"

"Well," said Lupin, laughing, "I received a bullet full in the chest ... or rather my pocket-book received a bullet.... Here, you can see the hole.... So I tumbled from the tree, like a dead man. Thinking that he was rid of his only adversary, he went back to the house. I saw him prowl about for two hours. Then, making up his mind, he went to the coach-house, took a ladder and set it against the window. I had only to follow him."

The doctor reflected and said:

"You could have collared him earlier. Why did you let him come up? It was a sore trial for Jeanne ... and unnecessary."

"On the contrary, it was indispensable! Mlle. Darcieux would never have accepted the truth. It was essential that she should see the murderer's very face. You must tell her all the circumstances when she wakes. She will soon be well again."

"But ... M. Darcieux?"

"You can explain his disappearance as you think best ... a sudden journey ... a fit of madness.... There will be a few inquiries.... And you may be sure that he will never be heard of again."

The doctor nodded his head:

"Yes ... that is so ... that is so ... you are right. You have managed all this business with extraordinary skill; and Jeanne owes you her life. She will thank you in person.... But now, can I be of use to you in any way? You told me that you were connected with the detective-service.... Will you allow me to write and praise your conduct, your courage?"

Lupin began to laugh:

"Certainly! A letter of that kind will do me a world of good. You might write to my immediate superior, Chief-inspector Ganimard. He will be glad to hear that his favourite officer, Paul Daubreuil, of the Rue de Surène, has once again distinguished himself by a brilliant action. As it happens, I have an appointment to meet him about a case of which you may have heard: the case of the red scarf.... How pleased my dear M. Ganimard will be!"

VII. A TRAGEDY IN THE FOREST OF MORGUES

The village was terror-stricken.

It was on a Sunday morning. The peasants of Saint-Nicolas and the neighbourhood were coming out of church and spreading across the square, when, suddenly, the women who were walking ahead and who had already turned into the high-road fell back with loud cries of dismay.

At the same moment, an enormous motor-car, looking like some appalling monster, came tearing into sight at a headlong rate of speed. Amid the shouts of the madly scattering people, it made straight for the church, swerved, just as it seemed about to dash itself to pieces against the steps, grazed the wall of the presbytery, regained the continuation of the national road, dashed along, turned the corner and disappeared, without, by some incomprehensible miracle, having so much as brushed against any of the persons crowding the square.

But they had seen! They had seen a man in the driver's seat, wrapped in a goat-skin coat, with a fur cap on his head and his face disguised in a pair of large goggles, and, with him, on the front of that seat, flung back, bent in two, a woman whose head, all covered with blood, hung down over the bonnet....

And they had heard! They had heard the woman's screams, screams of horror, screams of agony,....

And it was all such a vision of hell and carnage that the people stood, for some seconds, motionless, stupefied.

"Blood!" roared somebody.

There was blood everywhere, on the cobblestones of the square, on the ground hardened by the first frosts of autumn; and, when a number of men and boys rushed off in pursuit of the motor, they had but to take those sinister marks for their guide.

The marks, on their part, followed the high-road, but in a very strange manner, going from one side to the other and leaving a zigzag track, in the wake of the tires, that made those who saw it shudder. How was it that the car had not bumped against that tree? How had it been righted, instead of smashing into that bank? What novice, what madman, what drunkard, what frightened criminal was driving that motor-car with such astounding bounds and swerves?

One of the peasants declared:

"They will never do the turn in the forest."

And another said:

"Of course they won't! She's bound to upset!"

The Forest of Morgues began at half a mile beyond Saint-Nicolas; and the road, which was straight up to that point, except for a slight bend where it left the village, started climbing, immediately after entering the forest, and made an abrupt turn among the rocks and trees. No motor-car was able to take this turn without first slackening speed. There were posts to give notice of the danger.

The breathless peasants reached the quincunx of beeches that formed the edge of the forest. And one of them at once cried:

"There you are!"

"What?"

"Upset!"

The car, a limousine, had turned turtle and lay smashed, twisted and shapeless. Beside it, the woman's dead body. But the most horrible, sordid, stupefying thing was the woman's head, crushed, flattened, invisible under a block of stone, a huge block of stone lodged there by some unknown and prodigious agency. As for the man in the goat-skin coat he was nowhere to be found.

He was not found on the scene of the accident. He was not found either in the neighbourhood. Moreover, some workmen coming down the Côte de Morgues declared that they had not seen anybody.

The man, therefore, had taken refuge in the woods.

The gendarmes, who were at once sent for, made a minute search, assisted by the peasants, but discovered nothing. In the same way, the examining-magistrates, after a close inquiry lasting for several days, found no clue capable of throwing the least light upon this inscrutable tragedy. On the contrary, the investigations only led to further mysteries and further improbabilities.

Thus it was ascertained that the block of stone came from where there had been a landslip, at least forty yards away. And the murderer, in a few minutes, had carried it all that distance and flung it on his victim's head.

On the other hand, the murderer, who was most certainly not hiding in the forest—for, if so, he must inevitably have been discovered, the forest being of limited extent—had the audacity, eight days after the crime, to come back to the turn on the hill and leave his goat-skin coat there. Why? With what object? There was nothing in the pockets of the coat, except a corkscrew and a napkin. What did it all mean?

Inquiries were made of the builder of the motor-car, who recognized the limousine as one which he had sold, three years ago, to a Russian. The said Russian, declared the manufacturer, had sold it again at once. To whom? No one knew. The car bore no number.

Then again, it was impossible to identify the dead woman's body. Her clothes and underclothing were not marked in any way. And the face was quite unknown.

Meanwhile, detectives were going along the national road in the direction opposite to that taken by the actors in this mysterious tragedy. But who was to prove that the car had followed that particular road on the previous night?

They examined every yard of the ground, they questioned everybody. At last, they succeeded in learning that, on the Saturday evening, a limousine had stopped outside a grocer's shop in a small town situated about two hundred miles from Saint-Nicolas, on a highway branching out of the national road.

The driver had first filled his tank, bought some spare cans of petrol and lastly taken away a small stock of provisions: a ham, fruit, biscuits, wine and a half-bottle of Three Star brandy.

There was a lady on the driver's seat. She did not get down. The blinds of the limousine were drawn. One of these blinds was seen to move several times. The shopman was positive that there was somebody inside.

Presuming the shopman's evidence to be correct, then the problem became even more complicated, for, so far, no clue had revealed the presence of a third person.

Meanwhile, as the travellers had supplied themselves with provisions, it remained to be discovered what they had done with them and what had become of the remains.

The detectives retraced their steps. It was not until they came to the fork of the two roads, at a spot eleven or twelve miles from Saint-Nicolas, that they met a shepherd who, in answer to their questions, directed them to a neighbouring field, hidden from view behind the screen of bushes, where he had seen an empty bottle and other things.

The detectives were convinced at the first examination. The motor-car had stopped there; and the unknown travellers, probably after a night's rest in their car, had breakfasted and resumed their journey in the course of the morning.

One unmistakable proof was the half-bottle of Three Star brandy sold by the grocer. This bottle had its neck broken clean off with a stone. The stone employed for the purpose was picked up, as was the neck of the bottle, with its cork, covered with a tin-foil seal. The seal showed marks of attempts that had been made to uncork the bottle in the ordinary manner.

The detectives continued their search and followed a ditch that ran along the field at right angles to the road. It ended in a little spring, hidden under brambles, which seemed to emit an offensive smell. On lifting the brambles, they perceived a corpse, the corpse of a man whose head had been smashed in, so that it formed little more than a sort of pulp, swarming with vermin. The body was dressed in jacket and trousers of dark-brown leather. The pockets were empty: no papers, no pocket-book, no watch.

The grocer and his shopman were summoned and, two days later, formally identified, by his dress and figure, the traveller who had bought the petrol and provisions on the Saturday evening.

The whole case, therefore, had to be reopened on a fresh basis. The authorities were confronted with a tragedy no longer enacted by two persons, a man and a woman, of whom one had killed the other, but by three persons, including two victims, of whom one was the very man who was accused of killing his companion.

As to the murderer, there was no doubt: he was the person who travelled inside the motor-car and who took the precaution to remain concealed behind the curtains. He had first got rid of the driver and rifled his pockets and then, after wounding the woman, carried her off in a mad dash for death.

Given a fresh case, unexpected discoveries, unforeseen evidence, one might have hoped that the mystery would be cleared up, or, at least, that the inquiry would point a few steps along the road to the truth. But not at all. The corpse was simply placed beside the first corpse. New problems were added to the old. The accusation of murder was shifted from the one to the other. And there it ended. Outside those tangible, obvious facts there was nothing but darkness. The name of the woman, the name of the man, the name of the murderer were so many riddles. And then what had become of the murderer? If he had disappeared from one moment to the other, that in itself would have been a tolerably curious phenomenon. But the phenomenon was actually something very like a miracle, inasmuch as the murderer had not absolutely disappeared. He was there! He made a practice of returning to the scene of the catastrophe! In addition to the goat-skin coat, a fur cap was picked up one day; and, by way of an unparalleled prodigy, one morning, after a whole night spent on guard in the rock, beside the famous turning, the detectives found, on the grass of the turning itself, a pair of motor-goggles, broken, rusty, dirty, done for. How had the murderer managed to bring back those goggles unseen by the detectives? And, above all, why had he brought them back?

Men's brains reeled in the presence of such abnormalities. They were almost afraid to pursue the ambiguous adventure. They received the impression of a heavy, stifling, breathless atmosphere, which dimmed the eyes and baffled the most clear-sighted.

The magistrate in charge of the case fell ill. Four days later, his successor confessed that the matter was beyond him.

Two tramps were arrested and at once released. Another was pursued, but not caught; moreover, there was no evidence of any sort or kind against him. In short, it was nothing but one helpless muddle of mist and contradiction.

An accident, the merest accident led to the solution, or rather produced a series of circumstances that ended by leading to the solution. A reporter on the staff of an important Paris paper, who had been sent to make investigations on the spot, concluded his article with the following words:

"I repeat, therefore, that we must wait for fresh events, fresh facts; we must wait for some lucky accident. As things stand, we are simply wasting our time. The elements of truth are not even sufficient to suggest a plausible theory. We are in the midst of the most absolute, painful, impenetrable darkness. There is nothing to be done. All the Sherlock Holmeses in the world would not know what to make of the mystery, and Arsène Lupin himself, if he will allow me to say so, would have to pay forfeit here."

On the day after the appearance of that article, the newspaper in question printed this telegram:

"Have sometimes paid forfeit, but never over such a silly thing as this. The Saint-Nicolas tragedy is a mystery for babies.

"ARSÈNE LUPIN."

And the editor added:

"We insert this telegram as a matter of curiosity, for it is obviously the work of a wag. Arsène Lupin, past-master though he be in the art of practical joking, would be the last man to display such childish flippancy."

Two days elapsed; and then the paper published the famous letter, so precise and categorical in its conclusions, in which Arsène Lupin furnished the solution of the problem. I quote it in full:

"SIR:

"You have taken me on my weak side by defying me. You challenge me, and I accept the challenge. And I will begin by declaring once more that the Saint-Nicolas tragedy is a mystery for babies. I know nothing so simple, so natural; and the proof of the simplicity shall lie in the succinctness of my demonstration. It is contained in these few words: when a crime seems to go beyond the ordinary scope of things, when it seems unusual and stupid, then there are many chances that its explanation is to be found in superordinary, supernatural, superhuman motives.

"I say that there are many chances, for we must always allow for the part played by absurdity in the most logical and commonplace events. But, of course, it is impossible to see things as they are and not to take account of the absurd and the disproportionate.

"I was struck from the very beginning by that very evident character of unusualness. We have, first of all, the awkward, zigzag course of the motor-car, which would give one the impression that the car was driven by a novice. People have spoken of a drunkard or a madman, a justifiable supposition in itself. But neither madness nor drunkenness would account for the incredible strength required to transport, especially in so short a space of time, the stone with which the unfortunate woman's head was crushed. That proceeding called for a muscular power so great that I do not hesitate to look upon it as a second sign of the unusualness that marks the whole tragedy. And why move that enormous stone, to finish off the victim, when a mere pebble would have done the work? Why again was the murderer not killed, or at least reduced to a temporary state of helplessness, in the terrible somersault turned by the car? How did he disappear? And why, having disappeared, did he return to the scene of the accident? Why did he throw his fur coat there; then, on another day, his cap; then, on another day, his goggles?

"Unusual, useless, stupid acts.

"Why, besides, convey that wounded, dying woman on the driver's seat of the car, where everybody could see her? Why do that, instead of putting her inside, or flinging her into some corner, dead, just as the man was flung under the brambles in the ditch?

"Unusualness, stupidity.

"Everything in the whole story is absurd. Everything points to hesitation, incoherency, awkwardness, the silliness of a child or rather of a mad, blundering savage, of a brute.

"Look at the bottle of brandy. There was a corkscrew: it was found in the pocket of the great coat. Did the murderer use it? Yes, the marks of the corkscrew can be seen on the seal. But the operation was too complicated for him. He broke the neck with a stone. Always stones: observe that detail. They are the only weapon, the only implement which the creature employs. It is his customary weapon, his familiar implement. He kills the man with a stone, he kills the woman with a stone and he opens bottles with a stone!

"A brute, I repeat, a savage; disordered, unhinged, suddenly driven mad. By what? Why, of course, by that same brandy, which he swallowed at a draught while the driver and his companion were having breakfast in the field. He got out of the limousine, in which he was travelling, in his goat-skin coat and his fur cap, took the bottle, broke off the neck and drank. There is the whole story. Having drunk, he went raving mad and hit out at random, without reason. Then, seized with instinctive fear, dreading the inevitable punishment, he hid the body of the man. Then, like an idiot, he took up the wounded woman and ran away. He ran away in that motor-car which he did not know how to work, but which to him represented safety, escape from capture.

"But the money, you will ask, the stolen pocket-book? Why, who says that he was the thief? Who says that it was not some passing tramp, some labourer, guided by the stench of the corpse?

"Very well, you object, but the brute would have been found, as he is hiding somewhere near the turn, and as, after all, he must eat and drink.

"Well, well, I see that you have not yet understood. The simplest way, I suppose, to have done and to answer your objections is to make straight for the mark. Then let the gentlemen of the police and the gendarmerie themselves make straight for the mark. Let them take firearms. Let them explore the forest within a radius of two or three hundred yards from the turn, no more. But, instead of exploring with their heads down and their eyes fixed on the ground, let them look up into the air, yes, into the air, among the leaves and branches of the tallest oaks and the most unlikely beeches. And, believe me, they will see him. For he is there. He is there, bewildered, piteously at a loss, seeking for the man and woman whom he has killed, looking for them and waiting for them and not daring to go away and quite unable to understand.

"I myself am exceedingly sorry that I am kept in town by urgent private affairs and by some complicated matters of business which I have to set going, for I should much have liked to see the end of this rather curious adventure.

"Pray, therefore excuse me to my kind friends in the police and permit me to be, sir,

"Your obedient servant,

"ARSÈNE LUPIN."

The upshot will be remembered. The "gentlemen of the police and the gendarmerie" shrugged their shoulders and paid no attention to this lucubration. But four of the local country gentry took their rifles and went shooting, with their eyes fixed skyward, as though they meant to pot a few rooks. In half an hour they had caught sight of the murderer. Two shots, and he came tumbling from bough to bough. He was only wounded, and they took him alive.

That evening, a Paris paper, which did not yet know of the capture, printed the following paragraphs:

"Enquiries are being made after a M. and Mme. Bragoff, who landed at Marseilles six weeks ago and there hired a motor-car. They had been living in Australia for many years, during which time they had not visited Europe; and they wrote to the director of the Jardin d'Acclimatation, with whom they were in the habit of corresponding, that they were bringing with them a curious creature, of an entirely unknown species, of which it was difficult to say whether it was a man or a monkey.

"According to M. Bragoff, who is an eminent archæologist, the specimen in question is the anthropoid ape, or rather the ape-man, the existence of which had not hitherto been definitely proved. The structure is said to be exactly similar to that of *Pithecanthropus erectus*, discovered by Dr. Dubois in Java in 1891.

"This curious, intelligent and observant animal acted as its owner's servant on their property in Australia and used to clean their motor-car and even attempt to drive it.

"The question that is being asked is where are M. and Mme. Bragoff? Where is the strange primate that landed with them at Marseilles?"

The answer to this question was now made easy. Thanks to the hints supplied by Arsène Lupin, all the elements of the tragedy were known. Thanks to him, the culprit was in the hands of the law.

You can see him at the Jardin d'Acclimatation, where he is locked up under the name of "Three Stars." He is, in point of fact, a monkey; but he is also a man. He has the gentleness and the wisdom of the domestic animals and the sadness which they feel when their master dies. But he has many other qualities that bring him much closer to humanity: he is treacherous, cruel, idle, greedy and quarrelsome; and, above all, he is immoderately fond of brandy.

Apart from that, he is a monkey. Unless indeed ...!

A few days after Three Stars' arrest, I saw Arsène Lupin standing in front of his cage. Lupin was manifestly trying to solve this interesting problem for himself. I at once said, for I had set my heart upon having the matter out with him:

"You know, Lupin, that intervention of yours, your argument, your letter, in short, did not surprise me so much as you might think!"

"Oh, really?" he said, calmly. "And why?"

"Why? Because the incident has occurred before, seventy or eighty years ago. Edgar Allan Poe made it the subject of one of his finest tales. In those circumstances, the key to the riddle was easy enough to find."

Arsène Lupin took my arm, and walking away with me, said:

"When did you guess it, yourself?"

"On reading your letter," I confessed.

"And at what part of my letter?"

"At the end."

"At the end, eh? After I had dotted all the i's. So here is a crime which accident causes to be repeated, under quite different conditions, it is true, but still with the same sort of hero; and your eyes had to be opened, as well as other people's. It needed the assistance of my letter, the letter in which I amused myself—apart from the exigencies of the facts—by employing the argument and sometimes the identical words used by the American poet in a story which everybody has read. So you see that my letter was not absolutely useless and that one may safely venture to repeat to people things which they have learnt only to forget them."

Wherewith Lupin turned on his heel and burst out laughing in the face of an old monkey, who sat with the air of a philosopher, gravely meditating.

VIII. LUPIN'S MARRIAGE

"Monsieur Arsène Lupin has the honour to inform you of his approaching marriage with Mademoiselle Angélique de Sarzeau-Vendôme, Princesse de Bourbon-Condé, and to request the pleasure of your company at the wedding, which will take place at the church of Sainte-Clotilde...."

"The Duc de Sarzeau-Vendôme has the honour to inform you of the approaching marriage of his daughter Angélique, Princesse de Bourbon-Condé, with Monsieur Arsène Lupin, and to request...."

Jean Duc de Sarzeau-Vendôme could not finish reading the invitations which he held in his trembling hand. Pale with anger, his long, lean body shaking with tremors:

"There!" he gasped, handing the two communications to his daughter. "This is what our friends have received! This has been the talk of Paris since yesterday! What do you say to that dastardly insult, Angélique? What would your poor mother say to it, if she were alive?"

Angélique was tall and thin like her father, skinny and angular like him. She was thirty-three years of age, always dressed in black stuff, shy and retiring in manner, with a head too small in proportion to her height and narrowed on either side until the nose seemed to jut forth in protest against such parsimony. And yet it would be impossible to say that she was ugly, for her eyes were extremely beautiful, soft and grave, proud and a little sad: pathetic eyes which to see once was to remember.

She flushed with shame at hearing her father's words, which told her the scandal of which she was the victim. But, as she loved him, notwithstanding his harshness to her, his injustice and despotism, she said:

"Oh, I think it must be meant for a joke, father, to which we need pay no attention!"

"A joke? Why, every one is gossiping about it! A dozen papers have printed the confounded notice this morning, with satirical comments. They quote our pedigree, our ancestors, our illustrious dead. They pretend to take the thing seriously...."

"Still, no one could believe...."

"Of course not. But that doesn't prevent us from being the by-word of Paris."

"It will all be forgotten by to-morrow."

"To-morrow, my girl, people will remember that the name of Angélique de Sarzeau-Vendôme has been bandied about as it should not be. Oh, if I could find out the name of the scoundrel who has dared...."

At that moment, Hyacinthe, the duke's valet, came in and said that monsieur le duc was wanted on the telephone. Still fuming, he took down the receiver and growled:

"Well? Who is it? Yes, it's the Duc de Sarzeau-Vendôme speaking."

A voice replied:

"I want to apologize to you, monsieur le duc, and to Mlle. Angélique. It's my secretary's fault."

"Your secretary?"

"Yes, the invitations were only a rough draft which I meant to submit to you. Unfortunately my secretary thought...."

"But, tell me, monsieur, who are you?"

"What, monsieur le duc, don't you know my voice? The voice of your future son-in-law?"

"What!"

"Arsène Lupin."

The duke dropped into a chair. His face was livid.

"Arsène Lupin ... it's he ... Arsène Lupin...."

Angélique gave a smile:

"You see, father, it's only a joke, a hoax."

But the duke's rage broke out afresh and he began to walk up and down, moving his arms:

"I shall go to the police!... The fellow can't be allowed to make a fool of me in this way!... If there's any law left in the land, it must be stopped!"

Hyacinthe entered the room again. He brought two visiting-cards.

"Chotois? Lepetit? Don't know them."

"They are both journalists, monsieur le duc."

"What do they want?"

"They would like to speak to monsieur le duc with regard to ... the marriage...."

"Turn them out!" exclaimed the duke. "Kick them out! And tell the porter not to admit scum of that sort to my house in future."

"Please, father ..." Angélique ventured to say.

"As for you, shut up! If you had consented to marry one of your cousins when I wanted you to this wouldn't have happened."

The same evening, one of the two reporters printed, on the front page of his paper, a somewhat fanciful story of his expedition to the family mansion of the Sarzeau-Vendômes, in the Rue de Varennes, and expatiated pleasantly upon the old nobleman's wrathful protests.

The next morning, another newspaper published an interview with Arsène Lupin which was supposed to have taken place in a lobby at the Opera. Arsène Lupin retorted in a letter to the editor:

"I share my prospective father-in-law's indignation to the full. The sending out of the invitations was a gross breach of etiquette for which I am not responsible, but for which I wish to make a public apology. Why, sir, the date of the marriage is not yet fixed. My bride's father suggests early in May. She and I think that six weeks is really too long to wait!..."

That which gave a special piquancy to the affair and added immensely to the enjoyment of the friends of the family was the duke's well-known character: his pride and the uncompromising nature of his ideas and principles. Duc Jean was the last descendant of the Barons de Sarzeau, the most ancient family in Brittany; he was the lineal descendant of that Sarzeau who, upon marrying a Vendôme, refused to bear the new title which Louis XV forced upon him until after he had been imprisoned for ten years in the Bastille; and he had abandoned none of the prejudices of the old régime. In his youth, he followed the Comte de Chambord into exile. In his old age, he refused a seat in the Chamber on the pretext that a Sarzeau could only sit with his peers.

The incident stung him to the quick. Nothing could pacify him. He cursed Lupin in good round terms, threatened him with every sort of punishment and rounded on his daughter:

"There, if you had only married!... After all you had plenty of chances. Your three cousins, Mussy, d'Emboise and Caorches, are noblemen of good descent, allied to the best families, fairly well-off; and they are still anxious to marry you. Why do you refuse them? Ah, because miss is a dreamer, a sentimentalist; and because her cousins are too fat, or too thin, or too coarse for her...."

She was, in fact, a dreamer. Left to her own devices from childhood, she had read all the books of chivalry, all the colourless romances of olden-time that littered the ancestral presses; and she looked upon life as a fairy-tale in which the beauteous maidens are always happy, while the others wait till death for the bridegroom who does not come. Why should she marry one of her cousins when they were only after her money, the millions which she had inherited from her mother? She might as well remain an old maid and go on dreaming....

She answered, gently:

"You will end by making yourself ill, father. Forget this silly business."

But how could he forget it? Every morning, some pin-prick renewed his wound. Three days running, Angélique received a wonderful sheaf of flowers, with Arsène Lupin's card peeping from it. The duke could not go to his club but a friend accosted him:

"That was a good one to-day!"

"What was?"

"Why, your son-in-law's latest! Haven't you seen it? Here, read it for yourself: 'M. Arsène Lupin is petitioning the Council of State for permission to add his wife's name to his own and to be known henceforth as Lupin de Sarzeau-Vendôme.'"

And, the next day, he read:

"As the young bride, by virtue of an unrepealed decree of Charles X, bears the title and arms of the Bourbon-Condés, of whom she is the heiress-of-line, the eldest son of the Lupins de Sarzeau-Vendôme will be styled Prince de Bourbon-Condé."

And, the day after, an advertisement.

"Exhibition of Mlle. de Sarzeau-Vendôme's trousseau at Messrs. ——'s Great Linen Warehouse. Each article marked with initials L. S. V."

Then an illustrated paper published a photographic scene: the duke, his daughter and his son-in-law sitting at a table playing three-handed auction-bridge.

And the date also was announced with a great flourish of trumpets: the 4th of May.

And particulars were given of the marriage-settlement. Lupin showed himself wonderfully disinterested. He was prepared to sign, the newspapers said, with his eyes closed, without knowing the figure of the dowry.

All these things drove the old duke crazy. His hatred of Lupin assumed morbid proportions. Much as it went against the grain, he called on the prefect of police, who advised him to be on his guard:

"We know the gentleman's ways; he is employing one of his favourite dodges. Forgive the expression, monsieur le duc, but he is 'nursing' you. Don't fall into the trap."

"What dodge? What trap?" asked the duke, anxiously.

"He is trying to make you lose your head and to lead you, by intimidation, to do something which you would refuse to do in cold blood."

"Still, M. Arsène Lupin can hardly hope that I will offer him my daughter's hand!"

"No, but he hopes that you will commit, to put it mildly, a blunder."

"What blunder?"

"Exactly that blunder which he wants you to commit."

"Then you think, monsieur le préfet ...?"

"I think the best thing you can do, monsieur le duc, is to go home, or, if all this excitement worries you, to run down to the country and stay there quietly, without upsetting yourself."

This conversation only increased the old duke's fears. Lupin appeared to him in the light of a terrible person, who employed diabolical methods and kept accomplices in every sphere of society. Prudence was the watchword.

And life, from that moment, became intolerable. The duke grew more crabbed and silent than ever and denied his door to all his old friends and even to Angélique's three suitors, her Cousins de Mussy, d'Emboise and de Caorches, who were none of them on speaking terms with the others, in consequence of their rivalry, and who were in the habit of calling, turn and turn about, every week.

For no earthly reason, he dismissed his butler and his coachman. But he dared not fill their places, for fear of engaging creatures of Arsène Lupin's; and his own man, Hyacinthe, in whom he had every confidence, having had him in his service for over forty years, had to take upon himself the laborious duties of the stables and the pantry.

"Come, father," said Angélique, trying to make him listen to common-sense. "I really can't see what you are afraid of. No one can force me into this ridiculous marriage."

"Well, of course, that's not what I'm afraid of."

"What then, father?"

"How can I tell? An abduction! A burglary! An act of violence! There is no doubt that the villain is scheming something; and there is also no doubt that we are surrounded by spies."

One afternoon, he received a newspaper in which the following paragraph was marked in red pencil:

"The signing of the marriage-contract is fixed for this evening, at the Sarzeau-Vendôme town-house. It will be quite a private ceremony and only a few privileged friends will be present to congratulate the happy pair. The witnesses to the contract on behalf of Mlle. de Sarzeau-Vendôme, the Prince de la Rochefoucauld-Limours and the Comte de Chartres, will be introduced by M. Arsène Lupin to the two gentlemen who have claimed the honour of acting as his groomsmen, namely, the prefect of police and the governor of the Santé Prison."

Ten minutes later, the duke sent his servant Hyacinthe to the post with three express messages. At four o'clock, in Angélique's presence, he saw the three cousins: Mussy, fat, heavy, pasty-faced; d'Emboise, slender, fresh-coloured and shy: Caorches, short, thin and unhealthy-looking: all three, old bachelors by this time, lacking distinction in dress or appearance.

The meeting was a short one. The duke had worked out his whole plan of campaign, a defensive campaign, of which he set forth the first stage in explicit terms:

"Angélique and I will leave Paris to-night for our place in Brittany. I rely on you, my three nephews, to help us get away. You, d'Emboise, will come and fetch us in your car, with the hood up. You, Mussy, will bring your big motor and kindly see to the luggage with Hyacinthe, my man. You, Caorches, will go to the Gare d'Orléans and book our berths in the sleeping-car for Vannes by the 10.40 train. Is that settled?"

The rest of the day passed without incident. The duke, to avoid any accidental indiscretion, waited until after dinner to tell Hyacinthe to pack a trunk and a portmanteau. Hyacinthe was to accompany them, as well as Angélique's maid.

At nine o'clock, all the other servants went to bed, by their master's order. At ten minutes to ten, the duke, who was completing his preparations, heard the sound of a motor-horn. The porter opened the gates of the courtyard. The duke, standing at the window, recognized d'Emboise's landaulette:

"Tell him I shall be down presently," he said to Hyacinthe, "and let mademoiselle know."

In a few minutes, as Hyacinthe did not return, he left his room. But he was attacked on the landing by two masked men, who gagged and bound him before he could utter a cry. And one of the men said to him, in a low voice:

"Take this as a first warning, monsieur le duc. If you persist in leaving Paris and refusing your consent, it will be a more serious matter."

And the same man said to his companion:

"Keep an eye on him. I will see to the young lady."

By that time, two other confederates had secured the lady's maid; and Angélique, herself gagged, lay fainting on a couch in her boudoir.

She came to almost immediately, under the stimulus of a bottle of salts held to her nostrils; and, when she opened her eyes, she saw bending over her a young man, in evening-clothes, with a smiling and friendly face, who said:

"I implore your forgiveness, mademoiselle. All these happenings are a trifle sudden and this behaviour rather out of the way. But circumstances often compel us to deeds of which our conscience does not approve. Pray pardon me."

He took her hand very gently and slipped a broad gold ring on the girl's finger, saying:

"There, now we are engaged. Never forget the man who gave you this ring. He entreats you not to run away from him ... and to stay in Paris and await the proofs of his devotion. Have faith in him."

He said all this in so serious and respectful a voice, with so much authority and deference, that she had not the strength to resist. Their eyes met. He whispered:

"The exquisite purity of your eyes! It would be heavenly to live with those eyes upon one. Now close them...."

He withdrew. His accomplices followed suit. The car drove off, and the house in the Rue de Varennes remained still and silent until the moment when Angélique, regaining complete consciousness, called out for the servants.

They found the duke, Hyacinthe, the lady's maid and the porter and his wife all tightly bound. A few priceless ornaments had disappeared, as well as the duke's pocket-book and all his jewellery; tie pins, pearl studs, watch and so on.

The police were advised without delay. In the morning it appeared that, on the evening before, d'Emboise, when leaving his house in the motor-car, was stabbed by his own chauffeur and thrown, half-dead, into a deserted street. Mussy and Caorches had each received a telephone-message, purporting to come from the duke, countermanding their attendance.

Next week, without troubling further about the police investigation, without obeying the summons of the examining-magistrate, without even reading Arsène Lupin's letters to the papers on "the Varennes Flight," the duke, his daughter and his valet stealthily took a slow train for Vannes and arrived one evening, at the old feudal castle that towers over the headland of Sarzeau. The duke at once organized a defence with the aid of the Breton peasants, true mediæval vassals to a man. On the fourth day, Mussy arrived; on the fifth, Caorches; and, on the seventh, d'Emboise, whose wound was not as severe as had been feared.

The duke waited two days longer before communicating to those about him what, now that his escape had succeeded in spite of Lupin, he called the second part of his plan. He did so, in the presence of the three cousins, by a dictatorial order to Angélique, expressed in these peremptory terms:

"All this bother is upsetting me terribly. I have entered on a struggle with this man whose daring you have seen for yourself; and the struggle is killing me. I want to end it at all costs. There is only one way of doing so, Angélique, and that is for you to release me from all responsibility by accepting the hand of one of your cousins. Before a month is out, you must be the wife of Mussy, Caorches or d'Emboise. You have a free choice. Make your decision."

For four whole days Angélique wept and entreated her father, but in vain. She felt that he would be inflexible and that she must end by submitting to his wishes. She accepted:

"Whichever you please, father. I love none of them. So I may as well be unhappy with one as with the other."

Thereupon a fresh discussion ensued, as the duke wanted to compel her to make her own choice. She stood firm. Reluctantly and for financial considerations, he named d'Emboise.

The banns were published without delay.

From that moment, the watch in and around the castle was increased twofold, all the more inasmuch as Lupin's silence and the sudden cessation of the campaign which he had been conducting in the press could not but alarm the Duc de Sarzeau-Vendôme. It was obvious that the enemy was getting ready to strike and would endeavour to oppose the marriage by one of his characteristic moves.

Nevertheless, nothing happened: nothing two days before the ceremony, nothing on the day before, nothing on the morning itself. The marriage took place in the mayor's office, followed by the religious celebration in church; and the thing was done.

Then and not till then, the duke breathed freely. Notwithstanding his daughter's sadness, notwithstanding the embarrassed silence of his son-in-law, who found the situation a little trying, he rubbed his hands with an air of pleasure, as though he had achieved a brilliant victory:

"Tell them to lower the drawbridge," he said to Hyacinthe, "and to admit everybody. We have nothing more to fear from that scoundrel."

After the wedding-breakfast, he had wine served out to the peasants and clinked glasses with them. They danced and sang.

At three o'clock, he returned to the ground-floor rooms. It was the hour for his afternoon nap. He walked to the guard-room at the end of the suite. But he had no sooner placed his foot on the threshold than he stopped suddenly and exclaimed:

"What are you doing here, d'Emboise? Is this a joke?"

D'Emboise was standing before him, dressed as a Breton fisherman, in a dirty jacket and breeches, torn, patched and many sizes too large for him.

The duke seemed dumbfounded. He stared with eyes of amazement at that face which he knew and which, at the same time, roused memories of a very distant past within his brain. Then he strode abruptly to one of the windows overlooking the castle-terrace and called:

"Angélique!"

"What is it, father?" she asked, coming forward.

"Where's your husband?"

"Over there, father," said Angélique, pointing to d'Emboise, who was smoking a cigarette and reading, some way off.

The duke stumbled and fell into a chair, with a great shudder of fright:

"Oh, I shall go mad!"

But the man in the fisherman's garb knelt down before him and said:

"Look at me, uncle. You know me, don't you? I'm your nephew, the one who used to play here in the old days, the one whom you called Jacquot.... Just think a minute.... Here, look at this scar...."

"Yes, yes," stammered the duke, "I recognize you. It's Jacques. But the other one...."

He put his hands to his head:

"And yet, no, it can't be ... Explain yourself.... I don't understand.... I don't want to understand...."

There was a pause, during which the newcomer shut the window and closed the door leading to the next room. Then he came up to the old duke, touched him gently on the shoulder, to wake him from his torpor, and without further preface, as though to cut short any explanation that was not absolutely necessary, spoke as follows:

"Four years ago, that is to say, in the eleventh year of my voluntary exile, when I settled in the extreme south of Algeria, I made the acquaintance, in the course of a hunting-expedition arranged by a big Arab chief, of a man whose geniality, whose charm of manner, whose consummate prowess, whose indomitable pluck, whose combined humour and depth of mind fascinated me in the highest degree. The Comte d'Andrésy spent six weeks as my guest. After he left, we kept up a correspondence at regular intervals. I also often saw his name in the papers, in the society and sporting columns. He was to come back and I was preparing to receive him, three months ago, when, one evening as I was out riding, my two Arab attendants flung themselves upon me, bound me, blindfolded me and took me, travelling day and night, for a week, along deserted roads, to a bay on the coast, where five men awaited them. I was at once carried on board a small steam-yacht, which weighed anchor without delay. There was nothing to tell me who the men were nor what their object was in kidnapping me. They had locked me into a narrow cabin, secured by a massive door and lighted by a port-hole protected by two iron cross-bars. Every morning, a hand was inserted through a hatch between the next cabin and my own and placed on my bunk two or three pounds of bread, a good helping of food and a flagon of wine and removed the remains of yesterday's meals, which I put there for the purpose. From time to time, at night, the yacht stopped and I heard the sound of the boat rowing to some harbour and then returning, doubtless with provisions. Then we set out once more, without hurrying, as though on a cruise of people of our class, who travel for pleasure and are not pressed for time. Sometimes, standing on a chair, I would see the coastline, through my port-hole, too indistinctly, however, to locate it. And this lasted for weeks. One morning, in the ninth week, I perceived that the hatch had been left unfastened and I pushed it open. The cabin was empty at the time. With an effort, I was able to take a nail-file from a dressing-table. Two weeks after that, by dint of patient perseverance, I had succeeded in filing through the bars of my port-hole and I could have escaped that way, only, though I am a good swimmer, I soon grow tired. I had therefore to choose a moment when the yacht was not too far from the land. It was not until yesterday that, perched on my chair, I caught sight of the coast; and, in the evening, at sunset, I recognized, to my astonishment, the outlines of the Château de Sarzeau, with its pointed turrets and its square keep. I wondered if this was the goal of my mysterious voyage. All night long, we cruised in the offing. The same all day yesterday. At last, this morning, we put in at a distance which I considered favourable, all the more so as we were steaming through rocks under cover of which I could swim unobserved. But, just as I was about to make my escape, I noticed that the shutter of the hatch, which they thought they had closed, had once more opened of itself and was flapping against the partition. I again pushed it ajar from curiosity. Within arm's length was a little cupboard which I managed to open and in which my hand, groping at random, laid hold of a bundle of papers. This consisted of letters, letters containing instructions addressed to the pirates who held me prisoner. An hour later, when I wriggled through the port-hole and slipped into the sea, I knew all: the reasons for my abduction, the means employed, the object in view and the infamous scheme plotted during the last three months against the Duc de Sarzeau-Vendôme and his daughter. Unfortunately, it was too late. I was obliged, in order not to be seen from the yacht, to crouch in the cleft of a rock and did not reach land until mid-day. By the time that I had been to a fisherman's cabin, exchanged my clothes for his and come on here, it was three o'clock. On my arrival. I learnt that Angélique's marriage was celebrated this morning."

The old duke had not spoken a word. With his eyes riveted on the stranger's, he was listening in ever-increasing dismay. At times, the thought of the warnings given him by the prefect of police returned to his mind:

"They're nursing you, monsieur le duc, they are nursing you."

He said, in a hollow voice:

"Speak on ... finish your story.... All this is ghastly.... I don't understand it yet ... and I feel nervous...."

The stranger resumed:

"I am sorry to say, the story is easily pieced together and is summed up in a few sentences. It is like this: the Comte d'Andrésy remembered several things from his stay with me and from the confidences which I was foolish enough to make to him. First of all, I was your nephew and yet you had seen comparatively little of me, because I left Sarzeau when I was quite a child, and since then our intercourse was limited to the few weeks which I spent here, fifteen years ago, when I proposed for the hand of my Cousin Angélique; secondly, having broken with the past, I received no letters; lastly, there was a certain physical resemblance between d'Andrésy and myself which could be accentuated to such an extent as to become striking. His scheme was built up on those three points. He bribed my Arab servants to give him warning in case I left Algeria. Then he went back to Paris, bearing my name and made up to look exactly like me, came to see you, was invited to your house once a fortnight and lived under my name, which thus became one of the many aliases beneath which he conceals his real identity. Three months ago, when 'the apple was ripe,' as he says in his letters, he began the attack by a series of communications to the press; and, at the same time, fearing no doubt that some newspaper would tell me in Algeria the part that was being played under my name in Paris, he had me assaulted by my servants and kidnapped by his confederates. I need not explain any more in so far as you are concerned, uncle."

The Duc de Sarzeau-Vendôme was shaken with a fit of nervous trembling. The awful truth to which he refused to open his eyes appeared to him in its nakedness and assumed the hateful countenance of the enemy. He clutched his nephew's hands and said to him, fiercely, despairingly:

"It's Lupin, is it not?"

"Yes, uncle."

"And it's to him ... it's to him that I have given my daughter!"

"Yes, uncle, to him, who has stolen my name of Jacques d'Emboise from me and stolen your daughter from you. Angélique is the wedded wife of Arsène Lupin; and that in accordance with your orders. This letter in his handwriting bears witness to it. He has upset your whole life, thrown you off your balance, besieging your hours of waking and your nights of dreaming, rifling your town-house, until the moment when, seized with terror, you took refuge here, where, thinking that you would escape his artifices and his rapacity, you told your daughter to choose one of her three cousins, Mussy, d'Emboise or Caorches, as her husband.

"But why did she select that one rather than the others?"

"It was you who selected him, uncle."

"At random ... because he had the biggest income...."

"No, not at random, but on the insidious, persistent and very clever advice of your servant Hyacinthe."

The duke gave a start:

"What! Is Hyacinthe an accomplice?"

"No, not of Arsène Lupin, but of the man whom he believes to be d'Emboise and who promised to give him a hundred thousand francs within a week after the marriage."

"Oh, the villain!... He planned everything, foresaw everything...."

"Foresaw everything, uncle, down to shamming an attempt upon his life so as to avert suspicion, down to shamming a wound received in your service."

"But with what object? Why all these dastardly tricks?"

"Angélique has a fortune of eleven million francs. Your solicitor in Paris was to hand the securities next week to the counterfeit d'Emboise, who had only to realize them forthwith and disappear. But, this very morning, you yourself were to hand your son-in-law, as a personal wedding-present, five hundred thousand francs' worth of bearer-stock, which he has arranged to deliver to one of his accomplices at nine o'clock this evening, outside the castle, near the Great Oak, so that they may be negotiated to-morrow morning in Brussels."

The Duc de Sarzeau-Vendôme had risen from his seat and was stamping furiously up and down the room:

"At nine o'clock this evening?" he said. "We'll see about that.... We'll see about that.... I'll have the gendarmes here before then...."

"Arsène Lupin laughs at gendarmes."

"Let's telegraph to Paris."

"Yes, but how about the five hundred thousand francs?... And, still worse, uncle, the scandal?... Think of this: your daughter, Angélique de Sarzeau-Vendôme, married to that swindler, that thief.... No, no, it would never do...."

"What then?"

"What?..."

The nephew now rose and, stepping to a gun-rack, took down a rifle and laid it on the table, in front of the duke:

"Away in Algeria, uncle, on the verge of the desert, when we find ourselves face to face with a wild beast, we do not send for the gendarmes. We take our rifle and we shoot the wild beast. Otherwise, the beast would tear us to pieces with its claws."

"What do you mean?"

"I mean that, over there, I acquired the habit of dispensing with the gendarmes. It is a rather summary way of doing justice, but it is the best way, believe me, and to-day, in the present case, it is the only way. Once the beast is killed, you and I will bury it in some corner, unseen and unknown."

"And Angélique?"

"We will tell her later."

"What will become of her?"

"She will be my wife, the wife of the real d'Emboise. I desert her to-morrow and return to Algeria. The divorce will be granted in two months' time."

The duke listened, pale and staring, with set jaws. He whispered:

"Are you sure that his accomplices on the yacht will not inform him of your escape?"

"Not before to-morrow."

"So that ...?"

"So that inevitably, at nine o'clock this evening, Arsène Lupin, on his way to the Great Oak, will take the patrol-path that follows the old ramparts and skirts the ruins of the chapel. I shall be there, in the ruins."

"I shall be there too," said the Duc de Sarzeau-Vendôme, quietly, taking down a gun.

It was now five o'clock. The duke talked some time longer to his nephew, examined the weapons, loaded them with fresh cartridges. Then, when night came, he took d'Emboise through the dark passages to his bedroom and hid him in an adjoining closet.

Nothing further happened until dinner. The duke forced himself to keep calm during the meal. From time to time, he stole a glance at his son-in-law and was surprised at the likeness between him and the real d'Emboise. It was the same complexion, the same cast of features, the same cut of hair. Nevertheless, the look of the eye was different, keener in this case and brighter; and gradually the duke discovered minor details which had passed unperceived till then and which proved the fellow's imposture.

The party broke up after dinner. It was eight o'clock. The duke went to his room and released his nephew. Ten minutes later, under cover of the darkness, they slipped into the ruins, gun in hand.

Meanwhile, Angélique, accompanied by her husband, had gone to the suite of rooms which she occupied on the ground-floor of a tower that flanked the left wing. Her husband stopped at the entrance to the rooms and said:

"I am going for a short stroll, Angélique. May I come to you here, when I return?"

"Yes," she replied.

He left her and went up to the first floor, which had been assigned to him as his quarters. The moment he was alone, he locked the door, noiselessly opened a window that looked over the landscape and leant out. He saw a shadow at the foot of the tower, some hundred feet or more below him. He whistled and received a faint whistle in reply.

He then took from a cupboard a thick leather satchel, crammed with papers, wrapped it in a piece of black cloth and tied it up. Then he sat down at the table and wrote:

"Glad you got my message, for I think it unsafe to walk out of the castle with that large bundle of securities. Here they are. You will be in Paris, on your motor-cycle, in time to catch the morning train to Brussels, where you will hand over the bonds to Z.; and he will negotiate them at once.

"P. S.—As you pass by the Great Oak, tell our chaps that I'm coming. I have some instructions to give them. But everything is going well. No one here has the least suspicion."

He fastened the letter to the parcel and lowered both through the window with a length of string:

"Good," he said. "That's all right. It's a weight off my mind."

He waited a few minutes longer, stalking up and down the room and smiling at the portraits of two gallant gentlemen hanging on the wall:

"Horace de Sarzeau-Vendôme, marshal of France.... And you, the Great Condé ... I salute you, my ancestors both. Lupin de Sarzeau-Vendôme will show himself worthy of you."

At last, when the time came, he took his hat and went down. But, when he reached the ground-floor, Angélique burst from her rooms and exclaimed, with a distraught air:

"I say ... if you don't mind ... I think you had better...."

And then, without saying more, she went in again, leaving a vision of irresponsible terror in her husband's mind.

"She's out of sorts," he said to himself. "Marriage doesn't suit her."

He lit a cigarette and went out, without attaching importance to an incident that ought to have impressed him:

"Poor Angélique! This will all end in a divorce...."

The night outside was dark, with a cloudy sky.

The servants were closing the shutters of the castle. There was no light in the windows, it being the duke's habit to go to bed soon after dinner.

Lupin passed the gate-keeper's lodge and, as he put his foot on the drawbridge, said:

"Leave the gate open. I am going for a breath of air; I shall be back soon."

The patrol-path was on the right and ran along one of the old ramparts, which used to surround the castle with a second and much larger enclosure, until it ended at an almost demolished postern-gate. The park, which skirted a hillock and afterward followed the side of a deep valley, was bordered on the left by thick coppices.

"What a wonderful place for an ambush!" he said. "A regular cut-throat spot!"

He stopped, thinking that he heard a noise. But no, it was a rustling of the leaves. And yet a stone went rattling down the slopes, bounding against the rugged projections of the rock. But, strange to say, nothing seemed to disquiet him. The crisp sea-breeze came blowing over the plains of the headland; and he eagerly filled his lungs with it:

"What a thing it is to be alive!" he thought. "Still young, a member of the old nobility, a multi-millionaire: what could a man want more?"

At a short distance, he saw against the darkness the yet darker outline of the chapel, the ruins of which towered above the path. A few drops of rain began to fall; and he heard a clock strike nine. He quickened his pace. There was a short descent; then the path rose again. And suddenly, he stopped once more.

A hand had seized his.

He drew back, tried to release himself.

But some one stepped from the clump of trees against which he was brushing; and a voice said; "Ssh!... Not a word!..."

He recognized his wife, Angélique:

"What's the matter?" he asked.

She whispered, so low that he could hardly catch the words:

"They are lying in wait for you ... they are in there, in the ruins, with their guns...."

"Who?"

"Keep quiet.... Listen...."

They stood for a moment without stirring; then she said:

"They are not moving.... Perhaps they never heard me.... Let's go back...."

"But...."

"Come with me."

Her accent was so imperious that he obeyed without further question. But suddenly she took fright:

"Run!... They are coming!... I am sure of it!..."

True enough, they heard a sound of footsteps.

Then, swiftly, still holding him by the hand, she dragged him, with irresistible energy, along a shortcut, following its turns without hesitation in spite of the darkness and the brambles. And they very soon arrived at the drawbridge.

She put her arm in his. The gate-keeper touched his cap. They crossed the courtyard and entered the castle; and she led him to the corner tower in which both of them had their apartments:

"Come in here," she said.

"To your rooms?"

"Yes."

Two maids were sitting up for her. Their mistress ordered them to retire to their bedrooms, on the third floor.

Almost immediately after, there was a knock at the door of the outer room; and a voice called:

"Angélique!"

"Is that you, father?" she asked, suppressing her agitation.

"Yes. Is your husband here?"

"We have just come in."

"Tell him I want to speak to him. Ask him to come to my room. It's important."

"Very well, father, I'll send him to you."

She listened for a few seconds, then returned to the boudoir where her husband was and said:

"I am sure my father is still there."

He moved as though to go out:

"In that case, if he wants to speak to me...."

"My father is not alone," she said, quickly, blocking his way.

"Who is with him?"

"His nephew, Jacques d'Emboise."

There was a moment's silence. He looked at her with a certain astonishment, failing quite to understand his wife's attitude. But, without pausing to go into the matter:

"Ah, so that dear old d'Emboise is there?" he chuckled. "Then the fat's in the fire? Unless, indeed...."

"My father knows everything," she said. "I overheard a conversation between them just now. His nephew has read certain letters.... I hesitated at first about telling you.... Then I thought that my duty...."

He studied her afresh. But, at once conquered by the queerness of the situation, he burst out laughing:

"What? Don't my friends on board ship burn my letters? And they have let their prisoner escape? The idiots! Oh, when you don't see to everything yourself!... No matter, its distinctly humorous.... D'Emboise versus d'Emboise.... Oh, but suppose I were no longer recognized? Suppose d'Emboise himself were to confuse me with himself?"

He turned to a wash-hand-stand, took a towel, dipped it in the basin and soaped it and, in the twinkling of an eye, wiped the make-up from his face and altered the set of his hair:

"That's it," he said, showing himself to Angélique under the aspect in which she had seen him on the night of the burglary in Paris. "I feel more comfortable like this for a discussion with my father-in-law."

"Where are you going?" she cried, flinging herself in front of the door.

"Why, to join the gentlemen."

"You shall not pass!"

"Why not?"

"Suppose they kill you?"

"Kill me?"

"That's what they mean to do, to kill you ... to hide your body somewhere.... Who would know of it?"

"Very well," he said, "from their point of view, they are quite right. But, if I don't go to them, they will come here. That door won't stop them.... Nor you, I'm thinking. Therefore, it's better to have done with it."

"Follow me," commanded Angélique.

She took up the lamp that lit the room, went into her bedroom, pushed aside the wardrobe, which slid easily on hidden castors, pulled back an old tapestry-hanging, and said:

"Here is a door that has not been used for years. My father believes the key to be lost. I have it here. Unlock the door with it. A staircase in the wall will take you to the bottom of the tower. You need only draw the bolts of another door and you will be free."

He could hardly believe his ears. Suddenly, he grasped the meaning of Angélique's whole behaviour. In front of that sad, plain, but wonderfully gentle face, he stood for a moment discountenanced, almost abashed. He no longer thought of laughing. A feeling of respect, mingled with remorse and kindness, overcame him.

"Why are you saving me?" he whispered.

"You are my husband."

He protested:

"No, no ... I have stolen that title. The law will never recognize my marriage."

"My father does not want a scandal," she said.

"Just so," he replied, sharply, "just so. I foresaw that; and that was why I had your cousin d'Emboise near at hand. Once I disappear, he becomes your husband. He is the man you have married in the eyes of men."

"You are the man I have married in the eyes of the Church."

"The Church! The Church! There are means of arranging matters with the Church.... Your marriage can be annulled."

"On what pretext that we can admit?"

He remained silent, thinking over all those points which he had not considered, all those points which were trivial and absurd for him, but which were serious for her, and he repeated several times:

"This is terrible ... this is terrible.... I should have anticipated...."

And, suddenly, seized with an idea, he clapped his hands and cried:

"There, I have it! I'm hand in glove with one of the chief figures at the Vatican. The Pope never refuses me anything. I shall obtain an audience and I have no doubt that the Holy Father, moved by my entreaties...."

His plan was so humorous and his delight so artless that Angélique could not help smiling; and she said:

"I am your wife in the eyes of God."

She gave him a look that showed neither scorn nor animosity, nor even anger; and he realized that she omitted to see in him the outlaw and the evil-doer and remembered only the man who was her husband and to whom the priest had bound her until the hour of death.

He took a step toward her and observed her more attentively. She did not lower her eyes at first. But she blushed. And never had he seen so pathetic a face, marked with such modesty and such dignity. He said to her, as on that first evening in Paris:

"Oh, your eyes ... the calm and sadness of your eyes ... the beauty of your eyes!"

She dropped her head and stammered:

"Go away ... go ..."

In the presence of her confusion, he received a quick intuition of the deeper feelings that stirred her, unknown to herself. To that spinster soul, of which he recognized the romantic power of imagination, the unsatisfied yearnings, the poring over old-world books, he suddenly represented, in that exceptional moment and in consequence of the unconventional circumstances of their meetings, somebody special, a Byronic hero, a chivalrous brigand of romance. One evening, in spite of all obstacles, he, the world-famed adventurer, already ennobled in song and story and exalted by his own audacity, had come to her and slipped the magic ring upon her finger: a mystic and passionate betrothal, as in the days of the *Corsair* and *Hernani*.... Greatly moved and touched, he was on the verge of giving way to an enthusiastic impulse and exclaiming:

"Let us go away together!... Let us fly!... You are my bride ... my wife.... Share my dangers, my sorrows and my joys.... It will be a strange and vigorous, a proud and magnificent life...."

But Angélique's eyes were raised to his again; and they were so pure and so noble that he blushed in his turn. This was not the woman to whom such words could be addressed.

He whispered:

"Forgive me.... I am a contemptible wretch.... I have wrecked your life...."

"No," she replied, softly. "On the contrary, you have shown me where my real life lies."

He was about to ask her to explain. But she had opened the door and was pointing the way to him. Nothing more could be spoken between them. He went out without a word, bowing very low as he passed.

A month later, Angélique de Sarzeau-Vendôme, Princesse de Bourbon-Condé, lawful wife of Arsène Lupin, took the veil and, under the name of Sister Marie-Auguste, buried herself within the walls of the Visitation Convent.

On the day of the ceremony, the mother superior of the convent received a heavy sealed envelope containing a letter with the following words:

"For Sister Marie-Auguste's poor."

Enclosed with the letter were five hundred bank-notes of a thousand francs each.

IX. THE INVISIBLE PRISONER

One day, at about four o'clock, as evening was drawing in, Farmer Goussot, with his four sons, returned from a day's shooting. They were stalwart men, all five of them, long of limb, broad-chested, with faces tanned by sun and wind. And all five displayed, planted on an enormous neck and shoulders, the same small head with the low forehead, thin lips, beaked nose and hard and repellent cast of countenance. They were feared and disliked by all around them. They were a money-grubbing, crafty family; and their word was not to be trusted.

On reaching the old barbican-wall that surrounds the Héberville property, the farmer opened a narrow, massive door, putting the big key back in his pocket after his sons had passed in. And he walked behind them, along the path that led through the orchards. Here and there stood great trees, stripped by the autumn winds, and clumps of pines, the last survivors of the ancient park now covered by old Goussot's farm.

One of the sons said:

"I hope mother has lit a log or two."

"There's smoke coming from the chimney," said the father.

The outhouses and the homestead showed at the end of a lawn; and, above them, the village church, whose steeple seemed to prick the clouds that trailed along the sky.

"All the guns unloaded?" asked old Goussot.

"Mine isn't," said the eldest. "I slipped in a bullet to blow a kestrel's head off...."

He was the one who was proudest of his skill. And he said to his brothers:

"Look at that bough, at the top of the cherry tree. See me snap it off."

On the bough sat a scarecrow, which had been there since spring and which protected the leafless branches with its idiot arms.

He raised his gun and fired.

The figure came tumbling down with large, comic gestures, and was caught on a big, lower branch, where it remained lying stiff on its stomach, with a great top hat on its head of rags and its hay-stuffed legs swaying from right to left above some water that flowed past the cherry tree through a wooden trough.

They all laughed. The father approved:

"A fine shot, my lad. Besides, the old boy was beginning to annoy me. I couldn't take my eyes from my plate at meals without catching sight of that oaf...."

They went a few steps farther. They were not more than thirty yards from the house, when the father stopped suddenly and said:

"Hullo! What's up?"

The sons also had stopped and stood listening. One of them said, under his breath:

610

"It comes from the house ... from the linen-room...."

And another spluttered:

"Sounds like moans.... And mother's alone!"

Suddenly, a frightful scream rang out. All five rushed forward. Another scream, followed by cries of despair.

"We're here! We're coming!" shouted the eldest, who was leading.

And, as it was a roundabout way to the door, he smashed in a window with his fist and sprang into the old people's bedroom. The room next to it was the linen-room, in which Mother Goussot spent most of her time.

"Damnation!" he said, seeing her lying on the floor, with blood all over her face. "Dad! Dad!"

"What? Where is she?" roared old Goussot, appearing on the scene. "Good lord, what's this?... What have they done to your mother?"

She pulled herself together and, with outstretched arm, stammered:

"Run after him!... This way!... This way!... I'm all right ... only a scratch or two.... But run, you! He's taken the money."

The father and sons gave a bound:

"He's taken the money!" bellowed old Goussot, rushing to the door to which his wife was pointing. "He's taken the money! Stop thief!"

But a sound of several voices rose at the end of the passage through which the other three sons were coming:

"I saw him! I saw him!"

"So did I! He ran up the stairs."

"No, there he is, he's coming down again!"

A mad steeplechase shook every floor in the house. Farmer Goussot, on reaching the end of the passage, caught sight of a man standing by the front door trying to open it. If he succeeded, it meant safety, escape through the market square and the back lanes of the village.

Interrupted as he was fumbling at the bolts, the man turning stupid, lost his head, charged at old Goussot and sent him spinning, dodged the eldest brother and, pursued by the four sons, doubled back down the long passage, ran into the old couple's bedroom, flung his legs through the broken window and disappeared.

The sons rushed after him across the lawns and orchards, now darkened by the falling night.

"The villain's done for," chuckled old Goussot. "There's no way out for him. The walls are too high. He's done for, the scoundrel!"

The two farm-hands returned, at that moment, from the village; and he told them what had happened and gave each of them a gun:

"If the swine shows his nose anywhere near the house," he said, "let fly at him. Give him no mercy!"

He told them where to stand, went to make sure that the farm-gates, which were only used for the carts, were locked, and, not till then, remembered that his wife might perhaps be in need of aid:

"Well, mother, how goes it?"

"Where is he? Have you got him?" she asked, in a breath.

"Yes, we're after him. The lads must have collared him by now."

The news quite restored her; and a nip of rum gave her the strength to drag herself to the bed, with old Goussot's assistance, and to tell her story. For that matter, there was not much to tell. She had just lit the fire in the living-hall; and she was knitting quietly at her bedroom window, waiting for the men to return, when she thought that she heard a slight grating sound in the linen-room next door:

"I must have left the cat in there," she thought to herself.

She went in, suspecting nothing, and was astonished to see the two doors of one of the linen-cupboards, the one in which they hid their money, wide open. She walked up to it, still without suspicion. There was a man there, hiding, with his back to the shelves.

"But how did he get in?" asked old Goussot.

"Through the passage, I suppose. We never keep the back door shut."

"And then did he go for you?"

"No, I went for him. He tried to get away."

"You should have let him."

"And what about the money?"

"Had he taken it by then?"

"Had he taken it! I saw the bundle of bank-notes in his hands, the sweep! I would have let him kill me sooner.... Oh, we had a sharp tussle, I give you my word!"

"Then he had no weapon?"

"No more than I did. We had our fingers, our nails and our teeth. Look here, where he bit me. And I yelled and screamed! Only, I'm an old woman you see.... I had to let go of him...."

"Do you know the man?"

"I'm pretty sure it was old Trainard."

"The tramp? Why, of course it's old Trainard!" cried the farmer. "I thought I knew him too.... Besides, he's been hanging round the house these last three days. The old vagabond must have smelt the money. Aha, Trainard, my man, we shall see some fun! A number-one hiding in the first place; and then the police.... I say, mother, you can get up now, can't you? Then go and fetch the neighbours.... Ask them to run for the gendarmes.... By the by, the attorney's youngster has a bicycle.... How that damned old Trainard scooted! He's got good legs for his age, he has. He can run like a hare!"

Goussot was holding his sides, revelling in the occurrence. He risked nothing by waiting. No power on earth could help the tramp escape or keep him from the sound thrashing which he had earned and from being conveyed, under safe escort, to the town gaol.

The farmer took a gun and went out to his two labourers:

"Anything fresh?"

"No, Farmer Goussot, not yet."

"We sha'n't have long to wait. Unless old Nick carries him over the walls...."

From time to time, they heard the four brothers hailing one another in the distance. The old bird was evidently making a fight for it, was more active than they would have thought. Still, with sturdy fellows like the Goussot brothers....

However, one of them returned, looking rather crestfallen, and made no secret of his opinion:

"It's no use keeping on at it for the present. It's pitch dark. The old chap must have crept into some hole. We'll hunt him out to-morrow."

"To-morrow! Why, lad, you're off your chump!" protested the farmer.

The eldest son now appeared, quite out of breath, and was of the same opinion as his brother. Why not wait till next day, seeing that the ruffian was as safe within the demesne as between the walls of a prison?

"Well, I'll go myself," cried old Goussot. "Light me a lantern, somebody!"

But, at that moment, three gendarmes arrived; and a number of village lads also came up to hear the latest.

The sergeant of gendarmes was a man of method. He first insisted on hearing the whole story, in full detail; then he stopped to think; then he questioned the four brothers, separately, and took his time for reflection after each deposition. When he had learnt from them that the tramp had fled toward the back of the estate, that he had been lost sight of repeatedly and that he had finally disappeared near a place known as the Crows' Knoll, he meditated once more and announced his conclusion:

"Better wait. Old Trainard might slip through our hands, amidst all the confusion of a pursuit in the dark, and then good-night, everybody!"

The farmer shrugged his shoulders and, cursing under his breath, yielded to the sergeant's arguments. That worthy organized a strict watch, distributed the brothers Goussot and the lads from the village under his men's eyes, made sure that the ladders were locked away and established his headquarters in the dining-room, where he and Farmer Goussot sat and nodded over a decanter of old brandy.

The night passed quietly. Every two hours, the sergeant went his rounds and inspected the posts. There were no alarms. Old Trainard did not budge from his hole.

The battle began at break of day.

It lasted four hours.

In those four hours, the thirteen acres of land within the walls were searched, explored, gone over in every direction by a score of men who beat the bushes with sticks, trampled over the tall grass, rummaged in the hollows of the trees and scattered the heaps of dry leaves. And old Trainard remained invisible.

"Well, this is a bit thick!" growled Goussot.

"Beats me altogether," retorted the sergeant.

And indeed there was no explaining the phenomenon. For, after all, apart from a few old clumps of laurels and spindle-trees, which were thoroughly beaten, all the trees were bare. There was no building, no shed, no stack, nothing, in short, that could serve as a hiding-place.

As for the wall, a careful inspection convinced even the sergeant that it was physically impossible to scale it.

In the afternoon, the investigations were begun all over again in the presence of the examining-magistrate and the public-prosecutor's deputy. The results were no more successful. Nay, worse, the officials looked upon the matter as so suspicious that they could not restrain their ill-humour and asked:

"Are you quite sure, Farmer Goussot, that you and your sons haven't been seeing double?"

"And what about my wife?" retorted the farmer, red with anger. "Did she see double when the scamp had her by the throat? Go and look at the marks, if you doubt me!"

"Very well. But then where is the scamp?"

"Here, between those four walls."

"Very well. Then ferret him out. We give it up. It's quite clear, that if a man were hidden within the precincts of this farm, we should have found him by now."

"I swear I'll lay hands on him, true as I stand here!" shouted Farmer Goussot. "It shall not be said that I've been robbed of six thousand francs. Yes, six thousand! There were three cows I sold; and then the wheat-crop; and then the apples. Six thousand-franc notes, which I was just going to take to the bank. Well, I swear to Heaven that the money's as good as in my pocket!"

"That's all right and I wish you luck," said the examining-magistrate, as he went away, followed by the deputy and the gendarmes.

The neighbours also walked off in a more or less facetious mood. And, by the end of the afternoon, none remained but the Goussots and the two farm-labourers.

Old Goussot at once explained his plan. By day, they were to search. At night, they were to keep an incessant watch. It would last as long as it had to. Hang it, old Trainard was a man like other men; and men have to eat and drink! Old Trainard must needs, therefore, come out of his earth to eat and drink.

"At most," said Goussot, "he can have a few crusts of bread in his pocket, or even pull up a root or two at night. But, as far as drink's concerned, no go. There's only the spring. And he'll be a clever dog if he gets near that."

He himself, that evening, took up his stand near the spring. Three hours later, his eldest son relieved him. The other brothers and the farm-hands slept in the house, each taking his turn of the watch and keeping all the lamps and candles lit, so that there might be no surprise.

So it went on for fourteen consecutive nights. And for fourteen days, while two of the men and Mother Goussot remained on guard, the five others explored the Héberville ground.

At the end of that fortnight, not a sign.

The farmer never ceased storming. He sent for a retired detective-inspector who lived in the neighbouring town. The inspector stayed with him for a whole week. He found neither old Trainard nor the least clue that could give them any hope of finding old Trainard.

"It's a bit thick!" repeated Farmer Goussot. "For he's there, the rascal! As far as being anywhere goes, he's there. So...."

Planting himself on the threshold, he railed at the enemy at the top of his voice:

"You blithering idiot, would you rather croak in your hole than fork out the money? Then croak, you pig!"

And Mother Goussot, in her turn, yelped, in her shrill voice:

"Is it prison you're afraid of? Hand over the notes and you can hook it!"

But old Trainard did not breathe a word; and the husband and wife tired their lungs in vain.

Shocking days passed. Farmer Goussot could no longer sleep, lay shivering with fever. The sons became morose and quarrelsome and never let their guns out of their hands, having no other idea but to shoot the tramp.

It was the one topic of conversation in the village; and the Goussot story, from being local at first, soon went the round of the press. Newspaper-reporters came from the assize-town, from Paris itself, and were rudely shown the door by Farmer Goussot.

"Each man his own house," he said. "You mind your business. I mind mine. It's nothing to do with any one."

"Still, Farmer Goussot...."

"Go to blazes!"

And he slammed the door in their face.

Old Trainard had now been hidden within the walls of Héberville for something like four weeks. The Goussots continued their search as doggedly and confidently as ever, but with daily decreasing hope, as though they were confronted with one of those mysterious obstacles which discourage human effort. And the idea that they would never see their money again began to take root in them.

One fine morning, at about ten o'clock, a motor-car, crossing the village square at full speed, broke down and came to a dead stop.

The driver, after a careful inspection, declared that the repairs would take some little time, whereupon the owner of the car resolved to wait at the inn and lunch. He was a gentleman on the right side of forty, with close-cropped side-whiskers and a pleasant expression of face; and he soon made himself at home with the people at the inn.

Of course, they told him the story of the Goussots. He had not heard it before, as he had been abroad; but it seemed to interest him greatly. He made them give him all the details, raised objections, discussed various theories with a number of people who were eating at the same table and ended by exclaiming:

"Nonsense! It can't be so intricate as all that. I have had some experience of this sort of thing. And, if I were on the premises...."

"That's easily arranged," said the inn-keeper. "I know Farmer Goussot.... He won't object...."

The request was soon made and granted. Old Goussot was in one of those frames of mind when we are less disposed to protest against outside interference. His wife, at any rate, was very firm:

"Let the gentleman come, if he wants to."

The gentleman paid his bill and instructed his driver to try the car on the high-road as soon as the repairs were finished:

"I shall want an hour," he said, "no more. Be ready in an hour's time."

Then he went to Farmer Goussot's.

He did not say much at the farm. Old Goussot, hoping against hope, was lavish with information, took his visitor along the walls down to the little door opening on the fields, produced the key and gave minute details of all the searches that had been made so far.

Oddly enough, the stranger, who hardly spoke, seemed not to listen either. He merely looked, with a rather vacant gaze. When they had been round the estate, old Goussot asked, anxiously:

"Well?"

"Well what?"

"Do you think you know?"

The visitor stood for a moment without answering. Then he said:

"No, nothing."

"Why, of course not!" cried the farmer, throwing up his arms. "How should you know! It's all hanky-panky. Shall I tell you what I think? Well, that old Trainard has been so jolly clever that he's lying dead in his hole ... and the bank-notes are rotting with him. Do you hear? You can take my word for it."

The gentleman said, very calmly:

"There's only one thing that interests me. The tramp, all said and done, was free at night and able to feed on what he could pick up. But how about drinking?"

"Out of the question!" shouted the farmer. "Quite out of the question! There's no water except this; and we have kept watch beside it every night."

"It's a spring. Where does it rise?"

"Here, where we stand."

"Is there enough pressure to bring it into the pool of itself?"

"Yes."

"And where does the water go when it runs out of the pool?"

"Into this pipe here, which goes under ground and carries it to the house, for use in the kitchen. So there's no way of drinking, seeing that we were there and that the spring is twenty yards from the house."

"Hasn't it rained during the last four weeks?"

"Not once: I've told you that already."

The stranger went to the spring and examined it. The trough was formed of a few boards of wood joined together just above the ground; and the water ran through it, slow and clear.

"The water's not more than a foot deep, is it?" he asked.

In order to measure it, he picked up from the grass a straw which he dipped into the pool. But, as he was stooping, he suddenly broke off and looked around him.

"Oh, how funny!" he said, bursting into a peal of laughter.

"Why, what's the matter?" spluttered old Goussot, rushing toward the pool, as though a man could have lain hidden between those narrow boards.

And Mother Goussot clasped her hands.

"What is it? Have you seen him? Where is he?"

"Neither in it nor under it," replied the stranger, who was still laughing.

He made for the house, eagerly followed by the farmer, the old woman and the four sons. The inn-keeper was there also, as were the people from the inn who had been watching the stranger's movements. And there was a dead silence, while they waited for the extraordinary disclosure.

"It's as I thought," he said, with an amused expression. "The old chap had to quench his thirst somewhere; and, as there was only the spring...."

"Oh, but look here," growled Farmer Goussot, "we should have seen him!"

"It was at night."

"We should have heard him ... and seen him too, as we were close by."

"So was he."

"And he drank the water from the pool?"

"Yes."

"How?"

"From a little way off."

"With what?"

"With this."

And the stranger showed the straw which he had picked up:

"There, here's the straw for the customer's long drink. You will see, there's more of it than usual: in fact, it is made of three straws stuck into one another. That was the first thing I noticed: those three straws fastened together. The proof is conclusive."

"But, hang it all, the proof of what?" cried Farmer Goussot, irritably.

The stranger took a shotgun from the rack.

"Is it loaded?" he asked.

"Yes," said the youngest of the brothers. "I use it to kill the sparrows with, for fun. It's small shot."

"Capital! A peppering where it won't hurt him will do the trick."

His face suddenly assumed a masterful look. He gripped the farmer by the arm and rapped out, in an imperious tone:

"Listen to me, Farmer Goussot. I'm not here to do policeman's work; and I won't have the poor beggar locked up at any price. Four weeks of starvation and fright is good enough for anybody. So you've got to swear to me, you and your sons, that you'll let him off without hurting him."

"He must hand over the money!"

"Well, of course. Do you swear?"

"I swear."

The gentleman walked back to the door-sill, at the entrance to the orchard. He took a quick aim, pointing his gun a little in the air, in the direction of the cherry tree which overhung the spring. He fired. A hoarse cry rang from the tree; and the scarecrow which had been straddling the main branch for a month past came tumbling to the ground, only to jump up at once and make off as fast as its legs could carry it.

There was a moment's amazement, followed by outcries. The sons darted in pursuit and were not long in coming up with the runaway, hampered as he was by his rags and weakened by privation. But the stranger was already protecting him against their wrath:

"Hands off there! This man belongs to me. I won't have him touched.... I hope I haven't stung you up too much, Trainard?"

Standing on his straw legs wrapped round with strips of tattered cloth, with his arms and his whole body clad in the same materials, his head swathed in linen, tightly packed like a sausage, the old chap still had the stiff appearance of a lay-figure. And the whole effect was so ludicrous and so unexpected that the onlookers screamed with laughter.

The stranger unbound his head; and they saw a veiled mask of tangled grey beard encroaching on every side upon a skeleton face lit up by two eyes burning with fever.

The laughter was louder than ever.

"The money! The six notes!" roared the farmer.

The stranger kept him at a distance:

"One moment ... we'll give you that back, sha'n't we, Trainard?"

And, taking his knife and cutting away the straw and cloth, he jested, cheerily:

"You poor old beggar, what a guy you look! But how on earth did you manage to pull off that trick? You must be confoundedly clever, or else you had the devil's own luck.... So, on the first night, you used the breathing-time they left you to rig yourself in these togs! Not a bad idea. Who could ever suspect a scarecrow?... They were so accustomed to seeing it stuck up in its tree! But, poor old daddy, how uncomfortable you must have felt, lying flat up there on your stomach, with your arms and legs dangling down! All day long, like that! The deuce of an attitude! And how you must have been put to it, when you ventured to move a limb, eh? And how you must have funked going to sleep!... And then you had to eat! And drink! And you heard the sentry and felt the barrel of his gun within a yard of your nose! Brrrr!... But the trickiest of all, you know, was your bit of straw!... Upon my word, when I think that, without a sound, without a movement so to speak, you had to fish out lengths of straw from your toggery, fix them end to end, let your apparatus down to the water and suck up the heavenly moisture drop by drop.... Upon my word, one could scream with admiration.... Well done, Trainard...." And he added, between his teeth, "Only you're in a very unappetizing state, my man. Haven't you washed yourself all this month, you old pig? After all, you had as much water as you wanted!... Here, you people, I hand him over to you. I'm going to wash my hands, that's what I'm going to do."

Farmer Goussot and his four sons grabbed at the prey which he was abandoning to them:

"Now then, come along, fork out the money."

Dazed as he was, the tramp still managed to simulate astonishment.

"Don't put on that idiot look," growled the farmer. "Come on. Out with the six notes...."

"What?... What do you want of me?" stammered old Trainard.

"The money ... on the nail...."

"What money?"

"The bank-notes."

"The bank-notes?"

"Oh, I'm getting sick of you! Here, lads...."

They laid the old fellow flat, tore off the rags that composed his clothes, felt and searched him all over.

There was nothing on him.

"You thief and you robber!" yelled old Goussot. "What have you done with it?"

The old beggar seemed more dazed than ever. Too cunning to confess, he kept on whining:

"What do you want of me?... Money? I haven't three sous to call my own...."

But his eyes, wide with wonder, remained fixed upon his clothes; and he himself seemed not to understand.

The Goussots' rage could no longer be restrained. They rained blows upon him, which did not improve matters. But the farmer was convinced that Trainard had hidden the money before turning himself into the scarecrow:

"Where have you put it, you scum? Out with it! In what part of the orchard have you hidden it?"

"The money?" repeated the tramp with a stupid look.

"Yes, the money! The money which you've buried somewhere.... Oh, if we don't find it, your goose is cooked!... We have witnesses, haven't we?... All of you, friends, eh? And then the gentleman...."

He turned, with the intention of addressing the stranger, in the direction of the spring, which was thirty or forty steps to the left. And he was quite surprised not to see him washing his hands there:

"Has he gone?" he asked.

Some one answered:

"No, he lit a cigarette and went for a stroll in the orchard."

"Oh, that's all right!" said the farmer. "He's the sort to find the notes for us, just as he found the man."

"Unless ..." said a voice.

"Unless what?" echoed the farmer. "What do you mean? Have you something in your head? Out with it, then! What is it?"

But he interrupted himself suddenly, seized with a doubt; and there was a moment's silence. The same idea dawned on all the country-folk. The stranger's arrival at Héberville, the breakdown of his motor, his manner of questioning the people at the inn and of gaining admission to the farm: were not all these part and parcel of a put-up job, the trick of a cracksman who had learnt the story from the papers and who had come to try his luck on the spot?...

"Jolly smart of him!" said the inn-keeper. "He must have taken the money from old Trainard's pocket, before our eyes, while he was searching him."

"Impossible!" spluttered Farmer Goussot. "He would have been seen going out that way ... by the house ... whereas he's strolling in the orchard."

Mother Goussot, all of a heap, suggested:

"The little door at the end, down there?..."

"The key never leaves me."

"But you showed it to him."

"Yes; and I took it back again.... Look, here it is."

He clapped his hand to his pocket and uttered a cry:

"Oh, dash it all, it's gone!... He's sneaked it!..."

He at once rushed away, followed and escorted by his sons and a number of the villagers.

When they were halfway down the orchard, they heard the throb of a motor-car, obviously the one belonging to the stranger, who had given orders to his chauffeur to wait for him at that lower entrance.

When the Goussots reached the door, they saw scrawled with a brick, on the worm-eaten panel, the two words:

"ARSÈNE LUPIN."

Stick to it as the angry Goussots might, they found it impossible to prove that old Trainard had stolen any money. Twenty persons had to bear witness that, when all was said, nothing was discovered on his person. He escaped with a few months' imprisonment for the assault.

He did not regret them. As soon as he was released, he was secretly informed that, every quarter, on a given date, at a given hour, under a given milestone on a given road, he would find three gold louis.

To a man like old Trainard that means wealth.

X. EDITH SWAN-NECK

"Arsène Lupin, what's your real opinion of Inspector Ganimard?"

"A very high one, my dear fellow."

"A very high one? Then why do you never miss a chance of turning him into ridicule?"

"It's a bad habit; and I'm sorry for it. But what can I say? It's the way of the world. Here's a decent detective-chap, here's a whole pack of decent men, who stand for law and order, who protect us against the apaches, who risk their lives for honest people like you and me; and we have nothing to give them in return but flouts and gibes. It's preposterous!"

"Bravo, Lupin! you're talking like a respectable ratepayer!"

"What else am I? I may have peculiar views about other people's property; but I assure you that it's very different when my own's at stake. By Jove, it doesn't do to lay hands on what belongs to me! Then I'm out for blood! Aha! It's *my* pocket, *my* money, *my* watch ... hands off! I have the soul of a conservative, my dear fellow, the instincts of a retired tradesman and a due respect for every sort of tradition and authority. And that is why Ganimard inspires me with no little gratitude and esteem."

"But not much admiration?"

"Plenty of admiration too. Over and above the dauntless courage which comes natural to all those gentry at the Criminal Investigation Department, Ganimard possesses very sterling qualities: decision, insight and judgment. I have watched him at work. He's somebody, when all's said. Do you know the Edith Swan-neck story, as it was called?"

"I know as much as everybody knows."

"That means that you don't know it at all. Well, that job was, I daresay, the one which I thought out most cleverly, with the utmost care and the utmost precaution, the one which I shrouded in the greatest darkness and mystery, the one which it took the biggest generalship to carry through. It was a regular game of chess, played according to strict scientific and mathematical rules. And yet Ganimard ended by unravelling the knot. Thanks to him, they know the truth to-day on the Quai des Orfèvres. And it is a truth quite out of the common, I assure you."

"May I hope to hear it?"

"Certainly ... one of these days ... when I have time.... But the Brunelli is dancing at the Opera to-night; and, if she were not to see me in my stall ...!"

I do not meet Lupin often. He confesses with difficulty, when it suits him. It was only gradually, by snatches, by odds and ends of confidences, that I was able to obtain the different incidents and to piece the story together in all its details.

The main features are well known and I will merely mention the facts.

Three years ago, when the train from Brest arrived at Rennes, the door of one of the luggage vans was found smashed in. This van had been booked by Colonel Sparmiento, a rich Brazilian, who was travelling with his wife in the same train. It contained a complete set of tapestry-hangings. The case in which one of these was packed had been broken open and the tapestry had disappeared.

Colonel Sparmiento started proceedings against the railway-company, claiming heavy damages, not only for the stolen tapestry, but also for the loss in value which the whole collection suffered in consequence of the theft.

The police instituted inquiries. The company offered a large reward. A fortnight later, a letter which had come undone in the post was opened by the authorities and revealed the fact that the theft had been carried out under the direction of Arsène Lupin and that a package was to leave next day for the United States. That same evening, the tapestry was discovered in a trunk deposited in the cloak-room at the Gare Saint-Lazare.

The scheme, therefore, had miscarried. Lupin felt the disappointment so much that he vented his ill-humour in a communication to Colonel Sparmiento, ending with the following words, which were clear enough for anybody:

"It was very considerate of me to take only one. Next time, I shall take the twelve. *Verbum sap.*

"A. L."

Colonel Sparmiento had been living for some months in a house standing at the end of a small garden at the corner of the Rue de la Faisanderie and the Rue Dufresnoy. He was a rather thick-set, broad-shouldered man, with black hair and a swarthy skin, always well and quietly dressed. He was married to an extremely pretty but delicate Englishwoman, who was much upset by the business of the tapestries. From the first she implored her husband to sell them for what they would fetch. The Colonel had much too forcible and dogged a nature to yield to what he had every right to describe as a woman's fancies. He sold nothing, but he redoubled his precautions and adopted every measure that was likely to make an attempt at burglary impossible.

To begin with, so that he might confine his watch to the garden-front, he walled up all the windows on the ground-floor and the first floor overlooking the Rue Dufresnoy. Next, he enlisted the services of a firm which made a speciality of protecting private houses against robberies. Every window of the gallery in which the tapestries were hung was fitted with invisible burglar alarms, the position of which was known, to none but himself. These, at the least touch, switched on all the electric lights and set a whole system of bells and gongs ringing.

In addition to this, the insurance companies to which he applied refused to grant policies to any considerable amount unless he consented to let three men, supplied by the companies and paid by himself, occupy the ground-floor of his house every night. They selected for the purpose three ex-detectives, tried and trustworthy men, all of whom hated Lupin like poison. As for the servants, the colonel had known them for years and was ready to vouch for them.

After taking these steps and organizing the defence of the house as though it were a fortress, the colonel gave a great house-warming, a sort of private view, to which he invited the members of both his clubs, as well as a certain number of ladies, journalists, art-patrons and critics.

They felt, as they passed through the garden-gate, much as if they were walking into a prison. The three private detectives, posted at the foot of the stairs, asked for each visitor's invitation card and eyed him up and down suspiciously, making him feel as though they were going to search his pockets or take his finger-prints.

The colonel, who received his guests on the first floor, made laughing apologies and seemed delighted at the opportunity of explaining the arrangements which he had invented to secure the safety of his hangings. His wife stood by him, looking charmingly young and pretty, fair-haired, pale and sinuous, with a sad and gentle expression, the expression of resignation often worn by those who are threatened by fate.

When all the guests had come, the garden-gates and the hall-doors were closed. Then everybody filed into the middle gallery, which was reached through two steel doors, while its windows, with their huge shutters, were protected by iron bars. This was where the twelve tapestries were kept.

They were matchless works of art and, taking their inspiration from the famous Bayeux Tapestry, attributed to Queen Matilda, they represented the story of the Norman Conquest. They had been ordered in the fourteenth century by the descendant of a man-at-arms in William the Conqueror's train; were executed by Jehan Gosset, a famous Arras weaver; and were discovered, five hundred years later, in an old Breton manor-house. On hearing of this, the colonel had struck a bargain for fifty thousand francs. They were worth ten times the money.

But the finest of the twelve hangings composing the set, the most uncommon because the subject had not been treated by Queen Matilda, was the one which Arsène Lupin had stolen and which had been so fortunately recovered. It portrayed Edith Swan-neck on the battlefield of Hastings, seeking among the dead for the body of her sweetheart Harold, last of the Saxon kings.

The guests were lost in enthusiasm over this tapestry, over the unsophisticated beauty of the design, over the faded colours, over the life-like grouping of the figures and the pitiful sadness of the scene. Poor Edith Swan-neck stood drooping like an overweighted lily. Her white gown revealed the lines of her languid figure. Her long, tapering hands were outstretched in a gesture of terror and entreaty. And nothing could be more mournful than her profile, over which flickered the most dejected and despairing of smiles.

"A harrowing smile," remarked one of the critics, to whom the others listened with deference. "A very charming smile, besides; and it reminds me, Colonel, of the smile of Mme. Sparmiento."

And seeing that the observation seemed to meet with approval, he enlarged upon his idea:

"There are other points of resemblance that struck me at once, such as the very graceful curve of the neck and the delicacy of the hands ... and also something about the figure, about the general attitude...."

"What you say is so true," said the colonel, "that I confess that it was this likeness that decided me to buy the hangings. And there was another reason, which was that, by a really curious chance, my wife's name happens to be Edith. I have called her Edith Swan-neck ever since." And the colonel added, with a laugh, "I hope that the coincidence will stop at this and that my dear Edith will never have to go in search of her true-love's body, like her prototype."

He laughed as he uttered these words, but his laugh met with no echo; and we find the same impression of awkward silence in all the accounts of the evening that appeared during the next few days. The people standing near him did not know what to say. One of them tried to jest:

"Your name isn't Harold, Colonel?"

"No, thank you," he declared, with continued merriment. "No, that's not my name; nor am I in the least like the Saxon king."

All have since agreed in stating that, at that moment, as the colonel finished speaking, the first alarm rang from the windows—the right or the middle window: opinions differ on this point—rang short and shrill on a single note. The peal of the alarm-bell was followed by an exclamation of terror uttered by Mme. Sparmiento, who caught hold of her husband's arm. He cried:

"What's the matter? What does this mean?"

The guests stood motionless, with their eyes staring at the windows. The colonel repeated:

"What does it mean? I don't understand. No one but myself knows where that bell is fixed...."

And, at that moment—here again the evidence is unanimous—at that moment came sudden, absolute darkness, followed immediately by the maddening din of all the bells and all the gongs, from top to bottom of the house, in every room and at every window.

For a few seconds, a stupid disorder, an insane terror, reigned. The women screamed. The men banged with their fists on the closed doors. They hustled and fought. People fell to the floor and were trampled under foot. It was like a panic-stricken crowd, scared by threatening flames or by a bursting shell. And, above the uproar, rose the colonel's voice, shouting:

"Silence!... Don't move!... It's all right!... The switch is over there, in the corner.... Wait a bit.... Here!"

He had pushed his way through his guests and reached a corner of the gallery; and, all at once, the electric light blazed up again, while the pandemonium of bells stopped.

Then, in the sudden light, a strange sight met the eyes. Two ladies had fainted. Mme. Sparmiento, hanging to her husband's arm, with her knees dragging on the floor, and livid in the face, appeared half dead. The men, pale, with their neckties awry, looked as if they had all been in the wars.

"The tapestries are there!" cried some one.

There was a great surprise, as though the disappearance of those hangings ought to have been the natural result and the only plausible explanation of the incident. But nothing had been moved. A few valuable pictures, hanging on the walls, were there still. And, though the same din had reverberated all over the house, though all the rooms had been thrown into darkness, the detectives had seen no one entering or trying to enter.

"Besides," said the colonel, "it's only the windows of the gallery that have alarms. Nobody but myself understands how they work; and I had not set them yet."

People laughed loudly at the way in which they had been frightened, but they laughed without conviction and in a more or less shamefaced fashion, for each of them was keenly alive to the absurdity of his conduct. And they had but one thought—to get out of that house where, say what you would, the atmosphere was one of agonizing anxiety.

Two journalists stayed behind, however; and the colonel joined them, after attending to Edith and handing her over to her maids. The three of them, together with the detectives, made a search that did not lead to the discovery of anything of the least interest. Then the colonel sent for some champagne; and the result was that it was not until a late hour—to be exact, a quarter to three in the morning—that the journalists took their leave, the colonel retired to his quarters, and the detectives withdrew to the room which had been set aside for them on the ground-floor.

They took the watch by turns, a watch consisting, in the first place, in keeping awake and, next, in looking round the garden and visiting the gallery at intervals.

These orders were scrupulously carried out, except between five and seven in the morning, when sleep gained the mastery and the men ceased to go their rounds. But it was broad daylight out of doors. Besides, if there had been the least sound of bells, would they not have woke up?

Nevertheless, when one of them, at twenty minutes past seven, opened the door of the gallery and flung back the shutters, he saw that the twelve tapestries were gone.

This man and the others were blamed afterward for not giving the alarm at once and for starting their own investigations before informing the colonel and telephoning to the local commissary. Yet this very excusable delay can hardly be said to have hampered the action of the police. In any case, the colonel was not told until half-past eight. He was dressed and ready to go out. The news did not seem to upset him beyond measure, or, at least, he managed to control his emotion. But the effort must have been too much for him, for he suddenly dropped into a chair and, for some moments, gave way to a regular fit of despair and anguish, most painful to behold in a man of his resolute appearance.

Recovering and mastering himself, he went to the gallery, stared at the bare walls and then sat down at a table and hastily scribbled a letter, which he put into an envelope and sealed.

"There," he said. "I'm in a hurry.... I have an important engagement.... Here is a letter for the commissary of police." And, seeing the detectives' eyes upon him, he added, "I am giving the commissary my views ... telling him of a suspicion that occurs to me.... He must follow it up.... I will do what I can...."

He left the house at a run, with excited gestures which the detectives were subsequently to remember.

A few minutes later, the commissary of police arrived. He was handed the letter, which contained the following words:

"I am at the end of my tether. The theft of those tapestries completes the crash which I have been trying to conceal for the past year. I bought them as a speculation and was hoping to get a million francs for them, thanks to the fuss that was made about them. As it was, an American offered me six hundred thousand. It meant my salvation. This means utter destruction.

"I hope that my dear wife will forgive the sorrow which I am bringing upon her. Her name will be on my lips at the last moment."

Mme. Sparmiento was informed. She remained aghast with horror, while inquiries were instituted and attempts made to trace the colonel's movements.

Late in the afternoon, a telephone-message came from Ville d'Avray. A gang of railway-men had found a man's body lying at the entrance to a tunnel after a train had passed. The body was hideously mutilated; the face had lost all resemblance to anything human. There were no papers in the pockets. But the description answered to that of the colonel.

Mme. Sparmiento arrived at Ville d'Avray, by motor-car, at seven o'clock in the evening. She was taken to a room at the railway-station. When the sheet that covered it was removed, Edith, Edith Swan-neck, recognized her husband's body.

In these circumstances, Lupin did not receive his usual good notices in the press:

"Let him look to himself," jeered one leader-writer, summing up the general opinion. "It would not take many exploits of this kind for him to forfeit the popularity which has not been grudged him hitherto. We have no use for Lupin, except when his rogueries are perpetrated at the expense of shady company-promoters, foreign adventurers, German barons, banks and financial companies. And, above all, no murders! A burglar we can put up with; but a murderer, no! If he is not directly guilty, he is at least responsible for this death. There is blood upon his hands; the arms on his escutcheon are stained gules...."

The public anger and disgust were increased by the pity which Edith's pale face aroused. The guests of the night before gave their version of what had happened, omitting none of the impressive details; and a legend formed straightway around the fair-haired Englishwoman, a legend that assumed a really tragic character, owing to the popular story of the swan-necked heroine.

And yet the public could not withhold its admiration of the extraordinary skill with which the theft had been effected. The police explained it, after a fashion. The detectives had noticed from the first and subsequently stated that one of the three windows of the gallery was wide open. There could be no doubt that Lupin and his confederates had entered through this window. It seemed a very plausible suggestion. Still, in that case, how were they able, first, to climb the garden railings, in coming and going, without being seen; secondly, to cross the garden and put up a ladder on the flower-border, without leaving the least trace behind; thirdly, to open the shutters and the window, without starting the bells and switching on the lights in the house?

The police accused the three detectives of complicity. The magistrate in charge of the case examined them at length, made minute inquiries into their private lives and stated formally that they were above all suspicion. As for the tapestries, there seemed to be no hope that they would be recovered.

It was at this moment that Chief-inspector Ganimard returned from India, where he had been hunting for Lupin on the strength of a number of most convincing proofs supplied by former confederates of Lupin himself. Feeling that he had once more been tricked by his everlasting adversary, fully believing that Lupin had dispatched him on this wild-goose chase so as to be rid of him during the business of the tapestries, he asked for a fortnight's leave of absence, called on Mme. Sparmiento and promised to avenge her husband.

Edith had reached the point at which not even the thought of vengeance relieves the sufferer's pain. She had dismissed the three detectives on the day of the funeral and engaged just one man and an old cook-housekeeper to take the place of the large staff of servants the sight of whom reminded her too cruelly of the past. Not caring what happened, she kept her room and left Ganimard free to act as he pleased.

627

He took up his quarters on the ground-floor and at once instituted a series of the most minute investigations. He started the inquiry afresh, questioned the people in the neighbourhood, studied the distribution of the rooms and set each of the burglar-alarms going thirty and forty times over.

At the end of the fortnight, he asked for an extension of leave. The chief of the detective-service, who was at that time M. Dudouis, came to see him and found him perched on the top of a ladder, in the gallery. That day, the chief-inspector admitted that all his searches had proved useless.

Two days later, however, M. Dudouis called again and discovered Ganimard in a very thoughtful frame of mind. A bundle of newspapers lay spread in front of him. At last, in reply to his superior's urgent questions, the chief-inspector muttered:

"I know nothing, chief, absolutely nothing; but there's a confounded notion worrying me.... Only it seems so absurd.... And then it doesn't explain things.... On the contrary, it confuses them rather...."

"Then ...?"

"Then I implore you, chief, to have a little patience ... to let me go my own way. But if I telephone to you, some day or other, suddenly, you must jump into a taxi, without losing a minute. It will mean that I have discovered the secret."

Forty-eight hours passed. Then, one morning, M. Dudouis received a telegram:

"Going to Lille.

"GANIMARD."

"What the dickens can he want to go to Lille for?" wondered the chief-detective.

The day passed without news, followed by another day. But M. Dudouis had every confidence in Ganimard. He knew his man, knew that the old detective was not one of those people who excite themselves for nothing. When Ganimard "got a move on him," it meant that he had sound reasons for doing so.

As a matter of fact, on the evening of that second day, M. Dudouis was called to the telephone.

"Is that you, chief?"

"Is it Ganimard speaking?"

Cautious men both, they began by making sure of each other's identity. As soon as his mind was eased on this point, Ganimard continued, hurriedly:

"Ten men, chief, at once. And please come yourself."

"Where are you?"

"In the house, on the ground-floor. But I will wait for you just inside the garden-gate."

"I'll come at once. In a taxi, of course?"

"Yes, chief. Stop the taxi fifty yards from the house. I'll let you in when you whistle."

Things took place as Ganimard had arranged. Shortly after midnight, when all the lights were out on the upper floors, he slipped into the street and went to meet M. Dudouis. There was a hurried consultation. The officers distributed themselves as Ganimard ordered. Then the chief and the chief-inspector walked back together, noiselessly crossed the garden and closeted themselves with every precaution:

"Well, what's it all about?" asked M. Dudouis. "What does all this mean? Upon my word, we look like a pair of conspirators!"

But Ganimard was not laughing. His chief had never seen him in such a state of perturbation, nor heard him speak in a voice denoting such excitement:

"Any news, Ganimard?"

"Yes, chief, and ... this time ...! But I can hardly believe it myself.... And yet I'm not mistaken: I know the real truth.... It may be as unlikely as you please, but it is the truth, the whole truth and nothing but the truth."

He wiped away the drops of perspiration that trickled down his forehead and, after a further question from M. Dudouis, pulled himself together, swallowed a glass of water and began:

"Lupin has often got the better of me...."

"Look here, Ganimard," said M. Dudouis, interrupting him. "Why can't you come straight to the point? Tell me, in two words, what's happened."

"No, chief," retorted the chief-inspector, "it is essential that you should know the different stages which I have passed through. Excuse me, but I consider it indispensable." And he repeated: "I was saying, chief, that Lupin has often got the better of me and led me many a dance. But, in this contest in which I have always come out worst ... so far ... I have at least gained experience of his manner of play and learnt to know his tactics. Now, in the matter of the tapestries, it occurred to me almost from the start to set myself two problems. In the first place, Lupin, who never makes a move without knowing what he is after, was obviously aware that Colonel Sparmiento had come to the end of his money and that the loss of the tapestries might drive him to suicide. Nevertheless, Lupin, who hates the very thought of bloodshed, stole the tapestries."

"There was the inducement," said M. Dudouis, "of the five or six hundred thousand francs which they are worth."

"No, chief, I tell you once more, whatever the occasion might be, Lupin would not take life, nor be the cause of another person's death, for anything in this world, for millions and millions. That's the first point. In the second place, what was the object of all that disturbance, in the evening, during the house-warming party? Obviously, don't you think, to surround the business with an atmosphere of anxiety and terror, in the shortest possible time, and also to divert suspicion from the truth, which, otherwise, might easily have been suspected?... You seem not to understand, chief?"

"Upon my word, I do not!"

"As a matter of fact," said Ganimard, "as a matter of fact, it is not particularly plain. And I myself, when I put the problem before my mind in those same words, did not understand it very clearly.... And yet I felt that I was on the right track.... Yes, there was no doubt about it that Lupin wanted to divert suspicions ... to divert them to himself, Lupin, mark you ... so that the real person who was working the business might remain unknown...."

"A confederate," suggested M. Dudouis. "A confederate, moving among the visitors, who set the alarms going ... and who managed to hide in the house after the party had broken up."

"You're getting warm, chief, you're getting warm! It is certain that the tapestries, as they cannot have been stolen by any one making his way surreptitiously into the house, were stolen by somebody who remained in the house; and it is equally certain that, by taking the list of the people invited and inquiring into the antecedents of each of them, one might...."

"Well?"

"Well, chief, there's a 'but,' namely, that the three detectives had this list in their hands when the guests arrived and that they still had it when the guests left. Now sixty-three came in and sixty-three went away. So you see...."

"Then do you suppose a servant?..."

"No."

"The detectives?"

"No."

"But, still ... but, still," said the chief, impatiently, "if the robbery was committed from the inside...."

"That is beyond dispute," declared the inspector, whose excitement seemed to be nearing fever-point. "There is no question about it. All my investigations led to the same certainty. And my conviction gradually became so positive that I ended, one day, by drawing up this startling axiom: in theory and in fact, the robbery can only have been committed with the assistance of an accomplice staying in the house. Whereas there was no accomplice!"

"That's absurd," said Dudouis.

"Quite absurd," said Ganimard. "But, at the very moment when I uttered that absurd sentence, the truth flashed upon me."

"Eh?"

"Oh, a very dim, very incomplete, but still sufficient truth! With that clue to guide me, I was bound to find the way. Do you follow me, chief?"

M. Dudouis sat silent. The same phenomenon that had taken place in Ganimard was evidently taking place in him. He muttered:

"If it's not one of the guests, nor the servants, nor the private detectives, then there's no one left...."

"Yes, chief, there's one left...."

M. Dudouis started as though he had received a shock; and, in a voice that betrayed his excitement:

"But, look here, that's preposterous."

"Why?"

"Come, think for yourself!"

"Go on, chief: say what's in your mind."

"Nonsense! What do you mean?"

"Go on, chief."

"It's impossible! How can Sparmiento have been Lupin's accomplice?"

Ganimard gave a little chuckle.

"Exactly, Arsène Lupin's accomplice!... That explains everything. During the night, while the three detectives were downstairs watching, or sleeping rather, for Colonel Sparmiento had given them champagne to drink and perhaps doctored it beforehand, the said colonel took down the hangings and passed them out through the window of his bedroom. The room is on the second floor and looks out on another street, which was not watched, because the lower windows are walled up."

M. Dudouis reflected and then shrugged his shoulders:

"It's preposterous!" he repeated.

"Why?"

"Why? Because, if the colonel had been Arsène Lupin's accomplice, he would not have committed suicide after achieving his success."

"Who says that he committed suicide?"

"Why, he was found dead on the line!"

"I told you, there is no such thing as death with Lupin."

"Still, this was genuine enough. Besides, Mme. Sparmiento identified the body."

"I thought you would say that, chief. The argument worried me too. There was I, all of a sudden, with three people in front of me instead of one: first, Arsène Lupin, cracksman; secondly, Colonel Sparmiento, his accomplice; thirdly, a dead man. Spare us! It was too much of a good thing!"

Ganimard took a bundle of newspapers, untied it and handed one of them to Mr. Dudouis:

"You remember, chief, last time you were here, I was looking through the papers.... I wanted to see if something had not happened, at that period, that might bear upon the case and confirm my supposition. Please read this paragraph."

M. Dudouis took the paper and read aloud:

"Our Lille correspondent informs us that a curious incident has occurred in that town. A corpse has disappeared from the local morgue, the corpse of a man unknown who threw himself under the wheels of a steam tram-car on the day before. No one is able to suggest a reason for this disappearance."

M. Dudouis sat thinking and then asked:

"So ... you believe ...?"

"I have just come from Lille," replied Ganimard, "and my inquiries leave not a doubt in my mind. The corpse was removed on the same night on which Colonel Sparmiento gave his house-warming. It was taken straight to Ville d'Avray by motor-car; and the car remained near the railway-line until the evening."

"Near the tunnel, therefore," said M. Dudouis.

"Next to it, chief."

"So that the body which was found is merely that body, dressed in Colonel Sparmiento's clothes."

"Precisely, chief."

"Then Colonel Sparmiento is not dead?"

"No more dead than you or I, chief."

"But then why all these complications? Why the theft of one tapestry, followed by its recovery, followed by the theft of the twelve? Why that house-warming? Why that disturbance? Why everything? Your story won't hold water, Ganimard."

"Only because you, chief, like myself, have stopped halfway; because, strange as this story already sounds, we must go still farther, very much farther, in the direction of the improbable and the astounding. And why not, after all? Remember that we are dealing with Arsène Lupin. With him, is it not always just the improbable and the astounding that we must look for? Must we not always go straight for the maddest suppositions? And, when I say the maddest, I am using the wrong word. On the contrary, the whole thing is wonderfully logical and so simple that a child could understand it. Confederates only betray you. Why employ confederates, when it is so easy and so natural to act for yourself, by yourself, with your own hands and by the means within your own reach?"

"What are you saying?... What are you saying?... What are you saying?" cried M. Dudouis, in a sort of sing-song voice and a tone of bewilderment that increased with each separate exclamation.

Ganimard gave a fresh chuckle.

"Takes your breath away, chief, doesn't it? So it did mine, on the day when you came to see me here and when the notion was beginning to grow upon me. I was flabbergasted with astonishment. And yet I've had experience of my customer. I know what he's capable of.... But this, no, this was really a bit too stiff!"

"It's impossible! It's impossible!" said M. Dudouis, in a low voice.

"On the contrary, chief, it's quite possible and quite logical and quite normal. It's the threefold incarnation of one and the same individual. A schoolboy would solve the problem in a minute, by a simple process of elimination. Take away the dead man: there remains Sparmiento and Lupin. Take away Sparmiento...."

"There remains Lupin," muttered the chief-detective.

"Yes, chief, Lupin simply, Lupin in five letters and two syllables, Lupin taken out of his Brazilian skin, Lupin revived from the dead, Lupin translated, for the past six months, into Colonel Sparmiento, travelling in Brittany, hearing of the discovery of the twelve tapestries, buying them, planning the theft of the best of them, so as to draw attention to himself, Lupin, and divert it from himself, Sparmiento. Next, he brings about, in full view of the gaping public, a noisy contest between Lupin and Sparmiento or Sparmiento and Lupin, plots and gives the house-warming party, terrifies his guests and, when everything is ready, arranges for Lupin to steal Sparmiento's tapestries and for Sparmiento, Lupin's victim, to disappear from sight and die unsuspected, unsuspectable, regretted by his friends, pitied by the public and leaving behind him, to pocket the profits of the swindle...."

Ganimard stopped, looked the chief in the eyes and, in a voice that emphasized the importance of his words, concluded:

"Leaving behind him a disconsolate widow."

"Mme. Sparmiento! You really believe....?

"Hang it all!" said the chief-inspector. "People don't work up a whole business of this sort, without seeing something ahead of them ... solid profits."

"But the profits, it seems to me, lie in the sale of the tapestries which Lupin will effect in America or elsewhere."

"First of all, yes. But Colonel Sparmiento could effect that sale just as well. And even better. So there's something more."

"Something more?"

"Come, chief, you're forgetting that Colonel Sparmiento has been the victim of an important robbery and that, though he may be dead, at least his widow remains. So it's his widow who will get the money."

"What money?"

"What money? Why, the money due to her! The insurance-money, of course!"

M. Dudouis was staggered. The whole business suddenly became clear to him, with its real meaning. He muttered:

"That's true!... That's true!... The colonel had insured his tapestries...."

"Rather! And for no trifle either."

"For how much?"

"Eight hundred thousand francs."

"Eight hundred thousand?"

"Just so. In five different companies."

"And has Mme. Sparmiento had the money?"

"She got a hundred and fifty thousand francs yesterday and two hundred thousand to-day, while I was away. The remaining payments are to be made in the course of this week."

"But this is terrible! You ought to have...."

"What, chief? To begin with, they took advantage of my absence to settle up accounts with the companies. I only heard about it on my return when I ran up against an insurance-manager whom I happen to know and took the opportunity of drawing him out."

The chief-detective was silent for some time, not knowing what to say. Then he mumbled:

"What a fellow, though!"

Ganimard nodded his head:

"Yes, chief, a blackguard, but, I can't help saying, a devil of a clever fellow. For his plan to succeed, he must have managed in such a way that, for four or five weeks, no one could express or even conceive the least suspicion of the part played by Colonel Sparmiento. All the indignation and all the inquiries had to be concentrated upon Lupin alone. In the last resort, people had to find themselves faced simply with a mournful, pitiful, penniless widow, poor Edith Swan-neck, a beautiful and legendary vision, a creature so pathetic that the gentlemen of the insurance-companies were almost glad to place something in her hands to relieve her poverty and her grief. That's what was wanted and that's what happened."

The two men were close together and did not take their eyes from each other's faces.

The chief asked:

"Who is that woman?"

"Sonia Kritchnoff."

"Sonia Kritchnoff?"

"Yes, the Russian girl whom I arrested last year at the time of the theft of the coronet, and whom Lupin helped to escape."

"Are you sure?"

"Absolutely. I was put off the scent, like everybody else, by Lupin's machinations, and had paid no particular attention to her. But, when I knew the part which she was playing, I remembered. She is certainly Sonia, metamorphosed into an Englishwoman; Sonia, the most innocent-looking and the trickiest of actresses; Sonia, who would not hesitate to face death for love of Lupin."

"A good capture, Ganimard," said M. Dudouis, approvingly.

"I've something better still for you, chief!"

"Really? What?"

"Lupin's old foster-mother."

"Victoire?"

"She has been here since Mme. Sparmiento began playing the widow; she's the cook."

"Oho!" said M. Dudouis. "My congratulations, Ganimard!"

634

"I've something for you, chief, that's even better than that!"

M. Dudouis gave a start. The inspector's hand clutched his and was shaking with excitement.

"What do you mean, Ganimard?"

"Do you think, chief, that I would have brought you here, at this late hour, if I had had nothing more attractive to offer you than Sonia and Victoire? Pah! They'd have kept!"

"You mean to say ...?" whispered M. Dudouis, at last, understanding the chief-inspector's agitation.

"You've guessed it, chief!"

"Is he here?"

"He's here."

"In hiding?"

"Not a bit of it. Simply in disguise. He's the man-servant."

This time, M. Dudouis did not utter a word nor make a gesture. Lupin's audacity confounded him.

Ganimard chuckled.

"It's no longer a threefold, but a fourfold incarnation. Edith Swan-neck might have blundered. The master's presence was necessary; and he had the cheek to return. For three weeks, he has been beside me during my inquiry, calmly following the progress made."

"Did you recognize him?"

"One doesn't recognize him. He has a knack of making-up his face and altering the proportions of his body so as to prevent any one from knowing him. Besides, I was miles from suspecting.... But, this evening, as I was watching Sonia in the shadow of the stairs, I heard Victoire speak to the man-servant and call him, 'Dearie.' A light flashed in upon me. 'Dearie!' That was what she always used to call him. And I knew where I was."

M. Dudouis seemed flustered, in his turn, by the presence of the enemy, so often pursued and always so intangible:

"We've got him, this time," he said, between his teeth. "We've got him; and he can't escape us."

"No, chief, he can't: neither he nor the two women."

"Where are they?"

"Sonia and Victoire are on the second floor; Lupin is on the third."

M. Dudouis suddenly became anxious:

"Why, it was through the windows of one of those floors that the tapestries were passed when they disappeared!"

"That's so, chief."

"In that case, Lupin can get away too. The windows look out on the Rue Dufresnoy."

"Of course they do, chief; but I have taken my precautions. The moment you arrived, I sent four of our men to keep watch under the windows in the Rue Dufresnoy. They have strict instructions to shoot, if any one appears at the windows and looks like coming down. Blank cartridges for the first shot, ball-cartridges for the next."

"Good, Ganimard! You have thought of everything. We'll wait here; and, immediately after sunrise...."

"Wait, chief? Stand on ceremony with that rascal? Bother about rules and regulations, legal hours and all that rot? And suppose he's not quite so polite to us and gives us the slip meanwhile? Suppose he plays us one of his Lupin tricks? No, no, we must have no nonsense! We've got him: let's collar him; and that without delay!"

And Ganimard, all a-quiver with indignant impatience, went out, walked across the garden and presently returned with half-a-dozen men:

"It's all right, chief. I've told them, in the Rue Dufresnoy, to get their revolvers out and aim at the windows. Come along."

These alarums and excursions had not been effected without a certain amount of noise, which was bound to be heard by the inhabitants of the house. M. Dudouis felt that his hand was forced. He made up his mind to act:

"Come on, then," he said.

The thing did not take long. The eight of them, Browning pistols in hand, went up the stairs without overmuch precaution, eager to surprise Lupin before he had time to organize his defences.

"Open the door!" roared Ganimard, rushing at the door of Mme. Sparmiento's bedroom.

A policeman smashed it in with his shoulder.

There was no one in the room; and no one in Victoire's bedroom either.

"They're all upstairs!" shouted Ganimard. "They've gone up to Lupin in his attic. Be careful now!"

All the eight ran up the third flight of stairs. To his great astonishment, Ganimard found the door of the attic open and the attic empty. And the other rooms were empty too.

"Blast them!" he cursed. "What's become of them?"

But the chief called him. M. Dudouis, who had gone down again to the second floor, noticed that one of the windows was not latched, but just pushed to:

"There," he said, to Ganimard, "that's the road they took, the road of the tapestries. I told you as much: the Rue Dufresnoy...."

"But our men would have fired on them," protested Ganimard, grinding his teeth with rage. "The street's guarded."

"They must have gone before the street was guarded."

"They were all three of them in their rooms when I rang you up, chief!"

"They must have gone while you were waiting for me in the garden."

"But why? Why? There was no reason why they should go to-day rather than to-morrow, or the next day, or next week, for that matter, when they had pocketed all the insurance-money!"

Yes, there was a reason; and Ganimard knew it when he saw, on the table, a letter addressed to himself and opened it and read it. The letter was worded in the style of the testimonials which we hand to people in our service who have given satisfaction:

"I, the undersigned, Arsène Lupin, gentleman-burglar, ex-colonel, ex-man-of-all-work, ex-corpse, hereby certify that the person of the name of Ganimard gave proof of the most remarkable qualities during his stay in this house. He was exemplary in his behaviour, thoroughly devoted and attentive; and, unaided by the least clue, he foiled a part of my plans and saved the insurance-companies four hundred and fifty thousand francs. I congratulate him; and I am quite willing to overlook his blunder in not anticipating that the downstairs telephone communicates with the telephone in Sonia Kritchnoff's bedroom and that, when telephoning to Mr. Chief-detective, he was at the same time telephoning to me to clear out as fast as I could. It was a pardonable slip, which must not be allowed to dim the glamour of his services nor to detract from the merits of his victory.

"Having said this, I beg him to accept the homage of my admiration and of my sincere friendship.

THE GOLDEN TRIANGLE: The Return of Arsène Lupin

BY
MAURICE LE BLANC

CHAPTER I CORALIE

It was close upon half-past six and the evening shadows were growing denser when two soldiers reached the little space, planted with trees, opposite the Musée Galliéra, where the Rue de Chaillot and the Rue Pierre-Charron meet. One wore an infantryman's sky-blue great-coat; the other, a Senegalese, those clothes of undyed wool, with baggy breeches and a belted jacket, in which the Zouaves and the native African troops have been dressed since the war. One of them had lost his right leg, the other his left arm.

They walked round the open space, in the center of which stands a fine group of Silenus figures, and stopped. The infantryman threw away his cigarette. The Senegalese picked it up, took a few quick puffs at it, put it out by squeezing it between his fore-finger and thumb and stuffed it into his pocket. All this without a word.

Almost at the same time two more soldiers came out of the Rue Galliéra. It would have been impossible to say to what branch they belonged, for their military attire was composed of the most incongruous civilian garments. However, one of them sported a Zouave's *chechia*, the other an artilleryman's *képi*. The first walked on crutches, the other on two sticks. These two kept near the newspaper-kiosk which stands at the edge of the pavement.

Three others came singly by the Rue Pierre-Charron, the Rue Brignoles and the Rue de Chaillot: a one-armed rifleman, a limping sapper and a marine with a hip that looked as if it was twisted. Each of them made straight for a tree and leant against it.

Not a word was uttered among them. None of the seven crippled soldiers seemed to know his companions or to trouble about or even perceive their presence. They stood behind their trees or behind the kiosk or behind the group of Silenus figures without stirring. And the few wayfarers who, on that evening of the 3rd of April, 1915, crossed this unfrequented square, which received hardly any light from the shrouded street-lamps, did not slacken pace to observe the men's motionless outlines.

A clock struck half-past six. At that moment the door of one of the houses overlooking the square opened. A man came out, closed the door behind him, crossed the Rue de Chaillot and walked round the open space in front of the museum. It was an officer in khaki. Under his red forage-cap, with its three lines of gold braid, his head was wrapped in a wide linen bandage, which hid his forehead and neck. He was tall and very slenderly built. His right leg ended in a wooden stump with a rubber foot to it. He leant on a stick.

Leaving the square, he stepped into the roadway of the Rue Pierre-Charron. Here he turned and gave a leisurely look to his surroundings on every side. This minute inspection brought him to one of the trees facing the museum. With the tip of his cane he gently tapped a protruding stomach. The stomach pulled itself in.

The officer moved off again. This time he went definitely down the Rue Pierre-Charron towards the center of Paris. He thus came to the Avenue des Champs-Élysées, which he went up, taking the left pavement.

Two hundred yards further on was a large house, which had been transformed, as a flag proclaimed, into a hospital. The officer took up his position at some distance, so as not to be seen by those leaving, and waited.

It struck a quarter to seven and seven o'clock. A few more minutes passed. Five persons came out of the house, followed by two more. At last a lady appeared in the hall, a nurse wearing a wide blue cloak marked with the Red Cross.

"Here she comes," said the officer.

She took the road by which he had arrived and turned down the Rue Pierre-Charron, keeping to the right-hand pavement and thus making for the space where the street meets the Rue de Chaillot. Her walk was light, her step easy and well-balanced. The wind, buffeting against her as she moved quickly on her way, swelled out the long blue veil floating around her shoulders. Notwithstanding the width of the cloak, the rhythmical swing of her body and the youthfulness of her figure were revealed. The officer kept behind her and walked along with an absent-minded air, twirling his stick, like a man taking an aimless stroll.

At this moment there was nobody in sight, in that part of the street, except him and her. But, just after she had crossed the Avenue Marceau and some time before he reached it, a motor standing in the avenue started driving in the same direction as the nurse, at a fixed distance from her.

It was a taxi-cab. And the officer noticed two things: first, that there were two men inside it and, next, that one of them leant out of the window almost the whole time, talking to the driver. He was able to catch a momentary glimpse of this man's face, cut in half by a heavy mustache and surmounted by a gray felt hat.

Meanwhile, the nurse walked on without turning round. The officer had crossed the street and now hurried his pace, the more so as it struck him that the cab was also increasing its speed as the girl drew near the space in front of the museum.

From where he was the officer could take in almost the whole of the little square at a glance; and, however sharply he looked, he discerned nothing in the darkness that revealed the presence of the seven crippled men. No one, moreover, was passing on foot or driving. In the distance only, in the dusk of the wide crossing avenues, two tram-cars, with lowered blinds, disturbed the silence.

Nor did the girl, presuming that she was paying attention to the sights of the street, appear to see anything to alarm her. She gave not the least sign of hesitation. And the behavior of the motor-cab following her did not seem to strike her either, for she did not look round once.

The cab, however, was gaining ground. When it neared the square, it was ten or fifteen yards, at most, from the nurse; and, by the time that she, still noticing nothing, had reached the first trees, it came closer yet and, leaving the middle of the road, began to hug the pavement, while, on the side opposite the pavement, the left-hand side, the man who kept leaning out had opened the door and was now standing on the step.

The officer crossed the street once more, briskly, without fear of being seen, so heedless did the two men now appear of anything but their immediate business. He raised a whistle to his lips. There was no doubt that the expected event was about to take place.

The cab, in fact, pulled up suddenly. The two men leapt from the doors on either side and rushed to the pavement of the square, a few yards from the kiosk. At the same moment there was a cry of terror from the girl and a shrill whistle from the officer. And, also at the same time, the two men caught up and seized their victim and dragged her towards the cab, while the seven wounded soldiers, seeming to spring from the very trunks of the trees that hid them, fell upon the two aggressors.

The battle did not last long. Or rather there was no battle. At the outset the driver of the taxi, perceiving that the attack was being countered, made off and drove away as fast as he could. As for the two men, realizing that their enterprise had failed and finding themselves faced with a threatening array of uplifted sticks and crutches, not to mention the barrel of a revolver which the officer pointed at them, they let go the girl, tacked from side to side, to prevent the officer from taking aim, and disappeared in the darkness of the Rue Brignoles.

"Run for all you're worth, Ya-Bon," said the officer to the one-armed Senegalese, "and bring me back one of them by the scruff of the neck!"

He supported the girl with his arm. She was trembling all over and seemed ready to faint.

"Don't be frightened, Little Mother Coralie," he said, very anxiously. "It's I, Captain Belval, Patrice Belval."

"Ah, it's you, captain!" she stammered.

"Yes; all your friends have gathered round to defend you, all your old patients from the hospital, whom I found in the convalescent home."

"Thank you. Thank you." And she added, in a quivering voice, "The others? Those two men?"

"Run away. Ya-Bon's gone after them."

"But what did they want with me? And what miracle brought you all here?"

"We'll talk about that later, Little Mother Coralie. Let's speak of you first. Where am I to take you? Don't you think you'd better come in here with me, until you've recovered and taken a little rest?"

Assisted by one of the soldiers, he helped her gently to the house which he himself had left three-quarters of an hour before. The girl let him do as he pleased. They all entered an apartment on the ground-floor and went into the drawing-room, where a bright fire of logs was burning. He switched on the electric light:

"Sit down," he said.

She dropped into a chair; and the captain at once gave his orders:

"You, Poulard, go and fetch a glass in the dining-room. And you, Ribrac, draw a jug of cold water in the kitchen. . . . Chatelain, you'll find a decanter of rum in the pantry. . . . Or, stay, she doesn't like rum. . . . Then . . ."

"Then," she said, smiling, "just a glass of water, please."

Her cheeks, which were naturally pale, recovered a little of their warmth. The blood flowed back to her lips; and the smile on her face was full of confidence. Her face, all charm and gentleness, had a pure outline, features almost too delicate, a fair complexion and the ingenuous expression of a wondering child that looks on life with eyes always wide open. And all this, which was dainty and exquisite, nevertheless at certain moments gave an impression of energy, due no doubt to her shining, dark eyes and to the line of smooth, black hair that came down on either side from under the white cap in which her forehead was imprisoned.

"Aha!" cried the captain, gaily, when she had drunk the water. "You're feeling better, I think, eh, Little Mother Coralie?"

"Much better."

"Capital. But that was a bad minute we went through just now! What an adventure! We shall have to talk it all over and get some light on it, sha'n't we? Meanwhile, my lads, pay your respects to Little Mother Coralie. Eh, my fine fellows, who would have thought, when she was coddling you and patting your pillows for your fat pates to sink into, that one day we should be taking care of her and that the children would be coddling their little mother?"

They all pressed round her, the one-armed and the one-legged, the crippled and the sick, all glad to see her. And she shook hands with them affectionately:

"Well, Ribrac, how's that leg of yours?"

"I don't feel it any longer, Little Mother Coralie."

"And you, Vatinel? That wound in your shoulder?"

"Not a sign of it, Little Mother Coralie."

"And you, Poulard? And you, Jorisse?"

Her emotion increased at seeing them again, the men whom she called her children. And Patrice Belval exclaimed:

"Ah, Little Mother Coralie, now you're crying! Little mother, little mother, that's how you captured all our hearts. When we were trying our hardest not to call out, on our bed of pain, we used to see your eyes filling with great tears. Little Mother Coralie was weeping over her children. Then we clenched our teeth still firmer."

"And I used to cry still more," she said, "just because you were afraid of hurting me."

"And to-day you're at it again. No, you are too soft-hearted! You love us. We love you. There's nothing to cry about in that. Come, Little Mother Coralie, a smile. . . . And, I say, here's Ya-Bon coming; and Ya-Bon always laughs."

She rose suddenly:

"Do you think he can have overtaken one of the two men?"

"Do I think so? I told Ya-Bon to bring one back by the neck. He won't fail. I'm only afraid of one thing. . . ."

They had gone towards the hall. The Senegalese was already on the steps. With his right hand he was clutching the neck of a man, of a limp rag, rather, which he seemed to be carrying at arm's length, like a dancing-doll.

"Drop him," said the captain.

Ya-Bon loosened his fingers. The man fell on the flags in the hall.

"That's what I feared," muttered the officer. "Ya-Bon has only his right hand; but, when that hand holds any one by the throat, it's a miracle if it doesn't strangle him. The Boches know something about it."

Ya-Bon was a sort of colossus, the color of gleaming coal, with a woolly head and a few curly hairs on his chin, with an empty sleeve fastened to his left shoulder and two medals pinned to his jacket. Ya-Bon had had one cheek, one side of his jaw, half his mouth and the whole of his palate smashed by a splinter of shell. The other half of that mouth was split to the ear in a laugh which never seemed to cease and which was all the more surprising because the wounded portion of the face, patched up as best it could be and covered with a grafted skin, remained impassive.

Moreover, Ya-Bon had lost his power of speech. The most that he could do was to emit a sequence of indistinct grunts in which his nickname of Ya-Bon was everlastingly repeated.

He uttered it once more with a satisfied air, glancing by turns at his master and his victim, like a good sporting-dog standing over the bird which he has retrieved.

"Good," said the officer. "But, next time, go to work more gently."

He bent over the man, felt his heart and, on seeing that he had only fainted, asked the nurse:

"Do you know him?"

"No," she said.

"Are you sure? Have you never seen that head anywhere?"

It was a very big head, with black hair, plastered down with grease, and a thick beard. The man's clothes, which were of dark-blue serge and well-cut, showed him to be in easy circumstances.

"Never . . . never," the girl declared.

Captain Belval searched the man's pockets. They contained no papers.

"Very well," he said, rising to his feet, "we will wait till he wakes up and question him then. Ya-Bon, tie up his arms and legs and stay here, in the hall. The rest of you fellows, go back to the home: it's time you were indoors. I have my key. Say good-by to Little Mother Coralie and trot off."

And, when good-by had been said, he pushed them outside, came back to the nurse, led her into the drawing-room and said:

"Now let's talk, Little Mother Coralie. First of all, before we try to explain things, listen to me. It won't take long."

They were sitting before the merrily blazing fire. Patrice Belval slipped a hassock under Little Mother Coralie's feet, put out a light that seemed to worry her and, when he felt certain that she was comfortable, began:

"As you know, Little Mother Coralie, I left the hospital a week ago and am staying on the Boulevard Maillot, at Neuilly, in the home reserved for the convalescent patients of the hospital. I sleep there at night and have my wounds dressed in the morning. The rest of the time I spend in loafing: I stroll about, lunch and dine where the mood takes me and go and call on my friends. Well, this morning I was waiting for one of them in a big café-restaurant on the boulevard, when I overheard the end of a conversation. . . . But I must tell you that the place is divided into two by a partition standing about six feet high, with the customers of the café on one side and those of the restaurant on the other. I was all by myself in the restaurant; and the two men, who had their backs turned to me and who in any case were out of sight, probably thought that there was no one there at all, for they were speaking rather louder than they need have done, considering the sentences which I overheard . . . and which I afterwards wrote down in my little note-book."

He took the note-book from his pocket and went on:

"These sentences, which caught my attention for reasons which you will understand presently, were preceded by some others in which there was a reference to sparks, to a shower of sparks that had already occurred twice before the war, a sort of night signal for the possible repetition of which they proposed to watch, so that they might act quickly as soon as it appeared. Does none of this tell you anything?"

"No. Why?"

"You shall see. By the way, I forgot to tell you that the two were talking English, quite correctly, but with an accent which assured me that neither of them was an Englishman. Here is what they said, faithfully translated: 'To finish up, therefore,' said one, 'everything is decided. You and he will be at the appointed place at a little before seven this evening.' 'We shall be there, colonel. We have engaged our taxi.' 'Good. Remember that the little woman leaves her hospital at seven o'clock.' 'Have no fear. There can't be any mistake, because she always goes the same way, down the Rue Pierre-Charron.' 'And your whole plan is settled?' 'In every particular. The thing will happen in the square at the end of the Rue de Chaillot. Even granting that there may be people about, they will have no time to rescue her, for we shall act too quickly.' 'Are you certain of your driver?' 'I am certain that we shall pay him enough to secure his obedience. That's all we want.' 'Capital. I'll wait for you at the place you know of, in a motor-car. You'll hand the little woman over to me. From that moment, we shall be masters of the situation.' 'And you of the little woman, colonel, which isn't bad for you, for she's deucedly pretty.' 'Deucedly, as you say. I've known her a long time by sight; and, upon my word. . . .' The two began to laugh coarsely and called for their bill. I at once got up and went to the door on the boulevard, but only one of them came out by that door, a man with a big drooping mustache and a gray felt hat. The other had left by the door in the street round the corner. There was only one taxi in the road. The man took it and I had to give up all hope of following him. Only . . . only, as I knew that you left the hospital at seven o'clock every evening and that you went along the Rue Pierre-Charron, I was justified, wasn't I, in believing . . . ?"

The captain stopped. The girl reflected, with a thoughtful air. Presently she asked:

643

"Why didn't you warn me?"

"Warn you!" he exclaimed. "And, if, after all, it wasn't you? Why alarm you? And, if, on the other hand, it was you, why put you on your guard? After the attempt had failed, your enemies would have laid another trap for you; and we, not knowing of it, would have been unable to prevent it. No, the best thing was to accept the fight. I enrolled a little band of your former patients who were being treated at the home; and, as the friend whom I was expecting to meet happened to live in the square, here, in this house, I asked him to place his rooms at my disposal from six to nine o'clock. That's what I did, Little Mother Coralie. And now that you know as much as I do, what do you think of it?"

She gave him her hand:

"I think you have saved me from an unknown danger that looks like a very great one; and I thank you."

"No, no," he said, "I can accept no thanks. I was so glad to have succeeded! What I want to know is your opinion of the business itself?"

Without a second's hesitation, she replied:

"I have none. Not a word, not an incident, in all that you have told me, suggests the least idea to me."

"You have no enemies, to your knowledge?"

"Personally, no."

"What about that man to whom your two assailants were to hand you over and who says that he knows you?"

"Doesn't every woman," she said, with a slight blush, "come across men who pursue her more or less openly? I can't tell who it is."

The captain was silent for a while and then went on:

"When all is said, our only hope of clearing up the matter lies in questioning our prisoner. If he refuses to answer, I shall hand him over to the police, who will know how to get to the bottom of the business."

The girl gave a start:

"The police?"

"Well, of course. What would you have me do with the fellow? He doesn't belong to me. He belongs to the police."

"No, no, no!" she exclaimed, excitedly. "Not on any account! What, have my life gone into? . . . Have to appear before the magistrate? . . . Have my name mixed up in all this? . . ."

"And yet, Little Mother Coralie, I can't . . ."

"Oh, I beg, I beseech you, as my friend, find some way out of it, but don't have me talked about! I don't want to be talked about!"

The captain looked at her, somewhat surprised to see her in such a state of agitation, and said:

"You sha'n't be talked about, Little Mother Coralie, I promise you."

"Then what will you do with that man?"

"Well," he said, with a laugh, "I shall begin by asking him politely if he will condescend to answer my questions; then thank him for his civil behavior to you; and lastly beg him to be good enough to go away."

He rose:

"Do you wish to see him, Little Mother Coralie?"

"No," she said, "I am so tired! If you don't want me, question him by yourself. You can tell me about it afterwards. . . ."

She seemed quite exhausted by all this fresh excitement and strain, added to all those which already rendered her life as a nurse so hard. The captain did not insist and went out, closing the door of the drawing-room after him.

She heard him saying:

"Well, Ya-Bon, have you kept a good watch! No news? And how's your prisoner? . . . Ah, there you are, my fine fellow! Have you got your breath back? Oh, I know Ya-Bon's hand is a bit heavy! . . . What's this? Won't you answer? . . . Hallo, what's happened? Hanged if I don't think . . ."

A cry escaped him. The girl ran to the hall. She met the captain, who tried to bar her way.

"Don't come," he said, in great agitation. "What's the use!"

"But you're hurt!" she exclaimed.

"I?"

"There's blood on your shirt-cuff."

"So there is, but it's nothing: it's the man's blood that must have stained me."

"Then he was wounded?"

"Yes, or at least his mouth was bleeding. Some blood-vessel . . ."

"Why, surely Ya-Bon didn't grip as hard as that?"

"It wasn't Ya-Bon."

"Then who was it?"

"His accomplices."

"Did they come back?"

"Yes; and they've strangled him."

"But it's not possible!"

She pushed by and went towards the prisoner. He did not move. His face had the pallor of death. Round his neck was a red-silk string, twisted very thin and with a buckle at either end.

CHAPTER II RIGHT HAND AND LEFT LEG

"One rogue less in the world, Little Mother Coralie!" cried Patrice Belval, after he had led the girl back to the drawing-room and made a rapid investigation with Ya-Bon. "Remember his name—I found it engraved on his watch—Mustapha Rovalaïof, the name of a rogue!"

He spoke gaily, with no emotion in his voice, and continued, as he walked up and down the room:

"You and I, Little Mother Coralie, who have witnessed so many tragedies and seen so many good fellows die, need not waste tears over the death of Mustapha Rovalaïof or his murder by his accomplices. Not even a funeral oration, eh? Ya-Bon has taken him under his arm, waited until the square was clear and carried him to the Rue Brignoles, with orders to fling the gentleman over the railings into the garden of the Musée Galliéra. The railings are high. But Ya-Bon's right hand knows no obstacles. And so, Little Mother Coralie, the matter is buried. You won't be talked about; and, this time, I claim a word of thanks."

He stopped to laugh:

"A word of thanks, but no compliments. By Jove, I don't make much of a warder! It was clever the way those beggars snatched my prisoner. Why didn't I foresee that your other assailant, the man in the gray-felt hat, would go and tell the third, who was waiting in his motor, and that they would both come back together to rescue their companion? And they came back. And, while you and I were chatting, they must have forced the servants' entrance, passed through the kitchen, come to the little door between the pantry and the hall and pushed it open. There, close by them, lay their man, still unconscious and firmly bound, on his sofa. What were they to do? It was impossible to get him out of the hall without alarming Ya-Bon. And yet, if they didn't release him, he would speak, give away his accomplices and ruin a carefully prepared plan. So one of the two must have leant forward stealthily, put out his arm, thrown his string round that throat which Ya-Bon had already handled pretty roughly, gathered the buckles at the two ends and pulled, pulled, quietly, until death came. Not a sound. Not a sigh. The whole operation performed in silence. We come, we kill and we go away. Good-night. The trick is done and our friend won't talk."

Captain Belval's merriment increased:

"Our friend won't talk," he repeated, "and the police, when they find his body to-morrow morning inside a railed garden, won't understand a word of the business. Nor we either, Little Mother Coralie; and we shall never know why those men tried to kidnap you. It's only too true! I may not be up to much as a warder, but I'm beneath contempt as a detective!"

He continued to walk up and down the room. The fact that his leg or rather his calf had been amputated seemed hardly to inconvenience him; and, as the joints of the knee and thighbone had retained their mobility, there was at most a certain want of rhythm in the action of his hips and shoulders. Moreover, his tall figure tended to correct this lameness, which was reduced to insignificant proportions by the ease of his movements and the indifference with which he appeared to accept it.

He had an open countenance, rather dark in color, burnt by the sun and tanned by the weather, with an expression that was frank, cheerful and often bantering. He must have been between twenty-eight and thirty. His manner suggested that of the officers of the First Empire, to whom their life in camp imparted a special air which they subsequently brought into the ladies' drawing-rooms.

He stopped to look at Coralie, whose shapely profile stood out against the gleams from the fireplace. Then he came and sat beside her:

"I know nothing about you," he said softly. "At the hospital the doctors and nurses call you Madame Coralie. Your patients prefer to say Little Mother. What is your married or your maiden name? Have you a husband or are you a widow? Where do you live? Nobody knows. You arrive every day at the same time and you go away by the same street. Sometimes an old serving-man, with long gray hair and a bristly beard, with a comforter round his neck and a pair of yellow spectacles on his nose, brings you or fetches you. Sometimes also he waits for you, always sitting on the same chair in the covered yard. He has been asked questions, but he never gives an answer. I know only one thing, therefore, about you, which is that you are adorably good and kind and that you are also—I may say it, may I not?— adorably beautiful. And it is perhaps, Little Mother Coralie, because I know nothing about your life that I imagine it so mysterious, and, in some way, so sad. You give the impression of living amid sorrow and anxiety; the feeling that you are all alone. There is no one who devotes himself to making you happy and taking care of you. So I thought—I have long thought and waited for an opportunity of telling you—I thought that you must need a friend, a brother, who would advise and protect you. Am I not right, Little Mother Coralie?"

As he went on, Coralie seemed to shrink into herself and to place a greater distance between them, as though she did not wish him to penetrate those secret regions of which he spoke.

"No," she murmured, "you are mistaken. My life is quite simple. I do not need to be defended."

"You do not need to be defended!" he cried, with increasing animation. "What about those men who tried to kidnap you? That plot hatched against you? That plot which your assailants are so afraid to see discovered that they go to the length of killing the one who allowed himself to be caught? Is that nothing? Is it mere delusion on my part when I say that you are surrounded by dangers, that you have enemies who stick at nothing, that you have to be defended against their attempts and that, if you decline the offer of my assistance, I . . . Well, I . . . ?"

She persisted in her silence, showed herself more and more distant, almost hostile. The officer struck the marble mantelpiece with his fist, and, bending over her, finished his sentence in a determined tone:

"Well, if you decline the offer of my assistance, I shall force it on you."

She shook her head.

"I shall force it on you," he repeated, firmly. "It is my duty and my right."

"No," she said, in an undertone.

"My absolute right," said Captain Belval, "for a reason which outweighs all the others and makes it unnecessary for me even to consult you."

"What do you mean?"

"I love you."

He brought out the words plainly, not like a lover venturing on a timid declaration, but like a man proud of the sentiment that he feels and happy to proclaim it.

She lowered her eyes and blushed; and he cried, exultantly:

"You can take it, Little Mother, from me. No impassioned outbursts, no sighs, no waving of the arms, no clapping of the hands. Just three little words, which I tell you without going on my knees. And it's the easier for me because you know it. Yes, Madame Coralie, it's all very well to look so shy, but you know my love for you and you've known it as long as I have. We saw it together take birth when your dear little hands touched my battered head. The others used to torture me. With you, it was nothing but caresses. So was the pity in your eyes and the tears that fell because I was in pain. But can any one see you without loving you? Your seven patients who were here just now are all in love with you, Little Mother Coralie. Ya-Bon worships the ground you walk on. Only they are privates. They cannot speak. I am an officer; and I speak without hesitation or embarrassment, believe me."

Coralie had put her hands to her burning cheeks and sat silent, bending forward.

"You understand what I mean, don't you," he went on, in a voice that rang, "when I say that I speak without hesitation or embarrassment? If I had been before the war what I am now, a maimed man, I should not have had the same assurance and I should have declared my love for you humbly and begged your pardon for my boldness. But now! . . . Believe me, Little Mother Coralie, when I sit here face to face with the woman I adore, I do not think of my infirmity. Not for a moment do I feel the impression that I can appear ridiculous or presumptuous in your eyes."

He stopped, as though to take breath, and then, rising, went on:

"And it must needs be so. People will have to understand that those who have been maimed in this war do not look upon themselves as outcasts, lame ducks, or lepers, but as absolutely normal men. Yes, normal! One leg short? What about it? Does that rob a man of his brain or heart? Then, because the war has deprived me of a leg, or an arm, or even both legs or both arms, I have no longer the right to love a woman save at the risk of meeting with a rebuff or imagining that she pities me? Pity! But we don't want the woman to pity us, nor to make an effort to love us, nor even to think that she is doing a charity because she treats us kindly. What we demand, from women and from the world at large, from those whom we meet in the street and from those who belong to the same set as ourselves, is absolute equality with the rest, who have been saved from our fate by their lucky stars or their cowardice."

The captain once more struck the mantelpiece:

"Yes, absolute equality! We all of us, whether we have lost a leg or an arm, whether blind in one eye or two, whether crippled or deformed, claim to be just as good, physically and morally, as any one you please; and perhaps better. What! Shall men who have used their legs to rush upon the enemy be outdistanced in life, because they no longer have those legs, by men who have sat and warmed their toes at an office-fire? What nonsense! We want our place in the sun as well as the others. It is our due; and we shall know how to get it and keep it. There is no happiness to which we are not entitled and no work for which we are not capable with a little exercise and training. Ya-Bon's right hand is already worth any pair of hands in the wide world; and Captain Belval's left leg allows him to do his five miles an hour if he pleases."

He began to laugh:

"Right hand and left leg; left hand and right leg: what does it matter which we have saved, if we know how to use it? In what respect have we fallen off? Whether it's a question of obtaining a position or perpetuating our race, are we not as good as we were? And perhaps even better. I venture to say that the children which we shall give to the country will be just as well-built as ever, with arms and legs and the rest . . . not to mention a mighty legacy of pluck and spirit. That's what we claim, Little Mother Coralie.

We refuse to admit that our wooden legs keep us back or that we cannot stand as upright on our crutches as on legs of flesh and bone. We do not consider that devotion to us is any sacrifice or that it's necessary to talk of heroism when a girl has the honor to marry a blind soldier! Once more, we are not creatures outside the pale. We have not fallen off in any way whatever; and this is a truth before which everybody will bow for the next two or three generations. You can understand that, in a country like France, when maimed men are to be met by the hundred thousand, the conception of what makes a perfect man will no longer be as hard and fast as it was. In the new form of humanity which is preparing, there will be men with two arms and men with only one, just as there are fair men and dark, bearded men and clean-shaven. And it will all seem quite natural. And every one will lead the life he pleases, without needing to be complete in every limb. And, as my life is wrapped up in you, Little Mother Coralie, and as my happiness depends on you, I thought I would wait no longer before making you my little speech. . . . Well! That's finished! I have plenty more to say on the subject, but it can't all be said in a day, can it? . . ."

He broke off, thrown out of his stride after all by Coralie's silence. She had not stirred since the first words of love that he uttered. Her hands had sought her forehead; and her shoulders were shaking slightly.

He stooped and, with infinite gentleness, drawing aside the slender fingers, uncovered her beautiful face:

"Why are you crying, Little Mother Coralie?"

He was calling her *tu* now, but she did not mind. Between a man and the woman who has bent over his wounds relations of a special kind arise; and Captain Belval in particular had those rather familiar, but still respectful, ways at which it seems impossible to take offence.

"Have *I* made you cry?" he asked.

"No," she said, in a low voice, "it's all of you who upset me. It's your cheerfulness, your pride, your way not of submitting to fate, but mastering it. The humblest of you raises himself above his nature without an effort; and I know nothing finer or more touching than that indifference."

He sat down beside her:

"Then you're not angry with me for saying . . . what I said?"

"Angry with you?" she replied, pretending to mistake his meaning. "Why, every woman thinks as you do. If women, in bestowing their affection, had to choose among the men returning from the war, the choice I am sure would be in favor of those who have suffered most cruelly."

He shook his head:

"You see, I am asking for something more than affection and a more definite answer to what I said. Shall I remind you of my words?"

"No."

"Then your answer . . . ?"

"My answer, dear friend, is that you must not speak those words again."

He put on a solemn air:

"You forbid me?"

"I do."

"In that case, I swear to say nothing more until I see you again."

"You will not see me again," she murmured.

Captain Belval was greatly amused at this:

"I say, I say! And why sha'n't I see you again, Little Mother Coralie?"

"Because I don't wish it."

"And your reason, please?"

"My reason?"

She turned her eyes to him and said, slowly:

"I am married."

Belval seemed in no way disconcerted by this news. On the contrary, he said, in the calmest of tones:

"Well, you must marry again! No doubt your husband is an old man and you do not love him. He will therefore understand that, as you have some one in love with you . . ."

"Don't jest, please."

He caught hold of her hand, just as she was rising to go:

"You are right, Little Mother Coralie, and I apologize for not adopting a more serious manner to speak to you of very serious things. It's a question of our two lives. I am profoundly convinced that they are moving towards each other and that you are powerless to restrain them. That is why your answer is beside the point. I ask nothing of you. I expect everything from fate. It is fate that will bring us together."

"No," she said.

"Yes," he declared, "that is how things will happen."

"It is not. They will not and shall not happen like that. You must give me your word of honor not to try to see me again nor even to learn my name. I might have granted more if you had been content to remain friends. The confession which you have made sets a barrier between us. I want nobody in my life . . . nobody!"

She made this declaration with a certain vehemence and at the same time tried to release her arm from his grasp. Patrice Belval resisted her efforts and said:

"You are wrong. . . . You have no right to expose yourself to danger like this. . . . Please reflect . . ."

She pushed him away. As she did so, she knocked off the mantelpiece a little bag which she had placed there. It fell on the carpet and opened. Two or three things escaped, and she picked them up, while Patrice Belval knelt down on the floor to help her:

"Here," he said, "you've missed this."

It was a little case in plaited straw, which had also come open; the beads of a rosary protruded from it.

They both stood up in silence. Captain Belval examined the rosary.

"What a curious coincidence!" he muttered. "These amethyst beads! This old-fashioned gold filigree setting! . . . It's strange to find the same materials and the same workmanship. . . ."

He gave a start, and it was so marked that Coralie asked:

"Why, what's the matter?"

He was holding in his fingers a bead larger than most of the others, forming a link between the string of tens and the shorter prayer-chain. And this bead was broken half-way across, almost level with the gold setting which held it.

"The coincidence," he said, "is so inconceivable that I hardly dare . . . And yet the face can be verified at once. But first, one question: who gave you this rosary?"

"Nobody gave it to me. I've always had it."

"But it must have belonged to somebody before?"

"To my mother, I suppose."

"Your mother?"

"I expect so, in the same way as the different jewels which she left me."

"Is your mother dead?"

"Yes, she died when I was four years old. I have only the vaguest recollection of her. But what has all this to do with a rosary?"

"It's because of this," he said. "Because of this amethyst bead broken in two."

He undid his jacket and took his watch from his waistcoat-pocket. It had a number of trinkets fastened to it by a little leather and silver strap. One of these trinkets consisted of the half of an amethyst bead, also broken across, also held in a filigree setting. The original size of the two beads seemed to be identical. The two amethysts were of the same color and contained in the same filigree.

Coralie and Belval looked at each other anxiously. She stammered:

"It's only an accident, nothing else . . ."

"I agree," he said. "But, supposing these two halves fit each other exactly . . ."

"It's impossible," she said, herself frightened at the thought of the simple little act needed for the indisputable proof.

The officer, however, decided upon that act. He brought his right hand, which held the rosary-bead, and his left, which held the trinket, together. The hands hesitated, felt about and stopped. The contact was made.

The projections and indentations of the broken stones corresponded precisely. Each protruding part found a space to fit it. The two half amethysts were the two halves of the same amethyst. When joined, they formed one and the same bead.

There was a long pause, laden with excitement and mystery. Then, speaking in a low voice:

"I do not know either exactly where this trinket comes from," Captain Belval said. "Ever since I was a child, I used to see it among other things of trifling value which I kept in a cardboard box: watch-keys, old rings, old-fashioned seals. I picked out these trinkets from among them two or three years ago. Where does this one come from? I don't know. But what I do know . . ."

He had separated the two pieces and, examining them carefully, concluded:

"What I do know, beyond a doubt, is that the largest bead in this rosary came off one day and broke; and that the other, with its setting, went to form the trinket which I now have. You and I therefore possess the two halves of a thing which somebody else possessed twenty years ago."

He went up to her and, in the same low and rather serious voice, said:

"You protested just now when I declared my faith in destiny and my certainty that events were leading us towards each other. Do you still deny it? For, after all, this is either an accident so extraordinary that we have no right to admit it or an actual fact which proves that our two lives have already touched in the past at some mysterious point and that they will meet again in the future, never to part. And that is why, without waiting for the perhaps distant future, I offer you to-day, when danger hangs over you, the support of my friendship. Observe that I am no longer speaking of love but only of friendship. Do you accept?"

She was nonplussed and so much perturbed by that miracle of the two broken amethysts, fitting each other exactly, that she appeared not to hear Belval's voice.

"Do you accept?" he repeated.

After a moment she replied:

"No."

"Then the proof which destiny has given you of its wishes does not satisfy you?" he said, good-humoredly.

"We must not see each other again," she declared.

"Very well. I will leave it to chance. It will not be for long. Meanwhile, I promise to make no effort to see you."

"Nor to find out my name?"

"Yes, I promise you."

"Good-by," she said, giving him her hand.

"*Au revoir*," he answered.

She moved away. When she reached the door, she seemed to hesitate. He was standing motionless by the chimney. Once more she said:

"Good-by."

"*Au revoir*, Little Mother Coralie,"

Then she went out.

Only when the street-door had closed behind her did Captain Belval go to one of the windows. He saw Coralie passing through the trees, looking quite small in the surrounding darkness. He felt a pang at his heart. Would he ever see her again?

"Shall I? Rather!" he exclaimed. "Why, to-morrow perhaps. Am I not the favorite of the gods?"

And, taking his stick, he set off, as he said, with his wooden leg foremost.

That evening, after dining at the nearest restaurant, Captain Belval went to Neuilly. The home run in connection with the hospital was a pleasant villa on the Boulevard Maillot, looking out on the Bois de Boulogne. Discipline was not too strictly enforced. The captain could come in at any hour of the night; and the man easily obtained leave from the matron.

"Is Ya-Bon there?" he asked this lady.

"Yes, he's playing cards with his sweetheart."

"He has the right to love and be loved," he said. "Any letters for me?"

"No, only a parcel."

"From whom?"

"A commissionaire brought it and just said that it was 'for Captain Belval.' I put it in your room."

The officer went up to his bedroom on the top floor and saw the parcel, done up in paper and string, on the table. He opened it and discovered a box. The box contained a key, a large, rusty key, of a shape and manufacture that were obviously old.

What could it all mean? There was no address on the box and no mark. He presumed that there was some mistake which would come to light of itself; and he slipped the key into his pocket.

"Enough riddles for one day," he thought. "Let's go to bed."

But when he went to the window to draw the curtains he saw, across the trees of the Bois, a cascade of sparks which spread to some distance in the dense blackness of the night. And he remembered the conversation which he had overheard in the restaurant and the rain of sparks mentioned by the men who were plotting to kidnap Little Mother Coralie. . . .

CHAPTER III
THE RUSTY KEY

When Patrice Belval was eight years old he was sent from Paris, where he had lived till then, to a French boarding-school in London. Here he remained for ten years. At first he used to hear from his father weekly. Then, one day, the head-master told him that he was an orphan, that provision had been made for the cost of his education and that, on his majority, he would receive through an English solicitor his paternal inheritance, amounting to some eight thousand pounds.

Two hundred thousand francs could never be enough for a young man who soon proved himself to possess expensive tastes and who, when sent to Algeria to perform his military service, found means to run up twenty thousand francs of debts before coming into his money. He therefore started by squandering his patrimony and, having done so, settled down to work. Endowed with an active temperament and an ingenious brain, possessing no special vocation, but capable of anything that calls for initiative and resolution, full of ideas, with both the will and the knowledge to carry out an enterprise, he inspired confidence in others, found capital as he needed it and started one venture after another, including electrical schemes, the purchase of rivers and waterfalls, the organization of motor services in the colonies, of steamship lines and of mining companies. In a few years he had floated a dozen of such enterprises, all of which succeeded.

The war came to him as a wonderful adventure. He flung himself into it with heart and soul. As a sergeant in a colonial regiment, he won his lieutenant's stripes on the Marne. He was wounded in the calf on the 15th of September and had it amputated the same day. Two months after, by some mysterious wirepulling, cripple though he was, he began to go up as observer in the aeroplane of one of our best pilots. A shrapnel-shell put an end to the exploits of both heroes on the 10th of January. This time, Captain Belval, suffering from a serious wound in the head, was discharged and sent to the hospital in the Avenue des Champs-Élysées. About the same period, the lady whom he was to call Little Mother Coralie also entered the hospital as a nurse.

There he was trepanned. The operation was successful, but complications remained. He suffered a good deal of pain, though he never uttered a complaint and, in fact, with his own good-humor kept up the spirits of his companions in misfortune, all of whom were devoted to him. He made them laugh, consoled them and stimulated them with his cheeriness and his constant happy manner of facing the worst positions.

Not one of them is ever likely to forget the way in which he received a manufacturer who called to sell him a mechanical leg:

"Aha, a mechanical leg! And what for, sir? To take in people, I suppose, so that they may not notice that I've lost a bit of mine? Then you consider, sir, that it's a blemish to have your leg amputated, and that I, a French officer, ought to hide it as a disgrace?"

"Not at all, captain. Still . . ."

"And what's the price of that apparatus of yours?"

"Five hundred francs."

"Five hundred francs! And you think me capable of spending five hundred francs on a mechanical leg, when there are a hundred thousand poor devils who have been wounded as I have and who will have to go on showing their wooden stumps?"

The men sitting within hearing reveled with delight. Little Mother Coralie herself listened with a smile. And what would Patrice Belval not have given for a smile from Little Mother Coralie?

As he told her, he had fallen in love with her from the first, touched by her appealing beauty, her artless grace, her soft eyes, her gentle soul, which seemed to bend over the patients and to fondle them like a soothing caress. From the very first, the charm of her stole into his being and at the same time compassed it about. Her voice gave him new life. She bewitched him with the glance of her eyes and with her fragrant presence. And yet, while yielding to the empire of this love, he had an immense craving to devote himself to and to place his strength at the service of this delicate little creature, whom he felt to be surrounded with danger.

And now events were proving that he was right, the danger was taking definite shape and he had had the happiness to snatch Coralie from the grasp of her enemies. He rejoiced at the result of the first battle, but could not look upon it as over. The attacks were bound to be repeated. And even now was he not entitled to ask himself if there was not some close connection between the plot prepared against Coralie that morning and the sort of signal given by the shower of sparks? Did the two facts announced by the speakers at the restaurant not form part of the same suspicious machination?

The sparks continued to glitter in the distance. So far as Patrice Belval could judge, they came from the riverside, at some spot between two extreme points which might be the Trocadéro on the left and the Gare de Passy on the right.

"A mile or two at most, as the crow flies," he said to himself. "Why not go there? We'll soon see."

A faint light filtered through the key-hole of a door on the second floor. It was Ya-Bon's room; and the matron had told him that Ya-Bon was playing cards with his sweetheart. He walked in.

Ya-Bon was no longer playing. He had fallen asleep in an armchair, in front of the outspread cards, and on the pinned-back sleeve hanging from his left shoulder lay the head of a woman, an appallingly common head, with lips as thick as Ya-Bon's, revealing a set of black teeth, and with a yellow, greasy skin that seemed soaked in oil. It was Angèle, the kitchen-maid, Ya-Bon's sweetheart. She snored aloud.

Patrice looked at them contentedly. The sight confirmed the truth of his theories. If Ya-Bon could find some one to care for him, might not the most sadly mutilated heroes aspire likewise to all the joys of love?

He touched the Senegalese on the shoulder. Ya-Bon woke up and smiled, or rather, divining the presence of his captain, smiled even before he woke.

"I want you, Ya-Bon."

Ya-Bon uttered a grunt of pleasure and gave a push to Angèle, who fell over on the table and went on snoring.

Coming out of the house, Patrice saw no more sparks. They were hidden behind the trees. He walked along the boulevard and, to save time, went by the Ceinture railway to the Avenue Henri-Martin. Here he turned down the Rue de la Tour, which runs to Passy.

On the way he kept talking to Ya-Bon about what he had in his mind, though he well knew that the negro did not understand much of what he said. But this was a habit with him. Ya-Bon, first his comrade-in-arms and then his orderly, was as devoted to him as a dog. He had lost a limb on the same day as his officer and was wounded in the head on the same day; he believed himself destined to undergo the same experiences throughout; and he rejoiced at having been twice wounded just as he would have rejoiced at dying at the same time as Captain Belval. On his side, the captain rewarded this humble, dumb devotion by unbending genially to his companion; he treated him with an ironical and sometimes impatient humor which heightened the negro's love for him. Ya-Bon played the part of the passive confidant who is consulted without being regarded and who is made to bear the brunt of his interlocutor's hasty temper.

"What do you think of all this, Master Ya-Bon?" asked the captain, walking arm-in-arm with him. "I have an idea that it's all part of the same business. Do you think so too?"

Ya-Bon had two grunts, one of which meant yes, the other no. He grunted out:

"Yes."

"So there's no doubt about it," the officer declared, "and we must admit that Little Mother Coralie is threatened with a fresh danger. Is that so?"

"Yes," grunted Ya-Bon, who always approved, on principle.

"Very well. It now remains to be seen what that shower of sparks means. I thought for a moment that, as we had our first visit from the Zeppelins a week ago . . . are you listening to me?"

"Yes."

"I thought that it was a treacherous signal with a view to a second Zeppelin visit . . ."

"Yes."

"No, you idiot, it's not yes. How could it be a Zeppelin signal when, according to the conversation which I overheard, the signal had already been given twice before the war. Besides, is it really a signal?"

"No."

"How do you mean, no? What else could it be, you silly ass? You'd do better to hold your tongue and listen to me, all the more as you don't even know what it's all about. . . . No more do I, for that matter, and I confess that I'm at an utter loss. Lord, it's a complicated business, and I'm not much of a hand at solving these problems."

Patrice Belval was even more perplexed when he came to the bottom of the Rue de la Tour. There were several roads in front of him, and he did not know which to take. Moreover, though he was in the middle of Passy, not a spark shone in the dark sky.

"It's finished, I expect," he said, "and we've had our trouble for nothing. It's your fault, Ya-Bon. If you hadn't made me lose precious moments in snatching you from the arms of your beloved we should have arrived in time. I admit Angèle's charms, but, after all . . ."

He took his bearings, feeling more and more undecided. The expedition undertaken on chance and with insufficient information was certainly yielding no results; and he was thinking of abandoning it when a closed private car came out of the Rue Franklin, from the direction of the Trocadéro, and some one inside shouted through the speaking-tube:

"Bear to the left . . . and then straight on, till I stop you."

Now it appeared to Captain Belval that this voice had the same foreign inflection as one of those which he had heard that morning at the restaurant.

"Can it be the beggar in the gray hat," he muttered, "one of those who tried to carry off Little Mother Coralie?"

"Yes," grunted Ya-Bon.

"Yes. The signal of the sparks explains his presence in these parts. We mustn't lose sight of this track. Off with you, Ya-Bon."

But there was no need for Ya-Bon to hurry. The car had gone down the Rue Raynouard, and Belval himself arrived just as it was stopping three or four hundred yards from the turning, in front of a large carriage-entrance on the left-hand side.

Five men alighted. One of them rang. Thirty or forty seconds passed. Then Patrice heard the bell tinkle a second time. The five men waited, standing packed close together on the pavement. At last, after a third ring, a small wicket contrived in one of the folding-doors was opened.

There was a pause and some argument. Whoever had opened the wicket appeared to be asking for explanations. But suddenly two of the men bore heavily on the folding-door, which gave way before their thrust and let the whole gang through.

There was a loud noise as the door slammed to. Captain Belval at once studied his surroundings.

The Rue Raynouard is an old country-road which at one time used to wind among the houses and gardens of the village of Passy, on the side of the hills bathed by the Seine. In certain places, which unfortunately are becoming more and more rare, it has retained a provincial aspect. It is skirted by old properties. Old houses stand hidden amidst the trees: that in which Balzac lived has been piously preserved. It was in this street that the mysterious garden lay where Arsène Lupin discovered a farmer-general's diamonds hidden in a crack of an old sundial.

The Confessions of Arsène Lupin. By Maurice Leblanc. Translated by Alexander Teixeira de Mattos. III. *The Sign of the Shadow.*

The car was still standing outside the house into which the five men had forced their way; and this prevented Patrice Belval from coming nearer. It was built in continuation of a wall and seemed to be one of the private mansions dating back to the First Empire. It had a very long front with two rows of round windows, protected by gratings on the ground-floor and solid shutters on the story above. There was another building farther down, forming a separate wing.

"There's nothing to be done on this side," said the captain. "It's as impregnable as a feudal stronghold. Let's look elsewhere."

From the Rue Raynouard, narrow lanes, which used to divide the old properties, make their way down to the river. One of them skirted the wall that preceded the house. Belval turned down it with Ya-Bon. It was constructed of ugly pointed pebbles, was broken into steps and faintly lighted by the gleam of a street-lamp.

"Lend me a hand, Ya-Bon. The wall is too high. But perhaps with the aid of the lamp-post . . ."

Assisted by the negro, he hoisted himself to the lamp and was stretching out one of his hands when he noticed that all this part of the wall bristled with broken glass, which made it absolutely impossible to grasp. He slid down again.

"Upon my word, Ya-Bon," he said, angrily, "you might have warned me! Another second and you would have made me cut my hands to pieces. What are you thinking of? In fact, I can't imagine what made you so anxious to come with me at all costs."

There was a turn in the lane, hiding the light, so that they were now in utter darkness, and Captain Belval had to grope his way along. He felt the negro's hand come down upon his shoulder.

"What do you want, Ya-Bon?"

The hand pushed him against the wall. At this spot there was a door in an embrasure.

"Well, yes," he said, "that's a door. Do you think I didn't see it? Oh, no one has eyes but Master Ya-Bon, I suppose."

Ya-Bon handed him a box of matches. He struck several, one after the other, and examined the door.

"What did I tell you?" he said between his teeth. "There's nothing to be done. Massive wood, barred and studded with iron. . . . Look, there's no handle on this side, merely a key-hole. . . . Ah, what we want is a key, made to measure and cut for the purpose! . . . For instance, a key like the one which the commissionaire left for me at the home just now. . . ."

He stopped. An absurd idea flitted through his brain; and yet, absurd as it was, he felt that he was bound to perform the trifling action which it suggested to him. He therefore retraced his steps. He had the key on him. He took it from his pocket.

He struck a fresh light. The key-hole appeared. Belval inserted the key at the first attempt. He bore on it to the left: the key turned in the lock. He pushed the door: it opened.

"Come along in," he said.

The negro did not stir a foot. Patrice could understand his amazement. All said, he himself was equally amazed. By what unprecedented miracle was the key just the key of this very door? By what miracle was the unknown person who had sent it him able to guess that he would be in a position to use it without further instructions? A miracle indeed!

But Patrice had resolved to act without trying to solve the riddle which a mischievous chance seemed bent upon setting him.

"Come along in," he repeated, triumphantly.

Branches struck him in the face and he perceived that he was walking on grass and that there must be a garden lying in front of him. It was so dark that he could not see the paths against the blackness of the turf; and, after walking for a minute or two, he hit his foot against some rocks with a sheet of water on them.

"Oh, confound it!" he cursed. "I'm all wet. Damn you, Ya-Bon!"

He had not finished speaking when a furious barking was heard at the far end of the garden; and the sound at once came nearer, with extreme rapidity. Patrice realized that a watchdog, perceiving their presence, was rushing upon them, and, brave as he was, he shuddered, because of the impressiveness of this attack in complete darkness. How was he to defend himself? A shot would betray them; and yet he carried no weapon but his revolver.

The dog came dashing on, a powerful animal, to judge by the noise it made, suggesting the rush of a wild boar through the copsewood. It must have broken its chain, for it was accompanied by the clatter of iron. Patrice braced himself to meet it. But through the darkness he saw Ya-Bon pass before him to protect him, and the impact took place almost at once.

"Here, I say, Ya-Bon! Why did you get in front of me? It's all right, my lad, I'm coming!"

The two adversaries had rolled over on the grass. Patrice stooped down, seeking to rescue the negro. He touched the hair of an animal and then Ya-Bon's clothes. But the two were wriggling on the ground in so compact a mass and fighting so frantically that his interference was useless.

Moreover, the contest did not last long. In a few minutes the adversaries had ceased to move. A strangled death-rattle issued from the group.

"Is it all right, Ya-Bon?" whispered the captain, anxiously.

The negro stood up with a grunt. By the light of a match Patrice saw that he was holding at the end of his outstretched arm, of the one arm with which he had had to defend himself, a huge dog, which was gurgling, clutched round the throat by Ya-Bon's implacable fingers. A broken chain hung from its neck.

"Thank you, Ya-Bon. I've had a narrow escape. You can let him go now. He can't do us any harm, I think."

Ya-Bon obeyed. But he had no doubt squeezed too tight. The dog writhed for a moment on the grass, gave a few moans and then lay without moving.

"Poor brute!" said Patrice. "After all, he only did his duty in going for the burglars that we are. Let us do ours, Ya-Bon, which is nothing like as plain."

Something that shone like a window-pane guided his steps and led him, by a series of stairs cut in the rocks and of successive terraces, to the level ground on which the house was built. On this side also, all the windows were round and high up, like those in the streets, and barricaded with shutters. But one of them allowed the light which he had seen from below to filter through.

Telling Ya-Bon to hide in the shrubberies, he went up to the house, listened, caught an indistinct sound of voices, discovered that the shutters were too firmly closed to enable him either to see or to hear and, in this way, after the fourth window, reached a flight of steps. At the top of the steps was a door.

"Since they sent me the key of the garden," he said to himself, "there's no reason why this door, which leads from the house into the garden, should not be open."

It was open.

The voices indoors were now more clearly perceptible, and Belval observed that they reached him by the well of the staircase and that this staircase, which seemed to lead to an unoccupied part of the house, showed with an uncertain light above him.

He went up. A door stood ajar on the first floor. He slipped his head through the opening and went in. He found that he was on a narrow balcony which ran at mid-height around three sides of a large room, along book-shelves rising to the ceiling. Against the wall at either end of the room was an iron spiral staircase. Stacks of books were also piled against the bars of the railing which protected the gallery, thus hiding Patrice from the view of the people on the ground-floor, ten or twelve feet below.

He gently separated two of these stacks. At that moment the sound of voices suddenly increased to a great uproar and he saw five men, shouting like lunatics, hurl themselves upon a sixth and fling him to the ground before he had time to lift a finger in self-defense.

Belval's first impulse was to rush to the victim's rescue. With the aid of Ya-Bon, who would have hastened to his call, he would certainly have intimidated the five men. The reason why he did not act was that, at any rate, they were using no weapons and appeared to have no murderous intentions. After depriving their victim of all power of movement, they were content to hold him by the throat, shoulders and ankles. Belval wondered what would happen next.

One of the five drew himself up briskly and, in a tone of command, said:

"Bind him. . . . Put a gag in his mouth. . . . Or let him call out, if he wants to: there's no one to hear him."

Patrice at once recognized one of the voices which he had heard that morning in the restaurant. Its owner was a short, slim-built, well-dressed man, with an olive complexion and a cruel face.

"At last we've got him," he said, "the rascal! And I think we shall get him to speak this time. Are you prepared to go all lengths, friends?"

One of the other four growled, spitefully:

"Yes. And at once, whatever happens!"

The last speaker had a big black mustache; and Patrice recognized the other man whose conversation at the restaurant he had overheard, that is to say, one of Coralie's assailants, the one who had taken to flight. His gray-felt hat lay on a chair.

"All lengths, Bournef, whatever happens, eh?" grinned the leader. "Well, let's get on with the work. So you refuse to give up your secret, Essarès, old man? We shall have some fun."

All their movements must have been prepared beforehand and the parts carefully arranged, for the actions which they carried out were performed in an incredibly prompt and methodical fashion.

After the man was tied up, they lifted him into an easy-chair with a very low back, to which they fastened him round the chest and waist with a rope. His legs, which were bound together, were placed on the seat of a heavy chair of the same height as the arm-chair, with the two feet projecting. Then the victim's shoes and socks were removed.

"Roll him along!" said the leader.

Between two of the four windows that overlooked the chimney was a large fire-place, in which burnt a red coal-fire, white in places with the intense heat of the hearth. The men pushed the two chairs bearing the victim until his bare feet were within twenty inches of the blazing coals.

In spite of his gag, the man uttered a hideous yell of pain, while his legs, in spite of their bonds, succeeded in contracting and curling upon themselves.

"Go on!" shouted the leader, passionately. "Go on! Nearer!"

Patrice Belval grasped his revolver.

"Oh, I'm going on too!" he said to himself. "I won't let that wretch be . . ."

But, at this very moment, when he was on the point of drawing himself up and acting, a chance movement made him behold the most extraordinary and unexpected sight. Opposite him, on the other side of the room, in a part of the balcony corresponding with that where he was, he saw a woman's head, a head glued to the rails, livid and terror-stricken, with eyes wide-open in horror gazing frenziedly at the awful scene that was being enacted below by the glowing fire.

Patrice had recognized Little Mother Coralie.

CHAPTER IV
BEFORE THE FLAMES

Little Mother Coralie! Coralie concealed in this house into which her assailants had forced their way and in which she herself was hiding, through force of circumstances which were incapable of explanation.

His first idea, which would at least have solved one of the riddles, was that she also had entered from the lane, gone into the house by the steps and in this way opened a passage for him. But, in that case, how had she procured the means of carrying out this enterprise? And, above all, what brought her here?

All these questions occurred to Captain Belval's mind without his trying to reply to them. He was far too much impressed by the absorbed expression on Coralie's face. Moreover, a second cry, even wilder than the first, came from below; and he saw the victim's face writhing before the red curtain of fire from the hearth.

But, this time, Patrice, held back by Coralie's presence, had no inclination to go to the sufferer's assistance. He decided to model himself entirely upon her and not to move or do anything to attract her attention.

"Easy!" the leader commanded. "Pull him back. I expect he's had enough."

He went up to the victim:

"Well, my dear Essarès," he asked, "what do you think of it? Are you happy? And, you know, we're only beginning. If you don't speak, we shall go on to the end, as the real *chauffeurs* used to do in the days of the Revolution. So it's settled, I presume: you're going to speak?"

There was no answer. The leader rapped out an oath and went on:

"What do you mean? Do you refuse? But, you obstinate brute, don't you understand the situation? Or have you a glimmer of hope? Hope, indeed! You're mad. Who would rescue you? Your servants? The porter, the footman and the butler are in my pay. I gave them a week's notice. They're gone by now. The housemaid? The cook? They sleep at the other end of the house; and you yourself have told me, time after time, that one can't hear anything over there. Who else? Your wife? Her room also is far away; and she hasn't heard anything either? Siméon, your old secretary? We made him fast when he opened the front door to us just now. Besides, we may as well finish the job here. Bournef!"

The man with the big mustache, who was still holding the chair, drew himself up.

"Bournef, where did you lock up the secretary?"

"In the porter's lodge."

"You know where to find Mme. Essarès' bedroom?"

"Yes, you told me the way."

"Go, all four of you, and bring the lady and the secretary here!"

The four men went out by a door below the spot where Coralie was standing. They were hardly out of sight when the leader stooped eagerly over his victim and said:

"We're alone, Essarès. It's what I intended. Let's make the most of it."

He bent still lower and whispered so that Patrice found it difficult to hear what he said:

"Those men are fools. I twist them round my finger and tell them no more of my plans than I can help. You and I, on the other hand, Essarès, are the men to come to terms. That is what you refused to admit; and you see where it has landed you. Come, Essarès, don't be obstinate and don't shuffle. You are caught in a trap, you are helpless, you are absolutely in my power. Well, rather than allow yourself to be broken down by tortures which would certainly end by overcoming your resistance, strike a bargain with me. We'll go halves, shall we? Let's make peace and treat upon that basis. I'll give you a hand in my game and you'll give me one in yours. As allies, we are bound to win. As enemies, who knows whether the victor will surmount all the obstacles that will still stand in his path? That's why I say again, halves! Answer me. Yes or no."

He loosened the gag and listened. This time, Patrice did not hear the few words which the victim uttered. But the other, the leader, almost immediately burst into a rage:

"Eh? What's that you're proposing? Upon my word, but you're a cool hand! An offer of this kind to me! That's all very well for Bournef or his fellows. They'll understand, they will. But it won't do for me, it won't do for Colonel Fakhi. No, no, my friend, I open my mouth wider! I'll consent to go halves, but accept an alms, never!"

Patrice listened eagerly and, at the same time, kept his eyes on Coralie, whose face still contorted with anguish, wore an expression of the same rapt attention. And he looked back at the victim, part of whose body was reflected in the glass above the mantelpiece. The man was dressed in a braided brown-velvet smoking-suit and appeared to be about fifty years of age, quite bald, with a fleshy face, a large hooked nose, eyes deep set under a pair of thick eyebrows and puffy cheeks covered with a thick grizzled beard. Patrice was also able to examine his features more closely in a portrait of him which hung to the left of the fireplace, between the first and second windows, and which represented a strong, powerful countenance with an almost fierce expression.

"It's an Eastern face," said Patrice to himself. "I've seen heads like that in Egypt and Turkey."

The names of all these men too—Colonel Fakhi, Mustapha, Bournef, Essarès—their accent in talking, their way of holding themselves, their features, their figures, all recalled impressions which he had gathered in the Near East, in the hotels at Alexandria or on the banks of the Bosphorus, in the bazaars of Adrianople or in the Greek boats that plow the Ægean Sea. They were Levantine types, but of Levantines who had taken root in Paris. Essarès Bey was a name which Patrice recognized as well-known in the financial world, even as he knew that of Colonel Fakhi, whose speech and intonation marked him for a seasoned Parisian.

But a sound of voices came from outside the door. It was flung open violently and the four men appeared, dragging in a bound man, whom they dropped to the floor as they entered.

"Here's old Siméon," cried the one whom Fakhi had addressed as Bournef.

"And the wife?" asked the leader. "I hope you've got her too!"

"Well, no."

"What is that? Has she escaped?"

"Yes, through her window."

"But you must run after her. She can only be in the garden. Remember, the watch-dog was barking just now."

"And suppose she's got away?"

"How?"

"By the door on the lane?"

"Impossible!"

"Why?"

"The door hasn't been used for years. There's not even a key to it."

"That's as may be," Bournef rejoined. "All the same, we're surely not going to organize a battue with lanterns and rouse the whole district for the sake of finding a woman . . ."

"Yes, but that woman . . ."

Colonel Fakhi seemed exasperated. He turned to the prisoner:

"You're in luck, you old rascal! This is the second time to-day that minx of yours has slipped through my fingers! Did she tell you what happened this afternoon? Oh, if it hadn't been for an infernal officer who happened to be passing! . . . But I'll get hold of him yet and he shall pay dearly for his interference. . . ."

Patrice clenched his fists with fury. He understood: Coralie was hiding in her own house. Surprised by the sudden arrival of the five men, she had managed to climb out of her window and, making her way along the terrace to the steps, had gone to the part of the house opposite the rooms that were in use and taken refuge in the gallery of the library, where she was able to witness the terrible assault levied at her husband.

"Her husband!" thought Patrice, with a shudder. "Her husband!"

And, if he still entertained any doubts on the subject, the hurried course of events soon removed them, for the leader began to chuckle:

"Yes, Essarès, old man, I confess that she attracts me more than I can tell you; and, as I failed to catch her earlier in the day, I did hope this evening, as soon as I had settled my business with you, to settle something infinitely more agreeable with your wife. Not to mention that, once in my power, the little woman would be serving me as a hostage and that I would only have restored her to you—oh, safe and sound, believe me!—after specific performance of our agreement. And you would have run straight, Essarès! For you love your Coralie passionately! And quite right too!"

He went to the right-hand side of the fireplace and, touching a switch, lit an electric lamp under a reflector between the third and fourth windows. There was a companion picture here to Essarès' portrait, but it was covered over. The leader drew the curtain, and Coralie appeared in the full light.

"The monarch of all she surveys! The idol! The witch! The pearl of pearls! The imperial diamond of Essarès Bey, banker! Isn't she beautiful? I ask you. Admire the delicate outline of her face, the purity of that oval; and the pretty neck; and those graceful shoulders. Essarès, there's not a favorite in the country we come from who can hold a candle to your Coralie! My Coralie, soon! For I shall know how to find her. Ah, Coralie, Coralie! . . ."

Patrice looked across at her, and it seemed to him that her face was reddened with a blush of shame. He himself was shaken by indignation and anger at each insulting word. It was a violent enough sorrow to him to know that Coralie was the wife of another; and added to this sorrow was his rage at seeing her thus exposed to these men's gaze and promised as a helpless prey to whosoever should prove himself the strongest.

At the same time, he wondered why Coralie remained in the room. Supposing that she could not leave the garden, nevertheless she was free to move about in that part of the house and might well have opened a window and called for help. What prevented her from doing so? Of course she did not love her husband. If she had loved him, she would have faced every danger to defend him. But how was it possible for her to allow that man to be tortured, worse still, to be present at his sufferings, to contemplate that most hideous of sights and to listen to his yells of pain?

"Enough of this nonsense!" cried the leader, pulling the curtain back into its place. "Coralie, you shall be my final reward; but I must first win you. Comrades, to work; let's finish our friend's job. First of all, twenty inches nearer, no more. Good! Does it burn, Essarès? All the same, it's not more than you can stand. Bear up, old fellow."

He unfastened the prisoner's right arm, put a little table by his side, laid a pencil and paper on it and continued:

"There's writing-materials for you. As your gag prevents you from speaking, write. You know what's wanted of you, don't you? Scribble a few letters, and you're free. Do you consent? No? Comrades, three inches nearer."

He moved away and stooped over the secretary, whom Patrice, by the brighter light, had recognized as the old fellow who sometimes escorted Coralie to the hospital.

"As for you, Siméon," he said, "you shall come to no harm. I know that you are devoted to your master, but I also know that he tells you none of his private affairs. On the other hand, I am certain that you will keep silent as to all this, because a single word of betrayal would involve your master's ruin even more than ours. That's understood between us, isn't it? Well, why don't you answer? Have they squeezed your throat a bit too tight with their cords? Wait, I'll give you some air. . . ."

Meanwhile the ugly work at the fireplace pursued its course. The two feet were reddened by the heat until it seemed almost as though the bright flames of the fire were glowing through them. The sufferer exerted all his strength in trying to bend his legs and to draw back; and a dull, continuous moan came through his gag.

"Oh, hang it all!" thought Patrice. "Are we going to let him roast like this, like a chicken on a spit?"

He looked at Coralie. She did not stir. Her face was distorted beyond recognition, and her eyes seemed fascinated by the terrifying sight.

"Couple of inches nearer!" cried the leader, from the other end of the room, as he unfastened Siméon's bonds.

The order was executed. The victim gave such a yell that Patrice's blood froze in his veins. But, at the same moment, he became aware of something that had not struck him so far, or at least he had attached no significance to it. The prisoner's hand, as the result of a sequence of little movements apparently due to nervous twitches, had seized the opposite edge of the table, while his arm rested on the marble top. And gradually, unseen by the torturers, all whose efforts were directed to keeping his legs in position, or by the leader, who was still engaged with Siméon, this hand opened a drawer which swung on a hinge, dipped into the drawer, took out a revolver and, resuming its original position with a jerk, hid the weapon in the chair.

The act, or rather the intention which it indicated, was foolhardy in the extreme, for, when all was said, reduced to his present state of helplessness, the man could not hope for victory against five adversaries, all free and all armed. Nevertheless, as Patrice looked at the glass in which he beheld him, he saw a fierce determination pictured in the man's face.

"Another two inches," said Colonel Fakhi, as he walked back to the fireplace.

He examined the condition of the flesh and said, with a laugh:

"The skin is blistering in places; the veins are ready to burst. Essarès Bey, you can't be enjoying yourself, and it strikes me that you mean to do the right thing at last. Have you started scribbling yet? No? And don't you mean to? Are you still hoping? Counting on your wife, perhaps? Come, come, you must see that, even if she has succeeded in escaping, she won't say anything! Well, then, are you humbugging me, or what? . . ."

He was seized with a sudden burst of rage and shouted:

"Shove his feet into the fire! And let's have a good smell of burning for once! Ah, you would defy me, would you? Well, wait a bit, old chap, and let me have a go at you! I'll cut you off an ear or two: you know, the way we have in our country!"

He drew from his waistcoat a dagger that gleamed in the firelight. His face was hideous with animal cruelty. He gave a fierce cry, raised his arm and stood over the other relentlessly.

But, swift as his movement was, Essarès was before him. The revolver, quickly aimed, was discharged with a loud report. The dagger dropped from the colonel's hand. For two or three seconds he maintained his threatening attitude, with one arm lifted on high and a haggard look in his eyes, as though he did not quite understand what had happened to him. And then, suddenly, he fell upon his victim in a huddled heap, paralyzing his arm with the full weight of his body, at the moment when Essarès was taking aim at one of the other confederates.

He was still breathing:

"Oh, the brute, the brute!" he panted. "He's killed me! . . . But you'll lose by it, Essarès. . . . I was prepared for this. If I don't come home to-night, the prefect of police will receive a letter. . . . They'll know about your treason, Essarès . . . all your story . . . your plans. . . . Oh, you devil! . . . And what a fool! . . . We could so easily have come to terms. . . ."

He muttered a few inaudible words and rolled down to the floor. It was all over.

A moment of stupefaction was produced not so much by this unexpected tragedy as by the revelation which the leader had made before dying and by the thought of that letter, which no doubt implicated the aggressors as well as their victim. Bournef had disarmed Essarès. The latter, now that the chair was no longer held in position, had succeeded in bending his legs. No one moved.

Meanwhile, the sense of terror which the whole scene had produced seemed rather to increase with the silence. On the ground was the corpse, with the blood flowing on the carpet. Not far away lay Siméon's motionless form. Then there was the prisoner, still bound in front of the flames waiting to devour his flesh. And standing near him were the four butchers, hesitating perhaps what to do next, but showing in every feature an implacable resolution to defeat the enemy by all and every means.

His companions glanced at Bournef, who seemed the kind of man to go any length. He was a short, stout, powerfully-built man; his upper lip bristled with the mustache which had attracted Patrice Belval's attention. He was less cruel in appearance than his chief, less elegant in his manner and less masterful, but displayed far greater coolness and self-command. As for the colonel, his accomplices seemed not to trouble about him. The part which they were playing dispensed them from showing any empty compassion.

At last Bournef appeared to have made up his mind how to act. He went to his hat, the gray-felt hat lying near the door, turned back the lining and took from it a tiny coil the sight of which made Patrice start. It was a slender red cord, exactly like that which he had found round the neck of Mustapha Rovalaïof, the first accomplice captured by Ya-Bon.

Bournef unrolled the cord, took it by the two buckles, tested its strength across his knee and then, going back to Essarès, slipped it over his neck after first removing his gag.

"Essarès," he said, with a calmness which was more impressive than the colonel's violence and sneers, "Essarès, I shall not put you to any pain. Torture is a revolting process; and I shall not have recourse to it. You know what to do; I know what to do. A word on your side, an action on my side; and the thing is done. The word is the yes or no which you will now speak. The action which I shall accomplish in reply to your yes or no will mean either your release or else . . ."

He stopped for a second or two. Then he declared:

"Or else your death."

The brief phrase was uttered very simply but with a firmness that gave it the full significance of an irrevocable sentence. It was clear that Essarès was faced with a catastrophe which he could no longer avoid save by submitting absolutely. In less than a minute, he would have spoken or he would be dead.

Once again Patrice fixed his eyes on Coralie, ready to interfere should he perceive in her any other feeling than one of passive terror. But her attitude did not change. She was therefore accepting the worst, it appeared, even though this meant her husband's death; and Patrice held his hand accordingly.

"Are we all agreed?" Bournef asked, turning to his accomplices.

"Quite," said one of them.

"Do you take your share of the responsibility?"

"We do."

Bournef brought his hands together and crossed them, which had the result of knotting the cord round Essarès' neck. Then he pulled slightly, so as to make the pressure felt, and asked, unemotionally:

"Yes or no?"

"Yes."

There was a murmur of satisfaction. The accomplices heaved a breath; and Bournef nodded his head with an air of approval:

"Ah, so you accept! It was high time: I doubt if any one was ever nearer death than you were, Essarès." Retaining his hold of the cord, he continued, "Very well. You will speak. But I know you; and your answer surprises me, for I told the colonel that not even the certainty of death would make you confess your secret. Am I wrong?"

"No," replied Essarès. "Neither death nor torture."

"Then you have something different to propose?"

"Yes."

"Something worth our while?"

"Yes. I suggested it to the colonel just now, when you were out of the room. But, though he was willing to betray you and go halves with me in the secret, he refused the other thing."

"Why should I accept it?"

"Because you must take it or leave it and because you will understand what he did not."

"It's a compromise, I suppose?"

"Yes."

"Money?"

"Yes."

Bournef shrugged his shoulders:

"A few thousand-franc notes, I expect. And you imagine that Bournef and his friends will be such fools? . . . Come, Essarès, why do you want us to compromise? We know your secret almost entirely. . . ."

"You know what it is, but not how to use it. You don't know how to get at it; and that's just the point."

"We shall discover it."

"Never."

668

"Yes, your death will make it easier for us."

"My death? Thanks to the information lodged by the colonel, in a few hours you will be tracked down and most likely caught: in any case, you will be unable to pursue your search. Therefore you have hardly any choice. It's the money which I'm offering you, or else . . . prison."

"And, if we accept," asked Bournef, to whom the argument seemed to appeal, "when shall we be paid?"

"At once."

"Then the money is here?"

"Yes."

"A contemptible sum, as I said before?"

"No, a much larger sum than you hope for; infinitely larger."

"How much?"

"Four millions."

CHAPTER V
HUSBAND AND WIFE

The accomplices started, as though they had received an electric shock. Bournef darted forward:

"What did you say?"

"I said four millions, which means a million for each of you."

"Look here! . . . Do you mean it? . . . Four millions? . . ."

"Four millions is what I said."

The figure was so gigantic and the proposal so utterly unexpected that the accomplices had the same feeling which Patrice Belval on his side underwent. They suspected a trap; and Bournef could not help saying:

"The offer is more than we expected. . . . And I am wondering what induced you to make it."

"Would you have been satisfied with less?"

"Yes," said Bournef, candidly.

"Unfortunately, I can't make it less. I have only one means of escaping death; and that is to open my safe for you. And my safe contains four bundles of a thousand bank-notes each."

Bournef could not get over his astonishment and became more and more suspicious.

"How do you know that, after taking the four millions, we shall not insist on more?"

"Insist on what? The secret of the site?"

"Yes."

"Because you know that I would as soon die as tell it you. The four millions are the maximum. Do you want them or don't you? I ask for no promise in return, no oath of any kind, for I am convinced that, when you have filled your pockets, you will have but one thought, to clear off, without handicapping yourselves with a murder which might prove your undoing."

The argument was so unanswerable that Bournef ceased discussing and asked:

"Is the safe in this room?"

"Yes, between the first and second windows, behind my portrait."

Bournef took down the picture and said:

"I see nothing."

"It's all right. The lines of the safe are marked by the moldings of the central panel. In the middle you will see what looks like a rose, not of wood but of iron; and there are four others at the four corners of the panel. These four turn to the right, by successive notches, forming a word which is the key to the lock, the word Cora."

"The first four letters of Coralie?" asked Bournef, following Essarès' instructions as he spoke.

"No," said Essarès Bey, "the first four letters of the Coran. Have you done that?"

After a moment, Bournef answered:

"Yes, I've finished. And the key?"

"There's no key. The fifth letter of the word, the letter N, is the letter of the central rose."

Bournef turned this fifth rose; and presently a click was heard.

"Now pull," said Essarès. "That's it. The safe is not deep: it's dug in one of the stones of the front wall. Put in your hand. You'll find four pocket-books."

It must be admitted that Patrice Belval expected to see something startling interrupt Bournef's quest and hurl him into some pit suddenly opened by Essarès' trickery. And the three confederates seemed to share this unpleasant apprehension, for they were gray in the face, while Bournef himself appeared to be working very cautiously and suspiciously.

At last he turned round and came and sat beside Essarès. In his hands he held a bundle of four pocket-books, short but extremely bulky and bound together with a canvas strap. He unfastened the buckle of the strap and opened one of the pocket-books.

His knees shook under their precious burden, and, when he had taken a huge sheaf of notes from one of the compartments, his hands were like the hands of a very old man trembling with fever.

"Thousand-franc notes," he murmured. "Ten packets of thousand-franc notes."

Brutally, like men prepared to fight one another, each of the other three laid hold of a pocket-book, felt inside and mumbled:

"Ten packets . . . they're all there. . . . Thousand-franc notes . . ."

And one of them forthwith cried, in a choking voice:

"Let's clear out! . . . Let's go!"

A sudden fear was sending them off their heads. They could not imagine that Essarès would hand over such a fortune to them unless he had some plan which would enable him to recover it before they had left the room. That was a certainty. The ceiling would come down on their heads. The walls would close up and crush them to death, while sparing their unfathomable adversary.

Nor had Patrice Belval any doubt of it. The disaster was preparing. Essarès' revenge was inevitably at hand. A man like him, a fighter as able as he appeared to be, does not so easily surrender four million francs if he has not some scheme at the back of his head. Patrice felt himself breathing heavily. His present excitement was more violent than any with which he had thrilled since the very beginning of the tragic scenes which he had been witnessing; and he saw that Coralie's face was as anxious as his own.

Meanwhile Bournef partially recovered his composure and, holding back his companions, said:

"Don't be such fools! He would be capable, with old Siméon, of releasing himself and running after us."

Using only one hand, for the other was clutching a pocket-book, all four fastened Essarès' arm to the chair, while he protested angrily:

"You idiots! You came here to rob me of a secret of immense importance, as you well knew, and you lose your heads over a trifle of four millions. Say what you like, the colonel had more backbone than that!"

They gagged him once more and Bournef gave him a smashing blow with his fist which laid him unconscious.

"That makes our retreat safe," said Bournef.

"What about the colonel?" asked one of the others. "Are we to leave him here?"

"Why not?"

But apparently he thought this unwise; for he added:

"On second thoughts, no. It's not to our interest to compromise Essarès any further. What we must do, Essarès as well as ourselves, is to make ourselves scarce as fast as we can, before that damned letter of the colonel's is delivered at headquarters, say before twelve o'clock in the day."

"Then what do you suggest?"

"We'll take the colonel with us in the motor and drop him anywhere. The police must make what they can of it."

"And his papers?"

"We'll look through his pockets as we go. Lend me a hand."

They bandaged the wound to stop the flow of blood, took up the body, each holding it by an arm or leg, and walked out without any one of them letting go his pocket-book for a second.

Patrice Belval heard them pass through another room and then tramp heavily over the echoing flags of a hall.

"This is the moment," he said. "Essarès or Siméon will press a button and the rogues will be nabbed."

Essarès did not budge.

Siméon did not budge.

Patrice heard all the sounds accompanying their departure: the slamming of the carriage-gate, the starting-up of the engine and the drone of the car as it moved away. And that was all. Nothing had happened. The confederates were getting off with their four millions.

A long silence followed, during which Patrice remained on tenterhooks. He did not believe that the drama had reached its last phase; and he was so much afraid of the unexpected which might still occur that he determined to make Coralie aware of his presence.

A fresh incident prevented him. Coralie had risen to her feet.

Her face no longer wore its expression of horror and affright, but Patrice was perhaps more scared at seeing her suddenly animated with a sinister energy that gave an unwonted sparkle to her eyes and set her eyebrows and her lips twitching. He realized that Coralie was preparing to act.

In what way? Was this the end of the tragedy?

She walked to the corner on her side of the gallery where one of the two spiral staircases stood and went down slowly, without, however, trying to deaden the sound of her feet. Her husband could not help hearing her. Patrice, moreover, saw in the mirror that he had lifted his head and was following her with his eyes.

She stopped at the foot of the stairs. But there was no indecision in her attitude. Her plan was obviously quite clear; and she was only thinking out the best method of putting it into execution.

"Ah!" whispered Patrice to himself, quivering all over. "What are you doing, Little Mother Coralie?"

He gave a start. The direction in which Coralie's eyes were turned, together with the strange manner in which they stared, revealed her secret resolve to him. She had caught sight of the dagger, lying on the floor where it had slipped from the colonel's grasp.

Not for a second did Patrice believe that she meant to pick up that dagger with any other thought than to stab her husband. The intention of murder was so plainly written on her livid features that, even before she stirred a limb, Essarès was seized with a fit of terror and strained every muscle to break the bonds that hampered his movements.

She came forward, stopped once more and, suddenly bending, seized the dagger. Without waiting, she took two more steps. These brought her to the right of the chair in which Essarès lay. He had only to turn his head a little way to see her. And an awful minute passed, during which the husband and wife looked into each other's eyes.

The whirl of thoughts, of fear, of hatred, of vagrant and conflicting passions that passed through the brains of her who was about to kill and him who was about to die, was reproduced in Patrice Belval's mind and deep down in his inner consciousness. What was he to do? What part ought he to play in the tragedy that was being enacted before his eyes? Should he intervene? Was it his duty to prevent Coralie from committing the irreparable deed? Or should he commit it himself by breaking the man's head with a bullet from his revolver?

Yet, from the beginning, Patrice had really been swayed by a feeling which, mingling with all the others, gradually paralyzed him and rendered any inward struggle illusory: a feeling of curiosity driven to its utmost pitch. It was not the everyday curiosity of unearthing a squalid secret, but the higher curiosity of penetrating the mysterious soul of a woman whom he loved, who was carried away by the rush of events and who suddenly, becoming once more mistress of herself, was of her own accord and with impressive calmness taking the most fearful resolution. Thereupon other questions forced themselves upon him. What prompted her to take this resolution? Was it revenge? Was it punishment? Was it the gratification of hatred?

Patrice Belval remained where he was.

Coralie raised her arm. Her husband, in front of her, no longer even attempted to make those movements of despair which indicate a last effort. There was neither entreaty nor menace in his eyes. He waited in resignation.

Not far from them, old Siméon, still bound, half-lifted himself on his elbows and stared at them in dismay.

Coralie raised her arm again. Her whole frame seemed to grow larger and taller. An invisible force appeared to strengthen and stiffen her whole being, summoning all her energies to the service of her will. She was on the point of striking. Her eyes sought the place at which she should strike.

Yet her eyes became less hard and less dark. It even seemed to Patrice that there was a certain hesitation in her gaze and that she was recovering not her usual gentleness, but a little of her womanly grace.

"Ah, Little Mother Coralie," murmured Patrice, "you are yourself again! You are the woman I know. Whatever right you may think you have to kill that man, you will not kill him . . . and I prefer it so."

Slowly Coralie's arm dropped to her side. Her features relaxed. Patrice could guess the immense relief which she felt at escaping from the obsessing purpose that was driving her to murder. She looked at her dagger with astonishment, as though she were waking from a hideous nightmare. And, bending over her husband she began to cut his bonds.

She did so with visible repugnance, avoiding his touch, as it were, and shunning his eyes. The cords were severed one by one. Essarès was free.

What happened next was in the highest measure unexpected. With not a word of thanks to his wife, with not a word of anger either, this man who had just undergone the most cruel torture and whose body still throbbed with pain hurriedly tottered barefoot to a telephone standing on a table. He was like a hungry man who suddenly sees a piece of bread and snatches at it greedily as the means of saving himself and returning to life. Panting for breath, Essarès took down the receiver and called out:

"Central 40.39."

Then he turned abruptly to his wife:

"Go away," he said.

She seemed not to hear. She had knelt down beside old Siméon and was setting him free also.

Essarès at the telephone began to lose patience:

"Are you there? . . . Are you there? . . . I want that number to-day, please, not next week! It's urgent. . . . 40.39. . . . It's urgent, I tell you!"

And, turning to Coralie, he repeated, in an imperious tone:

"Go away!"

She made a sign that she would not go away and that, on the contrary, she meant to listen. He shook his fist at her and again said:

"Go away, go away! . . . I won't have you stay in the room. You go away too, Siméon."

Old Siméon got up and moved towards Essarès. It looked as though he wished to speak, no doubt to protest. But his action was undecided; and, after a moment's reflection, he turned to the door and went without uttering a word.

"Go away, will you, go away!" Essarès repeated, his whole body expressing menace.

But Coralie came nearer to him and crossed her arms obstinately and defiantly. At that moment, Essarès appeared to get his call, for he asked:

"Is that 40.39? Ah, yes . . ."

He hesitated. Coralie's presence obviously displeased him greatly, and he was about to say things which he did not wish her to know. But time, no doubt, was pressing. He suddenly made up his mind and, with both receivers glued to his ears, said, in English:

"Is that you, Grégoire? . . . Essarès speaking. . . . Hullo! . . . Yes, I'm speaking from the Rue Raynouard. . . . There's no time to lose. . . . Listen. . . ."

He sat down and went on:

"Look here. Mustapha's dead. So is the colonel. . . . Damn it, don't interrupt, or we're done for! . . . Yes, done for; and you too. . . . Listen, they all came, the colonel, Bournef, the whole gang, and robbed me by means of violence and threats. . . . I finished the colonel, only he had written to the police, giving us all away. The letter will be delivered soon. So you understand, Bournef and his three ruffians are going to disappear. They'll just run home and pack up their papers; and I reckon they'll be with you in an hour, or two hours at most. It's the refuge they're sure to make for. They prepared it themselves, without suspecting that you and I know each other. So there's no doubt about it. They're sure to come. . . ."

Essarès stopped. He thought for a moment and resumed:

"You still have a second key to each of the rooms which they use as bedrooms? Is that so? . . . Good. And you have duplicates of the keys that open the cupboards in the walls of those rooms, haven't you? . . . Capital. Well, as soon as they get to sleep, or rather as soon as you are certain that they are sound asleep, go in and search the cupboards. Each of them is bound to hide his share of the booty there. You'll find it quite easily. It's the four pocket-books which you know of. Put them in your bag, clear out as fast as you can and join me."

There was another pause. This time it was Essarès listening. He replied:

"What's that you say? Rue Raynouard? Here? Join me here? Why, you must be mad! Do you imagine that I can stay now, after the colonel's given me away? No, go and wait for me at the hotel, near the station. I shall be there by twelve o'clock or one in the afternoon, perhaps a little later. Don't be uneasy. Have your lunch quietly and we'll talk things over . . . Hullo! Did you hear? . . . Very well, I'll see that everything's all right. Good-by for the present."

The conversation was finished; and it looked as if Essarès, having taken all his measures to recover possession of the four million francs, had no further cause for anxiety. He hung up the receiver, went back to the lounge-chair in which he had been tortured, wheeled it round with its back to the fire, sat down, turned down the bottoms of his trousers and pulled on his socks and shoes, all a little painfully and accompanied by a few grimaces, but calmly, in the manner of a man who has no need to hurry.

Coralie kept her eyes fixed on his face.

"I really ought to go," thought Captain Belval, who felt a trifle embarrassed at the thought of overhearing what the husband and wife were about to say.

Nevertheless he stayed. He was not comfortable in his mind on Coralie's account.

Essarès fired the first shot:

"Well," he asked, "what are you looking at me like that for?"

"So it's true?" she murmured, maintaining her attitude of defiance. "You leave me no possibility of doubt?"

"Why should I lie?" he snarled. "I should not have telephoned in your hearing if I hadn't been sure that you were here all the time."

"I was up there."

"Then you heard everything?"

"Yes."

"And saw everything?"

"Yes."

"And, seeing the torture which they inflicted on me and hearing my cries, you did nothing to defend me, to defend me against torture, against death!"

"No, for I knew the truth."

"What truth?"

"The truth which I suspected without daring to admit it."

"What truth?" he repeated, in a louder voice.

"The truth about your treason."

"You're mad. I've committed no treason."

"Oh, don't juggle with words! I confess that I don't know the whole truth: I did not understand all that those men said or what they were demanding of you. But the secret which they tried to force from you was a treasonable secret."

"A man can only commit treason against his country," he said, shrugging his shoulders. "I'm not a Frenchman."

"You were a Frenchman!" she cried. "You asked to be one and you became one. You married me, a Frenchwoman, and you live in France and you've made your fortune in France. It's France that you're betraying."

"Don't talk nonsense! And for whose benefit?"

"I don't know that, either. For months, for years indeed, the colonel, Bournef, all your former accomplices and yourself have been engaged on an enormous work—yes, enormous, it's their own word—and now it appears that you are fighting over the profits of the common enterprise and the others accuse you of pocketing those profits for yourself alone and of keeping a secret that doesn't belong to you. So that I seem to see something dirtier and more hateful even than treachery, something worthy of a common pickpocket. . . ."

The man struck the arm of his chair with his fist:

"Enough!" he cried.

Coralie seemed in no way alarmed:

"Enough," she echoed, "you are right. Enough words between us. Besides, there is one fact that stands out above everything: your flight. That amounts to a confession. You're afraid of the police."

He shrugged his shoulders a second time:

"I'm afraid of nobody."

"Very well, but you're going."

"Yes."

"Then let's have it out. When are you going?"

"Presently, at twelve o'clock."

"And if you're arrested?"

"I sha'n't be arrested."

"If you are arrested, however?"

"I shall be let go."

"At least there will be an inquiry, a trial?"

"No, the matter will be hushed up."

"You hope so."

"I'm sure of it."

"God grant it! And you will leave France, of course?"

"As soon as I can."

"When will that be?"

"In a fortnight or three weeks."

"Send me word of the day, so that I may know when I can breathe again."

"I shall send you word, Coralie, but for another reason."

"What reason?"

"So that you may join me."

"Join you!"

He gave a cruel smile:

"You are my wife," he said. "Where the husband goes the wife goes; and you know that, in my religion, the husband has every right over his wife, including that of life and death. Well, you're my wife."

Coralie shook her head, and, in a tone of indescribable contempt, answered:

"I am not your wife. I feel nothing for you but loathing and horror. I don't wish to see you again, and, whatever happens, whatever you may threaten, I shall not see you again."

He rose, and, walking to her, bent in two, all trembling on his legs, he shouted, while again he shook his clenched fists at her:

"What's that you say? What's that you dare to say? I, I, your lord and master, order you to join me the moment that I send for you."

"I shall not join you. I swear it before God! I swear it as I hope to be saved."

He stamped his feet with rage. His face underwent a hideous contortion; and he roared:

"That means that you want to stay! Yes, you have reasons which I don't know, but which are easy to guess! An affair of the heart, I suppose. There's some one in your life, no doubt. . . . Hold your tongue, will you? . . . Haven't you always detested me? . . . Your hatred does not date from to-day. It dates back to the first time you saw me, to a time even before our marriage. . . . We have always lived like mortal enemies. I loved you. I worshipped you. A word from you would have brought me to your feet. The mere sound of your steps thrilled me to the marrow. . . . But your feeling for me is one of horror. And you imagine that you are going to start a new life, without me? Why, I'd sooner kill you, my beauty!"

He had unclenched his fists; and his open hands were clutching on either side of Coralie, close to her head, as though around a prey which they seemed on the point of throttling. A nervous shiver made his jaws clash together. Beads of perspiration gleamed on his bald head.

In front of him, Coralie stood impassive, looking very small and frail. Patrice Belval, in an agony of suspense and ready at any moment to act, could read nothing on her calm features but aversion and contempt.

Mastering himself at last, Essarès said:

"You shall join me, Coralie. Whether you like it or not, I am your husband. You felt it just now, when the lust to murder me made you take up a weapon and left you without the courage to carry out your intention. It will always be like that. Your independent fit will pass away and you will join the man who is your master."

"I shall remain behind to fight against you," she replied, "here, in this house. The work of treason which you have accomplished I shall destroy. I shall do it without hatred, for I am no longer capable of hatred, but I shall do it without intermission, to repair the evil which you have wrought."

He answered, in a low voice:

"I *am* capable of hatred. Beware, Coralie. The very moment when you believe that you have nothing more to fear will perhaps be the moment when I shall call you to account. Take care."

He pushed an electric bell. Old Siméon appeared.

"So the two men-servants have decamped?" asked Essarès. And, without waiting for the answer, he went on, "A good riddance. The housemaid and the cook can do all I want. They heard nothing, did they? No, their bedroom is too far away. No matter, Siméon: you must keep a watch on them after I am gone."

He looked at his wife, surprised to see her still there, and said to his secretary:

"I must be up at six to get everything ready; and I am dead tired. Take me to my room. You can come back and put out the lights afterwards."

He went out, supported by Siméon. Patrice Belval at once perceived that Coralie had done her best to show no weakness in her husband's presence, but that she had come to the end of her strength and was unable to walk. Seized with faintness, she fell on her knees, making the sign of the cross.

When she was able to rise, a few minutes later, she saw on the carpet, between her and the door, a sheet of note-paper with her name on it. She picked it up and read:

"Little Mother Coralie, the struggle is too much for you. Why not appeal to me, your friend? Give a signal and I am with you."

She staggered, dazed by the discovery of the letter and dismayed by Belval's daring. But, making a last effort to summon up her power of will, she left the room, without giving the signal for which Patrice was longing.

CHAPTER VI
NINETEEN MINUTES PAST SEVEN

Patrice, in his bedroom at the home, was unable to sleep that night. He had a continual waking sensation of being oppressed and hunted down, as though he were suffering the terrors of some monstrous nightmare. He had an impression that the frantic series of events in which he was playing the combined parts of a bewildered spectator and a helpless actor would never cease so long as he tried to rest; that, on the contrary, they would rage with greater violence and intensity. The leave-taking of the husband and wife did not put an end, even momentarily, to the dangers incurred by Coralie. Fresh perils arose on every side; and Patrice Belval confessed himself incapable of foreseeing and still more of allaying them.

After lying awake for two hours, he switched on his electric light and began hurriedly to write down the story of the past twelve hours. He hoped in this way to some small extent to unravel the tangled knot.

At six o'clock he went and roused Ya-Bon and brought him back with him. Then, standing in front of the astonished negro, he crossed his arms and exclaimed:

"So you consider that your job is over! While I lie tossing about in the dark, my lord sleeps and all's well! My dear man, you have a jolly elastic conscience."

The word elastic amused the Senegalese mightily. His mouth opened wider than ever; and he gave a grunt of enjoyment.

"That'll do, that'll do," said the captain. "There's no getting a word in, once you start talking. Here, take a chair, read this report and give me your reasoned opinion. What? You don't know how to read? Well, upon my word! What was the good, then, of wearing out the seat of your trousers on the benches of the Senegal schools and colleges? A queer education, I must say!"

He heaved a sigh, and, snatching the manuscript, said:

"Listen, reflect, argue, deduct and conclude. This is how the matter briefly stands. First, we have one Essarès Bey, a banker, rich as Crœsus, and the lowest of rapscallions, who betrays at one and the same time France, Egypt, England, Turkey, Bulgaria and Greece . . . as is proved by the fact that his accomplices roast his feet for him. Thereupon he kills one of them and gets rid of four with the aid of as many millions, which millions he orders another accomplice to get back for him before five minutes are passed. And all these bright spirits will duck underground at eleven o'clock this morning, for at twelve o'clock the police propose to enter on the scene. Good."

Patrice Belval paused to take breath and continued:

"Secondly, Little Mother Coralie—upon my word, I can't say why—is married to Rapscallion Bey. She hates him and wants to kill him. He loves her and wants to kill her. There is also a colonel who loves her and for that reason loses his life and a certain Mustapha, who tries to kidnap her on the colonel's account and also loses his life for that reason, strangled by a Senegalese. Lastly, there is a French captain, a dot-and-carry-one, who likewise loves her, but whom she avoids because she is married to a man whom she abhors. And with this captain, in a previous incarnation, she has halved an amethyst bead. Add to all this, by way of accessories, a rusty key, a red silk bowstring, a dog choked to death and a grate filled with red coals. And, if you dare to understand a single word of my explanation, I'll catch you a whack with my wooden leg, for I don't understand it a little bit and I'm your captain."

Ya-Bon laughed all over his mouth and all over the gaping scar that cut one of his cheeks in two. As ordered by his captain, he understood nothing of the business and very little of what Patrice had said; but he always quivered with delight when Patrice addressed him in that gruff tone.

"That's enough," said the captain. "It's my turn now to argue, deduct and conclude."

He leant against the mantelpiece, with his two elbows on the marble shelf and his head tight-pressed between his hands. His merriment, which sprang from temperamental lightness of heart, was this time only a surface merriment. Deep down within himself he did nothing but think of Coralie with sorrowful apprehension. What could he do to protect her? A number of plans occurred to him: which was he to choose? Should he hunt through the numbers in the telephone-book till he hit upon the whereabouts of that Grégoire, with whom Bournef and his companions had taken refuge? Should he inform the police? Should he return to the Rue Raynouard? He did not know. Yes, he was capable of acting, if the act to be performed consisted in flinging himself into the conflict with furious ardor. But to prepare the action, to divine the obstacles, to rend the darkness, and, as he said, to see the invisible and grasp the intangible, that was beyond his powers.

He turned suddenly to Ya-Bon, who was standing depressed by his silence:

"What's the matter with you, putting on that lugubrious air? Of course it's you that throw a gloom over me! You always look at the black side of things . . . like a nigger! . . . Be off."

Ya-Bon was going away discomfited, when some one tapped at the door and a voice said:

"Captain Belval, you're wanted on the telephone."

Patrice hurried out. Who on earth could be telephoning to him so early in the morning?

"Who is it?" he asked the nurse.

"I don't know, captain. . . . It's a man's voice; he seemed to want you urgently. The bell had been ringing some time. I was downstairs, in the kitchen. . . ."

Before Patrice's eyes there rose a vision of the telephone in the Rue Raynouard, in the big room at the Essarès' house. He could not help wondering if there was anything to connect the two incidents.

He went down one flight of stairs and along a passage. The telephone was through a small waiting-room, in a room that had been turned into a linen-closet. He closed the door behind him.

"Hullo! Captain Belval speaking. What is it?"

A voice, a man's voice which he did not know, replied in breathless, panting tones:

"Ah! . . . Captain Belval! . . . It's you! . . . Look here . . . but I'm almost afraid that it's too late. . . . I don't know if I shall have time to finish. . . . Did you get the key and the letter? . . ."

"Who are you?" asked Patrice.

"Did you get the key and the letter?" the voice insisted.

"The key, yes," Patrice replied, "but not the letter."

"Not the letter? But this is terrible! Then you don't know . . ."

A hoarse cry struck Patrice's ear and the next thing he caught was incoherent sounds at the other end of the wire, the noise of an altercation. Then the voice seemed to glue itself to the instrument and he distinctly heard it gasping:

"Too late! . . . Patrice . . . is that you? . . . Listen, the amethyst pendant . . . yes, I have it on me. . . . The pendant. . . . Ah, it's too late! . . . I should so much have liked to . . . Patrice. . . . Coralie. . . ."

Then again a loud cry, a heart-rending cry, and confused sounds growing more distant, in which he seemed to distinguish:

"Help! . . . Help! . . ."

These grew fainter and fainter. Silence followed. And suddenly there was a little click. The murderer had hung up the receiver.

All this had not taken twenty seconds. But, when Patrice wanted to replace the telephone, his fingers were gripping it so hard that it needed an effort to relax them.

He stood utterly dumfounded. His eyes had fastened on a large clock which he saw, through the window, on one of the buildings in the yard, marking nineteen minutes past seven; and he mechanically repeated these figures, attributing a documentary value to them. Then he asked himself—so unreal did the scene appear to him—if all this was true and if the crime had not been penetrated within himself, in the depths of his aching heart. But the shouting still echoed in his ears; and suddenly he took up the receiver again, like one clinging desperately to some undefined hope:

"Hullo!" he cried. "Exchange! . . . Who was it rang me up just now? . . . Are you there? Did you hear the cries? . . . Are you there? . . . Are you there? . . ."

There was no reply. He lost his temper, insulted the exchange, left the linen-closet, met Ya-Bon and pushed him about:

"Get out of this! It's your fault. Of course you ought to have stayed and looked after Coralie. Be off there now and hold yourself at my disposal. I'm going to inform the police. If you hadn't prevented me, it would have been done long ago and we shouldn't be in this predicament. Off you go!"

He held him back:

"No, don't stir. Your plan's ridiculous. Stay here. Oh, not here in my pocket! You're too impetuous for me, my lad!"

He drove him out and returned to the linen-closet, striding up and down and betraying his excitement in irritable gestures and angry words. Nevertheless, in the midst of his confusion, one idea gradually came to light, which was that, after all, he had no proof that the crime which he suspected had happened at the house in the Rue Raynouard. He must not allow himself to be obsessed by the facts that lingered in his memory to the point of always seeing the same vision in the same tragic setting. No doubt the drama was being continued, as he had felt that it would be, but perhaps elsewhere and far away from Coralie.

And this first thought led to another: why not investigate matters at once?

"Yes, why not?" he asked himself. "Before bothering the police, discovering the number of the person who rang me up and thus working back to the start, a process which it will be time enough to employ later, why shouldn't I telephone to the Rue Raynouard at once, on any pretext and in anybody's name? I shall then have a chance of knowing what to think. . . ."

Patrice felt that this measure did not amount to much. Suppose that no one answered, would that prove that the murder had been committed in the house, or merely that no one was yet about? Nevertheless, the need to do something decided him. He looked up Essarès Bey's number in the telephone-directory and resolutely rang up the exchange.

The strain of waiting was almost more than he could bear. And then he was conscious of a thrill which vibrated through him from head to foot. He was connected; and some one at the other end was answering the call.

"Hullo!" he said.

"Hullo!" said a voice. "Who are you?"

It was the voice of Essarès Bey.

Although this was only natural, since at that moment Essarès must be getting his papers ready and preparing his flight, Patrice was so much taken aback that he did not know what to say and spoke the first words that came into his head:

"Is that Essarès Bey?"

"Yes. Who are you?"

"I'm one of the wounded at the hospital, now under treatment at the home. . . ."

"Captain Belval, perhaps?"

Patrice was absolutely amazed. So Coralie's husband knew him by name? He stammered:

"Yes . . . Captain Belval."

"What a lucky thing!" cried Essarès Bey, in a tone of delight. "I rang you up a moment ago, at the home, Captain Belval, to ask . . ."

"Oh, it was you!" interrupted Patrice, whose astonishment knew no bounds.

"Yes, I wanted to know at what time I could speak to Captain Belval in order to thank him."

"It was *you*! . . . It was *you*! . . ." Patrice repeated, more and more thunderstruck.

Essarès' intonation denoted a certain surprise.

"Yes, wasn't it a curious coincidence?" he said. "Unfortunately, I was cut off, or rather my call was interrupted by somebody else."

"Then you heard?"

"What, Captain Belval?"

"Cries."

"Cries?"

"At least, so it seemed to me; but the connection was very indistinct."

"All that I heard was somebody asking for you, somebody who was in a great hurry; and, as I was not, I hung up the telephone and postponed the pleasure of thanking you."

"Of thanking me?"

"Yes, I have heard how my wife was assaulted last night and how you came to her rescue. And I am anxious to see you and express my gratitude. Shall we make an appointment? Could we meet at the hospital, for instance, at three o'clock this afternoon?"

Patrice made no reply. The audacity of this man, threatened with arrest and preparing for flight, baffled him. At the same time, he was wondering what Essarès' real object had been in telephoning to him without being in any way obliged to. But Belval's silence in no way troubled the banker, who continued his civilities and ended the inscrutable conversation with a monologue in which he replied with the greatest ease to questions which he kept putting to himself.

In spite of everything, Patrice felt more comfortable. He went back to his room, lay down on his bed and slept for two hours. Then he sent for Ya-Bon.

"This time," he said, "try to control your nerves and not to lose your head as you did just now. You were absurd. But don't let's talk about it. Have you had your breakfast? No? No more have I. Have you seen the doctor? No? No more have I. And the surgeon has just promised to take off this beastly bandage. You can imagine how pleased I am. A wooden leg is all very well; but a head wrapped up in lint, for a lover, never! Get on, look sharp. When we're ready, we'll start for the hospital. Little Mother Coralie can't forbid me to see her there!"

Patrice was as happy as a schoolboy. As he said to Ya-Bon an hour later, on their way to the Porte-Maillot, the clouds were beginning to roll by:

"Yes, Ya-Bon, yes, they are. And this is where we stand. To begin with, Coralie is not in danger. As I hoped, the battle is being fought far away from her, among the accomplices no doubt, over their millions. As for the unfortunate man who rang me up and whose dying cries I overheard, he was obviously some unknown friend, for he addressed me familiarly and called me by my Christian name. It was certainly he who sent me the key of the garden. Unfortunately, the letter that came with the key went astray. In the end, he felt constrained to tell me everything. Just at that moment he was attacked. By whom, you ask. Probably by one of the accomplices, who was frightened of his revelations. There you are, Ya-Bon. It's all as clear as noonday. For that matter, the truth may just as easily be the exact opposite of what I suggest. But I don't care. The great thing is to take one's stand upon a theory, true or false. Besides, if mine is false, I reserve the right to shift the responsibility on you. So you know what you're in for. . . ."

At the Porte-Maillot they took a cab and it occurred to Patrice to drive round by the Rue Raynouard. At the junction of this street with the Rue de Passy, they saw Coralie leaving the Rue Raynouard, accompanied by old Siméon.

She had hailed a taxi and stepped inside. Siméon sat down by the driver. They went to the hospital in the Champs-Élysées, with Patrice following. It was eleven o'clock when they arrived.

"All's well," said Patrice. "While her husband is running away, she refuses to make any change in her daily life."

He and Ya-Bon lunched in the neighborhood, strolled along the avenue, without losing sight of the hospital, and called there at half-past one.

Patrice at once saw old Siméon, sitting at the end of a covered yard where the soldiers used to meet. His head was half wrapped up in the usual comforter; and, with his big yellow spectacles on his nose, he sat smoking his pipe on the chair which he always occupied.

As for Coralie, she was in one of the rooms allotted to her on the first floor, seated by the bedside of a patient whose hand she held between her own. The man was asleep.

Coralie appeared to Patrice to be very tired. The dark rings round her eyes and the unusual pallor of her cheeks bore witness to her fatigue.

"Poor child!" he thought. "All those blackguards will be the death of you."

He now understood, when he remembered the scenes of the night before, why Coralie kept her private life secret and endeavored, at least to the little world of the hospital, to be merely the kind sister whom people call by her Christian name. Suspecting the web of crime with which she was surrounded, she dropped her husband's name and told nobody where she lived. And so well was she protected by the defenses set up by her modesty and determination that Patrice dared not go to her and stood rooted to the threshold.

"Yet surely," he said to himself, as he looked at Coralie without being seen by her, "I'm not going to send her in my card!"

He was making up his mind to enter, when a woman who had come up the stairs, talking loudly as she went, called out:

"Where is madame? . . . M. Siméon, she must come at once!"

Old Siméon, who had climbed the stairs with her, pointed to where Coralie sat at the far end of the room; and the woman rushed in. She said a few words to Coralie, who seemed upset and at once, ran to the door, passing in front of Patrice, and down the stairs, followed by Siméon and the woman.

"I've got a taxi, ma'am," stammered the woman, all out of breath. "I had the luck to find one when I left the house and I kept it. We must be quick, ma'am. . . . The commissary of police told me to . . ."

Patrice, who was downstairs by this time, heard nothing more; but the last words decided him. He seized hold of Ya-Bon as he passed; and the two of them leapt into a cab, telling the driver to follow Coralie's taxi.

"There's news, Ya-Bon, there's news!" said Patrice. "The plot is thickening. The woman is obviously one of the Essarès' servants and she has come for her mistress by the commissary's orders. Therefore the colonel's disclosures are having their effect. House searched; magistrate's inquest; every sort of worry for Little Mother Coralie; and you have the cheek to advise me to be careful! You imagine that I would leave her to her own devices at such a moment! What a mean nature you must have, my poor Ya-Bon!"

An idea occurred to him; and he exclaimed:

685

"Heavens! I hope that ruffian of an Essarès hasn't allowed himself to be caught! That would be a disaster! But he was far too sure of himself. I expect he's been trifling away his time. . . ."

All through the drive this fear excited Captain Belval and removed his last scruples. In the end his certainty was absolute. Nothing short of Essarès' arrest could have produced the servant's attitude of panic or Coralie's precipitate departure. Under these conditions, how could he hesitate to interfere in a matter in which his revelations would enlighten the police? All the more so as, by revealing less or more, according to circumstances, he could make his evidence subservient to Coralie's interests.

The two cabs pulled up almost simultaneously outside the Essarès' house, where a car was already standing. Coralie alighted and disappeared through the carriage-gate. The maid and Siméon also crossed the pavement.

"Come along," said Patrice to the Senegalese.

The front-door was ajar and Patrice entered. In the big hall were two policemen on duty. Patrice acknowledged their presence with a hurried movement of his hand and passed them with the air of a man who belonged to the house and whose importance was so great that nothing done without him could be of any use.

The sound of his footsteps echoing on the flags reminded him of the flight of Bournef and his accomplices. He was on the right road. Moreover, there was a drawing-room on the left, the room, communicating with the library, to which the accomplices had carried the colonel's body. Voices came from the library. He walked across the drawing-room.

At that moment he heard Coralie exclaim in accents of terror:

"Oh, my God, it can't be! . . ."

Two other policemen barred the doorway.

"I am a relation of Mme. Essarès'," he said, "her only relation. . . ."

"We have our orders, captain . . ."

"I know, of course. Be sure and let no one in! Ya-Bon, stay here."

And he went in.

But, in the immense room, a group of six or seven gentlemen, no doubt commissaries of police and magistrates, stood in his way, bending over something which he was unable to distinguish. From amidst this group Coralie suddenly appeared and came towards him, tottering and wringing her hands. The housemaid took her round the waist and pressed her into a chair.

"What's the matter?" asked Patrice.

"Madame is feeling faint," replied the woman, still quite distraught. "Oh, I'm nearly off my head!"

"But why? What's the reason?"

"It's the master . . . just think! . . . Such a sight! . . . It gave me a turn, too . . ."

"What sight?"

One of the gentlemen left the group and approached:

"Is Mme. Essarès ill?"

"It's nothing," said the maid. "A fainting-fit. . . . She is liable to these attacks."

"Take her away as soon as she can walk. We shall not need her any longer."

And, addressing Patrice Belval with a questioning air:

"Captain? . . ."

Patrice pretended not to understand:

"Yes, sir," he said, "we will take Mme. Essarès away. Her presence, as you say, is unnecessary. Only I must first . . ."

He moved aside to avoid his interlocutor, and, perceiving that the group of magistrates had opened out a little, stepped forward. What he now saw explained Coralie's fainting-fit and the servant's agitation. He himself felt his flesh creep at a spectacle which was infinitely more horrible than that of the evening before.

On the floor, near the fireplace, almost at the place where he had undergone his torture, Essarès Bey lay upon his back. He was wearing the same clothes as on the previous day: a brown-velvet smoking-suit with a braided jacket. His head and shoulders had been covered with a napkin. But one of the men standing around, a divisional surgeon no doubt, was holding up the napkin with one hand and pointing to the dead man's face with the other, while he offered an explanation in a low voice.

And that face . . . but it was hardly the word for the unspeakable mass of flesh, part of which seemed to be charred while the other part formed no more than a bloodstained pulp, mixed with bits of bone and skin, hairs and a broken eye-ball.

"Oh," Patrice blurted out, "how horrible! He was killed and fell with his head right in the fire. That's how they found him, I suppose?"

The man who had already spoken to him and who appeared to be the most important figure present came up to him once more:

"May I ask who you are?" he demanded.

"Captain Belval, sir, a friend of Mme. Essarès, one of the wounded officers whose lives she has helped to save . . ."

"That may be, sir," replied the important figure, "but you can't stay here. Nobody must stay here, for that matter. Monsieur le commissaire, please order every one to leave the room, except the doctor, and have the door guarded. Let no one enter on any pretext whatever. . . ."

"Sir," Patrice insisted, "I have some very serious information to communicate."

"I shall be pleased to receive it, captain, but later on. You must excuse me now."

VII
TWENTY-THREE MINUTES PAST TWELVE

The great hall that ran from Rue Raynouard to the upper terrace of the garden was filled to half its extent by a wide staircase and divided the Essarès house into two parts communicating only by way of the hall.

On the left were the drawing-room and the library, which was followed by an independent block containing a private staircase. On the right were a billiard-room and the dining-room, both with lower ceilings. Above these were Essarès Bey's bedroom, on the street side, and Coralie's, overlooking the garden. Beyond was the servants' wing, where old Siméon also used to sleep.

Patrice was asked to wait in the billiard-room, with the Senegalese. He had been there about a quarter of an hour when Siméon and the maid were shown in.

The old secretary seemed quite paralyzed by the death of his employer and was holding forth under his breath, making queer gestures as he spoke. Patrice asked him how things were going; and the old fellow whispered in his ear:

"It's not over yet . . . There's something to fear . . . to fear! . . . To-day . . . presently."

"Presently?" asked Patrice.

"Yes . . . yes," said the old man, trembling.

He said nothing more. As for the housemaid, she readily told her story in reply to Patrice' questions:

"The first surprise, sir, this morning was that there was no butler, no footman, no porter. All the three were gone. Then, at half-past six, M. Siméon came and told us from the master that the master had locked himself in his library and that he wasn't to be disturbed even for breakfast. The mistress was not very well. She had her chocolate at nine o'clock. . . . At ten o'clock she went out with M. Siméon. Then, after we had done the bedrooms, we never left the kitchen. Eleven o'clock came, twelve . . . and, just as the hour was striking, we heard a loud ring at the front-door. I looked out of the window. There was a motor, with four gentlemen inside. I went to the door. The commissary of police explained who he was and wanted to see the master. I showed them the way. The library-door was locked. We knocked: no answer. We shook it: no answer. In the end, one of the gentlemen, who knew how, picked the lock. . . . Then . . . then . . . you can imagine what we saw. . . . But you can't, it was much worse, because the poor master at that moment had his head almost under the grate. . . . Oh, what scoundrels they must have been! . . . For they did kill him, didn't they? I know one of the gentlemen said at once that the master had died of a stroke and fallen into the fire. Only my firm belief is . . ."

Old Siméon had listened without speaking, with his head still half wrapped up, showing only his bristly gray beard and his eyes hidden behind their yellow spectacles. But at this point of the story he gave a little chuckle, came up to Patrice and said in his ear:

"There's something to fear . . . to fear! . . . Mme. Coralie. . . . Make her go away at once . . . make her go away. . . . If not, it'll be the worse for her. . . ."

Patrice shuddered and tried to question him, but could learn nothing more. Besides, the old man did not remain. A policeman came to fetch him and took him to the library.

His evidence lasted a long time. It was followed by the depositions of the cook and the housemaid. Next, Coralie's evidence was taken, in her own room. At four o'clock another car arrived. Patrice saw two gentlemen pass into the hall, with everybody bowing very low before them. He recognized the minister of justice and the minister of the interior. They conferred in the library for half an hour and went away again.

At last, shortly before five o'clock, a policeman came for Patrice and showed him up to the first floor. The man tapped at a door and stood aside. Patrice entered a small boudoir, lit up by a wood fire by which two persons were seated: Coralie, to whom he bowed, and, opposite her, the gentleman who had spoken to him on his arrival and who seemed to be directing the whole enquiry.

He was a man of about fifty, with a thickset body and a heavy face, slow of movement, but with bright, intelligent eyes.

"The examining-magistrate, I presume, sir?" asked Patrice.

"No," he replied, "I am M. Masseron, a retired magistrate, specially appointed to clear up this affair . . . not to examine it, as you think, for it does not seem to me that there is anything to examine."

"What?" cried Patrice, in great surprise. "Nothing to examine?"

He looked at Coralie, who kept her eyes fixed upon him attentively. Then she turned them on M. Masseron, who resumed:

"I have no doubt, Captain Belval, that, when we have said what we have to say, we shall be agreed at all points . . . just as madame and I are already agreed."

"I don't doubt it either," said Patrice. "All the same, I am afraid that many of those points remain unexplained."

"Certainly, but we shall find an explanation, we shall find it together. Will you please tell me what you know?"

Patrice waited for a moment and then said:

"I will not disguise my astonishment, sir. The story which I have to tell is of some importance; and yet there is no one here to take it down. Is it not to count as evidence given on oath, as a deposition which I shall have to sign?"

"You yourself, captain, shall determine the value of your words and the innuendo which you wish them to bear. For the moment, we will look on this as a preliminary conversation, as an exchange of views relating to facts . . . touching which Mme. Essarès has given me, I believe, the same information that you will be able to give me."

Patrice did not reply at once. He had a vague impression that there was a private understanding between Coralie and the magistrate and that, in face of that understanding, he, both by his presence and by his zeal, was playing the part of an intruder whom they would gladly have dismissed. He resolved therefore to maintain an attitude of reserve until the magistrate had shown his hand.

"Of course," he said, "I daresay madame has told you. So you know of the conversation which I overheard yesterday at the restaurant?"

"Yes."

"And the attempt to kidnap Mme. Essarès?"

"Yes."

"And the murder? . . ."

"Yes."

"Mme. Essarès has described to you the blackmailing scene that took place last night, with M. Essarès for a victim, the details of the torture, the death of the colonel, the handing over of the four millions, the conversation on the telephone between M. Essarès and a certain Grégoire and, lastly, the threats uttered against madame by her husband?"

"Yes, Captain Belval, I know all this, that is to say, all that you know; and I know, in addition, all that I discovered through my own investigations."

"Of course, of course," Patrice repeated. "I see that my story becomes superfluous and that you are in possession of all the necessary factors to enable you to draw your conclusions." And, continuing to put rather than answer questions, he added, "May I ask what inference you have arrived at?"

"To tell you the truth, captain, my inferences are not definite. However, until I receive some proof to the contrary, I propose to remain satisfied with the actual words of a letter which M. Essarès wrote to his wife at about twelve o'clock this morning and which we found lying on his desk, unfinished. Mme. Essarès asked me to read it and, if necessary, to communicate the contents to you. Listen."

M. Masseron proceeded to read the letter aloud:

"*Coralie,*

"You were wrong yesterday to attribute my departure to reasons which I dared not acknowledge; and perhaps I also was wrong not to defend myself more convincingly against your accusation. The only motive for my departure is the hatred with which I am surrounded. You have seen how fierce it is. In the face of these enemies who are seeking to despoil me by every possible means, my only hope of salvation lies in flight. That is why I am going away.

"But let me remind you, Coralie, of my clearly expressed wish. You are to join me at the first summons. If you do not leave Paris then, nothing shall protect you against my lawful resentment: nothing, not even my death. I have made all my arrangements so that, even in the contingency . . ."

"The letter ends there," said M. Masseron, handing it back to Coralie, "and we know by an unimpeachable sign that the last lines were written immediately before M. Essarès' death, because, in falling, he upset a little clock which stood on his desk and which marked twenty-three minutes past twelve. I assume that he felt unwell and that, on trying to rise, he was seized with a fit of giddiness and fell to the floor. Unfortunately, the fireplace was near, with a fierce fire blazing in it; his head struck the grate; and the wound that resulted was so deep—the surgeon testified to this—that he fainted. Then the fire close at hand did its work . . . with the effects which you have seen. . . ."

Patrice had listened in amazement to this unexpected explanation:

"Then in your opinion," he asked, "M. Essarès died of an accident? He was not murdered?"

690

"Murdered? Certainly not! We have no clue to support any such theory."

"Still . . ."

"Captain Belval, you are the victim of an association of ideas which, I admit, is perfectly justifiable. Ever since yesterday you have been witnessing a series of tragic incidents; and your imagination naturally leads you to the most tragic solution, that of murder. Only—reflect—why should a murder have been committed? And by whom? By Bournef and his friends? With what object? They were crammed full with bank-notes; and, even admitting that the man called Grégoire recovered those millions from them, they would certainly not have got them back by killing M. Essarès. Then again, how would they have entered the house? And how can they have gone out? . . . No, captain, you must excuse me, but M. Essarès died an accidental death. The facts are undeniable; and this is the opinion of the divisional surgeon, who will draw up his report in that sense."

Patrice turned to Coralie:

"Is it Mme. Essarès' opinion also?"

She reddened slightly and answered:

"Yes."

"And old Siméon's?"

"Oh," replied the magistrate, "old Siméon is wandering in his mind! To listen to him, you would think that everything was about to happen all over again, that Mme. Essarès is threatened with danger and that she ought to take to flight at once. That is all that I have been able to get out of him. However, he took me to an old disused door that opens out of the garden on a lane running at right angles with the Rue Raynouard; and here he showed me first the watch-dog's dead body and next some footprints between the door and the flight of steps near the library. But you know those foot-prints, do you not? They belong to you and your Senegalese. As for the death of the watch-dog, I can put that down to your Senegalese, can't I?"

Patrice was beginning to understand. The magistrate's reticence, his explanation, his agreement with Coralie: all this was gradually becoming plain. He put the question frankly:

"So there was no murder?"

"No."

"Then there will be no magistrate's examination?"

"No."

"And no talk about the matter; it will all be kept quiet, in short, and forgotten?"

"Just so."

Captain Belval began to walk up and down, as was his habit. He now remembered Essarès' prophecy:

"I sha'n't be arrested. . . . If I am, I shall be let go. . . . The matter will be hushed up. . . ."

Essarès was right. The hand of justice was arrested; and there was no way for Coralie to escape silent complicity.

Patrice was intensely annoyed by the manner in which the case was being handled. It was certain that a compact had been concluded between Coralie and M. Masseron. He suspected the magistrate of circumventing Coralie and inducing her to sacrifice her own interests to other considerations. To effect this, the first thing was to get rid of him, Patrice.

"Ugh!" said Patrice to himself. "I'm fairly sick of this sportsman, with his cool ironical ways. It looks as if he were doing a considerable piece of thimblerigging at my expense."

He restrained himself, however, and, with a pretense of wanting to keep on good terms with the magistrate, came and sat down beside him:

"You must forgive me, sir," he said, "for insisting in what may appear to you an indiscreet fashion. But my conduct is explained not only by such sympathy or feeling as I entertain for Mme. Essarès at a moment in her life when she is more lonely than ever, a sympathy and feeling which she seems to repulse even more firmly than she did before. It is also explained by certain mysterious links which unite us to each other and which go back to a period too remote for our eyes to focus. Has Mme. Essarès told you those details? In my opinion, they are most important; and I cannot help associating them with the events that interest us."

M. Masseron glanced at Coralie, who nodded. He answered:

"Yes, Mme. Essarès has informed me and even . . ."

He hesitated once more and again consulted Coralie, who flushed and seemed put out of countenance. M. Masseron, however, waited for a reply which would enable him to proceed. She ended by saying, in a low voice:

"Captain Belval is entitled to know what we have discovered. The truth belongs as much to him as to me; and I have no right to keep it from him. Pray speak, monsieur."

"I doubt if it is even necessary to speak," said the magistrate. "It will be enough, I think, to show the captain this photograph-album which I have found. Here you are, Captain Belval."

And he handed Patrice a very slender album, covered in gray canvas and fastened with an india-rubber band.

Patrice took it with a certain anxiety. But what he saw on opening it was so utterly unexpected that he gave an exclamation:

"It's incredible!"

On the first page, held in place by their four corners, were two photographs: one, on the right, representing a small boy in an Eton jacket; the other, on the left, representing a very little girl. There was an inscription under each. On the right: "Patrice, at ten." On the left: "Coralie, at three."

Moved beyond expression, Patrice turned the leaf. On the second page they appeared again, he at the age of fifteen, she at the age of eight. And he saw himself at nineteen and at twenty-three and at twenty-eight, always accompanied by Coralie, first as a little girl, then as a young girl, next as a woman.

"This is incredible!" he cried. "How is it possible? Here are portraits of myself which I had never seen, amateur photographs obviously, which trace my whole life. Here's one when I was doing my military training. . . . Here I am on horseback . . . Who can have ordered these photographs? And who can have collected them together with yours, madame?"

He fixed his eyes on Coralie, who evaded their questioning gaze and lowered her head as though the close connection between their two lives, to which those pages bore witness, had shaken her to the very depths of her being.

"Who can have brought them together?" he repeated. "Do you know? And where does the album come from?"

M. Masseron supplied the answer:

"It was the surgeon who found it. M. Essarès wore a vest under his shirt; and the album was in an inner pocket, a pocket sewn inside the vest. The surgeon felt the boards through it when he was undressing M. Essarès' body."

This time, Patrice's and Coralie's eyes met. The thought that M. Essarès had been collecting both their photographs during the past twenty years and that he wore them next to his breast and that he had lived and died with them upon him, this thought amazed them so much that they did not even try to fathom its strange significance.

"Are you sure of what you are saying, sir?" asked Patrice.

"I was there," said M. Masseron. "I was present at the discovery. Besides, I myself made another which confirms this one and completes it in a really surprising fashion. I found a pendant, cut out of a solid block of amethyst and held in a setting of filigree-work."

"What's that?" cried Captain Belval. "What's that? A pendant? An amethyst pendant?"

"Look for yourself, sir," suggested the magistrate, after once more consulting Mme. Essarès with a glance.

And he handed Captain Belval an amethyst pendant, larger than the ball formed by joining the two halves which Coralie and Patrice possessed, she on her rosary and he on his bunch of seals; and this new ball was encircled with a specimen of gold filigree-work exactly like that on the rosary and on the seal.

The setting served as a clasp.

"Am I to open it?" he asked.

Coralie nodded. He opened the pendant. The inside was divided by a movable glass disk, which separated two miniature photographs, one of Coralie as a nurse, the other of himself, wounded, in an officer's uniform.

Patrice reflected, with pale cheeks. Presently he asked:

"And where does this pendant come from? Did you find it, sir?"

"Yes, Captain Belval."

"Where?"

The magistrate seemed to hesitate. Coralie's attitude gave Patrice the impression that she was unaware of this detail. M. Masseron at last said:

"I found it in the dead man's hand."

"In the dead man's hand? In M. Essarès' hand?"

Patrice had given a start, as though under an unexpected blow, and was now leaning over the magistrate, greedily awaiting a reply which he wanted to hear for the second time before accepting it as certain.

"Yes, in his hand. I had to force back the clasped fingers in order to release it."

Belval stood up and, striking the table with his fist, exclaimed:

"Well, sir, I will tell you one thing which I was keeping back as a last argument to prove to you that my collaboration is of use; and this thing becomes of great importance after what we have just learnt. Sir, this morning some one asked to speak to me on the telephone; and I had hardly answered the call when this person, who seemed greatly excited, was the victim of a murderous assault, committed in my hearing. And, amid the sound of the scuffle and the cries of agony, I caught the following words, which the unhappy man insisted on trying to get to me as so many last instructions: 'Patrice! . . . Coralie! . . . The amethyst pendant. . . . Yes, I have it on me. . . . The pendant. . . . Ah, it's too late! . . . I should so much have liked. . . . Patrice. . . . Coralie. . . .' There's what I heard, sir, and here are the two facts which we cannot escape. This morning, at nineteen minutes past seven, a man was murdered having upon him an amethyst pendant. This is the first undeniable fact. A few hours later, at twenty-three minutes past twelve, this same amethyst pendant is discovered clutched in the hand of another man. This is the second undeniable fact. Place these facts side by side and you are bound to come to the conclusion that the first murder, the one of which I caught the distant echo, was committed here, in this house, in the same library which, since yesterday evening, witnessed the end of every scene in the tragedy which we are contemplating."

This revelation, which in reality amounted to a fresh accusation against Essarès, seemed to affect the magistrate profoundly. Patrice had flung himself into the discussion with a passionate vehemence and a logical reasoning which it was impossible to disregard without evident insincerity.

Coralie had turned aside slightly and Patrice could not see her face; but he suspected her dismay in the presence of all this infamy and shame.

M. Masseron raised an objection:

"Two undeniable facts, you say, Captain Belval? As to the first point, let me remark that we have not found the body of the man who is supposed to have been murdered at nineteen minutes past seven this morning."

"It will be found in due course."

"Very well. Second point: as regards the amethyst pendant discovered in Essarès' hand, how can we tell that Essarès Bey found it in the murdered man's hand and not somewhere else? For, after all, we do not know if he was at home at that time and still less if he was in his library."

694

"But I do know."

"How?"

"I telephoned to him a few minutes later and he answered. More than that, to sweep away any trace of doubt, he told me that he had rung me up but that he had been cut off."

M. Masseron thought for a moment and then said:

"Did he go out this morning?"

"Ask Mme. Essarès."

Without turning round, manifestly wishing to avoid Belval's eyes, Coralie answered:

"I don't think that he went out. The suit he was wearing at the time of his death was an indoor suit."

"Did you see him after last night?"

"He came and knocked at my room three times this morning, between seven and nine o'clock. I did not open the door. At about eleven o'clock I started off alone; I heard him call old Siméon and tell him to go with me. Siméon caught me up in the street. That is all I know."

A prolonged silence ensued. Each of the three was meditating upon this strange series of adventures. In the end, M. Masseron, who had realized that a man of Captain Belval's stamp was not the sort to be easily thrust aside, spoke in the tone of one who, before coming to terms, wishes to know exactly what his adversary's last word is likely to be:

"Let us come to the point, captain. You are building up a theory which strikes me as very vague. What is it precisely? And what are you proposing to do if I decline to accept it? I have asked you two very plain questions. Do you mind answering them?"

"I will answer them, sir, as plainly as you put them."

He went up to the magistrate and said:

"Here, sir, is the field of battle and of attack—yes, of attack, if need be—which I select. A man who used to know me, who knew Mme. Essarès as a child and who was interested in both of us, a man who used to collect our portraits at different ages, who had reasons for loving us unknown to me, who sent me the key of that garden and who was making arrangements to bring us together for a purpose which he would have told us, this man was murdered at the moment when he was about to execute his plan. Now everything tells me that he was murdered by M. Essarès. I am therefore resolved to lodge an information, whatever the results of my action may be. And believe me, sir, my charge will not be hushed up. There are always means of making one's self heard . . . even if I am reduced to shouting the truth from the house-tops."

M. Masseron burst out laughing:

"By Jove, captain, but you're letting yourself go!"

"I'm behaving according to my conscience; and Mme. Essarès, I feel sure, will forgive me. She knows that I am acting for her good. She knows that all will be over with her if this case is hushed up and if the authorities do not assist her. She knows that the enemies who threaten her are implacable. They will stop at nothing to attain their object and to do away with her, for she stands in their way. And the terrible thing about it is that the most clear-seeing eyes are unable to make out what that object is. We are playing the most formidable game against these enemies; and we do not even know what the stakes are. Only the police can discover those stakes."

M. Masseron waited for a second or two and then, laying his hand on Patrice's shoulder, said, calmly:

"And, suppose the authorities knew what the stakes were?"

Patrice looked at him in surprise:

"What? Do you mean to say you know?"

"Perhaps."

"And can you tell me?"

"Oh, well, if you force me to!"

"What are they?"

"Not much! A trifle!"

"But what sort of trifle?"

"A thousand million francs."

"A thousand millions?"

"Just that. A thousand millions, of which two-thirds, I regret to say, if not three-quarters, had already left France before the war. But the remaining two hundred and fifty or three hundred millions are worth more than a thousand millions all the same, for a very good reason."

"What reason?"

"They happen to be in gold."

CHAPTER VIII
ESSARÈS BEY'S WORK

This time Captain Belval seemed to relax to some extent. He vaguely perceived the consideration that compelled the authorities to wage the battle prudently.

"Are you sure?" he asked.

"Yes, I was instructed to investigate this matter two years ago; and my enquiries proved that really remarkable exports of gold were being effected from France. But, I confess, it is only since my conversation with Mme. Essarès that I have seen where the leakage came from and who it was that set on foot, all over France, down to the least important market-towns, the formidable organization through which the indispensable metal was made to leave the country."

"Then Mme. Essarès knew?"

"No, but she suspected a great deal; and last night, before you arrived, she overheard some words spoken between Essarès and his assailants which she repeated to me, thus giving me the key to the riddle. I should have been glad to work out the complete solution without your assistance— for one thing, those were the orders of the minister of the interior; and Mme. Essarès displayed the same wish—but your impetuosity overcomes my hesitation; and, since I can't manage to get rid of you, Captain Belval, I will tell you the whole story frankly . . . especially as your cooperation is not to be despised."

"I am all ears," said Patrice, who was burning to know more.

"Well, the motive force of the plot was here, in this house. Essarès Bey, president of the Franco-Oriental Bank, 6, Rue Lafayette, apparently an Egyptian, in reality a Turk, enjoyed the greatest influence in the Paris financial world. He had been naturalized an Englishman, but had kept up secret relations with the former possessors of Egypt; and he had received instructions from a foreign power, which I am not yet able to name with certainty, to bleed—there is no other word for it—to bleed France of all the gold that he could cause to flow into his coffers. According to documents which I have seen, he succeeded in exporting in this way some seven hundred million francs in two years. A last consignment was preparing when war was declared. You can understand that thenceforth such important sums could not be smuggled out of the country so easily as in times of peace. The railway-wagons are inspected on the frontiers; the outgoing vessels are searched in the harbors. In short, the gold was not sent away. Those two hundred and fifty or three hundred millions remained in France. Ten months passed; and the inevitable happened, which was that Essarès Bey, having this fabulous treasure at his disposal, clung to it, came gradually to look upon it as his own and, in the end, resolved to appropriate it. Only there were accomplices. . . ."

"The men I saw last night?"

"Yes, half-a-dozen shady Levantines, sham naturalized French citizens, more or less well-disguised Bulgarians, secret agents of the little German courts in the Balkans. This gang ran provincial branches of Essarès' bank. It had in its pay, on Essarès' account, hundreds of minor agents, who scoured the villages, visited the fairs, were hail-fellow-well-met with the peasants, offered them bank-notes and government securities in exchange for French gold and trousered all their savings. When war broke out the gang shut up shop and gathered round Essarès Bey, who also had closed his offices in the Rue Lafayette."

"What happened then?"

"Things that we don't know. No doubt the accomplices learnt from their governments that the last despatch of gold had never taken place; and no doubt they also guessed that Essarès Bey was trying to keep for himself the three hundred millions collected by the gang. One thing is certain, that a struggle began between the former partners, a fierce, implacable struggle, the accomplices wanting their share of the plunder, while Essarès Bey was resolved to part with none of it and pretended that the millions had left the country. Yesterday the struggle attained its culminating-point. In the afternoon the accomplices tried to get hold of Mme. Essarès so that they might have a hostage to use against her husband. In the evening . . . in the evening you yourself witnessed the final episode."

"But why yesterday evening rather than another?"

"Because the accomplices had every reason to think that the millions were intended to disappear yesterday evening. Though they did not know the methods employed by Essarès Bey when he made his last remittances, they believed that each of the remittances, or rather each removal of the sacks, was preceded by a signal."

"Yes, a shower of sparks, was it not?"

"Exactly. In a corner of the garden are some old conservatories, above which stands the furnace that used to heat them. This grimy furnace, full of soot and rubbish, sends forth, when you light it, flakes of fire and sparks which are seen at a distance and serve as an intimation. Essarès Bey lit it last night himself. The accomplices at once took alarm and came prepared to go any lengths."

"And Essarès' plan failed."

"Yes. But so did theirs. The colonel is dead. The others were only able to get hold of a few bundles of notes which have probably been taken from them by this time. But the struggle was not finished; and its dying agony has been a most shocking tragedy. According to your statement, a man who knew you and who was seeking to get into touch with you, was killed at nineteen minutes past seven, most likely by Essarès Bey, who dreaded his intervention. And, five hours later, at twenty-three past twelve, Essarès Bey himself was murdered, presumably by one of his accomplices. There is the whole story, Captain Belval. And, now that you know as much of it as I do, don't you think that the investigation of this case should remain secret and be pursued not quite in accordance with the ordinary rules?"

After a moment's reflection Patrice said:

"Yes, I agree."

"There can be no doubt about it!" cried M. Masseron. "Not only will it serve no purpose to publish this story of gold which has disappeared and which can't be found, which would startle the public and excite their imaginations, but you will readily imagine that an operation which consisted in draining off such a quantity of gold in two years cannot have been effected without compromising a regrettable number of people. I feel certain that my own enquiries will reveal a series of weak concessions and unworthy bargains on the part of certain more or less important banks and credit-houses, transactions on which I do not wish to insist, but which it would be the gravest of blunders to publish. Therefore, silence."

"But is silence possible?"

"Why not?"

"Bless my soul, there are a good few corpses to be explained away! Colonel Fakhi's, for instance?"

"Suicide."

"Mustapha's, which you will discover or which you have already discovered in the Galliéra garden?"

"Found dead."

"Essarès Bey's?"

"An accident."

"So that all these manifestations of the same power will remain separated?"

"There is nothing to show the link that connects them."

"Perhaps the public will think otherwise."

"The public will think what we wish it to think. This is war-time."

"The press will speak."

"The press will do nothing of the kind. We have the censorship."

"But, if some fact or, rather, a fresh crime . . . ?"

"Why should there be a fresh crime? The matter is finished, at least on its active and dramatic side. The chief actors are dead. The curtain falls on the murder of Essarès Bey. As for the supernumeraries, Bournef and the others, we shall have them stowed away in an internment-camp before a week is past. We therefore find ourselves in the presence of a certain number of millions, with no owner, with no one who dares to claim them, on which France is entitled to lay hands. I shall devote my activity to securing the money for the republic."

Patrice Belval shook his head:

"Mme. Essarès remains, sir. We must not forget her husband's threats."

"He is dead."

"No matter, the threats are there. Old Siméon tells you so in a striking fashion."

"He's half mad."

"Exactly, his brain retains the impression of great and imminent danger. No, the struggle is not ended. Perhaps indeed it is only beginning."

"Well, captain, are we not here? Make it your business to protect and defend Mme. Essarès by all the means in your power and by all those which I place at your disposal. Our collaboration will be uninterrupted, because my task lies here and because, if the battle—which you expect and I do not—takes place, it will be within the walls of this house and garden."

"What makes you think that?"

"Some words which Mme. Essarès overheard last night. The colonel repeated several times, 'The gold is here, Essarès.' He added, 'For years past, your car brought to this house all that there was at your bank in the Rue Lafayette. Siméon, you and the chauffeur used to let the sacks down the last grating on the left. How you used to send it away I do not know. But of what was here on the day when the war broke out, of the seventeen or eighteen hundred bags which they were expecting out yonder, none has left your place. I suspected the trick; and we kept watch night and day. The gold is here.'"

"And have you no clue?"

"Not one. Or this at most; but I attach comparatively little value to it."

He took a crumpled paper from his pocket, unfolded it and continued:

"Besides the pendant, Essarès Bey held in his hand this bit of blotted paper, on which you can see a few straggling, hurriedly-written words. The only ones that are more or less legible are these: 'golden triangle.' What this golden triangle means, what it has to do with the case in hand, I can't for the present tell. The most that I am able to presume is that, like the pendant, the scrap of paper was snatched by Essarès Bey from the man who died at nineteen minutes past seven this morning and that, when he himself was killed at twenty-three minutes past twelve, he was occupied in examining it."

"And then there is the album," said Patrice, making his last point. "You see how all the details are linked together. You may safely believe that it is all one case."

"Very well," said M. Masseron. "One case in two parts. You, captain, had better follow up the second. I grant you that nothing could be stranger than this discovery of photographs of Mme. Essarès and yourself in the same album and in the same pendant. It sets a problem the solution of which will no doubt bring us very near to the truth. We shall meet again soon, Captain Belval, I hope. And, once more, make use of me and of my men."

He shook Patrice by the hand. Patrice held him back:

"I shall make use of you, sir, as you suggest. But is this not the time to take the necessary precautions?"

"They are taken, captain. We are in occupation of the house."

"Yes . . . yes . . . I know; but, all the same . . . I have a sort of presentiment that the day will not end without. . . . Remember old Siméon's strange words. . . ."

M. Masseron began to laugh:

"Come, Captain Belval, we mustn't exaggerate things. If any enemies remain for us to fight, they must stand in great need, for the moment, of taking council with themselves. We'll talk about this to-morrow, shall we, captain?"

He shook hands with Patrice again, bowed to Mme. Essarès and left the room.

Belval had at first made a discreet movement to go out with him. He stopped at the door and walked back again. Mme. Essarès, who seemed not to hear him, sat motionless, bent in two, with her head turned away from him.

"Coralie," he said.

She did not reply; and he uttered her name a second time, hoping that again she might not answer, for her silence suddenly appeared to him to be the one thing in the world for him to desire. That silence no longer implied either constraint or rebellion. Coralie accepted the fact that he was there, by her side, as a helpful friend. And Patrice no longer thought of all the problems that harassed him, nor of the murders that had mounted up, one after another, around them, nor of the dangers that might still encompass them. He thought only of Coralie's yielding gentleness.

"Don't answer, Coralie, don't say a word. It is for me to speak. I must tell you what you do not know, the reasons that made you wish to keep me out of this house . . . out of this house and out of your very life."

He put his hand on the back of the chair in which she was sitting; and his hand just touched Coralie's hair.

"Coralie, you imagine that it is the shame of your life here that keeps you away from me. You blush at having been that man's wife; and this makes you feel troubled and anxious, as though you yourself had been guilty. But why should you? It was not your fault. Surely you know that I can guess the misery and hatred that must have passed between you and him and the constraint that was brought to bear upon you, by some machination, in order to force your consent to the marriage! No, Coralie, there is something else; and I will tell you what it is. There is something else. . . ."

He was bending over her still more. He saw her beautiful profile lit up by the blazing logs and, speaking with increasing fervor and adopting the familiar *tu* and *toi* which, in his mouth, retained a note of affectionate respect, he cried:

"Am I to speak, Little Mother Coralie? I needn't, need I? You have understood; and you read yourself clearly. Ah, I feel you trembling from head to foot! Yes, yes, I tell you, I knew your secret from the very first day. From the very first day you loved your great beggar of a wounded man, all scarred and maimed though he was. Hush! Don't deny it! . . . Yes, I understand: you are rather shocked to hear such words as these spoken to-day. I ought perhaps to have waited. And yet why should I? I am asking you nothing. I know; and that is enough for me. I sha'n't speak of it again for a long time to come, until the inevitable hour arrives when you are forced to tell it to me yourself. Till then I shall keep silence. But our love will always be between us; and it will be exquisite, Little Mother Coralie, it will be exquisite for me to know that you love me. Coralie. . . . There, now you're crying! And you would still deny the truth? Why, when you cry—I know you, Little Mother—it means that your dear heart is overflowing with tenderness and love! You are crying? Ah, Little Mother, I never thought you loved me to that extent!"

Patrice also had tears in his eyes. Coralie's were coursing down her pale cheeks; and he would have given much to kiss that wet face. But the least outward sign of affection appeared to him an offense at such a moment. He was content to gaze at her passionately.

And, as he did so, he received an impression that her thoughts were becoming detached from his own, that her eyes were being attracted by an unexpected sight and that, amid the great silence of their love, she was listening to something that he himself had not heard.

And suddenly he too heard that thing, though it was almost imperceptible. It was not so much a sound as the sensation of a presence mingling with the distant rumble of the town. What could be happening?

The light had begun to fade, without his noticing it. Also unperceived by Patrice, Mme. Essarès had opened the window a little way, for the boudoir was small and the heat of the fire was becoming oppressive. Nevertheless, the two casements were almost touching. It was at this that she was staring; and it was from there that the danger threatened.

Patrice's first impulse was to run to the window, but he restrained himself. The danger was becoming defined. Outside, in the twilight, he distinguished through the slanting panes a human form. Next, he saw between the two casements something which gleamed in the light of the fire and which looked like the barrel of a revolver.

"Coralie is done for," he thought, "if I allow it to be suspected for an instant that I am on my guard."

She was in fact opposite the window, with no obstacle intervening. He therefore said aloud, in a careless tone:

"Coralie, you must be a little tired. We will say good-by."

At the same time, he went round her chair to protect her.

But he had not the time to complete his movement. She also no doubt had seen the glint of the revolver, for she drew back abruptly, stammering:

"Oh, Patrice! . . . Patrice! . . ."

Two shots rang out, followed by a moan.

"You're wounded!" cried Patrice, springing to her side.

"No, no," she said, "but the fright . . ."

"Oh, if he's touched you, the scoundrel!"

"No, he hasn't."

"Are you quite sure?"

He lost thirty or forty seconds, switching on the electric light, looking at Coralie for signs of a wound and waiting in an agony of suspense for her to regain full consciousness. Only then did he rush to the window, open it wide and climb over the balcony. The room was on the first floor. There was plenty of lattice-work on the wall. But, because of his leg, Patrice had some difficulty in making his way down.

Below, on the terrace, he caught his foot in the rungs of an overturned ladder. Next, he knocked against some policemen who were coming from the ground-floor. One of them shouted:

"I saw the figure of a man making off that way."

"Which way?" asked Patrice.

The man was running in the direction of the lane. Patrice followed him. But, at that moment, from close beside the little door, there came shrill cries and the whimper of a choking voice:

"Help! . . . Help! . . ."

When Patrice came up, the policeman was already flashing his electric lantern over the ground; and they both saw a human form writhing in the shrubbery.

"The door's open!" shouted Patrice. "The assassin has escaped! Go after him!"

The policeman vanished down the lane; and, Ya-Bon appearing on the scene, Patrice gave him his orders:

"Quick as you can, Ya-Bon! . . . If the policeman is going up the lane, you go down. Run! I'll look after the victim."

All this time, Patrice was stooping low, flinging the light of the policeman's lantern on the man who lay struggling on the ground. He recognized old Siméon, nearly strangled, with a red-silk cord round his neck.

"How do you feel?" he asked. "Can you understand what I'm saying?"

He unfastened the cord and repeated his question. Siméon stuttered out a series of incoherent syllables and then suddenly began to sing and laugh, a very low, jerky laugh, alternating with hiccoughs. He had gone mad.

When M. Masseron arrived, Patrice told him what had happened:

"Do you really believe it's all over?" he asked.

"No. You were right and I was wrong," said M. Masseron. "We must take every precaution to ensure Mme. Essarès' safety. The house shall be guarded all night."

A few minutes later the policeman and Ya-Bon returned, after a vain search. The key that had served to open the door was found in the lane. It was exactly similar to the one in Patrice Belval's possession, equally old and equally rusty. The would-be murderer had thrown it away in the course of his flight.

It was seven o'clock when Patrice, accompanied by Ya-Bon, left the house in the Rue Raynouard and turned towards Neuilly. As usual, Patrice took Ya-Bon's arm and, leaning upon him for support as he walked, he said:

"I can guess what you're thinking, Ya-Bon."

Ya-Bon grunted.

"That's it," said Captain Belval, in a tone of approval. "We are entirely in agreement all along the line. What strikes you first and foremost is the utter incapacity displayed by the police. A pack of addle-pates, you say? When you speak like that, Master Ya-Bon, you are talking impertinent nonsense, which, coming from you, does not astonish me and which might easily make me give you the punishment you deserve. But we will overlook it this time. Whatever you may say, the police do what they can, not to mention that, in war-time, they have other things to do than to occupy themselves with the mysterious relations between Captain Belval and Mme. Essarès. It is I therefore who will have to act; and I have hardly any one to reckon on but myself. Well, I wonder if I am a match for such adversaries. To think that here's one who has the cheek to come back to the house while it is being watched by the police, to put up a ladder, to listen no doubt to my conversation with M. Masseron and afterwards to what I said to Little Mother Coralie and, lastly, to send a couple of bullets whizzing past our ears! What do you say? Am I the man for the job? And could all the French police, overworked as they are, give me the indispensable assistance? No, the man I need for clearing up a thing like this is an exceptional sort of chap, one who unites every quality in himself, in short the type of man one never sees."

Patrice leant more heavily on his companion's arm:

"You, who know so many good people, haven't you the fellow I want concealed about your person? A genius of sorts? A demigod?"

Ya-Bon grunted again, merrily this time, and withdrew his arm. He always carried a little electric lamp. Switching on the light, he put the handle between his teeth. Then he took a bit of chalk out of his jacket-pocket.

A grimy, weather-beaten plaster wall ran along the street. Ya-Bon took his stand in front of the wall and, turning the light upon it, began to write with an unskilful hand, as though each letter cost him a measureless effort and as though the sum total of those letters were the only one that he had ever succeeded in composing and remembering. In this way he wrote two words which Patrice read out:

Arsène
Lupin.

"Arsène Lupin," said Patrice, under his breath. And, looking at Ya-Bon in amazement, "Are you in your right mind? What do you mean by Arsène Lupin? Are you suggesting Arsène Lupin to me?"

Ya-Bon nodded his head.

"Arsène Lupin? Do you know him?"

"Yes," Ya-Bon signified.

Patrice then remembered that the Senegalese used to spend his days at the hospital getting his good-natured comrades to read all the adventures of Arsène Lupin aloud to him; and he grinned:

"Yes, you know him as one knows somebody whose history one has read."

"No," protested Ya-Bon.

"Do you know him personally?"

"Yes."

"Get out, you silly fool! Arsène Lupin is dead. He threw himself into the sea from a rock; and you pretend that you know him?"

813. By Maurice Leblanc. Translated by Alexander Teixeira de Mattos.

"Yes."

"Do you mean to say that you have met him since he died?"

"Yes."

"By Jove! And Master Ya-Bon's influence with Arsène Lupin is enough to make him come to life again and put himself out at a sign from Master Ya-Bon?"

"Yes."

"I say! I had a high opinion of you as it was, but now there is nothing for me but to make you my bow. A friend of the late Arsène Lupin! We're going it! . . . And how long will it take you to place his ghost at our disposal? Six months? Three months? One month? A fortnight?"

Ya-Bon made a gesture.

"About a fortnight," Captain Belval translated. "Very well, evoke your friend's spirit; I shall be delighted to make his acquaintance. Only, upon my word, you must have a very poor idea of me to imagine that I need a collaborator! What next! Do you take me for a helpless dunderhead?"

CHAPTER IX
PATRICE AND CORALIE

Everything happened as M. Masseron had foretold. The press did not speak. The public did not become excited. The various deaths were casually paragraphed. The funeral of Essarès Bey, the wealthy banker, passed unnoticed.

But, on the day following the funeral, after Captain Belval, with the support of the police, had made an application to the military authorities, a new order of things was established in the house in the Rue Raynouard. It was recognized as Home No. 2 attached to the hospital in the Champs-Élysées; Mme. Essarès was appointed matron; and it became the residence of Captain Belval and his seven wounded men exclusively.

Coralie, therefore, was the only woman remaining. The cook and housemaid were sent away. The seven cripples did all the work of the house. One acted as hall-porter, another as cook, a third as butler. Ya-Bon, promoted to parlor-maid, made it his business to wait on Little Mother Coralie. At night he slept in the passage outside her door. By day he mounted guard outside her window.

"Let no one near that door or that window!" Patrice said to him. "Let no one in! You'll catch it if so much as a mosquito succeeds in entering her room."

Nevertheless, Patrice was not easy in his mind. The enemy had given him too many proofs of reckless daring to let him imagine that he could take any steps to ensure her perfect protection. Danger always creeps in where it is least expected; and it was all the more difficult to ward off in that no one knew whence it threatened. Now that Essarès Bey was dead, who was continuing his work? Who had inherited the task of revenge upon Coralie announced in his last letter?

M. Masseron had at once begun his work of investigation, but the dramatic side of the case seemed to leave him indifferent. Since he had not found the body of the man whose dying cries reached Patrice Belval's ears, since he had discovered no clue to the mysterious assailant who had fired at Patrice and Coralie later in the day, since he was not able to trace where the assailant had obtained his ladder, he dropped these questions and confined his efforts entirely to the search of the eighteen hundred bags of gold. These were all that concerned him.

"We have every reason to believe that they are here," he said, "between the four sides of the quadrilateral formed by the garden and the house. Obviously, a bag of gold weighing a hundredweight does not take up as much room, by a long way, as a sack of coal of the same weight. But, for all that, eighteen hundred bags represent a cubic content; and a content like that is not easily concealed."

In two days he had assured himself that the treasure was hidden neither in the house nor under the house. On the evenings when Essarès Bey's car brought the gold out of the coffers of the Franco-Oriental Bank to the Rue Raynouard, Essarès, the chauffeur and the man known as Grégoire used to pass a thick wire through the grating of which the accomplices spoke. This wire was found. Along the wire ran hooks, which were also found; and on these the bags were slung and afterwards stacked in a large cellar situated exactly under the library. It is needless to say that M. Masseron and his detectives devoted all their ingenuity and all the painstaking patience of which they were capable to the task of searching every corner of this cellar. Their efforts only established beyond doubt that it contained no secret, save that of a staircase which ran down from the library and which was closed at the top by a trap-door concealed by the carpet.

In addition to the grating on the Rue Raynouard, there was another which overlooked the garden, on the level of the first terrace. These two openings were barricaded on the inside by very heavy shutters, so that it was an easy matter to stack thousands and thousands of rouleaus of gold in the cellar before sending them away.

"But how were they sent away?" M. Masseron wondered. "That's the mystery. And why this intermediate stage in the basement, in the Rue Raynouard? Another mystery. And now we have Fakhi, Bournef and Co. declaring that, this time, it was not sent away, that the gold is here and that it can be found for the searching. We have searched the house. There is still the garden. Let us look there."

It was a beautiful old garden and had once formed part of the wide-stretching estate where people were in the habit, at the end of the eighteenth century, of going to drink the Passy waters. With a two-hundred-yard frontage, it ran from the Rue Raynouard to the quay of the river-side and led, by four successive terraces, to an expanse of lawn as old as the rest of the garden, fringed with thickets of evergreens and shaded by groups of tall trees.

But the beauty of the garden lay chiefly in its four terraces and in the view which they afforded of the river, the low ground on the left bank and the distant hills. They were united by twenty sets of steps; and twenty paths climbed from the one to the other, paths cut between the buttressing walls and sometimes hidden in the floods of ivy that dashed from top to bottom.

Here and there a statue stood out, a broken column, or the fragments of a capital. The stone balcony that edged the upper terrace was still adorned with all its old terra-cotta vases. On this terrace also were the ruins of two little round temples where, in the old days, the springs bubbled to the surface. In front of the library windows was a circular basin, with in the center the figure of a child shooting a slender thread of water through the funnel of a shell. It was the overflow from this basin, forming a little stream, that trickled over the rocks against which Patrice had stumbled on the first evening.

"Ten acres to explore before we've done," said M. Masseron to himself.

He employed upon this work, in addition to Belval's cripples, a dozen of his own detectives. It was not a difficult business and was bound to lead to some definite result. As M. Masseron never ceased saying, eighteen hundred bags cannot remain invisible. An excavation leaves traces. You want a hole to go in and out by. But neither the grass of the lawns nor the sand of the paths showed any signs of earth recently disturbed. The ivy? The buttressing-walls? The terraces? Everything was inspected, but in vain. Here and there, in cutting up the ground, old conduit pipes were found, running towards the Seine, and remains of aqueducts that had once served to carry off the Passy waters. But there was no such thing as a cave, an underground chamber, a brick arch or anything that looked like a hiding-place.

Patrice and Coralie watched the progress of the search. And yet, though they fully realized its importance and though, on the other hand, they were still feeling the strain of the recent dramatic hours, in reality they were engrossed only in the inexplicable problem of their fate; and their conversation nearly always turned upon the mystery of the past.

Coralie's mother was the daughter of a French consul at Salonica, where she married a very rich man of a certain age, called Count Odolavitch, the head of an ancient Servian family. He died a year after Coralie was born. The widow and child were at that time in France, at this same house in the Rue Raynouard, which Count Odolavitch had purchased through a young Egyptian called Essarès, his secretary and factotum.

Coralie here spent three years of her childhood. Then she suddenly lost her mother and was left alone in the world. Essarès took her to Salonica, to a surviving sister of her grandfather the consul, a woman many years younger than her brother. This lady took charge of Coralie. Unfortunately, she fell under Essarès' influence, signed papers and made her little grand-niece sign papers, until the child's whole fortune, administered by the Egyptian, gradually disappeared.

At last, when she was about seventeen, Coralie became the victim of an adventure which left the most hideous memory in her mind and which had a fatal effect on her life. She was kidnaped one morning by a band of Turks on the plains of Salonica and spent a fortnight in the palace of the governor of the province, exposed to his desires. Essarès released her. But the release was brought about in so fantastic a fashion that Coralie must have often wondered afterwards whether the Turk and the Egyptian were not in collusion.

At any rate, sick in body and depressed in spirits, fearing a fresh assault upon her liberty and yielding to her aunt's wishes, a month later she married this Essarès, who had already been paying her his addresses and who now definitely assumed in her eyes the figure of a deliverer. It was a hopeless union, the horror of which became manifest to her on the very day on which it was cemented. Coralie was the wife of a man whom she hated and whose love only grew with the hatred and contempt which she showed for it.

Before the end of the year they came and took up their residence at the house in the Rue Raynouard. Essarès, who had long ago established and was at that time managing the Salonica branch of the Franco-Oriental Bank, bought up almost all the shares of the bank itself, acquired the building in the Rue Lafayette for the head office, became one of the financial magnates of Paris and received the title of bey in Egypt.

This was the story which Coralie told Patrice one day in the beautiful garden at Passy; and, in this unhappy past which they explored together and compared with Patrice Belval's own, neither he nor Coralie was able to discover a single point that was common to both. The two of them had lived in different parts of the world. Not one name evoked the same recollection in their minds. There was not a detail that enabled them to understand why each should possess a piece of the same amethyst bead nor why their joint images should be contained in the same medallion-pendant or stuck in the pages of the same album.

"Failing everything else," said Patrice, "we can explain that the pendant found in the hand of Essarès Bey was snatched by him from the unknown friend who was watching over us and whom he murdered. But what about the album, which he wore in a pocket sewn inside his vest?"

Neither attempted to answer the question. Then Patrice asked:

"Tell me about Siméon."

"Siméon has always lived here."

"Even in your mother's time?"

"No, it was one or two years after my mother's death and after I went to Salonica that Essarès put him to look after this property and keep it in good condition."

"Was he Essarès' secretary?"

"I never knew what his exact functions were. But he was not Essarès' secretary, nor his confidant either. They never talked together intimately. He came to see us two or three times at Salonica. I remember one of his visits. I was quite a child and I heard him speaking to Essarès in a very angry tone, apparently threatening him."

"With what?"

"I don't know. I know nothing at all about Siméon. He kept himself very much to himself and was nearly always in the garden, smoking his pipe, dreaming, tending the trees and flowers, sometimes with the assistance of two or three gardeners whom he would send for."

"How did he behave to you?"

"Here again I can't give any definite impression. We never talked; and his occupations very seldom brought him into contact with me. Nevertheless I sometimes thought that his eyes used to seek me, through their yellow spectacles, with a certain persistency and perhaps even a certain interest. Moreover, lately, he liked going with me to the hospital; and he would then, either there or on the way, show himself more attentive, more eager to please . . . so much so that I have been wondering this last day or two . . ."

She hesitated for a moment, undecided whether to speak, and then continued:

"Yes, it's a very vague notion . . . but, all the same . . . Look here, there's one thing I forgot to tell you. Do you know why I joined the hospital in the Champs-Élysées, the hospital where you were lying wounded and ill? It was because Siméon took me there. He knew that I wanted to become a nurse and he suggested this hospital. . . . And then, if you think, later on, the photograph in the pendant, the one showing you in uniform and me as a nurse, can only have been taken at the hospital. Well, of the people here, in this house, no one except Siméon ever went there. . . . You will also remember that he used to come to Salonica, where he saw me as a child and afterwards as a girl, and that there also he may have taken the snapshots in the album. So that, if we allow that he had some correspondent who on his side followed your footsteps in life, it would not be impossible to believe that the unknown friend whom you assume to have intervened between us, the one who sent you the key of the garden . . ."

"Was old Siméon?" Patrice interrupted. "The theory won't hold water."

"Why not?"

"Because this friend is dead. The man who, as you say, sought to intervene between us, who sent me the key of the garden, who called me to the telephone to tell me the truth, that man was murdered. There is not the least doubt about it. I heard the cries of a man who is being killed, dying cries, the cries which a man utters when at the moment of death."

"You can never be sure."

"I am, absolutely. There is no shadow of doubt in my mind. The man whom I call our unknown friend died before finishing his work; he died murdered, whereas Siméon is alive. Besides," continued Patrice, "this man had a different voice from Siméon, a voice which I had never heard before and which I shall never hear again."

Coralie was convinced and did not insist.

They were seated on one of the benches in the garden, enjoying the bright April sunshine. The buds of the chestnut-trees shone at the tips of the branches. The heavy scent of the wall-flowers rose from the borders; and their brown and yellow blossoms, like a cluster of bees and wasps pressed close together, swayed to the light breeze.

Suddenly Patrice felt a thrill. Coralie had placed her hand on his, with engaging friendliness; and, when he turned to look at her, he saw that she was in tears.

"What's the matter, Little Mother Coralie?"

Coralie's head bent down and her cheek touched the officer's shoulder. He dared not move. She was treating him as a protecting elder brother; and he shrank from showing any warmth of affection that might annoy her.

"What is it, dear?" he repeated. "What's the matter?"

"Oh, it is so strange!" she murmured. "Look, Patrice, look at those flowers."

They were on the third terrace, commanding a view of the fourth; and this, the lowest of the terraces, was adorned not with borders of wall-flowers but with beds in which were mingled all manner of spring flowers; tulips, silvery alyssums, hyacinths, with a great round plot of pansies in the middle.

"Look over there," she said, pointing to this plot with her outstretched arm. "Do you see? . . . Letters. . . ."

Patrice looked and gradually perceived that the clumps of pansies were so arranged as to form on the ground some letters that stood out among the other flowers. It did not appear at the first glance. It took a certain time to see; but, once seen, the letters grouped themselves of their own accord, forming three words set down in a single line:

Patrice and
Coralie

"Ah," he said, in a low voice, "I understand what you mean!"

It gave them a thrill of inexpressible excitement to read their two names, which a friendly hand had, so to speak, sown; their two names united in pansy-flowers. It was inexpressibly exciting too that he and she should always find themselves thus linked together, linked together by events, linked together by their portraits, linked together by an unseen force of will, linked together now by the struggling effort of little flowers that spring up, waken into life and blossom in predetermined order.

Coralie, sitting up, said:

"It's Siméon who attends to the garden."

"Yes," he said, wavering slightly. "But surely that does not affect my opinion. Our unknown friend is dead, but Siméon may have known him. Siméon perhaps was acting with him in certain matters and must know a good deal. Oh, if he could only put us on the right road!"

An hour later, as the sun was sinking on the horizon, they climbed the terraces. On reaching the top they saw M. Masseron beckoning to them.

"I have something curious to show you," he said, "something I have found which will interest both you, madame, and you, captain, particularly."

He led them to the very end of the terrace, outside the occupied part of the house next to the library. Two detectives were standing mattock in hand. In the course of their searching, M. Masseron explained, they had begun by removing the ivy from the low wall adorned with terra-cotta vases. Thereupon M. Masseron's attention was attracted by the fact that this wall was covered, for a length of some yards, by a layer of plaster which appeared to be more recent in date than the stone.

"What did it mean?" said M. Masseron. "I had to presuppose some motive. I therefore had this layer of plaster demolished; and underneath it I found a second layer, not so thick as the first and mingled with the rough stone. Come closer . . . or, rather, no, stand back a little way: you can see better like that."

The second layer really served only to keep in place some small white pebbles, which constituted a sort of mosaic set in black pebbles and formed a series of large, written letters, spelling three words. And these three words once again were:

Patrice and
Coralie

"What do you say to that?" asked M. Masseron. "Observe that the inscription goes several years back, at least ten years, when we consider the condition of the ivy clinging to this part of the wall."

"At least ten years," Patrice repeated, when he was once more alone with Coralie. "Ten years ago was when you were not married, when you were still at Salonica and when nobody used to come to this garden . . . nobody except Siméon and such people as he chose to admit. And among these," he concluded, "was our unknown friend who is now dead. And Siméon knows the truth, Coralie."

They saw old Siméon, late that afternoon, as they had seen him constantly since the tragedy, wandering in the garden or along the passages of the house, restless and distraught, with his comforter always wound round his head and his spectacles on his nose, stammering words which no one could understand. At night, his neighbor, one of the maimed soldiers, would often hear him humming to himself.

Patrice twice tried to make him speak. He shook his head and did not answer, or else laughed like an idiot.

The problem was becoming complicated; and nothing pointed to a possible solution. Who was it that, since their childhood, had promised them to each other as a pair betrothed long beforehand by an inflexible ordinance? Who was it that arranged the pansy-bed last autumn, when they did not know each other? And who was it that had written their two names, ten years ago, in white pebbles, within the thickness of a wall?

These were haunting questions for two young people in whom love had awakened quite spontaneously and who suddenly saw stretching behind them a long past common to them both. Each step that they took in the garden seemed to them a pilgrimage amid forgotten memories; and, at every turn in a path, they were prepared to discover some new proof of the bond that linked them together unknown to themselves.

As a matter of fact, during those few days, they saw their initials interlaced twice on the trunk of a tree, once on the back of a bench. And twice again their names appeared inscribed on old walls and concealed behind a layer of plaster overhung with ivy.

On these two occasions their names were accompanied by two separate dates:

Patrice and Coralie, 1904
Patrice and Coralie, 1907

"Eleven years ago and eight years ago," said the officer. "And always our two names: Patrice and Coralie."

Their hands met and clasped each other. The great mystery of their past brought them as closely together as did the great love which filled them and of which they refrained from speaking.

In spite of themselves, however, they sought out solitude; and it was in this way that, a fortnight after the murder of Essarès Bey, as they passed the little door opening on the lane, they decided to go out by it and to stroll down to the river bank. No one saw them, for both the approach to the door and the path leading to it were hidden by a screen of tall bushes; and M. Masseron and his men were exploring the old green-houses, which stood at the other side of the garden, and the old furnace and chimney which had been used for signaling.

But, when he was outside, Patrice stopped. Almost in front of him, in the opposite wall, was an exactly similar door. He called Coralie's attention to it, but she said:

"There is nothing astonishing about that. This wall is the boundary of another garden which at one time belonged to the one we have just left."

"But who lives there?"

"Nobody. The little house which overlooks it and which comes before mine, in the Rue Raynouard, is always shut up."

"Same door, same key, perhaps," Patrice murmured, half to himself.

He inserted in the lock the rusty key, which had reached him by messenger. The lock responded.

"Well," he said, "the series of miracles is continuing. Will this one be in our favor?"

The vegetation had been allowed to run riot in the narrow strip of ground that faced them. However, in the middle of the exuberant grass, a well-trodden path, which looked as if it were often used, started from the door in the wall and rose obliquely to the single terrace, on which stood a dilapidated lodge with closed shutters. It was built on one floor, but was surmounted by a small lantern-shaped belvedere. It had its own entrance in the Rue Raynouard, from which it was separated by a yard and a very high wall. This entrance seemed to be barricaded with boards and posts nailed together.

They walked round the house and were surprised by the sight that awaited them on the right-hand side. The foliage had been trained into rectangular cloisters, carefully kept, with regular arcades cut in yew- and box-hedges. A miniature garden was laid out in this space, the very home of silence and tranquillity. Here also were wall-flowers and pansies and hyacinths. And four paths, coming from four corners of the cloisters, met round a central space, where stood the five columns of a small, open temple, rudely constructed of pebbles and unmortared building-stones.

Under the dome of this little temple was a tombstone and, in front of it, an old wooden praying-chair, from the bars of which hung, on the left, an ivory crucifix and, on the right, a rosary composed of amethyst beads in a gold filigree setting.

"Coralie, Coralie," whispered Patrice, in a voice trembling with emotion, "who can be buried here?"

They went nearer. There were bead wreaths laid in rows on the tombstone. They counted nineteen, each bearing the date of one of the last nineteen years. Pushing them aside, they read the following inscription in gilt letters worn and soiled by the rain:

HERE LIE
PATRICE AND CORALIE,
BOTH OF WHOM WERE MURDERED
ON THE 14th OF APRIL, 1895.
REVENGE TO ME: I WILL REPAY.

CHAPTER X
THE RED CORD

Coralie, feeling her legs give way beneath her, had flung herself on the prie-dieu and there knelt praying fervently and wildly. She could not tell on whose behalf, for the repose of what unknown soul her prayers were offered; but her whole being was afire with fever and exaltation and the very action of praying seemed able to assuage her.

"What was your mother's name, Coralie?" Patrice whispered.

"Louise," she replied.

"And my father's name was Armand. It cannot be either of them, therefore; and yet . . ."

Patrice also was displaying the greatest agitation. Stooping down, he examined the nineteen wreaths, renewed his inspection of the tombstone and said:

"All the same, Coralie, the coincidence is really too extraordinary. My father died in 1895."

"And my mother died in that year too," she said, "though I do not know the exact date."

"We shall find out, Coralie," he declared. "These things can all be verified. But meanwhile one truth becomes clear. The man who used to interlace the names of Patrice and Coralie was not thinking only of us and was not considering only the future. Perhaps he thought even more of the past, of that Coralie and Patrice whom he knew to have suffered a violent death and whom he had undertaken to avenge. Come away, Coralie. No one must suspect that we have been here."

They went down the path and through the two doors on the lane. They were not seen coming in. Patrice at once brought Coralie indoors, urged Ya-Bon and his comrades to increase their vigilance and left the house.

He came back in the evening only to go out again early the next day; and it was not until the day after, at three o'clock in the afternoon, that he asked to be shown up to Coralie.

"Have you found out?" she asked him at once.

"I have found out a great many things which do not dispel the darkness of the present. I am almost tempted to say that they increase it. They do, however, throw a very vivid light on the past."

"Do they explain what we saw two days ago?" she asked, anxiously.

"Listen to me, Coralie."

He sat down opposite her and said:

"I shall not tell you all the steps that I have taken. I will merely sum up the result of those which led to some result. I went, first of all, to the Mayor of Passy's office and from there to the Servian Legation."

"Then you persist in assuming that it was my mother?"

"Yes. I took a copy of her death-certificate, Coralie. Your mother died on the fourteenth of April, 1895."

"Oh!" she said. "That is the date on the tomb!"

"The very date."

"But the name? Coralie? My father used to call her Louise."

"Your mother's name was Louise Coralie Countess Odolavitch."

"Oh, my mother!" she murmured. "My poor darling mother! Then it was she who was murdered. It was for her that I was praying over the way?"

"For her, Coralie, and for my father. I discovered his full name at the mayor's office in the Rue Drouot. My father was Armand Patrice Belval. He died on the fourteenth of April, 1895."

Patrice was right in saying that a singular light had been thrown upon the past. He had now positively established that the inscription on the tombstone related to his father and Coralie's mother, both of whom were murdered on the same day. But by whom and for what reason, in consequence of what tragedies? This was what Coralie asked him to tell her.

"I cannot answer your questions yet," he replied. "But I addressed another to myself, one more easily solved; and that I did solve. This also makes us certain of an essential point. I wanted to know to whom the lodge belonged. The outside, in the Rue Raynouard, affords no clue. You have seen the wall and the door of the yard: they show nothing in particular. But the number of the property was sufficient for my purpose. I went to the local receiver and learnt that the taxes were paid by a notary in the Avenue de l'Opéra. I called on this notary, who told me . . ."

He stopped for a moment and then said:

"The lodge was bought twenty-one years ago by my father. Two years later my father died; and the lodge, which of course formed part of his estate, was put up for sale by the present notary's predecessor and bought by one Siméon Diodokis, a Greek subject."

"It's he!" cried Coralie. "Siméon's name is Diodokis."

"Well, Siméon Diodokis," Patrice continued, "was a friend of my father's, because my father appointed him the sole executor of his will and because it was Siméon Diodokis who, through the notary in question and a London solicitor, paid my school-fees and, when I attained my majority, made over to me the sum of two hundred thousand francs, the balance of my inheritance."

They maintained a long silence. Many things were becoming manifest, but indistinctly, as yet, and shaded, like things seen in the evening mist. And one thing stood in sharper outline than the rest, for Patrice murmured:

"Your mother and my father loved each other, Coralie."

The thought united them more closely and affected them profoundly. Their love was the counterpart of another love, bruised by trials, like theirs, but still more tragic and ending in bloodshed and death.

"Your mother and my father loved each other," he repeated. "I should say they must have belonged to that class of rather enthusiastic lovers whose passion indulges in charming little childish ways, for they had a trick of calling each other, when alone, by names which nobody else used to them; and they selected their second Christian names, which were also yours and mine. One day your mother dropped her amethyst rosary. The largest of the beads broke in two pieces. My father had one of the pieces mounted as a trinket which he hung on his watch-chain. Both were widowed. You were two years old and I was eight. In order to devote himself altogether to the woman he loved, my father sent me to England and bought the lodge in which your mother, who lived in the big house next door, used to go and see him, crossing the lane and using the same key for both doors. It was no doubt in this lodge, or in the garden round it, that they were murdered. We shall find that out, because there must be visible proofs of the murder, proofs which Siméon Diodokis discovered, since he was not afraid to say so in the inscription on the tombstone."

"And who was the murderer?" Coralie asked, under her breath.

"You suspect it, Coralie, as I do. The hated name comes to your mind, even though we have no grounds for speaking with certainty."

"Essarès!" she cried, in anguish.

"Most probably."

She hid her face in her hands:

"No, no, it is impossible. It is impossible that I should have been the wife of the man who killed my mother."

"You bore his name, but you were never his wife. You told him so the evening before his death, in my presence. Let us say nothing that we are unable to say positively; but all the same let us remember that he was your evil genius. Remember also that Siméon, my father's friend and executor, the man who bought the lovers' lodge, the man who swore upon their tomb to avenge them: remember that Siméon, a few months after your mother's death, persuaded Essarès to engage him as caretaker of the estate, became his secretary and gradually made his way into Essarès' life. His only object must have been to carry out a plan of revenge."

"There has been no revenge."

"What do we know about it? Do we know how Essarès met his death? Certainly it was not Siméon who killed him, as Siméon was at the hospital. But he may have caused him to be killed. And revenge has a thousand ways of manifesting itself. Lastly, Siméon was most likely obeying instructions that came from my father. There is little doubt that he wanted first to achieve an aim which my father and your mother had at heart: the union of our destinies, Coralie. And it was this aim that ruled his life. It was he evidently who placed among the knick-knacks which I collected as a child this amethyst of which the other half formed a bead in your rosary. It was he who collected our photographs. He lastly was our unknown friend and protector, the one who sent me the key, accompanied by a letter which I never received, unfortunately."

"Then, Patrice, you no longer believe that he is dead, this unknown friend, or that you heard his dying cries?"

"I cannot say. Siméon was not necessarily acting alone. He may have had a confidant, an assistant in the work which he undertook. Perhaps it was this other man who died at nineteen minutes past seven. I cannot say. Everything that happened on that ill-fated morning remains involved in the deepest mystery. The only conviction that we are able to hold is that for twenty years Siméon Diodokis has worked unobtrusively and patiently on our behalf, doing his utmost to defeat the murderer, and that

Siméon Diodokis is alive. Alive, but mad!" Patrice added. "So that we can neither thank him nor question him about the grim story which he knows or about the dangers that threaten you."

Patrice resolved once more to make the attempt, though he felt sure of a fresh disappointment. Siméon had a bedroom, next to that occupied by two of the wounded soldiers, in the wing which formerly contained the servants' quarters. Here Patrice found him.

He was sitting half-asleep in a chair turned towards the garden. His pipe was in his mouth; he had allowed it to go out. The room was small, sparsely furnished, but clean and light. Hidden from view, the best part of the old man's life was spent here. M. Masseron had often visited the room, in Siméon's absence, and so had Patrice, each from his own point of view.

The only discovery worthy of note consisted of a crude diagram in pencil, on the white wall-paper behind a chest of drawers: three lines intersecting to form a large equilateral triangle. In the middle of this geometrical figure were three words clumsily inscribed in adhesive gold-leaf:

The Golden
Triangle

There was nothing more, not another clue of any kind, to further M. Masseron's search.

Patrice walked straight up to the old man and tapped him on the shoulder:

"Siméon!" he said.

The other lifted his yellow spectacles to him, and Patrice felt a sudden wish to snatch away this glass obstacle which concealed the old fellow's eyes and prevented him from looking into his soul and his distant memories. Siméon began to laugh foolishly.

"So this," thought Patrice, "is my friend and my father's friend. He loved my father, respected his wishes, was faithful to his memory, raised a tomb to him, prayed on it and swore to avenge him. And now his mind has gone."

Patrice felt that speech was useless. But, though the sound of his voice roused no echo in that wandering brain, it was possible that the eyes were susceptible to a reminder. He wrote on a clean sheet of paper the words that Siméon had gazed upon so often:

Patrice and
Coralie
14 April,
1895

The old man looked, shook his head and repeated his melancholy, foolish chuckle.

The officer added a new line:

Armand
Belval

717

The old man displayed the same torpor. Patrice continued the test. He wrote down the names of Essarès Bey and Colonel Fakhi. He drew a triangle. The old man failed to understand and went on chuckling.

But suddenly his laughter lost some of its childishness. Patrice had written the name of Bournef, the accomplice, and this time the old secretary appeared to be stirred by a recollection. He tried to get up, fell back in his chair, then rose to his feet again and took his hat from a peg on the wall.

He left his room and, followed by Patrice, marched out of the house and turned to the left, in the direction of Auteuil. He moved like a man in a trance who is hypnotized into walking without knowing where he is going. He led the way along the Rue de Boulainvilliers, crossed the Seine and turned down the Quai de Grenelle with an unhesitating step. Then, when he reached the boulevard, he stopped, putting out his arm, made a sign to Patrice to do likewise. A kiosk hid them from view. He put his head round it. Patrice followed his example.

Opposite, at the corner of the boulevard and a side-street, was a café, with a portion of the pavement in front of it marked out by dwarf shrubs in tubs. Behind these tubs four men sat drinking. Three of them had their backs turned to Patrice. He saw the only one that faced him, and he at once recognized Bournef.

By this time Siméon was some distance away, like a man whose part is played and who leaves it to others to complete the work. Patrice looked round, caught sight of a post-office and went in briskly. He knew that M. Masseron was at the Rue Raynouard. He telephoned and told him where Bournef was. M. Masseron replied that he would come at once.

Since the murder of Essarès Bey, M. Masseron's enquiry had made no progress in so far as Colonel Fakhi's four accomplices were concerned. True, they discovered the man Grégoire's sanctuary and the bedrooms with the wall-cupboards; but the whole place was empty. The accomplices had disappeared.

"Old Siméon," said Patrice to himself, "was acquainted with their habits. He must have known that they were accustomed to meet at this café on a certain day of the week, at a fixed hour, and he suddenly remembered it all at the sight of Bournef's name."

A few minutes later M. Masseron alighted from his car with his men. The business did not take long. The open front of the café was surrounded. The accomplices offered no resistance. M. Masseron sent three of them under a strong guard to the Dépôt and hustled Bournef into a private room.

"Come along," he said to Patrice. "We'll question him."

"Mme. Essarès is alone at the house," Patrice objected.

"Alone? No. There are all your soldier-men."

"Yes, but I would rather go back, if you don't mind. It's the first time that I've left her and I'm justified in feeling anxious."

"It's only a matter of a few minutes," M. Masseron insisted. "One should always take advantage of the fluster caused by the arrest."

Patrice followed him, but they soon saw that Bournef was not one of those men who are easily put out. He simply shrugged his shoulders at their threats:

"It is no use, sir," he said, "to try and frighten me. I risk nothing. Shot, do you say? Nonsense! You don't shoot people in France for the least thing; and we are all four subjects of a neutral country. Tried? Sentenced? Imprisoned? Never! You forget that you have kept everything dark so far; and, when you hushed up the murder of Mustapha, of Fakhi and of Essarès, it was not done with the object of reviving the case for no valid reason. No, sir, I am quite easy. The internment-camp is the worst that can await me."

"Then you refuse to answer?" said M. Masseron.

"Not a bit of it! I accept internment. But there are twenty different ways of treating a man in these camps, and I should like to earn your favor and, in so doing, make sure of reasonable comfort till the end of the war. But first of all, what do you know?"

"Pretty well everything."

"That's a pity: it decreases my value. Do you know about Essarès' last night?"

"Yes, with the bargain of the four millions. What's become of the money?"

Bournef made a furious gesture:

"Taken from us! Stolen! It was a trap!"

"Who took it?"

"One Grégoire."

"Who was he?"

"His familiar, as we have since learnt. We discovered that this Grégoire was no other than a fellow who used to serve as his chauffeur on occasion."

"And who therefore helped him to convey the bags of gold from the bank to his house."

"Yes. And we also think, we know . . . Look here, you may as well call it a certainty. Grégoire . . . is a woman."

"A woman!"

"Exactly. His mistress. We have several proofs of it. But she's a trustworthy, capable woman, strong as a man and afraid of nothing."

"Do you know her address?"

"No."

"As to the gold: have you no clue to its whereabouts, no suspicion?"

"No. The gold is in the garden or in the house in the Rue Raynouard. We saw it being taken in every day for a week. It has not been taken out since. We kept watch every night. The bags are there."

"No clue either to Essarès' murderer?"

"No, none."

"Are you quite sure?"

"Why should I tell a lie?"

"Suppose it was yourself? Or one of your friends?"

"We thought that you would suspect us. Fortunately, we happen to have an alibi."

"Easy to prove?"

"Impossible to upset."

"We'll look into it. So you have nothing more to reveal?"

"No. But I have an idea . . . or rather a question which you will answer or not, as you please. Who betrayed us? Your reply may throw some useful light, for one person only knew of our weekly meetings here from four to five o'clock, one person only, Essarès Bey; and he himself often came here to confer with us. Essarès is dead. Then who gave us away?"

"Old Siméon."

Bournef started with astonishment:

"What! Siméon? Siméon Diodokis?"

"Yes. Siméon Diodokis, Essarès Bey's secretary."

"He? Oh, I'll make him pay for this, the blackguard! But no, it's impossible."

"What makes you say that it's impossible?"'

"Why, because . . ."

He stopped and thought for some time, no doubt to convince himself that there was no harm in speaking. Then he finished his sentence:

"Because old Siméon was on our side."

"What's that you say?" exclaimed Patrice, whose turn it was to be surprised.

"I say and I swear that Siméon Diodokis was on our side. He was our man. It was he who kept us informed of Essarès Bey's shady tricks. It was he who rang us up at nine o'clock in the evening to tell us that Essarès had lit the furnace of the old hothouses and that the signal of the sparks was going to work. It was he who opened the door to us, pretending to resist, of course, and allowed us to tie him up in the porter's lodge. It was he, lastly, who paid and dismissed the men-servants."

"But why? Why this treachery? For the sake of money?"

"No, from hatred. He bore Essarès Bey a hatred that often gave us the shudders."

"What prompted it?"

"I don't know. Siméon keeps his own counsel. But it dated a long way back."

"Did he know where the gold was hidden?" asked M. Masseron.

"No. And it was not for want of hunting to find out. He never knew how the bags got out the cellar, which was only a temporary hiding-place."

"And yet they used to leave the grounds. If so, how are we to know that the same thing didn't happen this time?"

"This time we were keeping watch the whole way round outside, a thing which Siméon could not do by himself."

Patrice now put the question:

"Can you tell us nothing more about him?"

"No, I can't. Wait, though; there was one rather curious thing. On the afternoon of the great day, I received a letter in which Siméon gave me certain particulars. In the same envelope was another letter, which had evidently got there by some incredible mistake, for it appeared to be highly important."

"What did it say?" asked Patrice, anxiously.

"It was all about a key."

"Don't you remember the details?"

"Here is the letter. I kept it in order to give it back to him and warn him what he had done. Here, it's certainly his writing. . . ."

Patrice took the sheet of notepaper; and the first thing that he saw was his own name. The letter was addressed to him, as he anticipated:

"*Patrice,*

"You will this evening receive a key. The key opens two doors midway down a lane leading to the river: one, on the right, is that of the garden of the woman you love; the other, on the left, that of a garden where I want you to meet me at nine o'clock in the morning on the 14th of April. She will be there also. You shall learn who I am and the object which I intend to attain. You shall both hear things about the past that will bring you still closer together.

"From now until the 14th the struggle which begins to-night will be a terrible one. If anything happens to me, it is certain that the woman you love will run the greatest dangers. Watch over her, Patrice; do not leave her for an instant unprotected. But I do not intend to let anything happen to me; and you shall both know the happiness which I have been preparing for you so long.

"My best love to you."

"It's not signed," said Bournef, "but, I repeat, it's in Siméon's handwriting. As for the lady, she is obviously Mme. Essarès."

"But what danger can she be running?" exclaimed Patrice, uneasily. "Essarès is dead, so there is nothing to fear."

"I wouldn't say that. He would take some killing."

"Whom can he have instructed to avenge him? Who would continue his work?"

721

"I can't say, but I should take no risks."

Patrice waited to hear no more. He thrust the letter into M. Masseron's hand and made his escape.

"Rue Raynouard, fast as you can," he said, springing into a taxi.

He was eager to reach his destination. The dangers of which old Siméon spoke seemed suddenly to hang over Coralie's head. Already the enemy, taking advantage of Patrice's absence, might be attacking his beloved. And who could defend her?

"If anything happens to me," Siméon had said.

And the supposition was partly realized, since he had lost his wits.

"Come, come," muttered Patrice, "this is sheer idiocy. . . . I am fancying things. . . . There is no reason . . ."

But his mental anguish increased every minute. He reminded himself that old Siméon was still in full possession of his faculties at the time when he wrote that letter and gave the advice which it contained. He reminded himself that old Siméon had purposely informed him that the key opened the door of Coralie's garden, so that he, Patrice, might keep an effective watch by coming to her in case of need.

He saw Siméon some way ahead of him. It was growing late, and the old fellow was going home. Patrice passed him just outside the porter's lodge and heard him humming to himself.

"Any news?" Patrice asked the soldier on duty.

"No, sir."

"Where's Little Mother Coralie?"

"She had a walk in the garden and went upstairs half an hour ago."

"Ya-Bon?"

"Ya-Bon went up with Little Mother Coralie. He should be at her door."

Patrice climbed the stairs, feeling a good deal calmer. But, when he came to the first floor, he was astonished to find that the electric light was not on. He turned on the switch. Then he saw, at the end of the passage, Ya-Bon on his knees outside Coralie's room, with his head leaning against the wall. The door was open.

"What are you doing there?" he shouted, running up.

Ya-Bon made no reply. Patrice saw that there was blood on the shoulder of his jacket. At that moment the Senegalese sank to the floor.

"Damn it! He's wounded! Dead perhaps."

He leapt over the body and rushed into the room, switching on the light at once.

Coralie was lying at full length on a sofa. Round her neck was the terrible little red-silk cord. And yet Patrice did not experience that awful, numbing despair which we feel in the presence of irretrievable misfortunes. It seemed to him that Coralie's face had not the pallor of death.

He found that she was in fact breathing:

"She's not dead. She's not dead," said Patrice to himself. "And she's not going to die, I'm sure of it . . . nor Ya-Bon either. . . . They've failed this time."

He loosened the cords. In a few seconds Coralie heaved a deep breath and recovered consciousness. A smile lit up her eyes at the sight of him. But, suddenly remembering, she threw her arms, still so weak, around him:

"Oh, Patrice," she said, in a trembling voice, "I'm frightened . . . frightened for you!"

"What are you frightened of, Coralie? Who is the scoundrel?"

"I didn't see him. . . . He put out the light, caught me by the throat and whispered, 'You first. . . . To-night it will be your lover's turn!' . . . Oh, Patrice, I'm frightened for you! . . ."

CHAPTER XI
ON THE BRINK

Patrice at once made up his mind what to do. He lifted Coralie to her bed and asked her not to move or call out. Then he made sure that Ya-Bon was not seriously wounded. Lastly, he rang violently, sounding all the bells that communicated with the posts which he had placed in different parts of the house.

The men came hurrying up.

"You're a pack of nincompoops," he said. "Some one's been here. Little Mother Coralie and Ya-Bon have had a narrow escape from being killed."

They began to protest loudly.

"Silence!" he commanded. "You deserve a good hiding, every one of you. I'll forgive you on one condition, which is that, all this evening and all to-night, you speak of Little Mother Coralie as though she were dead."

"But whom are we to speak to, sir?" one of them objected. "There's nobody here."

"Yes, there is, you silly fool, since Little Mother Coralie and Ya-Bon have been attacked. Unless it was yourselves who did it! . . . It wasn't? Very well then. . . . And let me have no more nonsense. It's not a question of speaking to others, but of talking among yourselves . . . and of thinking, even, without speaking. There are people listening to you, spying on you, people who hear what you say and who guess what you don't say. So, until to-morrow, Little Mother Coralie will not leave her room. You shall keep watch over her by turns. Those who are not watching will go to bed immediately after dinner. No moving about the house, do you understand? Absolute silence and quiet."

"And old Siméon, sir?"

"Lock him up in his room. He's dangerous because he's mad. They may have taken advantage of his madness to make him open the door to them. Lock him up!"

Patrice's plan was a simple one. As the enemy, believing Coralie to be on the point of death, had revealed to her his intention, which was to kill Patrice as well, it was necessary that he should think himself free to act, with nobody to suspect his schemes or to be on his guard against him. He would enter upon the struggle and would then be caught in a trap.

Pending this struggle, for which he longed with all his might, Patrice saw to Ya-Bon's wound, which proved to be only slight, and questioned him and Coralie. Their answers tallied at all points. Coralie, feeling a little tired, was lying down reading. Ya-Bon remained in the passage, outside the open door, squatting on the floor, Arab-fashion. Neither of them heard anything suspicious. And suddenly Ya-Bon saw a shadow between himself and the light in the passage. This light, which came from an electric lamp, was put out at just about the same time as the light in the bed-room. Ya-Bon, already half-erect, felt a violent blow in the back of the neck and lost consciousness. Coralie tried to escape by the door of her boudoir, was unable to open it, began to cry out and was at once seized and thrown down. All this had happened within the space of a few seconds.

The only hint that Patrice succeeded in obtaining was that the man came not from the staircase but from the servants' wing. This had a smaller staircase of its own, communicating with the kitchen through a pantry by which the tradesmen entered from the Rue Raynouard. The door leading to the street was locked. But some one might easily possess a key.

After dinner Patrice went in to see Coralie for a moment and then, at nine o'clock, retired to his bedroom, which was situated a little lower down, on the same side. It had been used, in Essarès Bey's lifetime, as a smoking-room.

As the attack from which he expected such good results was not likely to take place before the middle of the night, Patrice sat down at a roll-top desk standing against the wall and took out the diary in which he had begun his detailed record of recent events. He wrote on for half an hour or forty minutes and was about to close the book when he seemed to hear a vague rustle, which he would certainly not have noticed if his nerves had not been stretched to their utmost state of tension. And he remembered the day when he and Coralie had once before been shot at. This time, however, the window was not open nor even ajar.

He therefore went on writing without turning his head or doing anything to suggest that his attention had been aroused; and he set down, almost unconsciously, the actual phases of his anxiety:

"He is here. He is watching me. I wonder what he means to do. I doubt if he will smash a pane of glass and fire a bullet at me. He has tried that method before and found it uncertain and a failure. No, his plan is thought out, I expect, in a different and more intelligent fashion. He is more likely to wait for me to go to bed, when he can watch me sleeping and effect his entrance by some means which I can't guess.

"Meanwhile, it's extraordinarily exhilarating to know that his eyes are upon me. He hates me; and his hatred is coming nearer and nearer to mine, like one sword feeling its way towards another before clashing. He is watching me as a wild animal, lurking in the dark, watches its prey and selects the spot on which to fasten its fangs. But no, I am certain that it's he who is the prey, doomed beforehand to defeat and destruction. He is preparing his knife or his red-silk cord. And it's these two hands of mine that will finish the battle. They are strong and powerful and are already enjoying their victory. They will be victorious."

Patrice shut down the desk, lit a cigarette and smoked it quietly, as his habit was before going to bed. Then he undressed, folded his clothes carefully over the back of a chair, wound up his watch, got into bed and switched off the light.

"At last," he said to himself, "I shall know the truth. I shall know who this man is. Some friend of Essarès', continuing his work? But why this hatred of Coralie? Is he in love with her, as he is trying to finish me off too? I shall know . . . I shall soon know. . . ."

An hour passed, however, and another hour, during which nothing happened on the side of the window. A single creaking came from somewhere beside the desk. But this no doubt was one of those sounds of creaking furniture which we often hear in the silence of the night.

Patrice began to lose the buoyant hope that had sustained him so far. He perceived that his elaborate sham regarding Coralie's death was a poor thing after all and that a man of his enemy's stamp might well refuse to be taken in by it. Feeling rather put out, he was on the point of going to sleep, when he heard the same creaking sound at the same spot.

The need to do something made him jump out of bed. He turned on the light. Everything seemed to be as he had left it. There was no trace of a strange presence.

"Well," said Patrice, "one thing's certain: I'm no good. The enemy must have smelt a rat and guessed the trap I laid for him. Let's go to sleep. There will be nothing happening to-night."

There was in fact no alarm.

Next morning, on examining the window, he observed that a stone ledge ran above the ground-floor all along the garden front of the house, wide enough for a man to walk upon by holding on to the balconies and rain-pipes. He inspected all the rooms to which the ledge gave access. None of them was old Siméon's room.

"He hasn't stirred out, I suppose?" he asked the two soldiers posted on guard.

"Don't think so, sir. In any case, we haven't unlocked the door."

Patrice went in and, paying no attention to the old fellow, who was still sucking at his cold pipe, he searched the room, having it at the back of his mind that the enemy might take refuge there. He found nobody. But what he did discover, in a press in the wall, was a number of things which he had not seen on the occasion of his investigations in M. Masseron's company. These consisted of a rope-ladder, a coil of lead pipes, apparently gas-pipes, and a small soldering-lamp.

"This all seems devilish odd," he said to himself. "How did the things get in here? Did Siméon collect them without any definite object, mechanically? Or am I to assume that Siméon is merely an instrument of the enemy's? He used to know the enemy before he lost his reason; and he may be under his influence at present."

Siméon was sitting at the window, with his back to the room. Patrice went up to him and gave a start. In his hands the old man held a funeral-wreath made of black and white beads. It bore a date, "14 April, 1915," and made the twentieth, the one which Siméon was preparing to lay on the grave of his dead friends.

"He will lay it there," said Patrice, aloud. "His instinct as an avenging friend, which has guided his steps through life, continues in spite of his insanity. He will lay it on the grave. That's so, Siméon, isn't it: you will take it there to-morrow? For to-morrow is the fourteenth of April, the sacred anniversary. . . ."

He leant over the incomprehensible being who held the key to all the plots and counterplots, to all the treachery and benevolence that constituted the inextricable drama. Siméon thought that Patrice wanted to take the wreath from him and pressed it to his chest with a startled gesture.

"Don't be afraid," said Patrice. "You can keep it. To-morrow, Siméon, to-morrow, Coralie and I will be faithful to the appointment which you gave us. And to-morrow perhaps the memory of the horrible past will unseal your brain."

The day seemed long to Patrice, who was eager for something that would provide a glimmer in the surrounding darkness. And now this glimmer seemed about to be kindled by the arrival of this twentieth anniversary of the fourteenth of April.

At a late hour in the afternoon M. Masseron called at the Rue Raynouard.

"Look what I've just received," he said to Patrice. "It's rather curious: an anonymous letter in a disguised hand. Listen:

"'*Sir*, be warned. They're going away. Take care. To-morrow evening the 1800 bags will be on their way out of the country.

A FRIEND OF FRANCE.'"

"And to-morrow is the fourteenth of April," said Patrice, at once connecting the two trains of thought in his mind.

"Yes. What makes you say that?"

"Nothing. . . . Something that just occurred to me. . . ."

He was nearly telling M. Masseron all the facts associated with the fourteenth of April and all those concerning the strange personality of old Siméon. If he did not speak, it was for obscure reasons, perhaps because he wished to work out this part of the case alone, perhaps also because of a sort of shyness which prevented him from admitting M. Masseron into all the secrets of the past. He said nothing about it, therefore, and asked:

"What do you think of the letter?"

"Upon my word, I don't know what to think. It may be a warning with something to back it, or it may be a trick to make us adopt one course of conduct rather than another. I'll talk about it to Bournef."

"Nothing fresh on his side?"

"No; and I don't expect anything in particular. The alibi which he has submitted is genuine. His friends and he are so many supers. Their parts are played."

The coincidence of dates was all that stuck in Patrice's mind. The two roads which M. Masseron and he were following suddenly met on this day so long since marked out by fate. The past and the present were about to unite. The catastrophe was at hand. The fourteenth of April was the day on which the gold was to disappear for good and also the day on which an unknown voice had summoned Patrice and Coralie to the same tryst which his father and her mother had kept twenty years ago.

And the next day was the fourteenth of April.

At nine o'clock in the morning Patrice asked after old Siméon.

"Gone out, sir. You had countermanded your orders."

Patrice entered the room and looked for the wreath. It was not there. Moreover, the three things in the cupboard, the rope-ladder, the coil of lead and the glazier's lamp, were not there either.

"Did Siméon take anything with him?"

"Yes, sir, a wreath."

"Nothing else?"

"No, sir."

The window was open. Patrice came to the conclusion that the things had gone by this way, thus confirming his theory that the old fellow was an unconscious confederate.

Shortly before ten o'clock Coralie joined him in the garden. Patrice had told her the latest events. She looked pale and anxious.

They went round the lawns and, without being seen, reached the clumps of dwarf shrubs which hid the door on the lane. Patrice opened the door. As he started to open the other his hand hesitated. He felt sorry that he had not told M. Masseron and that he and Coralie were performing by themselves a pilgrimage which certain signs warned him to be dangerous. He shook off the obsession, however. He had two revolvers with him. What had he to fear?

"You're coming in, aren't you, Coralie?"

"Yes," she said.

"I somehow thought you seemed undecided, anxious . . ."

"It's quite true," said Coralie. "I feel a sort of hollowness."

"Why? Are you afraid?"

"No. Or rather yes. I'm not afraid for to-day, but in some way for the past. I think of my poor mother, who went through this door, as I am doing, one April morning. She was perfectly happy, she was going to meet her love. . . . And then I feel as if I wanted to hold her back and cry, 'Don't go on. . . . Death is lying in wait for you. . . . Don't go on. . . .' And it's I who hear those words of terror, they ring in my ears; it's I who hear them and I dare not go on. I'm afraid."

"Let's go back, Coralie."

She only took his arm:

"No," she said, in a firm voice. "We'll walk on. I want to pray. It will do me good."

Boldly she stepped along the little slanting path which her mother had followed and climbed the slope amid the tangled weeds and the straggling branches. They passed the lodge on their left and reached the leafy cloisters where each had a parent lying buried. And at once, at the first glance, they saw that the twentieth wreath was there.

"Siméon has come," said Patrice. "An all-powerful instinct obliged him to come. He must be somewhere near."

While Coralie knelt down beside the tombstone, he hunted around the cloisters and went as far as the middle of the garden. There was nothing left but to go to the lodge, and this was evidently a dread act which they put off performing, if not from fear, at least from the reverent awe which checks a man on entering a place of death and crime.

It was Coralie once again who gave the signal for action:

728

"Come," she said.

Patrice did not know how they would make their way into the lodge, for all its doors and windows had appeared to them to be shut. But, as they approached, they saw that the back-door opening on the yard was wide open, and they at once thought that Siméon was waiting for them inside.

It was exactly ten o'clock when they crossed the threshold of the lodge. A little hall led to a kitchen on one side and a bedroom on the other. The principal room must be that opposite. The door stood ajar.

"That's where it must have happened . . . long ago," said Coralie, in a frightened whisper.

"Yes," said Patrice, "we shall find Siméon there. But, if your courage fails you, Coralie, we had better give it up."

An unquestioning force of will supported her. Nothing now would have induced her to stop. She walked on.

Though large, the room gave an impression of coziness, owing to the way in which it was furnished. The sofas, armchairs, carpet and hangings all tended to add to its comfort; and its appearance might well have remained unchanged since the tragic death of the two who used to occupy it. This appearance was rather that of a studio, because of a skylight which filled the middle of the high ceiling, where the belvedere was. The light came from here. There were two other windows, but these were hidden by curtains.

"Siméon is not here," said Patrice.

Coralie did not reply. She was examining the things around her with an emotion which was reflected in every feature. There were books, all of them going back to the last century. Some of them were signed "Coralie" in pencil on their blue or yellow wrappers. There were pieces of unfinished needlework, an embroidery-frame, a piece of tapestry with a needle hanging to it by a thread of wool. And there were also books signed "Patrice" and a box of cigars and a blotting-pad and an inkstand and penholders. And there were two small framed photographs, those of two children, Patrice and Coralie. And thus the life of long ago went on, not only the life of two lovers who loved each other with a violent and fleeting passion, but of two beings who dwell together in the calm assurance of a long existence spent in common.

"Oh, my darling, darling mother!" Coralie whispered.

Her emotion increased with each new memory. She leant trembling on Patrice's shoulder.

"Let's go," he said.

"Yes, dear, yes, we had better. We will come back again. . . . We will come back to them. . . . We will revive the life of love that was cut short by their death. Let us go for to-day; I have no strength left."

But they had taken only a few steps when they stopped dismayed.

The door was closed.

Their eyes met, filled with uneasiness.

"We didn't close it, did we?" he asked.

"No," she said, "we didn't close it."

He went to open it and perceived that it had neither handle nor lock.

It was a single door, of massive wood that looked hard and substantial. It might well have been made of one piece, taken from the very heart of an oak. There was no paint or varnish on it. Here and there were scratches, as if some one had been rapping at it with a tool. And then . . . and then, on the right, were these few words in pencil:

> *Patrice and*
> *Coralie, 14*
> *April, 1895*
> *God will*
> *avenge us*

Below this was a cross and, below the cross, another date, but in a different and more recent handwriting:

> *14 April,*
> *1915*

"This is terrible, this is terrible," said Patrice. "To-day's date! Who can have written that? It has only just been written. Oh, it's terrible! . . . Come, come, after all, we can't . . ."

He rushed to one of the windows, tore back the curtain that veiled it and pulled upon the casement. A cry escaped him. The window was walled up, walled up with building-stones that filled the space between the glass and the shutters.

He ran to the other window and found the same obstacle.

There were two doors, leading probably to the bedroom on the right and to a room next to the kitchen on the left. He opened them quickly. Both doors were walled up.

He ran in every direction, during the first moment of terror, and then hurled himself against the first of the three doors and tried to break it down. It did not move. It might have been an immovable block.

Then, once again, they looked at each other with eyes of fear; and the same terrible thought came over them both. The thing that had happened before was being repeated! The tragedy was being played a second time. After the mother and the father, it was the turn of the daughter and the son. Like the lovers of yesteryear, those of to-day were prisoners. The enemy held them in his powerful grip; and they would doubtless soon know how their parents had died by seeing how they themselves would die. . . . 14 April, 1895. . . . 14 April, 1915. . . .

CHAPTER XII
IN THE ABYSS

"No, no, no!" cried Patrice. "I won't stand this!"

He flung himself against the windows and doors, took up an iron dog from the fender and banged it against the wooden doors and the stone walls. Barren efforts! They were the same which his father had made before him; and they could only result in the same mockery of impotent scratches on the wood and the stone.

"Oh, Coralie, Coralie!" he cried in his despair. "It's I who have brought you to this! What an abyss I've dragged you into! It was madness to try to fight this out by myself! I ought to have called in those who understand, who are accustomed to it! . . . No, I was going to be so clever! . . . Forgive me, Coralie."

She had sunk into a chair. He, almost on his knees beside her, threw his arms around her, imploring her pardon.

She smiled, to calm him:

"Come, dear," she said, gently, "don't lose courage. Perhaps we are mistaken. . . . After all, there's nothing to show that it is not all an accident."

"The date!" he said. "The date of this year, of this day, written in another hand! It was your mother and my father who wrote the first . . . but this one, Coralie, this one proves premeditation, and an implacable determination to do away with us."

She shuddered. Still she persisted in trying to comfort him:

"It may be. But yet it is not so bad as all that. We have enemies, but we have friends also. They will look for us."

"They will look for us, but how can they ever find us, Coralie? We took steps to prevent them from guessing where we were going; and not one of them knows this house."

"Old Siméon does."

"Siméon came and placed his wreath, but some one else came with him, some one who rules him and who has perhaps already got rid of him, now that Siméon has played his part."

"And what then, Patrice?"

He felt that she was overcome and began to be ashamed of his own weakness:

"Well," he said, mastering himself, "we must just wait. After all, the attack may not materialize. The fact of our being locked in does not mean that we are lost. And, even so, we shall make a fight for it, shall we not? You need not think that I am at the end of my strength or my resources. Let us wait, Coralie, and act."

The main thing was to find out whether there was any entrance to the house which could allow of an unforeseen attack. After an hour's search they took up the carpet and found tiles which showed nothing unusual. There was certainly nothing except the door, and, as they could not prevent this from being opened, since it opened outwards, they heaped up most of the furniture in front of it, thus forming a barricade which would protect them against a surprise.

Then Patrice cocked his two revolvers and placed them beside him, in full sight.

"This will make us easy in our minds," he said. "Any enemy who appears is a dead man."

But the memory of the past bore down upon them with all its awful weight. All their words and all their actions others before them had spoken and performed, under similar conditions, with the same thoughts and the same forebodings. Patrice's father must have prepared his weapons. Coralie's mother must have folded her hands and prayed. Together they had barricaded the door and together sounded the walls and taken up the carpet. What an anguish was this, doubled as it was by a like anguish!

To dispel the horror of the idea, they turned the pages of the books, works of fiction and others, which their parents had read. On certain pages, at the end of a chapter or volume, were lines constituting notes which Patrice's father and Coralie's mother used to write each other.

"*Darling Patrice,*

"I ran in this morning to recreate our life of yesterday and to dream of our life this afternoon. As you will arrive before me, you will read these lines. You will read that I love you. . . ."

And, in another book:

"*My own Coralie,*

"You have this minute gone; I shall not see you until to-morrow and I do not want to leave this haven where our love has tasted such delights without once more telling you . . ."

They looked through most of the books in this way, finding, however, instead of the clues for which they hoped, nothing but expressions of love and affection. And they spent more than two hours waiting and dreading what might happen.

"There will be nothing," said Patrice. "And perhaps that is the most awful part of it, for, if nothing occurs, it will mean that we are doomed not to leave this room. And, in that case . . ."

Patrice did not finish the sentence. Coralie understood. And together they received a vision of the death by starvation that seemed to threaten them. But Patrice exclaimed:

"No, no, we have not that to fear. No. For people of our age to die of hunger takes several days, three or four days or more. And we shall be rescued before then."

"How?" asked Coralie.

"How? Why, by our soldiers, by Ya-Bon, by M. Masseron! They will be uneasy if we do not come home to-night."

"You yourself said, Patrice, that they cannot know where we are."

"They'll find out. It's quite simple. There is only the lane between the two gardens. Besides, everything we do is set down in my diary, which is in the desk in my room. Ya-Bon knows of its existence. He is bound to speak of it to M. Masseron. And then . . . and then there is Siméon. What will have become of him? Surely they will notice his movements? And won't he give a warning of some kind?"

But words were powerless to comfort them. If they were not to die of hunger, then the enemy must have contrived another form of torture. Their inability to do anything kept them on the rack. Patrice began his investigations again. A curious accident turned them in a new direction. On opening one of the books through which they had not yet looked, a book published in 1895, Patrice saw two pages turned down together. He separated them and read a letter addressed to him by his father:

"*Patrice, my dear Son,*

"If ever chance places this note before your eyes, it will prove that I have met with a violent death which has prevented my destroying it. In that case, Patrice, look for the truth concerning my death on the wall of the studio, between the two windows. I shall perhaps have time to write it down."

The two victims had therefore at that time foreseen the tragic fate in store for them; and Patrice's father and Coralie's mother knew the danger which they ran in coming to the lodge. It remained to be seen whether Patrice's father had been able to carry out his intention.

Between the two windows, as all around the room, was a wainscoting of varnished wood, topped at a height of six feet by a cornice. Above the cornice was the plain plastered wall. Patrice and Coralie had already observed, without paying particular attention to it, that the wainscoting seemed to have been renewed in this part, because the varnish of the boards did not have the same uniform color. Using one of the iron dogs as a chisel, Patrice broke down the cornice and lifted the first board. It broke easily. Under this plank, on the plaster of the wall, were lines of writing.

"It's the same method," he said, "as that which old Siméon has since employed. First write on the walls, then cover it up with wood or plaster."

He broke off the top of the other boards and in this way brought several complete lines into view, hurried lines, written in pencil and slightly worn by time. Patrice deciphered them with the greatest emotion. His father had written them at a moment when death was stalking at hand. A few hours later he had ceased to live. They were the evidence of his death-agony and perhaps too an imprecation against the enemy who was killing him and the woman he loved.

Patrice read, in an undertone:

"I am writing this in order that the scoundrel's plot may not be achieved to the end and in order to ensure his punishment. Coralie and I are no doubt going to perish, but at least we shall not die without revealing the cause of our death.

"A few days ago, he said to Coralie, 'You spurn my love, you load me with your hatred. So be it. But I shall kill you both, your lover and you, in such a manner that I can never be accused of the death, which will look like suicide. Everything is ready. Beware, Coralie.'

"Everything was, in fact, ready. He did not know me, but he must have known that Coralie used to meet somebody here daily; and it was in this lodge that he prepared our tomb.

"What manner of death ours will be we do not know. Lack of food, no doubt. It is four hours since we were imprisoned. The door closed upon us, a heavy door which he must have placed there last night. All the other openings, doors and windows alike, are stopped up with blocks of stone laid and cemented since our last meeting. Escape is impossible. What is to become of us?"

The uncovered portion stopped here. Patrice said:

"You see, Coralie, they went through the same horrors as ourselves. They too dreaded starvation. They too passed through long hours of waiting, when inaction is so painful; and it was more or less to distract their thoughts that they wrote those lines."

He went on, after examining the spot:

"They counted, most likely, on what happened, that the man who was killing them would not read this document. Look, one long curtain was hung over these two windows and the wall between them, one curtain, as is proved by the single rod covering the whole distance. After our parents' death no one thought of drawing it, and the truth remained concealed until the day when Siméon discovered it and, by way of precaution, hid it again under a wooden panel and hung up two curtains in the place of one. In this way everything seemed normal."

Patrice set to work again. A few more lines made their appearance:

"Oh, if I were the only one to suffer, the only one to die! But the horror of it all is that I am dragging my dear Coralie with me. She fainted and is lying down now, prostrate by the fears which she tries so hard to overcome. My poor darling! I seem already to see the pallor of death on her sweet face. Forgive me, dearest, forgive me!"

Patrice and Coralie exchanged glances. Here were the same sentiments which they themselves felt, the same scruples, the same delicacy, the same effacement of self in the presence of the other's grief.

"He loved your mother," Patrice murmured, "as I love you. I also am not afraid of death. I have faced it too often, with a smile! But you, Coralie, you, for whose sake I would undergo any sort of torture . . . !"

He began to walk up and down, once more yielding to his anger:

"I shall save you, Coralie, I swear it. And what a delight it will then be to take our revenge! He shall have the same fate which he was devising for us. Do you understand, Coralie? He shall die here, here in this room. Oh, how my hatred will spur me to bring that about!"

He tore down more pieces of boarding, in the hope of learning something that might be useful to him, since the struggle was being renewed under exactly similar conditions. But the sentences that followed, like those which Patrice had just uttered, were oaths of vengeance:

"Coralie, he shall be punished, if not by us, then by the hand of God. No, his infernal scheme will not succeed. No, it will never be believed that we had recourse to suicide to relieve ourselves of an existence that was built up of happiness and joy. No, his crime will be known. Hour by hour I shall here set down the undeniable proofs. . . ."

"Words, words!" cried Patrice, in a tone of exasperation. "Words of vengeance and sorrow, but never a fact to guide us. Father, will you tell us nothing to save your Coralie's daughter? If your Coralie succumbed, let mine escape the disaster, thanks to your aid, father! Help me! Counsel me!"

But the father answered the son with nothing but more words of challenge and despair:

"Who can rescue us? We are walled up in this tomb, buried alive and condemned to torture without being able to defend ourselves. My revolver lies there, upon the table. What is the use of it? The enemy does not attack us. He has time on his side, unrelenting time which kills of its own strength, by the mere fact that it is time. Who can rescue us? Who will save my darling Coralie?"

The position was terrible, and they felt all its tragic horror. It seemed to them as though they were already dead, once they were enduring the same trial endured by others and that they were still enduring it under the same conditions. There was nothing to enable them to escape any of the phases through which the other two, his father and her mother, had passed. The similarity between their own and their parents' fate was so striking that they seemed to be suffering two deaths, and the second agony was now commencing.

Coralie gave way and began to cry. Moved by her tears, Patrice attacked the wainscoting with new fury, but its boards, strengthened by cross-laths, resisted his efforts:

At last he read:

"What is happening? We had an impression that some one was walking outside, in the garden. Yes, when we put our ears to the stone wall built in the embrasure of the window, we thought we heard footsteps. Is it possible? Oh, if it only were! It would mean the struggle, at last. Anything rather than the maddening silence and endless uncertainty!

"That's it! . . . That's it! . . . The sound is becoming more distinct. . . . It is a different sound, like that which you make when you dig the ground with a pick-ax. Some one is digging the ground, not in front of the house, but on the right, near the kitchen. . . ."

Patrice redoubled his efforts. Coralie came and helped him. This time he felt that a corner of the veil was being lifted. The writing went on:

"Another hour, with alternate spells of sound and silence: the same sound of digging and the same silence which suggests work that is being continued.

"And then some one entered the hall, one person; he, evidently. We recognized his step. . . . He walks without attempting to deaden it. . . . Then he went to the kitchen, where he worked the same way as before, with a pick-ax, but on the stones this time. We also heard the noise of a pane of glass breaking.

"And now he has gone outside again and there is a new sort of sound, against the house, a sound that seems to travel up the house as though the wretch had to climb to a height in order to carry out his plan. . . ."

Patrice stopped reading and looked at Coralie. Both of them were listening.

"Hark!" he said, in a low voice.

"Yes, yes," she answered, "I hear. . . . Steps outside the house . . . in the garden. . . ."

They went to one of the windows, where they had left the casement open behind the wall of building-stones, and listened. There was really some one walking; and the knowledge that the enemy was approaching gave them the same sense of relief that their parents had experienced.

Some one walked thrice round the house. But they did not, like their parents, recognize the sound of the footsteps. They were those of a stranger, or else steps that had changed their tread. Then, for a few minutes, they heard nothing more. And suddenly another sound arose; and, though in their innermost selves they were expecting it, they were nevertheless stupefied at hearing it. And Patrice, in a hollow voice, laying stress upon each syllable, uttered the sentence which his father had written twenty years before:

"It's the sound which you make when you dig the ground with a pick-ax."

Yes, It must be that. Some one was digging the ground, not in front of the house, but on the right, near the kitchen.

And so the abominable miracle of the revived tragedy was continuing. Here again the former act was repeated, a simple enough act in itself, but one which became sinister because it was one of those which had already been performed and because it was announcing and preparing the death once before announced and prepared.

An hour passed. The work went on, paused and went on again. It was like the sound of a spade at work in a courtyard, when the grave-digger is in no hurry and takes a rest and then resumes his work.

Patrice and Coralie stood listening side by side, their eyes in each other's eyes, their hands in each other's hands.

"He's stopping," whispered Patrice.

"Yes," said Coralie; "only I think . . ."

"Yes, Coralie, there's some one in the hall. . . . Oh, we need not trouble to listen! We have only to remember. There: 'He goes to the kitchen and digs as he did just now, but on the stones this time.' . . . And then . . . and then . . . oh, Coralie, the same sound of broken glass!"

It was memories mingling with the grewsome reality. The present and the past formed but one. They foresaw events at the very instant when these took place.

The enemy went outside again; and, forthwith, the sound seemed "to travel up the house as though the wretch had to climb to a height in order to carry out his plans."

And then . . . and then what would happen next? They no longer thought of consulting the inscription on the wall, or perhaps they did not dare. Their attention was concentrated on the invisible and sometimes imperceptible deeds that were being accomplished against them outside, an uninterrupted stealthy effort, a mysterious twenty-year-old plan whereof each slightest detail was settled as by clockwork!

The enemy entered the house and they heard a rustling at the bottom of the door, a rustling of soft things apparently being heaped or pushed against the wood. Next came other vague noises in the two adjoining rooms, against the walled doors, and similar noises outside, between the stones of the windows and the open shutters. And then they heard some one on the roof.

They raised their eyes. This time they felt certain that the last act was at hand, or at least one of the scenes of the last act. The roof to them was the framed skylight which occupied the center of the ceiling and admitted the only daylight that entered the room. And still the same agonizing question rose to their minds: what was going to happen? Would the enemy show his face outside the skylight and reveal himself at last?

This work on the roof continued for a considerable time. Footsteps shook the zinc sheets that covered it, moving between the right-hand side of the house and the edge of the skylight. And suddenly this skylight, or rather a part of it, a square containing four panes, was lifted, a very little way, by a hand which inserted a stick to keep it open.

And the enemy again walked across the roof and went down the side of the house.

They were almost disappointed and felt such a craving to know the truth that Patrice once more fell to breaking the boards of the wainscoting, removing the last pieces, which covered the end of the inscription. And what they read made them live the last few minutes all over again. The enemy's return, the rustle against the walls and the walled windows, the noise on the roof, the opening of the skylight, the method of supporting it: all this had happened in the same order and, so to speak, within the same limit of time. Patrice's father and Coralie's mother had undergone the same impressions. Destiny seemed bent on following the same paths and making the same movements in seeking the same object.

And the writing went on:

"He is going up again, he is going up again. . . . There's his footsteps on the roof. . . . He is near the skylight. . . . Will he look through? . . . Shall we see his hated face? . . ."

"He is going up again, he is going up again," gasped Coralie, nestling against Patrice.

The enemy's footsteps were pounding over the zinc.

"Yes," said Patrice, "he is going up as before, without departing from the procedure followed by the other. Only we do not know whose face will appear to us. Our parents knew their enemy."

She shuddered at her image of the man who had killed her mother; and she asked:

"It was he, was it not?"

"Yes, it was he. There is his name, written by my father."

Patrice had almost entirely uncovered the inscription. Bending low, he pointed with his finger:

"Look. Read the name: Essarès. You can see it down there: it was one of the last words my father wrote."

And Coralie read:

"The skylight rose higher, a hand lifted it and we saw . . . we saw, laughing as he looked down on us— oh, the scoundrel—Essarès! . . . Essarès! . . . And then he passed something through the opening, something that came down, that unrolled itself in the middle of the room, over our heads: a ladder, a rope-ladder.

"We did not understand. It was swinging in front of us. And then, in the end, I saw a sheet of paper rolled round the bottom rung and pinned to it. On the paper, in Essarès' handwriting, are the words, 'Send Coralie up by herself. Her life shall be saved. I give her ten minutes to accept. If not . . .'"

"Ah," said Patrice, rising from his stooping posture, "will this also be repeated? What about the ladder, the rope-ladder, which I found in old Siméon's cupboard?"

Coralie kept her eyes fixed on the skylight, for the footsteps were moving around it. Then they stopped. Patrice and Coralie had not a doubt that the moment had come and that they also were about to see their enemy. And Patrice said huskily, in a choking voice:

"Who will it be? There are three men who could have played this sinister part as it was played before. Two are dead, Essarès and my father. And Siméon, the third, is mad. Is it he, in his madness, who has set the machine working again? But how are we to imagine that he could have done it with such precision? No, no, it is the other one, the one who directs him and who till now has remained in the background."

He felt Coralie's fingers clutching his arm.

"Hush," she said, "here he is!"

"No, no."

"Yes, I'm sure of it."

Her imagination had foretold what was preparing; and in fact, as once before, the skylight was raised higher. A hand lifted it. And suddenly they saw a head slipping under the open framework.

It was the head of old Siméon.

"The madman!" Patrice whispered, in dismay. "The madman!"

"But perhaps he isn't mad," she said. "He can't be mad."

She could not check the trembling that shook her.

The man overhead looked down upon them, hidden behind his spectacles, which allowed no expression of satisfied hatred or joy to show on his impassive features.

"Coralie," said Patrice, in a low voice, "do what I say. . . . Come. . . ."

He pushed her gently along, as though he were supporting her and leading her to a chair. In reality he had but one thought, to reach the table on which he had placed his revolvers, take one of them and fire.

Siméon remained motionless, like some evil genius come to unloose the tempest. . . . Coralie could not rid herself of that glance which weighted upon her.

"No," she murmured, resisting Patrice, as though she feared that his intention would precipitate the dreaded catastrophe, "no, you mustn't. . . ."

But Patrice, displaying greater determination, was near his object. One more effort and his hand would hold the revolver.

He quickly made up his mind, took rapid aim and fired a shot.

The head disappeared from sight.

"Oh," said Coralie, "you were wrong, Patrice! He will take his revenge on us. . . ."

"No, perhaps not," said Patrice, still holding his revolver. "I may very well have hit him. The bullet struck the frame of the skylight. But it may have glanced off, in which case . . ."

They waited hand in hand, with a gleam of hope, which did not last long, however.

The noise on the roof began again. And then, as before—and this they really had the impression of not seeing for the first time—as before, something passed through the opening, something that came down, that unrolled itself in the middle of the room, a ladder, a rope-ladder, the very one which Patrice had seen in old Siméon's cupboard.

As before, they looked at it; and they knew so well that everything was being done over again, that the facts were inexorably, pitilessly linked together, they were so certain of it that their eyes at once sought the sheet of paper which must inevitably be pinned to the bottom rung.

It was there, forming a little scroll, dry and discolored and torn at the edges. It was the sheet of twenty years ago, written by Essarès and now serving, as before, to convey the same temptation and the same threat:

"Send Coralie up by herself. Her life shall be saved. I give her ten minutes to accept. If not . . ."

CHAPTER XIII
THE NAILS IN THE COFFIN

"If not . . ."

Patrice repeated the words mechanically, several times over, while their formidable significance became apparent to both him and Coralie. The words meant that, if Coralie did not obey and did not deliver herself to the enemy, if she did not flee from prison to go with the man who held the keys of the prison, the alternative was death.

At that moment neither of them was thinking what end was in store for them nor even of that death itself. They thought only of the command to separate which the enemy had issued against them. One was to go and the other to die.

Coralie was promised her life if she would sacrifice Patrice. But what was the price of the promise? And what would be the form of the sacrifice demanded?

There was a long silence, full of uncertainty and anguish between the two lovers. They were coming to grips with something; and the drama was no longer taking place absolutely outside them, without their playing any other part than that of helpless victims. It was being enacted within themselves; and they had the power to alter its ending. It was a terrible problem. It had already been set to the earlier Coralie; and she had solved it as a lover would, for she was dead. And now it was being set again.

Patrice read the inscription; and the rapidly scrawled words became less distinct:

"I have begged and entreated Coralie. . . . She flung herself on her knees before me. She wants to die with me. . . ."

Patrice looked at Coralie. He had read the words in a very low voice; and she had not heard them. Then, in a burst of passion, he drew her eagerly to him and exclaimed:

"You must go, Coralie! You can understand that my not saying so at once was not due to hesitation. No, only . . . I was thinking of that man's offer . . . and I am frightened for your sake. . . . What he asks, Coralie, is terrible. His reason for promising to save your life is that he loves you. And so you understand. . . . But still, Coralie, you must obey . . . you must go on living. . . . Go! It is no use waiting for the ten minutes to pass. He might change his mind and condemn you to death as well. No, Coralie, you must go, you must go at once!"

"I shall stay," she replied, simply.

He gave a start:

"But this is madness! Why make a useless sacrifice? Are you afraid of what might happen if you obeyed him?"

"No."

"Then go."

"I shall stay."

"But why? Why this obstinacy? It can do no good. Then why stay?"

"Because I love you, Patrice."

He stood dumfounded. He knew that she loved him and he had already told her so. But that she loved him to the extent of preferring to die in his company, this was an unexpected, exquisite and at the same time terrible delight.

"Ah," he said, "you love me, Coralie! You love me!"

"I love you, my own Patrice."

She put her arms around his neck; and he felt that hers was an embrace too strong to be sundered. Nevertheless, he was resolved to save her; and he refused to yield:

"If you love me," he said, "you must obey me and save your life. Believe me, it is a hundred times more painful for me to die with you than to die alone. If I know that you are free and alive, death will be sweet to me."

She did not listen and continued her confession, happy in making it, happy in uttering words which she had kept to herself so long:

"I have loved you, Patrice, from the first day I saw you. I knew it without your telling me; and my only reason for not telling you earlier was that I was waiting for a solemn occasion, for a time when it would be a glory to tell you so, while I looked into the depths of your eyes and offered myself to you entirely. As I have had to speak on the brink of the grave, listen to me and do not force upon me a separation which would be worse than death."

"No, no," he said, striving to release himself, "it is your duty to go."

He made another effort and caught hold of her hands:

"It is your duty to go," he whispered, "and, when you are free, to do all that you can to save me."

"What are you saying, Patrice?"

"Yes," he repeated, "to save me. There is no reason why you should not escape from that scoundrel's clutches, report him, seek assistance, warn our friends. You can call out, you can play some trick. . . ."

She looked at him with so sad a smile and such a doubting expression that he stopped speaking.

"You are trying to mislead me, my poor darling," she said, "but you are no more taken in by what you say than I am. No, Patrice, you well know that, if I surrender myself to that man, he will reduce me to silence or imprison me in some hiding-place, bound hand and foot, until you have drawn your last breath."

"You really think that?"

"Just as you do, Patrice. Just as you are sure of what will happen afterwards."

"Well, what will happen?"

"Ah, Patrice, if that man saves my life, it will not be out of generosity. Don't you see what his plan is, his abominable plan, once I am his prisoner? And don't you also see what my only means of escape will be? Therefore, Patrice, if I am to die in a few hours, why not die now, in your arms . . . at the same time as yourself, with my lips to yours? Is that dying? Is it not rather living, in one instant, the most wonderful of lives?"

He resisted her embrace. He knew that the first kiss of her proffered lips would deprive him of all his power of will.

"This is terrible," he muttered. "How can you expect me to accept your sacrifice, you, so young, with years of happiness before you?"

"Years of mourning and despair, if you are gone."

"You must live, Coralie. I entreat you to, with all my soul."

"I cannot live without you, Patrice. You are my only happiness. I have no reason for existence except to love you. You have taught me to love. I love you!"

Oh, those heavenly words! For the second time they rang between the four walls of that room. The same words, spoken by the daughter, which the mother had spoken with the same passion and the same glad acceptance of her fate! The same words made twice holy by the recollection of death past and the thought of death to come!

Coralie uttered them without alarm. All her fears seemed to disappear in her love; and it was love alone that shook her voice and dimmed the brightness of her eyes.

Patrice contemplated her with a rapt look. He too was beginning to think that minutes such as these were worth dying for. Nevertheless, he made a last effort:

"And if I ordered you to go, Coralie?"

"That is to say," she murmured, "if you ordered me to go to that man and surrender myself to him? Is that what you wish, Patrice?"

The thought was too much for him.

"Oh, the horror of it! That man . . . that man . . . you, my Coralie, so stainless and undefiled! . . ."

Neither he nor she pictured the man in the exact image of Siméon. To both of them, notwithstanding the hideous vision perceived above, the enemy retained a mysterious character. It was perhaps Siméon. It was perhaps another, of whom Siméon was but the instrument. Assuredly it was the enemy, the evil genius crouching above their heads, preparing their death-throes while he pursued Coralie with his foul desire.

Patrice asked one more question:

"Did you ever notice that Siméon sought your company?"

"No, never. If anything, he rather avoided me."

"Then it's because he's mad. . . ."

"I don't think he is mad: he is revenging himself."

"Impossible. He was my father's friend. All his life long he worked to bring us together: surely he would not kill us deliberately?"

"I don't know, Patrice, I don't understand. . . ."

They discussed it no further. It was of no importance whether their death was caused by this one or that one. It was death itself that they had to fight, without troubling who had set it loose against them. And what could they do to ward it off?

"You agree, do you not?" asked Coralie, in a low voice.

He made no answer.

"I shall not go," she went on, "but I want you to be of one mind with me. I entreat you. It tortures me to think that you are suffering more than I do. You must let me bear my share. Tell me that you agree."

"Yes," he said, "I agree."

"My own Patrice! Now give me your two hands, look right into my eyes and smile."

Mad with love and longing they plunged themselves for an instant into a sort of ecstasy. Then she asked:

"What is it, Patrice? You seem distraught again."

He gave a hoarse cry:

"Look! . . . Look . . ."

This time he was certain of what he had seen. The ladder was going up. The ten minutes were over.

He rushed forward and caught hold of one of the rungs. The ladder no longer moved.

He did not know exactly what he intended to do. The ladder afforded Coralie's only chance of safety. Could he abandon that hope and resign himself to the inevitable?

One or two minutes passed. The ladder must have been hooked fast again, for Patrice felt a firm resistance up above.

Coralie was entreating him:

"Patrice," she asked, "Patrice, what are you hoping for?"

He looked around and above him, as though seeking an idea, and he seemed also to look inside himself, as though he were seeking that idea amid all the memories which he had accumulated at the moment when his father also held the ladder, in a last effort of will. And suddenly, throwing up his leg, he placed his left foot on the fifth rung of the ladder and began to raise himself by the uprights.

It was an absurd attempt to scale the ladder, to reach the skylight, to lay hold of the enemy and thus save himself and Coralie. If his father had failed before him, how could he hope to succeed?

It was all over in less than three seconds. The ladder was at once unfastened from the hook that kept it hanging from the skylight; and Patrice and the ladder came to the ground together. At the same time a strident laugh rang out above, followed the next moment by the sound of the skylight closing.

Patrice picked himself up in a fury, hurled insults at the enemy and, as his rage increased, fired two revolver shots, which broke two of the panes. He next attacked the doors and windows, banging at them with the iron dog which he had taken from the fender. He hit the walls, he hit the floor, he shook his fist at the invisible enemy who was mocking him. But suddenly, after a few blows struck at space, he was compelled to stop. Something like a thick veil had glided overhead. They were in the dark.

He understood what had happened. The enemy had lowered a shutter upon the skylight, covering it entirely.

"Patrice! Patrice!" cried Coralie, maddened by the blotting out of the light and losing all her strength of mind. "Patrice! Where are you, Patrice? Oh, I'm frightened! Where are you?"

They began to grope for each other, like blind people, and nothing that had gone before seemed to them more horrible than to be lost in this pitiless blackness.

"Patrice! Oh, Patrice! Where are you?"

Their hands touched, Coralie's poor little frozen fingers and Patrice's hands that burned with fever, and they pressed each other and twined together and clutched each other as though to assure themselves that they were still living.

"Oh, don't leave me, Patrice!" Coralie implored.

"I am here," he replied. "Have no fear: they can't separate us."

"You are right," she panted, "they can't separate us. We are in our grave."

The word was so terrible and Coralie uttered it so mournfully that a reaction overtook Patrice.

"No! What are you talking about?" he exclaimed. "We must not despair. There is hope of safety until the last moment."

Releasing one of his hands, he took aim with his revolver. A few faint rays trickled through the chinks around the skylight. He fired three times. They heard the crack of the wood-work and the chuckle of the enemy. But the shutter must have been lined with metal, for no split appeared.

Besides, the chinks were forthwith stopped up; and they became aware that the enemy was engaged in the same work that he had performed around the doors and windows. It was obviously very thorough and took a long time in the doing. Next came another work, completing the first. The enemy was nailing the shutter to the frame of the skylight.

It was an awful sound! Swift and light as were the taps of the hammer, they seemed to drive deep into the brain of those who heard them. It was their coffin that was being nailed down, their great coffin with a lid hermetically sealed that now bore heavy upon them. There was no hope left, not a possible chance of escape. Each tap of the hammer strengthened their dark prison, making yet more impregnable the walls that stood between them and the outer world and bade defiance to the most resolute assault:

"Patrice," stammered Coralie, "I'm frightened . . . That tapping hurts me so!" . . .

She sank back in his arms. Patrice felt tears coursing down her cheeks.

Meanwhile the work overhead was being completed. They underwent the terrible experience which condemned men must feel on the morning of their last day, when from their cells they hear the preparations: the engine of death that is being set up, or the electric batteries that are being tested. They hear men striving to have everything ready, so that not one propitious chance may remain and so that destiny may be fulfilled. Death had entered the enemy's service and was working hand in hand with him. He was death itself, acting, contriving and fighting against those whom he had resolved to destroy.

"Don't leave me," sobbed Coralie, "don't leave me! . . ."

"Only for a second or two," he said. "We must be avenged later."

"What is the use, Patrice? What can it matter to us?"

He had a box containing a few matches. Lighting them one after the other, he led Coralie to the panel with the inscription.

"What are you going to do?" she asked.

"I will not have our death put down to suicide. I want to do what our parents did before us and to prepare for the future. Some one will read what I am going to write and will avenge us."

He took a pencil from his pocket and bent down. There was a free space, right at the bottom of the panel. He wrote:

"Patrice Belval and Coralie, his betrothed, die the same death, murdered by Siméon Diodokis, 14 April, 1915."

But, as he finished writing, he noticed a few words of the former inscription which he had not yet read, because they were placed outside it, so to speak, and did not appear to form part of it.

"One more match," he said. "Did you see? There are some words there, the last, no doubt, that my father wrote."

She struck a match. By the flickering light they made out a certain number of misshapen letters, obviously written in a hurry and forming two words:

"*Asphyxiated. . . . Oxide. . . .*"

The match went out. They rose in silence. Asphyxiated! They understood. That was how their parents had perished and how they themselves would perish. But they did not yet fully realize how the thing would happen. The lack of air would never be great enough to suffocate them in this large room, which contained enough to last them for many days.

"Unless," muttered Patrice, "unless the quality of the air can be impaired and therefore . . ."

He stopped. Then he went on:

"Yes, that's it. I remember."

He told Coralie what he suspected, or rather what conformed so well with the reality as to leave no room for doubt. He had seen in old Siméon's cupboard not only the rope-ladder which the madman had brought with him, but also a coil of lead pipes. And now Siméon's behavior from the moment when they were locked in, his movements to and fro around the lodge, the care with which he had stopped up every crevice, his labors along the wall and on the roof: all this was explained in the most definite fashion. Old Siméon had simply fitted to a gas-meter, probably in the kitchen, the pipe which he had next laid along the wall and on the roof. This therefore was the way in which they were about to die, as their parents had died before them, stifled by ordinary gas.

Panic-stricken, they began to run aimlessly about the room, holding hands, while their disordered brains, bereft of thought or will, seemed like tiny things shaken by the fiercest gale. Coralie uttered incoherent words. Patrice, while imploring her to keep calm, was himself carried away by the storm and powerless to resist the terrible agony of the darkness wherein death lay waiting. At such times a man tries to flee, to escape the icy breath that is already chilling his marrow. He must flee, but where? Which way? The walls are insurmountable and the darkness is even harder than the walls.

They stopped, exhausted. A low hiss was heard somewhere in the room, the faint hiss that issues from a badly-closed gas-jet. They listened and perceived that it came from above. The torture was beginning.

"It will last half an hour, or an hour at most," Patrice whispered.

Coralie had recovered her self-consciousness:

"We shall be brave," she said.

"Oh, if I were alone! But you, you, my poor Coralie!"

"It is painless," she murmured.

"You are bound to suffer, you, so weak!"

"One suffers less, the weaker one is. Besides, I know that we sha'n't suffer, Patrice."

She suddenly appeared so placid that he on his side was filled with a great peace. Seated on a sofa, their fingers still entwined, they silently steeped themselves in the mighty calm which comes when we think that events have run their course. This calm is resignation, submission to superior forces. Natures such as theirs cease to rebel when destiny has manifested its orders and when nothing remains but acquiescence and prayer.

She put her arm round Patrice's neck:

"I am your bride in the eyes of God," she said. "May He receive us as He would receive a husband and wife."

Her gentle resignation brought tears to his eyes. She dried them with her kisses, and, of her own seeking, offered him her lips.

They sat wrapped in an infinite silence. They perceived the first smell of gas descending around them, but they felt no fear.

"Everything will happen as it did before, Coralie," whispered Patrice, "down to the very last second. Your mother and my father, who loved each other as we do, also died in each other's arms, with their lips joined together. They had decided to unite us and they have united us."

"Our grave will be near theirs," she murmured.

Little by little their ideas became confused and they began to think much as a man sees through a rising mist. They had had nothing to eat; and hunger now added its discomfort to the vertigo in which their minds were imperceptibly sinking. As it increased, their uneasiness and anxiety left them, to be followed by a sense of ecstasy, then lassitude, extinction, repose. The dread of the coming annihilation faded out of their thoughts.

Coralie, the first to be affected, began to utter delirious words which astonished Patrice at first:

"Dearest, there are flowers falling, roses all around us. How delightful!"

Presently he himself grew conscious of the same blissful exaltation, expressing itself in tenderness and joyful emotion. With no sort of dismay he felt her gradually yielding in his arms and abandoning herself; and he had the impression that he was following her down a measureless abyss, all bathed with light, where they floated, he and she, descending slowly and without effort towards a happy valley.

Minutes or perhaps hours passed. They were still descending, he supporting her by the waist, she with her head thrown back a little way, her eyes closed and a smile upon her lips. He remembered pictures showing gods thus gliding through the blue of heaven; and, drunk with pure, radiant light and air, he continued to circle above the happy valley.

But, as he approached it, he felt himself grow weary. Coralie weighed heavily on his bent arm. The descent increased in speed. The waves of light turned to darkness. A thick cloud came, followed by others that formed a whirl of gloom.

And suddenly, worn out, his forehead bathed in sweat and his body shaking with fever, he pitched forward into a great black pit. . . .

CHAPTER XIV
A STRANGE CHARACTER

It was not yet exactly death. In his present condition of agony, what lingered of Patrice's consciousness mingled, as in a nightmare, the life which he knew with the imaginary world in which he now found himself, the world which was that of death.

In this world Coralie no longer existed; and her loss distracted him with grief. But he seemed to hear and see somebody whose presence was revealed by a shadow passing before his closed eyelids. This somebody he pictured to himself, though without reason, under the aspect of Siméon, who came to verify the death of his victims, began by carrying Coralie away, then came back to Patrice and carried him away also and laid him down somewhere. And all this was so well-defined that Patrice wondered whether he had not woke up.

Next hours passed . . . or seconds. In the end Patrice had a feeling that he was falling asleep, but as a man sleeps in hell, suffering the moral and physical tortures of the damned. He was back at the bottom of the black pit, which he was making desperate efforts to leave, like a man who has fallen into the sea and is trying to reach the surface. In this way, with the greatest difficulty, he passed through one waste of water after another, the weight of which stifled him. He had to scale them, gripping with his hands and feet to things that slipped, to rope-ladders which, possessing no points of support, gave way beneath him.

Meanwhile the darkness became less intense. A little muffled daylight mingled with it. Patrice felt less greatly oppressed. He half-opened his eyes, drew a breath or two and, looking round, beheld a sight that surprised him, the embrasure of an open door, near which he was lying in the air, on a sofa. Beside him he saw Coralie, on another sofa. She moved restlessly and seemed to be in great discomfort.

"She is climbing out of the black pit," he thought to himself. "Like me, she is struggling. My poor Coralie!"

There was a small table between them, with two glasses of water on it. Parched with thirst, he took one of them in his hand. But he dared not drink.

At that moment some one came through the open door, which Patrice perceived to be the door of the lodge; and he observed that it was not old Siméon, as he had thought, but a stranger whom he had never seen before.

"I am not asleep," he said to himself. "I am sure that I am not asleep and that this stranger is a friend."

And he tried to say it aloud, to make certainty doubly sure. But he had not the strength.

The stranger, however, came up to him and, in a gentle voice, said:

"Don't tire yourself, captain. You're all right now. Allow me. Have some water."

The stranger handed him one of the two glasses; Patrice emptied it at a draught, without any feeling of distrust, and was glad to see Coralie also drinking.

"Yes, I'm all right now," he said. "Heavens, how good it is to be alive! Coralie is really alive, isn't she?"

He did not hear the answer and dropped into a welcome sleep.

When he woke up, the crisis was over, though he still felt a buzzing in his head and a difficulty in drawing a deep breath. He stood up, however, and realized that all these sensations were not fanciful, that he was really outside the door of the lodge and that Coralie had drunk the glass of water and was peacefully sleeping.

"How good it is to be alive!" he repeated.

He now felt a need for action, but dared not go into the lodge, notwithstanding the open door. He moved away from it, skirting the cloisters containing the graves, and then, with no exact object, for he did not yet grasp the reason of his own actions, did not understand what had happened to him and was simply walking at random, he came back towards the lodge, on the other front, the one overlooking the garden.

Suddenly he stopped. A few yards from the house, at the foot of a tree standing beside the slanting path, a man lay back in a wicker long-chair, with his face in the shade and his legs in the sun. He was sleeping, with his head fallen forward and an open book upon his knees.

Then and not till then did Patrice clearly understand that he and Coralie had escaped being killed, that they were both really alive and that they owed their safety to this man whose sleep suggested a state of absolute security and satisfied conscience.

Patrice studied the stranger's appearance. He was slim of figure, but broad-shouldered, with a sallow complexion, a slight mustache on his lips and hair beginning to turn gray at the temples. His age was probably fifty at most. The cut of his clothes pointed to dandyism. Patrice leant forward and read the title of the book: *The Memoirs of Benjamin Franklin*. He also read the initials inside a hat lying on the grass: "L. P."

"It was he who saved me," said Patrice to himself, "I recognize him. He carried us both out of the studio and looked after us. But how was the miracle brought about? Who sent him?"

He tapped him on the shoulder. The man was on his feet at once, his face lit up with a smile:

"Pardon me, captain, but my life is so much taken up that, when I have a few minutes to myself, I use them for sleeping, wherever I may be . . . like Napoleon, eh? Well, I don't object to the comparison. . . . But enough about myself. How are you feeling now? And madame—'Little Mother Coralie'—is she better? I saw no use in waking you, after I had opened the doors and taken you outside. I had done what was necessary and felt quite easy. You were both breathing. So I left the rest to the good pure air."

He broke off, at the sight of Patrice's disconcerted attitude; and his smile made way for a merry laugh:

"Oh, I was forgetting: you don't know me! Of course, it's true, the letter I sent you was intercepted. Let me introduce myself. Don Luis Perenna, a member of an old Spanish family, genuine patent of nobility, papers all in order. . . . But I can see that all this tells you nothing," he went on, laughing still more gaily. "No doubt Ya-Bon described me differently when he wrote my name on that street-wall, one evening a fortnight ago. Aha, you're beginning to understand! . . . Yes, I'm the man you sent for to help you. Shall I mention the name, just bluntly? Well, here goes, captain! . . . Arsène Lupin, at your service."

The Teeth of the Tiger. By Maurice Leblanc. Translated by Alexander Teixeira de Mattos. "Luis Perenna" is one of several anagrams of "Arsène Lupin."

Patrice was stupefied. He had utterly forgotten Ya-Bon's proposal and the unthinking permission which he had given him to call in the famous adventurer. And here was Arsène Lupin standing in front of him, Arsène Lupin, who, by a sheer effort of will that resembled an incredible miracle, had dragged him and Coralie out of their hermetically-sealed coffin.

He held out his hand and said:

"Thank you!"

"Tut!" said Don Luis, playfully. "No thanks! Just a good hand-shake, that's all. And I'm a man you can shake hands with, captain, believe me. I may have a few peccadilloes on my conscience, but on the other hand I have committed a certain number of good actions which should win me the esteem of decent folk . . . beginning with my own. And so . . ."

He interrupted himself again, seemed to reflect and, taking Patrice by a button of his jacket, said:

"Don't move. We are being watched."

"By whom?"

"Some one on the quay, right at the end of the garden. The wall is not high. There's a grating on the top of it. They're looking through the bars and trying to see us."

"How do you know? You have your back turned to the quay; and then there are the trees."

"Listen."

"I don't hear anything out of the way."

"Yes, the sound of an engine . . . the engine of a stopping car. Now what would a car want to stop here for, on the quay, opposite a wall with no house near it?"

"Then who do you think it is?"

"Why, old Siméon, of course!"

"Old Siméon!"

"Certainly. He's looking to see whether I've really saved the two of you."

"Then he's not mad?"

"Mad? No more mad than you or I!"

"And yet . . ."

"What you mean is that Siméon used to protect you; that his object was to bring you two together; that he sent you the key of the garden-door; and so on and so on."

"Do you know all that?"

"Well, of course! If not, how could I have rescued you?"

"But," said Patrice, anxiously, "suppose the scoundrel returns to the attack. Ought we not to take some precautions? Let's go back to the lodge: Coralie is all alone."

"There's no danger."

"Why?"

"Because I'm here."

Patrice was more astounded than ever:

"Then Siméon knows you?" he asked. "He knows that you are here?"

"Yes, thanks to a letter which I wrote you under cover to Ya-Bon and which he intercepted. I told you that I was coming; and he hurried to get to work. Only, as my habit is on these occasions, I hastened on my arrival by a few hours, so that I caught him in the act."

"At that moment you did not know he was the enemy; you knew nothing?"

"Nothing at all."

"Was it this morning?"

"No, this afternoon, at a quarter to two."

Patrice took out his watch:

"And it's now four. So in two hours . . ."

"Not that. I've been here an hour."

"Did you find out from Ya-Bon?"

"Do you think I've no better use for my time? Ya-Bon simply told me that you were not there, which was enough to astonish me."

"After that?"

"I looked to see where you were."

"How?"

"I first searched your room and, doing so in my own thorough fashion, ended by discovering that there was a crack at the back of your roll-top desk and that this crack faced a hole in the wall of the next room. I was able therefore to pull out the book in which you kept your diary and acquaint myself with what was going on. This, moreover, was how Siméon became aware of your least intentions. This was how he knew of your plan to come here, on a pilgrimage, on the fourteenth of April. This was how, last night, seeing you write, he preferred, before attacking you, to know what you were writing. Knowing it and learning, from your own words, that you were on your guard, he refrained. You see how simple it all is. If M. Masseron had grown uneasy at your absence, he would have been just as successful. Only he would have been successful to-morrow."

"That is to say, too late."

"Yes, too late. This really isn't his business, however, nor that of the police. So I would rather that they didn't meddle with it. I asked your wounded soldiers to keep silent about anything that may strike them as queer. Therefore, if M. Masseron comes to-day, he will think that everything is in order. Well, having satisfied my mind in this respect and possessing the necessary information from your diary, I took Ya-Bon with me and walked across the lane and into the garden."

"Was the door open?"

"No, but Siméon happened to be coming out at that moment. Bad luck for him, wasn't it? I took advantage of it boldly. I put my hand on the latch and we went in, without his daring to protest. He certainly knew who I was."

"But you didn't know at that time that he was the enemy?"

"I didn't know? And what about your diary?"

"I had no notion . . ."

"But, captain, every page is an indictment of the man. There's not an incident in which he did not take part, not a crime which he did not prepare."

"In that case you should have collared him."

"And if I had? What good would it have done me? Should I have compelled him to speak? No, I shall hold him tightest by leaving him his liberty. That will give him rope, you know. You see already he's prowling round the house instead of clearing out. Besides, I had something better to do: I had first to rescue you two . . . if there was still time. Ya-Bon and I therefore rushed to the door of the lodge. It was open; but the other, the door of the studio, was locked and bolted. I drew the bolts; and to force the lock was, for me, child's play. Then the smell of gas was enough to tell me what had happened, Siméon must have fitted an old meter to some outside pipe, probably the one which supplied the lamps on the lane, and he was suffocating you. All that remained for us to do was to fetch the two of you out and give you the usual treatment: rubbing, artificial respiration and so on. You were saved."

"I suppose he removed all his murderous appliances?" asked Patrice.

"No, he evidently contemplated coming back and putting everything to rights, so that his share in the business could not be proved, so too that people might believe in your suicide, a mysterious suicide, death without apparent cause; in short, the same tragedy that happened with your father and Little Mother Coralie's mother."

"Then you know? . . ."

"Why, haven't I eyes to read with? What about the inscription on the wall, your father's revelations? I know as much as you do, captain . . . and perhaps a bit more."

"More?"

"Well, of course! Habit, you know, experience! Plenty of problems, unintelligible to others, seem to me the simplest and clearest that can be. Therefore . . ."

Don Luis hesitated whether to go on:

"No," he said, "it's better that I shouldn't speak. The mystery will be dispelled gradually. Let us wait. For the moment . . ."

He again stopped, this time to listen:

"There, he must have seen you. And now that he knows what he wants to, he's going away."

Patrice grew excited:

"He's going away! You really ought to have collared him. Shall we ever find him again, the scoundrel? Shall we ever be able to take our revenge?"

Don Luis smiled:

"There you go, calling him a scoundrel, the man who watched over you for twenty years, who brought you and Little Mother Coralie together, who was your benefactor!"

"Oh, I don't know! All this is so bewildering! I can't help hating him. . . . The idea of his getting away maddens me. . . . I should like to torture him and yet . . ."

He yielded to a feeling of despair and took his head between his two hands. Don Luis comforted him:

"Have no fear," he said. "He was never nearer his downfall than at the present moment. I hold him in my hand as I hold this leaf."

"But how?"

"The man who's driving him belongs to me."

"What's that? What do you mean?"

"I mean that I put one of my men on the driver's seat of a taxi, with instructions to hang about at the bottom of the lane, and that Siméon did not fail to take the taxi in question."

"That is to say, you suppose so," Patrice corrected him, feeling more and more astounded.

"I recognized the sound of the engine at the bottom of the garden when I told you."

"And are you sure of your man?"

"Certain."

"What's the use? Siméon can drive far out of Paris, stab the man in the back . . . and then when shall we get to know?"

"Do you imagine that people can get out of Paris and go running about the high-roads without a special permit? No, if Siméon leaves Paris he will have to drive to some railway station or other and we shall know of it twenty minutes after. And then we'll be off."

"How?"

"By motor."

"Then you have a pass?"

"Yes, valid for the whole of France."

"You don't mean it!"

"I do; and a genuine pass at that! Made out in the name of Don Luis Perenna, signed by the minister of the interior and countersigned . . ."

"By whom?"

"By the President of the Republic."

Patrice felt his bewilderment change all at once into violent excitement. Hitherto, in the terrible adventure in which he was engaged, he had undergone the enemy's implacable will and had known little besides defeat and the horrors of ever-threatening death. But now a more powerful will suddenly arose in his favor. And everything was abruptly altered. Fate seemed to be changing its course, like a ship which an unexpected fair wind brings back into harbor.

"Upon my word, captain," said Don Luis, "I thought you were going to cry like Little Mother Coralie. Your nerves are overstrung. And I daresay you're hungry. We must find you something to eat. Come along."

He led him slowly towards the lodge and, speaking in a rather serious voice:

"I must ask you," he said, "to be absolutely discreet in this whole matter. With the exception of a few old friends and of Ya-Bon, whom I met in Africa, where he saved my life, no one in France knows me by my real name. I call myself Don Luis Perenna. In Morocco, where I was soldiering, I had occasion to do a service to the very gracious sovereign of a neighboring neutral nation, who, though obliged to conceal his true feelings, is ardently on our side. He sent for me; and, in return, I asked him to give me my credentials and to obtain a pass for me. Officially, therefore, I am on a secret mission, which expires in two days. In two days I shall go back . . . to whence I came, to a place where, during the war, I am serving France in my fashion: not a bad one, believe me, as people will see one day."

They came to the settee on which Coralie lay sleeping. Don Luis laid his hand on Patrice's arm:

"One word more, captain. I swore to myself and I gave my word of honor to him who trusted me that, while I was on this mission, my time should be devoted exclusively to defending the interests of my country to the best of my power. I must warn you, therefore, that, notwithstanding all my sympathy for you, I shall not be able to prolong my stay for a single minute after I have discovered the eighteen hundred bags of gold. They were the one and only reason why I came in answer to Ya-Bon's appeal. When the bags of gold are in our possession, that is to say, to-morrow evening at latest, I shall go away. However, the two quests are joined. The clearing up of the one will mean the end of the other. And now enough of words. Introduce me to Little Mother Coralie and let's get to work! Make no mystery with her, captain," he added, laughing. "Tell her my real name. I have nothing to fear: Arsène Lupin has every woman on his side."

Forty minutes later Coralie was back in her room, well cared for and well watched. Patrice had taken a substantial meal, while Don Luis walked up and down the terrace smoking cigarettes.

"Finished, captain? Then we'll make a start."

He looked at his watch:

"Half-past five. We have more than an hour of daylight left. That'll be enough."

"Enough? You surely don't pretend that you will achieve your aim in an hour?"

"My definite aim, no, but the aim which I am setting myself at the moment, yes . . . and even earlier. An hour? What for? To do what? Why, you'll be a good deal wiser in a few minutes!"

Don Luis asked to be taken to the cellar under the library; where Essarès Bey used to keep the bags of gold until the time had come to send them off.

"Was it through this ventilator that the bags were let down?"

"Yes."

"Is there no other outlet?"

"None except the staircase leading to the library and the other ventilator."

"Opening on the terrace?"

"Yes."

"Then that's clear. The bags used to come in by the first and go out by the second."

"But . . ."

"There's no but about it, captain: how else would you have it happen? You see, the mistake people always make is to go looking for difficulties where there are none."

They returned to the terrace. Don Luis took up his position near the ventilator and inspected the ground immediately around. It did not take long. Four yards away, outside the windows of the library, was the basin with the statue of a child spouting a jet of water through a shell.

Don Luis went up, examined the basin and, leaning forwards, reached the little statue, which he turned upon its axis from right to left. At the same time the pedestal described a quarter of a circle.

"That's it," he said, drawing himself up again.

"What?"

"The basin will empty itself."

He was right. The water sank very quickly and the bottom of the fountain appeared.

Don Luis stepped into it and squatted on his haunches. The inner wall was lined with a marble mosaic composing a wide red-and-white fretwork pattern. In the middle of one of the frets was a ring, which Don Luis lifted and pulled. All that portion of the wall which formed the pattern yielded to his effort and came down, leaving an opening of about twelve inches by ten.

"That's where the bags of gold went," said Don Luis. "It was the second stage. They were despatched in the same manner, on a hook sliding along a wire. Look, here is the wire, in this groove at the top."

"By Jove!" cried Captain Belval. "But you've unraveled this in a masterly fashion! What about the wire? Can't we follow it?"

"No, but it will serve our purpose if we know where it finishes. I say, captain, go to the end of the garden, by the wall, taking a line at right angles to the house. When you get there, cut off a branch of a tree, rather high up. Oh, I was forgetting! I shall have to go out by the lane. Have you the key of the door? Give it me, please."

Patrice handed him the key and then went down to the wall beside the quay.

"A little farther to the right," Don Luis instructed him. "A little more still. That's better. Now wait."

He left the garden by the lane, reached the quay and called out from the other side of the wall:

"Are you there, captain?"

"Yes."

"Fix your branch so that I can see it from here. Capital."

Patrice now joined Don Luis, who was crossing the road. All the way down the Seine are wharves, built on the bank of the river and used for loading and unloading vessels. Barges put in alongside, discharge their cargoes, take in fresh ones and often lie moored one next to the other. At the spot where Don Luis and Patrice descended by a flight of steps there was a series of yards, one of which, the one which they reached first, appeared to be abandoned, no doubt since the war. It contained, amid a quantity of useless materials, several heaps of bricks and building-stones, a hut with broken windows and the lower part of a steam-crane. A placard swinging from a post bore the inscription:

BERTHOU
WHARFIN
GER &
BUILDER.

Don Luis walked along the foot of the embankment, ten or twelve feet high, above which the quay was suspended like a terrace. Half of it was occupied by a heap of sand; and they saw in the wall the bars of an iron grating, the lower half of which was hidden by the sand-heap shored up with planks.

Don Luis cleared the grating and said, jestingly:

"Have you noticed that the doors are never locked in this adventure? Let's hope that it's the same with this one."

His theory was confirmed, somewhat to his own surprise, and they entered one of those recesses where workmen put away their tools.

"So far, nothing out of the common," said Don Luis, switching on an electric torch. "Buckets, pick-axes, wheelbarrows, a ladder. . . . Ah! Ah! Just as I expected: rails, a complete set of light rails! . . . Lend me a hand, captain. Let's clear out the back. Good, that's done it."

Level with the ground and opposite the grating was a rectangular opening exactly similar to the one in the basin. The wire was visible above, with a number of hooks hanging from it.

"So this is where the bags arrived," Don Luis explained. "They dropped, so to speak, into one of the two little trollies which you see over there, in the corner. The rails were laid across the bank, of course at night; and the trollies were pushed to a barge into which they tipped their contents."

"So that . . . ?"

"So that the French gold went this way . . . anywhere you like . . . somewhere abroad."

"And you think that the last eighteen hundred bags have also been despatched?"

"I fear so."

"Then we are too late?"

Don Luis reflected for a while without answering. Patrice, though disappointed by a development which he had not foreseen, remained amazed at the extraordinary skill with which his companion, in so short a time, had succeeded in unraveling a portion of the tangled skein.

"It's an absolute miracle," he said, at last. "How on earth did you do it?"

Without a word, Don Luis took from his pocket the book which Patrice had seen lying on his knees, *The Memoirs of Benjamin Franklin*, and motioned to him to read some lines which he indicated with his finger. They were written towards the end of the reign of Louis XVI and ran:

"We go daily to the village of Passy adjoining my home, where you take the waters in a beautiful garden. Streams and waterfalls pour down on all sides, this way and that, in artfully leveled beds. I am known to like skilful mechanism, so I have been shown the basin where the waters of all the rivulets meet and mingle. There stands a little marble figure in the midst; and the weight of water is strong enough to turn it a quarter circle to the left and then pour down straight to the Seine by a conduit, which opens in the ground of the basin."

Patrice closed the book; and Don Luis went on to explain:

"Things have changed since, no doubt, thanks to the energies of Essarès Bey. The water escapes some other way now; and the aqueduct was used to drain off the gold. Besides, the bed of the river has narrowed. Quays have been built, with a system of canals underneath them. You see, captain, all this was easy enough to discover, once I had the book to tell me. *Doctus cum libro.*"

"Yes, but, even so, you had to read the book."

"A pure accident. I unearthed it in Siméon's room and put it in my pocket, because I was curious to know why he was reading it."

"Why, that's just how he must have discovered Essarès Bey's secret!" cried Patrice. "He didn't know the secret. He found the book among his employer's papers and got up his facts that way. What do you think? Don't you agree? You seem not to share my opinion. Have you some other view?"

Don Luis did not reply. He stood looking at the river. Beside the wharves, at a slight distance from the yard, a barge lay moored, with apparently no one on her. But a slender thread of smoke now began to rise from a pipe that stood out above the deck.

"Let's go and have a look at her," he said.

The barge was lettered:

LA

NONCHAL

ANTE.

BEAUNE

They had to cross the space between the barge and the wharf and to step over a number of ropes and empty barrels covering the flat portions of the deck. A companion-way brought them to a sort of cabin, which did duty as a stateroom and a kitchen in one. Here they found a powerful-looking man, with broad shoulders, curly black hair and a clean-shaven face. His only clothes were a blouse and a pair of dirty, patched canvas trousers.

Don Luis offered him a twenty-franc note. The man took it eagerly.

"Just tell me something, mate. Have you seen a barge lately, lying at Berthou's Wharf?"

"Yes, a motor-barge. She left two days ago."

"What was her name?"

"The *Belle Hélène*. The people on board, two men and a woman, were foreigners talking I don't know what lingo. . . . We didn't speak to one another."

"But Berthou's Wharf has stopped work, hasn't it?"

"Yes, the owner's joined the army . . . and the foremen as well. We've all got to, haven't we? I'm expecting to be called up myself . . . though I've got a weak heart."

"But, if the yard's stopped work, what was the boat doing here?"

"I don't know. They worked the whole of one night, however. They had laid rails along the quay. I heard the trollies; and they were loading up. What with I don't know. And then, early in the morning, they unmoored."

"Where did they go?"

"Down stream, Mantes way."

"Thanks, mate. That's what I wanted to know."

Ten minutes later, when they reached the house, Patrice and Don Luis found the driver of the cab which Siméon Diodokis had taken after meeting Don Luis. As Don Luis expected, Siméon had told the man to go to a railway-station, the Gare Saint-Lazare, and there bought his ticket.

"Where to?"

"To Mantes!"

CHAPTER XV
THE BELLE HÉLÈNE

"There's no mistake about it," said Patrice. "The information conveyed to M. Masseron that the gold had been sent away; the speed with which the work was carried out, at night, mechanically, by the people belonging to the boat; their alien nationality; the direction which they took: it all agrees. The probability is that, between the cellar into which the gold was shot and the place where it finished its journey, there was some spot where it used to remain concealed . . . unless the eighteen hundred bags can have awaited their despatch, slung one behind the other, along the wire. But that doesn't matter much. The great thing is to know that the *Belle Hélène*, hiding somewhere in the outskirts, lay waiting for the favorable opportunity. In the old days Essarès Bey, by way of precaution, used to send her a signal with the aid of that shower of sparks which I saw. This time old Siméon, who is continuing Essarès' work, no doubt on his own account, gave the crew notice; and the bags of gold are on their way to Rouen and Le Hâvre, where some steamer will take them over and carry them . . . eastwards. After all, forty or fifty tons, hidden in the hold under a layer of coal, is nothing. What do you say? That's it, isn't it? I feel positive about it. . . . Then we have Mantes, to which he took his ticket and for which the *Belle Hélène* is bound. Could anything be clearer? Mantes, where he'll pick up his cargo of gold and go on board in some seafaring disguise, unknown and unseen. . . . Loot and looter disappearing together. It's as clear as daylight. Don't you agree?"

Once again Don Luis did not answer. However, he must have acquiesced in Patrice's theories, for, after a minute, he declared:

"Very well. I'll go to Mantes." And, turning to the chauffeur, "Hurry off to the garage," he said, "and come back in the six-cylinder. I want to be at Mantes in less than an hour. You, captain . . ."

"I shall come with you."

"And who will look after . . . ?"

"Coralie? She's in no danger! Who can attack her now? Siméon has failed in his attempt and is thinking only of saving his own skin . . . and his bags of gold."

"You insist, do you?"

"Absolutely."

"I don't know that you're wise. However, that's your affair. Let's go. By the way, though, one precaution." He raised his voice. "Ya-Bon!"

The Senegalese came hastening up. While Ya-Bon felt for Patrice all the affection of a faithful dog, he seemed to profess towards Don Luis something more nearly approaching religious devotion. The adventurer's slightest action roused him to ecstasy. He never stopped laughing in the great chief's presence.

"Ya-Bon, are you all right now? Is your wound healed? You don't feel tired? Good. In that case, come with me."

He led him to the quay, a short distance away from Berthou's Wharf:

"At nine o'clock this evening," he said, "you're to be on guard here, on this bench. Bring your food and drink with you; and keep a particular look-out for anything that happens over there, down stream. Perhaps nothing will happen at all; but never mind: you're not to move until I come back . . . unless . . . unless something does happen, in which case you will act accordingly."

He paused and then continued:

"Above all, Ya-Bon, beware of Siméon. It was he who gave you that wound. If you catch sight of him, leap at his throat and bring him here. But mind you don't kill him! No nonsense now. I don't want you to hand me over a corpse, but a live man. Do you understand, Ya-Bon?"

Patrice began to feel uneasy:

"Do you fear anything from that side?" he asked. "Look here, it's out of the question, as Siméon has gone . . ."

"Captain," said Don Luis, "when a good general goes in pursuit of the enemy, that does not prevent him from consolidating his hold on the conquered ground and leaving garrisons in the fortresses. Berthou's Wharf is evidently one of our adversary's rallying-points. I'm keeping it under observation."

Don Luis also took serious precautions with regard to Coralie. She was very much overstrained and needed rest and attention. They put her into the car and, after making a dash at full speed towards the center of Paris, so as to throw any spies off the scent, took her to the home on the Boulevard Maillot, where Patrice handed her over to the matron and recommended her to the doctor's care. The staff received strict orders to admit no strangers to see her. She was to answer no letter, unless the letter was signed "Captain Patrice."

At nine o'clock, the car sped down the Saint-Germain and Mantes road. Sitting inside with Don Luis, Patrice felt all the enthusiasm of victory and indulged freely in theories, every one of which possessed for him the value of an unimpeachable certainty. A few doubts lingered in his mind, however, points which remained obscure and on which he would have been glad to have Don Luis' opinion.

"There are two things," he said, "which I simply cannot understand. In the first place, who was the man murdered by Essarès, at nineteen minutes past seven in the morning, on the fourth of April? I heard his dying cries. Who was killed? And what became of the body?"

Don Luis was silent; and Patrice went on:

"The second point is stranger still. I mean Siméon's behavior. Here's a man who devotes his whole life to a single object, that of revenging his friend Belval's murder and at the same time ensuring my happiness and Coralie's. This is his one aim in life; and nothing can make him swerve from his obsession. And then, on the day when his enemy, Essarès Bey, is put out of the way, suddenly he turns round completely and persecutes Coralie and me, going to the length of using against us the horrible contrivance which Essarès Bey had employed so successfully against our parents! You really must admit that it's an amazing change! Can it be the thought of the gold that has hypnotized him? Are his crimes to be explained by the huge treasure placed at his disposal on the day when he discovered the secret? Has a decent man transformed himself into a bandit to satisfy a sudden instinct? What do you think?"

Don Luis persisted in his silence. Patrice, who expected to see every riddle solved by the famous adventurer in a twinkling, felt peevish and surprised. He made a last attempt:

"And the golden triangle? Another mystery! For, after all, there's not a trace of a triangle in anything we've seen! Where is this golden triangle? Have you any idea what it means?"

Don Luis allowed a moment to pass and then said:

"Captain, I have the most thorough liking for you and I take the liveliest interest in all that concerns you, but I confess that there is one problem which excludes all others and one object towards which all my efforts are now directed. That is the pursuit of the gold of which we have been robbed; and I don't want this gold to escape us. I have succeeded on your side, but not yet on the other. You are both of you safe and sound, but I haven't the eighteen hundred bags; and I want them, I want them."

"You'll have them, since we know where they are."

"I shall have them," said Don Luis, "when they lie spread before my eyes. Until then, I can tell you nothing."

At Mantes the enquiries did not take long. They almost immediately had the satisfaction of learning that a traveler, whose description corresponded with old Siméon's, had gone to the Hôtel des Trois-Empereurs and was now asleep in a room on the third floor.

Don Luis took a ground-floor room, while Patrice, who would have attracted the enemy's attention more easily, because of his lame leg, went to the Grand Hôtel.

He woke late the next morning. Don Luis rang him up and told him that Siméon, after calling at the post-office, had gone down to the river and then to the station, where he met a fashionably-dressed woman, with her face hidden by a thick veil, and brought her back to the hotel. The two were lunching together in the room on the third floor.

At four o'clock Don Luis rang up again, to ask Patrice to join him at once in a little café at the end of the town, facing the Seine. Here Patrice saw Siméon on the quay. He was walking with his hands behind his back, like a man strolling without any definite object.

"Comforter, spectacles, the same get-up as usual," said Patrice. "Not a thing about him changed. Watch him. He's putting on an air of indifference, but you can bet that his eyes are looking up stream, in the direction from which the *Belle Hélène* is coming."

"Yes, yes," said Don Luis. "Here's the lady."

"Oh, that's the one, is it?" said Patrice. "I've met her two or three times already in the street."

A dust-cloak outlined her figure and shoulders, which were wide and rather well-developed. A veil fell around the brim of her felt hat. She gave Siméon a telegram to read. Then they talked for a moment, seemed to be taking their bearings, passed by the café and stopped a little lower down. Here Siméon wrote a few words on a sheet of note-paper and handed it to his companion. She left him and went back into the town. Siméon resumed his walk by the riverside.

"You must stay here, captain," said Don Luis.

"But the enemy doesn't seem to be on his guard," protested Patrice. "He's not turning round."

"It's better to be prudent, captain. What a pity that we can't have a look at what Siméon wrote down!"

"I might . . ."

"Go after the lady? No, no, captain. Without wishing to offend you, you're not quite cut out for it. I'm not sure that even I . . ."

And he walked away.

Patrice waited. A few boats moved up or down the river. Mechanically, he glanced at their names. And suddenly, half an hour after Don Luis had left him, he heard the clearly-marked rhythm, the pulsation of one of those powerful motors which, for a few years past, have been fitted to certain barges.

At the bend of the river a barge appeared. As she passed in front of him, he distinctly and with no little excitement read the name of the *Belle Hélène*!

She was gliding along at a fair pace, to the accompaniment of a regular, throbbing beat. She was big and broad in the beam, heavy and pretty deep in the water, though she appeared to carry no cargo. Patrice saw two watermen on board, sitting and smoking carelessly. A dinghy floated behind at the end of a painter.

The barge went on and passed out of sight at the turn. Patrice waited another hour before Don Luis came back.

"Well?" he asked. "Have you seen her?"

"Yes, they let go the dinghy, a mile and a half from here, and put in for Siméon."

"Then he's gone with them?"

"Yes."

"Without suspecting anything?"

"You're asking me too much, captain!"

"Never mind! We've won! We shall catch them up in the car, pass them and, at Vernon or somewhere, inform the military and civil authorities, so that they may proceed to arrest the men and seize the boat."

"We shall inform nobody, captain. We shall proceed to carry out these little operations ourselves."

"What do you mean? Surely . . ."

The two looked at each other. Patrice had been unable to dissemble the thought that occurred to his mind. Don Luis showed no resentment:

"You're afraid that I shall run away with the three hundred millions? By jingo, it's a largish parcel to hide in one's jacket-pocket!"

"Still," said Patrice, "may I ask what you intend to do?"

"You may, captain, but allow me to postpone my reply until we've really won. For the moment, we must first find the barge again."

They went to the Hôtel des Trois-Empereurs and drove off in the car towards Vernon. This time they were both silent.

The road joined the river a few miles lower down, at the bottom of the steep hill which begins at Rosny. Just as they reached Rosny the *Belle Hélène* was entering the long loop which curves out to La Roche-Guyon, turns back and joins the high-road again at Bonnières. She would need at least three hours to cover the distance, whereas the car, climbing the hill and keeping straight ahead, arrived at Bonnières in fifteen minutes.

They drove through the village. There was an inn a little way beyond it, on the right. Don Luis made his chauffeur stop here:

"If we are not back by twelve to-night," he said, "go home to Paris. Will you come with me, captain?"

Patrice followed him towards the right, whence a small road led them to the river-bank. They followed this for a quarter of an hour. At last Don Luis found what he appeared to be seeking, a boat fastened to a stake, not far from a villa with closed shutters. Don Luis unhooked the chain.

It was about seven o'clock in the evening. Night was falling fast, but a brilliant moonlight lit the landscape.

"First of all," said Don Luis, "a word of explanation. We're going to wait for the barge. She'll come in sight on the stroke of ten and find us lying across stream. I shall order her to heave to; and there's no doubt that, when they see your uniform by the light of the moon or of my electric lamp, they will obey. Then we shall go on board."

"Suppose they refuse?"

"If they refuse, we shall board her by force. There are three of them and two of us. So . . ."

"And then?"

"And then? Well, there's every reason to believe that the two men forming the crew are only extra hands, employed by Siméon, but ignorant of his actions and knowing nothing of the nature of the cargo. Once we have reduced Siméon to helplessness and paid them handsomely, they'll take the barge wherever I tell them. But, mind you—and this is what I was coming to—I mean to do with the barge exactly as I please. I shall hand over the cargo as and when I think fit. It's my booty, my prize. No one is entitled to it but myself."

The officer drew himself up:

"Oh, I can't agree to that, you know!"

"Very well, then give me your word of honor that you'll keep a secret which doesn't belong to you. After which, we'll say good-night and go our own ways. I'll do the boarding alone and you can go back to your own business. Observe, however, that I am not insisting on an immediate reply. You have plenty of time to reflect and to take the decision which your interest, honor and conscience may dictate to you. For my part, excuse me, but you know my weakness: when circumstances give me a little spare time, I take advantage of it to go to sleep. *Carpe somnum*, as the poet says. Good-night, captain."

And, without another word, Don Luis wrapped himself in his great-coat, sprang into the boat and lay down.

Patrice had had to make a violent effort to restrain his anger. Don Luis' calm, ironic tone and well-bred, bantering voice got on his nerves all the more because he felt the influence of that strange man and

763

fully recognized that he was incapable of acting without his assistance. Besides, he could not forget that Don Luis had saved his life and Coralie's.

The hours slipped by. The adventurer slumbered peacefully in the cool night air. Patrice hesitated what to do, seeking for some plan of conduct which would enable him to get at Siméon and rid himself of that implacable adversary and at the same time to prevent Don Luis from laying hands on the enormous treasure. He was dismayed at the thought of being his accomplice. And yet, when the first throbs of the motor were heard in the distance and when Don Luis awoke, Patrice was by his side, ready for action.

They did not exchange a word. A village-clock struck ten. The *Belle Hélène* was coming towards them.

Patrice felt his excitement increase. The *Belle Hélène* meant Siméon's capture, the recovery of the millions, Coralie out of danger, the end of that most hideous nightmare and the total extinction of Essarès' handiwork. The engine was throbbing nearer and nearer. Its loud and regular beat sounded wide over the motionless Seine. Don Luis had taken the sculls and was pulling hard for the middle of the river. And suddenly they saw in the distance a black mass looming up in the white moonlight. Twelve or fifteen more minutes passed and the *Belle Hélène* was before them.

"Shall I lend you a hand?" whispered Patrice. "It looks as if you had the current against you and as if you had a difficulty in getting along."

"Not the least difficulty," said Don Luis; and he began to hum a tune.

"But . . ."

Patrice was stupefied. The boat had turned in its own length and was making for the bank.

"But, I say, I say," he said, "what's this? Are you going back? Are you giving up? . . . I don't understand. . . . You're surely not afraid because they're three to our two?"

Don Luis leapt on shore at a bound and stretched out his hand to him. Patrice pushed it aside, growling:

"Will you explain what it all means?"

"Take too long," replied Don Luis. "Just one question, though. You know that book I found in old Siméon's room, *The Memoirs of Benjamin Franklin*: did you see it when you were making your search?"

"Look here, it seems to me we have other things to . . ."

"It's an urgent question, captain."

"Well, no, it wasn't there."

"Then that's it," said Don Luis. "We've been done brown, or rather, to be accurate, I have. Let's be off, captain, as fast as we can."

Patrice was still in the boat. He pushed off abruptly and caught up the scull, muttering:

"As I live, I believe the beggar's getting at me!"

He was ten yards from shore when he cried:

"If you're afraid, I'll go alone. Don't want any help."

"Right you are, captain!" replied Don Luis. "I'll expect you presently at the inn."

Patrice encountered no difficulties in his undertaking. At the first order, which he shouted in a tone of command, the *Belle Hélène* stopped; and he was able to board her peacefully. The two bargees were men of a certain age, natives of the Basque coast. He introduced himself as a representative of the military authorities; and they showed him over their craft. He found neither old Siméon nor the very smallest bag of gold. The hold was almost empty.

The questions and answers did not take long:

"Where are you going?"

"To Rouen. We've been requisitioned by the government for transport of supplies."

"But you picked up somebody on the way."

"Yes, at Mantes."

"His name, please?"

"Siméon Diodokis."

"Where's he got to?"

"He made us put him down a little after, to take the train."

"What did he want?"

"To pay us."

"For what?"

"For a shipload we took at Paris two days ago."

"Bags?"

"Yes."

"What of?"

"Don't know. We were well paid and asked no questions."

"And what's become of the load?"

"We transhipped it last night to a small steamer that came alongside of us below Passy."

"What's the steamer's name?"

"The *Chamois*. Crew of six."

"Where is she now?"

"Ahead of us. She was going fast. She must be at Rouen by this time. Siméon Diodokis is on his way to join her."

"How long have you known Siméon Diodokis?"

"It's the first time we saw him. But we knew that he was in M. Essarès' service."

"Oh, so you've worked for M. Essarès?"

"Yes, often. . . . Same job and same trip."

"He called you by means of a signal, didn't he?"

"Yes, he used to light an old factory-chimney."

"Was it always bags?"

"Yes. We didn't know what was inside. He was a good payer."

Patrice asked no more questions. He hurriedly got into his boat, pulled back to shore and found Don Luis seated with a comfortable supper in front of him.

"Quick!" he said. "The cargo is on board a steamer, the *Chamois*. We can catch her up between Rouen and Le Hâvre."

Don Luis rose and handed the officer a white-paper packet:

"Here's a few sandwiches for you, captain," he said. "We've an arduous night before us. I'm very sorry that you didn't get a sleep, as I did. Let's be off, and this time I shall drive. We'll knock some pace out of her! Come and sit beside me, captain."

They both stepped into the car; the chauffeur took his seat behind them. But they had hardly started when Patrice exclaimed:

"Hi! What are you up to? Not this way! We're going back to Mantes or Paris!"

"That's what I mean to do," said Luis, with a chuckle.

"Eh, what? Paris?"

"Well, of course!"

"Oh, look here, this is a bit too thick! Didn't I tell you that the two bargees . . . ?"

"Those bargees of yours are humbugs."

"They declared that the cargo . . ."

"Cargo? No go!"

"But the *Chamois* . . ."

"*Chamois*? Sham was! I tell you once more, we're done, captain, done brown! Old Siméon is a wonderful old hand! He's a match worth meeting. He gives you a run for your money. He laid a trap in which I've been fairly caught. It's a magnificent joke, but there's moderation in all things. We've been fooled enough to last us the rest of our lives. Let's be serious now."

"But . . ."

"Aren't you satisfied yet, captain? After the *Belle Hélène* do you want to attack the *Chamois*? As you please. You can get out at Mantes: Only, I warn you, Siméon is in Paris, with three or four hours' start of us."

Patrice gave a shudder. Siméon in Paris! In Paris, where Coralie was alone and unprotected! He made no further protest; and Don Luis ran on:

"Oh, the rascal! How well he played his hand! *The Memoirs of Benjamin Franklin* were a master stroke. Knowing of my arrival, he said to himself, 'Arsène Lupin is a dangerous fellow, capable of disentangling the affair and putting both me and the bags of gold in his pocket. To get rid of him, there's only one thing to be done: I must act in such a way as to make him rush along the real track at so fast a rate of speed that he does not perceive the moment when the real track becomes a false track.' That was clever of him, wasn't it? And so we have the Franklin book, held out as a bait; the page opening of itself, at the right place; my inevitable easy discovery of the conduit system; the clue of Ariadne most obligingly offered. I follow up the clue like a trusting child, led by Siméon's own hand, from the cellar down to Berthou's Wharf. So far all's well. But, from that moment, take care! There's nobody at Berthou's Wharf. On the other hand, there's a barge alongside, which means a chance of making enquiries, which means the certainty that I shall make enquiries. And I make enquiries. And, having made enquiries, I am done for."

"But then that man . . . ?"

"Yes, yes, yes, an accomplice of Siméon's, whom Siméon, knowing that he would be followed to the Gare Saint-Lazare, instructs in this way to direct me to Mantes for the second time. At Mantes the comedy continues. The *Belle Hélène* passes, with her double freight, Siméon and the bags of gold. We go running after the *Belle Hélène*. Of course, on the *Belle Hélène* there's nothing: no Siméon, no bags of gold. 'Run after the *Chamois*. We've transhipped it all on the *Chamois*.' We run after the *Chamois*, to Rouen, to Le Hâvre, to the end of the world; and of course our pursuit is fruitless, for the *Chamois* does not exist. But we are convinced that she does exist and that she has escaped our search. And by this time the trick is played. The millions are gone, Siméon has disappeared and there is only one thing left for us to do, which is to resign ourselves and abandon our quest. You understand, we're to abandon our quest: that's the fellow's object. And he would have succeeded if . . ."

The car was traveling at full speed. From time to time Don Luis would stop her dead with extraordinary skill. Post of territorials. Pass to be produced. Then a leap onward and once more the breakneck pace.

"If what?" asked Patrice, half-convinced. "Which was the clue that put you on the track?"

"The presence of that woman at Mantes. It was a vague clue at first. But suddenly I remembered that, in the first barge, the *Nonchalante*, the person who gave us information—do you recollect?—well, that this person somehow gave me the queer impression, I can't tell you why, that I might be talking to a woman in disguise. The impression occurred to me once more. I made a mental comparison with the woman at Mantes. . . . And then . . . and then it was like a flash of light. . . ."

Don Luis paused to think and, in a lower voice, continued:

"But who the devil can this woman be?"

There was a brief silence, after which Patrice said, from instinct rather than reason:

"Grégoire, I suppose."

"Eh? What's that? Grégoire?"

"Yes. Yes, Grégoire is a woman."

"What are you talking about?"

"Well, obviously. Don't you remember? The accomplice told me so, on the day when I had them arrested outside the café."

"Why, your diary doesn't say a word about it!"

"Oh, that's true! . . . I forgot to put down that detail."

"A detail! He calls it a detail! Why, it's of the greatest importance, captain! If I had known, I should have guessed that that bargee was no other than Grégoire and we should not have wasted a whole night. Hang it all, captain, you really are the limit!"

But all this was unable to affect his good-humor. While Patrice, overcome with presentiments, grew gloomier and gloomier, Don Luis began to sing victory in his turn:

"Thank goodness! The battle is becoming serious! Really, it was too easy before; and that was why I was sulking, I, Lupin! Do you imagine things go like that in real life? Does everything fit in so accurately? Benjamin Franklin, the uninterrupted conduit for the gold, the series of clues that reveal themselves of their own accord, the man and the bags meeting at Mantes, the *Belle Hélène*: no, it all worried me. The cat was being choked with cream! And then the gold escaping in a barge! All very well in times of peace, but not in war-time, in the face of the regulations: passes, patrol-boats, inspections and I don't know what. . . . How could a fellow like Siméon risk a trip of that kind? No, I had my suspicions; and that was why, captain, I made Ya-Bon mount guard, on the off chance, outside Berthou's Wharf. It was just an idea that occurred to me. The whole of this adventure seemed to center round the wharf. Well, was I right or not? Is M. Lupin no longer able to follow a scent? Captain, I repeat, I shall go back to-morrow evening. Besides, as I told you, I've got to. Whether I win or lose, I'm going. But we shall win. Everything will be cleared up. There will be no more mysteries, not even the mystery of the golden triangle. . . . Oh, I don't say that I shall bring you a beautiful triangle of eighteen-carat gold! We mustn't allow ourselves to be fascinated by words. It may be a geometrical arrangement of the bags of gold, a triangular pile . . . or else a hole in the ground dug in that shape. No matter, we shall have it! And the bags of gold shall be ours! And Patrice and Coralie shall appear before monsieur le maire and receive my blessing and live happily ever after!"

They reached the gates of Paris. Patrice was becoming more and more anxious:

"Then you think the danger's over?"

"Oh, I don't say that! The play isn't finished. After the great scene of the third act, which we will call the scene of the oxide of carbon, there will certainly be a fourth act and perhaps a fifth. The enemy has not laid down his arms, by any means."

They were skirting the quays.

"Let's get down," said Don Luis.

He gave a faint whistle and repeated it three times.

"No answer," he said. "Ya-Bon's not there. The battle has begun."

"But Coralie . . ."

"What are you afraid of for her? Siméon doesn't know her address."

There was nobody on Berthou's Wharf and nobody on the quay below. But by the light of the moon they saw the other barge, the *Nonchalante*.

"Let's go on board," said Don Luis. "I wonder if the lady known as Grégoire makes a practise of living here? Has she come back, believing us on our way to Le Hâvre? I hope so. In any case, Ya-Bon must have been there and no doubt left something behind to act as a signal. Will you come, captain?"

"Right you are. It's a queer thing, though: I feel frightened!"

"What of?" asked Don Luis, who was plucky enough himself to understand this presentiment.

"Of what we shall see."

"My dear sir, there may be nothing there!"

Each of them switched on his pocket-lamp and felt the handle of his revolver. They crossed the plank between the shore and the boat. A few steps downwards brought them to the cabin. The door was locked.

"Hi, mate! Open this, will you?"

There was no reply. They now set about breaking it down, which was no easy matter, for it was massive and quite unlike an ordinary cabin-door.

At last it gave way.

"By Jingo!" said Don Luis, who was the first to go in. "I didn't expect this!"

"What?"

"Look. The woman whom they called Grégoire. She seems to be dead."

She was lying back on a little iron bedstead, with her man's blouse open at the top and her chest uncovered. Her face still bore an expression of extreme terror. The disordered appearance of the cabin suggested that a furious struggle had taken place.

"I was right. Here, by her side, are the clothes she wore at Mantes. But what's the matter, captain?"

Patrice had stifled a cry:

"There . . . opposite . . . under the window . . ."

It was a little window overlooking the river. The panes were broken.

"Well?" asked Don Luis. "What? Yes, I believe some one's been thrown out that way."

"The veil . . . that blue veil," stammered Patrice, "is her nurse's veil . . . Coralie's. . . ."

Don Luis grew vexed:

"Nonsense! Impossible! Nobody knew her address."

"Still . . ."

"Still what? You haven't written to her? You haven't telegraphed to her?"

"Yes . . . I telegraphed to her . . . from Mantes."

"What's that? Oh, but look here. This is madness! You don't mean that you really telegraphed?"

"Yes, I do."

"You telegraphed from the post-office at Mantes?"

"Yes."

"And was there any one in the post-office?"

"Yes, a woman."

"What woman? The one who lies here, murdered?"

"Yes."

"But she didn't read what you wrote?"

"No, but I wrote the telegram twice over."

"And you threw the first draft anywhere, on the floor, so that any one who came along. . . . Oh, really, captain, you must confess . . . !"

But Patrice was running towards the car and was already out of ear-shot.

Half an hour after, he returned with two telegrams which he had found on Coralie's table. The first, the one which he had sent, said:

"All well. Be easy and stay indoors. Fondest love.

"CAPTAIN PATRICE."

The second, which had evidently been despatched by Siméon, ran as follows:

"Events taking serious turn. Plans changed. Coming back. Expect you nine o'clock this evening at the small door of your garden.

770

This second telegram was delivered to Coralie at eight o'clock; and she had left the home immediately afterwards.

CHAPTER XVI
THE FOURTH ACT

"Captain," said Don Luis, "you've scored two fine blunders. The first was your not telling me that Grégoire was a woman. The second . . ."

But Don Luis saw that the officer was too much dejected for him to care about completing his charge. He put his hand on Patrice Belval's shoulder:

"Come," he said, "don't upset yourself. The position's not as bad as you think."

"Coralie jumped out of the window to escape that man," Patrice muttered.

"Your Coralie is alive," said Don Luis, shrugging his shoulders. "In Siméon's hands, but alive."

"Why, what do you know about it? Anyway, if she's in that monster's hands, might she not as well be dead? Doesn't it mean all the horrors of death? Where's the difference?"

"It means a danger of death, but it means life if we come in time; and we shall."

"Have you a clue?"

"Do you imagine that I have sat twiddling my thumbs and that an old hand like myself hasn't had time in half an hour to unravel the mysteries which this cabin presents?"

"Then let's go," cried Patrice, already eager for the fray. "Let's have at the enemy."

"Not yet," said Don Luis, who was still hunting around him. "Listen to me. I'll tell you what I know, captain, and I'll tell it you straight out, without trying to dazzle you by a parade of reasoning and without even telling you of the tiny trifles that serve me as proofs. The bare facts, that's all. Well, then . . ."

"Yes?"

"Little Mother Coralie kept the appointment at nine o'clock. Siméon was there with his female accomplice. Between them they bound and gagged her and brought her here. Observe that, in their eyes, it was a safe spot for the job, because they knew for certain that you and I had not discovered the trap. Nevertheless, we may assume that it was a provisional base of operations, adopted for part of the night only, and that Siméon reckoned on leaving Little Mother Coralie in the hands of his accomplice and setting out in search of a definite place of confinement, a permanent prison. But luckily—and I'm rather proud of this—Ya-Bon was on the spot. Ya-Bon was watching on his bench, in the dark. He must have seen them cross the embankment and no doubt recognized Siméon's walk in the distance. We'll take it that he gave chase at once, jumped on to the deck of the barge and arrived here at the same time as the enemy, before they had time to lock themselves in. Four people in this narrow space, in pitch darkness, must have meant a frightful upheaval. I know my Ya-Bon. He's terrible at such times. Unfortunately, it was not Siméon whom he caught by the neck with that merciless hand of his, but . . . the woman. Siméon took advantage of this. He had not let go of Little Mother Coralie. He picked her up in his arms and went up the companionway, flung her on the deck and then came back to lock the door on the two as they struggled."

"Do you think so? Do you think it was Ya-Bon and not Siméon who killed the woman?"

"I'm sure of it. If there were no other proof, there is this particular fracture of the wind-pipe, which is Ya-Bon's special mark. What I do not understand is why, when he had settled his adversary, Ya-Bon didn't break down the door with a push of his shoulder and go after Siméon. I presume that he was wounded and that he had not the strength to make the necessary effort. I presume also that the woman did not die at once and that she spoke, saying things against Siméon, who had abandoned her instead of defending her. This much is certain, that Ya-Bon broke the window-panes . . ."

"To jump into the Seine, wounded as he was, with his one arm?" said Patrice.

"Not at all. There's a ledge running along the window. He could set his feet on it and get off that way."

"Very well. But he was quite ten or twenty minutes behind Siméon?"

"That didn't matter, if the woman had time, before dying, to tell him where Siméon was taking refuge."

"How can we get to know?"

"I've been trying to find out all the time that we've been chatting . . . and I've just discovered the way."

"Here?"

"This minute; and I expected no less from Ya-Bon. The woman told him of a place in the cabin—look, that open drawer, probably—in which there was a visiting-card with an address on it. Ya-Bon took it and, in order to let me know, pinned the card to the curtain over there. I had seen it already; but it was only this moment that I noticed the pin that fixed it, a gold pin with which I myself fastened the Morocco Cross to Ya-Bon's breast."

"What is the address?"

"Amédée Vacherot, 18, Rue Guimard. The Rue Guimard is close to this, which makes me quite sure of the road they took."

The two men at once went away, leaving the woman's dead body behind. As Don Luis said, the police must make what they could of it.

As they crossed Berthou's Wharf they glanced at the recess and Don Luis remarked:

"There's a ladder missing. We must remember that detail. Siméon has been in there. He's beginning to make blunders too."

The car took them to the Rue Guimard, a small street in Passy. No. 18 was a large house let out in flats, of fairly ancient construction. It was two o'clock in the morning when they rang.

A long time elapsed before the door opened; and, as they passed through the carriage-entrance, the porter put his head out of his lodge:

"Who's there?" he asked.

"We want to see M. Amédée Vacherot on urgent business."

"That's myself."

"You?"

"Yes, I, the porter. But by what right . . . ?"

"Orders of the prefect of police," said Don Luis, displaying a badge.

They entered the lodge. Amédée Vacherot was a little, respectable-looking old man, with white whiskers. He might have been a beadle.

"Answer my questions plainly," Don Luis ordered, in a rough voice, "and don't try to prevaricate. We are looking for a man called Siméon Diodokis."

The porter took fright at once:

"To do him harm?" he exclaimed. "If it's to do him harm, it's no use asking me any questions. I would rather die by slow tortures than injure that kind M. Siméon."

Don Luis assumed a gentler tone:

"Do him harm? On the contrary, we are looking for him to do him a service, to save him from a great danger."

"A great danger?" cried M. Vacherot. "Oh, I'm not at all surprised! I never saw him in such a state of excitement."

"Then he's been here?"

"Yes, since midnight."

"Is he here now?"

"No, he went away again."

Patrice made a despairing gesture and asked:

"Perhaps he left some one behind?"

"No, but he intended to bring some one."

"A lady?"

M. Vacherot hesitated.

"We know," Don Luis resumed, "that Siméon Diodokis was trying to find a place of safety in which to shelter a lady for whom he entertained the deepest respect."

"Can you tell me the lady's name?" asked the porter, still on his guard.

"Certainly, Mme. Essarès, the widow of the banker to whom Siméon used to act as secretary. Mme. Essarès is a victim of persecution; he is defending her against her enemies; and, as we ourselves want to help the two of them and to take this criminal business in hand, we must insist that you . . ."

"Oh, well!" said M. Vacherot, now fully reassured. "I have known Siméon Diodokis for ever so many years. He was very good to me at the time when I was working for an undertaker; he lent me money; he got me my present job; and he used often to come and sit in my lodge and talk about heaps of things. . . ."

"Such as relations with Essarès Bey?" asked Don Luis, carelessly. "Or his plans concerning Patrice Belval?"

"Heaps of things," said the porter, after a further hesitation. "He is one of the best of men, does a lot of good and used to employ me in distributing his local charity. And just now again he was risking his life for Mme. Essarès."

"One more word. Had you seen him since Essarès Bey's death?"

"No, it was the first time. He arrived a little before one o'clock. He was out of breath and spoke in a low voice, listening to the sounds of the street outside: 'I've been followed,' said he; 'I've been followed. I could swear it.' 'By whom?' said I. 'You don't know him,' said he. 'He has only one hand, but he wrings your neck for you.' And then he stopped. And then he began again, in a whisper, so that I could hardly hear: 'Listen to me, you're coming with me. We're going to fetch a lady, Mme. Essarès. They want to kill her. I've hidden her all right, but she's fainted: we shall have to carry her. . . . Or no, I'll go alone. I'll manage. But I want to know, is my room still free?' I must tell you, he has a little lodging here, since the day when he too had to hide himself. He used to come to it sometimes and he kept it on in case he might want it, for it's a detached lodging, away from the other tenants."

"What did he do after that?" asked Patrice, anxiously.

"After that, he went away."

"But why isn't he back yet?"

"I admit that it's alarming. Perhaps the man who was following him has attacked him. Or perhaps something has happened to the lady."

"What do you mean, something happened to the lady?"

"I'm afraid something may have. When he first showed me the way we should have to go to fetch her, he said, 'Quick, we must hurry. To save her life, I had to put her in a hole. That's all very well for two or three hours. But, if she's left longer, she will suffocate. The want of air . . .'"

Patrice had leapt upon the old man. He was beside himself, maddened at the thought that Coralie, ill and worn-out as she was, might be at the point of death in some unknown place, a prey to terror and suffering.

"You shall speak," he cried, "and this very minute! You shall tell us where she is! Oh, don't imagine that you can fool us any longer! Where is she? You know! He told you!"

He was shaking M. Vacherot by the shoulders and hurling his rage into the old man's face with unspeakable violence.

Don Luis, on the other hand, stood chuckling.

"Splendid, captain," he said, "splendid! My best compliments! You're making real progress since I joined forces with you. M. Vacherot will go through fire and water for us now."

"Well, you see if I don't make the fellow speak," shouted Patrice.

"It's no use, sir," declared the porter, very firmly and calmly. "You have deceived me. You are enemies of M. Siméon's. I shall not say another word that can give you any information."

"You refuse to speak, do you? You refuse to speak?"

In his exasperation Patrice drew his revolver and aimed it at the man:

"I'm going to count three. If, by that time, you don't make up your mind to speak, you shall see the sort of man that Captain Belval is!"

The porter gave a start:

"Captain Belval, did you say? Are you Captain Belval?"

"Ah, old fellow, that seems to give you food for thought!"

"Are you Captain Belval? Patrice Belval?"

"At your service; and, if in two seconds from this you haven't told me . . ."

"Patrice Belval! And you are M. Siméon's enemy? And you want to . . . ?"

"I want to do him up like the cur he is, your blackguard of a Siméon . . . and you, his accomplice, with him. A nice pair of rascals! . . . Well, have you made up your mind?"

"Unhappy man!" gasped the porter. "Unhappy man! You don't know what you're doing. Kill M. Siméon! You? You? Why, you're the last man who could commit a crime like that!"

"What about it? Speak, will you, you old numskull!"

"You, kill M. Siméon? You, Patrice? You, Captain Belval? You?"

"And why not? Speak, damn it! Why not?"

"You are his son."

All Patrice's fury, all his anguish at the thought that Coralie was in Siméon's power or else lying in some pit, all his agonized grief, all his alarm: all this gave way, for a moment, to a terrible fit of merriment, which revealed itself in a long burst of laughter.

"Siméon's son! What the devil are you talking about? Oh, this beats everything! Upon my word, you're full of ideas, when you're trying to save him! You old ruffian! Of course, it's most convenient: don't kill that man, he's your father. He my father, that putrid Siméon! Siméon Diodokis, Patrice Belval's father! Oh, it's enough to make a chap split his sides!"

Don Luis had listened in silence. He made a sign to Patrice:

"Will you allow me to clear up this business, captain? It won't take me more than a few minutes; and that certainly won't delay us." And, without waiting for the officer's reply, he turned to the old man and said slowly, "Let's have this out, M. Vacherot. It's of the highest importance. The great thing is to speak plainly and not to lose yourself in superfluous words. Besides, you have said too much not to finish your revelation. Siméon Diodokis is not your benefactor's real name, is it?"

"No, that's so."

"He is Armand Belval; and the woman who loved him used to call him Patrice?"

"Yes, his son's name."

"Nevertheless, this Armand Belval was a victim of the same murderous attempt as the woman he loved, who was Coralie Essarès' mother?"

"Yes, but Coralie Essarès' mother died; and he did not."

"That was on the fourteenth of April, 1895."

"The fourteenth of April, 1895."

Patrice caught hold of Don Luis' arm:

"Come," he spluttered, "Coralie's at death's door. The monster has buried her. That's the only thing that matters."

"Then you don't believe that monster to be your father?" asked Don Luis.

"You're mad!"

"For all that, captain, you're trembling! . . ."

"I dare say, I dare say, but it's because of Coralie. . . . I can't even hear what the man's saying! . . . Oh, it's a nightmare, every word of it! Make him stop! Make him shut up! Why didn't I wring his neck?"

He sank into a chair, with his elbows on the table and his head in his hands. It was really a horrible moment; and no catastrophe would have overwhelmed a man more utterly.

Don Luis looked at him with feeling and then turned to the porter:

"Explain yourself, M. Vacherot," he said. "As briefly as possible, won't you? No details. We can go into them later. We were saying, on the fourteenth of April, 1895 . . ."

"On the fourteenth of April, 1895, a solicitor's clerk, accompanied by the commissary of police, came to my governor's, close by here, and ordered two coffins for immediate delivery. The whole shop got to work. At ten o'clock in the evening, the governor, one of my mates and I went to the Rue Raynouard, to a sort of pavilion or lodge, standing in a garden."

"I know. Go on."

"There were two bodies. We wrapped them in winding-sheets and put them into the coffins. At eleven o'clock my governor and my fellow-workmen went away and left me alone with a sister of mercy. There was nothing more to do except to nail the coffins down. Well, just then, the nun, who had been watching and praying, fell asleep and something happened . . . oh, an awful thing! It made my hair stand on end, sir. I shall never forget it as long as I live. My knees gave way beneath me, I shook with fright. . . . Sir, the man's body had moved. The man was alive!"

"Then you didn't know of the murder at that time?" asked Don Luis. "You hadn't heard of the attempt?"

"No, we were told that they had both suffocated themselves with gas. . . . It was many hours before the man recovered consciousness entirely. He was in some way poisoned."

"But why didn't you inform the nun?"

"I couldn't say. I was simply stunned. I looked at the man as he slowly came back to life and ended by opening his eyes. His first words were, 'She's dead, I suppose?' And then at once he said, 'Not a word about all this. Let them think me dead: that will be better.' And I can't tell you why, but I consented. The miracle had deprived me of all power of will. I obeyed like a child. . . . He ended by getting up. He leant over the other coffin, drew aside the sheet and kissed the dead woman's face over and over again, whispering, 'I will avenge you. All my life shall be devoted to avenging you and also, as you wished, to uniting our children. If I don't kill myself, it will be for Patrice and Coralie's sake. Good-by.' Then he told me to help him. Between us, we lifted the woman out of the coffin and carried it into the little bedroom next door. Then we went into the garden, took some big stones and put them into the coffins where the two bodies had been. When this was done, I nailed the coffins down, woke the good sister and went away. The man had locked himself into the bedroom with the dead woman. Next morning the undertaker's men came and fetched away the two coffins."

Patrice had unclasped his hands and thrust his distorted features between Don Luis and the porter. Fixing his haggard eyes upon the latter, he asked, struggling with his words:

"But the graves? The inscription saying that the remains of both lie there, near the lodge where the murder was committed? The cemetery?"

"Armand Belval wished it so. At that time I was living in a garret in this house. I took a lodging for him where he came and lived by stealth, under the name of Siméon Diodokis, since Armand Belval was dead, and where he stayed for several months without going out. Then, in his new name and through me, he bought his lodge. And, bit by bit, we dug the graves. Coralie's and his. His because, I repeat, he wished it so. Patrice and Coralie were both dead. It seemed to him, in this way, that he was not leaving her. Perhaps also, I confess, despair had upset his balance a little, just a very little, only in what concerned his memory of the woman who died on the fourteenth of April, 1895, and his devotion for her. He wrote her name and his own everywhere: on the grave and also on the walls, on the trees and in the very borders of the flower-beds. They were Coralie Essarès' name and yours. . . . And for this, for all that had to do with his revenge upon the murderer and with his son and with the dead woman's daughter, oh, for these matters he had all his wits about him, believe me, sir!"

Patrice stretched his clutching hands and his distraught face towards the porter:

"Proofs, proofs, proofs!" he insisted, in a stifled voice. "Give me proofs at once! There's some one dying at this moment by that scoundrel's criminal intentions, there's a woman at the point of death. Give me proofs!"

"You need have no fear," said M. Vacherot. "My friend has only one thought, that of saving the woman, not killing her. . . ."

"He lured her and me into the lodge to kill us, as our parents were killed before us."

"He is trying only to unite you."

"Yes, in death."

"No, in life. You are his dearly-loved son. He always spoke of you with pride."

"He is a ruffian, a monster!" shouted the officer.

"He is the very best man living, sir, and he is your father."

Patrice started, stung by the insult:

"Proofs," he roared, "proofs! I forbid you to speak another word until you have proved the truth in a manner admitting of no doubt."

Without moving from his seat, the old man put out his arm towards an old mahogany escritoire, lowered the lid and, pressing a spring, pulled out one of the drawers. Then he held out a bundle of papers:

"You know your father's handwriting, don't you, captain?" he said. "You must have kept letters from him, since the time when you were at school in England. Well, read the letters which he wrote to me. You will see your name repeated a hundred times, the name of his son; and you will see the name of the Coralie whom he meant you to marry. Your whole life—your studies, your journeys, your work—is described in these letters. And you will also find your photographs, which he had taken by various correspondents, and photographs of Coralie, whom he had visited at Salonica. And you will see above all his hatred for Essarès Bey, whose secretary he had become, and his plans of revenge, his patience, his tenacity. And you will also see his despair when he heard of the marriage between Essarès and Coralie and, immediately afterwards, his joy at the thought that his revenge would be more cruel when he succeeded in uniting his son Patrice with Essarès' wife."

As the old fellow spoke, he placed the letters one by one under the eyes of Patrice, who had at once recognized his father's hand and sat greedily devouring sentences in which his own name was constantly repeated. M. Vacherot watched him.

"Have you any more doubts, captain?" he asked, at last.

The officer again pressed his clenched fists to his temples:

"I saw his face," he said, "above the skylight, in the lodge into which he had locked us. . . . It was gloating over our death, it was a face mad with hatred. . . . He hated us even more than Essarès did. . . ."

"A mistake! Pure imagination!" the old man protested.

"Or madness," muttered Patrice.

Then he struck the table violently, in a fit of revulsion:

"It's not true, it's not true!" he exclaimed. "That man is not my father. What, a scoundrel like that! . . ."

He took a few steps round the little room and, stopping in front of Don Luis, jerked out:

"Let's go. Else I shall go mad too. It's a nightmare, there's no other word for it, a nightmare in which things turn upside down until the brain itself capsizes. Let's go. Coralie is in danger. That's the only thing that matters."

The old man shook his head:

"I'm very much afraid . . ."

"What are *you* afraid of?" bellowed the officer.

"I'm afraid that my poor friend has been caught up by the person who was following him . . . and then how can he have saved Mme. Essarès? The poor thing was hardly able to breathe, he told me."

Hanging on to Don Luis' arm, Patrice staggered out of the porter's lodge like a drunken man:

"She's done for, she must be!" he cried.

"Not at all," said Don Luis. "Siméon is as feverishly active as yourself. He is nearing the catastrophe. He is quaking with fear and not in a condition to weigh his words. Believe me, your Coralie is in no immediate danger. We have some hours before us."

"But Ya-Bon? Suppose Ya-Bon has laid hands upon him?"

"I gave Ya-Bon orders not to kill him. Therefore, whatever happens, Siméon is alive. That's the great thing. So long as Siméon is alive, there is nothing to fear. He won't let your Coralie die."

"Why not, seeing that he hates her? Why not? What is there in that man's heart? He devotes all his existence to a work of love on our behalf; and, from one minute to the next, that love turns to execration."

He pressed Don Luis' arm and, in a hollow voice, asked:

"Do you believe that he is my father?"

"Siméon Diodokis is your father, captain," replied Don Luis.

"Ah, don't, don't! It's too horrible! God, but we are in the valley of the shadow!"

"On the contrary," said Don Luis, "the shadow is lifting slightly; and I confess that our talk with M. Vacherot has given me a little light."

"Do you mean it?"

But, in Patrice Belval's fevered brain, one idea jostled another. He suddenly stopped:

"Siméon may have gone back to the porter's lodge! . . . And we sha'n't be there! . . . Perhaps he will bring Coralie back!"

"No," Don Luis declared, "he would have done that before now, if it could be done. No, it's for us to go to him."

"But where?"

"Well, of course, where all the fighting has been . . . where the gold lies. All the enemy's operations are centered in that gold; and you may be sure that, even in retreat, he can't get away from it. Besides, we know that he is not far from Berthou's Wharf."

Patrice allowed himself to be led along without a word. But suddenly Don Luis cried:

"Did you hear?"

"Yes, a shot."

At that moment they were on the point of turning into the Rue Raynouard. The height of the houses prevented them from perceiving the exact spot from which the shot had been fired, but it came approximately from the Essarès house or the immediate precincts. Patrice was filled with alarm:

"Can it be Ya-Bon?"

"I'm afraid so," said Don Luis, "and, as Ya-Bon wouldn't fire, some one must have fired a shot at him. . . . Oh, by Jove, if my poor Ya-Bon were to be killed . . . !"

"And suppose it was at her, at Coralie?" whispered Patrice.

Don Luis began to laugh:

"Oh, my dear captain, I'm almost sorry that I ever mixed myself up in this business! You were much cleverer before I came and a good deal clearer-sighted. Why the devil should Siméon attack your Coralie, considering that she's already in his power?"

They hurried their steps. As they passed the Essarès house they saw that everything was quiet and they went on until they came to the lane, down which they turned.

Patrice had the key, but the little door which opened on to the garden of the lodge was bolted inside.

"Aha!" said Don Luis. "That shows that we're warm. Meet me on the quay, captain. I shall run down to Berthou's Wharf to have a look round."

During the past few minutes a pale dawn had begun to mingle with the shades of night. The embankment was still deserted, however.

Don Luis observed nothing in particular at Berthou's Wharf; but, when he returned to the quay above, Patrice showed him a ladder lying right at the end of the pavement which skirted the garden of the lodge; and Don Luis recognized the ladder as the one whose absence he had noticed from the recess in the yard. With that quick vision which was one of his greatest assets, he at once furnished the explanation:

"As Siméon had the key of the garden, it was obviously Ya-Bon who used the ladder to make his way in. Therefore he saw Siméon take refuge there on returning from his visit to old Vacherot and after coming to fetch Coralie. Now the question is, did Siméon succeed in fetching Little Mother Coralie, or did he run away before fetching her? That I can't say. But, in any case . . ."

Bending low down, he examined the pavement and continued:

"In any case, what is certain is that Ya-Bon knows the hiding-place where the bags of gold are stacked and that it is there most likely that your Coralie was and perhaps still is, worse luck, if the enemy, giving his first thought to his personal safety, has not had time to remove her."

"Are you sure?"

"Look here, captain, Ya-Bon always carries a piece of chalk in his pocket. As he doesn't know how to write, except just the letters forming my name, he has drawn these two straight lines which, with the line of the wall, make a triangle . . . the golden triangle."

Don Luis drew himself up:

"The clue is rather meager. But Ya-Bon looks upon me as a wizard. He never doubted that I should manage to find this spot and that those three lines would be enough for me. Poor Ya-Bon!"

"But," objected Patrice, "all this, according to you, took place before our return to Paris, between twelve and one o'clock, therefore."

"Yes."

"Then what about the shot which we have just heard, four or five hours later?"

"As to that I'm not so positive. We may assume that Siméon squatted somewhere in the dark. Possibly at the first break of day, feeling easier and hearing nothing of Ya-Bon, he risked taking a step or two. Then Ya-Bon, keeping watch in silence, would have leaped upon him."

"So you think . . ."

"I think that there was a struggle, that Ya-Bon was wounded and that Siméon . . ."

"That Siméon escaped?"

"Or else was killed. However, we shall know all about it in a few minutes."

He set the ladder against the railing at the top of the wall. Patrice climbed over with Don Luis' assistance. Then, stepping over the railing in his turn, Don Luis drew up the ladder, threw it into the garden and made a careful examination. Finally, they turned their steps, through the tall grasses and bushy shrubs, towards the lodge.

The daylight was increasing rapidly and the outlines of everything were becoming clearer. The two men walked round the lodge, Don Luis leading the way. When he came in sight of the yard, on the street side, he turned and said: "I was right."

And he ran forward.

Outside the hall-door lay the bodies of the two adversaries, clutching each other in a confused heap. Ya-Bon had a horrible wound in the head, from which the blood was flowing all over his face. With his right hand he held Siméon by the throat.

Don Luis at once perceived that Ya-Bon was dead and Siméon Diodokis alive.

CHAPTER XVII
SIMÉON GIVES BATTLE

It took them some time to loosen Ya-Bon's grip. Even in death the Senegalese did not let go his prey; and his fingers, hard as iron and armed with nails piercing as a tiger's claws, dug into the neck of the enemy, who lay gurgling, deprived of consciousness and strength.

Don Luis caught sight of Siméon's revolver on the cobbles of the yard:

"It was lucky for you, you old ruffian," he said, in a low voice, "that Ya-Bon did not have time to squeeze the breath out of you before you fired that shot. But I wouldn't chortle overmuch, if I were you. He might perhaps have spared you, whereas, now that Ya-Bon's dead, you can write to your family and book your seat below. *De profundis*, Diodokis!" And, giving way to his grief, he added, "Poor Ya-Bon! He saved me from a horrible death one day in Africa . . . and to-day he dies by my orders, so to speak. My poor Ya-Bon!"

Assisted by Patrice, he carried the negro's corpse into the little bedroom next to the studio.

"We'll inform the police this evening, captain, when the drama is finished. For the moment, it's a matter of avenging him and the others."

He thereupon applied himself to making a minute inspection of the scene of the struggle, after which he went back to Ya-Bon and then to Siméon, whose clothes and shoes he examined closely.

Patrice was face to face with his terrible enemy, whom he had propped against the wall of the lodge and was contemplating in silence, with a fixed stare of hatred. Siméon! Siméon Diodokis, the execrable demon who, two days before, had hatched the terrible plot and, bending over the skylight, had laughed as he watched their awful agony! Siméon Diodokis, who, like a wild beast, had hidden Coralie in some hole, so that he might go back and torture her at his ease!

He seemed to be in pain and to breathe with great difficulty. His wind-pipe had no doubt been injured by Ya-Bon's clutch. His yellow spectacles had fallen off during the fight. A pair of thick, grizzled eyebrows lowered about his heavy lids.

"Search him, captain," said Don Luis.

But, as Patrice seemed to shrink from the task, he himself felt in Siméon's jacket and produced a pocket-book, which he handed to the officer.

It contained first of all a registration-card, in the name of Siméon Diodokis, Greek subject, with his photograph gummed to it. The photograph was a recent one, taken with the spectacles, the comforter and the long hair, and bore a police-stamp dated December, 1914. There was a collection of business documents, invoices and memoranda, addressed to Siméon as Essarès Bey's secretary, and, among these papers, a letter from Amédée Vacherot, running as follows:

"*Dear M. Siméon,*

"I have succeeded. A young friend of mine has taken a snapshot of Mme. Essarès and Patrice at the hospital, at a moment when they were talking together. I am so glad to be able to gratify you. But when will you tell your dear son the truth? How delighted he will be when he hears it!"

At the foot of the letter were a few words in Siméon's hand, a sort of personal note:

"Once more I solemnly pledge myself not to reveal anything to my dearly-beloved son until Coralie, my bride, is avenged and until Patrice and Coralie Essarès are free to love each other and to marry."

"That's your father's writing, is it not?" asked Don Luis.

"Yes," said Patrice, in bewilderment. "And it is also the writing of the letters which he addressed to his friend Vacherot. Oh, it's too hideous to be true! What a man! What a scoundrel!"

Siméon moved. His eyes opened and closed repeatedly. Then, coming to himself entirely, he looked at Patrice, who at once, in a stifled voice, asked:

"Where's Coralie?"

And, as Siméon, still dazed, seemed not to understand and sat gazing at him stupidly, he repeated, in a harsher tone:

"Where's Coralie? What have you done with her? Where have you put her? She must be dying!"

Siméon was gradually recovering life and consciousness. He mumbled:

"Patrice. . . . Patrice. . . ."

He looked around him, saw Don Luis, no doubt remembered his fight to the death with Ya-Bon and closed his eyes again. But Patrice's rage increased:

"Will you attend?" he shouted. "I won't wait any longer! It'll cost you your life if you don't answer!"

The man's eyes opened again, red-rimmed, bloodshot eyes. He pointed to his throat to indicate his difficulty in speaking. At last, with a visible effort, he repeated:

"Patrice! Is it you? . . . I have been waiting for this moment so long! . . . And now we are meeting as enemies! . . ."

"As mortal enemies," said Patrice, with emphasis. "Death stands between us: Ya-Bon's death, Coralie's perhaps. . . . Where is she? You must speak, or . . ."

"Patrice, is it really you?" the man repeated, in a whisper.

The familiarity exasperated the officer. He caught his adversary by the lapel of his jacket and shook him. But Siméon had seen the pocket-book which he held in his other hand and, without resisting Patrice's roughness, whined:

"You wouldn't hurt me, Patrice. You must have found some letters; and you now know the link that binds us together. Oh, how happy I should have been . . . !"

Patrice had released his hold and stood staring at him in horror. Sinking his voice in his turn, he said:

"Don't dare to speak of that: I won't, I won't believe it!"

"It's the truth, Patrice."

"You lie! You lie!" cried the officer, unable to restrain himself any longer, while his grief distorted his face out of all recognition.

"Ah, I see you have guessed it! Then I need not explain . . ."

"You lie! You're just a common scoundrel! . . . If what you say is true, why did you plot against Coralie and me? Why did you try to murder the two of us?"

"I was mad, Patrice. Yes, I go mad at times. All these tragedies have turned my head. My own Coralie's death . . . and then my life in Essarès' shadow . . . and then . . . and then, above all, the gold! . . . Did I really try to kill you both? I no longer remember. Or at least I remember a dream I had: it happened in the lodge, didn't it, as before? Oh, madness! What a torture! I'm like a man in the galleys. I have to do things against my will! . . . Then it was in the lodge, was it, as before? And in the same manner? With the same implements? . . . Yes, in my dream, I went through all my agony over again . . . and that of my darling. . . . But, instead of being tortured, I was the torturer . . . What a torment!"

He spoke low, inside himself, with hesitations and intervals and an unspeakable air of suffering. Don Luis kept his eyes fixed on him, as though trying to discover what he was aiming at. And Siméon continued:

"My poor Patrice! . . . I was so fond of you! . . . And now you are my worst enemy! . . . How indeed could it be otherwise? . . . How could you forget? . . . Oh, why didn't they lock me up after Essarès' death? It was then that I felt my brain going. . . ."

"So it was you who killed him?" asked Patrice.

"No, no, that's just it: somebody else robbed me of my revenge."

"Who?"

"I don't know. . . . The whole business is incomprehensible to me. . . . Don't speak of it. . . . It all pains me. . . . I have suffered so since Coralie's death!"

"Coralie!" exclaimed Patrice.

"Yes, the woman I loved. . . . As for little Coralie, I've suffered also on her account. . . . She ought not to have married Essarès."

"Where is she?" asked Patrice, in agony.

"I can't tell you."

"Oh," cried Patrice, shaking with rage, "you mean she's dead!"

"No, she's alive, I swear it."

"Then where is she? That's the only thing that matters. All the rest belongs to the past. But this thing, a woman's life, Coralie's life . . ."

"Listen."

Siméon stopped and gave a glance at Don Luis;

"Tell him to go away," he said.

Don Luis laughed:

"Of course! Little Mother Coralie is hidden in the same place as the bags of gold. To save her means surrendering the bags of gold."

"Well?" said Patrice, in an almost aggressive tone.

"Well, captain," replied Don Luis, not without a certain touch of banter in his voice, "if this honorable gentleman suggested that you should release him on parole so that he might go and fetch your Coralie, I don't suppose you'd accept?"

"No."

"You haven't the least confidence in him, have you? And you're right. The honorable gentleman, mad though he may be, gave such proofs of mental superiority and balance, when he sent us trundling down the road to Mantes, that it would be dangerous to attach the least credit to his promises. The consequence is . . ."

"Well?"

"This, captain, that the honorable gentleman means to propose a bargain to you, which may be couched thus: 'You can have Coralie, but I'll keep the gold.'"

"And then?"

"And then? It would be a capital notion, if you were alone with the honorable gentleman. The bargain would soon be concluded. But I'm here . . . by Jupiter!"

Patrice had drawn himself up. He stepped towards Don Luis and said, in a voice which became openly hostile:

"I presume that you won't raise any opposition. It's a matter of a woman's life."

"No doubt. But, on the other hand, it's a matter of three hundred million francs."

"Then you refuse?"

"Refuse? I should think so!"

"You refuse when that woman is at her last gasp? You would rather she died? . . . Look here, you seem to forget that this is my affair, that . . . that . . ."

The two men were standing close together. Don Luis retained that chaffing calmness, that air of knowing more than he chose to say, which irritated Patrice. At heart Patrice, while yielding to Don Luis' mastery, resented it and felt a certain embarrassment at accepting the services of a man with whose past he was so well acquainted.

"Then you actually refuse?" he rapped out, clenching his fists.

"Yes," said Don Luis, preserving his coolness. "Yes, Captain Belval, I refuse this bargain, which I consider absurd. Why, it's the confidence-trick! By Jingo! Three hundred millions! Give up a windfall like that? Never. But I haven't the least objection to leaving you alone with the honorable gentleman. That's what he wants, isn't it?"

"Yes."

"Well, talk it over between yourselves. Sign the compact. The honorable gentleman, who, for his part, has every confidence in his son, will tell you the whereabouts of the hiding-place; and you shall release your Coralie."

"And you? What about you?" snarled Patrice, angrily.

"I? I'm going to complete my little enquiry into the present and the past by revisiting the room where you nearly met your death. See you later, captain. And, whatever you do, insist on guarantees."

Switching on his pocket-lamp, Don Luis entered the lodge and walked straight to the studio. Patrice saw the electric rays playing on the panels between the walled-up windows. He went back to where Siméon sat:

"Now then," he said, in a voice of authority. "Be quick about it."

"Are you sure he's not listening?"

"Quite sure."

"Be careful with him, Patrice. He means to take the gold and keep it."

"Don't waste time," said Patrice, impatiently. "Get to Coralie."

"I've told you Coralie was alive."

"She was alive when you left her; but since then . . ."

"Yes, since then . . ."

"Since then, what? You seem to have your doubts."

"It was last night, five or six hours ago, and I am afraid . . ."

Patrice felt a cold shudder run down his back. He would have given anything for a decisive word; and at the same time he was almost strangling the old man to punish him. He mastered himself, however:

"Don't let's waste time," he repeated. "Tell me where to go."

"No, we'll go together."

"You haven't the strength."

"Yes, yes, I can manage . . . it's not far. Only, only, listen to me. . . ."

The old man seemed utterly exhausted. From time to time his breathing was interrupted, as though Ya-Bon's hand were still clutching him by the throat, and he sank into a heap, moaning.

Patrice stooped over him:

"I'm listening," he said. "But, for God's sake, hurry!"

"All right," said Siméon. "All right. She'll be free in a few minutes. But on one condition, just one. . . . Patrice, you must swear to me on Coralie's head that you will not touch the gold and that no one shall know . . ."

"I swear it on her head."

"You swear it, yes; but the other one, your damned companion, he'll follow us, he'll see."

"No, he won't."

"Yes, he will, unless you consent . . ."

"To what? Oh, in Heaven's name, speak!"

"I'll tell you. Listen. But remember, we must go to Coralie's assistance . . . and that quickly . . . otherwise . . ."

Patrice hesitated, bending one leg, almost on his knees:

"Then come, do!" he said, modifying his tone. "Please come, because Coralie . . ."

"Yes, but that man . . ."

"Oh, Coralie first!"

"What do you mean? Suppose he sees us? Suppose he takes the gold from us?"

"What does that matter!"

"Oh, don't say that, Patrice! . . . The gold! That's the one thing! Since that gold has been mine, my life is changed. The past no longer counts . . . nor does hatred . . . nor love. . . . There's only the gold, the bags of gold . . . I'd rather die . . . and let Coralie die . . . and see the whole world disappear . . ."

"But, look here, what is it you want? What is it you demand?"

Patrice had taken the two arms of this man who was his father and whom he had never detested with greater vehemence. He was imploring him with all the strength of his being. He would have shed tears had he thought that the old man would allow himself to be moved by tears.

"What is it?"

"I'll tell you. Listen. He's there, isn't he?"

"Yes."

"In the studio?"

"Yes."

"In that case . . . he mustn't come out. . . ."

"How do you mean?"

"No, he must stay there until we've done."

"But . . ."

"It's quite easy. Listen carefully. You've only to make a movement, to shut the door on him. The lock has been forced, but there are the two bolts; and those will do. Do you consent?"

Patrice rebelled:

"But you're mad! *I* consent, *I*? . . . Why, the man saved my life! . . . He saved Coralie!"

"But he's doing for her now. Think a moment: if he were not there, if he were not interfering, Coralie would be free. Do you accept?"

"No."

"Why not? Do you know what that man is? A highway robber . . . a wretch who has only one thought, to get hold of the millions. And you have scruples! Come, it's absurd, isn't it? . . . Do you accept?"

"No and again no!"

"Then so much the worse for Coralie. . . . Oh, yes, I see you don't realize the position exactly! It's time you did, Patrice. Perhaps it's even too late."

"Oh, don't say that!"

"Yes, yes, you must learn the facts and take your share of the responsibility. When that damned negro was chasing me, I got rid of Coralie as best I could, intending to release her in an hour or two. And then . . . and then you know what happened. . . . It was eleven o'clock at night . . . nearly eight hours ago. . . . So work it out for yourself . . ."

Patrice wrung his hands. Never had he imagined that a man could be tortured to such a degree. And Siméon continued, unrelentingly.

"She can't breathe, on my soul she can't! . . . Perhaps just a very little air reaches her, but that is all. . . . Then again I can't tell that all that covers and protects her hasn't given way. If it has, she's suffocating . . . while you stand here arguing. . . . Look here, can it matter to you to lock up that man for ten minutes? . . . Only ten minutes, you know. And you still hesitate! Then it's you who are killing her, Patrice. Think . . . buried alive!"

Patrice drew himself up. His resolve was taken. At that moment he would have shrunk from no act, however painful. And what Siméon asked was so little.

"What do you want me to do?" he asked. "Give your orders."

"You know what I want," said the other. "It's quite simple. Go to the door, bolt it and come back again."

The officer entered the lodge with a firm step and walked through the hall. The light was dancing up and down at the far end of the studio.

Without a word, without a moment's hesitation, he slammed the door, shot both the bolts and hastened back. He felt relieved. The action was a base one, but he never doubted that he had fulfilled an imperative duty.

"That's it," he said, "Let's hurry."

"Help me up," said the old man. "I can't manage by myself."

Patrice took him under the armpits and lifted him to his feet. But he had to support him, for the old man's legs were swaying beneath him.

"Oh, curse it!" blurted Siméon. "That blasted nigger has done for me. I'm suffocating too, I can't walk."

Patrice almost carried him, while Siméon, in the last stage of weakness, stammered:

"This way. . . . Now straight ahead. . . ."

They passed the corner of the lodge and turned their steps towards the graves.

"You're quite sure you fastened the door?" the old man continued. "Yes, I heard it slam. Oh, he's a terrible fellow, that! You have to be on your guard with him! But you swore not to say anything, didn't you? Swear it again, by your mother's memory . . . no, better, swear it by Coralie. . . . May she die on the spot if you betray your oath!"

He stopped. A spasm prevented his going any further until he had drawn a little air into his lungs. Nevertheless he went on talking:

"I needn't worry, need I? Besides, you don't care about gold. That being so, why should you speak? Never mind, swear that you will be silent. Or, look here, give me your word of honor. That's best. Your word, eh?"

Patrice was still holding him round the waist. It was a terrible, long agony for the officer, this slow crawl and this sort of embrace which he was compelled to adopt in order to effect Coralie's release. As he felt the contact of the detested man's body, he was more inclined to squeeze the life out of it. And yet a vile phrase kept recurring deep down within him:

"I am his son, I am his son. . . ."

"It's here," said the old man.

"Here? But these are the graves."

"Coralie's grave and mine. It's what we were making for."

He turned round in alarm:

"I say, the footprints! You'll get rid of them on the way back, won't you? For he would find our tracks otherwise and he would know that this is the place. . . ."

"Let's hurry. . . . So Coralie is here? Down there? Buried? Oh, how horrible!"

It seemed to Patrice as if each minute that passed meant more than an hour's delay and as if Coralie's safety might be jeopardized by a moment's hesitation or a single false step.

He took every oath that was demanded of him. He swore upon Coralie's head. He pledged his word of honor. At that moment there was not an action which he would not have been ready to perform.

Siméon knelt down on the grass, under the little temple, pointing with his finger:

"It's there," he repeated. "Underneath that."

"Under the tombstone?"

"Yes."

"Then the stone lifts?" asked Patrice, anxiously. "I can't lift it by myself. It can't be done. It would take three men to lift that."

"No," said the old man, "the stone swings on a pivot. You'll manage quite easily. All you have to do is to pull at one end . . . this one, on the right."

Patrice came and caught hold of the great stone slab, with its inscription, "Here lie Patrice and Coralie," and pulled.

The stone rose at the first endeavor, as if a counterweight had forced the other end down.

"Wait," said the old man. "We must hold it in position, or it will fall down again. You'll find an iron bar at the bottom of the second step."

There were three steps running into a small cavity, barely large enough to contain a man stooping. Patrice saw the iron bar and, propping up the stone with his shoulder, took the bar and set it up.

"Good," said Siméon. "That will keep it steady. What you must now do is to lie down in the hollow. This was where my coffin was to have been and where I often used to come and lie beside my dear Coralie. I would remain for hours, flat on the ground, speaking to her. . . . We both talked. . . . Yes, I assure you, we used to talk. . . . Oh, Patrice! . . ."

Patrice had bent his tall figure in the narrow space where he was hardly able to move.

"What am I to do?" he asked.

"Don't you hear your Coralie? There's only a partition-wall between you: a few bricks hidden under a thin layer of earth. And a door. The other vault, Coralie's, is behind it. And behind that there's a third, with the bags of gold."

The old man was bending over and directing the search as he knelt on the grass:

"The door's on the left. Farther than that. Can't you find it? That's odd. You mustn't be too slow about it, though. Ah, have you got it now? No? Oh, if I could only go down too! But there's not room for more than one."

There was a brief silence. Then he began again:

"Stretch a bit farther. Good. Can you move?"

"Yes," said Patrice.

"Then go on moving, my lad!" cried the old man, with a yell of laughter.

And, stepping back briskly, he snatched away the iron bar. The enormous block of stone came down heavily, slowly, because of the counterweight, but with irresistible force.

Though floundering in the newly-turned earth, Patrice tried to rise, at the sight of his danger. Siméon had taken up the iron bar and now struck him a blow on the head with it. Patrice gave a cry and moved no more. The stone covered him up. The whole incident had lasted but a few seconds.

Siméon did not lose an instant. He knew that Patrice, wounded as he was bound to be and weakened by the posture to which he was condemned, was incapable of making the necessary effort to lift the lid of his tomb. On that side, therefore, there was no danger.

He went back to the lodge and, though he walked with some difficulty, he had no doubt exaggerated his injuries, for he did not stop until he reached the door. He even scorned to obliterate his footprints and went straight ahead.

On entering the hall he listened. Don Luis was tapping against the walls and the partition inside the studio and the bedroom.

"Capital!" said Siméon, with a grin. "His turn now."

It did not take long. He walked to the kitchen on the right, opened the door of the meter and, turning the key, released the gas, thus beginning again with Don Luis what he had failed to achieve with Patrice and Coralie.

Not till then did he yield to the immense weariness with which he was overcome and allow himself to lie back in a chair for two or three minutes.

His most terrible enemy also was now out of the way. But it was still necessary for him to act and ensure his personal safety. He walked round the lodge, looked for his yellow spectacles and put them on, went through the garden, opened the door and closed it behind him. Then he turned down the lane to the quay.

Once more stopping, in front of the parapet above Berthou's Wharf, he seemed to hesitate what to do. But the sight of people passing, carmen, market-gardeners and others, put an end to his indecision. He hailed a taxi and drove to the Rue Guimard.

His friend Vacherot was standing at the door of his lodge.

"Oh, is that you, M. Siméon?" cried the porter. "But what a state you're in!"

"Hush, no names!" he whispered, entering the lodge. "Has any one seen me?"

"No. It's only half-past seven and the house is hardly awake. But, Lord forgive us, what have the scoundrels done to you? You look as if you had no breath left in your body!"

"Yes, that nigger who came after me . . ."

"But the others?"

"What others?"

"The two who were here? Patrice?"

"Eh? Has Patrice been?" asked Siméon, still speaking in a whisper.

"Yes, last night, after you left."

"And you told him?"

"That he was your son."

"Then that," mumbled the old man, "is why he did not seem surprised at what I said."

"Where are they now?"

"With Coralie. I was able to save her. I've handed her over to them. But it's not a question of her. Quick, I must see a doctor; there's no time to lose."

"We have one in the house."

"No, that's no use. Have you a telephone-directory?"

"Here you are."

"Turn up Dr. Géradec."

"What? You can't mean that?"

"Why not? He has a private hospital quite close, on the Boulevard de Montmorency, with no other house near it."

"That's so, but haven't you heard? There are all sorts of rumors about him afloat: something to do with passports and forged certificates."

"Never mind that."

M. Vacherot hunted out the number in the directory and rang up the exchange. The line was engaged; and he wrote down the number on the margin of a newspaper. Then he telephoned again. The answer was that the doctor had gone out and would be back at ten.

"It's just as well," said Siméon. "I'm not feeling strong enough yet. Say that I'll call at ten o'clock."

"Shall I give your name as Siméon?"

"No, my real name, Armand Belval. Say it's urgent, say it's a surgical case."

The porter did so and hung up the instrument, with a moan:

"Oh, my poor M. Siméon! A man like you, so good and kind to everybody! Tell me what happened?"

"Don't worry about that. Is my place ready?"

"To be sure it is."

"Take me there without any one seeing us."

"As usual."

"Be quick. Put your revolver in your pocket. What about your lodge? Can you leave it?"

"Five minutes won't hurt."

The lodge opened at the back on a small courtyard, which communicated with a long corridor. At the end of this passage was another yard, in which stood a little house consisting of a ground-floor and an attic.

They went in. There was an entrance-hall followed by three rooms, leading one into the other. Only the second room was furnished. The third had a door opening straight on a street that ran parallel with the Rue Guimard.

They stopped in the second room.

"Did you shut the hall-door after you?"

"Yes, M. Siméon."

"No one saw us come in, I suppose?"

"Not a soul."

"No one suspects that you're here?"

"No."

"Give me your revolver."

"Here it is."

"Do you think, if I fired it off, any one would hear?"

"No, certainly not. Who is there to hear? But . . ."

"But what?"

"You're surely not going to fire?"

"Yes, I am."

"At yourself, M. Siméon, at yourself? Are you going to kill yourself?"

"Don't be an ass."

"Well, who then?"

"You, of course!" chuckled Siméon.

Pressing the trigger, he blew out the luckless man's brains. His victim fell in a heap, stone dead. Siméon flung aside the revolver and remained impassive, a little undecided as to his next step. He opened out his fingers, one by one, up to six, apparently counting the six persons of whom he had got rid in a few hours: Grégoire, Coralie, Ya-Bon, Patrice, Don Luis, old Vacherot!

His mouth gave a grin of satisfaction. One more endeavor; and his flight and safety were assured.

For the moment he was incapable of making the endeavor. His head whirled. His arms struck out at space. He fell into a faint, with a gurgle in his throat, his chest crushed under an unbearable weight.

But, at a quarter to ten, with an effort of will, he picked himself up and, mastering himself and disregarding the pain, he went out by the other door of the house.

At ten o'clock, after twice changing his taxi, he arrived at the Boulevard Montmorency, just at the moment when Dr. Géradec was alighting from his car and mounting the steps of the handsome villa in which his private hospital had been installed since the beginning of the war.

CHAPTER XVIII
SIMÉON'S LAST VICTIM

Dr. Géradec's hospital had several annexes, each of which served a specific purpose, grouped around it in a fine garden. The villa itself was used for the big operations. The doctor had his consulting-room here also; and it was to this room that Siméon Diodokis was first shown. But, after answering a few questions put to him by a male nurse, Siméon was taken to another room in a separate wing.

Here he was received by the doctor, a man of about sixty, still young in his movements, clean-shaven and wearing a glass screwed into his right eye, which contracted his features into a constant grimace. He was wrapped from the shoulders to the feet in a large white operating-apron.

Siméon explained his case with great difficulty, for he could hardly speak. A footpad had attacked him the night before, taken him by the throat and robbed him, leaving him half-dead in the road.

"You have had time to send for a doctor since," said Dr. Géradec, fixing him with a glance.

Siméon did not reply; and the doctor added:

"However, it's nothing much. The fact that you are alive shows that there's no fracture. It reduces itself therefore to a contraction of the larynx, which we shall easily get rid of by tubing."

He gave his assistant some instructions. A long aluminum tube was inserted in the patient's wind-pipe. The doctor, who had absented himself meanwhile, returned and, after removing the tube, examined the patient, who was already beginning to breathe with greater ease.

"That's over," said Dr. Géradec, "and much quicker than I expected. There was evidently in your case an inhibition which caused the throat to shrink. Go home now; and, when you've had a rest, you'll forget all about it."

Siméon asked what the fee was and paid it. But, as the doctor was seeing him to the door, he stopped and, without further preface, said:

"I am a friend of Mme. Albonin's."

The doctor did not seem to understand what he meant.

"Perhaps you don't recognize the name," Siméon insisted. "When I tell you, however, that it conceals the identity of Mme. Mosgranem, I have no doubt that we shall be able to arrange something."

"What about?" asked the doctor, while his face displayed still greater astonishment.

"Come, doctor, there's no need to be on your guard. We are alone. You have sound-proof, double doors. Sit down and let's talk."

He took a chair. The doctor sat down opposite him, looking more and more surprised. And Siméon proceeded with his statement:

"I am a Greek subject. Greece is a neutral; indeed, I may say, a friendly country; and I can easily obtain a passport and leave France. But, for personal reasons, I want the passport made out not in my own name but in some other, which you and I will decide upon together and which will enable me, with your assistance, to go away without any danger."

The doctor rose to his feet indignantly.

Siméon persisted:

"Oh, please don't be theatrical! It's a question of price, is it not? My mind is made up. How much do you want?"

The doctor pointed to the door.

Siméon raised no protest. He put on his hat. But, on reaching the door, he said:

"Twenty thousand francs? Is that enough?"

"Do you want me to ring?" asked the doctor, "and have you turned out?"

Siméon laughed and quietly, with a pause after each figure:

"Thirty thousand?" he asked. "Forty? . . . Fifty? . . . Oh, I see, we're playing a great game, we want a round sum. . . . All right. Only, you know, everything must be included in the price we settle. You must not only fix me up a passport so genuine that it can't be disputed, but you must guarantee me the means of leaving France, as you did for Mme. Mosgranem, on terms not half so handsome, by Jove! However, I'm not haggling. I need your assistance. Is it a bargain? A hundred thousand francs?"

Dr. Géradec bolted the door, came back, sat down at his desk and said, simply:

"We'll talk about it."

"I repeat the question," said Siméon, coming closer. "Are we agreed at a hundred thousand?"

"We are agreed," said the doctor, "unless any complications appear later."

"What do you mean?"

"I mean that the figure of a hundred thousand francs forms a suitable basis for discussion, that's all."

Siméon hesitated a second. The man struck him as rather greedy. However, he sat down once more; and the doctor at once resumed the conversation:

"Your real name, please."

"You mustn't ask me that. I tell you, there are reasons . . ."

"Then it will be two hundred thousand francs."

"Eh?" said Siméon, with a start. "I say, that's a bit steep! I never heard of such a price."

"You're not obliged to accept," replied Géradec, calmly. "We are discussing a bargain. You are free to do as you please."

"But, look here, once you agree to fix me up a false passport, what can it matter to you whether you know my name or not?"

"It matters a great deal. I run an infinitely greater risk in assisting the escape—for that's the only word—of a spy than I do in assisting the escape of a respectable man."

"I'm not a spy."

"How do I know? Look here, you come to me to propose a shady transaction. You conceal your name and your identity; and you're in such a hurry to disappear from sight that you're prepared to pay me a hundred thousand francs to help you. And, in the face of that, you lay claim to being a respectable man! Come, come! It's absurd! A respectable man does not behave like a burglar or a murderer."

Old Siméon did not wince. He slowly wiped his forehead with his handkerchief. He was evidently thinking that Géradec was a hardy antagonist and that he would perhaps have done better not to go to him. But, after all, the contract was a conditional one. There would always be time enough to break it off.

"I say, I say!" he said, with an attempt at a laugh. "You are using big words!"

"They're only words," said the doctor. "I am stating no hypothesis. I am content to sum up the position and to justify my demands."

"You're quite right."

"Then we're agreed?"

"Yes. Perhaps, however—and this is the last observation I propose to make—you might let me off more cheaply, considering that I'm a friend of Mme. Mosgranem's."

"What do you suggest by that?" asked the doctor.

"Mme. Mosgranem herself told me that you charged her nothing."

"That's true, I charged her nothing," replied the doctor, with a fatuous smile, "but perhaps she presented me with a good deal. Mme. Mosgranem was one of those attractive women whose favors command their own price."

There was a silence. Old Siméon seemed to feel more and more uncomfortable in his interlocutor's presence. At last the doctor sighed:

"Poor Mme. Mosgranem!"

"What makes you speak like that?" asked Siméon.

"What! Haven't you heard?"

"I have had no letters from her since she left."

"I see. I had one last night; and I was greatly surprised to learn that she was back in France."

"In France! Mme. Mosgranem!"

"Yes. And she even gave me an appointment for this morning, a very strange appointment."

"Where?" asked Siméon, with visible concern.

"You'll never guess. On a barge, yes, called the *Nonchalante*, moored at the Quai de Passy, alongside Berthou's Wharf."

"Is it possible?" said Siméon.

"It's as I tell you. And do you know how the letter was signed? It was signed Grégoire."

"Grégoire? A man's name?" muttered the old man, almost with a groan.

"Yes, a man's name. Look, I have the letter on me. She tells me that she is leading a very dangerous life, that she distrusts the man with whom her fortunes are bound up and that she would like to ask my advice."

"Then . . . then you went?"

"Yes, I was there this morning, while you were ringing up here. Unfortunately . . ."

"Well?"

"I arrived too late. Grégoire, or rather Mme. Mosgranem, was dead. She had been strangled."

"So you know nothing more than that?" asked Siméon, who seemed unable to get his words out.

"Nothing more about what?"

"About the man whom she mentioned."

"Yes, I do, for she told me his name in the letter. He's a Greek, who calls himself Siméon Diodokis. She even gave me a description of him. I haven't read it very carefully."

He unfolded the letter and ran his eyes down the second page, mumbling:

"A broken-down old man. . . . Passes himself off as mad. . . . Always goes about in a comforter and a pair of large yellow spectacles. . . ."

Dr. Géradec ceased reading and looked at Siméon with an air of amazement. Both of them sat for a moment without speaking. Then the doctor said:

"You are Siméon Diodokis."

The other did not protest. All these incidents were so strangely and, at the same time, so naturally interlinked as to persuade him that lying was useless.

"This alters the situation," declared the doctor. "The time for trifling is past. It's a most serious and terribly dangerous matter for me, I can tell you! You'll have to make it a million."

"Oh, no!" cried Siméon, excitedly. "Certainly not! Besides, I never touched Mme. Mosgranem. I was myself attacked by the man who strangled her, the same man—a negro called Ya-Bon—who caught me up and took me by the throat."

"Ya-Bon? Did you say Ya-Bon?"

"Yes, a one-armed Senegalese."

799

"And did you two fight?"

"Yes."

"And did you kill him?"

"Well . . ."

The doctor shrugged his shoulders with a smile:

"Listen, sir, to a curious coincidence. When I left the barge, I met half-a-dozen wounded soldiers. They spoke to me and said that they were looking for a comrade, this very Ya-Bon, and also for their captain, Captain Belval, and a friend of this officer's and a lady, the lady they were staying with. All these people had disappeared; and they accused a certain person . . . wait, they told me his name. . . . Oh, but this is more and more curious! The man's name was Siméon Diodokis. It was you they accused! . . . Isn't it odd? But, on the other hand, you must confess that all this constitutes fresh facts and therefore . . ."

There was a pause. Then the doctor formulated his demand in plain tones:

"I shall want two millions."

This time Siméon remained impassive. He felt that he was in the man's clutches, like a mouse clawed by a cat. The doctor was playing with him, letting him go and catching him again, without giving him the least hope of escaping from this grim sport.

"This is blackmail," he said, quietly.

The doctor nodded:

"There's no other word for it," he admitted. "It's blackmail. Moreover, it's a case of blackmail in which I have not the excuse of creating the opportunity that gives me my advantage. A wonderful chance comes within reach of my hand. I grab at it, as you would do in my place. What else is possible? I have had a few differences, which you know of, with the police. We've signed a peace, the police and I. But my professional position has been so much injured that I cannot afford to reject with scorn what you so kindly bring me."

"Suppose I refuse to submit?"

"Then I shall telephone to the headquarters of police, with whom I stand in great favor at present, as I am able to do them a good turn now and again."

Siméon glanced at the window and at the door. The doctor had his hand on the receiver of the telephone. There was no way out of it.

"Very well," he declared. "After all, it's better so. You know me; and I know you. We can come to terms."

"On the basis suggested?"

"Yes. Tell me your plan."

"No, it's not worth while. I have my methods; and there's no object in revealing them beforehand. The point is to secure your escape and to put an end to your present danger. I'll answer for all that."

"What guarantee have I. . . ?"

"You will pay me half the money now and the other half when the business is done. There remains the matter of the passport, a secondary matter for me. Still, we shall have to make one out. In what name is it to be?"

"Any name you like."

The doctor took a sheet of paper and wrote down the description, looking at Siméon between the phrases and muttering:

"Gray hair. . . . Clean-shaven. . . . Yellow spectacles. . . ."

Then he stopped and asked:

"But how do I know that I shall be paid the money? That's essential, you know. I want bank-notes, real ones."

"You shall have them."

"Where are they?"

"In a hiding-place that can't be got at."

"Tell me where."

"I have no objection. Even if I give you a clue to the general position, you'll never find it."

"Well, go on."

"Grégoire had the money in her keeping, four million francs. It's on board the barge. We'll go there together and I'll count you out the first million."

"You say those millions are on board the barge?"

"Yes."

"And there are four of those millions?"

"Yes."

"I won't accept any of them in payment."

"Why not? You must be mad!"

"Why not? Because you can't pay a man with what already belongs to him."

"What's that you're saying?" cried Siméon, in dismay.

"Those four millions belong to me, so you can't offer them to me."

Siméon shrugged his shoulders:

"You're talking nonsense. For the money to belong to you, it must first be in your possession."

"Certainly."

"And is it?"

"It is."

"Explain yourself, explain yourself at once!" snarled Siméon, beside himself with anger and alarm.

"I will explain myself. The hiding-place that couldn't be got at consisted of four old books, back numbers of Bottin's directory for Paris and the provinces, each in two volumes. The four volumes were hollow inside, as though they had been scooped out; and there was a million francs in each of them."

"You lie! You lie!"

"They were on a shelf, in a little lumber-room next the cabin."

"Well, what then?"

"What then? They're here."

"Here?"

"Yes, here, on that bookshelf, in front of your nose. So, in the circumstances, you see, as I am already the lawful owner, I can't accept . . ."

"You thief! You thief!" shouted Siméon, shaking with rage and clenching his fist. "You're nothing but a thief; and I'll make you disgorge. Oh, you dirty thief!"

Dr. Géradec smiled very calmly and raised his hand in protest:

"This is strong language and quite unjustified! quite unjustified! Let me remind you that Mme. Mosgranem honored me with her affection. One day, or rather one morning, after a moment of expansiveness, 'My dear friend,' she said—she used to call me her dear friend—'my dear friend, when I die'—she was given to those gloomy forebodings—'when I die, I bequeath to you the contents of my home!' Her home, at that moment, was the barge. Do you suggest that I should insult her memory by refusing to obey so sacred a wish?"

Old Siméon was not listening. An infernal thought was awakening in him; and he turned to the doctor with a movement of affrighted attention.

"We are wasting precious time, my dear sir," said the doctor. "What have you decided to do?"

He was playing with the sheet of paper on which he had written the particulars required for the passport. Siméon came up to him without a word. At last the old man whispered:

"Give me that sheet of paper. . . . I want to see . . ."

He took the paper out of the doctor's hand, ran his eyes down it and suddenly leapt backwards:

"What name have you put? What name have you put? What right have you to give me that name? Why did you do it?"

"You told me to put any name I pleased, you know."

"But why this one? Why this one?"

"Can it be your own?"

The old man started with terror and, bending lower and lower over the doctor, said, in a trembling voice:

"One man alone, one man alone was capable of guessing . . ."

There was a long pause. Then the doctor gave a little chuckle:

"I know that only one man was capable of it. So let's take it that I'm the man."

"One man alone," continued the other, while his breath once again seemed to fail him, "one man alone could find the hiding-place of the four millions in a few seconds."

The doctor did not answer. He smiled; and his features gradually relaxed.

In a sort of terror-stricken tone Siméon hissed out:

"Arsène Lupin! . . . Arsène Lupin! . . ."

"You've hit it in one," exclaimed the doctor, rising.

He dropped his eye-glass, took from his pocket a little pot of grease, smeared his face with it, washed it off in a basin in a recess and reappeared with a clear skin, a smiling, bantering face and an easy carriage.

"Arsène Lupin!" repeated Siméon, petrified. "Arsène Lupin! I'm in for it!"

"Up to the neck, you old fool! And what a silly fool you must be! Why, you know me by reputation, you feel for me the intense and wholesome awe with which a decent man of my stamp is bound to inspire an old rascal like you . . . and you go and imagine that I should be ass enough to let myself be bottled up in that lethal chamber of yours! Mind you, at that very moment I could have taken you by the hair of the head and gone straight on to the great scene in the fifth act, which we are now playing. Only my fifth act would have been a bit short, you see; and I'm a born actor-manager. As it is, observe how well the interest is sustained! And what fun it was seeing the thought of it take birth in your old Turkish noddle! And what a lark to go into the studio, fasten my electric lamp to a bit of string, make poor, dear Patrice believe that I was there and go out and hear Patrice denying me three times and carefully bolting the door on . . . what? My electric lamp! That was all first-class work, don't you think? What do you say to it? I can feel that you're speechless with admiration. . . . And, ten minutes after, when you came back, the same scene in the wings and with the same success. Of course, you old Siméon, I was banging at the walled-up door, between the studio and the bedroom on the left. Only I wasn't in the studio: I was in the bedroom; and you went away quietly, like a good kind landlord. As for me, I had no need to hurry. I was as certain as that twice two is four that you would go to your friend M. Amédée Vacherot, the porter. And here, I may say, old Siméon, you committed a nice piece of imprudence, which got me out of my difficulty. No one in the porter's lodge: that couldn't be helped; but what I did find was a telephone-number on a scrap of newspaper. I did not hesitate for a moment. I rang up the number, coolly: 'Monsieur, it was I who telephoned to you just now. Only I've got your number, but not your address.' Back came the answer: 'Dr. Géradec, Boulevard de Montmorency.' Then I understood. Dr.

Géradec? You would want your throat tubed for a bit, then the all-essential passport; and I came off here, without troubling about your poor friend M. Vacherot, whom you murdered in some corner or other to escape a possible give-away on his side. And I saw Dr. Géradec, a charming man, whose worries have made him very wise and submissive and who . . . lent me his place for the morning. I had still two hours before me. I went to the barge, took the millions, cleared up a few odds and ends and here I am!"

He came and stood in front of the old man:

"Well, are you ready?" he asked.

Siméon, who seemed absorbed in thought, gave a start.

"Ready for what?" said Don Luis, replying to his unspoken question. "Why, for the great journey, of course! Your passport is in order. Your ticket's taken: Paris to Hell, single. Non-stop hearse. Sleeping-coffin. Step in, sir!"

The old man, tottering on his legs, made an effort and stammered:

"And Patrice?"

"What about him?"

"I offer you his life in exchange for my own."

Don Luis folded his arms across his chest:

"Well, of all the cheek! Patrice is a friend; and you think me capable of abandoning him like that? Do you see me, Lupin, making more or less witty jokes upon your imminent death while my friend Patrice is in danger? Old Siméon, you're getting played out. It's time you went and rested in a better world."

He lifted a hanging, opened a door and called out:

"Well, captain, how are you getting on? Ah, I see you've recovered consciousness! Are you surprised to see me? No, no thanks, but please come in here. Our old Siméon's asking for you."

Then, turning to the old man, he said:

"Here's your son, you unnatural father!"

Patrice entered the room with his head bandaged, for the blow which Siméon had struck him and the weight of the tombstone had opened his old wounds. He was very pale and seemed to be in great pain.

At the sight of Siméon Diodokis he gave signs of terrible anger. He controlled himself, however. The two men stood facing each other, without stirring, and Don Luis, rubbing his hands, said, in an undertone:

"What a scene! What a splendid scene? Isn't it well-arranged? The father and the son! The murderer and his victim! Listen to the orchestra! . . . A slight tremolo. . . . What are they going to do? Will the son kill his father or the father kill his son? A thrilling moment. . . . And the mighty silence! Only the call of the blood is heard . . . and in what terms! Now we're off! The call of the blood has sounded; and they are going to throw themselves into each other's arms, the better to strangle the life out of each other!"

Patrice had taken two steps forward; and the movement suggested by Don Luis was about to be performed. Already the officer's arms were flung wide for the fight. But suddenly Siméon, weakened by pain and dominated by a stronger will than his own, let himself go and implored his adversary:

"Patrice!" he entreated. "Patrice! What are you thinking of doing?"

Stretching out his hands, he threw himself upon the other's pity; and Patrice, arrested in his onrush, stood perplexed, staring at the man to whom he was bound by so mysterious and strange a tie:

"Coralie," he said, without lowering his hands, "Coralie . . . tell me where she is and I'll spare your life."

The old man started. His evil nature was stimulated by the remembrance of Coralie; and he recovered a part of his energy at the possibility of wrong-doing. He gave a cruel laugh:

"No, no," he answered. "Coralie in one scale and I in the other? I'd rather die. Besides, Coralie's hiding-place is where the gold is. No, never! I may just as well die."

"Kill him then, captain," said Don Luis, intervening. "Kill him, since he prefers it."

Once more the thought of immediate murder and revenge sent the red blood rushing to the officer's face. But the same hesitation unnerved him.

"No, no," he said, in a low voice, "I can't do it."

"Why not?" Don Luis insisted. "It's so easy. Come along! Wring his neck, like a chicken's, and have done with it!"

"I can't."

"But why? Do you dislike the thought of strangling him? Does it repel you? And yet, if it were a Boche, on the battlefield . . ."

"Yes . . . but this man . . ."

"Is it your hands that refuse? The idea of taking hold of the flesh and squeezing? . . . Here, captain, take my revolver and blow out his brains."

Patrice accepted the weapon eagerly and aimed it at old Siméon. The silence was appalling. Old Siméon's eyes had closed and drops of sweat were streaming down his livid cheeks.

At last the officer lowered his arm:

"I can't do it," he said.

"Nonsense," said Don Luis. "Get on with the work."

"No. . . . No. . . ."

"But, in Heaven's name, why not?"

"I can't."

"You can't? Shall I tell you the reason? You are thinking of that man as if he were your father."

"Perhaps it's that," said the officer, speaking very low. "There's a chance of it, you know."

"What does it matter, if he's a beast and a blackguard?"

"No, no, I haven't the right. Let him die by all means, but not by my hand. I haven't the right."

"You have the right."

"No, it would be abominable! It would be monstrous!"

Don Luis went up to him and, tapping him on the shoulder, said, gravely:

"You surely don't believe that I should stand here, urging you to kill that man, if he were your father?"

Patrice looked at him wildly:

"Do you know something? Do you know something for certain? Oh, for Heaven's sake . . . !"

Don Luis continued:

"Do you believe that I would even encourage you to hate him, if he were your father?"

"Oh!" exclaimed Patrice. "Do you mean that he's not my father?"

"Of course he's not!" cried Don Luis, with irresistible conviction and increasing eagerness. "Your father indeed! Why, look at him! Look at that scoundrelly head. Every sort of vice and violence is written on the brute's face. Throughout this adventure, from the first day to the last, there was not a crime committed but was his handiwork: not one, do you follow me? There were not two criminals, as we thought, not Essarès, to begin the hellish business, and old Siméon, to finish it. There was only one criminal, one, do you understand, Patrice? Before killing Coralie and Ya-Bon and Vacherot the porter and the woman who was his own accomplice, he killed others! He killed one other in particular, one whose flesh and blood you are, the man whose dying cries you heard over the telephone, the man who called you Patrice and who only lived for you! He killed that man; and that man was your father, Patrice; he was Armand Belval! Now do you understand?"

Patrice did not understand. Don Luis' words fell uncomprehended; not one of them lit up the darkness of Patrice's brain. However, one thought insistently possessed him; and he stammered:

"*That* was my father? I heard his voice, you say? Then it was *he* who called to me?"

"Yes, Patrice, your father."

"And the man who killed him . . . ?"

"Was this one," said Don Luis, pointing to Siméon.

The old man remained motionless, wild-eyed, like a felon awaiting sentence of death. Patrice, quivering with rage, stared at him fixedly:

"Who are you? Who arc you?" he asked. And, turning to Don Luis, "Tell me his name, I beseech you. I want to know his name, before I destroy him."

"His name? Haven't you guessed it yet? Why, from the very first day, I took it for granted! After all, it was the only possible theory."

"But what theory? What was it you took for granted?" cried Patrice, impatiently.

"Do you really want to know?"

"Oh, please! I'm longing to kill him, but I must first know his name."

"Well, then . . ."

There was a long silence between the two men, as they stood close together, looking into each other's eyes. Then Lupin let fall these four syllables:

"Essarès Bey."

Patrice felt a shock that ran through him from head to foot. Not for a second did he try to understand by what prodigy this revelation came to be merely an expression of the truth. He instantly accepted this truth, as though it were undeniable and proved by the most evident facts. The man was Essarès Bey and had killed his father. He had killed him, so to speak, twice over: first years ago, in the lodge in the garden, taking from him all the light of life and any reason for living; and again the other day, in the library, when Armand Belval had telephoned to his son.

This time Patrice was determined to do the deed. His eyes expressed an indomitable resolution. His father's murderer, Coralie's murderer, must die then and there. His duty was clear and precise. The terrible Essarès was doomed to die by the hand of the son and the bridegroom.

"Say your prayers," said Patrice, coldly. "In ten seconds you will be a dead man."

He counted out the seconds and, at the tenth, was about to fire, when his enemy, in an access of mad energy proving that, under the outward appearance of old Siméon, there was hidden a man still young and vigorous, shouted with a violence so extraordinary that it made Patrice hesitate:

"Very well, kill me! . . . Yes, let it be finished! . . . I am beaten: I accept defeat. But it is a victory all the same, because Coralie is dead and my gold is saved! . . . I shall die, but nobody shall have either one or the other, the woman whom I love or the gold that was my life. Ah, Patrice, Patrice, the woman whom we both loved to distraction is no longer alive . . . or else she is dying without a possibility of saving her now. If I cannot have her, you shall not have her either, Patrice. My revenge has done its work. Coralie is lost!"

He had recovered a fierce energy and was shouting and stammering at the same time. Patrice stood opposite him, holding him covered with the revolver, ready to act, but still waiting to hear the terrible words that tortured him.

"She is lost, Patrice!" Siméon continued, raising his voice still louder. "Lost! There's nothing to be done! And you will not find even her body in the bowels of the earth, where I buried her with the bags of gold. Under the tombstone? No, not such a fool! No, Patrice, you will never find her. The gold is stifling her. She's dead! Coralie is dead! Oh, the delight of throwing that in your face! The anguish you must be feeling! Coralie is dead! Coralie is dead!"

"Don't shout so, you'll wake her," said Don Luis, calmly.

The brief sentence was followed by a sort of stupor which paralyzed the two adversaries. Patrice's arms dropped to his sides. Siméon turned giddy and sank into a chair. Both of them, knowing the things of which Don Luis was capable, knew what he meant.

But Patrice wanted something more than a vague sentence that might just as easily be taken as a jest. He wanted a certainty.

"Wake her?" he asked, in a broken voice.

"Well, of course!" said Don Luis. "When you shout too loud, you wake people up."

"Then she's alive?"

"You can't wake the dead, whatever people may say. You can only wake the living."

"Coralie is alive! Coralie is alive!" Patrice repeated, in a sort of rapture that transfigured his features. "Can it be possible? But then she must be here! Oh, I beg of you, say you're in earnest, give me your word! . . . Or no, it's not true, is it? I can't believe it . . . you must be joking. . . ."

"Let me answer you, captain, as I answered that wretch just now. You are admitting that it is possible for me to abandon my work before completing it. How little you know me! What I undertake to do I do. It's one of my habits and a good one at that. That's why I cling to it. Now watch me."

He turned to one side of the room. Opposite the hanging that covered the door by which Patrice had entered was a second curtain, concealing another door. He lifted the curtain.

"No, no, she's not there," said Patrice, in an almost inaudible voice. "I dare not believe it. The disappointment would be too great. Swear to me . . ."

"I swear nothing, captain. You have only to open your eyes. By Jove, for a French officer, you're cutting a pretty figure! Why, you're as white as a sheet! Of course it's she! It's Little Mother Coralie! Look, she's in bed asleep, with two nurses to watch her. But there's no danger; she's not wounded. A bit of a temperature, that's all, and extreme weakness. Poor Little Mother Coralie! I never could have imagined her in such a state of exhaustion and coma."

Patrice had stepped forward, brimming over with joy. Don Luis stopped him:

"That will do, captain. Don't go any nearer. I brought her here, instead of taking her home, because I thought a change of scene and atmosphere essential. But she must have no excitement. She's had her share of that; and you might spoil everything by showing yourself."

"You're right," said Patrice. "But are you quite sure . . . ?"

"That she's alive?" asked Don Luis, laughing. "She's as much alive as you or I and quite ready to give you the happiness you deserve and to change her name to Mme. Patrice Belval. You must have just a little patience, that's all. And there is yet one obstacle to overcome, captain, for remember she's a married woman!"

He closed the door and led Patrice back to Essarès Bey:

"There's the obstacle, captain. Is your mind made up now? This wretch still stands between you and your Coralie."

Essarès had not even glanced into the next room, as though he knew that there could be no doubt about Don Luis' word. He sat shivering in his chair, cowering, weak and helpless.

"You don't seem comfortable," said Don Luis. "What's worrying you? You're frightened, perhaps? What for? I promise you that we will do nothing except by mutual consent and until we are all of the same opinion. That ought to cheer you up. We'll be your judges, the three of us, here and now. Captain Patrice Belval, Arsène Lupin and old Siméon will form the court. Let the trial begin. Does any one wish to speak in defense of the prisoner at the bar, Essarès Bey? No one. The prisoner at the bar is sentenced to death. Extenuating circumstances? No notice of appeal? No. Commutation of sentence? No. Reprieve? No. Immediate execution? Yes. You see, there's no delay. What about the means of death? A revolver-shot? That will do. It's clean, quick work. Captain Belval, your bird. The gun's loaded. Here you are."

Patrice did not move. He stood gazing at the foul brute who had done him so many injuries. His whole being seethed with hatred. Nevertheless, he replied:

"I will not kill that man."

"I agree, captain. Your scruples do you honor. You have not the right to kill a man whom you know to be the husband of the woman you love. It is not for you to remove the obstacle. Besides, you hate taking life. So do I. This animal is too filthy for words. And so, my good man, there's no one left but yourself to help us out of this delicate position."

Don Luis ceased speaking for a moment and leant over Essarès. Had the wretched man heard? Was he even alive? He looked as if he were in a faint, deprived of consciousness.

Don Luis shook him by the shoulder.

"The gold," moaned Essarès, "the bags of gold . . ."

"Oh, you're thinking of that, you old scoundrel, are you? You're still interested? The bags of gold are in my pocket . . . if a pocket can contain eighteen hundred bags of gold."

"The hiding-place?"

"Your hiding-place? It doesn't exist, so far as I'm concerned. I needn't prove it to you, need I, since Coralie's here? As Coralie was buried among the bags of gold, you can draw your own conclusion. So you're nicely done. The woman you wanted is free and, what is worse still, free by the side of the man whom she adores and whom she will never leave. And, on the other hand, your treasure is discovered. So it's all finished, eh? We are agreed? Come, here's the toy that will release you."

He handed him the revolver. Essarès took it mechanically and pointed it at Don Luis; but his arm lacked the strength to take aim and fell by his side.

"Capital!" said Don Luis. "We understand each other; and the action which you are about to perform will atone for your evil life, you old blackguard. When a man's last hope is dispelled, there's nothing for it but death. That's the final refuge."

He took hold of the other's hand and, bending Essarès' nerveless fingers round the revolver, forced him to point it towards his own face.

"Come," said he, "just a little pluck. What you've resolved to do is a very good thing. As Captain Belval and I refuse to disgrace ourselves by killing you, you've decided to do the job yourself. We are touched; and we congratulate you. But you must behave with courage. No resistance, come! That's right, that's much more like it. Once more, my compliments. It's very smart, your manner of getting out of it. You perceive that there's no room for you on earth, that you're standing in the way of Patrice and Coralie and that the best thing you can do is to retire. And you're jolly well right! No love and no gold! No gold, Siméon! The beautiful shiny coins which you coveted, with which you would have managed to secure a nice, comfortable existence, all fled, vanished! You may just as well vanish yourself, what?"

Whether because he felt himself to be helpless or because he really understood that Don Luis was right and that his life was no longer worth living, Siméon offered hardly any resistance. The revolver rose to his forehead. The barrel touched his temple.

At the touch of the cold steel he gave a moan:

"Mercy!"

"No, no, no!" said Don Luis. "You mustn't show yourself any mercy. And I won't help you either. Perhaps, if you hadn't killed my poor Ya-Bon, we might have put our heads together and sought for another ending. But, honestly, you inspire me with no more pity than you feel for yourself. You want to die and you are right. I won't prevent you. Besides, your passport is made out; you've got your ticket in your pocket. They are expecting you down below. And, you know, you need have no fear of being bored. Have you ever seen a picture of Hell? Every one has a huge stone over his tomb; and every one is lifting the stone and supporting it with his back, in order to escape the flames bursting forth beneath him. You see, there's plenty of fun. Well, your grave is reserved. Bath's ready, sir!"

Slowly and patiently he had succeeded in slipping the wretched man's fore-finger under the handle, so as to bring it against the trigger. Essarès was letting himself go. He was little more than a limp rag. Death had already cast its shadow upon him.

"Mind you," said Don Luis, "you're perfectly free. You can pull the trigger if you feel like it. It's not my business. I'm not here to compel you to commit suicide, but only to advise you and to lend you a hand."

He had in fact let go the fore-finger and was holding only the arm. But he was bearing upon Essarès with all his extraordinary power of will, the will to seek destruction, the will to seek annihilation, an indomitable will which Essarès was unable to resist. Every second death sank a little deeper into that invertebrate body, breaking up instinct, obscuring thought and bringing an immense craving for rest and inaction.

"You see how easy it is. The intoxication is flying to your brain. It's an almost voluptuous feeling, isn't it? What a riddance! To cease living! To cease suffering! To cease thinking of that gold which you no longer possess and can never possess again, of that woman who belongs to another and offers him her lips and all her entrancing self! . . . You couldn't live, could you, with that thought on you? Then come on! . . ."

Seized with cowardice, the wretch was yielding by slow degrees. He found himself face to face with one of those crushing forces, one of nature's forces, powerful as fate, which a man must needs accept. His head turned giddy and swam. He was descending into the abyss.

"Come along now, show yourself a man. Don't forget either that you are dead already. Remember, you can't appear in this world again without falling into the hands of the police. And, of course, I'm there to inform them in case of need. That means prison and the scaffold. The scaffold, my poor fellow, the icy dawn, the knife . . ."

It was over. Essarès was sinking into the depths of darkness. Everything whirled around him. Don Luis' will penetrated him and annihilated his own.

For one moment he turned to Patrice and tried to implore his aid. But Patrice persisted in his impassive attitude. Standing with his arms folded, he gazed with eyes devoid of pity upon his father's murderer. The punishment was well-deserved. Fate must be allowed to take its course. Patrice did not interfere.

And Don Luis continued, unrelentingly and without intermission:

"Come along, come along! . . . It's a mere nothing and it means eternal rest! . . . How good it feels, already! To forget! To cease fighting! . . . Think of the gold which you have lost. . . . Three hundred millions gone for ever! . . . And Coralie lost as well. Mother and daughter: you can't have either. In that case, life is nothing but a snare and a delusion. You may as well leave it. Come, one little effort, one little movement. . . ."

That little movement the miscreant made. Hardly knowing what he did, he pulled the trigger. The shot rang through the room; and Essarès fell forward, with his knees on the floor. Don Luis had to spring to one side to escape being splashed by the blood that trickled from the man's shattered head.

"By Jove!" he cried. "The blood of vermin like that would have brought me ill-luck. And, Lord, what crawling vermin it is! . . . Upon my word, I believe that this makes one more good action I've done in my life and that this suicide entitles me to a little seat in Paradise. What say you, captain?"

CHAPTER XIX
FIAT LUX!

On the evening of the same day, Patrice was pacing up and down the Quai de Passy. It was nearly six o'clock. From time to time, a tram-car passed, or some motor-lorry. There were very few people about on foot. Patrice had the pavement almost to himself.

He had not seen Don Luis Perenna since the morning, had merely received a line in which Don Luis asked him to have Ya-Bon's body moved into the Essarès' house and afterwards to meet him on the quay above Berthou's Wharf. The time appointed for the meeting was near at hand and Patrice was looking forward to this interview in which the truth would be revealed to him at last. He partly guessed the truth, but no little darkness and any number of unsolved problems remained. The tragedy was played out. The curtain had fallen on the villain's death. All was well: there was nothing more to fear, no more pitfalls in store for them. The formidable enemy was laid low. But Patrice's anxiety was intense as he waited for the moment when light would be cast freely and fully upon the tragedy.

"A few words," he said to himself, "a few words from that incredible person known as Arsène Lupin, will clear up the mystery. It will not take him long. He will be gone in an hour. Will he take the secret of the gold with him, I wonder? Will he solve the secret of the golden triangle for me? And how will he keep the gold for himself? How will he take it away?"

A motor-car arrived from the direction of the Trocadéro. It slowed down and stopped beside the pavement. It must be Don Luis, thought Patrice. But, to his great surprise, he recognized M. Masseron, who opened the door and came towards him with outstretched hand:

"Well, captain, how are you? I'm punctual for the appointment, am I not? But, I say, have you been wounded in the head again?"

"Yes, an accident of no importance," replied Patrice. "But what appointment are you speaking of?"

"Why, the one you gave me, of course!"

"I gave you no appointment."

"Oh, I say!" said M. Masseron. "What does this mean? Why, here's the note they brought me at the police-office: 'Captain Belval's compliments to M. Masseron. The problem of the golden triangle is solved. The eighteen hundred bags are at his disposal. Will he please come to the Quai de Passy, at six o'clock, with full powers from the government to accept the conditions of delivery. It would be well if he brought with him twenty powerful detectives, of whom half should be posted a hundred yards on one side of Essarès' property and the other half on the other.' There you are. Is it clear?"

"Perfectly clear," said Patrice, "but I never sent you that note."

"Who sent it then?"

"An extraordinary man who deciphered all those problems like so many children's riddles and who certainly will be here himself to bring you the solution."

"What's his name?"

"I sha'n't say."

"Oh, I don't know about that! Secrets are hard to keep in war-time."

"Very easy, on the contrary, sir," said a voice behind M. Masseron. "All you need do is to make up your mind to it."

M. Masseron and Patrice turned round and saw a gentleman dressed in a long, black overcoat, cut like a frock-coat, and a tall collar which gave him a look of an English clergyman.

"This is the friend I was speaking of," said Patrice, though he had some difficulty in recognizing Don Luis. "He twice saved my life and also that of the lady whom I am going to marry. I will answer for him in every respect."

M. Masseron bowed; and Don Luis at once began, speaking with a slight accent:

"Sir, your time is valuable and so is mine, for I am leaving Paris to-night and France to-morrow. My explanation therefore will be brief. I will pass over the drama itself, of which you have followed the main vicissitudes so far. It came to an end this morning. Captain Belval will tell you all about it. I will merely add that our poor Ya Bon is dead and that you will find three other bodies: that of Grégoire, whose real name was Mme. Mosgranem, in the barge over there; that of one Vacherot, a hall-porter, in some corner of a block of flats at 18, Rue Guimard; and lastly the body of Siméon Diodokis, in Dr. Géradec's private hospital on the Boulevard de Montmorency."

"Old Siméon?" asked M. Masseron in great surprise.

"Old Siméon has killed himself. Captain Belval will give you every possible information about that person and his real identity; and I think you will agree with me that this business will have to be hushed up. But, as I said, we will pass over all this. There remains the question of the gold, which, if I am not mistaken, interests you more than anything else. Have you brought your men?"

"Yes, I have. But why? The hiding-place, even after you have told me where it is, will be what it was before, undiscovered by those who do not know it."

"Certainly; but, as the number of those who do know it increases, the secret may slip out. In any case that is one of my two conditions."

"As you see, it is accepted. What is the other?"

"A more serious condition, sir, so serious indeed that, whatever powers may have been conferred upon you, I doubt whether they will be sufficient."

"Let me hear; then we shall see."

"Very well."

And Don Luis, speaking in a phlegmatic tone, as though he were telling the most unimportant story, calmly set forth his incredible proposal:

"Two months ago, sir, thanks to my connection with the Near East and to my influence in certain Ottoman circles, I persuaded the clique which rules Turkey to-day to accept the idea of a separate peace. It was simply a question of a few hundred millions for distribution. I had the offer transmitted to the Allies, who rejected it, certainly not for financial reasons, but for reasons of policy, which it is not for me to judge. But I am not content to suffer this little diplomatic check. I failed in my first negotiation; I do not mean to fail in the second. That is why I am taking my precautions."

He paused and then resumed, while his voice took on a rather more serious tone:

"At this moment, in April, 1915, as you are well aware, conferences are in progress between the Allies and the last of the great European powers that has remained neutral. These conferences are going to succeed; and they will succeed because the future of that power demands it and because the whole nation is uplifted with enthusiasm. Among the questions raised is one which forms the object of a certain divergency of opinion. I mean the question of money. This foreign power is asking us for a loan of three hundred million francs in gold, while making it quite clear that a refusal on our part would in no way affect a decision which is already irrevocably taken. Well, I have three hundred millions in gold; I have them at my command; and I desire to place them at the disposal of our new allies. This is my second and, in reality, my only condition."

M. Masseron seemed utterly taken aback:

"But, my dear sir," he said, "these are matters quite outside our province; they must be examined and decided by others, not by us."

"Every one has the right to dispose of his money as he pleases."

M. Masseron made a gesture of distress:

"Come, sir, think a moment. You yourself said that this power was only putting forward the question as a secondary one."

"Yes, but the mere fact that it is being discussed will delay the conclusion of the agreement for a few days."

"Well, a few days will make no difference, surely?"

"Sir, a few hours *will* make a difference."

"But why?"

"For a reason which you do not know and which nobody knows . . . except myself and a few people some fifteen hundred miles away."

"What reason?"

"The Russians have no munitions left."

M. Masseron shrugged his shoulders impatiently. What had all this to do with the matter?

"The Russians have no munitions left," repeated Don Luis. "Now there is a tremendous battle being fought over there, a battle which will be decided not many hours hence. The Russian front will be broken and the Russian troops will retreat and retreat . . . Heaven knows when they'll stop retreating! Of course, this assured, this inevitable contingency will have no influence on the wishes of the great power of which we are talking. Nevertheless, that nation has in its midst a very considerable party on the side of neutrality, a party which is held in check, but none the less violent for that. Think what a weapon you will place in its hands by postponing the agreement! Think of the difficulties which you are making for rulers preparing to go to war! It would be an unpardonable mistake, from which I wish to save my country. That is why I have laid down this condition."

M. Masseron seemed quite discomforted. Waving his hands and shaking his head, he mumbled:

"It's impossible. Such a condition as that will never be accepted. It will take time, it will need discussion. . . ."

A hand was laid on his arm by some one who had come up a moment before and who had listened to Don Luis' little speech. Its owner had alighted from a car which was waiting some way off; and, to Patrice's great astonishment, his presence had aroused no opposition on the part of either M. Masseron or Don Luis Perenna. He was a man well-advanced in years, with a powerful, lined face.

"My dear Masseron," he said, "it seems to me that you are not looking at the question from the right point of view."

"That's what I think, monsieur le président," said Don Luis.

"Ah, do you know me, sir?"

"M. Valenglay, I believe? I had the honor of calling on you some years ago, sir, when you were president of the council."

"Yes, I thought I remembered . . . though I can't say exactly . . ."

"Please don't tax your memory, sir. The past does not concern us. What matters is that you should be of my opinion."

"I don't know that I am of your opinion. But I consider that this makes no difference. And that is what I was telling you, my dear Masseron. It's not a question of knowing whether you ought to discuss this gentleman's conditions. It's a question of accepting them or refusing them without discussion. There's no bargain to be driven in the circumstances. A bargain presupposes that each party has something to offer. Now we have no offer to make, whereas this gentleman comes with his offer in his hand and says, 'Would you like three hundred million francs in gold? In that case you must do so-and-so with it. If that doesn't suit you, good-evening.' That's the position, isn't it, Masseron?"

"Yes, monsieur le président."

"Well, can you dispense with our friend here? Can you, without his assistance, find the place where the gold is hidden? Observe that he makes things very easy for you by bringing you to the place and almost pointing out the exact spot to you. Is that enough? Have you any hope of discovering the secret which you have been seeking for weeks and months?"

M. Masseron was very frank in his reply:

"No, monsieur le président," he said, plainly and without hesitation.

"Well, then. . . ."

And, turning to Don Luis:

"And you, sir," Valenglay asked, "is it your last word?"

"My last word."

"If we refuse . . . good-evening?"

"You have stated the case precisely, monsieur le président."

"And, if we accept, will the gold be handed over at once?"

"At once."

"We accept."

And, after a slight pause, he repeated:

"We accept. The ambassador shall receive his instructions this evening."

"Do you give me your word, sir?"

"I give you my word."

"In that case, we are agreed."

"We are agreed. Now then! . . ."

All these sentences were uttered rapidly. Not five minutes had elapsed since the former prime minister had appeared upon the scene. Nothing remained to do but for Don Luis to keep his promise.

It was a solemn moment. The four men were standing close together, like acquaintances who have met in the course of a walk and who stop for a minute to exchange their news. Valenglay, leaning with one arm on the parapet overlooking the lower quay, had his face turned to the river and kept raising and lowering his cane above the sand-heap. Patrice and M. Masseron stood silent, with faces a little set.

Don Luis gave a laugh:

"Don't be too sure, monsieur le président," he said, "that I shall make the gold rise from the ground with a magic wand or show you a cave in which the bags lie stacked. I always thought those words, 'the golden triangle,' misleading, because they suggest something mysterious and fabulous. Now according to me it was simply a question of the space containing the gold, which space would have the shape of a triangle. The golden triangle, that's it: bags of gold arranged in a triangle, a triangular site. The reality is much simpler, therefore; and you will perhaps be disappointed."

"I sha'n't be," said Valenglay, "if you put me with my face towards the eighteen hundred bags of gold."

"You're that now, sir."

"What do you mean?"

"Exactly what I say. Short of touching the bags of gold, it would be difficult to be nearer to them than you are."

For all his self-control, Valenglay could not conceal his surprise:

"You are not suggesting, I suppose, that I am walking on gold and that we have only to lift up the flags of the pavement or to break down this parapet?"

"That would be removing obstacles, sir, whereas there is no obstacle between you and what you are seeking."

"No obstacle!"

"None, monsieur le président, for you have only to make the least little movement in order to touch the bags."

"The least little movement!" said Valenglay, mechanically repeating Don Luis' words.

"I call a little movement what one can make without an effort, almost without stirring, such as dipping one's stick into a sheet of water, for instance, or . . ."

"Or what?"

"Well, or a heap of sand."

Valenglay remained silent and impassive, with at most a slight shiver passing across his shoulders. He did not make the suggested movement. He had no need to make it. He understood.

The others also did not speak a word, struck dumb by the simplicity of the amazing truth which had suddenly flashed upon them like lightning. And, amid this silence, unbroken by protest or sign of incredulity, Don Luis went on quietly talking:

"If you had the least doubt, monsieur le président—and I see that you have not—you would dig your cane, no great distance, twenty inches at most, into the sand beneath you. You would then encounter a resistance which would compel you to stop. That is the bags of gold. There ought to be eighteen hundred of them; and, as you see, they do not make an enormous heap. A kilogram of gold represents three thousand one hundred francs. Therefore, according to my calculation, a bag containing approximately fifty kilograms, or one hundred and fifty-five thousand francs done up in rouleaus of a thousand francs, is not a very large bag. Piled one against the other and one on top of the other, the bags represent a bulk of about fifteen cubic yards, no more. If you shape the mass roughly like a triangular pyramid you will have a base each of whose sides would be three yards long at most, or three yards and a half allowing for the space lost between the rouleaus of coins. The height will be that of the wall, nearly. Cover the whole with a layer of sand and you have the heap which lies before your eyes . . ."

Don Luis paused once more before continuing:

"And which has been there for months, monsieur le président, safe from discovery not only by those who were looking for it, but also by accident on the part of a casual passer-by. Just think, a heap of sand! Who would dream of digging a hole in it to see what is going on inside? The dogs sniff at it, the children play beside it and make mudpies, an occasional tramp lies down against it and takes a snooze. The rain softens it, the sun hardens it, the snow whitens it all over; but all this happens on the surface, in the part that shows. Inside reigns impenetrable mystery, darkness unexplored. There is not a hiding-place in the world to equal the inside of a sand heap exposed to view in a public place. The man who thought of using it to hide three hundred millions of gold, monsieur le président, knew what he was about."

The late prime minister had listened to Don Luis' explanation without interrupting him. When Don Luis had finished, Valenglay nodded his head once or twice and said:

"He did indeed. But there is one man who is cleverer still."

"I don't believe it."

"Yes, there's the man who guessed that the heap of sand concealed the three hundred million francs. That man is a master, before whom we must all bow."

Flattered by the compliment, Don Luis raised his hat. Valenglay gave him his hand:

"I can think of no reward worthy of the service which you have done the country."

"I ask for no reward," said Don Luis.

"I daresay, sir, but I should wish you at least to be thanked by voices that carry more weight than mine."

"Is it really necessary, monsieur le président?"

"I consider it essential. May I also confess that I am curious to learn how you discovered the secret? I should be glad, therefore, if you would call at my department in an hour's time."

"I am very sorry, sir, but I shall be gone in fifteen minutes."

"No, no, you can't go like this," said Valenglay, with authority.

"Why not, sir?"

"Well, because we don't know your name or anything about you."

"That makes so little difference!"

"In peace-time, perhaps. But, in war-time, it won't do at all."

"Surely, monsieur le président, you will make an exception in my case?"

"An exception, indeed? What next?"

"Suppose it's the reward which I ask, will you refuse me then?"

"It's the only one which we are obliged to refuse you. However, you won't ask for it. A good citizen like yourself understands the constraints to which everybody is bound to submit. My dear Masseron, arrange it with this gentleman. At the department in an hour from now. Good-by till then, sir. I shall expect you."

And, after a very civil bow, he walked away to his car, twirling his stick gaily and escorted by M. Masseron.

"Well, on my soul!" chuckled Don Luis. "There's a character for you! In the twinkling of an eye, he accepts three hundred millions in gold, signs an epoch-making treaty and orders the arrest of Arsène Lupin!"

"What do you mean?" cried Patrice, startled out of his life. "Your arrest?"

"Well, he orders me to appear before him, to produce my papers and the devil knows what."

"But that's monstrous!"

"It's the law of the land, my dear captain. We must bow to it."

"But . . ."

"Captain, believe me when I say that a few little worries of this sort deprive me of none of the whole-hearted satisfaction which I feel at rendering this great service to my country. I wanted, during the war, to do something for France and to make the most of the time which I was able to devote to her during my stay. I've done it. And then I have another reward: the four millions. For I think highly enough of your Coralie to believe her incapable of wishing to touch this money . . . which is really her property."

"I'll go bail for her over that."

"Thank you. And you may be sure that the gift will be well employed. So everything is settled. I have still a few minutes to give you. Let us turn them to good account. M. Masseron is collecting his men by now. To simplify their task and avoid a scandal, we'll go down to the lower quay, by the sand-heap. It'll be easier for him to collar me there."

"I accept your few minutes," said Patrice, as they went down the steps. "But first of all I want to apologize . . ."

"For what? For behaving a little treacherously and locking me into the studio of the lodge? You couldn't help yourself: you were trying to assist your Coralie. For thinking me capable of keeping the treasure on the day when I discovered it? You couldn't help that either: how could you imagine that Arsène Lupin would despise three hundred million francs?"

"Very well, no apologies," said Patrice, laughing. "But all my thanks."

"For what? For saving your life and saving Coralie's? Don't thank me. It's a hobby of mine, saving people."

Patrice took Don Luis' hand and pressed it firmly. Then, in a chaffing tone which hid his emotion, he said:

"Then I won't thank you. I won't tell you that you rid me of a hideous nightmare by letting me know that I was not that monster's son and by unveiling his real identity. I will not tell you either that I am a happy man now that life is opening radiantly before me, with Coralie free to love me. No, we won't talk of it. But shall I confess to you that my happiness is still a little—what shall I say?—a little dim, a little timid? I no longer feel any doubt; but in spite of all, I don't quite understand the truth, and, until I do understand it, the truth will cause me some anxiety. So tell me . . . explain to me . . . I want to know . . ."

"And yet the truth is so obvious!" cried Don Luis. "The most complex truths are always so simple! Look here, don't you understand anything? Just think of the way in which the problem is set. For sixteen or eighteen years, Siméon Diodokis behaves like a perfect friend, devoted to the pitch of self-denial, in short, like a father. He has not a thought, outside that of his revenge, but to secure your happiness and Coralie's. He wants to bring you together. He collects your photographs. He follows the whole course of your life. He almost gets into touch with you. He sends you the key of the garden and prepares a meeting. Then, suddenly, a complete change takes place. He becomes your inveterate enemy and thinks of nothing but killing the pair of you. What is there that separates those two states of mind? One fact, that's all, or rather one date, the night of the third of April and the tragedy that takes place that night and the following day at Essarès' house. Until that date, you were Siméon Diodokis' son. After that date, you were Siméon Diodokis' greatest enemy. Does that suggest nothing to you? It's really curious. As for me, all my discoveries are due to this general view of the case which I took from the beginning."

Patrice shook his head without replying. He did not understand. The riddle retained a part of its unfathomable secret.

"Sit down there," said Don Luis, "on our famous sand-heap, and listen to me. It won't take me ten minutes."

They were on Berthou's Wharf. The light was beginning to wane and the outlines on the opposite bank of the river were becoming indistinct. The barge rocked lazily at the edge of the quay.

Don Luis expressed himself in the following terms:

"On the evening when, from the inner gallery of the library, you witnessed the tragedy at Essarès' house, you saw before your eyes two men bound by their accomplices: Essarès Bey and Siméon Diodokis. They are both dead. One of them was your father. Let us speak first of the other. Essarès Bey's position was a critical one that evening. After draining our gold currency on behalf of an eastern power, he was trying to filch the remainder of the millions of francs collected. The *Belle Hélène*, summoned by the rain of sparks, was lying moored alongside Berthou's Wharf. The gold was to be shifted at night from the sand-bags to the motor-barge. All was going well, when the accomplices, warned by Siméon, broke in. Thereupon we have the blackmailing-scene, Colonel Fakhi's death and so on, with Essarès learning at one and the same time that his accomplices knew of his schemes and his plan to pilfer the gold and also that Colonel Fakhi had informed the police about him. He was cornered. What could he do? Run away? But, in war-time, running away is almost impossible. Besides, running away meant giving up the gold and likewise giving up Coralie, which would never have done. So there was only one thing, to disappear from sight. To disappear from sight and yet to remain there, on the battlefield, near the gold and near Coralie. Night came; and he employed it in carrying out his plan. So much for Essarès. We now come to Siméon Diodokis."

Don Luis stopped to take breath. Patrice had been listening eagerly, as though each word had brought its share of light into the oppressive darkness.

"The man who was known as old Siméon," continued Don Luis, "that is to say, your father, Armand Belval, a former victim, together with Coralie's mother, of Essarès Bey, had also reached a turning-point of his career. He was nearly achieving his object. He had betrayed and delivered his enemy, Essarès, into the hands of Colonel Fakhi and the accomplices. He had succeeded in bringing you and Coralie together. He had sent you the key of the lodge. He was justified in hoping that, in a few days more, everything would end according to his wishes. But, next morning, on waking, certain indications unknown to me revealed to him a threatening danger; and he no doubt foresaw the plan which Essarès was engaged in elaborating. And he too put himself the same question: What was he to do? What was there for him to do? He must warn you, warn you without delay, telephone to you at once. For time was pressing, the danger was becoming definite. Essarès was watching and hunting down the man whom he had chosen as his victim for the second time. You can picture Siméon possibly feeling himself pursued and locking himself into the library. You can picture him wondering whether he would ever be able to telephone to you and whether you would be there. He asks for you. He calls out to you. Essarès hammers away at the door. And your father, gasping for breath, shouts, 'Is that you, Patrice? Have you the key? . . . And the letter? . . . No? . . . But this is terrible! Then you don't know' . . . And then a hoarse cry, which you hear at your end of the wire, and incoherent noises, the sound of an altercation. And then the lips gluing themselves to the instrument and stammering words at random: 'Patrice, the amethyst pendant . . . Patrice, I should so much have liked . . . Patrice, Coralie!' Then a loud scream . . . cries that grow weaker and weaker . . . silence, and that is all. Your father is dead, murdered. This time, Essarès Bey, who had failed before, in the lodge, took his revenge on his old rival."

"Oh, my unhappy father!" murmured Patrice, in great distress.

"Yes, it was he. That was at nineteen minutes past seven in the morning, as you noted. A few minutes later, eager to know and understand, you yourself rang up; and it was Essarès who replied, with your father's dead body at his feet."

"Oh, the scoundrel! So that this body, which we did not find and were not able to find . . ."

"Was simply made up by Essarès, made up, disfigured, transformed into his own likeness. That, captain, is how—and the whole mystery lies in this—Siméon Diodokis, dead, became Essarès Bey, while Essarès Bey, transformed into Siméon Diodokis, played the part of Siméon Diodokis."

"Yes," said Patrice, "I see, I understand."

"As to the relations existing between the two men," continued Don Luis, "I am not certain. Essarès may or may not have known before that old Siméon was none other than his former rival, the lover of Coralie's mother, the man in short who had escaped death. He may or may not have known that Siméon was your father. These are points which will never be decided and which, moreover, do not matter. What I do take for granted is that this new murder was not improvised on the spot. I firmly believe that Essarès, having noticed certain similarities in height and figure, had made every preparation to take Siméon's place if circumstances obliged him to disappear. And it was easily done. Siméon Diodokis wore a wig and no beard. Essarès, on the contrary, was bald-headed and had a beard. He shaved himself, smashed Siméon's face against the grate, mingled the hairs of his own beard with the bleeding mass, dressed the body in his clothes, took his victim's clothes for himself, put on the wig, the spectacles and the comforter. The transformation was complete."

Patrice thought for a moment. Then he raised an objection:

"Yes, that's what happened at nineteen minutes past seven. But something else happened at twenty-three minutes past twelve."

"No, nothing at all."

"But that clock, which stopped at twenty-three minutes past twelve?"

"I tell you, nothing happened at all. Only, he had to put people off the scent. He had above all to avoid the inevitable accusation that would have been brought against the new Siméon."

"What accusation?"

"What accusation? Why, that he had killed Essarès Bey, of course! A dead body is discovered in the morning. Who has committed the murder? Suspicion would at once have fallen on Siméon. He would have been questioned and arrested. And Essarès would have been found under Siméon's mask. No, he needed liberty and facilities to move about as he pleased. To achieve this, he kept the murder concealed all the morning and arranged so that no one set foot in the library. He went three times and knocked at his wife's door, so that she should say that Essarès Bey was still alive during the morning. Then, when she went out, he raised his voice and ordered Siméon, in other words himself, to see her to the hospital in the Champs-Élysées. And in this way Mme. Essarès thought that she was leaving her husband behind her alive and that she was escorted by old Siméon, whereas actually she was leaving old Siméon's corpse in an empty part of the house and was escorted by her husband. Then what happened? What the rascal had planned. At one o'clock, the police, acting on the information laid by Colonel Fakhi, arrived and found themselves in the presence of a corpse. Whose corpse? There was not a shadow of hesitation on that point. The maids recognized their master; and, when Mme. Essarès returned, it was her husband whom she saw lying in front of the fireplace at which he had been tortured the night before. Old Siméon, that is to say, Essarès himself, helped to establish the identification. You yourself were taken in. The trick was played."

"Yes," said Patrice, nodding his head, "that is how things must have gone. They all fit in."

"The trick was played," Don Luis repeated, "and nobody could make out how it was done. Was there not this further proof, the letter written in Essarès' own hand and found on his desk? The letter was dated at twelve o'clock on the fourth of April, addressed to his wife, and told her that he was going away. Better still, the trick was so successfully played that the very clues which ought to have revealed the truth merely concealed it. For instance, your father used to carry a tiny album of photographs in a pocket stitched inside his under-vest. Essarès did not notice it and did not remove the vest from the body. Well, when they found the album, they at once accepted that most unlikely hypothesis: Essarès Bey carrying on his person an album filled with photographs of his wife and Captain Belval! In the same way, when they found in the dead man's hand an amethyst pendant containing your two latest photographs and when they also found a crumpled paper with something on it about the golden triangle, they at once admitted that Essarès Bey had stolen the pendant and the document and was holding them in his hand when he died! So absolutely certain were they all that it was Essarès Bey who had been murdered, that his dead body lay before their eyes and that they must not trouble about the question any longer. And in this way the new Siméon was master of the situation. Essarès Bey is dead, long live Siméon!"

Don Luis indulged in a hearty laugh. The adventure struck him as really amusing.

"Then and there," he went on, "Essarès, behind his impenetrable mask, set to work. That very day he listened to your conversation with Coralie and, overcome with fury at seeing you bend over her, fired a shot from his revolver. But, when this new attempt failed, he ran away and played an elaborate comedy near the little door in the garden, crying murder, tossing the key over the wall to lay a false scent and falling to the ground half dead, as though he had been strangled by the enemy who was supposed to have fired the shot. The comedy ended with a skilful assumption of madness."

"But what was the object of this madness?"

"What was the object? Why, to make people leave him alone and keep them from questioning him or suspecting him. Once he was looked upon as mad, he could remain silent and unobserved. Otherwise, Mme. Essarès would have recognized his voice at the first words he spoke, however cleverly he might have altered his tone. From this time onward, he is mad. He is an irresponsible being. He goes about as he pleases. He is a madman! And his madness is so thoroughly admitted that he leads you, so to speak, by the hand to his former accomplices and causes you to have them arrested, without asking yourself for an instant if this madman is not acting with the clearest possible sense of his own interest. He's a madman, a poor, harmless madman, one of those unfortunates with whom nobody dreams of interfering. Henceforth, he has only his last two adversaries to fight: Coralie and you. And this is an easy matter for him. I presume that he got hold of a diary kept by your father. At any rate, he knows every day of the one which you keep. From this he learns the whole story of the graves; and he knows that, on the fourteenth of April, Coralie and you are both going on a pilgrimage to those graves.

822

Besides, he plans to make you go there, for his plot is laid. He prepares against the son and the daughter, against the Patrice and Coralie of to-day, the attempt which he once prepared against the father and the mother. The attempt succeeds at the start. It would have succeeded to the end, but for an idea that occurred to our poor Ya-Bon, thanks to which a new adversary, in the person of myself, entered the lists. . . . But I need hardly go on. You know the rest as well as I do; and, like myself, you can judge in all his glory the inhuman villain who, in the space of those twenty-four hours, allowed his accomplice Grégoire to be strangled, buried your Coralie under the sand-heap, killed Ya-Bon, locked me in the lodge, or thought he did, buried you alive in the grave dug by your father and made away with Vacherot, the porter. And now, Captain Belval, do you think that I ought to have prevented him from committing suicide, this pretty gentleman who, in the last resort, was trying to pass himself off as your father?"

"You were right," said Patrice. "You have been right all through, from start to finish. I see it all now, as a whole and in every detail. Only one point remains: the golden triangle. How did you find out the truth? What was it that brought you to this sand-heap and enabled you to save Coralie from the most awful death?"

"Oh, that part was even simpler," replied Don Luis, "and the light came almost without my knowing it! I'll tell it you in a few words. But let us move away first. M. Masseron and his men are becoming a little troublesome."

The detectives were distributed at the two entrances to Berthou's Wharf. M. Masseron was giving them his instructions. He was obviously speaking to them of Don Luis and preparing to accost him.

"Let's get on the barge," said Don Luis. "I've left some important papers there."

Patrice followed him. Opposite the cabin containing Grégoire's body was another cabin, reached by the same companion-way. It was furnished with a table and a chair.

"Here, captain," said Don Luis, taking a letter from the drawer of the table and settling it, "is a letter which I will ask you to . . . but don't let us waste words. I shall hardly have time to satisfy your curiosity. Our friends are coming nearer. Well, we were saying, the golden triangle . . ."

He listened to what was happening outside with an attention whose real meaning Patrice was soon to understand. And, continuing to give ear, he resumed:

"The golden triangle? There are problems which we solve more or less by accident, without trying. We are guided to a right solution by external events, among which we choose unconsciously, feeling our way in the dark, examining this one, thrusting aside that one and suddenly beholding the object aimed at. . . . Well, this morning, after taking you to the tombs and burying you under the stone, Essarès Bey came back to me. Believing me to be locked into the studio, he had the pretty thought to turn on the gas-meter and then went off to the quay above Berthou's Wharf. Here he hesitated; and his hesitation provided me with a precious clue. He was certainly then thinking of releasing Coralie. People passed and he went away. Knowing where he was going, I returned to your assistance, told your friends at Essarès' house and asked them to look after you. Then I came back here. Indeed, the whole course of events obliged me to come back. It was unlikely that the bags of gold were inside the conduit; and, as the *Belle Hélène* had not taken them off, they must be beyond the garden, outside the conduit and therefore somewhere near here. I explored the barge we are now on, not so much with the object of looking for the bags as with the hope of finding some unexpected piece of information and also, I confess, the four millions in Grégoire's possession. Well, when I start exploring a place where I fail to find what I want, I always remember that capital story of Edgar Allan Poe's, *The Purloined Letter*. Do you recollect? The stolen diplomatic document which was known to be hidden in a certain room. The police investigate every nook and corner of the room and take up all the boards of the floor, without results. But Dupin arrives and almost immediately goes to a card-rack dangling from a little brass knob on the wall and containing a solitary soiled and crumpled letter. This is the document of which he was in search. Well, I instinctively adopted the same process. I looked where no one would dream of looking, in places which do not constitute a hiding-place because it would really be too easy to discover. This gave me the idea of turning the pages of four old directories standing in a row on that shelf. The four millions were there. And I knew all that I wanted to know."

"About what?"

"About Essarès' temperament, his habits, the extent of his attainments, his notion of a good hiding-place. We had plunged on the expectation of meeting with difficulties; we ought to have looked at the outside, to have looked at the surface of things. I was assisted by two further clues. I had noticed that the uprights of the ladder which Ya-Bon must have taken from here had a few grains of sand on them. Lastly, I remembered that Ya-Bon had drawn a triangle on the pavement with a piece of chalk and that this triangle had only two sides, the third side being formed by the foot of the wall. Why this detail? Why not a third line in chalk? . . . To make a long story short, I lit a cigarette, sat down upstairs, on the deck of the barge, and, looking round me, said to myself, 'Lupin, my son, five minutes and no more.' When I say, 'Lupin, my son,' I simply can't resist myself. By the time I had smoked a quarter of the cigarette, I was there."

"You had found out?"

"I had found out. I can't say which of the factors at my disposal kindled the spark. No doubt it was all of them together. It's a rather complicated psychological operation, you know, like a chemical experiment. The correct idea is formed suddenly by mysterious reactions and combinations among the elements in which it existed in a potential stage. And then I was carrying within myself an intuitive principle, a very special incentive which obliged me, which inevitably compelled me, to discover the hiding-place: Little Mother Coralie was there! I knew for certain that failure on my part, prolonged weakness or hesitation would mean her destruction. There was a woman there, within a radius of a dozen yards or so. I had to find out and I found out. The spark was kindled. The elements combined. And I made straight for the sand-heap. I at once saw the marks of footsteps and, almost at the top, the signs of a slight stamping. I started digging. You can imagine my excitement when I first touched one of the bags. But I had no time for excitement. I shifted a few bags. Coralie was there, unconscious, hardly protected from the sand which was slowly stifling her, trickling through, stopping up her eyes, suffocating her. I needn't tell you more, need I? The wharf was deserted, as usual. I got her out. I hailed a taxi. I first took her home. Then I turned my attention to Essarès, to Vacherot the porter; and, when I had discovered our enemy's plans, I went and made my arrangements with Dr. Géradec. Lastly, I had you moved to the private hospital on the Boulevard de Montmorency and gave orders for Coralie to be taken there too. And there you are, captain! All done in three hours. When the doctor's car brought me back to the hospital, Essarès arrived at the same time, to have his injuries seen to. I had him safe."

Don Luis ceased speaking. There were no words necessary between the two men. One had done the other the greatest services which a man has it in his power to render; and the other knew that these were services for which no thanks are adequate. And he also knew that he would never have an opportunity to prove his gratitude. Don Luis was in a manner above those proofs, owing to the mere fact that they were impossible. There was no service to be rendered to a man like him, disposing of his resources and performing miracles with the same ease with which we perform the trivial actions of everyday life.

Patrice once again pressed his hand warmly, without a word. Don Luis accepted the homage of this silent emotion and said:

"If ever people talk of Arsène Lupin before you, captain, say a good word for him, won't you? He deserves it." And he added, with a laugh, "It's funny, but, as I get on in life, I find myself caring about my reputation. The devil was old, the devil a monk would be!"

He pricked up his ears and, after a moment, said:

"Captain, it is time for us to part. Present my respects to Little Mother Coralie. I shall not have known her, so to speak, and she will not know me. It is better so. Good-by, captain."

"Then we are taking leave of each other?"

"Yes, I hear M. Masseron. Go to him, will you, and have the kindness to bring him here?"

Patrice hesitated. Why was Don Luis sending him to meet M. Masseron? Was it so that he, Patrice, might intervene in his favor?

The idea appealed to him; and he ran up the companion-way.

Then a thing happened which Patrice was destined never to understand, something very quick and quite inexplicable. It was as though a long and gloomy adventure were to finish suddenly with melodramatic unexpectedness.

Patrice met M. Masseron on the deck of the barge.

"Is your friend here?" asked the magistrate.

"Yes. But one word first: you don't mean to . . . ?"

"Have no fear. We shall do him no harm, on the contrary."

The answer was so definite that the officer could find nothing more to say. M. Masseron went down first, with Patrice following him.

"Hullo!" said Patrice. "I left the cabin-door open!"

He pushed the door. It opened. But Don Luis was no longer in the cabin.

Immediate enquiries showed that no one had seen him go, neither the men remaining on the wharf nor those who had already crossed the gangway.

"When you have time to examine this barge thoroughly," said Patrice, "I've no doubt you will find it pretty nicely faked."

"So your friend has probably escaped through some trap-door and swum away?" asked M. Masseron, who seemed greatly annoyed.

"I expect so," said Patrice, laughing. "Unless he's gone off on a submarine!"

"A submarine in the Seine?"

"Why not? I don't believe that there's any limit to my friend's resourcefulness and determination."

But what completely dumbfounded M. Masseron was the discovery, on the table, of a letter directed to himself, the letter which Don Luis had placed there at the beginning of his interview with Patrice.

"Then he knew that I should come here? He foresaw, even before we met, that I should ask him to fulfil certain formalities?"

The letter ran as follows:

"*Sir,*

"Forgive my departure and believe that I, on my side, quite understand the reason that brings you here. My position is not in fact regular; and you are entitled to ask me for an explanation. I will give you that explanation some day or other. You will then see that, if I serve France in a manner of my own, that manner is not a bad one and that my country will owe me some gratitude for the immense services, if I may venture to use the word, which I have done her during this war. On the day of our interview, I should like you to thank me, sir. You will then—for I know your secret ambition—be prefect of police. Perhaps I shall even be able personally to forward a nomination which I consider well-deserved. I will exert myself in that direction without delay.

"I have the honor to be, etc."

M. Masseron remained silent for a time.

"A strange character!" he said, at last. "Had he been willing, we should have given him great things to do. That was what I was instructed to tell him."

"You may be sure, sir," said Patrice, "that the things which he is actually doing are greater still." And he added, "A strange character, as you say. And stranger still, more powerful and more extraordinary than you can imagine. If each of the allied nations had had three or four men of his stamp at its disposal, the war would have been over in six months."

"I quite agree," said M. Masseron. "Only those men are usually solitary, intractable people, who act solely upon their own judgment and refuse to accept any authority. I'll tell you what: they're something like that famous adventurer who, a few years ago, compelled the Kaiser to visit him in prison and obtain his release . . . and afterwards, owing to a disappointment in love, threw himself into the sea from the cliffs at Capri."

"Who was that?"

"Oh, you know the fellow's name as well as I do! . . . Lupin, that's it: Arsène Lupin."

THE END

Manufactured by Amazon.ca
Bolton, ON